Property Taxes

2017/18

Robert W Maas FCA FTII FIIT TEP
CBW Tax

Bloomsbury Professional

Bloomsbury Professional
An imprint of Bloomsbury Publishing Plc

Bloomsbury Professional Ltd
41–43 Boltro Road
Haywards Heath
RH16 1BJ
UK

Bloomsbury Publishing Plc
50 Bedford Square
London
WC1B 3DP
UK

www.bloomsbury.com

BLOOMSBURY and the Diana logo are trademarks of Bloomsbury Publishing Plc

British Library Cataloguing-in-Publication Data

A catalogue record for this book is available from the British Library.

ISBN: PB: 978 1 52650 140 0

Typeset by Phoenix Photosetting, Chatham, Kent
Printed and bound by CPI Group (UK) Ltd, Croydon, CR0 4YY

To find out more about our authors and books visit www.bloomsburyprofessional.com. Here you will find extracts, author information, details of forthcoming events and the option to sign up for our newsletters

Preface

The structuring of property transactions is one of the most difficult areas of tax planning. Each transaction needs to be considered individually. As few property transactions of any size are wholly financed by the taxpayer, the structure of a transaction is frequently dictated, or at least heavily influenced, by the requirements of third parties. Furthermore, the ease with which interests in land can be created or subdivided frequently means that the tax implications of a proposal on several different owners need to be considered.

VAT in particular can be extremely complex and getting it wrong can be expensive. I am finding in practice that I am spending a significant amount of time on VAT problems. Frequently, structuring a transaction slightly differently can give a vastly different VAT result. In the meantime there is no sign of a decrease in the number of VAT tribunal decisions and court cases that have to be considered.

There were no major changes in either of the two 2017 Finance Acts, although the new cash basis rules for property businesses seems to have required a massive amount of legislation. Both this and the new income tax property allowance are 'simplifications' aimed at helping people to cope with Making Tax Digital, albeit that HMRC's interpretation of 'simple' is questionable. There was also the new SDLT relief for first-time buyers, which is far more restrictive than the Chancellor suggested, and some tidying up of previous years' rushed changes. As always, the courts and tribunals were active in property matters too. I have also covered what we know about the proposal to extend NRCGT to commercial property as that is of obvious importance in advising non-residents.

I have tried in this book not only to explain the law – and to highlight areas where the law is not clear cut – but to put this into the context of the types of transaction that are likely to take place in practice. I hope that this will help property owners and developers and others who deal in property to understand the transaction, as well as pointing their professional advisers towards the relevant legislative provisions themselves.

I would like to thank readers of earlier editions who have drawn to my attention areas of the text that needed clarification. I welcome such help and hope that readers will continue to write to Bloomsbury Professional with suggestions for improvement. More than 50 years of experience of property taxation has taught me that there are always new things to be learnt in this field.

I would also like to take the opportunity of thanking others involved in the production of this book in particular Maggie O'Callaghan for typing the original manuscript, Jill Holland for typing the additional material for this edition and for most of the previous ones, and Tom Adcock and Nathan Steinberg for helpful comments on various aspects of the text.

RW Maas
London E1
January 2018

Contents

Table of Statutes

[All references are to paragraph numbers and appendices]

D

E

F

W

Table of Statutory Instruments and Other Guidance

[All references are to paragraph number]

I

Table of European Legislation

[*All references are to paragraph number*]

Primary Legislation

Secondary Legislation

Table of Cases

[*All references are to paragraph number*]

B

G

H

I

K

L

N

P

Q

R

S

T

U

Y

Z

Chapter 1

Introduction

1.1 Property transactions are different from most business operations for a number of reasons. As the unit cost is very high it is important to consider the structure of each individual transaction rather than the business as a whole. Because it is possible to make a very large profit on a single transaction, HMRC are likely to try very hard to contend that such profit is income rather than a capital gain – which in many cases is taxed less heavily – if there is any doubt as to the status of a transaction. For the same reason taxpayers frequently seek ways to transform a trading profit into a capital gain – or to try to arrange things so that it arises outside the UK – with the result that a large number of anti-avoidance provisions have been introduced over the years in an attempt to thwart such moves.

1.2 By means of leases and joint ownership it is easier than with most other types of asset to dispose of interests in a property whilst retaining a share in the ownership, or a reversionary or subsidiary interest in the property. Every site or building is unique, so that virtually every property transaction is different in one or more respects from every other. The needs and desires of landowners and developers differ considerably and the structure of a transaction may often need to be varied to accommodate the special wishes of, say, the vendor of part of a site who wants a lease in the redevelopment, of the landowner who wants to retain a share in the rental income from a development or who wants to exercise a degree of control over the appearance of the development, of the financier who wants temporarily to own the site to maximise his security, of the developer who may have a number of alternative ways of financing the development, or of the two owners of a property company whose ability to leave their funds in the company and whose needs for income may be vastly different.

1.3 The wide variety of uses to which property can be put, the volume of tax legislation aimed at property, and the propensity of landowners and developers to maintain a large degree of flexibility in relation to their holdings, in particular as regards the length of time for which they intend to retain a particular property, make tax planning both important and at the same time often very difficult. The problems are aggravated by the fact that the exact manner in which a transaction is structured can significantly affect the tax payable. Perhaps worse, it is relatively easy to walk unwittingly into tax traps by looking only at the end result of a series of transactions and missing the tax consequences of some of the steps leading up to that result.

1.4 A further problem is that the inter-relationship between different taxes is far more important when planning property transactions than with most types of business. In particular, VAT needs to be considered with care as some property disposals attract VAT whereas most do not, and expenditure is likely to consist of a mixture of exempt items, such as land purchases, and standard-rated ones, such as fees and building work. Furthermore, in those cases where receipts are normally exempt the taxpayer is sometimes entitled to opt to bring them into the scope of VAT if he so wishes. Whilst at first sight it is difficult to envisage anyone volunteering to be taxed if he does not have to be, it is likely to be sensible to make such an election in many cases. The position is further complicated by the fact that a structure that is attractive from a VAT point of view – or indeed a stamp duty land tax viewpoint – can often give rise to serious adverse income tax or corporation tax consequences. It is accordingly important, when considering tax on property transactions, to be able to take an overall view of all the problems involved.

1.5 The purpose of this book is to attempt to review the tax provisions that need to be considered in relation to property transactions and to relate them to one another. **Chapters 6** to **9** look at specific types of property transactions, the acquisition and disposal of property as a trading transaction, the holding of property as an investment – including the special rules that apply to Real Estate Investment Trusts (REITs), a semi-transparent listed property investment vehicle, the carrying out of property development, and the refurbishment of existing buildings. It is intended that each of these chapters should be able to stand on its own so that those not expert in tax can dip into them as required without having to peruse the entire book to ascertain the sorts of things that they need to think about. This inevitably involves a degree of duplication, as points dealt with elsewhere in the book which are of major importance to such types of transaction have also been examined in these four chapters in the specific context of the transaction involved. It is hoped that this element of duplication does not unduly distract the reader who wishes to read the book from cover to cover.

1.6 Clearly, in considering tax on property companies or property transactions, account needs to be taken of the general tax law. It is always difficult to determine how much of the tax system as a whole one needs to explain when dealing with a specialist area. It is hoped that this book will be useful to the property owner or developer without a detailed knowledge of tax as well as the tax practitioner and in achieving this aim a degree of compromise is inevitable. No attempt has been made to explain corporation tax or capital gains tax in any detail but sufficient of the basic principles have had to be included to enable the non-expert to see his property transactions in the context of his overall position. Clearly, however, these explanations of general principles should be looked on as guidelines and not as a detailed exposition of the general tax system; the reader will need to look elsewhere for the caveats and exceptions that there is not space enough to mention here.

1.7 **Chapters 11, 16, 17** and **18**, which deal with tax on chargeable gains, value added tax on residential and commercial property, inheritance tax (formerly capital transfer tax), respectively, are restricted to a consideration of the provisions of those taxes that either relate wholly to property or which tend to affect property far more than other assets. As such they are by no means exhaustive. No attempt has been made in these chapters to cover reliefs or anti-avoidance provisions that can apply to property as much as to other assets, but are not specific to property as such. Although there is no special tax regime for property, there are some taxes that are property-related. Stamp duty land tax (SDLT) and the annual tax on enveloped properties (ATED) are considered in **Chapters 19** and **20**. Council tax which is payable on residential property is considered in **Chapter 21** together with a brief summary of the uniform business rate which is payable on commercial property. Landfill tax is dealt with in **Chapter 22**. Aggregates levy, which might be considered as a tax on land, is felt to be outside the scope of this book, although a summary of the main features is included in **Chapter 23**.

1.8 The anti-avoidance provisions mentioned in **Chapter 15** are not specifically property related and the chapter is intended to flash warning lights, leaving the would-be tax avoider to refer elsewhere for a detailed consideration of the relevant provisions. Similarly, it needs to be borne in mind that the tax legislation contains a large number of other anti-avoidance provisions that are of general application. The applicability of such legislation needs to be considered before carrying out a complex property transaction.

1.9 Finally, for those not expert in tax, it may be helpful to put property tax in context in relation to the tax system as a whole. A basic distinction is drawn in tax law between property bought for resale and that bought as a long-term investment. The tax treatment of these two categories is very different. Accordingly, before considering what the tax effect of a property transaction is likely to be, it is important to ascertain whether it is a dealing (or trading) transaction or an investment transaction. This applies not only where property is acquired by individuals, but also where it is acquired by companies.

1.10 Irrespective of whether the building is bought for investment or resale the rental income produced from the building is taxed under the special rules that relate to UK property business income. These are considered in **Chapter 2**. To avoid rental income being converted into capital by the use of premiums for short leases, the legislation contains provisions designed to tax part of such a premium as if it were income. These are considered in **Chapter 3**.

1.11 There are two special areas of general tax law that are of particular relevance to property. The first is that most property transactions are financed partly by borrowings and the owner will want to ensure that he can obtain tax relief on such borrowings. The rules for the allowability of loan interest are considered in **Chapter 4**.

1.12 The second area is that much of the expenditure on buildings can qualify for capital allowances where the building is held as an investment. These allowances can be significant and can be set against the tax on the rental income produced by the building. The appropriate rules are considered in **Chapter 10**. Capital allowances are not in general available though where the plant is in a dwelling or other residence.

1.13 Useful decisions of the two former tax tribunals, the Special Commissioners (cited as STC (SCD)) and the VAT and Duties Tribunal (cited as VTD), and tax decisions of the First-tier Tribunal (cited as SFTD or TC), which replaced them from 1 April 2009, are highlighted in this book as well as court cases. It should, however, be borne in mind that First-tier Tribunal decisions are not binding even on another tribunal. Nevertheless the FTT generally seek to follow earlier FTT decisions unless they seem to be clearly wrong. This does not apply to decisions of the Upper Tribunal (cited as STC or UT), which are binding on the FTT. The Upper Tribunal hears appeals from the FTT (and sometimes directly from taxpayers in complex matters) and is a court of record of equivalent standing to the High Court. Traditionally the direct tax authorities have striven to settle cases without recourse to a tribunal so the volume of direct tax tribunal decisions is comparatively small. In contrast the VAT authorities seem to make little real attempt to settle matters informally so the volume of VAT tribunal cases is much larger. This has resulted in a large body of VAT tribunal decisions, some of which are contradictory. They have been included as they represent an argued interpretation of the law and as such are likely to be followed by other tribunals and the courts. Issues such as the distinction between a reconstruction, enlargement alteration or annex to a building depend very much on the facts and tribunals are the sole arbiters of fact. Where a court decision is made in relation to such matters previous tribunal decisions need to be approached with caution as the tribunal might not have reached the same decision if it had had the guidance on the law that the court decision has provided.

1.14 Most tax law applies throughout the UK. However, in recent years the government has devolved to the Scottish Parliament and the Welsh Assembly the right to raise some taxes. In the property context, this devolution applies to both SDLT (**Chapter 19**) and Landfill Tax (**Chapter 22**). The explanations in this book are limited to the laws passed by the UK Parliament. If the property is in Scotland, the Scottish Land and Buildings Transfer Tax (LBTT) will apply. Readers will have to look elsewhere to discover the details of LBTT.

It differs from SDLT in a number of respects. Similarly, if the property is in Wales, Welsh Land Transaction Tax (LTT) will apply on a transfer in place of SDLT. It is based on SDLT, but there are some differences, so again the reader will need to look elsewhere to discover what they are. Similarly with Landfill Tax, if the landfill site is in Scotland, the Scottish Landfill Tax (SLT) will apply. In Wales, Welsh Landfill Disposals Tax (LDT) is payable, not landfill tax.

Chapter 2

Rents

Introduction

2.1 Rents from land and property in the UK are taxed as income from a notional property business. Up to 2004/05 they were taxed under Schedule A but the *ITTOIA 2005* abolished that terminology (which had survived since the reintroduction of income tax in 1842) in relation to income tax for 2005/06 onwards and simply sets out the rules for taxing what it calls property income. The rules were altered radically in the 1990s, for income tax purposes from 6 April 1995 and for corporation tax from 1 April 1998. Between those dates there were two distinct systems, one for income tax and the other for corporation tax. Income tax is payable by individuals and trusts. It is also payable by overseas companies that invest in UK property but do not carry on a UK trade. Corporation tax is payable by UK companies and by non-UK trading companies.

2.2 This chapter is split into three sections:

1. The general rules (**2.3–2.80**).
2. Property income of non-UK residents (**2.81–2.87**).
3. Other matters, namely the treatment of service charges, dilapidations, rent-a-room relief for letting space in one's own residence, rents taxable as trading income, furnished holiday lettings and tipping rights (**2.88–2.159**).

The General Rules

2.3 Tax on property income is charged on every business that a person carries on for generating income from land in the UK and every transaction that the person enters into for that purpose other than in the course of a business (*ITTOIA 2005, s 265*; *CTA 2009, ss 205, 209*). A person's UK property interests are called a 'UK property business'.

2.4 The receipts of a UK property business are explicitly stated to include:

(*a*) receipts in respect of a licence to occupy or otherwise use land or in respect of the exercise of any other right over land; and

(*b*) rent charges and other annual payments reserved in respect of, or charged on or issuing out of, the land.

(*ITTOIA 2005, s 266, CTA 2009, s 207.*)

2.5 The right to use a caravan or a houseboat at only one location is treated as a right deriving from an estate or interest in land and is therefore part of the owner's UK property business (*ITTOIA 2005, s 266(4)*). For corporation tax a right to use a caravan or houseboat at only one location is treated as a right deriving from an estate or interest in land (*CTA 2009, s 207(4)*). However *CTA 2009, s 43* allows the operator of a caravan site to elect to treat caravan rents as trading income instead of UK property income. A caravan for this purpose is a structure designed or adapted for human habitation which is capable of being moved by being towed or being transported on a motor vehicle or trailer, or a motor vehicle designed or adapted for human habitation (but railway rolling stock and tents are specifically excluded from the definition). A structure composed of two sections separately constructed and designed to be assembled on a site by means of bolts, clamps or other devices is not prevented from being a caravan just because when assembled it cannot be lawfully moved on a highway by being towed or transported on a motor vehicle or trailer (*ITTOIA 2005, s 875; CTA 2009, s 1314*). A houseboat is defined as a boat or similar structure designed or adapted for use as a place of human habitation (*ITTOIA 2005, s 878(1)*; *CTA 2009, s 1319*).

2.6 In the case of furnished lettings, the amount payable for the use of the furniture as well as that for the use of the land is treated as income of the UK property business, and expenses in connection with the provision of the furniture are treated as expenses of that business. A furnished letting for this purpose is a lease or other arrangement under which a sum (or other consideration other than money) is payable in respect of the use of the premises (or caravan or houseboat) and the person entitled to the use of the premises is also entitled to the use of furniture in connection with that use. However, a trade which consists in, or involves, making furniture available for use in premises is not a furnished letting. It is not clear what this seeks to exclude. It appears to exclude a separate trade of leasing furniture, but, if so, it is odd that it was thought necessary, as it is hard to imagine anyone thinking that such an activity could fall within the above wording (*ITTOIA 2005, s 308*; *CTA 2009, s 248*).

2.7 The following activities are specifically excluded from the scope of a UK property business:

(*a*) profits arising from the occupation of land – these will normally constitute a trade (see **2.88**). This will exclude trades such as property dealing, operating hotels and those furnished lettings where there is a large degree of services (see **2.91** onwards);

(*b*) farming and market gardening – which are taxed as a trade by virtue of *ITTOIA 2005, s 9(1)*; *CTA 2009, s 36(1)* (see **23.9**);

(*c*) mines, quarries and other concerns which are taxed as a trade by virtue of *ITTOIA 2005, s 12*; *CTA 2009, s 39* (see **23.18**);

(*d*) the income from (and expenses of) tied premises – which is taxed as a trading receipt under *ITTOIA 2005, s 19*; *CTA 2009, s 42* (see **23.35**);

(*e*) rent receivable in connection with mines, quarries and other concerns which is taxed as a trade by virtue of *ITTOIA 2005, s 12*; *CTA 2009, ss 270–272* (see **23.20–23.24**);

(*f*) rent, etc. in respect of electric line wayleaves to the extent that this is taxable as trading income by virtue of *ITTOIA 2005, s 22*; *CTA 2009, s 45* (see **23.31**).

(*ITTOIA 2005, s 267*; *CTA 2009, s 208*.)

Although not specifically excluded in the property income legislation, a UK property business also does not include:

(*g*) annual interest, eg under a mortgage, which is taxable as interest income;

(*h*) profits from the occupation of woodlands managed on a commercial basis and with a view to the realisation of profits – which are exempt from tax (see **23.18**). Receipts from woodlands not meeting these requirements is probably not income at all for tax purposes.

2.8 If a non-UK company has both UK property transactions chargeable to corporation tax and UK property transactions chargeable to income tax it is treated as carrying on two separate UK property businesses, an income tax one and a corporation tax one. It is difficult to envisage such circumstances occurring. The obvious one is where the company is carrying on a trade in the UK through a branch and lets part of the trading premises (which would create a corporation tax UK property business) and also owns UK investment properties unconnected with the trade (which would give rise to an income tax UK property business). However, it would be odd to structure a company in this way. The trading operations would normally be carried on by a separate company to the investment transactions.

2.9 Despite the all-embracing nature of this charging section, rents can, in some cases, be assessable as trading income. Such cases are considered later in this chapter (see **2.88**).

2.10 Income tax on a UK property business is charged on (and payable by) the person receiving or entitled to the income (*ITTOIA 2005, s 271*). The word 'receiving' is odd. An agent may well 'receive' the income; however, unlike with interest, where they tax the agent as the person in receipt of the income, HMRC do not normally seek to tax an agent in relation to a property business (apart from the special provisions that used to apply for taxing non-residents). They will however tax the trustees of an interest in possession trust at the basic rate as a person in receipt of income, even though the beneficial owner of the rents is the life tenant. There is no corresponding provision for corporation tax purposes, but the basic corporation tax rules produce the same result. There is no corresponding provision for corporation tax. The person entitled to the income is normally the property owner. However HMRC accept that it is possible to split the right to income from the ownership of the property itself and pass the right to the rents to someone else. However, they say that this can only be done by a valid declaration or deed of trust (Trust, Settlements and Estates Manual, TSEM 9170). Gifting the right to income can of course have other tax consequences though. Where a property is jointly owned by spouses (or civil partners), the income is deemed to belong to them in equal shares, although they can, if they wish, jointly elect to be treated as entitled to the income in the proportions in which they actually own the property. (*ITA 2007, s 836*).

Computation of Profits

2.11 For 2017/18 onwards, the profits of a property business must be calculated in accordance with GAAP if either:

(*a*) the business is carried on at any time in the tax year by a company, an LLP, a corporate firm, ie a partnership in which a company is a partner or a trust;

(*b*) the cash basis receipts, ie the amounts which would be treated as income if the cash basis was used, exceed £150,000 (proportionately reduced if the business is carried on for part only of the tax year);

(*c*) the property business is carried on by an individual (P), a share of joint property income, ie income to which spouses or civil partners are treated as beneficially entitled in equal shares under *ITA* 2007, *s 836* (jointly held property) is brought into account in calculating the profits of a property business carried on by the other spouse (Q), and the profits of Q's property business are calculated in accordance with GAAP, ie one spouse cannot use the cash basis and the other the accruals basis unless a *s 837* election is made;

(*d*) a business premises renovation allowance (see **10.151**) is made at any time in calculating the profits of the property business and if those profits were to be calculated in accordance with GAAP for the tax year a balancing event (see **10.169**) would occur during that year; or

(*e*) an election (which must be made by the first anniversary of the normal self-assessment filing date for the tax year) is made to use the accruals basis

(*ITTOIA 2005, s 271A(1)–(11)* inserted by *F(No 2)A 2017, Sch 2, para 13.*) The Treasury has power by statutory instrument to amend condition (*a*) or the £150,000 figure in condition (*b*) (*ITTOIA 2005, s 271A(12)*).

2.12 In any other case, the profits of a property business for a tax year must be calculated on a cash basis (*ITTOIA 2005, s 271C*).

2.13 Calculating the profits in accordance with GAAP means calculating them in accordance with generally accepted accounting practice subject to any adjustment required or authorised by law in calculating profits for income tax purposes (*ITTOIA 2005, s 271B(1)*). This does not require a person to comply with the requirements of the Companies Act 2006 (or subordinate legislation) except as to the basis of calculation. Nor does it impose any requirement as to audit or disclosure (*ITTOIA 2005, s 271B(2)*).

2.14 The profits of a property business are calculated in the same way as the profits of a trade, subject to s 272 (see **2.16**) and 272ZA (see **2.17**) (*ITTOIA 2005, s 271E*).

2.15 Under the cash basis, receipts of the business are brought into account at the time they are received and expenses are brought into account when they are paid (*ITTOIA 2005, s 271D(2)*). This is subject to any adjustment required or authorised by law in calculating profits for income tax purposes (*ITTOIA 2005, s 271D(3)*). Special rules apply for premiums on leases (see **Chapter 3**).

2.16 Where profits are calculated on an accruals basis, ie in accordance with GAAP the special rules in *ITTOIA 2005, ss 243–255, 257* and *354* and *CTA 2009, ss 188–200* (post-cessation receipts) which apply on a discontinuance of a trade are specifically applied to the profits of a UK property business (*ITTOIA 2005, s 272*; *CTA 2009, ss 280–286*). It is unlikely that they will often apply. The post-cessation expenditure rules do not cover payments of rent under the privity of contract rules in respect of leases previously owned and assigned to a purchaser, the most likely type of post-cessation expense for a UK property business. They relate only to negligence, and product liability and similar claims and their related costs and to bad debts and related costs. One effect of calculating the profits of a UK property business under trading income rules is to apply all the trading income and Case I legal decisions, including that in *Odeon Associated Theatres Ltd v Jones* (see **9.4**) which was effectively excluded by the earlier Schedule A rules. Relief for 'pre-trading' expenditure in the seven years prior to the commencement of a UK property business can be claimed in the year that the business commences in the same way as with a trade (*ITTOIA 2005, s 57(2)*; *CTA 2009, ss 210(2), 61*). The specific relief for redundancy payments in *ITTOIA 2005, ss 76–80* and *CTA 2009, ss 76–81* and for training courses for employees and counselling services for employees in *ITTOIA 2005, ss 73–75* and *CTA 2009, s 73–75* are specifically applied to employees of a UK property business (*ITTOIA 2005, s 272; CTA 2009, s 210(2)*). So are the specific rules on apportionment (*ITTOIA 2005, s 203; CTA 2009, s 52, 1307*), business entertainment expenses (*ITTOIA 2005, ss 45–47; CTA 2009, s 1298*), expenditure involving crime (*ITTOIA 2005, s 55; CTA 2009, s 1304*), consideration for restrictive undertakings (*ITTOIA 2005, s 69; CTA 2009, s 69* formerly *FA 1988, s 73(2)*), deduction of emolument paid more than nine months after the end of the accounting year (*ITTOIA 2005, s 36–37; CTA 2009, s 1288; FA 1989, s 43*), expenses up to 5 April 2006 in connection with unapproved retirement benefit schemes (*ITTOIA 2005, ss 38–44; FA 1989, s 76* repealed by *FA 2004, s 326*) and expenditure in connection with the provision of security assets or services (*ITTOIA 2005, s 81)*(*ITTOIA 2005, s 272; CTA 2009, s 210(2)*).

2.17 Where profits are calculated on a cash basis the following trading income rules do not apply (*ITTOIA 2005*):

- s 30 — animals kept for trade purposes
- s 31 — relationship between rules prohibiting and allowing deductions
- s 35 — bad and doubtful debts
- s 36 — unpaid remuneration
- s 43 — profits calculated before end of nine-month period
- ss 48/49 — car hire
- s 50A — short-term hiring in and long-term hiring out
- s 50B — connected persons: application of s 48
- s 55B — rental rebates on leased plant
- s 57A — expenses incurred by traders on food and drink
- ss 60–67 — tenants under taxed leases
- s 68 — replacement and alteration of trade tools
- ss 92–94 — expenses connected with foreign trades
- s 95A — costs of setting up SAYE option scheme

- s 94AA deduction in relation to salaried members
- s 94D–94G expenditure on vehicles
- s 94H–94I use of home for business purposes
- s 98 acquisition of trade: receipts from transferor's trade
- ss 99–103 reverse premium
- ss 108–110 gifts of trading stock to charities, etc
- ss 111–129 herd basis

(*ITTOIA 2005, s 272ZA*.) In addition, *ITTOIA 2005, ss 291–294* (tenants under taxed leases: deductions) and *ss 296–298* (ICTA modifications) do not apply in calculating profits on a cash basis (*ITTOIA 2005, s 276A*).

2.18 Furthermore, where profits are calculated on a cash basis no deduction is allowed for –

(*a*) an item of a capital nature incurred on (or in connection with) the acquisition or disposal of a business or part of a business;

(*b*) an item of capital expenditure on (or in connection with) education or training;

(*c*) an item of a capital nature incurred on (or in connection with) the provision, alteration or disposal of land;

(*d*) an item of a capital nature incurred on (or in connection with) the provision, alteration or disposal of an asset for use in ordinary residential property (but see **2.19**); or

(*e*) an item of a capital nature incurred on (or in connection with) the provision, alteration or disposal of –

  (i) an asset that is not a depreciating asset,

  (ii) an asset not acquired or created for use on a continuing basis in the property business,

  (iii) a non-qualifying intangible asset, or

  (iv) a financial asset

(*ITTOIA 2005, s 307B(1)–(4)(6)(10)*.)

2.19 Head (*c*) does not prohibit a deduction for expenditure on an asset of a depreciating nature which (in being provided) is installed or otherwise fixed to qualifying land so as to become in law part of that land and which is not incurred on (or in connection with) a building; a wall, floor, ceiling, door, gate, shutter or window or stairs; a waste disposal system; a sewerage or drainage system; or a shaft or other structure in which a lift, hoist, escalator or moving walkway may be installed (*ITTOIA 2005, s 307B(5)*). If an asset is provided partly for use in ordinary residential property and partly for other purposes, such apportionment can be made as is just and reasonable for the purpose of applying head (*d*) (*ITTOIA 2005, s 307B(7)*). Ordinary residential property for the purpose of *s 307B* means a dwelling-house or part of a dwelling-house in relation to which an ordinary property business is carried on in the tax year and qualifying land is land other than ordinary residential property (*ITTOIA 2005, s 307B(8)*). An ordinary property business is so much of a UK property business as does not consist of the commercial letting of furnished holiday accommodation (or so much of an overseas property business as does not consist of such letting in one or more EEA States) (*ITTOIA 2005, s 307B(9)*).

2.20 An asset is a depreciating asset if (on the date the expenditure is incurred) it is reasonable to expect that the asset has a useful life of under 20 years (or its value will decline by 90% or more in that 20-year period). For this purpose, the useful life of an asset ends when it can no longer be of use to any person for any purpose as an asset of a business (*ITTOIA 2005, s 307B(11)(12)*). An intangible asset is something which is capable of being an intangible asset within the meaning of FRS 105. In particular, it includes an internally generated intangible asset and intellectual property (*ITTOIA 2005, s 307B(13)*). An intangible asset is non-qualifying unless (by virtue of having a fixed maximum duration) it must cease to exist within 20 years of the date the expenditure was incurred or if it consists of a right (whether conditional or not) to obtain an intangible asset without a fixed maximum duration by virtue of which (assuming the right is exercised at the last possible time) it must cease to exist within 20 years (*ITTOIA 2005, s 307B(14)(15)*). If the person carrying on a property business has an intangible asset which he licenses to another person, any licence or other right granted to the property business owner over that asset is non-qualifying (*ITTOIA 2005, s 307B(16)*). A financial asset is any right under (or in connection with) a financial instrument or an arrangement that is capable of producing a return that is economically equivalent to a return produced under any financial instrument (*ITTOIA 2005, s 307B(17)*). For this purpose a financial instrument has the same meaning as in FRS 105. Intellectual property means any patent, trade mark, registered design, copyright or design right, plant breeder's rights or rights under the *Plant Varieties Act 1997, s 7*; any such right under the law of a country or territory outside the UK; any information or technique having industrial, commercial or other economic value; and any licence or other right in respect of any of the above (*ITTOIA 2005, s 307B(20)*).

2.21 The reference in *s 307B* to acquisition, provision, alteration or disposal includes potential acquisition, provision, alteration or disposal (*ITTOIA 2005, s 307B(18)*). If there is a letting of accommodation only part of which is furnished holiday accommodation, such apportionment must be made as is just and reasonable in all the circumstances (*ITTOIA 2005, s 307B(19)*). An arrangement includes any agreement, understanding, scheme, transaction or series of transactions (whether or not legally enforceable). A building includes any fixed structure. A car has the same meaning as in *CAA 2001*. Provision includes creation, construction or acquisition (*ITTOIA 2005, s 307B(20)*).

2.22 In some cases all or part of disposal proceeds of an asset or capital refund must be brought into account as property business income (*ITTOIA 2005, s 307E(12)*). This applies in two cases:

(*a*) *Case 1*: Where the person receives disposal proceeds or a capital refund in relation to an asset for a tax year in which the cash basis applies and either–

- an amount of capital expenditure relating to the asset has been brought into account in calculating cash basis profits of the business, or
- an amount of relevant capital expenditure relating to the asset has been brought into account in calculating accruals basis profits either by way of a deduction under *ITTOIA 2005, ss 58* or *59* as applied by *s 272* (incidental costs of obtaining finance) or under *CAA 2001* (see below).

(*b*) *Case 2*: where disposal proceeds or a capital refund arise in relation to an asset in a tax year for which the property business profits were calculated on an accruals basis that year is subsequent to one in which the cash basis was used, and either–

- an amount of capital expenditure relating to the asset was paid in a tax year for which the cash basis was used, was brought into account in calculating cash basis profits, and would not have been qualifying expenditure had the cash basis not been used, or
- an amount of capital expenditure relating to the asset was brought into account in calculating accruals basis profits for a tax year by means of a deduction under *CAA 2001, ss 58* or *59* (as applied by *ITTOIA 2005, s 272*) or *s 311A*, and that tax year is before that in which the cash basis was last adopted

(*ITTOIA 2005, s 307E(1)–(8)*.)

2.23 For this purpose disposal proceeds means any proceeds arising from the disposal of an asset or any part of it, proceeds arising from the grant of any right in respect of the asset or any interest in it, and the amount of any damages, proceeds of insurance or other compensation received in respect of an asset (*ITTOIA 2005, s 307E(9)*). A capital refund means an amount that is in substance a refund of capital expenditure relating to an asset (*ITTOIA 2005, s 307E(10)*). Capital expenditure is expenditure of a capital nature incurred (or treated as incurred) on or in connection with the provision (including the creation, construction or acquisition), alteration or disposal of an asset or the potential provision, alteration or disposal of an asset (*ITTOIA 2005, s 307E(11)(24)*).

2.24 If only part of the capital expenditure has been brought into account in calculating profits (including expenditure brought into account under *CAA 2001*) the amount to be treated as income is proportionately reduced (*ITTOIA 2005, s 307E(13)*).

2.25 An amount does not need to be treated as income under *s 307E(12)* if (and to the extent that) it has already been brought into account as a property business receipt either under *s 307E(12)* or any other provision of *Part 3 of ITTOIA 2005* (other than *s 334D(4)* – assets not fully paid for (see **2.63**)) or it is brought into account as disposal value under CAA 2001 (*ITTOIA 2005, s 307E(14)(15)*). Any question as to whether (or to what extent) expenditure is brought into account in calculating property business profits is to be determined on such basis as is just and reasonable in all the circumstances (*ITTOIA 2005, s 307E(16)*). For the purpose of (*b*) in Case 1, relevant capital expenditure is capital expenditure which was incurred (or treated as incurred) by the taxpayer before the tax year in which he first used the cash basis and this cash basis deductible for that year (*ITTOIA 2005, s 307E(17)*). A person enters the cash basis for a tax year if the profits of the business for that year are calculated on a cash basis and those for the previous tax year were calculated on an accruals basis (*ITTOIA 2005, s 307E(18)*). Expenditure is cash basis deductible for a tax year if (on the assumption that it was paid in that year) it would have been deductible in calculating the profits for that year on a cash basis (*ITTOIA 2005, s 307E(19)*).

2.26 Expenditure is brought into account under *CAA 2001* if (and to the extent that) a capital allowance on plant and machinery is treated as an expense of the property business, or qualifying expenditure under those provisions is allocated to a pool for a relevant qualifying activity and is set-off against different disposal receipts (*ITTOIA 2005, s 307E(20)*). An activity is a relevant qualifying activity for this purpose if it is a qualifying activity within *CAA 2001, s 15(1)(b)–(da)* and the property business consists of or includes that activity (*ITTOIA 2005, s 307E(22)*). An amount of qualifying expenditure is set-off against different disposal receipts if it would have been unrelieved qualifying expenditure carried forward in the pool but for the fact that one or more disposal values in respect of other assets has at any time been brought into account in that pool (but for this purpose an amount is not to be regarded as not carried forward because the taxpayer enters the cash basis) (*ITTOIA 2005, s 307E(21)(23)*).

2.27 If at any time a person ceases to use an asset (or any part of it) for the purposes of a property business but does not immediately dispose of it, he is treated for the purposes of *s 307E* as disposing of it (or that part) at that time for an amount equal to its market value, namely the amount that would be regarded as normal and reasonable in the market conditions prevailing and between persons dealing with each other at arm's length (*ITTOIA 2005, s 307F(2)(8)*). If at any time there is a material increase in the taxpayer's non-business use of an asset (or any part of it) he is treated for the purposes of *s 307E* as disposing of the asset (or that part) at that time for an amount equal to the relevant proportion of its market value (as defined above). For this purpose there is an increase in the taxpayer's non-business use if the proportion of the taxpayer's use for the purpose of the property business decreases or the proportion of his use that is for other purposes increases. The relevant proportion is the difference between the proportion of the taxpayer's use of the asset (or part of the asset) that is non-business use and the proportion of his use that was non-business use before the increase referred to above (*ITTOIA 2005, s 307F(3)(4)*).

2.28 This provision does not apply to an overseas property business (see **2.112**) if the taxpayer ceases to be UK resident. Instead, he is treated for the purposes of *ITTOIA 2005, s 307E* as disposing of the asset at that time for its market value for *s 307E* purposes (*ITTOIA 2005, s 307F(5)(6)*). The move overseas is deemed to occur on the last day of the tax year for which the person is UK resident (or where split-year treatment applies on the last day of the deemed period of UK residence) (*ITTOIA 2005, s 307F(7)*).

2.29 Prior to 2017/18 the profits of a UK property business were computed in the same way as those of a trade (*ITTOIA 2005, s 272; CTA 2009, s 210(1)*). This means that they had to be prepared in accordance with generally accepted accounting practice, subject to any adjustment required or authorised by law (*ITTOIA 2005, s 25; CTA 2009, s 46*). For income tax purposes 'generally accepted accounting practice' (GAAP) meant generally accepted accounting practice with respect to accounts of UK companies that are intended to give a true and fair view, and had the same meaning in relation to individuals, entities other than companies and non-UK companies as it had in relation to UK companies (*ITTOIA 2005*). No definition was needed for corporation tax as the Companies Acts require the adoption of such principles. For income tax purposes, what was taxed was the profits or gains arising in the tax year (*ITTOIA 2005, s 270*).

2.30 HMRC have stated that accounts should be prepared to 5 April (or 31 March if the taxpayer is prepared to treat this as co-terminous with 5 April) and insist that the computation of profits or gains is time-apportioned over the fiscal year if accounts are prepared to a date other than 5 April (or 31 March). The exception to this is partnerships. UK property income of a partnership is included in the partnership tax return and therefore computed on the basis of the partnership's accounting year.

2.31 In *Kings v King (2004 STC (SCD) 186)* (see **5.26**) a property jointly owned and occupied by Mr and Mrs Kings was remortgaged and let out. The whole of the rental income was paid into Mr Kings' business bank account and Mr Kings alone was named as the landlord on the 'Agreement to Let' the property. The Special Commissioner held that 'Mrs Kings surrendered her entitlement to the rents received … and that Mr Kings alone is assessable to income tax on the rents received'. This suggests that where rents are paid into the bank account of one only of the joint owners – as probably happens quite frequently where the joint owners are husband and wife – great care may need to be taken to prevent the whole rents being treated as taxable on that person alone.

2.32 As indicated earlier, all of a person's UK properties together form his UK property business. A partnership is treated as a separate person for this purpose. There are no special rules for property let at less than a full rent, even if let at a nominal figure to a connected person – although in such a case it may be difficult to show that expenditure on the property was incurred wholly and exclusively for the purposes of the UK property business, and there could be employment income tax consequences for the tenant (see **23.50**). The disposal of a property does not forfeit relief for unrelieved losses in respect of that property; the loss can be carried forward against future UK property business income from other properties provided that the business itself continues. However, a partner is not able to set his share of a partnership UK property business loss against income from his personal properties, and vice versa. HMRC have said that where property is owned jointly (and, as will normally be the case, the letting activity does not amount to a partnership) and one of the joint owners takes responsibility for the overall supervision of the letting, if the name and address of that 'managing owner' is shown on the other co-owner's tax returns, questions relating to the letting will normally be made only to the managing owner (Tax Bulletin 25, October 1996). It is understood that they will also be content for a co-owner's share of the net letting income to be shown as a single figure in his return (other than of course for the managing owner).

2.33 HMRC regard expenditure incurred on legal and professional fees on the first letting or subletting of a property as capital unless the lease is for a year or less. Such expenses of renewing a lease will be revenue if the lease is for less than 50 years, but any part relating to a premium on the renewal is capital. HMRC give no guidance on how to split the fees between the premium and the rent (HMRC'S Property Income Manual, PIM2205). Presumably they expect a capitalised value to be calculated for the rent and the apportionment to be done between that figure and the premium. Where there is a change of tenant the new lease can normally be regarded as a renewal if it follows closely on the previous one and is on broadly similar terms. This does not apply if there is some other substantial use, such as owner occupation, between lettings or if a short lease is replaced by a long one (Property Income Manual, PIM2205).

2.34 There are also a few provisions that are excluded from applying for the purposes of a UK property business, namely *ITTOIA 2005, ss 60–67*; *CTA 2009, s 63* (deduction of taxable proportion of a premium). *Section 63* is not needed as there are separate UK property business rules giving relief for a premium paid. These are considered at **3.32–3.40**. Expenditure after 31 March 2008 on the provision or replacement of an integral feature in a building is not deductible if it is eligible for capital allowances (see **10.71**) (*ITTOIA 2005, s 55A*; *CTA 2009, s 263*).

2.35 There is also a special rule in relation to mutual business: *ITTOIA 2005, s 321; CTA 2009, s 260*). The transactions or relationships involved in mutual business are treated as if they were transactions or relationships between persons between whom no relationship of mutuality existed. Any surplus or deficit on such a business is regarded as a (taxable) profit or loss of a UK property business. The person in receipt of that profit, ie who is taxable on it, is the person who would be treated as the person entitled to the profit if the business were not a mutual one. This special rule is overridden by *Corporation Tax Act 2010 (CTA 2010), ss 642–648* in respect of co-operative housing associations.

2.36 Unfortunately the draftsman has opted not to define mutual business. It presumably means any type of mutual business. The effect of *ss 321* and *260* is, therefore, to exclude property income from the tax exemption for profits from mutual trading enunciated by the House of Lords in 1887 in *Styles v New York Life Assurance Co (2 TC 460)* to reflect the HMRC view that that decision does not apply to rental income.

2.37 HMRC accept that the use of different materials or building methods reflecting technological advances since the building was erected is still likely to be repairs. Where improvements were carried out prior to 1 April 2001, ESC B4 allowed a deduction in computing property income for the estimated cost of repairs obviated by the improvement or alteration, but this concession has been withdrawn. Some people are concerned that the effect of the withdrawal is to now make such expenditure capital. In some cases it may well do so, but it is probable that the decision in *Conn v Robins Bros Ltd (43 TC 266)* (see **9.9**) will give the same effect in most cases. Indeed it seems likely that ESC B4 was intended to apply the effect of that decision to property income and that it has been withdrawn as it is no longer needed now that such income is calculated using trading income principles. If the original steel frame of a building remains standing and it is reused HMRC accept that the rebuilding is not the replacement of the building (Tax Bulletin 26, December 1996).

2.38 It should be stressed that a UK property business is not a trade. The trading income rules on the computation of profits are simply adopted for quantifying the taxable amount of property income. Therefore the profits of a UK property business are not earned income and so do not become pensionable.

2.39 For income tax purposes a UK property business loss cannot be carried backwards or set against other income. It can only be carried forward against future UK property income. This could cause problems with bad debts. In the past where a debt for unpaid rent proved bad, relief was, in theory at least, given by adjusting the income for the year in which it was receivable. Under the current rules the bad debt is an expense of the year it becomes bad. If that is after the property is sold there may be no future income to set it against with the result that the relief is effectively lost. Curiously, if the taxpayer only owns one letting property he could be in a better position than if he owns several. This is because the disposal of that property will normally give rise to a cessation of the UK property business and *ITTOIA 2005, ss 96–100* or *ITA 2007, s 98(4)* gives relief for post-cessation bad debts against general income of the year in which it proves bad, whereas if the property business continues the bad debt will be an expense which can be relieved only against future income from that business. For corporation tax a UK property business loss can be set against any other income of the same accounting period or carried forward as if it were an expense of management (*CTA 2010, ss 62–64* formerly *ICTA 1998, s 392A*).

2.40 When a property business ceases is a question of fact. It is normally when the taxpayer's last let property is disposed of (or appropriated to a use other than letting). However if at that time he intends to acquire another property the business is likely to continue. If he does not in fact do so the business probably ceases when he abandons that intention. HMRC say that as a general rule of thumb the old business stops and a new one commences where there is an interval of more than three years and different properties are let in the taxpayer's old and new activities. Whist this is no more than guidance they say that the taxpayer would have to provide convincing evidence to show that the same business is carried on if the gap is more than three years (Property Income Manual PIM 2510). The basis for their three-year period is not readily apparent and should be challenged if the cessation results in a disallowance of losses.

2.41 Care sometimes needs to be taken to make clear in what capacity expenditure is incurred. In *Helena Partnerships Ltd (formerly Helena Housing Ltd) v HMRC (2012 STC 1584)* the parties managed to lose corporation tax relief for £104 million of repairs. Helena Housing Ltd is a registered social landlord. It was set up to acquire the housing stock of St Helens Metropolitan Borough Council. The housing required a substantial amount of repairs. This would incur a large amount of VAT, which would be irrecoverable as it related to the generation of VAT exempt rents. Accordingly a scheme was entered into under which the sale contract to Helena would provide for the property to be in a modern state of repair. The council would be obliged under the contract to modernise the stock at its own cost. It would then engage Helena to carry out the work required to meet that obligation. Not only did HMRC approve this scheme but the Office of the Deputy Prime Minister issued a press release praising the scheme as a method of VAT saving. Unfortunately no one considered the corporation tax consequence. This was that Helena carried out the repairs not to repair its houses but to meet its contractual obligation to the council. It was held that it was in reality carrying on two businesses, its rental business and a trade of providing services to the council. The cost of the repairs was an expense of its trading business and the sum that the council had contracted to pay it (which had been treated as a reduction in the acquisition price of the properties) was taxable income of that trade. The two cancelled one another out, but that left the rents received from tenants as taxable income of its rental business. Helena then claimed that the provision of social housing was charitable and accordingly that it was not taxable on its rents, but this was rejected by the FTT. The company, which by then had changed its name to Helena Housing Ltd appealed (unsuccessfully) on that issue only (*2012 STC 1584*), not on the repairs point. Happily the Court of Appeal judgment noted that whilst the company had created a £6 million corporation tax liability, it had saved £18 million in VAT to do so.

Loan Interest Payable

2.42 For income tax purposes loan interest is treated like any other expense up to 2017/18. *ICTA 1988, s 82*, which used to restrict the deduction for interest paid to non-residents in computing trading profits, was specifically excluded from applying to a UK property business and in any event was repealed by *ITTOIA 2005*, so such interest can be deducted. Where a swap, cap or other interest rate hedging contract is taken out the hedging costs will constitute deductions of the UK property business and any hedging gain will be taxable income of that business. Special rules apply after 2017/18. These are considered at **4.8**. The calculation should normally be on an accruals basis (Tax Bulletin 25, October 1996). Where a loan is both for a UK property business and a non-business qualifying purpose, relief obviously cannot be claimed both as a trading expense and as a charge on income. This used to be specifically stated in *FA 1995, Sch 6, para 17* but that provision was repealed by *ITTOIA 2005* for 2005/06 onwards, probably because the layout of *ITTOIA* makes it unnecessary.

2.43 For corporation tax purposes, loan interest is not deducted in calculating the income of a UK property business. Instead it is dealt with under the loan relationship rules. A net debit on loan relationships can be set against a UK property business profit, which normally creates the same overall result as if the interest had been deductible.

Expenditure on Energy-Saving Items (to 5 April 2015 only)

2.44 In computing the profits of a UK property business which includes a dwelling house, a deduction could be claimed for income tax purposes for capital expenditure during the period from 6 April 2004 to 5 April 2015 which was incurred in the provision of a qualifying energy saving item in the dwelling house, namely hot water system installation, draught proofing, solid wall insulation and floor insulation (*ITTOIA 2005, s 312* and *Energy-Saving Items Regulations 2007 (SI 2007 No 831)*). The regulations consolidated earlier ones. Curiously they substituted 'floor insulation' for 'loft insulation' which was in the original 2005 regulations. The Treasury had power by Regulation to add further descriptions of items or to remove or vary items and to impose such conditions as they thought appropriate. They did so in the *Energy-Saving (Deduction for Expenditure etc) Regulations 2004 (SI 2004 No 2664)*. These provided that the maximum deductions that could be claimed in any tax year was £1,500 per building irrespective of the number of dwelling houses contained in the building and irrespective of how many owners have an interest in the building. Where an interest was jointly held, or a number of people owned interests in the same building, the £1,500 limit (and, if necessary, an individual item of expenditure) had to be apportioned on a just and reasonable basis. This relief was broadened by *FA 2007, s 18*, the *Energy-Saving Items Regulations 2007 (SI 2007 No 831)* (which replaced the above regulations) from 6 April 2007 and the *Energy Saving Items (Income Tax) Regulations 2007 (SI 2007 No 3278)* which replaced them. The changes applied the £1,500 limit per dwelling-house in place of per building, so each flat in a block could qualify, and extended the relief to expenditure in a building that contains a dwelling house. The limitation to a single £1,500 where more than one person (who has an interest in the property) incurred expenditure still applied. The £1,500 limit had to be apportioned between them on a just and reasonable basis. This ensured work on the common parts in a block of flats could qualify. The relief could not be claimed if the item qualified for capital allowances. Nor could it be claimed for any expenditure in a building containing a dwelling house insofar as that expenditure was not for the benefit of the dwelling house. It is not wholly clear what this was intended to do. Presumably it was intended to ensure that, whilst expenditure on the common parts of buildings that benefit all of the flats in it qualified for relief, if part of the dwelling was used for non-residential purposes work which was for the benefit of that part only could not qualify. If the taxpayer received a contribution from a third party, that amount had to be excluded in calculating the expenditure eligible for relief. If expenditure was incurred in installing an energy-saving item in more than one dwelling, or in a building containing more than one dwelling, it had to be apportioned on a just and reasonable basis to all of the properties that benefitted from it. The expenditure also had to be apportioned if a dwelling was owned by several people and only one or some of them incurred the expenditure. Most people would think it just to apportion the whole of the expenditure to the person who incurred it but this does not appear to be the intent of the Regulation. At the time the item was installed, the dwelling house could not be in the course of construction and the taxpayer had to have an interest in the property, not be in the course of acquiring his interest or a further interest. The dwelling house could not be let as furnished holiday accommodation and the taxpayer could not claim rent-a-room relief in relation to the property (*ITTOIA 2005, ss 312–314*). If the above qualifying conditions were met in respect of some, but not all, of the expenditure it had to be apportioned on a just and reasonable basis. Expenditure incurred before the UK property business had begun was deductible only if the expenditure was incurred within the six months prior to commencement of the business (*ITTOIA 2005, s 313(5)*). The 2007 Regulations were replaced but not altered, from 6 December 2007 by the *Energy-Saving Items (Income Tax) Regulations 2007 (SI 2007 No 3278)*. These regulations made clear that duplicate relief could not be obtained by more than one person for the same expenditure, by excluding expenditure covered by a contribution from someone else.

2.45 A similar relief (*CTA 2009, ss 251–253*) was introduced for corporation tax by *FA 2007, s 17* and the *Energy-Saving Items (Corporation Tax) Regulations 2008, (SI 2008 No 1520)* but only for expenditure incurred in the period from 9 July 2008 to 31 March 2015. Curiously, the corporation tax regulations included cavity wall insulation and loft insulation even though the corresponding income tax regulations had ceased to do so.

Receipts and Payments on Sale of Land

2.46 For corporation tax purposes, receipts or payments of the purchaser relating to the period prior to the completion must be treated as having been received or paid by the vendor prior to completion. Only the balance of the receipt or payment is, of course, then treated as received by or paid to the actual recipient or payer (*CTA 2009, s 258*). *ICTA 1988, s 40(1)(2)* provided that where receipts or outgoings of the vendor are apportioned between the parties on a sale of land, the part attributable to the period falling after completion was similarly treated as being received or paid, as the case may be, by the purchaser immediately after the completion. This has not been re-enacted in

CTA 2009, probably because the revised wording makes it unnecessary to state it. Up to 2004/05 this provision also applied for income tax purpose, but was repealed by *ITTOIA 2005* in relation to income tax, presumably being felt to be so obvious that a specific provision is not required.

2.47 For both income tax and corporation tax, the amount apportioned to the vendor is treated as the same nature as the payment of the expense by the purchaser, ie it is regarded as an income payment by the vendor not capital (*ITTOIA 2005, s 320*; *CTA 2009, s 259*).

Alternative Accommodation

2.48 Where a person lets his own private residence, the cost of providing alternative accommodation for himself cannot, of course, be deducted (*Wylie v Eccott (6 TC 128)*; *Smith v Irvine (27 TC 381)*).

Capital Allowances/Wear and Tear Allowance

Machinery and Plant

2.49 Capital allowances can be claimed for machinery and plant used by a person entitled to rent or other receipts of a UK property business for the maintenance, repair or management of premises in respect of which the rent, etc. arises. This is achieved by treating the person's UK property business as a qualifying activity (*CAA 2001, s 15(1)(b)*). In the case of furnished holiday accommodation, the part of the UK property business (or deemed business) that consists of the commercial letting of such accommodation is treated for capital allowances as a separate trade, ie a second pool of plant and machinery in relation to such accommodation must be kept separate from the main UK property business pool (*CAA 2001, ss 15(1)(a), 249(1)*). Allowances can also be claimed for plant and machinery incorporated in the building itself only in relation to furnished holiday accommodation. These are considered at **10.17** onwards below.

2.50 Capital allowances on plant or machinery are not claimable in other buildings used for either furnished or unfurnished lettings of residential property (*CAA 2001, s 35*). Instead, for furnished lettings, an annual wear-and-tear allowance of 10% of the 'relevant rental amount' (see below) could be claimed up to 2015/16 (31 March 2016 for companies). An election to claim such an allowance had to be made by 31 January following the end of the tax year (two years after the end of the accounting period for corporation tax (*ITTOIA 2005, ss 308A, 308C(3); CTA 2009, ss 248A, 248E(3)*, both inserted by *Enactment of Extra-Statutory Concessions Order 2011; SI 2011/1037, Art 11*). The election could be made only if the dwelling-house contained sufficient furniture, furnishings and equipment for normal residential use and the taxpayer was responsible for that state of affairs. He was so responsible if he provided any of the furniture. In the case of a leasehold interest the lessee could claim only if a superior landlord was not eligible to claim a wear-and-tear allowance (*ITTOIA 2005, s 308B; CTA 2009, s 248B*). Where a wear-and-tear election was made, no deduction could be claimed for expenses on replacing or altering any tool or providing furniture, so far as it was attributable to the dwelling-house (*ITTOIA 2005, s 308C(1)(2); CTA 2009, s 248C(1)(2)*). The relevant rental amount was the rent and any other taxable receipts in respect of the dwelling-house, less deductible expenses (in relation to utilities, council tax or anything else the cost of which is normally borne by the lessee) that was attributable to the dwelling-house (*ITTOIA 2005, s 308C(4)–(6); CTA 2009, s 248C(4)–(6)*). The relief could not be claimed for furnished holiday lettings but capital allowances could be claimed for such a letting (see **2.122**) (*ITTOIA 2005, s 327(2)(c); CTA 2009, s 269(2)(3)* both inserted by *Enactment of Extra-Statutory Concession Order 2011, Art 11*). HMRC previously allowed relief for replacement of furniture, etc on a renewals basis in place of the 10% deduction but this concession was withdrawn from 6 April 2013 (HMRC Notice 7 December 2011). HMRC said that, in addition to the 10% allowance, a taxpayer could also deduct the net cost, ie less any sale proceeds for the old item, of renewing or repairing fixtures that were an integral part of the buildings, ie those that are not normally removed by either tenant or owner if the property is vacated or sold, eg baths, washbasins, toilets, central heating installations. They regarded expenditure on renewing such items as a revenue repair to the building. A taxpayer could not deduct the original cost of installing such fixtures or the extra cost of replacing a fixture with an improved version (Property Income Manual, para PIM 3010). A deduction for such replacements could also be claimed for unfurnished lettings, but no other capital allowances were due on such lettings. This 10% allowance applied only up to 2015/16 (31 March 2016 for companies) (*FA 2016, s 74(1)–(4)*). Where a company accounting period straddles 1 April, the parts falling before and after that date are treated as separate accounting periods for this purpose. The profits are apportioned between those periods on a time basis except where that would produce an unjust or unreasonable split, when a just and reasonable split must be used instead (*FA 2016, s 74(5)*). From 6 April 2016 a deduction is instead given for the cost for replacing fittings (see **2.35**).

2.51 For 2016/17 onwards (from 1 April 2016 for corporation tax) a deduction is allowed for expenditure incurred after 5 April 2016 (or 1 April 2016) on the replacement of domestic items in a dwelling-house if:

(*a*) the taxpayer carries on a property business in relation to land which consists of or includes the dwelling-house;

(*b*) a domestic item has been provided for use in the dwelling-house, the taxpayer incurs expenditure on replacing it, the new item is provided solely for the use of the lessee, and following the replacement the old item is no longer available for use in the dwelling-house;

(*c*) the only reason the expenditure is not deductible is that it is capital expenditure; and

(*d*) capital allowances are not claimable on the expenditure (in accordance with *ITTOIA 2005, ss 33 and 272* where the accruals basis is used or *s 307B* where a cash basis is adopted).

(*ITTOIA 2005, s 311A(1)–(6)*; *CTA 2009, s 250A(1)–(6),* inserted by *FA 2016, s 73* and amended by *F(No 2)A 2017, Sch 2, para 24*).

2.52 This deduction does not apply if the property business consists of or includes the commercial letting of furnished holiday accommodation (see **2.131**) and the dwelling-house constitutes some or all of that accommodation (*ITTOIA 2005, s 31A(7)*; *CTA 2009, s 250A(7)*). Nor does it apply if the person claims rent-a-room relief (see **2.116**) in relation to the dwelling-house in the same year (*ITTOIA 2005, s 311A(8)*).

2.53 For the purpose of **2.51**, where the new item is the same or substantially the same as the old, the whole of the expenditure on the new item can be deducted. In any other case the deduction is limited to what the taxpayer would have incurred had he replaced the old item by one the same or substantially the same (*ITTOIA 2005, s 311A(3)(d)*; *CTA 2009, s 250A(8)*). It is unclear how HMRC will seek to apply this in practice. It is probably not possible to find a washing machine substantially the same as one purchased eight years previously, as such items are generally improved and redesigned every year. If the taxpayer has to incur capital expenditure in connection with the disposal of the old item or the purchase of the new, eg the washing machine needs to be plumbed in, the deduction is increased by that incidental expenditure (*ITTOIA 2005, s 311A(10)*; *CTA 2009, s 250A(9)*). If the old item is disposed of in part-exchange for the new, it is only the cash element that is deductible. If the old item is disposed of in any other manner, the deduction is reduced by the amount or value of any consideration in money or money's worth that the taxpayer (or a connected person) receives, or is entitled to receive, in respect of it. If the old item is disposed of together with something else, the amount received is reduced by the value of that other thing (*ITTOIA 2005, s 311A(11)–(13)*; *CTA 2009, s 250A(10)–12)*).

2.54 For the purpose of these provisions a domestic item means an item for domestic use, such as furniture, furnishings, household appliances and kitchenware, but does not include anything which is a fixture, ie plant and machinery that is fixed in or to a dwelling-house so as to become in law part of that house, but including any boiler or water-filled radiator, whether or not so fixed, that is installed in the house as part of a space or water-heating system. A lessee means the person who is entitled to the use of the dwelling-house under a lease or any other arrangement under which a sum is payable in respect of the use of the house (*ITTOIA 2005, s 311A(14), (15)*; *CTA 2009, s 250A(13), (14)*). Read literally, nothing can ever qualify for a deduction if the lessee occupies the house with his family as the new item will not be provided solely for the use of the lessee; both parties will also envisage its use by his whole family. It should particularly be noted that the old item must no longer be available for use in the dwelling-house. The taxpayer may need to remove it from the property to ensure that the tenant cannot find an alternative use for it. There is nothing to stop it being used in another house owned by the landlord and subsequently being replaced again. There is no requirement to bring in a value of the old item if it is not disposed of for consideration in money or money's worth.

2.55 Capital allowances are normally treated as an expense in calculating the profits of the UK property business in the same way as with a trade *(CAA 2001, s 15)*. This is achieved by deeming that business for capital allowance purposes to be a trade.

Sea Walls

2.56 If the owner or tenant of any premises incurs expenditure (or if he is on a cash basis pays the expenditure) on making a sea wall or other embankment necessary to protect the premises against encroachment of the sea or of any tidal river he can treat one twenty-first of that expenditure as an allowable deduction from the rent for those premises for that and the next 20 years of assessment (*ITTOIA 2005, s 315 as amended by F(No 2)A 2017, Sch 2, para 25*; *CTA 2009, s 254*). Obviously a deduction cannot be claimed under this provision if capital allowances have been claimed for the expenditure under some other provision. If the whole of the taxpayer's interest in the premises is subsequently transferred (by operation of law or otherwise) to any other person, eg on a sale, the transferee takes over the entitlement to the deduction for future years. In the year of transfer it must be apportioned between the two in such manner as may be just. If part of the taxpayer's interest is transferred the transferee becomes entitled to such part of the deduction as is properly referable to that part of the premises (*ITTOIA 2005, s 316*; *CTA 2009, s 255*). If the expenditure was incurred by the tenant his interest will be deemed to have been transferred on the expiry of his lease:

(*a*) to any incoming lessee, if he makes a payment to the outgoing lessee in respect of the sea wall; or

(*b*) to his immediate landlord in any other case.

(ITTOIA 2005, s 317; CTA 2009, s 256.)

2.57 It is not clear what happens if the tenant is granted a new lease of the same premises on the expiry of his original lease. Although illogical, it appears that the right to the allowance will automatically devolve on the landlord as the tenant probably cannot make a payment to himself to bring himself within (*a*).

2.58 In the case of a company the allowances must be calculated for a year of assessment and apportioned between the accounting periods falling wholly or partly into that year (*CTA 2009, s 354(*5)).

2.59 A person who acquires a property with the benefit of a sea wall, etc. needs to enquire from the vendor whether any expenditure has been incurred in the previous 21 years which gave rise to a deduction under this provision as the benefit of these can pass to the purchaser.

Change of Accounting Basis

2.60 If a person carrying on a UK property business changes the way in which profits of the business are calculated for income tax purposes, the old basis was in accordance with the law or practice applicable to the period before the change, and the new basis accords with that for periods of account after the change, an amount by way of adjustment must be calculated. If this amount is positive, it is taxable as income; if it is negative, it is deductible in calculating the profits from the property business. The adjustment is treated as arising on the last day of the first period of account for which the new basis applies (except where it affects the calculation of any amount brought into account in respect of depreciation, when it is treated as arising only when the asset concerned is realised or written off). The detailed rules in *ITTOIA 2005, ss 227(3)–(6)* and *s 231* (adjustment income of trades) apply to calculate such income (*ITTOIA 2005, ss 329–334*).

2.61 Where the cash basis is used, *ITTOIA 2005, ss 239A* (spreading on leaving cash basis) and *s 239B* (election to accelerate change under *s 239A*) which apply to adjustment income of trades also apply to adjustment income of a property business (*ITTOIA 2005, s 334A* inserted by *F (No 2) A 2017, Sch 2, para 29*).

2.62 If a person carrying on a property business enters the cash basis for a year, ie his profits are calculated on a cash basis in the current year but on an accruals basis in the previous year and he would (apart from *CAA 2001, s 59(4A)*) have unrelieved qualifying expenditure for capital allowances purposes (see *CAA 2001, s 59(1)(2)*) relating to a relevant property business activity to carry forward from the previous tax year, a deduction is allowed in the current year for any cash basis deductible amount of the expenditure relating to each relevant property business activity (*ITTOIA 2005, ss 334B,*

334C(1)(3)). A cash basis deductible amount is any amount of the expenditure for which a deduction would be allowed in calculating the profits of the property business on a cash basis on the assumption that the expenditure was paid in the current tax year. The amount must be determined on such basis as is just and reasonable in all the circumstances (*ITTOIA 2005, s 334C(4)(5)*). For this purpose a relevant property business activity is an ordinary UK property business and a UK furnished holiday lettings business (as defined in *CAA 2001, ss 16, 17*) or an ordinary overseas property business and an EEA furnished holiday letting business (as defined in *CAA 2001, ss 17A* and *17B*) (*ITTOIA 2005, s 334C(6)*).

2.63 If at the time the taxpayer enters the cash basis for a tax year not all of the relevant capital allowance expenditure in earlier years has actually been paid for, this does not apply. Instead if the amount of the relevant expenditure that the person has actually paid exceeds the capital allowances given in respect of the expenditure, the difference must be deducted in calculating the profits for the current year. If the amount paid is less than the capital allowances given, the difference must be treated as property business income of the current year (*ITTOIA 2005, s 334D(1)(3)(4)*). Relevant expenditure for this purpose is expenditure on plant and machinery for which a deduction would be allowed in calculating cash basis profits (on the assumption that the expenditure was paid in the current tax year) and for which capital allowances have been claimed (*ITTOIA 2005, s 334D(2)*). Any question as to whether and to what extent expenditure is relevant expenditure must be determined on such basis as is just and reasonable in all the circumstances (*ITTOIA 2005, s 334D(5)*). If the amount of capital allowances given has been reduced under *CAA 2001, ss 205* or *207* (reduction where asset provided or used only partly for qualifying activity) the amount that the taxpayer has actually paid must be proportionately reduced (*ITTOIA 2005, s 334D(6)*).

2.64 If a taxpayer who enters the cash basis for a tax year is the successors (within *CAA 2001, s 266*) to another person who previously carried on the business and (as a result of an election under *s 266*) relevant plant or machinery is treated as sold by the predecessor to the successor at some time during the tax year, these provisions have effect in relation to the successor as if everything done to or by the predecessor had been done to or by the successor (and any expenditure actually incurred by the successor on acquiring the relevant plant or machinery is to be ignored for the purposes of calculating the profits of the property business for the tax year) (*ITTOIA 2005, s 334E*).

Charge to Tax on Post-cessation Receipts

2.65 Post-cessation receipts arising from a UK property business are chargeable to income tax so far as they are not otherwise chargeable to income tax or corporation tax. Tax is charged on the full amount of the receipts (subject to *ss 245, 255* and *257*, but as if *s 254(2A)* provided that, if the time immediately before the person permanently ceases to carry on the UK property business falls in a cash basis tax year, it must be assumed that the profits of the business are calculated on the cash basis) (*ITTOIA 2005, ss 349–351* as amended by *F (No 2) A 2017, Sch 2, para 30*). A post-cessation receipt is a sum received after the taxpayer permanently ceases to carry on a UK property business and which arises from the carrying on of the business before the cessation. If a partner in a firm ceases to be a partner but the partnership continues, the partner who leaves is treated as having ceased permanently to carry on the business for this purpose. If the time immediately before a person permanently ceases to carry on a UK property business falls in a cash-basis tax year (one for which the profits are calculated on the cash basis), a sum is to be treated as a post-cessation receipt only if it would have been part of the income of the property business had it been received at that time (*ITTOIA 2005, s 353* as amended by *F (No 2) A 2017, Sch 2, para 31*). *ITTOIA 2005, ss 82(6), 104(3), 109(2), 248, 249* and *250* (which deal with post-cessation receipts of a trade) apply also to a UK property business (*ITTOIA 2005, s 354(2)*).

2.66 If a person permanently ceases to carry on a UK property business and transfers to another person for value the right to receive sums arising from the transferor's UK property business, and the transferee does not subsequently carry on the transferred business, the transferor is treated as receiving a post-cessation receipt equal to the amount or value of the consideration if the transfer was at arm's length, or the value of the rights transferred as between parties at arm's length if it was not (*ITTOIA 2005, s 355*). Consideration received after the cessation of the property business is not a post-cessation receipt though (*ITTOIA 2005, s 355(4)*).

The Property Allowance

2.67 For 2017/18, an individual is entitled to a property allowance of £1,000 pa (*ITTOIA 2005, s 783BD(1)* inserted by *F (No 2) A 2017, Sch 3*). The Treasury have power by regulation to increase this figure (*ITTOIA 2005, s 783BD(2)*).

2.68 The individual qualifies for full relief for a tax year if his 'relevant property income' does not exceed the £1,000 property allowance for that year. Where this applies, the relievable receipts of the property business and any expenses associated with these receipts are not brought into account in calculating the income from his relevant property business (or businesses if he has more than one) (*ITTOIA 2005, ss 783BE, 783BF*). An individual's 'relevant property income' for a tax year is the relievable receipts for the tax year of the individual's relevant property business, ie the gross income not the profit (*ITTOIA 2005, s 783BC*).

2.69 If the relevant property income exceeds the £1,000 property allowance, the individual can elect for partial relief. Such an election must be made on or before the first anniversary of the normal self-assessment filing date for the tax year to which it relates (*ITTOIA 2005, s 783BK*). He can then deduct the property allowance from the income instead of deducting any 'relevant expenses', ie partial relief applies only to the extent that the deductible expenses of the property business (or businesses together) are below the £1,000 property allowance (*ITTOIA 2005, ss 783BG, 783BH*). The relevant expenses are all of the amounts to be brought into account as a deduction in calculating the profits of the property business for the tax year which are associated with the relevant receipts (*ITTOIA 2005, s 783BH(6)*). If the taxpayer has two or more property businesses, he can decide how he allocates the allowance between the businesses but cannot do so in such a way as to create a loss in one of the businesses and a profit in the other (*ITTOIA 2005, s 783BI*). As the relief results in the disallowance of all the expenses of all of the businesses, it is difficult to envisage many circumstances in which such an allocation will be necessary. The only obvious one is if one of the businesses has brought forward losses; the taxpayer may prefer to forfeit relief for the current year expenses of that business in order to utilise the losses, so would want to allocate as much of the £1,000 to his other property business as will eliminate the profits of that business.

2.70 An individual who is entitled to full relief can elect for it not to be given. Such an election must be made by the first anniversary of the normal self-assessment filing date for the year for which it is made (*ITTOIA 2005, s 783BJ*). It is difficult to envisage why a person should make such an election.

2.71 No property allowance will be given if in calculating the individual's liability to income tax for the tax year a tax reduction under *ITTOIA 2005, s 274A* (property business: relief for non-deductible costs of a dwelling-related loan – see **4.8**) is applied at Step 6 of the calculation in *ITA 2007, s 23* (tax reductions to which the taxpayer is entitled for the tax year) (*ITTOIA 2005, s 783BL*). This means that no property allowance is available if the individual is claiming relief for mortgage interest on a residential property.

2.72 Also no property allowance is given if rent-a-room relief is claimed for the tax year and either the rents exceed the £7,500 limit and the individual has not elected to apply the alternative method of calculating taxable profits (by not claiming expenses – see **2.122**) or the individual has elected for the rent-a-room relief not to apply (see **2.121**) ie, the property allowance cannot be used to top-up the rent-a-room allowance so as to give indirect relief for expenses (*ITTOIA 2005, s 783BM*).

2.73 The property allowance also does not apply if the individual's relevant property income includes either:

(a) a payment made by or on behalf of a person who is his employer or the employer of his spouse or civil partner,

(b) a payment made by or on behalf of a firm of which the individual is a partner or is connected with a partner, or

(c) a payment made by or on behalf of a close company in which the individual is a participator or an associate of a participator (as defined in *CTA 2010, ss 448* and *454*).

(*ITTOIA 2005, ss 783BN, 783BO, 783BP.*)

2.74 For the purpose of the property allowance, an individual's business is a 'relevant property business' if it is not a rent-a-room property business (one in which all of the receipts of the property business are rent-a-room receipts) in relation to the individual in the tax year (*ITTOIA 2005, s 783BA(1)(2)*). If an individual receives property income distributions from a property AIF (Alternative Investment Fund) or a REIT (see **7.38**) which are treated as profits of separate property business, that business is not a relevant property business (*ITTOIA 2005, s 783BA(3)(4)*).

2.75 The 'relievable receipts' of an individual's relevant property business for a tax year are the whole of the amounts brought into account as a receipt in calculating the profits of the business for the tax year, other than

(a) rent-a-room receipts, and

(b) non-relievable balancing charges, ie balancing charges under *CAA 2001*, which do not relate to a business or transaction which is carried on (or entered into),for the purpose of generating receipts which are relievable receipts of the property business.

(*ITTOIA 2005, s 783BB.*)

Income Tax UK Property Business Losses

2.76 An income tax UK property business loss is carried forward against any future income from that business (*ITA 2007, ss 118–123*). It cannot be set against income from other sources with the exception that a rental loss by a builder from a property held as trading stock can by concession be allowed as a trading expense instead of being carried forward as a UK property business loss (Business Income Manual, 51555). Where a taxpayer has only one letting property it may be difficult to determine when his UK property business ceases so that the losses cease to be relievable. It is probable that the sale of that property does not itself create a cessation provided that there is an intention to acquire further letting properties. On the other hand *ITTOIA 2005, s 264* states that 'a person's UK property business consists of every business which the person carries on for generating income from land in the UK' (and *ICTA 1988, s 15(1)* similarly stated that 'all the businesses and transactions carried on … by any particular person … so far as they are businesses or transactions the profits or gains of which are chargeable to tax under [Schedule A], are to be treated … as … a single business'). This appears to deem a person to have one single UK property business lasting throughout his entire life, irrespective of whether or not he owns property at any particular time. Such an interpretation would however render the specific incorporation of the rules on post-cessation income and expenses applicable only in rare circumstances which may induce the courts to refrain from a literal interpretation of *s 264*). HMRC's views on *ITTOIA 2005, s 9(2)* (and the corresponding corporation tax rule in *CTA 2009, s 36(2)*) (all farming in the UK treated as a single trade), a similar provision, may also apply here (see **23.9**). They consider that a significant gap in the activities brings the deemed trade to an end.

2.77 Where the UK property business includes an agricultural estate (see **2.47**) allowable expenses of which have been deducted in arriving at the loss, part of the UK property business loss can be set against any income of the taxpayer for the same or the next tax year (*ITA 2007, s 120*). The relevant part is the lower of the UK property business loss, the allowable agricultural expenses plus capital allowances (less balancing charges) or the taxpayer's 'relievable income' for the year (*ITA 2007 ss 118–124*). This relief must be claimed within 12 months of 31 January after the end of the year of loss, ie within approximately 22 months of the end of the tax year (*ITA 2007, ss 118–122*).

2.78 The allowable agricultural expenses are the disbursements or expenses attributable to the agricultural estate which are deductible in respect of maintenance, repairs, insurance or management of the estate, but excluding any loan interest (*ITA 2007, s 123(5)*). This will not necessarily include all the expenses in relation to the estate which are deductible in arriving at the loss. For example, rent of the land does not fall into either of the four heads specified but is an expense of the UK property business. Any allowable expenses attributable solely to part of the estate not used for the purposes of husbandry must also be excluded, as must be the non-husbandry part of expenses incurred partly for the agricultural part of the estate and partly for the non-agricultural part (*ITA 2007, s 123(6)(7)*).

2.79 An agricultural estate means land, including buildings, managed as one estate and including any land, houses or other buildings in the UK occupied wholly or mainly for the purposes of husbandry (*ITA 2007, s 123(4)*).

The relief can also be claimed if there are no allowable agricultural expenses but net capital allowances, ie less balancing charges (*ITA 2007, s 120*).

2.80 A loss cannot be set against other income if it arises directly or indirectly in consequence of (or in connection with) relevant tax avoidance arrangements entered into after 23 March 2010 (*ITA 2007, s 127A(1)(2)* inserted by *FA 2010, s 25*). These are arrangements (including any agreement or understanding, scheme, transaction or series of transactions whether or not legally enforceable) to which the taxpayer is a party and one of the main purposes of which is being in a position to make use of an annual investment allowance in reducing his tax liability by setting a property loss against general income (*ITA 2007, s 127A(4)(5)*). A loss must be attributed to an annual investment allowance as far as possible and once that has been exhausted to other capital allowance (*ITA 2007, s 127A(3)*). Similarly a loss attributable to agricultural expenses cannot be set against general income (to the extent of those expenses) if it arises directly or indirectly in consequence of (or in connection with) relevant tax avoidance arrangements (as defined above but by reference to allowable agricultural expenses) made after 12 March 2012 (*ITA 2007, s 127B* inserted by *FA 2012, s 10*).

2.81 A person's relievable income is his total income for the year after deducting UK property business losses brought forward (to the extent of the UK property business income) and after deducting relief under *s 379A(3)* for the balance of the previous year's loss (*ITA 2007, s 121(2)(3)*).

UK Property Business Losses of Companies

2.82 A UK property business loss of a company can be set against total profits of the accounting period (*CTA 2010, s 62*). It can also be surrendered to another group company under the group relief rules (*CTA 2010, s 99*). Alternatively, the loss can be carried forward and treated as a UK property business loss in the next accounting period (*CTA 2010, s 62*) but it cannot be surrendered as group relief in that later period (*CTA 2010, s 102*).

2.83 By concession a rental loss suffered by a builder from a property held as trading stock can be allowed as a trading expense instead of being carried forward as a UK property business loss (Business Income Manual, 51555).

2.84 If an investment company ceases to carry on its UK property business while remaining an investment company any unrelieved UK property business loss is not lost; it is carried forward as if it were a management expense (*CTA 2010, s 63*).

2.85 Except where the UK property business is carried on in the exercise of a statutory function paras **2.72** and **2.74** above do not apply to the extent (if any) that the UK property business is not carried on on a commercial basis. For this purpose a business (or part of a business) is carried on on a commercial basis if it is carried on either with a view to making a profit or so as to afford a reasonable expectation of profit. If there is a change in the manner in which the business (or part) is carried on, it is treated as being carried on throughout the accounting period of change in the way in which it is being carried on at the end of that accounting period (*CTA 2010, ss 64, 67*). It is not clear what happens in such a case. It appears that the loss cannot be carried forward at all. This contrasts with a trading loss incurred in such circumstances which can be carried forward against future profits from the trade under *ITA 2007, ss 77–79.*

2.86 If there is a change in the ownership of a company carrying on a UK property business to which any of *CTA 2010, ss 673, 676, 677–691* or *692–701* applies (broadly speaking, there is a major change in the nature or conduct of the business, or it is revived after the scale of the business has become negligible), a UK property business loss arising before the change of ownership cannot be carried forward to an accounting period beginning after the change in ownership. For this purpose the accounting period in which the change takes place is split into two, the second starting immediately after the change in ownership (*CTA 2010, ss 685, 702*).

2.87 A corporation tax property business loss is one of the categories of losses that HMRC has power to counteract under *F (No 2) A 2017, s 19* where a loss-related tax advantage would otherwise arise from relevant tax arrangements. Arrangements are relevant tax arrangements for this purpose if either–

(a) the purpose (or one of the main purposes) of the arrangements is to obtain a loss-related tax advantage, and

(b) it is reasonable to regard the arrangements as circumventing the intended limits of relief under the relevant provision or otherwise exploit shortcomings in the relevant provisions

(F (No 2) A 2017, s 19(3)–(5).)

In determining whether or not condition (*b*) is met, all the relevant circumstances must be taken into account, including whether the arrangements include any steps that are contrived or abnormal or lack a genuine commercial purpose (*F (No 2) A 2017, s 19(6)*). A tax-related advantage is a tax advantage as a result of a deduction (or increased deduction) under a provision mentioned in *s 19(8)* (such as *CTA 2010, s 62(3)* (losses of a UK property business) (*F (No 2) A 2017, s 19(7)*).

Non-Residents

2.88 A special scheme for rents payable to non-residents (called below the Non-Resident Landlords Scheme) was introduced to fit in with self-assessment for individuals. *ITA 2007, s 972* contains the enabling legislation for the new scheme and this is filled out by the *Taxation of Income from Land (Non-Residents) Regulations 1995 (SI 1995 No 2902)*. There are two options, to suffer tax by deduction at source or to opt into self-assessment. For the purpose of the Non-Resident Landlords Scheme an individual is non-resident if his usual place of abode is outside the UK. A trust or company is non-resident if it is managed and controlled outside the UK. A non-UK resident company is chargeable to income tax not corporation tax (except in relation to UK trading income and income ancillary to such trading income). It must therefore compute its taxable income in accordance with the income tax rules.

Deduction of Tax at Source

2.89 In the absence of any action by the landlord, the tenant or, if he pays his rent to a UK agent, that agent (or if there are several UK agents the last in the chain), must deduct tax at source from the rent at the 20% basic rate of income tax and account for it quarterly to HMRC, irrespective of whether the rent has been paid over to the landlord in that quarter. Payment into the landlord's UK account is not payment to an agent so the depositor has the obligation to deduct. A tenant is relieved of the obligation to account for tax where there is no agent if the gross rent is at the rate of £5,200 pa or less (*reg 3(5)*). He may need to take care as HMRC have said that there will be an obligation to account for tax if the rent is £100 per week and there are 53 rent days in the tax year (Taxline, March 1996, p 4). The deduction is based on the gross rents less specified expenses. Specified expenses means any amount paid in the quarter either by the tenant (or agent) or by another person at his direction that he can reasonably be satisfied are deductible under the UK property business rules (*reg 9*).

2.90 If the payer does not deduct tax when he should, HMRC nevertheless requires him to account to them for the sum that ought to have been deducted. It may not always be possible to recover the amount subsequently from the landlord. Great care needs to be taken where the tenant knows or suspects that the landlord's usual place of abode is outside the UK. However, HMRC have confirmed that the tenant would not be held liable for deducting tax at source if the landlord moves his usual place of abode outside the UK and the tenant is unaware that the move has taken place. In those circumstances HMRC could still assess the non-resident landlord. As the property is in the UK HMRC can readily enforce payment by obtaining judgment against the landlord and, if this is not complied with, instituting bankruptcy proceedings.

2.91 From the landlord's point of view the deduction of income tax creates a number of problems. Deduction at source is based on rents received by the agent (or paid by the tenant) whereas the landlord's UK property business liability is calculable on an accruals basis. Mortgage interest is rarely paid by the agent or at his direction. In the case of residential property it is normally paid direct by the landlord and with commercial property the agent is normally instructed to pay the rents into the landlord's bank account with the lender, against which the lender debits the interest by arrangement with the landlord. In either case it is unlikely to be a specified expense. Capital allowances on plant in a building, and in the case of furnished lettings up to 2015/16 the 10% wear and tear allowance, are also not specified expenses. It is notoriously difficult with repairs and some other types of expense to determine the extent to which they qualify as a UK property business deduction or are disallowable as capital. An agent or tenant is likely to be very cautious and give the benefit of any doubt to HMRC. He will be liable for a penalty if he takes into account something that HMRC think he ought not to have been reasonably satisfied was deductible. Accordingly deduction at source is likely to result in payment of excessive tax – and the need for the landlord to file a self-assessment return to reclaim the over-deduction. If the landlord is an individual, a possible advantage of deduction at source is that it is limited to basic rate tax; in practice, HMRC are likely to accept the deduction as satisfying the landlord's tax liability.

Self-Assessment

2.92 The alternative of opting in to self-assessment requires the consent of HMRC. This will not be given unless the non-resident has a satisfactory tax history, ie for a non-resident who wants to self-assess for 2016/17 onwards he has filed his tax return/accounts and paid the tax for all years up to 2014/15. A non-resident is automatically assumed to have a satisfactory tax history in the first year in which he invests in UK property. An application to self-assess needs to be made to HMRC as early as possible – for new purchases preferably well before completion. This is because the tenant or agent must deduct tax until he has been notified by HMRC not to do so. The application form must be completed by the landlord; it cannot be signed by the agent on his behalf. Permission to self-assess will be withdrawn if the non-resident incurs a tax surcharge or if he is tardy in supplying information to HMRC. Once it has been withdrawn, the non-resident will have to wait two years before being again allowed to self-assess.

2.93 Agents for a non-resident have to register with HMRC's Charities, Savings & International, Operations SO708, PO Box 203, BOOTLE L69 9AP), irrespective of whether they deduct tax at source or all their clients self-assess. The relevant application form can be downloaded from the HMRC website. Agents have to make a quarterly return of tax due (on a global basis) and a detailed annual return. They are also subject to audit by HMRC.

Service Charges

2.94 There is no special tax regime applying to service charges, or to sinking or reserve funds set up under service charge arrangements. The tax position will depend on identifying and applying the legal effect of the provisions of each individual lease, although in practice HMRC seem content to treat the amount as rent irrespective of its legal status (see **2.93**).

2.95 There are four main possibilities, although almost every lease is different, and the correct approach is not to try to ascertain into which of these categories the particular lease most nearly falls, but rather to identify the legal effect of that particular lease. The main possibilities are:

(*a*) the service charge is paid as additional rent;

(*b*) the service charge (including any reserve fund element) is paid under a covenant in the lease to reimburse to the landlord expenditure incurred by him;

(*c*) the service charge is payable to the landlord but the reserve fund element is payable to a trustee (who may be – and normally is – the landlord himself); and

(*d*) a separate management company takes on responsibility for maintaining the building and receives the service charge direct from the tenant.

2.96 The position is further complicated by *s 42* of the *Landlord and Tenant Act 1987,* which requires service charge monies to be held on trust for the tenants in the case of most, but not all, residential properties. *Section 42* overrides a provision in the lease in relation to such monies. Worse, it is not clear from the statute precisely what the terms of that statutory trust are (see **2.100**). Accordingly, the tax treatment of interest arising from the investment of such funds is likely to be different from that suggested by the terms of the lease.

2.97 Major tax problems are unlikely to occur in relation to service charges which merely recoup actual expenditure. The problems arise where a sinking or reserve fund is being built up. The VAT position can also be complex. This is considered at **16.165** onwards.

Additional Rent

2.98 Where the service charge is receivable as additional rent the receipt is clearly taxable as UK property business income in the same way as the basic rent and the landlord can deduct the actual expenditure to the extent that he can bring it within the UK property business rules (see **2.11** above). The effect will be to tax the landlord on money he receives in respect of contributions to a reserve fund or in respect of capital expenditure (as the definition of repairs under most service charge clauses will often include items that constitute improvements for tax purposes). Care may sometimes need to be taken to match receipts and payments where the service charge year is different from the landlord's accounting period – although it would be rare for any excess of service charge expenditure over service charge income falling in an accounting period to be so large as to exceed the total rents. If, although a landlord receives the service charge as additional rent, he is obliged by the lease to set aside the reserve fund element, this will in effect require him to appropriate his own (taxed) money for this purpose. If the reserve fund is required to be invested in such a case, the investment income will be income of the landlord and the tax payable on it will therefore be dependent on his tax position.

Under Covenant

2.99 Where the service charge is receivable under a covenant in the lease it is probably strictly assessable either as trading income or possibly as miscellaneous income. In practice the receipt is likely to be assessed as income of the UK property business although it does not strictly arise to the landlord 'by virtue of his ownership of an estate or interest in land'; it arises by virtue of the obligation to provide services that he has entered into. As a miscellaneous income loss cannot be carried back and cannot be set against non-miscellaneous income – such as rents – any attempt to assess as miscellaneous income needs to be resisted. The rules for losses on miscellaneous income are contained in *ITA 2007, ss 152–155* and *1016*.

Payable to a Trustee

2.100 If the reserve fund element of the service charge is payable by the tenant to a trustee the trust is a separate taxable entity, albeit that the sole trustee is normally the landlord, so the tax treatment of neither the contributions nor the income generated from their investment will be affected by the landlord's own tax position. As the trust will receive the sinking fund contributions as capital they would not themselves attract a tax charge. Income generated by the investment of the funds will belong to the trust and will be taxable. The tax rate depends on the form of the trust – which is not always readily apparent, ie is it a discretionary trust or an interest in possession trust? The rate on a discretionary trust is now 45%. With an interest in possession trust the trustees are taxable at the basic rate but each of the tenants will need to declare his share of the interest on his tax return. In the past HMRC were known to claim that the trust was an 'unincorporated association' and as such liable to corporation tax. As a trust is an entity recognised in law it is difficult to see how they could have substantiated such a claim It is interesting to note that in their 1991 consultative document on trusts HMRC stated (at 14.62):

> 'Any income and gains from the investment of the service charges are taxed under the normal trust rules. Often … liability is at the sum of the basic and additional rates because the trustees have the power to accumulate any income which is not needed to meet current expenditure or have some discretion as to how the fund income should be used.'

Different considerations may apply to service charges in residential property (see **2.73** onwards).

2.101 It also needs to be borne in mind that trusts have Inheritance Tax ('IHT') consequences and there is no exception in the IHT legislation for trusts set up under leases. There is probably no problem when money is paid into the trust as the tenant is fulfilling a contractual obligation and has no gratuitous intent to benefit anyone other than himself. If the trust is an interest in possession trust there will be a potential liability to IHT when the tenant disposes of his lease. This will bring about a cessation of his interest in possession, which will generate IHT on the difference between the disposal proceeds of the interest and the underlying value of the assets in the settlement attributable to that interest. The problem can be solved by the tenant attributing the appropriate proportion of the selling price to his interest in the reserve fund and reducing the amount attributable to his lease – although this may be unattractive to the purchaser from a CGT viewpoint. As the IHT is a liability of the trustees, and is thus in effect borne by the remaining tenants, consideration needs to be given to requiring the tenant, as a condition of giving him a licence to assign his lease, to reimburse any IHT payable.

2.102 If the trust was set up after 22 March 2006 or is a discretionary trust IHT charges can arise both on the application of the reserve fund monies and under the ten-yearly periodic charge if the life of the fund exceeds ten years. It is not at all clear how any IHT liability would be calculated. The rate depends on the rate payable by a deemed settlor at the time of creation of the settlement. Each tenant is probably the settlor of the amount he puts into the reserve fund – although it is unclear whether he 'settles' all his periodic payments at the time he signs the lease or if each payment is an additional settlement. Nor is it clear what assumptions are made as to the deemed settlor when the tenant is a company. HMRC do not in practice seem to take these IHT points but it is probably unsafe to assume that they will never do so.

Separate Management Company

2.103 Probably the most satisfactory approach from a tax point of view, where it is wished to maintain a reserve fund, is to have a separate management company to handle the management of the building. This is very common with residential property but rare with commercial lettings. The management company is almost certainly carrying on a trade of providing the services but the 'profit', ie the reserve fund, should be free of tax under the mutual trading principle provided that the requisite conditions are met. Mutual trading occurs where 'a member … makes a rateable contribution to a common fund, in which he and his co-partners are jointly interested … He pays according to an estimate of the amount which will be required for the common benefit' (*Styles v New York Life Assurance Co (2 TC 460)*). This is a good description of a service charge! The existence of a company does not destroy the mutuality but the receipt of service charges from a tenant who does not have an interest in the common fund probably does. This is why it is normal for each of the tenants to hold a share in the company. In theory, the ownership of the company is not important. What is important is to be able to demonstrate that, on a liquidation, any surplus assets will be returned to the contributors to the common fund. The receipt of investment income, such as bank interest from the investment of the sinking fund, will not destroy the mutuality. Such income will however be chargeable to corporation tax.

2.104 Where trading income is receivable from non-members it may be possible to separate those activities from the mutual activities. For example, if a company receives service charges for flats wholly from members and such charges from garages partly from members and partly from non-members, it may be possible to contend that the company is carrying on two distinct trading activities – servicing flats, which is a mutual trade, and servicing garages, the whole of the profit (if any) from which is chargeable to corporation tax. It is understood that HMRC are sometimes prepared to treat servicing the flats of shareholders as a mutual trade and servicing the flats of other tenants as a taxable activity.

2.105 The mutual trading concept does not apply to a UK property business itself as that business is not a trade; it is merely deemed to be one. Accordingly where, as is normal with residential flat management companies, the management company is also the landlord, eg it is entitled to the ground rents on long leases, the mutual trading concept cannot apply unless it can be established that the company is carrying on a trade of providing services separate from its right to receive the ground rents. In practice in the past where such a company claimed to be exempt under mutual trading HMRC normally accepted it. HMRC say that they accepted no tax was payable not under mutual trading principles but by concession. Where service charges received by occupier-controlled flat management companies were matched over a period of up to five years by admissible expenses no tax charge was normally imposed (Tax Bulletin 37, September 1998). This issue can normally be avoided by adopting a 31 March service charge year so that the receipts and expenditure in each year cancel out one another. In practice, HMRC do not seem to seek tax on any mismatch provided that the service charge rules do not contain provision to build up a reserve for future expenditure. The issue does not arise in a residential context because the *Landlord and Tenant Act 1987, s 42* requires residential service charge monies to be held in trust.

Deemed Trusts under the Landlord and Tenant Act 1987

2.106 *Section 42* of the *Landlord and Tenant Act 1987* provides that service charge monies received in relation to residential property are to be held on trust to carry out the work with any surplus being held on trust for the tenants. HMRC take the view that the correct accounting treatment in the light of this requirement is to treat the service charge monies as received as capital in the landlord's capacity as a trustee. Such monies will therefore not be income of the landlord. It seems questionable whether this is a correct interpretation but as it is wholly favourable to taxpayers it seems unlikely that anyone will challenge it.

2.107 Income generated from the investment of service charge monies (as defined in the *Landlord and Tenant Act 1985, s 180)* that must be held on statutory trusts under the *Landlord and Tenant Act 1987, s 42* is taxable on the trustees at the basic rate of income tax (*ITA 2007, s 480*). The exact nature of the trust created by *s 42* is unclear. It is also unclear who is the settlor. *Subsection 3(a)* appears to create a purpose trust, but such trusts are not recognised in English law (*Re Endacott [1959] 3 All ER 562*). Accordingly, in trust law, the trust may well be a resultant trust for the benefit of the settlor. Before the Special Commissioners in *Retirement Care Group Ltd v HMRC* (2007) STC (SCD) 539, the taxpayer contended that the income was not income which was to be accumulated. The Commissioner felt that the service charge and the income from it became a single fund and that the addition of the income to the fund amounted to an accumulation.

2.108 Where under the terms of a lease the landlord is entitled to receive the service charge without there being any requirement for him to put the monies into trust, the settlor of the *s 42* trust must be the landlord. Under the lease it is his money but the law requires him to take it and set up the trust. *Section 42(7)* provides that in certain circumstances the money is to revert to the person legally entitled to receive the service charge (which would normally be either the landlord or a separate management company or trust) and for that recipient to then pass the money to the landlord. Accordingly, if the landlord is the settlor, the trust must be a trust in which the settlor has retained an interest so that the income of that trust will be taxable on the settlor under *ITA 2007, ss 624–627*. That seems fairly tough on the landlord as the statute requires the trust to be created in this particular format. Nevertheless that seems to be the tax effect. If the landlord is not the settlor of the *s 42* trust, then presumably the tenant is the settlor. If that is the case, the trust is again one in which the settlor has retained an interest because of *s 42(3)(b)*. An alternative analysis is that the monies in the trust belong at all times to the tenants in equity, so that the income is taxable on the tenants at their tax rates. The landlord is taxable as a person in receipt of the income, but only at the basic rate.

2.109 The *Landlord and Tenant Act 1987* applies only to England and Wales. For *s 42* to apply a payment must be made under the terms of the lease. The Act defines a service charge as 'an amount payable by a tenant of a dwelling, as part of or in addition to rent, which is payable directly or indirectly for services, repairs, maintenance or insurance or the landlord's costs of management, and the whole or part of which varies or may vary according to the relevant costs'. There is an exception for an 'exempt' landlord as defined in *s 58(1)* of the Act (mainly registered social landlords, local authorities and charitable housing trusts) (Tax Bulletin 48, August 2000).

The Position of the Tenant

2.110 The position of the tenant is considered at **12.8** below. The structuring of service charges and reserve funds will depend largely on commercial considerations, taking into account whether a reserve fund is needed, the protection the tenants want for any such fund, the need of the tenants to obtain a deduction, and the importance to the landlord of not having to pay tax on money that he is required to set aside for a specific purpose.

Dilapidations

2.111 Where the landlord receives a payment from the tenant for dilapidations on the expiry of the lease the tax treatment is unclear. Logically the receipt is compensation for the fact that the tenant has not delivered back the premises in the same state and as a result has reduced the value of the landlord's interest in the property. It is therefore consideration for a part disposal of the property in accordance with *TCGA 1992, s 22*. However that is not the HMRC view. They say that the tax treatment depends on what the landlord does with the premises. If he disposes of the premises or occupies them himself, they agree it is a capital receipt chargeable to capital gains tax as it is compensation for failing to observe the terms of the lease as a result of which the property reverted to the landlord in a dilapidated condition. If he re-lets the premises and does not carry out the repairs, they consider it is a revenue receipt as it has the effect of filling a hole in the landlord's profits, ie it is compensation for the lower rent the property can now command (Property Income Manual PIM2020). It is hard to follow the logic of this. The hole is not a temporary one. There is a permanent diminution in the value of the premises and that diminution is as much a capital 'loss' if the premises are re-let as if they are sold or owner occupied. HMRC base their view on the Privy Council decision in *Raja's Commercial College v Gian Singh* (1976) TC 282. However that case had nothing to do with dilapidations. Raja had been a tenant of Mr Singh. He served a notice to quit which Raja disputed. They remained in occupation for six years. They agreed that Raja was entitled to damages for trespass and the dispute was whether or not this was taxable in Mr Singh's hands. That is the context in which the Privy Council said that the damages were taxable because they filled a hole left by the loss of rent. If the money is used towards the cost of repairs, the HMRC view is that it should be netted off against the expenditure as that expenditure has not been expended by the landlord to the extent that it has been made good by the former tenant (PIM2020). Again this seems questionable.

Income from Overseas Property

2.112 The profits from overseas properties are calculated in the same way as for UK ones, ie the taxpayer is treated as operating an overseas property business the income from which is calculated in the same manner as trading income (*ITTOIA 2005, s 265*; *CTA 2009, ss 206, 209*). If the land law in the country where the property is situated differs from that in the UK, they must be interpreted to produce the nearest possible result to the UK position (*ITTOIA 2005, s 363; CTA 2009, s 290)*.

2.113 The overseas property business in relation to overseas properties is separate from the UK property business for UK properties (*ITTOIA 2005, s 263(1); CTA 2009, s 204*). As the UK property business and the overseas property business are separate businesses, losses of one cannot be set against income from the other for income tax purposes (*ITTOIA, s 272(2)*). The special rules for EEA furnished holiday/lettings (see **2.103**) are not extended to overseas properties in other countries. Accordingly, such lettings will normally form part of the taxpayer's overseas property business. Capital allowances apply to an overseas property business in the same way as to a UK one (*CAA 2001, s 15(1)(d)*). For income tax purposes only, *ITTOIA 2005, ss 92–94*, which contain special rules to grant relief for expenses connected with foreign trades and travel between separate UK and foreign trades, do not apply to an overseas property business (*ITTOIA 2005, s 272(2)*). In most, if not all, cases this will deny relief for travelling expenses to visit the overseas property. This restriction does not apply for corporation tax.

2.114 The full income tax UK property business loss rules are applied to overseas properties but, of course, such losses can be set only against the profits of the overseas property business (*ITA 2007, s 118*).

2.115 For corporation tax purposes, a loss on the company's overseas property business can be carried forward against future income from that business. This does not apply to the extent that the business is not being carried on on a commercial basis. The rules at **2.55** above apply to a loss arising in such circumstances. These appear to disallow relief for the loss entirely (*CTA 2010, s 67*). A loss in an overseas property income business cannot be set against general income or surrendered under the group relief rules.

Rent-a-Room Relief

2.116 A special relief applies to the furnished letting of part of the only or main residence of an individual, including goods or services supplied in connection with the use of the residence (*ITTOIA 2005, ss 784–802*). This relief, which the government call 'rent-a-room', exempts the gross rent from income tax if it is less than £7,500 (£4,250 prior to 6 April 2016). If it exceeds that sum, the taxpayer is, in effect, allowed to claim a deduction in calculating the rent of such sum as will bring the aggregate deductions for expenses and interest up to £7,500. The rent must be assessable as either trading income or income of a UK property business (*ITTOIA 2005, s 786(1)(d)*). Meals, cleaning and laundry are expressed to be examples of goods and services used in connection with a residence (*ITTOIA 2005, s 786(2)*). If the receipts would otherwise be taxable as income of a property business the profits of which are calculated on a cash basis, any amount brought into account under *ITTOIA 2005, s 307E* (capital receipts under, or after leaving cash basis – see **2.22**) as a receipt of the property business must be treated as rent-a-room receipts (*ITTOIA 2005, s 786(6A)(6B)* inserted by *FA 2017, Sch 2, para 33*).

2.117 Although the relief is intended to apply only to residential accommodation some people think that it is drawn sufficiently broadly that it will also apply to a letting of a room in one's house for non-residential purposes. Accordingly it is sometimes suggested that the director of a family company might let a room in his house to his company for use as an office and escape tax on the rent. Anyone tempted to do this should be wary of simply not declaring the rent on the director's tax return. As HMRC have made clear that they do not accept this view (Tax Bulletin, Issue 12, August 1994), it would be wise to draw the treatment adopted to the attention of HMRC while at the same time claiming that it is not taxable. Apart from the intention of the legislation, there are two specific provisions that cast doubt on the above interpretation. *Section 787(1)* (defines a residence as 'a building, or part of a building occupied or intended to be occupied as a separate residence'. This may exclude a room intended to be occupied as an office from being part of the residence at all. That certainly is how the Revenue interpret the wording. *ITTOIA 2005, s 790(1)*, which deals with the position where there are joint owners of the property, refers to receipts 'in respect of the use of residential accommodation … in the residence'. It seems unlikely that the courts will hold that this allows a room to be let as commercial accommodation if there is a single owner but not if there are joint owners.

2.118 The relief does not apply if in the year of assessment the individual derives any taxable income other than rent-a-room receipts from a trade, letting or agreement from which he derives rent-a room receipts (*ITTOIA 2005, s 785*). It is not readily apparent what this exclusion is intended to cover. It seems to apply if another part of the residence is let unfurnished so that an amount is taxable as part of a UK property business. It would also apply if the services provided include any which are not similar to meals, cleaning and laundry. For example, if the rent includes use of a garden, such a facility would not appear to be either in respect of use of the furnished accommodation or the use of relevant goods or services. It is difficult to discern any logic in denying relief in either of these circumstances.

2.119 The property concerned must be a qualifying residence; that is, a property which is the individual's only or main residence at some time in the basis period for the year of assessment concerned (*ITTOIA 2005, s 786(1)(c)*). A residence is defined as a building, or part of a building occupied or intended to be occupied as a separate residence, or a caravan or house boat. Where a person has more than one residence, which is the main one is a question of fact. A building designed for permanent use as a single residence is to be treated as such notwithstanding that it is temporarily divided into two or more parts which are occupied as separate residences (*ITTOIA 2005, s 787(2)*). No guidance is given as to what is meant by temporarily divided. Suppose a person who owns a two-storey house puts a door at the foot of the stairs, lets the top part furnished to a family, and takes in a lodger in the bottom owner-occupied part. The property is undoubtedly occupied as two separate residences, one by the owner and the lodger and the other by the tenant family. If the door temporarily divides the property, the relief extends to the total rent received. If it does not, ie it either permanently divides it or divides it for longer than a short duration (whichever meaning the word temporary is intended to bear), the relief will apply only to the rent from the lodger. What if the upper part is let unfurnished? If the door divides the house temporarily, no relief at all is due. If it does not, relief is due on the rent from the lodger.

2.120 As mentioned in **2.116** above, the relief applies only if the gross rents do not exceed £7,500 pa (*ITTOIA 2005, s 789(4)*. The Treasury are empowered to alter this figure either upwards or downwards (*ITTOIA 2005, s 789(5)*). If, at any time in the basis period during which the property is the individual's only or main residence, sums accrue to some other person in respect of the use of residential accommodation in the residence (or in respect of goods or services supplied in connection with that use), the limit is reduced to half, ie £3,750 (*ITTOIA 2005, s 789(3)*). For example, if the rent is received jointly by husband and wife, each will be able to receive £3,750 tax free. This will also apply where only one spouse receives rent, by virtue of *ITA 2007, s 836* (which requires income from jointly held property to be attributed to spouses in equal shares), unless an election is made under *s 837.* Curiously, if the rent is received jointly by husband, wife and two children (who are either over 18 or bought a share of the house out of funds provided other than by their parents), each is entitled to £3,750, so increasing the total exempt amount in respect of the house to £15,000. The reason for this generosity on the part of the government where children are still living at home, is not readily apparent. However, it should be noted that if one of two joint recipients did not reside in the property (and thus could not qualify for 'rent-a-room' relief), the resident recipient would still only be entitled to £3,750 tax free.

2.121 Where the exemption applies and a loss is incurred, the loss will not be an allowable loss (*ITTOIA 2005, s 792*). Nor can capital allowances be claimed or a balancing charge be made (*ITTOIA 2005, s 793*). However, if a potential balancing charge plus the rent itself exceeds the £7,500 (or £3,750) figure, the balancing charge is brought into account to determine how much of the total is exempt (*ITTOIA 2005, s 788*). To preserve the benefit of a loss, an election can be made for the exemption from tax not to apply (*ITTOIA 2005, s 799*). Such an election has effect only for the year for which it is made; it does not affect the exemption for later years. It can also be withdrawn if this is beneficial – and it is discovered quickly, as both the election and a withdrawal need to be made within one year of the end of the year of assessment concerned (*ITTOIA 2005, s 799(3)*). HMRC have power to extend this time limit. Losses brought forward under *ITA 2007, ss 83–85* (or under *ITA 2007, ss 152–155* in relation to property related miscellaneous income) from years when 'rent-a-room' did not apply, can be carried forward for use in later years when an election for the exemption not to apply is in force.

2.122 Where the gross rents exceed the £7,500 or £3,750 limit, an election can be made to adopt a limited relief. Where, as will usually be the case, the receipts for rent and services are treated as derived from a single source, the taxable income of the basis period is deemed to be A minus B where A is the gross rents and B is the individual's limit for the year, ie £7,500 or £3,750 as the case may be (*ITTOIA 2005, ss 795–798, 800*). In other words the taxable income is the excess of the gross rents over £7,500. If the receipts are treated as derived from two or more sources, eg furnished letting and a trade of providing meals, the profits or gains of the basis period of each source are deemed to be C minus D. C is the gross income from the individual source and D is a fraction of the individual's limit for the year, namely the fraction that the gross income from that source bears to the aggregate gross income from all of the sources (*ITTOIA 2005, s 797*).

2.123 Where this election is made, no deduction can be claimed for expenses or loan interest. Nor can capital allowances be claimed (*ITTOIA 2005, ss 796(2), 797(2)*). There is no bar on HMRC raising a balancing charge though (*ITTOIA 2005, s 797(3)*). Clearly, the election should only be made if the expenses and interest are under the individual's limit for the year as the overall effect of the election is to substitute £7,500 (£3,750) for the aggregate of the actual expenses, capital allowances and other deductions.

2.124 The election must be made within one year after the end of the tax year for which it is to apply (*ITTOIA 2005, s 88(5)*). Once made it will also have effect for all future years until it is withdrawn (*ITTOIA 2005, s 88(2)*). Notice of withdrawal (which can apply to the first year if desired) must similarly be made within 12 months after the end of the tax year for which it is to have effect. A withdrawal will not prevent a fresh election being made for a subsequent year (*ITTOIA 2005, s 800(4)(5)*). If at any time while an election is in force, the rent drops below the £7,500 (or £3,750) limit, notice of withdrawal of the election is automatically deemed to have been given (*ITTOIA 2005, s 800(6)*).

Rents Taxable as Trading Income

2.125 Rents can be assessable as trading income in two circumstances. The first is where part of a trader's business premises is sublet. This is a concessional treatment to avoid the need to apportion outgoings. Statutorily rents are required to be taxed as part of a UK property business. For it to apply:

(*a*) the accommodation must be temporarily surplus to business requirements, ie it must have been used or intended for use in the business and it must not be evident that it has become permanently surplus to business requirements,

(*b*) the property must be used partly for the business and partly let – as the object of the concession is to avoid the need to apportion outgoings on the property between trading and UK property business expenses, and

(*c*) the rental income must be comparatively small (it is not clear in comparison with what).

(Tax Bulletin, Issue 10). In the past the concession was also given where premises formerly occupied in the trade were let temporarily pending their disposal but this treatment no longer appears acceptable.

2.126 The second is where services provided by the landlord are of sufficient substance that the landlord is carrying on a trade of providing serviced accommodation. There are no hard and fast rules as to what is necessary to constitute a trade. It is a matter of degree. Most Inspectors of Taxes will regard cleaning and lighting of the common parts as insufficient and will look for the provision of services to individual rooms. The provision of meals to tenants will generally attract trading income treatment. The provision of cleaning to individual rooms and making up beds will frequently do so. Where a range of services is not provided to individual rooms most Inspectors will resist a claim that a trade is being carried on, although some may be sympathetic if the landlord is engaged virtually full-time in managing his properties and provides at least some services to tenants such as small repairs, window cleaning, etc.

2.127 There are two leading cases, *Gittos v Barclay (55 TC 633)* and *Griffiths v Jackson (56 TC 583)* (see **2.128**), in both of which the activities were held not to constitute a trade. However, the services seem to have been of a relatively minor nature and the decisions are not surprising. Mrs Gittos owned a number of holiday villas which she let out furnished. The services provided seem to have been limited to preparing the villas for tenants and cleaning up after them. No services seem to have been provided for individual tenants whilst they were in occupation of their villa. Mr Jackson, who had a full-time job elsewhere, rented properties to students. He supplied linen, which was laundered once a month, for lets of 13 weeks or less but not for longer lettings. He provided occasional food and other services – primarily the stocking of fridges before a tenant took up occupation. Again, however, few or no services appear to have been provided to a tenant once his occupation of the property had commenced.

2.128 Following the decisions in *Gittos v Barclay* and *Griffiths v Jackson*, HMRC generally sought to re-categorise from trading to property business income many lettings which they had previously accepted as constituting a trade. It has also become virtually impossible to establish that a new furnished letting activity constitutes a trade. It should be borne in mind that those cases did not actually decide that furnished lettings for which services are provided cannot constitute a trade, but rather that, on the particular facts of those cases, those lettings did not do so. This was confirmed in Parliament by the then Chief Secretary to the Treasury, Peter Rees QC, an eminent tax barrister (see **2.138** below). Those cases nevertheless make it far more difficult than before to establish that the lettings constitute a trade where the landlord is not intimately involved in providing services to the tenants of the accommodation. It may be helpful to mention that in *Griffiths v Jackson* Vinelott J said that the real question is whether the activities constitute the letting of furnished rooms or the activities of a lodging housekeeper and the distinction between the two 'is no doubt a narrow one, more particularly in these days of self-service hotels and motels, but the principle is clear'. He went on to quote with approval Lord Russell of Kilowin in a rating case, *Westminster Council v Southern Railway Co ([1936] AC 511)*, who identified the main attributes of the keeper of a lodging house as the retention of a contractual right of access to the lodgers' rooms and control of the ingress and egress to and from the house.

2.129 It should also be mentioned that in *Nott v HMRC (2016 SFTD 628)* the FTT commented that:

> 'Perhaps because [*ITTOIA 2005*] *s 268* [which charges to income tax the profits of a "property business"] is, in effect, the starting position, consideration of the relevant case law shows that the normal badges of trade have not been found to be of particular assistance to the courts in addressing this issue [ie whether the exploitation of property by letting constitutes trading]. To take only some of the badges, in relation to income from letting property, a profit seeking motive, the number of lettings, the nature of the asset, and the nature of the financing could all be present in a typical property letting business without themselves pointing in the direction of trade.'

The Tribunal felt that the decisions in *Rotunda Hospital Dublin v Coman (7 TC 517)* and in *Griffiths* (see above) can best be regarded as demonstrating that a property owner who gives up occupation of his property in return for payment is very likely to be generating property income. Conversely, a property owner who remains in occupation is, all else being equal, more likely to be able to show that, if additional services are being provided, it is a package of services forming part of a trade from which his income derives. It held that the services provided by Mr Nott, while extensive, were in large part consistent with the services normally provided by a landlord of furnished holiday accommodation. It did not think that the provision of breakfast and daily cleaning which were offered for an additional fee were sufficient to change the profit derivation from the exploitation of property to a package of services comprising a trade.

2.130 When considering whether to push for trading income treatment it is important to be conscious of the VAT position. Whilst rents from letting residential accommodation are normally exempt from VAT, the provision of sleeping accommodation in a 'similar establishment' to a hotel, inn or boarding house, and the letting of 'holiday accommodation' in a house or flat, are both liable to VAT at the 20% standard rate (*VATA 1994, Sch 9, Group 1*). It is accordingly a difficult tightrope to walk to convince HMRC that the activities amount to a trade whilst keeping the income safe from VAT. Neither of the two above terms is exhaustively defined. Holiday accommodation is specifically stated to include all accommodation held out as such – a ploy that has often been used in the past to endeavour to take the property outside the protection of the *Rent Acts* (*Note 13* to *Group 1*). Premises in which furnished sleeping accommodation is provided and which are held out as being suitable for use by visitors or travellers is specifically stated to be a similar establishment to a hotel, etc. irrespective of whether or not meals are provided (*Notes 9* and *13* to *Group 1*).

Furnished Holiday Lettings

2.131 The widespread recategorisation in the 1980s of many serviced furnished lettings from trading income to UK property business income caused general disquiet. This was particularly so among seaside landladies (most of whom would in any event probably have succeeded in establishing an entitlement to trading income treatment), who had long enjoyed the benefits of trading income treatment and were often engaged full-time in their letting activities during the holiday season, and were relying on obtaining capital gains tax roll-over relief and retirement relief. The law was accordingly amended by *FA 1984, s 50* (now re-enacted in *ITTOIA 2005, ss 322–328* for income tax and *CTA 2009, ss 264–269* for corporation tax) to treat qualifying furnished holiday lettings as a trade for most tax purposes. In April 2009 HMRC acknowledged that this provision may not be compliant with European Law. Accordingly they would henceforth treat them as applying to qualifying furnished holiday accommodation anywhere in the EEA. Claims for the rules to apply for earlier years to properties in other EEA countries would be accepted within the normal time limits. Capital allowances could be claimed from the latest of the date the property was first used for qualifying lettings, the date on which the country in which it is situated joined the EEA and 1 January 1994. It is unclear what the significance of 1 January 1994 is. The furnished holiday letting rules date from 1984. The normal rule is that if the UK has failed properly to enact EC law a taxpayer can go back indefinitely. *FA 2011* created a new category of EEA furnished holiday lettings, which recognises this issue. This is considered at **2.135**.

2.132 A commercial letting of furnished holiday accommodation in the UK in respect of which the profits or gains are chargeable to income tax as part of a UK property business is to be treated as a trade for the purpose of the following provisions:

(*a*) *ITA 2007, ss 59–116* (loss relief) (to 5 April 2011 only see **2.127**);

(*b*) *CAA 2001* (the exclusion from capital allowances under *CAA 2001, s 35* does not apply as the definition of an ordinary property business in *CAA 2001, s 16* excludes holiday lettings);

(*c*) *ITTOIA 2005, s 312* (expenditure on energy saving items);

(*d*) *FA 2004, s 189(2)(ba)* (relevant earnings for pension purposes);

(*e*) *ITA 2007, s 836(3)* (jointly held property);

(*f*) *ITTOIA 2005, s 274B(4)* (exception from deductibility of finance costs (see **4.8**));

(*g*) *ITA 2007, s 399A(9)* (restriction on deductibility of interest on loans to invest in a partnership; and

(*h*) *ITTOIA 2005, s 307B* (cash basis: capital expenditure).

(*ITTOIA 2005, s 322(2)* as amended by *FA 2015, s 24(6) and F(No 2)A 2017, Sch 2, para 26.*)

For corporation tax a commercial letting of furnished holiday accommodation is treated as a trade for all purposes (*CTA 2010, s 65*).

Such a letting is also treated as a trade for the following capital gains tax provisions (for both CGT and corporation tax on chargeable gains):

(*a*) *TCGA 1992, ss 152–157* (roll-over relief on replacement of business asset);

(*b*) *TCGA 1992, s 165* (gifts of business assets);

(*c*) *TCGA 1992, s 169S(1)* (entrepreneurs' relief);

(*d*) *TCGA 1992, s 253* (relief for loans to traders); and

(*e*) *TCGA 1992, Sch 7AC* (exemptions for disposals by companies with substantial shareholding).

It should particularly be noted that this list does not include EIS reinvestment relief.

2.133 A UK property business which consists of the commercial letting of furnished holiday accommodation in the UK is treated as if it were a trade. Where part only of that business consists of such lettings, that part is treated as a trade for the purpose of the above provisions. Accommodation is not defined for this purpose. It will almost certainly include caravans and houseboats the income from which is taxed as income of a UK property business Although such income may well be taxed as trading income).

2.134 All such lettings made by a particular person, partnership or body of persons, eg a company, are to be treated as one trade (*ITA 2007, s 127; CTA 2010, s 65(3)*).

2.135 Similarly from 2011/12 if a person carries on an EEA furnished holiday letting business, it is treated as a trade for the purposes set out in **2.131** above (*ITTOIA 2005, s 322(2A); CTA 2009, s 264(2A)*). An EEA furnished holiday lettings business consists of the commercial letting of furnished holiday accommodation in one or more EEA countries (or of so much of an overseas property business as so consists) (*ITA 2007, s 1272ZA; CTA 2010, s 67A*). The trade is a single trade which consists of every commercial letting of furnished holiday accommodation included in the person's EEA furnished holiday letting business and the profits of which are chargeable to income tax (or corporation tax as the case may be) (*ITA 2007, s 127ZA(3); CTA 2010, s 67A(3)*). However *ITA 2007, ss 64–82* (setting off of losses against general income or against capital gains and carry back of early year losses) do not apply to an EEA furnished holiday letting business. Nor do *ITA 2007, ss 89–95* (terminal losses) (*ITA 2007, s 127ZA(4)*). The corresponding corporation tax loss provisions in *CTA 2010, ss 37–44* and *48–54* similarly do not apply to such a business (*CTA 2010, s 67A(5)*). If there is a letting of accommodation, only part of which is furnished holiday accommodation, a just and reasonable apportionment needs to be made (*ITA 2007, s 127ZA(5); CTA 2010, s 67A(5)). ITA 2007, s 836*, which treats income from property held in the joint names of married persons (or civil partners) who live together as arising to each in equal shares unless they elect otherwise, does not apply to EEA furnished holiday letting income (*ITA 2007, s 836*).

2.136 From 2011/12 onwards a loss on a furnished holiday letting cannot be set against general income. It can only be carried forward against future furnished holiday letting income from the same business (*ITA 2007, s 127(3A)*).

2.137 Apart from the restrictions on loss relief, it is difficult to think of any provision not on the list at **2.95** under which a person with furnished lettings would be at a disadvantage in having a deemed trade rather than a trade. It is equally difficult to see why the Chancellor at the time steadfastly resisted categorising furnished holiday letting as a trade but merely gave them the same major tax benefits as a trade attracts.

2.138 Although some Inspectors of Taxes have suggested that furnished holiday lettings cannot constitute a trade, as stated at **2.128** the then Chief Secretary to the Treasury, Peter Rees QC, an eminent tax barrister, made clear during the 1984 Finance Bill debates that at least in his view this is incorrect. '*Clause 49* … was designed to relieve the position which was thought to have been disturbed by two cases recently heard in the High Court. One is called *Gittos v Barclay* and the other *Griffiths v Jackson* … I do not believe that those cases established that the fruits of holiday lettings were never to be taxed under Case I of Schedule D [ie as trading income]. High Court judges have held that in certain circumstances such income should be taxed under Case VI of Schedule D, but there is an area of uncertainty by reference to the general tax law … *Clause 49* is not intended to overturn the general principles that may have to be applied where a holiday letting does not measure up to the tests as they eventually emerge … A proprietor of holiday lettings who does not satisfy the tests as laid down will still be at liberty to take his chance by reference to the general law … and I repeat that the two cases to which I have referred do not seem to me to have established that the fruits of holiday lettings are always to be taxed under Case VI of Schedule D or that they are never to be taxed under Case I' (Hansard, Standing Committee A, 5 June 1984, Cols 737/8). It is also worthy of note that HMRC's 'rent-a-room' press release of 18 June 1992 referred to 'Case I of Schedule D (the basis on which tax is charged when a taxpayer is regarded as carrying on a trade, which may be the case where substantial services are provided in connection with the furnished letting)'.

2.139 And later, 'The income tax from some caravan parks will be assessable under Case I of Schedule D – that is, when they are run consistently on a commercial basis, when a range of services is provided, and so on' (*Ibid* Col 739).

2.140 What is a commercial letting of furnished holiday accommodation? A letting is a commercial letting if it is on a commercial basis with a view to the realisation of profits (*ITTOIA 2005, s 323(2); CTA 2009, s 265(2)*). In *Brown v Richardson (1997 STC (SCD))* the Special Commissioners held that 'profits' means commercial, not tax-adjusted, profits so account had to be taken of interest payable (which at that time was not a deduction in calculating the profits but a charge on income deductible from total income). They decided that even though the properties had been let on a commercial basis the interest on the loans used to purchase them was so great that the appellant had not proved the letting was with the view to making a profit.

2.141 This case needs to be approached with caution. The taxpayer was claiming loss relief on a property which in the mortgage application he had described as a holiday home. The tribunal did not believe that the predominant reason for buying the property was to let it as furnished holiday accommodation and felt that the letting was primarily to obtain a contribution towards the running expenses of the property. That was the primary reason for their decision. Nevertheless HMRC believe the case supports their view that:

(*a*) profits, means commercial profits;

(*b*) a taxpayer's expressed intentions are not necessarily conclusive;

(*c*) where there is evidence to suggest a property was acquired primarily as a holiday or second home, the letting activity is likely to be with a view to generating income to offset costs rather than to realising profits; and (*d*) the size of a mortgage can be so large that the projected profitability is jeopardised or the commercial credibility of the scheme as a whole becomes questionable.

They say that in such cases they would 'expect a written business plan to be prepared at the outset' (Tax Bulletin, 31 October 1997). In the context of how small businesses normally operate, such an expectation is wholly unrealistic. This suggests that a lot of cases on the realisation of profit tests are likely to have to go before the Commissioners. A person lets accommodation if he permits another person to occupy it whether or not in pursuance of a lease (*ITTOIA 2005, s 323(1)*; *CTA 2009, s 265(1)*). Accommodation is furnished if the tenant is entitled to the use of furniture in connection with the use of the property (*ITTOIA 2005, s 325*; *CTA 2005, s 265(3)*).

2.142 Holiday accommodation is not specifically defined and would have its normal everyday meaning. However, it is specifically provided that accommodation is *not* to be treated as holiday accommodation unless:

(*a*) it is available for commercial letting to the public generally as holiday accommodation for periods which amount, in aggregate, to at least 210 days (140 days prior to 2012/13);

(*b*) the periods for which it is in fact let to the public generally as holiday accommodation under commercial lettings amount in aggregate to at least 105 days (70 days prior to 2012/13); and

(*c*) for a period comprising at least seven months (which need not be continuous but must include any month in which one of the 105 days in (*b*) above falls) it is not normally in the same occupation for a continuous period exceeding 31 days.

(*ITTOIA 2005, s 325*; *CTA 2009, s 267* both as amended by *FA 2011, Sch 14*.)

2.143 In the case of an individual (or other person who is not a company) the above tests must normally be met during the year of assessment (*ITTOIA 2005, ss 324, 325(2)*). If the accommodation is first let by the taxpayer as furnished accommodation in the current year of assessment the tests are applied by reference to the twelve months starting from the date on which the property was first let (not first available for letting) (*ITTOIA 2005, s 324(2)*). If it ceases to be let during the current year of assessment the tests are applied by reference to the 12 months ended on the date on which it was last let (*ITTOIA 2005, s 324(3)*). In the case of a letting by a company the tests are normally applied by reference to the period of 12 months ending with the last day of the accounting period. If the accommodation was first let, or ceased to be let, by the company as furnished accommodation in the accounting period, the tests are applied for the first, or last, 12 months of letting in the same way as with an individual (*CTA 2009, s 266*).

2.144 If, in a year of assessment or accounting period, a person lets furnished accommodation which is treated as holiday accommodation for *s 324* or *s 266* purposes ('the qualifying accommodation'), he can elect for the 70-day test under *s 325* or *s 267(3)* (see **2.102**(*b*)) to be applied to it and to any other accommodation specified in his claim which was let by him as furnished holiday accommodation during that year. Where such a claim is made, that other accommodation will be treated as holiday accommodation for the year if the number of days for which the qualifying accommodation and the other accommodation was let amounts on average to at least 105 days (*ITTOIA 2005, s 326*; *CTA 2009, s 268*). Qualifying accommodation cannot be specified in more than one claim in respect of any one year of assessment or accounting period (*ITTOIA 2005, s 326(5)*; *CTA 2009, s 268(5)*). However there is no reason why a single claim should not cover more than one property. Such a claim must be made within two years of the end of the tax year or accounting period to which it relates.

Example 2.1

Jack has two cottages, Westlea and Southlea, available for furnished holiday letting throughout the period 1 April to 30 October 2015. He actually lets Westlea for 180 days during this period and Southlea for 60 days.

Westlea qualifies as holiday accommodation but Southlea does not. If Jack elects for averaging, the days are aggregated, 180 + 60 = 240, and averaged over the two properties, 120 per property. Accordingly both properties will qualify as furnished holiday accommodation for 2015/16.

2.145 The wording in *ITTOIA 2005* and *CTA 2009* makes clear that any number of properties can be averaged. These averaging rules apply separately to UK and EEA holiday accommodation (*ITA 2007, s 326(7); CTA 2009, s 268(7)*).

2.146 From 2011/12 onwards if a person lets qualifying holiday accommodation during a year (or accounting period) and also lets it during the following year or the next two years, but it fails to meet the 105-days test in that following year (or following two years), and there was a genuine intention to meeting the letting conditions in those years, the taxpayer can elect to treat the accommodation as qualifying in that second or second and third years as the case may be (*ITA 2007, s 326A(1)(2); CTA 2009, s 268A(1)(2)*). In other words once a property qualifies as holiday accommodation in one year, it can be treated as doing so for up to two further years even though it does not meet the letting conditions. The election cannot trigger the right to so elect for a later year. If an election is not made for the second year it cannot be made for the third year either. The accommodation can meet the 105-days test in the first year so as a result of averaging properties under *s 326* can be treated as doing so in the second, but both a *s 326* and *326A* (or *s 268* and *268A*) election cannot be made in respect of the same year (*ITA 2007, s 326A(3),(4),(6); CTA 2009, s 268A(3),(4),(6)*). The election must be made on or before the first anniversary of the self-assessment filing date (31 January following the end of the tax year) or within two years of the end of a company's accounting period as the case may be (*ITA 2007, s 326A(5); CTA 2009, s 268A(5)*).

2.147 It should be noted that these provisions only apply to holiday lettings. They do not apply to student lettings or any other short-term furnished lettings. As nowadays people take holidays all over the country and not just at the seaside, it is likely to be difficult in many cases to determine whether or not a letting is a holiday let.

2.148 Once a property qualifies as holiday accommodation for a year, the whole of the income from letting it, not merely income from letting it for use as holiday accommodation, qualifies as part of the income of the deemed trade. It is not necessary to apportion the income between income from holiday use and income from letting for other uses outside the holiday season.

2.149 It should be noted that the test in **2.142**(*c*) above is not concerned with what happens during the remaining five months of the year. The property could be let to a single individual for the entire five months. It is also possible, at least in theory, for the property to be let to the same person for two continuous 30-day periods in the seven months provided that they are separated by a gap. However HMRC can be expected to scrutinise such a letting closely to ensure that such occupation by a single person is not 'normal' for the property.

2.150 Relief cannot be claimed under *ITA 2007, ss 72–74* in respect of a loss in a year of assessment if any of the accommodation in respect of which the trade is carried on in that year was first let by him as furnished accommodation (even though not as holiday accommodation) more than three years before the beginning of the year of assessment (*ITA 2007, s 127*), ie the trade is deemed for *s 381* purposes to start when furnished lettings began, not when letting as holiday accommodation began. There is no corresponding corporation tax provision. Naturally, relief cannot be given for a loss both as a deemed trading loss and under some other provision, eg against miscellaneous income (*ITA 2007, s 63*).

2.151 If an overseas property business consists of both an EEA furnished holiday letting part and other business or transactions, eg non-holiday lets and non-EEA holiday lets, the income from the two parts must be calculated separately if either capital allowances are claimed in relation to the EEA furnished holiday lettings, loss relief is claimed for either part, or the profits of the EEA furnished holiday lettings part are relevant UK earnings for pension purposes (*ITTOIA 2005, ss 328A(1)(2), 328B, CTA 2009, s 269A(1)(2)*).

2.152 From 1 April 2011 (6 April 2011 for income tax) there is a special rule for capital allowances on plant and machinery. This was introduced because a property can continuously come in and out of the furnished holiday letting regime if it meets the tests in **2.142** in some years but not in others. It applies to both UK and EEA furnished holiday letting businesses. If the person ceases to use the plant or machinery in a furnished holiday letting business without ceasing to use it in his UK (or overseas) property business (or vice versa) (and owns it as a result of having incurred capital expenditure on its provision for the purpose of his property business), he is treated:

(*a*) as having incurred capital expenditure on the provision of the plant or machinery for the purpose of the other activity equal to the market value of the plant at the date of cessation (or, if less, its original cost) on the day after ceasing to use it for the first activity;

(*b*) as owning the plant or machinery as a result of having incurred that notional expenditure; and

(*c*) as if the plant or machinery on or after that day were different plant and machinery.

(*CAA 2001, s 13B.*)

2.153 The intention behind this provision is to avoid balancing adjustments each time the furnished holiday letting business ceases. It seems to achieve this on the basis that no disposal value for the furnished holiday letting business falls to be brought into account until that business permanently ceases, and ceasing to meet the qualifying conditions without selling the property is a temporary cessation only. However it appears to operate erratically where the property is not a furnished holiday letting at the time the expenditure is acquired as when that property is next let as a furnished holiday letting, the figure that comes into the capital allowances pool is its market value at that time, not the actual expenditure. It is also unclear what happens when the letting business ceases. Presumably there is a disposal of both the actual plant and the notional plant. Where the plant is installed in the building, this does not matter as an ordinary property business cannot claim capital allowances on such plant. However it can claim capital allowances on other plant used for the purpose of the letting business such as equipment that it used for maintenance and repair of the properties.

2.154 For capital gains tax purposes, ie (*f*) to (*h*) at **2.132** above where in any year of assessment a person makes a commercial letting of furnished holiday accommodation, it is treated as having been used in that year only for the purposes of the trade of making such lettings (even if it is let for other purposes for part of the year) and that trade is deemed to have been carried on throughout the year (*TCGA 1992, ss 241, 241A*). This does not apply to any period in the year of assessment during which the accommodation is neither let commercially nor available to be so let, unless it is prevented from being so let or available by any works of construction or repair. For example, if it was used as a private residence for part of the year an apportionment would be necessary.

2.155 If a gain arises on the disposal of a property which was an individual's principal private residence and the base cost of that property was reduced by roll-over relief (because at the time of acquisition it was acquired as furnished holiday accommodation), the private residence exemption will not extend to the rolled-over gain. The latter is thus treated as the top part of the gain on the private residence and will be wholly taxed if it is less than the total gain on the disposal (*TCGA 1992, s 241*).

2.156 If part only of a property is let as holiday accommodation, such apportionments must be made as appear to HMRC, or, on appeal, the First-tier Tribunal, to be just and reasonable (*ITTOIA 2005, ss 328(3), 328A(3); CTA 2010, s 65(5), CTA 2009, s 269A(3); TCGA 1992, s 241*).

Tipping, etc Rights

2.157 A sum received for the grant of tipping rights on land has been held to be capital (*McClure v Petre (1988 STC 749)*). Once a site has been filled in it cannot again be exploited for tipping. Accordingly the owner has made a disposal of a valuable right attaching to the land, which is a capital disposal. Similarly a payment to acquire tipping rights is capital expenditure as a lasting benefit is obtained – albeit lasting only for a few years (*Rolfe v Wimpey Waste Management Ltd (1989 STC 454)*).

2.158 Although a person carrying on a trade of waste disposal cannot obtain tax relief for the cost of the site itself he can claim relief for expenditure incurred on either site preparation expenditure or expenditure on restoration after tipping has ended. Site preparation expenditure is written off over the useful life of the site. The amount deductible each year is:

$$\text{cumulative expenditure less part previous allowed} \times \frac{\text{volume of waste deposited in the period of account}}{\text{volume of waste deposited in the period + future capacity of the site}}$$

(*ITTOIA 2005, s 166*; *CTA 2009, ss 142–145*.)

Preparation includes expenditure on earthworks. A tipping licence under the *Control of Pollution Act 1974* or a waste management licence under the *Environmental Protection Act 1990* must have been held before tipping commenced to qualify for relief (*ITTOIA 2005, s 167*; *CTA 2009, s 144(1)*). Where expenditure was first incurred on the site before 6 April 1989 a portion of that expenditure can also qualify for relief, namely the part that the unused capacity of the site at 6 April 1989 bears to its total capacity including the part utilised before that date (*ITTOIA 2005, s 166(2)*; *CTA 2009, s 143(2),(3)*).

2.159 Restoration payments are normally deductible when they are paid, provided that the trade is still being carried on at that time. The payment must be incurred to comply with the conditions of the tipping or waste management licence or a *Town and Country Planning Act 1990, s 106* or similar agreement or a planning condition. (*ITTOIA 2005, s 168; CTA 2009, s 145*). Relief is not given to the extent that a capital allowance or a trading deduction has been given for the expenditure (*ITTOIA 2005, s 168(4)*). For expenditure after 20 March 2012 if the payment is made (directly or indirectly) to a connected person, the relief is deferred until the period of account in which the restoration work to which the payment relates is completed (*ITTOIA 2005, s 168(3); CTA 2009, s 145(3)* as amended by *FA 2012, s 53(2)(5)*). Also from that date, no deduction is allowed at all if the payment arises from arrangements to which the trader is a party if one of the main purposes of the payment is to obtain a deduction under *CTA 2009, ss 168* or *145* (*ITTOIA 2005, s 168(3A); CTA 2009, s 145(3A)*). Arrangement includes any agreement, understanding, scheme, transaction or series of transactions, whether or not legally enforceable (*ITTOIA 2005, s 168(7); CTA 2009, s 145(7)*).The taxpayer in *Dispit Ltd v HMRC (2007 STC (SCD) 194)* sought to deduct a provision for restoration payments but the Special Commissioners held that no deduction is due until an actual payment is made. Waste disposal activities is not defined in the rewritten legislation but will cover all or any of the collection, treatment, conversion and final depositing of waste materials (*ICTA 1988, s 91A*). HMRC have given guidance on what is site preparation expenditure and what revenue expenditure on the creation of internal cells in Tax Bulletin 34, April 1998 and Tax Bulletin 51, Feb 2001.

Chapter 3

Premiums

3.1 The consideration for the grant of a lease of land is not always simply an annual rent. The landlord may require payment of a capital sum for the grant of the lease. The rent would then normally be less than a market rent to take account of this capital sum (called a premium). In the absence of special provisions a landlord would effectively be able to convert income into capital by requiring a premium equal to the total of the annual market rents for the property, with the rent payable under the lease then being a nominal figure. This particularly applies to a short lease, where the tenant's cash flow position need not be seriously affected by, in effect, paying the whole of his rent in advance on signing the lease, particularly if the landlord is prepared to accept the premium by annual instalments. The legislation accordingly contains a number of special rules to prevent the avoidance of income tax by taking premiums and other capital payments in lieu of rent. This is done by treating part of the premium as additional rent.

Treatment of Premiums on Leases of up to 50 Years as Rent

3.2 If the payment of a premium is required under a lease the duration of which does not exceed 50 years (or otherwise under the terms subject to which such a lease is granted), part of the premium is taxed on the landlord as if it were rent. The taxable part is the amount of the premium reduced by one-fiftieth (2%) for each complete period of 12 months other than the first comprised in the term of the lease (*ITTOIA 2005, s 277*; *CTA 2009, ss 216, 217*). This effectively treats the taxable amount as income of the landlord's UK property business.

Example 3.1

Jane grants a lease on 1 July 2017 for the period of ten years seven months to 31 January 2027 at a rent of £100 pa and a premium of £50,000.

Jane is taxable on UK property business income for 2017/18 (in addition to the rent) on:

		£
Premium		50,000
Complete years	10	
Reduction	$\frac{10-1}{50} \times 50{,}000 =$	9,000
Additional rent		£41,000

3.3 The taxable amount can conveniently be expressed as 2% of the premium for each year by which the complete years in the term less 1 falls short of 50, ie in the above example the taxable amount could more directly be arrived at as:

2% × (50 – (10 – 1)) = 82% of £50,000 = £41,000

For the algebraically-minded the *Act* expresses it as:

$$P - \frac{(P \times Y)}{50}$$

where P is the premium and Y is the number of complete periods of 12 months (other than the first) comprised in the duration of the lease.

Deemed Premiums

3.4 If the terms subject to which a lease is granted impose an obligation on the tenant to carry out any work on the premises the lease is deemed to have required the payment of a premium (in addition to any actual premium payable) of a sum equal to the amount by which the value of the landlord's interest in the property immediately after the commencement of the lease exceeds what its then value would have been if the obligation to carry out the works had not been imposed on the tenant (*ITTOIA 2005, s 278*; *CTA 2009, s 218(1)–(3)*). The landlord's interest immediately after the commencement of the lease is a reversionary interest. Accordingly this effectively requires one to consider to what extent the value of the reversion will be increased by the expenditure when the lease falls in, and to discount this increase back to the commencement of the lease. In most cases where the tenant is required to fit out a shop or office this figure will be nil or very low, as at the expiry of the lease a new tenant would be likely to strip out the shopfront and most of the internal fittings and replace them in a different style, and an office would often need to be refurbished before it is re-let. A deemed premium may well arise, however, if the lease requires the tenant to erect a building or an extension or if it requires him to refurbish the premises and to make good dilapidations to the refurbished standard on the expiry of the lease. The VAT implications of such a provision are considered in **17.231**.

3.5 In practice HMRC rarely seek to assess deemed premiums under this provision where the work is fitting out. Where they do it is normally as a result of pressure from the tenant, who is seeking a deduction (see **12.47** below). A charge under it cannot arise if the work that has to be done by the tenant would have qualified as an expense of the landlord's UK property business if the expenditure had been incurred by the landlord, eg if it is repairs (*ITTOIA 2005, s 278(5)*; *CTA 2009, s 218(4), (5)*).

3.6 If under the terms subject to which a lease is granted a sum becomes payable by the tenant in lieu of all or part of the rent for any period, or as consideration for the surrender of the lease, such sum is again deemed to be an additional premium (*ITTOIA 2005, s 279*; *CTA 2009, ss 219, 220*). In such a case the income tax charge will be for the year of assessment in which the sum becomes payable by the tenant. In the case of a payment in lieu of rent, the taxable amount of the notional premium is calculated as if the duration of the lease were limited to that period.

Example 3.2

Karen granted a lease on 8 March 2012 for a term of 21 years at a rent of £10,000 pa with five-year reviews. It contains a right for the tenant to pay on any review date a capital sum equal to 400% of the reviewed rent instead of paying rent for the next review period. On the first review on 8 March 2017 the rent increased to £15,000 pa and the tenant opted to pay Karen £60,000 in lieu of the rent for the next five years.

Karen is deemed to have granted a five-year lease from 8 March 2017 for a premium of £60,000. She is therefore taxed as if she had received additional rent for 2017/18 of:

2% × (50 – (5 – 1)) = 92% of £60,000 =	£55,200

3.7 It should be borne in mind that this provision applies only where the payment in lieu of rent or to terminate the lease is made under the terms subject to which the lease is granted (although *ITTOIA 2005, s 281* or *CTA 2009, s 221* – see **3.8** below – will catch a payment on a variation). If the tenant negotiates a surrender of a lease during its term under which he agrees to make a payment to the landlord, the payment is not within the *sub-section*.

3.8 If a sum (other than rent) becomes payable by the tenant as consideration for the variation or waiver of any of the terms of a lease, the lease is deemed to have required the payment of an additional premium to the landlord. For the purpose of computing the tax on that notional premium the lease is deemed to commence at the time the variation or waiver takes effect, to cease at the time that it ceases to have effect, and to have become payable at the time the contract providing for the variation or waiver is entered into (*ITTOIA 2005, s 281*; *CTA 2009, s 221*).

3.9 A payment to induce a landlord to accept a surrender of a lease is almost certainly not within this provision as it seems to envisage the lease continuing. A payment to the landlord as part of a settlement of an action by the landlord for forfeiture following a breach has been held to be a payment for the waiver or variation of a term of the lease and thus a premium under *s 221* (*Banning v Wright (48 TC 421)*). Unlike with payments within *ss 277–280* (or *ss 218–220)*, a payment within *s 281* (or *s 221*) will not normally be envisaged in the original lease but will arise from a subsequent agreement.

3.10 If a lease requires a payment to be made not to the landlord but to some other person the amount to be taxed as income is calculated in the normal way. It is not, however, taxed on the landlord. It is assessed on the recipient as if he had himself been the landlord. This makes it a receipt of the recipient's UK property business (*CTA 2009, s 221(2)*). If he does not have any property income of his own, the effect of this deeming is also to deem him to carry on a UK property business. If the payment is for a variation or waiver (ie one within *ss 281* or *221*), it is taxed on the third party only if he is a connected person of the landlord (within *ITA 2007, s 993* – see Appendix 1). If he is not, it does not appear that it can be taxed as income at all.

3.11 If a premium is receivable by instalments the landlord can opt to pay the tax by instalments if he can satisfy HMRC that he would otherwise suffer hardship. The number and amount of the instalments is at the discretion of HMRC but they cannot be spread over more than eight years (*ITTOIA 2005, s 299*; *CTA 2009, s 236*). HMRC normally expect the monies received to be used to pay the tax and will generally agree to instalments coinciding with the receipt of the consideration.

3.12 If an instalment is paid late, HMRC charge interest only from the date the instalment fell due (Property Income Manual PIM1220).

Charge on Assignment of Lease Granted at an Undervalue

3.13 The above provisions apply only to premiums payable for the grant of a lease; they do not apply to a capital sum, often colloquially called a premium, payable on the assignment of a lease. Such a payment does not in general attract an income tax charge. There is, however, one exception. It would be relatively easy to avoid a charge under these rules by the landlord granting a lease to a connected person without asking a premium, with the connected person then collecting a capital sum from the prospective tenant for an assignment of the lease. *ITTOIA 2005, s 282* and *CTA 2009, s 222* are designed to prevent this.

3.14 If the terms subject to which a lease of a duration of 50 years or less is granted are such that, having regard to values prevailing at the time, the landlord could have demanded a premium (or a larger premium than he in fact received) for the grant of the lease if it had been negotiated at arm's length (the difference being called below the 'amount forgone'), an income tax charge will arise if the lease is subsequently assigned for a capital sum. The amount of this charge is the sum that would have been taxable under *s 277* or *s 34(1)* (see **3.2** above) if the lower of the amount received on the assignment (less any premium paid for the grant of the lease) or the amount forgone had been received as a premium for the grant of the lease. Such sum is taxed on the assignor as a receipt of his UK property business (or of a notional UK property business if he does not have a UK property business of his own) (*ITTOIA 2005, s 282(2)*; *CTA 2009, s 222(1)–(3)*). The assignor does not have to be connected with the lessor. If he has obtained a lease at an undervalue the *Act* assumes that the lease was not granted at arm's length and that it is accordingly reasonable to impose a charge on the assignor. If the grant of the original lease was at arm's length then prima facie the amount forgone will be nil as the lease will have been granted on arm's length terms.

3.15 If the amount received on an assignment is less than the amount forgone a further charge will arise on a subsequent assignment until the full amount of the amount forgone has been brought into account.

Example 3.3

On 1 January 2016, April granted a 20-year lease to her sister May at rent of £1,000 pa and a premium of £2,000. If the transaction had been at arm's length April could have demanded a premium of £15,000. On 8 January 2017, May assigned the lease to her niece June for a payment of £10,000. June occupied the premises for the purposes of her business. On 31 December 2017, she ceased trading and assigned the lease at arm's length for a payment of £20,000.

April is taxed under *s 34(1)* on the premium received of £2,000.

2% of (50 – 19) × £2,000		= £1,240
The amount forgone is		
Arm's length premium	15,000	
Premium received	2,000	
Amount forgone	£13,000	
		£1,240

May is taxed under *section 222* on the lesser of

Payment received	10,000		
Less premium paid	2,000	8,000	
Amount forgone		13,000	
2% × 31 × £8,000			= £4,960

June is taxed under *section 222* on the lower of

Payment received	20,000		
Less premium paid	10,000	10,000	
Amount forgone	13,000		
Less taxed on May	8,000	5,000	
2% × 31 × £5,000			= £3,100
April is taxed in 2015/16, May in 2016/17 and June in 2017/18. It will be seen that all the charges are based on the taxable proportion at the date the premium is granted.			
			£9,300

It will also be seen that the charges aggregate to:

2% × 31 × £15,000 = £9,300

3.16 If the original landlord or any assignor or assignee wishes to know where he stands he can submit to his Inspector of Taxes a statement showing whether or not a charge to tax arises or could arise under *ITTOIA 2005, s 282* or *CTA 2009, s 222* and, if so, the amount on which a charge may arise. If the Inspector is satisfied as to the accuracy of the statement he must certify its accuracy (*ITTOIA 2005, s 300*; *CTA 2009, s 237*). If he is not satisfied – and as he is not a valuer it is difficult to see how he can be satisfied – he does not appear to have to do anything. HMRC's Property Income Manual tells Inspectors to refuse to give a certificate unless all the parties concerned are in agreement with the determination (PIM1222). It is difficult to see any point in requesting such a certificate.

Charge on Sale of Land with Right to Reconveyance

3.17 When a person grants a lease of property he gives up the right to possession for the period of the lease and recovers that right at its expiry. By 1963, when the provisions on premiums were introduced, the draftsmen were beginning to appreciate the ingenuity of taxpayers, and realised that a person could obtain the same effect as granting a lease at a premium by selling his land and buying it back for a lower figure at a later date. *ITTOIA 2005, s 284* and *CTA 2009, s 224* are designed to prevent the avoidance of income tax on a premium for a short lease by the use of this device.

3.18 It operates where the terms subject to which an estate or interest in land is sold provide that it will be reconveyed at a future date to the vendor (or to a person connected with him within the terms of *ITA 2007, s 993* – see Appendix 1) or that it may be required to be so reconveyed. It imposes a charge to income tax on the vendor on the amount, if any, by which the sale price exceeds the price at which it is to be reconveyed, reduced (if the earliest date that it can be required to be reconveyed falls two years or more after the sale) by one-fiftieth for each complete year (other than the first) in the period between the date of sale and the earliest date of reconveyance (*ITTOIA 2005, s 284*; *CTA 2009, s 224*).

Example 3.4

Joseph sold a property for £180,000 on 1 June 2016 on terms that the purchaser would resell it to him for £120,000 on 1 June 2021.

Joseph will be charged to income tax on:

	£
Sale price	180,000
Reconveyance price	120,000
	60,000
Less 1/50th × (5 – 1) years	4,800
Taxable as income	£55,200

3.19 The taxable amount is treated as a receipt of the vendor's UK property business (or a notional UK property business if he does not have other property income) (*ITTOIA 2005, s 244(3)*; *CTA 2009, s 224(3)*). The amount is treated as received when the estate or interest is sold and is thus treated as income of the period in which that sale takes place. For this purpose the time of sale is either when an unconditional contract for sale is entered into, a conditional contract for sale becomes unconditional or an option or pre-emption right is exercised requiring the vendor to enter into an unconditional contract or sale (*ITTOIA 2005, s 286(6)*; *CTA 2009, ss 224(3), 226(6)*).

3.20 If the date of reconveyance is not fixed and the repurchase price varies with that date the price must be taken to be the lowest possible under the terms of the sale. If, when the reconveyance takes place the resale price is higher, the owner can claim (within six years after the date of the reconveyance) repayment of the excess of the tax paid over the amount payable based on the actual date of reconveyance (*ITTOIA 2005, ss 286(3), 301*; *CTA 2009, s 226(2)–(5)*). Presumably this claim needs to be made outside the tax return.

Example 3.5

Harry sold a property for £300,000 on 12 September 2017. The sale agreement provided that the tenant could resell the property to Harry at any time after five years and must resell it to him one month after the expiry of the fifteenth year if he has not done so earlier. The reconveyance price was expressed to be:

on a sale at end of year 5	£230,000
on a sale at end of year 15	£75,000

on a sale on intermediate date £230,000 less £15,500 for each complete year after the fifth.

The property was reconveyed at the beginning of year 9 for £183,500.

It must be assumed that the property will be reconveyed at the end of year 5 (the earliest date at which it can be reconveyed) for £75,000 (the lowest price at which it can be reconveyed).

Harry will therefore be charged to income tax for 2017/18 on:

	£
Sale price	300,000
Deemed reconveyance price	75,000
	225,000
Less 1/50th × (5 – 1) years	18,000
Taxable as income	£207,000

Following the reconveyance Harry can have the charge reduced to:

	£
Sale price	300,000
Reconveyance price	183,500
	116,500
Less 1/50th × (8 – 1) years	16,310
Taxable as income	£100,190

Clearly it is most unattractive to enter into that sort of an arrangement!

3.21 The legislation does not indicate how the tax is to be computed if the reconveyance price is not fixed. This would not happen in an avoidance situation as the owner would want to fix the amount of the difference between sale and repurchase price if that difference were a disguised premium. Suppose, however, that the owner of an historic building sells it with a right of first refusal to repurchase at market value in its current use in the event of the purchaser wishing to resell. He may be public spirited and require this right to prevent the building being sold to a developer. The transaction will be within *section 36*. However, the repurchase price is not known. Hopefully, HMRC would say that the earliest date the property could be reconveyed is the day after the sale, at which time the reconveyance price would be equal to the sale price so that no charge could arise. The risk is that they would say that the lowest price at which the property could be reconveyed, eg following a nuclear holocaust, is £1. Accordingly, income tax should provisionally be paid on the full sale proceeds. This would be disastrous, particularly as if tax is paid initially and the reconveyance does not take place within 51 years of the sale – in which case the tax payable would be nil – no claim for repayment can be made until such time, if any, as the reconveyance actually takes place. The Revenue stated in 1978 that they were not aware of any bona fide commercial transactions ever having taken place that could fall within *section 36*. It is to be hoped that this happy state of affairs will continue to prevail!

3.22 Without further anti-avoidance rules it would be possible to circumvent the above provisions by a sale coupled with a right to the grant of a long lease to the vendor at a future date for a premium of less than the sale price, or for no premium but at a nil or nominal rent. Accordingly it is provided that if the sale agreement provides for the grant of a lease (directly or indirectly out of the interest sold) to the vendor or to a connected person (within *ITA 2007, s 993* – see Appendix 1) the grant of the lease must be regarded as equivalent to a reconveyance of the interest sold at a price equal to the amount of the premium (if any) paid for the lease plus the value (at the date of the initial sale) of the right to receive a conveyance of the reversion immediately after the lease begins to run (*ITTOIA 2005, s 285; CTA 2009, s 225*). The difference between the price that the purchaser pays and the value of his interest after granting the lease is of course the cost of obtaining the use of the property for the period between his purchase and the grant of the lease, which is the sum that would have been demanded as premium if he had taken a lease instead of entering into the sale and leaseback transaction. There is an exemption from this provision where the lease is granted to the vendor (and begins to run) within one month of the sale. This is to ensure that normal commercial sale and leaseback transactions are not caught.

Rules for Ascertaining Duration of Leases

3.23 Without rules for ascertaining the duration of leases it would be possible to disguise a lease of under 50 years as a long lease by, for example, granting a 60-year lease with a break clause after 30 years, perhaps coupled with such an enormous increase in rent that the tenant is bound to exercise the break option. To prevent such manipulation the following rules must be applied to determine the duration of a lease for the purpose of *ss 276–286* and *215–247*.

(*a*) Where any of the terms of the lease make it unlikely that the lease will continue beyond a particular date and the premium paid was not substantially greater than it would have been had the term expired on that date the lease cannot be regarded as having a term longer than one expiring on that date (*ITTOIA 2005, s 303*; *CTA 2009, s 243(1) Rule 1*). For example, suppose a 55-year lease is granted containing a provision that the lease can be forfeited at any time after the 25th year if the tenant does not thereafter repaint the property once a week. It is improbable that the tenant will repaint weekly. Accordingly, it is likely that the lease will be forfeited a week after the expiry of the 25th year. The lease must therefore be regarded as being for 25 years plus a week.

(*b*) Where the terms of the lease include provision for the extension of the lease beyond a given date by notice given by the tenant, account may be taken of any circumstances making it likely that the lease will be extended (*ITTOIA 2005, s 303*; *CTA 2009, s 243(1) Rule 2*). For example, suppose a ten-year lease contains an option for the tenant to extend the lease for a further 15 years and on taking possession the tenant installs equipment having a life of 25 years which it is uneconomic to install for ten years only. It is likely that he will exercise the option to extend so the lease can be regarded as a 25-year lease. If the option to extend was exercisable by the landlord and not by the tenant the lease would be regarded as a ten-year lease even if it was obvious that there was an understanding that the lease would be extended.

(*c*) If the tenant (or a connected person within *ITA 2007, s 993* – see Appendix 1) is, or may become, entitled to a further lease of the same premises (or of premises including the whole or part of the same premises) the term of the lease can (but not must) be treated as not expiring before the term of the further lease (*ITTOIA 2005, s 303*; *CTA 2009, s 243(1) Rule 3*). For example, suppose a tenant enters into a lease for ten years for a premium and simultaneously enters into a further lease of the same premises for 89 years commencing on the expiry of the first lease. The first lease can be treated as a 99-year lease. It may be thought that this is an improbable transaction. However, if a landlord is taxed on part of a premium the tenant is entitled to a deduction (if he is carrying on a trade or subletting the premises) spread over the term of the lease and equal to the amount taxed on the landlord (see **12.46–12.50** below). Accordingly where a landlord does not mind being taxed on a premium, such as if he has losses or is a property dealing company, it would be attractive to the tenant to pay a premium for a very short lease. *Rule 3* was therefore introduced to stop the term of a lease being very short but being supplemented by a second lease, so that commercially the tenant had the security of a very long lease but the tax benefits of a very short one. Where it is appropriate to do so, all or part of any premium paid for either of the two leases can be attributed to the other (*ITTOIA 2005, s 306(5)*; *CTA 2009, s 246(5)*).

3.24 The rules in **3.23** above must be applied by reference to the facts which were known or ascertainable at the time of the grant of the lease. In the case of a payment for a waiver or variation of a term of a lease which is treated as a premium under *CTA 2009, 3 34(5)* (see **3.8** above) the facts known at the time the variation agreement is entered into need to be considered (*ITTOIA 2005, s 304(1)*; *CTA 2009, s 244(1)*). In applying the above rules it must be assumed that all parties concerned act as if they were at arm's length (even if they are in fact connected) (*ITTOIA 2005, s 304(2)*; *CTA 2009, s 244(2)*). If any benefits other than vacant possession and beneficial occupation of the premises, or the right to receive rent at a reasonable commercial rate in respect of the premises, are conferred by the lease (or in connection with its grant), or payments are made that would not be expected to be made by parties acting at arm's length if no other benefits had been conferred, it must be assumed that the benefits would not have been conferred (or the payments made) had the lease been for a term ending before its stated expiry so that s *243(1) Rule 1* (see **3.23**(*a*) above) cannot be applied so as to deem the lease to be for a shorter period than its expressed term. This does not apply if it can be shown that the benefits were not in fact conferred (or the payment made) for the purpose of securing a tax advantage by the use – or abuse – of the provisions relating to income tax on premiums for leases, etc. (*ITTOIA 2005, s 304(3)–(5)*; *CTA 2009, s 244(2)–(6)*).

3.25 *Sections 304* and *244* do not apply to leases granted before 13 June 1969 or a variation or waiver entered into before that date. Where any of the terms of such a lease include provision for the determination of the lease by either landlord or tenant it cannot be treated as being for a term extending beyond the earliest date on which it could be terminated by notice, and where any of the terms or any other circumstances make it unlikely that the lease will continue beyond a date, it cannot be treated as extending beyond that date. This is subject to the provisos that if the duration of a lease falls to be ascertained after it has come to an end it is not to be treated as for longer than the period for which it in fact subsisted, and if the duration falls to be ascertained during the subsistence of the lease the above rules must be applied in accordance with circumstances prevailing at the time, eg they cannot treat it as already having come to an end (*ITTOIA 2005, Sch 2, para 71*; *CTA 2009, Sch 2, para 46*). If the terms of a lease granted before 25 August 1971, or varied or waived before that date, provide for determination by notice given by the landlord, it cannot be treated as being for a term longer than one ending on the earliest date on which it could be so determined; the rules in **3.23**(*a*) above are modified by ignoring whether or not the premium is substantially greater than would be appropriate for a lease expiring on an earlier date, and those in **3.23**(*c*) above do not apply. The normal meaning of 'premium' is also modified in relation to such a lease (*ITTOIA 2005, Sch 2, para 70*; *CTA 2009, Sch 2, para 45*).

Power to Obtain Information

3.26 If HMRC believe that any person has information relevant to the ascertainment of the duration of a lease for these purposes, they can require him to give them such information on the matters that they specify as are in that person's possession. A solicitor cannot, however, be required (on a client matter) to do more than state that he was acting on behalf of a client and give the client's name and address (*ITTOIA 2005, s 305*; *CTA 2009, s 245*).

Ancillary Points

3.27 Where it appears to HMRC that the determination of a taxable amount under *ss 276–286* (or *ss 215–247*) may affect the tax liability of some other person, such as the tenant who will want to claim a deduction for the notional rent, they can notify that other person of the determination that they intend to make. If they do so the tenant, etc. has 30 days to object to the proposed determination. If he does not object he cannot later challenge the determination. If he objects and the calculation of the taxable amount cannot be resolved amicably between the landlord, the tenant, HMRC, and anyone else interested, the matter goes before the First-tier Tribunal. At this hearing all of the affected parties have a right to take part in the proceedings and all (and their successors in title) will be bound by the determination made by the Tribunal. HMRC are empowered to require any person to give such information as they may think necessary to decide whether a notification should be served on any person (*ICTA 1988, s 42; CTA 2009, s 240*).

3.28 Where a premium or other payment within *ss 276–286* or (or *ss 215–247*) is paid to a non-resident, the position is unclear. As the premium is deemed to be additional rent it is income of the landlord's UK property business. *Regulation 1(2)(a)* of the *Taxation of Income from Land (Non-Residents) Regulations 1995* (*SI 1995 No 2902*) requires tax to be deducted from 'any payment … which constitutes income of a Schedule A business carried on by a non-resident'.

3.29 The Regulations do not contain any specific rules regarding premiums. It was held in the employment income case of *CIR v Herd (66 TC 29)* that the reference to 'any payment' in the PAYE Regulations did not impose an obligation to deduct tax where part only of the payment was income. It may well be that the courts would interpret this regulation in the same way. However, HMRC have given no indication that the new rules were intended to remove the obligation to deduct tax from the income element of a premium on a lease. Interestingly, their booklet IR150 (Taxation of Rents) stated that tax has to be deducted 'from the income of your rental business' (para 542) but leaflet IR140 (Non-resident landlords) told the tenant only that he must deduct tax from rents. Both of these booklets have since been withdrawn but probably only because HMRC seem to have decided that taxpayers are not able to digest anything longer than two A4 pages.

3.30 For the purpose of the above provisions any sum (other than rent) paid on or in connection with the granting of a tenancy will be presumed to be a premium unless sufficient other consideration for the payment can be shown to have been given *(ITTOIA 2005, s 306; CTA 2009, s 246*).

3.31 *ITTOIA 2005, ss 306, 307* and *CTA 2009, s 247* contain definitions of a lease, premium and reversion. These are self-evident – with the possible exception of a premium, the normal meaning of which is extended to include any like sum payable either to the landlord, to his landlord, or to a connected person of either (within *ITA 2007, s 993* – see Appendix 1).

Deduction of Premium Paid

3.32 Where part of a premium or other payment to the landlord has become chargeable to income tax or treated as income of a UK property business under *ss 277* or *282* (or *ss 221* or *222*), or would have become so chargeable but for any exemption from tax, eg where the landlord is a charity, or but for the operation of *ss 287* and *227* themselves, the payer may be entitled to claim tax relief under either *ITTOIA 2005, ss 60–67* or *287–295* or *ICTA 1988, ss 227–230*. *Sections 60–67* are considered at **12.46–12.50** below. *Sections 287* and *227* apply where the tenant himself receives a premium or deemed premium in respect of the premises; for example, on the grant of a sublease. It limits the charge on the tenant (or the amount treated as income of his UK property business) under *ITTOIA 2005, ss 277, 279, 280, 281* and *282* (or *CTA 2009, ss 217, 219, 220, 221* or *224*) in relation to the premium he receives to the excess of the chargeable amount of that premium over the appropriate fraction of the amount chargeable on the superior interest (*ITTOIA 2005, s 288*; *CTA 2009, ss 227, 228*).

3.33 The amount chargeable on the superior interest is, of course, the amount on which the landlord is taxed. The appropriate fraction is the proportion of that amount that the length of the lease granted by the tenant bears to the length of the lease in relation to which he paid his premium, ie

$$\text{amount taxed on landlord} \times \frac{\text{length of lease for which tenant received premium}}{\text{length of lease for which tenant paid premium}}$$

3.34 In both cases the length of the lease is the period treated as the duration of the lease under *ss 277–281* or *ss 217–223* (which can be less than the term of the lease either because it is deemed under *ss 303* or *244* to have a specific duration or because the sum paid relates to a variation, waiver, etc. for less than the whole term of the lease), or the duration remaining at the date of the assignment where the charge is under *ss 282* or *222*.

Example 3.6

Leslie paid a premium of £80,000 on 6 April 2017 for a grant of a lease for a period of 40 years. She immediately granted a sublease for five years at a premium of £6,000.

Leslie is taxable as property income (in addition to her net rent received) on:

		£
Taxable portion of premium received		
2% × (50 – (5 – 1)) = 92% of £6,000		5,520
Less appropriate fraction of taxable portion of premium paid		
2% × (50 – (40 – 1)) = 22% of £80,000 =	£17,600	
17,600 × 5/40 =		2,200
		£3,320

3.35 If the sublease extends to part only of the premises only that part of the appropriate fraction of the amount chargeable on the superior interest which on a just apportionment relates to the part sublet can, of course, be deducted (*ITTOIA 2005, s 289*; *CTA 2009, s 229(2),(3)*).

3.36 If a person who pays a premium grants a sublease under which no premium is payable (or the premium on which is insufficient to enable full relief for the amount taxable on the landlord to be given) he is treated as paying additional rent for the premises, which is deemed to become due from day to day during the period in respect of which the amount chargeable on the landlord arose, equal in total to that amount (*ITTOIA 2005, ss 291–293*; *CTA 2009, ss 231–233*). In other words, the amount taxable on the landlord is spread on a day-to-day basis over the term of the lease (or rather its deemed term under *ss 277–282* or *ss 221* or *222*) and treated as rent payable by the tenant. If the tenant assigns his lease, the assignee takes over the right to the deduction for the unexpired period. In relation to leases granted after 1 April 2013 (6 April for income tax) no deduction is given if none would have been due but for deeming the lease to be shorter than its term in accordance with *ITTOIA 2005, s 303* or *CTA 2009, s 243, Rule 1* (see **3.23**(*b*) (*ITTOIA 2005, s 292(4A)–(4C)*; *CTA 2009, s 232(4A)–(4C)* inserted by *FA 2013, Sch 28, paras 2, 5*).

Example 3.7

Mary paid a premium of £60,000 on 18 May 2016 for a ten-year lease at a rent of £500 pa. She granted a sublease for five years from 1 July 2016 at a rent of £7,500 pa payable monthly in advance. She sold the lease to Mark for £55,000 on 31 December 2015.

Mary		£	£
Rent received 2016/17 10 months @ £625			6,250
Less rent paid		500	
notional additional rent			
2% × (50 – (10 – 1)) = 82% of £60,000 =	£49,200		
proportion attributable to period 18.5.2013–5.4.2014			
	$\frac{323}{10 \times 365 \text{ days}} \times 49{,}200 =$	4,354	
			4,854
			£1,396
Rent received 2017/18 8 months @ £625			5,000

	£	£
Less rent paid	500	
Less recovered from Mark on the assignment	187	
	313	
notional additional rent		
$\frac{270}{10 \times 365} \times 49{,}200 = 3{,}639$		
		3,952
		£1,048
Mark	£	£
Rent received 2017/18 4 months @ £625		2,500
Less rent paid (under apportionment on acquisition)	187	
notional additional rent		
$\frac{95}{10 \times 365} \times 49{,}200 = 1{,}281$		
		1,468
		£1,032

3.37 Where, as in *Example 3.6* above, full relief for the fraction of the amount chargeable on the landlord can be given against the premium on the sublease, no further relief can be given against the rent under that sublease. However, where relief is given against the taxable part of the premium on a sublease, but the taxable part of that premium is less than the taxable portion of the premium paid to the landlord that is attributable to the term of the sublease, relief for the balance can be given against the rent – but only to the extent of the proportion which that balance bears to the taxable portion of the premium paid that is attributable to the sublease (*ITTOIA 2005, s 293*; *CTA 2009, s 233(1)–(4)*).

Example 3.8

Suppose that Leslie in *Example 3.6* had granted her five-year sublease for a premium of £2,000 and a rent of £1,000 pa payable monthly in advance, and the ground rent payable under her lease was £100 pa payable annually in advance.

	£	£
Her taxable rent for 2017/18 would be		
Taxable portion of premium received		
2% × (50 – (5 – 1)) = 92% of £2,000	1,840	
Less appropriate fraction of taxable portion of premium paid (as before)	2,200	NIL
Excess	360	
Rent received		1,000
Less rent paid	100	
Notional additional rent		
$\frac{360}{2,200} \times \frac{17,600}{40 \text{ years}}$	72	172
		£828

Over the first five years Leslie will therefore obtain relief of £1,840 + (5 × £72) = £2,200, or 1/8th of £17,600, which is what one would expect as the sublease covers 1/8th of the length of Leslie's lease.

3.38 If the sublease extends to part only of the premises the relief due is calculated separately for that part and for the remainder (*ITTOIA 2005, s 294*; *CTA 2009, s 234*).

3.39 Where a person has granted a sublease for a term shorter than that of the headlease and subsequently grants a further sublease, relief is of course available against the premium or rent from that subsequent lease.

Example 3.9

Leslie in *Example 6* grants a second sublease for five years at a premium of £6,000 on the expiry of the sublease on 5 April 2020.

The position will be:

Relief in the first 5 years as in *Example 3.8*	
£1,840 + (5 × £72)	£2,200
Relief in year 6 against premium received as per *Example 3.6*	£2,200

Relief available to be given against premium/rent on subsequent leases for year 11 onwards	£13,200

3.40 No relief can be given under either *ITTOIA 2005, ss 60* or *287* (or *CTA 2009, ss 227–235* or *62–67*) (see **12.46**) in respect of an amount taxed on the landlord under *s 284* or *ss 224* or *225*. Relief used to be given for such a sum but it was found to be open to abuse – an artificial tax avoidance scheme exploited what was intended as an anti-avoidance provision to generate tax relief for the cost of land and buildings. Rather than seek to block this abuse the government opted to withdraw the relief completely.

Capital Gains Tax Relief

3.41 The grant of a lease at a premium is a part disposal for capital gains tax purposes. The value of the property undisposed of, namely the reversion on the lease, accordingly needs to be ascertained and the normal A/(A+B) formula used to arrive at the allowable cost (*TCGA 1992, s 42, Sch 8 para 2*). Where part of the premium has been taxed as property income that taxed amount obviously needs to be excluded from the capital gains tax computation. This is achieved by *TCGA 1992, Sch 8 paras 5 and 6*.

3.42 The basic rule is that the amount taxed as property income is excluded from capital gains tax, ie it is deducted from the premium, the net amount only being liable to capital gains tax (*TCGA 1992, Sch 8 para 5(1)*). For the purpose of applying the normal A/(A+B) formula that applies to part disposals in order to arrive at the part of the cost to be set against the premium, the gross premium still needs to be used in the denominator of the fraction (*TCGA 1992, Sch 8 para 5(1)*).

Example 3.10

Jane in *Example 3.1* (see **3.2** above) granted a lease at a premium of £50,000. Suppose the value of her freehold reversion following the grant of the lease was £140,000 and that the freehold property had originally cost her £160,000.

	£
Her chargeable gain will be	
Premium	50,000
Less part taxed as UK property business income (see *Example 3.3*)	41,000
	9,000

Less allowable cost

$$\frac{\text{part of premium subject to CGT}}{\text{entire premium + reversion}} \times \text{cost}$$

	$\frac{9{,}000}{50{,}000 + 140{,}000} \times £160{,}000$	7,579
Chargeable gain		£1,421

3.43 This treatment applies where the lease is granted out of a freehold or a long lease, ie one which is not a wasting asset – normally one of over 50 years. If a sublease is granted out of a lease which has 50 years or less to run at the time of granting the sublease (the length of the lease being determined in accordance with the rules set out in **11.32–11.49** below), a different approach is adopted. The amount which is taxed as UK property business income is deducted not from the consideration (the premium) but from the capital gain accruing on the receipt of the premium (*TCGA 1992, Sch 8 para 5(2)*). As will be seen from **11.42** below the capital gain in such circumstances is not calculated using the A/(A+B) formula and the special method of calculation makes the normal CGT treatment of the amount taxed as UK property business income inappropriate.

3.44 The deduction from the gain is limited to the amount of the capital gain; it cannot create or increase a capital loss (*TCGA 1992, Sch 8 para 5(2)*).

3.45 If income tax has been charged under *ITTOIA 2005, s 284* or *CTA 2009, ss 224, 225* (sale of land with right to reconveyance) (see **3.17** above) the amount charged to income tax is similarly excluded from the sale proceeds received unless the sale is a part disposal, when the sale proceeds are left unadjusted in the denominator of the part disposal fraction (*TCGA 1992, Sch 8 para 5(3)*) – or unless what is disposed of is the remainder of a lease, or a sublease out of a lease of 50 years or less, in which case the amount taxed as property income is deducted from the gain (but it cannot create or increase a capital loss) (*TCGA 1992, Sch 8 para 5(3)* proviso).

3.46 These rules displace *TCGA 1992, s 37* (exclusion of consideration chargeable to income tax) (*TCGA 1992, Sch 8 para 5(5)*). They apply where the income tax charge is on a deemed premium as well as where an actual premium is received (*TCGA 1992, Sch 8 para 5(4)*). These are both instances where a cash sum is received. The reason that *para 5(4)* does not include a deemed premium under *ITTOIA 2005, s 278* or *CTA 2009, s 218* (where the tenant is required to carry out works) is that the landlord would not have a capital gains tax disposal in such circumstances. Where a deemed premium arises under *s 278* or *s 218)* the amount on which the landlord is charged to tax is deemed to be enhancement expenditure attributable to his interest in the property, so capital gains tax relief will be obtainable on a subsequent disposal (*TCGA 1992, Sch 8 para 7*).

3.47 If the payer of a premium for a lease has granted a sublease and is entitled to treat part of the premium that he pays as additional rent under *ITTOIA 2005, ss 291–293* or *CTA 2009, ss 231–233* (see **3.36** above) any capital gains tax loss on the grant of the sublease is restricted by deducting from the loss the sum which he is entitled to claim as additional rent over the term of the sublease. This deduction can only eliminate the loss; it cannot convert it into a gain (*TCGA 1992, Sch 8 para 6(1)*).

Example 3.11

Leslie in *Example 3.8* (see **3.37** above) paid a premium of £80,000 on 6 April 2015 for a 40-year lease and received a premium of £2,000 on the same day for the grant of a five-year sublease.

Her capital gains tax computation on the premium received will be:

	£	£
Premium received		2,000
Less allowable portion of premium paid		
take percentage for a 40-year lease 95.457		
take percentage for a 35-year lease 91.981		
$\frac{95.457 - 91.981}{95.457} \times £80{,}000$		2,913
Loss		(913)
Restriction is made as follows:		
taxable portion of premium paid applicable to period of sublease	2,200	
taxable portion of premium received (92%)	1,840	
excess relievable against rents		360
Allowable loss		£(553)

3.48 Where a charge on property income arises under *ITTOIA 2005, s 282* or *CTA 2009, s 222* (see **3.14** above) in relation to the assignment of a lease granted at an undervalue, *TCGA 1992, s 37* (which excludes from capital gains tax amounts taxed as income) is not to apply (*TCGA 1992, Sch 8 para 6(2)*). The effect seems to be to subject the entire receipt to capital gains tax as well as charging part to income tax. It may be that the draftsman felt that where *ITTIOA 2005, s 282* or *CTA 2009, s 222* applies the grant of the lease would normally have been a transaction otherwise than at arm's length, so that the lessee's capital gains tax base cost would be the market value of the lease at the time it was granted, ie the open market premium that could have been charged. Accordingly the amount of the undervalue taxed under *ss 282* or *222* will already have been excluded from his capital gains tax computation. However, this would imply a capital gains tax charge on the lessor in relation to theundervalue, so there would still be double taxation overall.

'Premiums' for Assignments of Leases

3.49 A payment for an assignment of an existing lease is generally described as a premium. However, except in the unusual circumstances covered by *s 282* or *s 222* (see **3.14** above), such a payment will not attract an income tax charge on the landlord, and will generate no income tax relief for the tenant. The receipt by the assignor is chargeable to capital gains tax in the normal way. He will have made a complete disposal of his interest in the lease. See further **11.29–11.49** below. If the assignor pays the incoming tenant a capital sum to induce him to take the assignment, that sum was normally not taxable prior to 9 March 1999 (see **3.52**). It is now taxable if the assignor is connected with the landlord (but probably not otherwise), although spread over the period up to the first rent review. The new provisions do not address the problem of the assignor getting tax relief for the payment. He cannot normally obtain a deduction in calculating trading profits for the payment (unless he held the lease as trading stock) (see **12.47** below). He cannot treat it as allowable expenditure for the purpose of claiming a capital loss on the lease either, as it does not fit into the restrictive rules of *TCGA 1992, s 38(1)(2)*. This problem is considered further at **3.56**.

Surrender of Leases

3.50 The surrender of a lease will not normally attract an income tax charge under these rules even if the tenant makes a payment to the landlord for the surrender, unless that payment is under one of the terms subject to which the lease was granted (see **3.6–3.9** above). The landlord will of course be chargeable to capital gains tax on the receipt either under *TCGA 1992, Sch 8 para 3(2)* (see **11.36** below) or, more often, under *TCGA 1992, s 22(1)* as a capital sum derived from the landlord's interest in the property. The VAT aspects of reverse surrenders are dealt with at **17.10** onwards.

'Reverse Premiums'

3.51 The expression 'reverse premium' is frequently used to describe a payment by a landlord to a tenant to induce him either to enter into a lease or to increase the rent payable under an existing lease. The tax treatment of a reverse premium is likely to depend on the facts of each individual case and in particular on the category into which the transaction falls. If the payment is to an existing tenant to induce him to pay an increased rent the reverse premium is in effect paid in consideration of his disposing of his existing right to occupy the premises at a favourable rent. As such he will have a part disposal of his lease and will realise a capital gain on the reverse premium less an apportioned part of his base cost of the lease (*TCGA 1992, s 22(1)(c)*).

3.52 If the payment is to induce the tenant to enter into a new lease he starts with nothing. He is receiving the reverse premium as an inducement to persuade him to take on liabilities that he would not otherwise have undertaken. Such reverse premiums are normally taxable, if at all, as income under *ITTOIA 2005, s 101* or *CTA 2009, ss 96–100* formerly *FA 1999, Sch 6*.

3.53 *ITTOIA 2005, s 101* and *CTA 2009, ss 96–100* apply where:

(*a*) a person receives a payment or other benefit by way of inducement in connection with a transaction entered into by him or a person connected with him;

(*b*) that transaction is one under which the person receiving the payment or other benefit (or the connected person) becomes entitled to an estate or interest in (or a right in or over) land; and

(*c*) the payment or other benefit is paid or provided by either:

- (i) the person by whom that estate, interest or right is granted (or was granted at an earlier time) (the grantor),
- (ii) a person connected with the grantor, or
- (iii) a nominee of the grantor (or a connected person of his) or a person acting on the directions of the grantor or of a connected person (*ITTOIA 2005, s 99*; *CTA 2009, s 96*).

3.54 It should be particularly noted that:

(*a*) The payment must be by way of inducement. It is not clear what this means. For example, if a person is prepared to enter into a lease at £90,000 per annum and the prospective landlord suggests that instead he pays the prospective tenant £100,000 and the rent is increased to £115,000, it is not at all clear that the £100,000 is an inducement. It may be simply a commercial bargain under which one person is prepared to assume a liability to make a series of payments in consideration of an initial lump sum. When one purchases an annuity one would not normally describe the purchase price as an inducement to the insurance company to grant the annuity. The word 'inducement' implies an element of persuasion.

(*b*) It is not clear what is meant by 'other benefit'. HMRC have said that this has to be a benefit in money's worth and would not cover the granting of a rent-free period. However, they resisted requests for this to be spelt out in the legislation. It obviously needs to be a benefit that can be valued (and that value taxed) but even a rent-free period has a value to the tenant even though that value cannot be realised by a sale of the benefit.

(*c*) Persons are connected if they are connected within the meaning of *ITA 2007, s 993* (see Appendix 1) at any time when the relevant arrangements, ie any arrangements entered into in connection with the relevant transaction (either before, at the same time as, or after it), are entered into (*ITTOIA 2005, s 103*; *CTA 2009, s 100*). A payment to a third party who is not a connected person will not be caught. For example an individual could agree to take a lease if a payment is made to his fiancée, his nephew, his uncle or his common-law spouse. Whilst the opportunity for such payments may not arise often it is worth looking out for them.

(*d*) The recipient (or connected person) must become entitled to an estate or interest in land in consequence of the transaction. *Section 101* and *CTA 2009, ss 93–100* will not therefore apply if a person already has that interest, eg where the reverse premium is paid to vary the terms of an existing lease.

(*e*) The premium must be paid or provided by the landlord or a connected person of his. Situations can arise where an existing tenant is prepared to pay a landlord to accept a surrender of his lease. If the tenant enters into an agreement with the landlord and an unconnected third party that in consideration of the third party taking a new lease from the landlord the existing tenant will make a payment to the third party that payment will not fall within *s 101* or *Sch 6*. Similarly a payment by a tenant to a third party to induce him to take an assignment of an existing lease will not fall within the *section*. A payment by the landlord to induce the third party to take over an existing lease would do so though, unless the landlord himself initially took an assignment of his interest in the lease so that he is not the grantor of it.

3.55 There are a number of statutory exceptions.

(*a*) A receipt is not caught to the extent that it reduces the recipient's expenditure qualifying for capital allowances under *CAA 2001, s 532* (see **8.5**) (*ITTOIA 2005, s 100(1)*; *CTA 2009, s 97(1)* formerly *FA 1999,*

Sch 6 para 5). Where a tenant will carry out fitting out works it may be worth considering seeking a contribution to such costs instead of a reverse premium. Although this will restrict the tenant's capital allowances the resultant extra tax burden will be spread over a number of years and the landlord may be willing to increase the payment to reflect part of the benefit of his tax allowances if he can claim allowances under *CAA 2001, s 538* in relation to that contribution.

(*b*) A receipt by an individual which relates to premises occupied or to be occupied by him as his only or main residence is not caught (*ITTOIA 2005, s 100(2)*).

(*c*) A payment as consideration for the acquisition of an estate or interest in land under a sale and lease back within *ITA 2007, s 681A, CTA 2010, s 835* (see **12.15**), *ITA 2007, s 681AM, CTA 2010, s 847* (see **12.21**) or *ITA 2007, s 681BA, CTA 2010, s 850* (see **12.27**) is obviously not caught (*ITTOIA 2005, s 100(3)*; *CTA 2009, s 97(3),(4)*) as those provisions contain their own tax regime.

3.56 Where a reverse premium within *ss 101* (or *93–100*) is received for the purpose of a trade, profession or vocation carried on (or to be carried on) by the recipient it is taxed as a trading receipt of that trade (*ITTOIA 2005, s 101(2)*; *CTA 2009, s 98(2)*). In any other case it is treated as income of a UK property business. If the recipient already has a UK property business it is a receipt of that business (*ITTOIA 2005, s 311*; *CTA 2009, s 98(3)*). If a person has significant property income losses on other properties the diversion of a reverse premium to that person could be a means of utilising such losses. The effect in both cases is that the reverse premium is not normally taxed wholly in the year of receipt. It is normally spread on a straight-line basis over the lease term or, if shorter, the period to the review date on which the rent is first expected to be adjusted to a full market rent in accordance with UITF 12. If the landlord will accept reviews to say 95% of market rent this may allow the premium to be spread over the full lease term.

3.57 The reverse premium is taxed wholly in the year of receipt if one or more of the parties to the arrangements under which it is paid are connected persons (within *ITA 2007, s 993* – see Appendix 1) and the terms of those arrangements are not such as would reasonably have been expected if those persons had been dealing at arm's length, ie they differ to a significant extent from the terms which, at the time the arrangements were entered into, would be regarded as normal and reasonable in the market conditions then prevailing between persons dealing with each other at arm's length in the open market (*ITTOIA 2005, s 102*; *CTA 2009, s 99(1)–(3)*). The year of receipt for this purpose is the accounting year of the recipient in which the reverse premium is received. If the recipient receives it for the purposes of a trade, profession or vocation which has not yet commenced it is the accounting year in which the trade commences (*ITTOIA 2005, s 102(5)*; *CTA 2009, s 99(4),(5)*).

3.58 HMRC have given their own view on the interpretation of the legislation (Tax Bulletin 44, December 1999). They consider that:

(*a*) The following will be taxable inducements:

(i) contributions towards specific tenant's costs such as fitting out, start up or relocation;

(ii) sums paid to third parties to meet obligations of the tenant, such as rent to a landlord under an existing lease or a capital sum to terminate an existing lease; and

(iii) the effective payment of cash by other means, for example the landlord's writing off a sum which the tenant owes.

It is questionable whether a payment to a third party ((ii) above) constitutes a benefit to the tenant – or if it does whether the payment is the quantum of the benefit – particularly as the legislation contains no machinery for valuing non-cash benefits. HMRC do not deal with the more common case where the landlord takes an assignment of the prospective tenant's existing lease. Under that scenario, and indeed the payment of rent to the tenant's existing landlord, the 'benefit' to the tenant is virtually impossible to value in many cases as it is spread over an indefinite period and even then the cost cannot be quantified as this will depend on the ability to find a new tenant for the premises. Often a landlord takes an assignment of the prospective tenant's existing lease solely because he wants the tenant as an anchor tenant in his development and expects to be able to re-let the tenant's existing premises fairly easily. There is probably no benefit to the tenant in that event.

(*b*) The following are not caught because they do not involve any actual outlay:

(i) the grant of a rent-free period;

(ii) replacement by agreement of an existing lease at an onerous rent by a new lease at a lower rent; and

(iii) replacement by agreement of an existing lease by a new lease with less onerous conditions.

(*c*) The tenant does not receive a benefit if the landlord pays for tenant's fittings but reflects the expenditure in the rent.

(*d*) The payment by the tenant of fitting out costs or part of the building costs because he wants the work carried out to a specified standard is not caught even if the landlord reimburses all or part of the costs to him. (It is hard to imagine anyone thinking it might be.)

(*e*) A payment or other benefit to induce a person to buy a freehold building is not caught because a freehold cannot be 'granted', it can only be conveyed.

3.59 When this provision was originally introduced the government said that it was to clarify that law following the Privy Council decision in a New Zealand case, *CIR v Wattie (1998 STC 1160)* where an inducement payment to take a lease at a rent substantially above a market rate was held to be a capital receipt, albeit that it was admitted to be commercially, financially and mathematically linked to the rent. In practice, despite what the government said, the author cannot recollect having seen a pre-9 March 1999 reverse premium taxed as income. It is not by its nature income. It is not received in consideration of the tenant undertaking to provide services to the landlord. Admittedly a reverse premium has been held to be consideration for the provision of a service for VAT purposes (see **3.65**) but the VAT legislation deems anything done for a consideration and which is not a supply of goods to be a supply of services. This statutory fiction does not apply for income tax. The cases of *Gallagher v Jones (1993 STC 537)* and *Johnston v Britannia Airways Ltd (1994 STC 763)* emphasised that the starting point for the computation of profits for tax purposes is generally accepted accounting principles. The Accounting Standards Board's statement UITF 12 requires a reverse premium to be written off against profits over the term of the lease. Some people fear that this treatment will convert a reverse premium into profits even if it falls outside the scope of these provisions. This fear is probably unfounded. There is nothing in those cases to suggest that the accounting treatment can change the basic legal distinction between income and capital, and a reverse premium is by its nature a capital receipt. The reverse premium does not seem to come within the scope of property income as a receipt arising to a person from or by virtue of his ownership of an estate or interest in or right over such land (*ITTOIA 2005, s 264*; *CTA 2009, s 207(1)*) and neither can the lease premium rules be applied as the payment is not a 'premium required under a lease, or otherwise under the terms subject to which a lease is granted' (*ITTOIA 2005, s 277*; *CTA 2009, s 217(1)*). This view is supported by *ITA 2007, s 681B, CTA 2010, s 849* (see **12.25** below). This was introduced to impose an income tax charge on part of an amount received where a tenant under a short lease either took a reverse premium or sold his lease and took back a sublease at a higher rent. The *section* would hardly have been introduced if such a receipt was already within the charge to income tax.

3.60 A reverse premium that is not caught by *ss 101* (or *93–100*) and which is an inducement to take a new lease (as opposed to varying an existing one) does not seem to be within the scope of capital gains tax. This is charged on 'chargeable gains … accruing to a person on the disposal of assets' (*TCGA 1992, s 1(1)*). The author cannot see any asset that the tenant can have disposed of. The charge is extended by *TCGA 1992, s 22* to the case 'where any capital sum is derived from assets', but again it is not thought that this extension catches a reverse premium. The recipient of the premium does not derive it 'from' an asset. He derives it from agreeing to enter into a lease which has a negative market value. HMRC seem to accept that, apart from the special rules in *ITTOIA 2005, s 101* and *CTA 2009, s 96* (see **3.52**), the receipt is not taxable in such circumstances.

3.61 If the inducement is to take a new lease of premises already occupied by the tenant on the expiration of his existing lease, HMRC might contend that the receipt is in consideration of the tenant giving up his *Landlord and Tenant Act* rights deriving from the lease. However, it is difficult to envisage such a contention succeeding in the light of the decision in *Bayley v Rogers (53 TC 420)*, where it was held that a new lease granted following proceedings under the *Landlord and Tenant Act 1954* did not derive from the prior lease but was a separate asset.

3.62 The other provision that might need to be considered is *ITA 2007, ss 752–772* (*CTA 2010, ss 815–833* for corporation tax) (see **Chapter 14**). However, for this to apply, either:

(*a*) land, or property deriving its value from land, must be acquired with the sole or main object of realising a gain from disposing of the land; or

(*b*) land must be held as trading stock; or

(*c*) land must be developed with the sole or main object of realising a gain from disposing of the land when developed.

3.63 Assuming that the incoming tenant is intending to occupy the premises (so that condition (*a*) above will not apply) the receipt of a reverse premium will not normally fall into either of the two remaining categories.

3.64 As far as the payer is concerned, if he is a property dealer he should have no difficulty in obtaining a deduction for the reverse premium as a trading expense. If he holds the property as an investment, he will need to demonstrate that the payment constituted enhancement expenditure (see **11.8**(*b*) below). In many, if not most, cases it would clearly do so as the intention of making the payment is to enhance the investment value of the property. Similar considerations to those relating to payments to tenants to vacate premises would apply. These are discussed at **8.8** below. It may be more difficult to show that the expenditure is reflected in the state or nature of the asset at the time of its disposal though. It should particularly be noted that the legislation does not grant relief to the payer for a reverse premium taxed under *s 101* or *Sch 6*. Nor does it convert the payment to income as far as the payer is concerned. He can obtain a deduction only where the basic tax rules will permit this.

3.65 The VAT position on reverse premiums is considered at **17.10** onwards. Unfortunately the law is not clear-cut. Broadly speaking, a reverse premium does not attract VAT. However, it is necessary to consider carefully whether the receipt is merely intended as an inducement to take up the lease or whether the payer receives some benefit other than entering into the lease, for which all or part of the sum might constitute consideration.

Chapter 4

Relief for Interest Payable

4.1 Property owners frequently borrow funds to finance the acquisition of their properties or for carrying out works on them. In such circumstances it may be important to ensure that tax relief for the interest can be obtained. This is by no means automatic. The interest must sometimes meet specific conditions to attract a deduction for tax purposes.

4.2 For income tax purposes interest can be deducted either as a trading expense or as a UK property business expense. However, for 2017/18 onwards interest on a borrowing in connection with UK residential property is being phased out as a property business expense. Instead relief will be given at the basic rate only for such payments against the property business income (see **4.13**). If it cannot qualify as either it may still be deductible as an annual payment. As no deduction is in general allowed for mortgage interest on a person's own home, interest paid after 5 April 2000 on loans to acquire such properties is unlikely to be an annual payment (except on certain home income plans (see **4.24**)). Interest as such is not deductible for corporation tax purposes (*CTA 2009, s 1301A*); instead it is deductible as an element in the company's debit or credit on loan relationships. Interest paid by a company and UK source interest paid by any person to a non-UK resident normally has to be paid under deduction of income tax at 20% and the tax deducted paid over to HMRC (see **4.69**). For a non-resident with a UK borrowing, this effectively eliminates the benefit of the deduction. However withholding tax does not normally apply to a loan from one non-UK resident to another even though the interest on such a loan is deductible in calculating UK taxable income in the normal way.

Income Tax

Interest as a Trading or UK Property Business Expense

4.3 There are no special rules where the interest constitutes a trading expense or a UK property business expense. As with any other expense, to qualify as a deduction, the interest must be wholly and exclusively incurred for the purpose of the trade or property business (or overseas property business, where relevant). Provided it does so and does not fall foul of any of the other exclusions in *ITTOIA 2005, ss 32–37* it is deductible on an accruals basis in the same way as any other expense. This does not apply to interest in relation to residential property paid after 6 April 2017 (see **4.13**).

4.4 There can, however, be difficulties in determining to what the interest relates. In *Dixon v HMRC (2006 STC (SCD) 28)* the taxpayer purchased a newsagents business and dwelling house as a package for £134,500. £47,000 of the purchase price was apportioned to the house. The purchase price was satisfied as to £58,000 by the transfer of the purchaser's existing house to the vendor, as to £9,000 in cash and £67,500 by a mortgage. The taxpayer contended that the interest on the mortgage was a trading expense of the newsagency business. It was held that the purpose of the mortgage was to assist in the purchase of the package of assets, so 35% of the interest was for private use and only the remaining 65% was a business expense. This is a nasty decision. The whole of the interest would undoubtedly have been deductible if Mr Dixon had split the transaction, exchanging his house for the new house with £18,000 of equality money going towards the purchase of the newsagency and giving a charge on the house to the building society as additional security for a £67,500 loan to buy the newsagency.

4.5 Relief is also given under the normal rules for the incidental costs of obtaining finance by means of a loan or the issue of loan stock if the interest on the loan is deductible in calculating the profits of the property business (*ITTOIA 2005, s 58(1)*). The incidental costs for this purpose means expenses which are incurred on fees, commissions, advertising, printing and other incidental matters, and which are incurred wholly and exclusively for the purpose of obtaining the finance, providing security for it or repaying it (*ITTOIA 2005, s 58(2)*). Expenses incurred wholly and exclusively for the purpose of obtaining finance or providing security for it are incidental costs even if the finance is not in fact obtained (*ITTOIA 2005, s 58(3)*).

4.6 The following are excluded from being incidental costs of obtaining finance:

(*a*) currency losses;

(*b*) sums paid for the purpose of protecting against currency losses;

(*c*) the cost of repaying a loan or loan stock so far as attributable to its being repayable at a premium or having been obtained or issued at a discount; and

(*d*) stamp duty

(*ITTOIA 2005, s 58(4)*.)

This exclusion does not mean that such amounts are not deductible. It means that any deduction must be claimed under the normal trading expenses rule.

4.7 It is possible for interest to be capital. In a Privy Council case, *Wharf Properties Ltd v Commissioner of Inland Revenue (of Hong Kong) (1997) STC 351*, interest was held to be capital. The relevant head of the legislation prohibited the deduction of 'any expenditure of a capital nature'. Although the equivalent UK legislation, *CTA 2009, s 53* also refers to 'items of a capital nature', interest is dealt with separately under the loan relationship rules so this decision is not directly relevant to the UK. At least it was not until 2005! It may now be for income tax purposes as the equivalent provision in *ITTOIA 2005, s 33*, is simply: 'no deduction is allowed for items of a capital nature'. In any event, the decision is useful for what it says about accounting principles. If accounting principles give a choice of capitalising or expensing interest and the taxpayer chooses to capitalise it, HMRC are likely to insist on that choice being followed for tax purposes also and disallow relief for the interest. This does not necessarily apply if the taxpayer is a company because the loan relationship rules impose their own tax treatment of interest.

4.8 Where the cash basis is used, the 'cost of the loan' (which will include interest) that can be deducted in calculating the profits for a tax year is restricted to the 'non-adjusted deduction' (see **4.9**) multiplied by the 'relevant fraction' (see **4.9**).

If–

(*a*) a deduction for costs (such as interest) of a loan (a relevant loan) is allowed in calculating the profits of the property business (or would have been allowed but for *ITTOIA 2005, s 272A* (restriction of deduction of finance costs of residential property – see **4.8**);

(*b*) an amount of the principal of one or more such relevant loans is outstanding at the end time (the end of the tax year or, if earlier, the time the property business permanently ceases) (an outstanding relevant loan); and

(*c*) L exceeds V, where V is the sum of the values of the relevant properties and L is the total amount outstanding on relevant loans.

(ITTOIA 2005, ss 307C(1)–(5), 307D(1) inserted by *F(No 2)A 2017, Sch 2, para 23.)*

4.9 The non-adjusted deduction is the interest paid that would have been deductible but for this adjustment. The relevant fraction is –

$$\frac{V}{L}$$

(ITTOIA 2005, s 307D.)

4.10 For this purpose the total outstanding amount of relevant loans is the sum of the 'outstanding business amounts' of outstanding relevant loans.

This is:

$$\frac{X}{Y} \times A$$

Where A is the principal amount of the loan that is outstanding at the end time,

X is the amount of the deduction for costs of the loan that would have been deductible but for *ss 272A* and *307D*, and

Y is the amount that would have been deductible but for both the wholly and exclusively rule and *ss 272A* and *307D*.

(*ITTOIA 2005, s 307C(6)(7)*.)

4.11 A property is a relevant property if it is involved in the business at the end time (or was previously involved in the business at an earlier time in the tax year in which the business was carried on by the same person). A property is involved in the business for this purpose if it is a property whose exploitation forms the whole or part of the business (*ITTOIA 2005, s 307C(8)(10)*). The value of a relevant property is the sum of its market value at the time it is first involved in the property business plus improvement expenditure (ie capital expenditure incurred by the business owner in respect of the property as is not brought into account in calculating the profits of the business for any tax year) (*ITTOIA 2005, s 307(9)*). Its market value for this purpose is the price which the property might reasonably be expected to fetch in the market conditions then prevailing, and between persons dealing with each other at arm's length in the open market (*ITTOIA 2005, s 307C(14)*). Property means an estate interest or right in or over land (*ITTOIA 2005, s 307C(14)*).

4.12 The costs of a loan are interest on the loan, any amount in connection with the loan that is a return for the person receiving it which is economically equivalent to interest, and incidental costs of obtaining finance by means of the loan (as defined in *ITTOIA 2005, ss 58(2)–(4)* – see **4.5**) (*ITTOIA 2005, s 307C(12)(13)*). The wholly and exclusively rule of course means the rule in *ITTOIA 2005, ss 34* and 272ZA (see **2.17**) which prohibits a deduction for expenses not wholly and exclusively incurred for trade and for unconnected losses (*ITTOIA 2005, s 307C(14)*).

Restriction for Residential Lettings

4.13 From 2017/18 onwards, the deduction in calculating the profits of a property business for income tax purposes for the costs of a 'dwelling-related loan' will be reduced *(F(No 2)A 2015, s 24)*. The intention is to limit the deduction to the basic rate of tax. However the restriction will be phased in as follows:

2017/18	Full relief for 75% of the costs and basic rate relief on the rest
2018/19	Full relief for 50% of the costs and basic rate relief on the rest
2019/20	Full relief for 25% of the costs and basic rate relief on the rest
2020/21	Relief is at basic rate only.

This is achieved by a new *ITTOIA 2005, s 272A(1)–(4)*, which gradually withdraws completely relief for such a loan, and a new *s 274A* which effectively reinstates basic rate relief in most cases by granting a tax credit equal to the basic rate on the interest. The restriction does not apply to the commercial letting of holiday accommodation (*ITTOIA 2005, s 272B(4)*). Nor does it apply to corporation tax but, as the corporation tax rate will be at or below the basic rate of income tax, it would have been the effect in any event (*ITTOIA 2005, s 272A*).

4.14 A dwelling-related loan is so much of an amount borrowed for the purposes of the property business as is referable (on a just and reasonable apportionment) to the part of the business that is carried on for the purpose of generating income from land consisting of a dwelling-house or part of a dwelling-house or from an estate, interest or right in or over such land (*ITTOIA 2005, s 272B(2)*). Anything that is done in the course of a property business for creating (by construction or adaptation) a dwelling-house (or part of a dwelling-house) from which such income is to be generated must also be treated as done for the purpose of generating such income (*ITTOIA 2005, s 272B(3)*).

4.15 Costs in relation to a dwelling-related loan mean interest, any amount in connection with the loan that (for the recipient) is a return in relation to the loan which is economically equivalent to interest, and the incidental costs of obtaining finance (as defined in *ITTOIA 2005, s 58(2)–(4)* – see **4.5**) (*ITTOIA 2005, s 272B(5), (6)*). A dwelling-house includes any land occupied or enjoyed with it as its garden or grounds (*ITTOIA 2005, s 272B(7)*).

4.16 If an amount would be deductible in calculating the profits for income tax purposes of a property business for a tax year but for

ITTOIA 2005, s 272A, and a particular individual is liable to income tax on a percentage of those profits (which could be 100%), he is entitled to tax relief for that year on that percentage of that amount (the relievable amount) (*ITTOIA 2005, s 274A(1), (2)* inserted by *F(No 2)A 2015, s 24(5)*). A person has a relievable amount for a tax year if he has a current-year amount, a current-year estate amount or a brought-forward amount. A person who has more than one property business can have separate relievable amounts for each such business (*ITTOIA 2005, s 274A(1), (2)*). A person can have more than one property business if he has a UK property business and an overseas property business, or if he has a personal property business and a partnership property business. An individual's relievable amount for a tax year in relation to a property business is of course the aggregate of any current-year amount, current-year estate amount and brought-forward amount (*ITTOIA 2005, s 274A(3)*).

4.17 An individual has a current-year amount for a tax year if an amount would be deductible in calculating the profits for income tax purposes of the business for that year but for *s 274A* (Amount A) and the individual is liable for income tax on a percentage of those profits (greater than 0% and not exceeding 100%). The current-year amount is of course that percentage of amount A (*ITTOIA 2005, s 274A(4)*). An individual has a current-year estate amount if he is a beneficiary of a deceased estate, the estate has an interest in a rental business, the personal representatives of the deceased estate are liable to income tax on a percentage of the profits of that rental business, and the individual is liable to income tax on estate income treated as arising in the current year from an interest in the estate. The individual's current-year estate amount is his percentage interest of the personal representatives percentage interest in amount A (*ITTOIA 2005, s 274A(6)*). The brought-forward amount is considered at **4.21**.

4.18 If an individual is entitled to relief for a relievable amount for a tax year, the actual amount on which relief is given is the lower of:

(*a*) that relievable amount;

(*b*) the profits of the property business for income tax purposes (after any deduction for a brought-forward property business loss) or, if less, the share of the adjusted profits on which the individual is liable to income tax, plus any current-year estate amounts; and

(*c*) the individual's adjusted total income.

(*ITTOIA 2005, s 274AA(1)–(3)*.)

Where the limitation is by reference to adjusted total income (see **4.14**) the actual amount on which relief is to be given in relation to a property business is:

Adjusted total income sum of L for each relievable amount if there is more than one	× L (the lower of (a) or (b))

(*ITTOIA 2005, s 274AA(3).*)

In a simple case where a person has an interest in only one property business, the formula amount becomes:

Adjusted total income (L)	= adjusted gross income

Where there is more than one property business, the formula apportions the adjusted gross income amongst the different property businesses.

4.19 For this purpose the taxpayer's adjusted total income is his net income for the year (calculated as under *ITA 2007, s 23*) less so much of it as is savings income and dividend income, and less any allowances deducted for the year at step 3 of the *s 23* calculation (ie his personal allowance and any similar allowances) (*ITTOIA 2005, s 274AA(6)*).

4.20 The relief to be given is then that actual amount multiplied by the basic rate of tax for the year.

4.21 If a relievable amount (see **4.16**) exceeds the actual amount on which relief for the year is to be given (the amount at **4.18**), the difference is the individual's brought-forward amount for the following tax year in respect of the property business concerned (*ITTOIA 2005, s 274AA(4)*).

4.22 A special rule applies to rental income of an accumulation or discretionary trust. The income of such a trust is taxable at the 45% trust rate of tax. The trustees of a settlement have a relievable amount for a tax year in respect of a property business if they have a current-year amount or a brought-forward amount in respect of that business (or both). If they have both, it is the total of those amounts (*ITTOIA 2005, s 274B(1)–(3)*). The trustees of a settlement have a current-year amount if they have an amount A in relation to a percentage of the property business which is accumulated or discretionary income (within *ITA 2007, s 480*) (*ITTOIA 2005, s 274B(4),(6)*). The amount of the relief is L × the basic rate for the year where L is the lower of:

- the relievable amount;
- the profits for income tax purposes of the property business concerned after any deduction for brought-forward losses; and
- the share of the adjusted profits on which the trustees are liable for income tax and which (in relation to the trustees) is accumulated or discretionary income.

(*ITTOIA 2005, s 274C(1)(2).*)

If L is less than the relievable amount, the difference between the two figures is the brought-forward amount of the trustees for that property business for the following tax year (*ITTOIA 2005, s 274C(3)*).

4.23 Income tax relief for interest on a loan to invest in a partnership will also be restricted if the partnership carries on a property business and that business (or part of it) is carried on for the purpose of generating income from land consisting of a dwelling-house or part of a dwelling house (or an estate, interest or right in or over such land) (*ITA 2007, ss 399A*, inserted by *FA 2015, s 24(7)*). The restriction on higher rate tax relief is the same as for interest paid by a property business (see **4.13**) but basic rate relief is given on the full amount of interest (*ITA 2007, s 399B*).

Home Income Plans

4.24 The only interest on a loan to acquire property that qualifies as an annual payment – and as such can be set against general income – is that payable on some historic loans where the loan was taken as part of a home annuity or home income plan where at least 90% of the amount borrowed was used by the borrower to buy a life annuity on his own life or on the life of the survivor of himself and some other person or persons. The loan must have been made before 9 March 1999, the borrower or the annuitants must have been 65 or over at the time the loan was made; it must be secured on land in the UK or Eire; the borrower or one of the annuitants must own an interest in that land; the borrower or each of the annuitants must use the land as his only or main residence at the time the interest is paid; and the interest must be payable by the borrower or by one of the annuitants (*ICTA 1988, s 365*). The requirement that the property must be the main residence does not apply if, at the time it ceased to be the main residence, the intention of the borrower, or of each of the annuitants owning an interest in the land, was to take steps within the following 12 months with a view to disposing of his interest. Relief for the interest continues for the shorter of either that 12-month period or until the intention to dispose of the interest is abandoned (*ICTA 1988, s 365(1A)*). The tax relief is not based on current tax rates. It is given at a fixed rate of 23%. It is given for interest on the first £30,000 of borrowings only (*ICTA 1988, ss 365(3), 353(1A)–(1AB)* inserted by *ITA 2007, Sch 1 para 62*). MIRAS (Mortgage Interest Relief at Source) continues to apply to such loans where the borrowing is from a qualifying lender. This is a system of tax deduction at source that used to apply to mortgage interest up to 5 April 2000 when a loan to buy a principal private residence in the UK (but not the Republic of Ireland) was taken from a bank or building society. Where MIRAS applies to home income plan loans, no further tax relief will be due as it has already been given by reducing the monthly payments to the lending institution.

4.25 Relief is also given if the loan was made after 9 March 1999 in pursuance of a written offer by the lender before that date (or one evidenced by a note or memorandum made by the lender before that date) (*ICTA 1988, s 365(1AA)*. An interest payment under a pre-9 March 1999 home income plan will also qualify for relief if it is on a replacement loan made after 26 July 1999 as part of a scheme to replace a previous qualifying loan (*ICTA 1988, s 365(1AB)*. If the whole of a replacement loan is not used to replace the old one at least 90% of the non-qualifying amount must be used to buy an annuity on the life of the taxpayer or of the survivor of him and some other person, such as his spouse (*ICTA 1988, s 365(1AC)(1AD)*). This will allow the annuitant to top up both the loan and the annuity if his existing loan is under £30,000. If more than 10% of the extra borrowing is used for some other purpose no relief is given at all for the replacement borrowing – even up to the amount of the old loan.

4.26 Interest continues to qualify for relief even if the annuitant ceases to occupy the property provided that he had a qualifying home income plan at 9 March 1999 (*ICTA 1988, s 365(1)(d)*). This will allow relief to continue if the annuitant has to go into a nursing home or decides to move to a smaller house. This relaxation also applies if although the borrower (or one of the annuitants) did not occupy the property at 9 March 1999 he did so at some time in the previous year and at 8 March 1999 it was intended to take steps to sell the property within 12 months of its ceasing to be used as the principal residence (*ICTA 1988, s 365(1A)*).

Corporation Tax

4.27 Interest paid by a company qualifies for relief as a debit on loan relationships. This normally means that relief will be given for it on an accruals basis but there are major exceptions. The tax provisions on loan relationships apply both to interest paid (which is a debit on a loan relationship) and to interest received (which is a credit on a loan relationship). This makes the definitions a little difficult to follow as they are intended to embrace both borrower and lender. These rules also apply to other debits in respect of loans such as bad debts and financing costs and to other credits such as loan waivers.

What is a Loan Relationship?

4.28 A company has a loan relationship wherever:

(*a*) it stands in the position of a creditor or debtor as regards any money debt, and (*b*) that debt is one arising from a transaction for the lending of money (*CTA 2009, s 302(1),(2)*).

4.29 Broadly speaking, a money debt is one which falls to be settled either by the payment of money or by the transfer of a right to settlement under a debt which is itself a money debt (*CTA 2009, s 303(1),(2)*). Money is not restricted to sterling but covers any currency (*FA 1996, s 81(6)* now repealed). This provision was not re-enacted in *CTA 2009* as it was felt unnecessary to specifically say this.

4.30 A loan will almost always be a loan relationship. Unpaid purchase consideration is not a loan relationship, but could probably become one if the parties agreed to convert it into a loan (although this is not wholly clear). A money debt which is not a loan relationship – such as unpaid purchase consideration – is treated as a loan relationship if an instrument is issued by any person for the purpose of representing security for a money debt (*CTA 2009, s 303(3)*). Therefore a mortgage will always be a loan relationship. So will a money debt represented by a debenture or loan stock, eg where a property is transferred to a company in consideration of the issue of loan stock in the company.

4.31 Conversely a loan will not be a loan relationship to the extent that it arises from rights conferred by shares in a company. If company A acquires company B in consideration for issuing loan stock in itself in exchange for shares in company B, that loan stock will not be a loan relationship (*CTA 2009, s 303(3),(4)*).

4.32 Where interest on a money debt (see **4.29**) is payable by a company which is (or has been) the creditor in respect of it, but the debt did not arise from a loan relationship, eg it arose from unpaid consideration, that interest is to be treated as if it were payable under a loan relationship (*CTA 2009, ss 479(1),(2), 481(1)–(3)*). Other debits in respect of such a debt (ie other than those at **4.50**), such as writing it off if it proves bad, or any costs of creating the debt, are not brought within the loan relationship rules but are likely to be deductible under general principles. This provision will grant relief for interest on delayed completions – and tax interest received on such transactions or interest on compensation on a compulsory acquisition – on an accruals basis.

Trading Companies

4.33 Debits and credits (eg interest paid and received) are ascertained separately for trading and non-trading loan relationships. A trading loan relationship for this purpose is, of course, one to which the company is a party for the purpose of a trade which it carries on (*CTA 2009, s 297(1)–(3)*). Interest and other debits on trading loan relationships (net of any interest received on such relationships) are treated as trading expenses and credits on trading loan relationships as trade receipts (*CTA 2009, s 297(1)–(3)*). Although taxable rental income is calculated on trading principles, interest on a loan to acquire a property investment is on a non-trading loan relationship.

Investment and Other Non-trading Companies

4.34 Debits and credits on non-trading loan relationships are netted off. If there is a net credit (eg interest received in excess of interest paid) it is taxed as a profit arising from the company's loan relationships (*CTA 2009, ss 299, 301*). If there is a net debit (called a deficit on loan relationships) a claim can be made to treat the whole or any part of it in the following ways:

(*a*) set against profits of the company for the same accounting period;

(*b*) treated as eligible for group relief (unless the company is a charity – *s 83(5)*);

(*c*) carried back for up to three years; or

(*d*) carried forward against non-trading profits (which expression includes capital gains).

(*CTA 2009, ss 458, 459.*)

4.35 The claim must be made within two years after the end of the accounting period in which the deficit occurs (or the following accounting period if the claim is to carry forward under head (*d*)) or such longer period as HMRC may allow (*CTA 2009, s 460(1)*). Different claims can be made for different parts of the deficit but two claims obviously cannot be made in relation to the same amount (*CTA 2009, s 460(2),(3)*).

4.36 In the case of a claim under head (*a*) the profits against which the deficit is to be relieved must be identified in the claim (*CTA 2009, s 461(2),(3)*). In most cases it will not matter what profits are utilised. Any brought forward trading losses must be relieved in priority to setting a non-trading deficit on loan relationships against trading profits, but set-off of the non-trading deficit has priority to a claim to set off a trading loss of the same accounting period or to carry back a trading loss or a non-trading deficit on loan relationships of a later accounting period (*CTA 2009, s 461(5),(6)*).

4.37 If a non-trading deficit is carried back under head (*c*) it can be set only against profits and gains on loan relationships (*CTA 2009, s 463(1)–(3)*).

The carry back is against income of the three years preceding the beginning of the accounting period in which the deficit arises (*CTA 2009, s 463(2)–(4)*). Relief is given first against profits of the latest accounting period (*CTA 2009, s 462(4),(5)*). Brought forward losses or non-trading deficits, charges on income (both brought forward and for the accounting period), trading losses (both of the same accounting period and carried back from a later one), non-trading deficits of the same accounting period, and, in the case of an investment company, capital allowances under *CAA 2001, ss 15, 253* (see **10.2**), management expenses and charges on income (in both cases of the same or any other accounting period) must all be relieved in priority to the carried-back deficit on loan relationships (*CTA 2009, s 462(5)*).

4.38 If no claim is made the deficit is carried forward and treated as a non-trading debit of the next accounting period, but cannot be either utilised in that next period by set-off against income other than from non-trading profits or used in a group relief claim (*CTA 2009, s 457(1),(2*).

Calculation

4.39 For both trading and investment companies the credits and debits in respect of loan relationships for an accounting period are the amounts which in accordance with an 'authorised accounting method' (see **4.42**) when taken together fairly represent all profits, gains and losses of the company (including those of a capital nature) which arise from its loan relationships and related transactions and all interest under the company's loan relationships and all charges and expenses incurred by it for the purpose of its loan relationships and related transactions (*CTA 2009, ss 293, 307*). This includes interest, bad debts, financing costs and loan waivers. The HMRC view is that guarantee fees incurred in connection with a loan relationship do not fall within *section 84* unless the loan would not have been made without the guarantee (Tax Bulletin 26, December 1996). However, they may well be an expense deductible in calculating the income from the property business itself.

4.40 The charges and expenses to be brought into account are those incurred:

(*a*) in bringing any loan relationship into existence (eg the costs of raising loan finance);

(*b*) in entering into (or giving effect to) loan relationships or related transactions (eg stamp duty land tax on a mortgage);

(*c*) in making payments under loan relationships or in pursuance of loan relationships or related transactions (eg bank charges on interest payments or loan repayments); or (*d*) in taking steps for ensuring the receipt of payment under loan relationships or in accordance with loan relationships or related transactions (eg debt enforcement costs).

(*CTA 2009, s 307(4)*.)

4.41 The above expenses are allowable even where the proposed relationship proves abortive (*CTA 2009, s 329(1),(2)*). A related transaction means a disposal or acquisition (which includes a sale, gift, exchange, surrender, redemption or release) of rights or liabilities under the loan relationship (*CTA 2009, s 304(1),(2)*).

4.42 There are two alternate accounting methods that can be used under UK GAAP, the amortised cost (or accruals) basis and the fair value basis (*CTA 2009, ss 307–310*). Fair value, ie revaluation to market price, cannot normally be used where the parties are connected (*CTA 2009, ss 348–352*). In any event it is not normally appropriate to property transactions. Accordingly interest payable by property companies (except perhaps in relation to hedging transactions) must be accounted for on an accruals basis. The accruals basis used must:

(*a*) conform to generally accepted accountancy practice;

(*b*) not incorporate changes in valuations of loan relationships;

(*c*) allocate payments to the period to which they relate without regard to either the time of payment or receipt or the date the amount becomes due and payable;

(*d*) apportion payments between periods on a just and reasonable basis;

(*e*) assume (subject to authorised arrangements for bad debts (see **4.72**)) that every amount receivable under the loan relationship will be received in full as it becomes due;

(*f*) secure the making of adjustments for bad debts; and

(*g*) provide for the crediting of any debt released in the accounting period in which the release takes place.

(*CTA 2009, s 306(2)*.)

4.43 It is unlikely that a change in method during an accounting period will satisfy the condition of conforming to generally accepted accountancy practice. The accounting method used must be the same as that used in the company's statutory accounts unless that is not an authorised accounting method (*CTA 2009, s 307(2)*).

4.44 If there is any inconsistency or other material difference in the application of an authorised accounting method in respect of the same loan relationships for different accounting periods the debit or credit for earlier periods must be recomputed on the new basis and the difference treated as a debit or credit of the accounting period in which the change is made. A similar adjustment is made on a change of accounting method (*CTA 2009, s 314* and the *Loan Relationships and Derivative Contracts (Change of Accounting Practice) Regulations, SI 2004, No 3271*).

Special Computational Provisions

4.45 A payment that constitutes a distribution (see **4.96**) obviously is not a debit on a loan relationship (*CTA 2009, s 465(1)*).

4.46 If interest due to a connected person (within *CTA 2009, s 466*) is paid more than 12 months after the end of the accounting period in which it accrues it is not dealt with on an accruals basis but is allowed when paid. This does not apply if the lender is a UK company which has brought the full accrued amount into account as a credit on its loan relationships (*CTA 2009, ss 372–374*). It also does not apply where the lender is a non-UK company unless it is resident in a non-qualifying territory (within *TIOPA 2010, s 173*, ie one with which the UK does not have a double tax agreement), such as a tax haven, or it is effectively managed in a non-taxing non-qualifying territory, ie a non-qualifying territory in which companies are not liable to tax by reason of domicile, residence or place of management (*CTA 2009, s 374(1A),(3)*). Even where one of these exceptions would otherwise apply, the restriction also applies if the company is a close company and the other party is a participator, a person who controls a company which is a participator, an associate of any such person or a company controlled by a participator or in which a participator has a major interest (generally 40% or more) (*CTA 2009, s 375(1),(2)*) or if the other party is a company that owns 40% or more of the company or is the company's pension scheme (*CTA 2009, ss 377, 378*).

4.47 There is an exception to *s 375* where the lender is a collective investment scheme which is a CIS limited partnership or is a CIS-based close company (*CTA 2009, ss 375(3),(4), 376*). Neither *s 375* nor *s 377* applies if the lender is a company which is either resident in a non-qualifying territory or effectively managed in a non-taxing, non-qualifying territory (*CTA 2009, ss 375(4A), 377(4)*).

4.48 If the answer to the question whether any amount will become due under a loan relationship after the end of an accounting period, or the amount which will become due, or the time it will become due, depends on the exercise of an option by one of the parties to the relationship (or his associate within *ITA 2007, s 253(1)(2)* or *CTA 2010, s 448(1)(2)*) or is otherwise under the control of such a person, it must be assumed that he will exercise the option in the manner which (apart from taxation) is most advantageous to himself (*CTA 2009, s 420*).

4.49 The assumption under the accruals basis that an amount will be received in full as it becomes due is modified in relation to bad and doubtful debts provided that the accounting method requires the writing back of the debt or provision should it subsequently cease to be appropriate (*CTA 2009, s 322*).

4.50 This does not apply if the parties are connected. Persons are connected for this purpose if either:

(*a*) they are companies under common control (within *CTA 2010, s 449*) or one of which controls the other, or were in such a relationship at any time in the two years preceding the start of the relevant accounting period (there is an exception if the controller is the Crown, a government department, a foreign government or an international organisation), or

(*b*) the company is a close company and the other party to the loan relationship is a participator or an associate of a participator (or was so at some time within the two years preceding the start of the relevant accounting period), and is not one solely by reason of being a loan creditor (*CTA 2009, s 472*).

In such circumstances no relief is given for the bad debt even if it is a bona fide commercial loss (*CTA 2009, s 354(2)*). The only exception is if the creditor accepts shares in the debtor company in consideration of discharging the debt and the two companies would not have been connected had it not done so, ie if the debt was between unconnected persons but they become connected because the creditor agrees to take shares in satisfaction of the debt (*CTA 2009, s 356*). Even if the debt ceases to exist, eg it is waived, the debits brought into account in relation to it must be calculated as if it had continued in being, so no loss arises – but the notional continuation of the debt is not to give rise to a deduction for a notional continuing liability to pay interest on it (*CTA 2009, s 352*). This deeming will not, of course, create a notional debt in the following accounting periods. It is simply to disallow the write off in the current year. Not all debts constitute loan relationships so this rule will not necessarily disallow a bad debt if it arises other than by way of loan.

4.51 Conversely, where a liability to pay a sum is released, the amount released is a credit on the loan relationship for the accounting period in which the release takes place – except where the release arises from a voluntary arrangement under the *Insolvency Act* or the debtor and creditor are connected (within **4.50** above) (*CTA 2009, ss 322, 358, 359*).

4.52 Where the loan is not an arm's length one the debits and credits on the loan relationship must be calculated as though the transaction had been entered into on arm's length terms except where either:

(*a*) a deduction is being claimed for the acquisition at an undervalue of rights under a loan relationship; or

(*b*) the parties are members of the same group of companies (as defined in *TCGA 1992, s 170*).

(*CTA 2009, ss 444–446.*)

4.53 If a loan relationship is assigned within a group the transferor and transferee company are treated as if they were the same company (except for the purpose of determining which is to account for debits or credits (eg interest payments) not related to the assignment) (*CTA 2009, ss 335, 336*). This effectively means that both must adopt the same figure.

4.54 If a loan relationship is for an unallowable purpose no deduction is allowed for interest payable or other debits which (on a just and reasonable apportionment) are attributable to that unallowable purpose. A loan relationship has an unallowable purpose if one of its purposes is not amongst the business or other commercial purposes of the company. Any activities of the company that are not within the charge to corporation tax are also for unallowable purposes. HMRC give an example of a golf club borrowing to finance a new club house where income from members is non-taxable (as mutual trading). The interest would need to be apportioned to disallow the part attributable to the mutual activity. A transaction which has a tax avoidance purpose is also for an unallowable purpose unless that is not one of the main purposes for which the company entered into the transaction. Any purpose that consists in securing a tax advantage for the company or any other person (within *CTA 2010, s 1139*) is a tax avoidance purpose (*CTA 2009, ss 441, 442*).

4.55 This is likely to deny relief for some interest payments that were allowed under the previous rules. For example, if a close company buys a house for occupation by its director that may well be an unallowable purpose – although there is a reasonable argument that it is simply a method of remunerating the director, provided of course that as a result his total remuneration package is still a fair reward for his services. Money borrowed to be lent interest free to another company may well be for an unallowable purpose. Where a company is likely to enter into such transactions it may be sensible to amend the Articles of Association to give specific power to enter into that type of transaction to assist a contention that it forms one of the business purposes of the company.

4.56 If interest (or another debit on a loan relationship) is capitalised it is nevertheless allowed as a debit against profits, to be recognised under the normal accrual basis rules in the accounting period in which it would have fallen had it been a revenue item (*CTA 2009, s 320*).

4.57 Special rules apply to discounted securities. These are contained in *CTA 2009, ss 406–412.*

Alternative Finance Arrangements (Sharia Compliant Loans)

4.58 The return on alternative finance arrangements is treated for tax purposes in the same manner as loan interest for both income tax and corporation tax purposes. Alternative finance arrangements cover any arrangements entered into between two persons under which either:

(*a*) A financial institution buys an asset with the purpose of entering into the arrangement and sells it to the second, the amount payable by the second on his purchase exceeds the acquisition price paid by the institution, all or part of the sale price is not required to be paid until a later date than that of the sale, and the difference between the two purchase prices equates in substance to the return on an investment of money at interest (called an alternative finance return) (purchase and resale arrangements) (*ITA 2007, s 564C* inserted by *Taxation (International and Other Provisions) Act 2010 (TIOPA 2010), Sch 2*).

(*b*) A person deposits money with a financial institution, that money, together with money deposited with the institution by other people, is used by it with a view to producing a profit, from time to time the institution makes or credits a payment to the depositor (in proportion to the amount deposited by him) out of any profits resulting from the use of the money, and the payment so made (or credited) by the institution equate in substance to the return on an investment of money at interest (a profit share return) (deposit arrangements) (*ITA 2007, s 564E*).

(*c*) A financial institution acquires a beneficial interest in an asset and another person (the eventual owner) also acquires a beneficial interest in that asset and will make payments to the financial institution (amounting in aggregate to the consideration paid for its acquisition of its beneficial interest) to acquire its beneficial interest (whether or not in stages), will make other payments to the financial institution (whether in pursuance of a lease or otherwise), has the exclusive right to occupy or otherwise use the asset and is exclusively entitled to any income, profit or gain arising from (or attributable to) the asset, including in particular any increase in value (diminishing share ownership arrangements) (*ITA 2007, ss 564D, 564K*).

(*d*) They are entered into after 1 April 2007; they provide for one person (the 'bond-holder') to pay a sum of money ('the capital') to another (the 'bond-issuer'); they identify assets (or a class of assets) which the bond-holder will acquire for the purpose of generating gains directly or indirectly (the 'bond assets'); they specify a period at the end of which they cease to have effect (the 'bond term'); they require the bond issuer to undertake to dispose at the end of the bond term of any bond assets which are still in its possession, to make a repayment of the capital to the bond-holder during or at the end of the bond term (whether or not by instalments) and to pay to the bond-holder other payments (which do not exceed a reasonable commercial return on a loan of the capital) on one or more occasions; they are a listed security on a recognised stock exchange and they are wholly treated in accordance with international accounting standards as a financial liability of the bond-holder (investment bond arrangements) (*ITA 2007, s 564G*).

(*e*) They require a person (the 'principal') to appoint a financial institution as his agent (or, from 15 October 2009, one or both of the principal and agent are financial institutions); the agent uses money provided by the principal with a view to producing profit, and the principal is entitled to a specified extent to profits resulting from the use of the money with the agent being entitled to any additional profits (and possibly also to a fee); and payments in pursuance of the principal's entitlement equate, in substance, to the return on an investment of the money at interest (profit share agency arrangements) (*ITA 2007, s 564F*).

It should particularly be noted that, with the exception of (d), these all require the participation of a 'financial institution' (see **4.60**).

4.59 For the purpose of head (*a*), if the whole of the sale price is paid to the institution on one day (like a bullet mortgage or an endowment mortgage) the whole of the alternative finance return is deemed to accrue on that day. If the sale price is paid by instalments (like a repayment mortgage) the amount on each instalment that constitutes alternative finance return is an amount equal to the interest that would have been included in each instalment if the profit on the sale by the institution were the total interest payable on a loan by it to the purchaser equal to its purchase price, the instalments were part repayment of the principal with interest, and the loan were made on arm's length terms and accounted for under generally accepted accounting principles (*ITA 2007, s 564H*). This formula looks hard to apply working backwards, but is presumably the result on calculations done initially by the institution to calculate the return it requires, so it is likely in practice that the institution can identify the interest equivalent element in each payment. Simply spreading the overall return in proportion to each of the payments will not produce the correct answer.

4.60 Only the following qualify as financial institutions:

(*a*) a bank (as defined in *ICTA 1988, s 840A*);

(*b*) a building society (within the meaning of the *Building Societies Act 1986*);

(*c*) a wholly owned subsidiary of a bank or building society;

(*d*) a person licensed to carry on a consumer credit business or consumer hire business under *Part 3* of the *Consumer Credit Act 1974*;

(*e*) a 'bond-issuer', but only in relation to any bond assets which are rights under specified arrangements;

(*f*) a person authorised in a jurisdiction outside the UK to receive deposits or other repayable funds from the public and to grant credit for its own account;

(*g*) an insurance company; and

(*h*) a person who is authorised in a jurisdiction outside the UK to carry on a business which consists of effecting or carrying out contracts of insurance or substantially similar business (but not an insurance special purpose vehicle).

(*ITA 2007, s 564B*.)

Head (*e*) applies only from 1 April 2007 and heads (*g*) and (*h*) from 15 October 2009. It should be particularly noted that heads (*f*) and (*h*) require the foreign company to have some form of authorisation in its home country.

4.61 If an alternative finance return (ie within **4.58**(*a*)) is paid to or by an individual, trust or partnership (ie someone other than a company) in a foreign currency, and otherwise than for the purposes of a property business or a trade, profession or vocation, the calculations of the effective return (ie the institution's profit) and the part included in each instalment is done in the foreign currency and the amount in respect of each instalment is translated to sterling at the exchange rate for the day on which the instalment is paid (*ITA 2007, s 564J*).

4.62 It will be apparent that head (*a*) in **4.58** equates to a fixed rate mortgage and head (*b*) to a deposit of funds. Head (*c*) deals with increasing (or from the viewpoint of the institution, diminishing) ownership arrangements, head (*d*) covers alternative finance investment bonds, and head (*e*) agency profit sharing. A person does not have to be a Muslim to benefit from these provisions. It is the way that the arrangement is structured that qualifies for the relief, not the identity of the purchaser (ie the borrower equivalent) or the depositor (ie the investor equivalent).

4.63 For income tax purposes the alternative finance return or profit share return is treated as if it were interest. Accordingly, *ICTA 1988, ss 353, 365* (see **4.24** onwards) apply as if the arrangement involved making a loan and the alternative finance return were interest; and the alternative finance return or profit share return paid is treated as an expense of the payer's property business or trade. *ITTOIA 2005, s 58* (incidental costs of obtaining finance) applies as if it covered alternative finance arrangements (*TIOPA 2010, Sch 2, para 15*).

4.64 For corporation tax purposes, the arrangements are treated as a loan relationship to which the company is a party, with the institution's purchase price (or the deposit by the depositor as the case may be) being treated as a loan and the return as loan interest (*CTA 2009, ss 509–513*).

4.65 These provisions do not apply at all if the arrangements are not at arm's length and *TIOPA 2010, ss 146–217* (provisions not at arm's length – see **23.106**) requires the profits and losses of either party to be calculated on an arm's length basis, the person whose profits are increased as a result of that *Schedule* is the recipient of the return and he is not subject to income tax, corporation tax or a corresponding overseas tax on that return (*ITA 2007, s 564H*). In such a case, the person paying the return under the arrangements is not entitled to a deduction for the return, either in calculating profit or gains or against total income for income tax or corporation tax purposes (*ITA 2007, s 564Y*). It should be particularly noted that this is all or nothing. It is not the excess return over the arm's length figure that is disallowed; it is the total return.

4.66 As the return is treated for tax purposes as interest, *ITA 2007, ss 874–878* (deduction of tax at source – see **4.64**) requires UK tax to be withheld from the alternative finance return or profit share return paid to a non-resident in the same way as with interest (*TIOPA 2010, Sch 2, para 18*).

4.67 In the case of an alternative finance return, the institution's profit on the sale is of course excluded from the consideration for the sale and purchase of the asset for CGT purposes – so the purchaser's base cost is effectively the institution's original cost (*ITA 2007, s 564V(1)–(3)*). This does not, however, affect the operation of any provision of the *Tax Acts* or of *TCGA 1992*, providing for the consideration for a sale or purchase to be deemed to be a figure other than the actual consideration (*ITA 2007, s 564V(4)*). It is not wholly clear what this is intended to do. It seems unlikely that an institution will be a connected person of the 'borrower' and, even if it were, it seems unlikely that in that case either parliament wanted to give the borrower an uplift in his base cost or that the market value of the asset between purchase by the institution and its onward sale, which is likely to take place virtually simultaneously with the purchase, would have fallen significantly. A profit share is obviously not to be treated as a distribution for corporation tax purposes (*CTA 2009, Sch 1, para 97*).

Non-UK Companies

4.68 A non-UK company which is trading in the UK through a branch or agency is within the charge to corporation tax in respect of the income from that trade, and of investment income from property or rights held by or on behalf of the UK branch or agency (*CTA 2009, s 19*). Trading of course includes property dealing. Other UK income of a non-UK company is chargeable to income tax. Accordingly, if a non-UK company not trading in the UK owns property in the UK, interest paid is deductible from its UK rental income only if it meets the income tax tests set out in **4.3–4.26** above. It has been announced that property business profits of overseas companies will be moved from an income tax to a corporation tax regime from 6 April 2020.

Withholding Tax

4.69 Interest payable to a person whose usual place of abode is outside the UK is subject to UK withholding tax at 20% (*ITA 2007, s 874(1)(d)*). Interest payable by a company is subject to withholding tax at 20% (*ITA 2007, s 874(1)(a)–(c)*). Interest payable by anyone else to a non-UK resident also attracts UK withholding tax at 20% if it is taxable on the recipient as yearly interest arising in the UK (*ITA 2007, s 874(1)(d)*). However, under general principles of territoriality, the UK can tax a non-resident only on income arising in the UK. A non-resident will accordingly be chargeable to tax on interest only if the source of the interest is a UK source loan.

UK Source Loans

4.70 Unfortunately the rules as to what is and is not a UK source loan are not at all clear. It used to be generally accepted that a loan is a UK source loan if the borrower is resident in the UK, except where it is made under a specialty contract (ie under seal) and is executed abroad and governed by foreign law. A loan was in any event regarded as a UK source loan if it was secured on land in the UK. Following the abolition of exchange control HMRC were concerned at the ease with which UK companies could borrow overseas. They announced in 1982 that they had been reviewing the treatment of interest paid to non-residents and had taken fresh legal advice. This was to the effect that in the changed circumstances there could be no confidence that the courts would attach sufficient significance to the foreign speciality contract in itself as being a decisive factor. They therefore intended to contend in future that all borrowings by UK companies are UK source loans. The issue has been resolved from 17 July 2013. In determining whether a payment of interest arises in the UK, no account can any longer be taken of the location of any deed which records the obligation to pay the interest (*ITA 2007, s 874(6A)* inserted by *FA 2013, Sch 11, para 5*).

4.71 The House of Lords in *Westminster Bank Executor and Trustee Company (Channel Islands) Ltd v National Bank of Greece SA (46 TC 472)* held that the debt between the two companies had a non-UK source. Following this, albeit somewhat belatedly, HMRC have said that they regard the most important factors which would support a loan having a UK source as:

(*a*) the residence of the debtor, ie the place in which the debt will be enforced;

(*b*) the source from which the interest is paid;

(*c*) the place where the interest is paid; and

(*d*) the nature and location of the security for the debt.

Unfortunately, they go on to say that they are not prepared to comment in advance on where the source might be 'since the precise tax treatment depends on all the factors and on exactly how the transactions are in fact carried out' (Tax Bulletin, Issue 9, Nov 1993, p 100). Accordingly, little comfort can be drawn from the above statement. HMRC (FICO) have, however, told the author that they do not consider that a loan from one non-UK resident to another will have a UK source merely because it is secured on a UK property. In *Ardmore Construction Ltd (TC 3580)* the taxpayer sought to persuade the FTT not to adopt this multi-factorial approach based on a number of Commonwealth and Privy Council decisions but the Tribunal rejected these on the basis that English law differs from overseas laws.

4.72 Because of the uncertainty as to the withholding tax position, the cautious are likely to continue to borrow from UK lenders. If money is borrowed outside the UK, the loan agreement is specifically made enforceable in a country other than the UK, the interest is paid outside the UK and funded other than from the UK rents (or other UK income), and the loan is not secured on the UK property but is secured by non-UK assets, the interest is unlikely to have a UK source so no withholding obligation will arise. If it is secured by a mortgage on the UK property and the interest is paid out of the rents – as will normally be the case – there may be a risk that the loan will have a UK source, in spite of HMRC's current relaxed position, even if the borrower is non-UK resident and the rents are paid direct into his overseas bank account.

4.73 In practice, in the past HMRC did not normally seek to contend that a loan to a UK resident individual from a non-UK resident had a UK source and that income tax ought to have been accounted for – although they have taken the point in relation to borrowings by UK companies. This does not appear to be their current position so it would be unwise to assume that this practice will continue where UK tax relief is claimed for the interest.

4.74 Where an obligation to deduct tax from the interest arises it is likely that the non-UK recipient will resist it. Indeed loans to acquire UK properties normally contain a provision that if an obligation to deduct tax arises the interest rate specified is to be deemed to be a net rate after deduction of the withholding tax. This grossing up will significantly increase the cost of the loan.

4.75 The obligation under *ITA 2007, s 874* to deduct and pay over HMRC tax at the basic rate on the loan interest does not apply where the interest is payable in the UK and is on an advance from a bank which is within the charge to corporation tax in respect of the interest (ie a UK bank or the UK branch of an overseas bank) (*ITA 2007, s 879*). It is also not a problem if the lender is resident in a country with which the UK has a double taxation agreement exempting the resident of the other country from UK tax on interest – provided that the lender is prepared to claim the benefit of the double tax agreement (which is not always the case, even with banks) and that the claim for exemption is made to HMRC's Residency Unit before the first interest payment falls due. In *Mistletoe Ltd v Flood (2003 STC (SCD) 66)* the Special Commissioners held that the test whether the interest is payable in the UK needs to be applied at the date of each interest payment, not the date that the agreement was entered into.

4.76 The obligation to deduct tax does not apply to a payment by a company (or by a partnership of which any member is a company) if the company reasonably believes that the person beneficially entitled to the interest is either:

(*a*) a UK resident company or a partnership all of the partners of which are UK companies; or

(*b*) a non-UK company which carries on a trade in the UK through a branch or agency where the interest will be deductible in computing the UK taxable profits of that branch.

(*ITA 2007, ss 930, 933–938*.)

4.77 HMRC have power to require the deduction of tax in relation to a specified payee from payments made subsequent to their direction if they do not believe that either of the above qualifying conditions are met (*ITA 2007, 931(1)*). If neither of the above conditions is in fact satisfied the payer of the interest becomes liable for the tax that ought to have been deducted notwithstanding his reasonable belief that there was no obligation (and thus no right) to do so (*ITA 2007, s 938*). *Section 930* applies to payments of interest by local authorities and payments to local authorities, charities, approved pension schemes, personal equity plans, ISA managers and government departments and certain statutory bodies (*ITA 2007, ss 935–937*).

4.78 The EU Interest and Royalty Directive (Council Directive 2003/49/EC) prohibits an EU country from imposing tax on interest payments between associated companies in another EU country. Accordingly, *ITTOIA 2005, s 758* exempts from UK tax a payment of interest by a UK company (or a UK permanent establishment of an EU company) to an EU company if the two are 25% associates, ie one holds 25% or more of either the capital or voting rights in the other or a third company holds 25% of both, provided that HMRC have issued an exemption notice (*ITTOIA 2005, ss 759, 760*).

The obligation to deduct applies only to actual interest (including from 17 July 2013 interest paid in kind or by way of a voucher). It does not apply to the profit on a deeply discounted security which is taxed as income under *ITTOIA 2005, ss 427–460* (see **4.101**).

The Exemption Notice Procedure

4.79 To obtain an exemption notice, the EU recipient (or its authorised agent) has to send HMRC a certificate giving:

(*a*) proof of its residence;

(*b*) information as to its beneficial entitlement to the interest;

(*c*) details of the UK corporation tax to which the payer is subject;

(*d*) information establishing the 25% common ownership;

(*e*) a copy of the loan agreement; and

(*f*) a declaration certifying that it meets the conditions of *s 98*.

HMRC must either issue the certificate or refuse to do so within three months of receiving the application (*ITTOIA 2005, s 762* and the *Exemption from Tax for Certain Interest Payments Regulations 2004 (SI 2004 No 2622)*).

Special Relationships

4.80 If at the time the payment is made there is a special relationship (within the meaning of *Article 4(2)* of the *Directive*) between the two companies, or between one of those companies and another person, and owing to the special relationship the amount of interest exceeds an arm's length amount, the exemption does not apply to the excess (*ITTOIA 2005, s 763*). *TIOPA 2010, s 131* (which contains broadly similar rules to the transfer pricing provision on interest) applies to determine the arm's length amount – which could be nil (*ITTOIA 2005, ss 763, 764*). Unfortunately *Article 4(2)* of the *Directive (2003/49/EC)* does not contain a definition of a special relationship. It simply says what should happen where such a relationship exists. This restriction will not override any relief due under a double tax agreement. HMRC will show in the exemption certificate the amount of interest that qualifies for exemption where *s 763* applies.

4.81 The obligation to deduct tax applies only to payments of yearly interest. It is generally accepted that interest is yearly if it is on a loan for a period that is capable of exceeding 365 days (whether or not it in fact does so). Interest on late completions is yearly interest, even though it is normally very short term, as it is theoretically possible, although obviously highly improbable (except as part of a tax avoidance scheme), that the delay could extend to more than a year.

Thin Capitalisation

4.82 The changes to the transfer pricing rules made by the *Finance Act 2004* (see **23.95**) included a new restriction on the deductibility of interest on a loan made between two associated companies. The exemptions for small and medium-sized companies outlined at **23.95** of course apply for this purpose, but these do not apply where one of the parties is resident in a tax haven (or in another country with which the UK does not have a full double taxation treaty). These rules provide that in determining the arm's length price for interest on a loan (or a security) between associated companies, account needs to be taken of:

(*a*) whether the loan would have been made at all in the absence of a special relationship;

(*b*) whether the loan would have been smaller in the absence of such a relationship; and

(*c*) the rate of interest and other terms which would have been agreed in the absence of the special relationship.

(*TIOPA 2010, s 152*.)

4.83 For this purpose, in determining:

(*a*) the appropriate level or extent of the borrower's overall indebtedness;

(*b*) whether it might be expected that the loan, or a loan of a particular amount, would have been made; and

(*c*) the rate of interest and other terms that might be expected to be applicable to the transaction,

no account can be taken of any guarantee (or of any inference capable of being drawn from such a guarantee) provided by a company with which the borrower has a participatory relationship, ie where one of the companies directly or indirectly participates in the management, control or capital of another or the same person or persons so participate in both of them. A guarantee for this purpose includes any relationship, arrangement, connection or understanding (whether formal or informal) such that the lender has a reasonable expectation that in the event of a default by the borrower he will be paid by, or out of the assets of, one or more companies (*TIOPA 2010, ss 152, 154(5)*).

4.84 Some points to bear in mind are:

(*a*) The HMRC view is that if a company has a deficit on its balance sheet it would not have been able to borrow at all. This view is not necessarily correct.

(*b*) The answer is not necessarily all or nothing. For example, if a company takes a 100% borrowing from an associated company and it can be shown that in the absence of a special relationship it would have been possible to take a 60% loan, then interest on 60% will be allowable.

(*c*) If an arm's length loan is initially taken from an arm's length lender and is subsequently refinanced with an associated company on the same or better terms than could be obtained from that lender at the time of the refinancing, there is a strong inference that no adjustment falls to be made.

(*d*) The tests are applied by reference to the position 'at the time of the making or imposition of the actual provision' (*TIOPA 2010, ss 147, 152(2)*), ie when the loan was entered into, not when the interest is paid. Consider whether to have one long-term loan or a series of short ones. For example, if the initial borrowing can be readily justified it might be sensible to have a 20-year loan with a break clause if the property is sold. If there is a worry about the initial borrowing it might be better to have a two-year loan and renew it every two years. If the interest on the first loan cannot be justified that on the second or third might be, as the financial position of the company is likely to have improved.

(*e*) It is advisable to have a formal loan agreement with the lender being given a first charge on the property. A first charge will almost always support a borrowing of 60% to 80% of the value of the property.

(*f*) The provision only requires guarantees by companies to be ignored. There is no prohibition on taking account of guarantees by individuals or trusts.

(*g*) The provision is wider than the old *ICTA 1988, s 209(2)(d)* which required a 75% relationship. The transfer pricing rules apply where there is common control and also where two persons each control 40%.

Guarantees

4.85 If an arm's length loan (or other loan not restricted under *TIOPA 2010, s 152*) is guaranteed by another company, which is an 'affected person' in considering the arm's length provision, account must be taken of:

(*a*) whether the guarantee would have been provided at all in the absence of the special relationship;

(*b*) the amount that would have been guaranteed in the absence of that relationship; and

(*c*) the consideration for the guarantee and other terms which would have been agreed in the absence of that relationship.

(*TIOPA 2010, s 153.*)

Obviously, no account can be taken either of any guarantee given to the guarantor (*TIOPA 2010, s 153(5)*).

4.86 The then government believed that this restricts the deductibility of the interest paid by the borrower to interest on what would have been loaned in the absence of the guarantee or on the basis of a smaller guarantee. It is not wholly clear that it achieves this. It should be particularly noted that the restriction does not apply if the guarantee is given by an individual or a trust.

4.87 Where interest is restricted under *TIOPA 2010, s 153* the guarantor company is treated for transfer pricing purposes as if it had paid that disallowed interest. If there are two or more guarantors, the total deductible by all cannot of course exceed the disallowed interest, but the two can decide who claims what (*TIOPA 2010, ss 192–194*).

Deduction of Tax at Source

4.88 A UK company normally needs to deduct tax at source when making an interest payment to a non-UK lender. Where interest is disallowed, it is not chargeable to UK tax on the lender so the lender can reclaim the tax deducted at source on the disallowed amount. To avoid this procedure, before the interest payment is made either the lender (or the borrower on its behalf) can apply to HMRC for relief under *TIOPA 2010, s 174*, ie to agree the disallowable amount so that tax is not deducted from it (*TIOPA 2010, ss 181–184*).

4.89 Such a claim has two potential disadvantages, namely that it draws to the attention of HMRC the fact that the lender believes that the interest is disallowable and it means that the disallowance will have to be negotiated under time pressure.

Election for the Lender to Pay the Tax Instead

4.90 An election to pay the tax on disallowed loan interest can be made by the lender where:

(*a*) the actual provision forms part of a capital market arrangement;

(*b*) that arrangement involves the issue of a capital market investment;

(*c*) the securities representing that investment are issued wholly or mainly to independent persons; and

(*d*) the total value of the investments under the arrangement is at least £50 million.

The election is irrevocable and has effect throughout the terms of the arrangement. It is made by being included in the lender's tax return for the accounting period in which the arrangement is entered into (*TIOPA 2010, ss 199–204*).

4.91 This is intended to aid property securitisation issues. It would be difficult to do a securitisation if the company that acquires the properties has a significant doubt as to the allowability or otherwise of its interest payments. The election passes the risk to the lender so that the borrowing company will be 'clean'.

Anti-Avoidance

4.92 The exemption from withholding tax does not apply if the main purpose or one of the main purposes of any person concerned with the creation or assignment of the debt-claim in respect of which the interest is paid is to take advantage of the exemption from UK tax given to the recipient of the interest by *ITTOIA 2005, s 758* (*ITTOIA 2005, s 765*).

Capital Gains Tax

4.93 Interest cannot be claimed as a deduction against a capital gain (*TCGA 1992, s 38(3)*). Where the interest is substantial and exceeds the rental income it may sometimes be better to seek to establish that a property transaction is a trading transaction rather than a capital gain.

Interest under Development Agreements

4.94 Where a property development is financed by an institution, the development agreement sometimes provides that interest is to be calculated on the money advanced by the institution and that for the purpose of calculating the institution's interest in the property such interest is to be added to the development costs. Where this occurs the amount involved is often not interest and does not qualify for tax relief. It is a mere arithmetical figure. The easiest way to recognise whether interest is real or notional is to ascertain whether the institution has made a loan to the developer or whether it has undertaken to finance the building costs. If there is no loan, the 'interest' figure will not normally be real interest.

4.95 Where interest is physically payable under a development agreement it may be 'rolled up', ie it is not payable until the development is completed or sold. As interest paid more than twelve months after the accounting period to which it relates will in some cases not be allowed until it is paid (see **4.46**), the effect in such a case may well be to bunch the deduction into a single year, and care may sometimes need to be taken to ensure that the company has income available to obtain relief for the interest in that single year. This particularly applies to investment companies, where the disposal of the property is deemed to take place on the signing of the contract but the rolled-up interest would normally be paid out of the completion monies. It may be desirable to ensure that both dates fall into the same accounting period if there is any possibility that there will be insufficient income arising in the period when the interest would otherwise be paid to cover all the relief potentially available. In many cases rolled-up interest is not interest at all; it is notional interest as described in **4.94** above.

Interest as a Distribution

4.96 Interest paid by a company may be required to be treated as a distribution. Such interest will not be deductible for corporation tax purposes. In effect Parliament has decided that it should be treated as a dividend and not as interest at all. Interest – or other distributions out of assets of a company in respect of securities (which can include a simple loan) of the company – must be treated as a distribution if it is payable on securities under which the consideration given by the company for the use of the principal secured is to any extent dependent on the result of the company's business (or any part of it), or under which the consideration so given represents more than a reasonable commercial return for the use of the principal (*CTA 2010, ss 1000(E)(F), 1005, 1015(4)*). There are a number of exceptions.

4.97 The interest need not be treated as a distribution if:

(*a*) the recipient of the interest is itself chargeable to corporation tax (*CTA 2010, s 1032(1)*); and

(*b*) the consideration does not represent more than a reasonable commercial return for the use of the principal (if it does, only the excess is a distribution) (*CTA 2010, s 1000(E)(b)*).

The exemption does not apply if the recipient is entitled to an exemption from tax in respect of the interest, eg it is a pension fund or a charity (a non-resident company is not exempt from tax) (*CTA 2010, s 1032(2)*).

4.98 There used to be a problem if the value of the property fell and the principal of the loan, not merely the return, was dependent on the value of the property as could happen with a non-recourse loan secured on the property, ie one where the lender agreed to look only to the sale proceeds of the property for repayment of the loan. HMRC sometimes took the view that as the value of the property could in theory fall to a negligible amount, the principal secured was a negligible amount and a reasonable return on that negligible amount was itself a negligible figure. In such cases the amount of the principal secured is now treated for the purpose of *s 209(2)(d)* as equal to the consideration received by the company for the issue of the security, ie the amount of the loan (*CTA 2010, s 1008*). This relief does not apply if the security is one which to a significant extent reflects dividends on other distributions in respect of shares in one or more of the issuing company or any associated company (or reflects fluctuations in the value of such shares) (*ICTA 1988, s 209A*). Nor does it normally apply if hedging arrangements have been entered into that relate to some or all of the company's liabilities under the security (*CTA 2010, s 1013*).

4.99 Where a loan agreement includes a provision under which the lender is entitled to a share of the profit on a property development, the interest will fall within *CTA 2010, s 1000* onwards unless it is taken out by the above exception. This provision is accordingly of particular importance to property companies, especially as they are frequently tempted to borrow from overseas lenders.

4.100 Interest can also constitute a distribution if it is payable on redeemable securities issued in respect of shares in the company; on securities convertible directly or indirectly into shares in the company (unless issued on terms reasonably comparable with quoted securities), on equity notes (ie loans with no fixed redemption date or a date later than 50 years from the making of the loan) which are held by an associated company or one put in funds as directly or indirectly by the borrower; or on securities the terms of which are such that it is necessary or advantageous for a person who holds any of the securities to also have a proportionate holding of the shares of the issuing company (*CTA 2010, ss 1000(1)(C)(D)(F), 1003, 1015*). In the case of securities held by a non-UK company, this provision is sometimes overridden by the non-discrimination provision of the UK's many double taxation agreements.

Discounts

4.101 If a loan qualifies as a deeply discounted security the discount is taxed on the lender as income and, if the borrower is a company within the scope of corporation tax, allowed as a deduction to the borrower under the loan relationship rules spread over the life of the loan. However a discount is not interest, so income tax does not fall to be deducted at source from the discount. A loan is a deeply discounted security if at the time it is borrowed the amount payable on redemption exceeds (or might exceed) the issue price by more than 0.5% times the number of years in the period to redemption (up to a maximum of 30 years) (*ITTOIA 2005, s 430(1)(3)*). The deeply discounted securities legislation specifically provides that if the profit arises on the disposal of securities that are outside the UK, they are treated as arising from a source outside the UK (*ITTOIA 2005, s 428*). Unfortunately it is not clear what is meant by securities being outside the UK. A security does not need to be documented (*W T Ramsay Ltd v CIR, 1983 TC 101*). A loan is normally regarded as sourced where the debtor resides, so a deeply discounted security issued by a UK company to an overseas lender probably has a UK source. Nevertheless there is no requirement to withhold tax on the redemption of the security.

Example 4.1

Alpha Ltd borrows £100,000 for five years on terms that no interest is payable but that Alpha will pay the lender £120,000 at the end of the five years.

The loan is a deeply discounted security because £120,000 exceeds £100,000 plus 5 × 0.5% = £2,500. Accordingly Alpha can claim a deduction for the £20,000 discount spread over the five-year period.

4.102 If the redemption period is not a complete number of years each month or part of a month is treated as one-twelfth of a year (*ITTOIA 2005, s 430(2)*).

4.103 The lender is of course taxed on the discount as income, not as a capital gain. If the lender is not within the scope of corporation tax the tax charge arises on the redemption of the security, ie when the loan is repaid (*ITTOIA 2005, s 428*). If it is within the scope of corporation tax a deeply discounted security is taxed as a loan relationship. This normally effectively taxes the recipient annually on the discount spreads over the term of the loan. If the lender is non-UK resident the discount is not taxable unless the lender is within the scope of corporation tax in relation to the loan. This is because a non-resident is liable to income tax on UK source investment income (other than rental income) only to the extent that tax has been deducted at source (*ITA 2007, s 811*).

4.104 If the borrower is a company which is a connected person of the lender, or the borrower is a close company and the lender is a participator in the company, a deduction cannot be claimed each year; instead the whole amount of the discount is deductible in the accounting period in which the security is redeemed (ie the loan is repaid) (*CTA 2009, ss 407, 409*). However for many property transactions this may not matter unduly provided that the redemption of the loan falls into the same accounting period as that in which the trading profit or capital gain on the property disposal accrues.

Chapter 5

Investment or Dealing?

5.1 The tax treatment of a property transaction depends on whether it is an investment or a trading (dealing) transaction. It is therefore vital to determine what type of transaction is being entered into. Unfortunately this is by no means easy. It depends, in theory, on the motive for the acquisition of the property. This is not always clear. Worse, in practice it often depends on the taxpayer's ability to evidence what his motive was. Very few people naturally evidence their intentions in any sphere of activity. However, the tax differences between an investment and a dealing transaction can be of such moment that it is important to seek to ensure that the necessary evidence is available. In particular, in the case of a company, the courts tend to expect the directors to minute all of their decisions. Many companies, particularly family companies, do not hold regular board meetings and tend to minute only formal transactions such as the approval of the annual accounts. This attitude is very dangerous for a property company. Companies formed under the *Companies Act 2006* do not need to set out their objects in their constitution. Nevertheless it is advisable for a property investment company to set out its investment objective in its Articles of Association. Companies formed under earlier legislation had to set out their objects in the Memorandum of Association. Such companies clearly ought to have had investment as their main object.

5.2 Many people use three categories for property transactions – investment, dealing, and development. However, development is not really a separate category from an income and corporation tax point of view as development by itself is not an end; it is a means to an end. One either develops to generate income, in which case the motive for the acquisition of the property is investment, or develops to sell the completed building, in which case it is dealing. There are cases that indicate that it is also possible for a company to hold property neither as an investment nor as dealing stock (see **7.13**). There is also a concept of an adventure in the nature of trade, but as this is taxed as if it were a trade (*ICTA 1988, s 832(1)*) the distinction is irrelevant.

5.3 Broadly speaking, a property is bought as an investment if it is acquired in order to generate rental income. It will be bought as trading stock – and the transaction will be a dealing transaction – if it is acquired in order to make a profit from reselling it. Unfortunately this distinction is rarely clear cut. A purchaser hopes that an investment will increase in value. Accordingly (to some extent) every property can be said to have been bought with a view to reselling it at a profit. The purchase will nevertheless be as an investment if the main object was to generate income. A person who develops a building with the intention of selling it to produce a dealing profit may well let it before sale as he may be able to obtain a better price by selling it as a let building. Such a letting would not, however, transform it into an investment.

5.4 Some people believe that a single transaction cannot be a dealing transaction. This is a myth (see **5.30**). The conversion of a house into flats will normally be a dealing transaction even if the owner intends to occupy one of the flats as his residence. In such a case the way the transaction is structured can affect the tax position. Consideration needs to be given to separating out the owner's flat before the building work is done rather than after. Indeed the fact that a property is occupied as the owner's principal private residence does not prevent it having been acquired with a dealing motive. Where a person moves house frequently, making a significant gain on each transaction, it is not unknown for HMRC to seek to show that he is dealing in the properties and living in them only incidentally to his dealing motive.

The Basic Tests

5.5 There are a number of basic tests that HMRC and the courts will apply to determine whether a transaction is dealing or investment.

1. *The motive for the acquisition of the property.* This is the fundamental test. If it was to generate income the transaction is an investment; if it was to generate a profit on sale it is dealing. The remaining tests are needed because the motive is not always clear, or there is no evidence available to substantiate the professed motive, or the professed motive is not accepted by HMRC as the true motive. If a taxpayer claims that a property was bought as an investment – which in most, but not all, cases will produce a lower tax charge – but most of the remaining tests are indicative of dealing, HMRC will be unlikely to accept that the professed investment motive was the true intention in purchasing the property. The remaining tests are therefore important as either reinforcing or calling into question the professed motive on acquisition. The principles to be applied where there is more than one motive are set out at **5.27**.

2. *The evidence that is available to substantiate the claimed motive.* In general HMRC are unlikely to contend that a transaction, which the taxpayer claims to be dealing, is, in reality, investment. It is the purported investment transactions that they challenge. Accordingly where a property is bought as an investment it is sensible to seek to ensure that evidence is available to substantiate that investment intention.

In the absence of such evidence the courts will have to infer the intention from the remaining tests. Where a person purchases a property as an investment he might be expected to calculate the yield on letting and the yield after the first rent review. A calculation showing the capital value of the property on completion of development might suggest an intention to dispose of the completed development rather than to retain it. On the other hand the valuation may have been done to establish the mortgageability of the property for retention as an investment.

3. *The method of finance.* Property is by its nature a long-term investment. Accordingly if the funds to acquire or develop it are borrowed on a short-term basis this is normally indicative of an intention to dispose of the property rather than retain it. It should be borne in mind that an investor may well borrow short-term on a temporary basis if he feels that interest rates are likely to fall over the following year or so, with a view to replacing this with long-term borrowings later. A developer may borrow short-term to finance the development with a view to replacing this with long-term finance secured on the completed development.

4. *Whether the property is income producing.* If a property produces no income during the taxpayer's period of ownership it will be difficult to show that it was bought as an investment – unless of course it was bought for use as a private residence or for some other personal use where the return on the investment is the enjoyment of the property. If a property produces income but this merely equals (or is less than) the outgoings and interest on money used to acquire it, HMRC will look on it as non-income producing. If, although a property produces no income on acquisition, it is bought in the course of putting together a development site, the generation of income after the development could well have been the initial intention.

5. *The period of ownership.* Property investments are normally held for a period of several years. There is no hard and fast rule as to how long a property needs to be held to stamp it as an investment. A period of six years can normally be regarded as relatively safe. Four or five years is unlikely to provoke attack in most cases. If a property is held for less than about three years there is a significant risk that this will prompt HMRC to contend that it was bought for resale. It should be borne in mind, however, that length of ownership is only one of several factors to be looked at from which to draw an inference as to what the taxpayer's motive was at the time of his acquisition of the property. Where a property is developed the period of ownership after completion of the development is what needs to be looked at – unless the property was clearly held as an investment prior to redevelopment and the redevelopment was to enhance the price obtainable on its sale. If a property produces no net income up to the first rent review, a sale shortly after that rent review

could well be regarded as indicative of a dealing intention even though the property is retained for five or seven years after the letting.

6. *The reason for the disposal.* This is not nearly as important as the reason for the acquisition. Indeed it is not really an independent test at all. It can, however, be important to displace a dealing inference where a property which is claimed to be an investment is held for a relatively short period. If it can be shown that the reason for the sale is that the taxpayer can obtain a far better yield on an alternative investment, or he is being forced to raise money to reduce bank borrowings or to meet a specific requirement for a substantial cash sum, this is likely to displace the dealing inference that might otherwise be drawn from the short period of ownership.

7. *The expertise of the owner.* HMRC generally contend that a builder or a property developer is more likely to acquire property for dealing than as an investment. The logic of this is hard to discern. The expertise of a builder is just as likely to enable him to recognise attractive investments as attractive trading situations.

8. *Application for planning consent.* An application for planning consent prior to a sale could be indicative of a dealing intention particularly if the property was held for a relatively short period. On the other hand an application for planning consent may merely be a way of maximising the price obtained for an investment.

9. *A company's objects clause.* If the taxpayer is a company its objects clause is a major factor to look at. The directors can hardly contend that they were deliberately acting *ultra vires*. Accordingly the directors will find it difficult to show that they acquired a property as an investment if the company had no powers of investment. HMRC are under no such inhibition. Even if the company had such powers their existence will of course be neutral if it also had power to deal. Where the evidence as to the nature of a transaction is conflicting the courts will generally lean towards finding that the directors have done what they were empowered to do rather than acting outside the scope of their authority. Accordingly if the objects clause makes it clear that the company is an investment company the onus will effectively be on HMRC to demonstrate that a purported investment transaction was in fact a dealing transaction carried out in breach of the company's powers. Where the taxpayer is a trust the powers contained in the trust deed might similarly be a pointer to the nature of a transaction.

10. *The presentation in the owner's accounts.* Investments constitute fixed assets for accounting purposes. Dealing properties constitute current assets and are normally shown in the accounts as trading stock. Whilst the treatment in the accounts is not conclusive it is difficult for the

directors of a company to contend that a property is an investment if for many years they have approved accounts which have shown it in the balance sheet as trading stock. They were able to do so in *Albermarle 4 LLP v HMRC (2013 SFTD 664* – see **5.29**)

Decided Cases

5.6 The question as to whether a particular transaction is investment or dealing has spawned much litigation. Unfortunately about the only conclusions that can safely be drawn from the decided cases are that every case depends on its own individual set of facts and, possibly, that no matter how clear cut a case may seem, there is always the chance that the appeals Tribunal will come to a different conclusion. Nevertheless an examination of some of the decided cases may be helpful as they at least indicate some of the factors to which the courts have attached significance.

5.7 In *California Copper Syndicate Ltd v Harris (5 TC 159)* a company bought copper-bearing land in 1901 and resold it in two lots in 1902 and 1903 in exchange for the issue of shares in the purchaser company. It contended that the acceptance of shares rather than cash evidenced an initial investment intention. It was held that this was not a relevant factor. The Commissioners were entitled to find, as they had done, that the purchase of non-income producing land and its sale a year or two later was, by its nature, a dealing transaction. The receipt of the consideration otherwise than in cash could not change the nature of the transaction.

5.8 In *Tempest Estates Ltd v Walmsley (51 TC 305)* land forming part of a family estate was sold to a company as part of an estate duty planning exercise. The land was on the outskirts of Bolton and thought likely to have development value at some future date. Between 1946, when the land was bought by the company from the trustees of the estate, and 1956 there were minor sales, but in 1958 a significant part of the land was sold for development. This sale appears to have been treated as the realisation of an investment. There were further comparatively small sales but the general policy was not to sell land. In 1963 the company decided to pursue a more active development policy and purported to transfer three blocks of land from investment to dealing stock. It then sold that land. It was held that the initial purchase of the land in 1946 was a trading venture. The company's directors must have known that it was only a matter of time before the land would be disposed of or developed. The fact that the company was formed for the purpose of estate duty saving was not necessarily inconsistent with an acquisition of the land for trading purposes. It should particularly be noted that the bulk of the land was held for about 17 years. Normally, once land has been held for more than about six years – particularly if it has produced rental income, as happened with *Tempest*

Estates – one would feel fairly confident that the sale is the realisation of an investment. This case illustrates that all of the circumstances must be looked at. Furthermore the court had no hesitation in drawing an inference from letters written in 1958 as to the directors' intentions in 1946. This indicates that it is important not only to evidence one's intention on acquisition but also to take care that later correspondence does nothing to cast doubt on the initial professed intention.

5.9 This decision can be contrasted with that in *Rand v Alberni Land Co Ltd (7 TC 629)*, an earlier case. A company was formed to acquire land in Vancouver in order to develop and manage it with a view to ultimate sale, the land being held in trust for various people with different interests in it. Thus the company had a clear dealing purpose. It was held that the sales of land were capital gains as the real purpose of the company was to realise the full capital value of the respective interests in the land under the trust. Whilst this was undoubtedly the motive of the shareholders in forming the company it is difficult to ascribe such a motive to the directors as such. The motive of the major shareholder was also important in the *Simmons Properties* case (see **5.21** below), a later case than *Tempest Estates* (**5.8** above). It accordingly appears permissible to look at the circumstances surrounding the formation of a company to ascertain the true motive for the acquisition of the property. These can suggest that the directors' role was merely to put into effect a plan conceived by the shareholders so that the directors themselves had no motive in relation to the acquisition.

5.10 A word of warning. In *Balgownie Land Trust Ltd v CIR (14 TC 684)* the executors of a deceased estate held land with a direction under the will to realise it. They formed the company, transferred the land to it in exchange for shares, and distributed the shares to the beneficiaries. The company borrowed money to acquire further land. Some years later it sold most of the land. It was held to be dealing. Another company formed to acquire settled land, part of which it developed as building sites and sold as the opportunity arose, was similarly held to be dealing (*St Aubyn Estates Ltd v Strick (17 TC 412)*). These can be distinguished from *Alberni Land* (**5.9** above) insofar as the purchase and resale of further land in the *Balgownie* case stands as a trading transaction apart from the original land, and the development and splitting of land in the *St Aubyn* case could well have been deemed to be an appropriation of the land as trading stock if it had not been put into the company.

5.11 The importance of the motive at the time of acquisition is exemplified by the case of *Tebrau (Johore) Rubber Syndicate v Farmer (5 TC 658)*. A company was formed to acquire land for development as a rubber plantation. It bought two estates but found that it had inadequate finance to develop them. It therefore sold them to a second company mainly for shares. It was held, reversing the decision of the Commissioners, that there was no evidence that the land had been bought for resale, and that the profit was therefore capital. On the facts it is clear that the property was bought as a fixed asset. The decision illustrates that the subsequent frustration of the initial intention cannot change the nature of the transaction.

5.12 In February 1942 a company purchased three tenement properties in Glasgow for £20. At the time they were partly condemned as dangerous. The directors thought that a profit could be made out of the properties some day but were looking some years ahead. The company carried out some alterations and was then able to let the properties at rents fluctuating between £50 and £100 p.a. In 1949 the properties were sold and the company liquidated. It was held that the only reasonable conclusion was that the purchase was made with the intention of a resale at a profit when a suitable opportunity arose. It was therefore an adventure in the nature of trade. It did not matter that there was only a single transaction. Nor apparently did it make any difference that the rents represented a return of between 20% and 45% on the investment consistently for a period of six years – a factor which would normally be indicative that the property was bought as an investment (*CIR v Toll Property Co Ltd (34 TC 13)*).

5.13 By contrast, in *CIR v The Hyndland Investment Co Ltd (14 TC 694)* a company was formed in 1898 to acquire certain building land in Hyndland from its three shareholders, one of whom was a builder. It erected five tenements, which were completed and let by mid-1900. The investment turned out to be a poor one and the company had to raise additional finance. After the war, in 1920, the housing shortage created a demand for vacant houses and individual flats. Taking advantage of this demand the company sold a number of flats and houses – five in 1920, three in 1921, three in 1922, four in 1923 and one in 1926 – to improve its financial position. It was left with 24 flats, all in poor repair. It was held the company had not traded in disposing of the 16 flats. Significance was attached to the facts that the company had purchased one single block of property, so if it were trading it must have done so with regard to that block, that it continued after the sales to hold a large part of that investment, and that because of the company's circumstances it was expedient to sell part of the property to ease its financial position. This shows that evidence of an alternative reason for a sale can displace a dealing inference.

5.14 A company was incorporated in October 1933 to purchase 70 acres of land on the outskirts of Hull which the proprietor intended to develop as a garden suburb. It was accepted that this land was bought as trading stock. In 1934 it bought two further parcels of adjoining land. In 1935 it emerged that there were insoluble drainage difficulties and the garden suburb concept was abandoned in late 1936. There were a few small sales of land in 1936 and 1956 – the profits on which were treated as income. The land was shown as an investment in the company's accounts. It produced rental income but this was generally less than the expenses. In 1961 the land was compulsorily purchased by Hull Corporation. From 1952/53 onwards the company had been taxed as a property investment company and had submitted management expenses claims.

The company contended that although the land had initially been purchased as trading stock it had ceased to be held as such when the intention to develop was abandoned in 1936. It was held that the main question to be asked was what was the proper inference to be drawn from the way in which the company conducted its affairs in the 25 years from 1936 to 1961. The abandonment of a particular project of development does not involve abandoning altogether any idea of developing or otherwise dealing in land. There was accordingly no evidence that the land had ever ceased to be trading stock. The sale in 1961 was therefore made in the course of the company's trade (*Orchard Parks Ltd v Pogson (42 TC 442)*).

5.15 It should particularly be noted that no weight was given to the fact that HMRC had treated the company as an investment company for nine years, and little weight was given to the treatment in the company's accounts. The clear trading motive on acquisition seems to have been the prime influencing factor. This case should be contrasted with the later, non-property, one of *British-Borneo Petroleum Syndicate Ltd v Cropper (45 TC 201)*. In that case a company acquired an oil concession as trading stock. From 1935 onwards its principal source of income was royalties from this concession. There was no evidence of an appropriation from trading stock to investment. It surrendered its rights in 1964 for £900,000. It was held that this was a capital receipt. At some stage the concession had ceased to be held as trading stock. It did not matter when, as this was clearly more than six years before 1964, and HMRC were therefore out of time to raise an assessment.

5.16 In *Mitchell Bros v Tomlinson (37 TC 224)* two brothers decided to build houses for letting as an investment to make provision for their old age. By 1939 they had built or purchased some 60 houses, none of which were sold before 1947. Between 1942 and 1948 they bought a further 239 houses which they were able to purchase very cheaply because of wartime conditions. They sold 58 of these latter houses between 1946 and 1952. It was held that the brothers were carrying on a trade as property dealers. Although they originally had an investment intention it subsequently altered when conditions changed. It is not clear from the judgment if this change of intention applied so as to make the pre-1939 acquisitions trading stock or if it only affected the later acquisitions. It is probable that the Commissioners had in mind the later acquisitions only, ie they were holding that the fact that a person enters into property investment transactions does not frank all future property transactions with an investment intent.

5.17 *CIR v Reinhold (34 TC 389)* is an interesting decision. Mr Reinhold bought four houses in January 1945 and sold them in December 1947. He bought the properties for resale and had instructed his agent to sell whenever a suitable opportunity arose. The properties had produced no net income. His only previous property transaction was ten years earlier when he had bought a hotel and resold it at a profit before he completed the purchase. It is perhaps difficult to imagine anything more clearly trading. The property was bought for resale, was held for a short period only, and produced no net income. Nevertheless, it was held to be an investment.

Relevant factors were that the taxpayer was not a property agent and his business was not associated with the purchase and sale of land; and that the transaction was an isolated transaction. A transaction does not require to be unique in the life experience of a businessman to be treated as isolated so the transaction ten years earlier did not prevent it being so. So what? As the judgment makes clear, an isolated transaction can constitute a trade, particularly if it is entered into by a company where intention can be shown from the terms of its objects. However, Lord Keith felt that where an individual enters into an isolated transaction in a subject that is normally used for investment – land, houses, stocks and shares – the inference of trading is not to be so readily drawn in regard to a single transaction from an admitted intention to sell on the arrival of a certain pre-selected time.

> 'It is not, in my opinion, enough for the Revenue [HMRC] to show that the subjects were purchased with the intention of realising them some day at a profit. This is the expectation of most, if not all, people who make investments. Heritable property is a not uncommon subject of investment and generally has the feature, expected of investments, of yielding an income while it is being held. In the present case the property yielded an income from rents. It is said that it yielded no profit … the intention to resell at some date at a profit is not per se sufficient in this case to attract tax … Here the facts in my opinion are insufficient to establish that this is an adventure in the nature of trade' (Lord Keith at p 397).

This decision is hard to understand, but is worth remembering where an individual enters into an isolated transaction.

5.18 Another interesting case that the taxpayer was perhaps lucky to win is *Taylor v Good (49 TC 277)*. The taxpayer bought a property on impulse at an auction in July 1959 for £5,100. It was a large country house at which his mother had once worked. He had not decided what to do with it but had in mind the possibility of going to live in it. When he told his wife she refused to do this. Accordingly in September 1959, before completion of the purchase, he applied for planning permission for redevelopment. This was refused but granted on appeal in 1962. In 1963 he sold the land to a developer for £54,000.

In the High Court Megarry J said that part of the gain was capital and part income and remitted the case to the Commissioners to determine when trading commenced. The Court of Appeal held that the whole of the gain was capital as there was no evidence of an appropriation to dealing stock.

5.19 This case illustrates the supreme importance of the motive on acquisition. If the taxpayer had not been able to show that he did not start with a trading motive he would undoubtedly have lost as everything else pointed to a dealing transaction. He seems to have had no real motive on acquisition, which indicates that it is not necessary to demonstrate an investment motive, one merely needs to negate a trading one. The case also makes clear that one is not wholly safe by establishing that the property was not acquired with a dealing motive. It is still possible for there to be an appropriation to trading stock at a later date (although the *Simmons Properties* case (see **5.21** below) indicates that there must be a positive intention to appropriate).

5.20 *Marshall's Executors & Others v Joly (20 TC 256)* similarly illustrates that it is sufficient to demonstrate the absence of any motive. One of the three partners in a property dealing partnership died and his executors required the surviving partners to realise the unsold land, which they did over the following three years. It was held that there was no evidence to support a finding that the executors had carried on a trade. They were merely collecting in the assets of the estate. By contrast, in *Newbarns Syndicate v Hay (22 TC 461)* a member of a property dealing syndicate died and his executor took his place in the syndicate. It was held that on the particular facts of the case the executor was trading. Sales continued for many years after the death, the executor participated in annual meetings of the syndicate, and he had not pressed for the land to be sold and the deceased's share paid over to him.

5.21 *Lionel Simmons Properties Ltd (in liquidation) v CIR (53 TC 461)* is probably the most important case on the distinction between dealing and investment. It is one of the few to be heard by the House of Lords, it reversed the decision of the Commissioners on what is on the face of it primarily a question of fact and Lord Wilberforce gives a lucid analysis of the principles involved. Mr Simmons, a surveyor and thus a property expert, sought to build up, through his companies, a property investment portfolio which he ultimately intended to float as a public group. He formed a number of companies over a period of about eight years, each to develop and retain one or two properties. On occasions he sold properties, sometimes fairly shortly after development. However, such sales were in pursuance of a policy of trading up, ie he would sell one property to provide funds to acquire a larger one. The profits on such sales were credited to capital reserve. He later entered into arrangements with a quoted investment trust with the object of getting the financial backing to grow to a floatable size. In 1966, following the passing of the *Rent Act 1965* and the *Finance Act 1965*, he decided that there was no future for a property investment group, sold the properties, and liquidated all of the companies.

5.22 The Commissioners decided that some of the properties were trading stock and some investments. This was on the basis that they felt that as Mr Simmons was prepared to realise one development in order to find funds for another it was not until after completion of lettings that he could be in a position to decide finally whether to retain the property or not. Until the decision to hold was made, the Commissioners regarded the property as trading stock. This is difficult to reconcile with the Court of Appeal decision in *Taylor v Good* (**5.18** above) where it was made clear that having no intention on acquisition is not equivalent to having a possible trading motive. Nevertheless, the Court of Appeal in *Simmons* dismissed this because, in *Taylor v Good*, the Crown had accepted at Court of Appeal level that the purchase was not made for trading purposes whereas in *Simmons* the Commissioners were not satisfied that the properties were bought as investments. As the two do not seem inconsistent this distinction is somewhat obscure. The House of Lords (Lord Scarman dissenting) reversed the decision of both the Commissioners and the Court of Appeal, holding that a decision that any of the properties were trading stock was inconsistent with the primary facts found.

> 'One must ask, first, what the Commissioners were required or entitled to find. Trading requires an intention to trade: normally the question to be asked is whether this intention existed at the time of the acquisition of the asset. Was it acquired with the intention of disposing of it at a profit, or was it acquired as a permanent investment? Often it is necessary to ask further questions: a permanent investment may be sold in order to acquire another investment thought to be more satisfactory; that does not involve an operation of trade, whether the first investment is sold at a profit or at a loss. Intentions may be changed. What was first an investment may be put into the trading stock – and, I suppose, vice versa. If findings of this kind are to be made precision is required, since a shift of an asset from one category to another will involve changes in the company's accounts, and, possibly, a liability to tax … What I think is not possible is for an asset to be both trading stock and permanent investment at the same time, nor to possess an indeterminate status – neither trading stock nor permanent asset. It must be one or other, even though, and this seems to me legitimate and intelligible, the company, in whatever character it acquires the asset, may reserve an intention to change its character. To do so would, in fact, amount to little more than making explicit what is necessarily implicit in all commercial operations, namely that situations are open to review' (Lord Wilberforce).

It is interesting to note that at all levels the general investment motive of Mr Simmons was looked at to determine the motive of an individual company in acquiring an individual property. Also the decision to liquidate could not give rise to an inference of a trading motive as this did nothing more than put an end to Mr Simmons's investment plans. Frustration of a plan for investment, which compels realisation, even if foreseen as a possibility, cannot give rise to an intention to trade.

5.23 However, a Privy Council case, *Richfield International Land & Investment Co Ltd v Inland Revenue Commissioner (1989 STC 820)*, does need to be borne in mind. In 1972 the company acquired a number of properties which it let out and showed as investments in its accounts. In 1973 it sold a small property and treated the surplus as a capital gain. HMRC challenged this (presumably because of the short period of ownership) and the company agreed that it could be taxed as income. In 1978 it sold another fairly small property and treated the surplus as a trading profit – an indication that that particular property must have been appropriated to trading stock. In 1980 it sold the major property and treated the surplus as a capital gain. It was held that the property had become trading stock even though it was accepted that it had been acquired as an investment, had always been shown as an investment in the accounts, had been held for eight years, and had produced significant rental income throughout. The justification was that the company had accepted that the surpluses on the two small properties were taxable as trading profits. It is difficult to see how this shows evidence of an intention to appropriate the larger to trading stock, particularly in the face of the contrary treatment in the accounts. It is to be hoped that this case is merely an extreme example of the *Edwards v Bairstow & Harrison (36 TC 207)* principle, ie that the courts will not disturb a finding of fact unless it is so perverse that no reasonable tribunal could properly have arrived at it, rather than an undermining of the *Simmons* decision.

5.24 It is also worth mentioning a non-property case *Waylee Investment Ltd v Commissioner of Inland Revenue for Hong Kong (1990 STC 780)*. In that case a large Hong Kong listed company was in danger of collapse, which would have damaged public confidence in the economy of Hong Kong. Its bankers, believing that its fortunes could be restored with new management, subscribed for new shares which gave them effective control. The shares were acquired by Waylee, a subsidiary of the bank. In due course the company prospered. A little over two years later the company merged with another and in September 1979, four years after the acquisition of the shares, Waylee received an unsolicited offer for the shares, which it accepted. HMRC claimed that the shares had been acquired as trading stock. They had been held for a relatively short period. The bank had in its annual report after acquiring the shares expressed an intention to sell them as soon as conditions permitted. The rescue operation had taken place in the normal course of the bank's business. The Board of Review (the Hong Kong equivalent of the Special Commissioners) held that the shares had been acquired as a capital asset. The Privy Council affirmed this decision. The shares did not have the nature of trading stock; any attempt to sell them to meet depositor's demands would defeat the objective of showing the bank's confidence in the listed company, so they could not be regarded as circulating capital. The intention to sell as soon as conditions permitted did not necessarily label the shares as trading stock as this intention could be looked on merely as an expression of the bank's concern not to be seen to be involving itself in the management of the listed company on a long-term basis. It is also interesting to note that the court was prepared to attribute to the subsidiary the intentions of the bank itself.

5.25 Another Privy Council decision worth remembering is *Beautiland Co Ltd v Commissioner of Inland Revenue for Hong Kong (1991 STC 467)*. Two companies, Cheung Kong and Wheelock Marden, reached agreement in principle for the development of a number of properties owned by one or other of their groups. They incorporated Beautiland as a joint venture company for the purpose. One of the assets contributed to Beautiland by Cheung Kong was a 30% holding in Rostock Enterprises Ltd, which itself controlled a land-owning company. Two months later an offer to acquire 81% of Rostock was received by Cheung Kong from an unconnected third party and Beautiland sold most of its 30% holding to the third party in consequence of this offer. The Revenue assessed Beautiland as a share dealer. The Privy Council held that, in spite of the fact that it was clearly intended that Beautiland might trade in land, there was nothing in the joint venture agreement to indicate that the parties had in contemplation trading in the shares of subsidiary or associated companies. It followed that there could be no question of a separate contemplation of trading in land via shares. The shares acquired by Beautiland constituted its capital structure and there were no grounds for concluding that they were acquired as trading stock.

5.26 Mr Kings was a property dealer. In 1989/90 he experienced financial difficulties. To raise funds, on 1 March 1990 he and his wife moved from their private residence to one of the dealing properties with the intention of selling the private residence. They could not find a buyer so mortgaged the property and let it, using the capital raised to pay off Mr Kings' business overdraft (*Kings v King (2004 STC (SCD) 186*). Mr Kings claimed a deduction against his trading profit for the mortgage interest. The whole of the rents was paid into Mr Kings' business account. The Special Commissioners thought it possible for a jointly owned property to become trading stock of one partner alone, but held that there was no evidence to find that that had occurred. The mortgage interest was accordingly not a business expense. Curiously, he did find, however, that Mrs Kings had surrendered to her husband her entitlement to the rents and that accordingly they were taxable wholly on her husband, albeit as a property business receipt.

5.27 One particular area of difficulty is the tax treatment where, in order to obtain a particular piece of land, one has to acquire a package including other land that one does not want. In *Snell v Rosser, Thomas & Co Ltd (44 TC 343)* a building contractor wanted to buy a large house for conversion into flats for sale – clearly a trading venture. In order to obtain the house he also had to buy 5¾ acres of surrounding land. He resold this land at the first available opportunity. The profit on sale of the land was held to be trading as its acquisition was incidental to the acquisition of the stock in trade. By contrast, in a Privy Council decision (which carries the full weight of a decision of the Law Lords) three years earlier (*Iswera v Ceylon Commissioner of Inland Revenue ([1965] 1 WLR 663)*), it was held that where a taxpayer who wanted a particular piece of land on which to build a private residence had to buy a larger site and resell what she did not want, the sale of the surplus land was a transaction in the nature of trade, not an acquisition incidental to the acquisition of an investment.

5.28 The principles that must be applied where a person has more than one motive in acquiring land were reviewed by the Court of Appeal in *Kirkham v Williams (1991 STC 342)*:

(*a*) If on an objective analysis the transaction has all the characteristics of trading, that analysis must prevail.

(*b*) If the transaction is equivocal, the subjective intention of the taxpayer must be taken into account in weighing up whether the transaction is trading or not.

(*c*) If in an equivocal case the taxpayer's sole objective is non-commercial the transaction will not be a trading transaction.

(*d*) In all other cases the overall nature of the transaction is a question of fact to be determined by the Commissioners.

In *Kirkham v Williams*, Mr Kirkham contracted to buy land in Summer 1977 and in October 1977 applied for planning permission for redevelopment. Completion of the purchase was May 1978. The land was used by Mr Kirkham partly as offices and partly for storage in connection with his business. He also carried out some limited farming activities on the land. Planning permission for the erection of a dwelling house on the land was eventually obtained in August 1980. This was built by the taxpayer. It was never his intention to purchase the property as a residence for himself and his family. The land was sold in October 1982 and HMRC contended that it must, *inter alia*, have been acquired with the intention of disposing of it at a profit. Mr Kirkham contended that he had acquired it as a capital asset for use in his business. The General Commissioners found that the site was acquired principally to provide office and storage space for the taxpayer's business. They nevertheless held that it was a trading transaction. The Court of Appeal accepted that if the Commissioners had found that the subsidiary purpose for the acquisition of the site was trading they might be entitled to hold that the overall intention was trading. However, they were silent on what that purpose was; it seemed most likely that it was farming. Furthermore, even if it was trading the subsidiary purpose could not have been implemented concurrently with the primary purpose of providing office and storage space. Mr Kirkham could not develop the site unless he obtained planning permission and even then could not do so until he had been able to provide himself with storage and office space elsewhere. Accordingly the trading purpose was severely circumscribed and its implementation indefinite in point of time. In these circumstances, 'It was not open to the Commissioners, having made a finding which was apt to characterise the transaction as an acquisition of a capital asset, to deny it that character by reason of an intention thus circumscribed and indefinite' (Nourse LJ).

5.29 Although the production of income has long been regarded as one of the prime hallmarks of an investment, the absence of income is not necessarily fatal. In *Marson v Morton (59 TC 381)* Sir Nicholas Browne-Wilkinson, the Vice-Chancellor, was not deterred by the lack of income.

> 'It is true in the Reinhold case the Court of Session did rely on the fact that there would be income in rents as a relevant factor, and in my judgment it plainly is a relevant factor. But in my judgment in 1986 it is not any longer self-evident that unless land is producing income it cannot be an investment. The legal principle of course cannot change with the passage of time: but life does. Since the arrival of inflation and high rates of tax on income new approaches to investment have emerged putting the emphasis in investment on the making of capital profit at the expense of income yield. For example, the purchase of short-dated stocks giving a capital yield on redemption but no income has become commonplace … I can see no reason why land should be any different and the mere fact that land is not income-producing should not be decisive or even virtually decisive on the question whether it was bought as an investment.'

The facts of this case were somewhat strange. The taxpayer told an intermediary that he would be interested in investing in land. The intermediary subsequently introduced to him an opportunity to buy a site for £35,000. The taxpayer had no idea of the time-scale involved in property investment but thought it might be one or two years. He took no legal advice. He took no steps to sell the land but a few months later the intermediary said that he had a potential buyer and if the taxpayer sold he might double his money. He duly sold the land and received a cheque for £70,000. It was not until HMRC raised questions that he discovered that he had in fact bought the land not for £35,000 but for £65,000 with a £30,000 mortgage, and had sold it for £100,000 – or indeed that both vendor and purchaser were companies associated with the intermediary. The transaction has all the signs of trading; the land was bought with borrowed money, was held for a very short period, was always intended to be held for a fairly short period, and produced no income during the period of ownership. Nevertheless it was held by the General Commissioners to be an investment, a decision that the judge upheld as one which they were entitled to make.

5.30 There are a number of other decisions that are at least worthy of mention. *Emro Investments Ltd v Aller (35 TC 305)* illustrates that the accounting treatment adopted and a company's objects clause, although relevant, are not conclusive – the company, albeit ostensibly an investment company, was held to be trading. *Parkstone Estates Ltd v Blair (43 TC 246)* exemplifies the dangers of a company carrying on both dealing and investment activities. The company developed an industrial estate of twelve factories, one of which it let on a ten-year lease to an associated company and the remainder of which it sold. It was held that the company was trading and the let property was trading stock. If the let factory had been developed by another group company it would probably have been an investment. The fact that a property produces net rents in excess of borrowings is not necessarily conclusive of investment status. In *Parkin v Cattell (48 TC 462)* the taxpayer purchased a number of houses over a period of about eight years with controlled tenants and sold them as they became vacant. Although HMRC initially accepted these as investments they later had second thoughts. The transactions were held to be trading, the course of dealings indicating that the prime motive for the purchases was to obtain a profit on resale, not to reap the rental income. This decision needs to be borne in mind when considering the purchase of such controlled properties or the purchase of ground rents, although HMRC do not in practice challenge most such purchases and in many cases it will be possible to substantiate an investment intention. *Sugarwhite v Budd (1987 STC 491)*, which is considered in more detail in **14.73** below, emphasises that it is up to the taxpayer to prove his case. In that case a company contracted to buy a property but sub-sold it within a matter of weeks, so it never completed. The Commissioners, the High Court, and the Court of Appeal all held that there was no evidence before them to show that this was not a dealing transaction – even though it is difficult to envisage any set of circumstances which on the face of it gives such an indication of dealing. *Albermarle 4 LLP v HMRC (2013 SFTD 664)* emphasises the importance of oral evidence. The partnership claimed to have held the land as trading stock albeit that it had shown it in its accounts as an investment. The Tribunal felt that the documents were not conclusive either way but the oral evidence by two of the partners outweighed the points in HMRC's favour.

5.31 There are a number of decisions that make clear that a single purchase and sale can constitute a trade or an adventure in the nature of trade (which is taxed as a trade), eg *Reynolds' Executors v Bennett (25 TC 401)*; *Gray & Gillitt v Tiley (26 TC 80)*; *Burrell & Others v Davis (38 TC 307)*; *Turner v Last (42 TC 517)* – a single purchase sold in two lots; *Johnston v Heath (46 TC 463)*;

and *Clark v Follett (48 TC 677)*. In all of these cases there was a clear intention at the time of purchase to sell at a profit. Where a property is purchased jointly there is often a greater risk that HMRC will contend that it is bought for resale. Except within families or partnerships it is relatively unusual for people to want to enter into long-term investment relationships with a co-venturer.

5.32 Most people try to avoid being labelled as a property dealer in their own names for fear that this will mean that all future property transactions are also dealing. Whilst caution makes this a sensible approach, this worry is not wholly justified. It is perfectly possible for an individual to enter into investment transactions at the same time as he is dealing. In *Cooksey & Bibby v Rednall (30 TC 514)* two individuals jointly bought a farm in 1924 which they let. Between 1930 and 1940 they entered into a number of joint property transactions which were admitted to be dealing. The farm was sold in 1938. It was held that the Commissioner's finding that the profit on the farm was part of their trading profits could not be supported. This decision is of especial interest as it is a joint ownership case where the dealing inference might be expected to be strong. In *CIR v Dean Property Co (22 TC 706)* a partnership agreement recited that the partnership was being formed to acquire land for investment. It feu-ed most of it in lots to an associated company. The use of the description 'partnership' normally implies a trading intent – as partnership is the carrying on of business in common 'with a view of profit'. (It is safer to describe the relationship as being a joint investment.) Nevertheless the transactions were held to be investment. If an individual is regarded as a dealer in relation to some transactions only and he has other property that has fallen in value there may be a temptation to contend that all his property transactions are trading. Normally this temptation should be resisted. In *Hudson v Wrightson (26 TC 55)* the taxpayer's contention to this effect was accepted in part, the judge remitting the case to the Commissioners for them to determine which of his other properties were trading stock. In the event they decided that none of them were.

5.33 Particular problems arise with builders. Both HMRC and the courts seem reluctant to accept that a builder can ever invest in property – on the rather spurious ground that his expertise of itself implies an intention to resell at a profit rather than to generate income. HMRC tend to take a similar approach to other people in the property business such as estate agents, surveyors, architects, and developers. In *Spiers & Son Ltd v Ogden (17 TC 117)* a construction company acquired land on which it erected buildings which it let and subsequently sold. The sales were held to be part of its building trade. In *Sharpless v Rees (23 TC 361)* a builder bought land to run as a poultry farm as his health precluded his continuing as a builder. His health deteriorated further and he abandoned the idea and sold the land. The surplus on sale was held to be part of his building profits. Similarly in *Shadford v H Fairweather & Co Ltd (43 TC 291)* a building company abandoned a project to erect flats for letting and the surplus on selling the site was held to be part of its building profits. Even relatives of builders can be looked on with suspicion. In *Smart v Lowndes (52 TC 436)* a builder contracted to buy land but passed the benefit to his wife. The conveyance was in her name. The land had building potential and was sold six years later at a profit. HMRC successfully contended that the surplus was part of the husband's trading profit and that the wife was a nominee.

5.34 Even the generation of rental income over a number of years is not conclusive where the investor is a builder. In *J & C Oliver v Farnsworth (37 TC 51)* the surplus on a house built in 1929 and let for 24 years until its sale in 1953 was held to be part of the builder's trading profits. A similar decision applied where a building company built and let houses before the war and sold them over a period after the war as they became vacant (*James Hobson & Sons Ltd v Newall (37 TC 609)*). In *W M Robb Ltd v Page (47 TC 465)* a building company erected a factory in 1951 for occupation by another group company to which it let it. In 1962 the factory became unsuitable for the occupier's needs and a new one was built by the building company. The surplus on sale of the original factory was held to be part of the builder's trading profits.

5.35 Even after a builder has given up building, future profits on the sale of rented properties that he built in his active days are likely to be regarded as trading profits. This is exemplified by *Gladstone Development Co Ltd v Strick (30 TC 131)* – houses sold in 1945 but building ceased in 1939; *Speck v Morton (48 TC 476)* – houses sold in 1964 but building ceased in 1949; *Granville Building Co Ltd v Oxby (35 TC 245)* – house sold in 1950 shown as an investment in the accounts since 1942; and *Andrew v Taylor (42 TC 557)* – although here the taxpayer had a partial victory, it being held that sales between 1957 (when building ceased) and 1961 were trading but later sales were investments. The only clear victory for the taxpayer was *Harvey v Caulcott (33 TC 159)* where shops that had been let by the builder for around 30 years were held to be investments. There was also a partial victory in *West v Phillips (38 TC 203)* where the builder had initially split the properties he built between trading stock and investment. It was held that those originally designated as investments were not trading stock but those originally designated as stock retained that status when sold ten years after the taxpayer had ceased building. It must of course be realised that on a cessation of a trade stock which is not sold needs to be brought into account at market value. It is likely that this was not done in the builders' cases that went to appeal and that HMRC contended that the trade had not ceased because they were out of time to make the cessation adjustment. If a builder who contends that his trade has ceased brings his closing stock into account at market value HMRC are unlikely to attack subsequent sales of the properties. If he does not do so he ought not to be surprised that HMRC regard the trade as continuing after active building has ceased.

5.36 If it can be shown that the purchase and resale of land is not a trading transaction then, unless *ICTA 1988, s 776* (now, *CTA 2010, ss 815–833* for corporation tax and *ITA 2007, ss 752–772* for income tax, see **Chapter 14**) applies, it will not normally be taxable as income. In *Leeming v Jones (15 TC 333)* four people jointly purchased land with the intention of floating a company to which they would transfer it. The Commissioners decided that this did not amount to trading. HMRC claimed in the alternative that if the profit was not trading income it was taxable as miscellaneous income. It was held by the House of Lords that the charge on miscellaneous income 'sweeps up all sorts of annual profits and gains… but it has been settled again and again that that does not mean that anything that is a profit or gain falls to be taxed'. It must be an annual profit. Lawrence LJ in the Court of Appeal stated: 'In the case of an isolated transaction… there is really no middle course open. It is either an adventure in the nature of trade, or else it is simply a case of sale and resale of property.' These words were quoted with approval in the House of Lords.

5.37 When entering into property transactions that are designed to achieve some subsidiary objective, the risk that HMRC might contend that the transactions amount to property dealing should not be overlooked. This is what happened in *Rosemoor Investments v Inspector of Taxes (2002 STC (SCD) 325)*. Rosemoor was an investment company and a wholly owned subsidiary of a bank. The bank was approached by an arm's length company, Chelsea plc, with a scheme to provide cheap finance to Chelsea. The scheme was that Rosemoor should take a 999-year lease of six properties owned by the Chelsea group at a premium of £39.7 million. Rosemoor would lease back the properties to the vendor at a market rent under a 35-year lease. It would grant another Chelsea subsidiary an option to buy back the properties after five years for £48.5 million. The companies would jointly elect to pass the benefit of the capital allowances on the plant and machinery in the building to Rosemoor (see **10.65**). The transactions duly took place. HMRC contended that the transaction was property dealing as far as Rosemoor was concerned, with the result not only that its gain was taxable as income but also that it was not entitled to the capital allowances (see **6.9**). Fortunately for Rosemoor, the Special Commissioners held that Rosemoor was investing its money and was not trading.

5.38 Finally it should be mentioned that in *Mansell v CIR (2006 STC (SCD) 605)* the Special Commissioner (Mr Heller) drew a distinction between carrying on a trade and preparing to do so. In 1992 and 1993 Mr Mansell invested significant time and energy in becoming an expert on the development of motorway service stations. In late 1993 he identified a possible site for such a station. In April 1994 he entered into options to acquire the site. In March 1994 he engaged consultants to carry out a feasibility study on the site. He decided not to sell it straightaway because he began to realise the real worth of the site. In December 1994 negotiations began with Kuwait Petroleum but they bought an alternative site. Mr Mansell meanwhile was seeking planning permission for the land. The Commissioner felt that prior to December 1993 either Mr Mansell intended to realise a finder's fee but then abandoned that concept in favour of acquiring a land interest and turning it to account, or his ideas were nebulous and he had no specific concept for the realisation of profit until December 1993 when he decided to acquire the option and turn it to account. He held that for a trade to exist it is necessary that there be a fairly specific concept of the type of activity in the mind of the putative trader which is to be carried on. He based this largely on comments of Lord Millett in *Khan v Miah [2001] 1 All ER 20*, a partnership case, in which the Court of Appeal held that the parties did not become partners until trading commenced and that the trade (operating an Indian restaurant) was not being carried on at the relevant time as no food had been bought or bookings taken. Mr Heller accordingly held that Mr Mansell's trade had not commenced prior to 5 April 1994 so was not being carried on in 1993/94. This is a nasty decision in the context of property transactions. It is not at all unusual for a person to first identify a site and only then decide how he wants to exploit it. This author would have regarded Mr Mansell as having started his trade probably some time in 1993 when he first decided to look for sites and at the latest in March 1994 when he commissioned the feasibility study, having already entered into heads of agreement to take the options.

Chapter 6

Tax Aspects of Property Dealing

6.1 Property dealing (or trading) is the purchase of properties with a view to generating profits by reselling them. That is on a trade. The profits are taxed in the same way as the profits of any other trade. If it is carried on by an individual or a trust, the profit is subject to income tax at rates of up to 45%. If it is carried on by a company, the profit is liable to corporation tax at 20% (which will reduce to 19% from 1 April 2017 and to 17% from 1 April 2020). Property dealing by individuals is comparatively rare (other than when it happens by accident) as it is normally sensible to seek limited liability to minimise risk. However, property dealing by a limited liability partnership where the members are individuals is increasingly common, so income tax can be in issue.

Computation of Profits

6.2 Like any other trade profits are computed in accordance with generally accepted accounting practice subject to the proviso that an expense is deductible as a trading expense only if:

(*a*) it is wholly and exclusively laid out or expended for the purposes of the trade,

(*b*) it is not of a capital nature, and

(*c*) it does not fall within any of the other specific exclusions set out in *ITTOIA 2005* or *CTA 2009, ss 53, 54* or *68*.

Date of Disposal or Acquisition

6.3 In particular there are no special rules to determine the dates of disposal or acquisition of properties. This is not necessarily the contract date, which is the rule that applies for capital gains tax. Indeed, there is no compelling reason why a property dealer should not adopt the date of the purchase contract as the acquisition date and the date of completion of a sale as the disposal date. Many companies adopt such a policy. Clearly it would need to be followed consistently. Whilst some Inspectors of Taxes may challenge such a policy it is in accordance with the accounting concepts of prudence and not anticipating profits, which underlies the concept of the reliability of the reported profits. The company is under an obligation to complete the purchase of a property immediately it has contracted to buy it. It is therefore proper to recognise that liability in the company's accounts, which a policy of treating the purchase as taking place at the date of the contract does. When the company sells a property all it obtains by entering into a sale contract is a right to enforce completion subject of course to its establishing its title to the property. Unless the purchaser has the necessary funds that right is not worth very much. The tax cases, if not exactly littered with instances of things going wrong between contract and completion, certainly contain several examples of what can go wrong. For example, in *Magnavox Electronics Co Ltd (in liquidation) v Hall (59 TC 610)*, the purchaser was not able to raise the funds to complete the sale and the company took 13 months to find a new purchaser, and even then at a much reduced price. In *Zim Properties Ltd v Proctor (58 TC 371)*, the vendor was unable to demonstrate good title to the property and the purchasers accordingly refused to complete the transaction. It is also not unheard of for the parties to a contract to change their minds for one reason or another and for the contract to be discharged by mutual agreement. There are accordingly risks that accounts may reflect profits on 'sales' that never in fact take place if the disposal of a property is recognised immediately a contract is signed. In such circumstances it is more prudent to wait until completion has taken place before recognising the sale.

6.4 A word of warning. In *Smith v HMRC (2011 STC 1724)* the tribunal decided that accounting principles 'required the recognition of assets (as access to future economic benefits controlled by the entity) where there was sufficient evidence of the existence of those assets and they could be measured as monetary amounts with sufficient reliability'. That case concerned a building sub-contractor. Mr Smith would make a demand for payment. The contractor's quantity surveyor would then certify the work and he would be paid. He claimed to recognise income only when the certificate was issued, but the tribunal held that it should have been recognised when the demand for payment was made. This, of course, related to services, where UITF40 applies, but FRS 5 requires a transaction to be recognised when it is reasonably certain that it will take place, which will often be the contract date. However, it also requires consistency, so if a taxpayer feels that it is not reasonable to assume that a contract will proceed to completion, a consistent policy of adopting completion date should be acceptable.

6.5 This is not to say that it would not be equally proper and in accordance with generally accepted accounting practice to recognise a disposal when a contract is entered into. In the vast majority of cases the sale will have taken place before the accounts are finalised and if anything has gone wrong with the sale an appropriate adjustment can be made in the accounts to eliminate the false sale. It is, however, up to the taxpayer, not HMRC, to decide the accounting principles which he opts to adopt. Provided that these are generally accepted by the accounting profession as appropriate to the taxpayer's circumstances and that they are applied consistently it is well established that HMRC cannot require the taxpayer to prepare his accounts on some other basis (see, eg, *Symons v Weeks and Others (56 TC 630)* and *Heather v P-E Consulting Group Ltd (48 TC 293)*), although in determining the appropriate accounting basis it needs to be remembered that FRS 18 requires an entity to adopt the basis most appropriate to its particular circumstances. There are no accounting standards dealing specifically with the recognition of income other than UITF 40, which deals only with services.

6.6 In a Privy Council case, *Eckel v Board of Inland Revenue (1989 STC 305)*, which was concerned with similar legislation of Trinidad and Tobago, it was held that a property trading disposal did not take place on the contract date, but rather at the time of completion, as money can only be treated as a trade debt when the trader has done all that is required to earn it. The facts were somewhat special. The taxpayer had contracted to sell land to a company controlled by herself in 1970. The conveyances were in 1973 and 1974 and the Revenue raised assessments for those years. She initially claimed that she was not trading but before the Privy Council abandoned that claim and instead contended that the sale had taken place in 1970, which was by then out of time for assessment. In 1970 the taxpayer did not have legal title to the land; she obtained that later. It seems doubtful whether this decision can be used to require a trader to adopt completion rather than contract date if he chooses not to do so.

Stock in Trade

6.7 The land or properties owned by a property dealer at the end of his accounting year represent his stock in trade and work in progress. If the person is developing his sites the building costs are of course part of the cost of the stock in trade at the year end insofar as they relate to completed buildings, or part of the cost of work in progress on buildings still in the course of construction. Accordingly, such expenditure will not be deductible for tax purposes until the property is sold. Where money is borrowed for the construction of specific properties, some HMRC Officers contend that the interest on that borrowing is part of the cost of the building work and ought similarly to be added to the work in progress and not treated as an overhead expense of the company. This defers the obtaining of tax relief until the property is disposed of. For corporation tax the rules on loan relationships require the accruals basis to be used in respect of interest to allocate payments to the period to which they relate (see **4.77**(*c*)), which may well support a claim that the interest needs to be treated as a cost of acquisition of the stock of properties. Unfortunately, it is difficult in most cases to rebut a contention that where interest on a project-related loan constitutes a trading expense it should be treated as part of the cost of the stock. Where interest is not on a borrowing for a specific development but is an overhead of the business the deduction is normally claimable on an accruals basis like any other business expense.

6.8 If a property dealer erects houses on its land and grants long leases of them at a premium it will have made a part disposal of items that it holds as trading stock. It was held in *B G Utting & Co Ltd v Hughes (23 TC 174)* that to calculate its profits it must treat the premiums as income and must bring into account the reversionary interest retained at the lower of its cost or net realisable value, which is the normal method of valuing stock in trade. The cost of the reversionary interest was arrived at by adopting the formula:

$$\text{cost of reversion} = \text{expenditure on house} \times \frac{\text{market value of the reversion}}{\text{premium received} + \text{market value of the reversion}}$$

6.9 Where builders sell houses subject to the creation of ground annuals or feu duties, by contrast, the Courts have required the market value of the ground annuals to be brought into account as income (*CIR v John Emery & Sons (20 TC 213)*; *McMillan v CIR (24 TC 417)*). The logic is that in the *Utting* case (**6.7** above) the entire interest in the house was not disposed of whereas in the *Emery* case the entire interest was disposed of for a consideration consisting of an immediate cash sum plus the right to a stream of annual payments. To arrive at the true profit the market value of that right needs to be brought into account. Where a dealing company disposes of a property for a consideration part of which is unquantifiable and contingent (where *Marren v Ingles* – see **11.101** – would apply to a capital gain) it seems more likely that it would give rise to a part disposal along *Utting* lines than a disposal of the property and the acquisition of a chose in action.

Capital Allowances

6.10 A property dealer is not entitled to claim capital allowances in respect of expenditure on properties held as trading stock. This is because *CAA 2001, s 4(2)* provides that capital expenditure – which is what attracts allowances – does not include any sum which is allowed to be deducted in computing trading profits. Curiously, if a let property on which capital allowances are being claimed is appropriated to trading stock it appears that writing down allowances can continue to be claimed as the assets will form part of the asset pool and the appropriation is not a disposal event (although a subsequent cessation of the letting business would be). From 2017/18, it does not include any cash basis expenditure (other than on the provision of a car) either (*CAA 2001, s 4(2)(aa)* inserted by *F(No 2)A 2017, Sch 2, para 51*).

6.11 Where a property dealer lets a property (other than a residential one) which is held as trading stock the tenant may be entitled to claim capital allowances to the extent that he pays a premium for his lease. Where a building incorporates equipment that has become a landlord's fixture and neither the landlord nor any other person is entitled to claim capital allowances in respect of it, the lessee is deemed to have incurred expenditure on the fixture equal to the part of the premium that is attributable to it (*CAA 2001, s 184*) (see **10.59** onwards).

Losses

6.12 Provided that the trade is carried on on a commercial basis, a property dealing loss incurred by an individual can be set against general income for the tax year in which it arises or the previous tax year in the same way as any other trading loss. The taxpayer can choose which year's income to set it against. If it exceeds the income of one of those years, the balance can be set against the income of the other. Again, the taxpayer can choose which year's income should be utilised first. However, a loss cannot be used partly against income of each year so as to leave some taxable income to cover the individual's personal allowance or basic rate tax band. It must eliminate the whole of the taxable income of one year before the balance can be utilised against the other. This relief has to be claimed. A claim has to be made by 31 January two years after the loss-making year, ie within a year after the filing date of the tax return for the year in which the loss occurs (*ITA 2007, s 64*).

6.13 Alternatively, a loss incurred by an individual in the first tax years of the trade can be carried backwards and set against general income for the three tax years prior to that in which the loss arose. It is set against income of the earliest of those three years first. As with *s 63*, relief on any unused balance can be set against income of the second year only to the extent that the loss completely eliminates the income of the third (*ITA 2007, ss 72, 73*).

6.14 If the individual has insufficient taxable income to fully relieve the loss, he can elect to set it against any capital gains of the same or a subsequent year (*TCGA 1992, ss 261B, 261C*). As capital gains are taxed at a lower rate than income, it is not generally sensible to do this if the individual is likely to have taxable income within the next few years.

6.15 A trading loss can alternatively be carried forward and set against future profits from the same trade (*ITA 2007, s 83*). What is the same trade is a question of fact. In the case of property dealing, it is not always easy to determine. For example, suppose that an individual buys a large house, converts it to flats, sells the flats and uses the proceeds to buy and convert a second house. Both transactions are clearly the same trade. But suppose that there is a three-year gap between selling the last flat in the first house and buying the second house. It is less clear that there is a single continuing trade. If the first conversion generated a loss, the individual could be called upon by HMRC to demonstrate that he was looking to acquire a second house during the gap. He might be able to do this by, for example, producing agents' particulars of properties that he had looked at but had decided were not suitable for conversion. Suppose that after converting two houses the individual decided to buy a bare site and construct an office block on it. Is that the same trade as converting houses? It might be, for example, that the conversions may have been done to gain experience in building work with the intention of moving onto larger projects at an appropriate time. However, in this case a large gap between the two transactions would be likely to create a bigger problem than if the same type of development was carried on both before and after the gap.

6.16 A loss in the last 12 months of a trade can be carried back and set against profits of the trade for the three tax years preceding that in which the cessation occurs (*ITA 2007, ss 89–91*).

6.17 A loss incurred by a property dealing company can be carried forward and set against future profits from the trade. Alternatively it can be set against general income of the accounting period in which the loss is incurred or, if this is insufficient, of the prior twelve months (*CTA 2010, ss 37, 38*). If the dealing company is a member of a group its trading loss can be surrendered to another group company under the group relief provisions. The loss cannot, however, be set against profits of other group companies for an earlier or later accounting period. If the accounting period of the dealing company is not identical to that of the other group company to which it wishes to surrender its loss, the loss can only be set against the profits of the other company for its corresponding accounting period.

6.18 If the expenses of a property dealer in relation to a let property exceed the income the excess can be treated as a trading expense; it need not be carried forward to later years as a UK property business loss (Property Income Manual, PIM4300).

Transactions in Land: Anti-Avoidance

6.19 *ITA 2007, ss 517A–517U* and *CTA 2010, ss 356OA–356OT*, inserted by *FA 2016, ss 77–82*, enact a major anti-avoidance provision aimed at preventing property trading transactions being structured as investment transactions. A sale of the shares of a property dealing company can fall within these provisions, although they will not apply if the company pays corporation tax on the whole of its trading stock (as at the date of the sale). It is sensible to obtain a warranty from the purchaser of a controlling interest in the company that he will procure that this will happen. Such a warranty is not, of course, proof that the exemption will apply but, provided that the person giving it is a person of substance, it transfers the risk of an attack under the *section* to the purchaser.

6.20 A sale of a controlling interest of shares in a dealing company will automatically come within these provisions even if it can be demonstrated that there was no tax avoidance motive because the relevant provisions do not contain a motive test. The mere fact that the company holds land as trading stock is sufficient to trigger a charge. As the effect of these provisions applying is likely to be that the profit on the disposal of the shares will be taxed as income it is clearly vital to seek to obtain the protection of the exclusion. Unfortunately what the company does after it has been sold is not under the control of the vendor, but it is this that will determine the vendor's tax liability. The anti-avoidance provision is considered in detail in **Chapter 14**.

Special Provisions Affecting Property Dealers

6.21 In computing the profits of a property dealer, so much of the cost of woodland in the UK which is purchased in the course of his trade as is attributable to trees or saleable underwood growing on the land is to be disregarded. The part of the sale proceeds attributable to such trees is also disregarded if they have not been felled by the time the land is sold (*ITTOIA 2005, s 156*; *CTA 2009, s 134* – see **23.20** below).

6.22 Where a property dealer is taxed under *ITTOIA 2005, ss 277–282* or *285* or *CTA 2009, ss 219–221* (see **3.2–3.8** above) in respect of a premium received in relation to a lease of land which forms part of his trading stock the amount on which tax is so charged is excluded from his trading receipts (*ITTOIA 2005, s 158*; *CTA 2009, s 136*). Any amount taxed under *CTA 2009, ss 222–226* (see **3.13–3.22** above) is similarly excluded from trading receipts. If part of the tax assessed under *CTA 2009, s 225* is repaid by virtue of a claim *under CTA 2009, s 239* (see **3.20** above) the trading profits for the year in which the deemed premium was received – not that in which the claim is made – must be recomputed to exclude only the reduced figure (*CTA 2009, s 136(4),(5)*).

6.23 Except where he has trading losses brought forward – which cannot be set against property business income – it is accordingly generally of little concern to a trader to grant a lease within the above provisions as the aggregate of the property business income and trading profits will equal the trading profit that would otherwise have arisen if no part of the premium had been taxable. As a lessee can obtain relief in certain circumstances where part of a premium is taxable on the landlord (see **12.47** below) a property dealer may well be able to obtain a better price for the sale of a short lease that he holds if he grants a sublease for the term less one day than if he assigns the lease itself.

6.24 The *Finance Act 2016, ss 76* and *78* brought into the scope of UK tax profits realised by overseas persons from trading in and developing UK land after 5 July 2016. A non-resident is within the scope of UK income tax (or corporation tax in the case of a company) on the profits of a trade of dealing in or developing UK land (*ITTOIA 2005, s 6(1A)*; *CTA 2009, s 5(2)(a)* inserted by *FA 2016, ss 76(2), 78(11)*). Prior to 4 July 2016 the charge to tax arose only if the non-resident carried on the trade in the UK or, for corporation tax, carried it on in the UK through a UK permanent establishment. In practice HMRC rarely claimed that a non-resident's UK property trade was carried on in the UK, possibly because the concept of the place where a trade is carried on is fairly vague. It used to be accepted that it was where management and control took place but the courts began to look at where the real substance of the trade occurred. Furthermore, if the non-resident was based in a country with which the UK had a full double tax agreement (DTA), the DTA prevented HMRC from taxing the trade unless it was carried on through a permanent establishment in the UK. In the case of single property dealing, the property itself was trading stock so could not constitute a place 'through which' the trade was carried on. In the case of development for resale, most DTAs deemed a development site to be a permanent establishment if it existed for over 12 months (in some cases) or six months (for later agreements). Furthermore the DTAs with Jersey, Guernsey and the Isle of Man contained no such deeming (although they were amended at the time the new legislation was introduced to ensure that it did not breach those DTAs).

6.25 A non-resident's trade of dealing in or developing UK land consists of any activities of dealing in or developing UK land for the purpose of disposing of it, and any activities from which profits, gains or losses derive which are treated under *ITA 2007, Pt 9A* (or in the case of corporation tax, *CTA 2010, Pt 8ZB*) (transactions in UK land) (see **Chapter 14**) as profits or losses of the company's trade of dealing in or developing UK land (*ITTOIA 2005, s 6B(1)(2)*; *CTA 2009, s 5B(1), (2)*). Land for this purpose includes buildings and structures, any estate, interest or right in or over land, and land under the sea or otherwise covered by water (*ITTOIA 2005, s 6B(3); CTA 2009, s 5B(3)*). A disposal must be interpreted in accordance with *ITA 2007, s 517R* or *CTA 2010, s 356OQ* (see **Chapter 14**). UK land means land in the UK (*ITTOIA 2005, s 6B(4); CTA 2009, s 5B(4)*).

6.26 If a person has entered into an arrangement the main purpose (or one of the main purposes) of which is to obtain a tax advantage in relation to tax to which that person is chargeable (or would without the tax advantage be chargeable by virtue of *ITTOIA 2005, s 6(1A)* or *CTA 2009, s 5A* (as the case may be), the tax advantage must be counteracted by means of adjustments

(*ITTOIA 2005, s 6A(1), (3), (5)*: *CTA 2009, s 5A(1), (3), (5)*). Such adjustments can be made, by either HMRC or the taxpayer, by way of making or modifying an assessment or the amendment or disallowance of a claim or otherwise (*ITTOIA 2005, s 6A(4)*; *CTA 2009, s 5A(4)*). The adjustment is within the scope of self-assessment, ie the taxpayer is expected to volunteer it himself! This provision does not apply if the arrangement was entered into before 16 March 2016 (*FA 2016, ss 81(2), 82(2)*).

6.27 Obtaining a tax advantage for this purpose included obtaining it by virtue of any provisions of DTAs, but only where the tax advantage is contrary to the object and purpose of the DTA (*ITTOIA 2005, s 6A(2)*; *CTA 2009, s 5A(2)*). This seems designed to suggest that the provision will not normally override double tax agreements. However, it remains to be seen how other countries will interpret the object and purpose of their DTA. For example, the DTA with Germany deems a building site that lasts for over 12 months to be a DTA. If a German company buys and sells UK land and the UK claims the right to tax that land because it is in the UK, it is hard to see how such a claim can accord with the object and purpose of the DTA, which was to exempt German companies from such tax. A further oddity is that this protection for DTAs applies only where there is an arrangement; it does not apply for the purpose of *ss 5* or *6* themselves, unless a German company buying and selling UK land can itself constitute an arrangement.

6.28 For the purpose of this provision, arrangement includes any agreement, understanding, scheme, transaction or series of transactions whether or not legally enforceable (*ITTOIA 2005, s 6A(7)*; *CTA 2009, s 5A(6)*). A tax advantage for income tax purposes includes a relief or increased relief from tax; a repayment or increased repayment of tax; the avoidance or reduction of a charge to tax or an assessment to tax; the avoidance of a possible assessment to tax; the deferral of a payment, or advancement of a repayment, of tax; and the avoidance of an obligation to deduct or account for tax (*ITTOIA 2005, s 6A(6)*). The corporation tax legislation adopts the definition in *CTA 2010, s 1139* (*CTA 2009, s 5A(6)*). This is broadly the same as under *s 6A(6)*, but extends the scope to include some indirect savings.

6.29 Where a company was previously within the scope of corporation tax because it carried on the property dealing or development trade through a UK permanent establishment and it incurred expenses in relation to the trade which were not deductible for corporation tax but which would have been deductible in calculating the profits taxable under *CTA 2009, s 5(2)(a)* if the company had not already been carrying on the trade, *CTA 2009, s 61* (pre-trading expenses) has effect in relation to such expenses as if the company had started to carry on the trade at the time it came into charge to corporation tax under *CTA 2009, s 5(2)(a)* (see **6.24**). This relief does not, , apply if tax relief for the expenses was allowed by another country or territory (*FA 2016, s 80*).

Other Matters

6.30 HMRC rarely challenge the salaries drawn by the directors of trading companies (unless they do very little work in the business). A property dealing company is normally treated no differently to any other trading company in this respect, although the author has experienced cases where HMRC have questioned salary payments by property dealing companies where these are extremely large, particularly if they are accompanied by large pension contributions. Accordingly, the profits of a property dealing company can normally be withdrawn from the company by this route without difficulty. Furthermore, if high salaries are drawn the company can also set up a director's pension scheme and make substantial contributions to it. A property dealing company can usually easily justify a high salary for a full-time director as all, or the bulk, of the company's profit results from the work of that individual.

6.31 Following the removal of the cut-off point for employers' national insurance contributions, the increase in the rate of such contributions to 13.8% and the introduction of the special dividend tax rates, it is more attractive in arithmetical terms to extract profits from a family company by way of dividend rather than as salary. The proposed new system of taxing dividends for 2016/17 onwards makes dividends more expensive but in most cases will not alter this bias towards paying dividends rather than remuneration. Dividends can also give greater flexibility if shares are held by other adult family members as they split the income amongst the family. On the other hand if the company has non-family shareholders, the cost of paying dividends to such people can exceed the tax benefit from foregoing remuneration. Where shares are held by infant children (even if purchased from money deriving from someone other than the child's parents) the payment of dividends is likely to be regarded by HMRC as the creation of a settlement on the child if the company has not fully remunerated the parents for work done for the company.

6.32 It should be borne in mind that pension provision cannot be made against dividends, although £3,600 pa can be paid into a stakeholder pension scheme even if the individual has no earnings. Pensions are generally a highly attractive form of tax shelter.

Transactions Between a Dealing Company and an Associated Company (repealed from 31 January 2013)

6.33 Up to 31 January 2013, if a property dealing company (one dealing in land or buildings or one whose profits on the sale of land or buildings were part of its trading profits) became entitled to a deduction in computing its trading profits in respect of the depreciation in value of any right subsisting against an associated non-dealing company, and that depreciation was not brought into account in computing the trading profits of the associated company, the associated company was deemed to have received (on the last day of the period for which the dealing company claimed the deduction) income of an amount equal to that deduction (*ICTA 1988, s 774(1)(a),(4)*).

6.34 Similarly, if a dealing company made to an associated non-dealing company any payment in respect of which it was entitled to a deduction in computing its trading profits, the non-dealing company had to be treated as receiving miscellaneous income equal to that payment if it did not form part of its trading profits (*ICTA 1988, s 774(1)(b)*).

6.35 If the non-dealing company was carrying on a trade it could elect to treat the deemed receipt as trading income rather than miscellaneous income (*ICTA 1988, s 774(2)*). If it carried on more than one trade it could choose the trade which was to be deemed to be in receipt of the trading income.

6.36 The *section* did not apply to the writing off of a loan to the non-dealing company if it was carrying on a trade (or was formed to do so) and the loan was to meet expenditure which had proved abortive and for which the company was not entitled to claim tax relief. Nor did it apply to a payment to the non-dealing company to meet such expenditure (*ICTA 1988, s 774(3)*). It appears that a charge could still arise if the company was entitled to claim relief for the expenditure but had no income against which to set such relief – although in most cases the relief could then be given against the deemed income created by the section, thus negating the charge.

6.37 The sort of circumstance at which the *section* was probably aimed was where a dealing company owned shares in an associated company as part of its trading stock and wrote down the value of that stock, or where a dealing company lent money to an associated company which it wrote off as a bad debt (although it would be very rare that a property dealing company could establish a trading deduction for it). However, the wording of *sub-s (1)(b)* was very wide. It seemed to impose a charge on the purchase price of a property where a dealing company bought the property at market value from an associated investment company – although the author has never known HMRC to seek to apply the *section* in such circumstances and it would clearly be unreasonable for them to do so. It could also apply if an investment company granted a lease at a premium to an associated dealing company.

6.38 Two companies were associated for this purpose if one had control of the other or any person had control of both of them. A company had control of another if it had control either by itself or in conjunction with any person having control over it itself (*ICTA 1988, s 774(4)(d),(e)*). Control for this purpose meant the power of a person to secure:

(*a*) by means of the holding of shares or the possession of voting power in or in relation to that or any other body corporate, or

(*b*) by virtue of any powers conferred by the articles of association or other document regulating that or any other body corporate,

that the affairs of the first-mentioned body corporate were conducted in accordance with the wishes of that person (*CTA 2010, s 1124*). The author cannot ever remember the section having been invoked by HMRC. It was repealed by the *Statute Law (Repeals) Act 2013*, which was enacted to repeal a large number of obsolete legislative provisions.

Chapter 7

Tax Aspects of Property Investment

7.1 Property investment is the purchase of properties either with a view to generating income from the rents that they produce or with some other non-trading intention, such as to live in the property. Although the purchaser may well hope to be able to sell the property at some stage for more than its cost this expectation is incidental to the income generated from it or the enjoyment of it. Such properties are not trading stock to be bought and sold. They are capital assets held to generate a yield or to provide personal satisfaction. The profits on disposal of such properties are regarded as capital gains.

7.2 The tax rules for computing rental income are considered in **Chapter 2** and those for capital gains in **Chapter 11**. For an individual, there are no other special income tax or capital gains tax rules. If an individual purchases a property for occupation rent-free by a relative, the legislation does not impute notional income to either.

7.3 An individual (or trust) is not entitled to tax relief for the costs of managing his property portfolio. He can obtain tax relief for such costs only to the extent that he can show that they are wholly and exclusively incurred in generating the rental income and thus qualify as a deduction in calculating such income. No relief is due for managing the portfolio itself or for the work involved in carrying out improvements to the property (*ITA 2007, s 393(1)(a)*).

7.4 As an investment company is not carrying on a trade, for tax purposes it does not calculate profits; it calculates its total income from all sources and sets against that its management expenses, charges on income and debits on loan relationships. The main source of income of a property investment company will of course be its rents. It calculates the taxable rental income in accordance with the normal property business rules (see **Chapter 2**), by reference to income earned in its accounting period. If the company has other types of income, such as bank interest, it similarly calculates the taxable amount in accordance with the rules appropriate to that income – loan relationships in the case of bank interest. Having calculated the taxable income from each source these are then aggregated, together with capital gains, to form total profits. From this the company is entitled to deduct its management expenses.

Management Expenses

7.5 As indicated above, relief is due to a company for its management expenses. The legislation gives little guidance as to what is covered by the term 'management expenses'. Before the legislation was recast in *Finance Act 2004*, it used to say that it included commissions, but no longer does even that. Furthermore, the dividing line between 'management expenses' and 'property expenses' deductible in calculating the profits of a property business is not clear. There is undoubtedly an overlap between the two, which is dealt with by excluding from management expenses any expenses to the extent that they are otherwise deductible in computing profits *(CTA 2009, s 1219(3), (b))*.

7.6 Expenses of a capital nature cannot be treated as expenses of management (*CTA 2009, s 1219(3)(a), Camas plc v Atkinson, 2004 STC 860*). However, the law was changed in response to that case. Expenditure is also not deductible if it does not relate to the company's business of making investments or if the investments to which it relates are held by the company for an unallowable purpose, ie a purpose that is not a business or other commercial purpose of the company or the purpose of activities in respect of which the company is not within the charge to corporation tax (*CTA 2009, ss 1219(2), 1220*).

7.7 Any income of the company (other than franked investment income) which is derived from a source not charged to tax but arises from the company's investment business must be deducted from the management expenses (*CTA 2009, s 1222*). Capital allowances on plant and machinery can be added to management expenses if relief cannot be obtained under *CAA 2001, s 251* by deducting the allowances from income of the current accounting period (*CTA 2009, s 1233*). This effectively enables the allowances to be carried forward if they cannot be relieved in the year in which they were incurred. Charges on income that cannot be relieved in the accounting period are similarly carried forward by adding them to the unrelieved management expenses (*CTA 2009, s 1223*).

7.8 Management expenses are dealt with on an accruals basis. This is achieved by requiring the use of generally accepted accounting practice to calculate management expenses (*CTA 2009, ss 1224–1227*).

7.9 Prior to *Camas plc v Atkinson (2004 STC 860)*, which is considered at **7.10**, the only helpful cases on what is a management expense were *London and Northern Estates Co Ltd v Harris (21 TC 197)*, in which it was held that surveyor's fees paid by a property owning company were not an expense of management and *Southern v Aldwych Property Trust Ltd (23 TC 707)* in which the costs of advertising for tenants was similarly disallowed. In both of these cases the disputed expenditure would nowadays be deductible as a property business expense, ie they were expenses of managing the properties rather than of managing the company. HMRC invariably insist that all of the expenses of a property investment company should be analysed between expenses of managing its properties and expenses of managing the company itself, apportioning items such as directors' remuneration which relates to both functions. The property management expenses element is allowed as a deduction in calculating the profits of the property business. In the past if such expenses exceeded the rental income the excess had to be treated as a property business loss which, unlike management expenses, could not be relieved against non-property business income. However, the current corporation tax UK property business system allows such a set-off for companies (but not individuals or trusts) (see **2.50**) so the distinction no longer seems important.

7.10 Probably the most important case on management expenses is *Camas plc v Atkinson (2004 STC 860)*. That related to expenses of investigating the possibility of a share investment company expanding by merging with or taking over another company. HMRC sought to disallow the expense on the grounds that it was capital. The Court of Appeal held that the management expenses rules contained no distinction between capital and income. As stated above, this was reversed by what is now *CTA 2009, s 1219(3)(a)*. However, Carnwarth LJ (who gave the only judgment in the Court of Appeal) said in that case, referring to an earlier case, *Sun Life Assurance Society v Davidson (37 TC 330)*: 'It was common ground that the process of reaching a decision to purchase was management in the ordinary sense'. There is nothing in the speeches which supports the view that an activity which is part of that decision-making process ceases to be management, merely because it may also assist in the purchase if that is decided upon – still less if it is not. Unlike the provisions relating to trading expenses, there is no requirement that the expense should be 'wholly and exclusively related to management'. The rewrite of the legislation has not reversed this. There is still no 'wholly and exclusively' test. Instead, *CTA 2009, s 1219(2)(b)* looks merely at whether an investment is itself held for an unallowable purpose.

7.11 Following the Court of Appeal decision in *Camas v Atkinson* and the rewriting of the legislation, HMRC issued a guidance note on 15 June 2004 which makes the following helpful points:

(*a*) The fact that the investments of a company with investment business are held on capital account does not create a presumption that the expenses of managing those investments are themselves capital. Ordinary recurring expenditure which otherwise satisfies the statutory tests in is very unlikely to be of a capital nature (*para 3*).

(*b*) If expenses are debited in a statement of capital profits and losses in financial accounts that does not in itself exclude them from deduction as expenses of management (*para 4*).

(*c*) Expenditure on appraising and investigating investments will in general be revenue in nature (*para 6*).

(*d*) It is necessary to look at the immediate commercial effects of the expenditure rather than looking at its more distant purpose (*para 7*). It may be questionable whether this is necessarily correct as HMRC appear to derive it from trading income cases.

(*e*) In the case of abortive expenditure it is necessary to look at what the company would have got for its money if the expenditure had been successful (*para 7*). Again, HMRC derive this from trading income cases. In *Camas v Atkinson* Carnwarth LJ said:

> 'It is unnecessary to express a concluded view whether the fact that no acquisition occurred is in itself determinative. One can imagine cases where, following a firm commitment to purchase, expense is incurred in carrying it out, but some wholly unexpected event requires it to be aborted. If at the time it is incurred such expenditure is not an expense of management, it may be difficult to see why it should change its character thereafter. However, in this case, the lack of an actual purchase merely confirms the fact that there never was a firm decision to buy.'

(*f*) Expenditure up to the point at which a decision is made to acquire a particular investment will generally be non-capital; once the decision to acquire is made, the expenditure thereafter is capital in nature (*paras 8* and *9*). In *Camas v Atkinson* Carnwarth LJ said:

> 'I would not necessarily conclude that any expenditure thereafter [ie after a firm intention to acquire had been reached], even if the purchase proceeded, would have to be treated as costs of acquisition, rather than management. It must depend on the circumstances.'

(*g*) Once it has been decided to dispose of an investment, normally where a decision is taken to market it, HMRC regard costs incurred after that point as capital.

7.12 In order to claim a deduction for management expenses a company must show not only that it is resident in the UK but also that it qualifies as a company with investment business, namely 'any company whose business consists wholly or partly in the making of investments' (*ICTA 1988, s 130*). A company which never has any income may not be able to satisfy this definition. A property investment company will normally have no trouble in meeting these tests. However, it is possible for a company to be neither an investment nor a dealing company.

7.13 Until fairly recently there was no UK case law on what is an investment company although there were two Irish cases (where the definition is almost identical), *Howth Estate Company v Davies (2 ITC 74)* and *Casey v The Monteagle Estate Company Ltd (3 ITC 313)*. The question has now been considered by the UK courts in *Cook v Medway Housing Society Ltd (1997 STC 90)*. The company was a non-profit making company formed to acquire the housing stock of Rochester-upon-Medway City Council. HMRC disputed whether the Society's business consisted wholly or mainly in the making of investments. It was conceded by both sides that 'making investments' includes holding them and that the principal part of the company's income was derived from its property portfolio. It was held that 'the term "investment" means the laying out of moneys in anticipation of a profitable capital or income return'. The fact that the company was a not-for-profit one did not conflict with such an objective as the company could generate a profit to plough back into achieving the company's overriding objective. Accordingly the purpose and nature of the business was in principle that of holding investments. The judge went on to say 'In determining what is the business of a company for the purpose of *s 130*, it is necessary to have regard to the quality, purpose and nature of the company and its activities, and this includes the objects clause in the Memorandum of Association of the company … It is relevant to have regard to the actual activities carried on by the taxpayer at the relevant date, but if these are viewed without regard to the taxpayer's past history or future plans they may give only a partial and incomplete picture. The critical question is whether the holding of assets to produce a profitable return is merely incidental to the carrying on of some other business, or is the very business carried on by the taxpayer … The very business of the society is the provision of housing at a return below the market return, but none the less a return producing a profit'.

7.14 Another aspect was dealt with by Special Commissioners in *Tintern Close Residents Society Ltd v Winter (1995 Sp C 7)* and 12 similar cases. The company was incorporated 'to acquire, hold, manage, maintain and deal' with the Tintern Close estate. The Special Commissioner held that in looking at whether the business of a company consists wholly or mainly in the making of investments it is necessary to look at why the company was incorporated (was this to acquire assets in order to turn them into account for the purpose of profit so that it could be distributed to the shareholders), what its activities are, if it holds investments whether the purpose of doing so is to make money from them, and whether the purpose and motive of the operations indicate that its main business is to make investments. Applying these tests she decided that although the company held land (the common areas and the freehold reversion to the houses) it did not do so to make money and that its business, in the sense of its functions and activities, was to manage and administer Tintern Close not to make investments. It was accordingly not an investment company. HMRC have said that they agree with the Special Commissioner's approach and seek to explain it as confirming that the holding of investments incidental to the real purpose of a company does not necessarily involve it in carrying on a business of holding investments (Tax Bulletin Number 19, October 1995). By contrast it was held in *CIR v Tyre Investment Trust Ltd (12 TC 646)* that a company can make investments, and thus be an investment company, even though it never has any intention of turning them over.

7.15 The Special Commissioners have also held that the management company for the grounds of a residential development was not an investment company and in any event the principal part of its income was derived from members' annual subscriptions not from the making of investments (*White House Drive Residents Association v Worsley (1997 STC (SCD) 63)*). The annual subscriptions of such a company would normally be exempt from tax under either the mutual trading principle or HMRC's interpretation of the *Landlord and Tenant Act 1987* (see **2.71**), but in this case the company sought to deduct its management expenses from interest received, which is taxable.

7.16 An interesting case is that of *Macniven v Westmoreland Investments Ltd (1998 STC 1131).* The company had been incorporated in 1968 as a property holding company and was clearly an investment company from 1968 to 1988. It sold its last property in 1988 and used most of the proceeds to pay accrued interest on loans. It also purchased gilts with a comparatively small part of the proceeds in order to maintain its investment status. In January 1990 it bought a property from its shareholder as an investment as it was felt it would be more satisfactory for it to hold property investments HMRC accepted that the company was an investment company from 1990 but challenged its status in the interim – so as to disallow brought forward management expenses. They contended that the acquisition of the gilts and the new property were to display an investment activity when the company could have no main purpose of investment – as it had no funds to invest. The Special Commissioners held that the company made investments throughout and that as bank deposits were made in the course of its investment business the objectives of the company had never changed. The judge thought that the Commissioners were correct and this was upheld in both the High Court and the House of Lords.

Surplus Management Expenses

7.17 An investment company does not make 'losses' for tax purposes, although it can of course incur UK property business losses, which can be set against general income, and miscellaneous income losses, which can be used only against future income of that same type and cannot be set against other income of the company, even for the accounting period in which the loss was incurred. Clearly, however, an investment company's management expenses can exceed its profits (which are income plus taxable capital gains), so that in commercial terms it has a loss. Such a surplus of management expenses is carried forward and treated as if it were management expenses of the next accounting period. If the brought-forward surplus serves to increase a surplus in the next period it will also increase the amount carried forward in that year (*CTA 2009, s 1223*). In effect, a surplus of management expenses can be carried forward indefinitely until it is relieved. This is subject to the proviso that if the company were to cease to have an investment business, such as, for example, by becoming a trading company or by ceasing its business, any unrelieved management expenses at that stage would appear to be lost as the company would no longer be a company with investment business so the carry forward of management expenses would be to a period in which it is not possible to claim relief for them. They could not then be carried forward to a subsequent period in which the company might set up such a business as the right to carry forward is only from an accounting period in which the company has investment business. Where an investment company has charges on income which it has paid wholly and exclusively for purposes of its business, or capital allowances which cannot be relieved in the accounting period to which they relate, they can be added to the surplus management expenses and treated as management expenses of the next accounting period (*CTA 2009, ss 1221(2), (3), 1223*).

7.18 Unlike the loss of a dealing company, surplus management expenses cannot be carried back to an earlier accounting period. It should not be forgotten, though, that the capital allowances rules may allow unrelieved allowances to be carried back. In particular *CAA 2001, s 260(3)* allows capital allowances to be carried back to the extent that they cannot be relieved in the year to which they relate, and set against profits of any description of the preceding accounting period (or a part equal in length to the length of the current accounting period).

Charges on Income and Debits on Loan Relationships

7.19 As indicated above a deduction can be claimed for charges on income. This used to include annuities and other annual payments (including royalties and excluding payments in respect of loan relationships) but since 16 March 2005 has been limited to charitable donations (*CTA 2010, ss 189, 190*).

7.20 A deduction can also be claimed for deficits on loan relationships (see **4.52**), which will give relief for most interest payments.

Capital Allowances

7.21 A property investor is entitled to claim capital allowances on qualifying expenditure. Allowances are given, *inter alia*, for capital expenditure on:

(*a*) plant and machinery;

(*b*) industrial buildings (to 31 March 2011 only);

(*c*) commercial or industrial buildings in enterprise zones;

(*d*) qualifying hotels (to 31 March 2011 only);

(*e*) agricultural buildings and works (to 31 March 2011 only);

(*f*) dwelling-houses let on secured tenancies;

(*g*) mines and oil wells;

(*h*) research and development;

(*i*) certain fire safety works;

(*j*) certain works at sports grounds; and

(*k*) certain expenditure on security.

7.22 The legislation on capital allowances is considered in **Chapter 10**. It must be realised that much of the work on the construction of a modern building can constitute plant and machinery for capital allowance purposes. Where a building will not itself qualify for allowances under one of the above heads, such expenditure should be identified and the appropriate allowances claimed. Whilst most people now realise that allowances can be claimed in relation to a new building it is still frequently not appreciated that allowances are often also available on the purchase of a second-hand building.

Capital Gains of Companies

7.23 Capital gains (or chargeable gains as they are statutorily termed) of an investment company are calculated separately from its income, but added to the income to arrive at the taxable profits of the accounting period. The differences in the calculation rules – in particular for older companies rebasing to 31 March 1982, which will eliminate from tax most gains accruing prior to that date, and indexation – are likely to mean that capital gains will attract a lower effective rate of tax than income.

7.24 If an investment company enters into a sale and leaseback transaction to raise finance, HMRC are unlikely, in most cases, to claim that the sale is an indication that the property was bought for dealing purposes. They may well do so if the sale realises a substantial profit and the value of the lease taken back is low, so that the reality of the transaction is that the company has disposed of substantially the whole of its interest in the property. It would be difficult for them to establish a dealing motive if the company is left with the ability to generate a substantial profit rental under its leaseback.

7.25 For the purposes of taxation of capital gains, a sale and leaseback is regarded by HMRC as a part disposal even though the legal form of the transaction may be a complete sale combined with the grant of a lease. There is a part disposal of an asset where an interest or right is created by the disposal or where on making the disposal any description of the property remains undisposed of (*TCGA 1992, s 21(2)(b)*). It is not wholly clear that a sale and leaseback falls into either of these categories if the form of the transaction is looked on alone. The substance of the transaction is undoubtedly that the right to the leaseback is a right created by the disposal. It is in any event normally in the taxpayer's interest to accept that the transaction is a part disposal as this reduces the immediate capital gain. It must not, however, be overlooked that by applying the part disposal rules a sale and leaseback will give rise to a capital gain even if, as is often the case, the sale price does not exceed the cost. This is because it is necessary to value the leaseback, being the part of the asset deemed to be undisposed of. If the rent payable under the lease is less than the open market rent for the property, or the rent review pattern under the lease is less burdensome than is normal in the market, the lease will have a value. The capital gains tax base cost of the asset is then apportioned between the sale price of the interest sold and the value of the lease retained using the formula:

$$\text{base cost of interest sold} = \text{cost of entire interest} \times \frac{\text{sale price}}{\text{sale price} + \text{value of part retained}}$$

Close Investment-holding Companies

7.26 *Finance Act 1989, s 105(2)* introduced a new class of investment company, the close investment-holding company. Fortunately, most of the teeth of this animal were drawn prior to enactment, whereas the Chancellor's original concept of a close investment-holding company would have included all close property companies and would have subjected them to a very harsh tax regime. The legislation was repealed from 1 April 2015 by *FA 2014, Sch 1, para 4*. However, it has been re-enacted for the sole purpose of disallowing income tax loan interest relief on a borrowing to invest in such a company by *ITA 2007, s 393A*.

Definition

7.27 A close investment-holding company is a close company that does not fall within a number of exceptions (*CTA 2010, s 34(1)*). Fortunately the exceptions are sufficiently widely drawn that very few property companies are likely to be close investment-holding companies. A company will not be such a company during an accounting period if it exists wholly or mainly (see **7.25** below) for any one or more of the following purposes:

(*a*) Carrying on a trade on a commercial basis.

(*b*) Making investments in land or estates or interests in land where the land is (or is intended to be) let to anyone other than:

- a person who is connected with the company (within *ITA 2007, s 993* – see Appendix 1); or
- a person who is the spouse (or civil partner) of an individual who is connected with the company, or who is a relative (brother, sister, ancestor or lineal descendant) or the spouse of a relative of such an individual – or of the spouse of such an individual.

(*c*) Holding shares in (or securities of, or making loans to) one or more companies each of which is either:

- a 'qualifying company', ie one which is under the control of the relevant company or of another company that also controls the relevant company and which exists wholly or mainly for the purpose of carrying on a trade on a commercial basis or of making investments in land that fall within (*b*) above (or both); or
- a company which is under the control of the relevant company or under common control with it and which itself exists wholly or mainly for the purpose of holding shares in (or securities of, or making loans to) one or more qualifying companies.

(*d*) Co-ordinating the administration of two or more qualifying companies.

(*e*) Existing for the purpose of a trade or trades carried on on a commercial basis by either:

- one or more qualifying companies; or
- a company that controls the relevant company.

(*f*) The making by one or more qualifying companies (or by a company that controls the relevant company) of property investments falling within (*b*) above.

(*CTA 2010, s 34(2); ITA 2007, s 393A(1)-(4),(6)* inserted by *FA 2014, s 13.*)

7.28 Control for this purpose is as defined in *CTA 2010, s 450.* A company in liquidation will not be a close investment-holding company in the accounting period immediately following the winding-up if it was not one in the last accounting period prior to the winding-up, although it can be one in subsequent accounting periods if the liquidation extends over more than a year. (*CTA 2010, s 34(5); ITA 2007, s 393A(5)*). 'Where a trading company ceases to trade prior to commencement of winding up, it is the view of HMRC that the company will be a close investment holding company for the accounting period immediately before commencement of winding up and thus also immediately thereafter' (Tax Bulletin, Issue 3). Thus, care will need to be taken to ensure that the company continues to trade, if at all possible, until it is wound up in order that *CTA 2010, s 34(2)* will apply.

7.29 HMRC usually regard the expression 'wholly or mainly' as meaning more than 50%. Accordingly it is likely that a property company will be a close investment-holding company only if more than 50% of its properties fall within categories (i) and (ii) in head (*b*) above. This of course assumes that the properties are similar. If they are not, the 50% test may need to be applied to the overall rents or the overall value of the portfolio. It needs to be borne in mind that the status of a close company has to be determined accounting period by accounting period. Accordingly if a company acquires any such proscribed properties it will be necessary to check in each accounting period whether such properties form the major part of the assets in that accounting period. It is of course the purpose for the existence of the company as a whole that needs to be looked at though. 'Exists' implies the reason why the company is currently here, not why it was set up. A company whose only asset is a property with head (*b*)(i) or (ii) plus a large amount of cash may well be looking to invest that cash in investments that are not excluded items. If so the main reasons for the company's existence could well be to make those projected investments even though at the present time its income may derive solely from rent from a connected person.

Consequences of Close Investment-holding Company Status

7.30 A close investment-holding company could not claim the benefit of the small profits rate of corporation tax (but was still an associated company for the purpose of calculating the relief due to other companies) (*CTA 2010, s 18(b)*). The small profits rate of tax ceased to apply from 1 April 2015. A loan taken out by an individual to acquire the shares in, or lend to, such a company is not eligible for tax relief.

Other Matters

7.31 It is often difficult to obtain a deduction for remuneration paid to the directors of an investment company. Whilst HMRC rarely challenge remuneration paid to directors of a property dealing company, they frequently resist such a deduction included in the management expenses of an investment company. In what HMRC consider to be the leading case, *L G Berry Investments Ltd v Attwooll (41 TC 547)*, they allowed only £600 out of remuneration (in 1961 terms) paid of £1,800, although the circumstances there were unusual (see **7.28**). HMRC's general approach is first to insist on the remuneration being apportioned between remuneration for managing the company's properties and that for managing the company itself. The first part will then be compared with what an estate agent would charge for doing the work. This would normally be between 71/2% and 15% of the gross rent, depending on the work involved. Any excess would be disallowed unless the company can convince HMRC that the nature of the properties or the services provided to tenants are such that they involve far greater work than an estate agent would be prepared to undertake. As management of the properties is generally the major work involved in an investment company, HMRC would generally contend that only a very small salary is justifiable for managing the company itself. It is sometimes argued that a director is entitled to be remunerated for a significant amount of time that has been spent negotiating sales of properties, searching for new properties, or supervising the company's development programme. Whilst that is clearly correct, in the past there was a risk that such a salary might be regarded by HMRC as capital expenditure with the result that it would be taxable on the director but would not reduce the taxable income of the company. It was accordingly dangerous to pay such remuneration – although it was by no means clear that it was not properly deductible.

7.32 However, the case of *Camas v Atkinson* (see **7.10**) indicates that this approach is incorrect and ought to be resisted. It may also be worth noting that *Berry v Attwooll* did not go as far as the Court of Appeal. Furthermore, in that case the Commissioners (and the court) did not actually apply a 'wholly and exclusively' test. They asked themselves whether the sum of £1,800 had the quality of expenses of management and found that 'neither the company nor its directors and shareholders, nor its auditor, ever consciously determined that the directors should be remunerated for their services and incidental expenses as directors by paying them £600 each; all concerned were simply minded to cause the company to dispose of substantially the whole of its profits (using that word in a general sense) by paying directors fees'. They allowed the £600 because the Inspector of Taxes had indicated that he was prepared to allow £600 as an expense as he regarded it as the part of the remuneration that reasonably related to the services performed by the directors. The High Court held that the Commissioners had taken a correct view of the law.

7.33 Having said that, from 20 June 2007 a deduction can no longer be allowed for any particular expenses of management 'if any part of those expenses is incurred directly or indirectly in consequence of, or otherwise in connection with, any arrangements the main purpose, or one of the main purposes, of which is to secure the allowance of a deduction [as management expenses] or any other tax advantage'. (*CTA 2009, s 1248(1), (2)*). This appears to disallow the entire expense not merely the part paid to seek to secure a tax advantage. Accordingly claiming unjustifiable remuneration might result in the complete loss of relief for remuneration of the director concerned.

7.34 The option of paying substantial pension contributions for directors is also generally not open to an investment company, partly because of the small size of the salaries that HMRC will permit. Where a person has no other pension provision, up to £3,600 pa can be paid into a stakeholder pension scheme (a form of personal pension scheme) irrespective of whether or not the individual has earnings and irrespective of the source of any earnings. The reform of the pension scheme rules from 6 April 2006 aggravates the problem. Previously once a pension scheme was approved by HMRC contributions to it were automatically deductible. Now it is necessary to show that the remuneration is an expense of management of the company's investment business. This requires the remuneration package paid to a director (ie his salary plus pension contributions and any other benefits) to qualify as a management expense under normal principles.

Flat Management Companies

7.35 In blocks of flats it is common for the flats to be managed by a flat management company. This is generally owned by some or all of the leaseholders depending on how the company came about. In a new development, the developer will often transfer the freehold reversion to the company once all of the flats have been sold (or rather let on long leases, as it is not possible to have a freehold flat). In such cases each leaseholder is normally required to acquire a share in that company when he is granted his lease. For older blocks, ownership of the freehold reversion is often achieved under the leasehold enfranchisement legislation. This requires the agreement of the majority of the tenants, but as it involves cost, not all tenants choose to participate. In such a case the management company is likely to be owned only by those tenants that chose to participate in the enfranchisement.

7.36 HMRC have said that, in practice, a property management company, such as a flat management company, will not be required to complete tax returns where:

(*a*) its annual corporation tax liability is not expected to exceed £100;

(*b*) the company's business consists of the management, on a non-profit making basis, of a block of flats or apartments for the owners, lessees or tenants of the flats or apartments;

(*c*) the company's Articles of Association contain rules to ensure only the persons having an interest in the property under management own the shares in the company;

(*d*) the company is not entitled to receive any income from an interest in land; and

(*e*) the company pays no dividend or makes any other distribution of profit.

This does not prevent the company being taxed as trustee for the tenants on interest on service charge monies (HMRC press release 25 August 2006).

7.37 Where a flat management company is owned by the leaseholders (or the majority of them) it is not uncommon for them all to agree that the company should extend the term of their leases. It is normally assumed that this has no tax consequences, albeit that it shifts value from the company to the shareholders. Some people are concerned that HMRC might seek tax on the notional premium that could have been demanded for the lease. The lease extension is a transaction between connected persons in such circumstances and the CGT rules require such a transaction to be deemed to take place at market value. The author has never known HMRC to mount such a challenge. The fear is in any event probably misplaced – even where a premium is charged to other tenants who did not join in the enfranchisement process to extend their leases. The normal return on property is rent. Accordingly the arm's length consideration for the lease extension could take the form of a requirement to pay a market rent for an extended term. However, the property business income rules contain no provision to allow the actual rent to be increased to a market rent; so renting the property at below market rent has no tax consequences (other than possibly the disallowance of expenditure in generating the rents). As the extension to the lease does not require payment of a premium, HMRC would need to show that the extended lease is a sham, ie it does not reflect the real bargain between the parties, in order to impute a requirement for a premium into the lease. It would be very difficult for them to do this. The grant of the extended leases is of course a 'depreciatory transaction'. The effect of this is that any loss on the disposal of the freehold would be eliminated or restricted. However, as a sale of the freehold would not be in contemplation by the tenants, this is unlikely to be a significant problem.

Real Estate Investment Trusts

7.38 From 1 January 2007 a special tax regime applies to Real Estate Investments Trusts (REITs). A REIT is a property investment company that has elected into the REIT regime. This splits the income into REIT income (rents and gains from investment properties) and non-REIT, or general, income. The REIT income is exempt from corporation tax but taxable as income in the hands of the recipient. The general income bears corporation tax in the normal way (*CTA 2010, s 534(1)*). In the first five years only around 20 REITs were created and these were mainly focused on commercial property. The rules were significantly recast in the *Finance Act 2012* to make the REIT regime more attractive. The government is anxious to encourage REITs to provide housing.

The Qualifying Conditions

7.39 To qualify as a REIT a company must carry on property rental business, namely a property business (see **2.3**) or an overseas property business (see **2.120**) (*CTA 2010, s 519(1)*). The renting of tied premises is capable of being a property rental business for this purpose even though *CTA 2009, s 42(2)* requires such rent to be treated as trading income for other tax purposes (*CTA 2010, s 519(2)*). However, the following businesses do not qualify as a property rental business:

(*a*) The incidental letting of property (in the UK or elsewhere) which is held in connection with a trade in property (eg generating income from property dealing stocks).

(*b*) Letting of property which is held for administrative purposes in carrying on property rental business but is temporarily surplus to requirements, the space let is comparatively small compared to the space occupied for administrative purposes and the letting is for a term of three years or less.

(*c*) Letting of property if the property would fall in accordance with generally accepted accounting practice to be described as owner-occupied, but no account is to be taken of the fact that it may fall to be described as owner-occupied by reason only of the provision of services to an occupier who is in exclusive occupation of the property and is not connected (within *ITA 2007, s 993* – see **Appendix 1**) with a member of the group.

(*d*) The provision of services in connection with property outside the UK where those services would not form part of a property business if provided in connection with property in the UK.

(*e*) Entering into structured finance arrangements to which *CTA 2009, s 770(2) or ITA 2007, s 809BZM(2)* (structured finance arrangements) applies.

(*CTA 2010, ss 604,* the *REIT (Excluded Business) Regulations 2006* and the *REIT (Amendment of Schedule 16 to the Finance Act 2006) Regulations 2009 (SI 2009 No 1482).*)

7.40 In addition the following types of income or profit are excluded from being part of a property rental business:

(*a*) Income in connection with the operation of a caravan site the income from which is treated as trading income.

(*b*) Rent in respect of electric-line wayleaves.

(*c*) Rent in respect of the siting of a gas or oil pipeline.

(*d*) Rent in respect of the siting of a mast or similar structure designed for use in a mobile telephone network or other system of electronic communication.

(*e*) Rent in respect of the siting of a wind turbine.

(*f*) Dividends from another REIT (including stock dividends) (although from 17 July 2013, *CTA 2010, s 549A* (see **7.93**) treats such amounts as profits of a separate property rental business).

(*g*) Income arising out of an interest in an LLP where *CTA 2009, s 1273(4)* (winding up) applies.

(*CTA 2010, s 605* as amended by *FA 2010, Sch 19, para 11* and the *REIT (Excluded Business) Regulations 2006.*)

7.41 HMRC have power by regulation to amend *ss 604* and *605* and to add or delete items from them (*CTA 2010, ss 604(4), 605(3)*).

7.42 As well as having a property rental business a company which wishes to be taxed as a REIT must:

(*a*) be resident in the UK (and not also resident elsewhere);

(*b*) not be an open-ended investment company (OEIC);

(*c*) have all of its ordinary share capital listed on a recognised stock exchange (which excludes AIM and Plus Market companies as well as unquoted companies);

(*d*) not be a close company, or one excepted from being close only because it is controlled by a non-close company or because shares held by a close company are treated as being held by the public (with an exception for one which is close only by virtue of having as a participator an institutional investor (up to 16 July 2012 a limited partnership which was a collective investment scheme within *Financial Services and Markets Act (FSMA) 2000, s 235*));

(*e*) have only one class of issued ordinary share capital and have no issued shares that do not form part of its ordinary share capital (other than non-voting relevant preference shares – as defined in *CTA 2010, s 160(2)–(7)* – generally, non-convertible fixed rate shares) or shares which would be such but for carrying a right of conversion into shares or securities in the company; a share is non-voting for this purpose if either it carries no right to vote at a general meeting of the company or it carries a right to vote which is contingent on the non-payment of a dividend and which has not become exerciseable; and

(*f*) must not have a loan creditor who is entitled to an amount by way of interest which depends to any extent on the results of all or part of the company's business or on the value of any of the company's assets, or to an amount by way of interest that exceeds a reasonable commercial return on the consideration lent, or to an amount on repayment which exceeds the amount lent (unless it is an amount which is reasonably comparable with the amount generally repayable under the terms of issue of securities listed on a recognised stock exchange) – but for this purpose a loan is not regarded as depending on the results of the company's business by reason only that the terms of the loan provide for the interest to be increased in the event of the results improving or reduced in the event of their deteriorating.

(*CTA 2010, s 528* as amended by *FA 2012, Sch 4, para 4*.)

In the case of a Group REIT the above rules must be applied by reference to the principal company of the group.

7.43 For the purpose of (*d*) above, the following are institutional investors:

(*a*) the trustee or manager of an authorised unit trust (within *FSMA 2000, s 237(3)* or a unit trust scheme authorised in a territory outside the UK in an equivalent manner (within *FSMA 2000, s 237(1)(3))*;

(*b*) an open-ended investment company (OEIC) (within *FSMA 2000, ss 236(1), 262*) or a company incorporated outside the UK which under local law is equivalent to an OEIC (within *FSMA 2000, s 236(1))*;

(*c*) a person acting on behalf of a limited partnership which is a collective investment scheme (within *FSMA 2000, s 235*);

(*d*) the trustee or manager of a pension scheme within *FA 2004, s 150(1)*;

(*e*) a person acting in the course of a long-term insurance business which is authorised under *FSMA 2000* to carry on such business or which has an equivalent authorisation under the law of another country;

(*f*) a charity;

(*g*) a social landlord registered under the *Housing and Regeneration Act 2008, s 11* or its Scottish, Welsh or Northern Irish equivalent;

(*h*) a person who cannot be liable for corporation tax or income tax on the grounds of sovereign immunity;

(*i*) a UK REIT; or

(*j*) a person who is resident outside the UK and which is the equivalent of a UK REIT under the law of its territory of residence.

The Treasury have power to amend this list (*CTA 2010, s 528(4A),(4B)* inserted by *FA 2012, Sch 4, para 4*). They added (*i*) and (*j*) by the *REIT (Amendments to the Corporation Tax 2010 and Consequential Amendments) Regulations 2014 (SI 2014 No 518)*.

7.44 Throughout an accounting period the shares forming the company's ordinary share capital must also either satisfy the requirements of *CTA 2010, s 1137(2)(b)* (definition of 'listed') or be traded on a recognised stock exchange (*CTA 2010, s 528A(2)* inserted by *FA 2012, Sch 4, para 20*). In the case of a group REIT the principal company's ordinary share capital must be listed or quoted (*CTA 2010, s 528A(1)*). This condition is deemed to be met for the first three accounting periods in which the company is within the REIT regime if at the end of the third accounting period the shares (or the shares of the principal company in the case of a group REIT) are listed or they are traded on a recognised stock exchange during the three-year period (*CTA 2010, s 528B* inserted by *FA 2012, Sch 4, para 20*).

7.45 In addition to the above conditions the principal company of a Group REIT (see **7.113**) is required to prepare and send to HMRC for each accounting period financial statements in respect of the Group REIT (*CTA 2010, s 527(2)(e)*). These must be separate financial statements for each of its property rental business (ie its tax-exempt business), its property rental business in respect of its UK business (ie the business of UK members of the group and business in the UK of other members), and its residual (taxable) business.

7.46 The financial statements for the property rental business and residual business must each specify in relation to each member of the group:

(*a*) income (calculated in accordance with IAS);

(*b*) expenses (calculated in accordance with IAS);

(*c*) profits before tax excluding gains and losses on property (calculated in accordance with IAS); and

(*d*) assets (valued at the beginning of the accounting period in accordance with IAS and using fair value if there is a choice) disregarding liabilities secured against or otherwise relating to the assets.

7.47 The financial statement in respect of its UK business must specify in relation to each member its profits calculated in accordance with *CTA 2010, s 599* (which broadly requires the profits of a REIT to be calculated under the UK property business rules but allowing a deduction for interest and certain other costs). If there is a non-group minority shareholder in any group company (other than the principal company) both of the financial statements for the property rental business must exclude its share of income, gains, losses, assets and liabilities of that subsidiary (by reference to the minority shareholder's beneficial entitlement to profits available for distribution to equity holders) (*CTA 2010, ss 532, 533*).

7.48 HMRC have power by regulation to make further provisions in relation to the content and form of financial statements and to specify the time in which they must be submitted (*CTA 2010, s 533(5)*). They have done so by the *REIT (Financial Statements of Group REITs) Regulations 2006 (SI 2006 No 2864)* as amended by the *REIT (Financial Statements of Group REITs (Amendment) Regulations 2007 (SI 2007 No 3536)*. These require the expenses figure to show financing costs separately and to exclude intra-group financing costs in relation to the property rental business (but not the residual business). They also require financing costs of the UK property rental business to be separated from other financing costs of the property rental business. They also require a reconciliation between the audited accounts and the financial statements under *s 533(5)*. They also contain rules for the treatment of investments in non-group entities, joint ventures and open-ended investment companies. If a member of the group holds a beneficial interest in a non-corporate entity and has significant influence over that entity it must be treated as a member of the group. The regulations require the financial statements under *s 533(5)* to be submitted with the company's corporation tax return. From 1 January 2008 they also require changes in the value of hedging derivatives, and items outside the ordinary course of the company's business to be disclosed to reflect the provisions considered at **7.47**.

7.49 A company which meets the conditions in **7.42**(*a*) and (*b*) above and, from 17 July 2012, **7.43** can give written notice to HMRC stating that it wishes to be taxed as a REIT. Such a notice must specify the accounting period from which such treatment is to apply, must be given before the start of that period, must be accompanied by a statement that all of the conditions in **7.42** other than condition (*d*) are reasonably expected to be satisfied in respect of the company throughout the specified accounting period, and must contain such other information and documents as HMRC may by regulation prescribe (*CTA 2010, ss 524(1), 525*). In the case of a Group REIT (see **7.113**) the notice must be given by the principal company (*CTA 2010, s 523(1)*). Conditions (*c*)–(*f*) are additional conditions that must be met for a company to be a REIT in an individual accounting period (*CTA 2010, s 527*).

7.50 The company can be a close company (ie it need not meet (*d*) in **7.35**) for its first three years from the giving of the notice applying to become a REIT. If an accounting period straddles the end of the third year, condition (*d*) does still need to be met in the second part of the accounting period (*CTA 2010, s 527(5)–(8)*).

7.51 If a company does not expect to satisfy the condition that all of its shares must be listed on a recognised stock exchange (see **7.42**(*c*)) on the first days of an accounting period but reasonably expects to do so throughout the rest of the accounting period the company can qualify for the election but the statement mentioned above must confirm that the other conditions are reasonably expected to be satisfied throughout the accounting period and the quotation condition is reasonably expected to be satisfied in respect of the company for at least part of the first day of the accounting period and throughout the rest of that period (*CTA 2010, s 525(2)–(4)*). Prior to 17 July 2012 the company also had to certify that it would be a close company in its first accounting period. If the company was not a close company at the time it applied for REIT registration solely because it was not then a listed company the notice needed to be accompanied by a statement asserting that the other conditions were reasonably expected to be satisfied throughout its first accounting period, it expected to be a listed company for at least part of the first day of the specified accounting period and it expected to be non-close for all of it other than the first day (*CTA 2010, s 527(5)*). A company can take advantage of both of these relaxations (*CTA 2010, s 525(8)*).

7.52 Once such a notice has been given it will continue to apply to future accounting periods (*CTA 2010, s 526*). The company can opt out of the REIT regime at a later date by giving a further notice to HMRC specifying the date at the end of which the regime is to cease to apply to it. That date cannot be earlier than the date of which HMRC receive the notice (*CTA 2010, s 571*). In the case of a Group REIT (see **7.113**) the notice must of course be given by the principal company (*CTA 2010, s 571(1)*). If the company ceases to meet conditions (*a*)(*b*)(*e*) or (*f*) in **7.42** it automatically ceases to qualify for the REIT regime from the end of the accounting period prior to that in which the breach of the conditions occurred (*CTA 2010, s 578(1)(2)*). The company is, not surprisingly, required to notify HMRC of such a breach as soon as is reasonably practicable (*CTA 2010, s 578(3)*).

7.53 HMRC has power to ignore minor or inadvertent breaches of the REIT rules in **7.42** (*CTA 2010, ss 572–577* – see **7.80**) and to counteract a tax advantage (*CTA 2010, ss 545, 573* – see **7.89**). They can by regulation specify that a specific number of such breaches or counteracting action ought to disqualify the company from the REIT regime. HMRC can itself exclude a company from the REIT regime for breaches of *ss 573, 573B, 574, 575, 576* or *577* if either:

(*a*) the company has relied on a provision of *CTA 2010, ss 528* (conditions for company), *529* (property rental business) *530* (distribution of profits) and *531* (balance of business) more than four times in a ten-year period (*CTA 2009, s 577*);

(*b*) the company has been given two notices under *s 545* (seeking a tax advantage – see **7.89**) in a period of ten years (*CTA 2010, s 573(3)*);

(*c*) HMRC think that a breach of a requirement in *CTA 2010, s 529* (see **7.57**), *530* (see **7.58**) or *531* (see **7.61**) is so serious that the REIT regime should cease to apply to the company (*CTA 2010, s 574*); or (*d*) from 17 July 2012, *s 528(4)* (non-close company) was not met at some time in the first three years and at that time the company (or the group in the case of a group REIT) does not satisfy *s 528(4)* and has not done so for a period exceeding three years (or periods exceeding three years in aggregate) (*CTA 2010, s 573A(1)(2)*).

(*CTA 2010, s 572.*)

To exercise this power HMRC must give written notice to the company of its exclusion stating the reasons for it. The company has a right of appeal to the First-tier Tribunal. Such a notice takes effect from the end of the accounting period prior to that in which the event within (*a*) to (*c*) above applies (*CTA 2010, s 572(3)(4)*). Head (*d*) does not apply if the reason that *s 528(4)* is not met is because the principal company of a group REIT became a member of another group REIT (or a REIT became a member of a group REIT) (*CTA 2010, s 573A(3)*).

7.54 If a company ceases to carry on a business (or part of a business) which it carried on at a time when (*d*) above applied to the company and the business was transferred to another company (company X), head (*d*) must be taken to have applied to company X (and to any other transferee of the business from company X) (*CTA 2010, s 573A(4)(5)*). If HMRC give notice by virtue of head (*d*), the company or group is treated as having ceased to be a UK REIT on the first day of accounting period 1 or such later day as may be specified by HMRC (*CTA 2010, s 573A(8)*). Accounting period 1 is that which begins on entry into the REIT regime (*CTA 2010, s 609*), so the effect is that HMRC can treat the company as never having been a REIT. A breach of *s 528(4)* in the first three years is ignored in applying (*a*) above (*CTA 2010, s 577(8)*).

7.55 HMRC can also give a notice under *s 572(1)* if the condition in *s 528A* (further condition relating to shares – see **7.44**) would not be met in an accounting period but for *s 528B* (see **7.44**) and the company has benefited from the relaxation of the condition in *s 528A* in relation to three or more earlier accounting periods (*CTA 2010, s 573B(3)* inserted by *FA 2012, Sch 4, para 20*). Similar rules apply in relation to a group REIT (*CTA 2010, s 573B(1)(2)*). Neither of these provisions apply if the condition in *s 528A* is not met as a result of the REIT becoming a member of a group REIT or the group REIT becoming a member of another group REIT (*CTA 2010, s 573B(5)*). If a company ceases to carry on a business (or part of a business) which is carried on at any time during an accounting period in relation to which the company benefits from the relaxation of the conditions in *s 528A* and the trade is transferred to another company (company X), company X (and any further transferee from company X) is treated as having benefited from the relaxation of the conditions (*CTA 2010, s 573B(6)(7)*). If a notice is given under *s 572(1)* in these circumstances, the company (or group) is treated as having ceased to be a REIT on the first day of its first accounting period after becoming a REIT (ie it is treated as never having been a REIT) or such later day as may be specified by HMRC (*CTA 2010, s 573B(8)(9)*).

7.56 Even where a company is in the REIT regime, the regime will not apply in an individual accounting period unless throughout that period:

(*a*) its property rental business involves at least three properties;

(*b*) no single property represents more than 40% of the total value of the properties involved in its property rental business; and

(*c*) The whole of its UK REIT investment profits (see **7.97**) arising in the accounting period plus at least 90% of the rest of the profits of the company's property rental arising in the accounting period are distributed by way of dividend on or before the filing date for the company's tax return for that period under *FA 1998, Sch 18, para 14* (but a breach is ignored to the extent that compliance with this condition would be unlawful (under either UK law or the law of a foreign country prescribed in regulations made by HMRC) and a distribution that is taxed under *CTA 2010, ss 529, 551* (see **7.71**) is treated as having been made for the purpose of applying this test) *(CTA 2010, s 530(4))*. If the 90% distribution requirement is not met solely because the market value of a stock dividend is less than anticipated, the REIT will have six months from the accounting date (three months prior to 17 July 2012) to make good the shortfall (*CTA 2010, s 530 (6C)(6D)*).

(*CTA 2010, ss 529, 530* as amended by *FA 2013, Sch 19, para 2(3)*.)

Prior to 17 July 2013 the requirement at (*c*) was only to distribute at least 90% of the profits of the property rental business.

7.57 Distributions by way of dividend cover both cash dividends and share capital issued in lieu of cash (stock dividends) (*CTA 2010, s 554A*). The shares must be issued in consequence of the exercise by the holder of an option to choose either cash or shares (*CTA 2010, ss 554A(2), 1051*). The amount of the distribution in such a case is the cash equivalent under *ITTOIA 2005, s 412* (*CTA 2010, s 599A*). For CGT purposes the payment of such a stock dividend does not constitute a reorganisation of the company's share capital but the recipient is treated as acquiring the new shares for a consideration equal to their cash equivalent under *ITTOIA 2005, s 412* (*TCGA 1992, s 142A*).

7.58 In the case of a Group REIT (see **7.113**) the property rental businesses of the members of the group are treated as a single business and in place of requirement (*c*) above the whole of the group's UK REIT investment profits (see **7.97**) arising in the accounting period plus at least 90% of the rest of the group's UK profits arising in the accounting period must be distributed by the principal company by way of dividend on or before the filing date for its tax return (*CTA 2010, s 530(1)* as substituted by *FA 2013, Sch 19, para 1(2)*). The exception for an unlawful distribution applies but this test is applied to the part of the property rental business attributable to an individual member (*CTA 2010, s 530(1)*). Prior to 17 July 2013 the requirement was only to distribute at least 90% of the group's UK profits.

7.59 In applying *s 530* in relation to an accounting period, if the company delivered its tax return for that period showing the amount of the profits of its property rental business calculated in accordance with *CTA 2010, s 599* and at the time the return become final, those profits have been increased from the amount originally shown in the return, a distribution of those profits made within three months of that date is treated as having been made within the deadline in *CTA 2010, s 530(4)* – but only up to an amount equal to 90% of the increase in profits (*CTA 2010, s 530A(5)–(9)* inserted by *FA 2012, Sch 4, para 23*). Similarly in applying *s 530* in relation to a group REIT, if the principal company of the group delivered with its tax return the financial statement under *CTA 2010, s 532(2)(b)* (see **7.47**) showing the amount of the UK profits of the group arising in the accounting period and, at the time the principal company's return can no longer be amended, those profits have been increased from the original amount, any distribution of those profits made within the following three months is treated as having been made within the deadline in *CTA 2010, s 530(1)* – but only up to the 90% of the increase in profits (*CTA 2010, s 530A(1)–(4)*). *Section 340A* cannot be relied upon to satisfy the requirements of *CTA 2010, ss 530(1)(a)* or *530(4)(a)* to distribute the whole of the company's (or group's) UK REIT investment profits (*CTA 2010, s 530A(10)* inserted by *FA 2013, Sch 19, para 3*).

7.60 For the purpose of applying **7.56**(*a*) and (*b*):

(*a*) a reference to a property involved in a business means an estate, interest or right by the exploitation of which the business is conducted;

(*b*) a property is a single property if it is designed, fitted or equipped for the purpose of being rented, and it is available for rent on a commercial or residential unit separate from any other such unit;

(*c*) assets must be valued in accordance with IAS;

(*d*) where IAS offers a choice of valuation between cost and fair value, fair value must be used; and

(*e*) no account is to be taken of liabilities secured against (or otherwise relating to) assets, whether generally or specifically.

(*CTA 2010, s 529(4)*.)

7.61 In addition the profits from the company's tax-exempt business for the accounting period must be at least 75% of its total profits before tax for the accounting period, and at the beginning of the accounting period the aggregate value of the assets involved in the tax-exempt business (ie the property that would be shown as held if separate accounts were prepared for the company's exempt property business) and, from 17 July 2012, the cash and (from 17 July 2013) relevant UK REIT shares held in the residual business, must be at least 75% of the company's total assets (*CTA 2010, s 531(1)(5)*).

7.62 For this purpose profits must be calculated in accordance with international accounting standards but excluding realised and unrealised gains and losses on the disposal of property, changes in the fair value of hedging derivative contracts, and items which are outside the ordinary course of the company's business having regard to its past transactions. The assets must be valued in accordance with international accounting standards (IAS) and where IAS offers a choice of valuation the fair value must be used. Cash means money held on deposit (in any currency), gilts and any investments specified in regulations by HMRC (*CTA 2010, s 531(8)*). The test is based on gross assets, no account being taken of liabilities (*CTA 2010, s 531(4)(7)*). Relevant UK REIT shares are shares held by the company (or a member of a group REIT) in the principal company of another REIT or group REIT (*CTA 2010, s 531(9)* inserted by *FA 2013, Sch 19, para 4(5)*).

7.62A In the case of a Group REIT (see **7.113**) the aggregate amounts shown in the financial statements (see **7.45**) of income from tax-exempt business, income from non-tax-exempt business, assets involved in tax-exempt business and assets involved in non-tax-exempt business are used (*CTA 2010, s 531(2)(6)*). From 17 July 2013, a distribution falling within *CTA 2010, s 549A(6)* or *(8)* (see **7.97**) received by a REIT or by a member of a group REIT must be treated as profits of a property rental business in accordance with *CTA 2010, s 549A(1)*, notwithstanding *s 549A(5)* (that *s 549A* applies only to a distribution of exempt profits) (*CTA 2010, s 531(4A)* inserted by *FA 2013, Sch 19, para 4*).

The Effect of becoming a REIT

7.63 When a company comes into the REIT regime a new accounting period begins; the company's existing property rental business (called 'C (pre-entry)' is treated as ceasing. The assets involved in the business are treated as being disposed of at their market value and reacquired for the purpose of the tax-exempt property rental business (called 'C (tax-exempt)'(*CTA 2010, s 536(2)(3)*). This deemed disposal does not trigger a capital gain though (*CTA 2010, s 536(4)*). It does not trigger any capital allowances balancing adjustments either. Instead the tax-exempt business takes over the tax written down value of the assets.

7.64 In the case of a Group REIT (see **7.113**) the deemed disposal and reacquisition applies only to assets held by UK members of the group and where there is a minority interest in a subsidiary it does not apply to the percentage of its assets attributable to the minority shareholders (this is excluded from the group's financial statements – see **7.45**) (*CTA 2010, s 536(6)*). If a UK company becomes a member of an existing REIT there is similarly a deemed disposal and reacquisition at that time of the assets used for its property rental business (*CTA 2010, s 607(1)*). If it has a minority shareholder the part of the assets attributable to that shareholder is excluded (*CTA 2010, s 539(4)*).

7.65 While in the REIT regime the company is treated as carrying on two separate businesses, its tax-exempt business and its residual business (called 'C (residual)'), which comprises all other income and gains of the company. The tax-exempt business is completely ring-fenced (*CTA 2010, s 541(2)–(5)*). The profits of that business are not charged to corporation tax (*CTA 2010, s 534(1)(2)*). However, any losses of the business cannot be used against residual income, against income arising prior to the company becoming a REIT or against income arising after it ceases to be a REIT (*CTA 2010, s 541(4)(5)*). In the case of a Group REIT such ring-fencing applies both in relation to the group and in relation to each UK company in it (*CTA 2010, s 541(1)(a)*). If part of the profits of a subsidiary's property rental business is excluded from the group's financial statements (because it is attributable to an outside shareholder) that part is treated as profits of the group's residual business and so remains taxable (*CTA 2010, s 541(7)*).

7.66 Profits of the residual business are chargeable to corporation tax at the full 23% rate. The small companies rate cannot be used (*CTA 2010, s 534(3)*). It is not clear how this affects the small companies rate in associated companies. The tax-exempt business is treated as a separate company, not merely a separate business (*CTA 2010, s 534(3)*). Accordingly it may be that the REIT has to be regarded as comprising two associated companies, not one. In the case of a Group REIT (see **7.113**) the corporation tax charge applies only to UK resident members of the group. Where there is a minority interest in a company (so that the minority shareholder's interest in the rental income is treated as income of the group's residual business) those profits are treated as taxable profits of the individual subsidiary (*CTA 2010, s 534*).

7.67 Up to 16 July 2012 coming into the REIT regime triggered a special income tax charge. This was a proportion of the value of the assets treated as sold and reacquired (but ignoring any asset that had a negative market value. With corporation tax at the then rate of 28% the amount of the charge was 2% of such value. It was actually expressed as 2% divided by the rate of corporation tax at the time of entry. It was a notional amount of income chargeable to corporation tax as part of the residual income for the first accounting period that the REIT regime applied (*CTA 2010, ss 538, 539*).

7.68

Example 7.1

When a company entered the REIT regime in 2007 it had £100 million of rental property. The deemed income on entry was:

$$\frac{100{,}000{,}000}{30\%} \times 2\% = £6{,}666{,}667$$

Corporation tax on this at 28% = £1,866,667

which was 18.67% of £100m.

7.69 Although the amount was treated as income (taxable as miscellaneous income) it could not be offset by any loss, expense, etc; the tax on it had to be paid irrespective of the results of other activities of the company (*CTA 2010, s 538(5)*). This entry charge was abolished by *FA 2012, Sch 4, para 33*.

7.70 An irrevocable election could be made to pay the tax by instalments spread over four years, the first on the day the company entered the REIT and the next three on the anniversaries of that date. The effective rate was, however, increased to reflect notional interest on the instalments. The effective tax rate on each instalment was:

1st instalment	0.50%
2nd instalment	0.53%
3rd instalment	0.56%
4th instalment	0.60%
	2.19%

The Treasury had power to amend these figures in order to reflect changes in interest rates but any such change did not apply to companies that had already made the instalment election. If a company that made such an election ceases to be a REIT during the instalment period the outstanding instalments become immediately payable – without any reduction to reflect their premature payment (*CTA 2010, s 540*). This charge continues to apply to a company that entered the REIT regime before 17 July 2012 (*FA 2012, Sch 4, para 33(2)*).

7.71 In the case of a Group REIT the value of assets attributable to minority shareholders was ignored (*CTA 2010, s 539(4)*). The entry charge applied to assets held by non-UK group members (even though they were outside the scope of capital gains tax) if they carried on UK property rental business.

The tax charge on such a company was to income tax not corporation tax (*CTA 2010, s 538(4)*). If a company joined an existing Group REIT the entry charge applied as if it had become a REIT when it joined the group (*CTA 2010, s 607(1)*).

7.72 The Treasury have power to make regulations that apply where someone owns 10% or more of a REIT (*CTA 2010, s 554*). However, most of the regulations previously made under this power have now been incorporated into *CTA 2010*, so the remaining scope for regulation making is now much more restrictive. If a REIT makes a distribution to (or in respect of) a person who is beneficially entitled, directly or indirectly, to 10% or more of the dividends paid by the company (or to 10% or more of its share capital or of the voting rights in the company), and it has not taken reasonable steps to prevent the possibility of such a distribution being made, it is treated as receiving notional income taxable as miscellaneous income as part of its residual income arising in the accounting period in which the distribution is made.

7.73 The amount of the notional income is that given by the formula:

$$\frac{DO \times SO \times BRT}{MCT} + \frac{DP \times SP \times BRT}{MCT}$$

Where:

DO = the total amount of the C (tax-exempt) profits distributed by the company in respect of ordinary shares held by that person

SO = the percentage of the ordinary share capital held by that person that gave rise to the distribution

BRT = the basic rate of tax in force at the time the company distributed the income

MCT = the rate of corporation tax on the residual profits (or to the group residual profits in the case of a group REIT – see **7.113**)

DP = the total amount of profits distributed by the company in respect of preference shares and

SP = the total percentage of preference share capital held by the person concerned.

(*CTA 2010, ss 551, 552.*)

The regulations also require the company to provide details of the excess distribution to HMRC (*reg 11*). This provision neither seems to have been repealed nor included in *CTA 2010*. The regulation accordingly still appears to apply.

7.74

Example 7.2

John owns 12% of the ordinary shares and 4% of the preference shares of a REIT. The REIT pays John a dividend of £240,000 on its ordinary shares and £10,000 on its preference shares on 18 May 2014 in respect of its accounting year to 31 December 2013. The basic rate of income tax for 2010/11 is 20% and the rate of corporation tax is 28%.

The REIT is treated as receiving taxable income in its year to 31 December 2014 of

$$\left(£240{,}000 \times \frac{12}{100} \times \frac{20}{28}\right) + \left(£10{,}000 \times \frac{4}{100} \times \frac{20}{28}\right) = £(20{,}571 + 286) = £20{,}857$$

So it will have an additional tax liability at an average rate of 21.5% of £4,484.

The logic of this is not immediately apparent.

7.75 A tax charge also arises where the ratio of the REIT's tax-exempt profit (before capital allowances, brought forward losses and items taken into account under *CTA 2010, s 599(3)*, ie loan relationships, hedging derivatives and embedded derivatives in relation to the tax-exempt business) in an accounting period is less than 1.25 times its financing costs (and is not nil or a negative amount) (*CTA 2010, s 543(1)(3), 544 (1)–(3)*). Financing costs for this purpose are the aggregate of interest payable on borrowings, amortisation discounts related to borrowings, amortisation of premiums relating to borrowings, the finance expense implicit in payments made under finance leases, alternative finance returns (as defined in *CTA 2009, s 511*), and from 1 April 2014 periodic payments and receipts so far as they are from a derivative contract or other arrangement entered into to hedge a borrowing and are attributable to that hedge, and amortisation of discounts and premiums relating to such a derivative contract or arrangement (*CTA 2010, s 544(5)* as amended by the *REIT (Amendments to the Corporation Tax Act 2010 and Consequential Amendments) Regulations 2014 (SI 2014 No 518)*).

7.76 Prior to 17 July 2012 the legislation provided that matters do be taken into account in determining financing costs included costs giving rise to debit loan relationship (such as interest, but excluding exchange gains and losses), exchange gains or losses from debtor relationships in relation to debt finance (but not in relation to anything else), credits or debits on derivative contracts in relation to debt finance, the financing costs implicit in a payment under a finance lease, and any other costs arising from what under GAAP would be considered to be a financing transaction. The change excludes the costs of arranging loan finance and other accounting costs (Finance Bill 2012 Explanatory Notes). It also seems to exclude exchange differences. The Treasury has, however, been given power by regulation to amend the definition (*CTA 2012, s 544(6)*). HMRC have power to waive the charge in respect of an accounting period if they think that the company was in severe financial difficulties at some time during the accounting period, the result of failing to meet the 1.25 times test in that accounting period was because of circumstances that arose unexpectedly and in the circumstances the company could not reasonably have taken action to avoid the result being less than 1.25 (*CTA 2010, s 543(7)*).

7.77 The amount of the financing costs that exceed the 1.25 times limit must be treated as taxable income of the REIT's residual (taxable) business (*CTA 2010, s 543(4)(5)*). No loss, deficit, expense or allowance can be set against such notional profits (*CTA 2010, s 543(6)*). The amount charged to corporation tax is limited to 20% of the profits of the property rental business (*CTA 2010, s 543(3A)* inserted by *FA 2012, Sch 4, para 40*). The rule is modified in relation to Group REITS to exclude intra-group financing (*CTA 2010, s 544(3)*).

7.78

Example 7.3

In its year to 31 December 2017 the tax-exempt profits of a REIT after deduction of £800,000 financing costs are £500,000. However, the profits for *s 115* purposes require the financing changes deducted under *s 120* and any capital allowances to be added back, so the profits for *s 115* purposes are £1,300,000. The formula then gives the following result

$$\frac{1{,}300{,}000}{800{,}000} = 1.625$$

This exceeds 1.25 so no adjustment is necessary. Suppose though that the financing costs were £.8 million. The calculation would become

$$\frac{3{,}400{,}000}{2{,}800{,}000} = 1.214$$

The interest charge that would give a figure of 1.25 is £2 million. Accordingly £800,000 of the interest would be taxable.

7.79 In the case of a Group REIT (see **7.98**) the 1.25 figure is applied to:

$$\frac{\text{profits (adding back financing costs)}}{\text{financing costs (external)}}$$

where:

profits = the aggregate of the group UK property rental profits arising in the accounting period before capital allowances and financing costs

financing costs (all) = the financing costs incurred in respect of the group property rental business, and

financing costs (external) = the financing costs incurred in respect of:

(*a*) the group property rental business; and

(*b*) excluding intra-group costs.

(CTA 2010, s 544(1)–(3).)

7.80 If a company breaches one of the requirements in any of *CTA 2010, s 528(3)* (ie that it must be a listed company – see **7.42**(*c*)), *s 528(4)* (ie that it is not a close company – see **7.42**(*d*)), *s 528A* (further conditions relating to shares), *s 529* (property related business) (see **7.56**) *s 530* (distribution of profits) (see **7.56**) or *s 531* (balance of business) (see **7.61**) it must notify HMRC as soon as is reasonably practicable (*CTA 2010, s 561(1)–(3)*). When a company becomes aware of a breach it must tell HMRC the date on which the requirement first ceased to be met, the date, if any, on which it again was satisfied, details of the requirement that was breached, the nature of the breach and what, if anything, the company has done to avoid the breach occurring again (*CTA 2010, s 561(4)*). From 17 July 2012, such a notice does not have to be given if **7.42**(*d*) (non-close company) ceases to be met during the first three years but does have to be given in relation to the second part of a period that straddles the end of the three years (*CTA 2010, s 561(5)–(8)*).

7.81 A breach of *s 528(3)* will not put the REIT at risk of losing its tax-exempt status if it occurs because that company is taken over by another REIT and becomes a member of its group (*CTA 2010, s 562(1)(2)*). A breach of *s 528(4)* (non-close company) in the first three years is ignored. If that condition is not met on the first day of the second part of an accounting period that straddles the end of the three-year period, the company is treated as having ceased to be a REIT at that time. If the condition is met on that day but ceases to be met subsequently, it is treated as ceasing to be a REIT at the end of the accounting period preceding that in which the breach began (or at the end of the three-year period if later (*CTA 2010, s 562A(1)–(4)*). The breach is ignored if the reason that the condition ceases to be met is because the principal company of a group REIT becomes a member of another group REIT (or a REIT becomes a member of a group REIT) (*CTA 2010, s 562A(5)*). If the condition ceases to be met as a result of something done (or not done) by someone other than the company the breach can be ignored if the company remedies it by the end of the accounting period after that in which the breach began (*CTA 2010, s 562A(7)*). Prior to 17 July 2012, a breach of *s 528(4)* had the same consequences as a breach of *s 528(3)*, subject to the above provision allowing the correction of a breach caused by a third party. Any other breach of *s 528(3)* will forfeit the REIT status retrospectively to the start of the accounting period in which the breach occurs (*CTA 2010, s 562(5)*).

7.82 If *s 528A* (further conditions relating to shares) is not met in relation to an accounting period, the company (or group) is treated as having ceased to be a REIT at the end of the previous accounting period (*CTA 2010, s 562B(1)(2)* inserted by *FA 2012, Sch 4, para 18*). If the condition is not met as a result of the principal company of a group REIT becoming a member of another group REIT, or a REIT becoming a member of a group REIT, that breach is ignored (*CTA 2010, s 562B(3)*). However, if the condition in *s 528A(2)* (see **7.43**) is not met in relation to all of the first three accounting periods after becoming a REIT, the company (or group) is treated as ceasing to be a REIT at the end of the second accounting period – unless it is not met as a result of the company becoming a member of a group REIT (or the principal company of a group REIT becoming a member of another group REIT), in which case the breach is ignored (*CTA 2010, s 562C*).

7.83 A breach of condition (c) in *s 529* (see **7.56**(*c*)) that at least 90% of the tax-exempt profit is distributed within 12 months of the end of the accounting period will not put the REIT status at risk but attracts a corporation tax charge as part of the company's residual profits (*CTA 2010, s 564(2)*). This is on the shortfall in the required distribution (*CTA 2010, s 565*). Up to 16 July 2012 this charge could be avoided by distributing the shortfall within three months of the calculation of the company profits becoming final (ie before the enquiry window closes) (*CTA 2010, s 564(5)*). This proviso was abolished by *FA 2012, Sch 4, para 24*. It is no longer needed as a similar exclusion is now given by *s 530A* (see **7.59**).

7.84 The first two breaches of condition (a) or (b) of *s 529* within a ten-year period (that the company holds at least three properties and that no one of them exceeds 40% of its property portfolio) will not automatically forfeit the REIT status. They will do so if both conditions are breached simultaneously (except to the extent that the 40% condition cannot be met where the company has only two properties) (it is unclear how this could occur). They will also do so if the same requirement is breached for three consecutive accounting periods (*CTA 2010, ss 563, 575*).

7.85 A breach of *s 531(1)* (that at least 75% of the profits are tax exempt – see **7.61**) will not put the REIT status at risk if the tax-exempt profits exceed 50% of total profits for the accounting period (*CTA 2010, s 568(1)*). A breach of *s 531(5)* (that the REIT assets plus cash on the residual business exceed 75% of total assets will similarly not put the REIT status at risk if the proportion has not fallen below 50% (*CTA 2010, s 568(2)*). If a REIT is in breach of the condition in *CTA 2010, s 531(5)* for its first accounting period after becoming a REIT but meets the condition at the end of the second accounting period the breach is ignored (*CTA 2010, s 566(1)(2)*). For accounting periods beginning before 16 July 2012 a tax charge arose but this was abolished by *FA 2012, Sch 4, para 29*. The tax charge was the amount by which the sum given by the formula:

$$\frac{\text{market value of REIT assets at the end of the AP}}{\text{tax rate chargeable on residual income}} \times 2\%$$

exceeded the entry charge (*CTA 2010, ss 566, 567*). Effectively this imposed a further entry charge on the increase in value of the exempt business assets during the first accounting period. A breach of the condition in a later accounting period does not put the REIT status at risk (nor attract a tax charge) provided that the assets involved in the tax-exempt business are at least 50% of the company's total assets. However, if a breach of *s 531* continues for three consecutive accounting periods it cannot be considered minor and REIT status may be lost. Similarly two breaches of either condition in any ten-year period will put at risk the REIT status (although breaches in two consecutive periods will be considered a single breach for this purpose) (*CTA 2010, ss 568, 576*).

7.86 If during a ten-year period the company breaches at least two of the conditions in *ss 528–531* and the breaches are of different sections, the company can only rely on the regulations to escape action by HMRC under *CTA 2010, s 574* (see **7.53**) four times (*CTA 2010, s 577*).

7.87 If a REIT disposes of an asset used wholly and exclusively for the purpose of its tax-exempt business and keeps the proceeds in cash, the interest and other debits and credits on loan relationships arising from the funds must be treated as assets of its taxable residual business (*CTA 2010, s 547(1)(2)*).

7.88 If HMRC think that a REIT has tried to obtain a tax advantage (within *CTA 2010, s 1139* but including in particular entering into arrangements the sole or main purpose of which is to avoid or reduce the entry charge) for itself or another person they can by notice to the company counteract that advantage (*CTA 2010, s 545(1)–(5)*). A company does not of course obtain a tax advantage merely by virtue of becoming tax-exempt under the REIT rules, unless it does something which in HMRC's opinion is wholly or principally designed to create or inflate or apply a loss, deduction or expense or to have another effect of a kind specified by the Treasury by regulation for the purposes of *s 545* (*CTA 2010, s 545(6)*).

7.89 There is a right of appeal against such a notice to the First-tier Tribunal who can quash, affirm or vary the notice. Notice of appeal must be given within 30 days of the date on which the notice is given to the company (*CTA 2010, s 546(1)(2)*). In the case of a Group REIT (see **7.113**) this provision applies separately to each member of the group. Any appeal must be made by the group member on whom the assessment is made (*CTA 2010, ss 545(1), 546(1)*).

7.90 The Treasury can make regulations in relation to activities or situations which involve, or arise in connection with, a relationship between a REIT (or a member of a REIT group) and another person. They can do so only if they consider it expedient in the public interest and the statutory instrument is approved by a positive resolution of the House of Commons. The regulations cannot operate retrospectively. They can, in particular, treat a specified person or a person in specified circumstances, as forming part of a REIT group or provide for a specified provision which applies to members of a REIT group to also apply to a specified person or a person in specified circumstances (*CTA 2010, s 600*). This is aimed at companies that restructure to seek to exploit the REIT regime in circumstances that the government feel unacceptable (Finance Bill 2009 Explanatory Notes).

7.91 They have done so by the *REIT (Prescribed Arrangements) Regulations 2009 (SI 2009 No 3315)*. These apply if:

(*a*) an amount (the specified amount) falls to be (or ceases to be) taken into account as part of a REIT's tax-exempt or residual business; and

(*b*) the specified amount arises directly or indirectly from (or in consequence of) arrangements (whether or not part of other arrangements) which have the purpose (or one of the purposes) of allowing a REIT to meet one or more of the conditions of *CTA 2010, ss 529* (conditions for tax-exempt business – see **7.56** to **7.60**) or *530* (conditions for balance of business – see **7.60**),

(*regs 2,3*). There are exceptions for arrangements effected solely for genuine commercial purposes and arrangements made between persons dealing at arm's length (*reg 4*). Arrangements include any agreement, understanding, scheme, share reorganisation, transaction or series of transactions (whether or not legally enforceable) (*reg* 2). These regulations presumably still apply, albeit that they do not appear to have been updated to refer to *CTA 2010, ss 529* and *530* which replaced *FA 2006, ss 107* and *108*.

7.92 Where a REIT enters into such arrangements with a person ('the person in question'), the REIT, the person in question and any other person in which either the person in question or the REIT have a direct or indirect interest (unless it can be shown that the other person falls outside the scope of the arrangements) must be treated as forming a REIT group (*reg 5*). If such arrangements are entered into which take effect during the accounting period specified in a notice given under *CTA 2010, s 525* (see **7.52**) and it ceases to be a REIT by virtue of a notice under *CTA 2010, s 572* (transaction notice given by HMRC – see **7.54**) any corporation tax paid on the entry charge must be fully taken into account in assessing its overall liability to corporation tax (*reg 6*).

Distributions

7.93 A distribution out of the tax-exempt profits of a REIT is taxable income of the shareholder. It is treated as profits of a UK property business so far as (from 17 July 2013) it is a distribution of exempt profits (*CTA 2010, s 548* as amended by *FA 2013, Sch 19, para 5*). A distribution is of exempt profits so far as it falls within *CTA 2010, s 550(2)(a)(aa)(c)* or *(d)* (see **7.87**) (*CTA 2010, s 548(10)* inserted by *FA 2013, Sch 19, para 5*). In applying *CTA 2010, s 550* for this purpose in relation to a distribution made by the principal company of a post-cessation group or by a post-cessation company (ie a former REIT or group REIT – *CTA 2010, s 607(3)*), *s 350(1)* is to be read as referring to the post-cessation company or the principal company of the post-cessation group (*CTA 2010, s 548(11)* inserted by *FA 2013, Sch 19, para 5*). This deemed business is regarded as a separate business from any actual UK or overseas property business carried on by the shareholder, so losses in the actual business cannot be set against the deemed income. However, the tax-exempt business distributions from all of the REITs in which the shareholder has invested are regarded as a single business (*CTA 2010, s 549(3)–(5)*).

7.94 Paragraph **7.93** does not apply if the recipient is a dealer in respect of distributions (within *ICTA 1988, s 95*), a dealer in securities, or a member of Lloyd's (and the distribution relates to an asset of his premium trust fund or an ancillary trust fund) (*CTA 2010, s 549(1)*). The Act does not specify what happens in such a case. Presumably the deemed income is taxed as part of the recipient's trading profits. Nor does it apply in relation to a distribution falling within *CTA 2010, s 549A (6)* or *(8)* (see **7.97**) (distributions from one REIT to another) so far as that distribution is itself a distribution of exempt profits (*CTA 2010, s 548(9)* inserted by *FA 2013, Sch 19, para 5*).

7.95 A relevant distribution by a REIT does not attract a dividend tax credit to the extent that it is a distribution of exempt profits (*CTA 2010,* *s 549(2)* as amended by *FA 2013, Sch 19, para 6*). Nor from 16 December 2010 does *ITTOIA 2005, ss 409–414* (stock dividend income from UK resident companies) apply to such a distribution (*CTA 2010, s 549(2A)*). For this purpose a relevant distribution is a distribution from the REIT in respect of profits or gains of its property rental business. In the case of a group REIT, it is a distribution by the principal company of amounts shown in the financial statement under *CTA 2010, s 532(2)* (statement of group's property rental business – see **7.46**) as profits or gains of UK members and profits or gains of UK property rental business of non-UK members (*CTA 2010, s 549(3)*).

7.96 In relation to distributions after 17 July 2013, a relevant distribution does not include one falling within *CTA 2010, s 549A(6)* or *(8)* (see **7.97**) in so far as it is made out of exempt profits (*CTA 2010, s 549(3A)* inserted by *FA 2013, Sch 19, para 6*).

7.97 If a company receives a distribution falling within *CTA 2010, s 549A(6)* or *(8)* (called UK REIT investment profit) it must be treated (so far as it is a distribution of exempt profits) as profits of a property rental business carried on by the company in the UK which is separate from any other property rental business that it has (*CTA 2010, s 549A(1)(2)(5)* inserted by *FA 2013, Sch 19, para 6*). UK REIT investment profits are distributions made by the principal company of a group REIT to a shareholder which is either a REIT or a member of another group REIT and which is either:

(*a*) a distribution shown in its statement of group's property rental business (see **7.40**) as profits or gains of UK members of the group or of a UK property rental business of non-UK members of the group (*CTA 2010, s 549A(6)*); or

(*b*) a distribution in respect of profits or gains of the property rental business of the company (*CTA 2010, s 549A(8)*) (*CTA 2010, s 549A(1)(6)(8)* inserted by *FA 2013, Sch 19, para 6*).

References to profits of the property rental business or UK property rental business must be read as including UK REIT investment profits (including where the profits referred to are profits calculated in accordance with IAS or *CTA 2010, s 599*) (*CTA 2010, s 549A(3)*). *CTA 2010, s 549(2)* and (2A) (see **7.95**) apply in relation to UK REIT investment profits as they apply in relation to relevant distributions (*CTA 2010, s 549A(4)*). The reference to a distribution in *CTA 2010, s 549(6)* and *(8)* includes a distribution made by the principal company of a post-cessation group or post-cessation company, ie a company that was previously the principal company of a group REIT or was formerly a REIT (*CTA 2010, ss 549(7)(9), 607(3)*). A distribution received does not fall within *CTA 2010, s 549A(6)* or *(8)* if it is received in an accounting period which straddles 17 July 2013 (*FA 2013, Sch 19, para 13(3)(4)*).

7.98 The Treasury have power by Regulations to formulate a requirement for deducting tax from such distributions and for the collection and recovery of tax (*ITA 2007, ss 973, 974*). They have done so by the *REIT (Assessment, Collection and Recovery of Tax) Regulations 2006 (SI 2006 No 2867).* These require the REIT to deduct tax at the basic rate at the time of each distribution except to the extent that the REIT reasonably believes that the person beneficially entitled to the dividend is either:

(*a*) a UK resident company;

(*b*) an overseas company carrying on a trade in the UK through a permanent establishment (and the dividend forms part of its UK taxable income);

(*c*) a local authority, health service body or public office or department of the Crown;

(*d*) a charity (or the National Heritage Memorial Fund, the Historic Buildings and Monuments Commission for England, the British Museum or the Natural History Museum);

(*e*) a scientific research organisation within *CTA 2010, s 469*;

(*f*) a registered pension scheme (or Parliamentary pension fund or colonial etc pension fund within *ICTA 1988, s 613(4)*); or

(*g*) a partnership all of the partners of which are persons within the above heads or the European Investment Fund,

(*regs 3, 7*). This regulation making power was extended by *F(No 3)A 2010, Sch 4, para 2* to deal with the position where a REIT pays a stock dividend to a shareholder in lieu of a cash dividend (*CTA 2010, s 973(3A)(3B)*).

7.99 When a REIT makes a distribution out of its tax-exempt profits it must make a return to HMRC within 14 days of the end of the calendar quarter in which the distribution is made. The return must show the amount of the distribution and the income tax (if any) payable in respect of it. If it also makes a distribution out of other profits it must deliver with the return a reconciliation statement showing the amounts of that distribution which are attributable to each of *paras (a)–(e)* of *CTA 2010, s 550(2)* (see **7.101**) (*reg 4*).

7.100 The income tax deductible from distributions is payable at the same time as the return. It is payable without HMRC making any assessment (*reg 5*). Where a company deducts tax it must give the recipient a certificate showing the gross dividend, tax deducted and net dividend (*reg 6*). If the tax is not paid by the due date, or HMRC think that a distribution has been omitted from the return, or the amount declared is understated, they can make an assessment on the company to the best of their judgement (*regs 8, 9*).

7.101 If a REIT becomes aware of an error in such a return it must deliver an amended return without delay and an assessment or repayment necessary to correct the position can be made (*reg 11*).

Distributions made by a REIT must be attributed:

(*a*) firstly towards UK REIT investment profits;

(*aa*) secondly towards its 90% distribution requirement of the rest of its tax-exempt business;

(*b*) thirdly (if the company so determines) to distributions out of profits in respect of which corporation tax is payable;

(*c*) fourthly to the distribution of profits of the property rental business (ie the 10% balance of its tax-exempt income);

(*d*) fifthly to the distribution of capital gains of its tax-exempt business; and

(*e*) sixthly to other distributions.

(*CTA 2010, s 550(2)* as amended by *FA 2013, Sch 19, para 8*.)

Distributions within heads (*b*) and (*e*) are, of course, not part of the tax-exempt activities and are treated as dividends in the hands of the recipient carrying with them a 10% tax credit in the normal way. Prior to 17 July 2013, heads (*a*) and (*aa*) were combined as there was no separate concept of UK REIT investment profits.

Capital Gains

7.102 A gain on the disposal of an asset used wholly and exclusively for the REIT's tax-exempt business is not a chargeable gain. Nor is the part of a gain used partly for the purpose of the tax-exempt business, provided that the asset has been used partly in the tax-exempt business for at least a year (in aggregate) (*CTA 2010, s 535(1)–(5)*).

7.103 Gains accruing in respect of the REIT's residual business are taxed at the full corporation tax rate; the small companies' rate cannot apply (*CTA 2010, s 535(6)*).

7.104 If an asset which is used wholly and exclusively for the tax-exempt business begins to be used wholly and exclusively in the residual business it must be treated as disposed of (by the tax-exempt business) and, immediately reacquired (by the residual business) at its market value at that time (*CTA 2010, s 555(1)–(3)*). This does not apply for capital allowances purposes; instead the residual business takes over the then written down value (*CTA 2010, s 555(4)*).

The same rule applies in reverse where an asset used wholly and exclusively for the purpose of the REIT's residual business is moved into the tax-exempt business (*CTA 2010, s 557*).

7.105 In the case of a Group REIT (see **7.113**) these capital gains tax charges apply only in relation to UK resident group members. Where part of the gains of a subsidiary is excluded from the group's property rental business (because they relate to a minority shareholder in a subsidiary), that part of the gain is treated as a taxable gain of the member and as residual income (*CTA 2010, s 555(5)*).

7.106 If an asset which was used wholly and exclusively in the tax-exempt business is disposed of in the course of a trade, that disposal is treated as made in the residual business and thus attracts corporation tax (*CTA 2010, s 556(1)(2)*). For disposals after 16 July 2012 there is an exemption for a disposal by one company within a group REIT to another member of that group (*CTA 2010, s 556(2)*). At first sight this can never apply as a REIT cannot carry on a trade in its tax-exempt business. However, a property is deemed to have been disposed of in the course of a trade if it has been redeveloped by the REIT since acquisition, the cost of the development exceeds 30% of the fair value of the property (under IAS) at entry into the REIT regime (or at the date of its acquisition if later) and the company disposes of the property within three years of the completion of the development (*CTA 2010, s 556(3)*). Where such an asset was held at the time the company entered the REIT regime (and that was before 17 July 2012) the part of the tax paid on the entry charge that is attributable to the value of the property concerned at the time of entry can be reclaimed (*CTA 2010, s 556(4)*).

Leaving the REIT Regime

7.107 Where a company ceases to qualify as a REIT (whether because it gives notice under *s 571* is excluded by HMRC under *s 572* or ceases to qualify under *s 578*) its tax-exempt business is treated as ceasing immediately before it leaves the REIT regime. A new accounting period is deemed to start at that time. The assets held for the purpose of the tax-exempt business are treated (other than for capital allowance purposes) as disposed of at that time by the tax-exempt business at market value and immediately reacquired by a new post-cessation business (called C post-cessation) (*CTA 2010, ss 579, 580*). In the case of a Group REIT (see **7.113**) this provision applies in relation to each UK company that is a member of the group. Where a percentage of the assets of a subsidiary is excluded from the group financial statements (because they are attributable to a minority shareholder, that excluded amount is ignored in applying *s 131* (*CTA 2010, s 579(1)–(5)*). If a UK company ceases to be a member of the Group REIT, *s 131* applies to it as if it had ceased to be a REIT (*CTA 2010, s 579(6)*).

7.108 If the company voluntarily leaves the REIT regime by notice under *s 571* and it had been a REIT for less than ten years the gain on a disposal within two years after it leaves the regime of an asset formerly used for the purpose of the tax-exempt business is fully chargeable to corporation tax, ie any deemed disposal under *s 536(2)* (see **7.63**) (but only if it resulted in a gain) or *ss 555(2)* or *579(5)* is ignored and the chargeable gain is calculated by reference to original cost (*CTA 2010, s 581*).

7.109 If in such circumstances the company was required to leave the REIT regime under *ss 572* or *578*, HMRC have power to direct that either the REIT or corporation tax rules should apply with such modification as they may decide. In particular such a direction can alter the date at which the company would otherwise leave the REIT regime or can disapply or alter the tax-exemption for the period for which the company was a REIT. Such a direction can, in particular, prevent all or a specified part of a loss, deficit or expense from being set off or otherwise used in a specific manner (*CTA 2010, s 582(1)–(4)*).

7.110 There is a right of appeal to the First-tier tribunal against such a direction (*CTA 2010, s 582(6)*). On appeal, the tribunal can quash, affirm or vary the direction (*CTA 2010, s 582(7)*).

7.111 In the case of a Group REIT (see **7.113**) the reference in *s 581* to a disposal means a disposal by any member of the group (*CTA 2010, s 581(4)(6)*). *Sections 581* and *582* also apply to a disposal by a company that has left the group if either the Group had been a REIT for less than ten years or the company had been a member of the group for less than ten years (*CTA 2010, s 581(7)*). A direction by HMRC under *s 582(2)* can be given in relation to the group as a whole or to one or more members, but any appeal must be brought by the parent company (*CTA 2010, s 582(5)*).

7.112 The Explanatory Notes to the 2006 Finance Bill say: 'This rule is an anti-avoidance provision designed to prevent a REIT from artificially engineering its exit from the regime … The company may want to do this because they are facing a significant loss in the tax-exempt business that is not tax effective unless the company leaves the regime. If the company engineers its exit from the regime by breaking one of the six company conditions, the regime ceases to apply at the end of the previous accounting period – and the company will then be able to make use of the loss. This clause allows HMRC to set aside the normal cessation date or to prevent a loss from being set off.'

Group REITs

7.113 An entire group of companies can be brought into the REIT regime. The above rules apply to such a group in the same way as to a singleton company). In the rewrite the group rules have not been dealt with as a separate topic but are included within each individual provision. In applying the rules to a Group REIT reference to a company must (except where the context otherwise applies) be treated as reference to the group (*CTA 2010, s 518(1)*). There are, however, a number of specific modifications to the normal rules. These have already been considered above.

7.114 A company ('the principal company') and all its 75% subsidiaries form a group. If any of those subsidiaries themselves have 75% subsidiaries (within *CTA 2010, s 1154(3)*) the group includes such companies, and so on (*CTA 2010, s 606(1)*). A group cannot include a company (other than the principal company) which is not an effective 51% subsidiary (within *TCGA 1992, s 170*) of the principal company. Nor can it include an insurance company (within *ICTA 1988, s 431(2)*) an insurance subsidiary (ie a company 75% or more of which is owned by an insurance company or companies) or an open-ended investment company (*CTA 2010, s 606(2)(5)*). A company cannot be a member of more than one group. In such a case *TCGA 1992, s 170(6)* applies to determine the group of which it is a member (*CTA 2010, s 606(3)*).

7.115 The normal CGT no gain/no loss rule on transfers within a group does not apply to a disposal by or to a REIT (*TCGA 1992, s 171(2)(da)*). For the purpose of group relief (and the similar reliefs under *TCGA 1992, ss 171, 171A, 179A* and *179B*; *CTA 2009, ss 335–346* and *353–379* (loan relationships), *CTA 2009, ss 570–710* (derivative contracts), and *CTA 2009, ss 711–906* (intangible assets)) the Group property rental business (ie the tax-exempt business) must be treated as a separate group distinct from its pre-entry, residual and post-cessation business (*CTA 2010, s 601*).

7.116 If a non-resident UK member of a Group REIT has a property rental business in the UK ('the UK property rental business') whose profits would be chargeable to income tax as a UK property business, that UK property rental business must be treated as if it were chargeable to corporation tax (*CTA 2010, s 520*). For this purpose, a business is a property rental business if it would meet the conditions of *CTA 2010, s 519* (see **7.39**) if it were carried on by a UK company (*CTA 2010, s 519(4)*). Those profits are of course not also chargeable to income tax (*CTA 2010, s 520(3)*). References in the REIT legislation to a company's tax-exempt business refer only to the property rental business and reference to its residual business means only any other business carried on by the company in the UK (*CTA 2010, s 520(1)*).

7.117 The profits and gains of the UK property rental business are treated as being profits and gains of a UK resident member of the group for the purposes of *CTA 2010, ss 530(4)* (90% of the profits to be distributed as dividend – see **7.56**(*c*)), *548* (distributions liable to tax in hands of recipient – see **7.93**),

ITA 2007, ss 973, 974 (withholding tax – see **7.98**) and the Group REIT's financial statements (see **7.45**) (*CTA 2010, ss 530(2), 532(3), 548(1)*).

7.118 If a company disposes of an asset held in its REIT business to a 75% subsidiary which is outside its REIT group and then sells that subsidiary outside the group, and the purchaser elects to bring that subsidiary into its own REIT group it can do so even though conditions (*c*), (e) and (*f*) in **7.42** above may not be satisfied throughout the accounting period (conditions (*c*) to (*f*) up to 16 July 2012). In such circumstances there was no entry charge and no charge on the original movement of the asset out of the REIT trade. However, charges were imposed if the conditions were not met within six months of the acquisition of the subsidiary by the purchaser (*CTA 2010, s 558* as amended by *FA 2012, Sch 4, para 5*). A similar relaxation applies where a company in one REIT group is sold to another (*CTA 2010, s 559*).

Joint Ventures

7.119 A REIT can give a notice to treat the REIT and the joint venture company as if together they formed a Group REIT. The notice can be given only if:

(*a*) the REIT is carrying on a joint venture with another person;

(*b*) the joint venture takes the form of a company;

(*c*) the joint venture is carrying on a property rental business (within *CTA 2010, s 519*);

(*d*) the REIT is beneficially entitled to 40% or more of the profits available for distribution to equity holders in the joint venture company;

(*e*) the REIT is beneficially entitled to 40% or more of the assets of the joint venture company available to equity holders in the event of a winding up;

(*f*) the property rental business of the joint venture company does not involve property that in accordance with GAAP would fall to be described as owner-occupied (and for this purpose owner-occupied property included property held by the joint venture company and occupied by the REIT and property owned by the REIT and occupied by the joint venture company); and

(*g*) the income from and assets of the joint venture company's property rental business constitute at least 75% of its total income and assets (applying the definitions in *CTA 2010, s 531*– see **7.61**).

(*CTA 2010, ss 585, 586, 591, 598(3)*.)

A Group REIT can similarly give a joint venture look through notice provided that the above conditions are met by reference to the interests in the joint venture company held by one or more members of the group *(CTA 2010, ss 585(1), 586, 591, 598(3))*.

7.120 The notice must supply the name of the joint venture company and the accounting period from the beginning of which it is to apply. It must be given before the start of that accounting period. It can be given at the same time as the notice electing for into REIT regime or at any later time during which the company or group is a REIT (*CTA 2010, ss 586(6), 587(6)*).

7.121 The notice appears to be irrevocable. The REIT rules continue to apply to it unless and until the REIT ceases to hold a 40% interest in the joint venture company (*CTA 2010, s 590(1)(2)*).

7.122 Where such a notice has been given, the REIT must include the proportion of the profits and assets of the joint venture company to which it is beneficially entitled:

(*a*) within its own profits for the purpose of *s 530(4)* (see **7.56**(*c*));

(*b*) within its own profits for the purpose of *s 531(1)* (see **7.61**); and

(*c*) within the value of its own assets for the purpose of *s 531(5)* (see **7.61**).

(*CTA 2010, s 588(3)(6)*). It must also prepare financial statements incorporating its share of the income, expenses, gains, losses, assets and liabilities of the joint venture company or companies in the same way as a Group REIT (see **7.45**) (*CTA 2010, ss 588(3)(6)*).

7.123 In applying the profit to financing cost ratio under *s 543* (see **7.75**) the 1.25 limitation applies to

$$\frac{\text{profits} + \text{financing costs (JV)}}{\text{financing costs (external)}}$$

where

profits = the aggregate of the profits of the REIT's tax-exempt business before capital allowances, and the financing costs of its property rental business as claimed for tax purposes

financing costs (JV) = the aggregate of the REIT's share of the profits of the joint venture company (before capital allowances) and the REIT's share of the financing costs of that company's business

financing costs (external) = the sum of the financing costs of the REIT's tax-exempt business and the REIT's proportion of the financing costs of the UK property business of the joint venture company, but excluding in both cases financing costs between the two (*CTA 2010, s 588(3)(6)*).

7.124 The REIT's share of the joint venture company's profits and gains on properties of its tax-exempt business is exempt from corporation tax. For the purpose of applying the various tax charges and exemptions under the REIT provisions the joint venture company is treated as if it were the REIT, although any tax charges apply only to the REIT's share of its profits (*CTA 2010, s 588(3)(5)(6)*).

7.125 In the case of a Group REIT the principal company must include in its financial statements (see **7.45**) the percentage of income, expenses, gains, losses, assets and liabilities of the joint venture company which represent interest of a member of the REIT in the joint venture company. This percentage must be determined by reference to beneficial entitlement to profits available for distribution to equity holders (*CTA 2010, s 588(3)*).

7.126 In the same way as with a Group REIT member company, the REIT's share of the joint venture company's property rental income is included in the REIT's tax-exempt income and its share of any non-property rental business income is included in its residual business income (*CTA 2010, s 594(1)*). When a REIT acquired its interest in the joint venture company before 17 July 2012 an entry charge arose in the same way as when a company joined a UK Group REIT (see **7.64**). Similarly when it disposes of its interest *s 579* (effects of cessation – see **7.107**) applies in the same way as when a member of a Group REIT leaves the group (*CTA 2010, s 588(3)(5)*). If the joint venture company became the principal company of an existing REIT Group and gave a new look through notice no entry charge was payable (*CTA 2010, s 595*). *CTA 2010, s 588(3)–(6)* and *s 589(3)–(6)* (which are in the same terms) apply in particular for the purpose of interpreting *CTA 2010, s 549A(1)(a)(i)* and *(8)(a)(i)* (ie whether a company is a member of a group UK REIT) (*CTA 2010, s 588(7)* inserted by *FA 2013, Sch 19, paras 9, 10*).

7.127 Up to 16 July 2012, in the case of a non-UK resident joint venture company the rules in *CTA 2010, ss 538–540* (entry charge) (see **7.67**) and *CTA 2010, s 520* (see **7.116**) applied to the company with the substitution of a reference to the joint venture company for the non-UK group company (*CTA 2010, s 588(3)–(6)*).

7.128 Where a single company REIT carries on a joint venture with another person and the joint venture is conducted through a group of companies, the REIT can give a notice if:

(*a*) it is carrying on a joint venture with another person;

(*b*) the joint venture takes the form of a joint venture group (as defined);

(*c*) at least one member of the joint venture group is carrying on a property rental business;

(*d*) the venturing company (ie the REIT) is beneficially entitled to 40% or more of the profits available for distribution to equity holders in the principal company of the joint venture group; and

(*e*) the venturing company is beneficially entitled to 40% or more of the assets of the principal company of the joint venture group available to equity holders in the event of a winding up.

(*CTA 2010, s 587.*)

The REIT must, of course, include its share of the UK business to which it is beneficially entitled in its own profits (*CTA 2010, s 589(3)(6)*). The provisions modify the REIT conditions so as to apply them to the joint venture group (ie the REIT plus the group of companies which is a party to the joint venture (*CTA 2010, ss 588–590*).

7.129 Where a company which is a member of a group REIT enters into a joint venture with a company in another group of companies, the principal company of the group REIT (the venturing group) can give a 'joint venture group look through notice' provided that:

(*a*) the venturing group is carrying on a joint venture with another person;

(*b*) the joint venture takes the form of a joint venture group (as defined);

(*c*) at least one member of the joint venture group is carrying on a property rental business;

(*d*) the members of the venturing group (the one that includes the REIT) are, in aggregate, beneficially entitled to 40% or more of the profits available for distribution to equity holders in the principal company of the joint venture group; and

(*e*) the members of the venturing group are, in aggregate, beneficially entitled to 40% or more of the assets of the principal company of the joint venture group available to equity holders in the event of a winding up.

(*CTA 2010, s 587.*)

CTA 2010, ss 589–596 set out the modifications to the REIT conditions so as to apply them to the joint venture group (ie the group that includes the REIT plus the other joint venturers).

Take-overs

7.130 If a REIT (or a member of a Group REIT) becomes a member of a Group REIT (or of another Group REIT) *ss 536* (effect of entry), *538* (entry charge) and *579* (cessation of REIT regime) do not apply (*CTA 2010, ss 536(7), 538(6), 579(9)*). This ensures that if, as a result of a take-over, a company within the REIT regime continues within that regime the take-over does not trigger a second entry charge as if it were a company coming into the regime for the first time.

Manufactured Dividends

7.131 The rules on manufactured payments, which normally arise under sale and repurchase agreements where the temporary holder of a security makes a payment (the manufactured payment) to the transferor as compensation for the dividend that the transferor would have received in the absence of the transaction apply with amendment. The tax legislation seeks to equate the manufactured payment with the dividend it represents. For a manufactured payment which represents a distribution from a REIT to be equated with the dividend, the REIT distribution and any dividend from the taxable business have to be identified and treated separately. *CTA 2010, ss 785* and *786* amend the manufactured dividend rules to achieve this.

Chapter 8

Problems of Development

The Nature of the Transaction

8.1 Development can be either a trading or an investment operation. It is not a separate category taxed on its own. What determines its nature is whether it is intended to retain or sell the property after carrying out the development. If the intention is to let it and retain it to benefit from the rental flow, it is an investment. If it is intended to sell it, it is a trading or dealing transaction.

8.2 A sale of an interest as part of a financing operation to enable the balance to be retained as an investment will not necessarily make the transaction a trading transaction. Problems can sometimes arise where there is a mixed motive. It is 'not possible for an asset to be both trading stock and permanent investment at the same time, nor to possess an indeterminate status – neither trading stock nor permanent asset. It must be one or other' (Lord Wilberforce in *Simmons v CIR* (see **5.22** above)). Where there is a mixed motive on acquisition the dominant motive will usually determine the property's status (see *Kirkham v Williams*, **5.27** above). For example, a developer may want to create an office investment. He knows that to obtain planning permission he will need to incorporate a residential element in his scheme. He does not want to have a residential investment. He therefore buys the site with the intention that he will include flats in the development scheme which he will sell to occupiers. It is probable that the erection of the flats is a trading transaction following *Iswera v Ceylon Commissioner of Inland Revenue* (see **5.26**) although this is by no means certain. In that case the taxpayer had to acquire and resell land she did not want in order to obtain land that she did. This is not necessarily the same thing as being required to use for a purpose that the owner did not intend land that is bought as an investment. It is possible that would be regarded not as having formed an intention to deal in the flats but as a premature realisation of part of the investment. However, the sale of the flats is dealt with the fact of their sale will not affect the dominant investment motive for the remainder of the development.

8.3 Very few problems arise in practice where a property development is a trading transaction. The scope of allowable deductions in calculating trading income is very broad and it is difficult to envisage any expenditure attributable to the building or the development that will not meet the 'wholly and exclusively' requirement.

Interest Payable

8.4 The problems arise where the development is of an investment property. The first point to watch is the allowability of interest during the development period, especially where the development is being financed by an institution other than by way of a simple loan – as will normally be the case. Is the 'interest' really interest, ie is there a loan? If what is described as interest in the finance agreement is simply an arithmetical figure in a calculation it will not qualify for tax relief at all (see **4.94**). Even if interest is genuinely payable, in some cases tax relief will be due only when it is actually paid. If it is rolled up, the relief will be deferred (see **4.46**). Prior to 1 April 1996 relief on bank interest was not normally due until it was paid, although for corporation tax purposes interest paid to a bank carrying on a bona fide banking business in the UK (or to a UK stockbroker or discount house) was regarded as paid when it was debited to the company's account in the lender's books (*ICTA 1988, s 338(3)*). It was held in *MacArthur v Greycoat Estates Mayfair Ltd (1996 STC 1)* that this applied to both annual interest and to bank interest. Interest was probably not paid if it was debited to an overdrawn account though, at least if subsequent credits were not made to the account in the year to cover the charge (*Paton v CIR (21 TC 626)*). This was reaffirmed in *Minsham Properties Ltd v Price (1991 STC 718)*. The position is probably different if the lender makes a transfer from a fresh loan account to cover the interest debited to the original loan account. HMRC may well contend that the *Furniss v Dawson* principle applies in such circumstances, though, and that the reality of the transaction is that no payment of interest has been made. Although the legislation has been replaced by that on loan relationships, it can still be necessary in some circumstances to ascertain the date of payment, so these cases are not wholly obsolete. Where interest is rolled up it must be borne in mind that charges on income of an investment company cannot be carried back and deficits on loan relationships carried back cannot be offset against capital gains. Accordingly, on a sale, care may be needed to ensure that the interest payment does not occur in a later accounting period than that in which the capital gain crystallises. As the capital gain arises on the date of the sale contract and the interest will normally be paid on the redemption of the mortgage at completion, this can be a major problem if the two dates straddle the company's accounting date.

Capital Allowances

8.5 It must also be borne in mind that the structuring of a development can significantly affect the right to capital allowances. In general, the person who is entitled to claim such allowances is the person who incurs the qualifying expenditure. However, expenditure cannot be regarded as having been incurred by a person for capital allowances purposes to the extent that it has been, or is to be, met directly or indirectly by any other person (*CAA 2001, s 532*). Furthermore, if the person who incurs capital expenditure subsequently disposes of his interest in the building, he will cease to be entitled to capital allowances (although if the disposal is after 20 March 2007 the allowances already given will no longer be withdrawn by way of a balancing charge). If, as commonly happens, as part of a financing agreement the developer's initial interest in the property is sold to the institution, care may need to be taken to ensure that the developer retains the right to the allowances – particularly if the institution is a pension fund that cannot benefit from capital allowances. One possible route is to take advantage of *CAA 2001, s 538*. This provides that where, for the purpose of a trade carried on or to be carried on by him or by a tenant of land in which he has an interest, a person contributes a capital sum to expenditure on the provision of the asset, that contribution is to be treated as expenditure by him on the asset (with the expenditure by the person who incurred it being reduced accordingly). He will be entitled to claim allowances even though he does not own the asset. If the institution wants to own the property during the development phase for its own commercial protection, it may be possible for the developer to make a contribution to it. One point to watch is that the word 'contribution' implies part only of the cost. If the developer contributes 99% of the cost there is a risk that it would be held that he has not made a contribution to the cost but rather that he has met the expenditure on the asset. As he would not own the asset this would result in a complete loss of the right to claim capital allowances. A contribution of up to about two-thirds of the cost seems to be readily accepted by HMRC. A significantly higher contribution could be risky.

Site Assembly

8.6 A development often involves a site assembly. This can raise a number of points to watch. For example, an exchange of two pieces of land, such as giving site B to the owner of site A in exchange for site A, will be a disposal and an acquisition by both parties for both capital gains tax and stamp duty land tax purposes. The fact that no cash may change hands, or that only a small equalisation payment may be made, does not mean that tax can be ignored. Both parties may be crystallising large tax liabilities. Where the exchange involves the developer not merely swapping site B for site A but also agreeing to erect a building on site B at his own cost, the cost to him of site A is likely to depend on the exact terms of his agreement with the vendor. If the agreement is to exchange the sites and to erect a building on site B, the cost of site A is probably the value of site B plus the cost of erecting the building. If the agreement is to provide the vendor with site B with the completed building on it, the cost of site A is almost certainly the value of the land and building on site B, which may be substantially greater than the aggregate of the value of the site and the cost of erecting the building. The tax treatment of the difference between these two figures will also need to be considered. If site B was bought specifically to swap it for site A, its purchase, the erection of the building, and its swap for site A is probably a trading transaction, and the difference between the cost and the exchange value a dealing profit. If it was not bought specifically, consideration will need to be given as to whether it was initially acquired as trading stock or as an investment – and if the latter whether, when the decision to offer it in exchange for site A was taken, it may have been appropriated to trading stock.

8.7 Site assembly frequently involves not merely the purchase of land but also the need to obtain vacant possession of it. For a dealing company, a payment to a tenant to give up his tenancy should be allowable as a deduction in calculating trading income when the property is sold. The investment company needs to satisfy the fairly stringent conditions of *TCGA 1992, s 38* before such an expense can be deductible. The limited expenditure allowed under this provision is set out at **11.7** onwards.

8.8 The only one of the categories into which a payment to a tenant to secure vacant possession can fall is head *(b)*(i), enhancement expenditure. The obtaining of vacant possession certainly enhances the value of the investor's freehold; but is it reflected in the state or nature of the freehold at the time of the disposal? Often the answer to the question will be 'Yes', but by no means always, and sometimes it is by no means clear. Suppose a tenant had ten years to run on his lease and a payment is made to him to surrender it prematurely. If the developed building is sold 15 years later the payment will not be reflected in the nature of the freehold at that time as the lease would have expired in any event so that there would have been no need to make the payment to create the unencumbered freehold. However, the developed building will have a new tenant paying a significantly higher rent. The payment may well be reflected in the state of the freehold insofar as it enabled the development to be carried out and the new tenant installed. If, had the development been delayed until the original tenant's lease had expired, the new tenant could have been installed by the time of the disposal with his next rent review falling on the same date as his actual review, it is highly unlikely that the payment to the tenant can be said to be reflected in the state or nature of the developed building at the time of disposal. It may have made the development economically viable by reducing delays, but that, to the author, seems to be a different thing. If the tenant was a statutory tenant, either on a monthly tenancy or holding over on a lease that has expired, it will in many cases be unlikely that a payment to him to speed up his eviction will be reflected in the state or nature of the completed development when it is ultimately sold. To the extent that the payment represents statutory compensation that had to be paid to obtain vacant possession at all, rather than to obtain it at an earlier date than if proceedings for possession had been taken, there should be no problem.

8.9 If a tenant is not prepared to accept a payment to move out but instead insists on being provided with alternative accommodation, the cost of providing that accommodation is probably not enhancement expenditure for capital gains tax purposes. It is difficult to contend that it is incurred wholly and exclusively *on the asset*, ie the property being developed. Although the need to obtain vacant possession of the asset is the cause of the expenditure in buying the new property, as a separate distinct asset is obtained the courts are likely to regard the expenditure as incurred on the new property not the development one. If instead of buying alternative accommodation the developer makes a payment to a third party (which could be its wholly owned subsidiary) in consideration of the third party undertaking to rehouse the tenant this could well constitute enhancement expenditure on the development property. Another route might be to agree with the tenant a figure of compensation with a proviso that payment is to be satisfied by the provision of accommodation at a rent at under market value. In *Chaney v Watkis (58 TC 707)* the taxpayer bought a house, which was occupied by his mother-in-law, Mrs Williams. Some years later, in order to sell the house with vacant possession, he agreed to pay her a capital sum of £9,400. Before completion of the sale he decided to build an extension to his own house (at a cost far in excess of £9,400) to house his mother-in-law, and orally agreed with her that he should provide her with rent-free accommodation in his house for life in consideration of her releasing him from the obligation to pay the £9,400. It was held that, even though not paid as such, the £9,400 (or some lower figure) constituted enhancement expenditure. The basis of the decision was that the value of the new obligation undertaken (the provision of rent-free accommodation) was of equal value to the £9,400 that Mr Chaney had contracted to pay. The judge in fact remitted the case to the Commissioners to determine if this was the case. If they felt the value to be less than £9,400, only the lesser amount would be deductible as enhancement expenditure – presumably because by agreeing to accept the accommodation in lieu of the £9,400 Mrs Williams would be deemed to have waived her right to any difference between the £9,400 and the value of the accommodation.

8.10 Another problem with site assembly is that where land is held by a company, the controlling shareholders will sometimes not be prepared to permit the company to sell its land but would be willing to transfer the land to the developer by selling him all the shares in the company. The reason, of course, is that they hope to avoid one level of capital gains tax, ie they will pay tax only on the gain on their shares whereas if the company sells its land it will have a tax liability on the gain it makes and the after-tax amount of that gain will also reflect an increased gain to the shareholders on the disposal of their shares. The developer needs to bear very much in mind that the price he pays for the shares will not be deductible when he comes to calculate his gain on the ultimate disposal of the development. Where, as will normally be the case, the cost of the land is very much lower than its market value, the capital gains tax base cost of the owning company will be transferred to the developer, assuming that, after purchase, he transfers the land intra-group to the company that is assembling the site. The potential increase in his capital gains tax on disposal by having to take over a low base cost is a factor that the developer will normally wish to take into account – at least to some extent – in determining the price he is prepared to pay for the shares, ie this is likely to be lower than the price he would have paid for the land. How much lower is a matter for negotiation. It will depend on the developer's anxiety to have the land, on the potential tax saving for the vendors, and on the likelihood or otherwise of the developer wanting to dispose of an interest in the site either at the time of commencing development or the time of its completion. Where a company is purchased in order to acquire land that it owns, other factors may need to be considered. Does the company have losses that could be set against a capital gain if the property itself were sold? If so, it may be worthwhile purchasing the company and transferring the land in such a way that the capital gains tax exemption for intra-group transfers will not apply.

Obtaining Planning Consents

8.11 The costs of obtaining the planning consent on which the development is based will clearly form part of the deductible costs of the development. The abortive costs of unsuccessfully seeking planning consents, or of successfully seeking a planning consent which is subsequently abandoned, will not normally qualify as a deduction in calculating a capital gain. They will, of course, qualify as a trading expense in a dealing company. Sometimes, however, a developer will apply for consent in the knowledge that it is likely to be refused in order to narrow down the options open to the local authority when he puts in a revised application or to ascertain the planning criteria that are likely to be applied if he cannot obtain a sufficiently clear indication of this from the planning officers. The expenditure in such cases can be argued to be reflected in the state of the completed development as it did, and was intended to, facilitate the obtaining of the ultimate planning consent, which may well not have been obtained without the preliminary application having been made. Similarly, where an application for consent is made and then rejected, a lot of the work on preparing detailed plans and on site investigation may be work that would have been needed for the next application which may be successful. Accordingly, it can be argued that at least the cost of these works is reflected in the nature of the developed building. It must not be overlooked, though, that to qualify for a deduction, enhancement expenditure has to be wholly and exclusively incurred on the asset for the purpose of enhancing its value.

If there is a dual purpose the expenditure cannot qualify. It is arguable that expenditure on application A was for the purpose of enhancing the value of the site, even though in a different manner to the enhancement arising from application B. It is not certain that it is expenditure incurred 'on the asset' if the planning application for which it was incurred never reflects in an increase in value of the asset. Investigation of the circumstances of each individual case is needed to ascertain whether a claim for a deduction for part of the expenditure on abortive applications might be sustainable.

8.12 There is no requirement that the enhancement in value of the property must equal or exceed the amount of the expenditure. If expenditure of £10,000 results in a £2,000 increase in the value of the property the entire £10,000 appears to qualify as enhancement expenditure. 'Appears' because it is possible that the entire £10,000 is not 'expenditure reflected in the state … of the asset', only £2,000 of the expenditure being so reflected. However, the author has never known HMRC to seek to raise such a contention.

8.13 It is nowadays commonplace for a local authority to look for some specific benefit to the community as a condition for granting planning permission for a development of any substance. A planning authority is empowered to enter into legally binding agreements with a developer under the *Town and Country Planning Act 1990, s 106*. If a *s 106* agreement requires the developer to incorporate, say, an open space or a roadway in his development and transfer the land to the local authority, the tax treatment of the cost of that land – and of any works that the planning authority requires the developer to do on it – may need careful consideration. It is by no means clear that the cost of that land is reflected in the state or nature of the retained land. As mentioned above, expenditure probably does not need to be so reflected pound for pound. Even so it is difficult to argue that expenditure on land A is reflected in the state or nature of land B. It may well have increased the value of land B but that is not the appropriate test. Furthermore, the test of enhancement expenditure looks at the motive at the point it is incurred, and at that stage the motive would not normally have been to give the land to the local authority. It is doubtful if the gift to the local authority itself constitutes expenditure. It may, however, give rise to a capital gains tax loss which could be carried forward and set against the gain on ultimate disposal of the remainder of the land. An alternative argument is that the value of what has to be given under a *s 106* agreement is part of the price of obtaining planning consent. That value is satisfied by the work carried out or the value of the land given to the local authority, in the same way as the 'expenditure' in *Chaney v Watkis* (see **8.9** above) was the value of the consideration given in exchange for satisfying the obligation that had been entered into. There is no simple or straightforward answer. Each case needs to be looked at individually in the light of the knowledge that the problem of ensuring deductibility exists.

8.14 If the *s 106* agreement requires a payment to be made to the local authority, or work to be carried out on land owned by the local authority, the problem is eased as the developer will have incurred expenditure. Even then, however, it is possible that it could be held that it is not incurred 'on the asset', the developer's site, even though it is incurred for the purpose of enhancing its value. Where the *s 106* agreement is clearly a condition of obtaining planning permission it would be surprising if HMRC were to take such an argument. If the *section 106* agreement is entered into not to obtain the planning permission but to speed up its implementation there could be difficulties.

Rent-free Periods

8.15 A developer may well allow a tenant a rent-free period at the start of his lease. This should not give rise to tax problems provided that it is incorporated in the lease so that the landlord would never have been entitled to rent for that period. The VAT implications (see **17.230**) also need to be considered.

Appropriation from and to Trading Stock

8.16 Although most of the problems of development affect only investment companies there is one of special significance to dealers. If a property which was acquired as trading stock is developed and a tenant found, what happens if the property is not sold? If there is a positive decision to retain the property there will be an appropriation of it from trading stock to fixed capital. On such an appropriation tax becomes chargeable as if the property had been sold at its market value as trading stock and reacquired as a fixed asset at the same price (*TCGA 1992, s 161(2)*). Accordingly, corporation tax becomes payable on the trading profit realised by the deemed disposal. If there is a large gain, this can be a major problem, as the appropriation will not of course generate any money with which to pay the tax. If the property is transferred intra-group from dealing company A to investment company B the same treatment applies. A is deemed to have appropriated the property from trading stock to investment and to have then transferred it as an investment to B.

8.17 Many people fear that, if a property which is developed as trading stock is held for several years after development, HMRC may contend that there has in fact been an appropriation from trading stock – and so seek to collect tax on the then value of the property – even though a positive decision to appropriate it was not taken. In practice this is a very rare occurrence. In the light of the comments of Lord Wilberforce in *Simmons v CIR* (see **5.21** above), it seems doubtful whether the status of an asset can legally alter without any positive change of intention by the owner. Accordingly, the status probably cannot accidentally be altered – although it must be remembered that a positive decision does not need to be evidenced in writing but can be inferred from a course of action. This applies in particular where there is no written evidence or the evidence that does exist is equivocal. It must also be admitted that a case exists (*British-Borneo Petroleum Syndicate Ltd v Cropper (45 TC 201)* (see **5.15** above)) where a company successfully convinced the High Court that there had been an appropriation many years earlier which the then directors had not appreciated to be such. Furthermore, there is a Privy Council case (*Richfield International Land & Investment Co Ltd v Inland Revenue Commissioner of Hong Kong* (see **5.23** above)) where HMRC convinced the Hong Kong Commissioners and the Privy Council that an appropriation had taken place in spite of contrary treatment in the accounts.

8.18 Where a property held as trading stock is likely to be retained after development, consideration should be given to making an appropriation from trading stock before the development starts. Although this will crystallise a tax liability which will have to be funded from somewhere, the trading profit by reference to the value of the land prior to commencing development is likely to be substantially less than that on the completed development. The appropriation should either clearly be carried out by way of transfer to an investment company or care should be taken to evidence the decision to appropriate. At a minimum there should be a board minute resolving to appropriate the property as an investment, the company's objects clause should if necessary be changed to give it specific power to hold property as an investment, and the property should be taken out of trading stock and shown as a fixed asset in the accounts.

8.19 It is of course equally possible that a company might want to appropriate to trading stock property that it initially acquired as an investment. For example, if a property bought to produce rents has been held for a comparatively short period when a decision to develop and sell it is taken, it may be felt that it would be difficult to demonstrate the investment intention. A specific appropriation as trading stock would reinforce this intention and might be worth considering if the increase in value up to that time is significant. The tax treatment in this instance is similar. The company has a capital gains tax disposal at market value and an acquisition as trading stock at the same price. If the property is transferred intra-group from an investment company to a dealing company (which is acquiring it as dealing stock), the latter is deemed to have acquired it as an investment and immediately appropriated it to dealing stock. However, in each case an election can be made to bring the asset into trading stock at its market value reduced by the amount of the chargeable gain that would otherwise have arisen on the appropriation, in which case no tax charge will arise at the time of the appropriation (*TCGA 1992, ss 173(1), 161(1), (3)*). This election can also be made where an individual appropriates a property from investment to trading stock.

8.20 Now that the rate of tax on income and capital gains is the same for companies it is difficult to imagine circumstances where the election would not be beneficial. It even preserves the benefit of the indexation allowance up to the date of the appropriation. At worst it defers payment of the tax. It also forfeits the right to future indexation relief but that seems unlikely to be as significant as in the 1980s. As it is often easier to shelter income than capital gains from tax, the effect of transforming the capital gain into income in this way may well be to facilitate a reduction in the tax burden. The position is different for individuals, as taper relief can significantly reduce the effective tax rate on a capital gain and the election will forfeit that relief.

8.21 In theory at least, the election can equally be made where the value of the property has fallen since its acquisition as an investment. The effect then is to convert a capital gains tax loss into a trading loss, which is generally far more attractive. There must, however, be a genuine appropriation. An unsuccessful attempt to do this was made in *Coates v Arndale Properties Ltd (59 TC 516)*. In that case the transfer to a dealing company took place on the same day as the dealing company resold it to a third party and for a price of exactly £10,000 less than the ultimate selling price. The House of Lords had no hesitation in holding that the dealing company did not acquire the property as dealing stock; it acquired it as a tax avoidance device. *Section 173(1)* applies only where the acquisition is as dealing stock. On the facts, that decision is not surprising. In *Reed v Nova Securities Ltd (59 TC 516)* (which concerned a transfer to a share dealing company, but the principle is the same), the assets, which consisted of shares and debts, were transferred several years before any sale and at a price that was considered to be a fair market value. The company's claim in respect of the transfer of debts succeeded in the House of Lords, although that in respect of shares failed on the basis that it was clear that they had no value at the date of transfer and as such could not have been acquired in the course of the company's trade. The appropriation was also successful in *New Angel Court Ltd v Adam (2004 STC 779)*. In a unanimous decision the Court of Appeal commented that the mere fact that a group of companies sets out to avail itself of the opportunity of obtaining a fiscal advantage which Parliament has itself provided says nothing as to whether the requirement which Parliament has imposed as the condition of obtaining that fiscal advantage – that is to say that the asset in question must be acquired 'as trading stock' – has been fulfilled. Fiscal considerations must be put entirely on one side in considering whether an asset was acquired 'as trading stock' for the purposes of s *172(1)*; not only must the asset which has been transferred be 'of a kind which is sold in the ordinary course of the company's trade', but it must have been acquired by the taxpayer 'for the purposes of that sale with a view to resale at a profit'. They went on to conclude:

> 'The facts in the instant case were that … the price at which NAC acquired the properties was a proper market price; that following its

acquisition of the properties NAC set about selling them and succeeded in selling all but one of them; and that in doing so NAC made a real profit … The conclusion follows that NAC's acquisition of the properties was a trading transaction entered into for a trading purpose; and that NAC accordingly acquired the properties "as trading stock" within the meaning of s 173(1).'

These cases were heard after the *Ramsay* decision, so there is a good chance that a genuine appropriation from investment to trading stock, when the property had some value and before any attempt to find a purchaser had been made would be successful.

Structuring Development Projects

8.22 Most major developments require more finance than the developer can provide from his own resources. The person providing the development finance will normally have his own ideas as to how the transaction should be structured – especially to ensure that he has the best possible security over the property. Where a financing institution or other provider of funds seeks to dictate the development structure it is important to think through the tax consequences of its preferred structure. If this will involve extra tax, or bring forward the date when tax would otherwise be payable, it will increase the financing requirement. In these circumstances some sort of compromise on the structure can be in everyone's interest. For example, institutions prefer to hold the freehold interest in a site. This is better security than a lease and gives the holder the ability to take over the development if things go wrong. If the developer has contracted to acquire the site it may be relatively simple to pass over the benefit of the contract to the institution without generating a significant tax liability. If he has owned the site for several years and has fought to get planning permission for the development, a disposal of the freehold to the institution is likely to generate an immediate and large tax liability. In such circumstances the institution may well be content with a mortgage.

8.23 If the financier takes an equity interest in the project consideration needs to be given as to how this is to be done. If he takes it as part of the loan agreement this could result in a distribution when it is paid out which may not be attractive (see **4.79** above). The most satisfactory structure is frequently a joint venture between the developer and the financier. However, if the finance is provided from an overseas source there may well be a risk that the UK developer could be regarded by HMRC as an agent for the financier unless great care is taken. This would make him liable for the non-resident's tax on his share of the profits. It might be thought that the safest structure is a jointly-owned UK company. However, this can cause problems if the property is not sold immediately on completion of the development, as the two parties will normally have different requirements as to what is to be extracted from the company and how. It is too late to decide how the financier is to be paid out his share at the stage that the development is completed and the developer decides that he would rather like to keep the property as a long-term investment! At that stage the only way may be for the joint company to sell him the property and crystallise an unnecessary tax liability, or for him to buy in the other's shares which in the long term results in two taxable gains instead of only one. There is no 'best' structure. It will depend on the individual facts. It is, however, vital to think through the structure on day one.

VAT

8.24 Many people look at all of the taxes other than VAT and regard VAT, and often also SDLT, as alien imposts. That is extremely dangerous in the context of property tax. The principles of VAT are considered in **Chapters 16** and **17**. There are particular problems of VAT on development activity which are dealt with here and of VAT on refurbishments which are considered in **Chapter 9**.

8.25 Most property transactions are exempt for VAT purposes. This means that VAT is not charged on the sale proceeds or rent received but no relief can be claimed for VAT borne on expenditure. Most services, including professional fees and building work, are standard-rated, ie VAT at the 20% standard rate ('output tax') has to be added to the value of the services by the supplier. The effect is that, to the extent that he suffers VAT on his expenditure ('input tax') but cannot recover it from HMRC, VAT is an additional cost for the property developer.

8.26 New development – as opposed to refurbishment – is now either standard-rated or zero-rated. Zero-rating means that output tax is chargeable at the rate of nil per cent (instead of 20%), but, because the output is thus taxable, relief can be claimed for input tax suffered on expenditure. This is an ideal situation to be in. VAT does not have to be collected on behalf of HMRC but they will refund to the developer tax paid on his expenditure.

8.27 This privileged status is restricted to residential development and development for 'relevant' charitable purposes, ie for use by a charity otherwise than in the course of a business. Care needs to be taken with such development as a very wide meaning has been given to 'business' for VAT purposes. It is by no means self-evident when zero-rating applies.

Residential and Relevant Charitable Development

8.28 The items eligible for zero-rating are as follows:

1.

(*a*) The first grant (or assignment or surrender) by a person constructing a building of a major interest in (or in any part of) the building or dwelling or its site if it is either designed as a dwelling or number of dwellings or is intended for use solely for a relevant residential or relevant charitable purpose.

(*b*) The first grant (or assignment or surrender) by a person converting a non-residential building (or a non-residential part of a building) into one designed as a dwelling or number of dwellings or intended for use solely for a relevant residential purpose, of a major interest in (or in any part of) the building or dwelling or its site.

2. The supply in the course of construction of either:

(*a*) a building designed as a dwelling or number of dwellings or intended for use solely for a relevant residential or relevant charitable purpose, or

(*b*) any civil engineering work necessary for the development of a permanent park for residential caravans,

of any services relating to the construction other than the services of an architect, surveyor or any person acting as a consultant or in a supervisory capacity.

3. The supply to a registered housing association (within the meaning of the *Housing Association Act 1985* or its Northern Ireland extension) in the course of conversion of a non-residential building (or part of a building) into one designed as a dwelling or number of dwellings or intended for use solely for a relevant residential purpose, of any services relating to the conversion other than the services of an architect, surveyor or any other person acting as a consultant or in a supervisory capacity.

4. The supply of building materials to a person to whom the supplier is supplying services within heads 2 or 3 above which include the incorporation of the materials into the building in question (or its site).

(*VATA 1994, Sch 8, Group 5.*)

8.29 Building materials for the purpose of head 4 means goods of a description ordinarily incorporated by builders in a building of the same description (or its site) subject to a number of specified exceptions (which are set out in **8.76**) (*Group 5, Note 22*). For this purpose the incorporation of goods in a building includes their installation as fixtures (*Note 23*). The meaning of these concepts was considered by the Upper Tribunal in *Taylor Wimpey plc v HMRC (2017 STC 639)* (see **16.20A**).

8.30 There is a further zero-rated supply in relation to 'protected buildings' (listed buildings). This is considered in **9.19** below. A residential developer needs to seek to bring his outputs within *item 1* above. If he cannot do so, it may be that his builder can bring his outputs – which will form a large part of the cost of the development – within *items 2* or *3* so that he does not need to charge VAT to the developer.

8.31 The meaning of relevant residential and relevant charitable purposes is considered in **16.49** and **16.59** respectively. The de minimis exclusion for minor non-qualifying use applies for this purpose. This is considered at **16.126**.

8.32 To come within *item 1* the developer also needs to show that he is 'a person constructing a building'. This term is not defined. It obviously includes a builder constructing on his own land. HMRC accept that it also includes a person who commissions someone else to construct a building for him (C & E Notice 708, para 4.5). This used to be subject to a proviso that some supplies of services were made to him and he exercised some measure of control over the construction (such as control over design or planning) but this seems to have been dropped from the latest version of the Notice. This would normally cover the developer where he owns the land. If, however, he does not own the land, but has sold it to an institution on terms that he will carry out the development on the institution's behalf and on completion will be granted a lease, the position needs to be looked at closely. His agreement will normally be a building lease, which is an interest in land and will probably suffice to make him the person constructing the building. If the developer is purely a project manager, with the building contract being between the builder and the institution, the developer is unlikely to be a person constructing the building.

8.33 Even if the developer is the person constructing the building, the only outputs by him which qualify for zero-rating are grants by him of a major interest in all or part of the building. A major interest is the freehold or a lease for a term certain exceeding 21 years (*VATA 1994, s 96(1)*). In Scotland a lease of not less than 20 years is also a major interest (see **16.13**). Accordingly, the sale of the freehold of a relevant building will qualify for zero-rating. So will the grant of a lease for a term of over 21 years. Zero-rating will apply only to any premium received for the lease or, if there is no premium, to the first rental payment under the lease – so as to generate a zero-rated supply and bring about the ability to reclaim input tax in relation to the development. HMRC have indicated that it does not matter if the lease has a break clause, even one exercisable by either party, or terms that make it unlikely that it will in fact last for over 21 years. A lease for someone's life is not for a term certain and will not qualify for zero-rating. If a developer initially grants a lease of 21 years or less and on its expiry grants a new lease of over 21 years then, although the original lease will not qualify for zero-rating, the second ought to do so, provided that it is granted by the person who constructed the building (*C & E Commrs v Link Housing Association Ltd (1992 STC 718)* – see **16.17**). This may, however, not be of great comfort. Unless the first lease is very short HMRC are likely to contend that it determines whether or not the developer recovers the VAT he suffers on his development costs, even taking into account the decision in *C & E Commrs v Briararch Ltd (1992 STC 732)* – see **17.85**.

8.34 If it is not wished to grant leases to occupiers of over 21 years an overriding lease to the developer's subsidiary company for such a period might be considered, with it then granting shorter subleases to occupiers. This should at least enable VAT on the construction costs – and on the costs of subsequent refurbishments which remain the developer's liability as head landlord – to be recovered. It is possible that HMRC might seek to apply the abuse of rights doctrine (see **17.104**) to such a strategy.

8.35 Some people also perceive a risk that HMRC could contend that for direct tax purposes the development of a property with the intention of granting a long lease on completion is by its nature a trading transaction. This is probably unfounded as the intention at the time of the acquisition of the site or undeveloped property is to create a long-term investment and the grant of the lease is simply machinery to reduce the cost of that investment. Within a group of companies, this is clearly valid. The position is less clear if the developing entity is an LLP and a company owned by the members has to be set up to take the lease. However, if the initial intention is investment, the grant of the lease is not a change of intention. It is simply a means to maximise the gain on the investment by reducing the VAT cost. For those that do have a concern, the grant of a lease at a full market rent with upward only rent reviews should not create a trading risk because the value of the lease will be very low, with the bulk of the value of the property remaining with the developer. Reviews within the first five years creates SDLT complications (see **19.155**) so an earlier review, whilst theoretically better, may be unattractive.

8.36 Rents from residential properties are always exempt from VAT even if the option to tax (see **17.113** below) is exercised in respect of the building. The only exception is that the first rental payment under a lease can be zero-rated if there is no premium (*VAT 1994, Sch 8, Group 5, Note 14*). This is to trigger the right of recovery of VAT on the development costs. Rents for relevant charitable buildings are similarly always exempt with the exception that rents for an office building are taxable at 20% if the landlord exercises the option to tax, even though part of the building is used for relevant charitable purposes.

Other Development

8.37 All other development of new buildings is now potentially chargeable to VAT at the 20% standard rate.

8.38 The potential charge to tax arises because, although property disposals, assignments and grants of leases or licences are normally exempt from VAT unless the option to tax is exercised (see **17.1** below), there is a specific exclusion from exemption for a freehold disposal of either:

(a) a building which has not been completed and which is not a residential (or relevant charitable) one;

(b) a new building which is not a residential one;

(c) a civil engineering work which is in the course of being constructed; or

(d) a new civil engineering work.

8.39 A building or civil engineering work is new if it is disposed of within three years of completion. A disposal of a building prior to completion will always attract VAT. The detailed rules are considered in **17.23–17.26** below.

Need to Register for VAT

8.40 The need to register timeously for VAT is, and always has been, very important. There is no requirement to register until a person makes (or expects within the next 30 days to make) taxable supplies in excess of the registration limit. It might be thought in these circumstances that when the obligation to register arises the taxpayer would become entitled to recover the VAT on prior expenditure incurred in generating the taxable supply. Unfortunately this is not the case. *VATA 1994, ss 25(1), 26* allow a deduction for input tax for the VAT quarter in which the supply takes place. *Section 24(6)(b)* enables HMRC by regulation to grant a deduction for tax on the supply of goods or services taking place before the recipient is VAT-registered. This they have done in the *VAT Regulations 1995* (*SI 1995 No 2518*).

8.41 Unfortunately *reg 111(2)(c)* provides that no amount can be treated as input tax in respect of services which have been supplied to the taxable person more than six months before the date of the taxable person's registration. The *regulation* does give HMRC power to authorise the deduction of other input tax, and it is to be hoped that they will do so where a non-VAT registered person acquires land on which he is charged VAT and does not immediately register it. However, this is by no means certain and the best advice at present is that if a developer is not VAT-registered, for example, where a development property is acquired in a newly formed subsidiary, application for registration should be made immediately prior to the acquisition if VAT will be payable on the acquisition of the land. At the latest, application should be made at the time that construction commences in any other case. There is no similar restriction in respect of goods (other than goods disposed of before a person's registration), but HMRC could base the input tax on the value at the time of registration if that is less than the cost. However, the major part of the cost of a building is the labour element, which is the provision of a service. Indeed the entire building contract is normally regarded as a composite supply of labour and materials so the entire cost is a supply of services. See the case of *AJ & A Elliott (VTD 4926)*. It should also be realised that *reg 111* is permissive, not mandatory, ie it empowers HMRC to grant relief for earlier input tax, not requires them to do so. The four-year cap imposed by *VATA 1994, s 80(4)* also needs to be borne in mind. This normally requires input tax relief to be claimed within four years of the time the tax was incurred.

8.42 A person who is not required to register for VAT is nevertheless entitled to be registered if he can convince HMRC that he is carrying on a business and intends to make taxable supplies in the course or furtherance of that business (*VATA 1994, Sch 1, para 9*). A property developer who will make a taxable supply following completion of the building should accordingly apply to register for VAT as soon as he starts to incur input tax in relation to expenditure on the development. Not only will this avoid the loss of input tax relief for early expenditure but it will significantly assist the cash flow. This is because, once registered, the developer will be able to reclaim the input VAT he has suffered each quarter during the development phase (or, if he so chooses, each month). HMRC often register an intending trader subject to the condition that he will repay the input tax previously claimed should he not subsequently make any taxable supplies. The VAT tribunal in *ACS Hordern (VTD 8941)* held that this condition breached the *Sixth Directive* and is therefore unenforceable.

8.43 A person who intends to grant an exempt lease cannot qualify to register as an 'intending trader' as he does not intend to make taxable supplies. Accordingly in such cases it might be wise to decide whether or not to exercise the option to tax (see **17.126**) immediately an interest in the site for the building is acquired so as to create a right to register. In practice HMRC will not allow registration if the option to tax is not exercised and notified at the same time as the application for registration.

8.44 As far as the residential developer is concerned, HMRC will similarly normally register a person for VAT if he intends to make zero-rated outputs on completion of the development. In the past HMRC wanted some evidence that there was a genuine intention to carry out the development, such as sight of the construction contract or of the detailed planning consent. This is no longer necessary (see **17.211** below), at least in theory. Unfortunately the practice is somewhat different; if anything they now seem to require more information rather than less. The registration will be provisional. If, when the developer comes to make supplies, they are not zero-rated but exempt, the registration will be withdrawn and HMRC will reclaim the input tax refunded in error. It is accordingly most important to ensure that the first lease is zero-rated. If a developer has other income which will arise during the construction period and which will be exempt, he will need to agree with HMRC before he starts his development that the input tax he suffers should be directly attributed to the exempt and zero-rated outputs respectively. If he does not, the receipt of the exempt income will forfeit the right to reclaim input tax suffered on the development costs. Direct attribution is considered further in **Chapter 16** (see **16.230** onwards). A temporary exempt letting will not necessarily be fatal provided that there is evidence of an intention to make taxable (which includes zero-rated) supplies (*C & E Commrs v Briararch Ltd (1992 STC 732)*) (see **17.96**).

8.45 Where a number of different entities are involved, care needs to be taken to ensure that the costs arise in the right place. *Mr & Mrs Kelly t/a Ludbrook Manor Partnership* gives a salutary lesson. Mr and Mrs Kelly decided to use their house for a furnished lettings business. They formed a company, Happy Holidays Ltd (HHL) to operate the business. Before it could be marketed, substantial refurbishment work needed to be carried out. This was done by HHL Ltd, albeit that it did not have any interest in the land. The Kellys were then advised to use a partnership rather than a company. HHL invoiced the partnership for the costs of the building work. The FTT held that HHL had not carried on any economic activity so could not claim relief for the input tax on the building work. It could not have incurred the expense on behalf of the partnership as the partnership did not exist when the building work was done. HHL could not have sold the work to the partnership because it had nothing to sell. Similarly, there could not have been a TOGC as HHL had no business which it could transfer.

Building Work on Residential and Relevant Charitable Developments

8.46 The supply of building works in the course of the construction or demolition of a relevant residential or charitable building also qualifies for zero-rating, provided an appropriate certificate is obtained (see **16.98** below). This will enable the building contractor to zero-rate his charges to the developer irrespective of whether or not the developer is the person constructing the building and able to make zero-rated supplies. It will not, however, enable the developer to recover input tax on architects' and other fees which do not qualify for zero-rating. It may be possible in some cases for the builder to engage the architect and other professionals and supply the building to the developer. However, care would need to be taken to ensure that the supply is not a mixed supply which HMRC are entitled to dissect into its various elements. The contractual liability of the architect almost certainly needs to be to the contractor not to the developer, which would probably not be commercially acceptable in most cases, although the growth in the use of collateral warranties may make this acceptable where these are available.

Exclusion of Conversion, Reconstruction, Alteration, Enlargement or Annexe

8.47 *Note 16* to *Group 5* of *Schedule 8* provides that the construction of a building does not include:

(*a*) the conversion, reconstruction, or alteration of an existing building; or

(*b*) any enlargement of, or extension to, an existing building except to the extent that the enlargement or extension creates an additional dwelling or dwellings; or

(*c*) the construction of an annexe to an existing building (subject to an exception where it is to a relevant charitable building and is capable of functioning separately from it – see **16.98**).

Accordingly such items are VATable.

8.48 'Alteration' in the above context was held by the House of Lords to mean a structural alteration in *ACT Construction Ltd v C& E Commrs (1982 STC 25)*. The House of Lords held there that there is a two-stage test. One first needs to ask whether there is an alteration and, if there is, whether it is nevertheless excluded from zero-rating as repair or maintenance. This approach was considered further by Woolf J in the subsequent case of *Parochial Church Council of St Luke v C & E Commrs (1982 STC 856)*. In that case the church had been seriously damaged by arson. The Council took the view that prior to the fire the church had serious deficiencies and disadvantages so after the fire took the opportunity to redesign the church for modern needs. Woolf J thought that, as before zero-rating can apply there has to be a conversion, reconstruction or alteration, the decision will primarily depend on what is happening to the building as a whole. It is the nature of the whole operation that is important. If, however, it is possible to identify a separate subsidiary operation there is no reason why there should not be a different decision with regard to that part. Accordingly if as an integral part of alterations, rooms which previously existed have to be redecorated, the redecoration should be treated in the same way as the alteration. Woolf J felt that, although primarily regard must be had to the state of affairs which existed at the time the works commence, where the test is whether something is repair or maintenance it is also necessary to have regard to the church's condition prior to the fire, as without doing so it is impossible to say whether something different from what previously existed is being produced. He deduced the intention of Parliament to be that 'it is new works which are to be zero-rated and works which are designed to preserve or restore what had previously existed which are to be standard-rated'. In resolving the problem the motive for doing the work is irrelevant; the work must be judged from an objective standpoint. It is a question of fact or degree whether what is happening is the repair of the old building or the construction of a new one. HMRC say that the onus of determining whether building work is taxable at the standard or zero rate is on the supplier, ie the builder needs to be satisfied that he is carrying out works of construction of a relevant residential or charitable building rather than works in the course of the conversion, reconstruction, alteration or enlargement of an existing building to which he would need to add VAT at 20% (*VATA 1994, Sch 8, Group 5, Note 9*). If he guesses wrongly HMRC will of course hold him liable to pay the tax. They have, however, given some guidance – which of course has no legal force – as to how they interpret 'the construction of a building'.

8.49 HMRC consider that the builder or developer should ask himself 'Am I constructing an entirely new dwelling or other qualifying building (for which I have a valid certificate) or am I doing something to a building which already exists?' They have volunteered their own 'common-sense' views on some of what they presumably feel to be the more clear-cut situations.

(i) Where an existing building has been demolished to foundation level, the construction of a building making use of part or all the foundations of the former building (which can include the 'slab' of the ground floor) will continue to attract the zero-rating relief.

(ii) Where what remains of an existing building is limited to a single wall such as the front facade, the construction of a building making use of that single wall or facade (or a double facade on a corner site) will continue to attract the zero-rating relief but only if the retention of the facade is required under the planning consent.(Notice 708, para 3.2.1).

(iii) The building on to an existing house of another house to form two separate but semi-detached houses with no inter-connecting doors would qualify for zero-rating, provided that planning permission does not prevent its separate use, letting or disposal and the new building stands on its own land.

(iv) The building of a new house within an existing terrace of houses on the site of a house that has been totally demolished ('infilling') would qualify for zero-rating.

Although not mentioned in Notice 708, HMRC have in the past given the following as examples of things that they considered did not qualify for zero-rating:

(*a*) Where the outer walls of an existing building remain, even without floor or roof, any building operations in or around that shell.

(*b*) Where internal features are retained in addition to any part of the wall structure, as the building services involved would be supplied in the course of the reconstruction of an existing building.

(*c*) The building of an additional flat on top of an existing block.

(*d*) In the case of establishments like old people's homes, residential care homes, 'new' construction within the curtilage of the establishment may be loosely referred to as extensions or additions to the qualifying building; the test here is whether what is being built is an enlargement of any of the individual buildings on the site (the internal access test being crucial here). If it is, the work is standard-rated, if not, it is zero-rated. A walkway which is no more than a covered corridor, several metres in length, at a single floor level, whose main purpose is to provide shelter in bad weather when moving between adjacent buildings, is not regarded as internal access in such cases.

(C & E Leaflet 708/2/90, para 6 now withdrawn.)

8.50 HMRC felt able to give this guidance because they thought that anyone would say that the buildings resulting from (i) and (ii) were really new buildings whereas in (*a*) or (*b*) the old building was being reconstructed. The author is duly chastened but, whatever most people might say, does not think that the retention of a single facade with internal fireplaces attached to it (which falls within (*b*)) is any more a reconstruction than if the fireplaces were stripped out (to come within (ii)). The dividing line between (ii) and (*a*) has led to much litigation. Some further guidance on this area can be found at **16.98** onwards.

8.51 In practice, the VAT tribunals seem to take a more relaxed attitude than HMRC which may well be why the above guidance has been dropped. Indeed the High Court has held that the distinction between development that qualifies for zero-rating and that which is exempt is essentially a question of fact (see **8.56** onwards). In *B M Croxford (VTD 5730)* a bungalow and garage were constructed on the site of a derelict piggery utilising part of the walls of the old building. HMRC contended that the retention of more than one wall prevented the work constituting the construction of a new building but the tribunal held that the work was not the conversion of an existing building, as the greater part of the piggery had been demolished. The *London Diocesan Fund* wished to replace a church with a new one. The planning permission required the retention of the old church tower. In addition, about 10% of the old building was retained, the chancel being altered to form a chapel in the new church. The VAT tribunal held that the work on the tower was a separate project of repair, but even if it were included in the main project, that constituted the substantial demolition of the old church and the construction of a new church. This was upheld in the High Court (*C & E Commrs v London Diocesan (1993 STC 369)* – see **8.56** below). In *P S Thakkar t/a Meera Homes (VTD 6127)* a large detached house was developed as a home for the elderly. The planning permission described the work as extensions. The front wall of the house and the two inner walls supporting it were retained. So were parts of other walls which could be incorporated in the design. About 40% of the foundations were retained. The new building was much larger than the old and very different in appearance. The work was held to be the construction of a new building. The tribunal said that there could be no general rule as to how much had to survive to decide the question whether there was a new building or the alteration or enlargement of an existing one.

8.52 The VAT tribunal in *Ochil Developments Ltd (VTD 10017)* took an unusually robust view, holding that to decide the issue it was necessary to determine whether at the commencement of construction there was an existing building in the ordinary sense of the word. Applying this test it concluded that the roofless shell of a former building was not an existing building and therefore there had not been a reconstruction of an existing building. A similar result was reached in *AJ Penn (VTD 10312)* where a barn roof supported by scaffolding was held not to be an existing building. A feature of this case is that the taxpayer had at first intended to simply add an extra storey to an existing barn. However, it was discovered that the barn had no foundation and the existing walls could not safely be built on. It is interesting that the tribunal applied the test of whether there was an existing building not when the planning permission was obtained but only after the walls had been demolished and the roof put on temporary supports. This is probably incorrect (see **8.57**).

8.53 In *Joseph Samuel Developments (VTD 7177)* the VAT tribunal held that a new block of four flats at the rear of an existing block which used one wall of the block as a party wall, had independent foundations and independent gas and water supplies, but whose entrance was through the existing building, was an enlargement of the existing building – but that the construction of a two-storey block at the rear of an existing three-storey building incorporating part of that building and built partly over its flat roof but mainly on piers at first floor level was a new building as its appearance was very different to that of the existing building and its function was different to that of the existing building (there was also no internal access to the flat from the existing building and all services to it were independent of the existing building). From 21 July 1994, such a development should qualify for zero-rating (see **16.98**). The test of whether a derelict structure constitutes a building is essentially one of fact and degree. A structure that is so derelict as to have no potential and no future as a building is not susceptible to conversion, reconstruction, alteration or enlargement and cannot properly be described as an 'existing building'. Accordingly, held the tribunal in *J C Lewis*, the construction of a farmhouse on the site of a derelict barn utilising about 26% of the old walls and about 20% in volume of the internal walls, was a new building, albeit that it was similar in appearance to the original barn. This was upheld on appeal (*C & E Commrs v Lewis (1994 STC 739)*), the judge agreeing with the tribunal's approach of asking (a) whether there was an existing building, giving the word its ordinary popular meaning; and if so (b) was it susceptible to conversion, reconstruction, alteration or enlargement. In *Mr & Mrs Truran (VTD 7312)* the taxpayers demolished all of the internal walls and the roof of an existing building but under the terms of the planning permission retained all of the outer walls and re-used some of the roofing tiles. HMRC successfully argued that the shell that remained was still a building and thus the new flats constructed within that shell, and as an extension to it, constituted a reconstruction and enlargement of an existing building. In *Swan Developments (Land Co) Ltd (VTD 7394)* the external walls of an office block were demolished and new walls built. The company had then, floor by floor, replaced the offices with flats, retaining only the lift shaft, 60–70% of the floors and 60% of the pillars. The tribunal held that this amounted to a conversion of one sort of a building into another; it was not possible to say that the company had constructed a building as a whole, albeit that the part of the original building incorporated into the new building was small.

8.54 An interesting decision that casts doubt on **8.49**(*d*) is that in *Associated Nursing Services plc (VTD 11203)*. The company constructed a block of residential care units, ie self-contained flats for the elderly, with a communal lounge adjoining an existing nursing home. Planning consent was for an extension to the nursing home and the new block had internal access to the nursing home through the party wall. The new block was held to be a separate building qualifying for zero-rating. The tribunal looked first at its function following *C & E Commrs v Great Shelford Free Church (1987 STC 249)* and *C & E Commrs v Elliott (1993 STC 369* – see **8.52**). It held that this was different to the nursing home, which did not make use of the block of flats (although it is clear that the flats made use of the nursing home). It was therefore not an extension or annexation. Neither the planning permission nor the internal access could override the different nature of the two buildings. In addition it considered that a bystander observing the large size of the block relative to the nursing home would not have considered it an extension or annexation. A similar result was reached in *B A Siraj t/a Europa Builders (VTD 11742)* where a block of flats was erected adjacent to a large semi-detached house which had been converted into flats and a single external staircase gave access to both. Such a development is probably now zero-rated in any event (see **16.89**).

8.55 Unfortunately, there has been little consistency. The partial demolition of a slaughterhouse in poor condition and the creation of a dwelling-house (*M J Rasmussen (VTD 1741)*); the conversion of a barn into a house where during the conversion the barn was 'virtually flattened' in the October 1987 gale *(G Wilkins (VTD 5268))*; and the conversion of stables and outbuildings into a dwelling house retaining only one wall and part of another *(R H Gleed (VTD 2481))*, have all been held to be conversions. It does, however, appear that the trend is for VAT tribunals nowadays to give greater weight to the appearance of the finished building and the replication concept, whereas in the earlier cases they tended to concentrate on how much of the old building was incorporated into the new.

8.56 Fortunately, judicial guidance was given by the High Court on the appeals in *C & E Commrs v London Diocesan Fund; v Elliott and another (1993 STC 369)* and *v Penwith Property Co Ltd*, which were heard together. The High Court decision in these cases was given in March 1993. VAT tribunal decisions prior to that date (VTD 10180 and earlier) need to be approached with caution as they may not have adopted the correct legal principles. The *London Diocesan* case has already been mentioned in **8.51**. Mr and Mrs Elliott had carried out work on a residential nursing home. The 'new' building was almost three times the size of the old, the old building was virtually unaltered but the new one was different in appearance to the old and its dimensions made it the predominant building. The VAT tribunal held that notwithstanding internal access the work could not properly be described as an enlargement of the old building. McCullough J disagreed. Penwith constructed a house using the chimney stack and about 35% of the original outer walls of a derelict old one. The new house covered about twice the area of the old. The VAT tribunal held that reconstruction implied a degree of replication and this was more important than the question of how much of the old building was incorporated in the new one. They felt that a reasonable observer would conclude that the new building lacked the requisite degree of replication for the work to constitute a reconstruction. This was upheld.

8.57 McCullough J felt that the right approach is firstly to consider whether there is an existing building at the time the work commences. This means before any work, whether demolition or construction, begins. If there is not, the work can be zero-rated. If there is, it becomes necessary 'to consider the end result and ask whether the work done amounts to the conversion, reconstruction, alteration or enlargement of the original building in the sense in which those words are commonly used or whether the end result is a new building. If a number of buildings existed before the work began the question will be whether the work amounted to the conversion, reconstruction, alteration or enlargement of one or more of them. The matter is one of fact and degree'. He felt that in answering this second question it will in most cases be helpful to look at the finished work and ask how much of the original building has survived. If there is a stage in the works where all of the demolition has been done and none of the new work started it might be useful to consider how the site would then have looked. It is not normally helpful to consider the four words separately as the work may include elements of more than one, eg the main part of a derelict house may be *reconstructed*, its scullery and coal shed *converted* into a bathroom, its principal room *enlarged* by the addition of a bay window, and its surviving windows *altered* in style.

8.58 In the *London Diocesan* case McCullough J felt that the tower was probably part of the existing building but the tribunal had considered the position alternately on the basis that it was and was not. Although he felt that many tribunals would have reached a different conclusion, McCullough J could not say that the conclusion of the VAT tribunal was one that no tribunal, on the material before it, could properly have reached. Similarly, in the *Penwith* case McCullough J felt that, although the tribunal had asked the wrong questions, it was possible that had it asked itself the right ones it might still have held that the work was zero-rated and in that event it might have been impossible to say that such a decision was so unreasonable that it should be quashed. He felt that the tribunal in Mr and Mrs Elliot's case had misunderstood the facts. It had not realised that the planning permission required an interconnecting door; it had erred in finding that the new structure had itself all the facilities for an independent nursing home; and it had exaggerated the increase in area of the new building. On the facts the only reasonable conclusion was that there was an extension to an existing building which provided internal access to it.

8.59 Many of the subsequent VAT tribunal decisions have favoured the taxpayer. In *St John the Evangelist Parochial Church Council (VTD 11165)* a new parish centre was constructed adjoining a church. It was used for separate purposes to the church and had a separate heating system. However, a covered area was constructed between the two buildings. This was structurally independent of the church. HMRC's claim that this made the parish centre an extension or annexation to the church was rejected, but it was regarded as a borderline case. In *Ronald Jamieson (VTD 10939)* the construction of houses on the site of dilapidated farm buildings (cattle sheds, etc.) was held to be zero-rated albeit that most of the old stone walls were incorporated in the houses. What was there before – single-storey roofless buildings, without flooring, with empty openings for doors and windows, defective stonework, with no utilities, and the tops of the walls overgrown with grass – was not an existing building but a derelict ruin. In *Keep Design Ltd (VTD 11581)* two semi-derelict, boarded-up late Victorian terrace blocks of workmen's cottages were replaced by 15 modern starter homes. The party walls and brick spine of the cottages were retained. The tribunal felt that the work was more extensive than a mere alteration and was not a reconstruction of existing buildings because it did not replicate what was there before. Similarly in *Lucking Brothers (VTD 11595)* where a barn and a cattle shed were transformed into a house, retaining the timber frame of the barn and part of the walls and roof timber of the cattle shed, the tribunal considered that a casual observer who was shown the completed building and given a full explanation of the work involved would view it as a new building, not a conversion or reconstruction. It felt that the similarity in external appearance between the old and new buildings was not conclusive and the planning consent which required this of little significance. Again in *Josephine Lane (VTD 11710)* where a derelict lodge was replaced with a much larger house, retaining a facade, a gable end and chimney stack, the tribunal held that an informed layman inspecting the new building would be unlikely to connect it with the old lodge, so zero-rating applied. The incorporation of features of the original building was a requirement of the planning consent and as such was felt irrelevant as it did not reflect the taxpayer's wishes.

8.60 In *C & E Commrs v Marchday Holdings Ltd (1997 STC 272)* it was accepted by the Court of Appeal (in a split decision) that the construction of an office block on the site of a former industrial building was a new building albeit that it utilised about two-thirds of the concrete frame, 85% of the concrete floor slabs, some brick party walls, and the foundations of the old building. The retention of parts of the structure of the former building was relevant but did not of itself preclude the construction being a new building. It was unrealistic to ignore the cost of the work. The work as a whole was so extensive that the resulting office block was essentially a new building. Such 'conversions' are no longer able to constitute a new building from 1 March 1995 following the changes made by the *VAT (Construction of Buildings) Order 1995* (*SI 1995 No 280*) – see **16.32**.

8.61 Where four self-contained flats were constructed in the shell of a house, the interior of which was completely gutted, it was held that the construction work amounted to a conversion or alteration of an existing building (*Davies Investments (VTD 12308)*). In *St Albans Nursing Home Ltd (VTD 13488)* two adjoining detached houses were reconstructed and joined together to form a single building. It was held that the finished building had no affinity with the two previous ones in structure or appearance. The two houses had been completely transformed and their identities did not survive the construction work.

8.62 In *A R Carter (VTD 13828)* a cottage in need of substantial repair was transformed into a larger house. The completed building covered more than twice the area of the original, only about 12% of the walls derived from the cottage and there was a marked contrast between the house and the original cottage. The fact that in his planning application the taxpayer had stated he wanted to alter the existing building was dismissed on the basis that his intention at the time of the application was not conclusive evidence of the work that was actually done. In *G M & E A Flowers t/a Soar Valley Construction (VTD 13889)* the conversion of an old forge into a dwelling was held to have resulted in the creation of a new and different building. The conversion at the same time of a dairy and hay loft into dwellings was held to be an alteration as enough of the original remained for their identity to have survived the work. In *J S Bell (VTD 13448)* it was proposed to alter and enlarge two semi-detached cottages to a dwelling-house but, as work progressed, the condition of the buildings were found to be worse than expected. Very little could be used. The VAT tribunal accepted that the house was the construction of a new building, the old building having effectively been demolished piecemeal as work progressed.

8.63 On the other hand in *W J E Hurford (VTD 11422)* the tribunal held that a ruinous and unstable structure (a barn with no foundations whose roof had disintegrated and most of whose timbers had to be replaced) was an existing building as it would appear to a passer-by to be a building. In *WE Talbot & Sons (VTD 10968)* a house was regarded as a reconstruction albeit that it was over 70% larger than the old one and most of the retained features, 40% of the original external walls and of the roof, were required as a condition of planning consent. The tribunal felt that there was a recognisable house in existence at each stage of the development. It was irrelevant that the original house was uninhabitable or that the interior had been completely gutted and replaced; the test related to the principal structure of the building. This decision should be contrasted with that in *P S Thakkar* (see **8.51**) where on very similar facts it was held that there was a construction of a new building. In *S & H Shroufi (t/a Morris Grange Nursing Home) (VTD 14852)* where planning permission had been obtained for an extension, the tribunal held that that was what had been constructed; the extension was not a separate building, even though it had a separate entrance, was used for a different purpose to the rest of the building and the only internal access was through fire doors. Similarly in *Bruce Pugh (VTD 17013)*, a DIY builder case, the retention of part of the front wall (as part of the inner skin of the front wall of the new house) was sufficient to make the work reconstruction rather than the erection of a new building, albeit that the tribunal accepted that by any objective standard the incidental incorporation of part of the old was inconsequential.

8.64 Temporarily constructing a separate new building adjoining an existing one and subsequently joining them up will not necessarily prevent the new building being an extension. In *Graden Builders Ltd (VTD 12637)* the builders waited three months before constructing internal access between the two. The tribunal held that the new building was an extension as there had been throughout an intention that the two should be occupied together. In *Nidderdale Building Ltd (VTD 13158)*, a builder relying on a certificate provided by a director of his customer, following confirmation from the VAT office that construction of a new wing to a nursing home was zero-rated, did not charge VAT. After he had completed the new wing the customer engaged a different builder to construct a doorway linking the two buildings. Nidderdale was held liable to account for VAT as the new wing was an extension of the existing building. The decision may not be as harsh as it seems at first sight. The planning consent and the approved plans had included an internal access, which ought to have put Nidderdale on notice, and the new wing was not capable of operating separately as a nursing home – which the customer had said he intended – as it had no kitchen and no administrative accommodation.

8.65 However, in *D S Menzies (VTD 15733)*, a residential building that was erected without access to another a metre away and subsequently linked was held to be a separate building notwithstanding that the architect had suggested that, as the work had to be phased, it should be constructed as a separate entity; the planning permission was for 'additional accommodation', the linkage was done by the same builder who constructed the building (albeit under a separate contract) and the buildings were linked a mere 28 days after the construction. The VAT tribunal accepted that there was always an intention to link the two buildings but thought that the lack of funds might have prevented that happening for a substantial period and the building was usable as it was. The tribunal commented, 'it is also dangerous and productive of much uncertainty if, after works have been completed and invoiced, an alteration to a taxable status can occur because one building becomes linked with another'.

8.66 A similar result was reached in *JMB Strowbridge (VTD 16521)* where the appellant built a second nursing home adjacent to an existing one and subsequently removed the stud walls from both buildings making them into a single home. The tribunal held that the new building was an annexe but, as there was no internal access at the time of completion of the building work, it qualified for zero-rating. Mr Strowbridge originally intended to have a single building but decided to operate the two separately because he could not afford the VAT! By the time the building was completed five patients had died and in those changed circumstances it had become uneconomical to run the two separately. The tribunal accepted that the decision to merge the two buildings had not existed when the building was initially completed.

8.67 In the next case to come before the courts (as opposed to tribunals), *Cantrell & Others (t/a Foxearth Nursing Home) v C & E Commrs (2000 STC 100)* (called Wright & Fuller Ltd in the initial VAT tribunal), Lightman J indicated that the question whether the completed building works amounted to an enlargement, extension or annexe had to be asked as at the date of the supply. It had to be answered after an objective examination of the physical characteristics of the building or buildings before and after carrying out the works, having regard to similarities and differences in appearance, the layout, the uses to which they were physically capable of being put and the functions which they were physically capable of performing. The terms of planning permissions, the motives behind undertaking the works and the intended or subsequent actual use were irrelevant (except possibly to indicate the potential for use inherent in the building). Accordingly, in giving weight to a condition in the planning permission that the new structure was to be used only as part of the nursing home, and to the effect of the works on the nursing home enterprise as a whole and the function of the new structure, the tribunal had misdirected itself in law. In that case five separate buildings were linked together and a new building intended for use as a separate dementia unit designed to operate independently of the rest of the nursing home was built at one end with very limited internal access and a different appearance to the rest of the building. The tribunal held that the five buildings constituted an 'existing building' and that the new building was an extension. Lightman J remitted the case to the tribunal for rehearing where it found 'with considerable reluctance' that the new works constituted an annexe *(VTD 17804)*. The taxpayer appealed on the grounds that the tribunal had not followed the guidance of Lightman J. On appeal, Sir Andrew Morritt V-C felt that an annexe is an adjunct or accessory to something else. In the context of a building it must be 'a supplementary structure, be it a room, a wing or a separate building'. The fact that there is an association between the old and new building is not sufficient. He accordingly held that the new building was not an annexe; neither contiguity, common ownership nor inclusion in the building complex as a whole is sufficient to point to there being an annexe to the existing building (*Cantrell & another (t/a Foxearth Lodge Nursing Home) v C & E Commrs (No 2) (2003 STC 486)*). On the basis of this comment the FTT in *S Colchester (TC 2465)* held that the construction in that case was an annexe even though it met all four of the conditions in **16.32** to be a dwelling. They were entitled to look beyond the mere functionality of the new building in making the wider enquiry envisaged in that case; Mr Colchester's entire rationale for seeking planning consent for the new construction was based upon the shortcomings in the existing dwelling and the need to provide for additional facilities to be in common ownership and use. The Upper Tribunal *(2014 STC 2078)* agreed that the tribunal was required to look beyond the physical characteristics and functionality of the new building.

8.68 Similarly the construction in *Chacombe Park Development Services Ltd (VTD 19414)* was held to be neither an extension nor an annexe. In that case the existing building was a 45-bed care home in an L shaped structure. A new building was erected at one of the ends of the L to form a U shaped whole. There is a gap of 6½ feet between the two buildings and they are linked at ground and first floor level, the linking being intended only to create a fire escape. At each end of the link are secure, locked doors. The new building contains 32 en suite bed sitting rooms designed as permanent homes for elderly frail people in need of personal (but not nursing) care. Both buildings are in the same general style, as that was a condition of the planning consent, but the different uses strongly influenced the style of each building. The buildings are separately staffed. Although the new building has the appearance of being a wing of the old, the tribunal noted that 'it would be impossible to see the new work as being supplementary to the existing building'. The two are both designed and used for different purposes.

8.69 *Allen Water Developments Ltd (VTD 19131)* concerned the construction of a care home linked physically to an existing home by a corridor. Each home had its own staff and manager but there was a general manager having overall responsibility for both. The new home used excess kitchen capacity of the old. Applying the *Cantrell* tests the tribunal held that there were two separate buildings. It was influenced not only by the fact that the two functioned independently but also by the fact that the two structures in no way resembled one another, each had a different designer, and the linking corridor has been suggested by the Fire Officer and was used only for the delivery of meals from the old building (which needed to be reheated in the new). In *The Archdiocese of Southwark Commission for Schools and Colleges (VTD 18883)* a new building containing classrooms and lavatories was held to be an enlargement of the existing school not an annexe, although in any event the main access to it was through the existing building. Similarly in *Henshaws Society for Blind People (VTD 19373)* the construction of a residential unit containing 18 bedrooms and kitchen and dining rooms adjoining the entrance block of a school and linked to it only by fire doors, was held not to be either a separate building or an annexe but an extension to the existing college building. The tribunal thought that the two formed one single, unified cohesive structure albeit that the residential block was designed to function differently from the college.

8.70 The question in *Colchester Sixth Form College (VTD 16252)* was whether a five-storey building constructed in an area bounded on three sides by the existing college buildings was an annexe. The new building had its own water, heating and fire alarm systems and was capable of being used separately from the remainder of the college. It had its own entrance but in practice most students did not use this but accessed it via the old building. The tribunal accepted that in architectural terms an enlargement or extension could also be an annexe but felt that the scheme of the legislation could not support such a construction. Applying the two-stage test laid down in the *London Diocesan Fund* case, the tribunal decided that the new building was not an enlargement of the existing one as that remained unchanged. However, it provided an additional section to the college building with a real and substantial measure of integration with the existing building. It was accordingly an extension and did not qualify for zero-rating. The tribunal commented that even if they had classified it as an annexe it would still not have attracted zero-rating as the entrance to the new structure formed the main entrance to the college.

8.71 A new building within a synagogue complex that replaced an existing wooden structure was held to be a reconstruction of part of the existing building complex (*Yeshurun Hebrew Congregation (VTD 16487)*). The tribunal thought that if the existing building had to be looked at after the demolition of the wooden structure the new building would be an enlargement or extension of the existing building not an annexe. Similarly work carried out in two phases at a Gurudwara (a Sikh temple) were both held to be extensions to the *Gurudwara (Guru Norak Nishkan Sewak Jatha (Birmingham) UK (VTD 17499))*. In Phase I part of the Gurudwara was demolished and replaced by a new three-storey community block with internal access to the existing building. Phase II was the construction of a grand entrance porch surmounted by a new dome, which became the main entrance to the Gurudwara. The taxpayer also unsuccessfully contended that there was a single project for the construction of the temple which began in 1991 when a former Polish club was converted into a Gurudwara, and that the work started in 1993 (Phase I) and 1995 (Phase II) was part of that construction. This was dismissed as it was clear from the evidence that none of the work on either phases I or II was conceived prior to 1991.

8.72 The provision in issue in *M G & N Smith (VTD 17035)* was *Note 16* (see **8.47**), which zero-rates an extension to the extent it creates an additional dwelling. A new dwelling was built adjacent to an existing one. However, a small part of the upper floor utilised unused space within the old one with access to such space from the old building having been blocked off. In effect the works resulted in two semi-detached houses, albeit that part of the upper floor of one is carried upon part of the ground floor of the other. HMRC contended that *Note 16(b)* requires the additional dwelling to be contained wholly within the enlargement. They pointed out that the *Note* contains no apportionment provision. The tribunal rejected this. The natural meaning of the wording merely requires that an additional dwelling should be created. The use of the words 'except to the extent that' imputed the apportionment rule in *Note 11* (see **16.115**). Accordingly the extension was zero-rated. However, the work undertaken to incorporate part of the original dwelling in the new house should be standard-rated. *A & M Wright (TC 1523)* is a fascinating case. Mr and Mrs Wright lived in a large house in Devon for many years. They decided to undertake a speculative building project by turning their home into two semi-detached houses and living in one of them. However, the only way that they could achieve this was by building on each side of the existing house, creating a party wall within the existing house and constructing a new roof. The existing house was almost gutted, the existing internal walls, floors and windows all being removed. In addition the height was increased to create an extra floor. The floor space of the new house to be sold consisted roughly of 35% of the original house and 65% new construction. Mr and Mrs Wright sought registration as intending traders. HMRC refused to register them on the grounds that they were converting, reconstructing or altering an existing building and accordingly intending to make only exempt supplies. Mr and Mrs Wright contended that they were enlarging or extending an existing building to create an additional dwelling which would be a zero-rated supply. The tribunal first applied the *Cantrell* two-part test (see **8.67**), namely compare the building before and after the works were carried out by making an objective assessment of the physical characters of the building at the two points of time having regard (inter alia) to similarities and differences in appearance, the layout, and how the building is equipped to function and then ask whether the completed works amount to an enlargement of (or the construction of an extension or annexe to) the original building. It answered that there had been an enlargement or extension, not a conversion, reconstruction or alteration. It next asked whether the enlargement or extension had created an additional dwelling. It was clear that it had. It also thought that the fact that it incorporated part of the old dwelling did not prevent it being the 'construction of a building' for the purpose of *VATA 1994, Sch 8, Group 5, Item 1* as with *Jahansouz* (see **16.98**) where the Tribunal judge noted that *Note 16(b)* does not contain the word wholly. It then pointed out that the development consists partly of zero-rated new building and partly of an exempt supply of land (the part of the existing building incorporated into the new dwelling). Accordingly zero-rating would apply but only to the extent of the new work incorporated into the new dwelling.

8.73 *Note 16* was again in issue in *HMRC v Astral Construction Ltd (2015 STC 1033)*. This concerned the construction of a nursing home on the site of a derelict church and its outbuildings. The outbuildings and extensions to the church were demolished but the local authority required the existing original church to be retained. The area of the church was 315 sq m and the new building was 2,910 sq m. The church, with new extensions constructed at both ends, was incorporated to form one side of a square. The FTT, on the basis of *Marchday Holdings* (see **8.60**), felt that whether the work was an extension was not only a question of fact but also of degree. It felt that, viewing the final construction, the point had been reached where it would be a misnomer to describe the works as an extension. The church was dwarfed by the new building. An objective observer would see a large fully functioning care home of modern design that in an attractive way has incorporated an old and disused church. The Upper Tribunal agreed. *Chelmsford College Ltd (TC 2796)* concerned the construction of a new building, the Art and Design Block, erected close to the main college building and connected to it by a path at ground level and an enclosed footbridge at first floor level. HMRC said that the block was an extension of the main building; the college claimed that it was an annexe capable of functioning separately from it (see **16.98**). On the basis of the *Cantrell* tests the FTT decided that the new building was an annexe, not an enlargement. Unfortunately, as it shared a heating system with the main building and could not function effectively in winter without heating, the Tribunal also held that it was not capable of functioning separately. A similar decision was reached in *J3 Building Solutions Ltd*. This concerned an old coach-house in use as a dwelling. Planning permission was obtained to demolish part of the original coach-house and number of subsequent extensions and to create a new, larger, residence. The local authority regarded 'the whole scheme as a demolition of existing and re-build of a new dwelling'. HMRC said that as the old building has not ceased to exist (see note 18, Group 5, *VATA 1994, Sch 8*). The FTT took a somewhat odd view of note 18 (a building only ceases to be an existing building when demolished completely to ground level). It started from what it called 'the three-stage St Andrew's test' which derived from *Parochical Church Council of St Andrews (VATTR 2127)* and had been approved in *London Diocesan Fund* (a 1993 case – see **8.56**). This asks was there an existing building prior to the commencement of any works; was there still an existing building once any projected development has been carried out; and was the completed building to be described as the conversion, reconstruction, alteration or enlargement of that existing building? The Tribunal then held that if the answer to question 2 is no, the demolition work does not leave an existing building, Note 18 is irrelevant. This is unconvincing. It is hard to see how there cannot be an existing building after demolition if the demolition does not meet the Note 18 requirement. Accordingly this decision needs to be approached with caution because they sought to apply it only after deciding that the old building had ceased to exist. On appeal, the UT felt that the FTT had been hampered as neither side quoted relevant case law. A *Marchday*-type enquiry is no longer relevant as such, because Note 18 now provides its own answer as to whether or not the existing building continues to exist. On the facts of this case there remained an existing building throughout and it was incorporated into the new structure. That is an alteration, so Note 16 operates to exclude zero-rating. A similar decision was reached in *J3 Building Solutions Ltd (TC 5087)*. This concerned an old coach house in use as a dwelling. Planning permission was obtained to demolish part of the original coach house and all of a number of subsequent extensions and to create a new, larger, residence. The local authority regarded 'the whole scheme as a demolition of existing and re-build of a new dwelling'. HMRC said that as the old building has not ceased to exist (see *note 18, Group 5, Sch 8, VATA 1994*) the end product could not be a new building. The FTT took a somewhat odd view of *note 18* (a building only ceases to be an existing building when demolished completely to ground level).

8.74 *Leyton Sixth Form College (TC 3042)* undertook a major building and refurbishment project to cope with growing student numbers. An objective of the project was to give overall cohesion to the various buildings on the site. The project included the construction of a new building (Building C). The development included the construction of a wide and long atrium area, called The Street, which linked all the major buildings on the site and which is the main point of access to the college (for security reasons). The main access to the original main building is now through Building C, which adjoins it, by way of corridors at ground and first floor level. The FTT held that objectively Building C is an enlargement of the old main building, not an annexe. It looked at the way the buildings are used and, more particularly, the way the new building was intended to be used, as well as its appearance, layout and how it is equipped to function. They regarded the arrangement of the corridors as an important factor. It is integrated with the old building, not simply adjoined to it (see *Macnamara* – **16.100** and **16.105**). The new structure in Gateshead Jewish Nursery *(TC 3807)* was similarly held to be an enlargement of the existing building, not an annexe, as it was integrated into that building.

8.75 In *Litton & Thorner's Community Hall (TC 6101)* the dispute concerned a hall owned by a charity which was intended to be available for the local school to use and was available at other times as a community centre. Because of the range of uses proposed, it was essential that the hall contained reasonable storage space. The trustees decided to install ground source heat pumps, but did not appreciate how much space that needed. As a result, the heating equipment took over the planned storage space. They decided to add storage space onto the east side of the building. The builder recommended that a steel joist should be incorporated in the east wall to facilitate the building work for the envisaged storage space. This could not be added until planning consent was obtained and the necessary additional funds raised. It took the best part of five years before the storage space could be built. The FTT decided that the storage was an annex, not an enlargement of the building. This entitled the charity to zero-rating as it was to be used exclusively for charitable purposes. The FTT felt that the additional building neither looked nor felt like an extension. It was capable of functioning separately from the hall as it had its own external doors. The test is capability; it is irrelevant that it does not actually function on its own. Although the annex could be accessed from the hall, neither set of doors could be characterised as the main access as each was important for different reasons. Accordingly, the main access was not through the hall.

8.76 I have dealt with the cases on new residential buildings in **Chapter 8** as these seem to me to be a feature of development, those on listed buildings in **Chapter 9** as the work is normally in the course of a refurbishment, and what is a building in **Chapter 16**. This inevitably results in some cases that may be relevant to a particular issue being dealt with under one of the other heads. It might therefore be helpful to highlight the court decisions and also the relationship between court and tribunal decisions. These are accordingly summarised at **16.47**. VAT Tribunal decisions made before a court decision in the same area need to be approached with caution as the tribunal would not have had the benefit of the judges' views.

Fittings

8.77 Even if the building work qualifies for zero-rating, certain goods cannot be zero-rated by the builder (although they can still be zero-rated by the person constructing the building). These are:

(*a*) finished or prefabricated furniture other than furniture designed to be fitted in kitchens;

(*b*) materials for the construction of fitted furniture, other than kitchen furniture; and

(*c*) an electrical or gas appliance, other than:

   (i) one designed to heat space or water (or both) or to provide ventilation, air cooling, air purification or dust extraction; or

   (ii) a door entry system, waste disposal unit or machine for compacting waste which is intended for use in a building designed as a number of dwellings; or

   (iii) a burglar alarm, fire alarm, or fire safety equipment or an appliance designed solely for the purpose of enabling aid to be summoned in an emergency; or

   (iv) a lift or hoist,

(*d*) carpets or carpeting material.

(*VATA 1994, Sch 8, Group 5, Note 22.*)

This is intended to prevent taxable furniture being disguised as zero-rated building works.

8.78 The services supplied in conjunction with such goods must be separable from them. *D & C Hodson t/a Bordercraft Workshops (VTD 13897)* supplied fitted kitchen furniture individually manufactured to meet the precise measurements made by the client or his architect. They were usually fitted by a sub-contractor. If they did not fit, Hodson took them back and made the necessary adjustments. It was held that the service of ensuring that the units fitted was an intrinsic part of the supply of goods so zero-rating could not apply (see also *C & E v Jeffs and another* at **9.52**).

8.79 HMRC have indicated the sorts of items they consider are 'of a kind ordinarily installed by builders as fixtures'. These can be found in Annexes D and E to HMRC Notice 708. *Leisure Contracts Ltd (VTD 19392)* supply electrically powered covers for indoor swimming pools. The cover is fitted when the pool is installed and it is rare for a pool to be supplied without a cover. It was accepted that swimming pools are ordinarily incorporated in expensive houses. However, HMRC contended that the cover was excluded by **8.76**(*c*) as an electrical appliance. The tribunal felt this needed to await the ECJ decision in *Talacre Beach Caravan Sales Ltd*. In that case the ECJ subsequently held that although the sale of a fitted caravan was a single supply this did not mean that, if different tax rates are charged on different elements of that supply, it does not need to be dissected into those separate elements to calculate the tax due. The tribunal in *Rainbow Pools London Ltd (VTD 20800)* disagreed with that in *Leisure Contracts*, holding that the intrinsic nature of a pool cover is not an electrical appliance and the fact that it is powered by electricity does not turn it into one. In that case it found that a pool cover is ordinarily installed as fixtures as 90% of indoor pools installed in luxury houses have such a cover, but that moveable floors to cover the pool are so rare as to be extraordinary. However, the Upper Tribunal in *Taylor Wimpey* (see **16.20A**) thought that this case was wrongly decided. In *Tom Perry (VTD 19428)* the tribunal held that electric blinds designed to cover external glass automatically, to reduce the heating effect of sunlight inside the house (which had been designed to be energy efficient by using sunlight for warmth), were not items ordinarily incorporated in new houses and, even if that were wrong, they were electrical appliances not designed to provide air cooling.

The rules in relation to fixtures are considered in greater detail at **16.19**.

Phasing the Work

8.80 The timing of work can affect the VAT position. In *SA Whiteley (VTD 11292)* the taxpayer bought a house in 1988. He intended to modernise it, to replace an existing garage block with a new annexe containing office and staff accommodation, and to construct an indoor swimming pool. He was advised to seek planning approval in stages. Permission to develop the house was granted in June 1989 and work started. Permission to build the annexe was granted in March 1992 and work started in August 1992, the work on the house having been completed in August 1991. Permission for the swimming pool was granted in December 1992 and work commenced in February 1993. It was held that the taxpayer had constructed three separate buildings, not a single dwelling erected in stages. Accordingly the annexe and swimming pool could not qualify for zero-rating as being work carried out in the construction of the house.

8.81 In *St Mary's RC School (1996 STC 1091)* the construction of a school play area 13 years after the school opened was held by the tribunal to be the completion of the original building not an addition to it although this was reversed on appeal. There was a statutory requirement for a school to include recreation areas and these had been shown on the original plan. The construction had had to be deferred until a diversion order could be obtained in respect of a public right of way which crossed the land and further funding was needed to meet the cost both of that order and of the building work. The judge felt that the tribunal had not given sufficient weight to the temporal link and that a gap of 13 years was 'far too long'. In any event, lack of funds could not justify a time interval so as to be able to show that the work was continuous. In *The Trustees of the Sir Robert Geffery's School Charity (VTD 17667)* the charity built a new school in 1989 to 1991. It had planning permission for six classrooms only but the foundations were deliberately built strong enough to take an extra floor. A second storey was added when funds became available in 1998. The charity contended that these new classrooms were part of the original work, but the tribunal had no hesitation in holding that the building had been completed in 1991 and the new classrooms were the enlargement of an existing building. The tribunal was influenced by the comments in *Cantrell* (see **8.63**) that the test had to be applied at the date of the supply.

8.82 *Hoylake Cottage Hospital Charitable Trust (TC 925)* obtained planning permission in December 2003 for a new 60-bed nursing home. The permission did not make provision for a laundry and kitchen block. The intention was that future plans would include the development of a new day unit together with a kitchen and laundry block to serve the entire site. Temporarily the new nursing home would be serviced from the existing hospital buildings. HMRC accepted that the construction of the nursing home could qualify for zero-rating. The nursing home was completed in May 2009. The charity subsequently raised the funds for the kitchen and laundry block and work on it started in November 2010 with completion done by August 2011. The Tribunal held that the construction of the kitchen and laundry block was a continuation of the original development and should be zero-rated. In practice, the home had not been able to operate satisfactorily from the hospital kitchen. In all the circumstances a period of roughly 18 months (May 2009 to October 2010) was not an unreasonable delay. See also *Chipping Sodbury Town Trust (VTD 16641)* at **16.44**.

8.83 In *York University Property Company Ltd v HMRC (2015 SFTD 633)* the University obtained planning consent for the construction of a research building in two phases. Phase 1 was completed in 2004 and the building was occupied. The wall on one side of the building was designed to be easily removable when the finance to carry out Phase 2 became available. In 2011 the wall was removed and Phase 2 built. This effectively doubled the size of the building. HMRC contended that Phase 1 had produced a completed building and Phase 2 was therefore an extension to that building. The FTT said that there is no legally recognised concept of phasing. It needs to be determined whether the first phase resulted in a completed building or in the incomplete construction of a building that was completed by the Phase 2 works. This is a question of fact and degree. In this case they concluded that the Phase 2 works were an extension. The development in *Central Sussex College (TC 4151)* was also phased for want of finance. In fact Phase 2 was built largely at the same time as Phase 1 but that did not prevent the Tribunal from holding that Phase 1 created the building and Phases 2 and 3 were extensions to it.

Other VAT Issues

8.84 Where other work has to be done in connection with a residential development that other work might well be supplied in the course of construction of the residential development and thus itself qualify for zero-rating. In *C & E Commrs v Rannoch School Ltd (1993 STC 389)* the company built a new accommodation block at a school. It was a condition of planning consent that the company replace the sewage treatment plant serving the existing buildings. HMRC contended that the replacement sewerage system was a supply of civil engineering work and thus did not qualify for zero-rating. The High Court upheld the decision of the VAT tribunal that it was zero-rated as a supply in the course of construction of the new residential block, since it was supplied at the same time or shortly after and the new block could not be occupied until the plant was installed. In *Turner Stroud and Burley Construction Ltd (VTD 14454)* a riverside house was built with a boat dock underneath and a stairway connecting it to the living accommodation. It was held that the whole building, of which the dock was a necessary part, was designed as a dwelling; it was not designed partly as a dwelling and partly as a boat store.

8.85 In *Lonsdale Travel Ltd (VTD 12113)* a trader entered into two contracts, one with a developer to acquire a building in course of renovation and a second with a company controlled by him to carry out the renovation work, with the land contract being conditional on completion of the building works and the obligation to pay for the building work being concurrent with completion of the land contract. HMRC contended that there was no supply under the building contract as the arrangements meant that the renovation work had to be completed before either contract came into force, so the sale contract would relate to the completed building. This claim was rejected, the tribunal holding that the agreements were not shams and, except as regards the date of payment, the building agreement was wholly independent of the land contract and was in force before the works were completed.

Relief for Expenditure on Remediation of Contaminated and Derelict Land

8.86 Where a company acquires contaminated, or from 1 April 2009 derelict, land for the purposes of a trade or of a UK property business it is entitled to deduct 150% of the clean up costs in calculating its taxable profits (*CTA 2009, ss 1143–1179* as amended by *FA 2009, Sch 7, paras 1–4*). It should be noted that this relief does not apply to individuals or trusts. If the relief creates a loss, that loss can be used in the same way as any other trading (or property business) loss.

8.87 If the company prefers, it can surrender the loss in exchange for a repayable tax credit of 16% (or such other percentage as the Treasury may by Order specify) (*CTA 2009, s 1154*). As the corporation tax relief would be effectively at 30% (with a 20% corporation tax rate) or 27.5% (with a 19% rate), 16% cash in hand is a substantial discount. Assuming an interest rate of say 5%, the tax credit is beneficial only if the loss is unlikely to be relievable within the next 18 years. The administrative provisions in respect of this tax credit are dealt with at **8.102**. The amount that can be surrendered is obviously the lesser of the unrelieved loss or of 150% of the qualifying land remediation expenditure (see **8.92**). The unrelieved loss is the actual loss less any loss relief that the company is entitled to claim (whether or not it actually does so) under *CTA 2010, s 62(1)–(3)*(relief for a trading loss or a UK property business loss against total profits for the same or earlier accounting periods) or *s 403(1)* (group relief) (*CTA 2009, ss 1151, 1152*). No account is to be taken of property business losses or trading losses brought forward from an earlier accounting period or a trading loss carried back from the next one (*CTA 2009, s 1153(2)*). It is not wholly clear what this means. It is probably that the profits against which a loss is available for relief under *CTA 2010, ss 62, 37* or *99* must not be reduced by losses of another accounting period. In the case of a property business loss of an investment company the unrelieved loss is the lower of:

(*a*) the property business loss for the accounting period; or

(*b*) the amount which falls to be carried forward under *CTA 2009, s 1219(3)(a)* (which is an amalgam of property business losses and management expenses) but after deducting so much of that amount as is brought forward from an earlier accounting period.

8.88 The land must be in the UK (and acquired by the company for the purpose of its trade or property business) and at the time of acquisition all or part of the land must have been in a contaminated state (*CTA 2009, ss 1147, 1149(1)–(4)*). In the case of derelict land, if the land was held at 1 April 1998 and the dereliction occurred before that date this test is regarded as satisfied (*CTA 2009, ss 1147(3), 1149(3)*). The Treasury have power by statutory instrument to alter both of the above requirements (*CTA 2009, ss, 1147(3A), 1149(3A)*). The relief must be claimed (*CTA 2009, s 1149(6)*). It is given in the accounting period in which the expenditure is deductible under the normal corporation tax rules (*CTA 2009, s 1149(5)*). The relief cannot be claimed if the company itself or a person with a relevant connection was responsible wholly or partly, for the contamination (*CTA 2009, s 1150*). A person has a relevant connection for this purpose if he was connected to the company (within *ITA 2007, s 993* – see Appendix 1) either:

(*a*) at the time that something that gave rise to the contamination was done (or omitted to be done);

(*b*) at the time that the land was acquired by it; or

(*c*) when the relevant land remediation work was undertaken by the company (either directly or on its behalf).

(*CTA 2009, ss 1178, 1316.*)

8.89 The reason for this exclusion is not wholly apparent. Clearly a polluter ought to be expected to clean up his pollution without encouragement from the tax system as he already has a statutory obligation to do so. Nevertheless, where pollution occurred in the past when there was no such obligation one would have thought that the landowner should be encouraged to clean it up irrespective of who caused it. A company is also not entitled to relief if the land is contaminated or derelict wholly or partly as a result of something done (or not done) by someone else and that person, or a person connected with him, either holds any interest in the land (or right over it, or licence to occupy it or an option to acquire any such interest) or has previously sold the land (or otherwise disposed of any estate or interest in it) for a consideration which reflects, to any extent, the impact or likely impact on the value of the land of having to remedy the contamination or dilapidation (*CTA 2009, s 1150(a)(3)*).

8.90 The following constitutes relevant contaminated land remediation.

(*a*) The doing of any works (or taking any steps) in relation to the land in question, any controlled waters affected by that land or any adjoining or adjacent land for the purpose of:

  (i) preventing or minimising (or remedying or mitigating the effects of) any harm, or any pollution of controlled waters, by reason of which the land is in a contaminated state; or

  (ii) restoring the land or waters to its former state.

(*b*) Activities preparatory to such work which are undertaken by the company (either directly or on its behalf) for the purpose of assessing the condition of the land (or controlled waters or adjacent or adjoining land).

(*CTA 2009, s 1146.*)

8.91 For this purpose 'harm' means harm to the health of living organisms, interference with the ecological systems of which any living organism forms part, offence to the senses of human beings, or damage to property. Pollution of controlled waters means the entry into such waters of any poisonous, noxious or polluting matter or any solid waste matter (*CTA 2009, s 1179*). 'Controlled waters' has the same meaning as in *Part III* of the *Water Resources Act 1991* (or its Scottish or Northern Irish equivalents) (*CTA 2009, s 1179*). Controlled waters are affected by land in a contaminated state if (and only if) the land is in such a condition by reason of substances in, on or under it that pollution of those waters is being caused (or likely to be caused) (*CTA 2009, s 1179*). 'Substance' for this purpose means any natural or artificial substance, whether in solid or liquid form or in the form of a gas or vapour (*CTA 2009, s 1179*). The interest in the land that the company acquires must be a freehold or a lease of at least seven years (or, in the case of an assignment, for which there are at least seven years unexpired) (*CTA 2009, s 1178A*). The Treasury also have power to exclude activities from qualifying as remediation (*CTA 2009, s 1146(4)*). They have excluded the removal of material which contains (or may contain) Japanese Knotweed from the land to a licensed landfill site and also certain activities required by the *Building Act 1984*, the *Environmental Protection Act 1990* and some of the *Planning Acts* (where these impose a statutory obligation to remedy dilapidation or contamination) by the *Corporation Tax (Land Remediation Relief) Order 2009 (SI 2009 No 2037)*.

8.92 Qualifying land remediation expenditure is expenditure:

(*a*) on land all or part of which is in a contaminated or derelict state (see **8.93**);

(*b*) on relevant land remediation (see **8.90**) directly undertaken by the company or on its behalf;

(*c*) on employee costs (see **8.97**);

(*d*) on materials employed directly in that relevant land remediation (*CTA 2009, s 1172*)); or

(*e*) which is expenditure on sub-contracted land remediation (see **8.98**),

and would not have been incurred had the land not been in a contaminated state and which is not subsidised (see **8.98**) (*CTA 2009, s 1144*).

8.93 Land is in a contaminated state if (and only if), it is in a condition such that 'relevant harm' is being caused (or there is a serious possibility that it will be caused) because of something in, or under the land (*CTA 2009, s 1145(1),(2)*). Relevant harm is the death of (or significant injury or damage to) living organisms, significant pollution of controlled waters (within *Pt 3* of the *Water Resources Act 1991* or its Scottish and Northern Irish equivalent), a significant adverse impact on the ecosystem, or structural or significant damage to buildings or other structures, or interference with buildings or other structures that significantly compromises their use (*CTA 2009, ss 1145(1),(4), 1179*). Harm and pollution of controlled waters are as defined at **8.92**. From 1 April 2009 there is an exclusion where the contamination is by reason of the presence of living organisms, decaying matter derived from living organisms, air or water, or anything else present otherwise than as a result of industrial activity (*CTA 2009, s 1145(2)*). The Treasury can by order cut down the restrictions in *s 1145(2)* (*CTA 2009, s 1145(3)*). They have done so by the *Corporation Tax (Land Remediation Relief) Order 2009 (SI 2009 No 2037)* which allows the relief where the contamination is due to arsenic, arsenical compounds, Japanese Knotweed or radon. It provides, however, that the relief can apply only to that part of the land where such items are present and to expenditure for the purpose of remedying or mitigating the effect of relevant harm covered by such items. In the case of Japanese Knotweed the requirement that the contamination must have been present when the interest in land was acquired does not apply. The obvious example is cleaning up land which has previously formed the site of a gasworks, or chemical manufacture where the soil contains noxious substances and is unsuitable for housing or most commercial development until the land is reclaimed. However, the definition is very widely drawn. It will clearly cover the removal of asbestos in a building.

8.94 Relevant derelict land remediation means activities which comprise the doing of any works, the carrying out of any operations or the taking of any steps in relation to the land, provided that the purpose of the activities is a purpose specified by a Treasury order (*CTA 2009, s 1146A*). Where activities qualify as derelict land remediation, relevant preparatory activities (see **8.89**(*b*)) also qualify (*CTA 2009, s 1146A(1),(5)*). The Treasury have specified the removal of post-tensioned concrete heavyweight construction, building foundations and machinery bases, reinforced concrete pile caps, reinforced concrete basements and redundant services (ie pipes, wiring, cables, tunnels and other similar equipment or infrastructure used in relation to gas supply, water supply, drainage or sewerage, electricity supply and telecommunications) which are located below the ground (*Art 6, Corporation Tax (Land Remediation Relief) Order 2009, SI 2009 No 2037*). In *Dean & Reddyhoff Ltd v HMRC (TC 2767)* the company incurred expenditure on the construction of a marina and claimed relief for work on the construction of a sea wall on the seabed largely surrounding the marina on the basis that the work was for the purpose of protecting the marina buildings from harm by reason of wave, tidal surge and flood damage. HMRC retorted that the land was not in a contaminated state. The Tribunal broke the expenditure down into four elements, the sea wall, the additional sea wall adjoining the land, the plinth constructed on dry land on which the buildings stood, and the storm drains and culverts on the land to divert floodwater from the buildings. It dismissed the HMRC contention that the purpose of the relief is to bring 'brownfield' land in urban areas back into use. It felt that the purpose has to be discerned from the wording of the legislation. It decided that the foreshore is land, albeit that it is sometimes covered with seawater, but the seabed is not land. Accordingly the sea wall could not qualify, but the other items could. It felt that the additional sea wall qualified for land remediation relief as its purpose was to protect from the sea. However, the plinth and drainage was not on land in a contaminated state so could not qualify.

8.95 Land is in a derelict state if (and only if) the land is not in productive use and cannot be put into productive use without the removal of buildings or other structures (*CTA 2009, s 1145A*).

8.96 A nuclear site (one for which a nuclear site licence under the *Nuclear Installations Act 1965* is in force or previously existed and the period of responsibility of the licensee has not yet come to an end) is precluded from being land in a contaminated or derelict state (*CTA 2009, s 1145(2)–(4)*).

8.97 The employee costs attributable to relevant land remediation are the employee costs (salaries, employer's national insurance and pension contributions, but excluding benefits in kind) paid in respect of directors or employees directly and actively engaged in that relevant land remediation (*CTA 2009, s 1171(1),(2)*). Where a director or employee is partly engaged directly and actively in relevant land remediation his costs are apportioned unless he spends less than 20% of his total working time on such work (when no part of the costs are allowed) or over 80% of his time on such work (when the full costs are allowed) (*CTA 2009, s 1171(3),(4)*). Employees providing support services, such as secretarial or administrative services, cannot be directly and actively employed in relevant land remediation even if the whole of their time is devoted to supporting people who work full time in such tasks (*CTA 2009, s 1171(5),(6)*). A pension fund is defined as a scheme, fund or other arrangement established and maintained (whether in the UK or elsewhere) for the purpose of providing pensions benefits (*CTA 2009, s 1170(6)).*

8.98 Expenditure which would not have been incurred had the land not been in a contaminated state includes an increase in expenditure where the increase is incurred only by reason that the land is in a contaminated state, and also the costs of any works, operations or steps taken mainly for the purpose described in *para 3* (see **8.92**) (*CTA 2009, s 1173).* Expenditure is subsidised if a grant or subsidy is obtained in respect of it or it is otherwise met, directly or indirectly, by someone other than the company. A grant, subsidy or payment that is not allocated to particular items of expenditure must be allocated on a just and reasonable basis (*CTA 2009, s 1177*). Sub-contracted land remediation expenditure is of course a payment made to another person (the sub-contractor) in respect of relevant land remediation contracted out by the company to that person (*CTA 2009, s 1175(2)*). Up to 31 March 2009, except where the subcontractor was a connected person the whole of a sub-contractor payment qualified for relief even though it includes overheads and profits that would not qualify if incurred by the company itself (*CTA 2009, s 1176*). This provision was repealed by *FA 2009, Sch 7, para* 20. This may be because it was stating the obvious. The normal wholly and exclusively test presumably now applies. Where the company and the sub-contractor are connected (within *ITA 2007, s 993* – see **Appendix 1**) the payment is qualifying expenditure only to the extent of the sub-contractor's relevant expenditure, (ie expenditure incurred by the sub-contractor in carrying on the activities to which the sub-contractor payment relates which is incurred on employee costs or materials, is not of a capital nature, is not subsidised and is brought into account in determining the sub-contractor's expenditure) for a period for which accounts are drawn up and that ends not more than 12 months after the end of the paying company's period of account in which the sub-contractor payment is brought into account. Relief is also denied if the sub-contractor does not recognise the payment as income within the above period (*CTA 2009, s 1175*). This denies relief both on the part of the payment attributable to the sub-contractor's own profits and overheads and on any further amount that the sub-contractor carries forward in work in progress for over 12 months.

8.99 If qualifying land remediation expenditure (see **8.92**) is capital expenditure, the company can elect for it to be allowed as a deduction in computing profits unless it qualifies for capital allowances. Such an election will trigger the 150% relief under *para 12*. The deduction is given in the accounting period in which the expenditure is incurred. If the company has not commenced its trade at that time it is given in the accounting period in which the trade commences. The election must be in writing, must specify the accounting period in which it is made and must be given within two years after the end of the accounting period to which it relates (*CTA 2009, s 1147*).

8.100 Where a company claims a land remediation tax credit (see **8.102**) HMRC can, instead of paying it, set it (and interest on it) against any outstanding corporation tax liabilities. If the company owes PAYE and National Insurance for periods ending within the accounting period HMRC are not entitled to offset it against such tax but need not pay the tax credit until the PAYE has been paid. If the company's tax return for the relevant period is enquired into they do not have to repay the credit until the enquiry is completed (*CTA 2009, s 1155*). A land remediation tax credit is of course not income for any tax purposes (*CTA 2009, s 1156*). The loss surrendered for the credit obviously cannot be carried forward; nor can expenditure included in it be claimed as a deduction in calculating a capital gain in respect of the land (*CTA 2009, ss 1157, 1158*).

8.101 No enhanced deduction (or tax credit) can be claimed to the extent that a transaction is attributable to arrangements (which includes any scheme, agreement or understanding whether or not legally enforceable) entered into wholly or mainly for a disqualifying purpose. Nor can the election to treat capital expenditure as revenue be made for such expenditure. Arrangements are for a disqualifying purpose if their main object, or one of their main objects, is to enable a company to obtain:

(*a*) a deduction for capital expenditure which would not otherwise be allowed (or would otherwise have been smaller);

(*b*) land remediation relief to which the company would not otherwise be entitled; or

(*c*) a land remediation tax credit to which it would not otherwise be entitled.

(*CTA 2009, s 1169.*)

8.102 A land remediation tax credit carries the same interest as that on overpaid tax. Interest runs from the filing date (as defined in *FA 1998, Sch 18, para 14*) of the corporation tax return for the accounting period for which the credit is claimed (or from the date the return is actually filed if it is filed late). A claim for the tax credit must be made by being included in a company tax return (which will include an amended return) (*FA 1998, Sch 18, paras 10(2A)* and *83A*). The amount claimed must be quantified at the time the claim is made (*FA 1998, Sch 18, para 83I*). A claim can be withdrawn or amended but only by amending the tax return. A claim, amendment or withdrawal must be made by the first anniversary of the filing date for the company tax return (or within such later time as HMRC allow) (*FA 1998, Sch 18, paras 83J, 83K*). A fraudulent or negligent claim for a land reclamation tax credit attracts a penalty of up to 100% of the credit (*FA 1998, Sch 18, para 83*).

8.103 Special rules apply to insurance companies. These are not considered here. They are contained in *CTA 2009, ss 1159–1168*.

Chapter 9

Refurbishments

Income and Corporation Tax

9.1 If refurbishment work is carried out by a person who holds the building as dealing stock the expenditure will normally be revenue expenditure. It will be added to the cost of the building as stock-in-trade and will be deductible when the building is sold. Exceptionally, part may constitute repairs where the building has been let, but the costs of establishing the split will not always be justified.

Is the Expenditure Capital or Revenue?

9.2 Where a building is held as an investment, refurbishment work can be either revenue or capital. If it is capital it will normally constitute enhancement expenditure for capital gains tax purposes. The problems lie in differentiating between the two.

9.3 In general, works will be capital if they constitute improvements or the replacement of the entire asset. They will be revenue if they constitute repairs or the replacement of part of an asset. If by carrying out improvements the need for repairs is obviated the whole of the cost will nevertheless be capital; the notional figure of what the repairs would have cost cannot be deducted as a revenue expense (*William P Lawrie v CIR (34 TC 20)*; *Curtin v M Ltd (3 ITC 227)*). If, however, the improvements constitute the most practical way of restoring the building to its original condition they might be regarded as repairs (see **9.10** below). Unfortunately, the dividing line between improvements and repairs is often difficult to discern and the only real conclusion that can be drawn from the cases that have come before the courts seems to be that the decision in a particular case will depend upon its own individual facts. Nevertheless, it is helpful to consider the cases to try to bring out the main factors that need to be considered.

9.4 The two leading cases on the dividing line between repair and improvement are *Law Shipping Co Ltd v CIR (12 TC 621)* and *Odeon Associated Theatres Ltd v Jones (48 TC 257)*. In the *Law Shipping* case a company purchased a second-hand ship as it was about to start a voyage. When it reached port it was not allowed to leave until extensive work was carried out. It was held that the works were works of improvement. In effect the company had not bought a seaworthy ship; it had bought a dilapidated ship. The works were works of improvement as, when they were finished, the company had something of a different nature to that which it had purchased. In *Odeon Associated Theatres* the company acquired a number of cinemas during and immediately after the war. Due to wartime restrictions, repairs and redecorations, which would normally be done on a regular basis, had not been carried out. The state of disrepair on acquisition had, unlike in the *Law Shipping* case, not affected the price paid for the cinemas and the company operated them as cinemas for months to years before the repair work was carried out. It was held that the work was repairs not improvements.

9.5 It is likely that the two cases both represent extremes. In *Law Shipping* the ship could not be used as a ship at all (or virtually at all) without carrying out the works. In the *Odeon* case the works were desirable but not essential to enable the buildings to be used as cinemas. The repaired asset was the same asset as when it was in disrepair, not something different improved out of all recognition. Where works are carried out shortly after the acquisition of a building HMRC are likely to raise *Law Shipping* to demonstrate that they are capital. It is unlikely to be sufficient to defeat such a claim to show that the premises were usable on acquisition if subsequently the purchaser carried out refurbishment works before letting the premises or taking occupation. This suggests that they were not usable for the purpose for which he acquired them, which is much nearer the *Law Shipping* end of the line than the *Odeon* end. However, if the purchaser actually occupies the premises for several months before carrying out the work, HMRC's claim should be resisted strongly because this demonstrates that the premises were suitable for the use for which they were acquired and is much nearer the *Odeon* end of the line. In *Jackson v Laskers Home Furnishers Ltd (37 TC 69)*, a company took a lease of dilapidated premises at a peppercorn rent for the first year but under a lease containing a covenant to reinstate the premises. Even though the premises were usable, it is not surprising that the expenditure on reinstatement was held to be capital because, as in *Law Shipping*, it is clear that the premises were acquired cheaply in contemplation of the repairs needing to be carried out. This case is not authority for regarding dilapidations as capital if the premises were in reasonable repair when the lease was taken on by the trader.

9.6 The distinction between the two kinds of replacement is brought out by *Samuel Jones and Co (Devonvale) Ltd v CIR (32 TC 513)* and *O'Grady v Bullcroft Main Collieries Ltd (17 TC 93)*. In the *Samuel Jones* case a factory chimney became unsafe. It was demolished and replaced. It was held that the chimney was an integral part of the factory and the factory after the replacement was the same asset as before. Accordingly, the work was merely repairs. *Bullcroft* also involved a chimney. In this case it was a separate structure and not part of a building. It was demolished and a new chimney built a short distance away to replace it. It was held that the new chimney was not a repair of the old. It was a separate new asset. The cost was therefore capital.

9.7 Again the two cases are opposite ends of a line. The test applied in both was the same. Is the item replaced 'an entirety' or is it merely part of something larger? If it is an entirety, its replacement brings about a new asset. If it is not an entirety, its replacement is probably merely the repair of the larger asset which incorporates it. Unfortunately, it is not always easy to identify the entirety. In *Wynne-Jones v Bedale Auction Ltd (51 TC 426)* it was held that a cattle ring forming part of a large cattle mart was an entirety and could not be regarded as a mere part of the mart; in *Brown v Burnley Football & Athletic Co Ltd (53 TC 357)* it was held that a stand at a football ground was an entirety and not a mere part of the ground. However, in an Irish case, *Hodgkins v Plunder & Pollak (Ireland) Ltd (3 ITC 135)*, it was held that a weighbridge which was separate from the main factory building was not an entirety. It was a small part of the factory premises as a whole.

9.8 In *Auckland Gas Co Ltd v CIR [of New Zealand] (2000 STC 527)* the Privy Council made clear that what is a repair is not to be found by any rigid test or description but depends on a consideration of all the circumstances. For many years Auckland Gas had a mainly low-pressure network of underground cast iron pipes. These had a life of around 100 years but were prone to some major problems, leakage of gas and the entry of water, which occurred at joints in the pipes, fractures in the mains and corrosion of the pipes to individual premises. Auckland Gas developed a technique of inserting a polyethylene pipe into the existing cast iron mains and service pipes. Not only did this significantly reduce the maintenance problems but it enabled the gas to be transmitted at a much higher pressure. The courts accepted that if maintenance work had been done on the pipes the cost would have been deductible. But what had been done could not realistically be regarded merely as a repair of the network. 'For a leaky cast iron and steel low pressure system which it was not worthwhile renovating there had been substituted a system constructed of a new and different material, operating at a much higher pressure … The old mains and services no longer performed any function save protecting the polyethylene pipe against vibration and ground movement. That could not fairly be described as a method of fixing the faulty joints and corrosion.' Lord Nicholls pointed out that 'the desire to solve a maintenance problem is not inconsistent with carrying out work of a capital nature. The nature and extent of the work carried out not the physical assets are what is determinative of the character of the work. The fact that the method chosen is the cheapest and most effective is neutral. It does not deprive expenditure of its capital character.

Replacing an object may be cheaper and better than patching and mending.' By contrast in *Transco plc v Dyall (2002 STC (SCD) 199) (SpC 310)* the similar insertion of polyethylene pipes into existing cast iron gas mains was held to be a repair. In this case, the company had a policy of identifying pipes most at risk and inserting polyethylene into those pipes before a failure actually occurred. Furthermore, the replacement was not of whole pipes. Neither did it enable the pipeline system to transport a different type of gas or to function at a higher pressure, nor did it increase the useful life of the system.

9.9 Finally, it should perhaps be mentioned that whilst alterations, particularly structural alterations, are normally regarded as capital, this is not an inviolate rule. In *Conn v Robins Bros Ltd (43 TC 266)*, a company carried on business in premises which were over 400 years old. It carried out various works including strengthening a floor and replacing the shop front having eliminated a bow front. It was held that the whole of the work was repairs. In light of the age of the building and modern building techniques, structural alterations may be the most efficient and effective way of restoring the building to its original condition. Support for this principle can also be found in *Transco plc v Dyall (2002 STC (SCD) 199)* (see **9.8**).

9.10 In practice, the expenditure involved in most refurbishments will not fit wholly into one category. It is necessary to look in detail at the work done and analyse it between capital and revenue items. In most cases part of the capital items will qualify for capital allowances as plant and machinery, so the expenditure normally has to be split into three categories: repairs, plant and machinery, and other improvement work. HMRC issued a guidance note in October 2004 on the tax effect of work carried out to comply with the *Disability Discrimination Act 1995*. It is on the Gov.UK website (www. gov. uk) and gives some useful guidance on the capital/revenue divide.

Should Landlord or Tenant Incur the Expenditure?

9.11 It is sometimes optional whether expenditure on repairs is incurred by the landlord or occupier. In particular, where property is refurbished prior to letting and certain works are required by the tenant, it can sometimes be better from a tax point of view to allow him a rent-free period – and possibly pay a reverse premium to cover the costs – and leave him to carry out the work himself. As the test of whether an item is plant is whether it performs a business function, it is often difficult for the landlord to establish items as plant whereas if the tenant installs them for the specific needs of his own business, he may have a far stronger case. If all the work does not need to be carried out immediately, the tenant may also be in a stronger position than the landlord to claim that work carried out a few months later is repairs.

9.12 Where major works need to be carried out during the continuance of a lease, it should also be borne in mind that the tenant is likely to be in a position to claim tax relief at an earlier date than the landlord. The landlord's profit rental is more likely to be smaller, in relation to the cost of the works, than the tenant's profits. The tenant can also carry a trading loss backwards and, if it is a member of a group, can surrender it by way of group relief, whereas the landlord can only carry a UK property business deficiency forward – unless it is a company, when it has greater flexibility.

Where a registered social landlord, such as a housing association, takes over property in a dilapidated state from a Local Authority, it is common to enter into a VAT scheme to recover the VAT on the refurbishment costs (see **16.178**). This scheme puts the obligation to carry out the works onto the Local Authority and has the effect of converting repairs into capital for corporation tax purposes.

Effect on Time Apportionment

9.13 Following the rebasing of capital gains to 31 March 1982, it seems likely that most gains on properties will be calculated by reference to 31 March 1982 value, so that the old-time apportionment rules, which gave rise to a problem, will now not often apply. However, it should not be overlooked that they can sometimes still do so. Time apportionment no longer applies for individuals and trusts on disposals after 5 April 2008. It does still apply for corporation tax though. The difficulty is that the time apportionment rules required the gain on a pre-1965 property to be apportioned to blocks of expenditure by reference to their respective costs (*TCGA 1992, Sch 2, para 16(4)*), which could operate disadvantageously.

Example 9.1

A property cost £50,000 on 6 April 1945. A refurbishment was carried out in 1983 at a cost of £100,000 and the building was sold on 5 April 2010 for £1,000,000. If the refurbishment had not been carried out it would have realised £700,000. Indexation is ignored.

	£	£
Sale proceeds		1,000,000
Cost	50,000	
Enhancement expenditure	100,000	
		150,000
		£850,000

	£
Taxable (ignoring indexation)	
50/150 × £850,000 × 45/65ths	254,998
100/150 × £850,000	566,667
	£821,665

If the refurbishment had not been carried out the position would have been:

	£
Sale proceeds	700,000
Cost	50,000
	£650,000
Taxable 45/65ths	£450,000

The additional profit generated by the refurbishment was £200,000 but the chargeable gain has increased by £371,665.

If the taxpayer does not claim relief for the refurbishment costs the position would be:

	£
Sale proceeds	£1,000,000
Cost	50,000
	£950,000
Taxable 45/65ths	£657,692

9.14 The ideal position would therefore be to carry out the refurbishment but not to claim relief for the costs. Can this be done? The answer is unclear. The amount of a gain accruing on a disposal must be computed in accordance with *TCGA 1992, Part II (TCGA 1992, s 15(1))*. Unfortunately, that does not say how a gain is computed. It merely lays down how to arrive at the disposal consideration and the deductions. In particular *s 38* provides that 'the sums allowable as a deduction … shall be restricted to' specified types of expenditure. This wording does not seem apt to force someone to deduct an amount if he opts not to do so. *Paragraph 16(4)* of *Sch 2* refers to 'any of the expenditure which is allowable as a deduction in the computation'. If *s 38* does not force the taxpayer to claim expenditure, is it still allowable as a deduction in the computation if it is not claimed? HMRC's view is that as the *Act* does not require a claim, all expenditure falling within *s 38* must be deducted.

However, the Court of Appeal has held in the case of *Elliss v BP Northern Ireland Refinery Ltd (59 TC 474)*, which deals with capital allowances – where the legislation reads 'where a person incurs capital expenditure … there shall be made to him … an allowance' – that the taxpayer did not have to accept the allowances if he did not want them, and the wording of the legislation in that case seems far more mandatory than that of *s 38*. It seems doubtful that a taxpayer could be faulted for not claiming a deduction for expenditure if he does not want to. It is difficult to believe that, if he does not know the amount of all his expenditure, the legislature should have intended that he should be forced to undertake a lot of work to ascertain such information.

9.15 It should be remembered that the legislation provides a small measure of relief from this problem in some cases. If there is no initial expenditure (ie cost of the asset), or such expenditure is disproportionately small as compared with any of the items of enhancement expenditure (having regard to the value of the asset immediately before the enhancement expenditure was incurred), the gain can be apportioned to the blocks of expenditure by reference to the values at that time, and the part attributable to the initial acquisition of the asset treated as arising over the period from the time of that acquisition (*TCGA 1992, Sch 2, para 16(5)*). In practice, HMRC seem reluctant to accept that this provision can be used unless the cost is very small in comparison with enhancement expenditure. It should be particularly noted that the comparison is with cost, not the value of the building immediately before the enhancement expenditure is incurred, eg if a building cost £50,000 in 1950 and enhancement expenditure of £30,000 is incurred in 1986 when the value of the original building is, say, £400,000, the *section* would not apply, as although £30,000 may be small in relation to £400,000, it is not disproportionately small in relation to £50,000.

VAT

General Principles

9.16 Refurbishment, however major, is not the construction of a building. Accordingly the refurbishment of residential and relevant charitable buildings cannot attract zero-rating. Equally as the finished development will not be a 'new' building the disposal or grant of leases after development will be exempt from VAT. The 20% VAT charge that applies on the disposal of a new building (see **17.23** below) does not apply. Refurbishment for this purpose includes the extension, enlargement, or reconstruction of an existing building. The dividing line between the reconstruction of a building and the construction of a new one is not always clear. HMRC's guidance on this is set out in **8.49** above.

9.17 Accordingly, a developer carrying out a refurbishment is not normally in a position to claim relief for input tax he suffers on his expenditure unless he exercises the option to tax (see **17.126**). VAT on refurbishment costs is thus an additional cost of the development. Because of this, when carrying out a refurbishment, consideration needs to be given to making this election to bring the building into the VAT net. In theory, if the most likely tenant or purchaser for a building will be a taxable person he should not mind paying VAT on his rent or acquisition cost as he will be able to recover this from HMRC. The occasion of a major refurbishment calls for a review of an initial decision not to elect, as the tax at stake is likely to be significant. In most cases it is likely to make sense to make the election at that stage.

Listed Buildings

9.18 There is a common misconception that work on a listed building (or other protected building) is zero-rated if the building is a residential or relevant charitable one. In fact the zero-rating is now very limited. It applies only to the substantial reconstruction (or, up to 1 October 2012 only, approved alteration) of a protected building (*VATA 1994, Sch 8, Group 6*). A protected building is a building which is a listed building within the meaning of the *Planning (Listed Buildings and Conservation Areas) Act 1990* (or the corresponding Scottish or Northern Irish legislation) or a scheduled monument within the meaning of the *Ancient Monuments and Archaeological Areas Act 1979* (or the *Historic Monuments Act (Northern Ireland) 1971*). (*VATA 1994, Sch 8, Group 6, Note 1*). The building must be designed to remain as (or become) a dwelling (or a number of dwellings), or be intended for use for a relevant residential or relevant charitable purpose (see **16.49** and **16.59** below) after the reconstruction or alteration. A building is designed to remain as (or become) a dwelling only if each dwelling within it consists of self-contained living accommodation, there is no provision for direct internal access from the dwelling to any other dwelling (or part of one) and the separate use or disposal of the dwelling is not prohibited by a covenant, statutory planning consent or similar provision (*VATA 1994, Sch 8, Group 6, Note 2*). ESC 3.29 (which ignored minor non-qualifying use) applied to determine whether a building is used solely for a relevant charitable purpose but this was withdrawn from 1 April 2010. This is considered at **16.128**. The Upper Tribunal in *HMRC v Lunn (2010 STC 486)* considered *Note 2* in some detail. It felt that the wording, 'the separate use ... is not prohibited' means separate from another dwelling rather than distinct use, such as use by a separate household from that using the other dwelling. Accordingly a planning condition that a new dwelling within the curtilage of Radbrook Manor could be used only for purposes incidental or ancillary to the residential use of the Manor denied zero-rating for the new building. The First-tier Tribunal had taken the view that, as the new building consisted of self-contained living accommodation, its distinct use as a residence was not prohibited by the planning condition. The Upper Tribunal felt that the Tribunal decision in *Dr Nicholson* (see **16.37**) was out of line with other cases and had incorrectly applied the distinct use test.

9.19 A garage occupied with a dwelling and constructed at the same time as the dwelling (or on a substantial reconstruction of the dwelling) is regarded as part of it (*Note 2*). In *Grange Builders (Quainton) Ltd* a timber-framed barn was altered to become a garage. It was accepted that the barn was constructed at the same time as the house and was occupied with it. The tribunal accepted evidence that the barn had been used since 1996 or earlier exclusively as a garage for two cars. It was thought that the barn was probably originally constructed to hold carts or a gig. The first outbuilding for a motor vehicle was built in 1898, but coach-houses of older houses were adapted as garages from around that time. Customs contended that the barn was not constructed as a garage so could not fall within *Note 2*. The tribunal felt that a non-residential building converted to a building to store one or more motor vehicles can plainly be a garage, notwithstanding that it was not constructed as such. The tests in *Note 2* require only that:

(i) a building for the storage of a motor vehicle is occupied with a dwelling; and

(ii) that it was constructed at the same time as the dwelling.

There is no third requirement that it must have been constructed as a garage. Following this case, Customs have said that they now accept that zero-rating applies where a building was in use as a garage both before and after the reconstruction (Business Brief 11/05). It is difficult to draw such a proviso from the judgment, ie the fact that the Grange garage had been used as a garage for many years was not part of the reasoning behind the decision.

9.20 From 1 October 2012 the only item that qualifies for zero-rating is the first grant by a person substantially reconstructing (see **9.26**) a protected building (or by some other person if the benefit of the consideration accrues to the reconstruction) of a major interest (see **8.33** above) in, or in any part of, the building or its site. It should particularly be noted that it is only the owner of the building that can zero-rate his supply. The builder has to charge VAT.

9.21 Up to 30 September 2012 the following also qualified for zero-rating:

(*a*) The supply, in the course of an approved alteration (see **9.37**) of a protected building, of any services other than the services of an architect, surveyor or any person acting as consultant or in any supervisory capacity.

(*b*) The supply of building materials (which has the same meaning as in **8.28**) to a person by a supplier who *also supplies* to the same person *services* within *(a)* above which include the incorporation of the materials into the building.

(*VATA 1994 Sch 8, Group 6.*)

Zero rating for items 2 and 3 above was repealed by *FA 2012, Sch 26, paras 3, 7(3)*, subject to the following transitional rules.

9.22 In *Trevivian v HMRC (2015 SFTD 184)* (see **9.33**) the FTT felt that where a house is built with an integral garage, or is built without a garage and an attached garage is later added to the house, the alteration or construction of the garage is an alteration to the protected building. However, if the house is built without a garage and a detached garage is added subsequently, the garage is not within item 2. If the detached garage is added as part of a substantial reconstruction of the listed building, the addition of the garage is not itself an alteration but in relation to any subsequent alteration, the protected building includes the garage. Unfortunately they went on to find that the subsequent alterations altered the garage only, not the listed building

9.23 Zero-rating continued to apply until 1 October 2015 to a supply of services (other than excluded services) made in the course of an approved alteration to a protected building, and to a supply of building materials made in conjunction with services which include the incorporation of the materials into the building (or its site) in question, pursuant to a written contract entered into, or a relevant consent applied for, before 21 March 2012 (*FA 2012, Sch 27, para 7(4)*). For this purpose any works carried out that were not within the scope of the written contract (or the consent applied for) as it stood immediately before 21 March 2012 could not be regarded as made pursuant to the contract or consent (*FA 2012, Sch 27, para 7(8)*). Excluded services were the services of an architect, surveyor or other person acting as a consultant or in a supervisory capacity (*FA 2012, Sch 27, para 7(9)*).

9.24 For supplies between 1 October 2012 and 30 September 2015 a protected building was regarded as substantially reconstructed if either:

(*a*) at least 60% of the work carried out to effect the reconstruction (measured by reference to cost) were of such a nature that the supply of services (other than excluded services), materials and other items to carry out the works would, if supplied by a taxable person, have fallen within the above transitional rule; or

(*b*) at least 10% (measured by reference to cost) of the reconstruction of the protected building was completed before 21 March 2012 and at least 60% of the works carried out to effect the reconstruction would have come within (*a*) but for the requirement for a written contract to have been entered into, or relevant consent applied for, before that date.

9.25 An anti-forestalling charge applies on a 'pre-change' supply which was treated as taking place on or after 21 March 2015 and is 'linked to the post-change period' (*FA 2012, Sch 27, para 2*). A pre-change supply was a supply in the course of an approved alteration of a protected building, or of services, other than the services of an architect, surveyor or any person acting as consultant or in a supervisory capacity, and to the supply of building materials to a person to whom the supplier was supplying services in the course of an approved alteration of a protected building which included the incorporation of the materials into the building (or its site), which was treated as taking place before 1 October 2015 and, if it had taken place after that date, would have been taxable as a result of the amendments made by *FA 2012, Sch 26* (*FA 2012, Sch 27, paras 1, 3*). For this purpose a right to receive a supply included any option to receive it and any interest deriving from such an option (*FA 2012, Sch 27, para 3(3)*). A supply of services was linked to the post-change period if (and to the extent that) the services were carried out or provided after 30 September 2015. A supply of building materials was linked to the post-change period if (and to the extent that) they were incorporated into the building concerned (or its site) after 30 September 2012 (*FA 2012, Sch 27, para 5*). The amount of the anti-forestalling charge was of course an amount equal to VAT at 20% of the supply (reduced proportionately if it was not wholly linked to the post-change period) (*FA 2012, Sch 27, para 7*). The purpose of this provision was to prevent services being prepaid or goods purchased and delivered in advance. However, it seemed to require the builder to count the bricks on site but not yet used at close of business on 30 September 2012 and impose a VAT charge on their cost.

Substantial Reconstruction

9.26 A building is not to be regarded as substantially reconstructed unless, when the reconstruction is completed, the reconstructed building incorporates no more of the original building (ie as it was before construction began) than the external walls, together with other external features of architectural or historic interest (*Note 4* as substituted by *FA 2012, Sch 26, para 3*).

Prior to 1 October 2012 a building was substantially reconstructed if either:

(*a*) at least 60% (by cost) of the work carried out (excluding the cost of an architect, surveyor, etc.), would, if supplied by an independent contractor, be within (*a*) and (*b*) in **9.21** above; or

(*b*) the reconstructed building incorporates no more of the original building than the external walls, together with other external features of architectural or historic interest (*Note 4*).

The latter suggests either that the then government felt that we have no interiors worthy of preservation or that conservation is all very well but tax maximisation is far more important. To fall within head (*a*) at least 60% of the works carried out would have had to require listed building consent. In many cases it is only the exterior of a building that is listed, whereas the bulk of the building work is likely to be the interior. Accordingly this test is not always as easy to meet as it appears at first sight.

9.27 *Notes 1, 4, 6 12–14* and, up to 30 September 2012, *22–24* of *Group 5* (see **16.6** and **16.23–16.24** below) also apply for the purpose of *Group 6* (*VATA 1994, Sch 8, Group 6, Note 3*). Curiously the deemed disposal provisions where a building ceases to be used for a qualifying purpose (**16.122–16.123** below) do not apply to *Group 6*.

9.28 Most of the cases deal with what is an approved alteration, but there are a number where the issue is whether there was a substantial reconstruction. *TR Bates (VTD 2925)* and *Vivodean Ltd (VTD 6538)* both failed to meet the 60% test. So did *D Barraclough (VTD 2529)*, although the tribunal there felt that the renovation work carried out did not amount to reconstruction at all. *Belvedere Properties (Cheltenham) Ltd (VTD 18351)* failed because it produced no evidence to support either the 60% test or the shell/gutting test, and some of the work took place before the listed building consent was obtained. *ADJ Lee (VTD 5887)* failed because he had omitted to obtain the necessary listed building consent and he gave no evidence of the cost of the works, but the tribunal in any event felt that the works (which cost £900,000) pointed towards repairs and maintenance rather than reconstruction. In *WB Church (VTD 12427)* the tribunal felt that the works constituted the alteration of a listed building by the addition of an extension to, and the carrying out of various improvements and renovations to, an existing building, rather than a reconstruction. The issue in *Ian Mason (VTD 12406)* was not whether there had been a substantial reconstruction – Customs accepted that there had been – but how much of the input tax was disallowable because Mr Mason had himself occupied the building as a residence for a period prior to its being offered for sale.

9.29 The tribunal in both *Lordsregal Ltd (VTD 18535)* and *Southlong East Midlands Ltd (VTD 18943)* spelled out that the legislation imposes a two-stage test, namely has the building been substantially reconstructed and, if so, has the condition in Note 4 (the 60% test or the shell/gutting test) been met. In *Lordsregal* the tribunal defined 'substantially reconstructed' as a matter of impression based on the evidence. As the original building in that case was virtually uninhabitable and the evidence was that it might well have blown down in a severe storm, their overwhelming impression was that it was substantially reconstructed. It also felt that it met the 60% test. Customs contended that only 44% of the costs qualified. They arrived at this by going through the works line by line and differentiating between repairs and other work. The tribunal thought this the wrong test. The supplies must be 'in the course of' an approved alteration, which requires a broader perspective than taking each item in isolation and trying to categorise it. Supplies can be in the course of an approved alteration even though in other contexts they might be described as repairs. In *Southlong*, although the 60% test was met, the tribunal did not agree that this would automatically amount to substantial reconstruction. It felt that the ordinary meaning of 'reconstruction' is 'the construction anew of something that was already there'. It accordingly looked at the building as a whole both before and after the works and decided that the work, which cost £150,000, was not reconstruction at all but was more in the class of 'minor enlargement of the building and a modernisation of its interior'.

9.30 In *Dr NDF Browne (VTD 11388)* a VAT tribunal held that where the most effective repair or maintenance of an old building involved the use of modern methods or different building materials it was still a repair, not an alteration. A similar decision was reached in *C & E Commrs v Windflower Housing Association (1995 STC 860)* where a replacement roof was constructed to a higher specification and designed with a view to a possible future attic conversion. Even raising the roof pitch was held to be an integral part of the remainder of the work. In *C & E Commrs v C R Morrish (1998 STC 954)* the tribunal noted that the listed buildings legislation referred to 'works for alteration or extension of the building in any manner affecting its character as a building of special architectural or historic interest' and concluded that 'in any manner' gave 'alteration' a wide meaning that is not limited to structural alteration and so was able to distinguish the case from the *Windflower* one. It held that any items that altered the building in any manner that affected its character attract zero-rating. It also felt that the reconstruction works (after a severe fire) were too extensive to be excluded as repairs or maintenance, although it did disallow repairs to the outer walls under that head. On appeal Moses J said that the Tribunal had applied the wrong test. The statute requires consideration of three categories, reconstruction, alteration and repair and maintenance. Only alteration is zero-rated. If what was happening, viewed as a whole, was a supply in the course of rebuilding or reconstruction, it was standard-rated. The case was remitted to a fresh tribunal to find out whether there was any building in existence at all after the fire, as if there was not there could be no alteration. He gave a broad hint that Mr Morrish could then argue for zero-rating under what is now *Group 5* of *Sch 8*. The case appears to have been settled without the need for a further hearing.

9.31 In the case of *Vicar and Parochial Church Council of St Petroc Minor* (*VTD 16450*) work to stop damp penetration through part of the vestry wall of a listed church was held to be maintenance. Any element of alteration was an incidental result of such maintenance. This can be contrasted with the decision in *All Saints with St Nicholas Church, Icklesham (VTD 16321)* where the work to a church was held to be an approved alteration not repair or maintenance as it was the complete replacement of the existing lighting system. The vagaries of the legislation seem well illustrated by the decision in *C Mason (VTD 16250)*. Mr Mason replaced two lengths of boundary fence by walls. The first abutted the listed building and ran up to a hedge. The second ran from the other end of the hedge to some outbuildings. The first part of the wall was held to be part of the listed building but the second part was held to be a structure separate from the listed building so that its construction could not be an alteration of that building. It should, however, be noted that in *HMRC v Tinsley* (see **9.51**) Laddie J felt that the correctness of this decision must be in doubt following the *Zielinski Baker* case (see **9.47**).

9.32 The meaning of 'substantially reconstructed' was considered by the tribunal in *Cheltenham College Enterprises Ltd v HMRC ([2010] UKFTT 2010; [2010] SFTD 696).* The tribunal noted that there had been a divergence of views between different tribunals. It felt that the correct approach was to interpret the phrase 'substantially reconstructed', but bearing in mind that substantially normally means at least more than 50%. Having done so is then necessary to look at *Note 4* to determine whether, although the building has been substantially reconstructed using its everyday meaning, Parliament intended to exclude it from relief. It thought that the tribunal in *Barraclough* (see **9.28**) had applied the wrong test as it had looked at reconstruction as the initial test and then asked itself whether the reconstruction was substantial. The tribunal in *Cheltenham* felt that a building could be 'substantially reconstructed' without being 'reconstructed', so looking at the two words separately limited the relief more than Parliament had intended. It approved the approach taken in *Lordsregal* (see **9.29**) which had looked at the entire phrase. Applying this test it decided that in *Cheltenham* 'a substantial part of the building was substantially reconstructed (and in places wholly reconstructed)'. It then looked at the cost of the works, which was almost as much as that of a rebuild, to reinforce its view that the works amounted to a substantial reconstruction. The Tribunal in *Brunswick Properties Ltd (TC 3726)* held that the house there had not been substantially reconstructed despite meeting the 60% test. It categorised a large part of the work as ordinary repair or renovation following years of neglect, opining that 'it would need to be a truly exceptional case for repair as such to amount to reconstruction' for planning purposes.

9.33 The Tribunal in the later case of *Trevivian (2015 SFTD 184)* took a different view. They felt that in order for there to be a substantial reconstruction, there must be a reconstruction; something must be taken away and then put back. In that case there had been an earlier substantial reconstruction of the listed building in the 1980s. There was a further reconstruction in 2010. As part of that, a garage (which was built at the time of the 1980s reconstruction), which was about four yards from the house, was demolished and rebuilt. The Tribunal held that the garage was not part of the listed building. Accordingly its demolition and rebuilding could not be part of the reconstruction of the listed building; albeit that it was a reconstruction of the garage. The test is whether there has been an alteration *to* a protected building, not one *relating* to such a building. The other work in 2010 involved the demolition of outbuildings but left the dwelling itself unaffected. Accordingly the work was standard-rated.

9.34 It should be noted that whether or not a listed building qualifies for zero-rating will depend on its intended use after conversion. For example, the conversion of a listed windmill into a house can qualify but the conversion of a listed almshouse into offices would not do so, even if it had retained its residential use up to the time of conversion. At least this seems to be the intention, but it is a somewhat odd use of English to say that a windmill built in 1690 was 'designed to … become a dwelling' if work is carried out on it in 1990 to adapt it for use as a dwelling. It is 'intended' to become a dwelling after the substantial reconstruction. The substantial reconstruction is designed to change the building into a dwelling. It seems doubtful if the windmill itself was designed to become a dwelling. Conversely, the almshouse in the other example when built would have been designed to become a building for use for a relevant residential purpose, even though after the substantial reconstruction it would no longer be so used!

9.35 The timing of the work can be important. In *R W Gibbs (VTD 5596)* asbestos insulation was removed from pipework in the roof of a listed building. The owner had applied for listed building consent for the work but it was completed before the consent was formally granted. The VAT tribunal held, *inter alia*, that as consent had not been obtained at the time the work was carried out the work did not satisfy the definition of 'an approved alteration'. This was followed in *Alan Roper & Sons Ltd (VTD 15260)* where the tribunal said that a retrospective planning permission is in effect consent to retention of the alterations. A similar conclusion was reached in *Mr & Mrs Wells (VTD 15169)* where as the work progressed some of the planned (and approved) work proved impractical. Listed building consent for such modifications was applied for and granted retrospectively. It was held that zero-rating could not apply as such approval did not exist at the time the work was done. This seems very harsh. Other cases dealing with listed buildings can be found under the section on Do-It-Yourself Builders at **16.184**.

9.36 It was similarly held in *Dart Major Works Ltd (VTD 18781)*, where urgent demolition work was carried out with the approval of both the Conservation Officer and the Council's building control officer, who both felt that it should start as soon as possible because of the risk of collapse, with retrospective consent being subsequently granted, could not qualify. In that case the owners built a new house on the footprint of the old, using as much as possible of the salvaged materials, which enabled the tribunal to hold that it was not a reconstruction of the listed building and that the demolition work was a necessary part of the construction of the new house and thus qualified for zero-rating under the self-build rules (see **16.184**).

Approved Alterations

9.37 An approved alteration to a building is:

(*a*) works of alteration to a building used for ecclesiastical purposes (excluding use as a minister of religion's residence);

(*b*) works of alteration for which consent has been given under *Historic Monuments Act (Northern Ireland) 1971, s 10*; or

(*c*) works of alteration which cannot (or could not but for a Crown or Duchy interest) be carried out without consent under *Planning (Listed Buildings and Conservation Areas) Act 1990* (or the Scottish or Irish equivalents) or *Ancient Monuments and Archaeological Areas Act 1979, Part I*, and for which consent has been duly obtained (*VATA 1994 Sch 8, Group 6 Notes 6* to *8*).

Works of repair or maintenance cannot be an approved alteration though. Nor can an incidental alteration to the fabric of a building resulting from carrying out repairs or maintenance.

9.38 The objective is to prevent claims that, for example, the repair of a roof is an alteration because the use of modern building methods and materials has changed the pitch of the roof (VAT Information Sheet 10/95). This did not prevent the VAT tribunal in *N F Rhodes (VTD 14533*), where 65% of a roof was in disrepair so the entire roof was replaced, from holding that the remaining 35% of the cost that had been incurred for purely aesthetic reasons to restore the appearance of the whole roof qualified for zero-rating. In contrast in *Metropole (Folkstone) Ltd (VTD 19917)* the reinstatement of a balcony that had earlier been demolished for safety reasons, whilst clearly an alteration to the building as it stood before the balcony's construction, was held to be a repair to the building as a whole and thus not eligible for zero-rating. The new balcony was built of different materials to the old but to comply with the planning consent was designed to look identical as far as possible. In *ACT Construction Ltd v C & E Commrs (1982 STC 25)* the House of Lords held that the words repair and maintenance are not to be construed as being in antithesis to one another. The phrase 'repair or maintenance' is a single composite phrase and in many cases there may well be an overlap between repair and maintenance – and between 'structural alterations' and 'repair or maintenance'. The court decided to try to define the phrase saying that they are ordinary words in common use to be given their ordinary meaning. The relationship between alteration and repair was considered in *Parochial Church Council of St Luke v C & E Commrs (1982 STC 856* – see **8.44**). Where only part of any work is an approved alteration an apportionment must be made (*VATA 1994, Sch 8, Group 6, Note 5*). Similarly an apportionment is made if a service partly in relation to an approved alteration and partly for some other purpose (*Note 9*).

9.39 Even where listed building consent is obtained, HMRC have been known to claim that it was not needed and that therefore head (*c*) above is not met. For example, in *E C Owen (VTD 18660)* they sought an opinion from a different planning officer from the one who had granted the consent. In that case the tribunal made clear that whether it is needed is a question of fact for it to decide, and that the views of the planning department do not bind the tribunal.

9.40 The *Planning (Listed Buildings and Conservation Areas) Act 1990, s 6(2)* prevents a local authority from serving a building preservation order for five years from the date of issue of an immunity certificate by the Secretary of State for National Heritage. This is intended to give the owner an opportunity to carry out preservation work without the added burden of planning controls. However, it also means that **9.37**(*c*) cannot be satisfied, so a person applying for an immunity certificate in effect forfeits the VAT relief. This makes application for an immunity certificate unwise in many cases. Where an immunity certificate was issued before 1 March 1996, HMRC were, by concession, prepared to allow the relief as if condition (*c*) were met but now that they have highlighted the problem they expect applicants for immunity certificates to take into account the resultant loss of VAT relief (News Release 25/96).

9.41 First make sure that you have a building. *Calver Weir Restoration Project (2011 SFTD 1001)* was a charity which owned Calver Weir, a scheduled monument. The weir was constructed in the late eighteenth century to support the wheelhouse at Calver Mill (which has since been converted to dwellings so it is no longer dependent on the weir). The Tribunal held that the weir is not a building and that as *Note 1* to *Group 6* defines a '"Protected building" as a building which is … intended for use solely for a relevant charitable purpose' the charity fell at the first hurdle. At first sight this decision appears to give no effect to the inclusion of a scheduled monument within the zero-rating category. Most people would not regard a building as a 'monument'. However, the *Ancient Monuments and Archaeological Areas Act 1979* contains a definition of a monument which begins, 'any building, structure or work …'. Accordingly, it is possible that in referring to a building which is a scheduled monument, parliament intended to restrict the relief to the small number of scheduled monuments which consist of buildings. The wording is particularly odd as the *Ancient Monuments and Archaeological Areas Act 1979* specifically excludes a dwelling (other than a caretaker's flat) from being a scheduled monument. In the case of Calver Weir, the Tribunal also felt that even if the weir could have been a building, the bulk of the work was repair and maintenance, not alteration. In *E L Flood & Sons (TC 1842)* the planning authority required the bedroom ceilings to be returned to their original constituents of lathe and plaster instead of replacing damaged plasterboard ceilings that had been erected 40 years earlier. HMRC contended that this was a repair, but the tribunal held that it was an alteration as it arose solely from the authority's requirements, albeit that the current ceiling needed repairing.

9.42 HMRC take the view that an approved alteration must amount to an alteration of the building's fabric. This test was dismissed in *Mrs A Wynne Adams (VTD 18054)* where it was held that the demolition of an old retaining wall to prevent an eighteenth-century house from collapsing down a hill and the construction of a new one 2.5 metres nearer the house and with piles 12 metres deep to support it was an approved alteration not, as HMRC had contended, a repair. In *C & E Commrs v Viva Gas Appliances Ltd (1983 STC 819, [1983] 1 WLR 1445, [1984] 1 All ER 112, HL)* the House of Lords held that 'alteration' included any work upon the fabric of the building except that which was so slight or trivial as to be *de minimis*. HMRC accept that mains electrical wiring and lighting systems are part of the fabric of a building to the extent that they are in or on the structure of the building itself. Items that extend beyond the structure, such as wiring to floodlights in the grounds of churches will not attract zero-rating. Nor will electrical appliances that are attached to and serviced by the mains supply (Business Brief 7/00). In *E C Owen (VTD 18660)* the tribunal held that the construction of hand-built fitted wardrobes 12 feet high and 28 inches deep in a bedroom amounted to an alteration, applying the *Viva Gas* test. In *Chameleon Mirrors Ltd (VTD 20640)* the installation of slab mirrors was held to amount to an alteration. These are similar to a mirror tile but are much longer. The tribunal felt that HMRC had made the mistake of looking at the mirrors in isolation (they regarded the work as maintenance) rather than looking at the project as a whole).

9.43 When considering whether a supply in the course of an approved alteration of a protected building, and services other than the specified professional services, qualify for zero-rating (under *item (i)* in **9.19** above), the construction of a building separate from, but in the curtilage of, a protected building is not to constitute an alteration of that building (*VATA 1994, Sch 8, Group 6, Note 10*). The meaning of curtilage is considered in **13.9**(*d*) below. HMRC stated that the effect is to exclude from zero-rating such items as a new workshop in the grounds of a listed dwelling. This exclusion only prevents the new building qualifying for zero-rating under *Group 6*. It might, of course, still qualify for zero-rating in its own right under *Group 5* (residential and relevant charitable development). HMRC give as an example the erection of a new dwelling in the grounds of a listed hospital. It should be borne in mind, though, that *Group 5* is not apposite to cover the erection of a building which is not itself a dwelling but is designed for use with a dwelling, eg a residents' sun lounge in the garden of an old people's home.

9.44 In any event, what is a separate building is a question of fact. In *Martyn Arbib (VTD 11486)* the VAT tribunal held that a swimming pool building separated from the main house by a brick wall but connected by a walkway with a roof and open sides was not a separate building but an alteration to the house. The decision was upheld in the High Court. This decision can be contrasted with the later decision in *Collins and Beckett Ltd (VTD 19212)* where the facts were similar. In that case the covered walkway and the swimming pool were held to be an extension to the house but only the walkway qualified for zero-rating as photographs gave the impression of two buildings linked by a glazed corridor; the swimming pool was not itself a protected building and so was excluded by *Note 10*. In *Ventrolla Ltd (VTD 12045)* where a replacement window was claimed to be an improvement the tribunal held that the view of the planning authority that it was an alteration requiring listed building consent was not conclusive. There was no alteration to the fabric of the building and, even if the window was an alteration, it was an alteration to the window not the building. In *Barry Moore (VTD 18653)* it was similarly held that replacing a single-glazed window with a double glazed one was not an alteration.

9.45 In *C A Orme (VTD 9975)* a VAT tribunal held that the extent of the protected building could include buildings not physically attached to the main house but so close as to form an integral part of it. This was a question of fact and degree. However, a later tribunal held in *C M Lee (VTD 10662)* held that this cannot apply after 31 December 1991. A similar decision was reached in *PVR Nicholls (VTD 11115)*, where it was held that a door in the passageway between the two buildings, thus linking the two, did not justify the conclusion that the secondary building was affixed to the existing one so as to amount to an alteration to it rather than the construction of a separate building. The tribunal in *N Hardy (VTD 12776)* felt that the *Orme* principle still applied. In that case it was held that the outbuilding and the house together formed one dwelling which was a protected building. It was also accepted, applying *Pepper v Hart (1992 STC 898)*, that when the legislation was amended it had been Parliament's intention to preserve zero-rating for domestic buildings. A similar decision was reached in *G M Morfee (VTD 13816)* where work on a barn within the curtilage of a listed building (but not specifically mentioned in the listing) was held to be in the course of an approved alteration to the main building as the two constituted a single entity which was a protected building used as the owner's dwelling. However, in a more recent case *A J & L Kernahan (VTD 15203)* where conversion work was carried out on outbuildings to a listed farmhouse, the Tribunal relied on the *Orme* decision in holding that the outbuildings were not an integral part of the dwelling constituted by the main house. In *Dr A Heijn (VTD 15562)* it was accepted that converted outbuildings were within the curtilage of the house and formed part of the listed buildings but the work was held not to be eligible for zero-rating as there was insufficient evidence to show that before the work was carried out the outbuildings had been an integral part of the house so as to 'remain' part of the dwelling after the alteration.

9.46 The *Orme* decision was also followed in *D & L Clamp (VTD 16422)* where it was accepted that a converted barn was part of the main house, although as its separate use was prevented by a planning agreement the building work did not qualify for zero-rating. A curious decision was reached in *R G Powell (VTD 14520).* Mr Powell was a metalworker specialising in architectural metalwork. He was commissioned to cast and erect iron railings and gates to enclose a churchyard to discourage use of the churchyard by vagrants, etc. The church was a listed building. The railings were not affixed to the church but for part of the way were affixed to an existing stone wall. The tribunal held that the stone wall was a structure within the curtilage of the church so was part of the listed building. Accordingly the part of the railings attached to the wall was entitled to zero-rating but the balance was not. This decision seems curious because if the remainder of the railings were within the curtilage of the church it would be logical to regard their erection as much an alteration to the listed building as the part that altered an existing structure within its curtilage. It should, however, be mentioned that in *HMRC v Tinsley* (see **9.51**) Laddie J stated that the correctness of this decision must be in double following the *Zielinski Baker* case (see **9.37**). In *D L Wilson (VTD 15803)* where the taxpayer obtained listed building consent to reconstruct his garage the work was held to be the 'construction' of a separate building falling within *Note 10.*

9.47 The issue finally came before the courts in *C & E Commrs v Zielinski Baker & Partners Ltd (2004 STC 456)* where the House of Lords held (Lord Nicholls dissenting) that the building on which the work is carried out has to be a building that is designed to remain, or become, a dwelling house and it also has to be a listed building (2004 STC 456). The House of Lords decision in that case was handed down on 26 February 2004. Tribunal decisions prior to that date (VTD 18600 and earlier) need to be approached with caution as they may not have applied the correct legal principles. Zielenski Baker are property developers. In 1994 they were instructed to prepare and oversee a scheme for a development within the ground of a listed building. The scheme included some elements which were accepted as taxable. The disputed items were the conversion of an outbuilding into games and changing facilities and the construction of an adjoining indoor swimming pool. Zielenski Baker claimed that these should be zero-rated as approved alterations to a protected building. The outbuilding was (and always had been) linked to the house by a wall and was built at the same time as the house. Listed buildings consent was necessary for the works as the outbuilding was within the curtilage of a listed building, and this was duly obtained.

9.48 Lord Hoffmann dealt with the problem extremely succinctly: 'Note (1) (to *Group 6, item 2, Sch 8, VATA 1994*) defines a protected building by reference to two propositions both of which must be true. First it must be "a building which is designed to remain as or become a dwelling house".

Secondly, it must be a "listed building" … The actual outbuilding to which the alterations in this case were made was not designed to remain as or become a dwelling house. It was designed to be a games room, changing room and swimming pool. It therefore did not satisfy the first part of the definition'. Lord Walker of Gestingthorpe felt that the statutory fiction in the *Planning (Listed Buildings and Conservation Areas) Act 1980* that a listed building must be taken to include (as part of it) a separate structure built before 1 July 1948 within its curtilage could not reflect back onto 'a building' in the *VATA 1994* so as to extend the natural meaning of that simple expression. He felt not only that that gave an unnatural construction to the language but also that it did not fit easily with the European dimension which sought to limit zero-rating to a social housing objective. Lord Brown of Eaton-Under-Heywood pointed out that 'although part of a building may be a listed building, a part of a listed building cannot itself be a listed building' (*Shimizu (UK) Ltd v Westminster City Council [1997] 1 All ER 481*).

9.49 In *Lord and Lady Watson of Richmond (VTD 18903)* the taxpayers sought to distinguish themselves from *Zielenski Baker* on the grounds that the outbuilding was integral to the main building as it was built at the same time and it was linked to it by a high wall. Also it was converted into a guest bedroom, and as such could be readily adapted to become a dwelling in its own right. Sadly, none of this found favour with the tribunal. In *N P Smith (VTD 19064)* the work was carried out to an Oast house ancillary to a main house. Mr Smith sought to distinguish the case from *Zielenski Baker* on the grounds that the Oast house was itself a listed building. Sadly he failed because the planning permission prevented its use separate from the main house and, as it was nevertheless itself a dwelling, the tribunal held it could not form part of the main house so that the main house was not being altered. The taxpayer in *MIM Construction Ltd (TC 3504)* did manage to distinguish his case from *Zielenski Baker*. The new building was a stand-alone building within the curtilage of a large manor house with a number of outbuildings. Its use was held to be ancillary to the dwelling house but also ancillary to some of the other buildings. HMRC contended that that barred zero-rating, but the Tribunal held that once it was found to be ancillary to the dwelling, the work satisfied the statutory test.

9.50 In *K & G Levell (VTD 6202)* an old wall enclosed a kitchen garden of a listed building. A new building was erected on the outside of the wall in the style of a cart shed. The old wall was joined to the roof and gutters of the new building and although it formed the rear of, it was not part of, the supporting structure. It was held that the construction of the new building on its own separate foundation was not an 'alteration' of the wall and thus did not qualify for zero-rating. Alteration does not apparently need to be substantial. The VAT tribunal in *Wrencon Ltd (VTD 13968)* felt that the word had to be construed in the context of the planning law which required approval for any alteration which affected the building's character. This did not imply a structural alteration. It therefore felt that the painting of the outside walls which were previously unpainted was capable of qualifying for zero-rating. In that particular case they felt the work was repair as it was carried out in the context of general repairs and maintenance. *In C N Foley (VTD 13496)* changes to the height and ridges of the roof on a 13th century house were held to be alterations even though the change in the profile of the building viewed from below was slight. In *Dodson Bros (Thatchers) Ltd (VTD 13734)* re-thatching two listed buildings with Norfolk reed was held to be alterations as the different appearance of the thatch affected the character of the building. It is probably relevant that the roof was not in need of repair; in the first case it was wished to install a fire barrier and in the second it was wished to cure leakage around windows in the thatch. In *Parochial Church Council of Holy Trinity Church, Wolverhampton (VTD 13652)* works on the installation for the first time of electrical fittings was held to be an alteration to the building but where the work merely involved the repositioning of a light or where lights were installed on fittings such as the lectern rather than the fabric of the building zero-rating did not apply.

9.51 The correctness of some of this line of cases may be in doubt following *HMRC v Tinsley (2005 STC 1612)*. The case concerned the construction of a terrace at a protected building. The terrace came right up to and joined the house. Laddie J agreed with HMRC that, following the *Zielinski Baker* approach (see **9.47**), the alterations were done to the building not the house. Furthermore, the work carried out in the garden left it as part of the garden. HMRC conceded that each case needs to be considered on its facts. Just because work is carried out in a large part to an area of what is or was a garden, does not mean of itself that it is impossible for it to be considered as an alteration to the building. Mr Owen *(TC 3384)* lived in a listed building. He built a substantial garage abutting the house to house his collection of classic cars. He claimed that the work should be zero-rated as an approved alteration to the house. HMRC contended that as there had been no substantial reconstruction of the house, the construction of the garage did not fall within Group 6. They relied for support on a 2004 VAT Tribunal decision, *Sherlock and Neil Ltd (VTD 18793)*. The Tribunal held that the house was altered by the addition of an extension, which happened to be a garage. There is no need to read the final words of Note 2 (a dwelling includes a garage – see **9.19**) if, as in this case, the relevant tests are satisfied by the house. This decision conflicts with HMRC's published guidance, so casting doubt on its correctness.

9.52 In *C & E Commrs v Jeffs and another t/a J & J Joinery (1995 STC 759)* the appellants carried out joinery work off site to a customer's specific requirements and delivered it to the site where it was fitted by the customer's builders. The appellant made an initial site visit to take measurements and there was an implied obligation to make further site visits if any problems arose with their handiwork. HMRC's contention that the work was not entitled to zero-rating under what is now *item 2* of *Group 6* (see **9.19**) as it was a supply of goods without services was upheld by the court (reversing the decision of the VAT tribunal). Whether there is only a supply of goods or separate supplies of goods and services is a question of law, the answer to which is to be obtained by the application of common sense to the substance and reality of the matter as the court perceives it. In this case the services were nothing more than the normal obligations imposed by law upon any seller of goods. In *M E J Burgess and A P Holmes (VTD 14475)* the supply and fitting of individually-made display units in a shop, none of which were free-standing, was held to be a supply of services to which the goods were incidental. The tribunal accepted HMRC's view that the shop-fitting works were not dissimilar to the work of painting a room, where the paint is not a separate supply of goods!

9.53 In *Nick Hopewell-Smith (VTD 16725)* a barn was converted for use as residential accommodation ancillary to a Grade II listed farmhouse. It was 11 metres from the house and had been used for storage. After conversion the barn was physically capable of being occupied as self-contained living accommodation and there was no provision for internal access from the barn to the house. The tribunal noted that, although the planning consent prevented separate use, it did not prohibit the separate disposal of the house. Accordingly *VATA 1994, Sch 8, Group 6, Note 2(c)* (that separate use of the building is not prohibited – see **9.18**) did not apply as the two tests were expressed in the alternative. The building was in fact used by the family who occupied the house. The tribunal (Stephen Oliver QC) nevertheless held that the work qualified for zero-rating either because, notwithstanding that it was separated from the house, the barn could be described as a building designed to be part of a dwelling consisting of self-contained living accommodation or because it was such a dwelling in its own right.

9.54 The taxpayer was similarly lucky in *Hill Ash Developments (VTD 16747)*. Hill Ash carried out building work on a house and associated farm buildings purchased for use as a nursing home. The house was a listed building but the farm was not. The house was used as the nursing home. The listed building consent was for extension to the nursing home and conversion of agricultural buildings to form care flats and an administration block. The tribunal held that the disputed work was a conversion of the administration block and could not qualify for zero-rating as a supply in the course of construction of a dwelling under *VATA 1994, Sch 8, Group 5*. However, it did qualify for zero-rating as supplies in the course of approved alterations to a protected building. Although the administration block did not contain sleeping accommodation its use was so intimately bound up with the residential accommodation provided by the house and a new barn block as to constitute use for a relevant residential purpose following *Hardy* (see **9.45**). As the work did not involve the construction of a building it was unnecessary to decide whether the administration block was separate from the protected building.

9.55 In *Carson Contractors Ltd (TC 4679)* where a listed barn within the curtilage of a listed building was converted to provide additional living accommodation for the house, a *TCPA 1990, s 106* agreement called it an annexe and provided that it could only be used in conjunction with the main house as ancillary accommodation. The taxpayer contended that the accommodation was ancillary and thus part of the new house but the Tribunal held that it could not be ancillary as it was a separate dwelling. The Tribunal said that even if the two buildings together could be regarded as a single building, the test as to what is a dwelling looks at the motive of its design, not its use. As separate disposal of the new dwelling is prohibited by the planning consent, it no longer meets the definition of a protected building, albeit that it is listed. This seems a somewhat startling result but it is a decision of Hillier J, who is a very experienced chairman.

9.56 In the same way as for *Group 5*, the exclusion from zero-rating as an approved alteration for services consisting of the use of an item where there is no transfer of ownership but merely a transfer of an undivided share in the item, or possession of it, and for items which are acquired for use in a business but appropriated for private use (see **16.109**(*c*)), apply (*VATA 1994, Sch 8, Group 6, Note 11*).

Other Matters

9.57 I have dealt with the cases on new residential buildings in **Chapter 8** as these seem to me to be a feature of development, those on listed buildings in **Chapter 9** as the work is normally in the course of a refurbishment, and what is a building in **Chapter 17**. This inevitably results in some cases that may be relevant to a particular issue being dealt with under one of the other heads. It might therefore be helpful to highlight the court decisions and also the relationship between relationship between court and tribunal decisions. These are accordingly summarised at **16.47**. VAT Tribunal decisions made before a court decision in the same area need to be approached with caution as the tribunal would not have had the benefit of the judges' views.

Chapter 10

Allowances for Capital Expenditure

10.1 Capital allowances are granted in respect of capital expenditure incurred on qualifying assets. It is normally (although not always) necessary for the person claiming the allowances to own the asset and to have incurred the expenditure attracting the allowance. As the expenditure must be capital expenditure, allowances cannot be claimed in respect of expenditure on an asset that constitutes dealing stock (*CAA 1990, s 159(1)*). A detailed consideration of all the capital allowances rules is outside the scope of this work. This chapter deals with capital allowances only in the particular context of the ownership of property. In a property context, capital allowances can be claimable under the following provisions:

(*a*) Plant and Machinery (*CAA 2001, ss 11–270*) (see **10.2**).

(*b*) Industrial Buildings (*CAA 2001, ss 271–360*) (to 31 March 2011) (see **Appendix 4**).

(*c*) Agricultural Buildings and Works (*CAA 2001, ss 361–393*) (to 31 March 2011) (see **Appendix 4**).

(*d*) Qualifying Hotels (*CAA 2001, ss 271(3), 285(1), 317*) (to 31 March 2011) (see **Appendix 4**).

(*e*) Commercial Buildings in Enterprise Zones (to 31 March 2011) (*CAA 2001, ss 271(1), 281, 298, 299, 302, 303*) (see **Appendix 4**).

(*f*) Flat conversions (*CAA 2001, ss 393A–393W*) (to 5 April 2013) (see **Appendix 4**).

(*g*) Renovation of Business Premises (*CAA 2001, ss 360B–360Z4*) (see **10.165**).

(*h*) Research and Development (*CAA 2001, ss 437–451*) (see **10.191**).

(*i*) Certain Fire Safety Expenditure (to 31 March 2008) (*CAA 2001, ss 27, 29*) (see **Appendix 4**).

(*j*) Thermal Insulation of Existing Buildings (*CAA 2001, ss 27, 28*) (see **10.197**).

(*k*) Certain Expenditure on Sports Stadia (*CAA 2001, s 27(1), 30–32*) (to 5 April 2013) (see **10.199**).

(*l*) Cemeteries & Crematoria (*CTA 2009, s 146*) (see **10.200**).

(*m*) Dredging (*CAA 2001, ss 484–489*) (see **10.200**).

(*n*) Mines and Oil Wells (*CAA 2001, ss 394–436*) (see **10.200**).

(*o*) Certain expenditure on security (*CAA 2001, s 33*) (see **10.199**).

Capital allowances can, of course, also be claimed on equipment used in the management of property (see **2.32** above).

Plant and Machinery

Introduction

10.2 Much of the expenditure in relation to a modern building relates to items that constitute plant or machinery. A taxpayer is entitled, if he wishes, to isolate such expenditure and claim the appropriate capital allowances provided, of course, that he satisfies the appropriate conditions. This is relatively easy with a new building as the cost of plant is known. Accordingly the only issue is as to what constitutes plant. It is often not appreciated that capital allowances apply as much to a building that is purchased second-hand as to the construction of a new building. When a person buys the freehold of an existing building he is acquiring an amalgam of three things, the land, the building and the plant and machinery included in it. The overall cost can be apportioned between these three elements. On average around 12% of the purchase price of a non air-conditioned late 1970 office building is likely to qualify for capital allowances. In a modern air-conditioned building the eligible proportion will be far greater. An interesting article on the principles involved can be found in Taxline, February 1996.

10.3 In many cases (but not all) the allowance for plant is based solely on the price the purchaser pays for the building; the initial cost of installing the plant is irrelevant. Obviously the apportionment depends on valuation techniques and requires a knowledge of building construction, so needs to be done by an architect or quantity surveyor. There are substantial restrictions on what items in a building can constitute plant (see **10.75–10.82**). It is believed that this statutory limitation is in response to a claim by one of the major supermarket groups before the Special Commissioners that an entire supermarket and its adjoining car park qualifies as plant. A very helpful and comprehensive checklist of the items in a building that might qualify for capital allowances as plant or machinery was published in Taxation of 18 November 1993 (pages 148–150). Although this was prepared before the *Finance Act 1994* changes, most of the items are still relevant.

10.4 Normally, capital allowances can be claimed only where the taxpayer has incurred the capital expenditure on the plant and machinery for the purposes of a trade carried on by him (*CAA 2001, s 11(4)*). Allowances are also due where the expenditure was for the purposes of a profession, employment, vocation or office (*CAA 2001, ss 15(1)(e), 80*). From 6 April 2012 (1 April for corporation tax) capital allowances on fixtures in a purchased building can be claimed only if specified formalities are adhered to. These are considered at **10.107** onwards.

10.5 Of equal, if not greater, importance in a property context is that the leasing of plant or machinery otherwise than in the course of a trade qualifies for capital allowances – irrespective of whether or not the lessee is carrying on a trade – except where the machinery or plant is let for use in a dwelling house (*CAA 2001, ss 15(1)(h), 19*). *Section 15(1)(h)* is not restricted to cases where the letting is solely of plant or machinery; it will accordingly equally apply where a building which contains plant and machinery, such as lifts or central heating, is let so that the letting embraces such items. Indeed, leasing of plant or machinery as such would normally constitute a trade and would not need the extension provided by *section 15(1)(h)*, so the provision in practice applies primarily to the letting of buildings.

10.6 There is a specific exclusion for plant and machinery for use in a dwelling house (*CAA 2001, s 35*). HMRC have said that they consider study bedrooms in university halls of residence and similar buildings are dwelling houses but accept that communal areas, such as a kitchen or TV room for use by a number of occupants and stairs and corridors are not. Nor is an attic or basement which contains a boiler or air conditioning equipment as tenants do not have access to them (HMRC Brief 66/2008). HMRC subsequently said that from 22 October 2010 they consider that the distinctive characteristic of a dwelling house is its ability to afford to those who use it the facilities required for day-to-day private domestic existence. As far as university halls of residence are concerned, where the kitchen and dining facilities are physically separate from the study bedrooms and may not always be accessible to students, they are probably not dwelling houses, but cluster flats or houses in multiple occupation that provide the facilities necessary for day-to-day private domestic existence (such as bedrooms with en-suite facilities and a shared or communal kitchen/diner and sitting room) are dwelling houses (HMRC Brief 45/2010, Capital Allowances Manual CA11520). HMRC have said that this guidance applies for capital allowance purposes only. However, it is obviously a useful guide for other tax purposes.

Allowances Available

10.7 Expenditure on plant and machinery can qualify for either the annual investment allowance (AIA) or writing down allowance of 18% pa (20%

before 1 April 2012) on the reducing balance, ie on the written-down value at the beginning of the period. In the chargeable period bridging 1 April 2012 (6 April for income tax) the writing down allowance was calculated on a day-to-day basis (to two decimal places) (*FA 2011, s 10(9)(10))*. Balancing charges can arise where an asset is disposed of for a price in excess of the written-down value of all of the plant and machinery in that particular building (which will normally only occur on the sale of the building) and a balancing allowance can arise where the building is sold (but only in the comparatively rare circumstance where the part of the sale proceeds attributable to the plant is below its written-down value). Expenditure is normally pooled (see 10.20) to calculate the allowances. A separate pool must be retained for certain specified types of expenditure which attract a reduced writing down allowance of 8% (see **10.19**). If the balance of either pool falls below £1,000 an allowance equal to the whole of the pool can be claimed instead of the normal writing-down allowance (*CAA 2001, s 56A*).

10.8 The annual investment allowance (AIA) is given for qualifying expenditure up to a maximum of £200,000 (£25,000 prior to 1 January 2013, £250,000 prior to 1 April 2014 and £500,000 prior to 1 January 2016) (proportionately reduced or increased if the chargeable period is other than 12 months). (*FA 2013, s 7*). The Treasury have power by statutory instrument to amend the figures (*CAA 2001, s 51A(1),(4)–(6),(8)*). The allowances in the chargeable periods that bridge a change in rate are calculated separately for the two parts of that period and aggregated. However, relief for expenditure in the second part of the period is limited to the amount calculated for that period (*FA2014, Sch 2, para 1*).

10.9 The allowance for expenditure in the second deemed accounting period being limited to the maximum calculated for the period, ie the appropriate percentage of £200,000 (*FA 2014, Sch 2, para 4*).

Example 10.1

Widgets Ltd prepares accounts to 31 March each year. It incurred expenditure on plant and machinery of £400,000 in the nine months to 31 December 2015 and £120,000 in the three months to 31 March 2016.

The annual investment allowance for the year to 31 March 2016 is:

9/12 × £500,000 + 3/12 of £200,000

= £375,000 + £50,000 = £425,000

However, it can only claim £50,000 of the allowance against the post-31 March expenditure.

Example 10.2

Manufacturing Ltd also has a 31 March year end. Its expenditure is £40,000 up to 31 December 2015 and £70,000 in the following three months.

The allowance is again £425,000.

However, it can only claim £50,000 against the post-31 December 2015 expenditure.

As the expenditure in the first nine months was only £40,000, its annual investment allowance is limited to £90,000.

Note: The above apportionments have been done on the basis of months. Strictly, they ought to be done on the basis of days.

10.10 Where the annual investment allowance has to be shared (see below) only chargeable periods of a year or less are taken into account. If there is more than one such period, only that which gives rise to the greatest maximum amount is used. Any chargeable period that is longer than a year and which ends in 2016/17 is to be treated as a period of one year ended on its actual accounting date (*FA 2011, s 11(9)(10)*). In other words, if any of the relevant entities has a 12-month period, the AIA is calculated by using whichever accounting date falls earliest in 2016/17.

Example 10.3

Joe wholly owns three companies. They have different accounting dates, namely 28 February, 30 April and 30 September respectively, but all prepare accounts for 12 months.

The chargeable period that will give rise to the greatest allowance is the year to 28 February 2017, ie 11/12 × £500,000 plus 1/12 × £200,000. The annual investment allowance to be shared in the transitional year is accordingly £458,333 + £16,667 = £475,000.

There may be a trap here. Suppose, for example, the expenditure was as follows:

Company 1: £20,000 to 31 December 2015 and £30,000 thereafter

Company 2: £10,000 to 31 December 2015 and £12,000 thereafter

Company 3: £ 5,000 to 31 December 2015 and £20,000 thereafter

The actual allowance will be restricted to £51,667 because of the limitation on post-31 December 2015 expenditure. If the allowance could be based on the year to 30 April, the allowance would have been 8/12 × £500,000 plus 412 × £200,000 = £333,333 + £66,667 but there would have been no restriction as the post-31 December 2015 expenditure is below £66,667.

10.11 Similar rules applied on the transitions at 31 December 2012 and at 31 March 2014. For the latter, there were three deemed accounting periods applied to a period that straddled 1 April 2014 (6 April for income tax):

(a) the part (if any) of the straddling period as fell before 1 January 2013;

(b) the part (if any) of that period which fell between 1 January 2013 and 31 March 2014; and

(c) the part falling after 31 March 2014.

(FA 2014, Sch 2, para 1.)

The maximum allowance for expenditure in period (*a*) was what would have been due if the allowance had remained at £25,000. The maximum for expenditure in period (*b*) was that amount that would have been due if the allowance had remained at £250,000 *(FA 2014, Sch 2, paras 2, 3)*.

10.12 A trust and a partnership which includes a company or a trust as a partner, are not eligible for the AIA (*CAA 2001, s 38A(3)*). The AIA must be claimed. However, it is not necessary to claim the full allowance. If the claim is restricted the balance of the expenditure will qualify for a writing-down allowance. The AIA allows the full amount of the expenditure to be deducted from profits of the year to which it relates. It cannot be claimed in the chargeable period in which the trade or other qualifying activity is discontinued. Nor can it be claimed if the provision of the plant or machinery is connected with a change in the nature or conduct of the trade or business carried on by someone other than the person incurring the expenditure and the obtaining of an AIA is the main benefit (or one of the main benefits) which could reasonably be expected to arise from the making of the change (*CAA 2001, s 38B*).

10.13 These rules also apply where **10.14–10.18** below (groups of companies and multiple trades), which provide for a single allowance to be split between different persons or trades, applies. However, in applying those provisions, if there are different accounting periods involved, the single allowance is based on the one that gives the greatest allowance. If any of the periods exceeds 12 months, it must be treated for that purpose for 2012/13 to 2016/17 as if it were a period of 12 months ending on the date it actually ends (*FA 2013, Sch 1, para 5; FA 2014, Sch 2, para 5*).

10.14 A group of companies is entitled to only one AIA but can allocate this to group companies in any way it wishes. The *Companies Act 2006, s 1162* definition of a group applies for this purpose (*CAA 2001, s 51C*). A single company which carries on more than one trade or other qualifying activity can similarly decide how it wishes to allocate its AIA between those trades (*CAA 2001, s 51B*). If two or more groups of companies are both controlled by the same person in a financial year and related to one another, they must share a single AIA between them (*CAA 2001, s 51D*), as must other companies which are under common control and related to one another (*CAA 2001, s 51E*).

10.15 For this purpose a company or group is controlled by a person in a financial year if it is controlled by that person at the end of its chargeable period ended in that financial year. Control means the power to secure by means of the holding of shares or the possession of voting power in relation to the company or any other company, or as a result of any power conferred by the Articles of Association or other document regulating the company (or any other company) (or in the case of a company which is not a body corporate conferred by the constitution of the company), that the affairs of the company are conducted in accordance with the controller's wishes (*CAA 2001, s 51F*).

10.16 A company is related to another company in a financial year if either:

(*a*) at the end of the chargeable period of one or both of them ending in that financial year they carry on qualifying activities (ie activities that attract capital allowances) from the same premises; or

(*b*) more than 50% of the turnover of both companies for their chargeable period ending in that financial year is derived from qualifying activities within the same NACE classification,

(*CAA 2001, s 51G.*)

Groups of companies are related if any company in one group is related to any company in the other (*CAA 2001, s 51G(3)*).

10.17 The NACE classification is the first level (headings identified by an alphabetical code) of the common statistical classification of economic activities in the EC established by *Regulation (EC) No 1893/2006*. This is:

A. Agriculture, forestry and fishing.

B. Mining and quarrying.

C. Manufacturing.

D. Electricity, gas, steam and air conditioning supply.

E. Water supply, sewerage, waste management and remediation activities.

F. Construction (which includes demolition and construction installation activities).

G. Wholesale and retail trade and repair of motor vehicles and motor cycles.

H. Transportation and storage.

I. Accommodation and food storage activities (which includes hotels, other accommodation, restaurants, mobile food service and beverage serving activities).

J. Information and communication (which includes publishing, film production, broadcasting, computer programming and consultancy and data processing).

K. Financial and insurance activities.

L. Real estate activities.

M. Professional, scientific and technical activities.

N. Administrative and support service activities (which includes employment agencies, travel agencies, cleaning, landscape services, call centres and packaging activities).

O. Public administration and defence, compulsory social security.

P. Education.

Q. Human health and social work activities.

R. Arts, entertainment and recreation (which includes gambling and betting activities, sports, museums, and fitness facilities).

S. Other service activities (including membership organisations, repairing goods, dry-cleaning, laundering and other beauty treatment, funerals and physical well-being activities).

T. Activities of householders or employers and undifferentiated goods and services producing activities of households for own use.

U. Activities of extra territorial organisations and bodies.

It will be seen that some of these classifications are very widely drawn and will include very disparate activities.

10.18 A single AIA must also be shared where two or more qualifying activities are carried on by a single person (other than a company), controlled by the same person, and related to one another (*CAA 2001, s 51H*). For this purpose an activity is controlled by a person in a tax year if it is controlled by him at the end of the chargeable period for the activity which ends in that year.

In most cases this will be the end of the taxpayer's accounting year ending in the tax year. A qualifying activity carried on by a partnership is controlled by the person (if any) who controls the partnership. A person controls a partnership if he has the right to more than half its assets or more than half its income. If the partners between them control another partnership the two must be treated as controlled by the same person (*CAA 2001, s 51I*). Curiously this seems to ignore actual control such as voting control. The meaning of related is the same as at **10.10** (*CAA 2001, s 51J*). Additional rules apply where the allowance is restricted, and for short accounting periods and those exceeding 12 months (*CAA 2001, ss 51K–51N*).

10.19 All of the plant and machinery owned by a person is pooled. A writing-down allowance can be claimed on the balance of the pool at the start of the accounting period (or the basis period for the relevant year of assessment) plus the additions during that period that have not attracted AIA. The writing-down allowance is 18% pa on the reducing balance (20% prior to 2012/13 onwards) (*CAA 2001, s 56*). The writing down allowance is 8% pa (10% prior to 1 April 2012) for integral features (see **10.85**), long-life assets (see **10.139**) background plant (see **10.84**) and thermal insulation (see **10.197**). These are pooled together in a separate 'special rate pool'.

10.20 A balancing charge or allowance can also arise (*CAA 2001, s 56(6)(7)*). However, that will occur only if either the whole of the assets in the pool are sold or the sale proceeds of an asset exceeds the balance in the pool.

10.21 Some types of expenditure qualify for a 100% first-year allowance, ie the whole cost can be written off in the year the expenditure is incurred (see **10.147**, **10.160**, **10.163** and **23.189**). It is not necessary to claim the full amount but if a realised amount is claimed, the balance of the expenditure will qualify for writing-down allowances in later years.

10.22 If a building is sold to a connected person it may be difficult to avoid a balancing charge or allowance on the sale. An election to transfer at tax written-down value can be made only where a person succeeds to a trade that was previously carried on by a connected person within *ITA 2007, s 993* – see Appendix 1 (*CAA 2001, s 266*). An election cannot be made on the mere transfer of an asset. It may be possible to attribute a nominal sum to the plant and machinery in the sale contract and claim the protection of *CAA 1990, s 61*, but there is a risk that HMRC might regard such an apportionment as a sham (but see **10.94**(*a*)). It should be noted that the *Capital Allowances Act 2001* defines leasing as a qualifying activity; it does not deem it to be a trade. It should also be borne in mind that it may not matter unduly if the vendor incurs a balancing charge on a sale as the purchaser will, of course, become entitled to capital allowances.

10.23 There is an anti-avoidance rule where a company ceases to carry on a trade or part of a trade, another company begins to carry on the activities of that trade as its trade or part of its trade, and the predecessor ceases to carry on the trade (or part trade) as part of a scheme or arrangement, the main purpose or one of the main purposes of which is to entitle the predecessor to a balancing allowance in relation to plant or machinery on cessation of its trade (*CTA 2010, s 955*). The trade must be treated as never having ceased, with the successor being entitled only to the capital allowances that would have been due to the predecessor had it continued to carry on the trade (*CTA 2010, s 955(2)*). If the activities become a part of the successor's trade, that part must be treated as a separate trade (*CTA 2010, s 955(4),(6)*). This provision does not apply where *CTA 2010, s 940A* (company reconstructions without change of ownership) applies on the cessation (*CTA 2010, s 957(1)*). This provision effectively extends the scope of *s 940A* to situations where the two companies are not under common control.

10.24 Further anti-avoidance rules were introduced in *FA 2010*. For corporation tax purposes only, from 21 July 2009 where there is a 'qualifying change' in the person carrying on a trade and that change has an unallowable purpose the 'relevant excess' unused allowances at the time of the change can be used only against future profits from the same activities (*CAA 2001, s 212B*). The provision is aimed at cases where a company with a large pool of unclaimed capital allowances is sold into a new group principally to enable the new group to access those allowances by way of group relief.

10.25 A qualifying change occurs where a 75% subsidiary of one group of companies becomes a 75% subsidiary of a different group (*CAA 2001, s 212C*). The transfer of a trade to a partnership or a change in the holding proportions of a consortium or in the interests of partners can also be a qualifying change in some cases. The relevant excess is the excess of the tax written-down value of plant and machinery over its net book value (including the net investment in respect of finance leases (*CAA 2001, s 212K*). In ascertaining a relevant excess if a company has more than one capital allowance pool they must be aggregated and any deficit on one pool deducted from the excess on others (*CAA 2001, s 212O*). A change has an unallowable purpose if the main purpose (or one of the main purposes) of any arrangement made to bring about the change in ownership is to obtain a tax advantage by becoming able to utilise the capital allowances in relation to expenditure before (or on the day of) the change (*CAA 2001, s 212M*). If after the change in ownership the trade is amalgamated with that of another group company it must be treated as a separate trade from that of the other company (*CAA 2001, s 212P*).

10.26 Again for corporation tax purposes only, where capital expenditure is incurred after 8 December 2009 on the provision of plant or machinery, at the time it is incurred the asset is leased (or arrangements exist under which it is to be leased) and arrangements have been entered into in relation to payments under the lease that have the effect of reducing the value of the asset to the lessor, the lessor's qualifying expenditure on the asset for capital allowances purposes is restricted to that reduced value, V (*CAA 2001, s 228MA(1)(2)* inserted by *FA 2010, Sch 5, para 1*). This restriction applies where the lessor is treated as incurring capital expenditure under *CAA 2001, ss 67* (hire purchase etc) or *70A* (long funding leases). A lease includes any arrangements which provide for plant or machinery to be leased or otherwise made available by one person to another (*CAA 2001, s 228MA(8)*).

10.27 V is the present value of the lessor's income from the asset plus the present value of its residual value (reduced by the amount of any rental rebate (*CAA 2001, s 228MA(3)*). The lessor's income from the asset is the total of all of the amounts that have been received by the lessor (or it is reasonable to expect that the lessor will receive) in connection from the lease and any that have been (or it is reasonable to expect will be) brought into account by the lessor as income in computing profits chargeable to corporation tax (*CAA 2001, s 228MA(4)(a)*). For this purpose disposal receipts brought into account in calculating capital allowances are ignored (*CAA 2001, s 228MA(5)(a)*). The present value of both the lessor's income and the residual value must be calculated using the interest rate implicit in the lease (*CAA 2001, s 228MB(1)*). A rental rebate includes any sum payable to the lessee that is calculated by reference to the value of the asset when the lease terminates (*CAA 2001, s 228MC*).

10.28 Where plant or machinery is leased and a rental rebate is payable by the lessor after 8 December 2009 the deduction allowable in respect of the rebate is limited to the amount of the lessor's income from the lease (see **10.26**) (or, in the case of a finance lease, that amount excluding the finance charge) (*ITTOIA 2005, s 55B(1), CTA 2009, s 60A(1)*, both inserted by *FA 2010, Sch 5, para 2*). This does not apply if the lease is a long funding finance lease within *CAA 2001, s 148C* (which attracts a different treatment) (*ITTOIA 2005, s 55B(7); CTA 2009, s 60A(7)*). A rental rebate for this purpose is any sum payable to the lessee that is calculated by reference to the value of the assets when the lease terminates (*ITTOIA 2005, s 55B(2); CTA 2009, s 60A(2)*).

10.29 The income of the lessor from the lease is the total of all of the amounts receivable in connection with the lease that have been brought into account in calculating the lessor's income for income tax purposes (or for corporation tax purposes in the case of a company), but excluding disposal receipts brought into account under *CAA 2001, s 60(1)* and so much of any amount as represents charges for services, or qualifying UK or foreign tax, to be paid by the lessor (*ITTOIA 2005, s 55B(4)(a); CTA 2009, s 60A(4)(a)*). If the asset is acquired by the lessor in a transaction in relation to which an election is made under *CAA 2001, s 266* (election where predecessor and successor are connected persons) the provision applies as if the successor had been the lessor at all material times (and everything done to or by the predecessor had been done to or by the successor) (*ITTOIA 2005, s 55B(5); CTA 2009, s 60A(5)*). If the whole or part of a rental rebate is disallowed under this provision the amount disallowed (or if less, the excess of the rental rebate over the capital expenditure incurred by the lessor) can be treated as an allowable loss for capital gains purposes but can be used only against chargeable gains accruing to the lessor on the disposal of the asset (*ITTOIA 2005, s 55B(6), CTA 2009, s 60A(6)*).

10.30 If plant or machinery is subject to a lease, a capital allowance disposal event occurs after 8 December 2009 with the result that a disposal value falls to be brought into account for capital allowance purposes, and arrangements have been entered into that have the effect of reducing the disposal value of the asset insofar as it is attributable to rental payments under the lease, the disposal value must be determined as if the arrangements had not been entered into (*CAA 2001, s 64A* inserted by *FA 2010, Sch 5, para 3*). This does not apply if the arrangements trigger a tax charge under *CTA 2010, ss 752* or *753* (factoring of income) (*CAA 2001, s 64A(2)*).

Allowances Where the Cash Basis is Used

10.31 For 2017/18 onwards, if the profits of a trade or a property business carried on by a person are calculated on the cash basis, the person is not entitled to any capital allowances or liable to any balancing charge (*CAA 2001, s 1A(1)–(3)* inserted by *F(No 2)A 2017, Sch 2, para 50*). This does not apply to cars (*CAA 2001, s 1A(4)(5)*).

10.32 If a person carrying on a relevant activity incurs qualifying expenditure relating to an asset at a time when the profits from that activity are calculated on an accruals basis, he subsequently enters the cash basis for a tax year and no deduction would be allowed in respect of the expenditure in calculating profits for that year on a cash basis on the assumption that the expenditure was paid in that year, he is liable to a balancing charge for that year if one would have arisen had he remained on the accruals basis (or a disposal value must be brought into account in respect of the asset) (*CAA 2001, s 1A(6)–(8)*).

10.33 If a taxpayer who has incurred capital expenditure at a time when the profits of a trade or property business were calculated on a cash basis leaves the cash basis in a chargeable period, some or all of the expenditure was brought into account in calculating the cash basis profits and it would have been qualifying expenditure had an accruals basis applied at the time it was incurred, then (*a*) for the purposes of determining any entitlement of the taxpayer to an annual investment allowance or a first year allowance, he is treated as incurring the "unrelievable portion" of the expenditure in the chargeable period; and

(*b*) for the purposes of determining his available qualifying expenditure in a pool for the chargeable period, the whole of the expenditure must be allocated to the appropriate pool (or pools) in that chargeable period and the available qualifying expenditure in that pool must be reduced by the relievable portion of that expenditure.

(*CAA 2001, s 66A(1)(3)(4)* as amended by *F(No 2)A 2017, Sch 2, para 33.*)

For this purpose, the relieved portion of the expenditure is the higher of the amount of that expenditure for which a deduction was allowed in calculating the profits of the trade or property business and the amount for which a deduction would have been allowed if the expenditure had been incurred wholly and exclusively for the purposes of the trade or property business (*CAA 2001, s 66A(2)*). For the purposes of determining any disposal receipts, the expenditure must be regarded as qualifying expenditure (*CAA 2001, s 66A(5)*).

The Date Expenditure is Incurred

General Rule

10.34 The date on which expenditure is incurred is the date on which the obligation to pay it becomes unconditional (whether or not there is a later date on or before which the whole or any part of it is required to be paid), which is when the expenditure has a sufficient degree of certainty to require it to be reflected in business accounts (*CAA 2001, s 5(1)*). Normally this is likely to be the delivery date or the earlier time on which a liability to pay a deposit arises (to the extent of that deposit).

10.35 The government of the day said this is the time when 'the vendor will have completed his part of the contract and the purchaser's obligation to pay will be unconditional and absolute, although not necessarily immediate if the vendor is allowed a period of trade credit' (Mr John Moore, Hansard, Standing Committee B, 6 June 1985, Col 403). In practice, HMRC are likely to accept the adoption of the invoice date, as the obligation to pay will normally have become unconditional on or before that date. For large items of expenditure it could, however, be worth investigating whether an earlier date might meet the test if the invoice date is near the beginning of an accounting period. Where a contract provides for the purchaser to pay for goods on or within a prescribed time of delivery HMRC consider that the obligation to pay becomes unconditional when the asset is delivered (Tax Bulletin, Issue 8, Nov 1993, p 97).

Modification of General Rule

10.36 The general rule is modified in three cases.

1. The expenditure is treated as incurred at the end of the accounting period (or basis period) in which the asset became the property of the purchaser (or is otherwise attributed to him under the contract) if the obligation to pay contractually becomes unconditional as a result of the issue of a certificate (or some other event), and this occurs within a month after the end of that accounting period or basis period (*CAA 2001, s 5(4)*). This covers building work where under general law the bricks, concrete, etc. would become the property of the landowner when they are affixed to the land but the obligation to pay does not arise until the issue of an architect's certificate. It allows relief to be obtained in the accounting period in which the work is done where the architect's certificate is issued within the next month. It also covers test periods for plant where payment may not become due until a certificate has been issued by an engineer to the effect that it is working satisfactorily.
2. If, under (or by virtue of) any agreement, the whole or any part of an amount of capital expenditure is required to be paid on (or not later than) a date which is more than four months after that on which the obligation to pay becomes unconditional, the obligation to pay that part of the expenditure must be treated as becoming unconditional immediately before the expiration of that period – with the result that the capital allowances will not be due until that time (*CAA 2001, s 5(5)*).
3. If, under (or by virtue of) any agreement, the obligation to pay an amount became unconditional on a date earlier than that which accords with normal commercial usage, the expenditure can be treated as incurred on the date 'on or before which it is required to be paid', and *CAA 2001, s 5(5)* above is not to apply to it (*CAA 2001, s 5(6)*). This applies only where the sole or main benefit which might have been expected from the obligation becoming unconditional on the earlier date is to attribute the expenditure to an earlier accounting period than would otherwise have been the case (*CAA 2001, s 5(6)(b)*).

10.37 An example of the operation of Case (2) in **10.187** above may be helpful.

Example 10.4

Joe Bloggs Limited purchases a large item of equipment for £100,000. The supplier agrees to accept payment –

	£
deposit	10,000
on delivery	20,000
3 months after delivery	20,000
9 months after delivery	20,000
15 months after delivery	30,000

Joe Bloggs Limited prepares its accounts to 31 March. It pays the deposit on 1 September 2015. Delivery is on 28 February 2016 and the subsequent payments are all made on the due date.

Allowances due	£	£	£
Year to 31.3.2016 on deposit	10,000		
on payment on delivery	20,000		
on payment on 28 May	20,000	50,000	
writing-down allowance 18%		9,000	9,000
		41,000	
Year to 31.3.2017 on payment on 28.11.2016		20,000	
		61,000	
writing-down allowance 18%		19,980	10,980
		41,020	
Year to 31.3.2018 on payment on 28.05.2017		30,000	
		71,020	
writing-down allowance 18%		12,784	12,784
written-down value at 31.3.2018		58,236	

Consideration of the Rules

10.38 Where a purchaser cannot pay the full price immediately and agrees long credit terms with the supplier, it might be worth considering whether it is possible to use a hire purchase or similar agreement instead. This is because *CAA 2001, s 67* treats the expenditure under a HP contract which is payable after the time when the equipment is brought into use as being incurred when it is brought into use – curiously this 'in use' provision has not been amended in spite of the general abolition of the 'in use' rules. Under normal rules of construction this specific provision will override the general rule laid down by *CAA 2001, s 5*. This was confirmed when the legislation was introduced – 'We do not intend *clause 53* to affect the way in which *s 60* operates and has operated for many years and we do not think that it will' (Mr John Moore, Hansard, Standing Committee B, 6 June 1985, Col 409). The four-month period is long enough to cover a 100-day credit period so will cover the vast majority of normal trade credit periods. If expenditure is contemplated which attracts a longer period of trade credit, and the effect would be to defer relief for the expenditure until a later accounting period, it may be worth considering varying the credit period to reduce it to four months or, if longer, to terminate it at the end of the accounting period. However, *s 67* does not apply to fixtures to which the legislation described at **10.89–10.106** applies. Where an asset becomes a fixture it is treated as disposed of by the owner at that time unless he is also treated as the owner under that legislation (*CAA 2001, s 69*).

10.39 It should be noted that although the provision applies where the expenditure is required to be paid on or not later than a specified date over four months hence, it deems the expenditure to be incurred on that specific date, not on the date of payment if earlier. Accordingly, premature payment of the amount will not normally crystallise a right to allowances. It is doubtful if this was intended. If payment is to be made before the due date to bring the expenditure into an earlier accounting period, the contract should first be varied to terminate the permitted credit period on the proposed payment date.

10.40 Case (3) of **10.36** above is an anti-avoidance measure. It appears to be defective. It seems to proceed on the assumption that the date 'on or before which an amount is required to be paid' would be the date which accords with normal commercial usage, whereas it would normally be the date on which the obligation to pay becomes unconditional. Accordingly, the right to allowances would arise on the date of payment. It will, however, cover the situation where an agreement provides for the obligation to pay an amount to become unconditional at an early date but does not require payment until a later date, and it may be that it is merely intended to cover this limited type of case.

10.41 Where, as in most building contracts, a contract provides for retention of part of the price against satisfactory performance, the government takes the view that the obligation to pay the retention money does not become unconditional until the agreed period following the commissioning of the asset has passed and the machinery or plant concerned has been proved to be satisfactory. Accordingly, the right to allowances in respect of the retention moneys does not arise until that time (Hansard, Standing Committee B, 6 June 1985, Col 407).

10.42 If any other specific tax provision provides that expenditure eligible for capital allowances is to be treated as incurred on a date later than that determined under the above rules, *CAA 2001, s 5* obviously does not override that specific provision (*CAA 2001, s 5(7)*).

What is Plant and Machinery?

10.43 Clearly, the first problem is to identify what is plant and machinery. Neither term is defined. There have been no decided cases on what is meant by machinery, probably because it is generally self-evident whether or not a particular item is a machine. In a property context it will include such things as escalators, lifts, heating installation and air-conditioning installation. There have, however, been a large number of cases before the courts on what is plant. Interestingly, most of the disputed items have been building work or parts of buildings. The first, and perhaps still most quoted, attempt at a definition was made by Lindley LJ in 1887 in *Yarmouth v France (19 QBD 647).*

> 'Plant in its ordinary sense … includes whatever apparatus is used by a businessman for carrying on his business – not his stock-in-trade, which he buys or makes for sale; but all goods and chattels, fixed or movable, live or dead, which he keeps for permanent employment in his business.'

Yarmouth v France was a workman's compensation case. Applying his definition, Lindley LJ found that a horse was plant and the injured workman was thus entitled to compensation.

10.44 This test was amplified by Uthwatt J in *J Lyons & Co Ltd v Attorney-General ([1944] 1 All ER 477).*

> '… the question at issue may, I think, be put thus: Are the lamps and fitments properly to be regarded as part of the setting in which the business is carried on or as part of the apparatus used for carrying on the business? … the presence of lamps in this building is not dictated by the nature of the particular trade there carried on, or by the fact that it is for trade purposes that the building is used. Lamps are required to enable the building to be used where natural light is insufficient … In my opinion these lamps are not, in these circumstances, properly described as "plant", but are part of the general setting in which the business is carried on'.

10.45 The *J Lyons* case was not concerned with capital allowances – the allowances for both plant and machinery and industrial buildings were not introduced until April 1946 – but with war damage compensation. Nevertheless, Uthwatt J's distinction between the setting in which a business is carried on and apparatus used for carrying on the business has been adopted by the courts in tax cases as the correct test. During the 1960s and 1970s a functional test was applied – 'What purpose does the object in question fulfil?' – but it has been made clear in recent cases that this was simply a restatement of the 'setting' versus 'apparatus' test. In the *Wimpy* case (see **10.65** below) Hoffmann J indicated that there is in reality a two-part test. Is the item apparatus or part of the setting? If it is apparatus is it nevertheless part of the premises rather than plant? It will be part of the premises if after installation it would be more appropriate to describe the item as having become part of the premises than as having retained a separate identity. This is a question of fact and degree depending on, for example, whether the item visually retains a separate identity, the degree of permanence with which it is attached, the incompleteness of the structure without it, and whether it is likely to be replaced within a relatively short period.

10.46 The premises test has come into greater prominence in recent years as taxpayers have sought to push further and further the boundary between apparatus and setting. The test was formulated by Lord Lowry in *CIR v Scottish & Newcastle Breweries Ltd (55 TC 252)*:

> 'Something which becomes part of the premises, instead of merely embellishing them, is not plant, except in the rare case where the premises are themselves plant, like the dry dock in Barclay Curle.'

Vinelott J in *Hunt v Henry Quick Ltd (65 TC 108)* expressed this as 'whether it would be more appropriate to describe the item as having become part of the premises than as having retained a separate identity'. The rarity of the premises themselves being plant is reinforced by the fact that the decision of the Commissioners in favour of the taxpayer was reversed in each of *Gray v Seymours Garden Centre (Horticulture) (1995 STC 706)*, *Bradley v London Electricity plc (1996 STC 1054)*, *Attwood v Anduff Car Wash (1997 STC 1167)* and *Shove v Lingfield Park 1991 Ltd (2003 STC 1003)*. In the *Seymours Garden Centre* case Lord Lowry put the test succinctly:

> 'It is proper to consider the function of the item in dispute. But the question is what does it function as? If it functions as part of the premises it is not plant. The fact that the building in which a business is carried on is, by its construction, particularly well-suited to the business, or indeed was specially built for that business does not make it plant.'

And later,

> 'the fact that the planteria provides the function of nurturing and preserving the plants while they are there cannot transform it into something other than part of the premises in which the business is carried on'.

10.47 The list of items that have been held to be plant and those that have not is useful to demonstrate the wide range of items that people have felt might be plant. However, it must be stressed that, in applying the apparatus or setting test, it is necessary to look not only at the item itself but at the business that is being carried on. For example, in *CIR v Scottish & Newcastle Breweries Ltd (55 TC 252)*, a metal sculpture representing 'Seagulls in Flight', permanently affixed to the forecourt of a hotel in Liverpool, was held to be plant. This should certainly not be taken as an indication that all sculptures are plant. Indeed, very few sculptures are likely to meet the test of apparatus with which a business is carried on. This is not to say that the decision was wrong or anomalous, but merely that the contention put forward by the taxpayer, that the creation of the appropriate 'atmosphere' is a vital ingredient of its trade, would not be applicable to most businesses.

10.48 With this in mind the items that have been held to be plant by the courts include the following: movable partitions in the offices of shipping agents (*Jarrold v John Good & Sons Ltd (40 TC 681)*); a dry dock constructed by a company of shipbuilders and repairers (*CIR v Barclay, Curle and Co Ltd (45 TC 221)*); a swimming pool in a caravan park (*Cooke v Beach Station Caravans Ltd (40 TC 514)*); dockside grain silos of a grain importer (*Schofield v R & H Hall Ltd (49 TC 538)*); a hulk of a former sailing ship used for bunkering coal by a coal merchant (*John Hall, Junior & Co v Rickman (1906 1 KB 311)*); transformers and switchgear to bring power from the National Grid to a department store and window lighting in the store (*Cole Brothers Ltd v Phillips (55 TC 188)*); decor and murals in hotels and licensed premises (*CIR v Scottish & Newcastle Breweries Ltd (55 TC 252)*); decorative screens in the windows of a building society (*Leeds Permanent Building Society v Proctor (56 TC 293)*); light fittings, a specially designed suspended ceiling, wall panels, and cold water piping and tanks in a fast food restaurant (*Wimpy International Ltd v Warland (61 TC 51)*); decorative brickwork, murals, wall cladding for mirrors and light fittings in a fast food restaurant (*Associated Restaurants Ltd v Warland (61 TC 51)*); fixed storage platforms in a warehouse (*Hunt v Henry Quick Ltd & King v Bridisco Ltd (1992 STC 633)*); and a gazebo erected in the garden of a pub for the use of smokers (*Andrew v HMRC (2011 SFTD 145*).

10.49 Items held not to qualify as plant are a prefabricated laboratory and gymnasium in a school (*St John's School v Ward (49 TC 524)*); the canopy over the service area of a garage (*Dixon v Fitch's Garage Ltd (50 TC 509)*); a hulk of an old ferry boat used as a floating restaurant (*Benson v Yard Arm Club*

Ltd (53 TC 67)); false ceilings in a restaurant to conceal and partly to support pipes, wiring, etc. (*Hampton v Fortes Autogrill Ltd (53 TC 691)*); a stand at a football ground (*Brown v Burnley Football & Athletic Co Ltd (53 TC 357)*); light fittings and their associated wiring and cables in a department store (*Cole Brothers Ltd v Phillips (55 TC 188)*); an inflatable cover for a tennis court (*Thomas v Reynolds (59 TC 502)*); the shop front wall and floor tiles, suspended ceilings, raised floor areas, specially sited staircase and fire escape trap door in a fast food restaurant (*Wimpy International Ltd v Warland (61 TC 51)*); quarantine kennels forming a permanent structure (HMRC accepting that movable kennels were plant) (*Carr v Sayer (1992 STC 396)*); lighting affixed to storage platforms in a warehouse, which were themselves plant, to illuminate the space underneath (*Hunt v Henry Quick Ltd & King v Bridisco Ltd (65 TC 108)*); a planteria (a form of structure to protect growing plants and maintain their quality of growth) in a garden centre (*Gray v Seymours Garden Centre (Horticulture) (1995 STC 706)*); a structure housing a car wash (*Attwood v Anduff Car Wash (1997 STC 1167)*); an underground electricity substation (*Bradley v London Electricity plc (1996 STC 1054)*); an artificial all-weather race track (*Shove v Lingfield Park 1991 Ltd (2004 STC 805)*); decorative panels in a public house (*J D Wetherspoon v HMRC (2008 STC (SCD) 460)*); a valeting bay in a garage used to apply gloss coating to cars *(Rogate Services Ltd (TC 3449)* and a caravan purchased by the assistant warden of a caravan club in order to live on-site *Telfer v HMRC (TC 5350)*.

10.50 At first glance it is difficult to see the reasoning for some of these decisions even with an understanding of the 'setting' or 'apparatus' test. It may therefore be useful to look a little more closely at some of them. Partitioning in an office is normally part of the setting in which a business is carried on. The fact that it may be movable is irrelevant. The reason that *John Good & Sons Ltd* succeeded is that they were able to show not merely that their partitions were movable but also that they were in fact moved regularly. The demands of their business generated a need for extra space in certain departments in part of the year. The partitions were apparatus, as their function was to enlarge or reduce that space as required. HMRC initially applied the *John Good* decision to all movable partitions but have significantly hardened their attitude in recent years and now normally look to the reason for its being movable. The *Henry Quick* case does provide some authority for the contention that it is sufficient merely for the item to be movable. In that case storage platforms erected to form a mezzanine gallery for additional storage in a warehouse were held to be plant albeit that they were movable – in the sense that they could be demounted and re-erected elsewhere – but had in fact not been moved in the four years since installation and there was no evidence that they were installed as a temporary measure. The platforms were bolted to the floor and the wall, although it was found that this was to give them stability for safety reasons not with the intention of making them permanent structures. However, the decision that the platforms were plant was upheld on the *Edwards v Bairstow*

(36 TC 207) principle, the judge expressing doubt whether he himself would have regarded them as plant.

10.51 A dry dock is not simply a place where repairs can be carried out. It performs, at least in the case of the dock used by *Barclay, Curle & Co*, the functions of getting a ship from the river, securing it while it was under repair, and returning it to the river. Accordingly, it was not simply the setting for the trade but performed active functions in the operation of the trade.

10.52 The grain silos in *R & H Hall* were to hold the grain in a convenient position for delivery to purchasers and were thus part of the apparatus to transfer it from ship to lorry. They were not primarily intended to provide storage. If they had been they would probably have been held to be setting.

10.53 The swimming pool in the *Beach Station Caravan* case was not part of the setting in which the business was carried on, ie it was not there to enhance the appearance of the site but was one of the additional amenities provided to guests. At least that is how the author understands the decision. In the *Lingfield Park* case Hart J, commenting on the above case, explained that 'the reason why the swimming pools were plant was not because, as it happened, the business attraction lay in the customers themselves being able to use the water … but because the pools themselves (including the associated machinery) were part of the delivery system of the water'. In an Irish case, *O'Grady v Roscommon Race Committee (4 ITR 425),* a stand at a race track was held to be plant as it was 'part of the means to get people to go to that racecourse for viewing horses' and was thus very much akin to the *Beach Station* swimming pool. The contrary decision in the UK *Burnley Football Club* case was relied on by the Inspector and thus was effectively distinguished by the court.

10.54 A school gymnasium, even though movable, is part of the setting in which the business of the school is carried on; it is not itself part of the apparatus used in the business, although the equipment inside it is. The filling station canopy at *Fitch's Garage* was stated by the taxpayer to have been installed to provide shelter. It is an interesting speculation whether the taxpayer would have been more successful if its main purpose had been to attract customers. A similar canopy was held to be plant in an Irish case, *O'Culachain v McMullan Brothers (1991 1 IR 363)*, where evidence was given that, whilst the canopy undoubtedly provided shelter, the purpose of its erection was to provide an attractive setting for the sale of the company's products and to create the overall impression of efficiency and of financial solidarity and, most important of all, to attract customers.

10.55 In *Fortes Autogrill* the false ceiling was only in the public part of the restaurant. In these circumstances it is not surprising that it was held to be part of the setting. Following the *Scottish & Newcastle* case it may be that *Fortes* should have contended that in order to keep customers in a motorway restaurant for a meal rather than a snack it is important to provide a pleasant atmosphere. This argument was unsuccessful in the *Wimpy* and *Associated Restaurants* cases, with the exception of one specially designed stepped false ceiling with voids, where it was accepted by the Commissioners that its principal function was the creation of an atmosphere and that it was apparatus used in the trade and not a mere embellishment of the premises.

10.56 Both the *St John's School* and *Yard Arm Club* cases illustrate that the fact that something is movable does not stop it constituting part of the setting in which a business is carried on. Conversely, of course, the *Barclay, Curle* and *R & H Hall* cases illustrate that the fact that something is a fixed permanent structure does not preclude it from being plant and machinery. Such a structure might of course also qualify as an industrial building. In such a case the taxpayer would be able to choose which allowance to claim.

10.57 In *Carr v Sayer*, Sir Donald Nicholls made clear that plant 'does not convey a meaning wide enough to include buildings in general'. It is apt to cover equipment of any size and, 'if fixed, such equipment may readily be described as a structure, but … the equipment does not cease to be plant because it is so substantial that, when fixed, it attracts the label of a structure or, even, a building'. Furthermore, equipment does not cease to be plant merely because it also discharges an additional function of providing the place in which the business is carried out. 'Conversely, buildings … do not cease to be buildings and become plant simply because they are purpose-built for a particular trading activity … A purpose-built building … *prima facie* is no more than the premises on which the business is conducted.' He also pointed out that one of the functions of a building is to provide shelter and security for people using it and for goods inside it, so the fact that a purpose-built building performs such a function cannot make it plant. Accordingly, the quarantine kennels were not plant. He did, however, add a caveat that 'there may be cases where a structure, used for housing animals or birds, is so small or made of such ephemeral materials that, despite being fixed, it will be difficult to see clearly on which side of the boundary line the structure stands.' In *Seymours Garden Centre* Vinelott J emphasised 'It is true that a planteria fulfils the same function, the protection of plants between removal from the nursery and sale, which could be achieved without the use of any permanent structure – by glass and plastic cloches or by the use of straw bales, thermal blankets or, for that matter, bonfires during frosty nights. It does not follow that a structure erected to perform the same function must be plant.' This view was upheld by the Court of Appeal. He did not necessarily rule out glasshouses ever being plant though: 'It may be that a specialised glasshouse with integral heating, temperature and humidity controls, automatic ventilation, shade screens and other equipment could be considered to be … apparatus for carrying on a trade and not the premises in which the trade is carried on.' HMRC have said that they accept that in some cases a glasshouse unit and its attendant machinery are interdependent forming a single entity which will function as plant. Such units will be of an extremely sophisticated design including extensive computer controlled equipment without which the structure cannot operate and which will have been permanently installed during the construction of the glasshouse. Similarly, HMRC accept that polytunnels can be plant but normally only where crops are grown in the ground and the same ground cannot be continually re-used. (Capital Allowances Manual CA22090).

10.58 The *Anduff Car Wash* case emphasises that even a structure whose only purpose is to house plant is nevertheless premises in which the business is carried on. The judge there indicated that providing housing for machinery is a typical function of a building. Similarly the premises in *Rogate* were held not to be plant but simply a place where people worked. Even if that were wrong, as it had a floor, walls and a roof it was a building and thus precluded from relief by *CAA 2001, s 21* (see **10.59**). The *London Electricity* substation, although two metres underground, was a large structure, 12 metres × 18 metres, consisting of three levels connected by stairs. It was unmanned but personnel were required to visit it to carry out maintenance. London Electricity claimed that the substation and the equipment it housed was a single functioning entity. Alternatively it was a mere box (or series of boxes) housing the plant. In holding that the substation did not qualify as plant, and reversing the decision of the Special Commissioner, Blackburne J said 'the Special Commissioner failed to ask himself what plant-like function the structure as an entity performed in London Electricity's trading activity. If he had, the true and only reasonable conclusion he could have come to was that the structure functioned as the premises in which London Electricity's trading activity is carried on rather than the apparatus with which it was carried on. No plant-like function was identified for the structure as a whole.' This seems a harsh decision, bearing in mind that the substation was not occupied, was unsuitable for occupation, and was specially designed to house substantial apparatus. In the past HMRC have accepted that a structure built around plant whose sole purpose was to protect it from the elements was itself plant. This decision suggests that they are unlikely to do so any longer. The all-weather track installed at Lingfield Park was held clearly to be part of the premises (reversing the decision of the Commissioners), albeit that it was not a building serving the purpose of providing housing shelter or access.

10.59 In recent years the most important cases to come before the courts have been *Cole Brothers Ltd v Phillips* (Cole Brothers were the company in the John Lewis group that wanted group relief for the expenditure on the John Lewis store at Brent Cross) and *Wimpy International Ltd v Warland*. These could well be the last major cases in this area. The Court of Appeal in *Wimpy International* gave a strong indication that litigants will be wasting their time (and money) in bringing cases before the courts in this area in future. 'So what is to be done? The answer is, I think. that in these cases, the courts should be especially reluctant to upset the decisions of Commissioners, unless it can be shown not only that they have erred in law but also that their error is palpable. It is not enough to show that they may have applied the wrong test … or that they have not stated the test in the most precise language, or that they have omitted to refer to some factor which they ought to have taken into account. Where the judges have themselves failed to find a universal test the Commissioners are not to have their language examined too closely, or dissected line by line. So the cases will, I hope, be rare when it is held that the Commissioners have, on the face of it, applied the wrong test. Still rarer should be those cases where it is held that they must have applied the wrong test, because of their findings on the facts' (Lloyd LJ at p 105). Unfortunately the courts do not seem to have followed this guidance in practice, as in all of the subsequent cases won by HMRC the courts have reversed the decision of the Commissioners.

10.60 The *Cole Brothers Ltd v Phillips* case is interesting partly because it contains a thorough review of the authorities and partly because of the various submissions made. The company first contended that the electrical installation, which was the subject matter of the appeal, should be looked at as a whole. As part was clearly plant and everything was interdependent, the whole should be regarded as plant. This was rejected, primarily on the basis that the multiplicity of elements in the electrical system and the different purposes that they served effectively prevented them from being treated as a single entity. It is still worth considering putting forward such a contention whenever a large amount of expenditure clearly relates to plant but there is doubt as to whether the whole qualifies, as this approach was accepted in the House of Lords as likely to be a reasonable approach in some cases.

10.61 The second contention in the Court of Appeal, although not in the House of Lords, was that it was illogical to classify the transformers as plant but not the switchgear between those transformers and the Electricity Board's substation. In finding for the company Oliver LJ propounded the useful test that 'if the building had contained no electrical equipment other than that conceded or found to be plant, could it be argued that the switchboard which was introduced as the necessary control for that installation was not either itself plant or something the cost of which was incurred in the provision of plant?' This is a useful general test to apply to ancillary equipment.

10.62 The main area on which the company lost – specially designed interior lighting – illustrates the importance of presenting the facts properly before the Tribunal. This is the sole arbiter of fact. A finding of fact will be reversed only if there was no evidence on which the Tribunal could have reached its decision. In this case, while they had held that window lighting was apparatus to attract customers, the Commissioners had held that internal lighting was part of the setting in which the business was carried on. In the House of Lords the company put forward the *CIR v Scottish & Newcastle Breweries Ltd (55 TC 252)* argument – that the lighting was designed to provide a pleasing ambience for customers – but this does not appear to have been argued before the Special Commissioners, and was therefore not considered in detail by the House of Lords, who decided the case on the grounds that the Commissioners had not erred in reaching the decision they had made on the basis of the evidence before them.

10.63 It is a pity that this argument was not put forward in the first instance. The Commissioners placed emphasis on the fact that the building could not be used for any business without lighting. If it could have been shown that special lighting constituted plant, as it provided a function beyond merely providing light to make the building useable at all, it is likely that it would have qualified for allowances, even though it also formed part of the setting in which the business was carried on. It is significant to note that in the later case of *Wimpy International Ltd v Warland*, Hoffmann J reversed the decision of the Commissioners, and held that the light fittings there were plant. The company had given evidence that the lighting intensity was far greater than in a normal shop and was designed to create an atmosphere of brightness and efficiency to attract potential customers from outside. Similarly internal lighting was held to be plant in the *Associated Restaurants* case where the lights were specially positioned to create a specific atmosphere.

10.64 An interesting sidelight in the *Cole Brothers* case is that the case stated contains an analysis of the electrical installation showing the items that HMRC accepted as plant, as follows:

(*a*) Wiring, etc. to heating and ventilation equipment;.

(*b*) Wiring, etc. to fire alarm;

(*c*) Wiring, etc. to clocks;

(*d*) Public address system and staff location;

(*e*) Wiring, etc. to TV workshop and cash registers;

(*f*) Trunking for telephone system;

(*g*) Wiring, etc. to lifts;

(*h*) Wiring, etc. to escalators;

(*i*) Wiring, etc. to burglar alarm;

(*j*) Wiring, etc. to smoke detectors;

(*k*) Wiring, etc. to Electrical Appliance Department compactor room, etc;

(*l*) Emergency lighting system;

(*m*) Stand-by supply system;

(*n*) The fitments for the display of fittings for sale in the Lighting Department; and

(*o*) Additional sockets installed in the television sales area.

10.65 In the *Wimpy* hamburger restaurant case – and that of *Associated Restaurants*, which operated the Pizzaland restaurant chain, which was heard with it – the items that were held to be plant included carpets; a special stepped suspended ceiling with voids that was designed to create an environment suitable to the company's assessment of the public's current taste (a borderline item); fixed wall panels and mirrors; light fittings, where the lights were of a greater than normal intensity to create an atmosphere of brightness and efficiency; cold water piping and tanks, as fast food restaurants require a far greater water storage capacity than ordinary commercial premises; a brick-built plant room, erected because the trade of providing meals made it necessary to install machinery which could only be installed in a brick housing; decorative brickwork in Pizzaland shops, as the premises were complete without that purely decorative fixture (a borderline item); and fixed clay murals (which could not be removed without breaking them).

10.66 The categorisation of light fittings in both Wimpy and Pizzaland shops as plant should be contrasted with their treatment as premises in the *Cole Brothers* case. The distinction is that in *Cole Brothers* the evidence given was merely that they were specially designed, not that they performed a specific function in the trade, whereas in these later cases the evidence was that they were chosen and positioned in order to create a specific atmosphere. If *Cole Brothers* had conceded lighting in the aisles and contended that the lighting over the counters was intended specifically to attract customers' attention to what was on offer – as they claimed for window lighting – it is probable that the result would have been different. The categorisation in both Wimpy and Pizzaland shops of cold water tanks as plant is particularly interesting. HMRC have generally resisted such treatment in hotels, where a similar argument for abnormal capacity seems viable.

10.67 The then Minister indicated in a parliamentary statement in 1984 that basic lighting systems are not machinery or plant but that specialised lighting may qualify as plant where it performs a specific function and is not merely part of the trade's setting (Hansard, 15 February 1984, Col 203).

10.68 It is also interesting to see what was held not to be plant in the *Wimpy* and *Associated Restaurants* cases. The items held to form part of the premises were shop fronts; wall and floor tiles, artex on walls, and high quality ceramic tiles – even though they had a relatively short life – as the walls and floor surfaces of a shop need to be covered with something so the cladding could not be regarded as a mere embellishment; and suspended ceilings (with the one exception mentioned in **10.65** above). HMRC consider the replacement of a shop front to be a repair (see **12.57**), so this decision will apply only to the initial installation. It is also interesting to note that in the *Associated Restaurants* case, engineers' and architects' fees were apportioned and capital allowances granted on the proportion of the expenditure that related to allowable items. This accords with HMRC's normal practice, but does not seem to have been given judicial support before.

10.69 It is important to be aware of the distinction drawn in the *Wimpy* case between 'embellishments' which attract customers to the product, or create an ambience appropriate to the product, and those 'embellishments' which become part of the premises. The point needs to be made that the mere creation of an atmosphere conducive to the successful retail of a product is not of itself sufficient to sustain a claim to capital allowances. It is also important to be sensitive to the possible dangers in the lax presentation of the details of a refurbishment as there may no longer be a 'second chance' of getting it right in court. This was stressed in *J D Wetherspoon v HMRC (2008 STC (SCD) 460)* where the Special Commissioners phrased the question as whether the decorative panelling in issue there is more appropriately described as part of the premises in which the pub's trade is carried on or instead as an embellishment used to enhance the atmosphere of those premises. A factor that seemed to them helpful in answering that question (although not mentioned by Hoffmann J in Wimpy International) was 'the extent to which the panelling can be regarded as an unexceptional component which would not be an unusual feature of premises of the type to which the appellant is inviting the public'. That seems an odd test. Every restaurant needs extra capacity cold water tanks, which were held to be plant in the *Wimpy* case; indeed it seems to undermine the basic test of plant being what is needed specifically for the trade rather than for the building to be used at all. It is not surprising that using their test the Special Commissioners found that panelling is common in pubs, so the Wetherspoon panelling is an unexceptional component of a pub and thus part of the premises. In endorsing this decision the Upper Tribunal (*2012 STC 1450*) explained the Commissioners' view as being that ordinary panelling which simply turned what would otherwise have been an unpanelled room into a mainly panelled room had an effect upon the premises whereas the sculptures in *Scottish & Newcastle Breweries* were distinctive embellishments in their own right. It was in that context that the Tribunal in *Wimpy* allowed some wall panelling; but that was by no means unexceptional panelling, since it included finishings in bronze or silver mirrors or infills of melamine, hessian or a textured sandstone effect. The test is whether the panelling had retained its separate identity or lost it by becoming part of the premises.

10.70 It is worth considering carefully what items in a building might conceivably qualify as plant or machinery in the context of the occupier's particular trade. Where a building is not constructed for a particular occupier, none of the expenditure is likely to qualify as plant but much may qualify as machinery. In a purpose-built building anything installed especially for the needs of the trade should be examined with care. The fact that something is installed to meet the occupier's requirements does not, of course, prevent it being part of the setting in which the trade is carried on, but the fact that he has asked for it does raise a question mark over whether it might constitute apparatus. In some cases the architect may build in features that he perceives are needed for the trade without having to be specifically told to do so. It may be that the plans need to be examined with this in mind. It is also worth checking whether there was any correspondence (or notes of meetings) showing that the client asked the architect to include specific items. Following the phasing-out of agricultural buildings allowances HMRC and DEFRA together produced, as a special pilot exercise, additional guidance for the pig industry to illustrate the range of assets which qualify as plant or machinery (HMRC Brief 03/2010). The pig industry was chosen because it is a particularly heavy investor in buildings and structures with very short economic lives. There has been no follow-up on other sectors of agriculture. However, the list of qualifying and non-qualifying items may be helpful in other sectors. The list is not reproduced here as it is of limited interest but the Brief is on the HMRC website.

10.71 Where a person carrying on a qualifying activity incurs capital expenditure on alterations to an existing building which is incidental to the installation of machinery or plant, it is treated as part of the cost of the plant and machinery (*CAA 2001, s 25*). Installation costs and other costs ancillary to the machinery are in practice also regarded as forming part of the cost of the machinery. Many of the undisputed items in the *Cole Brothers* case (**10.64** above) were wiring to machinery, and thus ancillary to the machinery. Electrical wiring is not normally accepted by HMRC as constituting plant or machinery. It can therefore be important to break down such expenditure in great detail to separate out all amounts that are ancillary to machinery. The same applies to plumbing, where HMRC generally accept that hot water pipes are ancillary to the heating system but contend that the cost of cold water pipes is not eligible for capital allowances. As the cold water tanks and piping were regarded as plant in the *Wimpy* case and also in the *Associated Restaurants* case on the assumption that they were of a far greater capacity than would have been installed in a shop, it may well be that cold water piping and tanks in a hotel, or any other establishment where an abnormal amount of water is used, are plant. HMRC issued a guidance note in October 2004 on the tax effect of work carried out to comply with the *Disability Discrimination Act 1995*. This gives useful guidance in relation to alterations to buildings. It can be found on the Gov.UK website (wwwgov.uk).

10.72 In *J D Wetherspoon v HMRC (2008 STC (SCD) 460)* the Special Commissioners held that kitchen tiles, whilst reasonable for a busy pub kitchen, did not have sufficient nexus to the fryers, cookers and other plant that created the need for wipe-down walls and ceilings to be incidental to the installation of such items. They did think that the construction of individual cubicles or timber partitions and doors was incidental to the installation of toilets though, as the toilets could not be used properly without them. They also felt that pipework and drainage connected to a toilet is incidental to the installation of the toilet, although it might also be plant under **10.78**(1) below. The parties returned to the First-tier Tribunal *(2009 UKFTT 374(TC))* because they were unable to agree on the precise scope of the provisional findings. It was held that only tiling sufficient specifically to deal with splashing which might be expected to be caused by the usual functioning of qualifying plant could attract allowances as ancillary to the plant, and that the plastering to affix such tiles could not qualify. The cost of floor tiling in the toilets and an apportioned part of the costs of fully tiled walls was not ancillary to the toilets. The Upper Tribunal (*2012 STC 1450*) disagreed that the toilet cubicles qualified, but HMRC had not appealed on that point so the taxpayer won. They did, however, disallow the block work, ie the construction of the toilet block itself. The Tribunal felt that the focus of *CAA 2001, s 25* is on the point that if plant is installed in an existing building rather than a new one it may not fit, so alterations will need to be made to fit it. It might also apply to splash-back tiling to enable a new basin to be used without damaging the wall. However, it is unlikely to apply in a conversion or major refurbishment of a building. Where it applies, relief can be due even on expenditure that is disallowable because of *CAA 2001, s 21* (see **10.76**).

10.73 Interest on money borrowed specifically to finance the acquisition of plant is not ancillary to the cost of the plant and cannot qualify for allowances (*Ben-Odeco Ltd v Powlson (52 TC 459)*). An exchange loss, where a purchase of plant from abroad is in a foreign currency, may well qualify for allowances, however, depending of course exactly on how the transaction is structured (*Van Arkadie v Sterling Coated Materials Ltd (56 TC 479)*). A payment to cancel an option granted to a third party to buy an item of equipment from the taxpayer has been held to qualify for capital allowances on the basis that the buying out of the option was an integral part of the cost to the company of continuing to provide itself with that item of equipment (*Bolton v International Drilling Co Ltd (56 TC 449)*).

10.74 If machinery or plant is demolished and replaced, the demolition costs (less any sale proceeds received) are added to the cost of the replacement asset. If it is not replaced, the demolition costs are treated as if they were expenditure on the acquisition of machinery or plant (*CAA 2001, s 26*).

Restriction for certain fixtures, etc

10.75 Machinery and plant does not include any expenditure on the provision of:

(i) a building;

(ii) an asset in a building which is incorporated in it; or

(iii) an asset in a building which is of a kind normally incorporated into buildings – but which is not so incorporated in that particular building because it is movable for some other reason.

(*CAA 2001, s 21.*)

Head (iii) is obviously an anti-avoidance provision, although the concept that developers might substantially devalue the capital value of their building by not incorporating fixtures, in order to try to avoid a restriction on capital allowances, is so far-fetched that it is difficult to take it seriously. HMRC have expressed the view that 'a building' is anything with four walls and a roof provided that it is of a reasonably substantial size. Thus, while a wooden hut large enough to contain people is likely to be a building, a small dog kennel is not (IR Press Release 17.12.1993).

10.76 *Section 21* specifically provides that the following cannot be machinery or plant:

(*a*) walls, floors, ceilings, doors, gates, shutters, windows and stairs;

(*b*) mains services and systems for water, electricity and gas;

(*c*) waste disposal systems;

(*d*) sewerage and drainage systems;

(*e*) shafts or other structures in which lifts, hoists, escalators and moving walkways are installed; and

(*f*) fire safety systems.

There are, however, a great number of exceptions to these basic exclusions. These listed exclusions do not appear to add anything to the basic rule in **10.75**.

10.77 Similarly, machinery or plant does not include expenditure on the provision of:

(1) The following structures or other assets:

A. A tunnel, bridge, viaduct, aqueduct, embankment or cutting.

B. A way or hard standing (eg a pavement, road, railway or tramway), a park for vehicles or containers, or an airstrip or runway.

C. An inland navigation – including a canal, basin or a navigable river.

D. A dam, reservoir or barrage (including any sluices, gates, generators and other equipment associated with it).

E. A dock, harbour, wharf, pier, marina, jetty or any other structure at which vessels may be kept or merchandise or passengers shipped.

F. A dike, sea wall, weir or drainage ditch.

G. Any other structure other than an industrial structure, ie anything (other than a building) which is, or is to be, an industrial building or structure within *CAA 2001, ss 274–285* (or would be if that definition included an undertaking for the extraction of gas; and the provision of telecommunication, television or radio services). Following the repeal of industrial buildings allowance from 31 March 2011 the definitions in *ss 274–285* continue to have effect for this purpose (*FA 2008, Sch 27, para 33*).

(2) The acquisition of any interest in land – but not so as to exclude the acquisition of an interest in an asset which is so installed in, or affixed to, the land as to become in law part of it if that asset would itself constitute plant or machinery.

(3) Any works involving the alteration of land.

(*CAA 2001, ss 22, 24*.)

HMRC say that 'any substantial man-made asset' is a structure (IR Press Release 17.12.1993).

10.78 The exceptions to the exclusions, ie the items that are capable of being plant are:

1. Gas and sewerage systems which are provided mainly to meet the particular requirements of the trade or to serve particular machinery or plant used for the purposes of the trade. Prior to 1 April 2008 this head also excluded electrical (including lighting) and cold water systems. These are now eligible for allowances only as integral features (see **10.84**).

2. Up to 31 March 2008 only, space or water heating systems; powered systems of ventilation, air cooling or air purification; and any ceiling or floor comprised in such systems (unless it is intended to remain permanently in place). These are now eligible for allowances only as integral features (see **10.84**).

3. Manufacturing or processing equipment; storage equipment (including cold rooms); display equipment; and counters, checkouts and similar equipment.

4. Cookers, washing machines, dishwashers, refrigerators and similar equipment; washbasins, sinks, baths, showers, sanitary ware and similar equipment; and furniture and furnishings.

5. Hoists. Prior to 1 April 2008 this head also included lifts, escalators and moving walkways. These are now eligible for allowances only as integral features (see **10.84**).

6. Sound insulation provided mainly to meet the particular requirements of the trade.

7. Computer, telecommunication and surveillance systems (including their wiring and other links).

8. Refrigeration or cooling equipment.

9. Sprinkler equipment and other equipment for extinguishing or containing fire; fire alarm systems.

10. Burglar alarm systems.

11. Any machinery (including devices for providing motive power).

12. Strong rooms in bank or building society premises; safes.

13. Partition walls which are movable and intended to be moved in the course of the trade.

14. Decorative assets provided for the enjoyment of the public in the hotel, restaurant or similar trades.

15. Advertising hoardings; and signs, displays and similar assets.

16. Swimming pools (including diving boards, slides and structures on which such boards or slides are mounted).

17. A glasshouse which is constructed so that the required environment (ie air, heat, light, irrigation and temperature) for growing plants is provided automatically by means of devices which are an integral part of its structure. HMRC have agreed with the NFU that such a glasshouse is not a long-life asset in relation to expenditure incurred up to 31 December 2005 (Tax Bulletin 35, June 1998).

18. Cold stores.

19. Buildings provided for testing aircraft engines within the building.

20. Caravans provided mainly for holiday lettings (HMRC adopt the definition of 'caravan' in the *Caravan Sites and Control of Development*

Act 1960, s 29(1) (ie any structure designed or adapted for human habitation which is capable of being moved) Capital Allowances Manual CA22100).

21. A movable building intended to be moved in the course of the trade.
22. Expenditure on the alteration of land for the purpose only of installing machinery or plant.
23. Dry docks.
24. A jetty or similar structure provided mainly to carry plant or machinery.
25. Pipelines or underground ducts or tunnels with a primary purpose of carrying utility conduits.
26. Towers provided to support floodlights.
27. The provision of any reservoir incorporated into a water treatment works or the provision of any service reservoir or treated water for supply within any housing estate or other particular locality.
28. Silos provided for temporary storage and storage tanks.
29. Slurry pits or silage clamps.
30. Fish tanks or fish ponds.
31. Rails, sleepers and ballast for a railway or tramway.
32. Structures and other assets for providing the setting for any ride at an amusement park or exhibition.
33. Fixed zoo cages.

(*CAA 2001, s 23.*)

NB. An asset cannot come within 1 to 16 above if its principal purpose is to insulate or enclose the interior of the building or provide an interior wall, a floor or a ceiling which (in each case) is intended to remain permanently in place (*CAA 2001, s 23(4)*).

10.79 It should be stressed that if something falls within the above list it does not necessarily attract capital allowances. It is simply capable of doing so. The principles outlined in **10.2** to **10.74** above must be applied to determine whether or not the item is plant in the particular circumstances of the individual trade. The government believe that all items previously held by the courts to qualify as plant, fall within the above exceptions. Introducing the Finance Bill clause, the Minister, Stephen Dorrell, said, 'the clause's intention is to prevent further erosion of the tax base as a result of extension of entitlement to capital allowances. It will not remove entitlement to capital allowances for any taxpayer who is entitled to it under the present state of case law' (Standing Committee A 10.3.1994, Col 620). He did, however, also point out that 'decisions by the Special Commissioners are not case law'. He later said 'the purpose of the clause is not to rewrite capital allowance law but … to confirm that it is not normal for buildings, structures and works to be included as what most of us understand to be plant and machinery … I can give the Committee the clear undertaking that it is not our intention to change the capital treatment of any class of asset under the clause … Most of us would start with the proposition that plant and machinery does not include buildings, structures and works … Unfortunately, the Courts have ruled that many assets which would normally fall within those categories are already treated as plant and machinery' (Stephen Dorrell, SCA 10.3.1994, Col 632).

10.80 It seems doubtful whether many will agree with Mr Dorrell's assertion that 'the new rules will result in greater certainty for both taxpayer and the Revenue' (SCA 10.3.1994, Col 603). The items listed in **10.78** are presumably a definitive statement of what in a building the Revenue believe is likely to be plant. As such they should prove helpful in formulating capital allowances claims.

10.81 Where allowances for building work are claimed under *CAA 2001, s 25* (see **10.71**), the above restrictions do not apply as it is the machinery or plant installed in the building that triggers the allowance for the building alterations. Accordingly, for example, expenditure on a lift shaft to install a lift in an existing building should qualify for allowances (see Taxline, July 1995, p 3).

Attribution of overheads and preliminaries

10.82 HMRC accept that where a building incorporates plant or machinery the capital expenditure on the plant includes the proportion of the preliminaries or professional fees attributable to the provision of the part. One of the issues in *J D Wetherspoon v HMRC (2012 STC 1450)* was how such attribution should be made. The Commissioners first held that there was no basis in law for excluding preliminaries from *CAA 2001, s 25* incidental expenditure (as HMRC had contended). They went on to say that the allocation of preliminaries should be as accurate as reasonably possible. The extent of attribution or allocation required instead of a global apportionment depends on what is reasonable and proportionate, depending on the amount of money involved and the work necessary for a detailed exercise. There could not be any objection in principle to an apportionment which is inherently an estimate rather than an exact measurement of the cost properly attributable. The Upper Tribunal agreed. The decision records that the HMRC witness said that HMRC has various cost models for different types of building to see what percentage of preliminaries should be allocated to allowable and non-allowable expenditure. He added that normally in other cases a broad-brush approach is taken for practical purposes allowing 50%. Curiously they do not appear to have published these models, which would clearly be helpful to taxpayers, despite their professed desire to help taxpayers to get their tax right.

Background plant or machinery

10.83 Expenditure by a lessor on the provision of plant and machinery for leasing under a long-funding lease does not attract capital allowances (*CAA 2001, s 34A*). Instead it is the lessee who is entitled to the allowances (*CAA 2001, s 70A*). The definition of a long-funding lease is complex and is not considered here. It can be found in *CAA 2001, ss 71* onwards. There is an important exception in relation to property, namely that a lease of background plant and machinery cannot be a long-funding lease, so the lessor retains the right to the allowances (*CAA 2001, s 70R(3)*). Plant is background plant if it is affixed to (or otherwise installed in or under or on) any land which includes a building, it is background plant for the building if it is leased under a mixed lease (ie a single lease relating to both the land and the plant and the lease payments do not vary depending on the value from time to time of the plant (*CAA 2001, s 70R(2)*). Background plant for a building is any plant or machinery:

(*a*) which is of such a description that it could reasonably be expected to be installed in a variety of buildings of different description (ie it is not specific to a particular trade or limited types of trade); and

(*b*) its sole or main purpose is to contribute to the functionality of the building or its sites as an environment within which activities can be carried on.

(*CAA 2001, s 70R(4)*.)

10.84 The Treasury have power by order to prescribe items which are background plant, items which are capable of being background plant and items that cannot be background plant (*CAA 2001, s 70T*). They have duly done so by the *Capital Allowances (Leases of Background Plant or Machinery for a Building Order 2007) (SI 2007 No 303)* which prescribes that the following are deemed to be background plant or machinery:

(*a*) lighting installations including all fixed light fittings and emergency lighting systems;

(*b*) telephone, audio-visual and data installations incidental to the occupation of the building;

(*c*) computer networking facilities incidental to the occupation of the building;

(*d*) sanitary appliances and other bathroom fittings including hand driers, counters, partitions, mirrors, shower and locker facilities;

(*e*) kitchen and catering facilities for producing and storing food and drink for the occupants of the building;

(*f*) fixed seating;

(*g*) signs;

(*h*) public address systems; and

(*i*) intruder alarm systems and other security equipment including surveillance equipment.

The following may be background plant or machinery:

(*a*) heating and air conditioning installations;

(*b*) ceilings which are part of an air conditioning system;

(*c*) hot water installations;

(*d*) electrical installations that provide power to a building, such as high and low voltage switchgear, all sub-mains distribution systems and standby generators;

(*e*) mechanisms, including automatic control systems, for opening and closing doors, windows and vents;

(*f*) escalators and passenger lifts;

(*g*) window cleaning installations;

(*h*) fittings such as fitted cupboards, blinds, curtains and associated mechanical equipment;

(*i*) demountable partitions;

(*j*) protective installations such as lightning protection, sprinkler and other equipment for containing or fighting fires, fire alarm systems and fire escapes; and

(*k*) building management systems.

Plant used for any of the following purposes cannot constitute background plant or machinery:

(*a*) storing, moving or displaying goods to be sold in the course of a trade, whether wholesale or retail;

(*b*) manufacturing goods or materials;

(*c*) subjecting goods or materials to a process;

(*d*) storing goods or materials–

   (i) which are to be used in the manufacture of other goods or materials,

   (ii) which are to be subjected, in the course of a trade, to a process,

   (iii) which, having been manufactured or produced or subjected in the course of a trade to a process, have not yet been delivered to any purchaser, or

   (iv) on their arrival in the United Kingdom from a place outside the UK.

Expenditure on the provision or replacement of integral features

10.85 A writing down allowance at the reduced rate of 8% pa only (10% prior to 2012/13) is given for expenditure on the provision or replacement of an integral feature of a building or structure used for a qualifying activity (ie one that attracts capital allowances) as if the expenditure were capital expenditure or the provision of plant or machinery and the person who incurred the expenditure owned plant or machinery as a result of incurring it (*CAA 2001, ss 33A(1), 104D*).

The following are integral features:

(*a*) an electrical system (including a lighting system);

(*b*) a cold water system;

(*c*) a space or water heating system, a powered system of ventilation, air cooling or air purification, and any floor or ceiling comprised in such a system;,

(*d*) a lift, an escalator or a moving walkway; and

(*e*) external solar shading.

(*CAA 2001, s 33A(5).*)

The Treasury have power by statutory instrument both to add items to this list and to create exclusions (*CAA 2001, s 33A(7)*).

10.86 Any asset whose principal purpose is to insulate or enclose the interior of a building, or to provide an interior wall, floor or ceiling which is intended to remain permanently in place, does not qualify as an integral feature if it would otherwise have fallen into one of the above categories (*CAA 2001, s 33A(6)*).

10.87 Expenditure on the repair or replacement of an integral feature must be treated as capital expenditure if the amount of the expenditure exceeds 50% of the cost of replacing the feature at the time that the expenditure is incurred (*CAA 2001, s 33B(1)(2)*). If such expenditure is less than 50% but further expenditure is incurred on that same feature within the following 12 months, the expenditure must be aggregated to apply the 50% test (*CAA 2001, s 33B(3)(4)*).

10.88 Prior to 1 April 2008 some of the above items qualified as plant or machinery but others, such as lighting and cold water systems, did not or only partially did so. Although not brought within the definition of integral features, the 8% rate also applies to expenditure on the provision of solar panels from 6 April 2012 (1 April for corporation tax) (*CAA 2001, s 104A(1)(g)* inserted by *FA 2012, s 45(4)*).

Fixtures

Equipment which becomes Landlord's Fittings

10.89 The Court of Appeal held in *Stokes v Costain Property Investments Ltd (57 TC 688)* that where a tenant installed plant or machinery which became landlord's fittings, no one was eligible to claim capital allowances; the landlord because he had not incurred the expenditure and the tenant because he did not own the asset. This decision has been superseded by new rules now contained in *CAA 2001, ss 172–204* which are, in general, designed to allow the tenant to claim allowances in such circumstances.

10.90 The new provisions apply to expenditure on plant which is so installed or otherwise fixed in or to a building or any other description of land as to become in law part of the building or land (*CAA 2001, s 173(1)*). Any question as to whether an item has become part of a building is to be determined by the Special Commissioners. All persons whose tax position could be affected by the decision will be bound by it and accordingly have a right to attend and make representations at the hearing (*CAA 2001, s 204*).

10.91 In *Melluish v BMI (No 3) Ltd (1995 STC 964)* BMI, which leased assets to local authorities, sought to obtain capital allowances by an alternative route. It included a specific provision in its leases to local authorities that: 'As between the Lessor and the Lessee the Equipment hereby leased shall remain personal or movable property and shall continue in the ownership of the Lessor notwithstanding that the same may have been affixed to any land or building.' Although Vinelott J thought that this was effective to allow BMI to retain ownership of the assets in most cases, this was rejected by both the Court of Appeal and the House of Lords which held that 'the concept of a fixture which remained personal or movable property was a contradiction in terms and an impossibility in law'. The Court of Appeal did, however, consider that the equipment leasing rules applied irrespective of whether had the lessee acquired the assets, he would himself have been able to claim capital allowances. This was upheld by the House of Lords.

10.92 If at any time a person has claimed capital allowances otherwise than as plant and machinery in respect of expenditure relating, in whole or in part, to the construction, acquisition or provision of an asset, eg he claimed industrial buildings allowances, a later owner of the asset cannot claim plant and machinery allowances under these special rules relating to fixtures (*CAA 2001, s 9(1)*). This restriction does not apply if the original owner's claim was for industrial buildings allowances or scientific research allowance and the acquisition value for the current owner is fixed under *CAA 2001, ss 186, 187* (see **10.106** and **10.107**) (*CAA 2001, s 9(2)*). Similarly, once someone has claimed capital allowances under these special rules relating to fittings, a subsequent purchaser can only claim plant and machinery allowances in relation to that item; he cannot claim any other type of capital allowance (*CAA 2001, s 9(3)*). This restriction does not affect allowances for expenditure incurred before 24 July 1996 (*CAA 2001, Sch 3, para 10*). This is an anti-avoidance provision that seeks to prevent allowances being claimable by different people on the same expenditure.

Expenditure Incurred by the Tenant, etc

10.93 The basic rule is that if at the time when a person incurs capital expenditure on machinery or plant (either for the purpose of a trade carried on by him or for leasing otherwise than in the course of a trade) which becomes a fixture, he has an interest in the land (ie the freehold, a lease, an easement, an agreement to acquire an easement, or a licence to occupy the land), the fixture is to be treated for capital allowance purposes as belonging to him in consequence of his incurring the expenditure. This will give him an entitlement to claim capital allowances (*CAA 2001, ss 172–176*). A boiler or water-filled radiator installed in a building as part of a space or water heating system is specifically treated as a fixture for this purpose (*CAA 2001, s 176(1)*). If there are two or more persons to whom a fixture would be treated as belonging under this rule it is treated as belonging to the one, if any, who owns an easement, or if none does so, to a licensee, or if none is a licensee, to the owner of the interest which is not in reversion on any other of the interests (*CAA 2001,* *s 176(2),(3)*). In other words, where expenditure is incurred by two persons jointly, the asset is deemed to belong to whichever of them has the lesser interest. In *JC Decaux (UK) Ltd v Francis (Insp of Taxes) (1996 STC (SCD) 281)*, the taxpayer company leased various items of street furniture (including automatic public conveniences, electric information boards, bus shelters, etc.) to local authorities. The Special Commissioner dismissed the company's appeal for capital allowances on fixtures under what is now *CAA 2001, s 176* because the company would need to have an interest in the relevant land, in accordance with what is now *CAA 2001, s 173(1)*. The company did not have such an interest under English law, nor did its contractual rights to clean and maintain the equipment amount to a licence to occupy the land.

10.94 HMRC consider that a licence to occupy land 'will only arise where the claimant has an exclusive licence to occupy the land in question. A licence to occupy is a permission to enter and remain on a land for such a purpose as enables the licensee to exert control over the land. It is this level of control that suggests that a licence to occupy must be an exclusive licence' (Tax Bulletin 47, May 2000). They claim that the idea of exclusive occupation is supported in part by rating law that says that there can only be one occupier of land. The expenditure has to be actually incurred during the relevant period, ie the allowance is not given on earlier expenditure deemed to be incurred when the trade commenced. HMRC make no reference to the House of Lords decision in *Street v Mountford (1985 1 AC 809)* to the effect that an exclusive licence normally constitutes a lease. It is odd that HMRC should choose to express this view of exclusivity so soon after they abandoned exclusivity as an infallible test of when a licence exists for VAT purposes (see **17.81**).

10.95 It needs to be borne in mind that there are a number of anti-avoidance provisions that will deny or restrict relief for capital allowances where plant is leased under a finance lease. Although these are aimed at the lessor, if the right to allowances is switched to the lessee by virtue of *CAA 2001, ss 172–195* the restriction will still apply.

Right of a Purchaser of the Interest to Claim Allowances

10.96 The purchaser of an interest in a property can take over the right to allowances. If, after an item becomes a fixture:

(*a*) a person (called a 'purchaser' although it will include a person who acquires in any other manner) acquires an interest in the land (other than one created on his purchase); and

(*b*) the consideration he gives for that interest includes a capital sum which falls wholly or partly to be treated as expenditure on the provision of the fixture, that fixture is treated for capital allowance purposes as thereafter belonging to the purchaser (*CAA 2001, s 181*). For example, if a lessee to whom the fixture is treated as belonging sells his lease, the purchaser is entitled to contend that the price he pays includes a payment in respect of the fixture on which he is entitled to claim capital allowances. The purchaser can also claim the allowances in such circumstances if the fixture was leased to the vendor under an equipment lease and the purchaser paid a capital sum to the lessor to discharge the lessee's obligations under the lease (*CAA 2001, s 182*).

10.97 It is not clear what is meant by 'falls wholly or partly to be treated as expenditure on the provision of the fixture' ((*b*) of **10.84** above). It may be that this envisages the right to allowances passing to the purchaser only where part of the price he pays for the assignment of the lease is specifically attributed to the asset. It is more likely that it envisages an apportionment of the capital sum needing to be made where there is no such attribution. Such an apportionment would normally generate a balancing charge to the vendor. It would therefore be wisest to agree an apportionment on an assignment of a lease where the assignor has previously claimed allowances under these provisions or to agree that an appropriate election should be made under *CAA 2001, s 198* (see **10.127**) to prevent such a charge arising.

Election to Transfer Right to Allowances to an Incoming Lessee who Pays a Premium

10.98 If, after an item has become a fixture, a person who has an interest in the land and who is entitled to claim the allowance in respect of the fixture (or would be but for not being within the charge to tax) grants a lease at a premium, the lessor and lessee can jointly elect for the fixture to be treated as belonging to the lessee for capital allowance purposes in consequence of his incurring expenditure on its provision (*CAA 2001, s 183(1)*). The election must be made in writing within two years after the lease takes effect (and *not* two years after the end of the accounting period) (*CAA 2001, s 183(2)*).

10.99 Such an election cannot be made if the lessor and lessee are connected persons of one another (within *ITA 2007, s 993* – see **Appendix 1** (*CAA 2001, s 183(1)(d)*).

10.100 This provision allows a sublessee who pays a premium to attribute part of that premium to the fixture and claim capital allowances on it.

Right of an Incoming Lessee to Claim Allowances

10.101 If someone with an interest in the land but who is not entitled to capital allowances grants a lease at a premium, the landlord's fixtures included in the building are treated as belonging to the lessee, so that he will become entitled to claim the capital allowances. This does not apply if the asset had been used for the purpose of a trade by the lessor or a connected person of his (within *ITA 2007, s 993* – see Appendix 1) (*CAA 2001, s 184*). No election is necessary; the lessee has an automatic entitlement. This will cover the situation where a freeholder or a tenant installs equipment not for the purpose of a trade or for letting other than in the course of a trade and grants a lease at a premium. The obvious, and perhaps only, circumstance in which a person who intends to grant a lease can incur expenditure other than for letting is where he is a property dealer. As there is no requirement for him to have incurred *capital* expenditure this is probably what the provision is aimed at, ie it allows a person who pays a premium to a property dealer on the grant of a lease to attribute part of that premium to fixtures and claim capital allowances. The requirement that no one must have previously been entitled to allowances must particularly be noted. In *West Somerset Railway plc v Chivers (1995 (STC) SCD, 1 SpC 1)* the taxpayer leased from BR a railway line that had initially been built between 1862 and 1874 by the Bristol and Exeter Railway Co. It was held no allowances were due as it was for the taxpayer to show that no one had previously claimed allowances and no records existed to enable it to do so. The Special Commissioner thought the reference to claiming allowances included allowances under the *Customs and Inland Revenue Act 1878* and it was therefore probable that someone, such as BR or Great Western Railway, had become entitled to allowances at some stage!

10.102 If an interest in land in which the relevant land (or any part of it) is comprised is held by any person at the time that the purchaser acquires his interest in the relevant land (or the lease is granted over it) and that interest is not the one acquired by the purchaser within *CAA 2001, s 181* (see **10.71**) or by the lessee within *CAA 2001, s 184* (see **10.765**), for example it is one held by a superior landlord, then *ss 181* or *184* as the case may be is not to apply if:

(*a*) the person holding that interest falls to be treated under these provisions as the owner of the asset (other than under *CAA 2001, s 537* by virtue of having made a contribution to its cost), and

(*b*) he is entitled to capital allowances in respect of it (*CAA 2001, ss 181(2), 184(2)*).

This prevents multiple claims to an allowance in respect of a single asset.

Purchase of an Existing Building

10.103 Where machinery or plant is treated as belonging to a person ('the new claimant') under these provisions, the part (if any) of that person's expenditure in excess of the 'maximum allowable amount' does not qualify for allowances if the asset was previously treated under these rules as belonging to some other person ('the prior claimant') at a 'relevant earlier time' and the prior claimant claimed capital allowances and was required to bring a disposal value into account subsequent to 24 July 1996 (*CAA 2001, ss 185(1),(2), Sch 3, para 38*). The maximum allowable amount is the sum of the disposal value brought into account by the prior claimant and any installation costs (qualifying under *CAA 2001, s 25*) incurred by the new claimant (*CAA 2001, s 185(3)*). In plain English this means that on the purchase of an existing building the maximum sum eligible for allowances is the vendor's disposal value of the plant (or that of the previous owner if the vendor was not within the scope of UK tax), plus the original cost of any items for which he did not claim allowances and the original cost of any pre-24 July 1996 items, plus of course any additional expenditure incurred by the purchaser. Where there has been more than one deemed change of ownership of the asset the disposal value to be brought into account is obviously that on the latest change (*CAA 2001, s 185(4)*). The restriction applies even where the prior and new claimants are the same person (*CAA 2001, s 185(5)*).

10.104 A relevant earlier time is any time before the new claimant incurred his expenditure. An earlier time is to be disregarded (so that the restriction will not come into play) if in consequence of an intervening sale the asset had ceased to belong to any person, the sale was not a sale of the plant or machinery as a fixture and the vendor and purchaser on that sale were not connected with one another (within *ITA 2007, s 993* – see **Appendix 1**), ie only if the item has been removed from the building.

10.105 If a person claimed industrial building allowances (IBAs see **Appendix 4**) instead of plant and machinery allowances and he transfers (eg sells) the relevant interest in the building, the capital allowances claimable by the purchaser (or other transferee) or by any subsequent 'owner' of the plant under these provisions is restricted to the 'relevant amount' unless his acquisition was before 25 July 1996. This is the amount equal to the part of the consideration for the transfer (from the IBA claimant) which would have been attributable to the fixture if the IBA claimant had sold the building for an amount equal to its residue of expenditure under the IBA rules (*CAA 2001, s 186*). This effectively limits the amount eligible for plant and machinery allowances to the original cost of the relevant assets. The restriction does not apply if the fixtures have been severed from the building prior to the sale.

10.106 Similarly, where the vendor or a previous owner has at any time claimed scientific research allowance in respect of plant and machinery which is a fixture the purchaser (or transferee) can claim plant and machinery allowances only on 'the relevant amount'. The relevant amount is the proportion of the disposal value of the asset when it ceased to be used for scientific research that is attributable to the fixture (or if less, the proportion of the expenditure on which the scientific research allowance was claimed that is attributable to the fixture) (*CAA 2001, s 187*).

10.107 In relation to the purchase of a building (or other expenditure on fixtures) after 5 April 2012 (31 March for corporation tax) if the fixtures were treated as having been owned at a 'relevant earlier time' by a previous purchaser for the purpose of a qualifying activity, and a previous purchaser (not necessarily the same one) was entitled to claim a capital allowance in respect of his expenditure, the purchaser's expenditure on fixtures is deemed to be NIL, ie no capital allowance can be claimed, unless either:

(*a*) the pooling requirement is satisfied (see **10.109**);

(*b*) the fixed value requirement applies and is satisfied (see **10.110**); or

(*c*) the disposal value statement applies and is satisfied (see **10.116**).

(*CAA 2001, s 187A(3).*)

The Treasury say that this means that the pooling requirement needs to be satisfied in all cases and, in addition, one or other of the fixed value or disposal value statement requirements must be met (Finance Act 2012 Explanatory Notes). In most cases it will be the fixed value requirement. The pooling requirement did not normally apply prior to 5 April 2014 (1 April for corporation tax) though. This deeming does not of course affect the disposal value to be brought into account by the past owner (*CAA 2001, s 187B(6)*).

The Pooling Requirement

10.108 The pooling requirement is that the previous owner's expenditure was allocated to a pool in an accounting period beginning before the current owner's (ie the taxpayer claiming the allowance) purchase of the building, or a first-year allowance was claimed in respect of it (or of any part of it) (*CAA 2001, s 187A(4)*). Allocation to a pool does not require the previous owner to have claimed allowances. It does, however, require him to have quantified the amount eligible for allowances and included it in his capital allowances computation. This is likely to create major practical problems. A property investor with a heavy borrowing often does not claim allowances as his interest charges exceed the rents. Accordingly the cost of quantifying the potential allowances due is not justified. In the past the availability of allowances has not been a significant factor affecting the purchase price. Accordingly where allowances have not been claimed in the past – or have been claimed only on some of the cost – what is a purchaser to do? The eligible amount is unlikely to be readily ascertainable and the vendor is unlikely to want to incur heavy costs to ascertain it.

10.109 The purchaser can obviously pay the costs of ascertaining the figure but this must be done before the vendor submits his tax return for his accounting period in which the disposal takes place (the date of the contract). This gives a period of between one and two years to come up with a figure that the vendor can put into his tax computations. Clearly the purchase agreement needs to impose requirements on the vendor to include an amount in his capital allowance pool, to agree that amount with the purchaser, and to co-operate with the purchaser in ascertaining the figure. Where the vendor has claimed allowances but not necessarily all that might be available, the purchaser will need to consider whether to carry out detailed work to determine whether a further amount is available. If the first purchaser after 1 April 2014 does not need the allowances he is unlikely to want to do this, but if he does not do so the right to allowances on the extra items is lost completely in relation to all future purchasers.

The Fixed Value Requirement

10.110 The fixed value requirement applies if the past owner is (or was) required to bring a disposal value of the fixture into account in accordance with any of *CAA 2001, s 196* item 1 (cessation of ownership of the fixture under *CAA 2001, s 188* because of a sale of the qualifying interest (to which item 2 does not apply)), item 5 (deemed cessation of ownership of the fixture under *CAA 2001, s 190* because the the owner and the lessee have elected to treat part of a premium for a lease as for the purchase of the asset (in such a case the application or election must of course be by the landlord and the lessee)), or item 9 (permanent discontinuation of the business followed by the sale of the qualifying interest). These three occasions cover the sale of the property and the receipt of a premium for a long lease, which are the main situations in which a right to claim allowances will pass to someone else.

10.111 The fixed value requirement is that either–

(*a*) a relevant apportionment of the sale price has been made (see **10.113**); or

(*b*) the past owner (or lessee) was not entitled to claim capital allowances in respect of his expenditure on the fixture and the current owner has obtained a written statement (or copies):

- (i) from his vendor that a relevant apportionment of the sale price was not made and is no longer capable of being made (ie the conditions for *CAA 2001, s 187A(6)(a)* have not been met and are no longer capable of being met), and also
- (ii) from the last person entitled to claim capital allowances of the amount of the disposal value that he in fact brought into account.

(CAA 2001, s 187A(6)(b)(8).)

The onus is on the current owner to show whether the requirement applies and if it does, whether it is satisfied (*CAA 2001, s 187B(1)(a)*). The normal rules that apply to a *ss 198* or *199* election (such as it is irrevocable) apply to elections made under this provision (*CAA 2001, s 187B(2)*).

10.112 The vendor will not have been entitled to claim capital allowances if it either held the property as trading stock, is a pension fund, charity or other tax-exempt body, or is a non-business person. It appears that for the provisions to apply, such a person must have acquired the property from someone else, and that at some past time someone must have been entitled to claim allowances. If the vendor is the first owner of the property and is not entitled to claim allowances, *s 187A* does not apply at all and the purchaser will be entitled to claim the allowances. Where there was a previous owner entitled to claim allowances and the tax-exempt vendor has incurred further expenditure, *s 187A* applies only to the earlier expenditure; the purchaser is entitled to claim allowances by reference to the further expenditure by the vendor. It appears that the allowance in respect of the earlier owner's expenditure is limited to the disposal value that he brought into account.

10.113 A relevant apportionment of the sale price is made only if either:

(*a*) the past owner, or a purchaser from the past owner, has applied to the First-tier Tribunal to determine the part of the sale price attributable to fixtures within two years of the sale; or

(*b*) an election is made by the past owner and the purchaser under *CAA 2001, s 198* (see **10.127**) or *s 199* (see **10.130**) within two years of the sale – or if an application has been made under (*a*) before that application is determined or withdrawn (*CAA 2001, s 187A(7)*). The normal two-year time limit for making a *s 198* or *199* election is of course disapplied where an application is made to the tribunal and is pending at the end of that period (*CAA 2001, s 201 (1A)*). It should, however, be noted that the rules have been modified to require the notice of election to include either the unique taxpayer reference number (UTR) of both parties to it or, if one or both does not have a UTR, a statement to that effect (*CAA 2001, s 201(3)(f)*). HMRC consider that a person who is not entitled to claim capital allowances is nevertheless able to enter into a *s 198* or *199* election.

Head (*b*) above is likely to become the normal situation. It requires a *s 198* election to have been made or an application to have been made to the tribunal to determine the transfer value to enable such an election to be made.

10.114 The election cannot be made on a sale at an undervalue to a person not eligible to claim allowances or to certain dual resident companies, or on the vendor's business ceasing without the building being sold (*CAA 2001, ss 196, 198(1)*). In such cases, the disposal value statement route will need to be used. There is a particular problem where a building is bought from an LPA Receiver. The Receiver sells as agent for the company and, as he never became the owner of the asset, is not able to enter into the appropriate election. This can be done by the owner, but as he will not see the sale proceeds he has little incentive to co-operate in either making the election or in pooling the expenditure if this has not previously been done. Where a property is bought from a liquidator, the liquidator can pool and certify but insolvency practitioners do not normally want to spend time and money to assist a purchaser unless by doing so they will increase the sale price of the building.

10.115 A further problem is that many landlords, particularly non-residents, do not claim allowances because their rental income is largely covered by interest and other outgoings and the cost of establishing the allowances due is not justifiable where those allowances cannot be used. The expenditure clearly cannot be pooled until it has been quantified. Accordingly the purchaser either needs to persuade the vendor to establish the allowances due as a condition of the purchase, or he needs to incur the cost himself and hope that the vendor will be prepared to pool the amount and make the appropriate election. As the vendor needs to pool the expenditure in his tax computations for his accounting period in which the sale takes place (and in many cases the sale will itself bring the accounting period to an end), and those computations need to be submitted within 12 months of the end of the accounting period, urgent action may be needed, particularly where the help of a surveyor is needed to quantify the eligible expenditure.

The Disposal Value Statement Requirement

10.116 The disposal value statement requirement applies only if the past owner is (or was) required to bring a disposal value of the fixture into account under *CAA 2001, s 196*, item 2 (cessation of ownership under *CAA 2001, s 188* because of a sale of the qualifying interest where the sale is at an undervalue and either the purchaser is a dual-resident investing company which is connected with the former owner, or the purchaser's expenditure on the fixture cannot qualify for capital allowances or for R&D allowances). *Section 188* deals with the situation where a person ceases to have a qualifying interest in the fixture under *CAA 2001, s 176* (person with interest in land having fixture for purposes of qualifying activity), *s 181* (purchaser of land giving consideration for fixture), *s 182* (purchaser of land discharging obligations of equipment lessee), *s 182A* (purchaser of land discharging obligations of client under energy service agreement), *s 183* (incoming lessee where lessor entitled to allowances), or *s 184* (income lessee where lessor not entitled to allowances) (*CAA 2001, s 187A(10)*).

10.117 The disposal value statement is that within two years of the past owner's sale, the past owner made a written statement of the amount of the disposal value that he was required to bring into account and the current owner holds that statement or a copy of it (*CAA 2001, s 187A(11)*). It is for the current owner to show whether the disposal value requirement applies and is satisfied (*CAA 2001, s 187B(1)(b)*). This is aimed at 'a very small subset of disposal events' that may have occurred other than by way of an immediate sale (or lease) of the fixtures. HMRC give as an example a trader who ceases to trade but does not sell the property until some years later (Finance Bill 2012, Explanatory Notes).

10.118 It is possible for the current owner and the past owner to be the same person (*CAA 2001, s 187B(3)*). Accordingly a person is given a right to apply to the First-tier Tribunal to determine a dispute with himself, ie to determine the value of the fixtures (*CAA 2001, s 563*). This is needed to deal with the situation where the vendor is tax exempt and unwilling to join in an application to the Tribunal. 'A relevant earlier time' means any time (after 5 April 2012) before the earliest time when the current owner is treated as owning the fixture as a result of incurring the new expenditure. However, it does not include a time before that in which a person ceased to own the plant as a fixture as a result of a sale, if that sale was not a sale of the plant as a fixture and the buyer and seller were not connected persons (*CAA 2001, s 187B(4)(5)*).

10.119 If a business premises renovation allowance was made to the past owner in respect of the expenditure and a balancing event occurred in relation to that owner, the current owner cannot claim allowances on more than the 'maximum allowable amount', namely the proportion of the past owner's expenditure (less the premises renovation allowance minus any balancing charge) that the proceeds from the balancing event that is attributable to the fixture bears to the total proceeds from that event (*CAA 2001, s 186A(2)(3)* inserted by *FA 2012, Sch 10, para 6*). If the past owner's expenditure is less than (or equal to) the disposal proceeds, the current owner's maximum allowable amount is the part of the past owner's sale proceeds that is attributable to the fixture (*CAA 2001, s 186A(2)–(5)*). The current owner for this purpose means either the purchaser of the fixture from the past owner, or any other person who subsequently came to own it (*CAA 2001, s 186A(6)*).

10.120 These restrictions apply to expenditure incurred after 5 April 2012 (1 April for corporation tax) and to balancing events in relation to business premises renovation allowances arising after that date (*FA 2012, Sch 10, paras 11, 12*). If a fixture would be treated under *CAA 2001, s 187A(1)(b)* as having been owned at a time which both began and ended before 5 April 2012 by a person as a result of incurring capital expenditure on its provision, that period of ownership is ignored for the purpose of applying that provision (*FA 2012, Sch 10, para 13*). This apparently means that neither the pooling requirement nor the requirements to fix formally the value of fixtures apply in relation to such a period of ownership. As mentioned earlier, *CAA 2001, s 187A(3)(a)* (which imposes the pooling requirement) does not apply if the period for which the fixture is treated as having been owned by the past owner as a result of incurring the historic expenditure ends before 5 (or 1) April 2014 (*FA 2012, Sch 10, para 13(2)*). This is a small relief to cover the position where the property is sold to a non-business owner after 5 April 2012 who is unable to pool his expenditure. It is not wholly clear why it is needed.

Deemed Disposal by a Person who has Claimed Allowances

10.121 All of the above provisions are made subject to *CAA 2001, s 188*. This provides that when the person to whom a fixture is treated as belonging under the above provisions ceases to own the qualifying interest (ie the one that entitled him to claim capital allowances) the fixture must be treated as ceasing to belong to him at that time (*CAA 2001, s 188(1),(2)*). This will create a balancing charge or allowance if he has claimed capital allowances. It applies irrespective of whether cessation of ownership is by reason of its transfer, surrender, expiry or otherwise.

10.122 If the qualifying interest continues in existence (or would have continued but for having become merged in another interest) the former owner is treated as having sold the fixture (*CAA 2001, ss 189, 196*). The deemed price on such a sale will be as follows:

(*a*) If the cessation of ownership arises on an actual sale of the qualifying interest, the deemed price will be the part of the sale price which is treated as the purchaser's cost price of the fixture for capital allowance purposes (*CAA 2001, s 196(1)*). If the sale is at an undervalue, (*c*) below will apply instead, unless the purchaser is itself entitled to claim capital allowances (*CAA 2001, s 196(1)*). This prevents a sale at an artificially low price to a purchaser who is not within the scope of UK tax to avoid a balancing charge on the vendor. This deemed sale price will, in most cases, be 'the actual consideration … if any, for the fixtures which passes between the parties concerned, assuming that they are acting on an arm's length basis' (Hansard, 10 July 1985, Col 1186), ie if the parties agree to attribute a specific portion of the sale price for the interest to the fixture that is the figure that will normally be adopted. If they do not make such an attribution, an apportionment will need to be made by a valuer as provided for by *CAA 2001, ss 562–564*.

(*b*) If the cessation of ownership is a deemed cessation arising as a result of an election under **10.98** above for a lessee to claim allowances, the deemed price will be the part of the premium paid by the lessee which is treated for capital allowance purposes as expenditure by the lessee on the fixture (see **10.123** below).

(*c*) In any other case, the deemed price will be the portion of the price which, on a sale of the qualifying interest in the open market immediately prior to the cessation of ownership (and disregarding that cessation for valuation purposes), would fall for capital allowances purposes to be treated as expenditure by the purchaser on the provision of the fixture (see **10.123** below).

(*d*) If the qualifying interest does not continue in existence, eg the cessation of ownership is on the expiry or termination of a lease or licence, the deemed sale price is nil unless the former owner receives a capital sum by reference to the fixture, for example by way of compensation; in such a case it will be that sum.

(*CAA 2001, s 196, Table.*)

Disposal of Fixtures

10.123 If the taxpayer permanently discontinues his trade while the fixture is still owned (or deemed to be owned) by him, a disposal value needs to be calculated under *CAA 2001, s 61(2)*. If in such a case the fixture is severed from the land following the cessation, the sale proceeds of the fixture are not adopted as the disposal value (*CAA 2001, s 196, Table, item 6*). This is because the act of severing it from the land is likely to mean that the fixture has a scrap value only. The effect seems to be to bring *CAA 2001, s 196, Table, item 7* into play, so that the deemed disposal value is an apportioned part of the value of the building at the time of the cessation. If, following the severance, the building itself is sold the disposal value will be an apportioned part of the sale proceeds even though at that stage the fixture does not form part of the building (*CAA 2001, s 196, Table, items 9–11*). If a disposal value arises because the fixture ceases to be used wholly for the purpose of the deemed owner's trade, that disposal value will be the proportion of the sale price which would be attributable to the fixture if the deemed owner's interest in the land were sold in the open market (*CAA 2001, s 196, Table, item 12*). In other words, the purchaser cannot claim allowances on an amount greater than the original cost of the fitting (or its cost on its first acquisition after 11 July 1984 if there has been an intermediate purchase) if the vendor – or any previous owner since 11 July 1984 – claimed capital allowances.

10.124 The purchaser will normally be entitled to allowances under general principles on the amount of his expenditure on the asset (his cost price).

10.125 If a fixture ceases to belong to a deemed owner on the termination of a lease or licence it is treated as beginning to belong to the person who was the lessor or licensor (*CAA 2001, s 193*). This deeming will, however, only confer a right to capital allowances on the lessor if, and to the extent that, he has paid compensation to the lessee in respect of the fixture (as otherwise he will not have incurred capital expenditure on it) (*CAA 2001, s 196, Table, item 4*).

10.126 If there is a disposal or other event that requires a disposal value to be brought into account which would otherwise be less than the 'notional written-down value' of the machinery or plant, and that event is comprised in (or occurs in pursuance of) a scheme or arrangement which has tax avoidance as one of its main objects, the disposal value must be treated as if it were that notional written-down value (*CAA 2001, s 197(1)(2)*). The notional written-down value is arrived at by deducting from the cost the capital allowances that would have been claimable if that item were the only item of plant acquired by the owner (even if they were not in fact claimed). Tax avoidance for this purpose means obtaining a capital allowance (or greater allowance) or avoiding (or reducing) a balancing charge.

Election on Purchase of a Building

10.127 On the purchase of an existing building the purchaser and vendor can jointly elect that the disposal value should be some figure other than that given at **10.123**. The figure adopted must not exceed the lower of:

(*a*) the capital expenditure that was treated for capital allowance purposes as incurred by the vendor when he acquired the fixture; and

(*b*) the actual sale price of the entire qualifying interest in the building (or premium for the lease where *s 183* applies (see **10.98**)).

(*CAA 2001, s 198.*)

10.128 The balance of the expenditure is treated as attributable to the acquisition of the interest in the building. This obviously displaces the normal apportionment rule under *CAA 2001, ss 562–564* (see **10.122**(*a*)) (*CAA 2001, s 200(2)*). Where *CAA 2001, s 186* (see **10.106**), *187* (see **10.107**) or *197* (see **10.96**) applies that provision must of course be applied first. The election must be made in writing and contain the names of both parties and their tax district references and sufficient information to identify the machinery or plant concerned, the relevant land and the interest acquired by the purchaser (or particulars of the lease granted to him). The amount fixed by the election must be quantified at the time the election is made (but if later circumstances result in a reduction of the maximum permissible amount it is obviously reduced to reflect the new figure). The election must be made within two years of the purchaser acquiring his interest in the property and a copy of the election must be attached to both parties' tax returns. In the case of dispute each party is entitled to appear before the First-tier Tribunal and the Tribunal must determine the amount deemed to be the disposal value as a separate issue to any other question in the proceedings (*CAA 2001, ss 200, 201*).

10.129 HMRC say that since the rules on fixtures work on an asset by asset basis an election would need to be made in respect of each individual fixture. In practice they accept that the election can apply to a group of assets provided that it does not distort the tax computation. In particular they will accept an election covering all of the fixtures in a single property. They will not, however, accept a single election covering fixtures in more than one property (Tax Bulletin 35, June 1998).

10.130 The following will not be treated as a cessation of the deemed owner's interest in the fixture and will therefore not give rise to a balancing adjustment or a disposal value:

(*a*) A merger of the qualifying interest (the one that entitled the former owner to claim capital allowances) with another interest owned by the owner – the merged interest must be treated as the same interest as the qualifying interest.

(*b*) If the qualifying interest is a lease, a new lease being granted to the lessee on its termination – the new lease must be treated as the same interest as the qualifying interest.

(*c*) If the qualifying interest is a licence, a new licence to occupy the land being granted on its termination – the two licences must be treated as the same interest.

(*d*) If the qualifying interest is a lease, the lessee remaining in possession of the land after its termination with the consent of the lessor but without a new lease being granted – the qualifying interest is treated as continuing to subsist as long as the lessee remains in possession.

(*CAA 2001, ss 188(2), 189.*)

10.131 If at any time a fixture is permanently severed from the land, the fixture must be treated as ceasing at that time to belong to the deemed owner, so as to generate a balancing adjustment or disposal value to him, unless he in fact retains the ownership of the item following its severance (*CAA 2001, s 191*).

10.132 A similar election to that at **10.127** can be made when a lessee assigns his lease and the purchaser pays a premium to him. The amount apportioned to fixtures in such a case is of course limited to the premium paid (*CAA 2001, s 199*).

Expenditure Incurred by an Equipment Lessor

10.133 If someone ('the equipment lessor') incurs capital expenditure on machinery or plant for leasing which becomes a fixture and would have been treated as belonging to the lessee if he had incurred the expenditure, and an agreement is entered into for a lease, directly or indirectly from the equipment lessor to another person (the 'equipment lessee') for the purposes of a trade carried on (or to be carried on) by the equipment lessee (or for leasing other than in the course of trade), then the equipment lessor and lessee can jointly elect that the fixture should be treated for capital allowance purposes as belonging to the equipment lessor (and not to the lessee) in consequence of his having incurred the expenditure (*CAA 2001, s 177(1)*). In other words, where a tenant leases equipment which becomes a landlord's fixture, the leasing company and the tenant can elect that the leasing company should be entitled to the capital allowances so as to reflect the commercial bargain between them. The election must be in writing and made to the Inspector within two years after the end of the accounting period related to the incurring of the expenditure for corporation tax and by the normal time limit for amending a return for income tax (*CAA 2001, s 177(5)*). Such an election should always be made as the lessee cannot himself claim the allowances as he will not be the person who incurred the expenditure. The lessor and lessee must not be connected persons of one another (within (*ITA 2007, s 993* – see Appendix 1). A lease of assets which will become landlord's fixtures should accordingly never be made between connected persons as neither can become eligible to claim capital allowances. HMRC consider that an election cannot be made before the lessee's trade has started (Tax Bulletin, Issue 13, October 1994). The election cannot be made if the lease is of plant or machinery in a dwelling house (*CAA 2001, s 178*).

10.134 If the trade has not started by the time the lease is entered into, the election is to treat the fixture as belonging to the lessee from the later of the time the expenditure is incurred or the commencement of the trade (*CAA 2001, s 177(3)*). The requirements that the lease must be for a trade or leasing activity of the equipment lessee, that the equipment lessee must be within the scope of UK tax and that the asset would have belonged to the lessee if he had incurred the expenditure do not apply if:

(*a*) the machinery or plant is fixed to land that is not a building or part of a building;

(*b*) the equipment lessee has an interest in that land;

(*c*) the equipment lessor is entitled to sever the machinery from the land at the end of the lease and retain it;

(*d*) once severed the machinery or plant is capable of being used for the same purposes on a different set of premises; and

(*e*) the lease is an operating lease.

This recognises the reality that in such circumstances the asset belongs to the equipment lessee even though ownership may technically pass to the lessor during the period it is fixed to the land.

(*CAA 2001, ss 177, 179.*)

10.135 The requirements were relaxed for expenditure between 28 July 2000 and 1 January 2008 on a boiler, heat exchanger, radiator or heating control that was installed in a building as part of a space or water heating system where the agreement for the lease was approved by the appropriate Minister under the Affordable Warmth Programme. It was not necessary for the equipment to be used in a trade; it could be installed in a dwelling house, and the equipment lessee did not have to be taxable in the UK or to be entitled to claim capital allowances (*CAA 2001, s 180(1)*).

10.136 The equipment will be treated as ceasing to belong to the equipment lessor if he at any time assigns his rights under the equipment lease, or his financial obligations under the lease are at any time discharged on payment of a capital sum or otherwise (*CAA 2001, s 192(2)*). In the case of an assignment he is treated as having sold it to the assignee at the amount of the consideration for the assignment (*CAA 2001, s 196, Table, item 7*). This will generate a balancing adjustment or a disposal value. The assignee will be treated as if an election had been made under **10.133** above for him to be the equipment owner and will thus become the person entitled to claim the allowances in the future (*CAA 2001, s 194(2)*).

10.137 A capital sum received in discharge of the lessor's financial obligations under the lease, must be treated as the sale proceeds of the asset and will generate a balancing adjustment or a disposal value. If a capital sum is paid by the equipment lessee to be released from his obligations, ie in effect, he purchases the asset from the lessor, it will be treated as further expenditure on the provision of the asset and the fixture will be treated thereafter as belonging to the equipment lessee (so that he will be entitled to claim allowances on that payment) (*CAA 2001, s 195*). If the financial obligations of the equipment lessee become vested in some other person that person stands in the equipment lessee's shoes (*CAA 2001, s 192(3)*).

Supplementary

10.138 Where a person becomes the deemed owner of a fixture under any of the above provisions no other person (such as the person who actually incurred the expenditure) can claim capital allowances in respect of it (*CAA 2001, s 190(2)*). This does not affect the entitlement of a person who makes a 'contribution' to the expenditure to claim allowances (to the exclusion of the deemed owner) on the amount of that contribution under *CAA 2001, s 538*. Between 1 July 2004 and 22 April 2009 if plant was leased in circumstances where it was treated as not forming part of the land, the lessor entered into arrangements for the transfer to some other person of his right to receive some or all of the rentals and the consideration received by the lessor under that arrangement did not fall to be brought into account by him either as income or as a capital allowance disposal receipt, *ICTA 1988, s 785A* applied to that consideration. This taxed the consideration as income for the period in which it was received. *Section 785A* was unlikely to apply to plant which became fixtures in many cases because *ICTA 1988, ss 774A* and *774D* took precedence and were likely to apply in such circumstances (*ICTA 1988, s 785A(5A)*. *Section 785A* was repealed by *FA 2009, Sch 25, para 9* in relation to transactions after 22 April 2009.

10.139 If a lessee incurs capital expenditure for the purposes of his trade on machinery or plant which he is required under the terms of his lease to provide and that equipment is not so installed as to become in law part of the building (ie it is not a landlord's fitting), the item is deemed to belong to him (if it would not otherwise do so) as long as he continues to use it for the purpose of his trade. On the expiry of his lease it will be treated as belonging to the lessor (and the expenditure as having been incurred by him) (*CAA 2001, s 70*). The purpose of this latter assumption is to ensure that if the landlord sells the item he will suffer a balancing charge. The provision seems to be defective as it does not say what is to happen if the tenant ceases to use the item for the purpose of his trade while the lease is still subsisting.

Long-life Assets

10.140 The writing-down allowance on expenditure on long-life assets is limited to 8% pa (6% prior to 1 April 2008 and 10% before 1 April 2012). Machinery or plant constitutes a long-life asset if at the time when it was new it could reasonably be expected that it would have a useful economic life of at least 25 years (*CAA 2001, ss 90, 102*). This is not the useful life to the purchaser. It is the overall expected life of the asset, eg if the purchaser expects to use the asset for ten years, will then sell it to a purchaser who will use it for another ten years and who will then resell it for use for a further six years it will be a long-life asset. Long life assets are included in the special rate pool (see **10.19**).

10.141 Where expenditure is incurred on long-life assets such assets are of course separated out into a separate pool of plant and machinery. If all of such assets are disposed of, the pool – and the allowances – continues unless the trade ceases at the same time (*CAA 2001, ss 101–103*). This is the normal rule in respect of a plant and machinery pool. If a disposal value, eg on the disposal of an asset, falls to be brought into account by virtue of an event which is comprised in (or occurs in pursuance of) a scheme or arrangement which has avoidance of tax as one of its main objects, and that disposal value is less than the 'notional written-down value' of that plant and machinery, the disposal value must be treated as if it were equal to the 'notional written-down value'. This is the figure which would create neither a balancing allowance nor a balancing charge if the expenditure on the plant or machinery in question had been the only expenditure in the pool, the *de minimis* limits did not apply to that plant and the taxpayer had claimed all the allowance to which he was entitled. Avoidance of tax for this purpose means obtaining a capital allowance or deduction (or a greater allowance or deduction) or avoiding (or reducing) a balancing charge (*CAA 2001, s 104*). This is, of course, an anti-avoidance provision to prevent the allowances being accelerated by selling machinery at an undervalue or even at its second-hand market value, to a connected person to try to trigger a balancing allowance.

10.142 There are a number of important exclusions. In the context of property, fixtures in (or provided for use in) a building used wholly or mainly as a dwelling house, retail shop (or similar premises where retail trade or business, including repair work, is carried on), showroom, hotel or office, or for purposes ancillary to such a use will not be long-life assets (*CAA 2001, s 93*). This effectively limits the application of *s 90* to those fixtures in factories, warehouses and specialist buildings that will not fit into one of the above categories, ie mainly (but not exclusively) in those buildings which used to qualify for industrial buildings allowances (see **Appendix 4**). The then Chancellor perceived 6% pa writing-down allowance as roughly equivalent to the then 4% straight-line IBA. The idea was to discourage taxpayers from splitting their expenditure on such buildings between plant and machinery and IBA expenditure.

10.143 There is an exclusion for expenditure incurred before 1 January 2011 on the provision of a railway asset for use in a railway business. Apart from trains, a railway asset includes anything which is (or is to be comprised in) a railway track, railway station or light maintenance depot, and any apparatus falling to be installed in association with such an asset. A railway includes tramways and other systems of guided transport. A light maintenance depot means such a depot within *Part 1* of the *Railways Act 1993* or the equivalent of such a depot in relation to a tramway, etc. A railway business is limited to the provision of a service to the public for the carriage of goods or passengers in the UK or the Channel tunnel (*CAA 2001, s 95(3)*).

10.144 There is a *de minimis* exclusion. An individual or a partnership does not have to treat assets as long-life ones if the total expenditure on such assets during an accounting year does not exceed £100,000 (reduced proportionately for a period of less than a year) (*CAA 2001, s 99*). For this exclusion to apply the individual must devote substantially the whole of his time to carrying on his trade or profession. In the case of a partnership this exclusion does not apply unless all of the partners are individuals and at least half of them devote substantially the whole of their time to the business. Even where the *de minimis* limit applies, any expenditure on the provision of a share in an asset for leasing (including fixtures in a rental building), or a contribution towards the acquisition of such an asset, or expenditure on the provision of such an asset, will attract the 8% rate (10% before 1 April 2012) (*CAA 2001, s 98*).

10.145 Where expenditure under a single contract is payable by instalments it must be assumed that all of the expenditure is incurred at the time of the first instalment for the purpose of applying the limit (*CAA 2001, s 100(4)*).

10.146 These last two rules also apply for corporation tax. For corporation tax purposes a single £25,000 *de minimis* limit (£100,000 before 1 April 2012) is apportioned equally between the company and all of its associated companies (*CAA 2001, s 99(4)*). Accordingly if there are ten associated companies each would have a limit of £2,500 only (even if only one is likely to purchase long-life assets) so the *de minimis* limit will be of little practical effect.

Energy-Saving Plant and Machinery

10.147 A 100% first-year allowance can be claimed on expenditure on energy-saving plant and machinery that is unused and not second-hand (*CAA 2001, s 45A(1)*).

10.148 Plant or machinery is energy-saving if, either when the expenditure is incurred or when the contract is entered into, it is of a description specified by Treasury Order and meets the energy-saving criteria specified by the Treasury for plant and machinery of that description (*CAA 2001, s 45A(2)*). The Treasury have made such an Order, the *Capital Allowances (Energy-saving Plant and Machinery) Order 2001* (*SI 2001 No 2541*) as amended, most recently by the *Capital Allowances (Energy-saving Plant and Machinery) (Amendment) Order 2015 (2015 SI No 1508).*

10.149 This states that plant and machinery is energy-saving if:

(*a*) it falls within a technology class specified in the Energy Technology Criteria list dated 2 July 2015 published by the Department for Energy and Climate Change (DECC) (previously by that of 1 July 2014 or before 1 July 2014 fell within the appropriate lists dated 5 July 2013, 25 August 2011, 3 August 2010, 6 July 2009, 16 July 2008, 18 July 2007, 24 July 2006, 14 July 2005, 15 July 2004, 11 July 2003 and 26 March 2001 published by the Department for Environment, Food and Rural Affairs (DEFRA) or the Department of the Environment, Transport and Regions);

(*b*) it meets the energy-saving criteria set out in that list;

(*c*) it falls within one of the classes of:

- (i) boilers;
- (ii) motors and drivers;
- (iii) refrigeration;
- (iv) thermal screens;
- (v) heat pumps (from 5 August 2002);
- (vi) radiant and warm air heaters (from 5 August 2002);
- (vii) compressed air equipment (from 5 August 2002);
- (viii) solar thermal systems (from 5 August 2003) (provided that the system or the solar collector included in it is of a type included in the Energy Technology Products list);
- (ix) automatic monitoring and targeting equipment (from 5 August 2002) (but portable equipment must be of a type within one of the two above lists, and a component based fixed system within the class 'automatic monitoring and targeting equipment; in the Energy Technology Criteria list);
- (x) air-to-air energy recovery equipment (from 26 August 2004);
- (xi) compact heat exchangers (from 26 August 2004 to 8 October 2010 only);
- (xii) heating, ventilation and air conditioning equipment (zone controls prior to 6 July 2009) (from 26 August 2004);
- (xiii) uninterruptible power supplies (from 6 July 2009);
- (xiv) high speed hand air dryers (from 1 October 2011); and

(*d*) it is of a type that is specified in, and has not been removed from, the Energy Technology Products List dated 2 July 2015 published by DECC (or its predecessors or has been accepted for inclusion in that list (para 2.3).

10.150 The Energy Technology Products List is a novel concept for taxation purposes. It is not a static list, so will need to be specifically consulted at the time it is proposed to purchase an item that might be eligible. The idea is that manufacturers should send details of their products to DECC (except for CHP, lighting or pipe insulation). If DECC is satisfied that a product meets the published energy-saving criteria it will issue a letter of acceptance and add the product to the Products List from that date. If the application is rejected, DECC will indicate why and invite modification. A potential buyer of a product can then consult the Products List. If he buys an item on it, that purchase will attract the 100% allowance. As might be expected the list is very detailed. There are seven broad categories:

(*a*) boilers (with 13 sub-headings);

(*b*) combined heat and power (CHP);

(*c*) lighting;

(*d*) motors and drives (with five sub-headings);

(*e*) pipework insulation;

(*f*) refrigeration (with seven sub-headings); and

(*g*) thermal screens.

Within each category the manufacturer and the qualifying product (identified normally by its product number where the manufacturer makes a range of products) is shown. HMRC and DECC have set up a joint website, called the Enhanced Capital Allowance scheme, www.eca.gov.uk, which contains both the Products List and an application form for manufacturers to apply for certification of their products. It will be seen from **10.149** that CHP, lighting and pipework insulation are not specified in the Order. This is probably to allow for custom-built installations to qualify.

10.151 The Treasury are given power by Order to specify that in some cases the allowance is dependent on there being in force a relevant certificate of energy efficiency. Again this is done in the *Capital Allowances (Energy-saving Plant and Machinery) Order 2001, art 4* (as amended) which requires such a certificate in relation to 'combined heat and power' (or until 1 October 2011 only, a component-based fixed system within the technology class 'Automatic Monitoring and Targeting equipment') specified in the Energy Technology Criteria list. A relevant certificate of energy efficiency is issued by the Minister and certifies that the plant meets the efficiency requirements. Such a certificate can be revoked. If this is done it is treated as never having been issued. In such circumstances, if the taxpayer becomes aware that the certification has been revoked he must tell HMRC within three months and amend his tax return accordingly (*CAA 2001, s 45B*). The concept is that because a CHP unit is usually custom built it is not practicable to certify the product as such. What needs to be certified is the entire unit. This can be done off plan, but DECC clearly need the right to check that the actual installation has been carried out in accordance with the plan and to withhold the certificate if it has not.

10.152 Where plant is purchased which incorporates components, some of which are included in the Products List and some not, the Treasury is given power to require the cost to be apportioned with only the part of the cost attributable to qualifying components attracting the 100% allowance. The part of the price apportioned to such components is limited to the amount specified in the Treasury Order. If the expenditure is incurred in instalments each instalment must be apportioned pro rata (*CAA 2001, s 45C*). The Treasury has specified items within classes (i), (ii), (iii), (vi), (vii), (x) and (xii) in **10.149** and specified as the allowable limit the amount specified in the Energy Technology Products List for the qualifying components (*Capital Allowances (Energy-saving Plant and Machinery) Order 2001, art 5*).

10.153 It is common with combined heat and power units for these to be installed and operated by a supplier in return for an annual fee. In such a case the supplier will retain ownership of the equipment but will not have an interest in the building in which it is installed. Ownership of the equipment will normally pass to the client on the termination of the contract. It is of course possible for similar arrangements to be entered into in relation to other types of equipment than CHP units. The energy services agreement will not normally constitute a lease so the rules at **10.133** onwards will not apply. To encourage such service providers to use energy efficient equipment, *CAA 2001, s 180A* (inserted by *FA 2001, s 66* and *Sch 18, para* 2) deems the energy service provider to own the equipment as a result of incurring the expenditure on it, even though in law as the equipment is affixed to the land it is owned by the landowner (*CAA 2001, s 180A(1)*).

10.154 *Section 180A* applies where:

(*a*) an 'energy services agreement' (see **10.155**) is entered into;

(*b*) the 'energy services provider' (see **10.155**) incurs capital expenditure under that agreement on the provision of plant or machinery;

(*c*) the plant or machinery becomes a fixture;

(*d*) at the time it becomes a fixture its client has an interest in the land but the energy services provider does not;

(*e*) the plant or machinery is not provided for leasing and is not provided in a dwelling house;

(*f*) the operation of the plant or machinery is carried out wholly or substantially by the energy services provider (or a person connected with him);

(*g*) the energy services provider and the client are not connected persons; and

(*h*) the client and the energy services provider elect that *s 180A* should apply.

(*CAA 2001, s 180A(1)*.)

10.155 An energy services provider is a person carrying on a qualifying activity consisting wholly or mainly in the provision of energy management services (*CAA 2001, s 175A(2)*). An energy services agreement is an agreement entered into by an energy services provider and another person that makes provision, with a view to saving energy or using energy more efficiently, for:

(*a*) the design of plant or machinery (or of a system or systems incorporating plant or machinery);

(*b*) obtaining and installing it;

(*c*) operating it; and

(*d*) maintaining it,

where the amount of any payment in respect of its operation is linked (wholly or partly) to energy savings or increased energy efficiency resulting from the provision or operation of the plant or machinery (*CAA 2001, s 175A(1)*).

10.156 If the client would not have been entitled to an allowance under *CAA 2001, s 176* (see **10.93**) if he had incurred the expenditure on the equipment the above election cannot be made unless the plant belongs to a class specified by Treasury Order (*CAA 2001, s 180A (2)(3)*). The only class specified to date appears to be the technology class 'Combined Heat and Power' specified in the Energy Technology Criteria List (*Capital Allowance (Energy-saving Plant and Machinery) Order 2001, art 5*). The Criteria List is also to be found at www.gov.uk. *Section 176* deals only with fixtures used for a qualifying activity. The Order will therefore, for example, grant the 100% first-year allowance for CHP units provided to a local authority or NHS trust, which would not itself be eligible to claim the allowance as it is not a taxable entity.

10.157 If a person purchases a building in which plant is provided under an existing energy services agreement, and in connection with that purchase he pays a capital sum to the energy service provider to discharge the agreement, the purchaser is treated as the owner of the fixture as a result of incurring expenditure equal to the payment (unless immediately after the purchase some other person has a prior right to the fixture), and *CAA 2001, s 188* (see **10.121**) will apply to the energy services provider (*CAA 2001, s 182A*). It appears that this will trigger a balancing charge on the energy services provider but will not entitle the purchaser to the 100% allowance as at that stage the plant will be second hand.

10.158 If the energy services provider at any time assigns his rights under the energy services agreement, or the client discharges his obligations under the agreement (on payment of a capital sum or otherwise), the energy services provider is treated as ceasing to be the owner of the equipment (*CAA 2001,* *s 192A*). In the case of an assignment the assignee is treated both as having incurred expenditure on the equipment for a price equal to the consideration given by him and as being an energy services provider who owns the equipment under *section 180A* (*CAA 2001, s 195A*). If the client pays a capital sum to discharge his obligations he is treated as having purchased the equipment for that amount (*CAA 2001, s 195B*).

10.159 From 6 April 2012 (1 April for corporation tax) expenditure does not qualify for the energy-saving plant or machinery relief if a payment is made (or another incentive given) in respect of electricity or heat generated by the plant or gas or fuel produced by it under a scheme established by virtue of the *Energy Act 2008, s 41* (feed-in tariffs) or (from 1 April 2013) a corresponding scheme in Northern Ireland or *s 100* regulations (renewable heat incentives) or (from 1 April 2013) regulations under the *Energy Act 2011, s 113* (*CAA 2001, s 45AA(1)(5)* inserted by *FA 2012, s 45(3)* and amended by *FA 2013, s 67*). If subsequent to completing a tax return, the taxpayer becomes aware that it has become incorrect because of the operation of this provision, he must tell HMRC what amendment is needed to his tax return within three months of the day on which he became aware of that fact (*CAA 2001, s 45AA(3)(4)*). This restriction applies to expenditure on a combined heat and power system only where that expenditure occurs after 5 April (or 1 April) 2014 (*CAA 2001, s 45AA(6)*).

Environmentally Beneficial Plant or Machinery

10.160 A 100% first year allowance also applies to expenditure on environmentally beneficial plant or machinery (*CAA 2001, ss 45H–45J*). The item must be unused and not secondhand, must not be a long-life asset, and must not qualify for a 100% first-year allowance under some other provision. The item must be environmentally beneficial either at the time the expenditure is incurred or the time a contract for its provision is entered into (*CAA 2001, s 45H(1)(2)*).

10.161 Plant is environmentally beneficial if it is of a description specified by Treasury Order and meets the environmental criteria specified in the Order. The Treasury have power to make such Orders as they think appropriate to promote the use of technologies or products designed to remedy or prevent damage to the physical environment (*CAA 2001, s 45H(3)(a)*). They have done so by the *Capital Allowances (Environmentally Beneficial Plant and Machinery) Order 2003 (SI 2003 No 2076)* as amended several times, most recently by the *Capital Allowances (Environmentally Beneficial Plant and Machinery) (Amendment) Order 2015 (SI 2015 No 1509)*. The Order specifies plant falling within the Water Technology Criteria list dated 28 June 2015 or Water Technology Products list dated 7 July 2015 (or previously those dated 1 July 2014, 23 June 2013, 18 July 2007, 16 July 2008, 7 July 2009, 13 September 2010, 26 June 2011 and 17 September 2012) published by DECC which meets the environmental criteria specified in that list and which is of a type that has been specified in (and not removed from) the Water Technology Products list or has been accepted for inclusion in that list and is either:

(*a*) flow controllers;

(*b*) leakage detection equipment;

(*c*) meters and monitoring equipment (meters only prior to 11 August 2008);

(*d*) efficient taps (any taps prior to 11 August 2008);

(*e*) efficient toilets (any toilets prior to 11 August 2008);

(*f*) rainwater harvesting equipment (from 26 August 2004);

(*g*) water reuse systems (efficient membrane filtration systems for the treatment of waste water only between 22 September 2005 and 11 August 2008) (but see **10.162**);

(*h*) cleaning in place equipment (from 22 September 2005);

(*i*) efficient showers (from 22 September 2005);

(*j*) efficient washing machines (from 7 September 2006);

(*k*) small scale slurry and sludge dewatering equipment (from 7 September 2006);

(*l*) vehicle wash waste reclaim units (from 16 August 2007);

(*m*) water efficient industrial cleaning equipment (any efficient industrial cleaning equipment between 16 August 2007 and 11 August 2008 (but see **10.162**);

(*n*) water management equipment for mechanical seals (any such waste management equipment between 16 August 2007 and 11 August 2008 (but see **10.162**); and

(*o*) greywater recovery and reuse equipment (from 7 August 2013).

If a component of plant falls within items (*a*) to (*c*) (but the plant itself does not do so), the allowance is given on the amount specified in the list in relation to that component. It will be apparent that the only technology that the government intend to designate at the present is water technologies chosen for their potential to minimise water use or to improve water quality, such as metering and monitoring equipment, flow controllers, leakage detection equipment and efficient taps and toilets (Hansard SCB, 20 May 2003, Cols 170/171). The list can be found atwww. gov.uk.

10.162 As with energy technologies, the Treasury can provide that the allowance should not be given unless a relevant certificate of environmental benefit (see **10.151**) is in force (*CAA 2001, s 45I*). This is intended to cover items that are too specialised or complex to be included in the generic list of products. The detailed rules mirror those in *s 45A* (see **10.151**). The Treasury have power to provide for the apportionment of expenditure where some components of the plant qualify and some do not. The rules mirror those in *s 45C* (see **10.152**). They have set such a proviso for items within (*g*) (*m*) and (*n*) above. This will qualify for the allowance only if such a certificate is in force (*Article 5* of the *Order*).

Plant or Machinery for Gas Refuelling Station

10.163 A 100% first-year allowance can also be claimed for expenditure between 16 April 2002 and 31 March 2018 on plant or machinery for a gas refuelling station provided that the plant is unused and not second-hand (*CAA 2001, s 45E* as amended by *FA 2013, s 69* and the *Capital Allowances Act 2001 (Extension of First-year Allowances)(Amendment) Order 2015 (SI 2015 No 60)*). This covers plant for use solely for (or in connection with) refuelling vehicles with natural gas or hydrogen fuel. It includes storage tanks, any compressor, pump, control or meter used for or in connection with refuelling vehicles with such fuels, and equipment for dispensing such fuels to the fuel tank of a vehicle. The Treasury have power to extend the qualifying period (*CAA 2001, s 45E(1A)* inserted by *FA 2014, s 64*).

Electric Vehicle Charging Points

10.164 The 100% allowances also applies to expenditure between 23 November 2016 and 5 April 2019 (31 March 2019 for corporation tax) on plant or machinery for an electric vehicle charging point where that plant is unused, not second-hand and not excluded by *CAA 2001, s 46* (general exclusions) (*CAA 2001, s 45EA(1)(3)* inserted by *F(No 2)A 2017, s 38*). The plant must be installed solely for the purpose of charging electric vehicles (*CAA 2001, s 45EA(2)*). The Treasury have power to extend the relief beyond 2019 (*CAA 2001, s 45EA(4)*). An electric vehicle is defined as a road vehicle that can be propelled by electric power (whether or not it can also be propelled by another kind of power) and an electric vehicle charging point is defined as a facility for charging an electric vehicle (*CAA 2001, s 45EA(5)*).

Business Premises Renovation Allowance

10.165 This allowance is given only for expenditure between 11 April 2007 and 5 April 2017 (31 March 2017 for corporation tax)(*FA 2005, s 92* and *Business Premises Renovation Allowances (Amendment) Regulations 2012 (SI 2012 No 868)*). It applies to a person who (after that start date) incurs 'qualifying expenditure' in relation to a 'qualifying building' and has the 'relevant interest' in the building (*FA 2005, s 92* and *CAA 2001, s 360A*). The Treasury have power by Regulation to extend that period (*CAA 2001, s 360B(2)*).

10.166 The allowance is a 100% first-year allowance. A claim can be made to take a reduced allowance, in which case a writing down allowance of 25% of the qualifying expenditure (or such reduced amount as may be claimed) can be claimed in subsequent years (*CAA 2001, ss 360G, 360J(1)(4)*). The writing down allowance is proportionately increased or reduced if the chargeable period is more or less than a year (*CAA 2001, s 360J(2)*). The total initial and writing down allowances are limited to the amount of qualifying expenditure (*CAA 2001, ss 360J(3)(4), 360K*). No initial allowance can be claimed (and any allowance previously given is withdrawn) if the building does not constitute 'qualifying business premises' at the time that it is first used by the person with the relevant interest (or if it is not used by him the time when it is first suitable for letting as qualifying business premises) (*CAA 2001, s 360H*). No writing down allowance can be claimed if the person otherwise entitled to the allowance has granted a lease of over 50 years out of the relevant interest in consideration of the payment of a capital sum, or if the qualifying building does not constitute qualifying business premises at the end of the chargeable period. *ITTOIA 2005, s 303* (see **3.23**) applies for this purpose (without regard to *CAA 2001, s 360Z3(3)*, see **10.182**) (*CAA 2001, s 360I*). This is a nasty restriction as the lessee does not become entitled to claim the allowance. From 1 April 2014, expenditure does not qualify for relief if the qualifying building was used at any time during the period of 12 months ending with the day on which the expenditure was incurred (*CAA 2001, s 360B(3D)* inserted by *FA 2014, s 66(5)*). Accordingly, permitting temporary use by a charity – or it appears suffering unauthorised use by squatters – loses the relief completely.

10.167 Qualifying expenditure is capital expenditure incurred before 5 April 2017, which is:

(*a*) incurred on either:

- (i) the conversion of a qualifying building into qualifying business premises,
- (ii) the renovation of a qualifying building if it is (or will be) qualifying business premises, or
- (iii) repairs to a qualifying building (or where the building is part of a building, to the building of which the qualifying building forms part) to the extent that those repairs are incidental to expenditure within (i) or (ii); and

(*b*) which is incurred on:

(i) building works,

(ii) architectural or design services,

(iii) surveying or engineering services,

(iv) planning applications,

(v) statutory fees or statutory permits, or

(vi) expenditure on matters not falling within (i) to (v) but only up to 5% of the qualifying expenditure falling within items (i) to (iii).

(*CAA 2001, s 360B(1),(2A)–(2C)* as substituted by *FA 2014, s 66(2).*)

Prior to 1 April 2014, it was capital expenditure on, or in connection with, either

(*a*) the conversion of a qualifying building into qualifying business premises;

(*b*) the renovation of a qualifying building which either was or would become qualifying business premises; or

(*c*) repairs to a qualifying building (or a building of which the qualifying building formed part) to the extent that such repairs were incidental to expenditure within (a) and (b) – and of course to the extent that the cost was not deductible as revenue expenditure.

(*CAA 2001, s 360B(2)(4).*)

10.168 However, qualifying expenditure excludes: the acquisition of land or rights in or over land; the extension of a qualifying building (except to the extent required to provide a means of access to qualifying business premises); the development of land adjoining or adjacent to a qualifying building; and the provision of plant and machinery (unless it becomes a fixture as defined in *CAA 2001, s 173(1)* – see **10.54**) and, from 1 April 2014, unless it consists of one of the following items (*CAA 2001, s 360B(3)*). Allowable fixtures are:

(*a*) integral features (as defined in *CAA 2001, s 33A* – see **10.68**) or part of such a feature;

(*b*) automatic control systems for opening and closing doors, windows and vents;

(*c*) window cleaning installations;

(*d*) fitted cupboards and blinds;

(*e*) protective installations, such as lightning protection, sprinkler and other equipment for containing or fighting fires, fire alarm systems and fire escapes;

(*f*) building management systems;

(*g*) cabling in connection with telephone, audio-visual data installations and computer networking facilities, which are incidental to the occupation of the building;

(*h*) sanitary appliances, and bathroom fittings which are hand driers, counters, partitions, mirrors or shower facilities,

(*i*) kitchen and catering facilities for producing and storing food and drink for the occupants of the building;

(*j*) signs;

(*k*) public address systems; and

(*l*) intruder alarm systems.

(*CAA 2001, s 360B(3A)* inserted by *FA 2014, s 66(5)*.)

The Treasury have power by Regulation to amend the definition and to add or remove items from the list of allowable fixtures (*CAA 2001, s 360B(5)* as amended by *FA 2014, s 66(6)*).

10.169 From 1 April 2014, if any allowable expenditure exceeds that which it would have been normal and reasonable to incur on the works, services or other matters in the market conditions prevailing when the expenditure was incurred, and assuming the transaction as a result of which it was incurred was between persons dealing with each other at arm's length in the open market, no relief is given for that excess (*CAA 2001, s 360B(3B),(3C)*).

10.170 From 1 April 2014, if qualifying expenditure is incurred in a chargeable period and the works, services or other matters to which it relates are not completed or provided within 36 months from the date the expenditure was incurred (see **10.34**) the expenditure does not qualify for relief in that period to the extent that it relates to items still to be completed at the end of the three-year period (*CAA 2001, s 360BA(1),(2)*). All such adjustments and assessments must be made as are needed to give effect to this provision (*CAA 2001, s 360BA(3)*). If a person who has made a return becomes aware that it has become incorrect by virtue of this provision, he must tell HMRC what adjustments are needed within three months from the day on which he first became aware that something in the return had become incorrect (*CAA 2001, s 360BA(4),(5)*). The relief is not lost completely. The expenditure is treated as incurred at the time the works are completed or goods provided, so qualifying for relief in that later period (*CAA 2001, s 360BA(6)*).

10.171 A 'qualifying building' is a building or structure (or part of a building or structure), which:

(*a*) is situated in an area which is a disadvantaged area on the date on which the conversion or renovation work begins;

(*b*) was unused throughout the 12 months ending immediately before that date;

(*c*) had last been used either for the purposes of a trade, profession or vocation or as an office or offices (for any purpose);

(*d*) had not last been used as (or as part of) a dwelling; and

(*e*) in the case of part of a building or structure, had not been last occupied and used in common with any other part of the building (other than a part which itself was unused throughout the 12-month period or which had last been used as a dwelling).

(*CAA 2001, s 360C(1)*.)

10.172 The Treasury have power by Regulation to make further provision as to the circumstances in which a building is, or is not a qualifying building (*CAA 2001, s 360C(7)*). They have done so by the *Business Premises Renovation Allowances Regulations 2007 (SI 2007 No 945)* as amended by the *Business Premises Renovation Allowances (Amendment) Regulations 2012 (SI 2012 No 868)* and the *Business Premises Renovation Allowances (Amendment) Regulations 2014 (SI 2014 No 1687)* to exclude:

(*a*) expenditure incurred on, or in connection with, a qualifying building which is not in a disadvantaged area on the date the expenditure is incurred; and

(*b*) expenditure on a single project which, together with expenditure on that project in the previous three years, exceeds €20 million.

10.173 Up to 11 April 2012 the exclusion was for a trade in relation to which EU Commission Regulation EC/ 1628/2006 on the application of the EU Treaty to national regional investment aid did not apply. Expenditure is on a single project if it is incurred within the previous three years and together with the current expenditure would be treated as incurred as part of a single investment project for the purposes of the *General Block Exemption Regulation, Art 14(3)*.

10.174 The Treasury are also given power by Regulation to designate disadvantaged areas. If they do not do so the SDLT designation (see **19.172**) applies (*CAA 2001, s 360C(2)–(5)*). They initially designated as disadvantaged areas the 'areas specified as development areas by the Assisted Areas Order 2007' and the whole of Northern Ireland (*Business Premises Renovation Allowances Regulations 2007 (SI 2007 No 945)*). From 22 July 2014, they instead designated the 'areas specified as development areas by the Assisted Areas Order 2014' (*Business Premises Renovation Allowances (Amendment) Regulations 2014 (SI 2014 No 1687)*). The change brings in some new areas but excludes some areas that were previously designated. The Treasury subsequently designated further areas by the *Capital Allowances (Designated Assisted Areas) Order 2015 (SI 2015 No 2047)*.

10.175 The designated areas are summarised in **Appendix 3**. As indicated above, relief is due if the building was in a designated area at the time the conversion or renovation work began. However, the *2012 Regulations* (see above) deny relief for expenditure incurred after the designation is withdrawn. If the change in designation adds an area that was not designated when the work began no relief is due even on expenditure after the change in designation. If at the date that the work of conversion or renovation begins the building is situated partly in a disadvantaged area and partly outside, only the expenditure which (on a just and reasonable apportionment) is attributable to the part within the disadvantaged area qualifies for relief (*CAA 2001, s 360C(6)*). The legislation gives no guidance as to when a project begins. It may well be before the qualifying expenditure was incurred, as non-qualifying expenditure is nevertheless expenditure on the conversion or renovation. However, as the provision refers to 'work' it probably does not begin before any physical work on the building takes place.

10.176 In *Senix Investment Ltd v HMRC (2015 SFTD 501)*, the company bought a derelict church and converted it into a restaurant. The issue was whether the prior church use by the Weslyan Reform Union was use for the purpose of a trade, profession or vocation. The company said that an individual who carries on the self-employed activity as a minister of religion carries on a profession and the church was used for the purpose of that profession. They also said that the WRU carried on a trade, albeit that it was non-profit-making, as it would have aimed to generate income to meet its costs and it was clear from the WRU constitution that the church was run on business lines. The FTT agreed that the activities of the church amounted to a trade, so the church was a qualifying building.

10.177 'Qualifying business premises' are any building or structure (or part of a building or structure) which:

(*a*) constitute a qualifying building;

(*b*) are used, or available and suitable for letting for use, either for the purposes of a trade, profession or vocation or an office or offices; and (*c*) are not used, or available for use as (or as part of) a dwelling.

(*CAA 2001, s 360D(1)(2).*)

10.178 If qualifying business premises become temporarily unsuitable for use within (*b*) they are treated as remaining qualifying business premises during that temporary period (*CAA 2001, s 360D(3)*).

10.179 The Treasury have power by Regulation to amend the definition (*CAA 2001, s 360D(4)*). They have excluded from the definition premises where the person entitled to the relevant interest in the premises is carrying on a trade therein in the fishery and agricultural sector; the coal sector; steel sector; shipbuilding sector; synthetic fibres sector; transport sector or related infrastructure; or in the primary agricultural production sector; or which relates to the development of broadband networks or energy generation, distribution or infrastructure; or which is carried on by an undertaking which is subject to an outstanding recovery order made by the *Treaty on the Functioning of the European Union, Art 108(2)* or it is reasonable to assume would be regarded as an undertaking in difficulty for the purposes of the *General Block Exemption Regulation (Commission Regulation No 651/2014*) declaring certain categories of aid compatible with the internal market).

10.180 Many of the above terms are defined in the *General Block Exemption Regulation*. Prior to 22 July 2014, the exclusion for premises carrying on a trade in relation to which *EC Regulation 800/2008, Art 1(3)* (declaring certain categories of aid incompatible with the common market) applied, or which was subject to an outstanding recovery order under the EU treaty, or which it was reasonable to assume would be a firm in difficulty for the purpose of the EU guidelines on EU trade. Prior to 11 April 2012 the exclusion was for trades in relation to which *Regulation 1628/2006* on permitting state aid for national regional investment did not apply, and other premises which were used, or to be used, for the purpose of such a trade. The trades concerned covered fisheries and aquaculture, shipbuilding, the coal industry, the steel industry, synthetic and marketing of products which imitated or substituted for milk and milk products (*Business Premises Renovation Allowances Regulations 2007 (SI 2007 No 945)* as amended by the *Business Premises Renovation Allowances (Amendment) Regulations 2012 (SI 2012 No 868) and the Business Premises Renovation Allowances Regulations 2014 (SI 2014 No 1687)*).

10.181 'The relevant interest' in a qualifying building is the interest to which the person who incurred the qualifying expenditure was entitled when it was incurred (*CAA 2001, s 360E(1)*). If he was entitled to more than one interest, it is the one which was reversionary on all the others (*CAA 2001, s 360E(3)*). An interest does not cease to be the relevant interest merely because a lease or other interest is created above it (*CAA 2001, s 360E(2)*). If it is extinguished on the person entitled to it acquiring the interest on which it is reversionary, the merged interest becomes the relevant interest (*CAA 2001, s 360E(3)*). If a person incurs expenditure on the conversion of a qualifying building into qualifying business premises on terms that he will become entitled to an interest in the building on (or as a result of) the completion of the conversion, he is treated as having had that interest when he incurred the expenditure (so that it will be the relevant interest) (*CAA 2001, s 360F*).

10.182 If the relevant interest is a lease (or a tenancy or an agreement for lease the term of which has begun) and on its expiry or termination the lessee remains in possession with the consent of the lessor but without a new lease being granted to him, the lease is treated as continuing so long as the lessee remains in possession (and so the lessee will continue to hold the relevant interest) (*CAA 2001, ss 360Z3(2), 360Z4*). If on the termination of the lease the lessee is granted a new lease as a result of an option available to him under the terms of the original lease the second lease is treated as a continuation of the first (*CAA 2001, s 360Z3(3)*). If on the termination the lessor pays a sum to the lessee, the lease is treated as if it had come to an end by surrender for consideration of the payment, so the lessor's interest will become the relevant interest (*CAA 2001, s 360Z3(4)*). If a new lease is granted to a different tenant but he makes a payment to the previous lessee in connection with the transaction the two leases are treated as if they were a single lease that had been assigned in consideration for the payment (so the lessee under the second lease is treated as acquiring the relevant interest from the first) (*CAA 2001, s 360Z3(5)*).

10.183 No initial or writing down allowance can be made in respect of qualifying expenditure on a qualifying building if a relevant grant or relevant payment is made towards either that expenditure or any other expenditure incurred by any person in respect of the building and on the same investment project (*CAA 2001, s 360L(1)* as substituted by *FA 2014, s 66(8)*). A relevant grant or relevant payment for this purpose is a grant or payment which is a State aid (other than under *CAA 2001,* and whether or not it is one that is required to be notified to the European Commission) or a grant or subsidy which the Treasury by statutory instrument declares to be relevant for the purposes of the withholding of allowances under these provisions (*CAA 2001, s 360L(6),(7)*). A single investment project has the meaning given in the *EU General Block Exemption Regulations* (ie *Commission Regulation (EU) No 651/2014*) (*CAA 2001, s 360L(6)*).

10.184 If such a grant or payment is made after the allowance has been given or (within three years from the date the expenditure was incurred) a relevant grant or relevant payment is made towards any expenditure incurred by any person in respect of the same building and on the same single investment project, the allowance will be withdrawn. All such assessments and adjustments are to be made as is needed to give effect to the withdrawal. The taxpayers must notify HMRC of the adjustment needed within three months of first becoming aware that the claim has become incorrect because of this provision (*CAA 2001, s 360L(2)–(5)*). The rule prior to 1 April 2014 was that allowances could not be claimed in respect of expenditure to the extent that it was taken into account for the purposes of a relevant grant or relevant payment made towards that expenditure. (*CAA 2001, s 360L* as originally enacted). It should be noted that a partial grant or payment prohibits allowances on the entire amount of the expenditure to which it relates; allowances cannot be claimed on the balance.

10.185 A balancing adjustment (either allowance or charge) is made if a balancing event occurs within five years of the time when the premises were first used or suitable for letting (seven years for expenditure incurred before 1 April 2014). A sale or other event outside that five-year period has no effect on the allowance (*CAA 2001, s 360M* as amended by *FA 2014, s 66(9)*). A balancing allowance is given if either there are no proceeds from the balancing event or the proceeds are less than the residue of qualifying expenditure. A balancing charge is made if the proceeds exceed the residue of expenditure (but is limited to the allowances previously given). The allowance or charge is the difference between the residue of expenditure and the sale proceeds (*CAA 2001, s 360P*).

10.186 The balancing events are:

(*a*) a sale of the qualifying interest – the proceeds are the net sale proceeds;

(*b*) the grant of a lease of over 50 years in consideration of the payment of a capital sum – the proceeds are that sum unless it is less than the commercial premium (ie the premium that would have been received if the transaction had been at arm's length) in which case it is that commercial premium;

(*c*) the termination of the interest if it is a lease (other than by it merging with the interest reversionary on it) – the proceeds are nil unless the person entitled to the lease and a person entitled to any superior interest are connected persons, in which case the lessee is treated as receiving proceeds equal to the market value of the relevant interest at that time;

(*d*) the death of the person who incurred the relevant expenditure – he is treated as receiving proceeds equal to the residue of expenditure so no balancing adjustment (either charge or allowance) will arise;

(*e*) the qualifying building being demolished or destroyed – the proceeds are the net amount received for the remains of the qualifying building, together with any insurance money received and any other compensation received so far as it consists of capital sums; and the net cost of the demolition (any excess of its cost over any money received for the remains of the qualifying building) is added to the residue of qualifying expenditure; and

(*f*) the qualifying building ceasing to be qualifying business premises (without being demolished or destroyed) – the owner is deemed to receive proceeds equal to the market value of the relevant interest at that time.

(*CAA 2001, ss 360N, 360O, 360P.*)

10.187 The rules in **10.180** apply for this purpose. So do those in *ITTOIA 2005, s 303* (see **3.23**) for determining the length of a lease (and **10.180** does not apply for that purpose). It appears that where a building is demolished any amount received for the remains of the qualifying building is taken into account twice. It constitutes proceeds of the disposal but also reduces the amount of the demolition costs that can be added to the qualifying expenditure.

10.188 If the sum payable for the sale of the relevant interest in a qualifying building (or other proceeds from a balancing event) is attributable partly to assets representing expenditure qualifying for allowances, only so much of it as on a just and reasonable apportionment is attributable to the qualifying assets is brought into account (*CAA 2001, s 360Z2*). Such an apportionment will almost always be required as the disposal is likely to include the land on which the building stands.

10.189 It should be noted that where the sale or other balancing event occurred before 6 April 2012 (1 April for corporation tax) allowances were given only to the person who incurred the expenditure. The right to allowances could not be passed to a person who acquired the relevant interest even if he did so within the seven-year period so as to trigger a balancing charge on the person who incurred the expenditure. The right to allowances was lost. From that date a purchaser can claim allowances but only up to the 'maximum allowable amount'. This is the part of the vendor's expenditure (if any) for which he did not obtain allowances (or for which allowances were clawed back) (*FA 2001, s 186A* inserted by *FA 2012, Sch 10, para 6*). The detailed rules are considered at **10.120**.

10.190 Where the capital allowance or charge is to be given effect in calculating the profits of a person's trade (or profession or vocation) it is treated as a trading expense or receipt. If the building is let and the building is an asset of the owner's property business (as will normally be the case) it is treated as an expense or receipt of that business. In any other case it is given effect to by deeming the person to be carrying on a property business and treating it as an expense or receipt of that deemed business (*CAA 2001, ss 360Z, 360Z1*).

This deeming effectively negates the benefit of a balancing allowance as it will create a deemed loss in that deemed business and, unless the person is within the charge to corporation tax, such a loss is available only to offset against income of the property business in which it arises.

Research and Development

10.191 Where a person, while carrying on a trade, incurs expenditure of a capital nature on research and development related to the trade and directly undertaken by him or on his behalf (or incurs such expenditure while not trading and afterwards sets up a trade connected with the research), the entire expenditure can be written off against trading profits in the year it was incurred (or the year the trade commences if later) (*CAA 2001, s 441*). The allowance can be disclaimed in part but, if this is done, there does not appear to be an ability to claim the balance in a subsequent year (*CAA 2001, s 441(3)*). The expenditure is in effect treated as a trading expense of the year in which it is incurred. Scientific research means any activities in the fields of natural or applied science for the extension of knowledge. Research and development is defined in *CTA 2010, s 1138*. It adopts the definition that applies in accordance with generally accepted accounting practice but gives the Treasury power by Regulation to modify this (*CAA 2001, s 437(2)*).

10.192 It was held in *Gaspet Ltd v Elliss (60 TC 91)* that where a trader does not directly undertake the research there must be a contractual relationship of agency or something akin thereto between the trader and the person who carries out the research – although there is no requirement that the taxpayer must actually commission the research.

10.193 If property is purchased for the purpose of such research, it can qualify for the allowance in the same way as any other asset. However, the allowance cannot be claimed on expenditure incurred on the acquisition of, or of rights in or over, land – although it can still be claimed on building work. Where land is purchased or leased on which a building or structure (other than a dwelling) is standing, the price must be apportioned between the land and the building (including any machinery or plant forming part of the building), and allowances claimed only on the latter. Allowances can also no longer be claimed on the cost of a dwelling. Where part of a building is used as a dwelling, and part for research and development, an apportionment must be made unless the part of the cost apportionable to the dwelling does not exceed 25% of the total cost referable to the entire building (ie excluding the land), in which case there will be no restriction (*CAA 2001, ss 438, 440*). The clawback of allowances on a disposal is, of course, restricted to the sale proceeds of assets eligible for allowances.

10.194 A balancing charge will arise if the asset is subsequently disposed of by the owner (whether by sale or otherwise) either during, or after the discontinuance of, the trade; in the latter event the charge relates back to the date the trade ceased (*CAA 2001, s 442*). Where the expenditure was incurred before 1 April 1985 a balancing charge cannot arise if the asset is sold without ceasing to be used by the owner, eg on a sale and leaseback, but that anomaly has been corrected in relation to expenditure after that date. On transfers between connected persons the election described in **Appendix 4** at App 4.34 below can be made (*CAA 2001, s 569*).

10.195 The balancing charge is on the excess of the disposal value over the written-down value of the asset (or the amount of the allowances given if this is less than that excess). This amount is treated as trading income of the trade (*CAA 2001, s 442(3)*). The disposal value depends on the event giving rise to the clawback. If this occurs on a sale at or above market value the sale proceeds are used to calculate the clawback. If it occurs by the destruction of the asset the amount of any insurance monies or other compensation plus any monies received for the remains of the asset is used. Demolition costs are treated as an addition to the cost of the asset (*CAA 2001, s 445*). If the cessation of ownership occurs in any other way the market value of the asset is used (*CAA 2001, s 443(4)*). If the disposal value is less than the written-down value a balancing allowance will of course be given on the disposal. This can obviously only occur where the full 100% allowance has not been claimed (*CAA 2001, s 441(1)(b)*).

10.196 A small or medium-sized company (but not an unincorporated business) can deduct 230% of its expenditure on qualifying research and development in an accounting period (225% prior to 1 April 2015). If the accounting period is less than 12 months the £10,000 figure is reduced proportionately (*CTA 2009, s 1044*). A large company can deduct only 100% of its expenditure but in addition can claim a tax credit of 11%. However, in both cases qualifying research is limited to revenue expenditure and is unlikely to be incurred in a property context.

Thermal Insulation of Buildings

10.197 A trader who incurs expenditure after 1 April 2008 (6 April for income tax) on adding insulation against loss of heat to a building which is occupied by him for the purpose of his trade can claim capital allowances as if the expenditure were on plant and machinery, and as if it had belonged to him in consequence of his incurring the expenditure and had a disposal value of nil (*CAA 2001, s 280*). These allowances can also be claimed by a landlord who incurs expenditure on thermal insulation in respect of a let building (other than a dwelling house). The machinery or plant is treated as if it had been included in the lease of the building and as if its disposal value were nil (*CAA 2001, s 63(5)*). Again the relief only applies if at the time the expenditure is incurred the building is actually occupied by the trader or let by the landlord as the case may be.

10.198 The relief also extends to a furnished holiday letting business, a profession or vocation, a mining or transport undertaking, managing the investments of a company with investment business and special leasing of plant and machinery. It does not, however, apply if the expenditure is deductible as if it were a revenue expense under *CTA 2009, s 251* or *ITTOIA 2005, s 312* (see **2.28**). A more limited relief applied prior to 1 April 2008. The building had to be an industrial building and the taxpayer had to be carrying on either a trade or a property rental business (but the exclusion for dwelling houses did not apply).

Other Capital Allowances

10.199 Capital allowances are also given for expenditure in a number of other property-related categories. These are unlikely to affect most businesses and are not therefore considered in detail here. Expenditure by a trader on a sports stadium or sports ground used for the purpose of his trade could qualify for allowances as plant and machinery up to 5 April 2013 to the extent that it was carried out to comply with the terms of a safety certificate under the *Safety of Sports Grounds Act 1975*, to bring the ground up to the standards required by that *Act*, or to comply with the requirements of the local authority as to the terms that they would include in a safety certificate if it had been applied for or issued (*CAA 2001, s 30*). So could expenditure in respect of a regulated stand in taking steps to comply with either a safety certificate issued for the stand or the written requirements of the local authority on matters which would be taken into account in deciding to issue, or amend the terms of, a safety certificate (*CAA 2001, s 31*). Both of these providsions were repealed by *FA 2012, s 227*. Expenditure on an asset to improve the personal physical security of an individual who is the proprietor of, or a partner in, a business attracts capital allowances as plant. Allowances cannot be claimed for the cost of a dwelling or its grounds, but relief is due on items which become affixed to such a building (*CAA 2001, s 33*). This relief is intended to be very restricted. It is likely to apply only where there is a serious risk of a terrorist attack on the individual because of the nature of his business. A company is entitled to allowances on such expenditure under the general law, but an individual would, in the absence of specific legislation, be excluded because of the personal element of the expenditure.

10.200 Special schemes of allowances apply to capital expenditure on cemeteries and crematoria, including the cost of the land – they are broadly designed to write off the cost over the number of grave plots or memorial garden plots (*ITTOIA 2005, ss 169–172; CTA 2009, ss 146–149*); to capital expenditure on dredging in the course of a trade (*CAA 2001, ss 484–489*); and to qualifying expenditure in connection with the working of a mine, oil well or other source of mineral deposits of a wasting nature, or searching for, or on discovering and testing, deposits or winning access thereto, or on the construction of works which are likely to be of little value when the source is exhausted (*CAA 2001, ss 394–436*).

10.201 Up to 5 April 2011, allowances could also be claimed for expenditure on industrial buildings (as defined in the legislation), agricultural buildings and works, qualifying hotels, and commercial buildings in 1980 style enterprise zones. Flat conversion allowances were given up to 5 April 2013. The rules applicable to those allowances are summarised in **Appendix 4**.

Plant, etc Leased under a Finance Lease

10.202 Although not directly relevant to the property owner, as it is the lessor rather than the lessee who is entitled to the capital allowances, it should be mentioned that there are a number of anti-avoidance provisions in relation to plant and machinery leased under a finance lease. In some cases the assets will not qualify for capital allowances, although a straightforward lease providing for regular monthly or quarterly payments should not be affected. There are also special rules where the lessor and lessee are connected persons. A detailed consideration of these provisions is outside the scope of this book.

Chapter 11

Tax on Chargeable Gains

Introduction

11.1 Capital gains tax (CGT) is chargeable on gains accruing on the disposal of assets which are not taxable as income, for example as profits of a trade of property dealing (*TCGA 1992, ss 15, 37*). For individuals, other than basic rate taxpayers, and trusts the tax is charged at a flat rate of 28% on residential property and 20% on other assets (28% on disposals prior to 6 April 2016 and 18% on disposals prior to 23 June 2010). A basic rate taxpayer is taxable at 18% on residential property and 10% on other assets but only up to the unused portion of his basic rate income tax band. The 28% rate applies to gains above that level. The 28% and 18% rates also apply to carried interests in relation to investment management but this does not normally arise in a property context. Where an individual has unused basic rate band, this must first be utilised against any gains which attract entrepreneurs' relief (see **11.107**). Once this shortfall has been so utilised (or if there are no entrepreneurs' relief gains) the taxpayer can choose which gains should utilise that excess (*TCGA 1992, s 4BA* inserted by *FA 2016, s 83(14)*). The special residential property rate applies to both UK and non-UK residential property interests (other than those to which NRCGT applies) (*TCGA 1992, s 4BB(1)–(3)* inserted by *FA 2016, s 83(14)*).

11.2 There is an annual exemption of the first slice of taxable gain. This is £11,700 for 2018/19 £10,600 for 2011/12 and 2012/13, £10,900 for 2013/14, £11,000 for 2014/15, £11,100 for 2015/16 and 2016/17 and £11,300 for 2017/18). A husband and wife each have their own annual exemption. There is no similar exemption for companies and most trusts have an annual exemption of half that applicable to an individual, ie currently £5,650. Non-UK residents are not generally liable to CGT. Some non-resident companies, trusts and partnerships were brought within the charge to tax on gains from 6 April 2013 relating to residential properties valued at over £1 million (ATED related gains – see **11.160**), all non-residents are liable to tax on gains in relation to disposals of UK residential properties (NRCGT gains: see **11.181**) from 6 April 2015 and it is proposed to extend this charge to all UK property from 6 April 2019.

11.3 UK-resident companies (and overseas companies to the extent that they are trading in the UK through a permanent establishment) are not liable to capital gains tax, but are instead charged to corporation tax on chargeable gains, calculated as for capital gains tax purposes. An overseas company is chargeable to NRCGT at a rate of 20% (*TCGA 1992, s 4(3B)* inserted by *FA 2015, Sch 7, para 6*). However, it is proposed to move non-resident companies not the corporation tax regime from 6 April 2020. A company can also deduct an indexation allowance which is intended to compensate for inflation. This reflects the increase in the retail prices index since 1 April 1982. The allowance will be frozen at this level at 31 December 2017. The indexation allowance can only reduce or eliminate a gain. It cannot create or enhance a tax loss (*TCGA 1992, s 53(1)*). A UK company's capital gains are charged at the normal corporation tax rates. A company treats its chargeable gains as an additional source of income, and can offset against them trading losses, management expenses, loan relationships and charges on income. References in this chapter to capital gains tax (or to CGT) should, where appropriate, be taken as referring also to corporation tax on chargeable gains.

11.4 A special rule applies to sales and transfers within a group of companies. The price actually paid is ignored. Instead the asset is treated as having been acquired by the transferee at a price that would secure that neither a gain nor a loss would accrue to the transferor (*TCGA 1992, s 171(1)*). This is normally the transferor's cost plus its indexation allowance. Broadly speaking, a subsidiary needs to be at least 75% owned by the group for it to be regarded as a group company. It was held in *DMWSHNZ Ltd v HMRC (2014 STC 1440)* that the settlement of a debt is not the transfer of an asset. This was significant because *TCGA 1992, s 171A* provides that where one group company sells an asset outside the group at a loss and another sells one at a profit in the same accounting period, they can jointly elect that the asset should be treated as having been sold intra-group immediately before the outside sale, thus enabling the gain to be set against the loss. In this case one company had sold its asset some years earlier in exchange for the issue of loan notes. The gain crystallised on the sale of the loan notes, but did not become taxable until redemption and the company was seeking to set the past gain against a current loss. This decision was upheld by the Court of Appeal (*[2017] STC 1076*), which also pointed out that when the debt had been repaid, the obligation to pay had been discharged, so there were then no remaining creditor rights that could have been transferred to the issuer.

11.5 There is an anti-avoidance provision that will trigger tax on the gain at the time of transfer if the transferee leaves the group within six years of the transfer (*TCGA 1992, s 179*). Up to 18 July 2011 the gain was taxable in the company that left the group and was normally treated as a gain of the accounting period in which it left the group. Where a company leaves the group after that date by virtue of a disposal of the shares (of that company or its holding company) the gain is not taxed as such but is instead added to the consideration for the disposal (or a loss deducted from such consideration).

Accordingly if the gain on disposal is exempt under the substantial shareholdings exemption, this deeming also exempts tax on the gain on the asset transferred. The old rules continue to apply where the company leaves the group for any other reason. There is an exception where two or more associated companies leave the group at the same time and these include both the transferor and the transferee (*TCGA 1992, s 179(2)*). Companies are associated for this purpose only if together they would form a group, ie they are a sub-group within the main group (*TCGA 1992, s 179(2)*). It has been held that the test of association has to be held both at the time the asset was transferred and at the time that the transferee leaves the group (*Johnston Publishing (North) Ltd v HMRC (2008 STC 3116*). HMRC have said that they consider that where the companies are sister companies this means that the two companies concerned and their sub-group holding company must leave the group as a sub-group, but that it is not necessary for any other companies in the sub-group to do so (HMRC Brief 17.12.2008). From 19 July 2011 the requirement is that the companies must have been associated throughout the period from the transfer of the asset until immediately after they leave the group (*TCGA 1992, s 179(2)–(2ZB)*).

11.6 An individual can set a trading loss – but not a UK property business loss – against net capital gains of the same year of assessment to the extent that it cannot be relieved against income of that year (*ITA 2007, s 71* and *TCGA 1992, ss 261B, 261C*). Any excess trading loss can be set against capital gains of the following year if the trade is still being carried on in that year. Capital gains tax losses of earlier years must be utilised against capital gains in priority to trading losses and, unlike with brought forward capital losses, the claim for relief cannot be limited to preserve the benefit of the capital gains tax annual exemption. If the amount of capital gain available for offset is subsequently altered, eg because additional capital losses are established, the excess trading loss which this releases is converted into a capital gains tax loss – but ceases to be available for any relief at all if it is not utilised against future capital gains by the end of the year of assessment in which the trade ceases. The relief must be claimed at the time that a claim is made to set the trading loss against general income under *ITA 2007, s 64*, ie it cannot be claimed separately but the *s 64* claim must be expressed to extend to capital gains.

Calculation of Chargeable Gain

11.7 A chargeable gain is calculated by deducting from the disposal consideration (or in some cases deemed disposal consideration) the allowable deductions specified by the legislation. The allowable deductions are limited to:

(*a*)

- (i) the consideration (in money or money's worth) given by the taxpayer (or on his behalf) wholly and exclusively for the acquisition of the asset,
- (ii) the incidental costs (see **11.11** below) to the taxpayer of the acquisition (or, if the asset was not acquired by him, eg he created it, any expenditure wholly and exclusively incurred by him in providing the asset),

(*b*)

- (i) the amount of any expenditure ('enhancement expenditure') wholly and exclusively incurred on the asset by the taxpayer (or on his behalf) for the purpose of enhancing the value of the asset, being expenditure reflected in the state or nature of the asset at the time of the disposal,
- (ii) any expenditure wholly and exclusively incurred by the taxpayer in establishing, preserving or defending his title to, or to a right over, the asset, and

(*c*) the incidental costs (see **11.11** below) to the taxpayer of making the disposal.

(*TCGA 1992, s 38(1)*.)

11.7A For 2017/18 onwards, any amount taken into account by the taxpayer under *ITTOIA 2005, ss 96A* or *307E* (capital receipts under, or after leaving the cash basis – see) as the result of the operation of a deemed disposal under *ITTOIA 2005, ss 96A* or *307F* is to be excluded from the consideration for the disposal of the asset (*TCGA 1992, s 37(1A)–(1C)* inserted by *F(No 2)A 2017, Sch 2, para 44*).

11.8 For income tax purposes only, where an asset was acquired before 1 April 1982 its market value at that date must be used in place of cost. A company can adopt that market value or can calculate the gains by reference to original cost if that is likely to be more beneficial (*TCGA 1992, s 35*).

11.9 Where an individual disposes of the whole or part of a business (or of his partnership share in a business) or shares in a trading company, a relief, entrepreneurs' relief, applies, provided that the necessary qualifying conditions are met. This relief is considered at **11.107** onwards.

11.10 The meaning of a business asset is outside the scope of this book. Broadly speaking it was one used as a fixed asset of a trade. The Special Commissioner in *Patel v Maidment (2004 STC (SCD) 41)* held that an activity of letting flats did not qualify as a business asset, on the basis of the statement by Vinelott J in *Griffiths v Jackson* (see **2.128**) that 'it is a peculiar feature of UK tax law that the activity of letting furnished flats or rooms, while it may be a business and, in this case a demanding and time-consuming business, it is not a trade'. Whether that is correct in all cases seems questionable. The main function of a hotel is letting rooms furnished. Furthermore there is a Ministerial statement (see **2.138**) that *Griffiths v Jackson* does not establish that the fruits of holiday lettings were never to be taxed as a trade. Curiously though, between 6 April 2000 and 5 April 2008 a property which was let to a close trading company (even one wholly unconnected with the landlord) was a business asset. This was probably due to an accidental error in amending the wording of the legislation rather than a deliberate policy.

11.11 The incidental costs of the acquisition ((*a*)(ii) in **11.7** above) are limited to expenditure wholly and exclusively incurred by the taxpayer for the purpose of the acquisition, being either:

(i) fees, commission, or remuneration paid for the professional services of any surveyor or valuer, or auctioneer, or accountant, or agent or legal advisor;

(ii) costs of transfer or conveyance (including stamp duty); or

(iii) costs of advertising to find a seller.

11.12 The incidental costs of the disposal ((*c*) in **11.7** above) are similarly limited to expenditure wholly and exclusively incurred by the taxpayer for the purpose of the disposal being items within (i) or (ii) in **11.11** above, or:

(i) costs of advertising to find a buyer; or

(ii) costs reasonably incurred in making any valuation or apportionment required for the purposes of computing the chargeable gain, including in particular expenses reasonably incurred in ascertaining market value where required by *TCGA 1992*.

(*TCGA 1992, s 38(2)*.)

11.13 Head (ii) in **11.12** will only allow a deduction for costs of a valuation to enable a best estimate of the gain to be calculated and returned. It will not extend to subsequent costs in negotiating the value with the District Valuer or the Shares Valuation Division, or in litigating the amount of the valuation (*Caton (dec'd) v Couch (1997 STC 970)*). Accordingly, it is sensible to ensure that as much of the work as possible is done to arrive at the initial valuation, rather than estimating this and leaving the formal valuation to be done later. In *HMRC v Blackwell (2017 STC 1159)* – a non-property case) the Court of Appeal held that the 'state or nature' of Mr Blackwell's shares had to be identified by reference to the rights and obligations which those shares conferred on a shareholder pursuant to the company's Articles of Association. That state or nature is unaffected by the making or subsequent discharge of an agreement with a third party that fettered his dealing with the shares. The same would apply to property. If an obligation is personal to the owner and not inherent in his property rights, a payment to discharge that obligation would not be deductible. It is possible though that such a payment could be a selling expense in such a case but HMRC might be expected to challenge that.

Non-Deductible Expenditure

11.14 If expenditure cannot be brought within one of the above heads, no relief will be obtainable for it. Furthermore, there is a specific prohibition on deducting any payment of interest – other than certain interest payments by companies (see **4.88** above) (*TCGA 1992, s 38(3)*). There is also a specific prohibition on deducting:

(*a*) any expenditure allowable as a deduction for income or corporation tax purposes in computing the profits or gains or losses of a trade; and

(*b*) any expenditure which, if the assets to which the CGT computation relates had at all times been used as a fixed asset of a UK trade, would have been allowable as a deduction in computing the profits of that notional trade.

(*TCGA 1992, s 39.*)

11.15 In the context of property, *s 39* can, in particular, deny relief in some common circumstances. Where a liquidator or receiver has to pay arrears of rent to obtain a licence to assign a lease, the rent arrears cannot be deducted in calculating the gain arising on the assignment (*Emmerson v Computer Time International Ltd (50 TC 628)*). If the landlord will cooperate in such circumstances, an assignment of the lease with the arrears unpaid and the assignee undertaking to pay the arrears might be worth considering. It is possible that HMRC might contend that, as the liability to pay the rent was a liability of the assignor, the relieving him of this liability constitutes money's worth, and thus the payment of the arrears by the assignee is part of the consideration received by the assignor for the assignment. If the assignee were to enter into an agreement with the landlord under which the landlord waived the arrears in consideration of a payment to him by the assignee of the same amount, it would be difficult for HMRC to seek to tax this on the assignor. However, the assignee might find difficulty in bringing the payment into the categories of allowable deduction on a future disposal by him. It may be that it is a payment to acquire a separate asset, a right to take an assignment of the lease, which merges with the lease when the assignment takes place – so that *TCGA 1992, s 43* (assets derived from other assets) would treat the payment as part of the cost of acquiring the lease itself.

11.16 Where a person refurbishes a property prior to its disposal, a large part of the cost is likely to be repairs which, being of a revenue nature, would be excluded from CGT relief. Where a person carries out repairs on, or shortly after, acquiring a property and the cost of such repairs is excluded from being a deductible item under the UK property business rules, the amount disallowed should be claimed for CGT purposes as enhancement expenditure. However, the UK property business rules that applied before 6 April 1995 for income tax and 1 April 1998 for corporation tax differed from that laid down by the courts in relation to trading income (see **9.3** above) so, in theory at least, it is possible that expenditure which was not repairs under the property business rules would also be excluded from capital gains tax relief because of the different test propounded by *TCGA 1992, s 39(2)*. Where a seller would not be able to obtain a deduction for dilapidations, but the purchaser would be able to treat the cost as enhancement expenditure, it may be worth considering whether the work might be undertaken by the buyer with an appropriate adjustment being made to the price.

Contract – Date of Acquisition and Disposal

11.17 A further basic point that needs to be particularly borne in mind in relation to property is that for CGT purposes the date of acquisition or disposal of an asset is the date that the contract is entered into, not the date of the conveyance (*TCGA 1992, s 28(1)*). If the contract is conditional (in particular if it is conditional on the exercise of an option) the date of acquisition or disposal is the date that the condition is satisfied (*TCGA 1992, s 28(2)*). It has been held that in law there are only two types of conditional contract: a 'subject to contract' agreement and a contract where all the liabilities under the contract are conditional upon a certain event (*Lyon v Pettigrew (58 TC 452)* and *Eastham v Leigh London & Provincial Properties Ltd (46 TC 687)*). In the *Leigh London* case, a company agreed in 1962 to erect a building on land owned by a third party in consideration of the grant to it of a 125-year lease on completion. This is, of course, a fairly common building lease arrangement. The building was completed and the lease granted in 1964. HMRC contended that the 1962 agreement was two contracts, a building agreement and a conditional contract to grant the lease. It was held that the 1962 agreement was a single and absolute contract. The distinction is often described as a condition precedent and a condition subsequent; a condition precedent being something that has to happen before the contract can take effect at all; and a condition subsequent a condition that has to be fulfilled when carrying out the contract, ie something that does not strike at the root of the contract and non-compliance with which will not render the contract ineffective but will usually merely give rise to a claim for damages. The inclusion of a condition subsequent will not make a contract a conditional contract.

11.18 *Smith and Another v CIR (2004 STC (SCD) 60)* concerned the sale of a farm. An offer to buy the farm was accepted on 29 May 1991 and the sale was registered on 21 August 1991, the purchase price having been paid on 15 August 1991. However, the vendor continued to occupy the land, paying no rent but apparently with the agreement of the purchaser. In September 1999 the purchaser wrote a 'Letter of Understanding' which recorded, *inter alia*, that it was agreed that the vendor would flit and remove themselves from the land on 31 October 1999 'and thus complete the contract of sale'. The Special Commissioner had no hesitation in holding that as the contract was not conditional (or if it was, the condition was satisfied on 15 August 1991) the date of disposal was in 1991/92, not in 1999/00. The Letter of Understanding was firmly dismissed with the comment that 'it would be surprising if ex post facto a taxpayer could retrospectively rearrange his affairs so as to minimise his tax liabilities'. This seems to be based on the premise that, as the contract was completed in August 1991, a subsequent arrangement in relation to the subject of the contract cannot resurrect a completed contract but must be a fresh agreement.

11.19 If a contract is never completed it is generally accepted that there is no disposal for CGT purposes, ie the contract date merely fixes the date of disposal once completion has taken place. This is implicit in the judgments in *Magnavox Electronics Co Ltd (in liquidation) v Hall (59 TC 610)*. In that case a contract to dispose of a property was entered into in September 1978. The purchaser defaulted. As the company had trading losses which could be set against a capital gain arising in September 1978 but not against one in the next accounting period, the liquidator struggled to keep the contract alive. It was assigned to a new company controlled by the liquidator, varied (twice) to amend both the price and the completion date, and reassigned to a new purchaser in October 1979. It was held that the second variation was not effective to vary the contract and that the October 1979 completion was accordingly not under the September 1978 contract.

11.20 This does not, however, appear to be HMRC's view – notwithstanding that in *Magnavox Electronics Co Ltd (in liquidation) v Hall (59 TC 610)* case, the Case stated records that the solicitor for the Inland Revenue put forward the view that the words of the relevant provisions 'suggest that if a contract for sale is to be regarded as a disposal clear provision is necessary. In the absence of such provision it must be that disposal takes place when a sale is completed not when the contract is entered into' (*59 TC* at p 620). The decision in *Jones and another (Balls' Administrators) v Inland Revenue Commissioners*

(1997 STC 358), an inheritance tax case (see **18.70**), also gives support to the need for a contract to be completed before there could be a sale.

11.21 What happens if between contract and completion the taxpayer disposes of his interest in the property? In *Jerome v Kelly (2004 STC 887)* HMRC contended that the person who entered into the contract is liable for the tax on the disposal by the assignee of the contract. Fortunately, the House of Lords (reversing the decision of the Court of Appeal) held otherwise:

> 'Section 27(1) appears to be directed to a single limited issue, that is the timing of a disposal. It does not say that the contract is the disposal, but that a disposal effected by contract and later completed is to be treated, for taxing purposes, as made at the date of the contract. Its language is not so clear and compelling as to lead to the conclusion that Parliament must have intended to introduce a further statutory fiction as to the parties to a disposal.'

11.22 A far more worrying case is *Underwood v HMRC (2009 STC 239)*. Mr Underwood contracted to sell land to Paul Rackham Ltd for £400,000. On the same day Paul Rackham Ltd granted Mr Underwood an option to repurchase the land for £400,000 plus 10% of the increase in value up to the time of exercise of the option. Sixteen months later Mr Underwood exercised his option and immediately contracted to resell the land to a third party, Brickfields, for £600,000. The price payable under the option was accordingly £420,000. The same solicitor acted for all three parties. He decided that as the legal title had remained with Mr Underwood throughout, the simplest thing would be to prepare a transfer from Mr Underwood to Brickfields for £600,000 and for Mr Underwood to pay Rackham the £20,000 difference between the option price and the original sale price. Briggs J's analysis of the transaction was that Rackham had never paid Mr Underwood the £400,000 and accordingly the original sale contract had not been completed. Accordingly Mr Underwood's argument that he had received the £400,000 by way of set-off was 'an artificial and fallacious construct'. He thought that 'disposal is, after all, a concept to be addressed by the application of common sense'. His view of common sense seems to this author to be open to question. Fortunately that seems also to be the view of Rimer L J who, in granting leave to appeal to the Court of Appeal commented, 'The issues raised by the case are of considerable interest and would make an ideal topic for a moot … the court's determination of the issues raised by the appeal is likely to have an important relevance extending beyond the present case'. Sadly, the Court of Appeal agreed with HMRC. Lawrence Collins, LJ, having noted that 'it is necessary to identify, in a practical and commonsense way, what in law the parties were doing', went on to say, 'the true answer must be found in the true construction of the document or documents read in the light of all the relevant circumstances.

If the terms of the document are clear, that is the end of the question. If, however, there is any doubt or ambiguity upon the language used read in its proper context, it may be possible to resolve that doubt or ambiguity by reference to the inherent probabilities of businessmen entering into the transaction in one form rather than another'. He went on to say that 'there was no event which resulted in a disposal of the Property by Mr Underwood to Rackham Ltd under the 1963 contract or an acquisition by Rackham Ltd of the Property under that contract'. Lord Neuberger agreed, albeit 'with some regret'. He pointed out that:

> 'the fact that one can treat the payment of £20,000 as representing the performance of the two contracts does not lead to the conclusion that there was a disposal of the property … or … a disposal back. All that the netting off achieved was to free the property from Rackham Ltd's rights, which included an equitable interest. In other words, the fact that the two contracts … were "performed" on 30 November 1994 does not necessarily mean that the property was disposed of or acquired … on that date … artificiality can only be carried so far'. He distinguished the case from a sub-sale with a single conveyance on the basis that, 'The contractual arrangements between Mr Underwood and Rackham Ltd formed no part of the contractual chain, or what one might call the chain of equitable title, between the initial seller of the property (Mr Underwood) and its ultimate buyer (Brickfields). Thus Rackham Ltd, unlike the buyer/sub-seller in a sub-sale case, was not in a position to direct the sale of the property to Brickfields (or, thus, to turn the property to account'.

11.23 The normal rule set out in **11.17** is displaced where *TCGA 1992, s 22(1)* applies. This deems there to be a disposal where a capital sum is derived from assets notwithstanding that no asset is acquired by the person paying it. The section is expressed to apply in particular to:

(*a*) capital sums received as compensation for damage, loss or destruction of an asset or for any depreciation or risk of depreciation of an asset;

(*b*) capital sums received under a policy of insurance of the risk of damage, injury, loss or depreciation of assets;

(*c*) capital sums received in return for forfeiture or surrender of rights (or refraining from exercising rights); and

(*d*) capital sums received as consideration for the use or exploitation of assets.

In these four cases the time of disposal is the time when the capital sum is received (*TCGA 1992, s 22(2)*). A payment in money's worth is a capital sum for the purpose of *s 22* (*TCGA 1992, s 22(3)*).

11.24 It was held by the House of Lords in *Marren v Ingles (54 TC 76)* that where an asset is sold for an immediate payment plus a contingent right to future consideration that is unascertainable at the date of disposal, the value of the right to receive the contingent consideration is part of the disposal proceeds but that right is itself a separate asset, a chose in action, from which a capital sum is derived when the consideration is ascertained and paid. This decision was followed in *Marson v Marriage (54 TC 59)* where land was sold for development on terms that the vendor would receive a supplemental payment depending on how much of the land the purchasers were able to develop for residential development and the permitted density. It is not uncommon for land to be sold with an additional payment becoming due when planning permission is received for development. If the additional consideration is an amount that is fixed at the date of the contract HMRC consider that *TCGA 1992, s 48* applies. This provides that the consideration for a disposal is to be brought into account without regard to a risk of any part of the consideration being contingent – but if any part is subsequently shown to be irrecoverable, then on a claim being made to that effect, the tax payable is to be adjusted. HMRC did for a time consider that if a maximum figure was placed on unascertainable consideration, that took it out of the *Marren v Ingles* principle and into *s 48*. However, they now accept that is incorrect (HMRC Capital Gains Manual CG14889). It will be apparent that the precise nature of the additional consideration can affect the tax treatment. If it is a fixed, or otherwise ascertainable amount, tax is payable on the entire amount that is due to be received by reference to the contract date but will be revised if the amount is not received. If it is unascertainable the initial charge will be on the value of the chose in action with a further charge on the balance of the additional consideration when it is actually received. If the ultimate receipt is less than the initial value no adjustment can be made to the value of the additional compensation; but there will be an allowable loss on the disposal of the chose in action. A chose in action is not an interest in land and cannot therefore qualify for roll-over relief (see **11.93**) or for private residence exemption (CG64609) (see **13.3**). There are circumstances where the application of the *Marren v Ingles* principle can be disadvantageous. For example, principal private residence relief does not apply on the disposal of a chose in action and neither does roll-over relief. Accordingly care needs to be taken in structuring the transaction where one of those reliefs applies.

11.25 There is a potential problem where the value placed on the chose in action exceeds the amount realised on its disposal. This is that the loss on disposal of the chose in action cannot be carried back to the time of the original gain, so the taxpayer may be in the position of having to pay tax on a greater sum than he receives overall, and generating an allowable loss that can be used only against any future gain on other assets. In practice that would be rare, as the value initially placed on the chose in action is likely to be very small if, as is usually the case, there is significant uncertainty as to whether or when the additional consideration is likely to be received. Nevertheless, an election can be made to carry back to the year in which the disposal of the asset took place a loss on the chose in action (*TCGA 1992, s 279A*). The disposal of the original asset must be made by the person who owns the chose in action (ie the relief does not apply if the right has been assigned; the original disposal must have been in 1992/93 or later; it must have given rise to a gain; and the taxpayer must have actually had a capital gains tax liability in that year. However, once eligibility is established, the entire loss can be carried back and treated as a loss of that earlier year – so if it cannot be utilised in that earlier year can be utilised in any intervening year. The election must be made by the first anniversary of 31 January following the year in which the loss arises and is irrevocable (*TCGA 1992, s 279D*).

11.26 An interesting dispute arose in *Chaloner v Pellipar Investments Ltd (1996 STC 234)*. Pellipar owned three sites. It entered into a development agreement under which it would grant leases of two of the sites to a developer in consideration partly of the payment of premiums and partly of the developer developing the third site for the benefit of Pellipar. The issue was whether the value of the development of the third site was a capital sum received for the use or exploitation of assets within *TCGA 1992, s 22(1)(d)*. If it was, the 'disposal' date was the date of receipt. If it was not, then it was the date of the development agreement by virtue of *TCGA 1992, s 28(1)*. The judge felt that there is a basic distinction between a lease and a licence. A lease gives the right to actual possession; a licence gives a right to use the land with possession remaining with the owner. *Section 22(1)(d)* is apt to cover a licence but not a lease as possession is different from use. Accordingly the disposal took place at the date of the agreement.

11.27 A detailed consideration of all the capital gains tax rules is obviously outside the scope of this work. The object of this chapter is to look at those areas which particularly affect property. CGT in relation to private residences is considered separately in **Chapter 13**.

Leases

11.28 A lease of land is a wasting asset for CGT purposes if it is for less than 50 years. A lease for a longer period becomes a wasting asset when its duration reduces to 50 years (*TCGA 1992, Sch 8, para 1(1)*). If a lease is acquired subject to a sublease not at a rack rent and its value (estimated at the time of acquisition) at the expiration of the sublease will exceed its cost, it will not be a wasting asset until the sublease has expired (*TCGA 1992, Sch 8, para 1(2)*). Such a lease is in reality an appreciating asset until that time as the passage of the sublease will increase the value of the headlease.

11.29 In *Lewis v Walters (1992 STC 97)* the taxpayer unsuccessfully claimed that a 16-year lease of a flat should be regarded as a 66-year one, and thus not a wasting asset, as the then *Leasehold Reform Act 1967* gave the tenant a right to extend the lease for a further 50 years. The terms of the lease did not provide for the extension (see **11.38**(*a*) below) and, even if the statute could be interpreted as implying an additional term of the lease, the statutory right is not to an extended lease but to the grant of a 'new' tenancy, which would be a new and separate asset (see also **11.44**).

11.30 The cost of, and enhancement expenditure on, a wasting asset (less its estimated residual value) is normally written off on a straight-line basis over the anticipated life of the asset (*TCGA 1992, s 46*). However, the legislature felt that this treatment was inappropriate for leases of land, probably because it is well known that the value of a short lease drops at a far greater annual rate than the value of a longer one. Accordingly the rate at which the expenditure on a lease is deemed to waste away must be calculated by reference to a statutory table which writes off the cost progressively (*TCGA 1992, Sch 8, para 1(3)*).

11.31 In calculating the gain on the disposal of a lease it is necessary to exclude the proportion of cost given by the formula:

$$\frac{P(1) - P(3)}{P(1)}$$

and the proportion of the enhancement expenditure given by the formula:

$$\frac{P(2) - P(3)}{P(2)}$$

where:

P(1) = the table figure for the duration of the lease at the time of its acquisition;

P(2) = the table figure for the duration of the lease at the time when any item of enhancement expenditure is first reflected in the nature of the lease; and

P(3) = the table figure for the duration of the lease at the time of the disposal.

11.32 The table has yearly rests. Where the lease is not for an exact number of years, a twelfth of the difference between the figures for the number of whole years in the lease and the next higher number of complete years is added to that for the number of whole years for each extra month, any odd period of under 14 days being ignored and 14 days or more being treated as a month.

Example 11.1

On 18 June 2011, Penny took an assignment of a lease expiring on 31 December 2041 at a cost of £20,000. On 8 September 2013, she finished the building of an extension at a cost of £12,000. She sold the lease on 19 August 2017 for £30,000.

Duration of lease at 18.6.2011	30 years	6 months	12 days		
table figure	87.330 +	0.520*	+ NIL	=	87.850
Duration of lease at 8.9.2013	28 years	3 months	22 days		
table figure	85.053 +	0.293*	+ 0.098*	=	85.444
Duration of lease at 19.8.2017	24 years	4 months	12 days		
table figure	79.622 +	0.493*	+ NIL	=	80.115

* The monthly figures are calculated as follows:

Figure for 31 years		88.3710	(29)	86.2260	(25)	81.1000
Figure for 30 years		87.3300	(28)	85.0530	(24)	79.6220
		1.0410		1.1730		1.4780
1/12th		0.0867		0.0981		0.1232
	(×6)	0.5202	(×3)	0.2943	(×4)	0.4928

Penny's chargeable gain is accordingly:

		£	£	£
Disposal proceeds				30,000
Less cost		20,000		
Deduct non-allowable part	$\frac{87.850 - 80.115}{87.850}$	1,761	18,239	
Enhancement expenditure		12,000		
Deduct non-allowable part	$\frac{85.444 - 80.115}{85.444}$	748	11,252	29,491
Chargeable gain				£509

The same result can be arrived at more easily by simply deducting the reciprocal of the formula figure:

		£	£
Disposal proceeds			30,000
Less allowable cost	$\frac{80.115}{87.850}$ × £20,000	18,239	
allowable enhancement expenditure	$\frac{80.115}{85.444}$ × £12,000	11,252	29,491
			£509

11.33 The grant of a lease at an annual rent does not give rise to a disposal for capital gains tax purposes. The grant of a lease at a premium gives rise to a part disposal, the property undisposed of being the value, at the time of the grant of the lease, of the reversionary interest (*TCGA 1992, Sch 8, para 2*).

11.34 Strictly speaking, it is arguable that there is a part disposal – for a nil value – where no premium is received, as *para 2* does not necessarily override the general wording of *s 21* which provides that there is a part disposal whenever an interest in or right over an asset is created. Whilst such an interpretation would not create a deemed gain on the grant of the lease it would terminate the time apportionment period under *TCGA 1992, Sch 2, para 11(7)* if the property was acquired before 6 April 1965. The author has never known HMRC to adopt such an interpretation. This does not prevent a taxpayer raising it if it is in his interest to do so – which is likely to be very rare.

11.35 If, under the terms subject to which a lease is granted, a sum becomes payable by the tenant in lieu of all or part of the rent for any period or as consideration for the surrender of the lease, the lease is deemed for CGT purposes to have required the payment of a premium to the landlord (in addition to any actual premium) of that sum, for the period in relation to which it is payable (*TCGA 1992, Sch 8, para 3(2)*). Similarly, if a sum becomes payable by the tenant other than by way of rent as consideration for the waiver or variation of any of the terms of the lease, the lease is deemed to have required the payment of a premium (or additional premium) of that sum for the period from the time the variation takes effect to the time it ceases to have effect (*TCGA 1992, Sch 8, para 3(3)*). If the transaction is not at arm's length, the amount of the deemed premium under *para 3(3)* (although not the amount of a deemed premium under *para 3(2)*) is the sum that could have been required at arm's length for the variation.

11.36 A deemed premium under either *subpara (2)* or *(3)* (including one on surrender) is treated as becoming due, and thus assessable, at the date it is payable by the tenant and no recomputation is made even if earlier premiums have been received (*TCGA 1992, Sch 8, para 3*). If the landlord is himself a lessee under a lease of 50 years or less it must also be assumed that he had paid a premium (equal to the amount of the premium deemed to have been received by him) for the grant of the part of the sublease covered by the period in respect of which the premium (ie the deemed premium received) is deemed to have been paid (and that deemed consideration is treated as if it were enhancement expenditure incurred by the sublessee and attributable to that part of the sublease) (*TCGA 1992, Sch 8, para 3(5)*).

11.37 If a premium is deemed under *para 3(2)* or *3(3)* to have been received as consideration for the surrender of a lease, the gain on its grant is not recalculated. Instead, the 'premium' is treated as consideration for a separate transaction consisting of the disposal by the landlord of his interest in the lease (*TCGA 1992, Sch 8, para 3(4)*). This separate transaction is probably itself a part disposal of the landlord's interest in the property.

Duration of Leases

11.38 The legislation contains a number of special rules for determining the duration of a lease of land for CGT purposes. These rules are similar, but by no means identical, to those that apply for the purpose of the income tax charge on premiums (**3.23** above). They obviously need to be used in applying the wasting asset table but are not limited to this; they are of general application (*TCGA 1992, Sch 8, para 8(1)*).

(*a*) If the terms of a lease include provision for its determination by notice given by the landlord it cannot be regarded as extending beyond the earliest date on which it can be so determined (*TCGA 1992, Sch 8, para 8(2)*). This provision used to apply also to property business income but was found to give scope for avoidance and was repealed by *FA 1972, s 81(2)(a)*. It has presumably been retained for CGT purposes because there is no reason why a taxpayer should want to artificially shorten the term of his lease.

(*b*) If any of the terms of the lease or any other circumstances render it unlikely that the lease will continue beyond a date falling before the expiration of the term of the lease, it cannot be regarded as extending beyond that date (*TCGA 1992, Sch 8, para 8(3)*). This applies in particular if the lease provides for the rent to increase (or for the tenant's obligations to become in any other respect more onerous) after a given date, but includes provision for the determination of the lease on that date by notice by the tenant, and those provisions render it unlikely that the lease will continue beyond that date (*TCGA 1992, Sch 8, para 8(4)*). Hopefully, this final phrase will leave unaffected those leases where the tenant has an option to terminate the lease on a rent review.

(*c*) If the terms of a lease include provision for its extension beyond a given date by notice given by the tenant, it must be regarded as lasting for as long as it could be extended by the tenant 'but subject to any right of the landlord by notice to determine the lease' (*TCGA 1992, Sch 8, para 8(5)*). The meaning of the words in quotation marks is unclear. They are probably intended to make clear that the operation of (*a*) above is not displaced by this provision and takes precedence over it.

(*d*) The question as to what is the duration of a lease is to be decided by reference to the facts that were known or ascertainable at the time the lease was acquired or created (*TCGA 1992, Sch 8, para 8(6)*).

Meaning of 'Lease' and 'Premium'

11.39 For CGT purposes (unless the context otherwise requires) references to a lease must be taken to include:

(*a*) an underlease;

(*b*) a sublease;

(*c*) any tenancy or licence;

(*d*) an agreement for a lease (or for an underlease, sublease, tenancy or licence); and

(*e*) in the case of land outside the UK, any interest corresponding to a lease or to anything within (*a*) to (*d*) above.

(*TCGA 1992, Sch 8 para 10(1)(a)*.)

11.40 For the purpose of applying the rules in **11.28–11.39** above and **11.42** below (but not for any other capital gains tax purposes), a premium includes any like sum, whether payable to the intermediate or a superior landlord (and in Scotland includes a gross sum payable to any landlord or intermediate landlord on the creation of a sublease) (*TCGA 1992, Sch 8, para 10(2)(3)*). For such purposes any sum other than rent which is paid on (or in connection with) the granting of a tenancy must be presumed to have been paid by way of premium except in so far as other sufficient consideration for the payment is shown to have been given (*TCGA 1992, Sch 8, para 10(2)*), ie it is up to the parties to produce evidence to show that the payment is not a premium.

Grant of Sublease out of a Short Lease

11.41 The normal part disposal rules are modified for calculating a gain accruing on the part disposal of a lease which is a wasting asset (ie normally one with an unexpired term of 50 years or less) (*TCGA 1992, Sch 8, para 4(1)*). If the amount of the premium is at least that which would be obtainable if the rent payable under the sublease were the same as that payable under the lease – which will normally be the case only if both lease and sublease are entered into on arm's-length terms and either the rents are the same or the rent under the sublease is lower than that under the head lease – the deductible amount of the cost and enhancement expenditure is the fraction of such expenditure which, applying the wasting asset table, is to be written off over the term of the sublease (*TCGA 1992, Sch 8, para 4(2)(a)*).

Example 11.2

Sally paid a premium of £10,000 on 1 May 2017 for the grant of a ten-year lease. She granted a sublease for five years on 1 July 2017 at a premium of £6,000 and no profit rental.

Sally's chargeable gain (ignoring indexation) is as follows:

		£
Premium received		6,000
Less allowable portion of premium paid		
table percentage for a 10 year lease	46.695	
table percentage for a 9 years 10 month lease (ie the unexpired term at the time of the grant of the sublease)	46.105	
table percentage for a 4 years 10 month lease (ie the unexpired term of the head lease at the expiry of the sublease)	25.932	
proportion of premium for head lease relating to period of the sublease		
$\frac{46.105 - 25.932}{46.695} \times 10,000$		4,320
		1,680

Less deduction for part taxed as property business income (see **3.41** above)		
2% × (50 – (5 – 1)) × 6,000	£5,520	
deduct relief for premium paid (see **3.34** above)		
5/10 × 2% × (50 – (5 – 1)) × 10,000	4,600	1,420
Chargeable gain		260

11.42 If the premium is less than that which would be obtainable if the rent payable under the sublease were the same as that payable under the head lease – as will normally be the case where the head lessee is obtaining a profit rental (ie the rent under the sublease exceeds that under the headlease) as well as a premium – the above fraction must be multiplied by the premium and divided by the premium that would have been obtainable had the rents been the same (*TCGA 1992, Sch 8, para 4(2)(b)*). A valuation is obviously required to ascertain this notional premium.

Example 11.3

Suppose that Sally in *Example 11.2* had granted the sublease at a premium of £2,000 and a profit rental, and that the £6,000 figure in that example is the arm's length premium figure.

	£	£
Her chargeable gain (ignoring indexation) would become		
Premium received		2,000
Less allowable portion of premium paid		
$\frac{46.105 - 25.932}{46.695} \times \frac{2,000}{6,000} \times 10,000$		1,440
		560
Less deduction for part taxed as property business income		
2% × (50 – (5 – 1)) × 2,000	1,840	
deduct relief for premium paid,		
£4,100 but limited to	1,840	—
Chargeable gain		560

11.43 If the sublease does not extend to the whole of the land covered by the head lease the allowable expenditure must first be apportioned between the part of the premises covered by the sublease and the remainder of the premises (on the basis of their respective values) and the above rules applied to the fraction attributed to the part covered by the sublease (*TCGA 1992, Sch 8, para 4(3)*).

Other Points on Leases

11.44 Where a lease expires and the tenant is granted a new lease following proceedings under the *Landlord and Tenant Act 1954*, the new lease is not derived from the old but is a separate asset (*Bayley v Rogers (53 TC 420)*) (see also **11.29**).

11.45 Where part of a premium is taxed as income, the computation is modified to grant a measure of relief for this charge. The rules are considered in detail in **3.41** *et seq.* above.

11.46 Where a leaseholder acquires the freehold reversion or a superior lease and the two interests merge, HMRC consider that the wasting asset rules described in **11.28–11.39** above must be applied as if the lease had been disposed of on the date of the merger. The 'unwasted' balance of the cost can then be treated as part of the cost of the merged interest in accordance with *TCGA 1992, s 43*. Whilst this is logical, it is not clear that it is right as *TCGA 1992, Sch 8*, which contains the wasting asset rules, is expressed to apply in computing the gain accruing on the disposal of a lease and it is doubtful if its merger with the freehold reversion is such a disposal. Nevertheless, HMRC must be expected to firmly resist any claim to deduct the whole cost of the lease. If the superior interest is itself a lease of under 50 years, the unwasted part of the cost of the sublease and the cost of acquiring the head lease are aggregated and that aggregate treated as the cost of the merged asset, acquired at the date of the merger, for the purpose of applying the wasting asset rules to the merged lease.

Extension of Leases

11.47 It is not possible in law to vary a lease so as to extend its term. Accordingly, an extension normally takes the form of the surrender of the existing lease and the grant of a new one. In such circumstances the surrender is technically a disposal of the old lease for the sum of any payment received plus the value of the new lease (less any payment made). In practice HMRC do not regard the surrender of the old lease as a disposal provided that:

(*a*) the transaction is between unconnected parties bargaining at arm's length (or, if it is not, the terms of the transaction are equivalent to those that would have been made between such persons);

(*b*) the transaction is not part of (or connected with) a larger transaction;

(*c*) no capital sum is received by the lessee;

(*d*) the extent of the property in which the lessee has an interest under the new lease does not differ in any way from that under the old lease; and

(*e*) the terms of the new lease, other than in relation to its duration and the rent payable, do not differ from those of the old lease (ignoring any trivial differences) (HMRC Extra-Statutory Concession D39 and Tax Bulletin 41, June 1999).

Where any of these conditions are not met, capital gains tax needs to be considered. The safest thing may be to achieve the extension by the grant of an additional lease to take effect on the expiry of the existing one. Even where a transaction is at arm's length it should not automatically be assumed that all of the above conditions will be met. In particular the landlord may well take the opportunity to modernise some of the provisions of the lease, which would prevent (*e*) from being satisfied.

11.48 Where such a merger occurs the indexation allowance is, strictly speaking, calculable on the aggregate of the unwasted part of the cost of the lease and the cost of the superior interest from the date of acquisition of the superior interest, ie the date of the merger. By concession though, HMRC will allow indexation on the unwasted part of the cost of the lease to be calculated from the date of acquisition of that lease and on the superior interest from the date of acquisition of that interest (HMRC Extra-Statutory Concession D42). Where the owner of a lease of less than 50 years buys in an inferior interest, the cost of the inferior interest will probably constitute enhancement expenditure on the lease so no special rules are needed to cater for that situation.

Part Disposals of Land

11.49 It is often difficult to determine whether a holding of land is a single asset or a number of separate assets. For example, if two adjoining houses are purchased together, is the sale of one the complete disposal of a house or the part disposal of the pair? The calculations could in many cases produce significantly different results. HMRC have expressed the view that, unless it appears from the facts at the time of acquisition that more than one asset was acquired, a single acquisition of land, with or without buildings – whether obtained by purchase under one contract at an inclusive price, or by gift or inheritance as a whole – should be regarded as a single asset even though it may comprise distinguishable elements such as a house and garden, farmhouses, buildings, woodlands, cottages, etc. (CCAB Press Release, June 1968). It is debatable whether this view is correct in principle, at least where the different buildings are not within a single curtilage. If the assets are contiguous it may possibly be, but even that seems doubtful. If, however, a number of scattered parcels of land are purchased as a job lot it seems doubtful whether the mere fact that a single overall price is paid could suffice to constitute them a single combined asset. If separate prices are attributed to the different assets, the inference can be drawn from the above statement of HMRC's views that they would regard them as a number of separate purchases even though bought under a single contract.

11.50 This is probably an academic point as, in spite of their view of the legal position, HMRC have stated that even where there is a single inclusive price, in practice no objection is taken to treating individual houses as separate assets and apportioning the cost of a larger unit (such as a row of terraced houses) on the basis of such evidence as is available. Similarly, with a block of flats, no objection is normally taken to treating individual flats as separate assets if it appears that similar flats in the same ownership, or in the same locality, have commonly been sold singly as independent dwellings (CCAB Press Release, June 1968). HMRC have also said that where part of an estate is disposed of, eg on the sale of a field, they will accept that such part can be regarded as a separate asset and any fair and reasonable method of apportioning the total cost will be accepted (Statement of Practice D1). The taxpayer is not, of course, precluded from treating the sale as a part disposal if he wishes and the facts support a contention that the estate was a single asset. He will normally have to make up his mind which basis he wants to adopt at the time of his first disposal out of an estate, and use the same basis on subsequent sales of future parts.

Insurance Proceeds, etc.

11.51 If a building is destroyed – as opposed to damaged – and the insurance proceeds (or any other compensation) are used within a year of the receipt (or such longer time as HMRC may allow) to replace the building, an election can be made to treat the asset as having been disposed of at a no gain/no loss price with the excess of the insurance proceeds over such amount then being deducted from the cost of the new building (*TCGA 1992, s 23(4)*). If the whole of the insurance proceeds are not used to buy the replacement building but the part not reinvested is less than the amount of the gain (not the chargeable gain, ie before time apportionment for a company) the gain can be reduced to the amount not reinvested with the balance of the gain being deducted from the cost of the new property (*TCGA 1992, s 23(5)*). If a building is destroyed or irreparably damaged and all or part of any compensation or insurance proceeds is used to construct or otherwise acquire a replacement building situated elsewhere, both the old and new buildings are deemed to be assets separate from the land on which they stand or stood and the old building is regarded as destroyed (*TCGA 1992, s 23(6)*). This ensures that relief is not lost because the land is not destroyed, but also prevents the compensation being set against the land cost of the new building. Where the money is received by a lessee under a lease which is a wasting asset the sum can be set against the expenditure on the replacement building and no gain recognised but on a subsequent disposal of the asset the expenditure is set against what the base cost would have been had the asset been disposed of immediately after the replacement works (*TCGA 1992, s 23(8)*).

11.52 If the building is damaged rather than destroyed and the insurance proceeds (or any other compensation received) are used to restore the building, the receipt of the compensation again need not be treated as a part disposal of the asset (*TCGA 1992, s 23*). Instead, the insurance proceeds are deducted from the base cost. This treatment can also be adopted if all except a small amount of the compensation is used to restore the building. Strictly speaking this treatment can give rise to a problem on a subsequent disposal, as the original cost of the building would no longer be reflected in the state of the asset at the time of disposal, and would thus not constitute enhancement expenditure. For example, suppose a taxpayer, who had initially bought a site on which he erected a building at a cost of £200,000, receives insurance proceeds of £90,000 after a fire, and spends £95,000 on reconstruction. Logically the £90,000 should be deducted from the cost and the £95,000 added to it, giving a new base cost of £205,000. Strictly, however, a part of the original £200,000 will relate to work which has been destroyed and replaced by the new work. As such it ceases to qualify as enhancement expenditure. In practice HMRC are unlikely to take this point.

11.53 If the insurance proceeds are not wholly applied in restoring the building, the part so applied can be deducted from the new expenditure with only the balance being treated as disposal proceeds (*TCGA 1992, s 23(3)*). This does not apply if the part not reinvested is small or if the entire capital sum is small (even if no part of it is used to restore the building) as compared with the value of the asset. Instead it is deducted from the base cost of the asset so that any gain is deferred. If such sum exceeds the base cost of the asset the balance is of course taxable (*TCGA 1992, s 23(2),(3)*). There is no statutory definition of small. In *O'Rourke v Binks (65 TC 165)* the Court of Appeal said it is a question of fact and degree. HMRC have said that they regard an amount as small if either it does not exceed 5% of the total or it does not exceed £3,000 (Tax Bulletin 27, February 1997).

11.54 If a building is destroyed but no insurance proceeds are receivable, for example because it is uninsured, consideration might be given as to whether a capital loss can be established under *TCGA 1992, s 24(2)* on the grounds that the value of the asset has become negligible. Unfortunately this will rarely apply unless the building is destroyed by a nuclear holocaust, as the site will normally still have a value. To make this rule workable *s 24(3)* allows the building and land to be regarded as separate assets so as to trigger a claim under *s 24(2)*. Unfortunately it requires both land and buildings to be deemed to be sold and reacquired, so before making the election the premature crystallisation of the increase in value of the land needs to be weighed against the value of the loss on the building.

Small Part Disposals

11.55 If the consideration for the transfer or other disposal of part of a holding of land does not exceed 20% of the market value of the entire holding (as it subsisted immediately before the part disposal) the vendor can elect to deduct the disposal proceeds or other consideration from the base cost of the holding instead of calculating a gain on the disposal (*TCGA 1992, s 242(1), (2), (6)*).

11.56 The taxpayer cannot adopt this treatment if the consideration on the transfer exceeds £20,000 or if the consideration for all disposals of land by him in the year of assessment (other than disposals within *TCGA 1992, s 243* to an authority with compulsory powers under **11.57** below) exceeds £20,000 (*TCGA 1992, s 242(3)(4)*). It should be noted that all disposals of land, not merely small part disposals, need to be taken into account in applying this £20,000 test. Where the transfer is at an undervalue the £20,000 test must be applied by reference to the market value of the land disposed of (*TCGA 1992, s 242(5)*). In addition, this treatment cannot be used where the estate or interest in land is a wasting asset (*TCGA 1992, s 242(7)*) or where the transfer is a no gain/no loss transfer between spouses or members of a group of companies (*TCGA 1992, s 242(1)(b)*).

Part Disposal to Authority with Compulsory Powers

11.57 Where:

(*a*) a disposal of land forming part only of a holding is made to an authority exercising or having compulsory powers;

(*b*) the consideration for the transfer (or the market value if the transfer is not for full consideration – an unlikely event on a sale to a local authority, etc.) is small as compared with the market value of the entire holding immediately before the disposal; and

(*c*) the vendor had not taken any steps, by advertising or otherwise, to dispose of any part of the holding or to make his willingness to dispose of it known to any person,

the vendor can similarly elect to deduct the disposal proceeds from the base cost of the holding instead of calculating a gain on the part disposal (*TCGA 1992, s 243(1),(2)*).

11.58 For this purpose, proceeds will normally be regarded as small if they either do not exceed 5% of the value of the holding, or are £3,000 or less (as under **11.53**), there is no special time limit for making the claim, and a claim cannot be made if the estate or interest in land in question is a wasting asset (*TCGA 1992, s 243(4)*). An authority having compulsory powers is any body that either acquires the land compulsorily for the purpose for which it was acquired, or which had (or could have) been authorised to acquire it for that purpose. It also includes a person for whom some other body has (or could have) been authorised so to acquire it (*TCGA 1992, s 243(5)*). In other words, the relief will apply on any disposal under a compulsory purchase or under the threat of compulsory purchase, including, for example, a sale to a property developer in circumstances where, had the sale not taken place, the local authority would have been likely to acquire the land and resell it to the developer. It will also apply on many voluntary sales to local authorities even though no threat of compulsory purchase is made provided that the initial approach is from the local authority not the taxpayer. In practice *s 243* is likely to operate only where the £20,000 of proceeds limit in *s 242* is breached, as *s 242* is less restrictive.

Part Disposal – Consideration Exceeding Base Cost

11.59 If, on a transaction within either *ss 242* or *243*, the base cost of the entire holding is less than the consideration received on the part disposal (or is nil) the consideration cannot be deducted from the base cost. Instead the taxpayer can elect to deduct the base cost of the entire holding from the consideration for the part disposal, the balance of that consideration then being a chargeable gain (*TCGA 1992, s 244*). There is no special time limit for such an election.

Compulsory Acquisitions

11.60 Apart from the above relief for small part disposals there are a number of other provisions dealing with compulsory purchase of land.

Where an interest in land is acquired (otherwise than under a contract) by an authority possessing compulsory purchase powers, the time of the disposal and acquisition is the date on which the compensation for the acquisition is agreed or otherwise determined (variations on appeal being ignored for this purpose).

11.61 Where the land is acquired under contract the normal rules apply: the disposal takes place at the time the contract is entered into, or, if it is conditional, the date that the condition is satisfied.

11.62 Where land (or an interest in, or right over, land) is acquired under compulsory purchase powers (or is sold voluntarily in circumstances that the acquisition could have been made under compulsory purchase powers), the fact that the acquisition is made compulsorily must be ignored when considering whether the compensation ought to be apportioned and part treated as compensation for damage to, or for the loss of, an asset under *TCGA 1992, s 22(1)(a)*. So must any statutory provision treating the purchase price, compensation or other consideration as exclusively paid in respect of the land itself (*TCGA 1992, s 245(1)*). This provision was introduced to prevent the element of compensation for disturbance – which HMRC generally regard as a revenue receipt – being transformed into capital because under general law it is often merely an element in arriving at the price to be paid for the land on a compulsory acquisition.

11.63 It was held in *Stoke-on-Trent City Council v Wood Mitchell & Co Ltd (1979 STC 197)* that the effect of this provision is to treat compensation for loss of profits as a trading receipt, not as a capital sum. Accordingly, the local authority could not make a deduction for corporation tax in arriving at the amount of such compensation as that element of the compensation is itself a taxable amount. Following that case HMRC have adopted the stance that any element of compensation received for temporary loss of profits on a compulsory acquisition, or for losses on trading stock, or to reimburse revenue expenditure such as removal expenses, is revenue and should be regarded as taxable income. They will apply the same practice in those compensation cases where no interest in land is acquired – such as where compensation is paid due to damage, injury, or exploitation of land, or to the exercise of planning control (HMRC Statement of Practice SP 8/79).

11.64 If land (or an interest in land) is, or could have been, acquired compulsorily, and the compensation or purchase price includes an amount in respect of its severance from other land in which the vendor (in the same capacity) has an interest, or in respect of injurious affection of other land, the receipt must be treated as giving rise to a part disposal of that other land (*TCGA 1992, s 245(2)*). This is normally in the interest of the taxpayer, as it allows part of the base cost of the other land to be set against the compensation received.

Roll-over Relief on Compulsory Purchase

11.65 Where land is compulsorily acquired or is otherwise disposed of to an authority possessing compulsory purchase powers (ie a person who has been – or could be – authorised to acquire it compulsorily for the purpose for which it is acquired, or for whom another person has been – or could be – authorised so to acquire it), a claim for roll-over relief can be made in certain circumstances if the proceeds are used to acquire other land (*TCGA 1992, ss 243(5), 247(1), (8)*). HMRC consider that *s 247* also applies to a landlord where leasehold tenants exercise their statutory rights to acquire the freehold reversion or an extension of a lease of a property under the *Leasehold Reform Act 1967, Housing and Urban Development Act 1993* or the *Housing Acts 1985–1996* – as the leaseholder is an 'Authority' within *TCGA 1992, s 243(5)*, ie a person with compulsory purchase powers (HMRC Statement of Practice SP 13/93 and Tax Bulletin No 41, June 1999).

11.66 The taxpayer must not have taken any steps – whether by advertising or otherwise – to dispose of the land or to make his willingness to dispose of it known to the authority or to any other person (*TCGA 1992, s 247(1)(b)*). This presumably means willingness to dispose before any approach to acquire was made, and would hopefully not deny relief where a taxpayer was 'willing' to dispose of the land to the authority by private treaty because they had intimated an intention to exercise their compulsory purchase powers if he did not do so. It is understood that any steps taken by the taxpayer more than three years prior to the disposal will be ignored for the purposes of *TCGA 1992, s 247(1)(b)* (ICAEW Technical Releases 467, 477). The consideration for the disposal must be applied by the taxpayer in acquiring the new land (*TCGA 1992, s 247(1)(c)*). It must be acquired (or an unconditional contract for its acquisition entered into) within the period beginning 12 months before and ending three years after the disposal of the old land (see **11.95** below) or such longer period as HMRC may allow (*TCGA 1992, ss 247(5)(b), 152(3),(4)*). It is obviously sensible to approach HMRC within the time limit if the taxpayer needs to have it extended although the comments in **11.95** need to be borne in mind.

11.67 Where a roll-over relief claim is made, the consideration for the disposal is reduced to the CGT base cost of the old land (including indexation relief) and that for the acquisition of the new is reduced by the excess of the sale proceeds over that figure (*TCGA 1992, s 247(2)*), ie the gain that would otherwise have arisen on the old land is deducted from the cost of the new. If, because of time apportionment, it is not wholly chargeable gain, only the chargeable part need be deducted (*TCGA 1992, s 247(5)(a)*). If the whole of the consideration is not applied on the acquisition of the new land, the taxpayer is deemed to have reinvested the cost of the original land before reinvesting the gain realised on it, ie the whole of the amount not reinvested is taxable up to the amount of the gain. If it is less than the gain, roll-over relief is due on the balance of the gain (*TCGA 1992, s 247(3)*).

11.68 The relief cannot be claimed if the new land is a dwelling-house (or part of a dwelling-house, or an interest in, or right over, a dwelling-house) which qualifies for private residence relief under *TCGA 1992, ss 222–226* (see **13.3–13.45** below) at any time during the six years following its acquisition (*TCGA 1992, s 248(1)*). If a gain is rolled over into the cost of a dwelling-house which is not initially a principal private residence, but it subsequently becomes one in the six-year period, the gain on the original disposal must be recomputed to withdraw the relief.

11.69 If the gain is rolled over into land which is a depreciating asset, ie a lease of under 60 years, the gain is held over for ten years or until the earlier disposal of that lease, and will become taxable at the end of the hold-over period. If new land, which is not a depreciating asset, is acquired during the period that the gain is being held over, the gain can be switched to that new land instead. A switch cannot be made to another depreciating asset, however (*TCGA 1992, ss 154, 248(3)*).

11.70 If a claim for roll-over relief is made on a part disposal, a claim cannot also be made under *TCGA 1992, s 243* (see **11.57** above) to deduct the proceeds from the cost of the part undisposed of (*TCGA 1992, s 248(4)*). Where compensation includes an amount in respect of injurious affection to other land, a claim under *s 247* displaces the operation of *TCGA 1992, s 245(2)* (see **11.64** above) to the extent that roll-over relief is given for such an amount (*TCGA 1992, s 247(6)*).

Options

11.71 Options are very common in relation to property. For example, a developer who is assembling a site may make payments to property owners for an option over their land which would be exercised only if he can acquire all of the interests he needs for his development or is successful in obtaining planning consent for the development. This limits the developer's exposure in the event of the projected development proving abortive – as all he will have lost will be his option payments (leaving aside his time and costs of applying for planning consent) – and avoids his having to fund purchases of land many months in advance of his being in a position to carry out his development. A potential vendor is likely to find an option arrangement more attractive than a conditional contract for sale as it usually puts some money in his hand irrespective of whether or not the scheme proceeds.

11.72 For CGT purposes the grant of an option is regarded as the disposal of a separate asset to the land over which it is granted (*TCGA 1992, s 144(1)*). HMRC accept that roll-over relief on replacement of business assets is available in respect of gains on the grant of an option over land by reference to the underlying land (Tax Bulletin, February 1992). If the option is exercised, the grant and exercise are instead treated as a single transaction, the option money (ie the payment made for the grant of the option) being treated, as far as the purchaser is concerned, as part of the cost of the land acquired in pursuance of the option (*TCGA 1992, s 144(3)(a)*), and, as far as the vendor is concerned, as part of the sale proceeds (*TCGA 1992, s 144(2)*). The date of the combined transaction is determined by the sale of the land and not the grant of the option. In effect, an exercised option is a type of conditional contract, the exercise of the option normally being the event that makes the contract unconditional and thus fixing the date of the transaction (*TCGA 1992, s 28*).

11.73 Similar rules apply to a put option, ie one enabling the vendor to require the developer to purchase his land. On the exercise of the option the option money paid merges with the cost of the land. If the vendor pays option money to a purchaser for the right to put his land on to him – a very rare occurrence – the option money is deducted from the purchaser's cost of the land and treated as a selling expense of the vendor (*TCGA 1992, s 144(2)(b),(3)(b)*). Put options can be useful where the vendor is willing to sell his land but wishes to retain a degree of control over it when he does so. For example, he may wish to delay doing so until the next fiscal year if he has exhausted his capital gains tax annual exemption for the current year.

11.74 If possible cross options, ie those where the vendor has a right to require the developer to buy his land at a specified time and the developer has a simultaneous right to require the vendor to sell it to him, should be avoided where the purpose of the option is to defer the disposal date to a later tax year. For development land tax purposes HMRC sometimes contended that such an arrangement constituted an unconditional contract for sale as either party is able to enforce completion. Although it seems dubious whether this contention is correct as, in general, HMRC must tax the transactions that are entered into, not ignore the form of those transactions and look only to the overall effect, the taxpayer could be faced with a contentious appeal which can be both time-consuming and costly. If the options are successive rather than simultaneous, eg the vendor can require the developer to buy at any time during May 2016 and, in the event of his not doing so, the developer can require the vendor to sell at any time during June 2016, this will probably defeat such a contention even if it is raised, as there would be no single date on which both parties could force the sale. If the price payable for the land in pursuance of the option is undetermined, eg the higher of £50,000 or 70% of the open market value of the land on the date the option is exercised, this would also make it difficult for HMRC to say that there had been a contract for sale at the time the option was entered into as such a notional contract could well be void for uncertainty.

11.75 If a series of options is entered into solely to obtain the benefit of several years' capital gains tax annual exemptions for the vendor, the *Ramsay* principle needs to be borne in mind – although as the legislation itself effectively treats the grant and exercise of an option as a composite transaction, that principle may well have no practical effect in relation to options as it is difficult to envisage the courts regarding a series of, say, three annual sales of land with three separate conveyances as a single transaction. Nevertheless it is as well to consider whether any commercial benefits of a spreading arrangement are present in a particular case and if so to spell them out clearly in the agreement. For example, the developer's right to acquire the second tranche of land might be conditional on his having commenced building work or having installed an estate road so that the vendor can be satisfied that the remainder of his land will not be devalued if all of the options are not exercised. Where there is a series of options extending over several years it is difficult to avoid using put and call options while reassuring both parties that the whole of the land will be sold. It might be possible to use only call options if the price for the first part of the land is disproportionately high so that the developer is effectively forced to acquire the remainder because the price is so attractive – although this could possibly prompt a challenge as to whether the purchase price for the first tranche is wholly and exclusively incurred for the acquisition of that particular piece of land.

11.76 If an option is not exercised the landowner is taxable on the option money he receives in the year of receipt. In practice, in the past, HMRC generally waited a reasonable time to see whether it was exercised before raising an assessment although they would not wait for several years. There is no bar on their raising an assessment before the expiry of the option period (*Strange v Openshaw, 57 TC 544).* Now that the taxpayer has to self assess he will have to declare the option receipt, pay tax on it, and recover it if the option is exercised. The developer will obtain no tax relief for the option payment (unless he is a property dealer) if it lapses. If he sells the benefit of the option to another person, the grant and sale will be the acquisition and disposal of an asset (the option). An option is a wasting asset, so the cost depreciates on a time basis over the period for which it is capable of being exercised. Accordingly the part of the cost that is deductible on such a sale may be small. Care needs to be taken where expenditure in relation to the land is incurred as part of an option arrangement as is illustrated by *Garner v Pounds Shipowners and Shipbreakers (2000 STC 420).* The company granted a call option in September 1988 to buy land for £4m. It was paid £399,750 for the option but this was to be held by a stakeholder until the release had been secured of certain covenants over the land. The company subsequently paid £90,000 to secure the release of those covenants and the option money was paid over to it in May 1990.

The option was not exercised, expiring in January 1991. The company's claim that the option was not granted until May 1990 was dismissed; the option itself was an unconditional contract with the release of the covenants being a separate agreement. The Court of Appeal, reversing the decision of the High Court, held that the £90,000 was not deductible in computing the gain on the option. It was not incurred in granting the option or in establishing, preserving or defending title to it within *TCGA 1992, s 32*. On a proper construction of the documents the option was to acquire the land subject to the covenants not free of them. That was the bargain that the parties had chosen to make. This reasoning was upheld in the House of Lords. Mention should also be made of *Randall v Plumb (50 TC 392)* where the option agreement provided for the option money to be repaid if planning permission were not obtained within ten years. It was held that the consideration for the grant of the option was not the option money, but its current value taking the contingency into account. Nourse LJ in the *Pounds Shipowners* case felt that this followed from the fact that the judge in *Randall v Plumb (1995 STC 191)* had held that the contingency on which the option money was repayable did not fall within what is now *TCGA 1992, ss 48* or *49*. It followed that the position would be different where a contingency did fall within one of those provisions.

11.77 The abandonment of an option is specifically stated not to be the disposal of an asset (*TCGA 1992, s 144(4)*). Many people felt that this could be used to advantage by a landowner granting an option to an associated person and the developer acquiring the land subject to that option and paying the associated person a substantial sum to abandon his option. However, it was held in *Golding v Kaufman (58 TC 296)* that in the context of *section 144* the meaning of 'abandonment' is limited to the extinction of the option by lapse of time or otherwise than for valuable consideration, and it is not apt to describe the exploitation by the taxpayer of the rights conferred by the option as amounting to its abandonment. Accordingly, the receipt by the associated person would be chargeable to capital gains tax by virtue of *TCGA 1992, s 22* as a capital sum received in return for the surrender of a right.

11.78 An option binding the grantor to grant a lease for a premium is treated in the same way as an option for a sale even though when the option is granted the interest covered by it does not exist (*TCGA 1992, s 144(6)*). Where a disposal falls through and the vendor forfeits the purchaser's deposit, the forfeited deposit is treated in the same way as option money (*TCGA 1992, s 144(7)*), ie there is not a part disposal of the property but the complete disposal of a deemed separate asset – which will have no base cost, so the full amount of the forfeited deposit will be chargeable to CGT. *Section 144(7)* was in issue in *Hardy v HMRC ([2016] UKUT 322)*. Mr Hardy bought a prospective property off-plan. He was unable to complete the purchase and the vendor forfeited his deposit. He claimed a CGT loss of the amount of the deposit. The Upper Tribunal accepted that Mr Hardy had acquired a valuable right by entering into the purchase contract, namely the right to call for completion subject only to having performed his own obligations under the contract. However, on the basis of *Jerome v Kelly* (see **11.21**) that right did not constitute an asset. The right was conditional on the buyer performing his obligations under the contract; if he did so, he acquired an asset (the property) but if he did not do so, no asset came into existence. Even if that were wrong, *s 144(7)* looks not solely at the position of the seller. It looks at the deposit itself. It must accordingly apply to the buyer as well as the seller so prevented an asset being disposed of.

11.79 *TCGA 1992, s 17(1)* deems certain types of transaction to take place at a consideration equal to market value. These are gifts, transfers into settlement, distributions in specie by a company, other disposals not made by way of a bargain at arm's length, acquisitions for a consideration that cannot be valued, acquisitions in connection with a person's loss of office or employment or diminution of emoluments and transactions in consideration of, or recognition of, a person's services or past services in an office or employment or of any other service rendered by one person to another. It was held in *Mansworth v Jelley (2003 STC 53)* that where *s 17(1)* applies on the grant of an option the effect of the deeming under *s 144* (see **11.72**) is that the exercise of the option must also be treated as not at arm's length, and the market value of the asset at the date of exercise of the option (when *s 144* deems the transaction to take place) must be substituted as the cost of the asset. The effect of this decision is that if a purchaser exercises the option and immediately sells the land he will have no capital gains tax liability, but the vendor, who in most cases will have sold the land for its market value at the time of the grant of the option, will be taxable on the increase in value since that date even though he will never receive it.

11.80 *Finance Act 2003, s 158* inserted a new *TCGA 1992, s 144ZA* to restore the law to what it was generally believed to be before the *Mansworth v Jelley* decision. It disapplies the market value rule for determining the consideration for the sale except to the extent that it applies to determine the consideration for the option.

Example 11.4

Jack grants an option to his sister Jill for a consideration of £100, which gives her the right to acquire from him Whiteacre for £250,000. Jill exercises the option five years later when Whiteacre is worth £1.5m and immediately sells Whiteacre to a developer. When the option was granted, the value of the right to buy Whiteacre for £250,000 was £50,000.

Jill's gain before taper relief will be:

	£	£
Sale proceeds		1,500,000
Cost of option (its market value)	50,000	
Cost of Whiteacre	250,000	300,000
Gain		1,200,000

11.81 *Section 144ZA* itself created an opportunity for avoidance. For example, if a person were to grant a put option to a connected person for no consideration allowing that connected person to sell him an asset at an artificially low price that person would be able to pass the asset over to him without triggering CGT (if the sale price is equal to his cost) or even creating a capital loss (if the sale price is below his cost). *Section 144ZA* would not permit the market value to be substituted for the sale proceeds and although it would in theory allow an adjustment to the nil option price that option in fact has a nil value.

11.82 To thwart such transactions, *s 144ZA* is disapplied (except in relation to employment-related securities options) where the option is exercised after 1 December 2004 and its exercise is non-commercial (*TCGA 1992, s 144ZB(1)(2)* inserted by *FA 2005, Sch 5, para* 2). Instead, if the option is a put option (ie it binds the grantor to buy) the grantor's cost or acquisition of the asset (and his vendor's disposal consideration) is the market value of the asset at the time the option is exercised and if the option is a call option (ie it binds the grantor to sell) his consideration for the sale (and his vendor's acquisition cost) is again the market value of the asset at the time the option is exercised (*TCGA 1992, s 144ZB(4)(5)*). If the whole or any part of the underlying subject matter of the option (ie the asset that falls to be bought or sold on its exercise) is subject to any right or restriction which is enforceable by the person disposing of that underlying subject matter (or a person connected with him) that right or restriction must be ignored in arriving at the market value of the asset (and *TCGA 1992, s 18(6)(7)* which also contain rules to deal with such rights and restrictions are ignored) (*TCGA 1992, s 144ZB(6)(7)*). Nor, of course, is it a non-resident CGT disposal if *ITA 2007, s 517C* or *CTA 2010, s 356OC(1)* (transactions in land: see **14.6**) apply in relation to it so as to tax the gain as income (*TCGA 1992, s 14B(5)* inserted by *FA 2016, s 77(6)*).

11.83 The exercise of a put option is non-commercial for this purpose if the exercise price is less than the open market price of what is bought and the exercise of a call option is non-commercial if its exercise price exceeds the open market price of what is sold (*TCGA 1992, s 144ZC(1)(2)*). For this purpose, the exercise price means the amount or value of the consideration which under the terms of the option is receivable (under a put option) or payable (under a call option) as a result of the exercise of the option (and it does not include any consideration given for the acquisition of the option, whether directly from the grantor or from some other person) (*TCGA 1992, s 144ZC(3)*). The open market price is the price that the underlying subject matter might reasonably be expected to fetch on a sale in the open market at the time the option is exercised:

(*a*) ignoring any right or restriction to which it is subject which is enforceable by the person disposing of the underlying subject matter or a connected person;

(*b*) making no reduction in value because of an assumption that the whole of the asset is to be placed on the market at one and the same time; and

(*c*) if the underlying subject matter is or includes unquoted shares or securities assuming that there is available to a prospective purchaser all the information which a prudent prospective purchaser of that asset might reasonably require if he were proposing to purchase it from a willing seller by private treaty and at arm's length.

(*TCGA 1992, s 144ZC(4)–(7)*.)

11.84 Another special rule applies where arrangements are entered into that alter the value of the underlying subject matter between the grant and exercise of the option. It applies only if:

(*a*) *s 144ZB* would otherwise have applied;

(*b*) at the time the option is exercised the open market price (as defined in *ss 144ZC(4)–(7)*) of the underlying subject matter differs from its open market price at the time the option was granted;

(*c*) some or all of that change in the open market price results to any extent (directly or indirectly) from arrangements (defined to include any agreement, understanding, scheme transaction or series of transactions) to which the grantor of the option, a person who at any time holds the option or a person connected with either of such persons (called 'a relevant person') is or has been a party or which include one or more transactions to which a relevant person is or has been a party;

(*d*) the exercise of the option would not be non-commercial (within *s 1442C*) if the part of the change in the open market price which arises (directly or indirectly) from the relevant arrangements were ignored; and

(*e*) as a result (directly or indirectly) of the relevant arrangements either the grantor of the option or the person who exercises it might be expected to obtain an advantage in respect of chargeable gains either directly or indirectly in consequence of (or in connection with) the exercise of the option.

(*TCGA 1992, s 144Z(1)–(7)*.)

11.85 Arrangements for the purpose includes any agreement, understanding, scheme, transaction or series of transactions (whether or not legally enforceable) and 'an advantage' covers both a relief (or increased relief or repayment or increased repayment) from CGT or corporation tax and the deferral of any payment of that tax (or an advancement of any repayment) (*TCGA 1992, s 144ZD(8),(9)*).

11.86 In such circumstances *s 144ZA* (see **11.81**) applies instead of *s 144ZC*. This ensures that what is taxed is the full value of the option at the time of the grant plus the exercise price actually paid. The two together will roughly equal the value of the asset at the time of the grant of the option. HMRC give as an example if a person is granted an option to acquire for £100 an asset worth £1,000, the asset is devalued so that it is worth only £50 when the option is exercised but its value is subsequently restored to the £1,000 level. The value of the option would be in excess of £900 at the time of its grant so the person who granted it would be taxed by reference to a disposal price of a bit over £1,000 (the £900 plus value of the option plus, when it is exercised, the £100 exercise price).

Land Held at 31 March 1982

11.87 For disposals by individuals and trusts (but not companies) the intention is that only the gain arising since 31 March 1982 should be taxable – and only losses accruing after that date should be deductible. To achieve this, the base cost of assets held by an individual or trust is their value at 1 April 1982. For corporation tax, the legislation requires two calculations of the gain, one by reference to cost (or 6 April 1965 value if appropriate) and the second by reference to 31 March 1982 value:

1. If both calculations show a gain, the smaller gain is taxable.
2. If both show a loss, the smaller loss is allowable.
3. If one produces a gain and the other a loss, the transaction is treated as giving rise to neither a gain nor a loss.
4. If the sale proceeds are identical to either the cost or the 6 April 1965 value, the transaction is treated as giving rise to neither a gain nor a loss.

(*TCGA 1992, s 35*.)

11.88 As an alternative a company can make a once and for all election to treat every asset that it held at 31 March 1982 (but not some only) as having been acquired at its market value at that date. The historical cost will not then be relevant to the calculation of the gain. Such a claim can generate allowable losses where the 31 March 1982 value of the land exceeds its cost and it is sold at a loss. The claim must be made by the end of the accounting period after that in which the first disposal of pre-31 March 1982 assets takes place. For most companies this time limit will have passed.

11.89 The rebasing of capital gains tax to 31 March 1982 does not affect indexation for companies. A company has the option of calculating the indexation by reference to either the 31 March 1982 value or cost if this is more beneficial. A formal election to adopt the 31 March 1982 value is not required (*TCGA 1992, s 55(1)(2)*). If the gain itself is calculated by reference to the value at 31 March 1982, the indexation allowance must also be calculated by reference to that value, as the legislation deems the asset to have been acquired on that date.

Land Held at 6 April 1965

11.90 For corporation tax purposes only, where a gain is calculated by reference to cost and the asset was acquired before 6 April 1965, the gain is normally apportioned on a time basis over the period of ownership, the part apportioned to the period prior to 6 April 1965, when capital gains tax was introduced, not being taxable (*TCGA 1992, Sch 2, para 16*). This also applied for individuals up to 5 April 2008, but from that date a 5 April 1982 value has to be used in calculating a gain by an individual or trust. The taxpayer can instead elect to value the land at 6 April 1965 in which case the whole of the subsequent gain based on that value will be taxable. Such an election must be made within two years after the end of the year of assessment or accounting period in which the disposal occurs and is irrevocable (*TCGA 1992, Sch 2, para 17*). If the election produces a loss and time apportionment produces a gain, the transaction is treated as giving rise to neither a gain nor a loss. If the election produces a loss and the calculation by reference to actual cost shows a smaller loss, only that lesser amount is allowable (but it is not reduced by time apportionment) (*TCGA 1992, Sch 2, para 17(2)*).

11.91 Great care needs to be taken in connection with this election (and with the election for 31 March 1982 valuation referred to in **11.88** above) as, if the District Valuer does not agree with the taxpayer's 1965 valuation, the effect could well be to produce a larger taxable gain than under the time apportionment method – in particular it must be remembered that the asset must be valued as it stood in 1965 (or 1982) and if it was tenanted this could well reduce the value considerably if the tenant had a favourable lease or statutory security of tenure. In *Henderson v Karmel's Exors (58 TC 201)*, Mrs Karmel owned land which she leased under an informal arrangement to a partnership of which she was a partner. She received rent from the partnership. It was contended that the land should be valued at 6 April 1965 on the basis of vacant possession but it was held that all that she had at that date was the reversion in the land expectant on the determination of the tenancy – and as it was an agricultural tenancy this significantly devalued the land. In a Lands Tribunal Case, *Burman v Pembury Property Investment Co Ltd* (Estates Gazette, 21 September 1985), it was mentioned that, although at 6 April 1965 residential tenants had some security of tenure under the *Protection from Eviction Act 1964*, the Bill which became the *Rent Act 1965* was only published a couple of weeks before 6 April 1965 and had not then become law. As the District Valuer in that case assumed an open market rental value, this suggests that the protection to tenants was far less than under the *Rent Acts* – although it is possible that he merely overlooked the point. Where there has been a part disposal since 6 April 1965 and the time apportionment basis was adopted on that part disposal, an election to adopt a 6 April 1965 value cannot be made on a subsequent disposal of the remainder (*TCGA 1992, Sch 2, para 17(5)*). Particular problems arise with shares in companies, including property-owning companies. Each holding of shares has to be valued on its own (unless the related property rules apply to the valuation). The value of a minority shareholding is normally well below the appropriate proportionate part of the value of the company as a whole. Even where there was a strong prospect of a sale at 5 April 1965 this will normally be heavily discounted. Accordingly the sum of the value of all of the individual shareholdings will often be far less than the value of the company as a whole.

11.92 Time apportionment cannot be used on a disposal of land in the UK if the consideration received on the disposal exceeds the current use value at the time of disposal or if any material development of the land was carried out after 17 December 1973 (*TCGA 1992, Sch 2, para 9*). Instead a 6 April 1965 valuation must be adopted (*TCGA 1992, Sch 2, para 9(2)*). If time apportionment was used on a prior part disposal the tax on the part disposal must be recalculated on the valuation basis (*TCGA 1992, Sch 2, para 9(3)*). If the adoption of a 6 April 1965 value gives a greater gain than that over the entire period of ownership the actual gain (but without time apportionment) will be adopted as the chargeable amount instead (*TCGA 1992, Sch 2, para 9(4)*). Similarly, if it would produce a larger loss, only the actual loss is allowable. If it converts an actual gain into a loss, or vice versa, the transaction is treated as giving rise to neither a gain nor a loss. In *Morgan v Gibson (1989 STC 568)* it was held that time apportionment could not be used even if the land had 'hope value' at the time of acquisition so that the development value could not be viewed as an exceptional increase in value.

11.93 Where time apportionment applies the indexation relief must be deducted to arrive at the gain before time apportionment (*Smith v Schofield (1993 STC 268)*). This is anomalous as the result is part of the indexation (which relates to inflation since 1982) and is deemed to fall before 6 April 1965 so reducing the relief. The House of Lords reached this decision, reversing that of both the Commissioners and the Court of Appeal, with regret!

Special Reliefs

Roll-over Relief

11.94 Roll-over relief allows CGT on the disposal of certain types of assets used in a trade or profession to be deferred to the extent that the proceeds are invested in new qualifying assets (*TCGA 1992, s 152*). Land is one of the types of asset that qualify for CGT roll-over relief under *TCGA 1992, s 152*. So does any building or part of a building and any permanent or semi-permanent structure in the nature of a building. In both cases the asset must be both occupied and used only for the purposes of the trade (*TCGA 1992, s 155, Class 1*). A lessor of tied premises is deemed to occupy (as well as use) those premises only for the purposes of his trade (*TCGA 1992, s 156(4)*). The other types of assets that qualify for the relief are:

- Class 2: ships, aircraft and hovercraft
- Class 3: satellites, space stations and spacecraft (including launch vehicles)
- Class 4: goodwill
- Class 5: milk quotas
- Class 6: ewe and suckler cow premium quotas
- Class 7: payment entitlement under the EU single payment scheme and from 20 December 2013, under the basic payment scheme.
- Class 8: certain rights of a member of Lloyds

(*TCGA 1992, s 155* as amended by *FA 2014, s 61*.)

The disposal proceeds of an asset falling in any of these classes can be rolled-over into the acquisition of an asset falling into any class. The CGT cost of the new asset is reduced by the proceeds reinvested. The gain is the last part of the sale proceeds deemed reinvested, so if the full sale proceeds are not reinvested all or part of the gain on the old assets will remain taxable (*TCGA 1992, s 153*). Where the old asset was used for the purpose of the trade for part only of the period of ownership, or part only of the asset was used for the purpose of the trade, fairly common occurrences with property, relief is given on an appropriate proportion of the gain. It was held in *Richart v J Lyons & Co Ltd (1989 STC 665)* that, irrespective of whether or not the gain was calculated by reference to a 6 April 1965 valuation, in calculating the extent of this restriction the use of the properties throughout the actual period of ownership – not just the period from 6 April 1965 – needs to be taken into account. However, this decision does not apply for disposals after 5 April 1988 as *TCGA 1992, s 152(9)* now provides that 'period of ownership' is not to include any period before 31 March 1982.

11.95 To qualify for roll-over relief an unconditional contract for the acquisition of the replacement asset must be entered into within one year before or three years after the disposal of the old (*TCGA 1992, s 152(3)*). The Board have power to extend both of these time limits. If it is not possible to acquire the new asset within the statutory period it is obviously sensible to approach HMRC before the end of the three-year period and ask them to extend the time limit. Some Inspectors of Taxes seem willing to grant an extension, although the author was told by an Inspector that, in spite of Parliament reserving their decision to the Board, they have delegated to local Inspectors the power to grant (but not to refuse) an extension, but that an Inspector can only exercise this power in retrospect. In other words it is not permissible for an Inspector to agree in advance of the purchase of the new asset that he will grant an extension of the statutory period if the purchase has not taken place by the end of that period. If the taxpayer cannot acquire a replacement asset within the three-year period, however valid his reason may be, he must take the risk that when he does acquire it HMRC may at that stage contend that it was not bought within the statutory period. This is confirmed by HMRC's Capital Gains Manual which states at CG60640: 'No decision on a possible extension of time limit can be made until the old asset has been disposed of, the new asset has been acquired and all other conditions of relief are satisfied.' If an Inspector wishes to refuse the claim he must, however, refer it to the Board. Provided that they consider that a taxpayer has a good reason for not having met the three-year limit, the Board will normally extend the time limit if the new asset is bought within six years of the disposal of the old. Similarly, it is understood that they will normally extend the period of one year prior to the disposal to three years. In *R (on the application of Barnett) v CIR (2004 STC 21)* HMRC refused to extend the time limit and on judicial review the court held that this was a discretion for HMRC alone and the General Commissioners could not substitute their own view for that of HMRC. Mr Barnett sold his property on 22 April 1986 and acquired the new one on 27 July 1989, so he was only a few months outside the three-year period. HMRC did not feel that Mr Barnett had shown particular circumstances beyond his control that prevented the new property being acquired within the three-year period – there was nothing special about the property he acquired (from a company in which he had an interest) and he could easily have acquired a similar property elsewhere. It was held in the High Court in *Campbell Connelly & Co Ltd v Barnett (1992 STC 316)* that despite *TCGA 1992, s 28* the acquisition date of the new asset for roll-over relief purposes is the completion date, not the contract date, because the requirement that the asset must be brought into use immediately upon acquisition makes the contract date inappropriate. Although this was not explicitly confirmed by the Court of Appeal decision (*1994 STC 50*) it is implicit in the judgment there. It seems likely that the requirement that the disposal proceeds must be reinvested would similarly require the use of the completion date for the disposal.

11.96 Strictly speaking, if a person sells an asset and uses the proceeds to improve an existing property, roll-over relief is not due, as he will not have used the sale proceeds to acquire an asset. By concession, HMRC will allow roll-over relief in such circumstances (HMRC Extra-Statutory Concession D22). Relief will also be given for the cost of land on which the trader intends to erect a building, even though in such circumstances the asset is not immediately brought into use for the purposes of the trade, provided that the building work is carried out expeditiously and the building is brought into use for the purposes of the trade on completion (HMRC Extra-Statutory Concession D24). In *Steibelt v Paling (1999 STC 594)* Sir Richard Scott V-C questioned whether D24 is a concession at all. He felt it merely HMRC's view of the interpretation of *TCGA 1992, s 152(1)*. Accordingly the Commissioners were entitled to substitute their own views for those of HMRC on whether the D24 tests are met. Similarly, roll-over relief will be allowed if the proceeds from the old asset are used to acquire the freehold reversion of a property of which the trader already owns the lease (HMRC Extra-Statutory Concession D25). In *Watton v Tippett (1997 STC 893)* it was held that the gain on sale of half of a building could not be rolled over on to improvements to the other half, and in *Milton v Chivers (1995 Sp C 57)*, where a property was bought in anticipation of one trade and when it proved unsuitable was used for a different trade which was started eleven months after the acquisition of the building, it was held that there was not the necessary proximity between the acquisition of the building and the commencement of its use in the trade. If land is partitioned on the dissolution of a partnership it can be treated as a new asset of an individual partner provided that the partnership is dissolved immediately after the partition (HMRC Extra-Statutory Concession D23). It is understood that HMRC look for reinvestment of the net sale proceeds only and are also prepared to treat the acquisition expenses of the new asset as part of the cost of that asset for roll-over purposes. It appears that HMRC are prepared to treat a building as a separate asset from the land on which it stands for roll-over relief purposes (Taxline, Issue 10). This can be useful if only part of the proceeds are reinvested; the reinvested part may exceed the value of one of these elements on its own. There does not appear to be any legal basis for this treatment as *TCGA 1992, s 155* does not contain an equivalent provision to *s 24(3)* and *s 152(5)* clearly envisages a building including the land on which it stands.

11.97 The relief also applies where the asset is owned by an individual and the trade in which it is used is carried on by a company which is his personal company, ie one in which he can exercise at least 5% of the voting rights (*TCGA 1992, s 157*). The case of *Boparan v HMRC (2007) STC (SCD) 297* has highlighted a tax trap. In that case Mr Boparan and his wife owned a holding company which in turn owned 99% of a trading subsidiary. HMRC claimed that relief was not due as Mr Boparan could not exercise the voting rights in the subsidiary; he had to use his votes in the holding company to procure that company to exercise the votes in the subsidiary. The Special Commissioner agreed (albeit that he could see no logic in the law).

New Assets which are Depreciating Assets

11.98 Where the new asset is a depreciating asset, ie one with a predictable life of 60 years or less such as a short lease, the gain on the old asset is held over for a maximum of ten years or until earlier disposal; it does not reduce the cost of the depreciating asset (*TCGA 1992, s 154*). An effect of this provision in the case of a trade carried on by an individual is that the capital gains tax exemption on death will not apply to the gain as the asset is not deemed to be disposed of on death; that is simply the trigger for the tax charge. However, by concession, HMRC will treat the death as eliminating the held over gain (ESC D45). HMRC have also said that even though *TCGA 1992, s 155* treats land and buildings as separate assets they regard a building constructed on leasehold land where the lease has less than 60 years to run as a depreciating asset. Conversely, where plant or machinery has become part of a building which is itself not a depreciating asset, that plant will not be a depreciating asset either. Whether machinery has become part of a building will depend on the size and nature of the item, how it has become attached to the building and whether it can be removed without damage to the fabric of the building (Tax Bulletin, Issue 7).

Replacement of Business Assets by Members of a Group

11.99 In *Temperley v Visibell Ltd (49 TC 129)* a company bought a site on which to build a factory but later sold it and bought another site. It was held that relief was not due as it had never been used and occupied for the purposes of the trade. It was irrelevant that it had been bought with the intention of so using it if that intention never came to fruition. An important case is *Campbell Connelly & Co Ltd v Barnett (1994 STC 50)*. A subsidiary company sold the lease of its trading premises in 1984 and moved into its parent's trading premises. In January 1986 the company bought the freehold of another property as its new trading premises. Although the intention had been to buy the property with vacant possession, at the time of completion it was subject to a lease to A Ltd and an underlease to B Ltd. In September 1986 the parent company acquired B Ltd's underlease, and the subsidiary went into possession of the property. The contract date for both acquisitions was 13 December 1985. It was held that no roll-over relief was due. The subsidiary did not bring its freehold interest immediately into use for its trade on acquisition in January 1986; it was being used to generate rental income from it. It alternatively sought to argue that its acquisition of the freehold and its parent's acquisition of the underlease were together the acquisition of the new asset, and the eight-month gap should be ignored. The judge in the High Court felt that, although *TCGA 1992, s 175(1)* provides that for roll-over relief purposes all the trades carried on by members of a group must be treated as a single trade, as a matter of construction it could not be inferred from this that all members of a group should be treated as a single person. Accordingly, it was not permissible to treat two transactions by different legal entities as a single combined transaction. This reasoning was not referred to in the Court of Appeal decision which merely said that the acquisition by the parent was not out of the consideration obtained by the subsidiary for the disposal but presumably from its own resources. The judge probably meant no more by this than that an acquisition by one company could not be treated as having been made by another. In any event, *TCGA 1992, s 175(2A)* and *175(2AA)* now provide that the relief will apply on a disposal of an asset by one group company and the acquisition of an asset by another provided that the assets concerned are chargeable assets of the respective companies.

Grants

11.100 It was held in *Wardhaugh v Penrith Rugby Union FC (2002 STC 776)* that the receipt of a grant does not reduce the amount eligible for roll-over relief. The club sold its clubhouse for £315,109. It built a replacement one for £600,459 but received a grant of £490,000 towards its cost from the Sports Council, reducing the net cost to £110,459. It was held that the amount invested was £600,459, so the whole of the gain was eligible to be rolled over.

Roll-over Relief not Available

11.101 Land or buildings cannot qualify for roll-over relief where the trade is a trade of dealing or developing land unless the profit on sale would not form part of the trading profits, ie roll-over relief is due if the property is a fixed asset but not if it is trading stock (*TCGA 1992, s 156(2)(a),(3)*). It also cannot qualify for roll-over relief where the trade is one of providing services for the occupier of land in which the person carrying on the trade has an estate or interest (*TCGA 1992, s 156(2)(b)*). However, it is understood that HMRC accept that the relief can be claimed by the owner of a caravan site. Roll-over relief does not normally apply to non-trading companies but is extended to certain not-for-profit bodies by *TCGA 1992, s 158*. Where additional consideration is received on the grant of planning permission and the *Marren v Ingles* principle applies (see **11.24**) that additional consideration does not derive from an interest in land and thus does not qualify for roll-over relief.

11.102 If a company is entitled to roll-over relief under the intangible fixed assets rules in *CTA 2009* and either *CTA 2009, ss 898* (roll-over relief where pre-FA 2002 assets arises on or after 1 April 2002) *or 899* (roll-over relief where de-grouping charge on pre-FA 2002 assets arises on or after 1 April 2002) applies, the company is treated for CGT purposes as if the consideration for disposal of the old assets were reduced by the amount available for relief (*TCGA 1992, s 156ZA(1),(2)* inserted by *CTA 2009, s 1322*). This deeming does not of course apply to the other party to the transaction (*TCGA 1992, s 156ZA(3)*). If there is a disposal of an asset that both qualifies for CGT roll-over relief and is an intangible fixed asset for the purposes of *CTA 2009*, the period for re-investment under *TCGA 1992, s 152(3)* does not include any period beginning after 1 April 2002 (ie the CGT relief cannot apply), and Classes 4-7A (goodwill, milk quotas, ewe and suckler premium quotas, fish quotas, and entitlements under the single payment scheme or the EU basic payment scheme) do not apply as regards the acquisition of new assets that are chargeable intangible assets (*TCGA 1992, s 156ZB*). In other words, a company cannot roll over a gain on a CGT asset into an asset within the intangible asset regime. The two types of roll-over relief are completely separate. Prior to its amendment from 19 March 2014 by *FA 2014, s 62(1)*, there was a defect in the wording of this provision. That was corrected retrospectively by providing that where CGT roll-over relief was given against the acquisition of an intangible asset between 1 April 2009 and 19 March 2014, the cost of the new asset under the intangible asset rules is treated as reduced on 19 March 2014 by the CGT relief given (but not so as to reduce the tax written down value of the assets below nil) (*CTA 2009, s 870A* inserted by *FA 2014, s 62(2)*).

Roll-over Relief on Incorporation of a Business

11.103 A different form of roll-over relief applies where an individual, partnership, trust or other unincorporated entity transfers to a company a business as a going concern, together with the whole of the assets of the business (other than cash) wholly or partly in exchange for shares issued by the company to the person transferring the business (*TCGA 1992, s 162*). On a transfer wholly for shares the chargeable gains less allowable losses on the disposal of the assets is not charged to tax but is instead deducted from the cost of the shares, which will be their market value at the time of their issue. If the net gains exceed that cost the balance is of course taxed at the time of the incorporation. Where the transfer is partly for shares and partly for some other consideration, only the appropriate proportion of the net gains is deducted from the share element and the proportion attributed to the non-share element remains taxable. If the company takes over liabilities of the business as well as its assets HMRC do not regard the assumption of those liabilities as constituting 'other consideration' (ESC D32).

11.104 An election can be made to disapply *s 162*. The effect of disapplying it is to crystallise the gains on the disposal of the business. The election was introduced to cure a taper relief problem. Following the termination of that relief it is no longer likely to be helpful.

11.105 The word 'business' is wider than 'trade' so *s 162* is not limited to the incorporation of a trading activity. HMRC say, 'It is a question of fact whether a particular activity constitutes a business. It is not easy to draw the line, but we do not accept that the passive holding of investments or the holding of properties as an investment amounts to a business' (Capital Gains Manual CG65715). In *American Leaf Blending Co Sdn Bhd v Director General of Inland Revenue (1978 STC 561),* Lord Diplock said, 'In the case of a private individual, it may well be that the mere receipt of rents from property that he owns raises no presumption that he is carrying on a business', but as that case involved a company that was no more than an aside as the judges were not called on to address the position of an individual. The inheritance tax cases considered at **18.36** onwards are of no help as, for inheritance tax, a business is not relevant business property if it consists mainly of making or holding investments – although this certainly infers that holding investments can constitute a business at least in some circumstances. The mere holding of investments has been held to constitute a business for VAT purposes, but as VAT is a European tax it is probably unwise to assume that the courts will regard those cases as relevant to capital gains tax. Having said that, the tests set out in *C & E Commrs v Lord Fisher* (*1981 STC 238* – see **16.61**) have been adopted by the FTT in recent direct tax cases.

11.106 The ownership and renting of a large number of investment properties is likely to constitute a business if the proprietor (or, probably, his agent) is actively involved either in managing the properties or in searching for new properties. It is difficult to guess either the minimum number of properties that is likely to constitute a business or how much involvement is needed to constitute active involvement. This issue was considered by the Upper Tribunal in *Ramsay v HMRC ([2013] STC 1764).* Mr & Mrs Ramsay owned a single building divided into 10 flats of which five were occupied at the relevant time. They transferred the property to a company in exchange for shares. Mr & Mrs Ramsay managed the property, personally carrying out minor repairs, cleaning the common parts, maintaining the garden and cleaning vacant flats. It was agreed that they spent approximately 20 hours a week on the property. They had no other source of income. The FTT held that Mrs Ramsay was not carrying on a business. However, the Upper Tribunal disagreed and held that the activities carried out were sufficient in nature and extent to amount to a business.

> 'In my judgment the word "business" in the context of *s 162 TCGA* should be afforded a broad meaning. Regard should be had to the factors

referred to in Lord Fisher [See 16.565] which in my view … are of general application to the question whether the circumstances describe a business. Thus, it falls to be considered whether Mrs Ramsay's activities were a "serious undertaking earnestly pursued" or a "serious occupation", whether the activity was an occupation or function actively pursued with reasonable or recognisable continuity, whether the activity had a certain amount of substance in terms of turnover, whether the activity was conducted in a regular manner and on sound and recognised business principles, and whether the activities were of a kind which, subject to differences of detail, are commonly made by those who seek to profit by them. … overall, taking account both of the day-to-day activities, and the work undertaken by Mrs Ramsay in respect of the early refurbishment and redevelopment proposals, I conclude that the activities fall within the tests described in Lord Fisher. There remains, however, the question of degree. That is relevant to the equation because of the fact that in the context of property investment and letting the same activities are equally capable of describing a passive investment and a property investment or rental business. Although resolution of that issue will be assisted by consideration of the Lord Fisher factors, to those there must be added the degree of activity undertaken. There is nothing in the *TCGA* which can colour the extent of the activity which for the purpose of *s 162* may be regarded as sufficient to constitute a business, and so this must be approached in the context of a broad meaning of that term. Applying these principles, in this case I am satisfied that the activity undertaken in respect of the Property, again taken overall, was sufficient in nature and extent to amount to a business for the purpose of *s 162 TCGA*. Although each of the activities could equally well have been undertaken by someone who was a mere property investor, where the degree of activity outweighs what might normally be expected to be carried out by a mere passive investor, even a diligent and conscientious one, that will in my judgment amount to a business.'

Entrepreneurs' Relief

11.107 Entrepreneurs' relief applies to disposals by an individual after 5 April 2008 provided that the necessary conditions are met. It applies on a cumulative basis to the first £10 million of qualifying gains realised since 6 April 2008 (£1 million on disposals before 6 April 2010, £2 million on disposals before 23 June 2010 and £5 million on disposals before 6 April 2011). From 23 June 2010 the relief is given by imposing tax at a special rate of 10% on the qualifying gain. Prior to that date it was given by reducing the taxable gain on the asset by 4/9ths, giving an effective tax rate of 10% (5/9ths of 18%). (*TCGA 1992, s 169N(2)(3)*). This produced an effective tax rate of 10%. Where a taxpayer has part of his income tax nil rate band available, he must utilise this against gains qualifying for entrepreneurs' relief in priority to other gains (*TCGA 1992, s 4(6), (6A)* as amended by *FA 2016, s 83(8)*).

11.108 For the disposal of assets other than shares to qualify for entrepreneurs' relief the disposal must be either:

(*a*) a disposal of the whole or part of a business which has been owned by the individual for at least a year prior to the date of disposal; or

(*b*) a disposal of (or of an interest in) one or more assets which were formerly used in a trade that has ceased, provided that the business was owned by the individual for at least a year prior to the cessation of the business and the sale takes place within three years of that cessation.

(*TCGA 1992, s 169I(1)–(4)(8).*)

11.109 Although the legislation refers to a business, it defines a business as 'a trade profession or vocation … conducted on a commercial basis and with a view to the realisation of profits' (*TCGA 1992, s 169S(1)*). Accordingly the relief is limited to capital assets used in a trade. The relief of course applies only to assets (including goodwill) used for the purpose of the business. It cannot apply to shares and securities (although the relief at **11.7** might do so) or other assets that are held as investments (*TCGA 1992, s 169L*).

11.110 The relief also applies to the disposal of (or of interests in) shares or securities of a trading company (or the holding company of a trading group) but only if throughout the one-year period ending with the date of disposal (or the date the company ceased trading if earlier and such cessation occurred within the previous three years) if:

(*a*) the individual held at least 5% of the company's ordinary share capital (with only his proportionate share of joint holdings being counted);

(*b*) the individual was able to exercise at least 5% of the voting rights by virtue of that shareholding; and

(*c*) the individual was an officer (such as a director) or employee of the company (or of one or more members of its group if it is a holding company).

(*TCGA 1992, ss 169I(2)(c),(5)–(7), 169S(3)(4).*)

11.111 A property dealing company is a trading company and as such can attract the relief.

11.112 A word of warning. In *Chappell v HMRC (2009 STC (SCD) 11)* the taxpayer entered into a joint venture agreement with another person to carry out property ventures. The intention was clearly trading. The two joint venturers felt that their prospects of acquiring the first property that they were after would be enhanced if a particular individual were involved. Accordingly Mr Chappell sold 10% of his 50% interest in the joint venture to that individual. HMRC contended that the sale proceeds were trading income. The Special Commissioners disagreed. Mr Chappell did not enter into the joint venture intending to sell an interest in it. Accordingly the profit was a capital gain. However, it was not a gain on a trading asset as at the time of the sale the joint venture had not commenced its trade as, in the view of the Commissioner, 'it is impossible to commence a trade without acquiring trading assets'. Whilst that last concept is debateable, the case does emphasise that an intention to trade is not sufficient to make the disposal a disposal of part of a trade. As the Commissioner inferred that the joint venture was a partnership, and a partnership is tax transparent, the decision that the sale proceeds was not income might be construed as lucky. Had the joint venture acquired its first property prior to the sale would the sale (which would have effectively transferred the value of trading stock) still have been capital. Probably, yes, but *ITA 2007, ss 752–772* (see **Chapter 14**) would probably have been successfully invoked by HMRC.

11.113 Where entrepreneurs' relief applies in one of the above circumstances it can also apply to the disposal of other assets owned by the individual and which were in use for the purposes of the business throughout the year prior to the disposal of his interest in the partnership or of the shares, (or the cessation of the partnership's or the company's business). However, the disposal of such assets must be made as part of the withdrawal of the individual from participation in the business carried on by the partnership or company (*TCGA 1992, s 169K*). The amount qualifying for relief on such an associated disposal is restricted to such amount as is just and reasonable. If the asset was in use for the purposes of the business for part only of the period of ownership (regard must be had to the period of such use); only part of the asset was used in the business (regard must be had to that part); the individual was a member of the partnership or an officer or employee for only part of the period for which the asset was used in the business (regard must be had to the length of such period); or for all or part of the period (but ignoring any part falling before 6 April 2008) rent was paid for the use of the asset (regard must be had to the extent to which the rent was less than a market rent) (*TCGA 1992, s 169P; FA 2008, Sch 3, para 6*).

11.114 Whether or not a person is withdrawing from a business is a question of fact. However, on disposals after 18 March 2015, the individual must dispose of a holding of at least 5% of the company's ordinary share capital (and voting rights) and that disposal must not be by way of a capital distribution by the company (other than in a liquidation), or of securities constituting at least 5% of the value of the securities of the company, or at least of 5% interest in a partnership, and at the date of the disposal there must be no 'purchase arrangement'. A purchase arrangement for this purpose is an arrangement under which the individual or a connected person is entitled to acquire shares of the company (or of a company which is a member of a trading group of which the first company is a member – or of a company for which arrangements exist which it is reasonable to assume will result in its becoming a member of the same trading group). In the case of a partnership, a purchase arrangement is one under which the individual or a connected person is entitled to acquire any interest in the partnership or to increase his interest in the partnership (including acquiring or increasing a share of the profits or assets of the partnership or an interest in such a share (*TCGA 1992, s 169K(1)–(2); (3A)–(3C)*, inserted by *FA 2015, s 41*).

11.115 An interesting issue arose in *Stolkin v HMRC (292 SFTD 541)*. This concerned the interaction between enterprise investment roll-over relief and taper relief. Although the latter was abolished from 6 April 2008, the decision may also be applicable to entrepreneurs' relief. The taper relief rules provided that where an asset was used partly for business and partly for another purpose, it was to be treated as two separate assets. Mr Stolkin sought to claim his roll-over relief only against the deemed non-business asset (which attracted tax at a higher rate than the deemed business one). Both the Upper Tribunal and the Court of Appeal rejected this claim. They held that EIS relief applies in priority to taper relief. The first task is to calculate the overall gain on the sale of the real asset and apply EIS relief. It is to the net gain that taper relief applies. Entrepreneurs' relief adopts a slightly different approach to such mixed use assets. It deems the gain on the non-business part to be a chargeable gain (*TCGA 1992, s 169P(3)*). However, the reasoning in *Stolkin* seems equally applicable.

11.116 Entrepreneurs' relief can also apply on a disposal by a trust but only if the trust is an interest in possession trust, the beneficiary with the interest in possession carried on the business for the qualifying period and himself met all of the conditions at **11.7** in relation to shares in the company that he owned personally, and the interest in possession was not for a fixed term (*TCGA 1992, s 169J*). It should particularly be noted that in the case of a company this requires him to have held at least 5% of the company personally throughout the one-year period. If more than one beneficiary has an interest in possession in the same settled property and only one of them carries on the business (or meets the required conditions in the case of a company) only a proportion of the trust gains attracts the relief. This is, of course, the proportion that the qualifying beneficiary's share of the right to income bears to the aggregate shares of all of those beneficiaries (*TCGA 1992, s 169O*). The trust does not have a separate £10 million exemption. Its relief is limited to the unutilised balance of the life tenant's exempt amount and reduces the amount available for future use by the life tenant (*TCGA 1992, s 169N(7)(8)*).

11.117 The relief must be claimed; it is not automatic. In the case of a disposal by a trust the claim must be made jointly by the trustees and the beneficiary. The claim must be made by the first anniversary of 31 January following the end of the tax year in which the disposal takes place (*TCGA 1992, s 169M*). In the case of the disposal of a business any losses arising on the disposal must be netted against the gains before calculating the relief (*TCGA 1992, s 169N(1)*). It appears the disposal of assets under *s 169K* is a separate disposal to that of the business or shares so a claim could be made in relation to one only of the two disposals if one generates a loss and the other a gain (as *TCGA 1992, s 169H(2)* lists them separately as qualifying business disposals).

11.118 Capital gains tax retirement relief used to be given under *TCGA 1992, ss 163* and *164* but this was abolished for disposals after 5 April 2003. However, many of the rules were similar to those relating to entrepreneurs' relief, so some of the reasoning in the decided cases on this relief is likely to be relevant to entrepreneurs' relief too. As with entrepreneurs' relief, to qualify for retirement relief the taxpayer had to dispose of a business or part of a business. As with entrepreneurs' relief, relief on the disposal of shares in a personal company was limited to trading companies. This was one of the issues in *Hatt v Newman (2000 STC 113)* but sadly this was a taxpayer in person who did not appreciate the issue and the judge did not address it. Indeed he simply said:

> 'So far as the business of letting furnished rooms is concerned … as Vinelott J said in *Griffiths v Jackson (1983 STC 184)* [(see **2.83**)] … the principle that the letting of furnished rooms, while it may be a business, is not a trade, is "now too deeply embedded in the law to be altered except by legislation". In my judgment … Mr Hatt's appeal must fail.'

The Special Commissioners said:

> 'In relation to his claim for retirement relief, Mr Hatt has contended that the property was an asset of his business and that the lettings were a business activity. Whilst that may be so, there is ample authority to show that the business of letting furnished rooms is not a trade.'

As both recognised that Mr Hatt was carrying on a business, which is what is referred to in *TCGA 1992, s 163*, it is unfortunate that neither sought to address why they believed that 'business' in that section could not be given its normal meaning but had to be limited to a trade.

11.119 It was held that the sale of a field by a farmer who continued to farm on the bulk of the land was not the sale of part of a business. It was merely the sale of an asset of the business and did not qualify for relief (*McGregor v Adcock (51 TC 692)*). This decision was followed in *Mannion v Johnston (61 TC 598)* where Mr Johnston sold almost half of his farm and evidence was given that the reason was that he had become too infirm to continue the business on the same scale as before. While indicating that he did not feel the *McGregor v Adcock* decision was wholly satisfactory, the judge felt that he was bound by it. As he reversed the decision of the Commissioners it is clear that whether or not there has been a disposal of part of a business is a question of law, not one of fact or degree. If a farmer is still carrying on a business of farming after the sale he is unlikely to qualify for relief. These decisions suggest that a sale of one shop out of several would not be the sale of part of a business either – although it is worth bearing in mind in such a case that HMRC have in the past generally sought to establish that the opening of a new shop is a separate business for trading income purposes, not the expansion of the existing business.

11.120 In *Plumbly and others v Spencer (1999 STC 677)* the taxpayer was a full-time director and shareholder of a family business which paid him rent for the use of his land. On reaching the age of 60, the taxpayer disposed of his land and the company ceased to trade. The Court of Appeal held that full retirement relief was due as the land had been held for the purpose of a business carried on by the taxpayer's personal company. They felt it odd that the restriction which applied on a sale of a trading company could apparently be circumvented by the trading company simply becoming dormant and being retained. The corresponding entrepreneurs' relief provision, *TCGA 1992, s 169P(4)(d),* does not perpetuate that anomaly! Notwithstanding the general rule, that for capital gains tax purposes the disposal date is the time of the contract, HMRC practice was to adopt the completion date for calculating retirement relief provided that there was no undue delay between contract and completion.

11.121 Again, as with entrepreneurs' relief, where shares in a personal company or a partnership interest, were sold retirement relief could also be given for the gain on an associated disposal of assets used for the purpose of the company or partnership business. The associated disposal had to take place as part of the withdrawal of the individual concerned from participation in the company or partnership business, and immediately before the disposal of the shares or partnership interest (or the earlier cessation of the business) the asset had to have been in use for the purposes of that business (It was held in *Clarke v Mayo (1994 STC 570)* that the words 'immediately before' in this context can legitimately be construed as meaning 'sufficiently proximate in time to the material disposal or cessation so as to justify the conclusion that the transaction in question formed part of it'.) In that case the contract for the sale of the property (the associated disposal) was ten weeks before the cessation of the business, completion was four weeks before the cessation, and the sale of the shares took place a year after the cessation. It was nevertheless accepted that the sale of the property qualified for relief.

11.122 If there was a significant gap between sales of assets, the taxpayer could have difficulty in attracting relief – although he did so in *Jarmin v Rawlings (1994 STC 1005)*. Mr Rawlings was a dairy farmer owning 64 acres of land, farm buildings and a herd of 34 cows. He decided to give up dairy farming. In October 1988 he sold at auction his milking parlour and yard – an area of approximately 1.2 acres. Between then and completion of the sale in January 1989 he sold 14 cows. The remaining 20 were transferred to his wife's family farm for calving, and most were resold by the end of 1989. He had no financial interest in their milk after the transfer. Following the sale Mr Rawlings continued farming on the remaining land by rearing and finishing store cattle. This was far less labour-intensive. He was able to make his farm labourer redundant and halve his own working time. He retained, and leased out, his milk quota because he was advised that a sale would reduce the value of the land. The judge held that what had to be identified was the business. In this case it was the production and sale of milk. The Commissioners were entitled to hold that this was a different business to the rearing and finishing of store cattle. It made no difference that all the assets of the dairy farming business had not been sold; the key thing was that the activity had ceased. He also expressed the view that the reference in the legislation to the disposal of a business could not be intended to mean a capital gains tax disposal. Accordingly, it was not necessary to look only at what had been disposed of at the time of the auction; related transactions (albeit with different people) should also be taken into account, although events subsequent to completion probably could not.

11.123 The taxpayer was less fortunate in *Wase v Bourke (1996 STC 18)*. Mr Bourke decided to give up dairy farming. He sold his entire dairy herd at market value in March 1988. He retained a few young cattle which were fattened up and then sold. In February 1989 he sold his milk quota. He did not do so earlier as it was partly used up at the time he sold his herd whereas in 1989 it was 'clean' and therefore more valuable. The farm had become an arable farm and was being farmed by the taxpayer's wife. It was agreed that the dairy business had ceased to be carried on in March 1988. As the taxpayer was under 60 at that time relief was due only if in February 1989 he had disposed of all or part of his business. It was held that the business was the production and sale of milk and that had ceased in March 1988. Accordingly what was being sold a year later was simply an asset which had formerly been used in the business. The cessation of the farming and the later sale of the milk quota could not properly be described as amounting to a single transaction. Accordingly, no relief was due.

11.124 In *Barrett v Powell (1998 STC 283)*, Mr Powell farmed 326 acres of land, 100 of which he owned, 136 which he leased from Milton Keynes

Development Corp and 90 which he licensed from the Corporation. In March 1991 the Corporation paid him to surrender his lease but allowed him to continue farming the land under licence until they needed it. They terminated the licence in September 1991. Mr Powell continued to farm his 100 acres for another year and then ceased. The surrender of the lease was held to be the disposal of an asset of the business as the farming continued unchanged before and after that date. It is likely that retirement relief would have been granted if instead of surrendering the lease in 1990 Mr Powell had agreed to do so when called upon and the surrender had taken place in September 1991. A similar result was reached in *Purves v Harrison (2001 STC 267)*. Mr Harrison wished to dispose of his coach and minibus business. He could not find a purchaser at an acceptable price. In October 1989 he was approached by MPK Garages Ltd, which owned a neighbouring site, and asked whether he was prepared to sell the premises. He did so in anticipation of selling the business to another purchaser. That sale fell through and MPK allowed the business to remain in occupation on an informal licence. Mr Harrison was eventually able to sell the business in November 1990. It was held that the two sales could not in any real sense be regarded as a single disposal of the business. 'A continuing intention to dispose of the premises along with the remainder of the assets cannot alone suffice to create a sufficient connection between the two where, as here, the two disposals are to different persons and are separated by so many months.'

11.125 In *Todd v Fawcett (Sp C 438, 2005 STC (SCD) 97)* Mr Todd and his wife each gave part of their interest in a farming partnership to their three children. The farmland itself was not an asset of the partnership but was owned personally by Mr and Mrs Todd. On the same day as the gift, a large part of the land was sold to a residential developer. HMRC contended that as the decision to take a part of the land out of the partnership was made at the same time as the decision to make the gifts to the children the gift was not of an interest in the business but only in certain assets of the business, albeit that the property extraction in fact took place earlier than the gift. It was held that, as the gift to the children was of a part of the entire assets of the partnership at the date of the gift, it was a material disposal and accordingly the sale of the building land was an associated disposal qualifying for retirement relief.

EIS Reinvestment Relief

11.126 Capital gains realised by individuals can be rolled-over by reinvesting the gain in eligible shares in a qualifying unquoted trading company (*TCGA 1992, Sch 5B*). The relief can also be claimed by a settlement where either an interest in possession is held by an individual (or a charity) or all of the beneficiaries are individuals (or charities) (*TCGA 1992, Sch 5B, para 17*). Unlike with roll-over relief, it is not necessary to reinvest the entire proceeds;

it is only necessary to reinvest the gain and where not all the gain is reinvested relief can be claimed proportionate to the part of the gain reinvested. The full relief does not have to be claimed; the taxpayer can roll over a lesser amount, leaving a chargeable gain to utilise losses or his annual exemption. Eligible shares means shares forming part of the company's ordinary share capital other than any which carry a present or future preferential right to dividends, to redemption or to assets on a winding-up (*TCGA 1992, s 164N*).

11.127 Companies whose business consists primarily of certain specified property related activities are not qualifying companies. These proscribed activities are:

(*a*) property development;

(*b*) farming and market gardening;

(*c*) holding, managing or occupying woodland and other forestry activities or timber production;

(*d*) operating or managing hotels or comparable establishments or managing property used as a hotel or comparable establishment;

(*e*) operating or managing nursing homes or residential care homes or managing property used as a nursing home or residential care home.

(*ITA 2007, s 192* and *TCGA 1992, Sch 5B, para 19*.)

The Special Commissioner in *Maclean v HMRC (2007) STC (SCD) 350* held that the furnished holiday lettings in that case did not constitute a trade, but even if that was wrong, the trade could not be a qualifying trade as the facilities that would make it a trade were not provided during the winter months so the company's business could not consist primarily of its trading activities. It should be noted that HMRC pointed out that although furnished holiday lettings are deemed to be a trade for most tax purposes such deeming does not apply to reinvestment relief. Prior to 16 March 1998 the only property related exclusion was a company (or group) whose trade (or a substantial part of it) consisted in dealing in land. However, HMRC did not regard a trade of property development as excluded by this provision. Unfortunately the distinction between property development (for sale of the completed buildings, as investment does not in any event qualify) and property dealing is often hard to discern. A distinction has not traditionally been drawn between the two as they are taxed in the same way. Clearly, buying a property and reselling it in the same state is dealing. Equally clearly, buying a plot of land, erecting a building on it and selling it is development. The problem is where work is done on an existing building. Carrying out redecorations before reselling will not constitute development; gutting the building and reconstructing the interior will clearly do so. But where is the dividing line to be drawn? This is undoubtedly a question of fact and degree to be considered in relation to each individual building. If there are no structural alterations there is probably no development. If there are and this results in a different building, such as building a major extension or converting a house into two flats, that is probably development. The VAT cases on what is a new building (see **8.48** onwards) may be helpful as anything that results in the creation of such a building is almost certainly development. On the other hand it needs to be remembered that for VAT purposes a conversion, reconstruction or enlargement is statutorily prevented from resulting in a new building but such operations are normally likely to constitute development for reinvestment relief purposes.

Gifts to Settlor-interested Settlements

11.128 In two specific circumstances the capital gains tax that would otherwise arise on a gift can be held over. These are gifts of business assets (*TCGA 1992, s 165*) and gifts on which inheritance tax is chargeable – even at nil per cent (*TCGA 1992, s 260*). Both of these provisions enable an election to be made to treat the donor as disposing of the asset at a 'no gain, no loss' price and the donee as acquiring it at, in effect, the donor's capital gains tax base cost. In 2003 the government became concerned that these reliefs were being abused by transfers into a settlement in which the settlor had an interest, combined with action by the trustees to avoid the tax in some way. For example, a person with a second home might transfer it to a settlement. The trustees would grant the settlor's son or daughter the right to occupy the property for a period, so qualifying it as the child's principal private residence. The trust would then sell the property free of capital gains tax and distribute the proceeds to the settlor.

11.129 To combat such devices, a hold-over election under the above two provisions cannot be made if the disposal is to a settlement and either:

(*a*) a settlor has an interest in the settlement (or an arrangement subsists under which such an interest will or might be acquired by a settlor); or

(*b*) a chargeable gain would accrue on the disposal to the settlement, the allowable expenditure in calculating that gain falls to be reduced because a hold-over claim under *TCGA 1992, ss 165* or *260* was made on an earlier disposal (whether or not to the transferor), and immediately after making the disposal to the settlement the disposer has an interest in the settlement (or an arrangement exists under which he will or might acquire such an interest).

(*TCGA 1992, s 169B.*)

11.130 If the above conditions do not apply at the time of the disposal to the settlement, but they come to be satisfied at some time within the six years following the end of the tax year in which the disposal took place, a capital gain equal to the held-over gain is deemed to arise to the transferor at the time when condition (*a*) or (*b*) is first met. In addition, the CGT position of the settlement from the time that it acquired the asset has to be recalculated on the basis that the holdover relief was never due. This clawback of relief (or recalculation within the trust) does not apply if the transferor was an individual and died before condition (*a*) or (*b*) was satisfied (*TCGA 1992, s 169C*). It would be unusual for a person to acquire an interest in a settlement only after his death, but condition (*a*) is deliberately phrased to refer to 'a' rather than 'the' settlor. It is possible for there to be more than one settlor of a settlement, in which case the transferor will not necessarily be the person with the interest in possession. Alternatively, if the disposer is still in time to do so, he can revoke the hold-over relief claim (*TCGA 1992, s 169C(10)*). However, the time limit for revoking the claim is not extended. HMRC consider that, except where the legislation provides that a claim is irrevocable, a claim can be revoked provided that this is done before the expiry of the statutory time limit for making the claim. There is no special time limit for a claim under *s 165* or *s 260*, so the standard time limit of four years after the end of the tax year in which the disposal takes place will apply.

11.131 Neither of the above charges applies where either:

(*a*) the settlement is a maintenance fund for an historic building and the trustees have elected (or, for 2012/13 onwards, could have elected) under *ITA 2007, s 508* to be taxed on income of the settlement (in place of the settlor); or

(*b*) the settlement is a trust for a disabled person, ie one where during the lifetime of the disabled person at least half of the distributions by the trust (both income and capital) are for the benefit of that person, during his lifetime that person is entitled to at least half of the income arising in the trust (and no income can be applied for the benefit of any other person and no-one – not even the disabled person – has an interest in possession in the settlement) and if, at the time of the disposal to the settlement, one or more settlors has an interest in the settlement (or an arrangement exists under which he can acquire one) each such settlor is a disabled beneficiary (*TCGA 1992, s 169D(1)–(6)* as amended by *FA 2013, s 63*).

11.132 The above restriction against a settlor having an interest does not apply to the settlor's spouse (*TCGA 1992, s 169D(5)*). A 'disabled person' is a person who is either incapable of administering his property or managing his affairs by reason of a mental disorder (as defined in the *Mental Health Act 1983*) or is in receipt of a social security attendance allowance or disability living allowance (*TCGA 1992, s 169D(7)–(9)*). A trust which would satisfy head (*b*) in **11.131** but for the powers of the trustees under the *Trustee Act 1925, ss 32* and *33* is deemed to satisfy the head (*TCGA 1992, s 169D(10)* and *(11)*).

11.133 For the purpose of these provisions a person is a settlor in relation to a settlement if he is an individual and the settled property includes property originating from him, ie which either:

(*a*) he has provided directly or indirectly for the purposes of the settlement (or which someone else has provided in pursuance of reciprocal arrangements with him); or

(*b*) is property which wholly or partly represents that property or any part of it (including if it represents accumulated income from that other property).

(*TCGA 1992, s 169E.*)

11.134 An individual has an interest in a settlement if either:

(*a*) any property which is at any time comprised in the settlement (or any derived property) is (or will, or may, become) payable to or applicable for the benefit of the settlor or his spouse in any circumstances whatsoever; or

(*b*) the individual or his spouse enjoys a benefit derived directly or indirectly from any property comprised in the settlement or any derived property

(*TCGA 1992, s 169F(1)–(3).*)

'Spouse' does not include a widow or widower or a spouse from whom the individual is separated under a court order or a separation agreement or otherwise in circumstances that the separation is likely to be permanent (*TCGA 1992, s 169F(4)*). If the only circumstance in which an individual can receive a payment from the settlement is in the event of the death of a child of that individual where the child had become beneficially entitled to the property or any derived property at age 25 or under (or, if it is a marriage settlement, following the death of both parties to the marriage (and all or any of the children of the marriage)), the individual is regarded as not having an interest in the settlement (*TCGA 1992, s 169F(5)*). 'Derived property' is income from the original property, property directly or indirectly representing proceeds of the original property (or proceeds of income from that property) or income from property which is itself derived property (*TCGA 1992, s 169F(6)*).

11.135 An arrangement includes any scheme, agreement or understanding whether or not legally enforceable (*TCGA 1992, s 169G(1)*).

11.136 HMRC have power, by notice to require any of:

(*a*) a trustee (or former trustee) of a settlement;

(*b*) a beneficiary (or former beneficiary) of a settlement;

(*c*) a settlor in relation to the settlement; or

(*d*) a spouse of the settlor (or a person who was a spouse at some time subsequent to the disposal),

to give them such information as HMRC think necessary for the purpose of these provisions. They must allow at least 28 days for such information to be provided (*TCGA 1992, s 169G(2)–(5)*).

11.137 Where the tax on a gift of land, or any estate or interest in land (or shares or securities of a company controlled by the donor, or non-listed shares) is not held over under *TCGA 1992, ss 165* or *260* (whether because of the above restriction or because a decision was made not to make the election), the tax due can be paid by ten equal yearly instalments (*TCGA 1992, s 281* as amended by *FA 2004, Sch 21, para 6*). The first instalment is due on the date on which the tax on the gain would otherwise be payable. The instalments carry interest. The interest on each instalment must be paid with that instalment (*TCGA 1992, s 281(4)* and *(5)*). The relief must be claimed. The taxpayer can pay the outstanding tax (plus accrued interest) at any time before the outstanding instalments fall due. If the donee (or a subsequent donee) disposes of the asset for valuable consideration, all of the outstanding instalments immediately become payable (*TCGA 1992, s 281(6)* and *(7)*). If hold-over relief is clawed back under *TCGA 1992, s 169C* (see **11.130**), this instalment treatment can apply (by reference to the date of the disposal, not the time of the event that triggers the clawback) provided that at the time of the trigger event no part of the assets gifted have been disposed of. If any part of the assets gifted is subsequently sold, the tax on the whole of the gain (not merely on that part of the assets) will become immediately payable though (*TCGA 1992, s 281(8)* and *(9)*).

11.138 If the tax on a gift, or a sale at an undervalue, is not paid within 12 months of the date on which it became payable, HMRC can recover the tax from the donee. To do so, they must assess him to the tax within two years from the date on which it became payable. If the tax due from the donor is less than the tax on the gift (eg because he has paid some of it or has utilised losses against it), the donee can be assessed only on that lower amount. If the donee has died, the tax can be assessed on his personal representatives (*TCGA 1992, s 282(1)–(5)*). Tax arising on a claw-back of hold-over relief under *TCGA 1992, s 169C* (see **11.130**) can similarly be assessed on the trustees if the donor does not pay it (*TCGA 1992, s 282(5)* and *(6)*).

Roll-over Relief on Exchange of Joint Interests in Land

11.139 If two people own two interests in land jointly, a division of interests with one taking the entire interest in one plot and the other the entire interest in the second plot would result in a disposal by each of his half interest in one in consideration of receiving the half interest in the other. However, a form of roll-over relief applies in some such cases by deeming the exchange to be at a no gain, no loss price. If two or more persons jointly own land (or two or more separate holdings of land), one (the landowner) exchanges his interest (the relinquished interest) for that held by the other (or by another or others of the joint owners), and, as a consequence of the disposal (together with any related disposals), the landowner and each of the co-owners become the sole holder of part of the holding (or the sole owner of one or more of the holdings) the consideration for the disposal of the relinquished interest (and of the acquisition of the interest acquired) at such a price that would secure that neither a gain nor a loss arises on the disposal (*TCGA 1992, ss 248A(1)–(5), 248B(1)* inserted by the *Enactment of Extra-Statutory Concessions Order 2010 (SI 2010 No 157*). This applies from 1 April 2010 but before that the relief applied by concession (ESC D26). The wording was amended slightly from 1 March 2013 by the *Enactment of Extra-Statutory Concessions Order 2013 (SI 2013 No 234), para 2* as it was felt that the original wording did not accurately reflect the concession. It appears that all of the land needs to be in the UK (see *TCGA 1992, s 248B(7)(b)*). Spouses who live together are together treated as a landowner or a co-owner (*TCGA 1992, s 248A(7)(e)*).

11.140 This relief does not apply to the interest acquired (the acquired interest) if (or to the extent that) it is a dwelling-house or part of a dwelling-house (or an interest in or right over a dwelling-house) and any part of the gain accruing on a disposal of it by the landowner at any time in the six years from the acquisition of that acquired interest would be covered by principal private residence relief (*TCGA 1992, ss 248A(6), 248C(1)(2)*). If principal private residence relief did not apply at the date of acquisition of the acquired interest but it becomes the landowner's principal private residence at some time in the six-year period, the gain on the disposal of the relinquished interest has to be recalculated to withdraw the relief given on the acquisition (*TCGA 1992, s 248C(3)*).

11.141 If the consideration for the disposal of the relinquished interest (ie the value of the interest received in exchange plus any cash adjustment) exceeds its market value, but that excess is less than the amount of the gain (whether or not it is chargeable gain), the landowner can claim to reduce the gain to the amount of that excess (*TCGA 1992, s 248B(2)(a)*). If the gain is not a wholly chargeable gain the chargeable gain is reduced proportionately (*TCGA 1992, s 248B(2)(a)*).

11.142 The consideration for the acquisition is of course also reduced by the excess of the actual consideration for the disposal over the no-gain/no-loss price (or, in the case of *TCGA 1992, s 248B(2)*, where time apportionment for assets held at 6 April 1965 applies, by the amount by which the chargeable gain is reduced) (*TCGA 1992, s 248B(4)(b), (2)(b)(5)*).

11.143 If milk quota is associated both with the holding in which the relinquished interest is held and with the acquired interest the above rules apply to the milk quota as well (*TCGA 1992, s 248D*).

Roll-over Relief on Exchange of Joint Interests in Principal Private Residences

11.144 If:

(*a*) a person (the landowner) and one or more others jointly holds an interest in two or more dwelling-houses;

(*b*) one of them disposes of an interest in one or more of the houses (the relinquished interest) to the co-owner (or one or more of the co-owners);

(*c*) the consideration includes an interest in one of the other dwelling-houses (the acquired interest);

(*d*) as a consequence of the disposal (together with any related disposals) the dwelling-house in which the landowner acquires an interest becomes his only or main residence;

(*e*) each of the other dwelling-houses becomes the only or main residence of one (and only one) of the co-owners; and

(*f*) the whole of the gain on each of the residences is covered by principal private residence relief,

the parties can jointly elect for the disposal to be treated as taking place at a no-gain/no-loss price (*TCGA 1992, s 248C(1)–(7)* inserted by the *Enactment of Extra-Statutory Concessions Order 2010 (SI 2010 No 157)*. The same effect applied by concession (ESC D26) up to 31 March 2010. Spouses living together are treated as a single person for the purpose of this relief (*TCGA 1992, s 248E(8)(d)*). Where the election is made the acquired interest is treated as if it were acquired by the landowner at the time it was originally jointly acquired and for a consideration equal to the co-owner's original cost of the acquired interest (*TCGA 1992, s 248E(7)(b)*). It appears from *s 248E(8)(b)* that the properties must be in the UK.

11.145 It may be that there is a statutory way to achieve the same result. In *Jenkins v Brown (62 TC 226)* (sometimes called *Warrington v Brown*) six individuals each owned a farm. They conveyed the farms to trustees to be held for their joint benefit. As a result of the transfer each had an undivided unequal percentage share in the trust fund equal to the value of the farm he had put in. (It had previously been held in *Booth v Ellard (53 TC 393)* that putting property into such a pooling arrangement did not give rise to a disposal of the individual assets.) Subsequently three of the individuals took their farms out of the pool. It was held that this did not give rise to a disposal either. Whilst this decision is logical it was not based on the premise that there had never been a disposal of the beneficial interest in the farms, but rather that 'the measure of the beneficial interests of the settlors remained unaffected by the trust' as it was accepted that all of the farms had increased in value at the same rate whilst they were in the trust. It seems from this decision that if A has a property, Whiteacre, worth £100,000 and B has a property, Blackacre, worth £80,000 and £20,000 in cash, and they wish to exchange the properties, there would be no capital gains tax disposal if they enter into a pooling agreement covering both properties and the cash, and then dissolve the pool by B taking out Whiteacre and A the other assets.

Miscellaneous

11.146 It has been held by the courts that statutory compensation for disturbance under the *Agricultural Holdings Act 1948 (Davis v Powell (51 TC 492)* (or on the termination of a tenancy under the *Landlord and Tenant Act 1954 (Drummond v Austin Brown (58 TC 67)*) is not a capital sum derived from the lease or received in return for the surrender of rights. It derives from the statute, not from the lease. It is accordingly not within the scope of CGT. The dicta in the *Austin Brown* judgment make clear that the exemption applies only to the statutory compensation. If the tenant receives a capital sum to surrender his lease to his landlord this will be taxable.

11.147 In *Davis v Henderson (1995 STC (SCD) 308)* the landlord served a statutory notice to quit after which the tenant entered into negotiation with him and agreed to vacate on payment of the statutory compensation of £455,180 under the *Agricultural Holdings Act 1986* plus an amount of £520,000 additional compensation for giving early vacant possession. Mr Davis accepted that the £520,000 was taxable but disputed the £455,180, which had been calculated under the statutory formula. The Special Commissioners held that the tenancy was terminated 'by reason of' the notice to quit and he vacated the premises 'in consequence of' that notice. Accordingly the £455,180 was statutory compensation and exempt from tax. It should particularly be noted that Mr Davis insisted on service of the statutory notice to quit before starting negotiations and that he did not agree a single overall figure but accepted the statutory compensation provided he was separately compensated for early vacation.

11.148 HMRC accept that the decision in *Davis v Powell (51 TC 492)* applies to compensation for tenants' improvements under the *Agricultural Holdings Act 1986, s 64* or the *Agricultural Tenancies Act 1995, s 16*. They also accept that the surrender of a business tenancy before it comes to an end does not prevent the compensation being payable under the *Landlord and Tenant Act 1954, s 37* (Tax Bulletin Number 22, April 1996). If, following the expiry of a lease, the landlord serves a notice to quit and, to save time, the tenant agrees to accept a single payment in excess of the statutory compensation it may well be that the entire amount paid by the landlord, not merely that excess, will still be chargeable to CGT as consideration for the surrender of a right. In *Pennine Raceway Ltd v Kirklees Metropolitan Borough Council (1989 STC 122)* it was held that compensation under what is now the *Town and Country Planning Act 1990, s 107* on the revocation of planning permission was liable to capital gains tax. The value of the asset in question, Pennine's licence to use a racetrack, depreciated following the withdrawal of planning permission, and it was entitled to compensation in respect of that depreciation. Accordingly, in such circumstances the compensation derived from the asset, not from the statute and was caught under *TCGA 1992, s 22(1)*.

11.149 In calculating the consideration for the disposal of an asset for CGT purposes any money or money's worth charged to income tax as income of the person making the disposal is normally excluded (*TCGA 1992, s 37(1)*). There are two exceptions, both of which affect property. A balancing charge or an amount brought into account as disposal value of machinery or plant is not excluded – as the taxable amount merely claws back prior income or corporation tax allowances (*TCGA 1992, s 37(2)*). Secondly, where an asset is disposed of in consideration of a rent charge or a ground annual, the capitalised value of the rent charge or ground annual – or of any other right to a series of payments in the nature of income – must be treated as consideration for the disposal even though the income will be taxed as it is received (*TCGA 1992, s 37(3)*).

11.150 Where capital allowances have been claimed in respect of an asset and there is a CGT loss on disposal, it is restricted by the amount of the capital allowances (less any balancing charge) (*TCGA 1992, s 41*). This is reasonable, as the taxpayer will have had relief for the loss against income by virtue of the allowances. The effect is that a CGT loss cannot in practice arise on such assets, as even if the sale price is less than the written-down value a balancing allowance will arise rather than a capital gains tax loss. For 2017/18 onwards, if capital allowances have been made (or may be made) in respect of expenditure and those allowances include a deduction allowable in calculating profits on a cash basis under *ITTOIA 2005, ss 33A* or *307B* (see **2.18**), the capital allowances to be taken into account for this purpose are an amount equal to the total amount of expenditure which has qualified for capital allowances less any balancing charge to which the taxpayer is liable (*TCGA 1992, s 41(6A)* inserted by *F(No 2)A 2017, Sch 2, para 45*).

11.151 Freehold land cannot be a wasting asset for CGT purposes whatever its nature and whatever the nature of the buildings or works on it (*TCGA 1992, s 44(1)(a)*). This is in the taxpayer's interest, as only part of the cost of a wasting asset is deductible for CGT purposes.

11.152 If, on a sale at arm's length, the vendor grants a loan to the purchaser of all or part of the proceeds, and as a result of the purchaser's default on that loan the vendor repossesses the asset, he can elect to treat the gain on the sale as being limited to the amount actually received from the purchaser (less incidental costs of the disposal). The computation of the gain or loss on a later disposal will be made by reference to the original cost and date of acquisition of the asset (HMRC Extra-Statutory Concession D18). In other words, if the part of the proceeds actually received is less than the gain calculated by reference to the full proceeds, the taxpayer can opt to be taxed on the sum received (less incidental selling expenses) with no deduction for any part of the cost, leaving the cost to be relieved when the asset is resold. Property is, of course, the most common example of the type of asset where, in order to facilitate a sale, the vendor may agree to leave part of the purchase price on loan secured on the asset.

11.153 Where a mortgagee enforces his mortgage in any other circumstances, the CGT position will depend on whether or not he formally forecloses. If he does so the foreclosure results in the mortgagee taking the property in satisfaction of his debt. In such circumstances, if the mortgage debt is a chargeable asset he is treated as disposing of the debt and acquiring the property for the lesser of the amount of the mortgage outstanding and the market value of the property at the time of the foreclosure. This will be the base cost of the property on a subsequent sale. If the debt was not a chargeable asset he is (in effect) treated as acquiring the property for a sum equal to the greater of the market value of the property and the amount of the mortgage outstanding (*TCGA 1992, s 251(3)*). Foreclosure is a comparatively rare occurrence. What usually happens is that the mortgagee sells the property as agent for the borrower, accounting to him for any surplus and looking to him to make good from other sources any shortfall. In such circumstances the mortgagee is treated as selling the property as a nominee for the borrower (*TCGA 1992, s 26(2)*). The capital gains tax liability on the sale will then be a liability of the borrower, not of the mortgagee who actually sells the property to enforce his security.

11.154 Up to 5 April 2013, a grant payable to an individual by virtue of a scheme under the *Agriculture Act 1967, s 27* to give up occupation of an uncommercial unit was not to be treated for CGT purposes as part of the consideration accruing on the disposal of any asset (*TCGA 1992, s 249*). It was accordingly not liable to CGT. This provision was repealed by *FA 2012, Sch 39, para 49.*

Reliefs for Non-Resident Capital Gains Tax (NRCGT)

11.155 A number of CGT reliefs are adopted to apply to NRCGT (see **11.181**). Roll-over relief on the disposal of business assets will apply to an NRCGT gain only if the new asset is an interest in a UK residential property (*TCGA 1992, s 159A* inserted by *FA 2015, Sch 7, para 22*). A claim for hold-over relief can be made on a gift of a UK residential property to a non-UK resident (*TCGA 1992, s 167A* inserted by *FA 2015, Sch 7, para 26*). An election can similarly be made to override the deemed disposal under *TCGA 1992, s 168* (emigration of donee) or under *TCGA 1992, s 185* (deemed disposal of assets on company ceasing to be UK resident) if the asset will become subject to NRCGT (*TCGA 1992, ss 168A, 187B* inserted by *FA 2015, Sch 7, paras 28, 29*). If a gift of a residential property on which IHT is chargeable is made to a non-resident, a claim can be made to hold over the gain if the property will be within the scope of NRCGT (*TCGA 1992, s 261ZA* inserted by *FA 2015, Sch 7, para 35*). If the trustees of an overseas settlement realise an NRCGT gain or loss, it is apportionable to the beneficiaries in the same way as if it were a normal capital gain or loss (*TCGA 1992, Sch 4C, para 4(3)* inserted by *FA 2015, Sch 7, para 40*). HMRC can make a determination of an NRCGT gain (which makes the tax so determined collectible until it is displaced by a return) if it appears that a person was required to submit an NRCGT return and has not done so (*TMA 1970, ss 28G* inserted by *FA 2015, Sch 7, para 45*).

Milk Quotas

11.156 The Special Commissioners decided in *Cottle v Coldicott (1995) STC (SCD) 239* that milk quota is a separate asset from the land so that a disposal of such quota separate from the land is not a part disposal of the land. Quota acquired on the introduction of the scheme in 1984 has a nil base cost. Significance was attached to the fact that the quota was allocated by relation to a holding not to any particular parcel of land in that holding and that to treat a holding as an asset for capital gains tax purposes would cause a great many problems. It was also relevant that the taxpayer had claimed that the asset was the land and had sold the milk quota separate from leasing the land. The Special Commissioner decided that milk quota was an incorporeal asset separate from the land although it was normally required to be transferred with the land. He also held that it did not derive from the land.

11.157 The taxpayer in *Foxton re RCC (2005 STC (SCD) 661)* sought to overturn this decision arguing that as milk quota derives from land it is a right over land and its disposal is accordingly a part disposal of the land. The Commissioner dismissed this commenting that 'while milk quota is related to holdings of land that does not mean that it is the same asset as the holding because it can be dealt with separately'. Whether that is true is questionable. The normal practice where milk quota is sold is to grant a short lease to the purchaser (say 11 months) providing in it that the land will not be used for dairy production. The purchaser is then registered as holder of the quota in respect of the land comprised in the lease and the legislation treats the leased land and the purchaser's existing land as a single holding. On the termination of the lease, as the leased land will not have been used for dairy farming the legislation apportions the whole of the combined milk quota to the purchaser's own land. Accordingly, it seems probable that it is not actually possible to deal with quota separate from at least some interest in land. The Commissioners also pointed out that the CGT legislation recognises milk quota as a separate asset for roll-over relief purposes, which seems a much more convincing reason not to treat it as part of the land. Mr Faxton alternatively contended that as the quota was attached to the land and he was selling it with the consent of his own landlord he was selling it as agent for the landlord but this was dismissed as there was no evidence to support such a contention.

11.158 Milk Quota, or the EU Single Payment Scheme Payment Entitlement to give it the proper name, ceased in Northern Ireland, Scotland and Wales from 31 March 2015, but no new quota was allocated after 16 May 2014. In England, the Single Payment Scheme Entitlement was replaced by a new Basic Payment Scheme, which HMRC consider continues to reflect milk quota. They have accordingly said that they accept that Milk Quota became of negligible value in Northern Ireland, Scotland and Wales on 16 May 2014, so will accept CGT negligible value claims in relation to such quota. Where no such claim is made, a CGT loss will arise on 31 March 2015 when the asset ceased to exist. However, they do not accept that Milk Quota has become of negligible value in England and will reject any such claims. HMRC also say that they consider that Milk Quota should be pooled and treated as a single asset. Whether or not the pool is of negligible value may vary from case to case (HMRC Brief 18/2014).

Gains on High Value Properties (ATED-related CGT)

11.159 CGT on high-value properties owned by companies was introduced from 6 April 2013. The charge is part of then Chancellor Osborne's three-pronged attack on perceived (mythical in the eyes of most SDLT practitioners) avoidance of SDLT by the use of single-purpose vehicles (mainly companies). He believed that a person would put a house into a company so that when he came to sell the property he could instead sell the shares and pay 0.5% stamp duty instead of what was then 5% SDLT. The other two prongs are the 15% rate of SDLT where a property costing over £2 million is bought by a company (see **19.10**) and annual tax on enveloped dwellings (ATED) (see **Chapter 20**). All three charges are limited to residential properties valued at over £500,000 acquired or owned by companies and some other vehicles. Originally the CGT charge was to be limited to overseas companies, but it was decided to extend it to UK ones too as the tax rate – a flat rate of 28% – is significantly higher than the corporation tax rate.

11.160 A person (other than an excluded person – see below) is chargeable to CGT in respect of any ATED-related chargeable gain accruing to him in a tax year on a relevant high value disposal (*TCGA 1992, s 2B(1)* inserted by *FA 2013, Sch 25, para 4*). A person is excluded if he is an individual, the trustees of a settlement or the personal representatives of a deceased person and either the gain accrues on the disposal of a partnership asset and the person is a member of the partnership or it accrues on the disposal of property held for the purposes of a relevant collective investment scheme (one within *FSMA 2000, s 235*) and the person is a participant (within the meaning of *FSMA 2000, s 235*) in that scheme (*TCGA 1992, s 2B(2)(10)* inserted by *FA 2013, Sch 25, para 4*).

11.161 The tax is charged on the total amount of ATED-related chargeable gains (see **11.167**) accruing in the tax year on relevant high-value disposals (see **11.163**) after deducting ring-fenced ATED-related allowable losses in relation to that year (*TCGA 1992, s 2B(3)*). A loss cannot be carried back to an earlier tax year (*TCGA 1992, s 2B(5)*). Relief is not to be given more than once for the same loss (including corporation tax relief) (*TCGA 1992, s 2B(6)(7)*). The rate of tax is 28% (*TCGA 1992, s 4(3A)* inserted by *FA 2013, Sch 25, para 5*).

11.162 A gain or loss is ATED related if it falls within *TCGA 1992, Sch 4ZZA* (*TCGA 1992, s 288* inserted by *FA 2013, Sch 25, para 15*). An ATED-related gain is not defined in the legislation but it presumably means a gain calculated as being ATED-related under *TCGA 1992, Sch 4ZZA* (see below). Where an ATED-related gain arises to a UK company, it is, of course, taken out of the scope of corporation tax so that it is not taxed twice (*TCGA 1992, s 8(4A)* inserted by *FA 2013, Sch 25, para 6*). Where capital gains of a non-UK company fall to be apportioned to UK shareholders under *TCGA 1992, s 13* (attribution of gains to members of non-resident companies) an ATED-related gain is again taken out of the scope of *s 13*, to avoid double taxation (*TCGA 1992, s 13(1A)* inserted by *FA 2013, Sch 25, para 7*).

11.163 A disposal is a relevant high value disposal if:

(*a*) it is a disposal of the whole or part of a chargeable interest;

(*b*) the asset disposed of has at any time since 6 April 2013 been or formed part of a single-dwelling interest (see **20.8**);

(*c*) the taxpayer (or the responsible partner (see **20.24**) if the interest disposed of is a partnership asset, or the person with day-to-day control over the property if it is held for the purposes of a collective investment scheme) has been within the charge to ATED with respect to that single-dwelling interest on one or more days which are not relievable (ie to which an exemption does not apply) in relation to that interest; and

(*d*) the amount or value of the consideration for the disposal exceeds the threshold amount (normally £2 million – see **11.164**).

(*TCGA 1992, s 2C.*)

The ATED definitions apply to interpret this rule. In other words, if a property has never been within the scope of ATED, it will not be liable to CGT on disposal.

11.164 As indicated above, the threshold amount is normally £2 million. However, if the disposal is a part disposal or there has been one or more previous 'relevant disposals' the threshold amount is the appropriate fraction of £2 million. This is the consideration for the current disposal divided by the market value at the time of the disposal of a notional asset consisting of:

(*a*) the interest disposed of;

(*b*) if that is a part disposal, any part of the chargeable interest that continues to be owned by the taxpayer following that disposal;

(*c*) any chargeable interest (or part of a chargeable interest) which was the subject of a relevant related disposal; and

(*d*) any chargeable interest (or part of a chargeable interest) held by the taxpayer at the time of the current disposal which, had the taxpayer disposed of it at that time, would have been a relevant related disposal.

(*TCGA 1992, s 2D(1)–(4).*)

A relevant related disposal is any disposal by the taxpayer in the six years prior to the current disposal (ignoring any period prior to 6 April 2013) which meet conditions (*a*)–(*b*) in **11.134** and for which the single-dwelling interest then disposed of is the single-dwelling interest in relation to the current disposal (or another single-dwelling interest in the same dwelling) (*TCGA 1992, s 2D(7)*).

11.165 If the interest being disposed of is a part of the whole of a chargeable interest (or the whole of a part of such an interest) the threshold amount is the fraction of £2 million that the part disposed of bears to the whole interest. If the disposal is a part disposal or there has been a related disposal, the fraction at **11.164** must also be applied to that part (*TCGA 1992, s 2D(5)(6)*).

11.166 If a disposal would have been a relevant high value disposal but for being sold for less than the threshold amount, and had it been such a disposal an ATED-related loss would have accrued (other than to an excluded person – see **11.160**) and the cost and other allowable deductions exceeds the threshold amount, the disposal must be treated for the purpose of calculating the ATED-related loss (but not in calculating the non-ATED-related loss or gain) as being a relevant high value disposal, but the ATED-related loss on that disposal is restricted to the loss that would have arisen had the consideration for the disposal been £1 more than the threshold amount in relation to the disposal (*TCGA 1992, s 2E(1)(2)(4)*).

Example 11.5

Great Lettings Ltd sold a residential property for £1,980,000 in 2013/14. The property cost £2,200,000. The selling expenses were £150,000. The company will realise an ATED-related loss of:

	£	£
Deemed consideration		2,000,001
Cost	2,200,000	
Selling expense	150,000	2,350,000
Loss		(349,999)

Note. This and the following examples ignore the adjustment at **11.175** below.

11.167 If the single-dwelling interest was acquired prior to 6 April 2013, the value at 6 April 2013 is obviously used and the reference above to the costs and other allowable deductions exceeding the threshold amount must be taken to refer to the costs etc on the notional disposal (ie the assumed disposal that would have occurred had this legislation not been enacted and the property had been acquired at its market value at 5 April 2013) – see **11.168** (*TCGA 1992, s 2E(3)*).

11.168 If the interest disposed of was held by the taxpayer at 5 April 2013, the part of the gain occurring before 6 April 2013 (and, where the property was not within the scope of ATED for the entire time after that date, the part attributable to that period) is not within the charge to CGT (but if the taxpayer is a UK company, that part will remain chargeable to corporation tax in the normal way). This is achieved by providing that the ATED-related gain or loss is an amount equal to the relevant fraction of the notional post-April 2013 gain or loss, ie the gain or loss that would have accrued on the relevant high-value disposal had the taxpayer acquired the interest on 5 April 2013 for a consideration equal to its market value on that date (using the CGT not the corporation tax rules) (*TCGA 1992, Sch 4ZZA, para 3(1)–(3)*). The relevant fraction is:

$$\frac{CD}{TD}$$

Where CD is the number of days in the period from 6 April 2013 to the day before the date of the disposal which are ATED chargeable days (ie days for which ATED was chargeable), and

TD is the total number of days in that period

(*TCGA 1992, Sch 4ZZA, para 3.*)

Example 11.6

Houseco Ltd, a UK company, acquired a property for £1.5 million on 5 April 2004. Its value at 5 April 2013 was £2.5 million. The house was occupied by the shareholder of Houseco Ltd until 5 April 2017. It was thereafter let at arm's length. The property was sold for £4.1 million on 5 April 2022.

The ATED-related gain is:

	£
Sale proceeds	4,100,000
Value at 5 April 2013	2,500,000
	1,600,000
Chargeable fraction	
$\frac{4ths*}{9}$	711,111

*Strictly this should be done by reference to days but years have been used to simplify the illustration.

11.169 The non-ATED-related gain or loss, ie the part chargeable to corporation tax if the taxpayer is within the scope of UK tax, is then arrived at as follows:

1. Determine the pre-April 2013 gain or loss.
2. Determine the amount of the notional post-April 2013 gain remaining after the deduction of the ATED-related gain and reduce it by the notional indexation allowance. This is the fraction:

$$\frac{TD - CD}{TD}$$

(as defined in **11.138**) of an amount equal to the difference between the indexation allowance that would have applied had *TCGA 1992, s 2B* not been enacted and the gain had been chargeable to corporation tax, and the indexation allowance taken into account in determining the notional pre-April 2013 gain.
3. If there is a notional post-April 2013 loss, determine the loss remaining after deducting the ATED-related loss.
4. Add the amount of the gain at step 2 to the amount at step 1 (or deduct the loss calculated at step 3).

If the result is positive, that is the non-ATED-related gain; if it is negative, it is the non-ATED-related loss.

(*TCGA 1992, Sch 4ZZA, para 4.*)

Example 11.7

The non-ATED-related gain of Houseco Ltd in Example 11.6 is as follows, assuming the following indexation factors for a property purchased in April 2004:

	April 2013		0.344	
	April 2022 (assumed)		0.510	
		£	£	£
1.	Gain to 5 April 2013			
	Value at 5.4.2013		2,500,000	
	Less cost	1,500,000		
	indexation 0.344	516,000	2,016,000	
			484,000	

2.	Notional post 6 April 2013 gain as at **11.138**		1,600,000
	Less ATED-related part		711,111
			888,889
	Less notional indexation		
	£1,500,000 (original cost) × 0.510	765,000	
	Less used in part to 6 April 2013	516,000	
		249,000	
	Relevant fraction $\frac{9-4}{9}$ = 5/9ths		138,333
			750,556
3.	NIL		
4.	Non-ATED related gain		
	£484,000 + £750,556		1,234,556

11.170 The taxpayer can elect for *paras 3* and *4* not to apply, but to treat the entire gain or loss over the period of ownership to be treated as ATED-related (adjusting for such part of the post 5 April 2013 period for which it was not liable to ATED). Such an election must be made in the tax return for the year in which the first disposal of the interest or part of it takes place (or an amendment to that return) and is irrevocable (*TCGA 1992, Sch 4ZZA, para 5*). Where such an election is made, the gain is calculated as follows:

1. Determine the gain or loss (over the period of ownership (using CGT not corporation tax rules)).
2. The ATED-related gain or loss is the relevant fraction of that gain or loss (calculated as at **11.168** but assuming that the period of ownership started on 31 March 1982 (or, if later, the date of acquisition)).

(TCGA 1992, Sch 4ZZA (para 6(1)(2).)

Example 11.8

Suppose that Houseco Ltd in Example 11.6 had elected. The ATED-related gain would be:

	£
Disposal proceeds	4,100,000
Less cost	1,500,000
	2,600,000
ATED-related gain	
2/18ths	£288,888

11.171 The non-ATED-related gain is then the gain as calculated at **11.170** less the part of it which is ATED-related and less the notional indexation allowance on that balance. The notional indexation allowance in this instance is the indexation allowance computed for corporation tax purposes. If there is an ATED-related loss, that loss is simply deducted from the overall loss as indexation does not apply to losses (*TCGA 1992, Sch 4ZZA, para 6(3)–(6)*).

Example 11.9

The non-ATED-related gain of Houseco Ltd in Example 11.6 if the election is made is:

		£
Gain as above		2,600,000
Less ATED-related part		288,888
		2,311,112
Less indexation		
£1,500,000 × 0.510	765,000	
Appropriate fraction		
$\frac{18-2}{18} = 8/9\text{ths}$		680,000
		1,631,112

11.172 Where a gain arises, it cannot be sensible for a non-UK company to make a *para 5* election as it brings into tax part of the tax-free gain that accrued prior to 6 April 2013. For a UK company, the decision is more difficult. It is probably sensible to do both calculations. The election brings the gain over the entire period of ownership into the scope of ATED but the ATED-related fraction falls because the period prior to 6 April 2013 is wholly ATED-related. In the above example the difference is striking, ie:

	No election	*Election*
	£	£
ATED-related	711,111	288,888
Non-ATED-related	1,234,556	1,631,112
Indexation	654,333	680,000
Actual gain	2,600,000	2,600,000

Suppose that the entire use after 5 April 2013 in the above examples had been ATED-related. The position would have been:

	No election	*Election*
	£	£
ATED-related	1,600,000	1,300,000
Non-ATED-related	484,000	917,500*
Indexation	516,000	382,500
	2,600,000	2,600,000
*Gain	2,600,000	
Less ATED-related part 9/18ths		1,300,000
		1,300,000
Indexation		
765,000 × 9/18ths		382,500
		917,500

This shows that, even in a simple case, where there has been a significant period of ownership prior to 6 April 2013, an election might still be attractive.

11.173 If as a result of a claim under *FA 2013, s 106(3)* (to reduce the days for which ATED is payable – see **20.25**) there is an alteration in the number of ATED chargeable days, all such adjustments must be made to the CGT calculation as are necessary to reflect that reduction (*TCGA 1992, Sch 4ZZA, para 7*).

11.174 On disposals after 5 April 2015 the balance of the gain realised by a non-UK company is of course chargeable to NRCGT (see **11.150**) to the extent that it relates to the period after that date.

Tapering Relief

11.175 The ATED-related gain can be reduced by the relevant fraction (as calculated at **11.168** or **11.170** as the case may be) of the excess of the gain over five-thirds of the difference between the value of the consideration and the threshold amount (*TCGA 1992, s 2F*).

Example 11.10

In Example 11.6 the adjustment would be:

	£
Value of consideration	4,100,000
Threshold amount	2,000,000
	2,100,000
Relevant fraction 4/9ths	933,333
5/3rds thereof	1,555,555

As the gain of £711,111 does not exceed this figure, no adjustment is required.

This is because the relief is not actually a taper relief. It caps the gain at 1.667 times the consideration where it does not significantly exceed the £2 million figure. The relief can operate only where the base cost is less than £2 million as that is the only case in which the gain can exceed the excess of the proceeds over £2 million. It is most likely to apply where a property is purchased after 5 April 2013 at a cost of under £2 million, but increases in value so is brought within ATED by inflation.

11.176 ATED-related gains accruing on relevant high value disposals made by an EEA UCITS (as defined in *FSMA 2000, s 237*) which is not an open-ended investment company (as defined in *FSMA 2000, s 236(1)*) or a unit trust scheme (as defined in *FSMA 2000, s 237(1)*) are not chargeable gains under *TCGA 1992, s 2B* (*TCGA 1992, s 100A* inserted by *FA 2013, Sch 25, para 10*).

11.177 If an asset within the scope of ATED is appropriated to trading stock, the taxpayer cannot elect to roll-over the ATED-related part of the gain into stock under *TCGA 1992, s 161(3)*. That amount will be immediately taxable, although an election can still be made to roll-over the non-ATED-related part of the gain or loss (*TCGA 1992, s 161(3ZA, 3ZB)* inserted by *FA 2013, Sch 25, para 11*).

11.178 Similarly if an ATED-related gain or loss arises on an intra-group transaction, the transaction will not be deemed to be for a no gain/no loss consideration. It will be a taxable transaction (*TCGA 1992, s 171(2)(ba)* inserted by *FA 2013, Sch 25, para 12*). This provision seems to subject the entire gain to tax; not merely the ATED-related part.

11.179 Where a company emigrates from the UK, *TCGA 1992, s 185* deems a disposal and reacquisition of its assets at the time it ceases to be UK resident. *TCGA 1992, s 187* then allows the tax on this deemed disposal to be deferred for up to 10 years (or an earlier sale of the asset concerned). Where an ATED-related gain or loss would accrue on the deemed disposal, *s 185* is disapplied. Instead the ATED-related gain or loss is deemed to accrue at the time that the property is ultimately disposed of (in addition to the gain or loss that actually accrues after the company has ceased to be UK resident) (*TCGA 1992, s 187A(1)–(3)*) inserted by *FA 2013, Sch 25, para 13*). This does not affect the non-ATED-related portion of the gain (*TCGA 1992, s 187A(4)*). Accordingly it appears that the gain has to be calculated at the time of emigration with the tax on the non-ATED-related part then being held over under *s 187* and that on the ATED-related part being held over under *s 187A*.

11.180 In calculating a company's augmented profits for the purpose of the small companies rate of tax to determine whether they exceed the £300,000 lower limit or £1,500,000 marginal relief upper limit, ATED-related gains are included in the profits figure (*CTA 2010, s 32(1A)* inserted by *FA 2013, Sch 25, para 19*).

Non-resident CGT

11.181 From 6 April 2015, CGT (NRCGT) is charged on the disposal of UK residential property by non-residents (*TCGA 1992, s 14B* inserted by *FA 2005, Sch 7, para 11*). A person is a non-resident for this purpose if either:

(*a*) he is an individual and is not resident in the UK for the year in which the gain on the disposal accrues (or would accrue if there were a gain);

(*b*) he is an individual and any gain arising on the disposal would accrue in the overseas part of a tax year which is a split year as regards that individual;

(*c*) he is the personal representative of a deceased person and is treated as non-UK resident under *TCGA 1992, s 62(3)* (ie because the deceased was non-resident at the time of his death);

(*d*) it is a settlement which is not resident in the UK at any time during the tax year in which the gain on the disposal accrues; or (*e*) in any other case, the person is non-UK resident at the time at which any gain on the disposal accrues (or would accrue were there to be a gain).

(*TCGA 1992, s 14B(1)–(4)*.)

It is proposed to extend this charge to commercial and industrial property from 6 April 2019 and also to remove the current exemptions from the residential charge. Draft legislation for this change has not yet been published, but a summary of the proposals is given at **11.234** onwards.

11.182 A disposal is not a non-resident CGT disposal to the extent that any chargeable gains accruing to the person on the disposal would be chargeable to CGT under *TCGA 1992, s 10(1)* (non-resident with UK branch or agency) or *s 2(1C)* (corresponding provision relating to the overseas part of a split year) or would be chargeable to corporation tax as part of the person's chargeable profits by virtue of *TCGA 1992, s 10B* (non-resident company with a UK permanent establishment) (*TCGA 1992, s 14B(5)*).

11.183 A disposal of a UK residential property interest is a disposal of an interest in UK land (see **11.185**) (including one before 6 April 2015) where either:

(*a*) the land has at any time in the 'relevant ownership period' consisted of or included a dwelling; or

(*b*) the interest in UK land subsists under a contract for an off-plan purchase.

(*TCGA 1992, Sch B1, para 1(1)–(3)*.)

For this purpose, the relevant ownership period is the period from the day on which the person acquired the interest in UK land (or, if later, 6 April 2015) to the day before that on which the disposal occurs (*TCGA 1992, Sch B1, para 1(4)*). A contract for an off-plan purchase is a contract for the acquisition of land consisting of (or including) a building or part of a building that is to be constructed for use as a dwelling (see **11.186**) (*TCGA 1992, Sch B1, para 1(6)*). If the interest in land disposed of results from interests in UK land which the person acquired at different times, he is treated as having acquired the interest disposed of at the time he acquired the first of those interests (*TCGA 1992, Sch B1, para 1(5)*).

11.184 An interest in UK land is any estate, interest, right or power in or over land in the UK (or the benefit of an obligation, restriction or condition affecting the value of any such estate, etc) other than an excluded interest, namely:

(*a*) a security interest (ie an interest or right (other than a rent charge or, in Scotland, a feu duty) held for the purpose of securing the payment of money or the performance of any other obligation);

(*b*) a licence to use or occupy land;

(*c*) a tenancy at will or a manor; or

(*d*) such other description of interest or right that the Treasury may by Regulations provide.

(*TCGA 1992, Sch B1, para 2.*)

11.185 If a person grants a sell option binding him to sell an interest in UK land and a disposal of the land at the time of the grant would have been a disposal of a UK residential property interest, the grant of the option must be treated as the disposal of an interest in the land in question – but not so as to effect the operation of *TCGA 1992, s 144* (see **11.71**) (*TCGA 1992, Sch B1, para 3*).

11.186 A building is a dwelling at any time when it is used (or suitable for use) as a dwelling, or it is in the process of being constructed or adapted for such use. Land that at any time is (or is intended to be) occupied or enjoyed with a dwelling as a garden or grounds (including any building or structure on such land) must be regarded as being part of the dwelling at that time (*TCGA 1992, Sch B1, para 4(1),(2)*).

11.187 A building is not used (or suitable for use) as a dwelling when it is used as:

(*a*) residential accommodation for school pupils;

(*b*) residential accommodation for members of the armed forces;

(*c*) a home or other institution providing residential accommodation for children;

(*d*) a home or other institution providing residential accommodation with personal care for persons in need of such care by reason of old age, disability, past or present dependence on alcohol or drugs, or past or present mental disorder;

(e) a hospital or hospice;

(*f*) a prison or similar establishment;

(*g*) a hotel or inn or similar establishment;

(*h*) accommodation in any other institution that is the sole or main residence of its residents;

(*i*) a building within *Housing Act 2004, Sch 14, para 4* (a building which is occupied solely or principally by persons who occupy it for the purpose of undertaking a full-time course of further or higher education at a specified educational establishment (or at an educational establishment of a specified description), and where the person managing or having control of the building is the educational establishment in question (or a person specified in Regulations) (or under any provision in Scotland or Northern Ireland designated by the Treasury by Regulations as corresponding to *para 4*); and

(*j*) residential accommodation for students, but only if the accommodation includes at least 15 bedrooms, it is purpose-built for occupation by students (including converted for such use) and it is occupied by students on at least 165 days in the tax year.

(*TCGA 1992, Sch B1, para 4(1), (8).*)

Head (i) has to be applied year by year, ie if it meets the condition in a tax year, it is not residential accommodation for that year and if it does not do so, it is residential accommodation for the whole of that year (*TCGA 1992, Sch B1, para (4)*). Accommodation is occupied by students if it is occupied exclusively or mainly by persons who occupy it for the purpose of undertaking a course of education (other than as school pupils) (*TCGA 1992, Sch B1, para 4(9)*). The Treasury has power by Regulations to amend the cases where a building is to be regarded as not being used as a dwelling (*TCGA 1992, Sch B1, para 5*).

11.188 A building which (for any reason) becomes temporarily unsuitable for use as a dwelling must be treated as continuing to be suitable for such use (*TCGA 1992, Sch B1, para 4(10)*). This does not apply where the temporary unsuitability results from damage to the building if that damage was accidental (or otherwise caused by events beyond the control of the person disposing of the interest) and as a result of the damage the building was unsuitable for use as a dwelling for at least 90 consecutive days. This 90-day period must end at or before the end of the relevant ownership period (the day before the disposal – see **11.152**) but can begin before the start of that period (*TCGA 1992, Sch B1, para 6(1)–(4),(7)*). Damage is not, however regarded as accidental or beyond the person's control if it occurred in the course of work that was being done for the purpose of altering (or partly demolishing) the building which itself involved (or could be expect to involve) making the building unsuitable for use as a dwelling for 30 days or more (*TCGA 1992, Sch B1, para 6(6)*). Where the building is treated as not being a dwelling under this provision, work done in the 90-day period to restore it to suitability for use as a dwelling is not regarded as construction or adaptation of the building for such use (*TCGA 1992, Sch B1, para 6(5)*).

11.189 If a person disposes of an interest in UK land and a building which is in the relevant ownership period (see **11.183**) suitable for use as a dwelling (or has at any time so been), and it:

(*a*) has undergone complete or partial demolition or any other works during the relevant ownership period; and

(*b*) as a result of those works has (at any time before the completion of the disposal) either ceased to exist or become unsuitable for use as a dwelling,

the building is treated as also having been unsuitable for use as a dwelling throughout the period when the works were in progress and for any earlier period throughout which the building was (for reasons connected with the works) not used as a dwelling, provided that:

(i) as a result of the works, the building has either ceased to exist or become suitable for use as something other than a dwelling;

(ii) any planning permission or development consent required for the works, or for any change of use, with which they are associated, has been granted; and

(iii) the works have been carried out in accordance with any such permission or consent.

(*TCGA 1992, Sch B1, para 8(1)–(4)*.)

If conditions (i)–(iii) are not met, the building must be treated as remaining available for use as a dwelling throughout the period during which the works are taking place (*TCGA 1992, Sch B1, para 8(5)*). The building must also be treated as remaining suitable for use as a dwelling during any period in which either:

(*a*) it was undergoing any work, or put to a use, in relation to which planning permission or development consent was required but had not been obtained; or

(*b*) something was being done in contravention of a condition or requirement attached to a planning permission or development consent relating to the building.

(*TCGA 1992, Sch B1, para 8(6)*.)

Both of these requirements for planning permission and development consent to have been obtained can be treated as having been met if retrospective consent or permission is given subsequently (*TCGA 1992, Sch B1, para 9*).

11.190 A building is regarded as ceasing to exist from the time when it has either been demolished completely to ground level or been demolished to ground level except for a single façade (or in the case of a corner site, a double façade) which is retained as a condition or requirement of planning permission or development consent (*TCGA 1992, Sch B1, para 7*).

11.191 For the purpose of *Sch B1*, the completion of the disposal of an interest in land is regarded as occurring at the time of the disposal or, if the disposal is under a contract which is completed by a conveyance, the time of the conveyance (*TCGA 1992, Sch B1, para 10(1)*). A conveyance includes any instrument. 'Development consent' means development consent under the *Planning Act 2008* and 'planning permission' has the meaning given by the relevant planning legislation (*TCGA 1992, Sch B1, para 10*).

11.192 CGT is charged on the total amount of chargeable NRCGT gains accruing to a person in the tax year after deducting any allowable losses accruing to the person in the tax year from the disposal of UK residential property interests and any unused losses of previous years from the disposal of UK residential property (*TCGA 1992, s 14D(2)*). No other deductions can be made from NRCGT gains (other than carry back losses under *TCGA 1992, s 62(2AA)* (carry back of losses in year of death). Where split-year treatment applies to an individual, NRCGT losses in the overseas part of the year can be set against gains in the UK part, and where a person becomes UK resident unrelieved NRCGT losses of earlier years can be set against any future capital gains (*TCGA 1992, s 2(2A),(2B)* inserted by *FA 2015, Sch 7, para 3*). Where a person is taxable to both ordinary CGT and NRCGT for the same tax year, he is entitled to only a single CGT annual allowance for that year (*TCGA 1992, s 3(2)* inserted by *FA 2015, Sch 7, para 5*). Where it is necessary to determine from which chargeable gains a loss is to be deducted (or which losses are to be deducted from chargeable gains) this can be done in the way most beneficial to the taxpayer. The annual allowance can also be utilised in the most beneficial way (*TCGA 1992, s 4B* inserted by *FA 2015, Sch 7, para 7*).

11.193 A diversely held company can claim exemption from NRCGT. So can a unit trust scheme, an OEIC incorporated by virtue of regulations under *FSMA 2000, s 262*, and a company incorporated overseas which is the equivalent of an OEIC under its local law, if either it is a widely marketed scheme throughout the relevant ownership period or the investor in the scheme is an offshore fund, an OEIC or an authorised unit trust (the feeder fund) and the scheme is a widely marketed scheme throughout the alternative period, after taking into account the scheme documents relating to the feeder fund and the intended investors in the feeder fund, and the scheme and the feeder fund have the same manager. For this purpose, the relevant ownership period in relation to a unit trust scheme or OEIC is the period from the day on which the scheme acquired the interest in UK land which is the subject of the NRCGT disposal to the day on which that disposal occurs or, if shorter, the five years ending with the date of disposal. The alternative period in relation to such a scheme is the shorter of the relevant ownership period, and the period beginning when the feeder fund first became an investor in the scheme and ending with the date of disposal. A diversely held company is a company which is not a closely held company (see **11.195**). A company carrying on life assurance business (as defined in *FA 2012, s 56*) which makes a NRCGT disposal can also claim exemption if immediately before the time of the disposal the interest in UK land, which is the subject of that disposal, is held for the purpose of providing benefits to policyholders in the course of that business (*TCGA 1992, s 14F*).

11.194 Although *s 14F* requires the person to 'make a claim under this section with respect to the disposal', it does not actually indicate anything more about the claim or the machinery for making it.

11.195 If the company which makes an NRCGT disposal is a 'divided company' it must be treated for this purpose as closely held if the gain accruing on the disposal is primarily attributable to a particular division of the company and if that division were a separate company, it would be a closely-held one. A divided company is a cell company, ie one in which specific assets and liabilities of the company are ring-fenced and some of the shareholders have prior rights over that ring-fenced cell (*TCGA 1992, s 14G*). In addition, if arrangements are entered into the main purpose (of any party entering into them) is to avoid CGT by making the company widely-held, those arrangements must be disregarded. For the purpose of *ss 14F* and *14G* a company is a closely held company if either:

(*a*) it is under the control of five or fewer participants; or

(*b*) five or fewer participators together possess (or are entitled to acquire):

  (i) such rights as would, in the event of the winding up of the company on the basis set out in para 3, entitle them to receive the greater part of the assets of the company which would then be available for distribution among the participators; or

  (ii) such rights as would, in that event, so entitle them if there were disregarded any rights which any of them or any other person has as a loan creditor (in relation to the company or any other company).

(*TCGA 1992, Sch C1, para 2* inserted by *FA 2015, Sch 7, para 37.*)

The basis set out in *para 3* is that in the notional winding up of the company the part of the assets available for distribution among the participators which any person is entitled to receive is the aggregate of the part that he is entitled to receive and the part that he would be entitled to receive if any other company which is a participator (directly or indirectly) in the relevant company were also wound up and its assets distributed to its participators in proportion to their respective entitlement to the assets of that company (*TCGA 1992, Sch C1, para 3*).

11.196 For the purpose of determining whether five or fewer participators together possess or are entitled to acquire rights as set out in **11.195**(a) and (b), a person must be treated as a participator in the company if he is a participator in any other company which would be entitled to receive assets in the notional winding up of the relevant company (*TCGA 1992, Sch C1, para 4(1)(2)*). Except for the purpose of applying *para 3* above, no account is to be taken of a participator which is a company unless it possesses or is entitled to acquire the rights in a fiduciary or representative capacity (*TCGA 1992, Sch C1, para 4(3)(4)*). This is, of course, because *paras 3* and *4(2)* look through such a company and treat its participators as participators in the relevant company.

11.197 A company is treated as not being closely held if:

(*a*) it cannot be treated as closely-held except by taking as one of the five or fewer participators a person which is a diversely-held company; and

(*b*) it would not be closely held but for *para 2(3)* (**11.195**(b)) or *para 7(2)(d)* that person possesses or is entitled to acquire such rights as would entitle it on a winding up or in any other circumstances to receive the greater part of the assets of the company which would then be available for distribution among its participators, and would not fall into those paragraphs if the reference to participators did not include loan creditors which are diversely-held companies or qualifying institutional investors (a widely marketed unit trust scheme or OEIC, an investment-regulated pension scheme (or a scheme which would be one if it were a registered pension scheme) a company carrying on life assurance business, and a sovereign investment fund).

(*TCGA 1992, Sch C1, para 5(1)–(5)*.)

The Treasury have power by regulations to amend the definitions of qualifying institutional investor and qualifying pension scheme (*TCGA 1992, Sch C1, para 5(6), (7)*).

11.198 Where a participator in a company is a qualifying institutional investor (as defined above) any scheme or interest which it has as a participator in the company (in any of the ways set out in *CTA 2010, s 454(2)* or otherwise) is treated as a share or interest held by more than five participators for the purpose of determining whether or not the company is closely held (*TCGA 1992, Sch C1, para 6(1), (2)*). If a participator in a company is a general partner of a limited partnership which is a collective investment scheme (within *FSMA 2000, s 235*), its share or interest is treated as being held by more than five participators for the purpose of determining whether the company is closely held. This does not apply to any rights which would, in the event of the winding up of the company, entitle the general partner (or a participator in the general partner) to receive any assets of the company which would then be available for distribution among the participators. Nor does it apply to any rights which would, in such an event, so entitle the general partner (or a participator of it) if there were disregarded any rights which any person has as loan creditor (either in relation to the relevant company or any other company) (*TCGA 1992, Sch C1, para 6(3)–(9)*).

11.199 For the purpose of *Sch C1*:

(*a*) A person is treated as having control of a company if he exercises, is able to exercise, or is entitled to acquire, direct or indirect control over the company's affairs.

(*b*) A person is treated as having control of a company if he possesses (or is entitled to acquire) the greater part of its share capital, the greater part of the voting power, so much of the issued share capital as would entitle him to receive the greater part of the amount distributed if the whole of the company's income were distributed among the participators, or such rights as would entitle him to receive the greater part of the company's assets which would be available for distribution among the participators in the event of the winding up of the company or in any other circumstances (ignoring any rights that the person (or any other person) has as a loan creditor).

(*c*) If two or more persons together satisfy any of the above conditions, they must be treated as controlling the company.

(*d*) If a person possesses any rights or powers on behalf of another person (or can be required to exercise any rights or powers on the direction of (or on behalf of) another person) those rights or powers must be attributed to that other person.

(*e*) All the rights and powers of any associate of a person (including rights and powers exercisable jointly by any two or more associates of that person) must be attributed to that person. An associate of a person means a relative (spouse or civil partner, parent or remoter forebear, child or remoter issue, or brother or sister), the trustees of a settlement in relation to which the person is a settlor, or the trustees of a settlement in relation to which any relative (as defined above) of the person (living or deceased) was the settlor (*TCGA 1992, Sch 1C, paras 7, 8*).

11.200 A scheme (see **11.193**) is a widely marketed scheme at any time when:

(*a*) it produces documents (available to both investors and HMRC) which contain a statement specifying the intended categories of investor, an undertaking that units in the scheme will be widely available and an undertaking that units in the scheme will be marketed and made available sufficiently widely to reach the intended categories of investors (and in a manner appropriate to attract those categories);

(*b*) the specification of the intended categories of investors (and any other terms or conditions governing participation in the scheme) does not have a limiting or deterrent effect (ie an effect which limits investors to a limited number of specific persons (or specific groups of connected persons) or deters a reasonable investor (falling within one of the specified intended categories) from investing in the scheme); and

(*c*) units in the scheme are marketed and made available sufficiently widely to reach the intended categories of investors and in a manner appropriate to attract those categories of investors, and a person who falls within one of those intended categories can (upon request to the manager of the scheme) obtain information about the scheme and acquire units in it.

(*TCGA 1992, Sch C1, para 11(1)–(5).*)

A scheme does not fail to meet condition (c) by reason of it having at the time no capacity to receive additional investments (unless the capacity of the scheme to receive investments is fixed by the scheme document (or otherwise) and a pre-determined number of specific persons (or specific groups of connected persons) make investments in the scheme which collectively exhaust all (or substantially all) of that capacity) (*TCGA 1992, Sch C1, para 11(6)*).

11.201 If a gain or loss would accrue to a person on a deemed disposal of a UK property interest under *TCGA 1992, s 25(3)* (non-resident ceasing to carry on a trade in the UK through a branch or agency) and on the assumption that the disposal is a NRCGT disposal (and if the person is a company, any claim which it could make under *TCGA 1992, s 14F* is made), that gain or loss would be an NRCGT gain or loss, no gain or loss accrues to the person on that deemed disposal but the whole (or the corresponding part) of the gain or loss that would otherwise have accrued to that person under *s 25(3)* is deemed to accrue to him on a subsequent disposal (or part disposal) (in addition to any gain or loss that actually accrues on that subsequent disposal) and is treated as an NRCGT gain (or loss) chargeable to that person by virtue of *TCGA 1992, s 14D* (see **11.192**). In other words, instead of a deemed gain arising when the UK branch or agency ceases, the gain or loss is calculated at that time but is not crystallised until the property is actually disposed of. An election can be made to disapply this rule (so that the gain or loss is crystallised as normal under *s 25(3)*). If the person is a company, the election must be made within two years of the cessation of the trade through the branch or agency. If it is not, the normal four-year time limit applies (*TCGA 1992, s 25ZA* inserted by *FA 2015, Sch 7, para 13*).

11.202 If:

(*a*) a person makes an NRCGT disposal and all or part of the consideration is a right to unascertainable consideration (on account of its being referable in whole or in part, to matters which are uncertain at that time because they have not yet occurred);

(*b*) the whole or part of that unascertainable consideration is subsequently received; and

(*c*) the recipient would have been non-resident in relation to the original disposal had a gain on it accrued at the time of the receipt of the ascertained consideration,

(i) any amount by which the ascertained consideration exceeds the value of the right at the time of the original disposal is treated as consideration (or further consideration) accruing on the original disposal (or any deficit is treated as reducing the original consideration),

(ii) the value of the right brought into account at the time of the original disposal is taken to be nil, and

(iii) any resultant increase in the original gain is treated as accruing at the time of the receipt of the additional consideration (and any resultant decrease as a loss arising at the time of such receipt).

(*TCGA 1992, s 48A(1)–(4)* inserted by *FA 2015, Sch 7, para 14.*)

In other words, the *Marran v Ingles* rule (see **11.24**) is applied to calculate the gain on the initial disposal but when the consideration is ascertained, instead of there being a disposal of the chose in action, the original gain is recomputed as if the amount has never been unascertainable. However, any increase in the gain on the re-computation is then treated as a gain arising on the receipt of the additional consideration and any reduction in the original gain is treated as a loss arising at that time. It does not appear that such a loss can be carried back and set against the original gain. Consideration is not unascertainable for this purpose merely because the right to receive it is postponed or contingent (or because the right to receive it is postponed and is to be (or may be) to any extent satisfied by the receipt of property of one description or property of some other description that some person has a right to select the property or the description of property that is to be received) (*TCGA 1992, s 48A(5)*). A right is not to unascertainable consideration by reason only that either the amount or the value of the consideration has not been fixed if either the amount will be fixed by reference to the value and the value is ascertainable, or the value will be fixed by reference to the amount and the amount is ascertainable (*TCGA 1992, s 48A(6)*).

11.203 The starting point for calculating an NRCGT gain is the disposal proceeds of the entire interest in land. Where there has been mixed use of the interest (ie the land consists partly but not exclusively of one or more dwellings – such as a shop with a flat above) the NRCGT gain is the fraction of that overall gain that is attributable to the dwelling or dwellings on a just and reasonable apportionment (*TCGA 1992, Sch 4ZZB, para 9(1)–(5)* inserted by *FA 2015, Sch 7, para 39*). Where the interest (or the residential part of the interest) has been a dwelling for only part of the period of ownership, the NRCGT gain is the fraction of the total gain that the days that the property was a dwelling bears to the total period of ownership (in days) (*TCGA 1992, Sch 4ZZB, para 9(6)*).

11.204 For properties held at 5 April 2015, the NRCGT gain or loss is the relevant fraction of the notional post-April 2015 gain or loss. The relevant fraction is the number of days in the period from 6 April 2015 to the day before the date of disposal on which the property is wholly or partly a dwelling over the total number of days in that period. If the property is only partly a dwelling, that amount is then apportioned on a just and reasonable basis (*TCGA 1992, Sch 4ZZB, para 6(1)–(5)*). The notional post-April 2015 gain is, of course, the gain that would have accrued on the disposal if the property had been acquired at its market value at that date (*TCGA 1992, Sch 4ZZB, para 5(2)(a)*).

11.205 Where the land is held at 6 April 2015, the non-resident can elect instead to use either straight-line time apportionment or 'the retrospective basis of computation' (*TCGA 1992, Sch 4ZZB, para 2(1)*). Neither election can be made where the property is a high-value property, ie one within the scope of ATED-related CGT (including where an election has been made under *TCGA 1992, Sch 4ZZB, para 5*) (*para 2(2)(5)*). The election is irrevocable (*para 3(1)*). The election must be made in a standard tax return or in the NRCGT return relating to the disposal (or in an amendment to such a return) (*para 3(2)(3)*).

11.206 Where the election for straight-line time apportionment is made, the gain or loss is of course calculated over the entire period of ownership and apportioned on a time basis (by reference to days) between the periods before and after 5 April 2015 to find the NRCGT gain (*TCGA 1992, Sch 4ZZB, para 8*).

11.207 The retrospective basis of computation does not appear to be defined. However, it seems clear that the effect of the election is that the NRCGT gain becomes the actual gain or loss over the entire period of ownership (including the pre-6 April 2015 part). It is hard to see why a taxpayer should make such an election if there is a gain on the disposal. However, if there is a loss, the election will increase the NRCGT loss. Where the property was owned at 1 April 1982, the starting point is its value at that day (*TCGA 1992, Sch 4ZZB, para 9(7)*).

11.208 Where the NRCGT disposal is an off-plan purchase, the land that is the subject of the contract must be regarded as being (or including) a dwelling throughout the period of ownership of the contractual right, ie from the signing of the contract (*TCGA 1992, Sch 4ZZB, para 10*).

11.209 If the disposal is a high-value disposal (ie it will give rise to an ATED-related gain as well as an NRCGT gain) and the property was owned at 5 April 2015, the NRCGT gain or loss is the special fraction of the notional post-April 2015 gain or loss. This is the fraction that the number of days in the period from 6 April 2015 to the day before the date of disposal during which the property was (or included) a dwelling but not within ATED, bears to the total number of days in that period. The notional post-April 2015 gain is, of course, the gain that would have arisen had the property been acquired at its market value at 5 April 2015 (*TCGA 1992, Sch 4ZZB, para 13*).

11.210 If the property was acquired after 5 April 2015 (or the retrospective basis of computation election has been made) the calculation is the same but the ownership period obviously starts with the date of acquisition (or 31 March 1982 if the property was held at that date) and ends on the day before the disposal (*TCGA 1992, Sch 4ZZB, para 14*). Where a property comes into ATED only from 1 April 2016 and the property is owned on that date (and no election has been made to adopt the retrospective basis of computation) the calculation is done in two parts:

(*a*) calculate the notional post-April NRCGT gain or loss (that for the period from 6 April 2016 to the day before the date of disposal; and

(*b*) calculate the notional pre-April 2016 NRCGT gain or loss (that for the period from 6 April 2015 (or the date of acquisition) to 5 April 2016.

The resulting figures are added together to arrive at the NRCGT gain or loss on the disposal (*TCGA 1992, Sch 4ZZB, para 15*). The amount at (a) will be nil if the property is within ATED for the entire period from 6 April 2016 to the date of disposal. It should particularly be noted that time apportionment cannot be used. The property has to be revalued at both 5 April 2015 (unless the retrospective basis of computation election is made) and 5 April 2016 (unless the property is wholly within ATED from that date, so there will be no days in that period for which it is within the scope of NRCGT).

11.211 Although a capital gain realised by a non-UK resident is not normally chargeable to CGT unless it is an NRCGT gain or an ATED-related gain, there are some circumstances where it is taxable here, for example, *TCGA 1992*, apportions gains realised by a non-resident company to UK shareholders if they own over 10% of the company. The legislation accordingly needs to define how to arrive at the amount of a gain (or loss) that is neither NRCGT-related nor ATED-related. In a straightforward case, this is the sum of the notional pre-April 2015 gain (the gain assuming a disposal at market value at 5 April 2015) and the notional post-April 2015 gain, less the NRCGT gain included therein (*TCGA 1992, Sch 4ZZB, para 7*). For assets acquired after 5 April 2015 (or earlier acquisitions where the retrospective basis of computation election is made) it is the whole gain less the NRCGT gain (*TCGA 1992, Sch 4ZZB, para 9(5)*). Where time-apportionment is used, it is the part of the gain apportioned to the period up to 5 April 2015 (*TCGA 1992, Sch 4ZZB, para 8(1)*). Where part of the gain is ATED-related, it is the part of the gain remaining after deducting both the ATED-related gain and the NRCGT gain (*TCGA 1992, Sch 4ZZB, paras 1, 16–19*).

11.212 Some examples showing the inter-relationship between NRCGT and ATED-related CGT may be helpful.

Example 11.11

Kenhold Ltd, a Jersey company, owned a house in London which was acquired on 5 April 1998 at a cost of £800,000. The house was bought for occupation by its owner, Ken, when he visited London. The house was sold for £2 million on 5 May 2016. The house was valued at £1.2 million at 5 April 2012, £1.5 million at 5 April 2015, and £1.8 million at 5 April 2016.

ATED-related gain

	£
Disposal proceeds	2,000,000
Less value at 5 April 2015 (when it came into ATED)	1,500,000
Taxable gain	500,000

NRCGT gain

Special fraction

$$\frac{\text{months not within ATED}}{\text{period from 6 April 2015}} = \frac{0}{13}$$

Notional post-April 2015 gain

	£	£
Disposal proceeds		2,000,000
Less value at 5 April 2015	1,800,000	
Indexation .016	28,800	1,828,800
		170,200

As the special fraction is 0, there is no NRCGT gain. That is reasonable because the whole of the post-5 April 2015 gain is an ATED-related gain.

Example 11.12

Assume the same facts as in **Example 11.11**, but that Ken had moved out of the property on 5 May 2015 and it had then been let to an unconnected person.

ATED-related gain

		£
Disposal proceeds		2,000,000
Less value at 5 April 2015		1,500,000
		500,000
Period for which property was in ATED		
1 out of 13 months		
Taxable gain	£500,000 × 1/13th	38,461

NRCGT

Special fraction:	months not within ATED / Months from 6 April 2015	12/13
		£
Notional post-April 2015 gain (as before)		70,200
Chargeable gain £170,200 × 12/13ths		57,107

The same calculation is used if the property either was acquired after 5 April 2015, the taxpayer has elected for the whole of the gain or loss since acquisition to be treated as ATED-related (or has elected for the entire gain or loss to be treated as an NRCGT gain or loss), with the actual cost being used in place of the 5 April 2015 value (*TCGA 1992, Sch 4ZZB, para 14*).

Example 11.13

Lenco Ltd, a Guernsey company, owned a house in London which was acquired on 5 April 1998 at a cost of £300,000. The house was bought for occupation by its owner, Len, when he visited London. The house was sold for £800,000 on 5 May 2016. The house was valued at £550,000 at 5 April 2012, £600,000 at 5 April 2015 and £675,000 at 5 April 2016.

ATED-related gain

	£
Disposal proceeds	800,000
Less value at 5 April 2016	675,000
Taxable gain	125,000

NRCGT

	£		£
Notional post-April 2016 gain			
Disposal proceeds			800,000
Less value at 5 April 2016	675,000		
Indexation 0.003	202		£675,202
			£124,798
Special fraction			
months not within ATED / months within ATED	0/1	=	0
Chargeable gain			nil
Notional pre-April 2016 gain			
Value at 5 April 2016			675,000
Less value at 5 April 2015	600,000		
Indexation 0.013	7,800		607,800
			67,200
Special fraction	12/12	=	1
Taxable gain			£67,200

As the NRCGT chargeable gain is a fraction of the NRCGT gain that does not relate to the period for which an ATED-related gain arises, the calculation is no different where time apportionment is used. Time apportionment cannot be used to calculate an ATED-related gain.

Example 11.14

Suppose that Ken in **Example 11.12** elects to use time-apportionment.

NRCGT gain

	£	£
Disposal proceeds		2,000,000
Less cost	800,000	
Indexation 0.612	489,600	1,289,600
		710,400

Period from 6 April 2015	13 months
Period of ownership	97 months
Taxable portion of gain 13/97ths	95,208
Special fraction (as before) 12/13ths	
Chargeable gain £95,208 × 12/13ths	£87,884

As this is less than the £157,107 taxable under the valuation method, Ken should use time apportionment.

11.213 Where a disposal includes a non-ATED related element, the gain is calculated on the whole disposal proceeds. The non-ATED-related part is then calculated on a just and reasonable apportionment (*TCGA 1992, Sch 4ZZB, para 20*).

11.214 If the non-resident is a company the charge is to income tax, not to corporation tax. That means that the starting date is still 6 April 2015, not 1 April. However, the gain is calculated on corporation tax principles (*TCGA 1992, Sch 4ZZA, para 23*). The most important consequence of this is that a non-resident company can deduct the indexation allowance in calculating the gain.

11.215 Bearing in mind that ATED was designed to discourage people from holding properties in companies, it is odd that NRCGT should in contrast encourage such ownership, not only by imposing a lower tax rate (20% instead of 28%) but in addition should tax a lower gain if a company is used (because of the indexation allowance). The answer of course is the EU. ATED applies to both UK and non-UK companies; it does not discriminate. As NRCGT applies only to non-residents, EU law does not permit the UK to tax a company resident in another EU country more heavily than if the same investment were made by a UK company.

11.216 If it is necessary for the computation of an NRCGT gain to determine whether or not an asset is a wasting asset, the actual date of acquisition must be used, not 5 April 2015 (or 5 April 2016) (*TCGA 1992, Sch 4ZZB, para 24*). Similarly any restriction on a loss by reference to capital allowances must be calculated by reference to the original cost, not the 5 April 2015 value (*TCGA 1992, Sch 4ZZB, para 25*).

11.217 A group of non-UK resident companies can make a pooling election. This is not an election to offset losses in one company against gains in another; it is an election to be treated as being an NRCGT group (*TCGA 1992, s 188B* inserted by *FA 2015, Sch 7, para 30*). The election must be made by all of those members of the group who are qualifying members (*TCGA 1992, s 188A(1)(b)*). A qualifying member is a company that meets the qualifying conditions on the effective date of the election (the election needs to specify such a date from which it is to have effect). These are:

(*a*) it is not UK resident;

(*b*) it is a closely-held company (see **11.195**);

(*c*) it is not a company carrying on life assurance business;

(*d*) it does not hold any chargeable residential assets, ie an asset the disposal of which would be an NRCGT disposal but for already being within the scope of CGT because it is an asset of a UK branch or agency or a UK permanent establishment; and

(*e*) it holds an asset the disposal of which would be (or include) an NRCGT disposal.

(*TCGA 1992, s 188A(1)–(4)* inserted by *FA 2015, Sch 7, para 30.*)

The effective date cannot be more than 30 days prior to the date on which the election is made and is irrevocable (*TCGA 1992, s 188A(5)(6)*).

11.218 The companies which make a pooling election form an NRCGT group. That group continues to exist as long as at least one company continues to be a member of the group and to meet the qualifying conditions (*TCGA 1992, s 188B*).

11.219 Once a pooling election is in place, other group companies which meet the eligibility conditions can elect to join the group. If a company which holds an interest in a UK residential property and is eligible to join the group throughout a 12-month period does not elect to become a member of the group before the end of that 12-month period, it ceases to be eligible to join the group. If it subsequently disposes of all of the residential property interests it held at any time in that 12-month period and acquires another UK residential property interest (after the end of the 12-month period but not necessarily after it disposes of the earlier properties) it again becomes eligible to join the group (*TCGA 1992, s 188F*). This seems to be a rolling period. For example, suppose a company acquires residential property A in June 2015, but does not elect to join the group. In July 2017, it acquires residential property B. In August 2017 it sells property A. In August 2018 it sells property B and acquires a new residential property C. It cannot elect to join the group until it sells property A. However, by that time it cannot elect to join as it has held property B for 12 months without electing. It can elect to join the group from August 2018 following the sale of property B as it satisfies the eligibility conditions and has held property C, now its only residential property, for under 12 months.

11.220 A company will obviously cease to be a member of the NRCGT group if it ceases to be a member of the group or ceases to meet the qualifying conditions (*TCGA 1992, s 188G(1)*). Where it does so, it must be treated as having disposed of its residential property interests and re-acquired them at their market value immediately before it leaves the group (*TCGA 1992, s 188G(2)(6)*). This will obviously trigger a chargeable capital gain. This deemed disposal does not apply where either:

(*a*) the company ceases to be a member of the group in consequence of another member of the group ceasing to exist;

(*b*) all the companies which are members of the group cease to be members by virtue only of an event which causes the principal company of the group to cease to be a closely-held company (or causes the head of a sub-group of which they are members to cease to be a closely-held company or to become a member of another group); or

(*c*) the company ceases to be a member of the group by reason only of the fact that the principal company of the group becomes a member of another group (as defined in *TCGA 1992, s 170*).

(*TCGA 1992, s 188G(7)*.)

11.221 Where an NRCGT group exists, NRCGT is not payable on intra-group transfers but the transferee company stands in the transferor's shares for the purpose of determining whether or not an NRCGT gain or loss accrues on a subsequent disposal, the calculation of such gain or loss and the treatment for CGT purposes of any such gain or loss (*TCGA 1992, s 188C*). This applies only to NRCGT gains. There is still a disposal in relation to any other gain or loss that may arise on the disposal (*TCGA 1992, s 188C(6)*).

11.222 Where an NRCGT gain occurs in an NRCGT group, the 'relevant body' (ie all of the companies which are members of the group in a tax year) is chargeable to CGT in respect of chargeable NRCGT gains accruing to members of the group in that tax year) (*TCGA 1992, s 188D(1)(4)*). In calculating such chargeable gains, a deduction is allowed for any allowable NRCGT losses accruing to members of the group in that year, any unrelieved brought forward losses that accrued in a previous year to a member of the NRCGT group and any unrelieved allowable brought forward NRCGT losses which accrued to a company (while it was not a member of the group) if the company is a member of the NRCGT group in the tax year in which the gains accrue (*TCGA 1992, s 188D(2)(3)*).

11.223 Relief cannot be given more than once in respect of an NRCGT group loss (or part of a group loss) (*TCGA 1992, s 188E*).

11.224 Anything required or authorised to be done in relation to the relevant body is required or authorised to be done by all of the members of the NRCGT group in the tax year and any company which subsequently becomes a member of the NRCGT group (*TCGA 1992, s 188H*). The liability for any payment of tax or interest is a joint and several liability of all such companies (*TCGA 1992, s 188I*). The NRCGT group can if it wishes nominate a member of the group as the 'representative company'. That company then has the responsibility for doing anything required or authorised by the Act. Notice of the appointment of a representative company (and of any revocation of the nomination) needs to be given to HMRC before it takes effect (*TCGA 1992, s 188J*).

Administration

11.225 When an NRCGT disposal is made, the taxable person (or the relevant members of an NRCGT group) must submit a return to HMRC within 30 days of the completion of the disposal (an NRCGT return) (*TMA 1970, s 12ZB(1)–(3), (6)–(9)*). The return must contain the information prescribed by HMRC and must include a declaration that it is complete to the best of the person's knowledge and belief (*TMA 1970, s 12ZB(4)*). No return is, of course, required for an intra-group transfer in an NRCGT group (*TMA 1970, s 12ZB(5)*). Where a person makes two or more disposals which are completed on the same day and the contracts for which fall in the same tax year, they must be included in a single return (*TMA 1970, s 12ZC*). A return must be filed in respect of the grant of a call option even if the transaction completes (so the option and the sale become a single transaction under *TCGA 1992, s 144(2)*). In such a case, the consideration for the option must be disregarded in calculating the amount of CGT notionally chargeable at the completion date of the notional single transaction (*TMA 1970, s 12ZD*). A person does not need to give notice of chargeability to CGT to HMRC if the transaction that would otherwise trigger the requirement is an NRCGT disposal and an NRCGT return containing an advance self-assessment has been made before the notification deadline (*TMA 1970, s 7A*, inserted by *FA 2015, Sch 7, para 42*). A person is not required to make a return under *s 12ZB(1)* where the disposal is a no gain/no loss disposal under the CGT rules made after 5 April 2015 or on the grant of a lease after 5 April 2015 where there is no premium, the lease is not to a connected person (within *TCGA 1992, s 286*: see **Appendix 1**), and is under a bargain made at arm's length (*TMA 1970, s 12ZBA* inserted by *FA 2016, s 91*). A return can be submitted voluntarily in such a case if the taxpayer wants to do so. The Treasury has power by regulation, to add or remove circumstances in which this exclusion applies.

11.226 An NRCGT must include an assessment (an advance self-assessment) of the amount of tax notionally chargeable at the filing date (and if the taxpayer has made a prior return for the year, the amount of any increase in the amount notionally chargeable for the year) (*TMA 1970, s 12ZE*). The amount notionally chargeable at the filing date for an NRCGT return is the capital gains tax to which the taxpayer would be chargeable for the tax year concerned if:

(*a*) no NRCGT gain or loss accrues to him on any disposal by the taxpayer which is completed after the date of completion of the disposal to which the return relates;

(*b*) all allowable losses on prior or simultaneous NRCGT transactions which are available to be deducted are deducted;

(*c*) any other relief or allowance relating to CGT to which the taxpayer is entitled is to be taken into account (so far as it is available); and

(*d*) if the taxpayer is an individual, a reasonable estimate is made of whether or not income tax will be chargeable at the higher rate or the dividend upper rate in respect of the taxpayer's income for the tax year.

(*TMA 1970, s 12ZF(1)–(4).*)

The return must give particulars of the estimate at (*d*). A reasonable estimate is not regarded as an inaccuracy for penalty purposes (*TMA 1970, s 12ZF(5)(6)*). For this purpose, an estimate is reasonable if it is made on a basis that is fair and reasonable having regard to the circumstances in which it is made (*TMA 1970, s 12ZF(8)*). If the taxpayer is a relevant body on an NRCGT group, the references above to the taxpayer include any member of the NRCGT group (*TMA 1970, s 12ZF(7)*).

11.227 An advance self-assessment does not need to be included in the return if either:

(*a*) the taxpayer has been required to complete a normal UK tax return for either the year concerned or the previous year (and the notice has not been withdrawn);

(*b*) the taxpayer has been required to complete a company tax return specifying a period which includes the whole or part of the tax year concerned or the previous tax year; or

(*c*) the taxpayer has delivered an ATED return for the year to 31 March preceding the start of the relevant tax year (or a representative partner has done so).

(*TCGA 1992, s 12ZG.*)

The Treasury has power by regulations to prescribe further circumstances in which an advance self-assessment is not required (*TCGA 1992, s 12ZG(6)*).

11.228 Where a person is excluded from having to notify chargeability under **11.113** above, he is treated as having been required to file a tax return under *TMA 1970, s 8* (or *s 8A* if the person is the trustee of a settlement) (*TMA 1970, s 12ZH(1)–(3)*; *12ZE (1)–(3)*). The taxpayer can give a notice to HMRC specifying an NRCGT return which relates to the year and contains an advance self-assessment. That advance self-assessment is then deemed to be the self-assessment required by *TMA 1970, s 9*. If the taxpayer does not give such a notice by 31 January following the end of the tax year, the advance self-assessment for the disposal in the year with the latest completion date is treated as a self-assessment delivered under *s 8* (*TMA 1970, ss 12ZH(5), (6)* and *12ZI(5), (6)*). A notice must be given by 31 January in the tax year for the purpose of *s 9* (*TMA 1970, s 12ZH(8)*). It is hard to see any benefit in giving such a notice as it is bound to specify the last return and that will be deemed to be the relevant self-assessment if no notice is given. If notice is given and a later transaction relating to the same tax year occurs, the self-assessment attached to the NRCGT return for that transaction is deemed to amend the deemed *s 9* return (*TMA 1970, ss 12ZH(11)* and *12ZI(11)*).

11.229 A disposal of an interest in a residential property must be deemed to be an NRCGT disposal if, at the time of completion of the disposal, it is unclear whether the taxpayer will be non-UK resident for the tax year, but it is reasonable to expect that he will be (*TMA 1970, s 12ZJ(1), (2)*). If it later becomes clear that the disposal is not an NRCGT disposal, it must be treated as never having been such a disposal (and any necessary repayments or adjustments must be made) (*TMA 1970, ss 8* and *12ZJ(3)*). If it is not reasonable to suspect under *s 12ZJ(2)* that the disposal will be an NRCGT disposal and it later becomes clear that it is, an NRCGT return must be filed within 30 days of the day following that on which it became clear that the taxpayer was non-UK resident (*TMA 1970, s 12ZJ(4), (5)*).

11.230 The rules on amendment of an NRCGT tax return by a taxpayer (*s 12ZK*), correction of a return by HMRC (*s 12ZL*), and HMRC enquiries (*ss 12ZM, 12ZN*) are the same as for normal CGT returns.

11.231 If HMRC believe that a person should have submitted an NRCGT return but he has not done so, they can make a determination (to the best of the officer's information and belief) of the CGT that should have been assessed as the amount notionally chargeable (*TCGA 1992, s 28G(1), (2)* inserted by *FA 2015, Sch 7, para 45*). Notice of such a determination must be served on the taxpayer and it must state its date of issue. The amount is then regarded as a self-assessment – but can be superseded by filing the NRCGT return (*TCGA 1992, s 28G(3), (4)*). Where proceedings commenced for the recovery of the tax on a determination before the return is filed, those proceedings can continue as if they were for the recovery of the amount shown on the NRCGT return (*TCGA 1992, s 28G(5)*). A determination cannot be made more than three years from 31 January following the end of the tax year. A return to supersede the determination cannot be filed more than 12 months after the date of the determination (*TCGA 1992, s 28G(6)*).

11.232 HMRC can also make a determination if they discover that an amount of NRCGT should have been assessed but wasn't or the amount assessed has become insufficient (*TCGA 1992, s 29A(1), (2)* inserted by *FA 2015, Sch 7, para 47*). HMRC cannot make a discovery determination where an NRCGT return has been submitted unless either the under-assessment was brought about carelessly or deliberately by the taxpayer or a person acting on his behalf or, at the time when HMRC ceased to be entitled to enquire into the return (or notified the taxpayer of the completion of their enquiries), the HMRC officer could not reasonably have been expected, on the basis of the information made available to him before that time, to be aware of the under-assessment (*TCGA 1992, s 29A(3)–(5)*). The Act defines what information is made available to HMRC for this purpose (*TCGA 1992, s 29A(6), (7)*). These broadly follow the *TMA 1970, s 29* rules, but with the addition of information contained in an NRCGT return for the year or either of the previous two years. A challenge to the making of the determination can, however, only be raised on an appeal against the assessment (*TCGA 1992, s 29A(8)*).

11.233 The tax (or additional tax) shown in an advance self-assessment in a CGT return is payable on the filing date of the return. Any overpayment is repayable on the same date unless HMRC enquire into the return, in which case it is repayable on the completion of the enquiry (although HMRC have power to make an earlier repayment on account if they think it fit to do so (*TCGA 1992, s 59AA* inserted by *FA 2015, Sch 7, para 51*).

Chapter 12

Business Occupation of Property

12.1 The occupier of property needs to consider tax in four main areas – he wants a deduction for rent and similar payments of consideration for the use of the property; he wants a deduction for repairs; he wants to obtain allowances in relation to any capital expenditure he incurs on the property; and he needs to know whether, and how, receipts he obtains from his landlord – for example for a surrender or a variation of his lease or to induce him to take a lease – are taxable.

12.2 Capital allowances are considered in **Chapter 10**. A person who occupies property for the purpose of his business obtains relief for capital allowances by treating them as a deduction in arriving at his trading profit for tax purposes. Reverse premiums are considered at **3.51** above.

Relief for Rent, etc

12.3 Rent of business premises will normally satisfy the requirement of being wholly and exclusively incurred for the purposes of the tenant's trade and will be deductible in the same way as any other trading expense. There are, however, two possible problem areas. The first is where the lease is entered into in the course of a trade but, at the time that a payment of rent is made, the premises are no longer being used for trading purposes. The second is where there has been a sale and leaseback of the premises or some similar transaction.

12.4 Surprisingly, quite a number of cases have come before the courts on the deductibility of rent payable for a period after the premises have ceased to be used for business purposes, and on the treatment of a payment made to get rid of a lease which is no longer needed for the lessee's trade. In *CIR v Falkirk Iron Co Ltd (17 TC 625)*, the company leased a warehouse which became surplus to requirements. It could not find anyone to take over the lease but was able to sublet part of the premises. It was held that the difference between the rent paid and the rent received under the sublease was an allowable deduction against the company's trading profits. At the time the company moved out, the lease had about 2½ years unexpired, so the obligation to continue to pay the rent was of a comparatively short duration. In *Hyett v Lennard (23 TC 346)*, a trader took a 35-year lease of a shop in Oxford Street but closed the branch down after six years because it was unprofitable. He was able to sublet the premises for the remaining 29 years of the term but at a figure £1,000 below the rent which he had contracted to pay. It was held that the £1,000 difference was an allowable business expense in computing the profits of his trade, even though that particular branch had ceased.

12.5 The issue in *Herbert Smith v Honour (1999 STC 173)* was the timing of the deduction. The taxpayer, a firm of solicitors, occupied four separate offices. In January 1990 it leased new premises in which to house the entire firm. It moved the staff to those premises in December 1990. It was still, however, committed to pay rent under the four old leases. In its accounts to 30 April 1990 it made a provision for the difference between the rents payable on the old premises for the entire unexpired period of the lease (one had 16 years unexpired) less the amount that it estimated it could generate by subletting the buildings. In subsequent years it reviewed the provision and as a result increased it. HMRC accepted that accounting principles required the provision to be made but they contended that there was a rule of tax law which prohibited the anticipation of losses. This was rejected by the court which said that the overriding legal rule is what is the full amount of the profits for the year and, in general, accounts prepared in accordance with accepted principles of commercial accountancy are the guide to the amount of such profits. A supposed rule against anticipation of liabilities would be inconsistent with that basic principle. HMRC proposed to appeal the decision but subsequently abandoned their position and accepted that there is no tax rule against the anticipation of losses. Such a provision is probably no longer allowable following the introduction of FRS 12 (see **12.44**).

12.6 It is apparent from these cases that there is normally no difficulty where the rent continues to be paid. Problems arise, however, where a tenant who no longer requires business premises makes a payment to rid himself of the lease rather than continue paying the rent. Normally a lump sum paid to rid oneself of an onerous contract is a revenue expense if the payments which would have had to be made under the contract would have been deductible (*Anglo-Persian Oil Co Ltd v Dale (16 TC 253)*). However, the courts have been reluctant to apply this principle to rent and have striven to attribute a capital nature to such payments. Thus where a company paid its landlord a lump sum to induce him to take a surrender of its lease of a coal seam, the Court of Appeal held that the payment was capital as it was to get rid of a fixed capital asset, the lease, rather than to rid the company of the onerous burden of having to continue to make the rental payments (*Mallett v Staveley Coal & Iron Co Ltd (13 TC 772)*). In *Cowcher v Richard Mills & Co Ltd (13 TC 216)*, a retail company closed a shop in 1916. The landlord agreed to accept a surrender of the lease in consideration of the tenant paying £1,812 in annual instalments of £250 – which would take eight years to pay, a period longer than the unexpired term of the lease. After it had paid 4½ instalments the company made a single payment of £600 in satisfaction of the balance of £687 payable under the instalment arrangement. HMRC contended that the £600 was a capital payment. Rowlatt J thought that HMRC had been wrong to allow a deduction for the £250 pa and that the entire amount was capital following the *Staveley Coal* case. A payment to secure the cancellation of a 40-year lease with ten years unexpired was similarly held to be capital (*Union Cold Storage Co Ltd v Ellerker (22 TC 547)*). A capital payment to terminate a licence of a speedway stadium was also held to be capital as the licence, which at the time had five years to run, was a capital asset (*Dain v Auto Speedways Ltd (38 TC 525)*). In *West African Drug Co Ltd v Lilley (28 TC 140)* the business premises were destroyed by an earthquake when the lease had twelve years unexpired. The lessor claimed that not only was the company obliged to pay rent for the following twelve years but it also had an obligation to restore the premises. Even without the *Staveley Coal* decision it is likely that the obligation to rebuild would have been fatal to the claim, which was rejected by the court, that the payment by the company to rid itself of the lease was revenue. The payment to surrender a ten-year lease was similarly held to be capital in *Bullrun Inc v Inspector of Taxes (2000 STC (SCD) 384) (SpC 248)*.

12.7 The moral is clearly that a taxpayer should seek to sublet his business premises if they become surplus to requirements rather than try to surrender or assign the lease. Although no cases have come before the courts on the specific point, it would seem from the decision in *Hyett v Lennard* that the shortfall of rent paid over rent received would be a trading expense even if a premium is taken under the sublease – although part of that premium would of course be taxable under the UK property business provisions (**3.2** above). An interesting question is what happens if the tenant assigns the lease and the assignee subsequently defaults, a fairly common occurrence in recent years. The landlord will look to the assignor for the rent, under the doctrine of privity of contract. Rent payments by the assignor thereafter undoubtedly qualify for relief under the *Hyett v Lennard* principle albeit that any sum received from the assignee on the assignment was a capital receipt.

12.8 Difficulties can also arise with service charge payments if these include a contribution to a reserve fund. The main forms that service charge arrangements can take are considered in **2.63** above. If the service charge is payable as additional rent or under a covenant in the lease there should be no problem in the business tenant obtaining a deduction. If the reserve fund element is payable to trustees (or to the landlord as trustee), that payment is probably a capital payment for which the tenant is not entitled to a deduction. This is arguable, however. The payment can be said to be wholly and exclusively incurred for the purpose of giving the tenant the right to occupy the building, as it is something that he is obliged to pay under his lease to remain in occupation of the premises. Accordingly, whilst the payment is a capital receipt of the trust, it may nevertheless be revenue expenditure from the tenant's point of view. It probably depends on whether the tenant has a solely revenue motive (to continue to occupy the premises) or if part of his motive is that the reserve fund contribution will relieve him of future expenditure. If a management company is used which is a mutual trading company the tenant is almost certainly entitled to claim a deduction for the full service charge including the reserve fund element. The allowability of payments to a mutual trading company does not seem to have come before the courts but it seems implicit in *CTA 2009, s 101* that a trader will be entitled to a deduction for such payments.

12.9 A premium paid to obtain a renewal of a lease is, of course, capital, even if, in theory at least although not always in practice, the lease is very short – as it is to acquire an asset (*MacTaggart v B & E Strump (10 TC 17)*) – and even if it is payable by annual instalments (*Green v Favourite Cinemas (15 TC 390)*). In that case, the company leased a theatre for 21 years for an annual rent and a premium. The premium was payable by annual instalments. The landlord had the right to terminate the lease, in which case liability to pay future instalments would cease. It was held that the premium was capital expenditure. A payment to modify the terms of a lease has also been held to be capital (*Tucker v Granada Motorway Services Ltd (53 TC 92)*). In that case, the rent under a lease was based on gross takings. A payment was made to the landlord in consideration of his agreeing to amend the lease to allow tobacco duty to be deducted from the gross takings in calculating the rent. It was held that the payment was a once and for all payment for the purpose of making an identifiable capital asset (the lease) more valuable, and that it was therefore capital. If the lease is a short lease a premium attracts a measure of tax relief though (see **12.46**).

12.10 A rent based on profits is, of course, rent, not a distribution of profits. The profit relationship is merely an element in the calculation of the quantum of one of the expenses of earning that profit. Where a lease provided for rent to abate if profits were below a certain level this did not affect the nature of the payment as rent (*Union Cold Storage Co Ltd v Adamson (16 TC 293)*).

12.11 Where the tenant will obtain something additional to the mere use of the premises for his rental payments, these payments may well be found to constitute the purchase price of a capital asset being paid by instalments. In *Ainley v Edens (19 TC 303)*, a landlord carried out structural improvements to premises let on a 60-year lease and the tenant undertook to make 50 half-yearly payments 'by way of rent', which were expressed to represent repayment of the improvements with interest. They were held to be capital. In *CIR v Land Securities Investment Trust Ltd (45 TC 495)*, the landlord conveyed his interest in the property to the tenant in return for rentcharges of £96,000 pa for ten years. These significantly exceeded the previous rent. It was held that the annual payments were not revenue but were a cost of acquiring a capital asset, the reversionary interest. A company which leased premises under a long lease at a rent of £23,444 entered into a number of transactions which resulted in its rent increasing to £42,450 pa (compared with a rack rent for the premises of £60,000) and one of its subsidiaries becoming entitled to the freehold subject to a 22-year lease to the company's landlord at a nominal rent. The increase in the rent payable was held to be a payment to acquire a capital asset, the freehold, even though the acquisition was by another group company (*Littlewoods Mail Order Stores Ltd v McGregor (45 TC 519)*).

12.12 An interesting case on the deductibility of rent is *Allied Newspapers Ltd v Hindsley (21 TC 422)*. A newspaper company, through a subsidiary, bought a site adjoining its printing works and erected a building on it. The subsidiary rented the building to its parent at a rack rent. The parent sublet most of the building from time to time and only ever occupied a small part of it. The reason for the acquisition of the site was that it controlled the parent company's access to its printing works. It was held that the rent paid to the subsidiary was a trading expense, as, although the parent did not occupy the building, it had entered into the lease for the purposes of its trade.

Sale and Leasebacks, etc

12.13 There are two main anti-avoidance provisions that need to be considered where a sale and leaseback or similar transaction is undertaken as a result of which a trader ends up paying a higher rent than under his original lease; *ICTA 1988, ss 779* (now *ITA 2007, s 681A* onwards, *CTA 2010, s 834* onwards) and *780* (now *ITA 2007, s 681B* onwards, *CTA 2010, s 849* onwards).

Land Sold and Leased Back: ITA 2007, s 681A onwards; CTA 2010, s 834 onwards

12.14 These provisions date from 1964. They were designed to stop the owner of land from selling it and taking a leaseback at a rent that is artificially high in the early years in order to reduce his trading profit. They limit the amount of rent that is deductible by the payer.

12.15 The provisions apply where land (or any estate or interest in land) is transferred and as a result of:

(*a*) a lease of the land (or any part of the land) granted by the transferee to the transferor; or (*b*) any other transaction or series of transactions affecting the land or any estate or interest in the land,

the transferor (or an associated person) becomes liable (either at the time of the transfer or subsequently) to pay any rent under a lease of the land (or any part of the land) (*ITA 2007, s 681AA; CTA 2010, 835*). In other words it applies not only on a sale and leaseback but also on the sale of land followed by a lease of that land to the vendor or a person who is associated with him.

12.16 The deduction that can be made by the transferor (or the associated person as appropriate) in respect of rent under the lease is limited to 'the commercial rent' for the period for which the payment is made (*ITA 2007, s 681AD(3); CTA 2010, s 838(3)*). The commercial rent is the rent that might be expected to be paid under a notional lease of the land negotiated in the open market at the time when the actual lease was created. The notional lease must be deemed:

(*a*) to be of the same duration as the actual lease;

(*b*) to have the same terms as to maintenance and repairs as the actual lease; and

(*c*) to provide for rent payable at uniform intervals and either:

  (i) at a uniform rate, or

  (ii) if the rent payable under the actual lease is at a progressive rate (and such that the amount of rent payable for any year is never less than the amount payable for any previous year), a rent that increases by gradations proportionate to those provided by the actual lease (*ITA 2007, s 681AJ; CTA 2010, s 844*).

12.17 Paragraph (*c*)(ii) in **12.16** above of course covers the situation where the actual lease contains a rent review clause. It enables the notional lease to contain a similar clause. It should be noted that this can only be done where the reviews are upward-only reviews. If the rent could be reduced on a review the notional lease must be deemed to provide for rent to be paid at a fixed rate throughout the term of the lease. This is probably in the taxpayer's interest. The market rent under a lease for, say, 21 years with no reviews would be enormous. Nowadays such a lease is such a rarity that a landlord would want a very high rent to induce him to enter into it.

12.18 Where the rent deduction is restricted under *ITA 2007, s 681AD* or *CTA 2007, s 838* the amount disallowed can be carried forward and allowed in future years to the extent that the commercial rent in a later year (or where necessary later years) exceeds the actual rent (*ITA 2007, s 681AF; CTA 2010, s 840*). There must, however, be an actual payment of rent in the later year.

Example 12.1

A sells a property to X and leases it back for 15 years on terms that he will pay £50,000 pa rent for the first two years and £1 pa thereafter. The commercial rent on the basis of a 15-year lease without reviews is determined to be £9,000 pa. The deductions claimable by A are:

		Rent paid	*Brought forward*	*Total*	*Commercial rent*	*Deduction allowed*
		£	£	£	£	£
Year	1	50,000	–	50,000	9,000	9,000
	2	50,000	41,000	91,000	9,000	9,000
	3	1	82,000	82,001	9,000	9,000
Years	4–11	8	73,001	73,009	72,000	72,000
Year	12	1	1,009	1,010	9,000	1,010
	13	1	–	1	9,000	1
	14	1	–	1	9,000	1
	15	1	–	1	9,000	1

If the rent in years 3 to 15 had been nil instead of £1 no deduction would have been competent for any of those years as there would not have been a subsequent payment made to which the carried forward amount could be added.

12.19 Not only must there be a subsequent payment, but that payment must also be made by the transferor or a person who is associated with him. If the transferor assigns the lease to an associated person it appears that the associate can claim the benefit of the transferor's unrelieved payments. On a transfer to a non-associate the benefit of any unallowed payment is lost.

12.20 The following persons are associated persons of the transferor:

(*a*) An individual is associated with his spouse and any relative (brother, sister, ancestor or lineal descendent) or spouse of a relative of either the individual or his spouse.

(*b*) A trust is associated with the settlor (provided that he is an individual) and any person who is associated with the settlor.

(*c*) A person is associated with a company (or other body of persons) of which he has control (or of which persons associated with him have control, or of which he and persons associated with him together have control).

(*d*) A company is associated with another company that is under common control (within (*c*) above).

(*e*) In relation to a disposal by joint owners, those joint owners are associated with one another and with any person associated with any of them.

(*f*) If two persons each enter into a sale they are associated with one another and with any associated person of either of them if the two are acting in concert or the two transactions are in any way reciprocal. This is designed to cover the situation where A sells his building Greenacres to X; B sells his property Blackacres to X; A takes a lease of Blackacres; and B takes a lease of Greenacres. Although A and B may not be otherwise connected both will suffer a restriction on the deductibility of their rents as they are deemed to be associated.

(*g*) A company is associated with another if they both participate in (or one or both are incorporated for the purpose of) a scheme for the reconstruction of any company or companies or for the amalgamation of any two or more companies. This covers the situation where A sells its property; an unconnected company B takes a lease of the property; and B subsequently takes over A's trade on a reconstruction or amalgamation.

(*ITA 2007, s 681AM; CTA 2010, s 847.*)

12.21 The section also applies where land (or an estate or interest in land) is transferred and, as a result of a transaction or series of transactions, the transferor or a person associated with him becomes liable to make a payment (other than rent under a lease) which is in any way connected with the land, such as a rentcharge, for which tax relief is available (*ITA 2007, s 681AB; CTA 2010, s 836*). Where such a payment is made (whether or not rent is also payable) the commercial rent of the land cannot be based on an actual lease as one does not exist – or if it does, it does not reflect the whole terms of the arrangement. Instead it is the rent that might have been expected to be paid under a tenant's repairing lease (ie one where the lessee is under an obligation to maintain and repair the whole, or substantially the whole, of the premises comprised in the lease) negotiated in the open market at the time when the transaction under which the payments became due was effected and which is for a term equal to the term over which the payments are to be made (or which is for a term of 200 years if the payments are to be made in perpetuity or for a period in excess of 200 years) (*ITA 2007, s 691AK; CTA 2010, s 845*). It is interesting to note that in this case the rent under the notional lease does not have to be assumed to be at a uniform rate. The notional lease can contain whatever rent review pattern might be encountered in the open market.

12.22 In making the comparison between actual rent (or other payments) and the commercial rent, the following provisions apply.

(*a*) If a payment is made in respect of a future period commencing more than 12 months ahead, it must be treated as having been made for the 12 months from the date of payment (*ITA 2007, s 681AH; CTA 2010, s 842*).

(*b*) If a payment is expressed to be for a period which ends more than 12 months after the date of payment, only the part relating to the period ending within 12 months of that date can be treated as a payment for that year. No part of the payment can be treated as relating to any later period. Relief for that part would therefore be lost completely (*ITA 2007, s 681AF–681AH; CTA 2010, ss 840–842*). The reason for this is not readily apparent.

(*c*) If more than one payment is made for the same period the payments must be aggregated (*ITA 2007, s 681AG(2); CTA 2010, s 841(2)*). This includes an amount brought forward and deemed to have been paid at the time of the next subsequent payment (*ITA 2007, s 681AG(4); CTA 2010, s 841(4)*). If payments are made for overlapping periods they must be apportioned and the parts apportioned to the common period then aggregated (*ITA 2007, s 681AG(3); CTA 2010, s 841(3)*).

(*d*) If part of the rent is in respect of services, or of rates usually borne by the tenant, or of the use of an asset (eg furniture), the part applicable to such items is deductible in full and excluded from the rent for the purpose of comparing the actual and commercial rents. A split of the payment between rent and payments for services, etc. shown in the lease or agreement under which the payments are made is not to be regarded as conclusive of the part of the payment applicable to such items (*ITA 2007, s 681AI; CTA 2010, s 843*).

(*e*) If a premium was paid for the lease and the transferor is entitled to a deduction for notional rent under *ITTOIA 2005, ss 61–67* or *292–297* or under *CTA 2009, ss 63–67* or *232–234*, that notional rent is to be treated as having been paid from day to day as it becomes due (*ITA 2007, s 681AL(4); CTA 2010, s 846(4)*).

12.23 If, instead of selling or otherwise transferring land or an interest in land, the owner grants a lease or enters into any other transaction involving the creation of a new interest in land, it must be regarded as equivalent to his having transferred the land. If the original interest is a lease, a surrender or forfeiture must be treated as a transfer of the lease. Any other transaction or series of transactions affecting land (or an estate or interest in land) such that a person is the owner, or one of the owners, both before and after carrying out the transaction, but another person becomes or ceases to be a joint owner is also to be regarded as equivalent to a transfer, eg if A is the sole owner at step one and at the end of a series of transactions the land is owned jointly by A and B with A paying rent to B, A is regarded as having transferred an interest in land to B (*ITA 2007, ss 681AA(3)(4), 681AB(3)(4); CTA 2010, ss 835(3)(4), 836(3)(4)*).

12.24 References to a lease in the section include an underlease, sublease, tenancy or licence. In the case of land outside the UK they include any interest over the overseas land corresponding to a lease, tenancy or licence. Rent includes any other payment made under a lease (*ITA 2007, s 681AL; CTA 2010, s 846*).

Land Sold and Leased Back: Taxation of Consideration Received: ITA 2007, s 861B onwards; CTA 2010, s 849 onwards

12.25 This is aimed at preventing a tenant under a short lease from selling his interest for a capital sum and taking back a lease at a market rent. It was introduced following disquiet over a decision of the Special Commissioners. Although the decision was not reported (Special Commissioners' decisions have only been publicly reported since January 1995) the aggrieved taxpayers, Austin Reed, decided to seek to generate public support for their position and accordingly publicised the decision themselves. It adopts a different approach to *ITA 2007, s 861A* and *CTA 2010, s 834* insofar as instead of trying to limit the deductibility of the rent, it brings the capital sum into charge to tax.

12.26 The provisions apply where a lessee under a lease of land having 50 years or less to run and who is entitled to a deduction for the rent under the lease:

(*a*) either assigns his lease for a capital sum or surrenders it to his landlord in return for a capital sum; and

(*b*) takes a new lease (or an assignment of another lease) for a term not exceeding 15 years of (or including) the whole or any part of the land which was the subject of the original lease.

12.27 It provides that the whole of the rent payable under the new lease is to be deductible but that a proportion of the capital sum received is to be taxed as income (*ITA 2007, s 681BA; CTA 2010, s 850*). Where the rent is deductible as a trading expense the taxable amount is treated as trading income. In any other case it is taxed on the lessee as miscellaneous income (*ITA 2007, s 681BB(6)–(9); CTA 2010, s 851(6)–(8)*).

12.28 The taxable amount depends on the length of the lease. It is calculated by the following formula (*ITA 2007, s 681BB(4); CTA 2010, s 851(4)*).

$$\textit{capital sum} \times \frac{(16 - \textit{length} \text{ of new lease in years})}{15}$$

If the length of the lease is less than a year it is treated as a year, which leaves the recipient paying tax as income on the entire amount he receives.

Example 12.2

Lotsa Luck Ltd occupies a shop under a lease which has 30 years to run. It has no rent reviews and the rent is £4,000 pa The landlord would prefer a modern lease paying the market rent of £30,000 pa with five-yearly reviews. Lotsa Luck does not want to take on a commitment to such a rent for the full 30 years. It agrees with the landlord that it will surrender its existing lease for £450,000 provided that it is granted a new ten-year lease. The new lease is at £30,000 pa with a review after the fifth year.

Lotsa Luck will be treated as receiving additional trading income at the time it receives the £450,000 of

$$£450{,}000 \times \frac{(16 - 10)}{15} = £180{,}000$$

It will be able to deduct the full £30,000 pa rent that it pays under the new lease. The remaining £270,000 of the capital sum will be charged to capital gains tax.

Example 12.3

Winning Ways Ltd has a lease with 3 years 7 months unexpired. It assigns the lease to Harry Hopeful for £100,000, taking back a sublease for the full term at a market rent. Harry anticipates obtaining a new lease from the landlord when the existing lease expires.

Winning Ways will be taxed as income on

$$£100{,}000 \times \frac{(16 - 3^{7}/_{12})}{15} = £82{,}780$$

The remaining £17,223 will be taxed as a capital gain.

12.29 If the capital sum is payable by instalments the calculation is done separately for each instalment. It appears that the calculation proceeds on the basis that the new lease runs from its actual commencement date, not from the date of receipt of each instalment, so the taxable fraction will remain constant, ie the effect will simply be to spread the taxable amount rateably over each instalment (*ITA 2007, s 681BB(1); CTA 2010, s 851(1)*).

12.30 If the aggregate of the rent payable under the new lease in respect of any rental period that ends before the 15th anniversary of the lease exceeds the aggregate of the rent payable under that lease for the next following rental period, the term of the lease must be treated as ending on that date (*ITA 2007, s 681BF; CTA 2010, s 855*). A rental period means a quarter, month or other period in respect of which a payment of rent falls to be made under the lease.

Example 12.4

Alpha has a 30-year lease at a rent of £4,000 pa He surrenders it to his landlord for £100,000 and takes a new lease for 30 years at a rent of £20,000 pa for the first ten years and £4,000 pa thereafter.

The rent payable in the 40th quarterly rental period (£5,000) exceeds that payable in the 41st (£1,000), and accordingly the lease is treated as ending immediately after the 40th quarter, ie as being a ten-year lease.

Alpha is therefore taxed as income on:

$$£100{,}000 \times \frac{(16 - 10)}{15} = £40{,}000$$

12.31 If either the lessor or the lessee has power under the new lease to terminate it before the end of its term, or the lessee has power to vary his obligations under the lease so as to reduce the rent (or in any other manner beneficial to him), the lease must be treated as being for a term expiring on the earliest date on which such a power can be exercised (*ITA 2007, ss 681BG, 681BH; CTA 2010, ss 865, 857*). If both **12.30** and **12.31** could apply to a lease, whichever gives the shortest term takes precedence (*ITA 2007, s 681BE; CTA 2010, s 854*).

Example 12.5

Billy has a 25-year lease at £5,000 pa He surrenders it to his landlord for £100,000 and takes a new lease at the open market rental. The lease has five-yearly reviews. At any review date Billy can reduce the rent back to £5,000 on payment to the landlord of a sum of £80,000 if he exercises the right at the first review date, £60,000 at the next, £40,000 at the third or £20,000 at the final review date.

As Billy has power to reduce the rent at the end of year 5 the lease must be treated as for five years. Billy will thus be taxed as income on:

$$£100{,}000 \times \frac{(16 - 5)}{15} = £73{,}333$$

He will be taxed as a capital gain on the balance of £26,667.

If Billy actually reduces the rent on the first review he will not be able to obtain any reduction in the tax for the £80,000 payment that he makes (other than possibly as enhancement expenditure if he sells the lease).

12.32 Any rentcharge payable by the lessee which is secured on the whole or part of the property must be aggregated with the rent for the purpose of both *paras 2(a)* and *(b)* above (*ITA 2007, s 861BI; CTA 2010, s 858*).

12.33 If the new lease does not extend to the entire property which was the subject of the original lease, the amount to be used in the calculation of the income element is limited to the proportion of the capital sum which is reasonably attributable to the part of the property which was the subject of the original lease (*ITA 2007, s 681BC; CTA 2010, s 852*).

Example 12.6

Henry has a 20-year lease of 5,000 sq. ft. of office space. He surrenders it to his landlord for a payment of £80,000 and takes back a new ten-year lease of 1,000 sq. ft. of the premises.

The £80,000 is apportioned between the 4,000 sq. ft. surrendered and the 1,000 sq. ft. retained. This is a valuation exercise. Assume that the split is £65,000 for the part given up and £15,000 for the part retained (it is unlikely to be proportionate as the landlord gets vacant possession of part but not of the remainder).

Henry will be taxed as income on:

$$£15{,}000 \times \frac{(16 - 10)}{15} = £6{,}000$$

12.34 If instead of surrendering a lease the landlord and tenant agree to vary the terms of the original lease so that in return for a capital sum the tenant undertakes to pay a higher rent (for a period that ends within 15 years of the date on which the consideration is paid), he must be treated as having surrendered the original lease and having been granted a new lease (*ITA 2007, s 681BJ; CTA 2010, s 859*). If the consideration is payable by instalments the 15-year period runs from the date that the last instalment is paid. It is not clear what happens in such circumstances. For example, suppose that in return for £100,000 payable by five annual instalments the tenant agrees to pay an increased rent for the next 18 years. This 18-year period ends within 15 years after the date of payment of the last instalment. It is therefore deemed to be for a term not exceeding 15 years. Presumably it will be treated as being for a term of exactly 15 years as the increased rent is payable for 18 years. Accordingly, a fifteenth of the capital sum will presumably be taxed as income.

12.35 These provisions will also apply if the new lease is granted not to the original lessee but to a partner or associate of the lessee, or to an associate of a partner of the lessee (*ITA 2007, ss 681BA(4), 681BL; CTA 2010, ss 850(4), 861*). Associate for this purpose has the same meaning as in *ITA 2007, s 681DL* or *CTA 2010, s 882*. This is the same as in (*a*) to (*e*) (but not (*f*) and (*g*)) in **12.20** above.

12.36 Lease, lessee, lessor and rent are all defined in *ITA 2007, s 681BM* and *CTA 2010, s 862*.

Relief for Other Payments in Respect of the Premises

12.37 A trader can claim a deduction against his trading profits for the cost of repairs to the properties from which he operates. He cannot deduct expenditure on improvements. Nor can he deduct the cost of replacing the premises – although the replacement of part may well be deductible as constituting a repair of the whole. The court decisions on what constitutes repairs are considered in **9.3–9.10** above. The HMRC guidance on the expenditure on reinstatement of bomb damaged buildings in London Dockland and Manchester in 1996 is considered at **2.21**. With the exception of the reference to ESC B4 this applies equally to owner-occupied buildings as to rented ones (Tax Bulletin 26, December 1996).

12.38 Where a payment for dilapidations is made on the termination of a lease the payment should be deductible. HMRC apparently consider that if the payment is not used by the landlord for 'genuine repairs', or if the expenditure 'restores the building to its original state by rebuilding or dismantling items previously altered or added by tenants', it is disallowable (Taxline, Issue 12).

However, this seems of doubtful validity. It looks on dilapidations as deferred repairs. The distinction between income and capital, as far as the tenant who makes the payment is concerned, is whether the tenant obtains an enduring benefit from it. It seems improbable that a tenant obtains an enduring benefit from a payment he is obliged to make on the expiry of a lease under its terms.

12.39 Where part of a dwelling-house is used for the purposes of a trade or profession, *ICTA 1988, s 74(c)* used to limit the rent deductible for corporation tax purposes for the business portion to a maximum of two-thirds of the total, unless in any particular case it appeared that, having regard to all the circumstances, some greater sum ought to be deducted. It has been held that the two-thirds limitation applies only to rent and does not prevent the deduction of a larger proportion of rates (*Wildbore v Luker (33 TC 46)*). It would equally not apply to repairs although it is difficult to imagine circumstances in which repairs to a private house could meet the wholly and exclusively test necessary to qualify for a deduction. The restriction does not appear to have been carried through to either *ITTOIA 2005* or *CTA 2009.*

12.40 The cost to the owner of a beach cafe of erecting a barrier in front of the cafe as protection from the sea has been held to be capital expenditure (*Avon Beach & Cafe Co Ltd v Stewart (31 TC 487)*). So has the cost of constructing a new access road to a company's warehouse to meet complaints from neighbours regarding the use of the original access road (*Pitt v Castle Hill Warehousing Co Ltd (49 TC 638)*).

12.41 Replacement of shop fronts are normally dealt with on a renewals basis, ie the cost of a new shop front is treated as a revenue expense except to the extent that the work contains an element of improvement, which is capital. HMRC say this is because the replacement of a shop front is the repair of the shop (which is the entirety). The cost of adapting newly acquired premises may, however, be capital (Business Income Manual, BIM46935). HMRC consider that such expenditure is not machinery or plant (Capital Allowances Manual CA22110). This was confirmed in the *Wimpy* and *Associated Restaurant* cases (see **10.49**) where the Court of Appeal defined a shop front as part of the premises from which the business was carried on.

12.42 Expenditure by a tenant on making good dilapidations at the expiry of a lease is an allowable deduction if the work is of the nature of deferred repairs (Business Income Manual, BIM43260). So is a sum paid to the landlord by way of composition to the extent that it reflects deferred repairs. Where dilapidations are paid for by a new tenant as a condition of the grant of the lease (or by an existing tenant as consideration for the grant of a new lease, not in satisfaction of his obligations under the old) the payment will be capital. Expenditure will also be capital to the extent that it consists of rebuilding the premises, reinstatement of part of the premises previously demolished by the tenant, or demolishing a part added by the tenant. Even where the repairs qualify for a revenue deduction any element of improvement will, of course, also be capital.

12.43 An interesting point arose in *Southern Counties Agricultural Trading Society Ltd v Blackler (1999 STC (SCD) 200)*. The taxpayer occupied office premises for the purpose of its trade. It assigned its lease and paid the assignee a 'compensation payment' to reflect its belief that it had failed to meet its repairing obligations under the lease. The assignee agreed to indemnify the taxpayer against all claims resulting from any breach of any covenant in the lease. It was agreed that had the taxpayer engaged a third party to carry out the repairs the payment for remedying the dilapidations would have been a trading expense. However, the taxpayer had not paid the assignee to carry out the repairs. It had paid it to assume the taxpayer's liability to make good the dilapidations. It was also clear that the taxpayer wished to dispose of the lease and move to smaller premises. The Special Commissioners agreed with HMRC that the payment was of a capital nature to ensure the disposal of a disadvantageous asset.

12.44 HMRC in the past took the view that a provision for repairs was not deductible. This view was rejected by the Special Commissioners in *Jenners Princes Street Edinburgh Ltd v CIR (1998 STC (SCD)196)*. The company carried on a trade of retailers from a listed building. It spent an increasing amount on repairs. In 1994 it carried out a feasibility study on the possibility of a refurbishment to restore the building to its original condition and obviate the need for constant piecemeal repairs. This was completed during its accounting period to 31 January 1995. The company resolved to carry out the work and made a provision in those accounts for the estimated expenditure of £2.25m. The work was actually done in subsequent years. The Special Commissioners felt the HMRC position illogical. If they accepted, as they did, that 'expended' in *ICTA 1988, s 74(1)(a)* should be interpreted in the accountancy sense of including accruals, 'actually expended' in *s 74(1)(d)* must have a similar meaning. The adverb 'actually' qualifies the verb; it cannot change its meaning. HMRC gave notice of appeal but abandoned this in mid-1999. They were probably influenced by the fact that the accountancy profession had itself cut down significantly the scope for provisions in FRS 12. This permits a provision only where a business has a present obligation (legal or constructive) as a result of a past event, it is probable that expenditure will be required to settle that obligation, and a reliable estimate can be made of the amount of the obligation. It is probable that the provision in *Jenners* would not have met these conditions.

12.45 An interesting VAT issue arose in *I/S Fini v Skatteministeriet (Case C-32/03) (2005 STC 903)*. Fini leased premises for ten years from May 1988 from which it operated a restaurant, but closed the restaurant at the end of

1993. It could not find a replacement tenant. Accordingly, it remained VAT registered in order to reclaim the VAT is paid on its rent. The Danish VAT authorities refused to repay the VAT on the grounds that the property was no longer held for the purpose of making taxable supplies. The ECJ held that 'a person who has ceased an economic activity but who, because the lease contains a non-termination clause, continues to pay the rent and charges on the premises used for that activity is to be regarded as a taxable person and is entitled to deduct the VAT on the amounts paid'. This is based on the proposition that for the entire term of the lease the premises were directly and immediately linked to the economic activity for which it was entered into.

12.46 The distinction between capital and revenue is not necessarily all or nothing. In *Markets South West (Holdings) Ltd v HMRC ([2011] STC 1469)* the company incurred substantial costs in relation to an appeal against an enforcement notice under the *Town and Country Planning Act 1990.* It operated a market. It had various planning permissions. The local authority contended that these allowed the market to operate only on certain days of the week. The company contended that they contained no such restriction. The First-tier Tribunal held that the costs were capital expenditure. The Upper Tribunal looked more closely at the planning inspector's report and found that the company had contended that its existing permission entitled it to trade on all Wednesdays but if it did not the consent should be extended to do so. The Tribunal held that to the extent that the company had sought to enlarge the scope of the planning permission, the costs were capital but to the extent that it was defending what it believed to be its existing rights, it was revenue. It accordingly remitted the case to the First-Tier Tribunal to determine that issue.

Deduction in Respect of Premium Paid

12.47 Where a person pays a premium for the grant of a short lease (under 50 years) of premises used in connection with his trade, profession or vocation, he is allowed a deduction against profits even though the payment is capital. The deduction is based on the sum taxable on the landlord as income (**3.2** above) – or if he is exempt from tax, or not taxable on the premium because he can set it against a premium that he has himself paid, the sum on which he would otherwise have been taxable (*ITTOIA 2005, s 61*; *CTA 2009, s 63*). Relief is given not only for a premium paid but also for an amount of expenditure that gives rise to a charge on the landlord (or some other person) under *ITTOIA 2005, ss 278, 280* (**3.6** above); *281* (**3.8** above); or *282* (**3.14** above) or *CTA 2009, ss 218, 219, 220, 221* or *s 222*). In relation to leases granted after 1 April 2013 (6 April for income tax) no deduction is given if none would have been due but for deeming the lease shorter than its term in accordance with *ITTOIA 2005, s 303* or *CTA 2009, s 243, Rule 1* (see **3.23**(*b*)

(*ITTOIA 2005, s 61(5A)*; *CTA 2009, s 63(5A)* inserted by *FA 2013, Sch 28, paras 2, 5*).

12.48 The amount that is taxable on the landlord is spread on a day-to-day basis over the term of the lease – or the period treated as the term for the purpose of calculating the *ITTOIA 2005, s 281* or *CTA 2009, s 217* charge (or the period from the date of the assignment where the charge is under *ITTOIA 2005, s 282* or *CTA 2009, s 222*) – and treated as additional rent in respect of the property. The tenant is entitled to deduct each year the proportion of the additional rent that is attributable to the days falling within his accounting period or income tax basis period (*ITTOIA 2005, s 61(1),(4)*; *CTA 2009, s 62*). If only part of the land is used for business purposes then only the deemed additional rent in relation to that part is of course deductible (*ITTOIA 2005, s 61(5)*; *CTA 2009, s 63(3),(5)*). The relief is given to the person for the time being entitled to the lease (*ITTOIA 2005, s 61(1)*; *CTA 2009, s 63*). Accordingly, where a trader takes an assignment of a lease, he needs to check whether the original tenant paid a premium or other amount qualifying for relief, as if he did the assignee will acquire a right to a tax deduction based on that payment.

Example 12.7

The lessee in *Example 3.1* (**3.2** above) was Tarzan Enterprises Ltd, which acquired the lease for use in its trade. On 20 June 2018 Tarzan assigned the lease to X Plorer Ltd for £10,000. Tarzan Enterprises prepares its accounts to 31 December and X Plorer has a 30 June accounting date.

The term of the lease was ten years, seven months from 1 July 2013.

The amount taxable on the landlord, Jane, was £41,000.

The tenant is therefore entitled to a deduction of £3,874 pa, which will be given in the following periods:

To Tarzan Enterprises Ltd		£	£
Year to 31.12.2014 (from 1.7.2014)	$\frac{184}{365} \times £3,874$	1,953	
Year to 31.12.2015		3,874	
2 years to 31.12.2017	2 × £3,874	7,748	
Year to 31.12.2018 (to 20.6.2018)	$\frac{171}{365} \times £3,874$	1,815	15,390

To X Plorer Ltd

Year to 30.6.2018 (from 21.6.2018)	$\frac{10}{365} \times$ £3,874	106	
Year to 30.6.2019		3,874	
5 years to 30.6.2024	5 × £3,874	19,370	
Year to 30.6.2025(to 30.1.2025)	$\frac{7}{12} \times$ £3,874	2,260	25,610
			£41,000

It should particularly be noted that X Plorer Ltd's relief is not based on the payment it made to Tarzan but on Tarzan's original payment to Jane.

12.49 No relief is due for a 'premium' paid on the assignment of a lease (except in the unusual case where the initial lease was at an undervalue so that a charge arises on the assignor under *ITTOIA 2005, s 282*; *CTA 2009, s 222*). Accordingly, a trader who is asked to pay a premium for an assignment of a lease of less than 50 years ought to investigate the possibility of taking a sublease of the premises instead – unless, of course, he is in the lucky position of X Plorer Ltd in the above example where the relief due by taking an assignment exceeds the premium that he is paying. If the assignor is not prepared to grant a sublease it may be possible to find a third party, such as a property dealing company, who is prepared to take the assignment and grant a sublease. A property dealer is generally happy to grant a sublease as the amount on which it is taxed under the property business rules reduces its taxable trading profits so that its overall tax position is unaffected.

12.50 The relief is also given where a person is not in occupation of the land but deals with his interest in it as property employed for the purposes of his trade (*ITTOIA 2005, s 63*; *CTA 2009, s 65*). This is probably intended to cover tied houses of brewers, and similar properties. In such a case if a premium is received from a brewer's tenant, *ITTOIA 2005, s 288* and *CTA 2009, s 228* (see **3.35** above) applies to restrict the notional rent deductible by the brewer, and he cannot claim a deduction under both the trading and property business rules.

12.51 If the charge on the landlord arose under *ITTOIA 2005, s 278* or *CTA 2009, s 218* – on a deemed premium where the tenant was obliged to carry out work on the premises – no relief will be due for the deemed premium to the extent that the tenant was entitled to capital allowances on the expenditure (*ITTOIA 2005, s 60(5)*; *CTA 2009, s 62(5)*). This is achieved by requiring the calculation to be made as if the tenant had not had to carry out the work which attracted capital allowances. In practice, where part of the work qualified for capital allowances and part did not, it is likely in most cases that the non-capital allowances work on its own would have no value to the landlord, and thus would not generate a deemed premium to the landlord on that assumption, with the result that no relief at all would be due to the tenant.

Chapter 13

Private Residences

13.1 There are three main areas in which tax considerations can arise in connection with private residences; capital gains tax, the allowability (or in most cases non-allowability) of mortgage interest (which is dealt with at **4.4** above onwards), and the deduction of expenses against taxable income. It is also of course possible that the purchase and sale of a private residence could constitute trading. It was made clear in *Kirkham v Williams (1991 STC 342)* that where a person has more than one motive in acquiring land the subjective intention of the taxpayer must be looked at to determine whether the transaction is trading (see **5.28**). In the past HMRC claim to have had some success before the General Commissioners in characterising a transaction as trading where a person lived in a house for a short period and carried out substantial renovations during that time, but prior to *Kirkby v Hughes (1993 STC 76)* no such case had reached the High Court. The facts in that case were far more suggestive of trading than of the house having been acquired as a residence. The taxpayer, who was a building contractor and a bachelor, lived with his parents. In August 1978 he bought a four-bedroomed house which was unfit for occupancy. He renovated it and moved in temporarily while continuing to live mainly at his parents' home. He sold it in August 1981 at a substantial profit. In April 1981 he bought a vacant plot on which he built a four-bedroomed house. He intended to use it as his residence but never did. It was sold in August 1984. Part of the proceeds was used to buy a barn, which he converted into a four-bedroomed house which he lived in temporarily. It is clear that the Commissioners did not believe the taxpayer's claim that any of the three properties was intended to be his private residence. HMRC also contended in *Goodwin v Curtis* (see **13.5**) that the taxpayer was trading in private residences but this was rejected by the General Commissioners and HMRC did not appeal against the decision. Each case of course depends on its facts. In *A J Clarke v HMRC (TC 1461)* the FTT accepted that two houses were residences even though the first was bought with a short-term loan, was put on the market after six months and sold three months later; and the second (which the taxpayer built in the garden of the first) was occupied for only two years, including the development period during which Mr Clarke moved from room to room as each room was completed, and throughout the taxpayer had his former home available for his use (although he did not use it because of matrimonial problems).

13.2 Where a person lets part of his private residence or lets the whole whilst he is not using it himself the rent generated is of course taxable. However, no special problems arise compared with other lettings, with the possible exception that expenditure needs to be apportioned between that attributable to the letting and that to the private occupation. Clearly the method of apportionment will depend very much on the facts. Any reasonable method is likely to be acceptable provided that it represents a genuine attempt to arrive at the proportion of the total that is applicable to the letting. Problems can arise with holiday homes (where the letting season may be short) if the owner occupies a sizeable chunk of the prime time. In some cases the easiest solution is to bring in notional rent as a receipt and to claim the whole of the expenses. It should be borne in mind, however, that a large sum of expenses needs to be at risk before one should volunteer to pay tax on non-existent income. There is also a special income tax exemption for comparatively small amounts of rent (about £82 a week or £144 from 1 April 2016) received from letting part of a person's own home. This is designed to encourage people to take in lodgers. It is dealt with at **2.78–2.85**.

Capital Gains Tax Private Residence Exemption

13.3 A gain realised by an individual on the disposal of a dwelling-house or part of a dwelling-house which has been his only or main residence throughout his period of ownership, or throughout it except for all or part of the last 18 months (36 months up to 6 April 2014), is not a chargeable gain, ie it is not chargeable to capital gains tax (*TCGA 1992, ss 223, 223(1)*). The 18-month period is increased to 36 months where at the time of the disposal the individual (or his spouse or civil partner) is a disabled person (as defined in *FA 2005, Sch 1A*) or a long-term resident in a care home and the individual (or both the individual and his spouse where the spouse's disability attracts the relief) has no other relevant right in relation to a private residence (*TCGA 1992, s 225E(1)–(4)(8)* inserted by *FA 2014, s 58*). A care home is defined as an establishment that provides accommodation together with nursing or personal care (*TCGA 1992, s 225E(8)*). An individual is a long-term resident in a care home at the time of the disposal if at that time he is resident there and has either been resident there for at least three months or can reasonably be expected to be resident there for at least three months (*TCGA 1992, s 225E(5)*). An individual has a relevant right in relation to a private residence at the time of the disposal if:

(*a*) at that time he owns or holds an interest in another dwelling-house or part of a dwelling-house (or the trustees of a settlement own or hold an interest in another dwelling-house or part of a dwelling-house and the individual is entitled to occupy that dwelling-house (or part) under the terms of the settlement); and (*b*) the principal private residence exemption would have applied to any gain accruing to the individual (or trustees) on the disposal at that time of that interest (or would have done if an election has been made to treat that property as the individual's main residence).

(*TCGA 1992, s 225E(6)*.)

13.4 If the individual is within the scope of NRCGT and his period of ownership is deemed to start on 6 April 2015, periods before that date are ignored in determining when the house was the individual's private residence unless the taxpayer elects that this rule should not apply. Such an election must be made in the NRCGT return in respect of the disposal and must specify which days prior to 6 April 2015 the individual relies on as being a period the property was occupied as his residence (*TCGA 1992, s 223A(1)–(3)* inserted by *FA 2015, Sch 9, para 5*). Where such an election is made, the number of days of absence that can be ignored under *TCGA 1992, s 223(3)(a), (c)* or *(d)* (see **13.28**) must be reduced by any days that would have been ignored under that provision if the period of deemed ownership has started on the days specified in the election (*TCGA 1992, s 223A(4)–(6)*).

13.5 If an individual disposes of (or of an interest in) his only or main residence under a 'home purchase agreement' as a consequence of a change in the situation of his place of work or that of a co-owner of the property (being a change which is required by the employer of the individual or the co-owner) and under the terms of the agreement the individual receives a share of any profit made by the purchaser on its subsequent disposal of the property (and the receipt of that share would otherwise be treated as a disposal within *TCGA 1992, s 22* (capital sums derived from assets)) the receipt is treated as a gain attributable to the individual's sale of the property (but as accruing to him at the time it is received) (*TCGA 1992, s 225C(1) (2)*). This applies only if the share is received within three years of the initial disposal of the property by the individual (*TCGA 1992, s 225C(2) (a)*). A home purchase agreement is one made with the employer or a person operating under an agreement with the employer (such as a relocation company) which includes a term entitling the individual to receive a share of the profit (*TCGA 1992, s 225C(3)*). It should be noted that the change in the place of work must be 'required by' the employer; if the employer asks for a volunteer to move to another location the relief will not apply. It is not wholly clear why, but it is probably an anti-avoidance term, ie the individual must not be able to bring about the change. It should also be noted that the relief will not apply if the individual is forced to relocate because his spouse is required to move unless the spouse owns an interest in the property. This replaced an earlier concession, ESC D37.

What is a Residence?

13.6 Before looking at whether a property is a person's principal residence, it may need to be asked whether it is a residence at all. A residence is not defined in the legislation. However, the FTT is consistently adopting the principle that a residence is not a place where one lives; it has to be a place occupied as one's home with the intention of living there with a large degree of permanence or continuity or the expectation of continuity. This test needs to be applied not only to determine the principal residence. If a person occupies only one property, it is still a question of fact whether that occupation is such as to make the property his residence. If it is not, the relief will not apply. Mention should also be made of *Iles* (*TC 3565*) but only because the facts in that case were so extreme that it is unsurprising that the house was held not to be Dr Iles' residence. He occupied it for only 25 days; he had advertised it for sale prior to occupying it and had already accepted an offer on the flat and was dealing with the prospective purchaser's enquiries before contract, the flat had only two bedrooms for Dr and Mrs Iles and their two teenage daughters and one son (although the elder daughter was at university) and it was located 12 miles from Dr Iles' practice whereas the large houses he occupied before and after the flat were both within a mile of his practice.

13.7 HMRC have said that they do not attempt to impose a minimum period of occupation. They take the view that it is quality of occupation rather than the length of occupation which determines whether a dwelling-house is a person's residence (Tax Bulletin, Issue 12, August 1994). This approach was followed by the General Commissioners in *Goodwin v Curtis (1998 STC 475)*. Mr Goodwin completed his purchase of a farmhouse on 7 March 1985. At the same time he separated from his wife and he took up temporary residence there. On 11 April 1995 he advertised the property for sale and a sale was completed on 3 May 1995. In Autumn 1994, a company controlled by Mr Goodwin and a Mr Sharp contracted to buy a small cottage, Ayton, with the intention that they should use it as an office. They obtained planning consent but the company could not obtain finance so the purchase was completed on 3 April 1985 by Mr Goodwin personally. When Mr Goodwin sold the farmhouse he moved to Ayton as he had nowhere else to live. He immediately looked for a larger place to live in and bought a larger property, Stoneways, completion of which was on 26 July 1985. The Commissioners held that neither the farmhouse nor Ayton qualified for private residence relief. The judge felt that the test should be whether the property had been occupied by the taxpayer as his home. The Commissioners had distinguished between permanent residence and mere temporary accommodation. The judge thought that was a correct approach. The factors to be weighed up in reaching this decision were the degree of permanence, continuity and the expectation of continuity. The Commissioners were entitled to hold that both properties had been used as mere temporary accommodation and not as a residence.

13.8 The Court of Appeal noted that in *Levene v CIR (13 TC 486)* Viscount Cave had adopted the dictionary definition of 'reside' as 'to dwell permanently or for a considerable time, to have one's settled or usual abode, to live in or at a particular place', and felt the same approach is appropriate for capital gains tax (a VAT tribunal, whilst accepting this same meaning of residence, has given a more relaxed meaning to 'residential' though – see **17.28**). The property was also held not have been occupied as a residence in *Springthorpe v HMRC (TC 832)* where the Tribunal concluded that to the extent that the taxpayer did occupy the property, he did so for the purpose of renovating it rather than occupying it as his home which he expected to occupy with some degree of continuity. The Tribunal seem either to have set an extraordinarily high evidence threshold in that case or to have had serious doubts about the taxpayer's evidence as the facts set out in the decision are fairly suggestive of genuine occupation. The taxpayer again won in *Harte v HMRC (TC 1951)*, although the facts in that case appear so favourable to HMRC that it is surprising that it reached the tribunal. In *Dutton-Forshaw (TC 4644)*, the FTT cited a comment of Millet J in *Moore v Thompson* (see **13.9**): 'the need for permanence or continuity should not be overstated'. They felt this was consistent with the decision in *Goodwin v Curtis*. In that case Mr Dutton-Forshaw lived in the house for only around seven weeks and does not seem to have been registered on the electoral roll there. They placed importance on the fact that he registered his car at the flat and obtained a resident's parking permit, which he surrendered when he sold the flat.

Scope of the Dwelling-house

13.9 Dwelling-house is not defined. It probably means any building or part of a building which is used as a dwelling. Certainly the exemption is not limited to houses but extends to flats and other types of private residence. Indeed it has been held that a caravan jacked up and resting on bricks with water, electricity and telephone installed was a dwelling-house (*Makins v Elson (51 TC 437)*). The mere jacking-up of a caravan without connecting it to other facilities such as water, electricity or telephone may not suffice (*Moore v Thompson (61 TC 15)*). If the owner has a residence within a purpose-built hotel or other building which cannot be regarded as a dwelling-house, HMRC will allow the relief to be claimed for the rooms actually occupied as a residence whether or not they are self-contained (HMRC Capital Gains Manual, CG64320). The exemption applies to the disposal of the dwelling-house itself or any interest in it (*TCGA 1992, s 222(1)*). It also extends to land which the individual has for his own occupation and enjoyment with his residence as its garden or grounds up to an area (inclusive of the house) of half a hectare (approximately 1.23 acres), or such larger area as the appeal Commissioners may determine if they are satisfied that, regard being had to the size and character of the dwelling-house, that larger area is required for the reasonable enjoyment of the dwelling-house (or the part of the house owned by the individual owning the land) as a residence (*TCGA 1992, s 222(1)(b),(2),(3)*). For disposals prior to 19 March 1991 the exempt area was one acre. If the whole of the land owned with the house does not qualify for exemption the exempt part is the part which, if the remainder were separately occupied, would be the most suitable for occupation and enjoyment with the residence (*TCGA 1992, s 222(4)*).

13.10 There are a number of points to watch.

(*a*) Land occupied with a residence only qualifies for exemption if it is held for occupation as its garden or grounds. This applies even where the total area including the house does not exceed half a hectare. For example, if an individual occupies a house covering a quarter of an acre plus an adjoining half-acre plot which he has never used for any purpose that plot would not qualify for exemption. HMRC have been known to contend that if land is separated from a house by a wall or fence which does not contain a gate giving direct access from the house, it is not a garden or grounds for occupation with the residence. As a general principle this is undoubtedly wrong. However, it is probably fair to assume that, if land does not have direct access from the house, there is an inference that it is not garden or grounds of the house. In *Wakeling v Pearce (1995 STC (SCD) 96)* Mrs Wakeling owned property which comprised two non-contiguous parts about 30 feet apart. Her residence was on one. On the second she maintained a small garden, a washing line and garden shed. She allowed her grandchildren, friends and family to use it for relaxation. She sold this second part in two plots in 1987 and 1988 respectively. The Special Commissioner held that the fact that the land disposed of did not adjoin the residence was not fatal. The statutory requirement was merely that the land should be used with the residence as its garden. Mrs Wakeling had done that, albeit at a substantially reduced rate, up to the moment of sale. Accordingly, the exemption applied. HMRC decided not to appeal but only because of Mrs Wakeling's particular circumstances (Tax Bulletin, Issue 18, August 1995).

(*b*) The test as to whether land qualifies for the exemption is applied at the time of its disposal. Accordingly, if the individual sells the house but retains the land, even for only a day or two, the subsequent sale of the land cannot qualify for exemption, as at the date of sale it will not be owned for enjoyment with the house (as the house will at that time no longer be in the same ownership) (*Varty v Lynes (51 TC 419)*). HMRC did for a time sometimes claim that the extended relief did not apply, even on a simultaneous sale of the house and garden, after the cessation of occupation but now accept that this is misconceived (Tax Bulletin, Issue 12, August 1994). HMRC also regard this case as confirming that the use of the land other than at the date of disposal as irrelevant (Tax

Bulletin, Issue 18, August 1995). However, they accept that land which has traditionally been part of the grounds of a residence but which at the date of sale is unused or overgrown can nevertheless be included in the exemption (HMRC Capital Gains Manual, CG64360).

(*c*) It is extremely difficult to show that an area over half a hectare qualifies for relief if that area consists of land which is sold without the house being sold simultaneously. This is because it is hard to see how one can contend that land is required for the reasonable enjoyment of a house as a residence if one will continue to occupy it as a residence after having sold that land. The foregoing contention is not, however, impossible. In *Batey v Wakefield (55 TC 550)*, the taxpayer owned a house built on 1.1 acres of land. He had a bungalow for occupation by a caretaker built on the land. This was separate from the main house and had its own access from the road. When the taxpayer subsequently occupied the house full-time he no longer needed the caretaker and sold the bungalow together with 0.2 acres of the land. He managed to convince the General Commissioners not only that the sale of the bungalow was the sale of part of the dwelling-house, but also that the land wholly qualified for exemption even though it exceeded an acre and even though he could, and intended to continue to, reasonably enjoy the house without the 0.2 acres. In *Dickinson v HMRC (TC 3037)* part of the garden was sold to a developer. Prior to the contract date, the vendor allowed the developer onto the land to start foundation work on an informal basis. HMRC contended that at the contract date the land had ceased to be garden so PPR could not apply. The FTT held that for land to lose its character as garden or grounds, the change must be permanent; it cannot be transient or conditional. If the transaction had not progressed to completion, the land would have reverted to garden use. Accordingly it was still garden at the contract date.

(*d*) In *Lewis v Rook (1992 STC 171)* the Court of Appeal indicated that whilst, as in *Batey v Wakefield*, it is possible for a dwelling-house to consist of more than one building, this can only apply if the dwelling-house is 'appurtenant to, and within the curtilage of, the main house'. Balcombe LJ cited with approval Buckley LJ in *Methuen Campbell v Walters (1979 QB 525)*: 'For one corporeal hereditament to fall within the curtilage of another, the former must be so intimately associated with the latter as to lead to the conclusion that the former in truth forms part and parcel of the latter.' In their Tax Bulletin, Issue 12, August 1994 HMRC opine that a wall or fence separating two buildings will normally be sufficient to establish that they are not within the same curtilage.

The meaning of curtilage was explained by the Court of Session in 1951 in the case of *Sinclair-Lockhart's Trustees v Central Land Board (1 P&CR 320)*. 'The ground which is used for the comfortable enjoyment of a house or other building may be regarded in law as being within the curtilage of that house or building and thereby as an integral part of the same although it has not been marked off or enclosed in any way. It is enough that it serves the purpose of the house or building in some necessary or reasonably useful way.' For example, the garage of a house or a shed in the yard of shop premises would be in the same curtilage but two adjacent shops or houses would not normally be so comprised. If the owner of a factory was to develop land next door to the factory, even on the existing boundary of the factory, or was to use such land for storage purposes, the land would not normally be within the curtilage of the factory as it would not have previously been required for the comfortable enjoyment of the factory.

In *Lewis v Rook*, Lady Rook unsuccessfully claimed exemption for a gardener's cottage 190 yards from the main house. In *Markey v Sanders (60 TC 245)* exemption was similarly refused for a staff bungalow 130 metres from the main house. The taxpayer also lost in *Honour v Norris (1992 STC 304)* although the facts of that case were special and the decision unsurprising. Besides *Batey v Wakefield*, the taxpayer won in *Williams v Merrylees (60 TC 297)* where the disposal was of a lodge 200 metres from the main house, but on the *Edwards v Bairstow (36 TC 207)* principle as he had convinced the General Commissioners that the lodge was appurtenant to and within the curtilage of the main house. The judge held that, whilst he might not himself have reached that conclusion, it was not so unreasonable that he could overturn it.

(*e*) If a house and grounds are sold simultaneously but to different purchasers – for example, the house to someone who intends to occupy it and the grounds to a property developer – this probably also raises an inference that the land is not required for the reasonable enjoyment of the house as a residence. If the total area is under a half hectare there is unlikely to be a problem, as *s 222(1)(b)* looks to land owned for the vendor's enjoyment. If it exceeds a half hectare the test is narrower. It is necessary to show that the land is required for 'the reasonable enjoyment' of the house as a residence, ie anyone's enjoyment ignoring the particular circumstances of the vendor (*TCGA 1992, s 222(3)*).

(*f*) Whether or not an area of over half a hectare is required for the reasonable enjoyment of a house is normally best dealt with by the taxpayer's surveyor and the District Valuer rather than his accountant and the Inspector of Taxes. HMRC's demarcation line is that it is for the Inspector to determine what land is garden or grounds and for the District Valuer to then decide how much of it qualifies for relief (HMRC Capital Gains Manual, CG64353). As the appropriate area depends very much on local considerations, if agreement cannot be reached it is worthwhile considering taking an appeal before the General Commissioners. It is curious that Parliament has imposed on the Commissioners the burden of deciding the extent of the exemption bearing in mind that they have specifically precluded them from dealing with any dispute as to the value of land by requiring it to be referred to the Lands Tribunal (*TMA 1970, s 47(1)*).

(*g*) In their Tax Bulletin, Issue 2, February 1992, HMRC explain their view of what the exemption covers and the information they like to be given when a claim is made for the exemption to extend to an area of more than half a hectare. In particular, this quotes as guidance on the meaning of 'required' the words of Du Parcq J in *re Newhill Compulsory Purchase Order 1937, Payne's application* [*1938*] *2 All ER 163*: 'Required, I think, in this section does not mean merely that the occupiers of the house would like to have it, or that they would miss it if they lost it, or that anyone proposing to buy the house would think less of the house without it … 'Required' means, I suppose, that without it there will be such a substantial deprivation of amenities or convenience that a real injury would be done to the property owner.' When faced with such a restricted interpretation by an Inspector, the context in which Du Parcq was speaking should be borne in mind. The compulsory purchase legislation in 1937 prohibited a local authority from acquiring any 'park, garden or pleasure ground or any other land reasonably required for enjoyment with the house', and the land in question in the *Newhill* case was not garden land but 'other land'. One would expect the courts to have tried to give effect to a clear intention of Parliament that local authority compulsory purchase powers, which were given for the benefit of the community should be interpreted reasonably widely. It is not clear why the Tax Bulletin article does not mention more recent compulsory purchase cases, such as *R v Secretary of State ex parte Sharkey (1990 45 EG 113)*, where the courts have taken a far less restrictive approach to the word 'required'. It is in any event doubtful to what extent the courts will look at the compulsory purchase cases to aid the interpretation of *s 222* as the intention of Parliament in this case is almost certainly to exempt the whole of a house and its grounds but without extending that exemption to extraneous land. They did so in *Longson v Baker (2001 STC 6)* where Evans-Lombe J thought there is a sufficient analogy between the two statutory provisions that it was entirely legitimate for the Commissioner to take guidance from the *Newhill* case – but that Du Parcq J was emphasising that what the Commissioners are engaged in is an enquiry as to fact, namely what the permitted area of land should be.

(*h*) HMRC take the view that there are two distinct exemptions:

(i) the dwelling-house, including the land on which it stands and, where it consists of more than one building, the land between those buildings, and

(ii) its garden or grounds including any building in such grounds (HMRC Capital Gains Manual, CG64240).

Where there are several buildings they regard it as important to determine which buildings comprise the entity, 'the dwelling-house', partly because the extent of the dwelling-house can affect the extent of the grounds (eg if the dwelling-house includes a stable the paddock is probably grounds) and partly because land between buildings included in the dwelling-house qualifies for relief automatically outside the half hectare test (CG64242). Because of this distinction between house and garden, curtilage (see (*d*) above) is only relevant to determine the extent of the dwelling-house; it has no relevance to the identification of the permitted area of garden or grounds (CG64251). This is probably an oversimplification. To the extent that a garden falls within the curtilage of the house it will automatically qualify for relief even if it exceeds a half-hectare. HMRC say that the test whether or not a building is within the curtilage of the main house is whether it passes automatically on a conveyance of the house without having to be specifically mentioned (CG64248). The garden of a suburban house will normally meet this test. However, HMRC see a distinction between the curtilage of the main house and the curtilage of an estate (para 64249) and are specifically instructed to resist the argument that because a whole estate is contained within a single boundary, the whole estate should be regarded as within the curtilage of the main house. HMRC consider that an urban house will commonly have no curtilage beyond a small garden or yard (CG64291). HMRC also say that if a separate building is used wholly for business, private residence relief is excluded by *TCGA 1992, s 224(1)* and as such there is no need to consider whether it is in the curtilage of the main house (CG64261). It is doubtful if this is right. If it is within the curtilage and thus part of the main house it seems more correct to value the house (including the business building and land within the curtilage) and exclude from relief under *TCGA 1992, s 224(1)* the part of the overall gain which is attributable to the business building.

(*i*) A group of flats is regarded as a single dwelling-house if they are all occupied by the owner and his family, are within the same block and contiguous (CG64305). If they are in the same block but on different floors or separated by other flats, HMRC consider they will be a single dwelling only in exceptional circumstances (CG64305) and in such cases, HMRC consider length of occupation and use to be important factors. If access between the two is only via the street they do not accept they can constitute a single dwelling-house (CG64305). This is not necessarily correct.

(*j*) HMRC define a 'garden' as a piece of ground, usually partly grassed and adjoining a private house, used for growing flowers, fruit or vegetables, and as a place of recreation (CG64360). It seems improbable that constructing a pond, creating a patio, or even paving over the entire area as has happened with many suburban front gardens will cause the land to cease to be 'garden' as this definition suggests. Their definition of grounds is 'enclosed land surrounding or attached to a dwelling-house or other building serving chiefly for ornament or recreation', although unlike the definition of garden this is not intended as an exhaustive definition (CG64360). As a general rule, land surrounding the residence and in the same ownership is the grounds of the residence unless it is in use for some other purpose (CG64363). Paddocks and orchards are normally part of the grounds if there is no significant business use (CG64360). The land does not have to be exclusively used as garden or grounds (CG64360).

(*k*) Curiously HMRC seem to interpret occupation and enjoyment as legal terms, ie possession of the land without contested claims from third parties (CG64372 – although this has now been deleted from the manual). Such an interpretation of enjoyment seems inconsistent with the requirement for the Commissioners, who are normally concerned with facts more than law, to determine what area is required for the reasonable enjoyment of the house as a residence (*TCGA 1992, s 222(3)*). It is unlikely that they were intended to decide how much of the land is reasonably not subject to contested claims. It is equally unlikely that 'enjoyment' in *s 222(1)(b)* and *s 222(3)* were intended to have different meanings.

(*l*) What needs to be looked at in deciding what land qualifies for relief is the area required for the reasonable enjoyment of the dwelling-house; it is not permissible to take into account the particular requirements of the owner of the dwelling-house (*Longson v Baker (2000 STC (SCD) 244*). Accordingly, whilst in that case it was convenient for the taxpayer's purposes to have 7.56 hectares available to them on which to keep their horses, such a large area was not necessary or vital when stabling horses at a property.

(*m*) The house must actually be occupied. In *Shakoor (TC 2208)* (a penalty case) the dwelling-house was bought off-plan but building work took so long that the taxpayer lost patience and sold his interest in the uncompleted building. The FTT felt that any reasonable taxpayer would know that the property could not be his principal residence if he never occupied it. In *Gibson (TC 3021)* the taxpayer purchased his house in June 2003, intending to make it his family home with his then-girlfriend. Shortly after moving in they experienced problems with the roof timbers. They also considered extending the house and consulted an architect about the proposed extension. He said it would be cheaper to demolish the house and start again! Mr Gibson did just that. He demolished it completely and started rebuilding. He hoped to move into the new house by Summer 2005. The work took longer than expected, costs soared, and the relationship with his girlfriend became fraught. She refused both to move into the new house or get married. They decided to sell the house on completion, marry and get a smaller house. The FTT, on a split decision, held that the new house was not the same dwelling-house as the old and accordingly it had never been occupied as a main residence. The dissenting member opined that where a house is demolished and then reconstructed in order to achieve the same end as extending and remodelling the existing house more cost effectively, the new construction should be regarded as the same dwelling-house as the original.

Two or More Residences

13.11 Where a person has two or more residences at the same time, so that it is necessary to determine which is his main one for any period, he can conclude that question by notice in writing to HMRC given within two years from the beginning of that period (*TCGA 1992, s 222(5)(a)*), ie he can elect to which the exemption is to apply, but such an identification cannot apply for a period starting earlier than two years prior to the date of the election. HMRC consider that the election has to be made within two years of the acquisition of the second home. This was upheld in *Griffin v Craig-Harvey (1994 STC 54)*. The reasoning in that case is difficult to follow. *Section 222(5)* reads:

> 'So far as it is necessary … to determine which … is the individual's main residence for any period –
>
> (*a*) the individual may conclude that question by notice … given within two years from the beginning of that period …,
>
> (*b*) subject to paragraph (*a*) above, the question shall be concluded by … the Inspector, which may be as respects either the whole or specified parts of the period of ownership in question.'

The Special Commissioners held that 'that period' in (*a*) must relate to 'any period' in the introductory words, which most people would think is the natural construction. Vinelott J however, thought that was not even 'a possible construction', and that it must refer to the 'period of ownership' in (*b*) albeit both that the word 'that' normally refers to something that has gone before, not something that follows, and that (*b*) is in any event made subject to (*a*) so would not normally need to be even looked at where (*a*) applies. He supported his view by reference to Hansard. The Minister said in 1965 in introducing the provision, 'there is no provision for the case of a man who has one house and does not need to make any option but who later buys another house and then wishes to opt to treat the other as his principal residence. The effect of this Amendment is to keep open the option so that he can exercise a choice within two years from the time when he acquires the second house.' As the Minister talked of 'the effect' rather than 'the purpose' the taxpayer's construction would have the same effect, albeit that it would also have further effects, and the Minister gave no indication that the amendment was intended to deal solely with the circumstance he outlined. Accordingly it is not clear why Vinelott J felt that it resolves the ambiguity in the wording, a *sine qua non* for recourse to Hansard to be permissible under *Pepper v Hart (1992 STC 898).* In *Ellis v HMRC (2013 SFTD 144)* HMRC sought to contend that the election had no effect where the elected property was factually clearly not the main residence, but the FTT affirmed that once it was accepted that the property was a residence, the election is conclusive and HMRC cannot go behind it

13.12 The election can be varied at any time by giving a fresh notice. Again the variation cannot apply to any period over two years before the date of the new election. Vinelott J in *Griffin v Craig-Harvey* specifically accepted that if an election is made within two years of acquisition of the second property it can be varied at any time. He also specifically accepted that:

(*a*) if a person who has two residences acquires a third, an election between all three properties can be made within two years of acquiring the third;

(*b*) if a taxpayer owns three properties and ceases to use one of them as a residence, that cessation will trigger a fresh right of election between the other two;

(*c*) if a taxpayer with two houses transfers one to a settlement of which he is the life tenant the transfer will trigger a fresh right to elect (jointly with the trustees); and

(*d*) if a taxpayer has two houses one owned by himself and the other by a trust the transfer of the trust property to the taxpayer will trigger a fresh right to elect.

He declined to comment on what happens if a taxpayer who owns a residence and a let property begins to use the let property as a residence. Logically that triggers a new right to elect. In other words, it appears that where a taxpayer has more than one residence any event that results in his beginning or ceasing to use a property as a residence, or in a change of ownership of one of them, will trigger a fresh right to elect – but only with effect from the date of that event – provided that he occupies at least two properties as residences immediately after the event.

13.13 In the past HMRC often accepted an election made more than two years after the acquisition of a second residence as effective from two years prior to the date of the election. Such elections appear now to be invalid. It is difficult to know what to do in such a case. The safest thing is probably either to transfer one of the residences to a settlement and make a fresh election if the disposal can be achieved without triggering a capital gains tax charge, or to buy or rent a third residence and make a fresh election. However, either of these courses will incur costs (and it may be difficult to establish that a new property is in fact a residence) and it is likely that HMRC will consider themselves bound to honour past statements that elections were effective. HMRC's Capital Gains Manual tells staff that an invalid notice given on or before 16 October 1994 in favour of a residence in which a legal or equitable interest is held should be accepted as valid (CG64540). It is, however, unclear whether this is looking at all invalid notices or only at notices which were given because it was believed that a property held under licence triggered a need for an election. A Tax Bulletin article of 16 October 1994 stated that it did not (see **13.12**).

13.14 If no such election is made by the taxpayer the choice is to be made by the Inspector – whose choice can be different for different parts of the period of ownership – but subject to a right of appeal to the General or Special Commissioners within 30 days of the service on the taxpayer of notice of his determination of the question (*TCGA 1992, s 222(5)(b)*). There is a general principle that, where an officer of the Crown is given a discretion by Parliament, the exercise of which is subject to a right of appeal, he must exercise that discretion judicially, not according to his own whim (*Padfield v Ministry of Agriculture Fisheries and Foods ([1968] 1 All ER 694)*). Accordingly, the Inspector is almost certainly compelled to base his choice on what appears to him on his examination of the facts to be the main residence at a particular time. In this context, the first thing HMRC generally seem to look at is which property is registered as the main residence for council tax purposes (a second home attracts a discount on the tax). Other relevant factors are where is the individual registered to vote, are the bills for utilities in his name, what personal possessions are maintained at each property, how much time does he spend at each property and what is his normal postal address. Make sure that the address on HMRC's records is the one that the individual wants to be his main residence! Ask friends to write to him there and keep the envelopes. If, after making an election, the taxpayer acquires a further residence it is probable that the election will cease to apply as the acquisition of the new residence again makes it necessary to determine which is the taxpayer's principal residence. Accordingly, a fresh election ought to be made.

13.15 It must be borne in mind that a person can have two residences without owning them both. Thus, if a person rents a house on a monthly tenancy and also owns a holiday cottage it is important for him to elect to treat the cottage as his main residence, as he cannot realise a gain on the house (except to the extent that the landlord may make a payment to him to induce him to forego his statutory tenancy rights). If he does not elect, the determination by the Inspector would almost certainly be that the house is the main residence.

13.16 HMRC have stated that where in such circumstances the taxpayer was unaware that an election could be made they will extend the time limit for making the election under *s 222(5)(a)* to a reasonable time after the individual first becomes aware that he is entitled to make an election, and that they will then treat it as having effect from the date on which he acquired the second residence (HMRC Extra-Statutory Concession D21). This concession applies only if the taxpayer's interest in one of the properties has 'no more than a negligible capital value in the open market'.

13.17 HMRC considered at one stage that where a residence was occupied under a licence, eg a room in a hotel or club or a room in a relative's house, and the taxpayer owned another residence he needed to elect if he wanted the owned property to be treated (contrary to the facts) as his main residence. They no longer take this view. Where an election was made before 16 October 1994 on the basis of their earlier view it remains valid if it was to treat the owned property (or one of two or more owned properties) as the main residence. If it was to treat the property occupied under licence as the main residence, eg to preserve the benefit of losses on the owned properties, it ceased to be effective from 16 October 1994. Unfortunately it is not always easy to distinguish between a licence and a tenancy (which does trigger a need to elect). HMRC's Capital Gains Manual tells staff 'in most cases in which a residence is rented a tenancy exists' (CG64470). That is far too broad. The House of Lords in *Street v Mountford [1985] 1 AC 809*, probably the leading case in this area, held that a right to exclusive occupation of a residence is normally a lease (and thus a tenancy). It follows from this that payment of rent for shared premises may well be a licence to occupy – although it could in some cases be a lease. There is of course a large body of law on this area under the Landlord and Tenant legislation, as many landlords have sought to grant licences rather than leases to try to avoid the occupier gaining tenant's rights under that legislation.

13.18 If an individual acquires land and has a house built on it HMRC will regard the house or land as being the main residence for the period up to the date that the house is first occupied provided that this does not exceed 12 months. This concession also applies where a house is bought and is not immediately occupied because it is undergoing repairs or redecorations or the taxpayer is taking steps to dispose of his previous residence (Extra-Statutory Concession D49). The 12-month period can be extended to up to 24 months – but no longer – if there is a good reason for the delay, ie one that is outside the taxpayer's control. Where ESC D49 applies principal private residence relief is given on both houses; no *s 222(5)* election is required (Tax Bulletin, Issue 12, August 1994).

13.19 A husband and wife can only have one main residence between them whilst they are living together. Where a private residence election affects both it must be given by both (*TCGA 1992, s 222(6)(a)*). HMRC take the view that it does not affect both if only one has an interest in the properties concerned, ie they accept an election signed only by the husband where he owns both properties. Such an election could not affect the subsequent acquisition of another residence by the wife as that acquisition would make it necessary to determine anew what is the main residence and thus presumably render the election ineffective from that date. Where a couple marry and both spouses own a property, HMRC accept that a fresh two-year period begins with the marriage, but if one owns two properties and the other none they consider that a new two-year period does not apply. If the two jointly owned two properties prior to marriage, the marriage will trigger a fresh right of election as a joint election will need to be made following the marriage (Tax Bulletin, Issue 12, August 1994).

13.20 Where the disposal is an NRCGT disposal (ie a disposal by a non-resident – see **11.50**) the PPR election can still be made and valid, but the procedure is different (*TCGA 1992, s 222A(2), (3)* inserted by *FA 2015, Sch 9, para 3*). A *s 222A* notice cannot, however, vary an earlier *s 222* notice if that notice had effect to determine whether a property disposed of (in whole or part) before the NRCGT disposal was the person's main residence (*TCGA 1992, s 222A(4), (5)*).

13.21 A *s 224A* notice (including a notice of a variation) is not given in advance like the normal PPR election. It must be given in the NRCGT return in respect of the disposal of the property and cannot subsequently be varied (either by a new *s 224A* notice or by a *s 224* notice) (*TCGA 1992, s 222A(6)*).

13.22 Where a *s 224A* notice affects both the taxpayer and his spouse and both are required to make an NRCGT return in respect of the disposal of the dwelling-house in question, the notice is effective only if the taxpayer's spouse also elects for the property to be regarded as their main residence. If they are not both required to make an NRCGT return, the notice is effective as regards any period when they were living together as spouses or civil partners only if it is accompanied by a written notification from the other spouse agreeing to the terms of the notice in respect of that period (*TCGA 1992, s 222A(7)*).

13.23 A notice under *s 222A(2)* does not affect an election under *s 222(5)* (*TCGA 1992, s 222A(8)*). It is not clear what this means. It probably means that a *s 222A(2)* election can be made, notwithstanding that an election is in place to treat a different property as the person's main residence, but that the *s 222* election is in abeyance during the period to which the *s 222A* election relates.

13.24 From 2016/17 onwards, a dwelling-house (or part) must be treated as not being occupied as the individual's residence for the purpose of the private residence exemption at any time in the taxpayer's period of ownership which falls into a non-qualifying tax year (or a non-qualifying partial tax year) (*TCGA 1992, s 222B(1), (2)*). A tax year (or partial year) is a non-qualifying year for this purpose if neither the taxpayer nor his spouse (or civil partner) was resident for that tax year (or part of a tax year) in the country in which the house is situated, and the 'day count test' is not met for that tax year (or partial year) (*TCGA 1992, s 222B(3), (4)*). A partial tax year is one throughout which the taxpayer does not own the property, ie it is the year of acquisition or disposal (*TCGA 1992, s 222B(5)*). For this purpose an individual is resident in a non-UK country for a tax year (ie the UK tax year) if in that year either:

(*a*) he is liable to tax in the overseas country by reason of his domicile or residence, in respect of a period or periods making up more than half of the tax year; or

(*b*) he would be resident in that country for the tax year if the UK statutory residence test applied to that country (with references to that country substituted for the UK).

(*TCGA 1992, s 222B(6)–(9)*.)

For the purpose of the section, *TCGA 1992, s 11(1)(A)* (which ignores periods of residence in the UK for members of visiting forces and staff of designated headquarters) is of course disapplied for the purpose of these tests (*TCGA 1992, s 222B(10)*).

13.25 An individual meets the day count test in relation to a dwelling-house if he spends at least 90 days in it (not necessarily consecutively) during the year (or at least 90 × days in the partial tax year/days in the tax year, in the case of a partial year) (*TCGA 1992, s 222C(1)–(5)*). In applying this test if the individual has other qualifying houses in the same country, days spent in the other houses can be aggregated to arrive at the 90 days figure. A qualifying house is one owned by the taxpayer, his spouse or civil partner at the time of the occupation or by a person who is his spouse or civil partner at the time of the disposal (*TCGA 1992, s 222C(6)(9)*). A day spent in a house by the individual's spouse is counted towards the individual's 90-day target (but no day can be counted twice, eg if the individual is in one of the houses and the spouse in another on the same day, that counts as only one day) (*TCGA 1992, s 222C(7)*). A day counts as a day spent in a qualifying house if the individual (or spouse) is present at the house at the end of the day, or he is present in the house for some period during the day, and the next day has stayed overnight in the house (*TCGA 1992, s 222C(8)*). It is not clear what this is intended to cover.

Main Residence for Part only of Period of Ownership

13.26 If a house is an individual's only or main residence for part only of his period of ownership the capital gains tax exemption will apply to part of the gain (*TCGA 1992, ss 222(1), 223(2)*). This is the part which the length of the part (or the aggregate of the parts) of the period of ownership for which it was his main residence (inclusive in any event of the last 18 months (see **13.3** above) of his ownership) bears to the total length of his period of ownership, in both cases ignoring any period prior to 31 March 1982 (*TCGA 1992, s 222(7)*). In arriving at this fraction the house can be treated as occupied as the individual's main residence (even though factually it was not) during certain specified periods of absence provided that:

(*a*) it was his main residence at some time before the start of the period of absence and at some time subsequent to that period, ie it was the main residence prior (but not necessarily immediately prior) to the start of the period of absence and was reoccupied at some time between the end of that period and the time of its sale; and

(*b*) the individual had no other residence eligible for relief during that period of absence.

(*TCGA 1992, s 223(3)(7).*)

The property was also held not to be a residence in *Harte v HMRC (TC 1951)*, although the facts in that case were a bit extreme. Mr Harte owned his own house. He also owned a second property, which he inherited from his late father subject to his stepmother being entitled to live in it. She died on 20 May 2007. On 21 June 2007, Mr Harte transferred half of that property to his wife. The property was sold in October 2007. In August 2008, Mr Harte nominated the property as his main residence for the period 11–19 October 2007 only. His stepmother's furniture remained in the house until it was sold as did her clothes and other personal effects. There was no written evidence to suggest that Mr and Mrs Harte had ever occupied the property. Their own house was only six miles away. Mr Harte gave oral evidence that he had occupied the property from time to time, that the longest continuous period of occupation was three weeks, that there had been no need to furnish the property as his late stepmother's furniture was there and that he and his wife kept personal possessions in both of their properties.

13.26A *Higgins v HMRC (2017 SFTD 814)* dealt with an off-plan purchase. Mr Higgins entered into a contract to buy the lease of his apartment in October 2006. At that time the apartment did not exist. The apartment did not become occupiable until December 2009 and Mr Higgins did not become entitled to occupy it until he completed the purchase on 5 January 2010. He immediately moved in and used the apartment as his main residence. He contracted to sell it on 15 December 2011. HMRC contended that the apartment qualified as Mr Higgins' only residence from 5 January 2010 and that the gain attributable to the period from October 2006 to 5 January 2010 did not qualify for relief. The Tribunal gave this short shrift. The period of ownership will ordinarily begin on the date the taxpayer has the right to occupy. *TCGA 1992, s 22* (contract date is acquisition date) merely identifies the time of acquisition and disposal. That concept is not directly involved in determining the meaning of period of ownership. What is critical is that the period of ownership and the period of occupation coincide.

13.27 It should particularly be noted that it is necessary for the owner to reoccupy the property after the period of absence. If he sells the house without having done so – or if he reoccupies it but has a private residence exemption in force for a different property – the period of absence cannot be treated as a qualifying period. There is an exception from the need to reoccupy if the period of absence is due to work, ie falls within (*b*) or (*c*) below and the individual was prevented from resuming residence in the dwelling-house in consequence of the situation of the individual's place of work or a condition imposed by the terms of the individual's employment requiring the individual to reside elsewhere, being a condition reasonably imposed to secure the effective performance by the employee of his duties. (*TCGA 1992, s 223(3B)* inserted by the *Enactment of Extra-Statutory Concessions Order 2009, SI 2009 No 730*). The occupation of another residence by the individual (as of course will always be the case) during the period of absence would appear to debar relief by virtue of (*b*) above unless an election is made under *TCGA 1992, s 222(5)(a)* for the first house to be regarded as his main residence. This should particularly be borne in mind where the individual is working outside the UK. A house does not need to be in the UK to qualify for the private residence relief. Accordingly, it is arguable that in the absence of an election, the overseas house would qualify for relief and the period of absence from the UK house could not then be ignored. In practice HMRC do not seem to take this point. If the period overseas is sufficiently long for the individual to have ceased to be both resident and ordinarily resident in the UK it is in any event probable that his overseas house is not a property that is 'eligible for relief' under *TCGA 1992, s 223* as it would not have been within the scope of the *Act*. In such circumstances, provided that the individual sells the overseas house before returning to the UK, there is probably no problem.

13.28 The periods of absence in question in **13.26** above are:

(*a*) any period or periods not exceeding three years in aggregate (if they exceed three years this seems to mean that the house can be treated as the main residence for the first three); plus

(*b*) any period throughout which the individual (or his spouse or civil partner) worked in an employment or office all the duties of which were performed outside the UK (however long that period may be); plus (*c*) any period not exceeding four years (or periods which in aggregate do not exceed four years) throughout which the individual or his spouse or civil partner) was prevented from residing in the dwelling-house or part of the dwelling-house in consequence of the situation of his place of work or in consequence of any condition imposed by his employer requiring him to reside elsewhere which was reasonably imposed to secure the effective performance by the employee of his duties (again if the aggregate exceeds four years it appears that the first four will qualify for exemption).

(*TCGA 1992, s 223(3)* as amended by the *Enactment of Extra-Statutory Concessions Order 2009, SI 2009 No 730.*)

13.29 Although head (*b*), unlike (*a*) and (*c*), refers only to a single period it is probable that this is because there is no maximum. Accordingly each separate period meeting the head (*b*) test would wholly qualify for relief. It does seem, though, that if an individual loses his overseas employment any period spent overseas between employments will not fall within head (*b*) – although it can of course fall within head (*a*). It should also be noted that head (*b*) covers only offices and employments, it does not apply where a person is working full-time overseas as a self-employed individual or as a partner in a business. Furthermore all of the duties of an employment must be performed outside the UK; there is no exemption where any of the duties – even if they are merely incidental to the overseas duties – are performed in the UK.

13.30 It is curious that the relief under the second part of head (*c*) should have to depend on the reasonableness of the employer, over whom the individual of course has no control. It is probably intended to impose an objective test of whether an onlooker would consider the imposition by the employer a reasonable imposition, ie 'reasonably imposed' should be interpreted as 'imposed reasonably'. The reference in (*c*) to part of a dwelling-house presumably envisages that part being the entirety of the individual's residence as it is difficult to envisage it being possible for a person to occupy part of his house by reason of his work but impossible for him to occupy the rest of it. It should in any event be noted that his place of work must prevent the individual from occupying his house, not merely make it more convenient for him to live elsewhere. Fortunately, HMRC seem to take a relaxed view of this condition and do not expect a person to commute 100 miles a day even though it may be possible for him to do so.

13.31 It is irrelevant whether the house was unoccupied or let during the period of absence. Provided that the necessary conditions are met it is treated as the owner's private residence even if he had let it and could not therefore use it during that period. Prior to 6 April 2009, in the case of a husband and wife living together, absence due to the spouse's employment was treated as if it were as a result of the owner's employment (HMRC Extra-Statutory Concession D3). Where an individual claimed exemption for a period of absence within (*b*) or (*c*) above, ie where his employment prevented his residing in the house, the need for him to reoccupy the property was waived if he was unable to resume residence because the terms of his employment required him to work elsewhere (HMRC Extra-Statutory Concession D4). These concessions were given statutory effect from this date (see **13.27** and **13.28**).

13.32 Where an individual has different interests in a house at different times – for example where he first buys a lease and then buys the freehold reversion so that his interest becomes a freehold interest – his period of ownership starts from the first acquisition taken into account in arriving at the expenditure that is deductible for capital gains tax purposes (*TCGA 1992, s 222(7)*). If the initial interest is a mere tenancy which had no cost it may be worth investigating whether the taxpayer incurred legal fees or other incidental expenses on the acquisition as, if so, that would appear to enable the period of ownership to be extended to include the tenancy. In the case of a husband and wife living together, if one disposes of his interest to the other, including a disposal by way of a legacy on death (and presumably also under the statutory rules on an intestacy, although the Act specifically refers to a passing as legatee only), the transferee's period of ownership is treated as commencing when the transferor acquired his initial interest in the property and the property is treated as having been the transferee's main residence for any period for which it was the transferor's (*TCGA 1992, s 222(7)*). As *TCGA 1992, s 62* gives an uplifted base cost this can work unfairly where the interest in the property is inherited and the property was not the principal private residence of the deceased for his whole period of ownership. In such circumstances a deed of arrangement to put the property into an interest in possession trust for the surviving spouse may be worth considering. This has the same inheritance tax effect as a direct inheritance but avoids the capital gains tax problem.

13.33 If an individual ceases to live with his spouse (or civil partner) and subsequently disposes of (or of an interest in) the dwelling-house to the spouse, he can claim to treat the dwelling-house as continuing to be the husband's main residence until the disposal provided that:

(*a*) the disposal to the spouse is pursuant to an agreement between the two made in contemplation of (or in connection with) the dissolution or annulment of the marriage, judicial separation or separation in other circumstances such that the separation is likely to be permanent (or pursuant to a court order made on or in connection with such an event);

(*b*) in the period between the individual ceasing to reside in the house and the disposal to his spouse the house continued to be the only or main residence of the spouse; and (*c*) the individual has not elected for some other property to be treated as his main residence for any part of that period.

(*TCGA 1992, s 225B* inserted by the *Enactment of Extra-Statutory Concessions Order 2009, SI 2009 No 730.*)

This replaced Extra-Statutory Concession D6 which applied up to 5 April 2009. Condition (*c*) appears to deny relief for the entire period, not merely that part of it for which the election in relation to the other property applied. It should particularly be noted that this applies only where the house (or the husband's interest in it) is ultimately transferred to the wife. If it is sold and all or part of the proceeds paid to her the concession will not operate. In such a case it may be preferable to transfer the property to the wife and allow her to sell it.

13.34 Where a person resides in 'job-related' accommodation and also owns an interest in another property which he intends in due course to occupy as his main residence the property is regarded as his main residence during the time he is living in the job-related accommodation (*TCGA 1992, s 222(8)*). Accommodation is job-related for this purpose if either:

(*a*) it is provided to the person (or his spouse or civil partner) by reason of his employment and either:

  (i) it is necessary for the proper performance of his duties that he should reside there;

  (ii) the accommodation is provided for the better performance of the duties of the employment and it is one of the kinds of employment where it is customary for employers to provide living accommodation; or

  (iii) there is a special threat to the employee's security and the employee resides in the accommodation as part of special security arrangements.

(*b*) it is provided under a contract entered into at arm's length and requiring him (or his spouse or civil partner) to carry on a particular trade, profession or vocation and to live either on those premises or on other premises provided by that other person.

(*TCGA 1992, s 222(8A).*)

If the accommodation is provided by a company and the employee is a director (of that or an associated company) the individual must not have a material interest in the company and must be employed as a full-time working director (or the company must be non-profit making or a charity) (*TCGA 1992, s 222(8B)*). If head (*b*) applies, the living accommodation must not be provided either by a company in which the individual (or his spouse or civil partner) has a material interest, or by any person (or persons) together with whom the individual (or his spouse or civil partner) carried on a trade or business in partnership (*TCGA 1992, s 222(8C)*).

13.35 For disposals after 8 December 2009, if at any time during the period of ownership part of the dwelling-house was occupied by another person under an adult placement scheme (or a similar scheme in Scotland or Northern Ireland) that other person's occupation can be ignored. It does not amount to the use of that part of the dwelling-house by the owner being exclusively for the purpose of a trade (*TCGA 1992, s 225D*).

Restriction of Relief

13.36 Where part of a house is used exclusively for the purposes of a trade or business or of a profession or vocation, the gain on disposal must be apportioned and the exemption applied only to the non-business part (*TCGA 1992, s 224(1)*). If the house was used exclusively for business purposes for part only of the period of ownership, or if at any time in the person's period of ownership there is a change in what is occupied as his residence, for example because of a reconstruction or conversion of a building, the private residence exemption is restricted 'in such manner as the Commissioners concerned may consider to be just and reasonable' (*TCGA 1992, s 224(2)*). HMRC consider that in the context of the section time apportionment will normally be the appropriate method to use; they do not think it is normally appropriate to take into account changes in market value in apportioning gains to different periods (Tax Bulletin, Issue 12, August 1994).

13.37 The private residence exemption does not apply at all if the acquisition of the property was made wholly or partly for the purpose of realising a gain from disposing of it (*TCGA 1992, s 224(3)*). If, although the property was not acquired to realise a gain from disposing of it, any expenditure subsequent to the acquisition was incurred wholly or partly for the purpose of realising a gain from the disposal, the exemption does not apply to the part of the gain attributable to that expenditure. The Act gives no guidance as to how that part is to be calculated. It is probably the difference between the gain realised and the gain that would have been realised had the expenditure not been incurred. HMRC would in most cases probably accept an apportionment of the gain in the proportion that the tainted expenditure bears to the total expenditure using the formula in *TCGA 1992, Sch 2, para 16(4)* but there is no statutory right to this. The sort of thing the provision might apply to is where a person owning a leasehold house buys in the reversion in order to be able to sell a freehold or a person converts his house into two flats in order to obtain a higher price. The expenditure does not have to be capital expenditure. If a person redecorates his house to achieve a higher price on sale, this would appear, in theory at least, to bring the restriction into play. Surprisingly, HMRC do not in practice apply this restriction to expenditure incurred in obtaining planning permission for redevelopment or in obtaining the release of a restrictive covenant where that is the only relevant expenditure (Tax Bulletin, Issue 12, August 1994). Where all or part of a gain is excluded from the private residence exemption under this provision, it is nevertheless outside the scope of *ITA 2007, s 752* onwards (artificial transactions in land*)* by virtue of *ITA 2007, s 767* (see **14.64**). It could, however, still be taxable as trading income (which could apply where the house was acquired with a view to realising a profit on its disposal but probably not where the house was acquired with other motives and enhancement expenditure was incurred for such a motive).

13.38 As mentioned at **2.111** if the base cost of an individual's principal private residence was reduced by roll-over relief (because at the time of acquisition it was acquired as furnished holiday accommodation), the private residence exemption will not extend to the rolled-over gain. That amount is treated as the top part of the gain on the private residence and will be wholly taxed if it is less than the total gain on the disposal (*TCGA 1992, s 241*).

13.39 The relationship between private residence relief and business asset taper relief was considered in *Jefferies v HMRC ([2009] UK FTT 291; [2010] SFTD 189*). Mr and Mrs Jefferies sold a hotel, which has been used partly as a private residence. It was agreed that 65% related to the private residence element. HMRC claimed that the taxable gain had to be calculated by first deducting 65% of the gain as PPR leaving 35% (or £201,931) to be tapered. However, they claimed that for taper relief only 35% of the £201,931 could qualify for business asset taper relief as PPR did not remove part of the asset from the tax net, so the taper relief rules had to be applied by reference to the entire asset. They acknowledged that was an anomalous result. The Tribunal achieved a commonsense result by pointing out that the taper relief legislation provided for any apportionment to be done on a just and reasonable basis and the only such apportionment was to regard no part of the chargeable gain as relating to non-qualifying use.

House Owned by a Settlement

13.40 The capital gains tax private residence exemption also applies to a gain accruing to the trustees of a settlement if a house owned by the settlement was the only or main residence of a person entitled to occupy it under the terms of the settlement (*TCGA 1992, s 225*). It has been held that it is not necessary for the occupier to be specifically entitled under the trust deed to occupy the property. If the trustees of a discretionary trust, in exercise of their discretionary powers, allow a beneficiary to occupy a house owned by the trust (assuming that the trust deed gives them power to do so as will normally be the case) the exemption will apply (*Sansom & Another v Peay 52 TC 1*). Strangely, the exemption seems to apply even if the trustees charge the beneficiary a market rent for the property. HMRC take the view that a right to occupy the house rent-free gives the beneficiary an interest in possession in the house so the inheritance tax consequences will need to be considered. It may be possible to avoid this by leasing it to him for a nominal figure for a limited period, or by the trustees acquiring the house jointly with the beneficiary so that he is entitled to occupy it in his own right, and giving the right to live in the house to the youngest child of the beneficiary. In *Wagstaff (TC 3183)*, Mrs Wagstaff sold her residence to her son and daughter-in-law in 1996. HMRC accepted the sale was at an arm's length price. The sale was subject to an agreement that Mrs Wagstaff was entitled to continue to live in the flat at no cost for the remainder of her life or until her remarriage, subject to a payment of £5,000. In August 2005, she had a fall and as a result could not continue to occupy the flat so moved in with her son, leaving her belongings in the flat, until she found ground floor accommodation in June 2006. The flat was sold in March 2007. HMRC contended that the agreement did not fetter ownership of the flat. Mr & Mrs Wagstaff were free to sell it, albeit they could not give vacant possession. The FTT held that the agreement created a trust and the exemption applied.

13.41 It has been suggested that if a life interest is given to a number of beneficiaries only one of which occupies the property, the capital gains tax exemption nevertheless extends to the entire gain made by the settlement (Taxline, Issue 12, August 1994). The mere existence of a power in a will or trust deed to permit a beneficiary to occupy the house on such terms as the trustees think fit does not itself create an interest in possession in the property, but its exercise may do so. HMRC consider that using such a power either to allow non-exclusive occupation of the property or to create a contractual tenancy for full consideration will not give rise to an interest in possession. Nor will the creation of a lease for a term, or a contractual tenancy, for less than full consideration – although it will normally trigger a charge to inheritance tax under *IHTA 1984, s 65(1)(b)* (disposition by the trustees which reduces the value of relevant property). The creation of an exclusive or joint right of residence with the intention of providing the beneficiary with a permanent home will normally create an interest in possession even though it may be revocable (SP 10/79). An interest in possession will exist if a person has a present right to the present enjoyment of the property (*Pearson v CIR (1980 STC 318)*). Accordingly what is needed is to allow occupation without the creation of a right to occupy. Some guidance of what will not work can be drawn from inheritance tax cases on this area (see **13.69**). The additional relief for the last 36 months where the owner is a disabled person or a long-term resident of a nursing home (see **13.3**) also applies to a property owned by a settlement and occupied by such a person (*TCGA 1992, s 225E(7)* inserted by *FA 2014, s 58*).

13.42 Where the beneficiary occupies more than one residence any election as to which is to be treated as his main residence must be made jointly by him and the trustees (*TCGA 1992, s 225*). Unlike the relief for an individual's own residence, the relief is not automatic; it has to be claimed (*TCGA 1992, s 225*).

13.43 Relief can also be claimed by personal representatives when they dispose of a house which both before and after the deceased's death had been used as the only or main residence of an individual (or individuals) who under the deceased's will or the laws of intestacy is entitled to (or to an interest in possession in), the whole or at least 75% of the net proceeds of disposal of the house. If two or more people live in the house both before and after the death, the 75% figure applies to the aggregate of their interests. The net proceeds of disposal is the proceeds realised by the personal representatives less any incidental costs (but only if they qualify as deductible under *TCGA 1992, s 38(1)(c)*) and assuming that none of the proceeds are required to meet liabilities of the estate. If the qualifying beneficiary has more than one residence the election under *TCGA 1992, s 222(5)(a)* (see **13.11**) must be made jointly by the personal representatives and the beneficiary (*TCGA 1992, s 225A*). This statutory relief replaced an extra statutory concession (ESC D5). The idea is not to deny relief to someone because the house happens to be sold by the personal representatives rather than the legatee, but HMRC consider that there is no justification to allow the benefit of the relief to be obtained by someone who did not occupy the house as a residence.

13.44 Where an inherited property is disposed of by a beneficiary (other than the surviving spouse) the beneficiary's period of ownership is deemed to begin on the date of death so there will be a restriction of his principal private residence relief if, as will normally be the case unless he lived with the deceased, he does not go into immediate occupation from the date of death (Tax Bulletin, Issue 12, August 1994).

Restriction Where Hold-over Relief Claimed

13.45 If principal private residence relief under *TCGA 1992, s 223* is claimed by an individual or trustees private residence relief does not apply if at an earlier time there had been a gift of the property (or a sale at an undervalue) on which relief was claimed under *TCGA 1992, s 260* (hold-over relief on transfer attracting IHT), and all or part of the held over amount is reflected in a reduction in the trustees' capital gains tax base cost, (*TCGA 1992, s 226A(1)* and *(2)*).

13.46 If the hold-over relief claim under *s 260* is made after the disposal of the property the private residence relief is withdrawn retrospectively (*TCGA 1992, s 226A(3)*). Revoking the hold-over claim will restore the right to principal private residence relief (*TCGA 1992, s 226A(6)*). However, such a revocation cannot be made more than four years after the end of the tax year in which the gift on which *s 260* relief was claimed took place. Accordingly, it is too late to revoke a claim made in 2011/12 or earlier and a claim for 2012/13 ceases to be revocable after 5 April 2017.

13.47 If the gift on which the hold-over election was made (all of them if more than one) took place before 10 December 2003, partial private residence relief is allowed. The house is treated as qualifying for private residence relief up to 9 December 2003 but not thereafter. Nor can the last three years of ownership attract relief.

13.48 The loss of relief does not apply if the house is owned by the trustees of a maintenance fund for an historic building and the trustees have elected under *ITA 2007, s 508*) to be taxed on the income of the trust in place of the settlor for every tax year since the gift on which the hold over relief claim was made (*TCGA 1992, s 226B*).

House Occupied by a Dependent Relative

13.49 Up to 5 April 1988, the private residence exemption also applied to a gain accruing to an individual on the disposal of an interest in a house which was the sole residence of a dependent relative of his (or his wife) provided rent-free and without any other consideration. Where a house was occupied by a relative at that date the exemption continues as long as the relative continues to occupy the property (*TCGA 1992, s 226(1)*). Once the relative moves out, a later period of occupation by a dependent relative, or even by the same person, will not attract exemption. If the relative ceased to occupy the property before 5 April 1988 no period after that date can accordingly attract exemption. It should be noted that the house must have been the relative's only residence during the period for which the exemption is claimed. It is not sufficient for it to have been his main residence. The payment of outgoings such as rates or electricity which are liabilities of the occupier would not debar the relief. However, strictly speaking, the relative must not pay the ground rent as this is a liability of the landlord, the relieving of which would constitute consideration given by the relative. It would similarly be dangerous for the relative to pay for structural repairs which would normally be payable by the landlord under an arm's-length lease. HMRC have nevertheless stated that, even where the relative makes such payments, they are prepared to grant the relief by concession provided that no net income is receivable by the owner taking one year with another. Net income for this purpose will be computed in accordance with the rules for taxing income from property, with the exception that a deduction will be allowed for mortgage payments (including the capital element) (HMRC Extra-Statutory Concession D20). This is a major concession. Nevertheless, it would be sensible for the relative not to make such payments if this can be avoided as HMRC concessions can be – and sometimes are – withdrawn without warning.

13.50 A dependent relative is the mother of the individual (or of his spouse) if she is widowed or living apart from her husband or a single woman in consequence of dissolution or annulment of her marriage, or any other relative of the taxpayer or his spouse who is incapacitated by old age or infirmity from maintaining himself (*TCGA 1992, s 226(5)(6)*). It should be particularly noted that the mother must have been married at some time to qualify under the automatic test. If she was an unmarried mother she can qualify as a dependant only if she is incapacitated by old age or infirmity from maintaining herself. In practice, HMRC do not apparently take this point but will allow the relief to an unmarried mother or mother-in-law (HMRC Capital Gains Manual, CG65582).

13.51 Unlike the relief for the individual's own residence or that for a house owned by a trust, the relief for a house occupied by a dependant is not automatic; it must be claimed (*TCGA 1992, s 226(2)*). The relief is additional to that for the individual's own house but not more than one house can qualify for relief as the residence of a dependant of the taxpayer or his spouse at any one time (*TCGA 1992, s 226(3)*). The Inspector of Taxes is empowered to require a person claiming the relief to prove either that his spouse did not own a property occupied by a dependent relative during the period for which the relief is claimed or, if she did, that she relinquishes her right to claim relief in respect of it for that period (*TCGA 1992, s 226(4)*). As the relief must be claimed, if a loss arises on a house provided for a dependent relative there is no restriction on that loss as no claim for relief is competent (HMRC Capital Gains Manual, CG65084). Although this relief no longer applies, if it is wished to provide a house for a dependent relative this can be done by purchasing it through a settlement and utilising the relief described at **13.40**.

Let Properties

13.52 Where the private residence exemption applies to a house which has been wholly or partly let as residential accommodation at any time during the period of ownership, up to £40,000 of chargeable gain on the property, to the extent that it arises by reason of the letting, is exempt from tax. The exemption is the lower of the gain applicable to the letting period, the gain qualifying for the private residence exemption, or £40,000 (*TCGA 1992, s 223(4)*). Where a property is owned jointly by a husband and wife, it appears that each is entitled to his or her own £40,000 exemption in relation to his or her share. If a loss arises on the disposal it is disallowable to the extent that the basic private residence relief would have been due in the event of a gain, but there is no further restriction under *s 223* (CG65080).

13.53 In the past HMRC took the view that to qualify for this relief the letting must be to a person who occupies the property as a residence. However, in *Owen v Elliott (1990 STC 469)* the Court of Appeal held that there is nothing in *s 223(4)* to restrict the meaning of the words 'residential accommodation', so they must be interpreted in accordance with ordinary use of the English language. The fact that different wording is used in *TCGA 1992, s 222* to confine that relief to dwelling-houses has no bearing on *s 223(4)*. Accordingly the taxpayer was entitled to the relief. In the *Owen* case the taxpayer used his property as a guest house, living in an annex in the summer but occupying the property itself in winter. He accordingly used the whole house as his principal residence for part of each year. As during the remainder of the year the property was let to guests who used it as residential accommodation, ie they lived there albeit generally only for one or two weeks, he was entitled to relief under *s 223(4)*. To qualify for the exemption, the owner must be entitled to the private residence exemption under *s 222*, ie this extra relief applies only to the individual's own house and not to one occupied by a dependent relative. It is not clear whether this relief extends to properties owned by trustees. The section refers to a gain accruing to an individual, but the reference to *TCGA 1992, s 225* in *sub-s (1)(a)* would be otiose if the *section* cannot apply to trustees. HMRC's view is that it does apply to a house owned by a trust (CG64716). The intention is to encourage an occupier to let off surplus accommodation where the house has become too large for him. As some relief is given under *s 222* if a house has been a person's main residence 'at any time in his period of ownership', an individual who acquires a residential investment property ought to consider occupying it for a short period, and electing for it to be his private residence for that period. This will not only in many cases exempt a significant fraction of the gain from tax – as both the short period of occupation and the last three years will qualify for relief under *s 223* – but will also provide this extra exemption of up to £40,000 for the taxable part. There is no limit to the number of such exemptions that a person can claim under *s 223(4)*. However, it is, of course, necessary to establish that the property in question was occupied as a residence, not merely lived in for a period.

Use of an Office at Home

13.54 One area of difficulty – on which even the experts cannot agree – is whether, by claiming a deduction against income tax for part of the running costs of one's house because a room is used as an office, this will forfeit a corresponding proportion of the private residence exemption when the house is sold.

13.55 For expenditure to qualify as a deduction in computing trading profits it must be 'wholly and exclusively expended for the purpose of the trade, profession or vocation' (*ITTOIA 2005, s 34(1)*). To qualify as a deduction against salary it must be an expense which the employee is 'necessarily obliged' to expend 'wholly, exclusively and necessarily in the performance of' the duties of his employment (*ITEPA 2003, s 336(1)*). The capital gains tax exemption is restricted where part of the house is 'used exclusively for the purposes of a trade or business or of a profession or vocation' (*TCGA 1992, s 224(1)*). Some people feel that if the office is also used for some other purpose, eg at weekends or one day a year, this will prevent *s 224(1)* from coming into operation but that such use would not prevent the expenditure on, say, rates being wholly and exclusively for business purposes as it would have needed to be incurred had the business use been exclusive. The author personally finds this argument unconvincing. HMRC will normally only allow an income tax deduction for council tax and rates if a room is set aside for business purposes, and by claiming a deduction (which requires the expense to have been incurred wholly and exclusively for the purpose of the business) one seems to be effectively conceding that the room is used exclusively for such purposes. However, HMRC seem to take a more relaxed view. They tell their staff that, 'The exclusive use test is a stringent one and you should not usually seek any restriction to relief for a room which has some measure of regular residential use. But occasional and very minor residential use should be disregarded. For example, if a doctor keeps private possessions in a room used as her surgery the surgery should still be regarded as exclusively in business use' (CG64663).

13.56 There should be no problems in claiming a deduction against trading or professional income for expenses such as telephone and electricity that depend on usage. One uses electricity wholly and exclusively for heating and lighting the home 'office' during the period it is being occupied as an office. Accordingly, the claiming of the deduction does not imply exclusive use of the room for business purposes. This does not, however, apply to council tax, or repairs which are incurred irrespective of the period that the room is actually occupied for a particular purpose. Indeed it is doubtful if such expenses can strictly qualify as a deduction under general principles as one does not pay council tax for individual rooms, one pays it by virtue of occupation of the house as such. Similarly, one carries out repairs to maintain the value of the house as a unit. Accordingly, in allowing a claim for such expenses HMRC are probably making a concession. HMRC will generally allow the deduction of a modest sum (usually £1 to £5 per week) for 'use of home as office' in calculating trading profits in lieu of claiming specific expenses. Such a claim would not jeopardise the capital gains tax exemption as it does not imply a claim that a specific area of the home is used exclusively for business.

13.57 In many cases, even if capital gains tax is payable, the problem is not of great practical significance. Suppose a house bought for £50,000 is sold seven years later for £90,000, one-eighth having been used for business. One-eighth of the capital gain of £40,000 is £5,000 which may well be covered by the capital gains tax annual exemption. Even if the gain were £140,000 so that £17,500 would be taxable, if the annual exemption is not used against other gains the tax would be a maximum of £1,792 (28% of £6,400). This is equivalent to £256 p.a. over the period of ownership, which is equivalent to the income tax saving achieved by claiming an annual deduction for council tax of £640 at 40%.

13.58 Curiously, *s 224(1)* does not mention use for the purpose of an employment. It may be that such use is covered as it constitutes use for the employer's trade or business (the *section* merely talks of 'a trade' not the taxpayer's trade). Alternatively, it may be that no restriction is competent where an employee has an office at his home.

13.59 HMRC accept that where the duties of an employment requires an employee to work at home and he uses a room or rooms exclusively for work purposes he can deduct a proportion of the council tax (HMRC Press Release, 16 March 1993).

13.60 In practice it is difficult to obtain a deduction against salary for any expenses of working at home. HMRC tell their staff:

> 'It is not enough for the employee to demonstrate that he or she works from home, or even that there is an obligation placed on them to work at home. There needs to be something more; that there is an objective requirement resulting from the nature of the employment itself that requires some or all of the duties of the employment to be carried out at home and at no other place. Many employees do some of their work at home because they do not have time to complete it during the working day. That is a matter of personal choice and no deduction should be permitted. Some employees work at home because the place at which they usually work has limited opening hours and they need to work outside those hours. No deduction should be permitted in these cases. Even though the employer does not provide an alternative place at which all of the duties could be carried out there is no obligation that the work must be carried out at home … A deduction can only be permitted where the nature of the employment itself requires that the duties must be carried out at home and cannot be carried out in any other place.'

13.61 Mr Ainslie was semi-retired. He was employed by a firm of surveyors. He would not have been prepared to take the job if he had to travel every day to their offices and it was agreed that he should work from home. His contract of employment specifically stated, 'You will be required to work from your home.' He sought to attribute £4,000 of his salary as a fee for the use of his home. The Commissioner accepted that the employer had a contractual licence to use, through the taxpayer, the room he used at home for his work. However, they had not attributed any part of Mr Ainslie's salary to such use. The Commissioner accepted both that a room dedicated to office use was needed and this must have been obvious to the employer from the outset. Nevertheless, as no sum was attributed by the parties to such use, a deduction could not be made from Mr Ainslie's agreed salary to reflect it (*Ainslie v Buckley, 2002 STC (SCD) 132*).

13.62 For 2013/14 onwards, a fixed deduction can be claimed for the use of a person's home for the purpose of a trade (but not apparently a profession or vocation) instead of calculating the actual business element of the taxpayer's expenses (*ITTOIA 2005, s 94H*). The deduction for each month or part of a month for which the property is used is:

Number of hours worked*	Monthly deduction	Annual equivalent
25 or more	£10.00	£120.00
51 or more	£18.00	£216.00
101 or more	£26.00	£312.00

* hours spent wholly and exclusively on work done by the taxpayer, or an employee of the taxpayer, in the taxpayer's home wholly and exclusively for the purposes of the trade (*ITTOIA 2005, s 94H(3), (4), (4A*) inserted by *FA 2013, Sch 5* and amended by *FA 2016, s 24*). If a person has more than one home, the two are treated as if they were a single home for the purpose of this calculation (*ITTOIA 2005, 94H(5)*). The Treasury have power by regulations to amend these scale figures (*ITTOIA 2005, s 94H(6)*).

13.63 Where the trade is a partnership trade, the calculation is done separately for each partner who has business use of the home. For 2016/17 onwards, if one partner uses these scale figures all the partners must do so (*ITTOIA 2005, s 94H(5A)* inserted by *FA 2016, s 24*). For 2016/17 onwards, an hour cannot be counted twice where more than one person works in the home (*ITTOIA 2005, s 94H(4B)*). For example, suppose the taxpayer works at home for two hours a working day (40 hours a month) and an employee joins him for half-an-hour a day. The total eligible hours is 40 not 50. If the employee stays at the taxpayer's home for an extra three-quarters of an hour a day after the taxpayer leaves, so works at the home one-and-a-quarter hours a day, the extra three-quarters of an hour when he is there on his own is counted, bringing the number of hours up to 55 (assuming a 20 working day month).

13.64 If a person carries on a trade at any premises, those premises are used mainly for the purpose of the trade but are also used by the taxpayer as a home, and expenses in relation to the premises are incurred mainly (albeit not wholly and exclusively) for the purposes of the trade he can deduct the expenses from 2013/14 onwards less a fixed deduction to cover the private use element (*ITTOIA 2005, s 94I(1)–(3)* inserted by *FA 2013, Sch 5*). The deduction depends on how many people use the premises as a home or stay at the premises otherwise than in the course of the trade, namely:

Number of occupiers	Monthly reduction	Annualised figure
1	£350	£2,700
2	£500	£6,000
3 or more	£650	£7,800

(*ITTOIA 2005, s 94I(4)–(6).*)

Again, a part of a month counts as a month. It is not clear what is meant by 'stays at the premises'. It appears to mean spends one or more nights there but it is a little startling if Parliament feels that, if a small part of the business premises is used as a home, the taxpayer deserves to be penalised if he lets guests visit overnight. HMRC have power by statutory instrument to amend the figures (*ITTOIA 2005, s 94I(7)*). For 2016/17 onwards, if the trade is carried on in partnership, if one partner adopts this method all must do so (even if different partners occupy different premises) (*ITTOIA 2005, s 94I(6A)* inserted by *FA 2016, s 24(10)*).

Letting the House

13.65 HMRC seem to accept that if the owner moves out of the house and lets it, for example because he wishes to retain it as an investment or because it is an inopportune time to sell, the starting point for his UK property business is the value of the property at the date that he decides to let it (see example 2 in HMRC Business Income Manual, BIM45680). That means that he can mortgage the property up to that value (not merely up to its original cost) and obtain income tax relief against the rental income for the mortgage interest even if he does not use the funds raised in the business – because he is simply withdrawing the initial capital of his property business. It follows that if he chooses not to remortgage initially but does so at a later date he should be able to obtain tax relief for the interest on a borrowing up to the value of the property at the commencement of the letting activity – and should be entitled to relief on a higher amount if he can show that he uses the extra funds in the business.

Inheritance Tax

13.66 For most people the private residence forms their major asset. As it is non income-producing, a gift of an interest in the private residence appears attractive as it will not affect the donor's standard of living. Unfortunately in most cases the anti-avoidance rules on reservation of benefit (see **18.59**) prevent such a gift being effective. Indeed they can increase the tax liability as the effect is to treat the property as an asset of both the donor and the donee.

13.67 Because of the difficulties in generating an effective gift of an interest in one's principal private residence during one's lifetime, conventional planning is for the house to be owned jointly (as tenants in common) by husband and wife and for each to leave his share to the children by his will. This triggers an inheritance tax charge on that share, but in many cases, particularly where there is a mortgage on the property, this will fall within the £325,000 inheritance tax nil rate band. Accordingly if the remainder of the estate is left to the surviving spouse there will be little or no tax to pay. The surviving spouse can remain in occupation of the house by virtue of her ownership of the other half-share as joint owners are each entitled to use of the asset. The surviving spouse can make *inter vivos* gifts to the children of other assets which do not have reservation of benefit problems. In this way assets that are surplus to the surviving spouse's needs can be passed IHT-free to the children leaving only her half-share of the house and the assets she needs to meet her standard of living to suffer tax on her death to the extent that they exceed her own £325,000 nil rate band. Where the value of half of the house significantly exceeds £325,000 it is possible to limit the gift to the children to that level by providing that they are entitled to £325,000 to be satisfied by the transfer to them of such proportion of the private residence as is equal to that sum.

13.68 The only problem with this scenario is that in law joint owners hold the property on trust for sale which means that any one of them can apply to the court for an order that the property should be sold. The planning relies on the children forbearing from doing this. Unfortunately this does not always work. There have been cases where the children have forced a sale to get their hands on their share of the proceeds leaving the mother homeless, forced to move into a smaller house or forced to move into a residential home, thus thwarting the intention of the deceased spouse. The risk can be minimised in a number of ways. The easiest is for the first half-share of the property to be left not to the children but to a trust for their benefit – although under the rule in *Saunders v Vautier ([1835–42] All ER Rep 58)* if all the beneficiaries of a settlement are of legal capacity they can bring the settlement to an end, so the trust needs to include either infants or charities if the children are all adult. Provided that the trustees are not themselves the children and the trust deed is drafted carefully so that it would not put them in breach of trust to leave the surviving spouse undisturbed, they can normally be relied upon to respect the settlor's wishes.

13.69 An alternative approach was used by Mr and Mrs Evans. By her Will Mrs Evans left her half-share in the private residence in trust for her daughter.

Unfortunately she was not prepared to trust the trustees. She included a provision: 'While my husband … remains alive and desires to reside in the property and keeps the same in good repair … my trustees shall not make any objection to such residence and shall not disturb or restrict it in any way and shall not take any steps to enforce the trust for sale on which the property is held or to realise my share therein or to obtain any rent or profit from the property.' Furthermore she provided that only on the death of Mr Evans would the daughter become entitled to her mother's share of the property – although it was accepted that such wording did not actually postpone the interest of the daughter until her father's death. It was held that the provision preventing a sale, etc. was not merely an administrative provision. It conferred real benefit on the husband as by nullifying the rights of the trustees to exploit their half-share the Will effectively gave the husband the exclusive occupation of the property for the rest of his life. This was held to create a life interest in favour of the husband in the deceased wife's half-share. As a life tenant is treated for IHT purposes as owning the assets in which his interest subsists, the effect was that on Mr Evans' death IHT was payable on the whole value of the property not merely his half-share (*CIR v Lloyds Private Banking Ltd, 1998 STC 559*).

13.70 In *Woodhall v CIR (2000 STC (SCD) 558) (SpC 261)* the will required the trustees to permit all or any of the deceased's three children, Annie, Alan and Eric, to reside in the house. At the date of Alan's death he was the sole person residing there. HMRC claimed that he had an interest in possession in the house as he had a present right to present enjoyment, the test laid down in *Pearson v CIR (1980 STC 318)*. The executors claimed that Alan did not have a right to live in the house as the executors had discretion over which of the three children could live there. Alternatively if he had such a right Alan's interest could not exceed 50% as Eric also had a right to live there (Annie having died earlier). It was held that the will did not give the executors a dispositive power to decide who should occupy the house but merely an administrative power to permit such of the children as wanted to occupy the house to do so and if more than one jointly with the other. However, the Commissioner accepted that Alan had an interest in possession in only half of the house as Eric also had the right to live there. This may point to a way to reduce the IHT exposure. The larger the class of people entitled to live in the house the smaller the value passing on a death. Of course in practice no one wants to risk having to share occupation with strangers. Nevertheless instead of giving a right of occupation to A it would be sensible to give the right to A, his spouse whilst they are living together and the issue of A. Indeed if A is unmarried it might be possible also to include such other persons as A may from time to time nominate, with A having a power to revoke such nomination.

13.71 A similar decision was reached in *Faulkner v CIR (2001 STC (SCD) 112)*. In that case the will gave Mr and Mrs Harrison or the survivor of them a right to live in the house as long as they should wish. After Mrs Harrison's death Mr Harrison continued to occupy the house. On his death HMRC claimed IHT on the whole value of the house. The will trustees contended that he only had a licence to occupy. In the alternative they claimed that if he had an interest in possession he held it jointly with the residuary beneficiaries. The Special Commissioner held that the will did not give the trustees any dispositive power to decide whether the Harrisons should occupy the house and in what way, whether by licence or otherwise; on the contrary it directed them to permit the Harrisons to occupy the house. They were entitled to claim the right of occupation, which amounted to an interest in possession. The interest in possession was not shared with the residuary beneficiaries; they were not able to claim any interest in the house at the time when Mr Harrison had the right to occupy it.

13.72 The taxpayer was successful in *Judge (exor of Walden decd) v HMRC (2005 STC (SCD) 863).* The deceased's will left his house on trust for sale (with the consent of his widow during her lifetime) and provided that the trustees should permit her the use and enjoyment of the property 'for such period or periods as they shall in their absolute discretion think fit'. HMRC contended that this meant that there should be no sale of the house so long as the widow wished to reside there, so that she had an interest in possession. It was held that he did not have an interest in possession as she did not have the right as against the trustees to occupy the property for any period because the trustees had an absolute discretion as to whether or not they would permit her to do so. The wording whilst preventing the trustees from selling the house does not of course prevent them from evicting the widow and renting it out, so it does not fully protect the widow.

13.73 *Wolff v Wolff (2004 STC 1633)* is a salutary lesson for the tax planner. Mr and Mrs Wolff entered into a reversionary lease scheme to seek to avoid inheritance tax. Under this, they granted a 125-year lease of their house to their two daughters starting on 4 June 2017 at a peppercorn rent. In late 2001 they went to a different solicitor to reconsider their wills. He pointed out to them, which they had not previously appreciated, that from June 2017 (when they would both be about 80) they had no right to stay in the house and would be at the mercy of their daughters or their successors in title – and if the daughters allowed them to remain in the house free of charge, that would create a reservation of benefit which would negate the IHT saving they were hoping for and render the scheme pointless. As a result, Mr and Mrs Wolff applied to the court to set aside the lease on the grounds that they did not understand its effect when they entered into it. Luckily the judge agreed that the Wolffs made a mistake as to the legal effect of the transaction and, as it was a serious mistake, it gave rise to the equity of setting the lease aside. Luckily his initial reaction was that their mistake was as to the consequences of their transaction, not to its effect, as that would not have given grounds to set it aside.

13.74 The decision in *Cook and another (executors of Watkins, decd) v CIR (2002 STC (SCD) 318)* seems particularly harsh, although it should be stressed that it was the executors, not HMRC, who had contended for an interest in possession. Mrs Watkins died on 12 December 1999. Her house consisted of two flats one of which was let and the other of which was occupied by her and her husband. Her will contained a direction to the trustees that her husband might use that flat as his principal place of residence provided that he paid all of the outgoings. On Mrs Watkins' death Mr Watkins, who was 89, went to live with his daughter. He returned to the flat on several occasions and made limited use of it, but also removed personal items. His daughter considered that her father was living permanently with her. Mr Watkins was admitted to hospital on 4 January 2000. Later in January the executors changed the locks so that Mr Watkins had no access to the flat. Mr Watkins died in hospital on 10 February 2000. It was held that Mr Watkins had an interest in possession in the property. There is a presumption that a person will accept a legacy unless the contrary was proved, and the Special Commissioners felt that the evidence in favour of a disclaimer was not strong enough to displace that presumption. It may be that this is a peculiarity of Scottish law and would not apply to an English life tenancy. HMRC's Inheritance Tax Manual states (at IHT35046): 'Where there is an alimentary life rent which has been enjoyed it should be maintained that … such a benefit cannot be renounced.'

13.75 It is almost a standard practice where property is held as tenants in common by a husband and wife and they have children for the wills of each to provide that an amount of assets equal to the IHT nil rate band should go to the children or a trust for the benefit of the children. Where the major asset is the matrimonial home there are various ways to achieve this without forcing (or risking forcing) a sale of the house. One common way is for the house to be transferred to the surviving spouse subject to her giving an undertaking to make a payment equal to the nil rate band to the children's trust when the house is sold. If the house is not sold the debt to the trustees ought to be deductible in calculating the IHT on the death of the second spouse. This is what Mrs Phizackerley did. Unfortunately when her husband died HMRC refused to allow a deduction for the debt on the basis that when the house was initially acquired it was acquired as joint tenants with money provided wholly by Mr Phizackerley and the joint tenancy was subsequently severed so creating a gift by Mr Phizackerley to his wife. The IHT legislation denies a deduction for a debt if the consideration for the debt consisted of property derived from the deceased. The debt due by Mr Phizackerley's estate was part consideration for the transfer to him by Mrs Phizackerley's executors of her half share in the house and that half share was property 'derived from' Mr Phizackerley. The Special Commissioner agreed (*Phizackerley v HMRC (2007 STC (SCD) 328)*). Most commentators seem to have adopted the view that this trap only applies where the joint tenancy is severed subsequent to purchase. As the Special Commissioner felt it unnecessary to decide whether the disposition that triggered the problem was a gift of cash or a gift of a share in the property it is hard to see why the problem does not arise in any case where one spouse provides all of the funds for the acquisition of the house and both spouses own property as tenants in common. A tenancy in common enables the first spouse to die to dispose of his interest in the house to the children rather than it passing automatically to the surviving spouse, so is probably the most common method of joint ownership. Accordingly it is probably safest to avoid using a debt or charge in such circumstances, albeit that the alternative may be to give the children or trustees a right in the property. An alternative approach is to leave the children an interest in the matrimonial home equal to the nil rate band plus the additional residence nil rate band (see **18.111**). This has the advantage that it gifts the growth in value of the interest too, but it makes the conveyancing a bit messy.

Deed of Variation

13.76 *IHTA 1994, s 142* provides that where, within two years after a person's death, any of the dispositions made on death (whether by will or on an intestacy) are varied by an instrument in writing made by the persons who would benefit from the disposition, the change is treated as having been made by the deceased. Certain formalities need to be complied with where such a deed of variation is entered into. *Soulter's Executing v CIR (2002 STC (SCD) 385)* concerned such a deed of variation. Miss Soulter owned a property which was occupied jointly by herself and her friend Miss Greenlees. In her will Miss Soulter granted her friend a free liferent and use and occupation of the house as long as she wished to reside there. Miss Soulter died in November 1999 and Miss Greenlees died a year later, having occupied the house in the interim. The two sets of executors entered into a deed of arrangement under *IHTA 1984, s 142* to remove the liferent provision in Miss Soulter's will. It was held that as the liferent ceased on Miss Greenlees' death her executors had nothing that they could vary. The deed merely pretended that Miss Greenlees' liferent did not happen. It did, and it ceased, and there is accordingly no content in the purported variation. This seems to be based on the premise that for a variation to be effective the asset has to exist at the time a deed of variation is entered into because *s 142(1)* refers to 'an instrument in writing made by the persons … who benefit … under the disposition'. The decision is hard to follow. Although Miss Greenlees' executors were not persons who benefited, Miss Greenlees herself was, and it is normally accepted that executors can act on behalf of the deceased.

13.77 HMRC apparently accept that where property is held under a joint tenancy it is possible to sever the joint tenancy after death (ie to turn it into a tenancy in common) as part of a deed of arrangement.

Income Tax Charge on Pre-owned Assets

13.78 An annual income tax charge applies from 2005/06 onwards in relation to 'pre-owned assets'. Although it is a charge to income tax, it is an inheritance tax anti-avoidance provision and is imposed only where inheritance tax has been avoided. It applies where an individual occupies land (either alone or jointly) and at some time after 17 March 1986 (the date of introduction of the inheritance tax reservation of benefit rules) either:

(*a*) that individual owned an interest in that land (or in other property the proceeds of the disposal of which were directly or indirectly applied by another person towards the acquisition of an interest in the land) and has disposed of all or part of that interest other than by an excluded transaction; or

(*b*) that individual had directly or indirectly provided any of the consideration given by another person for the acquisition of an interest in the land (or of other property which funded the acquisition of an interest in the land).

(*FA 2004, Sch 15, para 3*.)

13.79 The income tax charge is on the 'appropriate rental value' less any payments which in pursuance of a legal obligation are made by the individual during the taxable period to the owner of the land in respect of its occupation by that individual (*FA 2004, Sch 15, para 4(1)*). This allows a deduction for rent actually paid. It should be noted that it must be paid under a legal obligation; a voluntary payment will not suffice. It must also apparently be paid in the tax year (or the part of it during which the property is occupied); a payment in a subsequent year will not qualify.

13.80 The appropriate rental value is

$$\text{Rental value of the land} \times \frac{\text{value at the valuation date of interest previously disposed of}}{\text{value of the land at the valuation date}}$$

(*FA 2004, Sch 15, para 4(2)*.)

Where the property previously disposed of was the same as that currently occupied, the numerator and denominator will be the same, so the charge will be on the rental value of the land. However, where what was originally disposed of was not an interest in the entire land or a lesser interest than that currently owned, the formula limits the charge to the proportion of the current rental value that relates to the amount initially disposed of. Where what was gifted in the original disposal was not the land but some other asset, such part of the value of the land occupied as can reasonably be attributed to the property originally disposed of is used in place of the value of the interest previously disposed of. If the original disposal was a sale at an undervalue, the amount to be included in the numerator in the above formula is obviously part only of the value, namely the part of the value at the time of the original sale that was represented by the undervalue (*FA 2004, Sch 15, para 4(2), (4)*). The valuation date is such date as the Treasury prescribe by Regulation in relation to the year. They have prescribed 6 April in the tax year (or the date the land was first used by the individual if later (*Charge to Income Tax by Reference to Enjoyment of Previously Owned Assets Regulations 2005, SI 2005/724, reg 2*). The Regulation can also provide for a value to be arrived at by reference to an earlier valuation date subject to any prescribed adjustments (*FA 2004, Sch 15, para 4(5)(a), (b)*).

13.81 The rental value of the land is the rent which would have been payable for the period for which the property is occupied if it had been let to the individual at an annual rent equal to its annual value (*FA 2004, Sch 13, para 4(3)*). This is the rent which might reasonably be expected to be obtained on a letting of the land from year to year (on the basis that the only amounts that can be deducted in respect of services provided by the landlord are amounts in respect of the cost to the landlord of providing services other than the repair, insurance or maintenance of the property) if the tenant undertook to pay all taxes, rates and charges usually paid by a tenant and the landlord undertook to bear the cost of the repairs, insurance and any other expenses necessary for maintaining the property in a state to command the rent (*FA 2004, Sch 15, para 5*). To avoid having to ascertain that rental value each year, the Treasury have been given power by Regulation to provide for that value to be based on the rents for an earlier year subject to any prescribed adjustments (*FA 2004, Sch 15, para 4(5)(b)*). They have done so in the Regulations mentioned at **13.80**. These provide that the rental value need not be ascertained annually but needs to be revalued every five years (*reg 4*). Where the property was held at 6 April 2005 this required a revaluation at 6 April 2010 and will require another at 6 April 2015.

13.82 Similar rules apply to chattels, which would include furniture in a house if that was gifted with the house (*FA 2004, Sch 15, paras 6, 7*).

13.83 The charge does not apply if the previous disposal of the property was:

(*a*) a disposal of the individual's whole interest in the property (except for any rights expressly reserved by him over the property) by either an arm's length transaction or by a transaction such as might be expected to be made at arm's length between persons not connected with each other;

(*b*) a transfer to the individual's spouse (or under a court order to a former spouse);

(*c*) a gift into a settlement in which his spouse or former spouse has an interest in possession;

(*d*) a disposition in favour of his spouse or a child of either for the maintenance of that other person falling within *IHTA 1984, s 11*; or

(*e*) an outright gift to an individual which fell wholly within *IHTA 1984, s 19* (annual exemption) or *s 20* (small gifts).

(*FA 2004, Sch 15, para 10(1)*.)

13.84 Nor does it apply if the event that triggers the charge is a contribution to the cost of the acquisition of an interest in land by another person and either:

(*a*) the other person was the donor's spouse (or former spouse if the contribution was made under a court order);

(*b*) the contribution was made to a settlement in which the individual's spouse or former spouse has an interest in possession;

(*c*) the contribution was an outright gift of money and was made at least seven years before the earliest date on which the individual met the condition in *s 3(1)(a)*, ie first occupied the land; or

(*d*) the contribution was a disposition for maintenance of family within *IHTA 1984, s 11* or an outright gift within *IHTA 1984, ss 19* or *20*.

(*FA 2004, Sch 15, para 10(2)*.)

13.85 The exemptions in **13.83**(*c*) and **13.84**(*b*) do not apply after the interest in possession of the spouse or former spouse has come to an end otherwise than on her death (*FA 2004, Sch 15, para 10(3)*).

13.86 The charge also does not arise if the value of the property is included in the taxpayer's estate for IHT purposes, namely:

(*a*) If the relevant property, ie the property previously disposed of or the property representing the consideration provided, is part of the taxpayer's estate for IHT purposes (*FA 2004, Sch 15, para 11(1)* and *(9)*).

(*b*) If other property which derived its value from the relevant property and whose value, so far as attributable to that relevant property, is not substantially less than the value of the relevant property is included in the taxpayer's estate. If the value is substantially less, the income tax charge is not on the full rental value but on such proportion of that value as is reasonable to take account of the amount included in the taxpayer's estate (*FA 2004, Sch 15, para 11(1)* and *(2)*).

(*c*) If the property (or other property that derived its value from it) falls to be treated as subject to a reservation of benefit (see **18.81**) (or would do so but for one of the exemptions in *FA 1986, ss 102(5)(d)–(l)* (gifts to charities, to political parties, to housing associations for national purposes etc, to maintenance funds for historic buildings and to employee trusts), *102B(4)* (see **18.94**(*c*)) or *102C(3)* or *Sch 20, para 6* (see **18.85** and **18.95**)). For the purpose of applying this exemption where the taxpayer made a contribution towards the cost of someone else's acquisition of a property, it has to be assumed that a gift of money can give rise to a reservation of benefit (in spite of *FA 1986, Sch 2, para 2(2)(b)* which precludes it from doing so). In the case of a gift to a maintenance fund the fund must obviously also continue to meet the appropriate qualifying conditions. Again, if the reservation relates to property that derives its value from the relevant property but whose value is substantially less than that of the relevant property the rental charge is reduced (*FA 2004, Sch 15, para 11(3)–(5), (8)* and *(10)*).

However, if the value of the taxpayer's estate is reduced by an 'excluded liability' the exemption applies only to the extent that the value of the property exceeds the excluded liability. An excluded liability is one where the creation of the liability and any transaction by virtue of which the taxpayer's estate came to include the relevant property (or property derived from it) were associated operations within *IHTA 1984, s 268* (*FA 2004, Sch 15, para 11(6)* and *(7)*). Suppose, for example, a person sold his house to a trust for £500,000 leaving the proceeds outstanding and settled the loan account for the benefit of his children. The house is now worth £600,000. The £500,000 is an excluded liability so a benefit charge will arise on five-sixths of the rental value of the house.

13.87 There are a number of exemptions where the taxpayer is either non-resident or non-domiciled in the UK:

(*a*) the charge does not apply if the taxpayer is not UK resident during the year;

(*b*) if the taxpayer is resident in the UK but not domiciled here (or deemed domiciled here for IHT purposes), the charge does not apply to non-UK property; and

(*c*) if the taxpayer is resident and domiciled (or deemed domiciled) in the UK, the charge does not apply to property which is excluded property within *IHTA 1984, s 48(3)(a)* (ie non-UK property held by a settlement where the settlor was non-UK domiciled at the time he created the settlement).

(*FA 2004, Sch 15, para 12.*)

It is arguable that in the situation where a trust within (*c*) owns shares in an offshore company which itself owns a UK property and the taxpayer is a life tenant of the trust the charge does not apply as the shares in the offshore company are deemed to be part of the taxpayer's estate (and thus the exemption in **13.86**(*a*) above applies) albeit that in determining the amount of IHT payable on death, no account is to be taken of the value of such property (*IHTA 1984, s 3(2)*). HMRC seem likely to resist such an argument, though.

13.88 There is also a *de minimis* exemption. No charge arises if the appropriate rental value for a tax year does not exceed £5,000. If a taxpayer is chargeable in respect of both land and chattels (or intangible property) the £5,000 figure applies to the aggregate of the charge for the year (*FA 2004, Sch 15, para 13*).

13.89 The Treasury have power by regulation to confer further exemptions (*FA 2004, Sch 15, para 14*). They have exempted a disposal of part of an interest in land where the disposal was by a transaction made at arm's length with an unconnected person (or if it was made before 7 March 2005 and there was no consideration in money or readily convertible assets (as defined for employment income purposes) it was made by a transaction such as might be expected to be made between unconnected persons acting at arm's length) (*reg 5*). This lets out equity release plans for the elderly. The Minister announced in July 2005 that relief against double taxation would be introduced to cover the situation where a potentially exempt transfer crystallises on the death of the donor where the gift was of a debt owned by donor, the debt was consideration for the acquisition of an asset from that donor and the full value of the asset (or of property derived from it) is chargeable to IHT as part of the donor's estate. The appropriate regulations do not yet appear to have been published.

13.90 A variation or disclaimer under a deed of arrangement within *IHTA 1984, s 144*, or a disposal under one of the other transactions within *IHTA 1984, s 18* (compliance with testator's request under *IHTA 1984, s 143* or an election by the surviving spouse under *Administration of Estates Act 1925, s 47A*), is disregarded if it is not treated for IHT purposes as a transfer of value by the taxpayer (*FA 2004, Sch 15, para 16*). For example, suppose a deceased father left his house to his surviving spouse. By a deed of arrangement within *s 144* she redirected the house to her son. Later, she occupies the house. As *s 144* deems the disposal to have been effected by the deceased, it is not a pre-owned asset of the surviving spouse.

13.91 If the taxpayer is chargeable to income tax both under *Sch 15, para 3* (land) (or *para 6* – chattels) and under *para 8* (intangible property, such as a lease) by reference to intangible property which derives its value, in whole or in part, from the land (or chattel) he is not taxed twice; instead whichever head of charge produces the larger taxable amount applies (*FA 2004, Sch 15, para 18*).

13.92 If a person is already taxable on a benefit in kind in relation to the property under *ITEPA 2003* because he occupies the property by reason of his employment, the ITEPA charge takes priority and the charge under *Sch 15* is limited to any excess over the ITEPA charge (*FA 2004, Sch 15, para 19*). The two will normally be different as the ITEPA charge is in most cases largely based on the cost of the property not its rental value (see **23.51**).

Election to Apply IHT

13.93 The charge can be avoided completely by electing to treat the property as subject to a reservation of benefit for IHT purposes. The election must be made in such manner as may be prescribed. The Treasury have prescribed that it must be made in writing using form IHT 500 (*Income Tax Benefits Received by Former Owner of Property) (Election for Inheritance Tax Treatment) Regulations 2007 (SI 2007 No 3000)*). It must be made on or before the filing date for the individual's tax return for the first year in which the charge would otherwise arise – although if a reasonable excuse can be established HMRC can extend the time limit. The election can be withdrawn or amended at any time during the life of the taxpayer but this must be done by the filing date of the tax return to which the charge relates (*FA 2004, Sch 15, paras 21–23*). It should particularly be noted that once a taxable benefit has arisen it is too late to elect even in respect of a subsequent year (unless there is a reasonable excuse). For example, suppose a taxpayer decided not to elect for 2005/06 but accepted the charge. In 2009/10 he changed his mind. He will have to continue to pay the charge.

13.94 This means that the election needed to be made by 31 January 2007 where the taxpayer occupied the property during 2005/06. If he did not do so but first occupied it in 2013/14, the election would have needed to be made by 31 January 2015. HMRC have power to accept a late election (*FA 2004, Sch 15, para 23(3)*). However, they have said that they will do so only if the taxpayer can show that an event beyond his control prevented him making the election by the due date. They also envisage that they would accept a late election where the taxpayer can show that he was unaware – and could not reasonably have been aware – that he was liable for a tax charge under the provision and he elects within a reasonable time of becoming aware. They also say that the taxpayer will have to show that the failure to elect is not the result of either taking active steps to avoid both the charge and the IHT gift with reservation rules or wishing to avoid committing himself pending clarification of the effects of the election (Guidance Notes 13.6.2007 and 26.10.2007).

13.95 Where the full value of the property does not attract the rental charge, only the chargeable proportion (see **13.80**) (of the value at the date of death or ceasing to occupy the property, not of the value at the time of the gift) is brought into the taxpayer's estate. If the property is disposed of during the taxpayer's lifetime, any property which is substituted for it must also be treated as subject to a reservation (*FA 2004, Sch 15, para 21*).

13.96 HMRC have said that, in their view, none of the variants of the home loan or double trust scheme that were being used in 2005 succeeded in circumventing the reservation of benefit rules. However, they recommended that taxpayers who entered into such schemes and have taken the view that the pre-owned asset rules apply should continue to do so. If HMRC's view ultimately proves correct, they will refund the income tax paid (with interest) irrespective of any time limits for repayment that might otherwise apply (HMRC Notice, 6 March 2012). This suggests that they intend to take a test case or cases to the Tribunal.

Chapter 14

Artificial Transactions in Land – CTA 2010, Part 8ZB; ITA 2007, Part 9A

14.1 *CTA 2010, Pt 8ZB* (and its income tax equivalent *ITA 2007, Pt 9A*) constitute one of the main anti-avoidance provisions. They have rewritten and extended earlier anti-avoidance rules. They apply to disposals after 4 July 2016 (*FA 2016, ss 81(1), 82(1)*) although they replace earlier legislation aimed broadly at the same sort of transaction. They are directed specifically at property transactions. Their purpose is to prevent property dealing profits being disguised as capital. They will not normally apply to a straight purchase and sale of a property; that is likely to be taxable already as a dealing profit if the conditions necessary to bring the provisions into play are met, and operate only where a profit is not taxable as income, ie where the gain would otherwise either be taxable as a capital gain or be outside the scope of UK tax completely. They introduce new *ss 517A* to *517U* into *ITA 2007* and *ss 356OA* to *356OT* into *CTA 2010*. These provisions apply both to UK residents and to non-residents.

14.2 The provisions apply if either:

(*a*) a person acquiring, holding or developing land in the UK;

(*b*) a person who is associated with such a person at a relevant time; or

(*c*) a person who is a party to, or concerned in, an arrangement which

- (i) is effected with respect to all or part of the land; and
- (ii) enables a profit or gain to be realised by any indirect method or by any series of transactions,

realises a profit or gain from a disposal of the land and one of four conditions are met (*ITA 2007, s 517B(1)–(3); CTA 2010, s 356OB(1)–(3)*).

14.3 The four conditions are:

A. The main purpose (or one of the main purposes) of acquiring the land was to realise a profit or gain from disposing of the land.

B. The main purpose (or one of the main purposes) of acquiring any property deriving its value from the land was to realise a profit or gain from disposing of the land.

C. The land is held as trading stock.

D. If the land has been developed, the main purpose (or one of the main purposes) of developing the land was to realise a profit or gain from disposing of the land when developed.

(*ITA 2007, s 517B(4)–(7)); CTA 2010, s 356OB(4)–(7).*)

14.4 For the purpose of **14.2**(*b*) above, a relevant period is any time in the period from the time the activities of the project begin to six months after the disposal at **14.2** (*ITA 2007, s 517B(8); CTA 2010, s 356OB(8)*). The project for this purpose means all activities carried out for the purposes of dealing in or developing the land and any other purposes mentioned in conditions A–D (*ITA 2007, s 517B(9); CTA 2010, s 356OB(9)*). A person, A, is associated with another person, B, if A is connected to B within *ITA 2007, ss 993–994* (or *CTA 2010, s 1122* as the case may be) (see **Appendix 1**) or A is related to B (*ITA 2007, s 517B(10); CTA 2010, s 356OB(10)*).

14.5 A is related to B, for this purpose:

(*a*) Throughout any period for which A and B are consolidated for accounting purposes, ie.their financial results for a period are comprised in group accounts (or are required to be comprised in group accounts, or would be required but for an exemption). Group accounts for this purpose are accounts prepared under the *Companies Act 2006, s 399* or any corresponding provision of the law of a territory outside the UK.

(*b*) On any day on which the participation condition is met. This condition is met on a day if, within the period of six months beginning with that day, one of the parties participates (directly or indirectly) in the management, control or capital of the other, or the same person or persons directly or indirectly participates in the management, control or capital of both.

(*c*) On any day on which the 25% investment condition is met in relation to them. This is met if one of them has a 25% investment in the other or a third person has a 25% investment in each of them. *TIOPA 2010, s 259NC* applies for the purposes of determining whether a person has a 25% investment in another person for this purpose as it applies for the purposes of *TIOPA 2010, s 259NB(2)* and *TIOPA 2010, ss 157(2), 158(4), 159(2)* and *160(2)* (which contain definitions used for *s 259NA*) obviously also apply.

(*ITA 2007, s 517U(1)–(7); CTA 2010, s 356OT(1)–(7).*)

14.6 Where the provision applies, the profit or gain must be treated for income tax purposes as profits of a trade carried on by the chargeable person. If the chargeable person is non-UK resident, the trade is his trade of dealing in or developing UK land (see below). The profits are treated as arising in the tax year in which the profit or gain is realised (*ITA 2007, s 517C(3); CTA 2010, s 356OC(3)*) (*ITA 2007, s 517C(1)–(4); CTA 2010, s 356OC(1)–(4)*). The provision does not apply to the extent that the profit or gain would be taxed as income apart from the section. Accordingly the majority of land transactions by UK residents will not be affected by the provision. It should be noted that this provision does not treat the deemed gain as miscellaneous income. It treats it as a trading profit or loss. This probably means that a loss is a normal trading loss which will qualify for sideways loss relief. It also needs to be appreciated that the four conditions at **14.3** are all indicia of trading. The provision cannot apply, however complex the transactions entered into may be, unless the acquisition of the land itself was for trading. The only exception to this is Condition B at **14.3** where the vehicle holding the land was itself acquired with an intention to trade it. It should also be noted that *ss 517B* and *356OB* require someone to hold or develop the land itself. They are not concerned with indirect realisations. As such they are unlikely to apply very often, as the profit will already arise from a trading transaction. It is only in circumstances where that trading profit is diverted, or partly diverted, to someone else that the provision can apply.

14.7 This provision applies to capital gains as well as income gains (*ITA 2007, ss 517C(5); CTA 2010, s 356OC(5)*). This is not intended to bring investment transactions within the scope of income taxation. One of the four conditions or trading intentions, at **14.3** must still be met. This provision is intended simply to ensure that, if the vehicle through which the land is held is a capital asset, the fact that a capital gain arises on that asset does not prevent the section from applying.

Disposals of Property Deriving its Value from Land

14.8 Similarly:

(*a*) if a person realises a profit or gain from a disposal of property which (at the time of the disposal) derives at least 50% of its value from land in the UK;

(*b*) that person is a party to (or concerned in) an arrangement concerning some or all of that land (the project land); and

(*c*) the main purpose (or one of the main purposes) of the arrangement is to deal in or develop the project land and realise a profit or gain from a disposal of property deriving the whole or part of its value from that land,

the 'relevant amount' must be treated for income tax purposes as profits of a trade carried on by that person arising in the year in which the profit or gain arises, except to the extent that such amount is already taxable as income (*ITA 2007, ss 517D, 517E(1)–(4); CTA 2010, ss 356OD, 356OE(1)–(4)*). The 50% limitation is intriguing. Suppose a company owns two properties, one of which it intends to retain and let and the other to develop and sell. It appears that if a shareholder sells his shares, the provision will not apply if the investment property is worth more than the trading property, but it will do so – albeit that it will only tax the part of the proceeds of sale of the shares that is apportioned to that property – if it is worth more than the investment property. And what if a trading property was developed into two houses, one of which was sold prior to the sale of the shares? It appears that if the value of the investment property plus the cash from the sale of the first house together exceed the value of the second house, the provision does not apply.

14.9 The relevant amount is so much (if any) of the profit or gain as is attributable (on a just and reasonable apportionment) to the relevant UK assets, ie any land in the UK from which the property derives any of its value (at the time of the disposal) (*ITA 2007, s 517E(5), (6); CTA 2010, s 356OE(5), (6)*). Again the section applies to gains which are capital in nature as well as to those which are income (*ITA 2007, s 517E(7); CTA 2010, s 356OE(7)*).

14.10 This provision is the one aimed at disposals of shares, interests in trusts or partnerships and similar indirect disposals of the land. There are a few points to note. First, the conditions at **14.2** and **14.3** do not apply to such a disposal. Instead the main purpose test at **14.8**(*c*) above is what determines whether or not the provision applies. It will be noted that, unlike its predecessor, the legislation does not contain an exclusion for the disposal of shares in a property trading company. The reason is that the exclusion where an amount is already taxable as income applies irrespective of on whom it is taxable. What is taxed is 'the relevant amount'. This is the proportion of the profit or gain realised from a disposal of the shares or other property that is attributable (on a just and reasonable apportionment) to the UK land from which the shares or other asset derives its value (*ITA 2007, s 517E(1), (5), (6); CTA 2010, s 356OE(1), (5), (6)*). The exclusion then provides that 'sub-section(1) does not apply to an amount so far as it would (apart from this section) be brought into account as income in calculating profits (of any person) for corporation tax purposes or for income tax purposes' (*ITA 2007, s 517E(3); CTA 2010, s 356OE(3)*).

14.11 This is badly worded.

Example 14.1

Take a simple example. Joe owns 100% of the shares in Joe's Properties Ltd, a property dealing company. He sells the shares for £500,000. At that time the company owns trading stock worth £400,000 and £180,000 of cash and debtors. The purchaser is only prepared to pay Joe £500,000 because the company will have an £80,000 corporation tax liability when it sells the properties.

The calculation seems to be:

	£
Gain on shares (assuming £1 cost)	500,000
Proportion of gain attributable to UK land:	
$\frac{400,000}{580,000} \times 500,000$	344,828
Less gain taxable on the company when it sells the property	(400,000)
Taxable under *s 517E*	NIL

There are two obvious problems. First, the £400,000 is not part of the relevant amount, so it is hard to see how it can be excluded from that amount. Secondly, the use of the word 'would' rather than 'will' is confusing. 'Would' suggests conditionality whereas one would expect an amount to be excluded only if it will be taxed as income at some stage. The answer may well be that as the test has to be applied at the time the shares are disposed of the only thing that can realistically be looked at is what at that date appears likely to occur in the future. This approach differs from that of the predecessor legislation where the exclusion was conditional on the stock subsequently being sold in the ordinary course of the company's business.

14.12 It is hard to envisage a circumstance in which this provision can ever apply because the purpose at **14.8**(*c*) is, by definition, a trading purpose. Accordingly, the land has to be trading stock of the underlying vehicle (even if the vehicle itself does not realise that it is and incorrectly believes it to be an investment). As it is trading stock, the exclusion at *ss 517E(3)* and *356OE(3)* will apply. Accordingly, there cannot be a tax charge on the property referred to at *ss 517E(1)* and *356OE(1)* (ie the shares or ownership interest in the vehicle owning the land).

14.13 These provisions apply to losses in the same way as to gains, so references to a gain include a loss (*ITA 2007, s 517F; CTA 2010, s 356OF*).

The Chargeable Person

14.14 The chargeable person under both *ss 517C* and *517E* (or *ss 3560C* and *3560E*) is normally the person who realises the profit or gain. However (except in relation to fragmented activities (see **14.16**), if all or any part of the profit or gain accruing to a person is derived from value provided directly or indirectly by another person, that other person is the chargeable person (irrespective of whether or not the value is put at the disposal of the recipient of the gain); and if all or any part of the profit or gain accruing to a person is derived from an opportunity of realising a profit or gain provided directly or indirectly by another person, that other person is the chargeable person (*ITA 2007, s 517G; CTA 2010, s 356OG*). For corporation tax purposes, the reference to another person is limited to another company (*CTA 2010, s 356OG(4), (6)*).

14.15 In determining who has provided value or an opportunity, a partnership or partners in a partnership can be regarded as a person or persons distinct from the individuals or other persons who are for the time being partners; the trustees of a settlement can be regarded as persons distinct from the individuals or other persons who are for the time being the trustees; and personal representatives can be regarded as persons distinct from the individuals or other persons who are for the time being personal representatives (*ITA 2007, s 517P; CTA 2010, s 356OO*).

Fragmentation

14.16 If a person (P) (limited to a company for corporation tax) disposes of land in the UK, any of conditions A–D at para **14.3** are met, and a person who is associated with P at a relevant time has made a relevant contribution to the development of the land or any other activities directed towards realising a profit or gain from the disposal of the land, the profit or gain realised by P from the disposal must be taken to be what it would have been if R were not a distinct person from P (and as if everything done by, or in relation to, R had been done by P) (*ITA 2007, s 517H(1)–(3); CTA 2010, s 356OH(1)–(3)*). R's activities are referred to as 'fragmented activities'.

14.17 For this purpose the relevant time is any time in the period beginning when the activities of the project (ie all activities carried out for the purposes of dealing in or developing the land and any other purpose mentioned in conditions A–D (see **14.3**)) began, and ending six months after the disposal. Contribution means any kind of contribution, including, for example, the provision of professional or other services or a financial contribution (including the assumption of a risk). Any contribution made by P to the activities is a 'relevant contribution' unless the profit made (or to be made) by P in respect of the contribution is insignificant having regard to the size of the project. R is associated with P if R is connected with P by virtue of *ITA 2007, ss 993* and *994* (or *CTA 2010, ss 1122* and *1123* for corporation tax) or is related to P within *ITA 2007, s 517U* or *CTA 2010, s 356OT* (see **14.5**) (*ITA 2007, s 517H(6)–(10); CTA 2010, s 356OH(6)–(10)*).

14.18 The scope of this provision is not clear.

Example 14.2

John buys a property for £400,000 because he believes that the area is being upgraded and he will be able to sell it at a profit in a couple of years' time. He takes a mortgage of £300,000 and borrows another £50,000 from his brother, Jack. John agrees to pay interest to Jack at the same rate as on the mortgage.

John sells the house two years later for £700,000. He declares a dealing profit on his tax return of:

	£	£
Sale proceeds		450,000
Less cost	400,000	
Loan interest – bank	24,000	
– Jack	4,000	428,000
Profit		22,000

John has disposed of land in the UK. He held it as trading stock. Jack seems to have made a relevant contribution, ie a financial contribution, by lending the £50,000. Accordingly John's profit on the disposal is £26,000 (£22,000 plus Jack's 'profit'). Jack is presumably not taxable on his interest as it has been deemed to have been earned by John and has already been taxed on John.

Example 14.3

Fred is offered an opportunity to acquire a development site. He engages his wife Fiona, who is an architect, to design a building for the site. She charges Fred her normal fees.

Fred, not Fiona is taxable on Fiona's fees, even though these arise in the course of her profession as an architect and would be a valid deduction for Fred but for *s 517JH*, unless the couple can show that Fiona's fees are insignificant. There is no indication in the legislation as to what is meant by insignificant. The architect's fees are normally around 5% of the cost of a project, which hopefully is insignificant in the context of the size of the project (which is presumably the value of the developed property).

Example 14.4

Ben bought a building site that he thought was ripe for housing development. He obtained planning consent but only for a much smaller number of houses than he had anticipated. He engaged his brother, Bob, to do the building work. Because Ben had overpaid for the hope value in the land, he made a loss on the development of £100,000. Bob made a building profit of £250,000.

It appears that, as the building costs are obviously not insignificant in relation to the sales, Ben is taxable on £150,000 even though he has lost £100,000 and Bob has a tax-free profit of £250,000 (less his cost of labour and material).

Presumably as no MP raised any objection in Parliament to this weird legislation, those three examples represent the real intention of Parliament (as opposed to whatever intention the courts may discern from the legislation). In the last example, Ben could well be forced into bankruptcy, in which case the only economic effect of the legislation will be to relieve Bob from tax on his building profit. The exemption where an amount is already taxable in *s 517E(1)* (or *s 356OE(1)*) does not appear to apply to *s 517H* (or *s 356OH*) because *s 517H* (and *s 356OH*) deals only with a disposal of land; it does not relate to a disposal of property deriving its interest from land, and *s 517C* (or *s 356OC*) does not contain a corresponding exemption.

14.19 Any amount which is paid (directly or indirectly) by R to P for the purposes of meeting, or reimbursing the cost of income tax (or corporation tax, as the case may be) which P is liable to pay as a result, is not to be taken into account in calculating profits or losses of either R or P for any income or corporation tax purposes and is not to be regarded as a distribution for corporation tax purposes (*ITA 2007, s 517H(4), (5); CTA 2010, s 536OH(4), (5)*).

Calculating and Assessing the Gain

14.20 The profit or gain from a disposal of any property under all of the above provisions must be calculated on the principles applicable to the calculation of trading profits, subject to any modifications that may be appropriate. Any apportionment (whether of income, expenditure or any other amount) that is required to be made for the purpose of these provisions must be made on a just and reasonable basis (*ITA 2007, ss 517I, 517J; CTA 2010, ss 356OI, 356OJ*).

14.21 If an arrangement has been entered into, the main purposes (or one of the main purposes) of which is to enable a person to obtain a relevant tax advantage that advantage is to be counteracted by means of adjustments. Such adjustments can be made by way of making an assessment, modifying an assessment, amending or disallowing a claim or otherwise (*ITA 2007, s 517K(1), (3), (4); CTA 2010, s 356OK(1), (3), (4)*). A relevant tax advantage is an advantage in relation to income tax (or corporation tax as the case may be) chargeable in respect of amounts treated as profits of a trade under these provisions. For income tax purposes a tax advantage includes for this purpose a relief or increased relief from tax, a repayment or increased repayment of tax, the avoidance or reduction of a charge to tax or an assessment to tax, the avoidance of a possible assessment to tax, the deferral of a payment of tax or advancement of a repayment of tax and the avoidance of an obligation to deduct or account for tax. For corporation tax purposes, tax advantage is defined by reference to *CTA 2010, s 1139*, which is slightly different, namely: a relief or increased relief from tax; a repayment of tax or increased repayment of tax; the avoidance or reduction of a charge to tax on an assessment to tax; the avoidance of a possible assessment to tax; the avoidance or reduction of a charge or assessment to a charge under the CFC rules; or the avoidance or reduction of a charge or assessment to a charge in relation to the bank levy (*CTA 2010, s 356OK(6)*). References to obtaining a relevant tax advantage include obtaining such an advantage by virtue of any provisions of double tax arrangements (but only in a case where the relevant tax advantage is contrary to the object and purpose of the provisions of the double tax agreement (*ITA 2007, s 517K(2), (5), (6); CTA 2010, s 356OK(2), (5), (6)*). It should be noted that for corporation tax purposes, a tax deferral does not constitute a tax advantage. Also 'double tax arrangements' is not defined for income tax purposes, whereas for corporation tax it is defined as arrangements which have effect under *TIOPA 2010, s 2(1)* (*CTA 2010, s 356OK(6)*). However, this is probably because *ITA 2007, s 1023* already contains the identical definition so it does not need to be defined again. This provision does not apply if the arrangement was entered into before 16 March 2016 (*FA 2016, ss 81(3), 82(3)*).

Exemptions

14.22 If *s 517C* applies because Condition D is met (land is developed with the purpose of realising a gain from its disposal when developed: see **14.3**) and part of the profit or gain is fairly attributable to a period before the intention to develop was formed, *s 517C* has effect as if the person had not realised that part of the profit or gain. Similarly, if *s 517E* applies (property deriving its value from land: see **14.8**) and part of the profit or gain is fairly attributable to a period before the person mentioned in *s 517D* was a party to, or concerned in, the arrangement in question, *s 517E* has effect as if the person had not realised that part of the profit or gain. In applying this exclusion, account must be taken of the treatment of a person who appropriates land as trading stock (*ITA 2007, s 517L; CTA 2010, s 356OL*).

14.23 These provisions do not apply to a gain accruing to an individual if the gain is exempt from CGT as a result of principal private residence relief (see **13.3**) or would be so exempt but for *TCGA 1992, s 224(3)* (residences acquired partly with a view to making a gain) (*ITA 2007, s 517M*). It is, of course, a question of fact when a decision to develop a property for sale is made. Indeed, if a property held for many years as an investment is developed and sold, it is questionable whether the main purpose of the development is to realise a gain from disposing of the land when developed. It may well be simply to maximise the capital gain by selling it in the form that will generate the largest possible gain. Leaving that aside, in most cases an intention to develop is unlikely to be formed until planning permission has been obtained because it is hard to see how one can intend to do something that the law does not permit one to do. Accordingly a change of intention will tax the development profit but is unlikely to tax the increase in the value of the land brought about by the grant of planning consent. It is also relevant that in the real world people tend to obtain planning permission first and it is only when they have done so that they decide whether to sell on the land with planning consent or to carry out the development themselves.

Interpretation

14.24 If it is necessary to determine the extent to which the value of any property or right is derived from any other property or right for the purpose of these provisions,

(*a*) value can be traced through any number of companies, partnerships, trusts and other entities or arrangements; and

(*b*) the property held by a company, partnership or trust must be attributed to the shareholders, partners, beneficiaries or other participants at each stage in whatever way is appropriate in the circumstances.

(*ITA 2007, s 517N(1)–(3); CTA 2010, s 356OM(1)–(3)*.)

For this purpose a partnership includes an entity established under the law of a country or territory outside the UK which has a similar nature to a partnership, and 'partners' in relation to such an arrangement must be construed accordingly. A trust includes arrangements which have effect under the law of a country or territory outside the UK under which persons acting in a fiduciary capacity hold and administer property on behalf of other persons, and 'beneficiaries' in relation to such arrangements, is to be construed accordingly (*ITA 2007, s 517N(4), CTA 2010, s 356OM(4)*).

14.25 In determining whether *ss 517C* or *517E* applies, account must be taken of any method, however indirect, by which any property or right is transferred or transmitted or the value of any property or right is enhanced or diminished. The occasion of the transfer or transmission of any property or right, however indirect, and the occasion when the value of any property or right is enhanced can be occasions on which those provisions apply. They apply in particular to:

(*a*) sales, contracts and other transactions made otherwise than for full consideration or for more than full consideration;

(*b*) any method by which any property or right (or the control of any property or right) is transferred or transmitted by transferring share capital or other rights in a company, rights in a partnership or an interest in settled property;

(*c*) the creation of an option affecting the disposition of any property or right and the giving of consideration for granting it;

(*d*) the creation of a requirement for consent affecting such a disposition and the giving of consideration for granting it;

(*e*) the creation of an embargo affecting such a disposition and the giving of consideration for releasing it; and

(*f*) the disposal of any property or right in the winding up, dissolution, or termination of a company, partnership, or trust.

(*ITA 2007, s 517O; CTA 2010, s 356ON.*)

14.26 An arrangement includes any agreement, understanding, scheme, transaction or series of transactions, whether or not legally enforceable. Any number of transactions can be regarded as constituting a single arrangement if a common purpose can be discerned in them (or there is other sufficient evidence of a common purpose) (*ITA 2007, s 517Q; CTA 2010, s 356OP*).

14.27 References to a disposal of any property include any case in which the property is effectively disposed of (whether wholly or partly) by one or more transactions or by any arrangement. Reference to a disposal includes a part disposal. In particular, there is a part disposal where, on a disposal, any form of property derived from the asset remains undisposed of (including where an interest or right in or over the asset is created by the disposal, as well as where it subsists before the disposal) (*ITA 2007, s 517R; CTA 2010, s 356OQ*).

14.28 Reference to land includes: buildings and structures; any estate, interest or right in or over land; and land under the sea or otherwise covered by water. References to property deriving its value from land include: any shareholding in a company which derives its value directly or indirectly from land; any partnership interest which derives its value directly or indirectly from land; any interest in settled property which derives its value directly or indirectly from land; and any option, consent or embargo affecting the disposition of land (*ITA 2007, s 517S; CTA 2010, s 356OR*).

14.29 For the purposes of *s 517B(1)* (see **14.2**) and *s 517D(1)* (see **14.8**) it does not matter whether the person realising the profit or gain in question realises it for himself or for another person. If, for example, by a premature sale, a person directly or indirectly transmits the opportunity of realising a profit or gain to another person, the first person realises the other's profit or gain for him (*ITA 2007, s 517T; CTA 2010, s 356OS*).

14.29A From 8 March 2017, these provisions have effect (so far as they would not otherwise have done so) in relation to amounts that are recognised in GAAP accounts drawn up for any period of account beginning after that date (or in the part of a straddling period after 7 March 2017 of accounts beginning before that date (*F(No 2)A 2017, s 39(1)*). GAAP accounts for this purpose are accounts drawn up in accordance with generally accepted accounting practice and recognised means recognised as an item of profit or loss.

Transitional

14.30 If a person disposes of land, or of property deriving the whole or part of its value from land, to a person who is associated with him at the relevant time, the disposal is made between 16 March 2016 and 4 July 2016, and a person obtains a relevant tax advantage as a result of the disposal, that tax advantage is to be counteracted by means of adjustments (which can be made by way of making an assessment, the modification of an assessment, amendment or disallowance of a claim or otherwise). For this purpose a relevant tax advantage is an advantage in relation to tax to which the person in question is charged or chargeable (or would be chargeable if the advantage were not obtained) by virtue of *ITTOIA 2005, s 6(1A)* (profits of a trade of dealing in or developing UK land arising to a non-UK resident) or *ITA 2007, ss 517C* or *517E* or *CTA 2010, ss 356OC* or *356OE.*

14.31 Where property is disposed of under a contract (including a conditional contract) the date of the disposal is the date of the contract, not the date the property is conveyed or transferred (*FA 2016, ss 81(4)–(10); 82(4)–(10)*). For the purpose of this provision: 'arrangements' includes any scheme, agreement or understanding (whether or not legally enforceable); disposal has the same meaning as in *ITA 2007, s 517R* (or *CTA 2010, s 356OQ*) (see **14.27**); a tax advantage has the same meaning as in *ITTOIA 2005, s 6A* (or *CTA 2010, s 1139*); a person is associated with another person if he is connected with that other person (within *ITA 2007, ss 993* and *994*) or is related to that other person (within *ITA 2007, s 517U*: see **14.17**) (*FA 2016, ss 81(11)–(13), 82(11)–*

(13)). The relevant time where the person is chargeable under *ITTOIA 2005, s 6(1A)* (or *CTA 2009, s 5(1A)*) is the time the disposal is made and where he is chargeable under *ITA 2007, ss 517C* or *517E* (or *CTA 2010, ss 356OC* or *356OE*) is any time in the period when the activities of the project (ie the project described in *ITA 2007, s 517B(9)* or *CTA 2010, s 356OB(9)* (see **14.4**) or the activities mentioned in *s 517D(2)(a)* or *s 356OD(2)(a)* (see **14.8**)) began and ending six months after the disposal mentioned in *ss 517B* or *517D* (or *ss 356OB* or *356OD*) (*FA 2016, ss 81(11)–(15), 82 (11)–(15)*).

14.32 If a person has entered into an arrangement the main purpose (or one of the main purposes) of which is to obtain a tax advantage for himself by virtue of any provision of double tax arrangements, that advantage must be counteracted by means of adjustments (either by assessment, modification of an assessment, amendment or disallowance of a claim or otherwise), but only if the relevant tax advantage is contrary to the object and purpose of the provisions of that double tax agreement. A tax advantage is as defined at **14.21**. A relevant tax advantage in relation to income tax *to which the company is chargeable* is one by virtue of *s 6(1A)* (profits of a non-resident from a trade of dealing in or developing UK land) (*ITTOIA 2005, s 6A; CTA 2009, s 5A*). The reference to the company in the phrase in italics above (which is in *ITTOIA 2005, s 6A(5)* rather than 'the person' is probably a mistake.

14.32A These transitional rules do not apply to exempt receipts after 8 March 2017 from these provisions (*F(No 2)A 2017, s 39*). The government felt that where contracts entered into before 5 July 2016 had not been completed by 8 March 2017, there is a risk that tax avoidance is involved, so they felt that the time had come to apply the new provisions to such contracts.

Disposals before 5 July 2016

14.33 The prior provisions, *CTA 2010, ss 815–833* and *ITA 2007, ss 752–772*, applied primarily (but by no means exclusively) in two circumstances: on the disposal of shares in a property company and where a UK resident passed the opportunity to make a trading profit on UK land to an overseas company. The first case to come before the courts in connection with the predecessor legislation, *ICTA 1988, s 776, Yuill v Wilson (52 TC 674)*, concerned the passing of the opportunity to make a profit to an overseas company. There the land was initially held as trading stock by a UK company and this may well have been the reason for *s 776* applying at all. If land was acquired direct from an unconnected vendor by a non-UK resident company it seems doubtful whether the *sections* could impose a tax charge on a UK resident shareholder of the acquiring company (although an indirect charge might be sustained in relation to a gain that he made on his shares) as the fact that the overseas company was chargeable to UK tax on its gain as income would seem to prevent the sale proceeds being a capital sum (a prerequisite for the section to apply) even though HMRC may have had no means to recover that tax liability from the company. See, however, *Sugarwhite v Budd* (**14.73** below) where a tax charge was imposed on the vendor.

14.34 A major practical problem with *ss 815* and *752* was that they were not one of the provisions the operation of which is dealt with by an HMRC Head Office section, but were handled by the local network, and many Inspectors of Taxes seemed unclear as to their scope. Many appeared to think that any large gain from the disposal of property, or of something deriving its value from property, must be caught by the *sections*. This was by no means the case. For the *sections* to apply a person had to realise 'a gain of a capital nature' in one of three specified circumstances. If none of those three circumstances were present the *sections* could not apply however large the gain and however short the period of ownership might be.

When did the Sections Operate?

14.35 The three circumstances, one of which was necessary to bring the *sections* into operation, were where either:

(*a*) land, or property deriving its value from land, was acquired with the sole or main object of realising a gain from disposing of the land (*CTA 2010, s 819(2)(a)(b); ITA 2007, s 756(3)(a),(b)*); or

(*b*) land was held as trading stock (*CTA 2010, s 819(2)(c); ITA 2007, s 756(3)(c)*); or

(*c*) land was developed with the sole or main object of realising a gain from disposing of the land when developed (*CTA 2010, s 819(2)(d); ITA 2007, s 756(3)(d)*).

14.36 Even where one of these circumstances was present the *section* did not apply unless, in addition, a gain of a capital nature was obtained from the disposal of the land either:

(i) by the person acquiring, holding or developing the land, or by a connected person (within *ITA 2007, s 993* – see Appendix 1); or

(ii) where any arrangement or scheme was effected as respects the land which enabled a gain to be realised by any indirect method, or by any series of transactions, by a person who was a party to (or concerned in) the arrangement or scheme.

(*CTA 2010, ss 819(3), 820; ITA 2007, ss 756(4), 757.*)

14.37 Land was initially defined as including buildings and any estate or interest in land or buildings (*ICTA 1988, s 776(13)(a)*). A reference to land also had to be construed as including part of the land, for example if a person acquires five acres of land with the object of realising a gain from its disposal and sells one acre, he cannot claim that he did not have such a motive in acquiring the one acre as it was part of the larger area and the motive related to that larger area. This definition seems to have disappeared on the tax law rewrite, probably because it already applied under the *Interpretation Act 1978*.

14.38 There was no exhaustive definition of 'property deriving its value from land', but this was stated to include:

(*a*) any shareholding in a company (or any partnership interest or interest in a settlement) deriving its value directly or indirectly from land; and

(*b*) any option, consent or embargo affecting the disposition of land.

(*CTA 2010, s 833(2); ITA 2007, s 772.*)

14.39 Land was to be treated as disposed of if the property in the land or control over the land was effectively disposed of. The legislation envisaged that this could take place by one or more transactions, or by means of an arrangement or scheme, concerning either the land or property deriving its value from the land, and embraced all such transactions (*CTA 2010, s 816; ITA 2007, s 753*).

14.40 *CTA 2007, s 819(2)((a)(b)* and *ITA 2007, s 756(3)(a),(b)* can accordingly be restated as either:

(*a*) any interest in land or buildings; or

(*b*) any shareholdings in a land-owning company; or

(*c*) any option or embargo affecting the disposition of land; or

(*d*) any other asset deriving its value directly or indirectly from land, is acquired with the sole or main object of realising a gain by either:

  (i) disposing (directly or indirectly) of the land; or

  (ii) disposing of any interest in the land or any buildings on it; or

  (iii) transferring control over the land, such as disposing of over 50% of a land-owning company.

14.41 If a minority shareholding in a land-owning company was acquired with the object of disposing of that holding, or of an enlarged holding which was insufficient to give control, *ss 819(2)(a)(b)* and *753(3)(a),(b)* did not apply, although the transaction may well have been a trading transaction and thus taxable as income under different provisions. This was so even if the sale took place on an occasion when other shareholders also sold shares so that a controlling interest passed, unless the original minority acquisition was made as part of an arrangement to transfer a controlling interest. What matters was the taxpayer's motive in acquiring his minority holding. The position was not as clear if the charge was under *ss 819*(2)(c) or *753(3)(c)*(see **14.45** below).

14.42 The motive test applied solely at the time of acquisition. If property was acquired as a long-term investment and the owner subsequently changed his mind and decided to sell it, the increase in value after the change of mind was not within *ss 819(2)(a)(b)* or *756(3)(a),(b)* as the property was acquired with an investment motive (although as the property would probably then have become trading stock it may well have been within *ss 819(2)(c)* or *756(3)(c)*).

14.43 *Sections 819(2)(a)(b)* or *756(3)(a),(b)* was unlikely in practice to apply on a straightforward purchase and sale of land, because if land was acquired with the sole or main object of realising a gain from disposing of it the transaction was a trading transaction under general principles – or in the case of an isolated transaction an adventure in the nature of trade – and taxable under the rules that relate to trading income. The profit on disposal would not therefore be a gain of a capital nature. Where it did apply was where land, or more likely property deriving its value from land, was acquired with the intention of transferring control over the land by some indirect means.

14.44 It should be noted, however, that the motive of acquiring to resell did not need to be the motive of the taxpayer. It could be the motive of a third party (*Winterton v Edwards (52 TC 655)* – see **14.68** below).

14.45 *Sections 819(2)(c)* and *756 (3)(c)* call for a little explanation. It is a question of fact whether land is held as trading stock. The test in this case was applied at the time of disposal, not the date of acquisition. If land was held as trading stock it was caught even though it may have been acquired for some other purpose and appropriated as trading stock. Curiously, the *sections* did not exclude the increase in value prior to appropriation as trading stock in such circumstances. It may be that the draftsman felt that such increase would automatically be excluded by the computation (see **14.52** below).

14.46 It should particularly be noted that where land was held as trading stock the *sections* automatically applied. There was no motive test. Accordingly if a controlling interest in a company owning land as trading stock (and which derived its value from that land) was disposed of (so that the land was deemed to have been disposed of) the *sections* automatically came into operation even though the sale may have been the bona fide realisation of a long-term investment in the shares. Under *ss 820* and *757* (see **14.36** above) the gain of a capital nature needed to be made by the person holding, acquiring or developing the land, or by a connected person. A person acquiring property deriving its value from land, eg shares in a property dealing company, accordingly could not be taxed under that *para* unless he was a connected person of the company which held the land as trading stock. A shareholder was not automatically a connected person of the company. He was only connected if he controlled the company either alone or together with persons who were connected with him (*ITA 2007, s 993(6)* – see **Appendix 1**). However, if two or more persons acted together to exercise control of a company they were regarded as connected in relation to the company so that their holdings needed to be aggregated under *s 993(6) (ITA 2007, s 993(7))*. Although a minority shareholder was not within *ss 820* or *757* if he sold his shares in isolation, what if he joined in a sale of the entire company? He was probably again outside the scope of the provision as joining in a sale agreement was not the exercise of control over the company. However, an agreement by all of the shareholders of a property dealing company to sell their shares in the company to a third party may well have been an arrangement effected as respects the land owned by the company which enabled a gain to be realised by an indirect method by a person who was a party to the arrangement, and thus within *ss 820* or *757(2)*. The courts have given a very wide interpretation to 'arrangement' in other contexts and based on this it may well be that a mere agreement to sell together could constitute an arrangement.

14.47 There was an exemption from the charge under s*s 820* and *757* on a disposal of shares in a company that owned land as trading stock (or a holding company that owned (directly or indirectly) at least 90% of the ordinary shares of such a company). All of the land held as trading stock at the date of the disposal of the shares had to be disposed of subsequently both 'in the normal course of its trade by the company that held it' and 'so as to procure that all opportunity of profit in respect of the land arose to that company' (*CTA 2010, s 828; ITA 2007, s 766*). It was normal when selling a property dealing company to ask the purchaser for a warranty that the trading stock would be sold in the normal course of trade by the company so as to procure that all opportunity of profit would accrue to the company. The vendor was very much in the hands of the purchaser on this. If, for example, the purchaser subsequently procured that the company transfer a site at cost to another company in its group this would deprive the vendor of his exemption under *ss 828* or *766* – not just in respect of the value of that site but in relation to the entire sale proceeds of the shares. This illustrates the importance not only of obtaining such a warranty but also of ensuring that whoever gives it was of sufficient substance that the money would be available if a claim needed to be made under it. It is to be hoped that the requirement that 'all opportunity of profit in respect of the land' must arise to the vendor is not interpreted too literally. A purchaser would not (in most cases) exist for the land unless he saw some opportunity of profit for himself in acquiring the land! The intention was obviously to deny the exemption only where some artificial transaction was entered into to direct part of the profit due to the company to a third party. Obviously if the company owned property other than the trading stock, the exemption applied only to so much of the value of the shares as derived from the trading stock; the part deriving from the other property could give rise to a charge under the *section* if it fell within one of the other paragraphs of *ss 819(2)* or *756(3)*.

14.48 This exemption applied only where the charge was within **14.36**(i). There was no exemption where the charge was under **14.36**(ii) because an arrangement or scheme had been entered into. As indicated above it is possible that a sale by all of the shareholders of a company constituted an arrangement. Fortunately, HMRC did not seem to take this point and accepted that the *section* is not intended to catch innocent transactions.

14.49 The motive test under *ss 819(2)(d)* and *756(3)(d)* where land was developed was applied at the time that the intention to develop the land was formed. Any increase in value occurring before that time was specifically excluded from the scope of the *section* (unless of course it was already within one of the other sub-paragraphs). The calculation of the amount to exclude had to take account of the tax treatment where a person appropriates land as trading stock (*CTA 2010, s 827(3); ITA 2007, s 765(3)*). This is a somewhat strange wording. Why merely take account of that treatment instead of adopting it? It is also unfortunate that there is no legislation as to the treatment to adopt in calculating the income of a trade in such circumstances. The legislation provides for the appropriation to be at market value for capital gains tax purposes (*TCGA 1992, s 161*) but this would not automatically apply for calculating trading profits also. In *Ridge Securities Ltd v CIR (44 TC 373)* it was held that the appropriation should take place at market value by analogy with the rule in *Sharkey v Wernher (36 TC 275)*, which deals with the situation where property is appropriated from trading stock. However, the *Ridge Securities* case is a High Court decision that did not go to appeal. It should also be borne in mind that it was concerned with an artificial avoidance device which could conveniently be thwarted by deeming an appropriation to trading stock at market value. Nevertheless in practice it is likely that HMRC regarded *ss 827(3)* and *765(3)* as requiring an appropriation at market value. If the *ss 815* or *752* gain was calculated on the assumption that the land was appropriated to trading stock that assumption also had to be made for capital gains tax purposes (*TCGA 1992, s 161(6); ITA 2007, s 770*).

The Meaning of a 'Gain of a Capital Nature'

14.50 As indicated earlier, not only did one of the three circumstances have to exist but also a gain of a capital nature had to be realised to bring the section into operation. A gain of a capital nature was one that, apart from *ss 815* or *752*, did not fall to be included in any computation of income for the purposes of the *Tax Acts* (*CTA 2010, s 833(1); ITA 2007, s 772(1)*). Accordingly, if a gain could be taxed as income under some other provision it was to be taxed under that provision, not under *ss 815* or *752*. *Sections 815* and *752* could only operate if the gain would escape tax or be taxed as capital if the *section* did not exist. In many cases a transaction that HMRC sought to tax under *ss 815* or *752* was trading income. In such a case a *ss 815* or *752* assessment was not competent. As the motive test under *ss 819(2)(a)(b)* and *756(3)(a)(b)* was the same as that for trading it is difficult to envisage a circumstance where a simple purchase and sale of land could fall within *ss 815* or *752*. It is either a capital gain or a trading profit depending on whether or not it was bought for resale.

The Effect of the Section

14.51 Where *ss 815* or *752* did apply the gain had to be treated as income which arose when the gain was realised and which for corporation tax purposes was taxable as miscellaneous income (*CTA 2010, ss 818(1); ITA 2007, ss 755(1), 756(2)*). It would normally have been treated as income of the person by whom the gain was realised (*CTA 2010, s 8211(1); ITA 2007, s 759(1)*). A gain was not realised until the recipient could effectively enjoy or dispose of it (*CTA 2010, s 829(2); ITA 2007, s 768(2)*).

14.52 Because the *provision* could often apply to a series of transactions designed to transfer land by indirect means it was difficult to lay down rules for the calculation of the gain. The *Act* did not attempt this. It required the adoption of 'such method of computing a gain … as is just and reasonable in the circumstances' (*CTA 2010, s 822(2); ITA 2007, s 760(2)*). In considering what was a just and reasonable computation it required to be taken into account:

(*a*) the value of what is obtained for disposing of the land; and

(*b*) the need to allow as a deduction only such expenses as were attributable to the land disposed of.

14.53 As further guidance the draftsman indicated that account should be taken of:

(*a*) the way in which trading profits are computed if the transaction is the acquisition of a freehold and the grant of a lease out of it (for such purposes the reversion is treated as trading stock and a proportionate part of the cost of the land is attributed to it – see *Utting v Hughes (23 TC 174)*, **6.8** above); and

(*b*) the adjustment made in calculating trading income under *CTA 2009, s 136* and *ITTOIA 2005, s 158*, which allows a deduction in computing trading profits for any part of a premium taxed as UK property income or as property business income.

There was no requirement to take these two factors into consideration; it was merely permissible to do so, although a court would undoubtedly expect them to be applied unless there was a good reason for not doing so.

14.54 In calculating the gain any necessary apportionments of income or expenditure had to be made by such method as was just and reasonable in the circumstances, and any valuations that were needed to give effect to the *section* had to be made (*CTA 2010, s 822; ITA 2007, s 760*).

A Gain Obtained for Another Person

14.55 A charge under *ss 815* or *752* could arise where the person holding, acquiring or developing the land or a connected person, or a person who was a party to a scheme or arrangement affecting the land, obtained the gain not for himself but for some other person (*CTA 2010, s 819(3); ITA 2007, s 756(4)*). For this purpose, partnerships, trusts and deceased estates could be regarded as persons distinct from the persons who were for the time being partners, trustees or personal representatives (*CTA 2010, s 825; ITA 2007, s 763*). A gain was obtained for someone by some other person if that other person directly or indirectly transmitted the opportunity of making that gain to the person who received it, whether by a premature sale or otherwise (*CTA 2010, s 819(4); ITA 2007, s 756(5)*). This was probably not an exhaustive definition. If the gain arising to A was derived from value provided indirectly by B (eg if something was done to pass value out of land owned by B into that owned by A) it is likely that B obtained the gain for A. In such circumstances the charge to tax was on the person who transmitted the opportunity to make the gain (B), not on the person who received it (*CTA 2010, s 821(3); ITA 2007, s 759*). If part of the gain accruing to a person was derived from value (or an opportunity to realise a gain) provided by another person that person was taxable on that part and the recipient of the gain was taxable on the balance (*CTA 2010, s 821(5); ITA 2007, s 759*).

14.56 When a person was assessed in respect of a gain that he had made for another he was given a right to recover the tax from that other person, although if, as was probably normally the case, that other person was not resident in the UK that right might not be worth much (*CTA 2010, s 829(3); ITA 2007, s 768(3)*). To enable him to do so he could require HMRC to issue him with a certificate specifying the amount assessed and the tax paid. Such a certificate was conclusive evidence of any facts stated in it. For this purpose, but not for *s 752* generally, the tax attributable to income so assessed was calculated by treating the income as the highest part of the payer's income (*ITA 2007, s 768(6)*), but leaving out of account any payment for compensation for loss of office, profit on insurance policies or a premium on a lease (*ITA 2007, ss 768(6), 1012*). If the person assessed does not pay the tax within six months of its due and payable date HMRC can recover the tax from the recipient of the gain (or at least can try to do so). This does not prejudice their right to recover it from the person assessed (*CTA 2010, s 829(4); ITA 2007, s 768(4)*). Irrespective of whether or not the recipient of the gain reimburses the tax to the payer it is to be treated as having been paid by the recipient of the gain for the purpose of calculating his capital gains tax liability. This enables the amount taxed under *ss 815* or 752 (and expenditure taken into account in calculating the amount assessable) to be excluded from the calculation of the capital gain by virtue of *TCGA 1992, ss 37–39; (TCGA 1992, ss 37(5), 39(4)*).

Ancillary Points

14.57 In applying *ss 815* and *752*, any number of transactions could be regarded as a single arrangement or scheme if a common purpose could be discerned in them. They could also be so regarded if, although the transactions did not themselves display a common purpose, there was sufficient other evidence of their having been carried out for a common purpose (*CTA 2010, s 820(3); ITA 2007, s 757(3)*). Account was also to be taken of any method, however indirect, by which any property or right was transferred or transmitted or the value of any property or right was enhanced or diminished. Any such transaction could give rise to a charge under *ss 815* or *752 (CTA 2010, s 823(2); ITA 2007, s 761(1)*). The Act gave the following examples of the sort of thing that the draftsman had in mind.

(*a*) A sale, contract, or other transaction at an undervalue or an overvalue.

(*b*) The transfer of (or of control over) property or a right over land by assigning share capital or other rights in a company, or by assigning rights in a partnership or an interest in settled property.

(*c*) The creation of any option, consent, or embargo affecting the disposition of any property or right, either for full value or otherwise, and any payment for the release of the embargo or the giving of the consent.

(*d*) The disposal of any property or right over land on the winding-up of a company or the termination of a partnership or trust (*CTA 2010, s 823(3); ITA 2007, s 761(3)*).

14.58 In considering the motive or intentions of any person, the objects and powers of a company as set out in its memorandum of association, or the objects and powers of any partnership or trust as set out in the partnership or trust deed, were not conclusive (*ICTA 1988, s 777(4)*). There was no corresponding provision in *CTA 2010* or *ITA 2007*, probably because it can be implied from *s 762(3)*. What needed to be looked at is what in fact happened. If what happened was within the section, it was taxable even though it may have been *ultra vires*. As HMRC has always adopted this approach to company objects clauses and partnership deeds, it is not clear why it was felt necessary to spell it out in this instance.

14.59 Value could be traced through any number of companies, partnerships and trusts to ascertain whether and to what extent the value of any property was derived from some other property or right. At each stage of this exercise the property held by a company, partnership or trust could be attributed to the shareholders, partners, or beneficiaries in whatever manner was appropriate in the circumstances (*CTA 2010, s 824; ITA 2007, s 762*).

14.60 Where, under the settlement provisions, income of a trust was treated as income of the settlor, a *s 752* gain realised by the trust was of course to be treated as income of the settlor *(CTA 2010, s 817; ITA 2007, s 754*). This also applied in any other circumstances where income was deemed to belong to some other person.

14.61 *Sections 815* and *725* applied to non-UK residents if all or any part of the land was situated in the UK (*CTA 2010, s 819(1); ITA 2007, s 759(8)*).It is difficult to envisage only part of the land being in the UK. One instance in which this can occur is that both UK and non-UK land were taken into account in determining whether a company derived its value from land. Where the person entitled to the consideration was not resident in the UK, HMRC could require the payer to deduct income tax at the basic rate from the consideration and pay it over to them (*ITA 2007, s 944*). They could apparently require such a deduction even if the recipient was not the taxable person (because the gain was provided for him by another). Of course, they needed to know about the transaction before the payment was made. In practice this was likely to mean that the provision would only operate where the consideration was payable by instalments such that the whole amount has not been paid over by the time HMRC considered the transaction. HMRC did find out in advance in *Entergy Power Development Corp v Pardoe (2000 STC 286)* but this did not help them. They issued what would now be *s 944* notices to a number of different potential purchasers of a company including Entergy. It was held that a person cannot be entitled to any consideration until a contract exists. Accordingly a notice issued in advance of the contract was invalid. The court accepted that this means that it was virtually impossible for HMRC to issue directions where contract and completion take place on the same day, but felt that the wording of the section indicated that Parliament had intended to give HMRC power to intervene only once an entitlement to a contractual receipt arose.

14.62 These provisions could not apply to land situated outside the UK *(CTA 2010, s 819(1)(c); ITA 2007, s 759(8))*.

14.63 In the past HMRC frequently raised an assessment under these provisions and a capital gains tax assessment – and sometimes a trading income assessment as well – in respect of the same gain. In *Lord Advocate v McKenna (1989 STC 485)* it was accepted that HMRC are entitled to raise alternative assessments in this way. However, if no appeals are made they are not entitled to seek to enforce payment of the tax due under both assessments. They must select which assessment to pursue. An attempt to enforce payment of all three alternate assessments was described by Scott LJ in the Court of Appeal as 'vexatious and oppressive' in *CIR v Wilkinson (1992 STC 454)*.

Exemption for Principal Private Residence

14.64 *Section 752* onwards could not apply to a gain accruing to an individual on a disposal of his principal private residence if the gain on disposal would be exempt if it were a capital gain (*ITA 2007, s 767*). It is somewhat surprising that the capital gains tax definition of a principal residence – which enables the taxpayer to elect which of two or more residences should be regarded as the main one – was adopted. It is not clear what happens where the gain was partly exempt, eg because a property was a principal residence for part only of a person's period of ownership or because it was used partly for business purposes. Where a gain on a main residence was chargeable to capital gains tax solely by virtue of *TCGA 1992, s 224*, which denies the private residence exemption to the extent that a gain is attributable to acquisition or enhancement expenditure incurred for the purpose of realising a gain from the disposal, the exemption from *s 752* still applies. The position is unclear in relation to property held by trusts. *ITA 2007, s 767* referred specifically to a gain accruing to an individual. However it also referred to *TCGA 1992, ss 222–226*, and *s 225* can only apply to trustees. It is anybody's guess how the courts will interpret this ambiguity if called upon to do so.

Decided Cases

14.65 A number of cases reached the courts in relation to these provisions. The first was *Yuill v Wilson (52 TC 674)*. Mr Yuill controlled two UK companies which owned land as trading stock. They sold the land to two Guernsey companies at market value. Planning consent for redevelopment was obtained and the Guernsey companies resold their land to a UK company at the enhanced market value. It was held by the House of Lords that Mr Yuill, as the guiding spirit behind the scheme, had provided the Guernsey companies with the opportunity to make a capital profit. He was therefore taxable on the gain of the Guernsey companies under what is now *ITA 2007, s 756(4)* (see **14.55**). The terms on which the land was sold by the Guernsey companies were peculiar. The full price was payable on completion on 25 March 1974. However, the agreement provided that the vendors would lend back almost 95% of the consideration to the purchaser. In the event of nationalisation of the land within three years of the sale the bulk of the purchase price (approximately 70%) was to be repaid. Roughly two-thirds of that sum would be repayable on nationalisation in year four and one-third in year five. The House of Lords held that the Guernsey companies had received on completion only the £248,000 that did not have to be lent back. They set the whole of the cost of the land and selling expenses (not merely a proportionate part thereof) against that £248,000. The effect was to produce a loss for 1973/74. Accordingly, no *s 756(4)* charge could arise in that year. A charge would, however, arise in 1976/77 when the possibility of having to repay the top third of the consideration no longer existed. Further charges would similarly arise in 1977/78 and 1978/79.

14.66 This case is of interest for a number of reasons. The calculation of the gain by setting the whole of the cost against the part of the consideration actually received is surprising. It appears to be based on the concept that, until it is known, if part of the sale proceeds needs to be repaid it is proper to make full provision for that possibility, however remote, it may appear. It is interesting that Mr Yuill, who never owned the land, was taxed rather than his UK companies which transferred their land to the Guernsey companies. On the face of it they are the persons who passed the opportunity of gain to Guernsey. To tax Mr Yuill seems to be drawing aside the corporate veil with a vengeance. He may have been the guiding force behind the transactions but the potential gain was never his. The transactions were all at market value. It is surprising that a sale at full market value can be regarded as a transfer of an opportunity to make a gain simply because at some later date the market value of the land increased.

14.67 When HMRC raised their assessment for 1976/77 Mr Yuill somewhat cheekily returned to court (*Yuill v Fletcher (58 TC 145)*). He claimed that the House of Lords ought to have valued the rights conferred on the vendor companies under their contracts and brought this into the computation as money's worth. Alternatively, if those rights were incapable of being valued in 1973/74 they should have been valued in 1974/75. This claim was based on comments that had been made in the Court of Appeal in the earlier case. In the High Court, Mr Justice Walton held that the House of Lords had already decided the matter on the same facts in *Yuill v Wilson* and he was bound by the method of calculation that they had laid down. He also expressed scepticism as to whether the rights were capable of being valued. If they were not they could not constitute money's worth. The decision was unanimously upheld in the Court of Appeal.

14.68 The next case was *Winterton v Edwards and Byfield v Edwards (52 TC 655)*. The major shareholder in a property company, Mr Lyon, acquired two sites outside the company. The two minority shareholders protested. Mr Lyon accordingly agreed that he would pay them a share (corresponding to their interest in the company) of the profit on the developments. He duly paid over their shares in two instalments, one in 1970/71 and the other in 1971/72. HMRC assessed the minority shareholders, Mr Winterton and Mr Byfield, on the sums of £41,395 and £45,995 that they had respectively received from Mr Lyon. It was held that conditions *(2)(a)* and *(2)(c)* (now *s 756(3)(a)(b)(d)*) both applied – the land had been both acquired and developed with the object of realising a gain from disposing of it. It did not matter that the motive had been Mr Lyon's and that Mr Winterton and Mr Edwards never themselves had any interest in the land at the time it was acquired or when the decision to develop it was taken. A scheme had been effected which enabled a gain of a capital nature to be realised. (A complex scheme was effected by Mr Lyon who did not want to pay income tax on his share of the gain.) Mr Winterton and Mr Byfield were persons 'concerned in' the scheme insofar as they benefited from it. Accordingly, all of the conditions for the provisions to operate existed and the assessment was upheld.

14.69 The concept enunciated in *Winterton v Edwards* that the motive did not have to be in the mind of the taxpayer was also applied in *Page v Lowther (57 TC 199)*. A substantial long-established family trust held 2.6 acres of land in Kensington. They decided that it should be redeveloped. However, they felt a social responsibility to ensure that the development was in keeping with the tone of the area and were not prepared to simply sell the land to a small developer. A major development company was interested in carrying out the development but unwilling to pay the price for the land that the trustees required. To resolve these commercial problems the trustees sold a long lease of the land to the development company. The developer undertook that when it granted underleases to occupiers it would procure that the occupier paid a premium to the trustees, calculated on a formula. It was held that land had been developed within *s 776(2)(c)* (now *ITA 2007, s 756(3)(c)*), albeit that the motive was the developer's, not the trustees', and that the agreement under which the occupiers of houses were to pay premiums constituted an arrangement to which the trustees were parties. The provisions accordingly applied. The trustees were simply seeking to obtain the market value for their land. They appear to have been caught because they tied the premium to the development. It is not certain that the *section* would have applied if they had sold the lease initially for an agreed price payable by instalments as and when the developer himself took premiums from the occupiers. It is probable that in such a case the trustees would realise their gain before the development commenced – although *Yuill v Wilson* perhaps casts doubt on this. It may be that the trustees would not realise their gain until they receive the money in which case the gain would arise after commencement of the development and would thus still be caught. The taxpayers also put forward the alternative argument that they had not sought to avoid tax and *s 776* had to be construed in the light of *sub-s (1)*, 'This section is enacted to prevent the avoidance of tax…'. However, Mr Justice Warner felt that this did not entitle one to treat as ambiguous words which are in themselves clear, and, as the transaction fell squarely within the wording of *sub-s (2)*, he had to find in favour of HMRC. He also thought it tenable to take the view that the trustees had in fact avoided tax 'albeit perhaps unwittingly'.

14.70 There is also a Special Commissioners case, *Newman v Pepper (2000 STC (SCD) 345)*. This is an oddity. Denis Newman acquired a farm in 1963. In 1982 he executed a trust deed conveying the land other than the farmhouse to bare trustees to hold it as to one-eighth for each of his five children and three-eighths for himself. Two days later on 9 July 1982 the trustees granted an option to a firm of builders, Wates, to buy the land. It was common ground that the date of the formation of the first intention to develop the land was 9 July 1982. The option was exercisable after 1 August 1983. It enabled Wates to buy either the whole of the land or such part as by that time Wates had obtained planning permission for. The option defined the purchase price as 15% of the sale price of all of the buildings to be constructed on the land (subject to certain adjustments) subject to a minimum of £50,000 per developable acre. In July 1985 Wates assigned the benefit of the option to McAlpine Homes and Canberra Developments Ltd. In November 1985, McAlpine and Canberra exercised the option in relation to part of the land which was the subject of outline planning permission. That land was duly transferred, McAlpine paying £528,483 and Canberra £186,017, a total initial consideration of £714,500. In February 1986 McAlpine and Canberra entered into a deed of partition of the land. In May 1986 the trustees released Canberra from its remaining obligations under the option agreement for a payment of £175,000.

14.71 At some stage a purported CGT hold-over election in relation to the gift by Denis Newman on the creation of the settlement was made. Colin Newman, one of the sons and one of the trustees, did not dispute this election at a meeting with the Inspector of Taxes in September 1987. However, when the case came before the Commissioners, Colin denied that he had ever signed the hold-over election. He claimed that it was a forgery (and presumably as a result part of the gain should have been taxed in 1982). The Commissioner rejected this contention. He also rejected a further claim that as McAlpine had entered into a mortgage containing a standard clause that it would 'pay and discharge all future rent, rates, taxes, duties, charges, assessments, impositions and outgoings whatsoever', the CGT and *s 776* tax liabilities should be assessed on McAlpine not Newman. He similarly rejected a claim that the tax should have been assessed on the trustees not the beneficiaries even though they were mere nominees. The only thing the Commissioner said about *s 776* in his judgment was: 'In relation to the Revenue computations of the taxpayers' liabilities …

in relation to income tax assessable pursuant to *s 776*, I find, insofar as such computations relate to factual issues and hold, insofar as such computations relate to questions of law, that such computations by the Revenue are correct.' It does not appear that any arguments were raised (by a taxpayer in person) in relation to whether the trading income rules rather than *s 776* ought to have applied. HMRC did not raise *s 776* assessments for 1986/87, which suggests that they did not regard the receipts from Canberra as within *s 776*. That would be logical, as in the event those receipts were not based on the value of the land when developed; it was only the receipts from McAlpine (and possibly the interim receipts from Wates) that were.

14.72 The taxpayer won one appeal under these provisions. In *Chilcott v CIR (55 TC 446)* a property-dealing company, Kolinol, agreed to sell its only property under an arrangement whereby it received shares in Minet Holdings. The shareholders then sold their shares to Trafalgar House for a consideration to be satisfied by the transfer later of shares in Minet Holdings (ie the shares that Kolinol, by then a subsidiary of Trafalgar, would receive from Minet). There was clearly an arrangement. However, it was held that at the time of the sale of the shares in Kolinol it did not own land as trading stock and accordingly circumstance *(2)(b)* (see **14.4**(*a*)) did not apply. As neither *(2)(a)* nor (*c*) (see **14.4** (*a*) and (*c*)) was in issue the gain on the shares could not be within *what is now ITA 2007, s 755* even though it was clear that the gain made by the shareholders of Kolinol derived from the value of the property.

14.73 The only other case to have reached the courts on these provisions (leaving aside *Entergy Power Development Corp v Pardoe* (see **14.61**) which was concerned with a specific detailed aspect of the legislation) is *Sugarwhite v Budd (60 TC 679)*. Mr Sugarwhite bought a property in 1973 for £20,000. He endeavoured to sell it but was unable to find a purchaser. He mentioned his predicament to a solicitor who introduced him to a Bahamian company that was prepared to buy the property for £25,000. The Bahamian company sub-sold the property to a second Bahamian company at a profit of £6,500. It was then sold to a third Bahamian company at a profit of £1,000 and finally to a UK company at a profit of a further £1,000. Mr Sugarwhite was asked to convey the property direct to the ultimate purchaser, which he did. He had a couple of years previously sold another property to a Bahamian company introduced to him by the same solicitor. HMRC assessed Mr Sugarwhite under *s 776(8)* (see **14.55**) as having provided the opportunity of realising a gain to the three Bahamian companies. Mr Sugarwhite claimed firstly that he was not a party to an arrangement within *s 776* as he had merely entered into an arm's length sale of the property. The Special Commissioner held, however, that there had been an arrangement to enable the Bahamian companies to make a profit from the property and that as Mr Sugarwhite had signed the conveyance he was party to this. This illustrates the dangers of becoming involved with sub-sales of property without completion. A vendor of a property who is asked to convey direct to a third party needs to be very wary, particularly if it is apparent at completion that some of the funds are going to non-UK companies.

14.74 Mr Sugarwhite's second contention was that in any event the Bahamian companies had not made a gain 'of a capital nature' as the transactions were clearly dealing transactions. None of the Bahamian companies had held the property for more than a few weeks and they had not had to pay for the property as they never completed the sub-purchase. It was held that it was for Mr Sugarwhite to produce evidence to show the motive of the Bahamian companies in acquiring the land. He had not done so. Even if he was not in a position to demonstrate the motive of the companies he could have produced the solicitor who effected the introduction, who might have been able to throw more light on the motive. The Court of Appeal indicated that if the taxpayer 'was unwilling or unable to adduce evidence' to show that the transaction was not entered into for tax avoidance purposes it was open to the Commissioner to accept that as being a possibility. Accordingly it was impossible for him to be certain that the transaction was a trading transaction – as a transaction designed solely to avoid tax is not trading – and he was therefore entitled to find that the profits made could have been gains of a capital nature. This emphasises that, however obvious the nature of a transaction may appear to be, it is not safe to assume that it will appear so clear cut to the Commissioners, and as the onus is on the taxpayer to displace an assessment it is important to bring evidence to demonstrate what in fact occurred.

Advance Clearance of Proposed Transactions

14.75 There was a clearance procedure whereby a taxpayer can put details of a transaction or a proposed transaction before HMRC and require him to say whether he was satisfied that the section did not apply to the transaction. If the Inspector stated that he was so satisfied HMRC could not subsequently raise an assessment on the taxpayer under the *section* in respect of the transaction unless the particulars given in the clearance application were not such as to make full and accurate disclosure of all facts and considerations that were material to be known to the Inspector in making his decision (*CTA 2010, s 831; ITA 2007, s 770*). If the Inspector was not satisfied this did not mean that he would raise an assessment under *ss 815* or *752* if the transaction went ahead. It could merely mean that he did not understand the transaction, or that he could not make up his mind and wanted the opportunity to consider it afresh when the taxpayer submitted his tax return, or that he did not have enough information to make a decision and, as Parliament has felt it proper not to provide him with power to request additional information, felt that it would be wrong to ask the taxpayer to supply this voluntarily.

14.76 The clearance procedure applied only where the gain arose by virtue of *CTA 2010, s 819(2)(a),(b)* or *(c)* or *ITA 2007, s 756(3)(a),(b), or (d).* There was no clearance procedure where the land was held as trading stock. In practice many local Inspectors of Taxes did in the past give a clearance on the sale of shares in a property dealing company but this had no statutory effect – and because the exemption under *ss 828* and *766* (see **6.12** above) depended on what happened to the company's trading stock after the sale HMRC were not in a position to give a clearance, as this had to be a major unknown factor.

14.77 The procedure was that a person who considered that one of the above provisions might apply to a gain of a capital nature which he either had obtained or would obtain from a proposed transaction could supply to the Inspector to whom he submitted his income or corporation tax return written particulars showing how the gain would arise (or had arisen). The Inspector then had to notify him, within 30 days from his receipt of those particulars, whether he was satisfied that the *section* did not apply (*CTA 2010, s 831; ITA 2007, s 770*).

14.78 This clearance procedure was very unsatisfactory. As indicated above, there was no power for the Inspector to seek further information from the taxpayer. The taxpayer had to guess what information the Inspector was likely to feel he needed to arrive at a decision. If clearance was refused, the taxpayer did not know whether this might merely be because he has guessed wrongly or whether the Inspector really thought the provisions applied. The author once had a clearance refused and later learned that this was because he had not thought to tell the Inspector a company's motive for purchasing the factory that it had bought 20 years earlier and used for its manufacturing activity since then (which fact he did think to tell him) but had – incorrectly as it turned out – expected that the Inspector would assume that it was bought for the purpose for which it was, in fact, used. The second problem is that HMRC did not have to tell the taxpayer why a clearance was refused, and normally did not do so. Because of both these factors it was wise to try to discuss the transaction informally with HMRC before submitting a formal clearance application.

14.79 Another problem was that on a sale of shares in a company each shareholder was statutorily required to make his own individual application to his own tax district. This could result in delays, as the shareholder's Inspector normally consulted the company's Inspector – or perhaps simply referred the application to him for a decision. It could also lead to inconsistencies, with one shareholder being given a clearance and another refused it on the same facts. It was also unclear to what extent, if at all, the courts might hold an application for clearance against the taxpayer if it was refused and he nevertheless proceeded with the transaction. Unlike with the clearances under *CTA 2010, s 731* or *ITA 2007, s 682* (transactions in securities), which can be made by any taxpayer, and *TCGA 1992, s 138* which can be made by any company concerned in a reorganisation, the only taxpayer entitled to apply for *ss 831* or *770* clearance was one 'who considered that' these provisions may apply, which appears to require the taxpayer to prejudge the issue.

14.80 Because of these problems the decision as to whether or not to apply for clearance was difficult. This was not a clearance that the author personally applies for as a matter of course simply to be on the safe side where he did not feel that *ss 815* or *752* applied. A refusal of clearance might well not be of significance, but would create unnecessary worry for the taxpayer. The new legislation contains no clearance procedure at all.

Power to Obtain Information

14.81 HMRC are empowered to require any person to furnish them with such particulars as they think necessary for the purpose of *ss 815* or *752*. They must allow him at least 30 days to supply the particulars (*CTA 2010, s 832(1)(2); ITA 2007, s 771(1)(2)*). In particular, they can ask for details of:

(*a*) transactions or arrangements with respect to which the person acted on behalf of others;

(*b*) transactions or arrangements which in HMRC's opinion should properly be investigated (even though the person on whom the notice is served may consider that a charge under *ss 815* or *752* cannot arise); and

(*c*) whether the person to whom the notice is given has taken any part in any transactions or arrangements of a description specified in the notice (*CTA 2010, s 832(3); ITA 2007, s 771(3)*).

14.82 A lawyer is not to be deemed to have taken part in any transaction for the purposes of (*c*) by reason only that he has given professional advice to a client in connection with the transaction. Furthermore, a solicitor (acting for a client) cannot be compelled to do more than state that he was acting on behalf of a client in a transaction and give the name and address of the client (*CTA 2010, s 832(5)–(7); ITA 2007, s 771(5)(6)*). An accountant or other professional adviser can be required to disclose full details of transactions entered into by clients. It may well be that the mere giving of professional advice does not constitute taking part in a transaction, but the information that HMRC can ask for under *sub-s (1)* is not limited to the transactions set out in *sub-s (2)*. In *Essex v CIR (53 TC 720)* a notice was served under *s 778*. Mr Essex appealed on the grounds that the notice was invalid as it did not indicate the transactions as to which information was required, and that the wording was so obscure that the notice was burdensome and oppressive. It was held that the notice was valid. It did not have to specify individual transactions and there was no evidence that Mr Essex had in fact found the notice unintelligible or burdensome.

Other Artificial Transactions

14.83 Another way for HMRC to attack artificial transactions is to seek to apply what is known as the *Ramsay* or *Furniss v Dawson* principle. This is a principle of construction first enunciated by the courts in *W T Ramsay Ltd v CIR (1981 STC 174)*, significantly expanded in *Furniss v Dawson (55 TC 324)*, and broadened again in *MacNiven v Westmoreland Investments Ltd (2001 STC 237)*, three House of Lords cases. This states that when it is sought to attach a tax consequence to a transaction the courts must first identify the legal nature of the transaction. If that emerges from a series or combination of transactions intended to operate as such that series may be regarded as a whole. Having identified the legal nature of a transaction the courts must then relate this to the language of the statute. HMRC sought to apply the *Ramsay* principle to a property transaction in *CIR v Bowater Property Developments Ltd (1988 STC 476)*. The company negotiated to sell land outside its group for £202,500. It contracted to sell the land to five group companies with the intention that they would resell it to the proposed purchaser. This would avoid development land tax (which no longer exists) as that incorporated a *de minimis* exemption of £50,000 for each company. The proposed sale fell through but the companies later sold the land to a different purchaser. It was held that the *Ramsay* principle did not apply as there was not a pre-ordained series of transactions as the ultimate purchaser was not known at the time of the sales to the subsidiaries. This case might well now be decided differently following the *Westmoreland Investments* case.

14.84 An alternative approach was taken by HMRC in *Hitch v Stone (2001 STC 214)*. The purported transactions in that case were very complex. They were designed to avoid both capital gains tax and development land tax. HMRC claimed that some of the documents were shams and thus of no effect. If such documents were ignored the transactions became the disposal of the land realising a substantial capital gain. HMRC took an 'all or nothing' approach. They did not claim that if they were wrong the *Ramsay* principle in any event applied. They lost in the High Court but, on appeal, the documents were held to be shams.

Chapter 15

Use of Overseas Companies to Acquire UK Properties

15.1 Because of the large potential profits to be made from many property transactions, and a general aversion towards paying tax, taxpayers are often tempted to seek to avoid UK tax on property transactions by routing these through an overseas company. Unfortunately it is not as simple to avoid UK tax in this way as many people think. There are a number of tax considerations that need to be borne in mind.

(*a*) For UK tax purposes it is irrelevant where a company is incorporated (unless it is in the UK); what matters is where it is resident. This is generally the country from which central management and control is exercised. For example, a Panamanian registered company which is controlled from the UK is regarded as a UK resident company for UK tax purposes. Management and control is normally exercised by the directors but they may be mere puppets of the shareholders or may have effectively delegated their powers to one of their number (or even to somebody else). In such cases the courts are likely to hold that control is exercised not by the directors but by whoever makes the decisions. As a company is normally controlled by its directors it is normally resident in the country in which the directors usually hold their board meetings. Such meetings ought to be held regularly and proper minutes maintained. The courts generally attach considerable weight to board minutes. Clearly the minutes must demonstrate that the decisions are made at board meetings – and that these do not merely rubber stamp decisions taken elsewhere – and all major decisions need to be minuted. With the exception of a few very old companies, a company that is incorporated in the UK will always be resident in the UK even if it is controlled and managed elsewhere (*FA 1988, s 66*). A helpful current analysis of the relevant law can be found in *Wood v Holden (2006 STC 443)*. This is relevant to property companies as it is directed to the situation where very few decisions need to be made by a company, which is typical of single property companies. The overseas companies in that case were part of a tax avoidance scheme. They were managed by a Netherlands Trust Company. The High Court (and Court of Appeal) reversed the decision of the Special Commissioners. The key facts were held to be that the directors of the company 'were not by-passed, nor did they stand aside since their representatives signed or executed the documents'. The fact that the decisions accorded with a plan made by UK accountants so the directors made the decisions they were expected to make did not create an inference that the accountants or anyone else dictated to the directors what decisions they should make. The facts in the later case of *Laerstate BV v HMRC (2009 SFTD 551)* where a Dutch company was held to be UK resident albeit that directors' meetings were held in the Netherlands were such that it was clear that a UK resident director had made the major decisions here and they had been merely ratified in the Netherlands. It accordingly does not cast doubt on *Wood v Holden*.

(*b*) A non-UK resident company which trades in the UK is chargeable to UK tax on its UK trading profits. The purchase and resale of a single property is in many cases a dealing transaction. Accordingly, if a non-UK company enters into such a transaction in the UK it may well have a tax liability here – although if it has no UK assets HMRC may have difficulty in enforcing the liability unless it is resident in another EU country. The country of residence is unlikely to enforce payment, as by convention one country is not normally prepared to enforce payment of another country's tax debts, although the UK is increasingly entering into treaties with other countries for the mutual enforcement of tax debts, so it is unwise to rely on this. The position is different in the EU, where there is an EU Directive on the mutual enforcement of tax debts. It must also be borne in mind that (except in relation to rental income where special rules apply – see **2.55**) an overseas company can be taxed in the name of any agent that it has in the UK and the agent will then be personally liable for the tax. Great care may need to be taken to ensure that there is no one in the UK who could be deemed to be an agent. If there is, the agent can be assessed even though he may not himself receive the sale proceeds of the property. There is an exception for a broker and for an agent who is not 'an authorised person carrying on the regular agency' of the non-resident. The phrase in quotation marks is not defined (*TIOPA 2010, Sch 6; ITA 2007, ss 818–824*).

Whether or not a trade of property dealing is carried on in the UK where the only properties dealt in are UK ones is not clear. It used to be thought that a trade is carried on in the place where contracts for sales are entered into. However it is nowadays accepted that this is only one of the factors that the courts should take into account, albeit an important one. It is probable that trading in land or buildings situated in the UK, and the development of such land, will be regarded as taking place in the UK, particularly where the legal title can be perfected only by registering the sale in a UK Land Registry. If a UK property is bought and split, eg into flats, and all the resulting parts are sold to genuine non-UK residents for use as holiday homes or *pieds-à-terre* the position is less clear cut. If the overseas resident is a company controlled by, or held for the benefit of, UK residents that might tip the balance back to UK trading. In most cases this has become an academic question since 5 April 2016 as there are now specific provisions designed to ensure that profits from dealing in UK land are taxed in the UK. These are considered in Chapter 14.

There is a further problem, namely that *TIOPA 2010, s 130* provides that the permanent establishment article of a double tax treaty does not prevent income of a person resident in the UK from being taxable here. In other words the treaty protects only the profit of the overseas entity itself from tax. It will not prevent the UK taxing a shareholder under *ITA 2007, ss 720–730* (see (*c*) below) or, if the overseas entity is a transparent one, from taxing UK partners or proprietors on their share of the entity's profit.

In the case of development for resale it also needs to be remembered that most of the UK's double tax agreements extend the definition of a permanent establishment to include a building site or construction or installation project that lasts for more than 12 months (in some cases six months). Some double tax agreements are even more extensive. For example the agreement with Australia treats an Australian entity as having a permanent establishment in the UK if it undertakes a supervisory or consultancy activity in the UK connected with such a building site owned by someone else. Some of the older agreements, such as those with Jersey and Guernsey, do not contain a specific building site provision but these agreements have been amended to allow the UK to tax UK dealing profits made by a resident of those Islands. In any event it is by no means clear that the courts will not interpret the expression 'other fixed place of business' so as to regard a building site as such a place on the basis that the site duration in later agreements might be simply a relaxation of the basic position, rather than an extension to it. Furthermore the new legislation is intended to override double tax agreements.

(*c*) If the overseas company would be a close company if it were UK resident there are a number of anti-avoidance provisions that need to be borne in mind.

(i) UK resident shareholders can be taxed on capital gains realised by the non-UK company (*TCGA 1992, s 13*). The gain is apportioned amongst the shareholders in proportion to their interests in the company and the part apportioned to a UK resident to whom more than 25% of the gain is attributed (10% prior to 6 April 2012) is treated as a gain realised by him (with no relief for any losses realised by the overseas company other than those arising in the same company in the same year of assessment). It does not matter that the shareholder has not received the money and may well not be in a position to force the company to pay it to him; he must find the tax out of his own resources.

(ii) A UK resident who has made a transfer of assets, in consequence of which income (including property dealing profits) arises to an overseas company, can be taxed on that income if he has power to enjoy it or receives a payment representing it. 'Power to enjoy' is very widely defined (*ITA 2007, ss 720–730*). However, simply residing in the property does not itself generate income so this will not be a problem if the overseas company was formed solely to hold the property and does not have, and never has had, other income-producing assets.

(iii) A UK resident who has not made such a transfer can be taxed as income on anything that he receives from an overseas company or settlement if its income derives from a transfer by a third party (*ITA 2007, s 732*).

The House of Lords indicated in *Vestey v CIR (54 TC 503)* that what is now *ITA 2007, ss 720–730* (and *731*) can normally apply only where the person who made the transfer of assets, or his spouse, is the person who has the power to enjoy, or receives, the capital payment, which is why *s 732* was introduced. If the beneficiary is, say, a child of the transferor, *s 732* rather than those provisions will normally apply. A mere power to enjoy does not bring about a charge under that section. A detailed consideration of these provisions – which need to be considered when contemplating any overseas transaction – is outside the scope of this book.

(*d*) It should also be remembered that:

(i) the personal tax return now asks (part of Question 5): 'If you … have, or could have received (directly or indirectly) income, or a capital payment or benefit, from a person abroad as a result of any transfer of assets read the notes.' On the face of the guidance, it is virtually impossible to answer 'No' to that question if the taxpayer has an interest in any overseas entity. The question requires a 'Yes' answer even if *ITA 2007, s 739* (which provides exemptions from *ITA 2007, ss 720–730* and *732*) applies or if the only income of the overseas entity is UK income which has borne tax. Answering 'Yes' without volunteering an explanation is likely to trigger an enquiry into the return. It will in most cases be difficult to state that a taxpayer could not have received income from the foreign company. In addition the Foreign Supplementary Page to the return contains a question: 'If you have omitted income … because you are claiming an exemption in relation to a transfer of assets, enter the total amount omitted (and give details in the

"Any other information" box).' Although many people believe that this question is non-statutory, as going beyond the information to which HMRC are statutorily entitled, it emphasises the extent to which HMRC are likely to want to probe the use of overseas entities.

(ii) HMRC have power to require a person to make a return of assets acquired by him (*TMA 1970, s 12(2),(3)*). The request for a statement of assets acquired used to form part of the income tax return but no longer does. Nevertheless, the power is still there. If a person is asked to make such a return what matters is beneficial ownership. If the shares in a Jersey company are registered in the names of Jersey residents as nominees, they have to be nominees for someone and if that someone is a UK individual he needs to declare his beneficial ownership if called upon to make a return;

(iii) HMRC are notified by the Stamp Taxes Office of most transactions in UK land and try to tie these in with taxpayer's files; and

(iv) one of the main activities of HMRC's Special Investigations section is to ensure that tax is paid on transactions in land in the UK (particularly London) by non-UK residents where this is due.

15.2 A non-UK resident company is not liable to UK corporation tax in respect of chargeable gains on UK land which it holds as an investment (unless it is an asset of a UK business). Accordingly, if non-UK residents wish to invest in UK land they should use an overseas company and ensure that they can demonstrate that it is controlled and managed outside the UK. They also need to be able to demonstrate that the transaction is, in fact, an investment and not a dealing transaction. The development of property to sell after development is normally dealing, not investment. A non-UK resident could equally well from a CGT point of view enter into UK investments in his own name but this is unattractive from an inheritance tax viewpoint.

15.3 A UK resident who sets up an overseas investment company is caught by *TCGA 1992, s 13* (see **15.1**(*c*)(i) above). If the overseas company is owned by an overseas trust a deferral of UK income tax can be achieved whilst the funds remain in the trust, but only if the taxpayer, his spouse, his children and his grandchildren are not potential beneficiaries. Capital gains of a non-UK settlement (and of a company controlled by it) are treated as realised by the settlor and therefore taxable on him if he is domiciled and resident or ordinarily resident in the UK. This applies not only where the settlor and his spouse are beneficiaries but also if any child of his (including an adult child), or the spouse of such a child, or a grandchild (or spouse of a grandchild), or certain companies are potential beneficiaries. There is an exemption where the settlement was created before 17 March 1998 if the beneficiary is an infant.

15.4 Neither of these provisions apply if the shareholder of the company or the settlor of the trust is non-UK domiciled. It has been common for a foreigner who comes to the UK to hold his UK house through a foreign company. Assuming that he retains a non-UK domicile, this has inheritance tax advantages as the shares will be a non-UK asset, and therefore outside the scope of UK inheritance tax, whereas the property itself is within the scope of that tax if owned by an individual. HMRC have indicated that in such circumstances they will in some circumstances seek to show that the individual is a 'shadow director' of the overseas company and accordingly taxable here in respect of the occupation of the property under *ITEPA 2003, ss 97–113* (see **23.60**). Whether they could succeed in such a claim obviously depends on the facts – and probably, whatever the law may be, on the common reluctance of foreigners to engage in litigation with other people's Revenue authorities. Great care accordingly needs to be taken before adopting this structure – although both of the alternative options, holding the property personally or through an overseas trust, have their own tax problems. HMRC have won a case in the House of Lords, *R v Allen (2001 STC 1537)* but it was accepted by the defendant in that case (it was a criminal case) that he was a shadow director. His argument was mainly that the benefit in kind rules did not apply to a shadow director. This was unanimously dismissed by the court. It also needs to be borne in mind that holding an expensive house through a company triggers a liability to ATED and other tax issues (see **Chapter 20**).

15.5 A non-UK resident company is liable to UK income tax (not corporation tax) on rental income from UK properties. None of the UK's double taxation agreements grant an exemption from tax on rents. A non-UK company investing in UK property should normally seek to provide the whole of the finance for the property by way of loan so that it has the largest possible amount of allowable interest to set against the UK income. The income tax rules as to what interest is allowable, not their corporation tax counterparts, need to be met. There is no reason in principle why the borrowing should not be from another non-UK associated company – or even from the shareholder if he is a non-UK resident. This overcomes the problem of security, although possibly at the cost of an interest disallowance. However, HMRC tend to look closely at borrowings by non-UK companies to invest in UK properties. Where these form part of a back-to-back arrangement, eg where the loan is secured on a deposit of cash outside the UK, they often seek to disallow the interest on the basis that it is not incurred wholly and exclusively for the purpose of the property business. In practice it is normally possible to negotiate a lesser disallowance than HMRC contend for. In most cases where borrowings are secured on additional assets or guaranteed by a shareholder the security or guarantee is needed because the loan exceeds that which a bank would normally lend on the security of the property alone. Accordingly the part of the interest relating to that amount ought to be readily justifiable. This is discussed in greater depth at **4.67** onwards.

15.6 It needs to be borne in mind that a tenant or a UK agent of the landlord who collects the rent may have an obligation to deduct tax from the rent if the landlord's usual place of abode is outside the UK. 'Usual place of abode' is primarily a factual test and is thus a little easier for the tenant to identify than the landlord's place of residence. There may also be a requirement for the tenant to deduct tax from the taxable part of any premium or deemed premium that he pays (see **Chapter 3**). As explained at **2.89** the landlord can ask HMRC to authorise the tenant or agent not to deduct tax, but to instead allow the landlord to file UK tax returns.

Chapter 16

Value Added Tax on Residential Property

Introduction

16.1 Value added tax (VAT) on property is possibly the most complex area of VAT law. There are two separate sets of VAT rules, one for residential and certain charitable property and the other for other types of property and land. Initially there was a single set of rules under which new buildings were either exempt or zero-rated, and repairs, refurbishments, etc. attracted VAT at the standard rate, which is 20% Prior to 4 January 2011 it was 17.5%. Zero-rating is very attractive. It means that the supply of the building or services concerned is taxable at a rate of 0%. Although this effectively exempts the supply from VAT, since the supply is nominally 'taxable' it enables input VAT incurred on expenditure in relation to the supply to be recovered, whereas input tax in respect of exempt supplies is irrecoverable and therefore an additional cost to the property owner. Cases referred to below with VTD or TC citations are VAT tribunal and First-tier (Tax) Tribunal decisions respectively. It should be borne in mind that these do not have the same authority as court or Upper Tribunal decisions. The distinction between the two is set out at **1.13**.

16.2 This chapter deals with VAT on residential and relevant charitable property (see **16.55**). **Chapter 17** deals with VAT on commercial property. The special VAT issues that relate to refurbishments and to property development are not dealt with here. They are dealt with in **Chapter 8** (Problems of Development – see **8.24–8.80**) and **Chapter 9** (Refurbishments – see **9.16–9.56**) respectively. It does, however, need to be borne in mind that some of the concepts used in VAT apply to both the residential and commercial rules.

16.3 VAT is not solely a UK tax. It is a European Community tax, and as such has to comply with EC law. In particular, the UK VAT legislation has to give effect to the *EC Council Directive of 28 November 2006 (2006/112/EC)* which is officially known as the Principal VAT Directive or often simply the VAT Directive. This replaced *Council Directive 77/388*, popularly known as the *Sixth Directive*. There are some permitted derogations from the Directive and also a number of other directives that amend the VAT rules. Derogations are areas where the European Commission has agreed with the UK government that the UK does not need to comply with a particular rule. These are normally fairly minor departures from the strict EU law where the UK wishes to adopt a simplified procedure for administrative convenience. However, when the UK joined the EU it was granted a major derogation, namely that it could retain the then existing zero-rating for certain types of supplies. The UK was forced to drop its zero-rating of commercial and industrial development from 1 April 1989, because this was held to be in breach of that permitted derogation which allows zero-rating only for 'clearly defined social reasons and for the benefit of the final consumer'.

16.4 The effect of standard-rating is that the developer either has to add 20% (17.5% prior to 4 January 2011) to his selling price and account for that tax to HMRC or treat his selling prices as VAT-inclusive and account for 16.67% of that price (14.89% prior to 4 January 2011). In most cases, he will obviously seek to adopt the former course assuming, of course, that he realises that he has a liability. Whether this reduces the price that he can obtain for the building is likely to depend on the purchaser's VAT position.

16.5 If the purchaser is a fully taxable person, he will be able to recover the VAT from HMRC. In such circumstances there is no reason to think that the imposition of VAT will affect the price that he is prepared to pay for the building. If he is not a taxable person, or is partially exempt, all or part of the VAT will represent a real additional cost. Whether this will reflect in the price of the building is likely to depend on the building itself and other potential tenants. It is unlikely, for example, that a bank which wants a branch in a new shopping centre will decide to forego the additional custom that it perceives it can obtain there because of the imposition of the VAT. Similarly the developer is unlikely to want the bank so badly that he will accept a lower price from it than he can obtain by selling to a retailer. Accordingly, the bank will have to face up to paying the market price. However, the market price of an office development in the centre of the City of London is likely to be determined primarily by demand by banks and financial institutions, which are generally partially exempt and can recover only a comparatively small proportion of their input tax. There is a risk that opting in such a building could depress its market price. In practice, whether or not VAT is chargeable does not seem to significantly affect the market price of a building, albeit that it may limit the number of potential purchasers.

Zero-Rated Supplies of Residential and Certain Charitable Buildings

16.6 Zero-rating applies only to certain supplies of, or in connection with, residential and some charitable buildings. The eligible items are:

1. (*a*) The first grant of a major interest by a person constructing a building which is either designed as a dwelling or intended for use solely for a relevant residential or relevant charitable purpose.

   (*b*) The grant by a person converting a building from non-residential to residential use of a major interest in the building.

2. The supply in the course of construction of a dwelling (or building intended for a relevant residential or charitable use) of construction work on the building.

3. The supply to a housing association in the course of conversion of a non-residential building into a dwelling (or relevant residential building) of construction work on the building.

4. The supply of building materials in conjunction with the services supplied at (2) and (3) above.

16.7 There are obviously a number of caveats. The detailed rules are as follows:

1. (*a*) The first grant (or assignment or surrender – *Note 1, Group 5*) by a person constructing a building of a major interest in (or in any part of) the building, dwelling or its site if it is either:

      (i) *designed as* a dwelling or number of dwellings; or

      (ii) *intended for use solely* for either a relevant residential purpose, or a relevant charitable purpose.

   (*b*) The grant (or assignment or surrender), by a person converting a building, of a major interest in any part of the building, dwelling or its site deriving from the conversion of a non-residential building (or a non-residential part of a building) into one designed as a dwelling or number of dwellings or one intended for use solely for a relevant residential purpose.

2. The supply in the course of the construction of either:

   (*a*) a building which is

      (i) designed as a dwelling or number of dwellings; or

      (ii) intended for use for a relevant residential or charitable purpose; or

   (*b*) any civil engineering work necessary for the development of a permanent park for residential caravans,

   of any services related to the construction other than the services of an architect, surveyor, or other person acting as a consultant or in a supervisory capacity.

3. The supply to a relevant housing association in the course of conversion of a non-residential building (or part of a building) into one either:

   (*a*) designed as a dwelling or number of dwellings; or

   (*b*) intended for use solely for a relevant residential purpose,

   of any services related to the conversion other than the services of an architect, surveyor or any person acting as a consultant or in a supervisory capacity.

4. The supply of building materials to a person to whom the supplier is also supplying services within heads 2 or 3 above which include the incorporation of the materials into the building in question (or its site). For this purpose 'building materials' means goods of a description ordinarily incorporated by builders in a building of the same description (or its site) subject to a number of specified exceptions (which are set out in **8.76** above) (*Note 22, Group 5*) and the incorporation of goods in a building includes their installation as fittings (*Note 23*).

(*VATA 1994, Sch 8, Group 5.*)

16.8 Each of the above heads is obviously subject to a number of qualifications which are considered in detail below. Zero-rating under *item 1* applies if a person constructing the building is beneficially interested in the consideration for the grant of the major interest even though he is not the person who grants that interest (*VATA 1994, Sch 10, para 40*). This ensures that zero-rating is not lost where the land is registered in the name of joint owners (who technically have an interest not in the land, but in its sale proceeds) or a nominee. It seems odd at first sight that if such a provision is felt necessary for VAT purposes, to cater for the separation of legal from beneficial ownership, a similar rule has not been enacted for income and corporation tax purposes. The reason is probably that direct taxes are imposed on the beneficial owner of an asset, so the distinction is relatively unimportant, whereas VAT is imposed on transactions, where the identity of the owner is less important than the legal nature of the transaction.

16.9 *Items 2* and *3* in **16.6** do not apply to a supply of services within *VATA 1994, Sch 4, para 1(1)* (the transfer of an undivided share in property or the transfer of the possession of goods (which includes the grant assignment or surrender of a major interest in land)). Nor do they apply where by (or under) the directions of a person carrying on a business goods held or used for the purpose of the business are put to private use or otherwise used for a purpose other than for the purpose of the business within *Sch 4, para 5(4)* (*VATA 1994, Sch 8, Group 5, Note 20*). An interesting issue arose in *J M Associates (VTD 18624)*. J M builds conservatories. It markets to people who are buying a newly built house. Work on the conservatory begins when the new house is complete or complete subject to snagging, ie prior to its first occupation. J M claimed that its supply was construction work in the course of construction of the building. The tribunal disagreed. It thought the work the alteration or enlargement of an existing building – but commented that the position might well be different if a developer were to permit J M's work to commence prior to completion of the building. HMRC apparently consider that scaffolding normally involves two separate supplies, a zero-rated supply of erecting and dismantling the scaffolding, and a standard rated supply of the hire of the scaffolding. This was upheld by the VAT tribunal in *Pharaoh Scaffolding (VTD 20741)*. The Tribunal placed importance on the fact that de facto control of the scaffolding passed to the customer. The HMRC view seems to derive from the VAT tribunal decision in *R & M Scaffolding Ltd (VTD 18226)*. In an earlier case though, *GT Scaffolding Ltd (VTD 18226)*, where HMRC claimed that there was a single standard-rated supply, the tribunals held that there was a single zero-rated supply as possession of the scaffolding had not been passed to the customer.

16.10 The first grant of a lease that constitutes a major interest allows the whole of the input tax on the development to be recovered by attributing it wholly to the taxable first grant. HMRC say that this is so even where the value of the first grant does not represent full equity in the property, such as in shared ownership schemes run by housing associations (Business Brief 23/2006).

16.11 However, HMRC point out that by granting a long lease the developer is using the asset as a capital asset for the purpose of a business, with the result that a capital goods scheme adjustment (see **17.205**) will arise should an exempt grant be made of the building during the following ten years. They also say that if the developer grants long leases of all of the flats in a block and subsequently sells the freehold the proceeds of sale of the freehold is partly the sale of the (exempt) interests in the leases but mainly the (zero-rated) sale of the common parts that have not been subject to any previous supply. Accordingly there is unlikely to be any need for a capital goods scheme adjustment. This author finds it hard to follow the logic of this as the leases together will themselves carry all of the rights over the common parts so that the landlord has little or no right over such parts which can be disposed of but has an obligation to maintain them. Accordingly, the rights over the common parts in reality have a negative value. However, as HMRC's interpretation favours the taxpayer, there is little point in seeking to challenge its view. The only item that Business Brief identifies where an adjustment might be required is the grant of a lease of a relevant residential building followed by a sale of the freehold. In such a case the sale of the freehold will be exempt (as it is the second grant of a major interest in the building).

16.12 It should particularly be noted that zero-rating applies only to buildings, not a structure which is not a building but is used for a relevant charitable purpose. In *Culver Weir Restoration Project (TC 1310)* (see **9.26**) and *Wheeled Sports 4 Hereford Ltd (TC 1059)* a weir and a skate park respectively were both held to be standard rated as they were not buildings.

Caravans and Houseboats

16.13 Zero-rating also applies to:

(*a*) Caravans which exceed the limit of size of a trailer for the time being permitted to be towed on roads by a motor vehicle having a maximum gross weight of 3,500 kilos and which either:

  (i) were manufactured to standard BS 3632:2005 or BS 3632:2015 approved by the British Standards Institution (BSI), or

  (ii) are second-hand and which were manufactured to a previous version of the BSI standard and were occupied before 6 April 2013.

(*b*) Houseboats, namely boats or other floating decked structures designed or adapted for use solely as places of permanent habitation and not having means of (or capable of being readily adapted for) self-propulsion.

(*c*) The transfer of an undivided share in such a caravan or houseboat or of the possession of the caravan or houseboat.

(*d*) The putting to private use (or making available to any person for such use) by a person carrying on a business of such a caravan or houseboat.

(*VATA 1994, Sch 8, Group 9; Sch 4, paras 1(1), 5(4)* as amended by the *VAT (Caravans) Order 2015, SI 2015 No 1949.*)

However, such zero-rating does not extend to removable contents other than goods of a kind mentioned in item 4 of Group 5 (the supply of building material to a person to whom the supplier is supplying services which include the incorporation of the materials into the building or its site in question. Nor does it apply to the supply of accommodation in a caravan or houseboat (*VATA 1994, Sch 8, Group 9, Note*).

16.14 It should be noted that the other notes to *Group 5* do not apply to *Group 9*. They will, however, apply where relevant, to the civil engineering works for the development of a caravan park for residential caravans as the zero-rating for such parts is under *Group 5*. In respect of such works, a caravan is not a residential caravan if residence in it throughout the year is prevented by the terms of a covenant, statutory planning consent or similar permission (*VATA 1994, Sch 5, Group 5, Note 19*). It was held in *Oak Tree Motor Homes Ltd (TC 4445)* that a motor home is not a caravan for the purposes of *Group 5*. Although the definition of a caravan is based on that in the *Caravans Act 1960*, which includes a motor home, *VATA 1994* has not done this. For the purposes of *Group 9*, a caravan does not include a vehicle that has the ability to move under its own power. In *C Jenkin & Son Ltd (2017 UKUT 239 (TCC))* the company supplied caravans to members of the travelling community eligible for housing benefit for use as their homes on pitches granted by local authorities. The occupier paid a separate pitch fee to the local authority. The leasing agreement was couched in terms of a tenancy of real property. HMRC raised an assessment to recover input tax on the basis that the tenancy was an exempt supply of an interest in land, not the zero-rated supply under *Sch 9* which the company had assumed. The Tribunal held that it was neither! It could not be a supply of an interest in land because the company did not have such an interest. It was a supply of accommodation in a caravan, which is specifically excluded from zero-rating. It was accordingly a standard-rated supply. The UT disagreed. It said that the supply of a caravan without the right to occupy it on a site is not a supply of accommodation; it is a supply of a caravan. The company could not supply the pitch and services because it had no control over them. Consequently, it was making zero-rated supplies by the leasing of caravans. In *Thermo Timber Technology Ltd (TC 5013)* the company supplied mobile timber-framed structures to both schools and holiday operators. It claimed to be able to zero-rate them as caravans, ie 'any structure designed or adapted for human habitation which is capable of being moved from one place to another (whether by being towed, or by being transported on a motor vehicle or trailer)'. This was dismissed on the basis that although the structure contained toilet and kitchen facilities, they were designed as classrooms. Although the use to which the structure was put was irrelevant, their adaption would have been done differently if they were being supplied as holiday homes. In *Scandinavian Log Cabins Direct Ltd (TC 5312)* what was being supplied was a flatpack kit for the construction of a log cabin. The company contended that constituted a kit for a caravan. HMRC accepted that when assembled the kit produced a caravan but contended that what was being supplied was not a caravan but materials to build a caravan. The taxpayer drew the Tribunal's attention to a 1964 purchase tax case, *Betterways Panels Ltd v CCE [1964] 1 All ER 948,* where the court had held that a flatpack furniture kit was equivalent to furniture. Accordingly the FTT held that what was being supplied was a zero-rated caravan. *Cottingham Park Lodges Ltd (TC 5576)* sold a package of items to a prospective occupier of its caravan park; a wooden lodge (which qualified as a zero-rated caravan, removable contents (standard-rated) and a licence to occupy the site (exempt). The Tribunal accepted that these were separate supplies, so the issue was the apportionment of the sale price. The company claimed that it purchased the lodge at a discount and did not seek to make a profit on its sale. Its business model was to resell the lodge at cost to be able to let the land. Fortunately, in one case it had let the land without the lodge (with the tenant buying the lodge direct from the manufacturer) and the Tribunal felt that that letting validated the apportionment. It accepted that the company's apportionment was a fair and reasonable one, although largely on the basis that HMRC had not been able to suggest a more reasonable apportionment.

What is a Major Interest in Land?

16.15 For the purposes of *item 1* in **16.6** above, a major interest is the freehold or a lease for a term of over 21 years (*VATA 1994, s 96(1)*). The word 'over' should particularly be noted. A lease for 21 years exactly is not a major interest. It also needs to be borne in mind that the date from which a lease runs is frequently earlier than the date the lease is executed, eg a lease for 21 years and 1 month from 25 March 2012 which is executed on 30 May 2012 is not a major interest. A lease must actually be for 'a term certain exceeding 21 years'. A term certain is a fixed period. A lease for the life of the tenant would not be for a term certain and could not qualify for zero-rating – probably even if it were expressed to be for a minimum period of 21 years and a day. There are no anti-avoidance provisions to prevent a person granting a 22-year lease with an option for either party to terminate it after seven years, instead of granting a seven-year lease. HMRC appear to have accepted this device (an old version of C&E Notice 742A, para 11), although the fact that this is not repeated in the current Notice 708 may cast doubt on whether they are still of that view. In theory there is no reason why both parties should not have the option to terminate the lease prematurely. It should, however, be borne in mind that the HMRC have put forward for direct tax purposes the argument that cross-options are equivalent to a contract for sale and if this argument is valid – which seems doubtful but cannot be wholly dismissed – the use of cross-options in leases may be equally vulnerable to attack by HMRC. In *C S & J M Isaac (VTD 14656)* the VAT tribunal accepted that a deed of rectification which purported to extend the leases beyond 21 years was effective to do so, but the facts were unusual. In Scotland a lease of not less than 20 years is a major interest. Scottish land law does not permit the creation of a longer lease.

Who is a Person Constructing a Building?

16.16 To qualify for zero-rating the supply, ie the sale or the grant of the lease, must be made by a person constructing the building. This expression is not defined in the legislation. HMRC consider that it covers not only a person who himself constructs a building on his own land, such as a speculative builder, but also a landowner who commissions a builder to erect a building on land that he owns (Notice 708, para 4.5.1). In other words, a property developer or other landowner who engages an architect to design a building and hires a contractor to erect it will be a person constructing a building, but one who hires another person to provide a complete package of erecting a building on his land will not – although he may be if, as would almost always be the case, he has at least a right of veto over the design. VAT tribunals seem to have taken a far more restrictive approach, however. Where a land-owning company and an associated building company jointly sold houses, the land-owning company having obtained the planning permission, designed the houses, and constructed roads and sewers, the land-owning company was held not to be 'a person constructing a building' even though the building company invoiced it for the building work (*Monsell Youell Developments Ltd (VTD 538)*). A similar decision was reached in *Permacross Ltd (VTD 13251)* where infrastructure work was carried out prior to selling residential building plots. In *Hulme Educational Foundation (VTD 625)* a landowner which leased its site to a developer was held not to be a person constructing a building, the tribunal holding that the construction must be physically done by the person concerned (or by his servants or agents) or that person must himself directly enter into a contract or arrangement for another to do the physical construction work. *Cameron New Homes Ltd (VTD 17309)* was also held not to be a person constructing a building. It had carried out extensive work on the land, including remediation, shuttering the site ready for foundation work, altering the vehicular access and excavating for the foundations of the houses at the time it sold the building. It was nevertheless held that these works were preparatory. There was not a building under construction but merely a building site.

16.17 It was held in *C & E Commrs v Link Housing Association Ltd (1992 STC 718)* that 'a person constructing' should be construed to mean simply 'the constructor of a building' so that a person would be covered by the expression irrespective of whether the building had been completed or was still under construction. The phrase is purely descriptive. Indeed HMRC's usual contention that the first supply after completion of a building determines whether input tax is recoverable is inconsistent with the logic of their contention that a person ceases to be the person constructing a building when construction is completed. Link was held to be entitled to zero-rate in 1989 sales of buildings that it had constructed over 20 years earlier. HMRC say that the *Link* decision applies only in respect of input tax incurred in relation to disposal costs (Business Brief 15/92). This is questionable. There is no obvious reason why it should not apply, for example, to input tax on refurbishment work carried out to enable the building to be sold at a realistic price. It probably would not apply to repairs whilst a tenant is in occupation, as the work would relate to the exempt rents not the zero-rated disposal.

16.18 HMRC have also expressed the view that the disposal of, or the grant of a major interest in, a partially completed building qualifies for zero-rating provided that the work has progressed beyond ground level (Notice 708, para 2.3.1). This is surprisingly generous, as most people would not describe the foundations and the first course of bricks as a building at all. HMRC also say that a person who acquires a major interest in an uncompleted building and continues the construction of it will also be regarded as a person constructing the building (para 15.5). This appears to give scope for avoidance. For example, a person who intends to construct and sell a building should consider leaving a little bit of the construction work undone, as the purchaser may be prepared to pay a higher price if, by finishing it himself, he becomes entitled to zero-rate his supply. Within a group of companies there may be scope for transferring the property to another group company during the construction period to double up the value of zero-rated supplies. This would not work if a group registration exists. Obviously such devices are vulnerable to attack – although in the current state of the law, if the *Ramsay* and *Furniss v Dawson* principles apply to VAT at all, the obtaining of a higher price on a sale, albeit only because of an improvement in the purchaser's tax position, is probably a commercial motive that will prevent the principle operating. However, they did not initially consider that the person constructing (or converting) status could apply to a person who acquires a completed building under a TOGC (transfer of a business as a going concern). They now accept that the transferee inherits the person constructing status and is capable of making a zero-rated first major interest grant provided that no such grant has yet been made by the transferor; the transferee would suffer an unfair VAT disadvantage if its first major interest grants were treated as exempt (eg a developer restructures its business by transferring it to an associated company via a TOGC); and the transferee would not obtain an unfair VAT advantage by being in a position to make zero-rated supplies (eg by recovering input tax on a refurbishment of an existing building (HMRC Brief 27/2014)). Fairness and unfairness are of course in the eye of the beholder. It appears that this relaxation is very restrictive and will apply only where denying person constructing status would breach the EU principal of neutrality.

Fixtures

16.19 *Article 6* of the *VAT (Input Tax) Order 1992* (*SI 1992 No 3222*), as substituted by the *VAT (Input Tax) (Amendment) Order 1995* (*SI 1995 No 281*), disallows input tax relief to a developer where, for the purpose of making a grant of a major interest in a building or its site which will be a zero-rated supply, he incorporates in the building or its site goods which do not constitute building materials. Building materials for this purpose means goods which would be zero-rated under either *VATA 1994, Sch 8, Group 5, item 1* or *2* (see **16.13** and **8.29**) or *Group 6 item 2* (see **9.19**). Even where goods fall within that head it disallows input tax in respect of finished or prefabricated furniture (other than where designed to be fitted in kitchens) or materials for such furniture, domestic electrical or gas appliances (other than for space and/or water heating) and carpets or carpeting material. This disallowance is colloquially known as 'the builders' block'. The VAT tribunal in *Edmond Homes Ltd (VTD 11567)* held that fitted units to hold wash hand basins, which contained a door which hid the pipework beneath the basin and formed a small storage area under it, were not prefabricated furniture as their prime function was to support the basins and their use as a cupboard was purely incidental. Following this decision HMRC accept that input tax relating to all base units incorporating a wash hand basin installed in bathrooms, cloakrooms and bedrooms of new dwellings is recoverable by the housebuilder, and where such units are installed by a building contractor in new dwellings, they are zero-rated. This includes vanity or vanitory units incorporating a work surface or shelf. They still consider that other base units are fitted furniture, as are wall units such as bathroom cabinets (Business Brief 3/94). HMRC's view is that an item is incorporated in a building if it is fixed to a building or its site in such a way that its fixing or removal would either require the use of tools or result in either the need for remedial work to the fabric of the building or substantial damage to the goods themselves (VAT Information Sheet, 5/00, December 2000, para 4). Goods are ordinarily incorporated in a building if in the ordinary course of events they would normally be incorporated in the construction of a building of that generic type. They do not sub-divide generic types, eg a large detached house is in the same category as a small terraced house, or ask if the goods themselves are the norm, eg a tap would be regarded as ordinarily incorporated whether it is chromium or gold-plated (para 5).

16.20 It should be particularly noted that, under *item 4*, the materials must be supplied to the person to whom the supply of services is made, and they must be used or installed as part of the building work. These requirements are tighter than the previous rule that they needed to be supplied 'in connection with' such work.

16.20A The meanings of 'incorporates in a building' in the Order, 'ordinarily incorporated by builders in a building of the same description' in the definition of building materials in Note 22 of Group 5 and installation as fittings in Note 23 of Group 5 (see **16.7**) ordinarily incorporated were considered by the Upper Tribunal in *Taylor Wimpey plc v HMRC (2017 STC 639)*. It said that this is not the same question as the land law question as to whether something becomes a fixture or remains a chattel. It thought that an item is incorporated in a building if it becomes either a fixture or a fitting. It felt that installed as fittings means, in substance, chattels that are attached to a building where the degree of attachment is not sufficient (on the facts of the particular case) to constitute the item a fixture. Merely plugging an item into the buildings power supply is not, on its own, sufficient but 'fixing the item in a manner designed to be other than temporary, either to a physical part of the structure or to a supply of electricity, gas or water or means of ventilation or drainage' is necessary. This would exclude white goods that are free-standing and attached to the building by means only of a removable plug or other temporary attachment to the mains services in circumstances where the equipment is, of its nature, portable in the ordinary course but would be expected to include (to the extent they do not become fixtures) a built-in oven, a surface hob, an extractor hood, a wired and plumbed-in washing machine or dishwasher, stand-alone washer driers and tumble driers attached in a non-temporary manner to ventilation, and refrigerators, freezers and fridge-freezers if they are installed in a location with some reasonable expectation of permanence in the sense of the expected life of the item. 'Ordinarily installed by builders' means articles which one would expect a builder to install as a matter of course; items which a prospective purchaser viewing the house would express surprise if they were not there. The test is whether the installation or incorporation of the item by builders is either commonplace or not out of the ordinary. The prevalence of its installation must be greater than that it is not exceptionally installed and greater than merely sometimes installed. The comparison is with what is normally expected in a similar type of property, e.g. normally installed in houses, normally installed in apartment blocks, etc. However, there is no proper distinction for this purpose between luxury homes and other less luxurious dwellings.

16.21 Gas fires (*F Booker Builders & Contractors Ltd (VTD 446)*); night storage heaters forming part of an all-electric heating system (*Robert Dale & Co (Builders) Ltd (VTD 1347)*); mechanical ventilator units installed for sound-proofing (*British Airports Authority (No. 5) (VTD 447)*); a warden call system and alarm switch in sheltered housing (*Garndene Communications Systems Ltd (VTD 2253)*); a ventilation system needed because a house had been designed to be as draughtproof as possible (*C H Wigmore (VTD 6040)*); and a domestic sprinkler system (*P&M Bates (VTD 20948)*), have all been held to be articles of a type ordinarily installed by builders as fittings. In *C H Wigmore*, the tribunal held that 'ordinarily' did not mean invariably, but commonly or usually, and one had to look at the generic description to which the article belonged – in that case ventilation systems – and decide whether, when such a system was needed, it would ordinarily be installed by a builder. In the *Garndene* case and the later case of *McCarthy & Stone plc (VTD 7014)* the tribunal looked at the category of house, in both cases sheltered housing, and determined what a builder would normally install in such housing. In *2S Airchangers Limited (VTD 12495)* HMRC argued that as the company's ventilation system was a technological innovation it could not be something 'ordinarily' installed by builders. The tribunal retorted that ventilation systems were ordinarily installed by builders in new dwellings and the company's system fell into that generic category. In *John Price (TC 634)* the tribunal held that roller blinds are ordinarily installed by builders in a dwelling-house (in spite of HMRC having said in Notice 431NB that they did not qualify). HMRC subsequently said that they will not change their policy, ie they do not accept the decision. The cover over an indoor swimming pool (but not a moveable floor over such a pool) was held to qualify in *Rainbow Pools London Ltd (VTD 20800* – see **8.79**) but the Upper Tribunal in *Taylor Wimpey* (see **16.20A**) felt that this was a wrong decision.

16.22 Trees and shrubs planted in a landscaping scheme for new housing developments were held to qualify in *Rialto Homes plc (VTD 16340)*. Following this case HMRC have expressed the view that for such 'soft landscaping' to be eligible for zero-rating:

(*a*) the work must be carried out at the same time as, or immediately after, the construction of the building; and

(*b*) the landscaping work must be connected with the construction in that it produces in its results a whole with it (they accept that all planting carried out within the plot of a house will meet this condition to the extent that it is detailed on a landscaping plan approved by a planning authority under a planning condition). They consider that:

(i) screening planted along roadside verges,

(ii) work within the plot of a specific house that is not on such a landscaping scheme,

(iii) work performed after completion of the construction such as the replacement of trees and shrubs which die or become damaged or diseased, and

(iv) work carried out outside the plot of a specific house,

do not fall within *item 4* and remain standard-rated (Business Brief 7/00).

16.23 Even though they may be items of a kind ordinarily installed by builders as fixtures, *VATA 1994, Sch 8, Group 5, Note 22* disallows input tax relief – thus effectively negating the benefit of zero-rating – for finished or prefabricated furniture (other than that designed to be fitted in kitchens), materials for the construction of such furniture, electrical or gas appliances other than those designed to provide space or water heating, and carpets or carpeting material. Extractor fans (*H C Moss (Electrical) Ltd (VTD 2020)*), electrically operated Venetian blinds (*Frank Haslam Milan & Co Ltd (VTD 3857)*); a two-way communications speech unit in sheltered accommodation (*Garndene Communications Systems Ltd (VTD 2253)*); door entry systems, fire alarm systems and extractor fans in sheltered accommodation (*McCarthy & Stone plc (VTD 7014)*); wet and dry bollards (units incorporating an electrical and gas supply – and a sink in the case of wet bollards, plumbed in and immovable) in a school laboratory (*Sheldon School (VTD 15300)*), and wall-mounted banks of staff lockers in a nursing home (*Birmingham Council for Old People (VTD 15437)*) have all fallen foul of this restriction. So has an Aga cooker which the taxpayer claimed was intended to provide space heating for the kitchen which was designed without heating because of the cooker (*Richard Custin (VTD 19739)*).

16.24 In *C & E Commrs v McLean Homes Midland Ltd (1993 STC 335)* it was held that built-in wardrobes utilising an outer wall and two internal walls to which were fitted shelving and a door were not fitted furniture at all; they were part of the fabric of the building. The decision in *McLean Homes Midland Ltd* does not give *carte blanche* to zero-rate all fitted furniture. It was distinguished in two more recent tribunal decisions, although in both cases the facts were somewhat out of the ordinary. In *S H Wade (VTD 13164)*, the tribunal held that wardrobes, which the supplier had originally treated as standard-rated but which accountants acting for receivers of the supplier had subsequently considered should have been zero-rated, were 'fitted furniture' and their supply did not qualify for zero-rating. In *S Leon (t/a Custom Bedrooms) (VTD 13200)*, the tribunal held that the fact that two walls of a bedroom were commonly used as part of the wardrobe did not prevent supplies of items used in the construction of the wardrobe from being materials for the construction of 'fitted furniture', within what is now *VATA 1994, Sch 8, Group 5, Note 22(a)(b)*.

16.25 Following these cases HMRC have summarised their view of what they call 'this complex area', namely:

(*a*) suppliers of zero-rated construction services can generally also zero-rate the supply of building materials incorporated into the building;

(*b*) but not if they are materials for the construction of fitted furniture, other than kitchen furniture;

(*c*) the service of incorporating finished, prefabricated and fitted furniture into qualifying buildings is zero-rated when supplied in the course of construction of that building, even though the cost of the materials themselves are not – a fair and reasonable apportionment can be made;

(*d*) free-standing items of furniture are not items incorporated into a building so will always be standard-rated;

(*e*) furniture is not defined; it is very much a matter of impression, but beds, chairs, bookcases, sideboards, dining tables, cupboards (with some exceptions), dressing tables, bedside cabinets, chests of drawers, linen chests, etc. are furniture and therefore standard-rated even if they form part of a range of matching units;

(*f*) airing cupboards, under-stair storage cupboards or other similar basic storage facilities which are formed by becoming part of the fabric of the building are not furniture and can qualify for zero-rating;

(*g*) so can baths, WCs, wash hand basins, etc. and items which provide storage capacity as an incidental result of their primary function, such as shelves formed as the result of constructing simple box work over pipes;

(*h*) simple bedroom wardrobes (as in *McLean Homes (Midland)*) installed on their own are not furniture so can qualify for zero-rating, but more elaborate wardrobes – however fitted – are furniture, as are simple bedroom wardrobes installed as part of a larger installation of furniture in a room, eg as part of a matching range;

(*i*) the characteristics of a simple wardrobe are that it includes a space bordered by the walls, ceilings and floor (an element to bridge over a bed or create a dressing table would disqualify the construction from being simple); the sides and back would be formed by using three walls of the room or two walls and a stub wall (but the installation of a cupboard in the corner of a room where one side is a closing end panel would not qualify); on opening the wardrobe, one should see the walls of the building which would normally be bare or painted plaster (back panelling would exclude the item); and it will have no more than a single shelf running the full length of the wardrobe, a rail for hanging clothes and a closing door or doors (ie internal features such as divisions, drawers, shoe racks, etc. would disqualify it);

(*j*) where wash hand basins installed in bathrooms or cloakrooms are supported by basin units rather than pedestals, the basin unit will not be furniture if it is a boxlike structure entirely below the line of the top of the basin and contains a shelf and a covering door or doors with the only storage space being directly beneath the basin itself; and

(*k*) more elaborate units, with other storage space constructed on either or both sides of the basin, are furniture, as are wall units such as bathroom cabinets.

(Business Brief 12/97) Notice 708 gives detailed guidance at paras 13.5.2, 13.5.3, 13.6 and 13.8.1 on what HMRC consider does and does not constitute building materials ordinarily incorporated into a building.

16.26 Six weeks after the issue of this Business Brief, the VAT tribunal in *Moores Furniture Group Ltd (VTD 15044)* held that a bedroom wardrobe where the back and sides were formed by an outside wall and two internal walls qualified for zero-rating. HMRC unsuccessfully claimed that the fact that the doors were decorative and designed to blend with the rest of the room took it out of (*i*) above. It also held that a similar wardrobe, where one wall was a specially constructed stub wall, was also zero-rated. However, if a closing end panel made of chipboard was used instead of a stub wall the same wardrobe became standard-rated furniture. The tribunal took note of Business Brief 12/97 on the basis that 'although not binding on the tribunal I do not believe that the Commissioners own published guidelines … can be ignored' in deciding against HMRC that the stub wall was acceptable. While this gives Business Briefs a status that they do not deserve, it is gratifying to see HMRC held bound by their own published material. The tribunal in *Coopers Fire Ltd (TC 2570)* held that fire curtains met the ordinarily incorporated test. They are one of a range of fire barrier products a builder may use in the ordinary way. The curtains in this case were electronically raised and the fire broke the current, causing the curtain to fall by gravity. The tribunal said that the exclusion for domestic electrical appliances (see **16.19**) did not apply as the electricity was ancillary to the essential function, which operates without electricity.

16.27 It should not be overlooked that fixtures which do not qualify for zero-rating under *Group 8* could qualify under some other provision. In

Softley Limited t/a Softley Kitchens (VTD 15034) zero-rating was allowed under *Group 12, item 2(g)*, equipment and appliances designed solely for use by a handicapped person. The company sold a range of kitchens specifically for disabled persons. In designing the kitchen it took into account the design of the customer's wheelchair and particular disabilities. HMRC's claim that the company was not making a supply of goods, but a composite supply of goods and services of which the services were the predominant element, was rejected by the tribunal. It was a supply of goods with the services of design and fitting being integral to that supply. The low level fittings were suitable only for use by a disabled person – although some items were held to be VATable as there was insufficient evidence to distinguish them from items that would normally be supplied to a customer who was not disabled. Some taxpayers have tried an alternative approach of seeking to at least reduce the VAT by separating the furniture from the fitting service. In *I & P Ramsey t/a Kitchen Format (VTD 12393)* the taxpayer contended that he was selling kitchen furniture and arranging for a self-employed fitter to fit it. Unfortunately, the agreement with the customer was to supply and install, and the installation was guaranteed by Kitchen Format. In the light of this agreement the tribunal felt it was clear that the entire supply was by Kitchen Format and that the fitters supplied their services to Kitchen Format and not to the customer. A similar conclusion was reached in the later case of *M Wilson and others t/a M & S Interiors (VTD 17494)*.

16.28 An interesting argument was raised in *Talacre Beach Caravan Sales Ltd v C & E Commrs (2004 STC 817)*. The supply of a caravan was zero-rated if it exceeded the size permitted for the use on roads of a trailer drawn by a motor vehicle having an unladen weight of less than 2030 kilogrammes (the scope of the zero-rating has since been changed) (*VATA 1994, Sch 8, Group 9, item 1*). However, the zero-rating is specifically stated not to extend to removable contents other than goods of a kind mentioned in *item 4* of *Group 5* (see **16.6**). Talacre contended that the sale of a fully fitted caravan including its contents is a single supply for VAT purposes as the furniture is ancillary to the caravan. Accordingly the exclusion did not apply as there was no supply of the contents (they being deemed to be subsumed in the sale of the caravan). Lindsay J disagreed. He did not believe that the authorities on what is a supply pointed to a general rule that 'is necessarily determinative even where there is a convincing reason to disapply it'. He felt that there might be circumstances in which, even within a single transaction, different treatments may be applicable. As he could see no social reason why Parliament should not have felt fit to standard-rate removable furniture he held that 'a finding that a static caravan and its removable contents are supplied by … one single transaction does not, of itself, require the removable contents to be given the zero-rating attributable to the caravan'. The ECJ agreed (*Case C251/05, 2006 STC 1671*), holding that the fact that there is a single supply of which the principal element is exempt with a right of recovery (the technical analysis of zero-rated) does not prevent the UK levying VAT on the part of the supply that does not qualify for that exemption. The question of what is fitted furniture in a caravan was looked at closely in *Colaingrove Ltd v HMRC (2014 STC 1457)*. For those interested, reference should be made to the judgement in that case.

16.29 The moral of *Queen Mary, University of London (QMU) (TC 1094)* is that, with property in particular, the whole tax system needs to be considered. QMU needed a new building for its biology department. It set up a subsidiary, Queen Mary Developments (QMD), to carry out the construction. The new building would incorporate substantial amounts of plant. As QMU could not claim capital allowances, it entered into an agreement with Lloyds Bank to share the benefit of the allowances with Lloyds. To claim the allowances, Lloyds needed an interest in the land, so QMU leased the site to Lloyds and Lloyds granted an underlease back to QMU. Lloyds bought the plant from QMD and made it available to QMU under the leaseback on payment of a rent based on its financing costs. Lloyds opted to tax. QMU contended that the reality of the transaction was that there was not a supply of land; it was the provision of plant and machinery on advantageous terms and that around 24% of such plant qualified for zero-rating as builders fixtures. As such QMU was in a similar position to *Argents Nurseries Ltd* (see **17.6**); it was a letting of permanently installed equipment. The Tribunal held that Lloyds made a single supply to QMU which it would be artificial to split (per *Card Protection Plan Ltd v CCE*, see **17.15**). It defined that supply as a 'supply of credit limited to its use of the plant and machinery provided as a package through QMD, and dressed up as a lease of the land', but accepted that it was a supply of the use of permanently installed plant and machinery. However, as it was a single supply, on the basis of *Talacre Beach* (see **16.28**) it could not be split into a zero-rated and taxable element. It was fully taxable. *Colingrove* later returned to the court with a different issue, namely whether a veranda which is bolted to the caravan and sometimes also fixed to the land on which it is sited, is zero-rated as part of the caravan or a separate taxable supply (*Colingrove Ltd v HMRC, 2015 STC 1013*). The FTT held that the veranda was not subordinate to the caravan, nor was it integral to it. The Upper Tribunal held that where the veranda is sold with the caravan, it is a single supply. There is nothing in the ECJ decision in *Talacre* to displace the Card Protection Plan principle to determine the nature of a supply. *Talacre* then requires one to see if there is anything in domestic law to exclude the veranda from zero-rating. The Tribunal could see nothing to do so.

Demolition

16.30 *Item 2* in **16.6** above excludes supplies in the course of the demolition of a building (demolition previously qualified for zero-rating). However, HMRC have said that 'where the contract for the construction of a zero-rated building also extends to the demolition of any building on the site', they regard the demolition as being done 'in the course of' the construction of the new zero-rated building and thus qualifying for zero-rating. This requires a single contract to cover both the demolition and construction. (Hansard, 16 May 1989, Col 76). However, the Minister was quoting HMRC's leaflet 708/2/89, and it is noted that para 3.3.4 of the latest (February 2008) edition of Notice 708, which supersedes that leaflet, states that:

> 'work is closely connected to the construction of a building when it allows the construction of the building to take place, such as if you demolish existing buildings and structures as part of a single project to construct a new building or buildings in their place'.

This seems to represent belated recognition that demolition is generally carried out by a specialist demolition contractor rather than by the builder who is to construct the new building, as a project can presumably embrace a number of distinct contracts with different contractors.

Civil Engineering Works

16.31 Since 1989, the only civil engineering work qualifying for zero-rating is that necessary to develop a permanent park for residential caravans. This exception is intended to zero-rate concrete pitches, roads, drains, sewers and the installation of mains water and electricity on permanent residential caravan parks to give occupiers of pitches the same benefit as occupiers of a dwelling-house. Whether it achieves this is unclear, as in *Stonecliff Caravan Park (VTD 11097)* the company developed a residential caravan park by installing roads, lighting and services and constructing brick skirtings for mobile homes (which were delivered to the site in two sections and assembled there). A purchaser of a mobile home entered into a pitch agreement under which he was permitted for a weekly fee to station his mobile home on the site and enjoy certain communal facilities. The tribunal held that the sales of mobile homes were zero-rated, as sales of caravans and the brick skirtings were an integral part of the sale of the home, so that the input tax on them was attributable to a zero-rated supply. However, the rest of the work was attributable to the pitch agreement which was exempt as the grant of a licence to occupy land, albeit that the work included the construction of individual pitches and the costs of connecting water and other services to the individual homes. This decision was accepted as correct in law in *C & E Commrs v Harpcombe Ltd (1996 STC 726)* where it was held that there were two separate supplies, the zero-rated sale of a mobile home and an exempt site licence, and the expenditure on providing the concrete base to the pitch related to the latter. In *P C Eccles (VTD 13372)* a claim by the taxpayer that site preparation work related wholly to the sale of mobile homes was rejected. The tribunal held that this work was essential to the exempt letting of pitches as well as to the zero-rated sales of mobile homes. In *Tingdene Developments Ltd (VTD 16546)* the tribunal again held that the concrete bases related to the exempt supply of pitches but accepted that work such as roadside kerbs, road surfacing, tree planting and other work not immediately related to the company's contractual obligations under the pitch agreements were directly referable to the taxpayer's aim of attracting new buyers in the same way as advertising and thus attributable to the sales of caravans. The construction of a civil engineering work does not, of course, include the conversion, reconstruction, alteration or enlargement of such a work (*VATA 1994, Sch 8, Group 5, Note 15*).

What is a Building Designed as a Dwelling?

16.32 A building is designed as a dwelling or a number of dwellings only if the following conditions are met in relation to each dwelling:

(*a*) it consists of self-contained living accommodation;

(*b*) there is no provision for direct internal access from the dwelling to any other dwelling or part of a dwelling;

(*c*) the separate use of the dwelling, or its separate disposal, is not prohibited by the terms of any covenant, statutory planning consent or similar provision; and

(*d*) statutory planning consent has been granted in respect of it, and its construction or conversion has been carried out in accordance with that consent.

(*Sch 8, Group 5, Note 2*.)

HMRC's view is that to come within (*a*), the dwelling must have the basic elements of living; they would expect there to be a kitchen, bathroom, sleeping area and living area. At a minimum they would expect two rooms, one a bathroom and the other providing the other facilities. In the case of a studio flat, they would expect to see, at the very least, in the living/sleeping room an area that could be used for the purpose of food preparation (a sink, storage for cups and utensils, etc, a worktop, space for a fridge and a means of cooking). If no cooking appliance is installed, they would expect there to be an appropriate connection for such an appliance (VAT Information Sheet 2/14). They accept that (*b*) can be met if the only access is a fire door connecting the dwellings, but would expect this to be fitted with an appropriate fire door lock and intended to be secured at all times other than in the event of a fire or a fire test. The door must not be capable of being routinely opened to allow occupants to move freely from one dwelling to another (VAT Information Sheet 2/14). They also say that condition (*b*) would be met notwithstanding a prohibition on the sale of individual flats arising as a result of a financial agreement (such as a mortgage) or an agreement to let the accommodation to students of a particular university or school (VAT Information Sheet 2/14).

16.33 Conditions (*a*) and (*c*) should be particularly noted. These have provided a great deal of work for the tribunals. If a dwelling is constructed in the grounds of another it is not uncommon for the planning permission to require that the two can only be sold together. The planning condition reflects a test that has in the past been applied by HMRC and accepted by the VAT tribunals. In *J K Lund (VTD 12926)* HMRC refused a VAT refund on the grounds that the building had been constructed unlawfully. Evidence was produced from the planning authority that, although the extent of rebuilding had been greater than provided for in the planning permission, it had decided during the course of the works not to object to it. The tribunal therefore found that the work was lawful – a pyrrhic victory for the taxpayer as they also found it was work of reconstruction. It appears that, under the new test, such acquiescence by the planners would be insufficient. This provision is apparently to prevent 'granny flats' and similar new homes, or flatlets belonging to existing buildings, from attracting zero-rating (VAT Information Sheet 10/95). This should be contrasted with the decision in *A I Davison* (see **16.189**) where the work was lawful but the tribunal held that head (*d*) was not met as the planning permission, although permitting the construction of the dwelling, had not been granted in respect of a dwelling.

16.34 In *Oldrings Development Kingsclere Ltd (VTD 17769)* a studio room constructed as a single-storied self-contained building some forty foot from the main house was held to be a building constructed as a dwelling because it was designed to be large enough and to contain facilities for it to be occupied as a granny or teenager's studio or for a variety of other purposes albeit that it was to be used initially to indulge the taxpayer's wife in her hobby of painting. The meaning of a dwelling is also considered in some of the cases referred to at **16.94**. In *JFB & FR Sharples (VTD 20775)* a *s 106* agreement provided that the freehold interest on the land on which sheltered accommodation was built could not be disposed of separately from the freehold interest in the Hall in whose grounds they were built, other than a disposal by Mr & Mrs Sharples to their self-invested pension plan (SIPP). The tribunal held that there was no prohibition on the separate disposals of the dwellings as they could be disposed of by granting a long lease. Even if that were wrong the permitted disposal to the SIPP meant that there was no 'prohibition', as that meant absolutely prevented, not prevented with exceptions. The planning consent in *Steven Lunn (VTD 20981)* stated that the new house could only be used for purposes either incidental or ancillary to the residential use of the main house. The tribunal held that it is possible for an ancillary use to be a separate use. It also rejected HMRC's contention that separate disposal was implicitly prohibited. Other tribunals have taken a tougher lien on planning consent though. See, for example, **16.189**.

16.35 *M J Watson (TC 780)* is a sad tale. Mr Watson obtained planning permission for an extension to his father's property for him and his family. During the course of construction the local authority's building control department decided that the work amounted to a new building and insisted it should have a separate entrance. HMRC refused to refund the VAT under the DIY Builders Scheme on the basis that the planning consent was for an extension, not a separate building. Mr Watson applied for retrospective planning consent for the development that had actually taken place. The local authority granted this but only to the time that the changes were made. The Tribunal held that the relief was not due as under head (*d*) planning permission has to exist at the time that development starts. The relief would have been due had the amended permission been backdated to the date of the original application. The Tribunal was pretty scathing about the local authority!

16.36 Equally sad is *Sheila Anne Searle (TC 1521)*. Mrs Searle wished to construct two adjoining houses next to her own for her two adult daughters. The local authority would grant planning permission for only one house. After much negotiation they granted permission for 'Erection of chalet style bungalows to provide two residential units for two related families'. The plans included an internal access door between the two dwellings but this was blocked up prior to completion of the second dwelling and never unblocked. Mrs Searle also entered into a *s 106* contract that if either or both dwellings ceased to be occupied by herself and members of her family the building could thereafter be used only as a single dwelling. It was held that Mrs Searle could not recover VAT under the DIY Builders Scheme. Firstly there was direct access between the two dwellings because, even though the door was blocked up, it could be unblocked without the need for planning consent (as it already had it). Secondly the *s 106* agreement prohibited the disposal of the two dwellings separately. Thirdly the work was not carried out in accordance with the planning consent as this did not provide for the blocking of the internal access. This is particularly unfortunate because if Mrs Searle had built a single house for occupation by the two families, she would have been able to recover the VAT. HMRC seem to accept that a fire door which cannot be used except in the case of fire does not constitute access to the adjoining building (see **16.32**).

16.37 An interesting issue in relation to (*c*) arose in *Dr R W Nicholson (VTD 19412)* a DIY builder case. Dr Nicholson purchased a one-acre site containing a 17th century listed barn and a number of derelict unlisted farm buildings. When he bought the site the barn had planning permission for conversion to a dwelling-house. Dr Nicholson obtained a different permission for 'conversion of existing barn and outbuildings to farm dwelling and annexe'. The development consisted of a southern wing and a northern wing (the latter formed from the existing barn). The two wings were connected by a single storey structure at the north end of which was a garage for the north wing and at the south end of which was a kitchen for the south wing with internal access to the remainder of that wing. There was no internal access between the two wings. What was created, therefore, was two dwellings. HMRC contended that the south wing is an annex to the north wing. It cannot be treated as a separate building because the planning consent prohibits its use except 'for purposes incidental to the enjoyment of the dwelling-house as such'. The tribunal held that this restriction does not 'prohibit the separate use or disposal of the building' within *note 2(c)* to *Group 5*. Although it would be impractical to sell the two separately the condition would not prevent Dr Nicholson selling one wing to a relative. Separate use of one dwelling can be 'only incidental' to the use of another. Accordingly what has been created from the conversion is a single building consisting of two dwellings the input tax on both of which was recoverable.

16.38 A word of caution. In *Gill Cartagena (VTD 19454)*, a different tribunal held that a virtually identical planning condition prohibited separate use. The Upper Tribunal in *HMRC v Lunn (2010 STC 486)* (see **9.18**) indicated that the Tribunal in *Dr Nicholson* seems to have applied an incorrect test, so it probably can no longer be relied upon. The Tribunal in *Mrs M E Wendels (TC 737)* held that a condition 'that the occupation of the dwelling shall be limited to a person solely or mainly employed or last employed in the cattery business [carried on in adjoining land] or a widow or widower of such a person or any resident dependants' was not a restriction on the separate use or disposal (from the cattery) of the building. In *Brims Construction Ltd (TC 2455)* HMRC argued that *Wendels* (and a similar case, *Ian Phillips, TC 2456)*) had been wrongly decided and that the case of *Holden v HMRC (TC 2043)*, where the planning restriction was that the flat should be occupied only in conjunction with the operation of the adjacent photographic studio, supported the view that use and occupation of accommodation amount to the same thing. The tribunal agreed with that in *Holden*. So did that in *R Drummond*, a DIY housebuilder case *(TC 2456)*. However, the tribunal in *R Burton (TC 2522)* supported the *Wendels* decision. It held that 'prohibited' is a strong word and a condition that limited occupation to present or past employees of the adjoining family business did not prohibit the separate use or disposal of the building from the business. On appeal (*2016 UKUT 20*) at the Upper Tribunal Barling J disagreed. He pointed out that 'in construing a condition in a planning permission the whole consent needs to be considered, and a strict or narrow approach is to be avoided in favour of one which is benevolent, applies commonsense and, where appropriate, takes account of the underlying planning purpose for the condition as evidenced by the reasons expressed'. He also noted: 'There is no question that the limitation in the condition is in sufficiently mandatory and clearly defined terms to be capable of amounting to a prohibition' and held that what is prohibited is separate use from the fishery. Although the wording of the condition was expanded beyond the fishery workers, each such occupant still had to have a specific link with the fishery; it is that link which is crucial. Barling J said that he was in complete agreement with the approach and analysis of the FTT in *Swain (TC 2719)* which means that he agreed that the approach in some of the other cases, particularly that in *Wendels*, was erroneous. The FTT in *Roy Shields (TC 2818)* also supported the *Wendels* interpretation. Unfortunately the Upper Tribunal disagreed *(2015 STC 643)*. The condition in that case was that 'the occupation of the dwelling shall be limited to a person solely employed by the equestrian business'. It held that 'a condition of planning permission for a dwelling that requires it to be occupied by a person who works at a specific location prohibits the use of the dwelling separately from the specific location'. Accordingly any use separate from the equestrian business is prohibited by the planning consent. The Tribunal held that *Phillips (TC 2456)* and *Bull (TC 2510)* had been wrongly decided and thought that the conditions in *Wendels* and *Burton* were more widely expressed. As *Burton* in the Upper Tribunal has disowned *Wendels*, *Burton* may now be the only case that can be safely relied on. In a later case, *Boggis (TC 5519)*, the planning condition was that the house could be occupied only by persons employed in the equestrian activity at the site (or a widow or widower of such a person) or for purposes ancillary to the residential use of Avil's Farmhouse. The FTT held that this did not permit occupation other than in conjunction with the equestrian business or the farm or farmhouse. It applied a purposive construction. On a strict reading, it is hard to see how occupation by a widow of a former employee who herself had never worked on the farm would not be separate from the use of the farm. In *A & P Treanor (TC 5591)*, which concerned a live/work unit, the Tribunal dismissed the taxpayer's appeal saying that the issue had now effectively been settled by the Upper Tribunal decision in *Burton*. A similar decision was reached in *Campbell (TC 5621)*. In that case, by the time the matter came before the FTT, the local authority had withdrawn the planning restriction, but the Tribunal held that the determining factor is that it applied when the work was carried out. In *Summit Electrical Installations Ltd (TC 6006)* (see **16.58**) a planning condition that the units could only be occupied by students of Leicester University and De Montfort University was held not to prevent separate use as that required the building to be linked to some specific other piece of land.

16.39 *Pearson (TC 2735)*, a DIY builder case, involved the conversion of a barn to form a live/work unit. The planning consent prohibited the occupation of the residential part by any person other than the occupier of the work part. Accordingly, said HMRC, head (*c*) (see **16.30**) is not satisfied, as separate use is not permitted. The Tribunal posed the question, separate from what? It decided that the condition could not apply where, as in this case there was no physical separation between the two elements and held that in reality the appellant had undertaken a residential conversion. Unfortunately, HMRC then refused to refund most of the tax, contending that the Tribunal decision meant that Lady Pearson's suppliers should have charged her VAT at 5% and, whilst HMRC would refund that, she would have to recover the excess from her suppliers – although sadly they could not themselves recover it from HMRC as the transactions were over four years old. Lady Pearson returned to the FTT *(TC 4005)*. The FTT held that HMRC should have raised the issue at the original Tribunal hearing and, not having done so, they were obliged to comply with the original Tribunal ruling that the whole of the tax was repayable. In *HMRC v Barkas (2015 STC 1341)* the consent for a live/work unit provided that 'the workshop/office … shall only be used/operated by the occupiers of the dwelling hereby granted permission'. The Upper Tribunal held that neither the use of the term live/work unit nor any other part of the application sought a permission which prohibited separate use or disposal of the residential part (which was a separate building within the same curtilage) and nothing in the consent itself prohibited it. HMRC had obtained a letter from the local authority, which said that it did not consider that the two could be sold separately but the Tribunal held that they had misconstrued the position. The FTT had pointed out that the restriction on the use of the work unit did not prevent it being left empty. In *Edmont Ltd (TC 4676)*, another DIY Builder case, the planning restriction for the new house was: 'To retain the whole of the land together as one parcel and in one ownership and not to alienate any part of the land or any building erected thereon without the prior consent in writing of the Council … not to use or permit any other person to use the land or any part thereof for any purpose other than the commercial equestrian business or for agriculture or forestry'. It was held that this did not prohibit separate use because anyone working locally in agriculture could live in the dwelling. Disposal was similarly not prohibited as the inclusion of the provision for Council consent contemplated granting such permission.

16.40 *Mark Catchpole (TC 1995)* built a house in an unusual format. It comprised two seemingly totally separate buildings linked only by timber decking and being only one metre away from one another. The second contained only bedrooms and a shower room. HMRC contended that Mr Catchpole could not recover any input tax as a DIY builder as neither unit could be 'occupied as separate units of accommodation at any time' under the planning consent. The tribunal first noted that both parties agreed that there was only one property and one dwelling. The question was therefore whether one dwelling could consist of two buildings. It decided that it could. However, did that mean that the works undertaken constituted 'the construction of a building designed as a dwelling'? This depends on whether the *Interpretation Act 1978* rule that unless the context otherwise requires the singular includes the plural, applies. The tribunal could see nothing in the legislation to override that presumption.

16.41 In *Simon Jones (TC 1804)*, a DIY housebuilder case, Mr Jones purchased land containing agricultural buildings with planning permission to convert the barn into a house and outbuildings into an office. The *s 106* agreement prohibited the owner of the land from allowing the office to be used by anyone other than the occupier of the house and up to three staff. HMRC contended that this prevented the separate use or disposal of the house. Mr Jones disagreed. He could sell the house on its own albeit that he would not then be able to use the office. A purchaser of the house could occupy it as the *s 106* agreement prevented use of the office without the house, not use of the house without the office. The Tribunal agreed with Mr Jones.

16.42 The tribunal in *University of Bath (VTD 14235)* held that whether a building was designed as a dwelling or number of dwellings had to be considered in relation to the building as it was originally constructed. Individual student rooms without toilets, showers or kitchen facilities were not dwellings; nor were blocks of rooms with a shared kitchen. It also held that a building could not be intended for use solely as student accommodation if it was always envisaged that the rooms would be let to other people during vacation periods. A similar decision was reached in *University Court of the University of St. Andrews (VTD 15243*). In contrast, in the later case of *Denman College (VTD 15513)* (heard by a three-man tribunal chaired by Stephen Oliver QC), student accommodation blocks each consisting of eight study-bedrooms containing a bathroom and shower unit were held to be residential accommodation even though the blocks did not contain cooking facilities. In *Agadus Israel Housing Association Ltd (VTD 18798)* the issue was whether the eight residential units in a third-floor extension constructed for the charity were self-contained. HMRC contended that they did not contain adequate facilities. The units were intended for people with Alzheimer's disease and were designed to allow flexible independent living for the residents. The extension contains a hallway which gives access to a communal room, a visitor's lavatory, a cleaning room and office space for the charity's staff, as well as to the residential unit. Each unit consists of a bedsitting room with an en suite shower room. Each has its own door with a lock and key (held by the residents and their family and friends, although the charity's Chief Executive also has a key). The tribunal noted that in each unit 'there is also the facility to have a microwave cooker, a refrigerator and a kettle' and held that 'in our view, in the twenty-first century, premises with their own front door, en suite bathing facilities and the ability to cook with a microwave cooker and a kettle are self-contained living accommodation'. HMRC appear to apply a stricter test though (see **16.32**).

16.43 Head (*d*) in **16.32** was in issue in *Cavendish Green Ltd (2017 SFTD 197)*. The company built a boundary wall. At the time it thought it was covered by a General Consent, but it was too high. Retrospective planning consent for the wall was obtained subsequently but after the disposal of the building plot. The FTT held that the wall was sufficient to constitute the entire site as a building designed as a dwelling which is in the course of construction. Unfortunately when the company came to sell the land, the purchaser wanted a bespoke house so a new planning consent was obtained. This made no reference to the boundary wall which already existed and was covered by the earlier retrospective consent. The FTT held that zero-rating could not apply as at the time of the disposal there was no planning consent for a building of which the wall formed part.

16.44 It is specifically provided that the construction (or conversion of) a building designed as a dwelling includes the construction of (or conversion of) a garage, provided that the dwelling and the garage are constructed (or converted) at the same time and the garage is intended to be occupied with the dwelling (or with one of them if there are more than one) (*VATA 1994, Sch 8, Group 5, Note 3*). In *Chipping Sodbury Town Trust (VTD 16641)* the Trust demolished two cottages and replaced them with semi-detached houses. It was a condition of the planning permission that two car parking spaces be provided for each house. A certificate of practical completion in respect of the houses was issued on 22 December 1997. At that time work on pathways was in abeyance as the Trust was seeking planning permission for the construction of garages. This was duly obtained and the pathing was completed at the same time as the construction of the garages. It was held that the garage had not been constructed at the same time as the houses so did not qualify for zero-rating. In *Bowley (TC 4800)* planning consent was given for a house and garage. The certificate of practical completion for the house was issued in June 1994 and the house was occupied from that date. However, work on the garage block was not completed until February 2014, almost 20 years later, albeit that the foundation work had been commenced in April 2013 and a reinforced floor slab laid in September 1994. The FTT held that the garage had been constructed at the same time as the house as they were a single continuous building project

16.45 An interesting issue arose in *Civilscent Ltd (2009 UKFTT 102(TC); TC 70 2009 SFTD 233)*. The company built three blocks containing 97 flats in all. The planning permission contained a provision that the whole of the parking on the site was to be provided and retained permanently for occupiers of the flats. In the event it was possible to provide only 22 parking spaces. The company let a number of the flats on 125-year leases between late 2005 and early 2006. At that time the parking had not been created. Leases of 11 of the parking spaces were granted in 2007 to existing tenants. Both parties relied on the ECJ decision in *Skatteministeriet v Henrikson (1990 STC 768)* – see **16.50**. The tribunal decided that the real issue was whether the grant of parking space leases was sufficiently closely linked to the grants of the flat leases as to constitute a single economic transaction. It decided that they were not. It did not regard the facts that the grant of the leases were separate transactions, that a separate price was paid for each, or that there was a significant delay between the two transactions as determinative. However, it felt that there needs to be at least an arrangement or understanding on the part of both parties that the elements of a single economic package will be completed; a mere possibility is not enough. In contrast in *Palmers of Oakham v HMRC (TC 959)* it was held that a garage built in March/Dec 2006 was constructed at the same time as a house built in March 2009. The Tribunal distinguished the position from that in both *Chipping Sodbury Town Trust (VTD 16641)* and *SA Whitely (VTD 11292)* (see **8.72**) on the grounds that in those cases the later buildings were built under separate planning permission. In the *Palmers* case a single planning consent for the house and garage was granted in 2003. Funds for the development were not immediately available. The work on the garage was started to keep the planning permission alive and was done in stages as funds became available. The house was built when more funds were raised.

16.46 HMRC accept that extra-care dwellings, ie self-contained flats, houses, bungalows or maisonettes that are sold or let with the option for the occupant to purchase varying degrees of care to suit his or her needs as and when they arise, are buildings designed as dwellings and thus eligible for zero-rating. This is so even if the building has been designated for planning as Class C2 (residential institutions). They do not consider that the classification for planning purposes is determinative as to the nature of the building (HMRC Brief 47/2011). This does not apply to accommodation where the occupant needs care or supervision of a type typically provided by an institution.

16.47 I have dealt with the cases on new residential buildings in **Chapter 8** as these seem to me to be a feature of development, those on listed buildings in **Chapter 9** as the work is normally in the course of a refurbishment, and what is a building in this chapter. This inevitably results in some cases that may be relevant to a particular issue being dealt with under one of the other heads. It might therefore be helpful to highlight the court decisions and also the relationship between court and tribunal decisions. VAT Tribunal decisions made before a court decision in the same area need to be approached with caution as the tribunal would not have had the benefit of the judges' views.

- *ACT Construction Ltd v C & E Commrs* – meaning of 'alteration' and 'of repair or maintenance' – see **8.48** and **9.38** – decision 3.12.1981 – exercise caution in relying on VTDs prior to VTD 1500
- *Parochial Church Council of St Luke v C & E Commrs* – relationship between 'alteration' and 'repair or maintenance' – see **8.48** – decision 28.7.1982 – exercise caution in relying on VTDs prior to VTD 1500
- *C & E Commrs v Viva Gas Appliances Ltd* – whether an alteration – see **9.42** – decision 24.11.1983 – exercise caution in relying on VTDs prior to VTD 1500
- *C & E Commrs v Great Shelford Free Church* – whether enlargement of existing building – see **8.54** – decision 3.4.1987 – exercise caution in relying on VTDs prior to VTD 2379
- *C & E Commrs v Link Housing Association Ltd* – who is a person constructing a building – see **16.17** – decision 10.7.1992 – exercise caution in relying on VTDs prior to VTD 7996

- *C & E Commrs v McLean Homes Midland Ltd* – goods normally incorporated by a builder – see **16.24** – decision 16.2.1993 – exercise caution in relying on VTDs prior to VTD 10313
- *C & E Commrs v Rannoch School* – whether works in the course of construction of a building – see **8.84** – decision 19.2.1993 – exercise caution in relying on VTDs prior to VTD 10313
- *C & E Commrs v London Diocesan Fund* – meaning of conversion reconstruction alteration or enlargement – see **8.51** – decision 24.3. 1993 – exercise caution in relying on VTDs prior to VTD 10328
- *C & E Commrs v Windflower Housing Association* – whether roof replacement repair or improvement – see **9.30** – decision 16.6.1995 – exercise caution in relying on VTDs prior to VTD 13466
- *C & E Commrs v St Mary's RC School* – whether work in the course of construction of a building – see **8.81** – decision 21.6.1996 – exercise caution in relying on VTDs prior to VTD 14423
- *C & E Commrs v Arnold* – when is a building substantially completed – see **16.193** – decision 30.7.1996 – exercise caution in relying on VTDs prior to VTD 14426
- *C & E Commrs v Marchday Holdings Ltd* – whether a new building – see **8.60** decision 11.12.1996 – exercise caution in relying on VTDs prior to VTD 14714
- *C & E Commrs v Morrish* – whether conversion, reconstruction, alteration or enlargement – see **9.30** – decision 1.7.1998 – exercise caution in relying on VTDs prior to VTD 15643
- *Cantrell & others t/a Foxearth Nursing Home v C & E Commrs* – see **8.67** – decision 28.1.2000 – exercise caution in relying on VTDs prior to VTD16503
- *C & E Commrs v Zielinski Baker & Partners Ltd* – whether alterations to a residential building – see **9.47** – decision 26.2.2004 – exercise caution in relying on VTDs prior to VTD 18601
- *C & E Commrs v Tinsley* – whether alterations to a residential building – see **9.51** – decision 10.6.2005 – exercise caution in relying on VTDs prior to VTD 19112

What is a Dwelling?

16.48 There is no statutory definition of a dwelling as such. HMRC's view is that the word should be given its day-to-day meaning of a place where someone lives (see **16.90**). This was also the view expressed by Lord Millett in a housing case, *Uratemp Ventures Ltd v Collins* (see **16.95**).

Relevant Residential Purpose

16.49 A building *is used for a relevant residential purpose* if it is used as either:

(*a*) a home or other institution providing residential accommodation for children;

(*b*) a home or other institution providing residential accommodation with personal care for persons in need of personal care by reason of:

- (i) old age;
- (ii) disablement;
- (iii) past or present dependence on alcohol or drugs; or
- (iv) past or present mental disorder;

(*c*) a hospice;

(*d*) residential accommodation for students or school pupils;

(*e*) residential accommodation for members of any of the armed forces;

(*f*) a monastery, nunnery or similar establishment; or

(*g*) an institution which is the sole or main residence of at least 90% of its residents.

(*VATA 1994, Sch 8, Group 5, Note 4.*)

16.50 A building is, however, not to be regarded as used for a relevant residential purpose if it is used as:

(i) a hospital;

(ii) a prison or similar institution (eg a borstal establishment would not be covered by (*a*)); or

(iii) an hotel, inn or similar establishment (*Note 4*).

16.51 The distinction between a hospital and a home or other institution providing personal care was in issue in *Hospital of St John & St Elizabeth (VTD 19141)*. The hospital built a Centre for occupation by elderly people with mental illness in conjunction with a local NHS hospital trust. It successfully contended that its purpose was to care for such people not to treat them. The residents all suffered from dementia. There was no cure for their disease; the aim was to provide them with a home for life and to maximise the quality of their lives. Accordingly the construction of the centre qualified for zero-rating as being an institution providing personal care.

16.51A In *Pennine Care NHS Trust (TC 4998)*, the FTT concluded that 'personal care' is a term that must reflect current times; it may go beyond the basics of feeding and washing and in the context of mental health the inclusion of the type of bespoke and specialist care provided by the Unit does not trespass into the arena of a 'hospital or similar institution'. After mulling this over for almost two years, HMRC have said that they now accept that personal care may incorporate a high level of medical treatment if it is essential to the accommodation that is being provided. Care homes, as distinct from hospital, may be set up to provide an extended period of in-house treatment or to offer treatment that assists recovery or rehabilitation. A care home may have a treatment centre that occupies a building or a distinct part of a building, in which case that treatment centre will be subject to zero-rating if it is to be used solely (at least 95%) by the residents of the care home (HMRC Brief 2/2017).

16.52 If a number of buildings are constructed simultaneously on the same site and are intended for use together as a unit solely for a relevant residential purpose each of them is to be treated as intended for use solely for such a purpose (*Note 5*). This will ensure relief for nursing homes, etc. where there are separate accommodation blocks and a communal dining or recreation room in a different building. It is important to note that the buildings must be constructed at the same time. *Note 5* will not allow zero-rating for a later addition to a nursing home which is a separate building to the main home and not of itself capable of being a dwelling. For the definition of a 'dwelling', see **16.32** onwards above. HMRC will by concession treat buildings as constructed at the same time if the original planning permission covers their installation but the construction is phased over a limited period (VAT Information Sheet 10/95). No guidance is given as to what is a limited period, although the cases considered at **8.73** may give some guidance as to what is not! The issue in *St Andrew's Property Management Ltd (VTD 20499)* was whether *Note 4* allows zero-rating where one institution is built within another or whether *Note 5* permits zero-rating only where the buildings are constructed at the same time. St Andrew's Healthcare, which is a charity, provides health and care services primarily for patients with mental health problems. The charity constructed a new building in the hospital grounds for the purpose of accommodating and treating young people who have both learning difficulties and challenging behaviour. These are not medical issues. It is a secure building in which the young people are housed full-time. The average stay is three years. The building is the residents' only home while they are there. The tribunal had no difficulty in holding that the building qualified as an institution providing care within *Note 4*. Accordingly *Note 5* was not relevant. It deals with a different situation. The issue in *TGH (Commercial) Ltd (TC 4851)* was whether a building, Holme Terrace, which it was constructing for a charity, was used for a relevant residential purpose. HMRC had accepted that the property consisted of a number of dwellings but, although that would give the zero-rating, TGH did not accept it because to do so would have implications for other work on the site. The FTT held that the building, which housed a workshop used to maintain a number of relevant residential buildings, qualified for zero-rating as it was constructed at the same time as at least one of the residential buildings. An interesting twist is that HMRC appealed the decision and, worried at having to bear HMRC's costs, the company then withdrew its appeal. The Upper Tribunal (*2017 UKUT 0116 (TCC)*) held that the effect of the withdrawal is that there was nothing left for it to decide, so the FTT decision must stand in spite of HMRC's wish for the UT to clarify the position. In *St George's Augustinian Care (TC 5316)*, a communal building in a retirement village was held not to qualify for zero-rating. The fact that a resident of an apartment in the retirement village has a right to use facilities contained in a wholly separate building does not make those facilities part of his dwelling.

16.53 HMRC have given some guidance in relation to the construction and sale of 'independent living' units within the grounds of a residential care home. They say that in order for either the construction or the sale to qualify for zero-rating the units need to be either 'designed as dwellings' or intended for use solely for a relevant residential unit. HMRC do not think they meet either of these tests. Although they may have the physical characteristics of a dwelling, there is normally a planning stipulation that they cannot be used separately from the care home. That will prevent them being dwellings. Even where personal care is provided to occupants of the units they consider that either such care is not provided as an institution would provide personal care or, if that is wrong, it is provided as part of the existing home or institution. They also say that the units are not 'an institution which is the sole or main residence of at least 90% of its residents' because the units are not institutions (HMRC Brief 66/2007).

16.54 There are a number of points that should be noted.

1. A building used as a residence for children can qualify even if all that is provided is the accommodation. A home or other institution providing accommodation for the elderly, disabled, etc. will qualify only if personal care is provided in addition to the accommodation. It is not wholly clear if such personal care has to be provided in the accommodation itself, but it probably does.

2. It should be noted that (*b*) in **16.49** above requires not only that personal care be provided but also that the inmates be in need of such care. No guidance is given as to what constitutes personal care. Clearly the provision of a full cleaning and nursing service, such as in a nursing home, will qualify. It is unlikely that the mere provision of a warden

with residents doing everything else themselves would do so – although in such circumstances it may well be that the residents' rooms would constitute dwellings and thus qualify for zero-rating under *item 1(a)* in **16.6** above instead of *item 1(b)*.

3. The dividing line between a hospice (qualifying for zero-rating) and a hospital (which is standard-rated) is not clear. Both provide medical care. As the intention seems to be to allow zero-rating where an institution is a person's permanent home, but to deny it where a person may stay there for a few days only, it is likely that a hospice will be limited to an institution that provides care for those whose illness is perceived to be incurable.

4. It appears that a rooming house let to a school on a lease of over 21 years as student accommodation will qualify for zero-rating even if the school lets it out to others during the vacation period, as the test is whether the building is 'intended for use as residential accommodation for students'.

5. The wording 'hotel, inn or similar establishment' should be contrasted with that used in *VATA 1994, Sch 9, Group 1, item 1*, ie 'hotel, inn, boarding house or similar establishment'. This suggests that a boarding house could qualify for zero-rating provided that the 90% test in head (*g*) in **16.49** above is met – although it is debatable whether a boarding house constitutes an 'institution'. If it does not, it will not come within head (*g*). A property supplying accommodation and breakfast for homeless and unemployed people has been held to be a similar establishment to a hotel (*Namecourt Ltd (1984 VATTR 22) (VTD 1560)*), as has accommodation for long-term residents in a guest house (*Mrs R I McGrath (1992 STC 371)*).

6. The word 'institution' is not defined. In *Cathal McAlister (VTD 18011)* the tribunal thought that it must mean a building used by an organisation or a body so that it could be described as an institutional building. However, they feel that the word refers to a single building not to the aggregation of buildings that formed the institution.

16.55 It was held in *Urdd Gobaith Cymru (Welsh League of Youth) (VTD 14881)* that residential accommodation need not imply permanence. *Urdd Gobaith* is an educational establishment to foster use of the Welsh language. It built lodging accommodation to be used wholly by students and teachers attending its courses. The average stay by a student was four days. The tribunal felt that while 'a residence' implies a degree of permanence, 'residential accommodation' does not; it merely signifies lodging, sleeping or overnight accommodation. It also felt that if Parliament had intended to exclude short-term accommodation, the legislation would have said so. HMRC have said that they accept this decision and have changed their policy to reflect it (Business Brief 6/98). HMRC point out that a building which was not residential under their old definition, but is residential under the new, cannot be 'converted' into a residential building, so input tax on such a 'conversion' is now irrecoverable. They did, however, allow zero-rating by concession where conversion commenced (or was contracted for) before 9 June 1998 when they pointed out this fact.

16.56 The reduced rate also applies to the supply of services of installing mobility aids for use in domestic accommodation by a person who at the time of the supply is 60 or over and the supply of such mobility aids by the installer. 'Mobility aids' covers grab rails, ramps, stair lifts, bath lifts, built-in-shower seats and showers containing such seats and walk in baths fitted with sealable doors (*VATA 1994, Sch 7A, Group 10* inserted by the *VAT (Reduced Rate) Order 2007 (SI 2007 No 1601)*).

16.57 In *Derby YMCA (VTD 16918)*, the YMCA owned a hostel and youth centre consisting of a complex of three buildings. It converted part of the first floor of one of these consisting of 15 hotel-style bedrooms into ten self-contained flatlets plus the provision of a staff room and ancillary laundry and toilet facilities. HMRC accepted that the YMCA was a relevant housing association within *item 3* (see **16.7**) and that the building was not designed as a dwelling or a number of dwellings for the purpose of *Note 7* (see **16.90**). However, they contended that the test was not whether it was a dwelling but rather whether it was used as a dwelling; the living accommodation was clearly the residence of most of the recipients. Alternatively they contended that the building was not used for a relevant residential purpose because it was similar to a hotel. The tribunal held that the building was a non-residential part of a building within *Note 7*; it was not designed as a dwelling, nor physically adapted for use as a dwelling, nor used for a relevant non-residential purpose (and not as a building similar to a hotel). However, it also held that the new self-catering flatlets were not used for a relevant residential purpose within *Note 4(g)* (see **16.49**). Accordingly, zero-rating was denied. In the High Court Evans-Lombe J, upholding the conclusion of the tribunal, commented that 'It is the intrinsic nature of the enterprise, as established by evidence of what is actually being performed in order to advance it, that is important in arriving at a conclusion whether or not a particular undertaking constitutes a business. It does not seem to me that the principle of tax neutrality assists in that process'.

16.58 It is possible for a building to qualify for zero-rating both as a dwelling (because the test is based on design) and as a building intended for use for a relevant residential purpose (because that test is based on use). In such a case, which provision to use is up to the taxpayer (VAT Information Sheet 2/14). This is so even if during construction the user gave the builder a certificate that the building was intended to be used for a relevant residential purpose. The planning permission does not necessarily determine the VAT treatment. This was the position in *Summit Electrical Installations Ltd (TC 6006)*. Summit was a sub-contractor. It was engaged by Create Construction Ltd to put electrical installations in a block of student studio flats. The developer of the site issued a certificate to Create that it intended to use the building for a relevant residential purpose. HMRC contended that in those circumstances, Summit had to charge VAT to Create. Summit had not done so on the basis that it was supplying building work for residential accommodation. The FTT held that the accommodation was residential, so Summit's services were correctly zero-rated.

Relevant Charitable Purpose

16.59 *Use for a relevant charitable purpose* is use by a charity otherwise than in the course or furtherance of a business (*VATA 1994, Sch 8, Group 5, Note 6*). The obvious example is a church. It does not appear that the charity needs to be a UK charity – although it should be borne in mind that, for income tax purposes, an overseas charity has been held not to be within the definition of a 'body which must apply its income for charitable purposes only', on the basis that those words imply a UK charity (*Camille & Henry Dreyfus Foundation Inc v CIR (36 TC 126)*). The ECJ held in *Persche v Finanzamt Ludenscheid* (Case C-318/07)(2009 STC 586) that a provision which allows a donation to a charity in one member country but denies it to a similar charity in another is likely to infringe the EC principle of free movement of capital, so it would probably be discriminatory to limit charitable VAT reliefs To UK charities. Where a charity does not carry on a business, its office premises will also fall within this head. If some of its activities constitute the carrying on of a business for VAT purposes the appropriate part of its office premises will qualify. An apportionment needs to be made, the part that is to be used for non-business purposes qualifying for zero-rating (see **16.90** below). In many cases the problems of making such an apportionment will be awesome. In *St Dunstan's Roman Catholic Church Southborough (VTD 15472)* the VAT tribunal held that the construction of a double garage within the curtilage of the church for use by the priest was for use by the charity for a relevant charitable purpose even though the priest might use his car partly for his pastoral work and partly for personal journeys. Minor non-qualifying use can be ignored under ESC 3.29. This is outlined at **16.129**.

16.60 The courts have held that a wide meaning needs to be given to the word business in the context of VAT (see, for example, *C & E Commrs v Royal Exchange Theatre Trust (1979 STC 728)*). In *C & E Commrs v Morrison's Academy Boarding Houses Association (1978 STC 1)*, quoted with approval in the *Royal Exchange Theatre Trust* case, it was pointed out that the words 'commerce' or 'profit' are not used in association with the word 'business' and that, if activities are 'predominantly concerned with the making of taxable supplies to consumers for a consideration', the taxpayer is in the 'business' of making taxable supplies. Neill J in the *Royal Exchange Theatre Trust* case considered that the activities must include some sort of commercial element for a business to exist, although the VAT tribunal in *Hunmanby Bowling Club* (see **16.80** below) did not follow this.

16.61 In *C & E Commrs v Lord Fisher (1981 STC 238)*, Gibson J accepted six indicia put forward by the Crown on the basis of previous cases to determine whether activities constitute a business, namely:

(*a*) whether the activity is a 'serious undertaking earnestly pursued';

(*b*) whether it is an occupation or function actively pursued with reasonable or recognisable continuity;

(*c*) whether it has a certain measure of substance as measured by the quarterly or annual value of taxable supplies made;

(*d*) whether it is conducted in a regular manner and on sound and recognised business principles;

(*e*) whether it is predominantly concerned with the making of taxable supplies for a consideration; and

(*f*) whether the taxable supplies are of a kind which, subject to differences of detail, are commonly made by those who seek to profit by them.

Lord Fisher organised shoots on his estate for his friends who contributed to the costs. The judge thought that 'the sharing of the costs of a sporting or other pleasure activity does not by itself turn an activity of pleasure and social enjoyment into a business'. In *HMRC v Longridge on the Thames (2016 STC 236)* (see **16.71**) Andrew LJ commented that the Fisher criteria omit reference to the connection or proportionality of the payment to the service (as required by *European Commission v Finland (C-246/08)* and while those criteria have a role to play they cannot displace the approach required by CJEU jurisprudence. In *Finland* the CJEU said that the scope of the term 'economic activities' is very wide and that it is objective in character, in the sense that the activity is considered per se and without regard to its purpose or results. However, the receipt of a payment does not per se mean that a given activity is economic in nature. In that case the provision of legal aid by *Finland* was held not to be an economic activity even though a litigant was required to make a contribution to the cost based on his means.

16.62 An interesting case on what is a business is that of *Cardiff Community Housing Association Ltd (VTD 16841)*. The Association is a charity. It provides social housing for persons in need. It is a non-profit making organisation dependent wholly on Government and public grants. It claimed the construction of an office block for its own use qualified for zero-rating. HMRC contended that, as it was in receipt of rental income from its properties, the charity was carrying on a business so the office would not be used for a relevant charitable purpose. The rents represented about 20% of the charity's income. The tribunal found the decision difficult but on balance felt that the charity was carrying out a function on behalf of the state in the same way as the Institute of Chartered Accountants (*ICAEW v C & E Commrs,*

1997 STC 1155) which did not amount to an economic activity. It was therefore not carrying on a business. The tribunal also found that the charity carried out its activities as a body governed by public law so that its activities were outside the scope of VAT by virtue of *Article 4(5)* of the *EC Sixth Directive*. In the later case of *Riverside Housing Association (2006 STC 2072)* where HMRC instructed leading counsel, the tribunal (Colin Bishopp) said that it found itself unable to agree with the Tribunal in Cardiff that there is no exploitation when the income derived from an activity must be utilised in the business rather than put to any other purpose. It thought it an 'inevitable conclusion' that the letting of property in return for payment is an economic activity. It also held that even though Riverside carried on activities which are in the public interest and which are supported by public money it is not a public body; it is a private sector organisation which happens to undertake functions on behalf of the state. This was upheld by Lawrence Collins J who referred to the tribunal decision in Cardiff Community Housing but concluded, "It is true that there are cases on either side of the line, but I am wholly persuaded that on the evidence and in the light of the trend of the decisions the tribunal was entitled to come to its well-reasoned decision that the activities of Riverside are in the course or furtherance of a business". He added that he would have come to the same decision as the tribunal on the facts. *Morley Retreat Conference House (VTD 17265)* is a registered charity offering facilities for retreats and conferences. It runs on a non-profit making basis and, as its supplies are exempt, is not registered for VAT. It constructed a chapel and claimed that the construction work should be zero-rated, as it was supplied in the course of the construction of a building intended solely to be used for a relevant charitable purpose. It was held that the chapel was used as part and parcel of the business run by Morley, albeit that no charge was made for its use.

16.63 In *Yarburgh Children's Trust (2002 STC 207)* a building owned by the trust, which is a charity, was used by a playgroup run by a separate charity at a concessionary rent. The trust contended that such use was otherwise than in the course of a business. Patten J felt that the balance of authority, particularly the ECJ decision in *Wellcome Trust Ltd v C & E Commrs (Case C-155/94, 1996 STC 945)* that share disposals by trustees formed part of the normal management of trust assets and were not carried out in furtherance of any business, was against treating an activity as an economic one merely because it results in a consideration or produces income. He accepted an HMRC submission that the motive of the person who makes the supply cannot dictate the tax treatment of the transaction but felt that excluding such motive does not allow the tribunal to disregard the observable terms and features of the transaction in question and the wider context in which it is carried out. He felt that the tribunal needs to ascertain such things as the nature of the activities carried on by the person alleged to be in business, the terms upon which and manner in which those activities are carried out and the nature of the relationship between the parties to the transaction. The mere fact of the letting at a rent is not sufficient in itself to render that transaction an economic activity. The playgroup's occupation of the building was not in the furtherance of a business. The overwhelming impression is that the play-school was a co-operative venture run by trained staff with the benefit of help provided by parents. The tribunal was entitled to conclude that no business user was involved.

16.64 This decision was followed in *St Paul's Community Project Ltd (VTD 18466)*, another charity, where the facts were similar. HMRC sought to distinguish the cases on the grounds that St Paul's ran a day nursery, not a play group, that the opening hours were longer than in Yarborough and that the parents probably paid greater fees to St Paul's than in Yarborough. The tribunal thought none of those factors significant. Nor did they think that the fact that in Yarborough the management of the playgroup was in the hands of a committee of parents whereas in St Paul's parents were in a minority on the committee was a basis for distinguishing the two cases.

16.65 The comment of Patten J that the mere fact of letting at a rent is not sufficient in itself to render the letting an economic activity was followed by the tribunal in *Ardenglen Developments Ltd (VTD 19906)*. Ardenglen Housing Association Ltd (AHA) proposed building an annexe to one of its properties to create additional office accommodation which could be let out to local community groups. One of the proposed providers was ERDF. It was discovered that AHA did not qualify for ERDF funding. It accordingly incorporated Developments, which would qualify, to construct the annexe. The annexe itself met the conditions for zero-rating. Developments duly carried out the development after which it granted a 20-year lease (the land is in Scotland) to AHA which in turn granted a 20-year lease to a charity. The rent from Developments to AHA was £19,596 pa, reviewable every five years and that from AHA to the charity was £23,980 reviewable every five years. HMRC contended that Developments intended to use the building to generate rent from AHA, which is an economic activity so it could not contend that the building would be used solely for a relevant charitable purpose. The tribunal pointed out that 'intended use' relates to the building not the supply. 'Intended' looks to the future, ie what is to be done with the building following its supply. As with *Yarborough* where the lease came about only to satisfy the requirement for lottery funding, the lease came about only to satisfy the funding requirement. Accordingly the lease and the sublease were isolated one-off transactions to enable the project to be carried into effect and as such did not give rise to AHA carrying on an economic activity of letting the building. The use intended by Developments of the building was solely its occupation by the charity in a way that was consistent with AHA's aims. In Yarborough the letting was at a clear undervalue whereas Developments lease to AHA appears to have been a market rent, but the tribunal do not appear to have placed any significance on that.

16.66 In *Donaldson's College (VTD 19258)*, a Scottish case, HMRC argued that The Yarborough Children's Trust and St Paul's Community cases have both been wrongly decided and, being decisions of an English High Court judge, they were not binding in Scotland so the tribunal should decline to follow them. That case concerned a school for deaf children. The tribunal found that it was for all practical purposes controlled by central government and that it was not carrying on a business. It agreed with the College that the HMRC approach of using the *Lord Fisher case* (see **16.61**) as a checklist was inappropriate and that the true test is 'whether the activity is predominantly concerned with providing taxable supplies for a consideration'. It is depressing that HMRC seem so contemptuous of the High Court that they would rather seek to establish that tax law is different in England and Scotland than to accept defeat in the courts with good grace. It does, however, seem clear that they have no intention of allowing a taxpayer to plead Yarborough and St Paul's, however similar the facts may be, so to do so one will have to pursue the claim to a tribunal. Despite the above stricture the Lord Fisher tests have been adopted in a number of later cases, including non-VAT cases, so seem to be generally agreed as appropriate tests, albeit not necessarily conclusive of the question.

16.67 In *The Sheiling Trust (Ringwood Waldorf School) (VTD 19472)* the tribunal (Edward Sadler and John Brown) formulated the following guidance from the various cases on whether an activity is a business for VAT purposes.

1. A wide-ranging enquiry must be made with the objective of discovering the intrinsic nature of the activity; that enquiry should extend to the features of the activity, and the manner and context in which it is carried out, including the relationship between all the parties.

2. To comprise a 'business', the activity must have 'economic content' – its intrinsic nature must be economic (and not, for example, social or charitable).

3. The fact that in the carrying out of the activity a supply is made for a consideration is not in itself sufficient to give the activity such 'economic content'.

4. The fact that in the carrying out of the activity no profit is made (or there is no intention to make a profit) is not in itself sufficient to enable the activity to be characterised as having no such 'economic content': in particular, an activity may have 'economic content' where it is carried out by way of making supplies which are of a kind that are made commercially, even if in the case under review they are made for no profit.

5. The motive of the person carrying out the activity does not dictate its tax treatment (and in particular, whether or not it is a business for VAT

purposes): that treatment must be ascertained from the nature of the activity rather than its purpose.

6. If the activity is undertaken by a charity, then the fact that the activity is a means whereby the charity carries out its charitable objects is not in itself sufficient to enable the activity to be characterised as having no 'economic content': but that fact is relevant to the intrinsic nature of the activity and therefore to the question of whether or not the activity has 'economic content'.

7. The six indicia or 'tests' first referred to in the Lord Fisher case are useful tools which can be employed in the analysis of an activity to determine whether it is a business, but they are no more than tools and should not be applied as a comprehensive and rigid code.

The school is a 'contribution school' under which parents of the children are required to contribute to the well-being of the school community both by contributing financially and by contributing their particular skills to assist the school. The tribunal held that the charity was not carrying on a business so the building work was for a relevant charitable purpose.

16.68 The question in *Quarriers (VTD 20660)* was whether Quarriers, a Scottish charity would use its new national epilepsy centre in the course or furtherance of a business. This provides hi-tech diagnostic facilities, treatment, therapeutic advice and information each year to about 350 people with epilepsy who live in a comfortable home environment for about eight weeks during their assessment. The charity is financed primarily by payments from local Health Authorities. HMRC contended that Quarriers carries on an economic activity as its supplied services for a consideration to the NHS. It is not undertaking a function of the NHS but is filling a gap left by the NHS. Quarriers contended that engaging in the marketplace is not the correct test of whether it is making supplies for a consideration. The correct test is the predominant concern test formulated in the *Morrison's Academy* case (see **16.60**). The activities of Quarriers were not economic; they provided a unique service which was not financially independent. The service is subsidised by Quarriers in furtherance of its charitable objects. There is no direct link between the cost of the services provided to a particular individual and the charges made to a Health Board or Local Authority. The tribunal agreed. It felt that the activities of the new epilepsy centre are not in any sense a trading or commercial activity that might justify being described as economic. They do not have the mark of a business activity. The charges made by Quarriers are not determined by reference to going rates in the market, as there is no market as such, but essentially by reference to what Health Boards are prepared to pay for the unique service provided by Quarriers. This case was closely followed by a second *Quarriers (VTD 20670)* in which the tribunal again held that Quarriers was not carrying on a business activity in running a school, unique in West and Central Scotland, for children with severe emotional difficulties. Again the school was non-profit making, heavily subsidised by Quarriers, but partly financed by charges to local authorities which were fixed in advance by reference to the estimated costs of operating the school, not by reference to the cost of the actual service supplied to an individual child.

16.69 The taxpayer similarly won in *Jenfield Swifts Football Club (VTD 20689)*. The Club is non-profit making, is located in a deprived area of Perth with few facilities, and has received the enthusiastic support of the local authority. It is a Community Amateur Sports Club. Its income derives from gate receipts, takings from a tea hut which operates only when games are played, pitch fees from other teams and charges of £5 or £7.50 that (by arrangement with its landlord) the Club makes to various community associations to use the clubhouse from time to time. The tribunal had no hesitation in accepting that the Club performs and operates for purposes beneficial to the community, or in holding that it was similar to a village hall. It had considered the decision in Quarriers and 'could neither fault it nor improve upon it' and added that although the facts in *Jenfield* were slightly different 'the tests were the same as those ably set out therein on a wide ranging discussion of authority, with which we agree'. The FTT in *Eynsham Cricket Club (TC 6047)* took a different view. It held that whilst a community amateur sports club is capable of being a charity for VAT purposes, Eynsham is not a charity because it has a subsidiary social purposes and so is not established exclusively for charitable purposes. It went on to hold that the new pavilion was intended for use as a village hall or similar activity and held that it was. However, as it was not a charity, that could not help it. This is an odd result. Use by a charity as a village hall qualifies for zero-rating, but it is that use as a village hall which prevents the club from being a charity.

16.70 The issue in *Wakefield College (2016 STC 1219)* was whether the building was used solely for a relevant charitable purpose. It was agreed that the delivery of grant funded education is not a supply. However, in some cases the College charges fees to students. These are a small minority of the total but they are (in the FTT's view) 'of reasonable substance'. The fees seem to have been around 19% of the College's income. The College contended that such students were subsidised and that the teaching of those students was not possible without the grant, but the Tribunal thought that the terms of the grant meant that 'it makes very good business sense to take on the fee paying students as well'. Accordingly teaching the fee paying students constituted a business, so zero-rating could not apply. The building cost £29 million so the loss of VAT relief was very significant. In the Upper Tribunal Wakefield accepted that it was carrying on a business in relation to those students that paid full fees but said that the FTT had not considered whether such business use is de minimis. The Tribunal remitted the case to the FTT to consider that. The FTT then held (largely on the basis of *Commission v Finland (Case*

C-246/08) where the Advocate-General said that there was no direct link where the payment was only part payment of the fees set by national legislation and the proportion payable was also dependent on the recipient's income) that the varying factors such as age, previous academic achievements, receipt of benefits, low income and personal factors that *Wakefield* took into account in deciding what to charge an individual student, combined with the fact that the overall contribution that students make to the cost of running the college is small, meant that the fees from students are not 'consideration'.

16.71 In *HMRC v Longridge on the Thames (2016 STC 2362)*, a charity which provided water-based courses, activities and facilities for young people, a building comprising toilet, changing and shower facilities on the ground floor and space for training courses and meetings above was held to be intended for use solely for relevant charitable purposes. The charity charged fees for attendance at courses but these were heavily subsidised. The FTT concluded that the intrinsic nature of the charity's activity or enterprise is not that of a business. It was heavily influenced by the fact that the activities were largely provided by volunteers. The UT agreed it had applied the correct test but said that the *Finland* case applies where the amount a recipient paid was determined by reference to two factors, the cost of the supply and the extent of the recipient's resources. However, it does not apply where that link is broken. The fact that fees charged to some students represented less than the cost of the supply because that cost was in part defrayed by grant funding did not have the consequence that the fees did not amount to consideration for the supply. Accordingly the college's supplies to students were made in the course or furtherance of a business. The Court of Appeal disagreed. It felt that the way UK law had developed has not followed the development of EU law. 'In determining whether a person carries on economic activity, there is no doubt there is no exception for activities carried on for the benefit of the public. Likewise, the fact that the provider does not seek to make a profit is also irrelevant'. Under EU law, economic activity entails a permanent activity in return for remuneration (*Landesanstalt fur Landwirtschaft v Franz Gotz (C-408/06)*). Andrew J said that the correct approach is to start from the general rule and ask if there is evidence either that there was no direct link between the service and the payment or other evidence, which shows that there is no economic activity.

16.72 In *French Education Property Trust Ltd (TC 4762)* where one charity leased a school to another charity which operated the school, the FTT, having considered both *Yarburgh* (see **16.63**) and *Longridge*, said that they were not compelled to find that there had been an economic activity simply on the basis that there had been the letting of a property for rent. Instead the wider circumstances must be considered. Unfortunately they went on to hold that although the rent was not intended to show a profit, it was intended to recover its costs (other than the part covered by donations) and the way the arrangement was structured amounted to an economic activity. In *Capernwray Missionary Fellowship of Torchbearers v HMRC (TC 3750)* Capernwray Missionary Fellowship of Torchbearers is a charity. It occupies Capernwray Hall. It built a conference hall as a separate building. This comprised dormitory bedrooms on the ground floor (which are occupied by those attending courses) a large lecture room on the first floor and a few smaller rooms on the top floor. The charity runs a bible school in the Conference Hall for 30 weeks in the year and a number of shorter courses at other times. The winter bible school lasts 22 weeks and the summer school, eight weeks. Over 80% of the charity's income is from fees from those attending courses, of which 75% is from the bible schools. The charity sets its fees to just cover its costs. It relies heavily on unpaid volunteers. Without these, the fees would have to be about 25% higher. The FTT held that the sleeping accommodation was not intended for a relevant residential purpose as the attendees were not students. It also held that it was not intended for a relevant charitable purpose because under the Lord Fisher tests, the bible school is a serious undertaking earnestly pursued, pursued with continuity, has a measure of substance and is conducted on solid business principles as it sets its fees to cover its costs. The first floor was used for a large extent for religious preaching and for worship which is not intrinsically of an economic nature. However, it was also intended for use in the economic activity so the Conference Hall as a whole was not intended for use for a relevant charitable purpose. It should be noticed that HMRC relied largely on the 2009 CJEU decision in *Commission v Finland (Case C- 246/08),* which said that the term 'economic activity' is wide and has to be considered without regard to its purpose or result. However, the Tribunal felt that the Lord Fisher tests are still helpful in determining whether an activity is of an economic nature.

Use as a Village Hall, etc

16.73 Use of a building as a village hall or similarly in providing social or recreational facilities for a local community is also a relevant charitable purpose (*VATA 1994, Sch 8, Group 5, Note 6*). In *Jubilee Hall Recreation Centre Ltd v C & E Commrs (1999 STC 381),* the Court of Appeal interpreted the scope of this provision restrictively. It felt that its purpose was to extend the relief to the case where the local community is the final consumer in respect of the services. It would not include a building intended for economic activities unless such activities are an ordinary incidence of the use of the building by a local community for social, including recreational, purposes. This introduces considerations of scale and locality. The scale of Jubilee Hall's commercial activities went far beyond the normal activities of a village hall. The court also doubted, without deciding, whether an area covering much of Central London could aptly be described as a 'local community' or whether people who worked in an area and lived elsewhere are part of its local community. In *C & E Commrs v St Dunstan's Educational Foundation (1999 STC 381),* heard at the same time, the Court of Appeal held that a sports centre constructed primarily for use as one of the facilities of a fee-paying school could not be brought within the scope of zero-rating merely by allowing its use by the local community when not in use by the school. Beldam LJ also doubted whether the word 'use' in this context includes the activity of leasing the building to a third party, in this case the local authority, although it appears to have been accepted that allowing the school to occupy, for no consideration, would not of itself have denied the relief. In *Bennachie Leisure Centre Association (VTD 14276)* the tribunal held that a building which was part of a larger complex and contained a central area marked out for badminton, with changing rooms, toilets, crèche, club room, office, kitchen, tea room, craft shop, thrift shop, fitness rooms and equipment store was similar to a village hall as it was suitable for both social and recreational use and was not intended for other purposes to a material extent. The building was intended to service ten parishes within a six-mile radius, which the tribunal felt comprised a local community. However, as this case was decided before the Court of Appeal decision in *Jubilee Hall*, it needs to be approached with caution.

16.74 In *Aspex Visual Arts Trust (VTD 16419)* a former chapel which had been converted into an art gallery and artists studios was held not to be similar in character to a village hall; it did not cater for the wide range of activities associated with village halls and attracted visitors from a large geographical area. The VAT tribunal in *The London Federation of Clubs for Young People (VTD 17079)* thought that a village hall is a place where a considerable variety of activities may take place but went on to say, 'But a building to which the local community (with or without others) has access and where a variety of activities may take place is not necessarily a village hall' and would not necessarily involve use in a way similar to that of village halls. It went on to find that the charity's recreation centre was neither used solely for relevant charitable purposes nor used solely as a village hall. Its expression of regret at being compelled to dismiss the appeal was somewhat diluted by going on to indicate that it would award costs against the charity should HMRC wish to apply for them! In *Hanbury Charity (VTD 20126)*, which built a community centre including, at the behest of the planning authority, a nursery, HMRC conceded that the present use of the community centre matched the multi-purpose characteristic of village halls but contended that it was not a village hall on the odd basis that its use was immaterial as the use had to be relevant to the purpose of the charity (which was an educational charity). It also contended that the relief for village halls was a specific relief for specific types of charitable bodies such as village hall community associations. It then contended that the relief applied only if the charity itself operates the village hall whereas Hanbury had delegated the running to a management committee of local residents. All of these contentions were dismissed as being a gloss on the legislation which was not justified either by the legislation itself or by the decided cases. HMRC finally contended that as owner the charity could terminate at any time the use of the hall by the local community! The tribunal pointed out that the charity was given a sum of money by the Leicester Diocesan Board of Education for the sole purpose of constructing a community hall on the charity's land for the benefit of the local community and there was a planning condition that the sale proceeds could only be used for a community hall.

16.75 A swimming pool was held not to be similar to a village hall in *The South Molton Swimming Pool Trustees (VTD 16495).* The tribunal placed no relevance on the fact that a swimming pool was not similar in appearance to a village hall as the provision is concerned with use not appearance. However, it differed from a village hall in that all the activities were organised by the trustees not by the local community. In any event the pool was run as a well-organised business operation and drew custom from a much wider area than a local community. In *Southwick Community Association (VTD 16441)* a community centre was held not to be similar to a village hall because membership of the association was not limited to people living in Southwick and its immediate area but included affiliated groups which included branches of national organisations. This seems a harsh decision but it was followed 'regrettable though the financial consequences are to SACA', in *South Aston Community Association and another (VTD 17702)* where the tribunal held that 'Fircroft College is not providing facilities … for a local community. It is providing facilities in the course or furtherance of a business carried on by it to anyone in need, whether they be local or not, who may care to come and sign up for a course offered by the college'. A day centre for the elderly annexed to a residential care home was similarly held not to be the provision of facilities solely for a local community in *Beth Johnson Housing Association (VTD 17095).*

16.76 In *Ledbury Amateur Dramatic Society (VTD 16845)* a building intended as a community theatre was held to be for a use similar to a village hall in providing social or recreational facilities for the local community. HMRC had argued that the theatre was not similar to a village hall because ownership and management were vested in a particular charity whose object was to provide for the needs of a limited section of the population (those interested in theatre) whereas a village hall is normally managed by local trustees; that the supplies of building work were not made to the final consumer but to the trustees who carried on an economic activity by charging entrance fees to the public; and the use of the theatre for the trustees' own purposes was substantial (24 days a year!). In *Sport in Desford (VTD 18914)* the use of a clubhouse of a sport and dance club was held to be similar to a village hall. The tribunal felt this was essentially a question of fact. It did not feel it material that the majority of the activities were sports activities, as these constitute social or recreational facilities.

16.77 The judge in *C & E Commrs v Yarburgh Children's Trust (2002 STC 207)* felt that it is not enough to show that the building in question was intended to be used for an activity which could take place in a village hall and is available to members of the local community. What needs to be shown is that the building is, or fulfils the role of, a village hall or other building designed for public use in the provision of social or recreational facilities for the local community. In that case the use of the building was restricted by the terms of the *Children Act 1989*. Accordingly, the building was not used as a village hall. As the judge decided that the building was used by a charity otherwise than in the furtherance of a business, the village hall point was not, however, relevant to the decision itself. In *Nutley Hall Ltd (VTD 18242)* a community hall built in the grounds of a home for people with learning difficulties was held not to be a village hall. The planning permission in that case restricted the use to teaching, leisure and social activities ancillary to the nursing home. The tribunal felt that it operated as an integral part of the activities of the home, which went well beyond the use ordinarily made of a village hall.

16.78 In *New Deer Community Association (2016 STC 507)*, the FTT said that to meet the legislative test, a principal feature of the building would need to be a large multipurpose hall where members of different households could meet to undertake shared activities. The building in that case provided changing facilities and storage space for a sports ground. Although the facilities were provided for the local community, the only place where the community could meet was a small kitchen/committee room occupying 4.4% of the space. The Tribunal concluded that only the 4.4% was for use similar to a village hall. Agreeing, the Upper Tribunal pointed out the test is whether the use or intended use of a building is similar to the use of a building as a village hall (not whether the building is similar). It felt that the approach in *Caithness Rugby Football Club* (see below) was the correct one. It also said it is clear that something more than mere use for the provision of social or recreational facilities for the local community is required. The question is whether the activities to be conducted in the building are similar to the type of social or recreational activities that one would expect to be conducted in a village hall for the benefit of a local community. New Deer did not use the building in providing social or recreational facilities; it used it as an adjunct to the social or recreational facilities provided for the local community by the sports pitch. It also felt that the design of the building was relevant to the extent that it dictated what uses were reasonably practicable. In *Caithness Rugby Football Club (2016 STC 2028)*, a clubhouse and changing rooms on a sports ground was held to be similar to a village hall. In that case it was shown that the clubhouse was used extensively by the local community for non-rugby activities. 90% of the use was by groups other than the rugby club. Furthermore, unlike with *New Deer*, the changing rooms (which occupied 50% of the building) were discrete from the main hall area. In contrast, in *Witney Town Bowls Club (TC 4598)*, the construction of a new clubhouse, even though it was specifically designed so as to be capable of being used to provide meeting space for other community use, was held not to be similar to a village hall, partly on the ground that the clubhouse was managed by the Club's Management Committee and partly because it was primarily used for the purposes of the club. The Upper Tribunal firmly rejected an HMRC claim that the *Jubilee Hall* case (see **16.73**) was persuasive authority that use as a village hall required direction or control over the use of the building by the local community. Although that is a relevant consideration, it is not a decisive one.

16.79 There have also been a number of earlier tribunal decisions in relation to sports pavilions which are probably still relevant. *In Roy Meadows (VTD 11817)*, a builder constructed a building containing changing rooms, a shower room, a referee's room and a kitchen for a junior football club. The VAT tribunal held that the building was unsuitable for business use and was used by the club in a way similar to a village hall, ie for providing recreational facilities for a segment of the local community. It felt that this was probably a charitable objective under the *Recreational Charities Act 1958*, albeit that the club was not a registered charity, and adjourned the case for the club to produce further evidence that the building was provided for charitable purposes.

16.80 In contrast, in *Hunmanby Bowling Club (VTD 12136)* where the club erected a pavilion building, the tribunal held that even if the club was a recreational charity, it used the pavilion in the course of a business because it made charges, albeit at well below a commercial rate, to non-members. The club's total income of around £1,000 p.a. was used to maintain the bowling green, not the pavilion, so this seems a harsh decision. It illustrates that requirements for zero-rating need to be strictly complied with. VAT tribunals can sometimes interpret this provision rigidly. In *Ormiston Charitable Trust (VTD 13187)* the trust erected a sports pavilion and changing room. The facilities were aimed mainly at children aged 5–15 but there were also weekly fitness classes for mothers and occasional events for fathers. There was also use by local sports clubs. HMRC successfully argued that this mix of social and recreational facilities was not such as could be expected to be carried on in a village hall and the facilities were provided only for a particular section of the local community.

16.81 The VAT treatment of work to a village hall or similar community project can also be affected by the financing. If a local authority owns the hall and uses its own funds to carry out the work to it, it is not making a supply. If it owns the hall and receives funds from other bodies that will use the hall such funds are likely to be consideration for such use. If a person who provides the funds will not use the hall, the receipt may be a donation outside the scope of VAT but only, say HMRC, if such funds are freely given and neither the donating party nor a particular third party benefits. If the local authority uses its own funds to finance the work, the normal VAT rules will apply. If it uses donated funds, it will normally be able to recover the VAT under *VATA 1994,* *s 33* provided that it incurs the expenditure itself. Sometimes a voluntary group will approach a local authority for assistance. The local authority will set up a project fund into which funds raised locally, grants received by the local group and any subsidy from the local authority is paid. In many such cases it will be the voluntary group that owns the hall. If the local authority carries out work to the hall and gives this work away, it can recover the VAT under *s 33*. If, however, it receives a benefit, that is likely to be a business supply. If it simply acts as agent for the voluntary group, the supply of building work will be to the voluntary body not to the local authority, and the local authority will not be able to recover the VAT. If it charges the voluntary group for arranging the work, its charge will be a supply taxable at the standard rate (Notice 749 para 11(4)).

Who can Zero-Rate?

16.82 A supply within *item 1(a)(ii)* in **16.6** above – of a building intended for use for a relevant residential or charitable purpose – can be zero-rated only if the person to whom the supply is made (ie the purchaser, lessee or customer) is the person who will use the building for the relevant purpose and he has given to the supplier a certificate stating that the building is intended for use for a qualifying purpose (*VATA 1994, Sch 8, Group 5, Note 12*). Similarly a supply in the course of construction of a building intended solely for relevant charitable purposes and the related supply of materials can be zero-rated under *items 2* and *4* respectively only if made to a person who intends to use the building for the charitable purpose and who certifies that fact. A subcontractor cannot zero-rate his supplies to the main contractor even if the contractor holds a certificate of intended use from the charity (see *ME Smith (Electrical Engineers) Ltd (VTD 13594)*). It should be noted that, strictly speaking, the certificate must be given *before* the supply is made. If this is not done, the building is not eligible for zero-rating. Accordingly, a failure to supply the certificate cannot be corrected later, although in practice HMRC may not take the point. Normally the solicitor acting in the transaction is likely to ensure that this certificate has been given.

16.83 The certificate must be in a form to be laid down by HMRC. They have in fact laid down separate forms for residential and relevant charitable development. The requirement for this certificate is because the vendor or lessor is not himself in a position to judge to what use the purchaser or lessee intends to put the building. If HMRC are to forgo tax based on some person's intention, they want that intention stated in writing so that they have some comeback if what transpires does not accord with that intention.

16.84 If such a certificate is incorrect, the certifier lays himself open to a penalty equal to the tax undercharged as a result of the incorrect certificate (*VATA 1994, s 62*). Technically, the issue of the certificate does not appear to absolve the supplier from responsibility for getting his VAT position right. Accordingly, if he has any doubt about whether he is entitled to zero-rate the supply, it is wise to obtain an indemnity or check the position with HMRC, not simply rely on the certificate. HMRC have said that they will not, however, seek to recover any tax due from the supplier if he takes all reasonable steps to check the validity of the declaration and then, in good faith, zero-rates the supply (C & E Notice 48, ESC 3.11). In *Paul Butland t/a Harrogate Site Services (VTD 6531)* planning permission had been granted for the conversion of a listed building into a nursing home but the owner had made a fresh application to use the building as a hotel. This was granted in November 1989. The builder started work in August 1989 and zero-rated the work because he claimed that he understood that it was to be converted into a nursing home. The VAT tribunal held that he was liable to account for the tax and did not accept that he was unaware of the proposed hotel use.

16.85 Whether or not HMRC still feel themselves bound by that undertaking not to seek to recover the tax where a builder acted in good faith, seems questionable in the light of *HMRC v Fenwood Developments Ltd (2006 STC 644)*. Fenwood constructed a mental nursing home for Pastoral Homes Ltd in 2000. Pastoral certified that it intended to use the home for a relevant residential purpose. The home is registered with the local authority as a nursing home. Pastoral's philosophy was one of providing a care-based system to its female patients, most of whom were the victims of severe sexual or physical abuse, and it intended them to live as normally as possible. It took only patients for whom ordinary psychiatric hospitals could do no more, and aimed to provide them with a home, if necessary, for life. Many of its residents had been 'sectioned' under the *Mental Health Act 1983*. Pastoral did not provide any diagnostic services; it offered accommodation for women who no longer needed, or could no longer benefit from, hospital treatment. HMRC visited the home after Pastoral had been sold to a larger group. After discussion with the new manager as to how they then operated, they took the view that 'it is an institution which is both similar to a hospital and similar to a prison' and promptly assessed Fenwood for the VAT, not Pastoral for a penalty. Fortunately the tribunal disagreed. It did not feel that Pastoral was similar to either a prison or a hospital. For good measure, it also held that in looking at use after completion, not intended use at the time of supply, HMRC applied the wrong test and accordingly their assessments must have been made arbitrarily and therefore not to best judgment. Despite the tribunal's strictures HMRC appealed to the High Court. This upheld the tribunal's decision, including that the assessment was not made to HMRC's best judgment so was liable to be set aside on that ground even if it were otherwise correct in law.

16.86 HMRC assessed the developer in *Trustees of the Institute for Orthodox Christian Studies, Cambridge (TC 4622)*, but that may have been because the contract provided that the Institute would pay the VAT in addition to the purchase price if the vendor had to account for output tax. In that case the certificate was held to be invalid as the Tribunal held that the Institute intended to use the building for business purposes. This was partly because it intended to let rooms to students and partly because, although its supplies of education were heavily subsidised and there was no intention to make a profit, the fees charged to students were a significant part of the charity's income and the intrinsic nature of education is an economic activity.

16.87 What happens if HMRC do not agree that the work qualifies for zero-rating and refuse to recognise the validity of the certificate? That is what happened in *Church of Christ the King (VTD 12783)*. The church purchased a warehouse to which it intended to carry out extensive building work in three stages. HMRC contended that the work was a conversion, reconstruction, alteration or enlargement of an existing building and did not qualify for zero-rating. They further contended that, although stages one and two had been completed and the building was partially in use, the VAT tribunal was not entitled to hear the charity's appeal as the work was a single project which had not yet been completed and the tribunal was not entitled to hear an appeal relating to future supplies. The tribunal agreed. It also considered that it had no jurisdiction to hear an appeal against HMRC's refusal to recognise the zero-rating certificates and that, in any event, such a certificate related only to the intended use of a new building and was not apt to cover construction work which did not relate to a new building. The charity would therefore have to pay over VAT to the builder but could come back to the tribunal when it had completed stage three – assuming that the unexpected VAT bill leaves it with sufficient funds to do so – and seek to show that the work should be zero-rated.

16.88 On 30 March 1990 HMRC entered into a concordat with the Committee of Vice Chancellors and Principals of the Universities of the UK (CVCP) which contained a concession allowing a university to certify student accommodation as a relevant residential building if it is 'a new building clearly intended primarily for use as student accommodation for ten years from the date of completion'. The concordat, and therefore presumably the concession, was subsequently unilaterally withdrawn by HMRC. HMRC refused to allow this concession to Greenwich Property Ltd, a wholly owned subsidiary of the University of Greenwich on two grounds, that the concession applied only if the university itself made the accommodation available in the vacation period, and that they were entitled to refuse to apply a concession where they believed it was being used for the avoidance of tax. The company applied for judicial review – *R (on the application of Greenwich Property Ltd) v C & E Commrs (2001 STC 618) ([2001] EWHC Admin 230)*. The judge thought that the purpose behind the concession was to enable the universities to make profitable use of their student accommodation in vacations and still get the benefit of zero-rating. Thus 'solely' meant solely in term time. There was nothing in the wording of the concession to indicate that the university could not use a third party. The judge also dismissed the tax avoidance point as there was nothing in the concession to stipulate that it could not be used for tax avoidance. In any event he did not regard the scheme adopted as tax avoidance albeit that it included some artificial elements.

16.89 Following comments in the High Court in *Help the Aged* in 1997, HMRC formed the view that where an educational establishment has charitable status, the supply and installation of lifts to facilitate the movement of disabled staff and pupils between floors is zero-rated by virtue of *VATA 1994, Sch 8, Group 12, item 17* if the building concerned is used for the provision of permanent or temporary residence or as a day-centre for disabled people. They have subsequently changed their mind, and now consider that zero-rating applies only to lifts in residential accommodation, as educational institutions normally do not provide care in a day centre. They will apply their original view by concession where a contract for the installation of a lift in non-residential accommodation was entered into before 31 March 2005 (Business Brief 3/05). The wording of *item 17* seems more apt to support their original view than their current one. This is 'the supply to a charity of providing a permanent or temporary residence or day-centre for handicapped persons of services necessarily performed in the installation of a lift for the purpose of facilitating the movement of handicapped persons between floors within that building'. *Friends of the Elderly (VTD 20597)* installed a new lift in a care home. The work on the lift shaft included structural alterations. HMRC challenged, unsuccessfully, whether the architects' fees in relation to the design and supervision of construction of the lift shaft were 'necessarily performed' in the installation of the lift. They contended that installation is the activity of installing and installing does not include the supervision or planning of the activity. The tribunal held that 'all the services without which the lift could not have been finally installed are included'.

Conversions

16.90 In applying *items 1(b)* and *3* in **16.6** above, a building (or part of a building) is non-residential if either:

(*a*) it is neither designed nor adapted for use as a dwelling or number of dwellings or for a relevant residential purpose; or

(*b*) it is designed or adapted for such a purpose but it was constructed more than ten years before the grant of the major interest and no part of it has been used as a dwelling or for a relevant residential purpose in the ten years immediately preceding the grant.

(*VATA 1994, Sch 8, Group 5, Note 7*). *Note 7A* applies this same test for the purpose of *item 3*. The taxpayer in *A and T Johnson (VTD 20506)* sought to contend that once a property had been declared unfit for human habitation under the *Housing Act 1985* it ceased to be a residential building, so its conversion into a residence ought to qualify for zero-rating, but the tribunal held that the building had clearly still been 'designed as a dwelling'. It is up to the taxpayer to demonstrate that the building had not been used as a dwelling in the relevant period. HMRC have said that for the purpose of (*b*) above if a house has been illegally occupied by squatters this will not disqualify it from being treated as empty (Notice 708, Chapter 5). Where part of a house was lived in during the ten-year period zero-rating cannot apply unless that part was a self-contained dwelling (para 1.5). They also say that the charge does not enable a developer to recover input tax incurred before 1 August 2001 if the house is sold after that date as such tax was incurred in relation to an exempt supply (para 2.5). This appears questionable. The sale triggers zero-rating, so on the face of it although when he incurred the input tax the developer intended to use it in making an exempt supply he surely would have changed his intention on 1 August 2001 in which case *reg 109* (see **16.245**) would give a right to repayment.

16.91 A garage occupied with a dwelling is not a non-residential building if it is separate from the dwelling (*Note 8*). In *John Clark (TC 552)*, a DIY housebuilder case, the Tribunal held that *Notes 7A* (see above) and *8* should be read together, so that where only 20% of the previous building was a garage, the other 80% could attract zero-rating. Whilst this seems logical, the Tribunal itself noted that it was disagreeing with the Tribunals in *Sally Cottam (VTD 20036)* (see **16.190**) and *Podolsky (TC 387)*, both of which had held that if part of the building had been used as a garage, none of it could attract zero-rating. Where part of a building is residential and part is not, the conversion of the non-residential part does not fall within *item 1(b)* or *3* unless it creates an additional dwelling or dwellings (*Note 9*). For example, if a building contains a shop with a flat above, the conversion of the shop into a second flat can qualify for zero-rating. The conversion of the shop to residential use, so that the entire building is used as a single residence, will not qualify, however. HMRC say that there are a small number of charities which provide accommodation for rent that cannot recover VAT on conversions because they are prevented by legal constraints from selling their converted properties (and thus cannot grant a major interest in the completed building), and do not qualify as DIY builders as the receipt of rents means that they are carrying on a business. HMRC will consider refunds of VAT by concession to such bodies on an individual basis (News Release 15/96). The Tribunal in *Dunlop (TC 4147)* agreed with the *John Clark* approach. In that case, a former washhouse, part of which had subsequently been used as a garage was converted to a house. The Tribunal held that *Note 8* prevented the garage from being a dwelling, albeit that it was not occupied with a dwelling at the time of conversion, as it was occupied with a dwelling at some time within the previous10 years (see *Note 7A*) and thus was itself deemed to be a residential building. The reasoning is not convincing.

16.92 Problems frequently arise with pubs. Although these often contain living accommodation for the publican, that accommodation is sometimes not self-contained but shares some facilities with the pub. Conversion of the pub to a house will not fall within *item 1(b)* because the building as a whole is not a non-residential building, and the non-residential part will not normally be converted into a dwelling but merely into part of a dwelling as the other part already exists. The problem is well illustrated by the tribunal decision in *Calam Vale Ltd (VTD 16869)*. The company converted a pub into two dwellings. The conversion involved the division of the building vertically. Accordingly each of the dwellings included both an old residential and old commercial element. The company unsuccessfully argued that no part of the pub was previously a dwelling under *Note 2* as it was not self-contained, but the tribunal agreed with HMRC that a dwelling for this purpose simply means a place where someone lives. The cases considered in the following paragraphs suggest that the interpretation is not that simple though. The tribunal in *Alexandra Countryside Investments* (see **16.93**) indicated that it felt that *Calam Vale* had been wrongly decided. The question was considered by the Court of Appeal in *C & E Commrs v Blom-Cooper (2003 STC 669)*. The court held that the clear purpose and effect of *Note 9* (see **16.91**) in conjunction with note 7 (see **16.90**) is to give a restricted meaning to the expression 'converting … a non-residential part of a building'. If before conversion the building already contains a residential part the conversion of a non-residential part will not be treated as 'converting … a non-residential part for the purposes of section 35(1D) unless the result of that conversion is to create an additional dwelling'. This was a do-it-yourself builder case so was concerned with the interpretation of *VATA 1994, s 35(1D)* (see **16.186**) rather than *Sch 8, Group 5* but the wording is almost identical.

16.93 In *C & E Commrs v Jacobs (2004 STC 1682)* a former boarding school was converted into a dwelling-house. HMRC contended that the school use was for a relevant residential purpose either as 'an institution which is the sole or main residence of at least 90% of its residents' or 'residential accommodation for school pupils' (see **16.49**). The tribunal dismissed the first on the basis that it was only used as a residence during term time, the children having their main residences elsewhere; and the second on the grounds that the purpose of the totality of the building was to educate the children and the building as a whole was not used as residential accommodation within **16.49**(*d*). On appeal, Evans-Lombe J felt that this whole building approach was incompatible with the Court of Appeal decision in *Blom-Cooper* (see **16.92**). He accordingly held that VAT was irrecoverable to the extent that it related to the conversion of the headmaster's flat and the boys' accommodation (including kitchens, dining room and lavatories, as well as bedrooms). He felt, however, that the VAT in relation to the three staff flats that were created in the conversion was recoverable, notwithstanding that two of them utilised in part what had previously been staff bedsits, as the flats constituted additional dwellings within *Note 9* (see **16.91**) and the note seemed to him to allow recovery even where the additional dwelling may have been created from a part that was formerly residential. HMRC have said that they do not consider that the Court of Appeal decision has any impact on cases where a building which is part residential and part non-residential is converted into dwellings and the number of dwellings post conversion exceeds that pre conversion. They consider that zero-rating will not apply to any dwelling derived in whole or in part from the conversion of the residential part because *VATA 1994 Sch 8, Group 5 items 1(b)* and *3(a)* (see **16.7**) restrict the zero-rating to the dwellings derived from the conversion of the non-residential part (Business Brief 22/2005). The *Jacobs* case and Business Brief 22/2005 were both reviewed by the FTT in *Alexandra Countryside Investments Ltd (TC 2751).* Like *Calam Vale*, this was a conversion of a pub containing a manager's flat into two dwellings. Disagreeing with HMRC, the tribunal felt that the legal principles set out by the Court of Appeal in *Jacobs* were equally applicable to the almost identical wording of *Sch 8, Group 5.* It felt that *Calam Vale* was wrongly decided in the light of those principles. In accordance with Ward LJ's analysis in *Jacobs*, '*Note 9* has to be construed so that the result of the conversion is to create in the building an additional dwelling or dwellings. One counts the number of dwellings in the building before conversion and again after conversion. If there are more on the recount *note 9* is satisfied'. The tribunal in *Languard New Homes Ltd (TC 4917)* agreed with that in Alexandra. However, the FTT in *DM & DD Macpherson (TC 4756)* distinguished that case from *Jacobs* on the basis that *Jacobs* was a DIY house builder case and the wording of the legislation is not identical, dismissed the *Alexandra Countryside Investments* reasoning, and reverted to the *Calum Vale* analysis. The Upper Tribunal in a disappointingly brief decision (*2017 STC 1925*) has endorsed the FTT's decision in MacPherson and reversed that in *Languard New Homes* the appeal of which it heard at the same time, albeit 'with some hesitation'. They dismissed Jacobs on the basis that 'the point at issue here was not addressed by the Court of Appeal in Jacobs as their focus was on the question whether the additional dwelling required by Note (9) had to be created out of the non-residential part of the building or would still satisfy Note (9) if it were created out of former residential parts'. The problem in the current cases is *Note 7.* The former non-residential part of the public house in Languard 'has not been converted into a dwelling because it has been converted into part of a dwelling'. The non-residential part of the building (which is what has to be converted for zero-rating to apply) cannot include any space that was residential because a non-residential part and a part which already contains a dwelling are mutually exclusive concepts. It is to be hoped that one of the taxpayers will appeal to the Court of Appeal. The application of *Note 7* is unclear and needs either to be revisited by parliament or looked at more thoroughly by a higher court. The distinction that HMRC draw between a horizontal conversion (zero-rated) and a vertical conversion (standard-rated) has no logic. In both cases, additional dwellings are being created and there is little doubt that the literal construction adopted by the Tribunal does not reflect the purpose behind the legislation.

16.94 The meaning of a non-residential building was in issue in *Look Ahead Housing Association (VTD 16816)*. The Association owned two buildings which had originally been town houses but had been used as bedsits since 1946. It converted them into self-contained flats. It was not disputed that the bedsits were not self-contained. HMRC contended that the buildings were not non-residential before conversion. They argued that the purpose of the legislation was to promote the creation of new housing and that this had not occurred here, the buildings having been used as dwellings both before and after the conversion. The tribunal felt that the provisions had to be construed in the context of UK law not UK social policy. It held that, giving the word its ordinary meaning, a 'dwelling' would contain facilities for all the major activities of life, particularly sleeping, cooking, eating and toilet facilities (see *University of Bath* – **16.42**). The bedsits did not have the characteristics of dwellings and thus were 'non-residential' as defined in *Note 7*.

16.95 However, in *Amicus Group Ltd (VTD 17693)* on virtually identical facts the tribunal refused to follow this decision. They agreed with HMRC that it had been wrongly decided in the light of the House of Lords decision in *Uratemp Ventures Ltd v Collins ([2001] 3 WLR 806)*, a Housing Act case. Lord Millett had said there that 'the supposed requirement that cooking facilities must be available for premises to qualify as a dwelling derives from cases directed to the question whether the tenancy constituted a 'separate' dwelling when it included shared accommodation or facilities'. The tribunal felt that 'such considerations are far removed from VAT on construction of buildings where the distinction is made between dwellings and other buildings, rather than between separate and other dwellings'. The ordinary English meaning of a dwelling is 'a place where one lives, regarding and treating it as a home' and a bedsit with shared kitchen and bathroom facilities satisfies this definition. The Amicus decision was followed in *Kingscastle Ltd (VTD 17777)* where one of seven rooms on the upper floor of a coaching inn had been occupied by the landlord as his living accommodation. That room was held to be a dwelling.

16.96 In *Merlewood Estates Ltd (VTD 20810)* the owner of five blocks of flats decided to construct new flats in the roof spaces and to grant a major interest of each new flat. It argued that it was converting a 'non-residential part' of a building into a building designed as a number of dwellings. None of the existing tenants had access to the roof space. It was effectively empty space. HMRC contended that the roof space of an existing building was integral to the residential part of the building. It had to have a roof and if the roof is pitched the pitch creates a void. It was artificial to separate the void from the rest of the building. Accordingly the void was residential even though it was not lived in. The tribunal disagreed. Integral is not part of the statutory test. Some meaning has to be given to the words 'non-residential part'. *Note 7(a)* to *Group 5* (see **16.82**) states that a part of a building is non-residential if it is not designed for use as a dwelling. The roof space was not designed for such use. Accordingly the conversion was entitled to zero-rating.

Housing Associations

16.97 For the purpose of *item 3* in **16.7**, the following are 'relevant housing associations':

(*a*) a registered social landlord under the *Housing Act 1996*; or

(*b*) a registered housing association within the *Housing Associations Act 1985* (in Scotland) or the *Housing (Northern Ireland) Order 1992.*

(*VATA 1994, Sch 8, Group 5, Note 21.*)

From 1 April 2010 a private registered provider of social housing is also a relevant housing association (*VATA 1994, Sch 8, Group 5, Note 21*). Until the coming into force of a provision defining such a person the expression means a person (other than a local authority) listed in the register under the *Housing and Regeneration Act 2008, Pt 2, Ch 3.*

Conversion, Reconstruction and Alteration

16.98 Unless it falls within *items 1(b)* or *3* (see **16.6** above), or relates to a listed building, building work cannot be zero-rated if it consists of the conversion, reconstruction or alteration of an existing building. Nor can the enlargement of, or extension to, an existing building, except to the extent that it creates an additional dwelling or dwellings. This will allow the zero-rating of additional self-contained flats on top of an existing block of flats and probably also the types of additional flats considered at **8.54** and **8.55** above (VAT Information Sheet 10/95 & Notice 708, para 3.2.4). An 'alteration' in this context was held by the House of Lords to mean a structural alteration (*ACT Construction Ltd v C & E Commrs, 1982 STC 25*). This was also the issue in *A K Jahansouz (TC 637*). Mr Jahansouz owned the freehold of a building consisting of two flats. He also owned the top flat. He removed the roof and constructed a third flat. This had its own entrance through a lobby on the second floor. HMRC contended that the work was a loft conversion but the Tribunal held that it was an enlargement of the property by the creation of a new dwelling in it. Further tribunal decisions that may be useful are considered at **16.184** onwards (Do It Yourself Builders). A fascinating case in the same sort of area is *A & M Wright (TC 1523)*, which is considered at **8.72**. In *Capital Focus Ltd (TC 5193)* the company converted a commercial property into a house for multiple occupation (HMO) with 10 bedrooms (some only en-suite) and a communal kitchen. HMRC contended that none of the individual rooms constituted a dwelling. The FTT held that whilst *Sch 7A* excluded a HMO from being a dwelling (see **16.154**), *Sch 8* does not do so. It refers to a building consisting of a dwelling or number of dwellings and in this case the building itself satisfied that test as it itself consisted of self-contained accommodation which clearly contains the basic elements of living.

Annexes

16.99 Similarly, zero-rating does not apply to an annexe to an existing building unless the whole or part of that annex is intended for use solely for a relevant charitable purpose, and:

(*a*) it is capable of functioning independently from the existing building; and

(*b*) the only or main access to the annexe is not via the existing building (and that to the existing building is not via the annexe). (*Group 5, Notes 16* and *17* as amended by the *VAT (Construction of Buildings Order 2002) (SI 2002 No 1101)*).

The aim is to give the same tax treatment to a discrete facility housed in an annexe to the main building as to one in a separate building. The annexe must be capable of functioning independently of the existing building and be capable of use even if the connection to the main building is closed. The change does not give tax-free treatment to enlargements of charity buildings by the creation of additional floorspace for a single activity (VAT Information Sheet 10/95). Nor can the enlargement of, or extension to, an existing building qualify, except to the extent that it creates an additional dwelling or dwellings. In *Leyton Sixth Form College (TC 3042)* (see **8.74**), the FTT held that if the new building were an annexe (it actually held that it was an enlargement) it was not capable of functioning independently from the existing building, because it contained the plant room which provided heating and water for both buildings. It is questionable whether that is correct. On the face of it, the 'annexe' is capable of functioning independently, which is the statutory test; it is the original building that can no longer do so.

16.100 'Annexe' is not defined in the legislation. In *Macnamara* (see **16.105**), Stephen Oliver QC said: 'the term annexe connotes something that is adjoined but either not integrated with the existing building or of tenuous integration'. Annexes intended for use solely for relevant charitable purposes are reinstated into the zero-rating Class by note (17) only if they are capable of functioning independently and if the main access to the annexe is not via the existing building and the main access to the existing building is not via the annexe'. In *Yeshurun Hebrew Congregation* (see **8.71**) the tribunal described an annexe as 'not itself a principal building but a supplementary building, connected or associated with the main building and fulfilling a subordinate role in relation to that building'.

16.101 Clearly a person who carries out such operations is not a person constructing a building for the purpose of *item 1* in **16.6** above. It is not clear if a restrictive covenant is a 'similar permission' to a planning consent. It is probably not. Certainly, in normal terminology it does not seem very similar. It has sometimes been suggested that head (*b*) in **16.99** above can be circumvented by erecting the new building without internal access to the adjoining one and subsequently creating such access. This ploy failed in *Highacre Construction Co Ltd (VTD 5772)*. Highacre owned a nursing home to which it wished to add an extension. A new company, M Ltd, bought the site of the extension and contracted with Highacre for it to construct it. Although the plans envisaged connecting doors, these were bricked up. Highacre zero-rated its invoices to M Ltd. M Ltd subsequently bought the nursing home from Highacre and inserted the connecting doors between the two buildings. The tribunal held that the only purpose of blocking up the internal door spaces had been to justify zero-rating the work and that in those circumstances it was permissible to look at the terms of the planning permission, which had clearly envisaged the two buildings being operated as a single entity, to determine the nature of the building work – which they held to be an enlargement of the original building. In any event the lack of internal access did not stop the addition of a self-contained flat to an existing house from being an enlargement in *J W Cooper & Sons (VTD 2402)* or in *Assetcope Ltd (VTD 4656)*. However, such an extension would now be zero-rated (see **16.98** above).

16.102 A similar result was reached in *Raymond Symonds (VTD 9050)* where a customer engaged a builder to build a new house adjoining an existing one. It was self-contained with its own access and services. The customer subsequently engaged another builder to break through the party wall. It was held that the customer's intention was always that the two houses should subsequently be adapted to form a single dwelling. Accordingly, the work done by the first builder was not eligible for zero-rating as it was merely the first stage of a clear and declared plan to convert and enlarge an existing house. This decision seems to put a builder in an impossible position as he will not necessarily know that the customer has an intention to join the two houses in such circumstances.

16.103 The opposite happened in *Carrophil Ltd (VTD 10190)*. The company constructed a Sunday school room for a church on the site of the former vestry. It adjoined the church on two sides. Double doors which had provided access from the church to the vestry – and therefore provided access to the schoolroom – remained in place at the time of practical completion of the work. A month later the architect gave instructions for these doors to be sealed and on the schoolroom side they were covered with plasterboard. HMRC contended that the schoolroom was an extension to the church with internal access. The VAT tribunal held that there was no internal access. The closing of such access, albeit as an afterthought and albeit after practical completion, was done on the instructions of the architect and was sufficiently connected with the rest of the work to be part of the construction of the schoolroom. Looking at whether the schoolroom was a taxable enlargement of the church or a zero-rated extension, the tribunal held that an educated layperson, looking at the completed work, would conclude that the church had been extended to provide accommodation for the Sunday school. Similarly in *Woodley Baptist Church (VTD 17833)* the construction of a youth club above the church hall was held to be an enlargement not an annexe, largely on the basis of the definitions enunciated in *Macnamara* (see **16.105**). The construction of a new sports hall was similarly held to be an extension not an annexe in *Thomas Rotherham College (VTD 17841)*. Similarly in *W B Evans t/a BSEC (VTD 18432)* new changing rooms at the side of an outside sports hall were held not to be an annexe. There was direct access between the two and the new building was too well integrated with the old. However, HMRC accepted that as the occupier (YMCA) was a charity the part of the changing rooms designed as a washroom for handicapped persons qualified for zero-rating under *VATA 1994, Sch 8, Group 12, item 12* (the supply to a charity of a service of providing … a washroom or lavatory for use by handicapped persons in a building … used principally by a charity for charitable purposes).

16.104 In contrast, in *Castle Caereinion Recreation Association (VTD 18303)* a new multi-purpose room built on top of a village hall was held to be an annex, although the building of a committee room on the ground floor was held to be an extension. Both had their own entrances, but what was fatal in relation to the committee room was that it also had internal access to the hall. In *Torfaen Voluntary Alliance (VTD 18797)* the tribunal accepted that work carried out to a church hall constituted an annexe. The new and the old part of the building were in a different style, the exterior appearance of the two was different, the two buildings were functionally independent and had separate entrances. Although the planning permission required connecting double doors, these were kept locked and were opened only on request, so the tribunal accepted that they were not the 'main access' to either building. The tribunal commented that in applying the 'capable of functioning independently' test, 'one would normally discount toilets and other services', although that was not relevant to the case. Unfortunately the tribunal in *Henshaws Society for Blind People (VTD 19373)* (see **8.66**) took a different view and held that a construction that extended over the first floor of an existing building was incapable of functioning separately from it 'of necessity having some services in common with it'.

16.105 The VAT tribunal (Stephen Oliver QC) in *BT Macnamara (VTD 16039)* observed that the exclusion from zero-rating of enlargements, extensions and annexes was expressed in order of their degree of integration with the existing building. An enlargement is structural work which produced an overall increase in the size or capacity of the existing building, extension denotes a lesser degree of integration with the existing building, being the addition of a new section or wing, while an annexe merely adjoined the existing building with the degree of integration being tenuous. In that case a new building containing classrooms and a laboratory was constructed in a gap between parts of two existing school buildings. Although the tribunal noted that the work involved no conversion or alteration to an existing building and that there was no enlargement of any individual building, the effect of the project was to produce an additional section or part of 'the building'. The degree of integration made it an extension of the existing 'building'. Even if that were wrong it was an annexe. The tribunal stated that 'the term annexe connotes something that is adjoined but either not integrated with the existing building or of tenuous integration'. This definition has been accepted as a useful and correct analysis in subsequent cases. It should, however, not be overlooked that an annexe was defined differently by the High Court in *Cantrell and Others (t/a Foxearth Lodge Nursing Home) v CCE (2000 STC 100)* (see **8.67**) where a collection of buildings was looked at as a single building. There, Sir Andrew Morritt said that an annex is an adjunct or an accessory to something else so must be a supplementary structure; the fact that there is an association between the old and new structure is not sufficient.

16.106 *Kids Church (VTD 18145)* presented the tribunal with an interesting dilemma. The charity was offered a lease of part of a disused warehouse as a children's activity centre. It would have been prohibitively expensive to make the premises fit for any purpose involving children. The charity therefore erected fireproof partition walls between its part of the warehouse and the remainder, laid a new concrete floor to its part and installed new wiring there. It described the work as the creation of an internal annexe. The VAT tribunal decided that it could not be an annexe as there was no relationship between its use and that of the rest of the warehouse. Even if it was an annexe the only access to it was through the warehouse. It was clearly not an enlargement of the warehouse or an extension to it. As the warehouse remained it could not be a reconstruction. Accordingly it had to be a conversion or alteration of the existing building.

16.107 In *Trustees of Elim Church, Tamworth (VTD 19190)* a nursery used separately from the church with the only access between the two being a locked security door was held not to be an annexe because there was 'substantial structural integration'. The tribunal also felt there was functional integration because the church could use the nursery's lavatories and kitchen, albeit that it had never actually done so and, somewhat contradictory, the tribunal added that as the lavatories were in the nursery it was the nursery that was capable of functioning independently rather than the church. In *East Norfolk Sixth Form*

College (VTD 20816) it was held that a new two storey classroom block was an annexe but did not qualify for zero-rating as it was not capable of being used on its own, as it did not contain toilet facilities and those being taught in classrooms need lavatories. Similarly in *Treetops Hospice Trust (TC 1350)* where a new building (approximately the same size of the old) was linked by two lockable (albeit normally unlocked) doors, the work was held to be an extension. The tribunal commented that even if it had been an annexe, it was not capable of functioning independently from the existing building as it did not have separate kitchen and bathing facilities. A similar decision was reached in *TL Smith Properties Ltd and Tregwilyn Lodge Ltd (TC 1375)* where a new nursing home building was held to be an enlargement of the adjoining existing dementia care home.

16.108 It is often very difficult to determine whether building work which utilises part of the fabric of an existing building is a conversion, reconstruction or alteration or the creation of a completely new building. There have been a large number of decided cases on this point. As this is a question that is primarily of concern in the context of development, these cases are considered in **Chapter 8** at **8.47** onwards. Zero-rating also applies to certain alterations to listed buildings used for residential and relevant charitable purposes. These are considered in **Chapter 9** (Refurbishments) at paragraphs **9.16** onwards.

What is a Building?

16.109 A building is not defined. The Act does, however, say that a building ceases to be a building only if:

(*a*) it is demolished completely to ground level; or

(*b*) the part remaining above ground level consists of no more than a single facade (or if it is a corner site, a double facade), the retention of which is a condition or requirement of a statutory planning consent or similar permission (*Group 5, Note 18*).

This prevents the restoration of a derelict cottage being regarded as the construction of a building where the useable parts of the walls are incorporated into a new house unless *item 1(b)* or *3* (see **16.6** above) applies. It effectively (but unsuccessfully judging from later decisions) seeks to override the test that VAT tribunals have devised of whether looking at the building an onlooker would say that it is a new building or a reconstruction of what was there before. HMRC interpret 'ground level' as permitting cellers, basement and a concrete slab to remain from the previous construction (Notice 708, para 3.2.1). It is understood that where two derelict cottages are converted into one, and one of them was occupied at some time since VAT was introduced on 1 April 1973 but the other was not, HMRC do not consider that zero-rating applies.

HMRC have indicated that a letter from the rate office, water board, electricity board or Post Office stating that they have had no contact with the property since 1 April 1973 will be satisfactory evidence that the property has not been occupied since that date (Tolley's Practical VAT, June 1996). Notice 708, para 3.2.3 states that: 'In determining whether a building has been demolished completely to ground level, you can ignore the retention of party walls that separate one building from another building that is not being demolished'. It is not clear if this is an HMRC concession or is based on a presumption that the party wall does not form part of the building. The Notice has no statutory effect.

16.110 Head (*b*) in **16.109** was in issue in the First-tier Tribunal in *Almond v Revenue and Customs Commrs ([2009] UKFTT 177 (TC), [2010] STI 1399 (TC 132)*. A single facade was retained but the planning permission did not specify this in terms. It did, however, require the building to be carried out in accordance with the planning application, plans and drawings and these showed the retention of the facade. This was held to satisfy the statutory requirement. It was also in issue in *John Clark (TC 552)*, a DIY housebuilder case. The planning permission there required the restoration of two walls but one of them collapsed during the course of the building work, so the final building retained only one. The Tribunal held that the collapsed façade was one required to be maintained 'even if it requires to be reconstructed to have to do so'. In *M Samuel (TC 872)* 'on account of some extraordinary quirk of planning law, the local planning authority considered that local planning policies meant that consent … could only be given if it was framed as an application for an extension of the existing building … it appears that the planners would have been perfectly happy to grant permission for a new building … but that in that situation the new house would have had to be much smaller …'. Because of this technicality they required the retention of two adjoining walls. The Tribunal thus had to decide whether the site of the building was a corner site. They agreed with HMRC that this phrase 'required that the building be located at the corner of a road, or in some other location that could sensibly be said to satisfy the 'corner site' requirement; it was not simply a reference to the two walls being at the corner of the building as 'double façade' covered that'. The Tribunal in *Reeves (TC 4980)* held that a façade is 'the face or front of a building towards a street or other open place' (OED). In that case what had been retained was a gable wall, and that is not a façade. Accordingly, the building did not cease to be an existing building.

16.111 This provision was in issue in *R M & S L Midgley (VTD 15379)*. The appellants wished to renovate and extend a dilapidated house. They obtained the necessary planning permission and started work. If things had gone to plan the work would have been VATable. However, it was discovered that with one exception all of the walls of the original house were unstable and had to be demolished. The work continued. When it was nearly finished application for planning permission for the changed work was made and granted retrospectively. The house was clearly an existing building when the work began. The tribunal held that on the demolition of the walls (but not before then) it ceased to be an existing building as it then came to satisfy **16.109**(*b*) above. The effect was that work up to that time was standard-rated but thereafter it was zero-rated, so an apportionment would be required. It is interesting to note that HMRC accepted that the retrospective planning consent satisfied the planning consent condition. This contrasts with their approach to listed building consent under *Group 6* (see **9.18**). The taxpayer was less lucky in *Mark Tinker (VTD 18033).* Mr Tinker demolished the kitchen and bathroom of his house and replaced them with a new kitchen and bathroom. Later he demolished the remainder of the house and rebuilt the relevant rooms attached to the new kitchen and bathroom. The tribunal held that such a two-stage demolition did not result in a new building as at no stage did an existing building cease to exist. A similar result was reached in *G D Gilder (VTD 18143).* Mr Gilder, who suffered from multiple sclerosis, lived in a bungalow which was not suitable for his needs. He wished to demolish it and build a new one. However, he had nowhere else to live. Accordingly he built the new bungalow as an 'extension' to the old, moved into the extension and demolished the original bungalow. It was held that the new bungalow was an extension of the old even though there was never any intention for the two to be occupied together. In *D Pollock and D Heath (VTD 20380)* the then planning consent agreed to the retention of a corner façade but had not required it. The tribunal held that **16.109**(*b*) above was not satisfied. In *M Lennon & Co Ltd (TC 4488)* the appellant bought an end of terrace house with permission to convert it into flats. It decided to demolish the house instead. Its structural engineer told it that if the building was demolished completely, the party wall would collapse. They accordingly retained half of the front façade to prevent that happening. The Tribunal held that the reason for retaining the half-façade was irrelevant. The statutory test was clear. A similar decision was reached in *Baxmoor Construction Ltd (TC 4851)* where the building was substantially demolished except for a small section of the façade before being substantially rebuilt. The planning consent did not require the retention of that part and the FTT could see no basis on which it could infer a condition that it had to be retained.

16.112 In *Maierhofer v Finanzamt Augsburg-Land (2003 STC 564) (Case C-315/00)* the claimant constructed prefabricated buildings and leased them to the German government for housing asylum seekers. The buildings were sometimes erected on land leased by the claimant and sometimes on land leased by the government. The buildings were assembled in ten days on concrete aprons. At the end of the lease term they were dismantled and re-erected elsewhere. Was this the letting of immovable property? Yes, said the ECJ, the buildings are not mobile and cannot be easily dismantled or easily moved. They also decided that it is irrelevant to the question whether the lessor makes available to the lessee both the land and the building or merely the building. Unfortunately, 'No' said the VAT tribunal in *The University of Kent (VTD 18625)*. The University hired 12 'sleep units' to accommodate an overflow of students. It first claimed that the units were 'caravans' but this was dismissed on the basis that the units were not self-contained as they did not have cooking facilities and thus were not akin to a dwelling. (This seems of doubtful validity – see **16.94** for alternative views.) The University then claimed that the letting to them was a letting of immovable property. The units could not be moved by hand and were connected to mains electricity, water and drainage. The tribunal felt that moveable is a matter of degree. In this case they could be disconnected and moved with a lorry and crane in an hour and a half. This was not sufficient to make them immovable.

16.113 The VAT Tribunal in *Adath Israel Synagogue (VTD 20809)* held that a wall surrounding a cemetery, designed by an architect who managed its construction, was not a building. In *W R Dunster (TC 727)* the Tribunal held that a prototype zero-carbon home suitable for construction on land designed as a flood plane was a dwelling but not a building. The structure floated when the water level was high and rested in the river bed when it was low. The structure was attached to a pontoon which was itself attached to the land via 12ft poles. The Tribunal held that a building must be connected with the land in such a way as to become part of it. They held that the structure was a houseboat. Unfortunately this was a DIY builders case and that scheme does not extend to houseboats.

16.114 There were two issues in *BS Design & Management Ltd (TC 3622)*. The building, a corner building, was demolished apart from the party wall and the two corner facades. The first issue was whether that was correct. HMRC contended that the rear facade had also been retained, but the Tribunal was satisfied by photos of the construction work in progress that it had been demolished and rebuilt using the old bricks. This emphasises the importance of photographs during the course of the work to demonstrate what took place if the operations are unusual (in this case supporting the facades while the back wall was being rebuilt). The second issue was that the planning permission did not specifically require the retention of the facades; it required the work to be carried out in accordance with the approved plans which included the retained facades. HMRC contended that Note 18 permits the retention of a facade only where it is a specific condition of the permission granted, imposed by the person granting it. In this case the council did not make it a requirement that the facades must be retained; they merely consented to the applicant's desire to retain them. The Tribunal firmly stated:

> 'there is nothing in the statute which suggests that the motivation of the planning authority is remotely relevant to the application of Note 18, or that the retention of the façade must be set out as an explicit condition

of the consent. The legislation is drafted in objective terms and the sole issue to be determined is whether the retention of the facades is a requirement of the planning consent'.

A similar decision was reached in *The Trustees of the Eaton Mews Trust (TC 1943)*. In contrast in *Boxmoor Construction Ltd (TC 3951)* the Tribunal held that there was no evidence to show that the planning consent required the retention of the retained features. Indeed, as the consent had been for extensions and alterations, whereas the building had been virtually demolished, it seemed unlikely that it would have included such a requirement.

Miscellaneous

16.115 There are provisions for apportionment where part of a building qualifies for zero-rating and part does not (*Group 5, Notes 10* and *11*). These are likely to give rise to immense practical problems of valuation where, for example, there is a sale as a single transaction of an office building with penthouse flats on top. Is the notional residential building to be valued as if it were floating in mid-air, or is the building to be valued as if it were wholly residential and the value of the lower floors then ignored? Whilst such problems can no doubt give valuers many pleasurable hours, it needs to be remembered that a taxpayer who resolves this valuation dilemma in a different way to HMRC could find himself faced with a misdeclaration penalty. A dispute will not, in the normal course of events, arise until HMRC do a VAT inspection. Clearly, in such circumstances it would be advisable to tell HMRC, at the time the VAT liability arises, that a valuation has been adopted in the return, and the amount and effect of such valuation, so as to give them an early opportunity to challenge it. This should hopefully provide a reasonable excuse defence against any possible misdeclaration penalty.

16.116 HMRC accept that there will be some rough edges in these apportionment rules and announced that they will ignore a simple office incorporated into a residential building. This will cover, for example, an office for the matron in a nursing home. It is not clear how many offices this will stretch to. One would hope that it will allow as many as necessary for the efficient running of the residential building, but it will be wise to check with HMRC in each individual case. By concession, since 1990 HMRC allowed universities (and other Higher Education Institutes) to ignore vacation use when determining whether student accommodation is intended for use solely for a relevant residential purpose. They also allowed dining rooms and kitchens to be zero-rated as residential accommodation for students and school pupils if they were used predominantly by the living-in-students. Both of these concessions were withdrawn from 1 April 2015. However, taxpayers with student accommodation that has been zero-rated under this concession can continue to rely on it when determining whether there has been a change of use in the ten-year claw-back period. Where a building was in the course of construction at 1 April 2015, and the work was being zero-rated in reliance on the concession, they can also continue to rely on it (including in relation to construction work after that date provided that there has been a meaningful start to the construction of the building (or the first building if a single development consists of more than one) and the works are expected to progress to completion without interruption). They can also continue to rely on it for the purpose of zero-rating the first grant of a major interest in new student accommodation if a meaningful deposit (eg on exchange of contracts) has been paid before that date, or an agreement for lease or purchase has been signed before that date and a meaningful start to the construction has taken place. Entering into an option is not sufficient though (Technical Note, 31 January 2014 and HMRC Brief 14/2014).

16.117 Furthermore HMRC take the view that 'solely for a relevant residential or relevant charitable purpose' can incorporate a de minimis margin. Accordingly HMRC accept that the statutory condition is satisfied if 95% or more of the building is used for charitable purposes (HMRC Brief 32/2010). HMRC say that 'Any method may be used to calculate the qualifying use of the building, so long as it is fair and reasonable' (HMRC Brief 32/2010). This is considered in more detail at **16.128**.

16.118 The issue came before the VAT tribunal in *University Court of the University of St Andrews (VTD 19054)*. HMRC took the stance that use of university buildings outside the academic term is ignored in apportioning by concession, and also by concession they allow an apportionment beyond the strict legal entitlement in respect of certain structural work, but it is not open to the tribunal to review the exercise of such discretions. The tribunal took the view that *Note 10* grants zero-rating only to parts or areas of a building which are intended solely for a relevant residential purpose; it does not permit partial zero-rating in respect of parts or areas having a mixed use. The building in question was a facilities building, whose purpose was to meet the social needs of students residing in the 12 accommodation blocks built with it. The building included a gym, music room, kitchen and dining room, conference room, projection room, bar, shop and common room. HMRC had agreed zero-rating for the kitchen and dining room, music room, gym and kitchen chef's office. It was agreed that the bar and shop (and it appears the common room) did not qualify. The tribunal felt that a corridor that was the means of access to the gym and music room, the toilets provided for students and the first-aid room qualified for zero-rating, as they would be needed even if the building had not included the non-residential areas. It agreed with HMRC that the other disputed areas (cleaning materials store, a corridor to allow rear access to the kitchen and the bar and shop, staff room, staff changing room, office and reception areas, lobby and cloakroom) were mixed-use, and it was solely up to HMRC to agree any concessionary treatment.

16.119 Zero-rating of time-shares, or where residence in a building throughout the year (or the use of the building or part of it as the grantee's principal private residence) is prevented by the terms of a covenant, statutory planning consent or similar permission, is prohibited by *VATA 1994, Sch 8, Group 5, Note 13*. This is intended to prevent holiday accommodation being brought within the scope of zero-rating by selling or leasing it, ostensibly without limitation of usage, in circumstances where there is a legal bar on it being used as a permanent residence. The scope and perhaps even the validity of this provision is questionable. In *Mrs BA Ashworth (VTD 12924)* the VAT tribunal held that, in the appellant's case, the exclusion was inconsistent with *Article 13B(b)(1)* of the *EC Sixth Directive* and the discriminatory effect was not objectively justified. It therefore decided that Mrs Ashworth's occupation of the property was exempt, not standard-rated. Mrs Ashworth lived in the property for 11 months a year and stayed with her daughter for the month of February during which her lease of her lodge prohibited occupation. The tribunal was influenced partly by the fact that the lodge (at a marina) did not have the attributes of a holiday site but mainly by the fact that it was clearly occupied as the appellant's home not as holiday accommodation. A similar result was reached in *Livingstone Homes UK Ltd (VTD 16649)*. The company developed new detached dwellings on substantial plots at a holiday resort in Scotland. The feu disposition of each plot was made subject to a condition that all houses on the development were to be used only as holiday dwellings and for no other purpose. The VAT tribunal held that the effect of this provision did not preclude the house being used as a principal private residence within *VATA 1994, Sch 8, Group 5, Note 13(ii)* (residence throughout the year prevented by the terms of any permission) as there was nothing to prevent a person from living in the house throughout the year and having no other home. However, the tribunal in *Loch Tay Highland Lodges Ltd (VTD 18785)* felt that *Livingstone* had been wrongly decided, as the fact that a house was a person's principal private residence did not take it outside *Note 13*. The principal residence is not determined solely by reference to the amount of time spent there (*Frost v Fellham* – see **4.33**). The later Tribunal in *Trathen and Goode (TC 898)* followed the decision in *Loch Tay*, commenting that, 'We regard *Livingstone* as illogical since it gives no effect to the words 'only and for no other purpose', since all purposes other than holiday use are excluded and one such purpose must be residence when not on holiday'.

16.120 If the major interest granted is a lease of over 21 years, zero-rating applies only to the premium paid, as the intention is that all rents of residential accommodation should be exempt from VAT. The draftsman believed that, in order to trigger the right to repayment of input VAT, the first supply after the construction of the building needs to be a zero-rated supply. An exempt supply would forfeit the relief. Accordingly, if no premium is payable the first payment of rent due under the lease is treated as consideration for a zero-rated supply so as to preserve the right to repayment of input VAT (*VATA 1994, Sch 8, Group 5, Note 14*). Following the *Briararch* decision (see **17.96** below) this provision is apparently ineffective in achieving its aim. HMRC seem unlikely to take this point, however.

16.121 Other points to note are as follows:

(*a*) The construction of a civil engineering work does not cover the conversion, alteration or enlargement of such a work (*Note 15*).

(*b*) A caravan is not a residential caravan if residence in it throughout the year is prevented by the terms of a covenant, statutory planning consent or similar permission (*Note 19*).

(*c*) The reference to services in *items 2* and *3* do not include a transfer of an undivided share in goods or the transfer of the possession of goods, which are deemed to be supplies of services by *VATA 1994, Sch 4, para 1(1)*. Nor does it include the appropriation of goods to a non-business purpose which is similarly deemed to be a supply of services under *Sch 4, para 5(4)* (*Note 20*).

(*d*) The special rule in *VATA 1994, s 30(3)*, which allows goods to be imported free of VAT if their sale will qualify for zero-rating, does not apply to VAT on goods incorporated in buildings which are zero-rated under *Group 5* (*Note 22*).

Where a charity uses premises in a village hall or similarly in providing social or recreational facilities for a local community, the premises are treated as being used for a relevant charitable purpose irrespective of whether the occupier is using them for such a purpose (*VATA 1994, Sch 10, para 36(6)*).

Change of Use of Residential and Charitable Buildings

16.122 *VATA 1994, Sch 10, para 1* imposes a VAT charge if subsequent to one of the zero-rated transactions in **16.6** above, and within ten years of the completion of the building, it is used for a non-qualifying purpose. The relevant legislation is contained in *VATA 1994, Sch 10*.

16.123 The provisions apply wherever there is an increase in the part of the premises that is not used for a relevant residential purpose or a relevant charitable purpose in the ten-year period or the owner disposes of his entire interest in the building during the period and as a result of the increase the non-qualifying proportion exceeds the maximum non-qualifying proportion at any earlier time in the ten-year period (*VATA 1994, Sch 10, paras 35, 36(1)–(3)* as amended by *VAT (Buildings and Land) Order 2011; SI 2011, No 86*). If only a proportion of the use of the premises is for a relevant residential or charitable purpose and that use is not confined to a part of the premises which is used solely for such a purpose, the same proportion of the premises is regarded as being used for relevant resident or charitable purposes (*VATA 1994, Sch 10, para 36(4)(5)*). In *Balhousie Holdings Ltd (2017 SFTD 126)* the company constructed three care homes via subsidiaries. On completion they did a sale and leaseback to raise the funds to run the homes. HMRC took the view that the sale and the leaseback were separate transactions and that the sale triggered the VAT charge. The FTT disagreed. They felt that para 36 requires a taxpayer to relinquish all and every interest in the relevant property and that this is not the case with a sale and leaseback transaction.

16.124 The provisions treat the owner as making a taxable supply (to himself) immediately prior to the increase. The value of that supply is:

$$R2 \times Y \frac{(120 - Z)}{(120)}$$

where:

R1 is the maximum previous non-exempt part of the premises,

R2 is the new non-exempt part of the premises,

Y is the amount that yields an amount of VAT chargeable on it equal to the VAT which would have been chargeable on the relevant zero-rated supply (or the aggregate amount if there was more than one supply) had the premises not been intended for a relevant residential or charitable purpose, and

Z is the number of whole months since the day on which the premises were completed.

R2 is replaced in this formula by (R2 – R1) for changes after the first.

16.125 Prior to 1 March 2011 the provisions applied where:

(*a*) one or more such zero-rated supplies relating to a building had been made to a person;

(*b*) within ten years from the date on which the building was completed a person granted an interest in (or right over, or licence to occupy) the building – or to be more precise any part of the building to which the intended use that gave rise to zero-rating was attributable; and

(*c*) the building (or part of a building) was not intended for use for a relevant residential or charitable purpose after the grant referred to in (*b*).

(*VATA 1994, Sch 10, paras 36(1)–(3)*.)

16.126 The grant of the interest had to be treated as a taxable supply (in the course or furtherance of a business) which was not zero-rated under *VATA 1994, Sch 8, Group 5*. (*VATA 1994, Sch 10, para 36(4)*). Prior to 1 June 2002, the effect was to trigger a tax charge on that grant – which expression, of course, covers a disposal as well as a lease. From that date the charge is on a proportion of the VAT that would have been chargeable if the original supply had not been zero-rated. The proportion is 10% of such VAT for each year or part of a year unexpired in the ten-year period up to the time of the trigger event (*VAT (Construction of Buildings) Order 2002* (*SI 2002 No 1101*)). For example, if after 4¾ years the building is sold for a non-qualifying use, 60% of the VAT will be clawed back (as the use qualified for only four full years).

16.127 Similar rules applied where the owner simply alters the use of the building within the ten-year period, such as turning an old people's home into a hotel without making a disposal. In such circumstances he is deemed to make a taxable supply to himself at the time he first uses the building for the non-qualifying purpose. A change from one qualifying use to another, such as the sale of a nursing home to a charity to be used as a non-fee-paying school, will not trigger the charge. The amount on which VAT is charged is not the value of the building at the time of the change of use or the value at the date the original zero-rated supply was made. It is a notional amount, the VAT payable on which is equal to the VAT that would have been payable on the original supply had it been taxable (*VATA 1994, Sch 10, para 37*).

16.128 The change in approach was to create uniformity. The pre-1 March 2011 rules worked erratically in HMRC's view. HMRC give an example of a £5 million building consisting of five floors used by a charity wholly for its own non-business activities with a change of use of one floor after five years. If the charity itself used the floor for business purposes, it triggered a VAT charge of £100,000 (which would qualify as input tax if the business is a taxable business). If the charity rented the floor to another charity, there was no charge as the property continued to be used for relevant charitable purposes. If it was let to another charity for business purposes, the tax charge was calculated by reference to a premium and rent charged. It is unclear why HMRC regarded this as anomalous as on those examples it triggered a charge wherever the premises ceased to be used for charitable purposes. Under the new rules the charge would always be:

20% (one floor) × 5,000,000 × 60/120 (months) = £500,000

VAT on this at 20% is £100,000.

This is the same as the figure produced in most cases by the previous rules! Further examples can be found in VAT Information Sheet 04/11, which is available on the HMRC website.

These deemed disposal provisions do not apply on a change of use where the zero-rating for protected buildings rules applied (see **9.18** onwards).

16.129 HMRC announced in July 2009 that they consider that the word 'solely' as used in the phrase 'used solely for a relevant charitable purpose', can incorporate an appropriate de minimis margin and that in order to avoid unnecessary disputes in marginal cases they will accept that the statutory condition is satisfied if the relevant use of the building by the charity is 95% or more. In the light of this change of view they withdrew ESC 3.29 (which allowed a 10% de minimis in three defined circumstances) as being no longer necessary (HMRC Briefs 39/2009 and 32/2010).

16.130 In practice from 21 March 2007 HMRC did not enforce a change of use charge on such buildings even if it brought the non-qualifying use beyond the 10% de minimis concession if that change of use was not anticipated at the time that zero-rating was obtained. If it was apparent that at the time the zero-rating was obtained it was intended that qualifying use would exceed 10% at some time during the ten-year period HMRC consider that the original supply should never have been zero-rated (HMRC Brief 29/07). As the ESC was conditional on the building continuing to be used for the qualifying purpose throughout the ten-year period, they presumably will enforce the change of use charge if the building ceases to be used completely for the qualifying purpose. HMRC have not indicated whether they apply this practice to their new de minimis interpretation.

16.131 It should be noted that no relief is given for any VAT paid at the time of construction on building and other costs. In many cases such VAT will have been reclaimed as inputs of a taxable business at that stage, but it is possible to envisage circumstances in which it was not reclaimable, such as if the building was occupied by a charity which was not carrying on a business. In such circumstances the charge on change of use can be penal.

16.132 For many years there was a problem with Academies. These are State funded schools that provide free education but a part of the initial capital expenditure is provided by a private sector sponsor. An Academy is normally set up as a charity so the construction costs should in theory qualify for zero-rating. An Academy has to enter into an agreement with the Secretary of State under the *Education Act 1996, s 579*. This agreement requires the Academy to integrate into its local community. However, community use of its premises is non-charitable use, so can forfeit or restrict the VAT recovery. The government have addressed this from 1 April 2011 in *VATA 1994, s 33B*, which allows the proprietor of the Academy to claim a refund of input VAT from HMRC in the same way as local authorities (*VATA 1994, s 33A* inserted by *FA 2011, s 76*).

Reduced Rate on Energy Saving Materials, etc

16.133 The supply of services of installing:

(*a*) insulation for walls, floors, ceilings, roofs or lofts, or for water tanks, pipes or other plumbing fittings;

(*b*) draught stripping for windows and doors;

(*c*) central heating system controls (including thermostatic radiator valves);

(*d*) hot water system controls;

(*e*) solar panels;

(*f*) wind turbines;

(*g*) water turbines;

(*h*) ground source heat pumps (from 1 June 2004);

(*i*) air source heat pumps (from 7 April 2005);

(*j*) micro combined heat and power units (from 7 April 2005);

(*k*) boilers designed to be fuelled solely by wood, straw or similar vegetal material (from 1 January 2006),

in residential accommodation is chargeable at a reduced rate of 5%. The 5% rate also applies to the supply of the materials themselves provided that they are supplied by the person who installs them. (*VATA 1994, Sch 7A, Group 2, Items 1* and *2* as amended by *FA 2013, s 193*). Prior to 1 August 2013 the 5% rate also applied to installing such energy-saving materials in a building intended for use solely for a relevant residential purpose. Although not directly concerned with this provision, it is worth noting that in *Colaingrove Ltd (TC 2534)* HMRC argued that the supply of the use of a caravan and the supply of fuel to it was a single standard-rated supply of fully serviced holiday accommodation. The FTT held that, as in *EC v France (Case C-94/09)*, the French undertaker's case, the ECJ had confirmed that French legislation applying a reduced rate of VAT to the transportation of a body in a vehicle met the EU law on reduced rates, the reduced rate under *VATA 1994, Sch 7A, Group 1* (fuel and power for domestic use) applied to the fuel element, irrespective of the fact that there was a single overall supply.

16.134 This legislation was in issue in *Beco Products Ltd (VTD 18638)*. Beco manufactures insulating construction blocks, 'Wallform'. These are hollow polystyrene blocks. HMRC accepted that installing such blocks in isolation from other building work attracts the 5% rate. Walls can be built out of the blocks by filling them with concrete. HMRC contended that an extension so constructed would not qualify for the reduced rate. However, if one contractor erects the blocks on site and a separate contractor fills them with concrete, the first can charge the 5% rate but the second cannot do so. The tribunal agreed. In *Pinevale Ltd (TC 2283)* the FTT held that insupolycarbonate roofing panels for a conservatory attached to a house, and radiation reflector strips, were energy-saving materials as they had been shown to achieve a demonstrable reduction in heat loss as compared with double glazing. It also accepted that the expression insulation for roofs can fairly be read, where (as in *Pinevale*) the product functions as the roof and thereby keeps the inside of the conservatory wind and water proof, as being just as much insulation for roofs as where something is supplied to be affixed to an existing roof. The Upper Tribunal disagreed (*2014 STC 2217*). It said that the test in **16.133** is exhaustive. A material which is insulation for a roof under (*a*) is not the same thing as the roof itself. The test presupposes that there is a roof to which the insulating material is applied. *Wetheralds Construction Ltd (TC 5552)* supplied a Solid Roof System which it fitted to customers' conservatories. It involved attaching insulated panels to the existing roof structure and then covering the roof with waterproof tiling. The FTT held this to be a reduced rate supply. It was not the replacement of the roof as in *Pinevale*. The essential character of the supply was of insulation of the existing roof, not a roof replacement.

16.135 *Envoygate (Installations) Ltd and Richvale Ltd (TC 3361)* involved the replacement of box sash windows and the supply and fitting of draught stripping for windows made at the same time. HMRC contended that there was a single supply of sash windows. The Tribunal held that there were two separate supplies and that of the draught stripping attracted the 5% rate. Over 85% of customers purchased both together and the draught stripping was roughly 50% of the total price. *Itchen Sash Windows Renovation Ltd (TC 3645)* was concerned with the supply of weather stripping, a process designed to significantly reduce heat loss, noise, dust and sash rattle. HMRC accepted that this attracted the reduced rate. However, for the stripping to work effectively, it was often necessary to renovate the windows. HMRC contended that where this was done, the weather stripping was subsumed into a standard-rated supply of window renovation. The FTT held that the two were separate supplies, but that the renovation was not ancillary to the weather stripping so the renovating work was VATable at the standard rate.

16.136 The reduced rate now applies to all residential and relevant charitable buildings. It should be noted that the 5% rate applies to materials only if they are supplied by a person who provides a service of installation. It does not apply to the purchase of materials for DIY installation.

16.137 The 5% reduced rate also applies to supplies to a 'qualifying person' of services of installing:

(*a*) gas-fired room heaters that are fitted with thermostatic controls;

(*b*) electric storage heaters;

(*c*) closed solid fuel fire cassettes;

(*d*) electrical dual immersion water heaters with foam-insulated hot water tanks;

(*e*) gas-fired boilers;

(*f*) oil-fired boilers; or

(*g*) radiators;

in that person's sole or main residence and the supply of the materials themselves provided that they are supplied by the person who installs them (*VATA 1994, Sch 7A, Group 3, Items 1* and *2*).

16.138 The reduced rate only applies, however, if the consideration for the supply is funded by a grant made under a scheme which:

(*a*) has as one of its objectives the funding of the installation of energy-saving materials in the homes of qualifying persons; and

(*b*) disburses, directly or indirectly, its grants in whole or in part out of funds made available to it in order to achieve that objective by either the UK Government, the EC, a local authority or under an arrangement approved by the Director General of Electricity Supply or of Gas Supply (*VATA 1994, Sch 7A, Group 3, Note 2*).

16.139 A qualifying person is one who is:

(*a*) aged 60 or over; and

(*b*) in receipt of either council tax benefit, disability living allowance, disability working allowance, any element of child tax credit other than the family element, working tax credit, housing benefit, income based Job Seeker's Allowance, income support, or disablement pension or war disablement pension at the increased rate (*VATA 1994, Sch 7A, Group 3, Note 6*).

16.140 The 5% rate also applies to the following supplies made to a qualifying person and funded under an approved scheme (ie one within (*b*) in para **16.138**):

(*a*) connecting or reconnecting a mains gas supply to the qualifying person's sole or main residence (together with the supply of the necessary goods);

(*b*) installing, maintaining or repairing a central heating system in the qualifying person's sole or main residence (together with the supply of the necessary goods);

(*c*) installing any of the following qualifying security goods in the qualifying person's sole or main residence (together with the supply of the necessary goods):

(i) locks or bolts for windows;

(ii) locks, bolts or security chains for doors;

(iii) spy holes;

(iv) smoke alarms; and

(*d*) installing, maintaining or repairing a renewable source heating system in the qualifying person's sole or main residence (together with the supply of the necessary goods).

(*VATA 1994, Sch 7A, Group 3, Items 3–6, 8A, 8B, 9, 10, Note 5.*)

16.141 The reduced rate also applies to the leasing of goods (to anyone) that form the whole or part of a central heating system installed in the sole or main residence of a qualified person, and the supply of goods that form the whole or part of such a system if immediately before being supplied they were leased under arrangements such that the consideration for the supplies consisting in the leasing of the goods was in whole or part funded by a grant under a relevant scheme (*VATA 1994, Sch 7A, Group 3, Items 7* and *8*). Leasing of goods can qualify if the consideration is a payment becoming due only by reason of the termination (whether by the passage of time or otherwise) of the leasing of the goods, even apparently if that payment will not be funded by a grant under a relevant scheme (*VATA 1994, Sch 7A, Group 3, Note 1*).

16.142 Residential accommodation in **16.133** has a special meaning for the purpose of the reduced rate, namely:

(*a*) a building or part of a building that consists of a dwelling or a number of dwellings;

(*b*) a building or part of a building used for a relevant residential purpose;

(*c*) a caravan used as a place of permanent habitation; or

(*d*) a houseboat.

(*VATA 1994, Sch 7A, Group 2, Note 2.*)

16.143 Use for a relevant charitable purpose has the same meaning as in **16.59**. Use for a relevant residential purpose has the same meaning as in **16.49**. (*VATA 1994, Sch 7A, Group 1, Note 7, Group, 2 Note 3*).

16.144 HMRC have issued guidance on these provisions. They consider that 'installation' means putting in place, which involves some process by which materials like draught stripping are permanently fixed in place although some products, such as loft insulation, may simply need to be unrolled and positioned in place to be installed. Necessary minor building works such as planning doors or enlarging loft hatches are covered by installation. If the grant does not cover the full cost it is only the part covered by the grant that qualifies. For example if the grant is £700 and the cost of the installation is £1,000, 70% of the cost is VATable at 5% and the remaining 30% at 20%. In *Case C-161/14 European Commission v UK (2015 STC 1767)*, the CJEU held that this relief is incompatible with EU law to the extent that the supplies cannot be considered as part of a social policy. The UK accordingly needs to review this relief but has said that it will not amend the law before 1 April 2016.

Reduced Rate on Residential Conversions and Renovations

16.145 The 5% reduced rate also applies to supplies in respect of certain residential conversions. These are:

(*a*) the supply in the course of a qualifying conversion (see **16.146**) of qualifying services (see **16.153**) relating to the conversion (*VATA 1994, Sch 7A, Group 6, item 1*);

(*b*) the supply of building materials by a person who is supplying qualifying services in the course of a qualifying conversion where those services include the incorporation of such materials in the building concerned or its immediate site (*VATA 1994, Sch 7A, Group 6, item 2*);

(*c*) the supply in the course of the renovation or alteration (or extension) of qualifying residential premises (see **16.146**) of qualifying services related to that renovation or alteration, provided that the conditions at **16.159** are met (*VATA 1994, Sch 7A, Group 7, item 1*);

(*d*) the supply of building materials by a person who is supplying qualifying services in the course of such a renovation or alteration where those services include the incorporation of such materials in the building concerned or its immediate site (*VATA 1994, Sch 7A, Group 7, item 2*).

16.146 A qualifying conversion is any of the following:

(*a*) A conversion of premises consisting of a building (or part of a building):

  (i) where after the conversion the premises contain a number of single household dwellings that is different from the number of such dwellings before the conversion (but is not less than one); and

  (ii) where there is no part of the premises being converted that is a part that after the conversion contains the same number of single household dwellings as before the conversion (whether zero, one or two or more).

(*VATA 1994, Sch 7A, Group 6, Note 3.*)

This is called a changed number of dwellings conversion (*VATA 1994, Sch 7A, Group 7, Note 2(a)*).

(*b*) A conversion of premises consisting of a building or part of a building where:

(i) before the conversion the premises being converted do not contain any multiple occupancy dwellings;

(ii) after the conversion they contain only a multiple occupancy dwelling or two or more such dwellings; and

(iii) the use to which those premises are intended to be put after the conversion is not to any extent use for a qualifying residential purpose (which although separately defined in *Sch 7A, Group 6, Note 6* is the same thing as a relevant residential purpose for zero rating purposes – see **16.48**).

(*VATA 1994, Sch 7A, Group 6, Note 5.*)

This is called a house in multiple occupation conversion (*VATA 1994, Sch 7A, Group 6, Note* 2).

(*c*) A conversion of premises consisting of a building or two or more buildings (or part of a building or two or more parts of buildings or a combination of a building or two or more buildings and a part of a building or two or more parts of buildings) where:

(i) the use to which the premises being converted were last put before the conversion was not to any extent use for a relevant residential purpose and those premises are intended to be used solely for a relevant residential purpose after the conversion; and

(ii) if the qualifying residential purpose is an institutional purpose (ie it is not residential accommodation for students or school pupils or for members of the armed forces) the premises being converted are intended to form after the conversion the entirety of an institution used for that purpose.

(*VATA 1994, Sch 7A, Group 6, Note 7.*)

This is called a special residential conversion (*VATA 1994, Sch 7A, Group 6, Note* 2). In the case of a special residential conversion the 5% rate applies only if the supply is made to the person who intends to use the premises for the qualifying residential purpose and before the supply is made that person has given a certificate to the supplier stating that the conversion is a special residential conversion. The certificate must be in a form to be laid down by HMRC (*VATA 1994, Sch 7A, Group 6, Note 8*). This is of course similar to the rules on zero-rating of relevant residential or charitable buildings (see **16.81–16.89**). HMRC are empowered to specify the form of certificate in a notice published by them. They have done so in an Annex to VAT Information Sheet 4/01 (May 2001). It is reproduced in Notice 708, Chapter 18.

In all three cases any necessary statutory planning consent and statutory building control approval needed for the conversion must also have been granted – presumably before the relevant supply takes place (*VATA 1994, Sch 7A, Group 6, Note 10*).

16.147 HMRC give as an example of (*a*) in **16.146** the installation of a lift in a block of flats consisting of four floors each with four flats. On the first three floors the footprint of each flat is changed but on the fourth floor three penthouse flats are created from the original four. Only the work to convert the top floor will be eligible for the 5% rate because it is only in this part of the building that the number of dwellings changes. Suppose, however, the first floor is converted into five flats as well. The overall number of flats in the building will not have changed but the 5% rate can nevertheless apply to the conversion work done on the ground and third floor as the number of dwellings on both has changed (VAT Information Sheet 4/01, para 2.4 and Notice 708, para 7.3.1). In other words they interpret 'premises' as being different to the building in which those premises are situated, whereas in everyday parlance most people would regard the two as synonymous. Furthermore they interpret the 'premises being converted' as meaning only the part of the premises affected by the conversion work. Whilst this is a generous interpretation it could give rise to problems. For example suppose a building consists of four flats each consisting of one maisonette flat. The top flat is converted so that it can be used as a single flat with that on the third floor. If the premises being converted is the third and fourth floor then the whole work qualifies for relief as two dwellings are converted into one. On the other hand if the third floor is not part of the premises being converted then none of the work will qualify for the 5% rate as the conversion creates only part of a dwelling.

16.148 HMRC's interpretation found favour with the VAT tribunal in *Wellcome Trust (VTD 18417)*. The trust owned an investment property containing seven flats. After the conversion it contained only four. The second floor was a single flat prior to the conversion. Although substantial structural work was carried out, including moving the staircase and lift well and lowering the ceiling by about two feet, after conversion the second floor still contained a single flat. The Trust contended that as the second floor had given up part of its space to the third they should be regarded together as premises. HMRC contended that the second floor could not satisfy head (*a*)(*ii*) at **16.146**. The converted second-floor apartment contained enough of the old flat to contain the same number of dwellings – although it might be different if the new were 50% smaller than the old rather than 5% smaller as had happened. They also said that their examples in Information Sheet 4/01 'were helpful but not determinative'. Although the tribunal felt note 3 difficult to interpret and apply, they agreed with HMRC.

16.149 In *Opal Carleton Ltd (TC 635)* the company developed student accommodation for the use of a university in the early 1970s. It zero-rated its supply as relating to relevant residential accommodation. The building was later reconfigured to reduce the units of accommodation from 223 to 145 but upgrade the units to include in each a bathroom pod and kitchenette. Opal claimed that the building had been converted from student accommodation to single household dwellings so the building work qualified for the reduced rate. The Tribunal disagreed. Looking at the position in the round the building was let as halls of residence and is still halls of residence. Accordingly the building works were for the upgrading of the student units, which are a relevant residential purpose not a dwelling. It is not open to Opal to choose which heading suits it best. The fact that the units might now qualify as dwellings does not prevent their being for a relevant residential purpose.

16.150 *Cordery Build Ltd (TC 2068)* was concerned with the conversion of a block of 36 bedsits used as sheltered accommodation for the elderly into one bedroom flats for sale to any individual. Each bedsit was self-contained with washing and kitchen facilities. There was a communal laundry and lounge. Each unit had a bell cord to contact the landlord's call centre, who would in turn notify their onsite estate manager of any emergency. The conversion involved removing the bell cords, erecting a wall to create a separate bedroom and living room and enlarging the kitchen to accommodate a washing machine. The company contended that prior to conversion the building was in use for a relevant residential purpose and after the conversion it was 36 separate dwellings. The Tribunal agreed with HMRC that to constitute an institution, a building must have an element of organisation present. It thought that pre-conversion the property was 'sheltered housing' and not an institution. Accordingly the conversion was not a qualifying conversion or a changed number of dwellings conversion.

16.151 The work in *Nabarro (TC 3757)* was the demolition of a 'granny flat' at the side of the house and the addition of two storeys to the house. The question was whether there was initially one house (including the granny flat) or two. There was no direct access to the house from the flat, but they were linked by an open area covered with corrugated sheeting. Each was treated separately for council tax and the two had separate house numbers. The taxpayer contended that they were two separate dwellings in one building, so the conversion changed the dwellings in the building from two to one. The FTT agreed that there were two dwellings but was sceptical as to whether they were contained in a single building. It was swayed by the fact the council seemed to have regarded the two as a single building.

16.152 An example of (*b*) in **16.146** above might be the conversion of a house into bed-sits. If a three-storey house is converted into a ground floor flat for the owner and two floors of bed-sits it does not appear that any of the work would qualify. If the entire building is the premises being converted it will not qualify as after the conversion it will contain a single household dwelling (the flat), not contain only multiple occupancy dwellings. If only the first and second floor are the premises it will not qualify as prior to conversion those two floors on their own would not have been a single household dwelling but only part of such a dwelling.

16.153 Curiously, if the conversion is done in two stages, first to a ground-floor flat and a combined first- and second-floor flat, and then the conversion of the larger flat into bed-sits, the first conversion would qualify under head (*a*) and the second under (*b*). The large flat does not actually need to be used as such, as the test is whether it is 'designed' for occupation by a single household, not whether it is intended that it should actually be occupied for such a purpose. Suppose, at a later date, the ground floor flat is converted into bed-sits. If those are self-contained and do not share facilities with those on the other two floors, that appears to be a qualifying conversion. If, however, they are not, but create additional bedrooms that will share the facilities on the other floors, the conversion will not qualify as it will simply increase the size of an existing multiple occupancy dwelling not create a new one. Head (*b*) does not allow the reverse situation, ie the conversion of a multiple occupancy dwelling into flats, but this is probably because it is unnecessary to do so as such a conversion falls within head (*a*).

16.154 A single household dwelling is one that is designed for occupation by a single household and which:

(*a*) consists of self-contained living accommodation;

(*b*) has no provision for direct internal access from the dwelling to any other dwelling or part of a dwelling;

(*c*) is not prohibited from being used separately by the terms of any covenant, statutory planning consent or similar provision; and

(*d*) is not prohibited from being separately disposed of by any such terms.

(*VATA 1994, Sch 7A, Group 6, Note 4.*)

This definition is similar, but not identical, to that of a dwelling for zero-rating purposes, the only practical difference being that for zero-rating purposes planning consent must also have been granted and the construction or conversion carried out in accordance with that consent. The requirement for any necessary planning permission does also apply for the 5% rate (see **16.146**) but there is no obligation to actually comply with it. There is also an obligation to obtain any necessary building control consent, which does not apply to zero-rating.

16.155 A multiple occupancy dwelling is one that is designed for occupation by persons not forming a single household, is not to any extent used for a relevant residential purpose and which meets conditions (*a*) to (*d*) above (*VATA 1994, Sch 7A, Group 6, Note 4*). A building is designed for occupation of a particular kind both if it was originally constructed for such occupation (and not later adapted for a different kind of occupation) and if it is so designed as a result of adaptation (*VATA 1994, Sch 7A, Group 6, Note 4*). *Dr R W Nicholson (VTD 19412)* (see **16.37**) provides a useful twist on the interpretation of head (*c*). The Upper Tribunal in *HMRC v Lunn (2010 STC 486)* (see **9.18**) considered the meaning of 'separate use' in the context of the identical wording in *VATA 1994, Sch 8, Group 6, Note 2*.

16.156 Where part of a supply of services qualifies for the reduced rate and part does not, an apportionment needs to be made to determine the extent to which the 5% rate applies (*VATA 1994, Sch 7A, Group 6, Note 1*). A qualifying conversion includes any garage works (the construction of a garage or a conversion of a non-residential building (ie one neither designed nor adapted as a dwelling or dwellings or for a qualifying residential purpose), or non-residential part of a building, that results in a garage) related to the conversion. Garage works are related if they are carried out at the same time as the conversion and the resulting garage is intended to be occupied with one of the dwellings (or the institution or other accommodation in the case of a special residential conversion) resulting from the conversion (*VATA 1994, Sch 7A, Group 6, Note 7*).

16.157 A supply of qualifying services consists of:

(*a*) carrying out works to the fabric of the building; or

(*b*) carrying out works within the immediate site of the building in connection with the means of providing water, power, heat, drainage, security or access for the building or in connection with the provision of means of waste disposal to the building.

(*VATA 1994, Sch 7A, Group 6, Note 11.*)

16.158 In the case of the conversion of part of a building the works must of course relate to that part or to the provision of water, etc to that part (*VATA 1994, Sch 7A, Group 6, Note 11*). The incorporation, or installation as fittings, in the building of any goods is not carrying out works to the fabric of a building unless such goods are building materials (as defined in *VATA 1994, Sch 8, Group 5, Notes 22* and *23* – see **8.78**) (*VATA 1994, Sch 7A, Group 6, Notes 11, 12*). HMRC say that supplies by architects, surveyors or any person acting in a supervisory capacity, the supply of goods on hire, landscaping and work to outbuildings that remain outbuildings do not qualify for the 5% rate (VAT Information Sheet 4/01, para 3.1 and Notice 708, para 7.6). This is presumably because they do not regard them as 'the carrying out of works'.

16.159 Services in connection with the renovation, alteration or extension of qualifying residential premises (ie within **16.145**(*c*) or (*d*)) qualify for the 5% rate if either of the following conditions are satisfied:

(*a*) The premises concerned (or where those premises are a building which, when last lived in, formed a relevant residential unit, any of the other buildings which formed part of that unit) have not been lived in during the two years ending with the commencement of the relevant works (three years prior to 1 January 2008).

(*b*) If it has, it was not lived in during an earlier period of two years, the person whose occupation brought that period to an end acquired a major interest in the dwelling for a consideration during the unoccupied period (and at a time when it had been unoccupied for at least two years) the supply was made to that person, and the relevant works are carried out during the period of 12 months from the date of the acquisition of the building (where there are joint owners only one needs to have lived in the building).

(VATA 1994, Sch 7A, Group 7, Note 3.)

16.160 'Qualifying residential premises' means a single household dwelling or a multiple occupancy dwelling (see **16.155**) or a building (or part of a building) which, when it was last lived in, was used for a relevant residential purpose (VATA 1994, Sch 7A, Group 7. Note 2). The relevant works for this purpose are of course the works that attract the 5% rate (*VATA 1994, Sch 7A, Group 7, Note 3*). The 5% rate applies only if:

(i) any statutory planning consent or building control approval needed for the renovation or alteration has been obtained (*VATA 1994, Sch 7A, Group 7, Note 4*); and

(ii) where the premises in question are a building (or part of a building) which, when it was last lived in, was used for a relevant residential purpose, the building (or part) must be intended to be used solely for such a purpose after the renovation or alteration and, before the supply is made, the recipient of the supply must give the supplier a certificate stating that intention (*VATA 1994, Sch 7A, Group 7, Note 4A*).

'Qualifying services' has the same meaning as at **16.153** (*VATA 1994, Sch 7A, Group 7, Note 4*).

16.161 Test (*b*) above is intended to allow a person to buy an empty property, move in and refurbish it around himself. However, it is very restrictive, particularly if planning permission is required for the refurbishment. The refurbishment must be 'carried out', which presumably means completed rather than started, within 12 months of acquiring the house. It should also be noted that he must acquire the property for a consideration, although not necessarily an open market consideration. Acquisition as a gift or as a dividend in specie from a company will not enable the owner to qualify for the 5% rate – although it will still qualify if the taxpayer does not move into the property prior to the refurbishment as the alternative test, (*a*), does not look at what happened on the acquisition. Curiously, as the supply must be to the owner, a subcontractor cannot use the 5% rate where test (*b*) applies although he can do so under test (*a*). This is confirmed by HMRC in VAT Information Sheet 4/01, para 3.5. and Notice 708, para 8.3.4. Occupation by squatters in the three-year period will not deny relief (Notice 708, para 8.3.3).

16.162 HMRC said when the legislation was introduced that the relief will cover the conversion of a house into flats or flats into a house; the conversion of relevant residential purpose buildings (such as a nursing home) or non-residential buildings into single household dwellings; the conversion of houses in multiple occupation (ie where the accommodation is not self-contained such as bed-sits, shared houses and flats and bed and breakfast establishments with a mix of short and long stay residents) into single household dwellings; and the conversion of a building which may have been lived in, such as a pub with staff accommodation, which does not qualify as a single household dwelling into houses or flats (VAT Information Sheet 4/01, paras 2.2 and 2.11). They also say that conversion includes all works of repair, maintenance or improvement to the fabric of the building where the work forms an intrinsic part of changing the number of dwellings (para 2.4). They also say that the relief applies even if the property was originally a dwelling but was converted to some other use and is reconverted back to a dwelling (para 2.7). HMRC consider that conversion into a number of dwellings means that a building is converted into semi-detached houses, terraced housing, maisonettes or flats (para 2.9), albeit though most people would regard two semi-detached houses or a terrace of houses as made up as separate buildings.

16.163 HMRC have said that a dwelling that has been used for storage or a purpose other than living accommodation for three years will 'usually' be treated as empty for the purpose of the reduced rate (VAT Information Sheet 4/01, para 1.2 and Notice 708, Chapter 8). They emphasise that it is the VAT registered trader's responsibility to hold proof that the supply qualifies for the reduced rate. They will accept letters from empty property officers in local authorities or other evidence such as the electoral roll, council tax data, and other sources of reliable information which show on the balance of probabilities that the building had been unoccupied for three years prior to the commencement of the work (para 1.5). HMRC also say that 'renovation' (see **16.145**(*c*)) includes any work of repair, maintenance (eg redecoration) or improvement (eg an extension or the installation of double glazing) carried out to the fabric of the building (para 1.3). Most of the cases to date have concerned DIY builders and are considered at **16.184** onwards.

Rents

16.164 Rents from residential properties are always exempt. The only exception is the first rental payment under a lease, which can be zero-rated if there is no premium. Rents for relevant charitable buildings are also always exempt, with the exception that rents for an office building will be taxable if the landlord elects to waive the exemption ('exercises the option to tax'). Rents for commercial buildings are normally exempt but an election can be made to bring them into the scope of VAT (see **17.110**).

Service Charges

16.165 An area that frequently causes problems is service charges payable under leases. Unfortunately this is an area where the legal status of the payment is often difficult to ascertain and HMRC have made a number of concessions. Whilst, in general, concessions are helpful, there is in this area a tendency for local HMRC officers to want to apply them as a matter of course even where they are not necessarily in the interests of the landlord levying the service charge or the tenant paying it. It is accordingly sometimes necessary to remember that a taxpayer is entitled to be taxed in accordance with the application of the law to his particular lease, whatever HMRC's normal treatment of similar transactions may be. Many of the problems that have arisen in the past in relation to service charges in relation to commercial property will disappear if the option to tax (see **17.126**) is exercised. However, as many landlords are reluctant to exercise this option, they are likely to continue to exist in practice for some time.

16.166 Normally a service charge will be nothing more than a method of calculating the rent payable under the lease, ie the rent will be the aggregate of a fixed (and normally periodically reviewed) sum plus an additional amount varying with the expenditure on providing the specific services which the lease obliges the landlord to supply. This will always be the position where the lease requires the service charge to be paid as additional rent. It may not legally always be so where it is payable under a covenant in the lease. In such cases the lease may need to be studied carefully to ascertain whether the service charge is part of the consideration for the use of the premises or if it is consideration for the covenant by the landlord to provide specific services. If it is the latter then legally it will be liable to VAT at 20%. However, HMRC, probably in an attempt to adopt a standard policy towards service charges, ignore the legal niceties and say that provided the service charge 'is connected with the external fabric or the common parts of the building or estate as opposed to the demised areas of the property of the individual occupants' and it is paid for by all the occupants through a common service charge, it attracts the same VAT status as the rent (Notice 742, paras 11.2 and 12.1). In effect they regard the service charge as additional rent regardless of how it is reserved under the lease.

16.167 One area where this does cause problems in practice is with serviced offices, ie where a person lets out on a short-term basis the use of an office, normally with shared use of support staff such as a receptionist, telephonist and secretary. It might be thought that as this is very similar to a hotel, the VAT treatment would be the same. Unfortunately it is not. Instead HMRC's approach is to treat it as a straightforward lease. This can result in a significant loss of input tax relief. Most of the customers are likely to be VAT-registered traders who could reclaim input tax on the fee they pay. Unfortunately such things as repairs, equipment leasing for shared equipment, reception and switchboard, and costs of the support staff are regarded by HMRC as costs of the 'common parts', and the proportion of the daily charge relating to such items as part of the rent – and thus exempt from VAT (C & E Notice 742, para 11.7). In most such cases it will be attractive to exercise the option to tax rents for the future. If a separate charge is made for the services of the receptionist and telephonist, it is unlikely that HMRC could deem this to be part of the consideration for the supply of the premises. This might therefore be an alternative way to turn that part of the charge into a taxable supply.

16.168 The VAT tribunal in *Suffolk Heritage Housing Association Ltd (VTD 13713)* held that, where a separate charge for heating based on the estimated cost of the heating supply was made to tenants of sheltered accommodation, this was sufficient to secure zero-rating; the heating was not an integral part of the exempt rent. HMRC said in February 1996 that they were appealing against this decision. The appeal has not yet been reported or, presumably, heard. In any event, HMRC consider that the decision was reliant on the specific form of the tenancy agreement. All the tenants took the heating supply. Although in theory they need have not done so, HMRC did not consider that this was a real option – if it had been, they would have accepted that the heating was a separate supply.

16.169 The decision of the tribunal in *Tower Hamlets Housing Action Trust (VTD 17308)* casts doubt on the traditional HMRC approach. The issue in dispute was whether there should be an apportionment for the supply of telephone equipment and photocopying services from the supply of office accommodation under a tenancy agreement. The tribunal thought the matter to be one of impression. As far as the telephones were concerned, the payment would not depend on the amount of use by the tenant of the telephone. They therefore did not regard the provision of telephone equipment as an aim in itself but as a means of better enjoying the principal service of the provision of the property.

> 'As a matter of commercial reality, one would expect to find telephone equipment in a serviced office just as one would expect to find furniture. It is an essential feature of a serviced office that telephones are provided.'

The telephone was accordingly part of the exempt supply of accommodation. Photocopying on the other hand was different. It would have been paid for per copy. It is difficult to see how such a supply could be ancillary to the supply of the accommodation and is an aim in itself that has no connection with the property.

16.170 Whilst HMRC's approach is often beneficial to tenants, it gives rise to two problem areas. Firstly, if services are supplied to a tenant's individual flat or office, HMRC regard that part of the service charge as a separate supply from the accommodation. The effect is that they consider that VAT at 20% needs to be added to that part of the service charge (assuming of course that the landlord's total supplies exceed the registration limit) except to the extent that it relates to zero-rated items such as electricity when the benefit of the zero-rating can be passed on to the tenant. Where a charge to the tenant for services in his individual office is specifically linked to his usage of those services, this treatment is probably correct regardless of how the charge is described in the lease, as the landlord will either be making a separate supply of the services or will be making a mixed supply of the services and the accommodation – which for VAT purposes would need to be broken down into its component elements. Where, however, the services supplied to individual offices or flats are not based on usage, it is most probable that the landlord is making a composite supply of serviced accommodation and that the entire consideration for that supply is rent. This was accepted by the VAT tribunal in *Business Enterprises (UK) Ltd (VTD 3161)* in relation to the use of furniture. In practice it would be fairly unusual for a landlord to provide services to individual offices without charging separately for them – with the exception of heating which is zero-rated in any event and would thus not generate a VAT charge. This difficulty is therefore more apparent than real, although it is a major problem in relation to the use of furniture.

16.171 Difficulties can, however, still arise in apportioning the expenditure between the exempt and taxable supplies. In *Sovereign Street Workspace Ltd (VTD 9550)*, where HMRC contended that maintenance of the property related wholly to the exempt licence to occupy, the VAT tribunal accepted that part could be attributed to the taxable supplies because part of the building was used to provide taxable supplies such as the telephone answering service, mail handling and an information and advice service supplied to tenants. Despite this normal approach, HMRC seem to have successfully argued in *First Base Properties Ltd (VTD 11598)* that cleaning of both individual offices and common parts of a building were part of the exempt supply of the premises.

16.172 The second problem is that whilst the tenant of residential premises is, in general, content for the service charge in respect of common parts to be treated as rent, the tenant of commercial premises may well be unenthusiastic. The tenant will be left bearing the VAT suffered on his share of the service charge expenditure – but will not be able to treat it as input tax as he would have done had he incurred the expenditure direct. Accordingly, where all of the tenants are themselves taxable persons a way needs to be found to enable the service charge to be a taxable supply. Whilst this increases the tenant's initial outlay – as it increases the payment he must make to the landlord – the recovery of the tax from HMRC leaves him overall better off.

16.173 One way that ought to achieve this is for the lease specifically to separate the charge for services from that for accommodation. However, the practice of providing for a service charge to be paid as additional rent is designed to make it easier for the landlord to enforce payment and it may be unattractive to him to forfeit this benefit. Another possibility is for the service charge not to be payable to the landlord at all but to a third party, which could be a subsidiary of the landlord. However, care would need to be taken with the wording of the relevant provision to ensure that the subsidiary is itself providing the relevant services, and not merely making arrangements for their provision. It would also probably weaken the landlord's right to enforce payment and may also cause a nuisance if the landlord sells his interest in the shopping centre, industrial estate or whatever.

16.174 Paragraph 11.5 of Notice 742 (May 2012 edition), which relates to commercial premises, states:

> 'if you are responsible for providing services to the occupants of a building in which you have no interest, your services will always be standard-rated as they are not part of the supply of the accommodation itself.' If the lease provides for the service charge to be paid to a separate company which will itself provide the services, the supplies by that company should fall into this head. However, paragraph 11.5 also says that:
>
> 'If your contract is to arrange for the services and to collect the service charge on the landlord's behalf as a managing agent, then your supply is to the landlord and not to the occupants. Your supply is still standard-rated.'

If the landlord covenants to provide the services under the lease this limitation will probably apply (although, as indicated at **16.166**, it does not necessarily reflect the law). The tenants will of course want the landlord bound to provide the services so it may not be practicable to put the responsibility on a management company, although there is no tax reason why the landlord should not guarantee the management company's obligations. It may alternatively be possible to structure the service charge arrangements in such a way that the landlord – or more likely his managing agent – incurs the service charge expenditure as agent for the tenants. This will enable him to pass on to the tenants the right to recover the input tax paid. HMRC stated in 1973 when VAT was introduced that even where such an arrangement was not spelled out in the lease, the landlord could elect to treat himself as agent for the tenants in respect of service charge expenditure provided that he maintained a separate bank account for each property and the service charge was designed solely to recover expenditure (C&E Press Release 21 March 1973). The landlord would, however, need to register himself as agent, so this method is probably only practical where the service charge expenditure is above the registration limit. As HMRC do not mention this method in their Notice 742, it may no longer be acceptable and should not be adopted without the prior agreement of HMRC.

16.175 In the past little consideration has been given to this problem, particularly as there was little incentive for the landlord to seek to provide the benefit of recoverability to his tenants. However, the increase in the size of service charges in recent years and the broadening of the scope of the services that the landlord may provide in, for example, a shopping centre, resulting in a far greater proportion of the expenditure bearing VAT than before, has made tenants far more conscious of their loss of input tax relief. At the same time tenants are increasingly looking on service charges and rent together as the cost of occupying the property, so that anything that the landlord can do to reduce the cost of the service charge is likely to lessen tenant resistance to a rent increase. It is accordingly in the landlord's own interest to seek to eliminate the tenants' loss of input tax relief.

16.176 The problem has been aggravated by the decision in *Trustees of Nell Gwynn House Maintenance Fund v C & E Commrs (1999 STC 79)* although that case was decided on the wording of the leases used. The service charge of a block of flats was payable to trustees. The dispute was whether the trustees were obliged to account for VAT on the provision by them of staff. It seems to have been accepted either that VAT was not chargeable in relation to other items or that the input tax on other items equalled the output tax leaving nothing to be assessed. In the House of Lords it was agreed that there is a distinction between the case where A pays B for services to be provided by B and the case where A puts B in funds so that B can arrange for C to provide the services. In the first it is the provision of the services which constitutes the supply. In the second it is the arranging for services to be supplied. Here the trustees were supplying the staff, as they employed them. The fact that they did so as trustees did not prevent them from contracting as employers with the staff to carry out the services and so themselves supplying those services to the tenant. The House of Lords also rejected an argument based on *Glawe Spiel und Unterhaltungsgerate Aufstellungsgesellschaft mbH & Co KG v Finanzamt Hamburg-Barmbek-Uhlenhorst (Case C–38/93) (1994 STC 543)* that the consideration for the services provided by the trustees was not the gross amount receivable by the trustees but only the fee that they were entitled to retain for themselves. It felt that the commercial reality is that when the trustees take the money from the maintenance fund to pay the staff to carry out the trustees' obligations under the lease, they receive that money beneficially in consideration of the services provided. Furthermore, once it was accepted that the trustees employed the staff, the amount received by the trustees could not be 'expenses paid out in the name and for the account of' the tenants excludable under *Article 11(3)(c)* of the *EC Sixth Directive.*

16.177 Various mandatory service charges paid by the occupants of residential property (including the owner of a freehold interest) are, by concession, treated as exempt even though the payment is made to a separate management company or the service was otherwise not supplied by the landlord. The charges concerned are for the upkeep of the common areas of an estate or block of flats, the provision of a warden, superintendent, caretaker or people performing a similar function connected with the day-to-day running of the estate or block, and the general maintenance of the exterior – including painting or window cleaning of individual dwellings if the residents cannot refuse this. The concession does not extend to optional services supplied personally to a resident, such as carpet cleaning and shopping. Nor does it apply to non-domestic property or to holiday accommodation (Business Brief 3/94 and C & E Notice 742, para 12.2). A taxpayer does not have to take the benefit of a concession. He is entitled to be taxed in accordance with the law.

16.178 In the *Nell Gwynn* case, the trustees submitted as an alternative that the grant of the lease and the provision for the supply of maintenance services all formed part of a single economic transaction and the trustees, like the landlord, should be treated as the grantor so that their part of the supply would be exempt. The House of Lords rejected this argument (which was based on *Article 13(B)(b)* of the *EC Sixth Directive*) as the letting of the properties was not done by the trustees and although there was a close link between the letting of the properties and the receipt of the service charges, the supply of the services was by a different taxpayer and was quite distinct from the exclusion under the Directive for the letting of the land. In the light of the concession referred to above, introduced five years before the House of Lords hearing, it is a little surprising that HMRC were so insistent on not applying that concession to earlier years.

16.179 *Clarence Holdings Ltd (VTD 17289)* dealt with timeshares. The company had set up a trust to which it had granted a long lease. Under this the company reserved the right to require the trustees to grant weekly occupancy licenses (the timeshares). The company sells to an owner such a weekly licence to occupy. The owner automatically also becomes a member of an Owners Club. The Owners Club undertakes the maintenance and administration of the estate for which it makes an annual charge to the individual owners. It was held that the annual maintenance fee was not part of the consideration for the right to occupy. It was a separate supply of services provided by the Owners Club. It is curious that HMRC took this case to the tribunal as it seems hard to distinguish from the *Nell Gwyn* case.

16.180 In *Canary Wharf Ltd (VTD 14513),* the company was head-lessee of an office building. Most of its premises were sublet on 25-year occupational underleases. A management company (a member of Canary Wharf Ltd's VAT group) was a party to the underleases. These required the management company to provide services to the common parts and the estate and to manage the car parking. In return the under-lessees covenanted with the management company to pay service charges. The management company had its own offices and employed over 230 staff. It invoiced the under-lessees direct. HMRC contended that the management services were part of a single (exempt) composite supply made by the landlord. This was rejected by the VAT tribunal which held that the management company provided a separate (taxable) supply. It also felt that the group registration did not affect the fact that the supplies were in reality by the management company to the under-lessees. The tribunal seems to have been influenced by the obvious substance of the management company, although it is unclear why that should affect the legal analysis.

16.181 The decision of the ECJ in *RLRE Tellmer Property sro v Financni reditelstvi v Usti nad Labem (C-572/07) (2009 STC 2006)* casts doubt on the HMRC practice. RLRE owns a number of buildings in which apartments are let. It invoices its tenants separately for cleaning of the common parts by its own caretaking staff. The issue before the ECJ was whether the cleaning was a separate taxable supply or part of the exempt supply of letting. The ECJ's answer was that 'The letting of immovable property … essentially consists in the conferring by a landlord on a tenant, for an agreed period and in return for payment, of the right to occupy property as if that person were the owner and to exclude any other person from enjoyment of such a right … Thus even if the cleaning services of the common parts of an apartment block accompany the use of the property let, they do not necessarily fall within the concept of letting … It is, moreover, undisputed that the cleaning services of the common parts of an apartment block can be supplied in various ways, such as, for example, a third party invoicing the cost of the service direct to the tenants or by the landlord employing his own staff for the purpose or using a cleaning company.

It should be noted that, in this case, RLRE Tellmer Property invoiced the cleaning services to the tenant separately from the rent. Also 'since the letting of apartments and the cleaning of the common parts of an apartment block can, in circumstances such as those at issue in the main proceedings, be separated from each other, such letting and such cleaning cannot be regarded as constituting a single transaction within the meaning of the case law of the court'. It held that 'the letting of immovable property and the cleaning service of the common parts of the latter must, in circumstances such as those at issue in the main proceedings, be regarded as independent, mutually divisible operations, so that the said service does not fall within that provision' (*Article 13B(b)* of the *Sixth Directive*, now *Article 135* of the *VAT Directive*). However, following the case HMRC quickly sought to distinguish it. They say that 'Tellmer itself provided both the property leasing and the cleaning service to the tenants. However, the tenants had the choice of making an independent contract within a third party to provide the cleaning services … , Similarly the UK only treats leasing of property and related service charges as a single supply where the services are provided by the lessor (or his agent) as a condition under the lease agreement.

16.182 HMRC consider that the findings in *Tellmer* are consistent with existing UK policy (HMRC Brief 67/2009). This seems questionable. In most cases, tenants are simply required to pay the service charge; the tenants as a group may well have the ability to tell the managing agents which contractor they wish to use. The landlord is normally indifferent. *Field Fisher Waterhouse (2011 SFTD 1015)* challenged whether the services supplied by landlords under a lease agreement with their tenants is an element of a single exempt supply of land or a separate taxable supply of services. The FTT referred the issue to the CJEU which commented:

> 'the leasing of immovable property and the supplies of services linked to that leasing, such as those at issue in the main proceedings, may constitute a single supply from the point of view of value added tax. The fact that the lease gives the landlord the right to terminate it if the tenant fails to pay the service charges supports the view that there is a single supply, but does not necessarily constitute the decisive element for the purpose of assessing whether there is such a supply. On the other hand, the fact that services such as those at issue in the main proceedings could in principle be supplied by a third party does not allow the conclusion that they cannot, in the circumstances of the dispute in the main proceedings, constitute a single supply'.
>
> (*Field Fisher Waterhouse v HMRC Commrs (C-392/11).*)

The case does not appear to have come back to the tribunal to apply that guidance, which suggests that it settled. In *Honourable Society of Middle Temple v HMRC (2011 SFTD 1088)* the supply of cold water by the landlord to its tenants was held to be a separate supply. In that case the water was itemised separately on the rent invoice. The tenants had no practical alternative to taking their supply of water from the landlord (as it owned the underground pipes through which it flowed). The Tribunal held that they were separate supplies because 'the letting of property and the supply of water are treated differently in our VAT system. Objectively, the supply of water can be made by a third party, Thames Water, under a separately metered system'. Sadly the Upper Tribunal disagreed *([2013] All ER (D) 127)*. The tenants of premises in the Inn had no choice but to obtain water from the taxpayer. As both accommodation and water were essential if they were to occupy and use the premises, the tenants must be assumed to require a combination of those two elements if the premises were to fulfil their economic purpose. The leasing of the premises and the supply of the water to those premises under the lease form a single economic supply which it would be artificial to split because, from the point of view of the typical tenant, both the premises and the water were equally indispensable and inseparable.

16.183 The CJEU was again asked to revisit the principle in *Case C-42/14 Minister Finansow v Wojskowa Agencja Mieszkaniowa w Warszawie (2015 STC 1419)*. The court affirmed that, 'the letting of immovable property and the provision of water, electricity and heating as well as refuse collection accompanying that letting must, in principle, be regarded as constituting several distinct and independent supplies … unless the elements of the transaction, including those indicating the economic reason for concluding the contract, are so closely linked that they form, objectively, a single, indivisible economic supply which it would be artificial to split'. The court laid down a number of principles.

(*a*) If the tenant has the right to choose his suppliers and/or the terms of use of the goods or services at issue, the supplies relating to those goods or services may, in principle, be considered to be separate from the letting.

(*b*) If the tenant can determine his own consumption of water, electricity or heating, which can be verified by the installation of individual meters and billed according to their consumption, supplies relating to those services may, in principle, be considered to be separate from the letting.

(*c*) Services such as the cleaning of the common parts of a building under joint ownership, should be regarded as separate from the letting if they can be organised by each tenant individually or by the tenants collectively and if the supply of those goods and services is itemised separately from the rent on invoices addressed to the tenant. But the fact that the tenant has the right to obtain those services from the provider of his choice is also not in itself decisive.

(*d*) If an immovable property offered for letting appears objectively, from an economic point of view, to form a whole with the supplies that accompany it, they can be considered to constitute a single supply with the letting. The same may apply to the letting of turnkey offices, ready for use with the provision of utilities and certain other supplies, and to immovable property which is let for short periods (in particular for holidays or for professional reasons) and offered with those supplies, which are not separable.

(*e*) If the landlord himself is not able to choose freely and independently, particularly of other landlords, the suppliers and the terms of use of the goods and services provided with the letting, the supplies at issue are generally inseparable from the letting. This is particularly so when a landlord who owns part of a multi-dwelling building is required to use suppliers designated by his co-proprietors collectively.

Do-It-Yourself Builders

16.184 *VATA 1994, s 35* enables tax to be refunded on the supply of goods to persons constructing new homes (or buildings for use solely for a relevant residential or relevant charitable purpose) or converting non-residential premises to residential otherwise than in the course of a business. The work must be lawful (*VATA 1994, s 35(1), (1A)*). Lawful is not defined, but *reg 201 of the VAT Regulations 1995* requires the claimant to produce, *inter alia*, documentary evidence that planning permission for the building has been granted and *s 35(4)* applies the notes to *Sch 8, Group 5*, for construing the section. There are two separate claim forms, VAT 431NB for new houses and VAT 431C for conversions. It should be stressed, however, that it applies only to conversions from non-residential to residential. In *T Brennan (TC 4709)* Mr Brennan obtained several planning consents to extend his house. He contended that the work was so extensive that he had, in effect, created a new-build house. The Tribunal disagreed and pointed out that even if he had achieved that, there could not be a new building as the original had not been demolished to ground level. The provision also applies to buildings to be used for relevant residential purposes (see **16.49** above) and relevant charitable purposes (see **16.59** above) which are built by charities and voluntary bodies.

16.185 In *Mr and Mrs Watson (VTD 18675)*, the taxpayers converted a barn into two dwellings (see **16.187**) intending to live in them. To recover some of the cost, when the buildings were completed they let them out, although their intention by then was that at some stage their children would live in them. It was held that the test as to whether the works were carried out in the course or furtherance of a business had to be applied at the time it was completed, and at that stage the intention was that the dwellings should be used in a letting business. This contrasts with the later decision in *M P Curry (VTD 20077)*. Mr Curry saw an advertisement for a house, 12 The Close, with the benefit of planning permission for the construction of another house on part of the land. He acquired it with the intention of living at No 12 and building and selling the new house (No 14). He duly moved into No 12 in May 2003. In September 2003 he bought the bricks for the new house. In April 2004 he changed his plan and decided to live in No 14 and sell No 12. At the time neither house was saleable as there was a problem over the garages and until this was resolved a boundary could not be delimited. No 14 was completed in August 2004 and let for a year to friends from South Africa who were coming temporarily to the UK. This tenancy was extended to around April 2007, ie the friends rented the house for a little under three years. The tribunal considered that the business limitation has to be looked at at the time of construction. They also felt that whilst deliberately letting a property for a long period is carrying on a business it is 'inappropriate to suggest that a person is carrying on a business of letting property if he decides that he must let the property for a short period because his other plans have been undermined by factors outside his control'. They then went on to hold that even though when the project started Mr Curry intended to build No 14 to sell, his change of mind during the construction prevented that intention being a business as there would never be any supplies in the course of the business. This decision may need to be approached with caution though, as it is prefaced with the comment that there was virtually no discussion of the legal issues during the hearing so the decision was based on the tribunal's own consideration of the legal position. In *Mr Andrews and Mrs Boakes (TC 2737)* the taxpayers converted two derelict cottages together used as a care home into a single dwelling. It was held that relief was not due as the care home was used for a relevant residential purpose.

16.186 HMRC sought to deny relief to *Newtonbutler Playgroup Ltd (VTD 13741)*, a charity, on the basis that the provision of playgroup facilities amounted to a business and was thus not a relevant charitable purpose. HMRC's view was based on the fact that parents were invited to make a weekly contribution towards the cost of refreshments. The tribunal accepted that this was not consideration for admission to the building and allowed the refund claimed. In *Mr D L & Mrs G D Rawson (VTD 7921)*, a VAT tribunal held that the supply of a fence surrounding the house qualified for zero-rating as being in the course of constructing the dwelling house, but the supply of further fences to keep out deer did not so qualify, as the expense had to be related to the house in some way and not made for other purposes. An interesting case is that *of Shinewater Association Football Club (VTD 12938).* The club charged a small annual membership fee to cover its administrative costs. It used a playing field owned by the National Playing Fields Association. The club arranged for a new pavilion to be constructed, funded partly by a loan from the NPFA and partly from funds raised by the club. Most of the construction work was by club members on a voluntary basis. The club, and others licensed by the NPFA to use the ground, was entitled to occupy the pavilion under a licence from the NPFA. The club claimed a refund under *VATA 1994, s 35* on the materials used for construction of the pavilion. HMRC rejected this on the grounds both that the supply was made in the course of a business and that the pavilion was not intended for use solely for a relevant charitable purpose. The tribunal allowed the club's appeal. The construction was undertaken in furtherance of the ownership rights of NPFA, not as part of Shinewater's business, and the pavilion facility was substantially provided to the local community in the same way as a village hall.

16.187 These provisions also apply to the conversion of a non-residential building (or non-residential part of a building) into a building designed as a dwelling (or dwellings), a building intended for use solely for relevant residential purposes or something that would fall into one of those categories if different parts of the building were treated as separate buildings (*VATA 1994, s 35(1A)(c), (1D)*). The notes to *VATA 1994, Sch 8, Group 5* (see **16.6** to **16.121** above) apply for this purpose. In particular statutory planning consent in respect of the dwelling must have been granted and the separate use and disposal of the dwelling must not be prohibited by the terms of any covenant, statutory planning consent or similar provision (*Note (2)* – see **16.32**). *Mr & Mrs G D King (VTD 15961)* were denied relief for converting a derelict property into their family home. They contended that, before becoming derelict, the building had been used as a commercial guest house, but it was held that it had been used as a home for elderly guests (not a nursing home) which was held to be a relevant residential purpose (as being within **16.49**(*b*)(i) above). Similarly, relief was denied for the refurbishment of a derelict croft which had not been used as a residence since before April 1973. Unfortunately the owner allowed casual use from time to time in 1975 and 1978 to young relatives although the croft lacked sanitation and was too cold to be occupied in winter. Such casual use was held to be use as a residence (*James Halcro-Johnston (VTD 17147)*). Another helpful case is *Dr R W Nicholson (VTD 19412)* which is considered at **16.37**, although the decision is questionable in the light of the Upper Tribunal decision in *HMRC v Lunn (2010 STC 486)*(see **9.18**). *Simon Jones (TC 2180)*, where the taxpayer had purchased agricultural buildings with planning consent for conversion to a residence, also succeeded. The FTT there held that a condition not to use or resell the residence separately from the adjoining offices, contained in a *s 106* agreement with the local authority entered into by the previous owner, did not bind Mr Jones not to sell the house separate from the office, albeit that if he were to do so he could not continue to use the office or let it to anyone other than the occupier of the house. Accordingly, the relief was due. See also **16.38** in relation to separate use.

16.188 *Mr J A Moore (VTD 15972)* acquired three barns for conversion into five dwellings. He decided instead to convert them into a single dwelling with a swimming pool and workshop. The East barn was converted into a dwelling in 1994 and Mr Moore moved in. At that time the North and West barns were in the process of being converted into the swimming pool and workshop.

These formed a separate building five feet from the East barn. It was held that that gap was fatal. The two barns had been converted into a separate building which was not used as a dwelling. The tribunal held that a building designed as a dwelling-house must mean a single building; it could not embrace two buildings (contrast this with **16.105**; it seems that a building in VAT law can mean 'building' or 'buildings' depending on which interpretation will defeat the taxpayer!). *Julie Wade (TC 1351)* owned a property consisting of a house which had been extended and which was attached to a barn. She converted the extension and the barn together into a dwelling separate from the main house. A peculiarity was that she was advised to apply for planning consent to convert the extension into a separate dwelling and when she had got this to apply (without implementing the permission) to incorporate the barn into that dwelling. HMRC argued first that the barn was a garage and thus residential, so there could be no conversion into a residential property. The tribunal thought this a question of fact. It accepted that the barn had been used primarily for storage and concluded that it was a barn, not a garage. HMRC secondly contended that as the planning permission was to incorporate the barn into a dwelling (albeit a non-existent one) it was already part of a dwelling before conversion (see **17.53**) and even if that were wrong, the conversion of the barn had to create a dwelling, not part of a dwelling. The tribunal rejected both arguments. *VATA 1994, s 35(1D)* specifically envisages part only of a building being non-residential and the Court of Appeal in *C & E Commrs v Jacobs (2004 STC 1682)* – see **16.93** had held that an additional dwelling did not have to be created wholly from the non-residential part. It accordingly allowed recovery of the VAT to the extent that it related to the conversion of the barn (but not that relating to the conversion of the extension as that was already residential). *Charles Smith (TC 5510)* began converting a barn into additional living accommodation for his home. Part way through, someone suggested that if he installed a steel frame he could turn the barn into a house in its own right. HMRC were happy to refund to Mr Smith the 5% VAT which they said the builder should have charged on that qualifying conversion, but not the full 17.5% that he had in fact charged. The FTT held that they had to refund the full 17.5% on work done prior to the change of intention as the builder correctly charged 17.5% on such work because at the time he could not have known that it would have been used for a qualifying conversion.

16.189 When is planning consent not planning consent? *Mr A I Davison (VTD 17130)* applied for planning permission to construct a double garage within the curtilage of a large house. The application was subsequently amended to increase the size of the building and add first floor living accommodation. The planning authority accepted the changes as not making a material amendment and told Mr Davison that he could proceed without needing further permission. Unfortunately, HMRC and the VAT tribunal thought otherwise. The tribunal accepted that the new building was a dwelling but held that zero-rating did not apply because the planning permission has not been granted in respect of it as a dwelling. Jack Wilson was granted planning permission for a two-storey extension to his house. On closer inspection, he discovered the structure was unsound and that he would have to demolish the building and reconstruct a new one. He discussed this with the Local Authority's Building Controls Manager who agreed to the work provided that the two external corner walls were retained. This was confirmed in a letter from the council, which confirmed that the works ultimately carried out were included in the original planning application. HMRC refused repayment on the grounds that the works did not conform with the planning consent that was in fact granted. The Tribunal concluded that the works 'had the necessary permission of the planning authority', given at the meeting with the Building Controls Manager. The retention of the walls arose from an 'other similar permission' to planning consent. Although this conforms with common sense, the reasoning of the Tribunal is questionable. The words 'other similar permission' are included in *Note 4(2)(c) of Sch 9, Group 6* (separate use or disposal not prohibited) but not in *Note 4(2)(d)*, which firmly states: 'statutory planning consent has been granted in respect of that dwelling and its construction or conversion has been carried out in accordance with the consent' (see **16.32**). *Nigel Williams (TC 5571)* was granted planning permission for an extension of a house. Preparatory work showed that the extension would be unsafe and he was advised to demolish the existing building. The work went ahead on the basis that retrospective planning permission for a new house would be granted. It was held that zero-rating could not apply as the necessary planning consent has to exist at the time the work is carried out, not merely be in effect at that time. The Tribunal in *Master Wishmakers Ltd (TC 5624)* followed the decision in *Williams*. In *Swindell (TC 5626)* the planning consent allowed the taxpayer to let any part of the land (farmland) for up to 12 months. Mr Swindell contended that this would enable him to let it indefinitely for successive 12-month periods, which would have the same economic effect as a sale, but the Tribunal felt that disposal is an absolute concept that cannot be equated to a series of leases (and were, in any event, sceptical as to whether the condition enabled building on the land to be so let). In *Quitic Ltd (TC 5694)* the restriction was withdrawn by the planning authority in the course of the construction of the building. The FTT held that the condition whether the construction has been carried out in accordance with the planning permission can be tested only when the building is completed. As at that stage, the planning permission permitted separate occupation, the building met all the tests for being a separate dwelling.

16.190 In contrast, in *Sally Cottam (VTD 20036)* where the taxpayer was told by the local authority that planning permission was not required – which prompted HMRC to claim that no relief was available as planning consent is requisite for the relief – the tribunal (Stephen Oliver QC) reasoned that the local authority must have meant either that a general consent applied or that they were granting consent and allowed the claim. A further interesting point in that case was that the relief does not apply to the conversion of a garage occupied with a dwelling. The building in question was an outhouse a comparatively small part of which was used as a garage. Stephen Oliver used a three stage test, is the end product a dwelling? (Yes); what is being converted? (A single building with several uses); and is that building in its entirety a garage? (No). The Tribunal in *John Clark (TC 552)* (see **16.91**) felt this approach to be an incorrect one though.

16.191 The provision also covers the situation where a person engages a builder to carry out the conversion provided that the conversion work is lawful and the contractor is not acting as an architect, surveyor or consultant or in a supervisory capacity (*VATA 1994, s 35(1C)*). In such a case the relief extends to the building work involved, not merely the cost of materials included in such work. It is not clear what the exclusion for acting as architect, etc. means. It clearly excludes the cost of engaging an architect. But what if a builder is engaged on a design and build basis? It appears to deny relief for the entire cost of the work but is probably intended merely to exclude the element that relates to the prohibited activities, assuming that these are segregable. The dispute in *R Hall (TC 5368)* hinged on the date of completion. The FTT said that it will always be a matter of fact and degree as to whether and when any particular building project has been finished. This is not necessarily the date on the Certificate of Completion from Building Control. That is the date that the work to satisfy the Building Regulations has been done, but the building project may well still be ongoing.

16.192 There is a very tight time limit for the claim. *Section 35(2)* gives HMRC power to refuse a claim unless it is made in such time and form as they may by regulation prescribe. They have prescribed three months after the completion of the building in *reg 201* of the *VAT Regulations*. They have also prescribed that the claim must be accompanied by a certificate of completion obtained from a local authority or such other documentary evidence of completion as is satisfactory to HMRC. Mr Martin was unhappy with his builder's quote for levelling the site of the garden, spreading topsoil and creating paths. He accordingly did this himself. Unfortunately the local authority issued a completion certificate when the builder left the site in April 2000. Mr Martin finished the garden work in July 2001 and immediately put in his claim, which was promptly rejected on the grounds that the house had been completed when it was habitable and ready for occupation in April 2000. The tribunal were unsympathetic to Mr Martin's contention that if that was the date of completion it would be impossible to recover the VAT on the garden work even though the garden was clearly part of the house. They thought three months gave ample time to complete such work! *(G M Morris, VTD 17860)*.

16.193 HMRC say that a building is completed when it has been finished in accordance with the original plans or in accordance with the Building Regulations. If in doubt, the date when a certificate of completion is issued by the local authority can be used (Notice 719, para 3.9). The *VAT Regulations 1995 (SI 1995 No 2518), reg 201* requires a certificate of completion in support of the claim, so in practical terms a claim cannot be made before this is issued. HMRC's insistence that such a certificate is not conclusive, however, was upheld in *C & E Commrs v Arnold (1996 STC 1271)* where the judge, reversing the decision of the VAT tribunal, held that the tribunal had no jurisdiction to review the operation of an extra-statutory concession. In that case the work was substantially completed by August 1983 when the taxpayer went into occupation. The certificate of completion was not issued until November 1994. HMRC had decided that the building was completed before 21 April 1994 so that the concession did not apply. In *Dr B N Purdue (VTD 13430)* the date of the certificate was held to be conclusive that the building had been completed, work after that date being held not to be part of the conversion.

16.194 A do-it-yourself builder cannot recover any part of the VAT he incurs on materials for renovating a house that has been empty for over three years. Any conversion services supplied to him by a builder will attract the 5% rate (see **16.159**). A do-it-yourself builder will be able to reclaim the VAT on the conversion of a non-residential building into a house (but not on a changed number of dwellings conversion) – because this was already within *VATA 1994, s 35(1)(c)* (see **16.186**) – and also on the renovation of a house that has been empty for ten years – because the new *Note 7* (see **16.91**) treats such a building as currently being non-residential (VAT Information Sheet 4/01, Part 5 and Notice 719, Chapter 7).

16.195 An interesting point arose in the First-tier Tribunal in *Jennings v Revenue and Customs Commrs ([2010] UKFTT 49 (TC), [2010] STI 2154 (TC 00312))*. Mrs Jennings arranged the construction of a log cabin. She paid directly for some of the materials as the builder could not afford to do so. HMRC refused to refund the VAT on those materials because the planning permission provided that the cabin could only be used as holiday accommodation. They contended that *VATA 1994, Sch 8, Group 5, Note 13* (see **16.119**) prevented the DIY Builders relief from applying. The Tribunal disagreed. The purpose of the relief is to put a private individual in the same position as someone who had paid a builder; the reference across to that note was simply for interpretation. HMRC have said that they accept this decision. They have never in the past applied the scheme to holiday homes because the supply by a developer attracts VAT at the standard-rate but they now accept that claims for VAT incurred on building materials for holiday homes meet the necessary criteria. They will also allow relief where the work involves the conversion of a previously non-residential building into a home (HMRC Brief 29/2010).

16.196 *Paola Sassi v Revenue and Customs Commrs ([2009] UKFTT 280 (TC)(TC 224))* is an interesting First-tier Tribunal decision. Ms Sassi is an expert in sustainable architecture and teaches a course at Cardiff University.

She sought accommodation in Cardiff. She found a plot with planning permission for a single home. She thought it would be more environmentally friendly to build two flats than one house and resolved to construct a 'super-insulated, zero-heating' building. It was always her intention to live in one flat and let out the other. HMRC refused to refund VAT on the expenditure on the let flat claiming that the development was carried out in the course of a business. The Tribunal considered the indicia set out in *C & E Commrs v Lord Fisher (1981 STC 238)* (see **16.61**) and decided that this was not a case of someone building to let. The letting had to be put into context. Ms Sassi's project included designing and creating a sustainable building for use not only as a dwelling but also for research. They did not think that such overall activity amounted to carrying on a business.

Other Residential Issues

Registered Social Landlords

16.197 A registered social landlord is a not-for-profit body whose members include representatives of both the social housing tenants and the local authority. It is normally a housing association. A 'VAT arrangement' has developed to exploit the fact that a local authority can reclaim VAT on repairs and improvements, whereas the registered social landlord cannot. Suppose, for example, a local authority has housing stock valued at £1 million, and £10 million of expenditure is needed to bring it up to modern standards. It will sell the properties to the registered social landlord for £11 million, subject to its undertaking to expend £10 million on bringing the properties up to standard. It will then enter into a separate agreement with the registered social landlord engaging it to carry out the work that it has undertaken to provide. The registered social landlord will pay £1 million to the local authority and satisfy the balance of the purchase price by carrying out the work. It charges the local authority VAT on the £10 million, which enables it to recover its own input tax on the works. The local authority recovers from HMRC the VAT that it has been charged because the building work is solely referable to its commitment to upgrade the housing.

16.198 While this seems to be acceptable for VAT purposes, it needs to be realised that for corporation tax purposes the effect of such an arrangement is that the registered social landlord has acquired the properties for £11 million (HMRC Press Release 20.8.2004). If it had bought them for £1 million and upgraded them itself, at least some of the expenditure would have created a revenue deduction for repairs, so the loss of corporation tax relief (then at either 19%, 30% or somewhere in between) needs to be weighed against the VAT saving.

16.199 The above came into existence in early 2002. It is not affected by the decision in *South Liverpool Housing Ltd (VTD 18750)*. That relates to an earlier government scheme under which a local authority applied for a grant to bring its properties up to standard but could not itself benefit from it. It had to transfer the properties to a registered social landlord and the grant was paid by the Housing Corporation to that registered social landlord. In such circumstances, Liverpool City Council had no obligations to carry out the work. Whilst the tribunal accepted that the acceptance of obligations could constitute consideration, the only obligations undertaken by South Liverpool Housing were obligations to the tenants, so the tribunal had little difficulty in finding that the only persons to whom it could have made a supply was the tenants. As this was an exempt supply, the input tax on the works was irrecoverable.

Church and Memorial Refund Scheme

16.200 Although not part of the VAT system, the government introduced a system of grants, the Listed Places of Worship Grant Scheme, from 1 April 2001 to counter criticism of the imposition of VAT on repairs to churches and war memorials. This is administered by the Department for Culture, Media and Sport (DCMS). The grant reimburses the VAT on such repairs. From 22 March 2006 the scheme includes VAT on professional fees of architects and surveyors as well as some fixtures and fittings. Details of the scheme can be found on the Listed Places of Worship Grant Scheme website, www.lpwscheme.org.uk. The scheme was revamped in 2012 following the abolition of the reduced rate on alterations to listed buildings. The government has said that it will continue at least for the life of the current parliament, ie until May 2015. However, the total grants are capped. The scheme was extended from 1 October 2013 to cover works to some fittings and to professional fees directly related to eligible building work. From the same date, applications can be made by religious and charitable groups whose main purpose is to conserve, repair and maintain redundant listed places of worship that are not in private ownership (DEFRA press release 16.9.2013). A similar grant scheme applies to VAT paid in respect of the construction, renovation and maintenance of memorials, such as statues, monuments and similar constructions. The memorial must be solely for the purpose of commemorating people, events or animals, must bear a commemorative subscription and be accessible to the public for at least 30 hours per week. It will give a full VAT refund. Details of the scheme can be found on the Memorial Grant website, www memorialgrant.org.uk. The scheme does not apply to private expressions of remembrance, such as headstones; nor to gardens, although minor landscaping around a memorial in the course of the construction may be eligible.

Effect of VAT Changes on Arbitration of Rent for Agricultural Holdings

16.201 In *Mason v Boscawen (2009 STC 624),* the High Court held that the VAT element of rent of a farm tenancy which had been opted into VAT was part of the rent. The effect of this is that a change in the rate of VAT would alter the amount of the rent. The *Agricultural Holdings Act 1984, Sch 2, para 4* provides that a change in the rent of an agricultural holding triggers a right to arbitration but only if there has not been an alteration in the rent in the previous three years. To avoid the problems that this ultimately creates *para 4(2)* has been amended to provide that a change in the amount of rent is not to trigger a need for (or a right to) a fresh arbitration if it arises from the exercise of an option to tax under *VATA 1994, Sch 10,* the revocation of such an option, or a change in the rate of VAT applicable to grants of interests in, or rights over, land in respect of which such an option has effect (*para 4(2)(d)* inserted by *FA 2009, s 79*).

Some General VAT Issues

Registration

16.202 VAT is charged on the supply of goods or services in the UK made by a taxable person in the course or furtherance of a business carried on by him (*VATA 1994, s 4*). A taxable person is someone who is either registered or required to be registered under *VATA 1994* (*VATA 1994, s 2*). A person is required to be registered if his aggregate taxable supplies in the previous 12 months exceed the registration limit or his supplies within the next 30 days is expected on their own to exceed that limit (*VATA 1994, Sch 1, para 1*). The registration limit from 1 April 2016 is £83,000. Supplies made other than in the course of a business, such as an individual selling a piece of land that he holds as an investment, are outside the scope of VAT, even if that individual carries on a taxable business, provided that the land is not used in connection with that business. What is registered is the person, not the business. Accordingly if a person carrying on a trade of, say, dealing in goods buys a property which he lets out (which will make it an asset of a property rental business) he needs to aggregate the turnover of the two businesses to determine if he needs to register – and if he is already registered for the dealing business the income and expenses of the property rental business need to be included in his VAT returns (although, subject to the option to tax, they will normally be VAT exempt income and generate irrecoverable input tax). A non-UK resident who carries on a business in the UK, such as letting UK property, is required to register for VAT if he makes taxable supplies in the UK at a time after 30 November 2012 irrespective of the size of his turnover unless he has an office or other fixed business establishment in the UK. If he has a UK fixed establishment in the UK, the normal £83,000 threshold applies – even if it applies, if the supplies of rental income are not made through that fixed establishment, that limit will not apply to those supplies (*VATA 1994, Sch 1A, para 1* inserted by *FA 2012, Sch 28, para 1*).

16.203 A person who is not registered and not required to register can ask to be registered. If he does so, HMRC must register him provided that he satisfies them either that he makes taxable supplies (however small) or that he is carrying on a business and intends to make taxable supplies in the course or furtherance of that business (*VATA 1994, Sch 1, para 9*). A person who makes only exempt supplies is not entitled to be registered. HMRC are wary of registering people on the basis that they intend to make taxable supplies, as they are concerned about the risk of fraud. Accordingly they require such an 'intending trader' to evidence his intention. Volunteering is important because input tax incurred prior to registration is not normally recoverable unless the taxpayer is a taxable person at the time the expenditure is incurred. There are two exceptions. Input tax on goods can be claimed if they were supplied within four years prior to registration and on services within the six months prior to registration (HMRC Notice 700, paras 11.2 and 11.3). For pre-incorporation supplies of a company or other body corporate, the goods or services must have been supplied to someone who became a member, officer or employee of the company (para 11.4). This may be too restrictive. In *Kopalnia Odkrywkowa Polski Trawertyn P Granatowicz, M Wasiewicz, spotka jass na v Dyrector Izby Skorbowej W Poznaniu (2012 STC 1085)* the CJEC held that national legislation cannot preclude either the partners or a partnership from being able to exercise the right to deduct input tax on investment costs incurred by those partners before the creation of the partnership for the purposes of, and with a view to, its economic activities. In that case two individuals acquired an open-cast stone quarry in December 2006 which they contributed in kind to a partnership which they set up in April 2007. It also held that this right to deduct was not affected by the fact that the invoice was not in the name of the partnership.

16.204 HMRC initially wanted strong evidence of a future intention to make taxable supplies by way of business before registering a property owner or developer for VAT. In 1990 they stated that they will register a person if he or his professional adviser writes to HMRC advising them that either:

(*a*) a feasibility study has been commissioned which will have to be paid for;

(*b*) he either holds title to the land, is negotiating for its purchase, or holds an option to purchase it;

(*c*) he has commissioned an architect to seek planning permission or has instructed some other professional person with the intention of selling or letting the property;

(*d*) if a sale or lease of a residential or relevant charitable building is contemplated (see **8.28** above), he has obtained the necessary certificate from the customer; or

(*e*) if a zero-rated sale of a substantially reconstructed listed building is contemplated, he has obtained the listed building consent.

(C & E Press Release 25 September 1990.)

The author's experience suggests that this statement was somewhat tongue-in-cheek and that documentary evidence to back up such a statement is still required. HMRC has subsequently said that following the abolition of the self-supply charge 'local VAT offices may require more detailed information before allowing intending trader registration' (Business Brief 8/96). In practice they normally seem to look for a signed contract to buy the property or a signed building contract before being prepared to register a property company and, where supplies will be taxable only if the option to tax is exercised, expect the notice of the exercise of the option to be submitted at the same time as the application for registration. They are worried about the risk of registering someone who has no real intention to make taxable supplies. Although the *VAT Regulations 1995, reg 108* provides for a clawback of VAT where the intention changes, the decision of the European Court of Justice in *Intercommunale voor Zeewaterontzilting v Belgian State (1996 STC 569)* casts doubts on its validity, so they may have good reason to be concerned (see **16.249**). Where a person intends to exercise the option to tax HMRC require this to be done before they will register him if he would not otherwise be a taxable person.

16.205 The legal position on intention is set out clearly in the First-tier Tribunal decision in *Macaw Properties Ltd (TC 1863)*. Macaw acquired a large freehold estate in 1999 for £2.1m. The estate included a large mansion house (containing over 25 rooms) and an extremely large stable block. It was Grade I listed and on English Heritage's Buildings at Risk register. The company contended that it had always intended to use the house and grounds as a high class hotel and to convert and let out the stable block for commercial use. HMRC said that the company has not provided sufficient objective evidence to confirm its alleged intention. The Tribunal noted that in *Rompelman v Minister van Financien (Case 268/83) ([1985] ECR 655)* the ECJ had indicated that a subjective intention to make taxable supplies is sufficient to vest a transaction carried out in pursuance of that intention with the character of an economic activity. However, it had added that a tax authority can require that the declared intention is supported by objective evidence. The Tribunal accordingly examined carefully what evidence was available. It decided that the first objective evidence of an intention to operate a hotel was a letter of 3 April 2006 and thought from that letter that the intention had been formed sometime earlier. The first objective evidence to make taxable supplies of the stable block was a letter of 23 October 2004, which indicated that the intention had been formed much earlier. It accordingly held that Macaw had the intention of making taxable supplies of the stable block before 23 October 2004 and of the main house from 1 January 2006. Prior to that time its intentions were uncertain. Accordingly, input tax was recoverable only from those dates. A subsidiary point in relation to the stable block related to the option to tax. This was accepted by HMRC with effect from 5 March 2008. However, it later transpired that Macaw had made an earlier exempt supply of the block, so HMRC's permission was needed to opt to tax (see **17.133**). Accordingly, the option was invalid. HMRC argued (as they had previously done unsuccessfully in *Beaverbank Properties Ltd (VTD 18099)* – see **17.178** that Macaw could not form an intention to make taxable supplies until it received that permission. This was held not to be the correct test. The test is whether the company 'could reasonably have entertained the expectation that HMRC would agree to the necessary option to tax becoming effective'. The Tribunal concluded that it was at all relevant times reasonable to suppose that HMRC would agree to this provided that a fair and reasonable attribution of input tax was made.

16.206 HMRC have long taken the view that a nominee is agent for its principal and both must register for VAT because they consider that supplies are made both to and by the nominee, but the nominee (qua nominee) does not carry on a business. *VATA 1994, s 47(2A)* treats a supply to an agent who acts in his own name as also being onward supplied to his principal. However, this approach was rejected by the tribunal in *Lester Aldridge (VTD 18864)*. This was a firm of solicitors; the firm negotiated a 25-year lease of offices for its business. It chose to hold this through a nominee company, Lester Aldridge Nominees Ltd (LANL). The firm guaranteed the lease, paid the rent and took all other action that was required to ensure compliance with the terms of the lease. The tribunal held that the true nature of the arrangement between the landlord, LANL, and Lester Aldridge was such that the landlord could properly be regarded as making a supply to Lester Aldridge.

Who Bears the VAT?

16.207 *VATA 1994, s 89* provides that (unless the contract provides otherwise) on a change in the rate of VAT, or exempt items becoming taxable, the contract price under contracts then in existence must be adjusted to reflect that change. It was not originally clear that this applied where an exempt item became taxable as a result of the exercise of an option to tax. Accordingly the rule was amended to make it clear that, if the option to tax is exercised, the provisions do apply (*VATA 1994, s 89(3)*). The landlord is thus entitled to collect the VAT from the tenant, unless the lease refers specifically to the rent being inclusive of any VAT. As *s 89* provides for the contract price to be varied, the effect seems to be that the rent is increased by 20% and whatever remedies, such as distraint or forfeiture, are available to the landlord to recover rent will apply also to the VAT. This applies only if the lease is silent regarding VAT. If the lease provides that the rent stated is inclusive of all taxes, the landlord would have to bear the VAT if he opts to charge tax. See also **17.128**, which considers the position where an option to tax in relation to a commercial property has been exercised.

Time of Supply

16.208 In February 1989, HMRC issued Guidance Notes on their interpretation of the time of supply rules for property and their views on prepayments. The time of supply rules were particularly important at that time, insofar as if a supply fell before 1 April 1989, it was likely to be zero-rated or exempt, whereas if it fell after that date it could be taxable. They are also of importance where the rate of tax changes, such as when it was increased from 15% to 17.5% on 1 April 1991 and from 17.5% to 20% from 4 January 2011.

16.209 The time of supply is normally the earlier of:

(*a*) the date the services are performed or goods are delivered or made available to the customer;

(*b*) the date of payment; and

(*c*) the date a tax invoice is issued.

(*VATA 1994, s 6.*)

16.210 In the view of HMRC it is not possible to issue a tax invoice in respect of a zero-rated supply because *Regulation 20* of the *VAT Regulations 1995* states that 'Regulations 13, 14 … shall not apply to any zero-rated supply'. *Regulation 13* provides that 'Save as otherwise provided in these Regulations … a registered taxable person making a taxable supply to a taxable person shall provide him with a tax invoice'. *Regulation 14* specifies what a tax invoice must contain. *VATA 1994, s 6(15)* defines a tax invoice as 'such an invoice as is required under *para* 2*(1)* of *Sch 11* to this Act or would be so required if the person to whom the supply is made were a taxable person'. *Paragraph 2(1)* states that Regulations 'may require taxable persons supplying goods or other services to other taxable persons to provide them with invoices (to be known as 'tax invoices')'.

16.211 It is by no means certain that HMRC's view is correct. *Regulation 20* removes the obligation to issue a tax invoice for a zero-rated supply, but does not seem to actually prevent the issue of such an invoice.

16.212 HMRC take the view that the date a building is made available is the date of the transfer of title to the property, ie the completion date, not the contract date, where they are different. It could be argued that if a purchaser or lessee is allowed into occupation at an earlier date, the property should be held to have been made available at that time but the Court of Session held in *Cumbernauld Development Corporation v C&E Commrs (2002 STC 226)* that the time of supply was the date on which title was given to the purchaser, which in Scotland is the date that the feu disposition is given. In that case, the corporation exchanged sites with a golf club. It gave the club occupation of the site on 1 May 1996, but it was not until 6 March 1997 that the feu dispositions for the two sites were exchanged. It was held that the legislation is concerned with the supply of goods and the 'goods' in that case was the major interest in land (see **16.214**). That expression must be interpreted to mean ownership of the land and not any lesser interest such as a right or mere licence to occupy. Until exchange the club had no more than a personal right against the corporation to receive a conveyance in the form of a feu disposition. In *Leser Landau (VTD 13644)* land was acquired by compulsory purchase and was vested in the purchasing authority in March 1992. The amount of the compensation was still to be determined. The taxpayer sought to register as an intending trader in March 1993 and to waive exemption so as to recover VAT on the costs of determining the consideration. The VAT tribunal upheld HMRC's refusal to register him, as the disposal had taken place in March 1992. The fact that it was impossible to calculate the tax at that date did not defer the tax point until it became ascertainable; there was no reason in principle why tax should not be accounted for on an estimated amount.

16.213 HMRC also consider that one cannot make available what does not exist. Accordingly, if title to a property is transferred before the building is completed, all that can be made available at that time is what is actually in existence on the day the title is transferred. They also say this would normally be the work which has been certified by the architect as having been completed. It is arguable that this is wrong, as there would also be materials on site, work since the architect inspected, etc. Furthermore, an architect values the work done. He does not value the building in its partially completed state. It is also of course possible to make available the right to have the building completed, which would be a standard rated supply. However, the completion of the work would still be a separate taxable supply.

16.214 The grant, assignment or surrender of a major interest in land (the freehold or a lease of over 21 years) is deemed to be a supply of goods for VAT purposes (*VATA 1994, Sch 4, para 4*). However, each receipt of rent is deemed to be a separate supply occurring at the earlier of its receipt or the issue of a tax invoice for such rent (*VAT Regulations 1995, reg 85(1)*). The landlord can, if he wishes, at the beginning of any period issue a tax invoice for the rent due for a period of up to a year showing, in addition to the usual requirements, the dates each payment falls due for payment, the VAT-exclusive amount payable on each date and the rate of tax and VAT payable on each date. If he does so, the tax point for each payment is the earlier of the due date and the date the rent is actually received. A change in the rate of VAT after the issue of such an invoice invalidates it for subsequent due dates (*reg 85(2)(3)*). A lease of 21 years or less is a supply of services (*VATA 1994, s 5(2)(b)*) but identical tax point rules apply to those in respect of major interests as the supplies under the lease will be continuous services (see **16.222**).

16.215 If an interest in land is compulsorily purchased and at the normal time of supply under *VATA 1994, s 6* (see **16.209**) the person entitled to compensation does not know the amount he is due to receive for his land he is instead deemed to make a supply each time that he receives a payment from the purchasing authority (*VAT Regulations 1995, reg 84(1)*).

16.216 Similarly if a person grants or assigns the freehold interest and at the time of the grant or assignment that total consideration is not determinable he must be treated as making a number of separate supplies, the first at the time fixed by *section 6* and later ones at the earlier of the date that a part of the consideration which was not initially determinable is received or a VAT invoice is issued in respect of it (*VAT Regulations 1995, reg 84(2)*).

16.217 This does not apply to the sale of a new commercial building or civil engineering work (ie one constructed within the prior three years) which is standard-rated under *VATA 1994, Sch 9, Group 1, item 1(a)* if either:

(*a*) the grantor;

(*b*) any person who, with the intention or expectation that occupation of the land on a date at some time within ten years after completion of the building would not be wholly or mainly for eligible purposes, provides finance for the grantor's development of the land (or has entered into any agreement or understanding to do so); or

(*c*) a person connected with either (within *CTA, 2010, s 1122*),

intends or expects to occupy the land at some time within ten years after completion of the building without being in occupation of it wholly or mainly for eligible purposes (*VAT Regulations 1995, reg 84(3)(4)*). From 15 August 2009, a company is not connected with another merely because both are under the control of the Crown, a government department or the Northern Ireland department (*VAT Regulations 1995, reg 85(5)(f)*). *VATA 1994 Sch 10, paras 3A(8)* to *(13)* (see **17.159–17.163**) applies to define eligible purpose and occupation and *VATA 1994 Sch 9, Group 1, note 2* (see **17.26**) applies to determine when a building is completed. Providing finance has the same meaning as in *VATA 1994 Sch 10, para 3A(4)* (see **17.145**) but obviously excludes paying the purchase price for the building. The grantor's interest in the land means the acquisition by the grantor of an interest in it and includes the construction of the building or works (*VAT Regulations 1995, reg 84(5)*). This is an anti-avoidance provision to prevent arrangements under which the selling price is fixed in such a way that it cannot be determined until after the end of the ten-year period.

16.218 If a contract provides for retention of part of the consideration pending full and satisfactory performance of the contract (or of part of it), a supply is treated as taking place at the earliest of the release of the retention money or the issue of a tax invoice (*VAT Regulations 1985, reg 89*). This will obviously apply to retentions under building contracts. Where services, or a combination of goods and services, are supplied in the course of the construction, alteration, demolition, repair or maintenance of a building or civil engineering work under a contract which provides for payment to be made periodically or from time to time, such as on the issue of: an architect's certificate, those services are treated as separately and successively supplied at the earlier of (*a*) each time a payment is received, (*b*) each time the supplier issues a tax invoice, or (*c*) in relation to certain supplies in respect of exempt land (to the extent they have not previously been treated as supplied) the day on which the services are performed. The supplies covered by head (*c*) are those where, at the time the services were (or are) performed, either:

(i) it was (or is) the intention or expectation of either the supplier, or of a person responsible for financing the supplier's cost of providing the services and goods, that the relevant land (ie the land on which the building, etc. to which the services relate is constructed) would become or continue to be exempt land (whether immediately or eventually); or

(ii) the supplier had, or has, received (and used in making the supply) a supply of services or goods, the time of supply for which was itself determined under head (*c*) above (or but for the issue of a VAT invoice would have been).

(*VAT Regulations 1995, reg 93(1)–(3).*)

The regulation contains detailed rules to amplify head (*c*) (*reg 93(4)–(14)*). These are virtually identical to the tests in *VATA 1994, Sch 10, para 3A(3)–(14)* with the substitution of a reference to the 'supplier' for the 'developer'. The reference to the provision of funds obviously excludes funds made available to the supplier by paying him all or part of the consideration for the supply itself (ie paying for the work does not constitute making funds available to the supplier to finance his costs of making the supply) (*reg 93(6)*). The supplier's costs of providing the services and goods is the amount payable by the supplier for supplies of goods and services to him to be used in making the supply plus his own staff and other internal costs of making the supply (*reg 93(7)*). This definition displaces that in **17.158**.

16.219 Head (*c*) in **16.217** is of course an anti-avoidance provision. It is intended to stop exempt taxpayers setting up an in-house construction company which would sub-contract all of the work to an arm's length builder, pay the builder out of funds provided to it by another group company and not invoice its parent company for the work for many years. The government's first attempt to combat this was to create a deemed supply after 18 months. This accidentally caught a large number of innocent situations – as arm's length building disputes can take well over 18 months to resolve with payment and invoicing being left in abeyance in the interim – and in a group situation virtually invited an 18 month delay in billing. The new *reg 93* is far better targeted. It still suffers from the problem that it is unclear when building services 'are performed' HMRC say that this is when the work is completed. That will normally be when a certificate of practical completion is issued but in a case of 'unusual delay' they will look at when the work was actually completed. A subcontractor will need to make up his own mind when his work is completed but HMRC say he should ignore the need to carry out any 'snagging' work that takes place after the main work is completed. HMRC also warned that leaving a small aspect of the contracted work undone would be varying the contract and 'could be seen by the Courts as a criminal act' as all the work that the contractor had 'genuinely agreed' to do would have been completed. (VAT Information Sheet 7/99). It is questionable whether in many cases that would be a correct analysis of the position. They have not repeated it in Notice 708. Probably a greater worry is why the draftsman should have referred to 'the date on which those services were performed', which suggests something happening on a single day, if he meant the date that a series of continuous services extending over several months was completed. The wording of the Regulations is more appropriate to each day's work being a separate supply.

16.220 If the supplier gives an authenticated receipt containing the particulars required by a tax invoice, such receipt can be treated as a tax invoice provided that no tax invoice is issued (*reg 13(4)*). The authenticated receipt must be issued within 30 days after the time that the supply is deemed to take place (*reg 13(5)*). In *Crosstyle plc (VTD 7169)*, a company made a progress payment in July but the authenticated receipt was dated 1 August. The VAT tribunal left open the question whether the date on the authenticated receipt had to be treated as the date of supply even if it was incorrect as, even if it did, the company had a reasonable excuse for claiming input tax relief in the wrong period. In practice, HMRC generally accept claims made before a receipt is issued provided that the claimant subsequently obtains a receipt (Notice 700, para 24). Although *reg 29(2)* provides that a person must hold a tax invoice or a comparable document, such as an authenticated receipt, before it can claim input tax relief, it is difficult to envisage either that this can override the date fixed by *reg 93*, or that the general rule in *VATA 1994, s 6(6)*, that the date of issue of a tax invoice is substituted as the time of supply if it is issued within 14 days of the normal time of supply, can override the specific rule of *reg 93*. Indeed in *Sprowston Hall Hotel Ltd (VTD 7253)* another VAT tribunal specifically held that *reg 93* displaced what is now *VATA 1994, s 6(5)* – and by inference also *VATA 1994, s 6(6)* which merely modifies that provision. HMRC say that where a contract is terminated early, before the terms have been fulfilled, eg because of the insolvency of the contractor, the supply is considered to have been completed on the day that the work ceased (Business Brief 4/96), on the basis that 'that date is the basic tax point for those supplies where *VATA 1994, s 6* applies'. This is questionable. *Regulation 93* overrides the normal tax point rules. Once a service is identified as coming within that provision, the only possible tax points are the dates of payment and the date of issue of an invoice. The termination of the contract or completion of the services is not expressed to be a tax point.

16.221 The receipt of a deposit will often constitute a supply. In *Jelson Holdings Ltd (VTD 6632)* a developer agreed in August 1990 to sell a plot of land and construct an industrial building on it. It required a deposit of £160,000 against the building work and this was paid to its solicitor. On 20 September 1990 it was released to the company although the work was not due to be completed until December. The VAT tribunal held that the deposit had been released with the purchaser's consent and the tax point occurred on 20 September. In the tribunal's view a deposit paid solely as security (which would not constitute a supply) would be returned to the payer on performance of the contract and would not form part of the contract price. On this analysis it would seem that the receipt of a deposit by the vendor of a property would create a tax point at the latest at the date of contract, when it ceases to be security and becomes payment of part of the price. HMRC say that where development land is sold, particularly by a developer to a registered social landlord, and the deposit is held by a stakeholder and not released to the vendor (or vendor's agent) until completion, the release creates the tax point and at that point construction will normally have progressed beyond foundation level so the supply (assuming it is for residential development) can normally be zero-rated. Where the deposit is made available to the landlord at the time of exchange when the land is still bare land the deposit can still be zero-rated if it is clear from the contract or agreement that what will be supplied at completion, or at the time of the grant, will be partly completed dwellings, as the VAT liability of the deposit is determined by the anticipated nature of the supply (HMRC Brief 36/2009).

16.222 'Continuous supplies', ie where services are supplied for a period for a consideration the whole or part of which is determined or payable regularly or from time to time are treated as separately and successively supplied at the earlier of the time of the issue of a VAT invoice which includes the supply or the time that a payment is received (*reg 90*). Where a continuous supply (other than one which is exempt under *Group 1* of *Sch 9* or would be exempt but for an election to charge VAT) or a supply within *reg 85* in relation to a long lease (see **16.214**) or one within *reg 86(1)–(4)* (supplies of water, gas, power, heat, refrigeration or ventilation) is made and:

(*a*) the supplier and recipient are connected (within *CTA 2010, s 1122*);

(*b*) they are both members of a group of companies but are not within a single VAT group;

(*c*) the supply is taxable (either at 20% or 5%); and

(*d*) it cannot be shown that the recipient is a fully taxable person (ie entitled to recover the whole of the tax as input tax),

there is a deemed tax point 12 months after the supplies commenced and at the end of each subsequent 12 months (*VAT Regulations 1985, reg 94B(1)–(5.* This does not apply if a tax point has already arisen in that 12-month period or if the supplier receives payment or issues a tax invoice within six months of the end of the period (*reg 94B(5)(6)*). HMRC have power to allow a different period end date to that specified above for such category of supply as they believe can be adequately identified or to change the end date (*reg 94B(5)(c),(8)*). From 15 August 2009 two companies are not connected for the purpose of (a) above if they would otherwise be connected merely because they are both under the control of the Crown, a government department or the Northern Ireland department (*VAT Regulations 1995, reg 94B(4) as substituted by the VAT (Amendment) (No 3) Regulations 2009, SI 2009 No 1967*). This is, of course, an anti-avoidance provision to prevent a tax point being delayed indefinitely. It is questionable to what extent it is needed as HMRC normally take the view that the approval of statutory accounts which include an intra-group current account balance, is equivalent to payment as the creditor is entitled to call for the money.

Place of Supply

16.223 *Regulation 5* of the *VAT (Place of Supply of Services) Order 1992* (*SI 1992 No 3121*) deems most services in relation to land to be supplied where the land is situated. It applies to:

(*a*) the grant, assignment or surrender of any interest in (or right over) land, a personal right to call for or be granted any interest in or right over land, or a licence to occupy land or any other contractual right exercisable over (or in relation to) land;

(*b*) any works of reconstruction, demolition, conversion, reconstruction, alteration, enlargement, repair or maintenance of a building or civil engineering work; and (*c*) services such as are supplied by estate agents, auctioneers, architects, surveyors, engineers and others involved in matters relating to land.

This gives effect to *Article 45* of the *VAT Directive (Article 9* of the *Sixth Directive)*, which states that the place of supply of services connected with immovable property, including the services of estate agents and experts, and of services for preparing and co-ordinating construction works, such as the services of architects and of firms providing on-site supervision, shall be the place where the property is situated (*Article 9(2)(a)*).

16.224 Where advice is given in relation to land outside the UK, it can be difficult to determine whether it falls within the *Order* – in which case it is outside the scope of UK VAT, but there may well be an obligation to register for VAT in the country in which the land is situated if that is another EC country – or if it is a *VATA 1994, Schedule 5* consultancy service, which is outside the scope of UK VAT but with a right to recover input tax and no obligation to register in the other country. If work within the *Order* is carried out by a non-UK person on land in the UK, and the recipient of the supply is VAT-registered, he is required to account for the VAT under the reverse charge procedure and there is no requirement for the non-resident to register for VAT in the UK (*VATA 1994, s 8(6); Sch 5, paras 9, 10*). However, this reverse charge procedure is not standard throughout the EU, eg it does not apply in Ireland.

16.225 The *Order* was held to apply in the case of *Mechanical Engineering Consultants Ltd (VTD 13287)*, where a UK company trading as consulting engineers was engaged by a Swiss company to manage, supervise and guarantee the commissioning of a waste incinerator complex in the UK. The UK company claimed that the incinerator, which was bolted to a cradle structure attached to the land, was not part of the land, but the VAT tribunal held that it was a fixture, and thus part of the land. The *Order* was also held to apply to accountancy and book-keeping services in *Aspen Advisory Services Ltd (VTD 13489)* although the facts there were unusual. The company entered into a contract with a Channel Islands company for management of property in the UK. It delegated day-to-day management of the property to a project manager but itself provided the accountancy and book-keeping services. The VAT tribunal held that all of the services were carried out under the terms of the property management agreement and that it would be artificial to divide the services under that contract into those relating to land and those not relating to land. There was a single composite supply. Accordingly this decision does not indicate that accountancy and book-keeping are of themselves within the *Order* solely because they are accounting for land transactions. Indeed, *W H Payne & Co 490) (VTD 13668)* suggests they are not. The appellant partnership supplied accountancy, book-keeping and taxation services to several overseas companies which owned property in the UK, in relation to agreeing and accounting for their UK tax liabilities on the rents. It was held that the UK properties were not fixed establishments of the overseas companies and that the partnership was making a supply to the overseas companies of *VATA 1994, Sch 5* services which were deemed to be supplied outside the UK.

16.226 The ECJ considered the treatment of timeshares in *RCI Europe v HMRC (Case C-37/08) (2009 STC 2407).* RCI charged three types of fee; an enrolment fee, an annual subscription and an exchange fee, payable on requesting an exchange for the owner's unit (which RCI treated as a returnable deposit). It was held that the services provided by RCI Europe was the facilitation of rights relating to a particular property, and the property with which those services are connected is that of the owner who wishes to make an exchange. This applied to all three types of fee. If the timeshare is in Spain the place of supply is accordingly Spain.

16.227 The issue of timeshares again came before the ECJ in *Macdonald Resorts Ltd v HMRC (2011 STC 412) (Case C-270/09).* This deals with the place of supply in relation to a timeshare scheme. Macdonald Resorts Ltd sold timeshare rights in both the UK and Spain. It operated a timeshare exchange scheme. The owner of a timeshare right who did not wish to utilise it himself could deposit his right into a pool in exchange for points on payment of an enhancement fee. A person who did not own timeshare rights could purchase points. Points could be exchanged for a week's use of a different property on payment of a transaction fee. There was also an annual management fee to remain a member of the scheme, which was based on the points held by the member. Macdonald Resorts Ltd contended that the fees either related to the letting or leasing of immovable property or were for services connected with such property. Accordingly the place of supply was where the property was situated. HMRC claimed that the fees were for membership of the scheme and as such not directly related to immovable property. Accordingly the place of supply was in the UK where Macdonald Resorts Ltd was situated. A problem with the company's analyses was what happens where a person who owned timeshare rights in a UK property exchanged the points attributable to that property for the use of a property in Spain? The court held that all of the different types of fee must be classified as being for the right to temporarily use a property. As such they are taxable where the property for which points are exchanged is situated. This is an awkward decision insofar as it means that the place of supply on acquisition of the points cannot be determined until the points are used, which may be a year or more later. The logic of the court is that the acquisition of the points is not an aim in itself for the customer. The acquisition of the points is a 'preliminary transaction' in order to be able to exercise the right to the temporary use of a property. In these circumstances VAT cannot be charged on the fee paid at the time the points are acquired; that fee is simply a payment on account for the real service and the VAT on it cannot be charged until the customer converts the points into the right to use a specific property.

16.228 A different approach was taken in *Fortyseven Park Street Ltd (2017 SFTD 35)*. The company sold fractional interests in the property to investors. By virtue of his ownership of his interest the customer was entitled to occupy the property. However, he entered into an agreement with the company limiting his right to occupy and entitling him to exchange his right to occupy the property for occupational rights in other properties. The company contended that it was granting an exempt interest in land. HMRC contended that the customer does not acquire an interest in land capable of falling within the land exemption but is provided with a taxable service of the right to participate in a plan comprising a number of benefits which includes the provision of an opportunity to occupy a residence. The FTT thought it quite clear that the customer is paying the price in return for the right to occupy a residence under the terms of the membership agreement, albeit that such rights can be exercised only once a successful reservation is made. Looking at the commercial and economic realities, the customer is acquiring the occupancy rights and his other membership benefits are ancillary to those rights. There is sufficient reciprocal performance and a sufficiently direct link between the price and the occupation for this to be a letting of immovable property. However, that letting is excluded from exemption because it is the provision of sleeping accommodation in a similar establishment to a hotel (see **17.27**).

16.229 An interesting issue arose in *Muster Inns Ltd v HMRC (2014 SFTD 1035)*. Muster Inns decided to refurbish its pub. It engaged Amberley Construction Ltd to do the building work. Amberley was based in Guernsey. It engaged UK workers and by agreement with Muster those were housed in the pub, as was the director of Amberley who supervised the work. He was also allowed use of a desk in Muster's office. Amberley billed for the work from its office in Guernsey. HMRC contended that Amberley did not have a business establishment in the UK, so was not entitled to be VAT registered. The Tribunal agreed. Although it had facilities at the pub with the necessary structure in terms of having human and technical resources to supply the services, that did not have sufficient permanence and stability to constitute a business establishment. Accordingly Muster must be treated as both supplying and receiving the service under the reverse charge rules.

Partial Exemption

16.230 Property companies will increasingly be partly exempt for VAT purposes. Some of their turnover (such as sales of new buildings and rents and sale proceeds of opted-in properties) are standard-rated; some (such as sales of new houses) are zero-rated; and some (such as sales of 'old' buildings and rents from non opted-in properties) are exempt. In such circumstances, unless one of the *de minimis* limits applies, there is a restriction on the input tax that can be reclaimed under the *VAT Regulations 1995* (*SI 1995 No 2518*). A business is partially exempt where it makes both taxable and exempt supplies. The position is different where it makes business and non-business supplies (see **17.207**). It was held in *E C Commission v Spain (Case C-204/03) (2006 STC 1087)* and *E C Commission v France (Case C-243/03) (2006 STC 1098)* that a country cannot limit the right to deduct the full input tax suffered by excluding from relief the part of the expenditure made good by a subsidy.

16.231 There is no restriction if the exempt input tax (ie the tax on purchases of exempt items) is less than £625 per month on average either for the return period or the taxpayer's tax year (*VAT Regulations 1995, reg 106*)).

16.232 Where the above *de minimis* limits do not apply, the input tax must be apportioned between exempt and taxable supplies. This is normally done by direct attribution, ie:

(*a*) expenditure that is incurred in generating taxable supplies must be attributed to such supplies – the VAT being recoverable in full;

(*b*) expenditure incurred in generating exempt supplies must similarly be attributed to such supplies – so no part of the VAT will be recoverable; and

(*c*) VAT on expenditure that cannot be specifically attributed, eg on general overheads, is apportioned in the ratio, rounded up to the nearest whole number, that taxable supplies made by the taxpayer bears to the value of all his supplies (*reg 101(2)(d)(4)*). For this purpose sales of capital goods used in the business and, where they are incidental to the taxpayer's business activities, zero-rated supplies in respect of buildings, exempt supplies of land or buildings, freehold disposals of new buildings, surrenders of interests in land, or disposals taxable only by virtue of the exercise of the option to tax (see **17.112**), are ignored, as are financial services within *Sch 9, Group 5* (*reg 101(3)*). Prior to 1 April 1992 the apportionment was in the ratio that the VAT on taxable supplies bore to the VAT on total supplies. This often worked unfairly, particularly where a property company made mainly zero-rated supplies of buildings, as most of the inputs related to such supplies were themselves zero-rated and thus generated no input tax. The ECJ held in *NCC Construction (Danmark A/S v Skatteministeriat (Case C-174/08) (2010 STC 432)* that the sale by a building business of buildings constructed on its own account cannot be regarded as 'incidental' to its building business where that activity constitutes the direct, permanent and necessary extension of its business.

16.233 HMRC can permit the use of an alternative method of arriving at deductible input tax. They can also require a taxpayer to use such special method as they may require (*reg 102*). All special method directions or approvals must be in writing and any input tax not covered by the special method must be apportioned rateably between taxable and other supplies (*VAT Regulations 1995, reg 102(5)–(8)*). In *HMRC v London Clubs Management Ltd (2012 STC 388)* the company operated casinos. It sought to apportion its residual input tax between exempt (gaming) and taxable (restaurant) supplies on the basis of floor area occupied. The Court of Appeal upheld the finding of the FTT that this was an acceptable basis, but stressed both that the apportionment is highly fact specific and that the courts are bound by findings of fact by the FTT (which the court felt 'remarkably benign' in that case). In *Finanzamt Hildersheim v BLC Baumarkt GmbH & Co KG (2013 STC 521; Case C-511/10)* the taxpayer built and let a building that was partly exempt residential and partly taxable commercial. It sought to apportion the input tax by reference to floor space but the German tax authorities insisted that it must be by reference to turnover. The ECJ confirmed that a country can allow an apportionment other than by reference to turnover, but only if the method used allows a more precise determination of the deductible proportion.

16.234 An interesting issue arose in *Antonio Jorge Lda v Fazenda Publica (Case C-536/03) (2008 STC 2533)*. The Portuguese tax authorities contended that in apportioning VAT on overheads for a property development company the value of work in progress should be included in the denominator of the calculation at (*c*) in **16.232**. The ECJ held that this is contrary to the Directive. 'The event giving rise to tax, its chargeability and the possibility of deduction are linked to the actual provision of services … . It is contrary to the system to allow the determination of the extent of the deduction to take into account transactions not yet performed and which may never actually take place, whilst the chargeable event for the tax, and as a result the right to deduct, depend on a transaction actually having been carried out'.

16.235 In applying the partial exemption formula input tax attributable to certain exempt supplies can be treated as relating to taxable supplies (*reg 105*). These include the granting of a lease or licence to occupy premises provided that the input tax attributable to all such supplies in the year is less than £1,000 and the only exempt input tax incurred by the taxpayer is on supplies falling within *reg 105*. This will rarely help property companies. It is intended to prevent a trading company becoming partly exempt solely because it sublets its premises. An interesting point fell for consideration by the European Court of Justice in *Regie-Dauphinoise-Cabinet A Forest SARL v Ministre du Budget (Case C-306/94) (1996 STC 1176)*. The company was a property management company. In the course of its business it obtained advances from property owners. It was entitled to retain the interest it generated from such funds. It contended that the interest was incidental to its business of property management and therefore, by virtue of *Article 19(2)* of the *EC Sixth Directive* (now *Article 174* of the *VAT Directive)*, should be excluded from the partial exemption calculation. The ECJ said that the investment of the monies constituted the direct, permanent and necessary extension of the taxable activity but was not incidental to the management activity; it was a consequence of the advance made by owners. Accordingly it gave rise to an input tax restriction.

16.236 If a property developer makes both taxable and exempt supplies, it will often not be known at the time of purchase of materials what type of supply they will be used for. HMRC initially said that they would allow input tax relief to be claimed on a provisional basis provided that the developer maintains sufficiently detailed records to show what the materials are used for and refunds any VAT that turns out to be non-deductible. Alternatively, he can defer claiming input tax relief until the materials are actually used and the deductibility of the VAT established. Their current view is that if the taxpayer knows from the outset what supplies he intends to make he should attribute input tax on speculative costs to those supplies from the outset. In other cases input tax on speculative supplies should be regarded initially as residual as there is no firm intention to use them to make either taxable or exempt supplies. If a speculative project is aborted the input tax will remain residual. When the taxpayer proceeds with a development he will then have a clear intention to make one or other type of supply and the allowable input tax should be adjusted under *regs 108* or *109* (see **16.245**) (VAT Information Sheet 8/01).

16.237 In *HDG Harbour Development Group Ltd (VTD 9386)* the company made a zero-rated grant of a lease in 1987 and subsequently received exempt rents from the building subsequent to 1 August 1989. It incurred expenditure subsequent to that date on legal fees in respect of a party wall dispute and on a claim by the builder for increased costs in respect of the construction of the building. The VAT tribunal rejected the contention that these costs related to the initial construction of the building, holding that they were 'totally new matters arising in a way unconnected with the original development' and thus could only be attributed to the exempt rents.

16.238 In *Mr & Mrs George Vitzthum (VTD 11076)* it was held that it is implicit in the definition of input tax in what is now *VATA 1994, s 24(1)* that the use of the goods or services has to be for an authorised business purpose. Accordingly, where a double garage was constructed partly for storage of business stock and partly as office space for a business carried on from the taxpayer's home, but the planning consent limited its use to storing private motor vehicles and other domestic purposes, the tax on the construction costs could not be input tax.

16.239 A salutary tale on apportionments between exempt and taxable supplies is to be found in *C & E Commrs v University of Wales College of Cardiff (1995 STC 611)*. The college constructed two buildings for a new engineering faculty. With the approval of HMRC it entered into a lease and leaseback arrangement in order to recover VAT incurred on the construction cost from 1 April 1989. Under this it granted leases in April 1992, after completion of the building work, to a wholly-owned subsidiary and opted to tax the rents. It claimed that virtually the whole of the input tax was attributable to the taxable lease, albeit that the college had used the buildings for its own partly exempt purposes between 1990 and 1992 HMRC said that the apportionment had to be based on the use when the input tax was incurred. At that date the lease had not been entered into. On the basis of the 'income' of the faculty in 1989, they considered that 51% was attributable to taxable supplies and 49% to exempt ones. The court upheld this test. HMRC had power under the *VAT Regulations 1995 (SI 1995 No 2518)*, *reg 102* to direct an approach that gives a fair and reasonable attribution of the tax for the accounting period, and under *reg 107* this could be adjusted by reference to the longer period of the college's VAT year. However, nothing occurring after the end of that longer period could subsequently alter the attribution. This is the sort of case where it is vital to try to agree a special method of attribution of input tax with HMRC under *reg 102* in advance of the first supply.

16.240 *St Helens School Northwood Ltd (2007 STC 633)* built a new sports complex. It let the complex outside school hours for a fairly nominal sum to a subsidiary, St Helens Enterprises Ltd, which exploited the complex commercially. It attempted to apportion its input tax in the ratio of hours of school use in the first year to hours of SHEL's use. This was rejected on the basis that *reg 102* looks only at supplies by the taxable person, so it is not permissible to take into account use by a third party. Warren J agreed but could see no reason why the projected use by SHEL could not be taken as a proxy for the use (for VAT purposes) of the building by the school in granting the licence. However, he also agreed with HMRC that the physical use of the complex is not necessarily a fair and reasonable proxy for the use of the premise. He felt that what needs to be looked for is the economic use and pointed out that had the school not granted the licence at all the whole of the input tax would have been attributable to the school's exempt supplies. Furthermore, the sports complex is used for the purpose of those supplies not because there is a supply to parents of the physical use (by their daughters) of the complex but because the availability of the complex is part of the package of benefits which constitutes the exempt supply by the school to the parents. He concluded that on the facts the overwhelming economic use of the complex by the school is in relation to the provision of educational services. It was also clear that the income generated by the licence to SHEL was never intended to meet a scheme of the capital costs on which the disputed input tax arose. He concluded that the standard method produces a more fair and reasonable apportionment which reflects the economic use than the school's proposed special method.

16.241 The decision in *C & E Commrs v Wiggett Construction Ltd (2001 STC 933)* is interesting. The company targets housing associations. In December

1995, it incurred input tax on the purchase of a plot of derelict land in Manchester. In December 1996, it entered into four agreements with a housing association. The first was to sell it the land, the second to construct a building on it, the third was a variation of the building contract, and the fourth an agreement for the construction of additional flats. The company accepted that the land sale was exempt. However, it claimed that the four contracts formed an integral package and together formed the bargain between the parties. It would never have entered into the land sale agreement without having the building contracts. The land sale attracted roughly 20% of the total consideration. The company contended that 80% of the input tax on the purchase of the land related to the construction contract. HMRC not unnaturally contended that it related solely to the land sale. The VAT tribunal found in favour of the company. It was held that it was entitled to reach that conclusion on the evidence. It had applied the correct tests that the input tax had to be objectively linked to the taxable transaction, that the link must be direct and immediate, and the input must be a cost component of the taxable transaction.

16.242 HMRC returned to the fray in *C & E Commrs v Southern Primary Housing Association Ltd (2004 STC 209).* The company bought a property for £435,000 plus VAT. It did not opt to tax the property. It resold it to a housing association for £481,000 and at the same time entered into an agreement with the housing association to build residential units on the property for £1.87m. The issue was again whether the VAT paid on the acquisition of the property fell to be attributed wholly to the exempt supply of the property or partly to the zero-rated supply of the building work. HMRC sought to contend that the *Wiggett Construction* case had been incorrectly decided as it breaches the well established principle of neutrality as there should be no difference between a taxpayer who buys and sells a piece of land and also contracts to provide building services on a different piece of land and one who contracts to build on the land on which he sells. Sir Donald Ratten felt that HMRC's comparison was an invalid one. The tribunal applied the direct and immediate link and the cost component tests enunciated by the ECJ in the *BLP* case (see below) and decided that, looked at objectively, the facts as a whole showed that the sale of the land and the building contract were part of one overall commercial transaction. The Court of Appeal held that whether or not the facts amounted to a 'use' was a question of law and that the fact that the two transactions were commercially linked did not mean that those transactions were 'directly and immediately' linked to the development contract. 'There is nothing about the development contract as such which makes the land purchase and sale essential. If the housing association had already owned the land … the inputs of the development contract would have just been the costs of carrying it out'. The cost of buying the land was not a cost of the development contract itself. HMRC did not appeal this decision. In HMRC Brief 57/2009, commenting on the decision, they say that there are some basic requirements that must apply before a supply can exist. The recipient must receive some benefit, he must supply some consideration and the consideration must be paid in return for the benefit. Conclusions on what the cost components of any supply are will flow from a careful analysis of the supply.

16.243 In *St James Court Hotel Ltd (VTD 17487)* the company constructed two restaurants in order to comply with a franchise agreement to enable it to operate as a Crowne Plaza hotel. It sublet these to restaurant operators and did not opt to waive exemption for the rents. It contended that it had used the inputs exclusively in making a taxable supply of construction services to the tenants as an inducement to them to enter into the lease or, alternatively, that it had used them both in making taxable supplies of hotel services and an exempt supply of letting. The tribunal dismissed both claims; the first on the basis that there was no evidence that an inducement had been offered to tenants, and in carrying out the work the hotel simply decided to offer its restaurant premises for lease rather than to run it themselves, and the second on the basis that the expenses were directly incurred in fulfilling its contractual obligations under the agreement for lease. The tribunal commented that if the Hotel had run the restaurant itself there would clearly have been a direct link to the supplies, but stressed that there has to be an objective link between the supplies and the taxable transactions. It is clear from *BLP Group plc v C & E Commrs (Case 4-4/94, 1995 STC 424)* that this excludes situations where the causal chain has been broken by an exempt supply. *Goldmax Resources Ltd (VTD 18219)* is a sad illustration of such a break. Goldmax bought a property intending to convert it to residential property and sell the converted building to a housing association. Unfortunately the rules of the Housing Association made it impossible for Goldmax to carry out the building work. Goldmax introduced another builder, from which it obtained a management fee, and sold the land to the housing association. It was held that there were two distinct contracts and that input tax on the land could not be an input of the management fee. In *Bridgeworth Golf Club v HMRC ([2010] SFTD 94)* the Tribunal held that, although the refurbishment of the bar and kitchen were directly attributable to the taxable supplies from the bar and restaurant, the refurbishment of the lounge where the drinks and food were consumed was not wholly related to such supplies, as the use of the clubhouse by the members 'is an intrinsic part of their membership and inseparable from the exempt supplies of sporting services'. In this case the club admitted that it could not survive without lounge and dining facilities and these had to be at their most attractive to build up the membership. Mention should also be made of *Bedale Golf Club (TC 4619)* where a bar refurbishment was held to be attributable partly to the exempt supply of facilities for playing sport because the area was used for the presentation of golfing awards. In contrast, in *The Queen's Club (TC 6119)*, refurbishment expenditure was held to be attributable wholly to the taxable supply of catering as HMRC could identify no specific sports-related use of the Club's restaurant and bars. The question in *Durham Cathedral (TC 5477)* was whether work on a bridge which gave access for visitors to the cathedral was solely attributable to the non-business purpose of worship or whether it was also used in making the taxable supplies in the cathedral's gift shop. The Tribunal held that the expenditure was attributable to the activities of the cathedral as a whole, so a proportion of it was used in making the taxable supplies.

16.244 An interesting issue arose in *Community Housing Association Ltd v HMRC (2009 STC 1324)*. Community Housing Association ('CHA') is a registered social landlord. Prior to 2006 it engaged surveyors and other professionals, suffering VAT on their fees and also engaged builders who could zero-rate their supplies. In 2006 it realised that it could avoid the VAT by setting up a subsidiary, CHA Ventures Ltd ('Ventures') to undertake all future development activity on CHA sites, so that Ventures would provide a zero-rated design and build service to CHA. CHA also transferred to Ventures all construction projects which it had on hand. The dispute was over the professional fees already paid by CHA in relation to such projects. CHA 'reinvoiced' Ventures in respect of such fees. CHA claimed that it had changed its intention in respect of such fees; it previously intended to use them to create exempt buildings but now intended to use them to make taxable supplies to Ventures. The VAT tribunal disagreed. Passing the obligation to pay for the supplies to Ventures could not change the nature of the supplies themselves. However, Sales J felt that the tribunal had misdirected itself, albeit possibly as the result of the 'somewhat misleading' invoice description of there having been a 're-supply' of professional services. What CHA had actually supplied to Ventures for consideration was 'the benefit of the assignment/novation of these contracts'. That is clearly a supply of services and is a taxable supply. HMRC's analysis that CHA had continued to use the services with the intention of making exempt supplies of social housing, despite the interposition of Ventures, involved taking a general, overarching approach which is incompatible with established law such as in *BLP Group plc v Customs & Excise Commrs (Case C-4/94) (1995 STC 424)* and *C & E Commrs v Southern Primary Housing Association Ltd* (see **16.220**) that the right to deduct input tax arises in respect of goods and services which have a direct and immediate link with taxable transactions. This means that the proper focus of analysis needs to be the immediate supply by CHA to Ventures rather than the ultimate supply of social housing by CHA to tenants. The past professional services were clearly a cost component of CHA's taxable supply to Ventures.

16.245 Where input tax has been attributed to taxable supplies because the taxpayer intended to use the item in making such supplies, and at some time within the next six years he changes his mind and uses or decides to use the item to make exempt supplies, he must account for an amount equal to that input tax on the return for the period in which the exempt use takes place or the intention to make the taxable supply is abandoned, and thus repay such input tax to HMRC (*reg 108*). There are similar provisions for adjustment if input tax which was initially treated as relating to exempt supplies subsequently becomes attributable to taxable supplies (*reg 109*). Where a housebuilder cannot sell a property there is a temptation to let it on a temporary basis until the property market improves and a sale becomes feasible. The letting will make the housebuilder partly exempt as he now intends to use the costs of building the house to make both taxable (zero-rated) and exempt (residential property letting) supplies. This may bring about an adjustment to previously recovered VAT in accordance with *reg 108*. This is dealt with at **17.74**. In *Cooper & Chapman (Builders) Ltd v C & E Commrs (1993 STC 1)*, the company converted a house into self-contained furnished flats which it advertised as holiday accommodation and recovered VAT on the building costs. It subsequently received an offer to take a lease of the whole block as an exempt supply. It was held that the input tax had to be apportioned between what had actually been used for making holiday lettings and what related to the exempt supply of the tenancy. In *The Really Useful Group plc (VTD 6578)*, the company commenced refurbishment of office premises for its own use. It subsequently decided to sell them instead and agreed a sale on terms that required it to complete the refurbishment work. Its claim that, in fulfilling its obligation to complete the refurbishment work, it was continuing to use the supplies for the purpose of its business was rejected by the VAT tribunal, which applied *reg 108* to require the repayment to HMRC of the whole of the input tax.

16.246 In *Royal and Sun Alliance Insurance Group v C & E Commrs (2003 STC 832)*, Royal & Sun Alliance (RSA) (through another member of its VAT group) rented five properties which the landlords had opted to tax. It decided to sublet the properties. It did not know whether it would be beneficial to itself opt to tax until it could identify the VAT characteristics of its future subtenants. It made no claim for input tax relief in relation to the rent paid. When it found sub-tenants, RSA exercised the option to tax. It contended that once it made the election it became entitled to reclaim the VAT paid on the rent in the earlier years, and claimed repayment of such VAT under *reg 109*. It originally intended to use the inputs to make exempt supplies but being unable to do so, within the six-year period it formed an intention to use the inputs in making taxable supplies. It manifested this intention by the option to tax. HMRC contended that the inputs (the rents) were consumed each quarter so that by the time the option to tax was exercised the inputs could no longer be used by RSA in making any supplies. By a majority the House of Lords agreed. RSA did not have an initial intention to use the inputs relating to the lease in supplying a mixture of services. It was trying to keep its options open. *Regulation 109* is predicated on a definite intention to make exempt supplies followed by a change of plan. *Regulation 85* (see **16.238**) derives from *VATA 1994, s 6(14)* which gives HMRC 'power to make regulations … with respect to the time at which … a supply is to be treated as taking place … where it is a supply … for a consideration the whole or part of which is determined or payable periodically … and … the regulations may provide for goods or services to be treated as separately and successively supplied at prescribed times or intervals'. That is what *reg 85* does. The same goods or services are not being supplied over and over again. The structure of the legislation is to treat the landlord as granting rights of occupation in successive units of months, quarters or whatever. Accordingly a change of plan about the use to be made of the leases in the future is not a change of intention about the use of the leases in the past. Once a quarter has passed it is no longer possible to use or intend to use the supply for that quarter for anything at all.

16.247 Following this case, HMRC issued guidance in this area. They now accept that a taxpayer can have an intention to make taxable supplies before an option is in place but consider that 'clear documentary evidence of taxable intention is essential'. This seems questionable; it is for the VAT tribunal to decide questions of fact and there is no logical reason why they cannot do so on the basis of oral evidence alone. HMRC instance as acceptable evidence a document accepting a bank loan on the basis that taxable supplies will be made. They stress, however, that if a taxpayer is keeping his options open as to whether or not to elect (which the Royal & Sun Alliance did) there is not an intention to make taxable supplies. They go on to say that they recognise that property developers often look at many sites in connection with a taxable project and that it may be onerous to opt them all. As projects progress they consider that the weight of evidence needed to substantiate a continuing intention to make taxable supplies will increase. They view the lack of an option as strong evidence that the taxpayer is merely keeping his options open and that the necessary intention does not exist (Business Brief 14/04).

16.248 Mention should also be made of the decision of the CJEC in *Sveda UAB v Valstybine mokesciu inspekcija prie Lietuvos Respublikos finansu ministerijos (Case C-126/14) (2016 STC 447)*. The taxpayer undertook with the Lithuanian Ministry of Agriculture to construct a Baltic mythology recreational and discovery path which would be open to the public free of charge. The project was 90% grant-aided. Sveda sought to deduct input tax on the construction work, which the tax authority denied on the basis that the path was not used in making taxable supplies. The business of Sveda included the provision of accommodation, food and beverages. Sveda contended that it intended to use the path in connection with future supplies of food, drink and souvenirs from shops that it would establish at each end of the path. The Court held that there was an entitlement to deduct the input tax which was paid for the acquisition or production of capital goods for the purpose of a planned economic activity which are intended for use by the public free of charge and may enable taxable transactions to be carried out, provided that a direct and immediate link is established between the expenses associated with the input transactions and transactions giving rise to the right to deduct (or with the person's economic activity as a whole). This illustrates that to come at least within the partial exemption rules the primary purpose of the expenditure does not need to be the economic activity, provided that a direct and immediate link can be established with the activity. This principle is also well illustrated in the UK case of *Roald Dahl Museum and Story Centre (TC 3445)*. In that case the charity built an exhibition space to house Roald Dahl's writing hut. The FTT held that the fact that a couple of copies of an explanatory book was attached to the exhibit and the book was on sale in the Museum's gift store was sufficient to create a right to deduct.

16.248A In *Direktor na Direktsia Obzhalvane I danachro-osiguritelna praktika Sofia v Iberdrola Immobiljaria Real Estate Investments (CPC C-132/16)*, the municipality of Tsarevo (Bulgaria) obtained a building permit to construct a waste-water pump station to serve a holiday village. Iberdrola purchased several parcels of land in the village to build 300 holiday apartments. It agreed with the municipality for Tsarevo that it would construct the pump station. Without the pump station, Iberdrola could not use its apartments. Bulgaria refused a deduction for input tax on the costs of the pump station. The CJEC held that Iberdrola was entitled to deduct input tax in respect of a supply of services consisting of the construction or improvement of a property owned by a third party when that third party enjoys the results of those services free of charge and where those services are used by the taxable person and the third party in the context of their taxable activities – but only insofar as those services do not exceed what is necessary to allow that taxable person to carry out its taxable output transactions and where their cost is included in the price of those transactions. This decision confirms HMRC's practice of allowing input tax on work done on land which is transferred to a local authority in compliance with a planning obligation (see **17.232**).

Change of Intention

16.249 The statutory basis for *reg 108* is open to question. In *Intercommunale Voor Zeewaterontzilting in Liquidation v Belgian State (Case C-110/94) (1996 STC 569)* it was held that, where the tax authority has accepted that a company which has declared an intention to commence an economic activity giving rise to taxable transactions has the status of a taxable person, the status of taxable person cannot be withdrawn retrospectively (except in cases of fraud or abuse) if as a result of a feasibility study it is decided not to move to the operational stage with the result that the economic activity envisaged has not given rise to taxable transactions. In *Belgium v Ghent Coal Terminal (Case C-37/95) (1998 STC 260)* Ghent Coal bought land in 1980 and carried out improvements to it, on which it recovered the VAT, between 1981 and 1983. In March 1983 the City of Ghent required Ghent Coal to exchange the land (that was then in the course of development) for another site owned by the city. Accordingly, the original land was never used for the purpose of Ghent Coal's business. The Belgium VAT authorities required Ghent Coal to refund the input tax it had claimed on the aborted development work. The ECJ held that *Article 17* of the *Sixth Directive* (now *Article 167* of the *VAT Directive*) must be construed as allowing a taxable person acting as such to deduct the VAT payable by him on purchases for the purpose of development intended to be used in connection with taxable transactions. The right to deduct remains acquired where, by reason of circumstances beyond his control, the taxable person has never made use of the goods or services to carry out taxable transactions. A similar decision was reached in *Finanzamt Goslar v Breitsohl (Case C-400/98) (2001 STC 355)* (see **17.163**).

16.250 HMRC contend that *reg 108* does not concern the appellant's right to deduct input tax. It is merely an adjustment of the deductible amount under *Article 20(1)* of the *Sixth Directive* (now *Article 185* of the *VAT Directive).* The VAT Tribunal in *Tremerton Ltd (VTD 15590)* accepted this. However, it is questionable whether an adjustment because of a change of intention falls within *Article 20(1).* It is also questionable whether *Article 20(1)* will allow different adjustment periods to be adopted in different circumstances. It is more apt to cover simply the annual adjustment under *reg 107.*

16.251 In *WEH Key (VTD 15354),* Mr Key converted some residential buildings into dwellings in 1990 at a time when a sale would have been exempt. In 1994 he let them as holiday lets – a taxable activity on which he accounted for VAT. In 1994 he sold the dwellings – now zero-rated (see **8.28** above) and at the time zero-rated by concession. HMRC contended that throughout Mr Key had an intention to make exempt supplies and this was upheld by the tribunal – in the absence of Mr Key, who was not represented. It is unclear to the writer how a taxpayer can make a taxable (zero-rated) supply of his entire interest in a building without first forming an intention to make such a supply. It also seems to be unclear how he can make a taxable supply without 'using' those services which created the item being supplied in making that taxable supply, which is of itself sufficient to trigger the attribution of the input tax to the taxable supply under *reg 109.* There seems no reason why the same principle cannot be applied in reverse. If a person initially intends to make a taxable supply and ultimately makes an exempt one within the six-year period, perhaps there is no obligation to repay the input tax initially recovered on the basis that there has not been a change of intention; circumstances have merely frustrated that intention being achieved.

16.252 Following the *RSA* case (see **16.246**), HMRC have given some guidance on change of intention in Business Brief 14/04. They stress that VAT incurred on day-to-day costs that has been attributed to exempt supplies (as happened in *RSA*) cannot be adjusted once an option to tax is put in place. They also say that where a business incurs VAT on costs without knowing what supplies will be made, such as costs relating to acquiring land for property development when it is not yet clear what type of project (if any) will take place, those costs cannot be directly attributed to either taxable or exempt supplies and should be regarded as residual (ie as within **16.232**(*c*)). If a project is firmed up, or costs are used in a different project in which taxable or exempt intentions are known, 'then payback or clawback may apply'.

16.253 The position may well be different if, at the time the input tax was incurred, the person was not VAT registered and had no intention of making supplies at all. *Waterschap Zeeuws Vlaanderen v Staatssecretaris van Financien (Case C-378/02) (2005 STC 1298)* concerned a Dutch public water authority. It constructed a sewage plant which it used as a public authority and was not therefore a taxable person in respect of it. Five years later it sold the sewage plant to a foundation which was established for the promotion of the environment in Dutch Flanders and leased it back for nine years. The ECJ held that the sale to the foundation was a taxable transaction, but that there was no right to deduct any of the tax paid on construction as, at the time of the supply to it, it was not a taxable person, so *Article 20* of the *Sixth Directive (now Articles 184–186* of the *Principal Directive)* (which gives the right to deduct on a change of intention) cannot apply to that supply.

Payment of Another Party's Costs

16.254 Agreements in relation to property frequently provide for the tenant to bear the landlord's costs, eg on an assignment. In such circumstances HMRC consider that, as the legal advice or other supply was to the landlord, the tenant is not entitled to reclaim the VAT on such costs (Notice 742B, para 15, now withdrawn). Accordingly the tax invoice should be issued by the solicitor, etc. to the landlord so that he can reclaim the VAT, and the tenant should be required to bear only the VAT-exclusive amount (or if the landlord is partly exempt the amount not reclaimable from HMRC). This concept has been upheld by a VAT tribunal in *Francis Jackson Homes Ltd (VTD 6352)*, where the company was not allowed relief for the input tax on the vendor's legal and estate agency fees which it had agreed to pay on an acquisition of land, and by the High Court in *Turner v C & E Commrs (1992 STC 621)*. Redrow Group plc successfully surmounted this problem by using a tripartite agreement between itself, its customer and an estate agent *(C & E Commrs v Redrow Group plc (1999 STC 161))*. It operated an incentive scheme under which, if a customer purchased one of its houses, it would pay the fees of estate agents instructed to sell the purchaser's existing house. Redrow chose the estate agent; it instructed the agent; the agent was required to report progress to Redrow; it had to agree the price with Redrow; the instructions could not be changed without the agreement of Redrow; and Redrow were contractually liable as principal for the agent's fees unless the house owner did not proceed with his proposed purchase of a house from Redrow. The House of Lords held that the transactions between Redrow and the estate agents were a supply of services for a consideration to Redrow. They did what Redrow instructed them to do, for which they charged a fee that was paid by Redrow. The matter has to be looked at from the standpoint of the person who is claiming an input tax deduction. Was something being done for him for which, in the course or furtherance of his business, he had to pay a consideration which attracted VAT? The fact that at the same time someone else (the purchaser) also received a service as part of the same transaction does not deprive Redrow of its right to deduct. The service supplied to a person might well consist of the right to have services rendered to a third party. The grant of such a right is itself a supply of services. It is sufficient for Redrow to be entitled to deduct input tax if it received something of value in return for the payment of the agent's fee and what it obtained was for the purposes of its business.

16.255 The importance of the contractual relationship was emphasised by the tribunal in *Ashfield District Council v C & E Commrs (2001 STC 1706)*. The Council made housing improvement grants to home-owners. It also helped the home-owner to find a suitable contractor, supervised the contractor and paid the grant money direct to the contractor. It was held that the Redrow principle could not apply as the contractual relationship was between the home-owner and the contractor, not the Council and the contractor and that the Council paid the contractor as agent for the home-owner. Accordingly it could not reclaim the VAT on the contractor's charges.

16.256 HMRC also regard the payment of the costs as part of the consideration for an assignment, etc. (Law Society Press Release 28 October 1992). For example, suppose that a lease provides that a tenant can assign his lease subject to his landlord's consent and subject to his paying the landlord's costs which came to £300 plus £60 VAT. If the tenant pays the full £360 he cannot recover the VAT. In addition the landlord is deemed to have made a supply of services to the tenant for £360. If the tenant is exercising a right under the lease, which will be the case where he has an absolute right to assign or where the landlord's consent is not to be unreasonably withheld, this supply is made under the lease and will not attract VAT unless the rent under the lease is VATable. If the assignment is a result of the landlord exercising his discretion, HMRC regard the supply as separate from the lease so it will attract VAT. As the solicitor supplies his services to the landlord, the landlord is presumably entitled to treat the £60 that the tenant has paid as input tax – and to set it against the £60 he owes HMRC on his own deemed supply.

16.257 HMRC are prepared to treat the lender as agent of the borrower – for the purpose of bad debt relief only and not for any other purpose – in relation to costs relating directly to the sale of the property and which would have ordinarily been incurred by the borrower had he arranged the sale himself (Business Brief 24/94). This will allow the lender to claim bad debt relief for such costs to the extent that they are not recovered from the borrower (or the sale of the property) – as *reg 9(3)* of the *VAT (Bad Debt Relief) Regulations 1986* (*SI 1986 No 335*) treats the latest supply as giving rise to the bad debt. The same treatment applies to expenditure on repairs and maintenance. If the lender uses its own in-house estate agency or legal department to deal with the sale, it can treat itself as making a supply as principal to the lender – provided that it accounts for output tax on that notional supply.

16.258 HMRC are not prepared to grant similar relief for costs incurred on services provided to the lender as principal, such as legal fees for taking possession, locksmith fees for securing the property, or the cost of pursuing a claim against a valuer for negligence. The VAT on such items is input tax attributable to the exempt loan. Nor are they willing to grant relief for costs in relation to letting the property; they regard these as supplied to the borrower and nothing to do with the lender. Costs incurred by a *Law of Property Act 1925* receiver in respect of the sale are covered by the concession, but only if the VAT element of such costs has been borne by the lender, ie not if the borrower has claimed the VAT as input VAT. Where the lender incurs expenditure on completing the construction of a partially completed building, or on major refurbishment of a property prior to sale, they are prepared to treat the charge of such costs to the borrower as a supply by the lender to the borrower (and thus potentially eligible for bad debt relief) if the sale of the building is either a taxable supply or a transfer of a going concern or, in the case of building (but not refurbishment) costs, if the property is the subject of a taxable letting and output tax on the rents has been paid over to HMRC. They are not prepared to grant bad debt relief for such costs where the sale or letting of the building is exempt (Business Brief 24/94).

Payments by Guarantors

16.259 A similar problem arises in respect of payments of rent by a guarantor where the option to tax has been exercised and the guarantor is called on to pay the rent. The supply under the lease is to the tenant not to the guarantor, and accordingly the guarantor is not entitled to recover the VAT as input tax. *Kenwood Appliances Ltd (13876)* was the assignee of a lease granted to M Ltd and it had itself re-assigned it to F Ltd. F Ltd became insolvent and defaulted. The landlord recovered the rent from the guarantor of M Ltd's obligations, who in turn sought indemnity from Kenwood. Kenwood argued that as each payment of rent was a separate supply which was deemed under the *VAT Regulations 1995, reg 85* to take place at the date of payment, and M Ltd's obligation which the guarantor settled arose under its lease, the supply was a supply to M Ltd. The VAT tribunal held that the deemed separate supply was a supply to the person entitled at the relevant time to enjoyment of the rights under the lease, namely F Ltd (which it appears was not VAT-registered at the time). Payments by a vendor of property who guarantees the rent it will fetch are dealt with at **17.142**.

Apportionments on Completions

16.260 HMRC have agreed with the Law Society that apportionments of rent on the completion of a sale of a landlord's interest in tenanted property are outside the scope of VAT (Law Society's Gazette, 1 May 1991).

Statutory Compensation

16.261 Compensation paid to a tenant under the *Landlord and Tenant Act 1954* or the *Agricultural Holdings Act 1986* is outside the scope of VAT (C & E Notice 742, para 10.7). However, compensation negotiated in lieu of these statutory rights, or a top-up payment to supplement it, is a standard-rated supply of services by the tenant irrespective of the VAT status of the property.

Payments under Planning Act Agreements

16.262 Property developers enter into a wide variety of agreements with planning authorities and water or sewage undertakings under, for example, *Town and Country Planning Act 1990, s 106* and similar enactments to provide the authority with a 'planning gain' in connection with the grant of planning permission. HMRC's view on the VAT effect of such agreements is as follows.

(*a*) If a developer vests for no monetary consideration a new road or a new sewer or ancillary works in the local authority, etc. there is not a supply to the authority (so no VAT needs to be accounted for) but input tax in relation to the construction of such works is part of the cost of the main development, and therefore deductible, unless the supplies in relation to the development will be exempt supplies (C & E Notice 742, para 8.1).

(*b*) Similarly, if the developer provides other building work or other services free or at a nominal charge under a *section 106* agreement, the provision of those services is not a taxable supply but the input tax in relation to them is normally recoverable as part of the cost of the main development (C & E Notice 742, para 8.3).

(*c*) Payments in money to the local authority under such an agreement are not consideration for taxable supplies, other than a payment to a water company to supply mains water and sewerage services (C & E Notice 742, para 8.5).

Joint Ownership

16.263 Where the benefit of the consideration for the grant of a major interest accrues to the person constructing the building, but that person is not the grantor, he is deemed to be the person making the grant for the purpose of determining whether zero-rating applies (*VATA 1994, Sch 10, para 40,* formerly *para 8(1)*). This is intended to cover joint ownerships and, presumably, nominees. In law, joint ownership is normally a trust for sale with the joint owners being the beneficiaries. Accordingly, they will in legal terms grant leases as trustees but, in their capacity as trustees, would not be the person constructing the building. *Sch 10, para 7* ensures that the benefit of zero-rating is not lost because of this technicality. It was held by the VAT tribunal in *GW & JA Green (VTD 9016)* that joint owners were jointly registrable for VAT (see **17.51**).

16.264 HMRC take the view that joint ownership of property constitutes a partnership between the joint owners. Accordingly, they consider that it is not possible for one joint owner to exercise the option to tax and for the other not to do so. Conversely, if one of the joint owners is a taxable person because of his other activities, his share of the income from the jointly-owned properties need not be aggregated with his individual supplies. It will be interesting to see if a VAT tribunal is prepared to impose a late registration penalty if joint owners who ought to have registered for VAT, eg if they are developing the building, register individually and not as a partnership. HMRC's position was upheld by the VAT tribunal in *GW & JA Green (VTD 9016)* on the basis that the supply of the building was made jointly and there was no basis for dividing the value of the supplies between them. This does not seem to justify deeming two individuals to constitute a separate 'person', however.

Partnerships

16.265 In contrast, it is specifically provided that a registration of persons carrying on a business in partnership can be in the name of the firm (*VATA 1994, s 45*). In practice, partnerships are always registered as a firm.

16.266 *Fengate Developments (VTD 18308)* was a property development partnership between Mr Darlow and his second wife, Mrs Darlow. Darlows was a partnership between Mr Darlow and his first wife, Mrs Brawn, which traded as potato merchants. A cold store had been constructed on Fengate's land. This was leased to Darlows. Fengate had elected to waive exemption. Situated at the corner of the Fengate land was an undeveloped plot (the Red Land). This was transferred from Mr and Mrs Darlow to Mr Darlow and Mrs Brawn for £125,000 as tenants in common. At the time the value of the Red Land was £250,000. £125,000 was paid by Mrs Brawn to Fengate and a further

£125,000 was paid to Fengate by Mr Darlow, the entire £250,000 coming out of Darlows. Fengate's accounts showed a disposal of the land for £250,000. Fengate contended that it had not made a supply of the land at all. The intention of the parties was that the transfers should give effect to a sale by Mr Darlow to Mrs Brawn of part of her partnership interest (ie that in the Red Land) for £125,000. The £125,000 paid by Mr Darlow was simply a capital contribution by him to Fengate and that by Mrs Brawn was a capital contribution to Fengate by Mrs Darlow (being money due to her personally but paid into Fengate at her direction). The tribunal dismissed this contention. Although Mrs Darlow could have sold an interest in part of her Fengate partnership share to Mrs Brawn, Mrs Brawn could have realised that interest only on a dissolution of Fengate. What effectively happened (on the basis of the documentation) was that the Red Land ceased to be an asset of the Fengate partnership and became a personal asset of Mr Darlow and Mrs Brawn (or possibly an asset of Darlows). Accordingly there had been a taxable supply of the land by Fengate for £250,000.

Joint Ventures

16.267 A joint venture is different from a partnership. It is where two or more people agree to act jointly, but without binding one another. The supplies will normally be made by one of the joint venturers, but the profits are shared between the two. HMRC do not like joint ventures. They tell staff, 'there are obvious revenue risks in this situation [one could be under the registration limit] which emphasise the importance of only allowing this practice if the parties specifically request it and then only if you are certain that a true joint venture exists' (VAT Manual, Vol V1-5, Sec 3, para 2.23). They say that 'the characteristics of a 'true' joint venture are that two or more venturers agree to act in concert, fulfilling agreed obligations and inputting resources which are later correspondingly reflected in the level of benefit which they receive'. Joint ventures are fairly common with property development. With a joint venture, it can be difficult to discern if one of the joint venturers makes supplies to the other or if each is simply performing his obligations under the agreement. For example, suppose that a property developer buys land and enters into an agreement with a surveyor that the surveyor will obtain planning permission for redevelopment and the property will then be sold with the surveyor being entitled to 20% of the profit. If this is a joint venture, no VAT is payable on the surveyor's profit share, as he receives it not as consideration for providing his services but simply as a division of profits (which is outside the scope of VAT). It is accordingly important to be able to establish that a joint venture exists to avoid HMRC seeking to treat a profit share as consideration for the provision of services. An illustration of the problems that can arise where a joint venture is not properly documented can be found in *Maritsan Development Ltd v HMRC (TC 1971).* In that case HMRC concluded that one of the venturers was providing services to Maritsan and insisted that it issue a VAT invoice. Maritsan has to argue the case before the Tribunal to get the invoice set aside.

Options

16.268 The grant of an option to acquire land is the exempt grant of a right over land. Accordingly, it may be possible to reduce substantially the tax on the disposal of a new building by attaching most of the price to the option and requiring a comparatively small price to be paid for the building itself.

Charities

16.269 Where a person bequeaths a dwelling or land to a charity, HMRC have expressed the view that 'any supply of the property flowing from the bequest would normally be outside the scope of VAT so a charity would not be able to claim input VAT on the expenses of the sale' (Business Brief 12/92). This is because HMRC's legal advice is that such assets are not 'goods which have been donated for sale' which qualify for zero-rating under *VATA 1994, Sch 8, Group 15, Item 1*. This was the issue in *Pondini Ltd v The Treasury of the Isle of Man (TC 3295)*. Although this concerned the IOM legislation, it is identical to that in the UK. It was pointed out there that note IF (which dates from 2000) excludes from the meaning of goods 'anything that is not goods even though provision made by or under an enactment provides for a supply of that thing to be treated as a supply of goods'. Accordingly the disposal was not zero-rated.

Receivers

16.270 It was held in *re John Willment (Ashford) Ltd (1979 STC 286)* that a receiver appointed under a debenture is obliged to account to HMRC for the VAT on supplies made by him since not to do so would make the company, whose agent he was, liable for a criminal offence. In *Sargent v C & E Commrs (1995 STC 398)*, it was held that, notwithstanding the de-criminalisation of VAT offences, this principle not only still applies but applies equally to a receiver appointed under a fixed mortgage of a property, ie a *Law of Property Act 1925* receiver. The justification is that the VAT element in rents collected by the receiver constitute 'outgoings … affecting the mortgaged property', which the receiver is required to discharge under *Law of Property Act 1925, s 109(8)*. The Court of Appeal rejected HMRC's alternative submission that *reg 9* of the *VAT Regulations 1995*, which enables HMRC to treat any person carrying on the business of a company in liquidation or receivership as the taxable person, is wide enough to cover a *Law of Property Act* receiver who, by collecting rents from one property, carries on part of the company's business. See **16.236** above for the VAT position on selling costs of a property incurred by a receiver.

Exchanges of Land

16.271 Care needs to be taken where a transaction involves an exchange of land. This occurred in *Cumbernauld Development Corporation (VTD 14630).* Cumbernauld wished to dispose of a site, the access to which was blocked by the club house and car park of a golf club. It entered into an agreement with the golf club under which the club transferred the land to Cumbernauld and Cumbernauld provided it with a club house, leisure facilities, car parking and an enlargement of the golf course adjoining on land owned by Cumbernauld. The golf club also agreed to allow preferential use of its course by local residents. The land transferred by the golf club was worth £120,000 ignoring any ransom element. The cost to Cumbernauld of carrying out the works on the adjoining land was £3 million. The agreement was expressed to be for nil consideration but the parties accepted that there had been supplies for a consideration. The question before the tribunal was the value of the supply by the golf club to Cumbernauld of the access land.

16.272 The tribunal held that the £120,000 figure could not be used, as the value of the access land to Cumbernauld was far greater. As the subjective value of the supply is the value attributed by the recipient to what is received (*Empire Stores Ltd v C & E Commrs (Case C-33/93) (1994 STC 623)*), the consideration is the value of the land to Cumbernauld. This is not necessarily £3 million. Some elements of the package, such as the need to allow local residents on the course and the increased costs of maintenance of the larger course, might have a negative value that should be deducted from the figure. The case was therefore adjourned to allow the parties to try to agree a value.

References to 'Grant'

16.273 The word 'grant' has given rise to difficulties. It is specifically stated to include an assignment or surrender and also the supply made by a person to whom an interest is surrendered where he is paid to accept the surrender (*VATA 1994, Sch 9, Group 1, Notes 1 & 1A*). HMRC have said that it means a transfer of title or the execution of a lease and does not cover rental payments under existing leases even though such payments are deemed to be supplies. The VAT status is normally determined at the time of a grant.

However, *VATA 1994, s 96(10A)* provides that, where the grant of an interest, right, licence or facility gives rise to supplies made at different times after the making of the grant and the question whether any of those supplies is zero-rated or exempt depends on the nature of the grant, that question is to be determined at the time of the supply not by reference to the time of the grant. For example, the VAT status of rents will depend on whether the option to tax has been exercised at the time each payment of VAT fell due, not on whether it had been exercised at the time the lease was entered into. This provision has retrospective effect to the introduction of VAT.

16.274 *Section 96(10A)* does not apply so as to make exempt a supply that arises from the prior grant of a freehold interest, but does not prevent such a supply from being exempt (*VATA 1994, s 96(10B)*). This is an anti-avoidance provision. It is intended to ensure that where the transfer of a freehold of a commercial building is standard-rated because the building is less than three years old a subsequent supply arising from a grant outside the three-year period will also be standard-rated (and where the original sale of a freehold is exempt any further supply arising from the grant will also be exempt).

Work Required under Statutory Powers

16.275 Local authorities have statutory powers to require a property owner to carry out specified works to his premises. Where the owner does not comply with the notice, the local authority can carry out the work itself and recover the cost from the property owner. Where they do this, the supply by the builder is to the local authority. In recovering the cost the local authority is not making a supply to the landowner; it is merely exercising a statutory power. However, the local authority, having incurred the VAT, is entitled to recover it from HMRC under *VATA 1994, s 33* (Business Brief 19/98). On this basis it is probably entitled to recover only the VAT-exclusive amount from the property-owner, although that may depend on the precise wording of the statute involved. If the property-owner asks the local authority to arrange for the work to be done and send him the bill, there will in contrast be a supply to the local authority by the builder and an onward VATable supply by the local authority to the property-owner.

Serviced Building Plots and Partially Completed Buildings

16.276 At what stage does a building plot become a building? This can be an important question because the construction of a building by a do-it-yourself builder and the zero-rating for residential development require the construction of a building or the trader to be a person constructing a building. The view of

HMRC (and its predecessor HM Customs) has always been that a sale or other disposal of a partially completed building attracts the same VAT liability as that of a completed building but someone cannot be a person constructing a building until some building work on the structure has taken place. This was the issue in *Stapenhill Developments Ltd (VTD 1593)*. The company acquired a site on which it intended to erect houses. It carried out drainage work for the entire site. It did some work on the foundations for a block of terraced houses but then discovered that the ground was too wet and decided to abandon that work and move to a higher part of the site. Its bankers then intervened and forced a sale of the land. The company contended that the sale should be zero-rated as 'the granting by a person constructing a building of a major interest in … the building or its site' (see **16.7(1)**(*a*) above). HMRC contended that the sale was exempt as a supply of land. Although neither attracts tax, exemption of course affects the deductibility of input tax. The tribunal held that the legislation does not require a completed building to be upon the land but it is a matter of substance and degree whether what has been done is sufficient to make someone a person constructing a building. It held that the supply was exempt. It also held that the word 'site' needs to be interpreted in the context of a reasonable plot of land surrounding a building. Although HMRC take this case as authority for saying that site development work is not sufficient to bring about a 'building' it is arguable whether the tribunal went that far. The company in that case did not even suggest that the drainage works were sufficient; it relied on the foundation work. The tribunal thought that an enquirer would have had to be told, 'We were digging foundations for some houses but they were in the wrong place and we have abandoned them'. No building work had taken place on the higher land so nothing had been done at all on the actual proposed building.

16.277 In *M E Conway (VTD 11725)* Mr Conway constructed foundations on a site that he was told was to be used for the construction of zero-rated dwellings. Unfortunately the plans were changed and garages and workshops were constructed instead. In holding that Mr Conway needed to account for VAT the tribunal commented, 'If it could be shown that residential development had been authorised and started he might have been able to claim zero-rating for his work'. In *Cameron New Homes Ltd (VTD 17309* – see **16.16**) where the excavations for the foundations had been done and the trenching shuttered but no concrete had yet been poured into them it was held that at the time of sale 'there was nothing on the land that was recognisably a building under construction … The works had not passed beyond preparatory works'. The tribunal there felt that it was not necessary for it to decide where the line should be drawn as the works there clearly fell on the wrong side of it.

16.278 HMRC's view is that, 'You can zero-rate the sale of … land that will form the site of a [residential] building provided a building is clearly under construction' (Notice 708, para 4.7.4). They used to say in Notice 742A,

'Construction of a building begins when it progresses above the level of the building's foundations', but this seems to have disappeared from the current version. In none of the above cases had the foundations for a building that was erected by the purchaser been constructed so it is doubtful whether they actually support HMRC's view. Indeed, this view no longer seems tenable following the decision in *D & S Virtue t/a Lammermuir Game Services (VTD 20259)*. The tribunal there felt the relevant test as to whether work is done in the course of the construction of a building designed as a dwelling is:

(*a*) the services must be connected with the construction of a building;

(*b*) services which facilitate or have a substantial connection with the construction, such as preparatory or site clearance work or ground or earthworks, are connected with the construction of the building;

(*c*) there must be a temporal connection between those services and the construction of the building; and

(*d*) whether there is such a connection is a question of fact or degree.

Under these tests, starting to dig a trench for the foundations may well be enough. HMRC seem to accept that demolition can also be enough provided that this immediately precedes the start of work on the new building.

16.279 Nevertheless, most people try to work within the HMRC view. The first brick laid above the foundations is often referred to as 'the golden brick' as it is the laying of that brick which will trigger the right to zero-rate the onward sale of a residential development site. Most people consider it safer to lay the whole of the first level of bricks. It needs to be borne in mind that in the *Stepenhill* case the tribunal defined site as being limited to the area on which a single dwelling was to be constructed, so laying one brick on an entire development site is probably not sufficient to enable the whole site to be zero-rated.

16.280 Where an existing building is demolished and a new one constructed the position is clearer as *VATA 1994, Sch 8, Group 5, Note 18* specifically provides that a building only ceases to be an existing building if it is 'demolished completely to ground level' (or the part above ground level consists of no more than a single façade (or double façade on a corner site) whose retention is a planning condition). This statutory provision is considered at **16.96** onwards.

16.281 What happens where a site is sold when site preparation work has been done but no work has been carried out above ground level? The early cases seem to have simply accepted that there is a single sale of a serviced site. However, HMRC subsequently formed the view that 'where the freehold sale of land is ancillary to the supply of new or part completed civil engineering works, this is a single standard rated supply. But where the new or part completed civil engineering works are incidental to the supply of land, the supply is treated as an exempt supply of land (subject to the option to tax) and a standard rated supply of civil engineering works. This policy allows the supplier to reclaim input tax on the construction of the civil engineering works which would not otherwise be possible'. This policy was challenged successfully in *D & S Virtue t/a Lammermuir Games Services (VTD 20259)* (from which the above quotation is taken). In that case Lammermuir obtained planning consent, carried out the site preparation work (which was work on the overall site but did not include any work on individual house plots) and advertised building plots for sale as serviced building plots. The tribunal held that the commercial reality is that there was a single supply of land and thought there were insuperable difficulties in ascertaining a value to be attributed to the services element.

16.282 Following this case HMRC changed their view and now accept that the supply of a serviced building plot is a single exempt supply of land by the landowner (HMRC Brief 64/2007). They go on to say that where the landowner can demonstrate that these services are being received in the course of construction of a building designed as dwellings the supply of civil engineering works to the landowner can be zero-rated. This will normally apply only where:

(*a*) the landowner holds sufficient planning consent to demonstrate that the work is in the course of the construction of a dwelling;

(*b*) the civil engineering work is closely connected with, or facilitates, the construction of buildings; and

(*c*) the construction of the building will follow on closely after the completion of the civil engineering works.

This requires the landowner to have a firm intention to sell the serviced plots once the civil engineering work is completed, that a purchaser can only construct a residential building on the plot and that any purchaser is ready to begin actual construction of the buildings as soon as possible.

16.283 This statement in relation to the works is obviously welcome; it prevents irrecoverable VAT on the works pushing up the cost of the finished house. However, it is difficult to reconcile it with HMRC's view that the sale of the serviced land is exempt not zero-rated. If the civil engineering work is in the course of construction of a building then logically the land containing such work ought to be a partially constructed building (except perhaps in the situation of *Lammermuir* itself where the work was solely to the overall site and no ground work had taken place at all on individual building plots).

16.284 HMRC consider that the construction of a building is completed at a given moment in time. That point is determined by a combination of when a Certificate of Completion is issued in accordance to approved plans and specifications, the scope of the planning consent and whether the building is habitable or fit for purpose (Notice 708, para 3.3.2). They consider that 'snagging' carried out after the building has been 'completed' can be zero-rated if it is carried out by the builder under the building contract. Otherwise it is standard-rated.

16.285 The tribunal decision in *Mr & Mrs Jones (VTD 20426)*, a do-it-yourself builder case, casts doubt on this. Mr & Mrs Jones built their own house. They engaged a plasterer. They discovered significant faults and took the view that the work was wholly unacceptable and all of the plasterwork would have to be redone. This had not physically been done by the time that they obtained the Certificate of Completion and they moved into the house before it was done. HMRC contended that by the time the replastering was done, the house had been completed, so the house was an existing building and the replastering an alteration. The tribunal disagreed. The Certificate merely records that the substantive requirements of the Building Regulations have been satisfied. To the naked eye the old plasterwork was obviously inadequate and dangerous so the construction project could not be regarded as finished until the new plasterwork was installed. Accordingly, its replacement, albeit by a different plasterer, was carried out in the course of construction of the dwelling.

Chapter 17

Value Added Tax on Commercial Property

17.1 Transactions in land and commercial or industrial buildings are in general exempt from VAT. There are three main exceptions.

1. The disposal of a commercial or industrial building within three years of its construction – which is taxable at the 20% standard rate (see **17.25** below).
2. Specified, mainly leisure-related, types of property which are taxed at the 20% standard rate (see **17.27** below).
3. A disposal where the option to bring exempt disposals of land and buildings into the charge to tax has been exercised (see **17.126** below).

17.2 *VATA 1994, Sch 9, Group 1,* which contains the exemption for land, is intended to ensure that sales of new non-residential buildings are subjected to VAT at 20% by excluding such sales from exemption (see **17.25**).

17.3 The exemption applies to the grant of any interest in, or right over, land, or any licence to occupy land (including an assignment of such an interest or right, or in Scotland any personal right to call for or be granted any such interest or right) other than:

(*a*) a freehold disposal of:

- (i) a building which has not been completed and which is not a residential one; or
- (ii) a new building which is not a residential one; or
- (iii) a civil engineering work which is in the course of being constructed; or
- (iv) a new civil engineering work; or

(*b*) the grant of certain specified, mainly leisure-related, activities (see **17.27** below).

As is usual there are a number of 'Notes' which modify these basic provisions.

17.4 *Schedule 9, Group 1* gives effect to *Article 13B(6)* of the *Sixth Directive*, which states that 'Member States shall exempt the following under conditions which they shall lay down for the purpose of ensuring the correct and straightforward application of the exemptions and preventing any possible evasion, avoidance or abuse: … (*b*) the leasing or letting of immovable property excluding [the items in **17.1**(2) above]. Member States may apply further exclusions to the scope of this exemption … (*g*) the supply of buildings or parts thereof and of the land on which they stand …'.

17.5 This has given rise to a great deal of litigation in the ECJ. It was held in *Fonden Marselisborg Lystbadehavn v Skatteministeriet (Case C-428/02) (2006 STC 1467)* that the concept of letting immovable property includes the letting of water-based mooring berths for pleasure boats and land site for storage of boats on park land (although this was a pyrrhic victory as it was also held that the term vehicle includes a boat so the exclusion at **17.27**(vi) would probably take such moorings out of the exemption). In the later case of *Leichenich v Peffehoven (2013 STC 846; Case C-532/11)* the ECJ held that the concept of the leasing and letting of immovable property included the leasing of a houseboat (including the space and landing stage contiguous therewith) which was fixed (by attachments which were not easily removable) to the bank and bed of a river, stayed in a demarcated and identifiable location in the river water and was used exclusively for the permanent operation of a restaurant/discotheque at that location. The letting constituted a single exempt supply; it was not necessary to distinguish between the letting of the houseboat and that of the landing.

17.6 The UK legislation does not contain definitions of either a building or civil engineering works. However, *Article 12(2)* of the *EU Directive* at 28 November 2006 which replaced the Sixth Directive (and is generally called the *Principal Directive*) (formerly *Article 4(3)* of the *Sixth Directive*) defines a building as 'any structure fixed to or in the ground' and *Article 135(2)* (formerly *Article 13B(b)*) excludes from the exemption for the leasing or letting of immovable property 'lettings of permanently installed equipment and machinery' and also 'hire of safes', neither of which appears to have been incorporated into UK legislation, in addition to the items listed at **17.27**. This was in issue in *Argents Nurseries Ltd (VTD 20045)* which concerned 'Poly Tunnels' used by nurseries. HMRC contended that a lease of Poly Tunnels was an exempt grant of an interest in land whereas the taxpayer believed them to be a taxable lease of plant and equipment. The tribunal agreed that the Poly Tunnels were structures fixed to the ground. However, it also felt that they were permanently installed equipment and machinery and as such excluded from zero-rating. It seems to have been influenced by the capital allowance meaning of plant. A similar decision was reached in *Queen Mary, University of London (TC 1094)* (see **16.27**).

17.6A It should be borne in mind that VAT is payable only on a supply of goods or services for consideration by a taxable person acting as such (Principal VAT Directive (2006/112/EC) Act 2(1)(a)). If there is no consideration – such as on a gift – VAT is not payable as there is no supply. This principle needs to be approached with a degree of caution though as HMRC are adept at identifying some service as consideration for what the taxpayer thought was a gift. If HMRC can identify something as consideration, it might trigger a right to substitute market as the quantum of the consideration. A gift could, of course, lead to a claw-back of input tax. In *Minister Finansow v Posnania Investment SA (2007 All ER(D) 106)*, the CJEC held that VAT was not payable where a company transferred a property to a local authority in satisfaction of a tax liability.

Surrender of Leases

17.7 The surrender of an interest in land is exempt from VAT. Before 1 March 1995, a surrender was taxable and *Note 1* excluded from the normal exemption for an assignment, an assignment to one's landlord. This was an anti-avoidance provision designed to thwart avoidance of tax on a surrender. Both of these exclusions were held by the European Court of Justice to be in breach of the *EC Sixth Directive* in *Lubbock Fine & Co v C & E Commrs (1994 STC 101)*. This was a reference to the Court by the London VAT Tribunal.

It was held that the words 'letting of immovable property' in *Article 13B* cover the case where a tenant, for consideration, surrenders his lease and returns the immovable property to his immediate landlord because 'where a given transaction, such as the letting of immovable property, which would be taxed on the basis of the rents paid, falls within the scope of an exemption provided for by the *Sixth Directive*, a change in the contractual relationship, such as termination of the lease for consideration, must also be regarded as falling within the scope of that exemption'. It was further held that the power in *Article 13B(b)* to apply further exclusions from exemption enable a country to tax other types of letting, but does not allow it to tax a transaction terminating a lease where the grant of that lease was compulsorily exempt (ie to break down the relations created by a lease into exempt and taxable parts). As it was not necessary for the decision, the Court declined to decide whether the surrender of a lease of buildings for consideration paid by the landlord to the tenant was a compulsorily exempt supply under *Article 13B(g)*. The opinion of the Advocate General was that it was not, as by a surrender a tenant cannot transfer to the landlord the power of disposal of the building as a landlord can sell his building even when it is let.

17.8 HMRC initially took the view that the European Court decision applied only where a payment was made by the landlord to the tenant, although the Court had said that *Article 13B(b)* does not permit the UK 'to tax the consideration paid by one party to the other in connection with the surrender of the lease' which is equally apt to cover a payment by the tenant to the landlord to accept a surrender although as indicated above they declined to specifically rule on it. Their view was that such a 'reverse surrender' was a supply made by the landlord of accepting an obligation to refrain from an act (enforcing his rights under the lease) which is not the grant of an interest in land and is thus a taxable supply (Business Brief 16/94). However, in September 1994 in *Marbourne Ltd (VTD 12670)*, a VAT tribunal held that the *Lubbock Fine* principle applied to a reverse surrender, albeit to do so it had to introduce the novel concept of a supply by the tenant for a negative consideration. The tribunal in *Central Capital Corporation Ltd (VTD 13319)* declined to follow the decision in *Marbourne Ltd*. It held that the relevant supply of land was made by the landlord but that, applying the European Court of Justice's decision in *Lubbock Fine & Co*, the supply by the landlord qualified for exemption under *Article 13B(b)* of the *EC Sixth Directive*. Since the original grant of the lease was not taxable, the subsequent 'reverse surrender' of that lease was also not taxable. HMRC originally intended to appeal against the *Marbourne* decision, but instead the government decided to exempt reverse surrenders. Accordingly *Note 1* now states that a grant 'includes an assignment or surrender and the supply made by the person to whom an interest is surrendered when there is a reverse surrender'.

Reverse Premiums

17.9 The ECJ considered the VAT position on reverse premium in two cases, *C & E Commrs v Mirror Group plc (Case C-409/98, 2001 STC 1453)* and *C & E Commrs v Cantor Fitzgerald International (Case C-108/99, 2001 STC 1453)*. It would be nice to be able to say that following those cases the law is clear. Unfortunately that is not the case. Each case will need to be looked at on its individual merits. That is clearly unsatisfactory with a self-assessed tax. The only safe solution is likely to be to ask HMRC to rule on each transaction, assuming of course that they are prepared to do so.

In *Cantor Fitzgerald* it was the assignor, not the landlord, who made a payment to Cantor Fitzgerald to induce it to take an assignment of the lease. The VAT tribunal held that the reverse premium fell within the *Lubbock Fine* decision. HMRC appealed to the High Court which referred the question to the ECJ *(1998 STC 948)* because it felt that the scope of the principle laid down in the *Lubbock Fine* case was unclear. The ECJ ruled in favour of HMRC. It held that the relevant supply is a supply of services, namely agreeing to accept an assignment of a lease of property from a lessee. Such a supply is not the letting of immovable property. The supplier had no interest in the property at the time of the supply. This differs from the *Lubbock Fine* case. Lubbock Fine assigned its right to occupy the property back to the landlord which is why the court ruled that transaction to be exempt.

17.10 Mirror Group plc entered into two agreements with Olympia and York Canary Wharf Ltd. The first was an agreement for lease of five floors at One Canada Square. The second granted Mirror Group an option to take an extra four floors. The agreement for lease provided for an inducement payment of approximately £12 million, £6.5 million to be payable on occupation of the five floors and the completion of fitting-out work that Mirror Group plc had undertaken under the lease, and the remaining £5.5m to be put into escrow and repaid to the extent that Mirror Group plc did not take up the option space. The VAT tribunal held that 'so much of the inducement as can be ascribed to Mirror Group's undertaking to enter into the lease' was exempt and the balance taxable. The High Court then referred the case to the ECJ,which ruled that the *Lubbock Fine* principle does not apply as Mirror Group did not have an interest in land and it left it to the UK courts to decide if Mirror Group made a supply of anything:

> 'It must be noted that a taxable person who only pays the consideration in cash due in respect of a supply of services, or who undertakes to do so, does not himself make a supply of services for the purposes of Article 2(1) of the Sixth Directive. It follows that a tenant who undertakes, even in return for payment from the landlord, solely to become a tenant and to pay the rent does not, so far as that action is concerned, make a supply of services for consideration if the landlord, taking the view that the presence of an anchor tenant in the building containing the leased premises will attract other tenants, were to make a payment by way of consideration for the future tenant's undertaking to transfer it business to the building concerned. In those circumstances, the undertaking of such a tenant could be qualified as a taxable supply of advertising services.'

17.11 The *Cantor Fitzgerald* case was not a true reverse premium, as in that case it was the assignor, not the landlord, who made a payment to Cantor Fitzgerald to induce it to take an assignment of the lease. The VAT tribunal held that the reverse premium fell within the *Lubbock Fine* decision. HMRC appealed to the High Court which referred the question to the ECJ (*1998 STC 948*) because it felt that the scope of the principle laid down in the *Lubbock Fine* case was unclear. The ECJ ruled in favour of HMRC. It held that the relevant supply is a supply of services, namely agreeing to accept an assignment of a lease of property from the lessee. Such a supply is not the letting of immovable property. The supplier had no interest in the property at the time of the supply. This differs from the *Lubbock Fine* case. Lubbock Fine assigned its right to occupy the property back to the landlord, which is why the court ruled that transaction to be exempt.

17.12 The ECJ judgment leaves two important questions unanswered; namely, in what circumstances can the supply be a supply of services and what happens if one party to the transaction has exercised the option to tax? The recipient of a reverse premium could legitimately take the view that it is not VATable, and risk a penalty if HMRC subsequently discover the receipt of the premium and find a way to tax it. The safest route is probably to tell HMRC of the receipt of the premium and make the case that it is not taxable. This is likely to trigger an assessment and start the interest clock running though.

17.13 The ECJ pointed out that it was for the UK courts to ascertain whether Mirror Group made a supply of services for consideration to the landlord and, if it did, what that supply was. It seems inherently improbable that the administrator of Olympia and York Canary Wharf Ltd would have paid Mirror Group £6.5 million purely to be an anchor tenant of Canary Wharf, occupying five floors, plus a further £4.1 million if it exercised an option to take three further floors. Indeed the evidence seems to be merely that 'given its high profile, Mirror Group commanded 'anchor tenant' status', which is far from indicating that it was being paid to be an anchor tenant. It is hard to see why Olympia and York Canary Wharf should need an 'anchor tenant' for Canary Wharf as the company was trying to promote Canary Wharf as a financial centre. In that context, a letting to Mirror Group was not an 'anchor' letting but seems more likely to be a desperate measure to let the building to anyone prepared to move to it. Furthermore, even if the £6.5 million was in respect of Mirror Group becoming an anchor tenant, why pay the further £4.1 million when that objective had already been achieved by the initial letting? Unfortunately the company seems to have agreed before the Commissioners that it was paid solely for being an anchor tenant and the UK courts did not allow it to re-open that question.

17.14 Be that as it may, even if part of the reason for the payment was to persuade Mirror Group to become anchor tenant, it is most improbable that this was the sole motive in the eyes of the administrator. It is likely that he also wanted simply to let the space – and would have offered at least part of the reverse premium to anyone who would take the space. This in turn raises the question of whether a dual motive suggests two separate supplies. Even if it does, can this question be looked at solely from the viewpoint of the supplier or does one need also to look at it through the customer's eyes? It is most improbable that Mirror Group thought that it was being paid partly to induce it to enter into the lease and partly for a supply of advertising services that it was making to Canary Wharf. Indeed, the Advocate General (Tizzane) suggested that what needs to be looked at is not motive but rather:

> 'The contract's economic purpose, that is to say, the precise way in which performance satisfies the interests of the parties. In the case of a lease … this consists in the transfer by one party to another of an exclusive right to enjoy immovable property for an agreed period. It goes without saying that this purpose is the same for all the parties to the contract and thus determines its content. On the other hand, it has no connection with the subjective reasons which have led each of the parties to enter into the contract, and which obviously are not evident from its terms.'

17.15 If motive is irrelevant, it may be that it is not possible to have a situation where a reverse premium is both to induce someone to act as anchor tenant and to induce him to enter into the lease. One or the other of these elements must predominate; ie the contract's economic purpose must either be letting of the property or advertising.

The ECJ in *Card Protection Plan (Case C-349/96, 1999 STC 270)* stated that:

> 'First … every supply of services must normally be regarded as distinct and independent and, second, that a supply which comprises a single service from an economic point of view should not be artificially split … the essential features of this transaction must be ascertained in order to determine whether the taxable person is supplying the customer, being a typical consumer, with several distinct principal services or with a single service. There is a single supply in particular in cases where one or more elements are to be regarded, by contrast, as ancillary to a principal service if it does not constitute for customers an aim in itself, but a means of better enjoying the principal service supplies.'

17.16 Can this principle also apply where there are offsetting services, as in the Mirror Group case, ie if Mirror Group was obtaining negative consideration for becoming a tenant and at the same time receiving actual consideration for the advertising service of becoming 'anchor tenant'? Is it necessary to ask whether these comprise a single service from an economic point of view and, if so, which is the principal one? Alternatively, must a split always be made, as part of the receipt relates to a supply by Mirror Group and part does not? It will be interesting to see how the UK courts approach this problem. Furthermore, if an undertaking to be an anchor tenant rather than merely to be a tenant is a separate supply of services, what else can fall into this category? Might agreeing to be the tenant of most of a building be a separate supply? It seems unlikely, yet it is hard to discern any real difference between being an anchor tenant and being the main tenant. It should also be noted that the court did not actually say that such a service is a separate supply, but merely that it 'could be'. Common sense suggests that it will be fairly unusual, except perhaps in relation to shopping centres where the anchor tenant may be important to attract customers to other tenants, for the anchor tenant exception to apply.

In the vast majority of cases, the primary economic purpose will be to let the building.

17.17 The second question is perhaps easier. The crux of the Mirror Group case was the nature of the supply by Mirror Group in consideration of the reverse premium. Leaving aside the anchor tenant point, the ECJ said that Mirror Group did not make a supply at all. The receipt of the reverse premium was part of the 'consideration' that it gave for the supply of the lease to it by the tenant, albeit that it was, in effect, negative consideration. It must follow from this that, if Mirror Group had opted to tax in respect of the building but Olympia and York Canary Wharf Ltd had not done so, VAT would not have been payable on the reverse premium. Olympia and York would not have been a taxable person and Mirror Group would have made no supply. The ECJ was not concerned with the VAT position of the landlord as the appellant was Mirror Group Ltd. It is therefore not surprising that it did not address the dilemma that if there was no supply by the tenant it must follow either that there was no supply at all or that the reverse premium was negative consideration for the supply by the landlord. *Article 13(C)* of the *Sixth Directive* (now *Article 137* of the *Principal Directive*), the *vires* for the option to tax, is not very helpful. It merely states that 'Member States may allow taxpayers a right of option for taxation in cases of (a) letting and leasing of immovable property', which brings us to UK domestic law. *VAT Act 1994, Sch 10, para 2(1)* states that:

> 'where an election under this paragraph has effect in relation to any land, if and to the extent that any grant made in relation to it at a time when the election has effect by the person who made the election … would … fall within *Group 1* of *Schedule 9*, the grant shall not fall within that group'.

17.18 It seems clear that VAT is not charged on consideration; it is charged on supplies and the consideration is merely the value placed on that supply. It seems to follow from this that if the sole supply is the grant of the lease the reverse premium must be an element in valuing that grant. It is accordingly clear that the reverse premium cannot be outside the scope of VAT. Either the reverse premium must be VATable or the value of the supply must be determined under *VATA 1994, s 19(3)*, ie supplies for a consideration not wholly consisting of money. The effect of this might well be that only part of the rent under the lease is VATable as the consideration for the lease would then be the difference between the rent payable over the term of the lease and the reverse premium received. The mind boggles at the problems this would create. Accepting that the reverse premium is itself taxable would afford a pragmatic solution, although taxing part only of the rent would be a more logical, albeit fairly horrific, interpretation of the legislation.

17.19 Unfortunately Mirror Group's victory turned out to be a pyrrhic one. They had agreed at the VAT tribunal that the payment had been in return for acting as anchor tenant. In these circumstances the court refused either to remit the case to the tribunal or to arrive at its own view of the apportionment required. To do either would be to allow Mirror Group an opportunity to reargue a question of fact contrary to the agreed statement of facts which would not be fair bearing in mind that UK law gives no appeal on a question of fact (*Trinity Mirror plc (formerly Mirror Group Newspapers Ltd) v C & E Commrs (2003 STC 518)*).

17.20 HMRC initially took this to mean that the ECJ found in favour of HMRC and that 'the normal commercial reality of such transactions (ie reverse premiums) means that there will be a supply of services where, in return for a payment made to him, a prospective tenant affords the advantage of agreeing to be bound by the obligations that he has to fulfil'. They leapt onto a comment of the Vice Chancellor in the high court that 'the ECJ did not hold, and it does not follow, that the provision by a tenant of advantages to a landlord through the medium of obligations incurred under a tenancy agreement cannot constitute a supply of services by a tenant to a landlord'. That may be so, but it is hard to imagine that the ECJ were seeking to draw a distinction between agreeing to pay the rent under a lease and agreeing to the other tenants' obligations under it. Whilst it is possible for a lease to impose obligations that give a specific benefit to the landlord, in which case such obligations are unlikely to be 'solely to become a tenant', it seems likely that in most cases they will not do so. Fortunately, HMRC subsequently changed their view and now 'accept that lease obligations to which tenants are normally bound do not constitute supplies for which inducement payments on entering leases are consideration'. Accordingly 'the majority of such payments are likely to be outside the scope of VAT as they are no more than inducements to tenants to take leases and to observe the obligations in them. There will be a taxable supply only where a payment is linked to benefits a tenant provides outside normal lease terms'. They gave as examples of taxable cases: carrying out building works to improve the premises, carrying out, fitting out, or refurbishment works for which the landlord has responsibility, and acting as anchor tenant (Business Brief 12/05). Unfortunately, this leaves a prospective tenant who receives a reverse premium in a position of uncertainty. HMRC's published view is that it is not 'normally' taxable. In such circumstances the best approach where the only obligation undertaken is to become a tenant under a standard commercial lease is to take the view that the receipt is not taxable, tell HMRC that one has done so and expect them to raise an assessment which will have to be litigated.

17.21 HMRC have produced a helpful table to determine the tax liability in relation to payments in respect of leases where no option to tax has been exercised (C & E Manual Vol V1-8, 5.15):

(a)	*Surrender*	
	Landlord pays tenant to surrender the existing lease	Exempt supply by the tenant
(b)	*Assignment*	
	Landlord pays tenant to assign the existing lease	Exempt supply by the tenant
(c)	*Reverse surrender*	
	Tenant pays landlord to take back the lease	Exempt supply by the landlord
(d)	*Reverse assignment*	
	Tenant pays third party to take away lease	Standard rated supply by the third party
(e)	*Reverse premium*	
	Landlord pays a prospective tenant to accept	Standard rated supply by the the lease prospective tenant.

Head (*a*) reflects the decision in *Lubbock Fine* (see **17.7**) and head (*c*) that in *Central Capital Corporation* (see **17.8**). Both are now specifically exempted under *VATA 1994, Sch 9, Note 1* (see **17.8**). Head (*b*) is also a specific exemption in *Note 1*. Head (*d*) reflects the decision in *Cantor Fitzgerald* (see **17.9**). It is questionable whether head (*c*) is wholly correct. It reflects the decision in *Mirror Group* (see **17.10** onwards) but, as indicated above, Business Brief 12/05 accepted that in many cases a reverse premium is exempt.

17.22 It also needs to be borne in mind that in *British Eventing Ltd v HMRC (2011 SFTD 18)* (see **17.139**) the First-tier Tribunal held that the assignment of a lease is not a supply of an interest in land at all if the lease has a negative value. This means that the payment cannot be attributed to the lease – which makes it VATable as it must then be consideration for something else. In that case HMRC contended that a reverse premium of £340,000 could not in any event be a cost component of a lease with a value of only £10. The argument that it is not a supply is unconvincing. It depends on a deeming provision (*VATA 1994, Sch 4, para 5*) which applies on a disposal of assets, but such deeming is only necessary where the transaction would not otherwise be a supply, so it seems a circular argument.

Freehold Disposal of New Buildings, etc

17.23 It is important to note that head (*a*) in **17.6** above denies exemption only on the disposal of a freehold interest in a new building. Exemption will still apply to a premium for the grant of a long lease (subject to the operation of the option to tax considered at **17.156** below).

17.24 The reference in (*a*)(i) and (ii) in **17.3** above to a residential building is the author's shorthand not the draftsman's. It means a building designed as a dwelling or number of dwellings or intended for use for a relevant residential purpose or relevant charitable purpose. These expressions have the same meaning as in *Group 8* (see **16.49** and **16.59** above) (*Note 3*).

17.25 It should be noted that VAT is payable on the disposal of a building only if this takes place while the building is 'new', ie within three years of the building being completed (*Notes 4* to *6*). A sale of a non-residential building prior to the time it is completed will always attract VAT.

17.26 A building is to be taken to be completed when either an architect issues a certificate of practical completion in relation to it or it is first fully occupied (*Note 2*). The certificate of practical completion is normally issued when the structural work is finished but fitting-out work still needs to be done. Accordingly the building is not necessarily fit for occupation at that stage. A civil engineering work is completed when either an engineer issues a certificate of practical completion or it is first fully used (*Note 2*). Clearly, the earlier a building is completed the better it is likely to be, so as to start the three-year period running. If no completion certificate is issued it could be many years after completion before the building is fully let, and the three-year period would not start to run until that time. It is therefore important to ensure that the architect or engineer issues a completion certificate at the earliest practical date. It could be argued that it is better for a new building to remain taxable as long as possible to ensure the recoverability of input tax on the construction costs. However, the option to tax rents will enable this to be achieved by way of the grant of a lease to a connected person if the building remains unsold and unlet for longer than three years.

Leisure-Related Activities

17.27 The miscellaneous items that attract tax at 20% are:

(i) the grant of any interest, right or licence consisting of a right to take game or fish except where at the same time the freehold of the land over which its right is exercisable is sold to the same purchaser (see also **17.28**);

(ii) the provision in an hotel, inn, boarding house or similar establishment of sleeping accommodation, etc. or of accommodation in rooms which are provided in conjunction with sleeping accommodation, or which are provided for the purpose of a supply of catering (see also **17.29–17.43**);

(iii) the grant of any interest in, right over or licence to occupy holiday accommodation (see also **17.44**);

(iv) the provision of seasonal pitches for caravans, and the grant of facilities at sites to persons for whom such facilities are provided (see also **17.48**);

(v) the provision of pitches for tents and of camping facilities;

(vi) the grant of facilities for parking a vehicle (see also **17.51**);

(vii) the grant of any right to fell and remove standing timber;

(viii) the grant of facilities for housing an aircraft or mooring a ship (which includes anchoring or berthing – *Note 15*);

(ix) From 1 October 2012, the grant of facilities for the self storage of goods;

(x) the grant of a right to occupy a box, seat or other accommodation at a sports ground, theatre, concert hall or other place of entertainment;

(xi) the grant of facilities to a person who uses them wholly or mainly to supply hairdressing services; and

(xii) the grant of facilities for playing any sport or participating in any physical recreation (subject to the exemption in **17.55**).

17.28 Where the land is leased, head (i) charges VAT on the portion of the rent attributable to the sporting rights if these are 'valuable'(*VATA 1994, Sch 9, Group 1, Note 8*). HMRC take the view that such rights are valuable where their rental value exceeds 10% of the total rent under the lease (Notice 742, para 6.2). The basis for this arbitrary figure is not known. It is probably pragmatism! Part of a premium for the grant of a lease similarly has to be apportioned to the value of sporting rights. It should be borne in mind that the VAT charge would apply not merely to the grant of a lease over, for example, a shooting moor. It can also apply on the grant (or presumably the assignment) of a lease of a farm, if the rights to take game are of significant value. If the grant of an interest in or right over land (or a licence to occupy land) includes a valuable right to take game or fish, the consideration must be apportioned and VAT charged on the gaming or fishing element (*VATA 1994, Sch 9, Group 1, Note 8*). No guidance is given as to what is meant by 'valuable'. The ECJ held in *Walderdorff v Finanzamt Waldviertel (Case C-451/06)* that a right granted to an angling club to fish in two ponds for a period of ten years was not a leasing or letting of immovable property as it did not confer the right to occupy the immovable property concerned and to exclude any other person from it; it merely gave the VATable right to fish from the ponds.

17.29 It is specifically provided that for the purpose of head (ii) a similar establishment includes premises in which there is provided furnished sleeping accommodation, whether with or without the provision of board or facilities for the preparation of food, which are used by or held out as being suitable for use by visitors or travellers (*VATA 1994, 9 Sch, Group 1, Note 9*). In spite of this the tribunal in *International Student House (VTD 14420)* thought that the provision of sleeping accommodation did not necessarily indicate that the premises were similar to a hotel, particularly where the accommodation was not held out for use by visitors or travellers. It considered that a characteristic of a hotel, inn or boarding house was that it was concerned with the business of providing accommodation. The appellant in that case was a charity providing accommodation in London for students of different nationalities with a view to furthering international friendship and co-operation. It had a selective admissions policy which aimed to create a group of resident students from different nationalities. The tribunal regarded these as important factors to distinguish the accommodation from that provided by a hotel. A property supplying accommodation and breakfast for homeless people has been held to be a similar establishment (*Namecourt Ltd (VTD 1560)*), as has accommodation for long-term residents in a guest house (*Mrs R I McGrath, 1992 STC 371*). So has the provision of long-stay accommodation to local authorities to house homeless persons where the accommodation was self-contained apartments in a hotel building with minimal additional services being provided (*Mr & Mrs C Ward, TC 2179*). However, in *Atlas Property London Ltd (TC 3797)* the Tribunal took a different view, although it is not clear if it was referred to these two earlier cases. Atlas owned a number of houses, which it had converted into self-contained units of fairly basic living accommodation for temporarily homeless people which it let to local authorities. The length of stay varied from a few days (although that was not the norm) to up to two years. HMRC calculated an average at eight months. Very few services were provided, basically the minimum to meet the council's and health and safety requirements. The Tribunal noted that the length of stay was highly unusual for a hotel, there were few 'hotel-like' services provided, and the accommodation supplied was very different to that in serviced flats. The level of service in that case, albeit minimal, appears to have been greater than that provided by Mr and Mrs Ward though. *Principal and Fellows of Lady Margaret Hall (TC 4181)* involved a scheme to seek to turn student accommodation into a taxable supply by the use of a separate company to provide the accommodation. The FTT held that the company was acting as an agent for the college. However, if they were wrong, they would have held that the accommodation was not similar to a hotel, etc because the effect of the geographical proximity of the building in which the accommodation is contained is that students are brought together for college life, use of the library, eating and access to on-site academies, which are not features normally found in hotels.

17.30 It was held in *Dinaro Ltd (t/a Fairway Lodge) (VTD 17148)* that a hostel building providing accommodation for vulnerable adults requiring support and supervision was not an establishment similar to a hotel. Having regard to the hostel residents' average length of stay and their need for supervision, the residents could not be regarded as travellers. In *Acorn Management Services Ltd (VTD 17338)*, by contrast, the provision to US universities of accommodation for students and faculty members attending courses in the UK was held to be similar to and in competition with a hotel. The accommodation was paid for in full by the university before the students arrived; the average stay was 15 weeks; cleaning was carried out by contractors once a week and laundry was left to the students. In *Look Ahead Housing and Care Ltd (VTD 17613)* hostels providing short term accommodation for the homeless and rough sleepers were held to be similar to a hotel. HMRC had argued that it was an exempt supply of welfare services. The tribunal were influenced by the fact that the hostel provided 'furnished sleeping accommodation with a supply of catering'. It felt that the transients could properly be described as visitors. The company made a charge for accommodation. It's staff were not trained to provide counselling or medical help and referred people to outside agencies where this was required. A similar decision was reached in *North East Direct Access Ltd (VTD 18267)* which housed homeless single men including especially those suffering from disabilities and addiction. The case was distinguished from *Dinaro Ltd* as there was a lesser degree of care and the residents were not restricted to those needing care.

17.31 In *B J Group (VTD 18234)* the company let out rooms. There was a dispute over the status of 14 rooms let to corporate tenants for use by their staff and guests. The rooms were let at a daily rate. B J Group claimed that the rooms were let on assured shorthold tenancies. It did not provide meals or a bar but had check-in and check-out facilities and provided a maid service to clean the rooms during the week and a laundry service. The rooms had cooking facilities. They were normally occupied only for a few days at a time. The VAT tribunal held that the lettings were of a similar establishment to a hotel even though the head-lease restricted the use of the building to single self-contained flats. Mr & Mrs Holding *(VTD 19573)* make available for occupation by members of the public three rooms in their house plus two further rooms in a bungalow in their garden. They have two long-term lodgers. They do not advertise the accommodation but rely on word of mouth. As a result occupation by transient visitors is sporadic. It was held that they do not operate a boarding house as the long-term visitors only eat with them about once a week so they do not normally provide 'board'. Their establishment is also not similar to a hotel etc, as they do not compete with the hotel sector in the provision of accommodation. This seems a harsh result. The intention was clearly to provide board and lodging, albeit that in the period looked at by the tribunal they had little success in finding customers.

17.32 It will be noted that head (ii) leaves the hiring of meeting rooms in a hotel exempt. In *Simon Packford (VTD 11626)* it was the practice of a hotel to make a charge for the continued use of a function room where a wedding or private party continued into the evening after the reception and meal were finished. The VAT tribunal held that the supply was neither integral nor incidental to the supply of catering as that supply had finished before the paid room hire started. It adjourned the case to allow the taxpayer to produce clear evidence of the purpose for which the room was provided, the inference being that the charge is likely to be exempt. In contrast, the tribunal in the case of *Willerby Manor Hotels Ltd (VTD 16673)* on similar facts, declining to follow *Packford* on the grounds that it had been decided before the CJEC decision in *Card Protection Plan Ltd*. The tribunal held that 'the hire of a function room for an evening reception is a supply ancillary to those of wedding reception facilities and is integral to the reception arrangements: it is a means of better enjoying the principal service supplied'. Accordingly, the company 'had made a composite supply of a standard-rated package of wedding reception facilities, the main ingredient in which was a supply of catering'.

17.33 The room hire was similarly found to be a single composite supply of wedding facilities in *Chewton Glen Hotels Ltd (VTD 20686)*. Indeed the tribunal there held that even where minimal additional services were supplied (so that it is realistic to regard those additional elements as a better means of enjoying the principal service of the room hire) that does not mean that the room hire is an exempt supply. This seems an extraordinary conclusion. The tribunal based it on the *Tempco* (see **17.87**) and *Card Protection Plan* cases. However, it is hard to reconcile it with either. In *Card Protection Plan* the ECJ said it is necessary to identify the essential features of the transaction to determine whether or not a single service is being supplied. In *Tempco* it said that a transaction comprising the letting of immovable property, which is essentially a relatively passive activity, linked simply to the passage of time and not generating any significant value needs to be distinguished from other activities which are either industrial or commercial in nature. Once the essential characteristic is identified as room hire in accordance with *Card Protection Plan* that identification surely puts it into the category of a relatively passive activity; if the ancillary features were sufficient to take the transaction out of being a relatively (not a wholly) passive activity it is hard to see how the essential characteristic could be room hire. It is equally hard to see how room hire of itself can be other than an exempt supply (as it does not fall within the leisure related exceptions). Chewton Glen is licensed for weddings. The room hire for the wedding is often accompanied by the service of drinks in the same room. The tribunal also found that the right to use the room brings with it the opportunity to take photographs in the grounds, the right to use the hotel's toilets and other common areas and limited use of its reception services. If such facilities are enough to transform the simple hire of a room into a taxable supply it is difficult to envisage any circumstances in which room hire can qualify for exemption.

17.34 HMRC's view is that the provision of a package of wedding services (eg use of rooms for a ceremony, wedding breakfast and wedding party) is a single standard-rated supply regardless of whether the catering is supplied by the taxpayer or someone else (Notice 709/3/13, para 4.4). The basis for the last part of this is unclear as it has long been established that HMRC cannot aggregate supplies by two separate people and regard the two as a single supply. However, the decision in *Drumtochty Castle (TC 2111)* does lend support to HMRC's view, as it starts from the premise that the supply of the accommodation is not a supply of an interest in land. Accordingly it is a standard-rated supply in the same way as a supply of catering. The Tribunal in *Willant Trust Ltd (TC 4172)* said that to be exempt, the client must occupy the land in question as if he or she were the owner, and the supplier's involvement must be relatively passive. It held that the client did not occupy as owner as it had to use the caterer and the disco provider nominated by the supplier and the supplier was closely involved in the planning of the wedding so its involvement was not passive.

17.35 HMRC say that where a meeting or other function room is provided under either an eight-hour conference delegate rate (use of conference room plus meals) or a 24-hour conference delegate rate (use of conference room plus meals and overnight sleeping accommodation) the supplies should be treated as separate supplies (so the conference room element will be exempt). This does not apply when the primary purpose is a supply of catering (so a room for a wedding reception would not be exempt) or if the hotel itself organises and runs the conference (Business Brief 1/06). Prior to January 2006 they accepted that an apportionment could be made where the eight-hour rate applied but thought that under a 24-hour rate there was a single supply of the hotel facilities.

17.36 Head (ii) reflects *Article 135* of the *EC VAT Directive* (formerly *Article 13(B)(b)1* of the *EC Sixth Directive*) which excludes from exemption the 'provisions of accommodation, as defined in the laws of the Member States, in the hotel sector or in sectors with a similar function'. In *Blasi v Finanzamt Munchen I (Case C-346/95) (1998 STC 336)* the ECJ stated that while exemptions must be construed strictly, exclusions from them were not to be, and the words 'sectors with a similar function' should be broadly construed. Their purpose is to ensure that the provision of temporary accommodation in competition with the hotel sector is subject to tax. It is likely that 'similar establishment' will similarly be given a wide meaning. Or perhaps not! In *Leez Priory (VTD 18185)* where the priory with its 13 bedrooms was available for hire for weddings it was held not to be similar to a hotel as, although it provided food, drink, accommodation and other hospitable services identically to a hotel, it did not do so for travellers but only for wedding guests. That did not help the taxpayer though, as it was held that the taxpayer was making a taxable supply of wedding functions, not separate supplies of a licence to use the property and other services. A similar decision was reached in *Best Images Ltd (TC 480)*. Mr Bains let out two large elaborately furnished rooms for wedding facilities. He did not provide food, flowers, dancers or music. He occasionally provided beer and soft drinks. He seems to have provided little else other than tables and chairs, although he would attend the wedding 'to introduce proceedings, to defuse any arguments, to deal with illness'. He also, of course, cleaned the building. It was held that 'the supply made was not the passive letting of land within Article 13 of the [Sixth] Directive'. The Tribunal was strongly influenced by the comment of the Advocate General in *Blasi* that the exclusions from exemption 'entail more active exploitation of the immovable property'. The ECJ itself did not endorse this test. *Blasi* was concerned with whether Germany was entitled to define short-term letting of residential property as similar to accommodation in a hotel. The court agreed with the Advocate General that a test of six months as being short-term was reasonable. Furthermore the Directive did not itself refer to 'the passive letting of land'. It referred to 'the provision of accommodation, as defined in the laws of the Member States, in the hotel sector or sectors with a similar function', and the provision of a furnished room without much else bears little relationship to the hotel sector.

17.37 In *Acrylux Ltd v HMRC [2009] UKFTT 223; [2009] SFTD 763)* where the taxpayer let out a house and its grounds for special events, generally for a weekend, on a self-catering basis (with the hirer being responsible for cleaning and tidying up the property at the end of the weekend) with Acrylux doing virtually nothing other than recommending local suppliers to the hirer, the supply was held to be the provision of sleeping accommodation in a similar establishment to a hotel. This was in spite of the fact that the taxpayer simply hired out the house for the hirer to do with it as he wished; he was not required to use any part as sleeping accommodation – although the Tribunal felt that it 'seems to deny the reality of what is one of the main facilities that the appellant offers … it is not just a venue for wedding receptions or parties. It is a venue that offers sleeping accommodation as part of the package and, indeed, as an important part of the package'. It seems to place a very wide interpretation on the words to equate the provision of accommodation with no ancillary services as 'similar to' a hotel. The Tribunal went on to hold that even if they were wrong the hire of the property was the provision of holiday accommodation as the building 'is advertised or held out as suitable for holiday or leisure use'. That also seems to be stretching the wording virtually to breaking point.

17.38 *Drumtochty Castle Ltd (TC 2111)* was hired out for functions, primarily weddings. The customer would pay a facility fee in return for which he obtained exclusive use of the entire castle, including its 11 bedrooms, for an agreed period. The appellant provided cutlery, crockery, glassware and table linen for the wedding breakfast and recommended local caterers, but the client was left to make his own arrangements with the caterers. The appellant would also introduce the client to other third parties, such as the local vicar, photographers, florists and beauty parlours and would itself offer additional services such as horse and carriage hire or extra sleeping accommodation on which it charged VAT. The appellant charged VAT on the part of the facility fee attributable to afternoon tea on the first day and bed and breakfast accommodation. It regarded the rest of the facility fee as being an exempt licence to occupy the castle. HMRC contended that there was a single supply falling within head (ii) above. Alternatively, there was a single supply of a wedding package. The tribunal held that the arrangement did not constitute or include the grant of a licence to occupy the castle and its grounds. They did not give the client the right to exclude others, such as the company or its staff. The company was simply actively exploiting the castle as part of an overall package of supplies, which they described as a wedding package. In *Blue Chip Hotels Ltd (2017 UKUY 0204 TCC)*, the FTT held that the supply on its own of the use of a room licensed for weddings was not a licence to occupy land because the licence itself has a value, so what was being acquired was the right to hold a wedding at the hotel. The UT agreed, but for a different reason. 'The Tamerisk Room had to be a seemly and dignified venue for such proceedings and BCH had to meet the obligations imposed on it by the Approved Premises Regulations, such as making a responsible person available and supervising the use of the room. … That was … a more complicated service than simply making the property available to the customer for a period … By its active exploitation of the Tamerisk Room, BCH added significant value to the supply of the room.'

17.39 Where a supply within head (ii) is made to an individual for a period exceeding four weeks and throughout that period the accommodation is provided for the use of the individual (either alone or together with others who occupy the accommodation with him otherwise than at their own expense (directly or indirectly)) after the first four weeks VAT is chargeable only on the value of the facilities other than the right to occupy the accommodation. The VATable amount must, however, be at least 20% of the total price of the accommodation for that period (*VATA 1994, Sch 6, para 9*). HMRC were for a time by concession prepared to treat a period of accommodation as continuous if the guest left for an occasional weekend or holiday or the guest was a student who left during the vacation but returned to the same accommodation for the following term. This concession was withdrawn from 1 April 2015. After that date such a break starts a new 28-day period and full VAT will have to be paid during that period (Technical Note, 31 January 2014). The *Afro Caribbean Housing Association Ltd (VTD 19450)* had an agreement with the British Refugee Council to provide temporary accommodation to asylum seekers under which it enters into licences with the individuals but is paid by BRC. The tribunal agreed with HMRC that no supply of services was made to the individuals, but held that the supply to BRC was the provision of accommodation to individual asylum seekers. As such it fell within *para 9*.

17.40 Fortified by the *Blasi* decision *Colaingrove Ltd (VTD 16187)*, which operated caravan parks, sought to persuade the VAT tribunal that the exclusion of seasonal pitches from exemption was not authorised by EC law. The tribunal accepted that it was unrealistic to treat the provision of caravan pitches as having a similar function to the hotel sector but noted that some versions of the text indicated that 'accommodation' was intended to have a wider meaning than its normal one of accommodation of persons. In any event the tailpiece of *Article 13B(b)(1)* of the *Sixth Directive*, 'Member States may apply further exclusions to the scope of this exemption', gave the UK a large degree of discretion to limit the scope of the exemption and the exclusion for seasonal caravan pitches was consistent with those for camping sites and car parking sites. The Court of Appeal agreed that the tailpiece gives the UK a wide discretion which validates the exclusion (*Colaingrove Ltd v C & E Commrs, 2004 STC 712*).

17.41 This wide discretion is emphasised by the ECJ decision in *Amengual Far v Amengual Far (Case C-12/98)* to the effect that it allows Member States (in that case Spain) to subject to VAT lettings of immovable property and by way of exception to exempt only lettings of immovable property to be used as dwellings.

17.42 Interestingly head (ii) also seems to leave the supply of timeshare accommodation exempt even though it ought logically to fall into the leisure-related activities category. In *Macdonald Resorts Ltd v HMRC (2011 STC 412) (Case C-270/09)* the ECJ held that the use of such rights constitutes the letting of immovable property. However, both the court and the Advocate General pointed out that a Member State has a discretion (under what is now *Article 135* of the *VAT Directive*) to apply further exclusions to the exemption for the leasing and letting of immovable properties. That case is considered at **16.207**.

17.43 The case of *ND & RC Roden (TCF 2300)* highlights what the FTT described as a 'very nasty VAT trap for an unwary taxpayer'. The Rodens' purchased (primarily for renting out) a long lease of an apartment in a hotel complex with a proviso that they would not let the property other than through the hotel's letting agent. The FTT held that the rents received were VATable as being for use as a hotel etc, but the purchase of the property was for an exempt purpose so the VAT thereon was irrecoverable unless the option to tax was exercised.

17.44 Head (iii) includes the grant of an interest in a dwelling which is excluded from zero-rating under *VATA 1994, Sch 8, Group 5, Note 13* (see **16.119**) because for example the grantee is not entitled to reside in it (or part of it) throughout the year (*VATA 1994, Sch 9, Group 1, Note 11(a)*). It also includes a supply made in pursuance of a tenancy, lease or licence under which the grantee is permitted to erect and occupy holiday accommodation (*Note 11(b)*). It does not, however, include a freehold disposal of a building which is not a new building or the grant of a tenancy, lease or licence which is made for a consideration in the form of a premium (*Note 12*). It is not clear if *Note 12* excludes from tax the rent payable as well as the premium. It seems likely that the intention is merely to exclude the premium.

17.45 It is important to properly identify what is being supplied. Attempts have been made with holiday accommodation to split the transaction into an exempt sale of land and a taxable supply of building work. The attempt succeeded in *Lower Mill Estates* (see **17.122**) where a customer bought a plot and could then decide either to use Lower Mills associated building company or instruct his own builder to erect his holiday chalet. It failed in *Fairway Lakes Ltd v HMRC (2016 UKUT 340)* where they seem to have got the contracts the wrong way round. A customer would instruct Fairway to erect a holiday lodge, which it did from a prefabricated pitch. An associated company would then grant a lease of the land on which the lodge stood to the customer who bought a lodge from Fairway. HMRC cannot normally discern a single transaction where supplies are made by different persons, but in this case they successfully contended that what the customer was buying from Fairway was a (fully VATable) composite supply of the erection of the unit plus an undertaking to procure that the landowner would grant a lease to the customer. The split in *Kings Leisure Ltd (TC 4877)* was also unsuccessful. This related to static caravans. Kings Leisure licensed a site to the customer and an associated company, Autoclassic Ltd, sold the customer a caravan to place on the land. A base was needed between the land and the caravan. This was constructed by Kings Leisure. The customer paid his money wholly to Autoclassic which in turn made a commission payment to Kings Leisure. The issue was whether as part of that payment Kings Leisure had sold the base to Autoclassic so as to create a taxable supply by Kings Leisure so that it could recover the input VAT on the building costs. The FTT held that the only identifiable supply by Kings Leisure to Autoclassic was of the right to sell mobile homes from its site. The construction of the bases was not an input of that supply; it was an input of the exempt letting of the pitch to the eventual customer.

17.46 The rules on holiday accommodation were extended in 1989 to ensure that the provision of accommodation in a tent provided by the site operator is taxable, as well as the granting of a site on which to pitch one's own tent (as previously) – which seems to be somewhat scraping the barrel on broadening the tax base! A houseboat includes a residential houseboat (*Note 10*). In *Mrs D G Everett (VTD 11736)* HMRC adopted the stance that, if a houseboat is capable of self-propulsion, it is designed or adapted for use for recreation or pleasure, but this was rejected by the tribunal, which held that the phrase does not embrace a home. It must be remembered that holiday accommodation includes any accommodation advertised or held out as such or, after 1 February

1991, as suitable for holiday or leisure use (*Note 13*). Much residential property in London has been held out as such in recent years in an attempt to thwart the *Rent Acts*. Such a device is unlikely to be successful and creates an unnecessary VAT liability. In *Poole Borough Council (VTD 7180)* it was held that 'accommodation' in this context is not confined to living accommodation and that a licence to use a beach hut which provided that the hut was not to be used for living accommodation, but for pleasure only, was standard-rated as the hut was capable of being used for cooking, eating, shelter, changing clothes, etc. and thus 'accommodated' the typical requirements of holiday makers. The letting or sale of a new chalet situated at a holiday or leisure park is standard-rated irrespective of whether it is advertised as holiday accommodation and its occupation during winter months was prohibited by the planning authority. This provision has, however, been held to breach the *EC VAT Directive* where in reality the accommodation was a long-term residence (see **16.119** above). The freehold sale or the receipt of a premium (but not the rent) for the lease of such a building which is not new – presumably within the definition in **17.25** above although the Order does not say so – remains exempt.

17.47 It should not be overlooked that for VAT to be payable, a person has to be a taxable person. This is well illustrated by the CJEC case of *Slaby v Minister Finansow (Case C 180/10) (2011 STC 2230)*. Mr Slaby bought agricultural land in 1996 intending to farm it. He did so and accounted for Polish VAT under the agricultural flat rate scheme. In 1997 the land was redesignated for holiday home development. Mr Slaby carved up the land into 64 plots and began to sell them from 2000 onwards. The court held that VAT was not payable if Mr Slaby sold the land in his private capacity but would be payable if he sold in a business capacity. It emphasised that the change in status was beyond Mr Slaby's control. It said that taking active steps for the purpose of concluding the sales would be indicative of a business. It is not clear on what basis Poland sought to tax the sales. A sale of land is exempt under the VAT Directive. It seems to stretch the legislation unduly to contend that a sale of land zoned as holiday accommodation amounts to the (taxable) provision of such accommodation.

17.48 The granting of facilities for camping in caravans has always been taxable and the wording also makes clear that the provision of seasonal pitches for caravans and the grant of facilities by a third party at a site where the pitch is licensed from someone else are taxable. From 1 March 2012, a seasonal pitch is defined as a pitch on a holiday site or a non-residential pitch on any other site. There is an exception for an employee pitch, namely a pitch on a holiday site occupied by an employee of the site operator as that person's principal place of residence during the period of occupancy, eg a caretaker's caravan. A holiday site is a site (or part of a site) which is operated as a holiday or leisure site. A non-residential pitch is a pitch which is provided for less than a year or provided for a longer period and is subject to an occupation restriction and which (in either case) is not intended to be used as the occupant's principal place of residence during the period of occupancy. An occupation restriction is a covenant, statutory planning consent or similar permission, the terms of which prevent the person to whom the pitch is provided from occupying it by living in a caravan at all times throughout the period for which it is provided (*Notes 14, 14A* as substituted by the *VAT (Land Exemption) Order 2012, SI 2012 No 58*). Prior to that date the non-residential pitch exclusion was for a seasonal pitch namely a pitch which was provided for a period of less than a year, or which although provided for a longer period could not legally be occupied by living there in a caravan throughout the period (such as where planning consent limits use of a site to the summer months) (*Note 14* as originally enacted).

17.49 In *Ticklock Ltd (TC 573)* the planning consent provided that the site could be used 'as a holiday park only'. Accordingly the agreement with purchasers of caravans contained a provision that 'under no circumstances shall the chalet be used as a main residence but shall only be occupied for holiday and recreational purposes'. The Tribunal construed this wording as clearly restricting permanent occupancy and held that the lease related to a seasonal pitch. It is hard to follow this. The owner was entitled to occupy his caravan for recreational purposes for 365 days in the year. If he lived relatively nearby but, for example, liked to swim in the sea, he could use his chalet every day without it becoming his main residence. By concession, 'where a site owner can distinguish the utilities – electricity, gas and water – going to the caravans from those which are being used elsewhere on the site for swimming pools and so on, if he divides the amount by the number of caravans and designates it separately in his bills to those caravans, no VAT will be charged on the utility charges, or on the rates for the current year' (Hansard, Standing Committee G, 16 May 1989, Cols 96–97). In *Tallington Lakes Ltd (VTD 19972)* the company let out pitches on terms that 'in accordance with the planning permission no mobile home shall be occupied during the month of February' but the lease specifically permitted the caravan to be occupied as a private residence. The tribunal held as a fact that at no time had the local authority sought to enforce the February exclusion and that it was too late for them to take enforcement action. They also found that a large number of occupiers in fact occupied their caravans throughout the year as their residences. Accordingly, the planning condition led lapsed, so the pitches were not seasonal pitches and qualified for exemption. The High Court held that the tribunal had misconstrued the planning law and that the restriction was still enforceable at the time of the case so standard-rates applies (*2008 STC 2734*).

17.50 By concession HMRC allowed a site owner to treat the recharge of business rates as outside the scope of VAT. They also allowed the zero-rating of water and sewerage charges where actual consumption could not be identified. Both concessions were withdrawn from 1 January 2012. Zero-rating continues to apply if actual consumption can be identified, such as through metering (HMRC Technical Note 14.12.2010).

17.51 The VAT charge on the grant of facilities for parking a vehicle applies not only to the operation of a car park but, in HMRC's view, also on the lease of lock-up garages separate from a residence. The validity of a similar provision of Danish law under the *Sixth Directive* was upheld by the European Court of Justice in *Skatteministeriet v Henriksen (1990 STC 768)* subject to the caveat that if the letting of a garage is 'closely linked' with the letting of residential property 'so that the two lettings constitute a single economic transaction', the letting of the garage is exempt. HMRC have sometimes in the past allowed exemption only if the two lettings are contained in a single lease, but the ruling of the European Court seems to go wider than that. A different tribunal reached the same decision in *Barry Hopcraft (VTD 18590)*. Vehicle for this purpose must be interpreted as covering all means of transport, including boats *(Fonden Marselisborg Lystbadehavn v Skatteministeriet (Case C-428/02; 2006 STC 1467)*.

17.52 Care may need to be taken with nomenclature. *K T Routledge (VTD 18395)* had a piece of land in Leicester which he used to run a basketball club. Between the club and Leicester FC was a piece of land which Mr Routledge licensed to the football club on match days. It had once been a car park but now was rough concrete and suitable only to provide clear access to the football stadium for fans and emergency vehicles. It had not been used as a car park since the 1970s and the lease of the land to Mr Routledge did not permit it to be used as a car park; nor did his lease to the football club. None of this prevented HMRC contending that Mr Routledge had leased facilities for parking vehicles, apparently primarily on the grounds that the land was identified 'as The Granby Hall car park', its old 1970s use. Fortunately the Tribunal found that it was no longer a car park.

17.53 In *C & E Commrs v Trinity Factoring Services Ltd (1994 STC 504)* the company asked tenants whether they wished to use the garage for parking a vehicle – in which case they charged VAT – or for storage – in which case they did not. It was held that the purpose of the letting had to be determined by the terms of the lease and where a lease of a garage was silent it was a necessary implication that a grant of facilities for parking a vehicle had been made. In *G W and J A Green (VTD 9016)* the taxpayers jointly invested in lock-up garages with the aid of borrowings serviced out of rental income. They contended that they were not letting the garages in furtherance of any business. The VAT tribunal held that the activities had the characteristics of a business and that VAT was payable. It also rejected a claim that each of the taxpayers was separately registrable. The supplies were made by them as joint owners and there was no basis for dividing the value of the supplies between them. They were therefore registrable jointly. The use of land for storage of caravans on a short-term basis was held to be the grant of facilities for parking a vehicle in *A C Slot (VTD 15076)* on the basis that, although the principal purpose of a caravan might be to provide accommodation, a caravan designed to be towed on roads was a vehicle. In *A & A Newall (VTD 18074)* caravans were stored long term and moved only when the owners took a vacation. Indeed some of the caravans had had their wheels removed. This was nevertheless regarded as parking a vehicle.

17.54 The charge can even apply to a simple sale of land. In *C & E Commrs v Venuebest Ltd (2003 STC 433)* the company let a vacant site to a partnership. There was no restriction on what the partnership did with the land. Venuebest had previously used the land in its business of car hire. The partnership used it for a pay and display car parking business. It was held that the nature of the land pointed to its likely use being for car parking and as such use was not prohibited under the lease there was a 'plain implication' that it was being let to be used as a car park so the transaction was the grant of facilities for parking a vehicle; it did not matter that the people who would ultimately use the land for that purpose (the customers of the partnership) were not the people to whom the grant was made.

17.55 Vehicle Control Services Ltd (VCS) (*Vehicle Control Services Ltd v HMRC, 2013 STC 892*) sought to avoid VAT by turning excess parking charges into damages for trespass. The company operated car parks on behalf of owners. Its contract with the landowner entitled it to retain all parking enforcement charges. The FTT held that the company had no contractual relationship with people who used the car park, so the fees were derived from its contract with the landlord. Although it is possible to bring an action for trespass without having exclusive occupation of the land, occupation is essential; a mere right of access, which is what the company had, is not enough. The Court of Appeal disagreed. It said that the company had power to enter into a contract with the motorist because the landowner had allowed it to. It had offered the motorist use of a parking space subject to complying with specified conditions. Accordingly the money VCS collected from motorists for breach of those conditions was not consideration arising from the landowner. Furthermore VCS's agreement with the landowner gave it the right to evict trespassers, so there was no impediment to the parking charge being damages for trespass. HMRC then challenged the deduction of input tax. They argued that the expenditure had to be apportioned between taxable and out-of-the-scope supplies in the same way as with taxable and exempt supplies (*Vehicle Control Services Ltd v HMRC, 2017 STC 11*).

17.56 Curiously, although the lease of a car park is the grant of facilities for parking a vehicle it appears that the lease of a hotel is not the provision of sleeping accommodation etc. At least that is what the VAT tribunal decided in *Asington Ltd (VTD 18171)*. Asington leased seven furnished flats to a company,

TCP, which let them to its customers as furnished sleeping accommodation. The tribunal agreed that the provision by TCP was use as an establishment similar to a hotel but held that Asington's supply to TCP was the exempt supply of an interest in land.

17.57 A grant of 'facilities for the self-storage' of goods is excluded from **17.27**(ix) if either:

(*a*) the person making the grant is connected (within *CTA 2010, s 1122*) with any person who uses the 'relevant structure' for the self storage of goods and makes the grant in circumstances where the 'relevant structure' used is, or forms part of, a capital item (one within the capital goods scheme – see **17.205** – where the adjustment period has not come to an end);

(*b*) the grant is made to a charity and it does not use the relevant structure (in whole or in part) in the course of a business; or

(*c*) if the relevant structure is part of a building, its use for the storage of goods is by the person or persons to whom the grant is made and is ancillary to his use of the building for other purposes.

(*VATA 1994, Sch 9, Group 1, Notes 15C, 15E, 19,* inserted by *FA 2012, Sch 26, para 5(5).*) A facility for the self-storage of goods means the use of a relevant structure for the storage of goods by the person (or persons) to whom the grant of facilities is made (*Note 15A*). Live animals are not goods for this purpose (*Note 15A*). Use by a person with the permission of the person to whom the grant is made is treated as use by that grantee (*Note 15B*). A relevant structure means a container or other structure that is fully enclosed, or a unit or building (*Note 15D*).

17.58 The fact that self-storage is brought within the scope of VAT suggests that ordinarily storage is the grant of a licence over land. The CJEU had to consider this in *Minister Finansow v R R Donnelley Global Turnkey Solutions Poland sp 200 (C-155/12) (2014 STC 131)*. The company stored goods in Poland for non-Polish traders. The service was described by the court as a complex one. It involved the admission of goods to a warehouse, placing them on shelves, storing the goods, packaging them, issuing them, unloading and loading them and, in some cases, repackaging them into individual sets. The court said that the storage of goods must, in principle, be considered to constitute the principal supply, and the reception, placement, issuing, unloading and loading of the goods amounted to only ancillary supplies. However, repackaging is an independent principal supply. Where the transaction is a single supply of storage, it comes within Art 47 of the VAT Directive (place of supply of services connected with immovable property) only if the recipients of the service are given a right to use all or part of expressly specific immovable property. If the recipients have no right of access to the part of the property where their goods are stored (or that immovable property does not constitute a central and essential element of the supply of services) it is not a service connected with land, so the place of supply would be the place where the recipient is established, not the location of the warehouse.

17.59 The grant of facilities for sport or recreation (item xi) is exempt if the grant of the facilities is for either:

(*a*) a continuous period exceeding 24 hours; or

(*b*) a series of ten or more periods where:

- (i) each period is in respect of the same activity carried on at the same place;
- (ii) the interval between each period is at least a day but under 15 days;
- (iii) consideration is payable by reference to the whole series and is evidenced by a written agreement;
- (iv) the grantee has exclusive use of the facilities; and
- (v) the grantee is a school, a club, an association or an organisation representing affiliated clubs or constituent associations.

(*VATA 1994, Sch 9, Group 1, Note 16.*)

17.60 Head (*b*) will cover for example the regular use of a football pitch by a club once a week or once a fortnight for its home games or licensing a school to use a swimming pool once a week. It should, however, be noted that the use must not only be regular but also exclusive. Note 16 was considered by the VAT Tribunal in *Polo Farm Sports Club (VTD 20105)*. This related to the grant of a long term licence to use hockey pitches between 8.00am and 9.30pm each day. The planning consent prohibited the use of floodlights after 9.30pm and in addition the club did not want its pitches used after that time because it was in a residential area. The taxpayer thought that the supply was taxable, but HMRC considered it exempt. At issue was item (*a*) and (*b*)(ii) above. The tribunal held that the use was not continuous within (*a*). The tribunal could not work out a rational basis for the two conditions which seem anomalous. It was therefore thrown back on the wording used and held that (*b*)(ii) did not apply as the interval between each period was 10½ hours. This is itself an anomalous result as a long term licence is clearly the sort of thing that ought to be exempt. In *Goals Soccer Centres plc (TC 2253)* the taxpayer let soccer pitches to a team but also separately offered them an opportunity to participate in a league. HMRC contended that this was a single supply of participation in a football competition and in a sports league. The FTT pointed out that the two supplies could be used separately, eg the team could leave the league but continue to hire the pitch, and felt it inappropriate to treat the two as a single supply.

17.61 In *Threshfield Motors Ltd (VTD 16699)* the company argued that it did not provide mooring facilities but only granted a licence to occupy bare land which would become a mooring facility only if the licensee installed mooring equipment such as pontoons, ropes, chairs and gangways. The VAT tribunal held that it was still providing mooring facilities.

17.62 Head (xii) (facilities to supply hairdressing services) does not apply to a grant of facilities which provides for the exclusive use by the grantee of a whole building, a whole floor, a separate room or a clearly defined area, unless the person making the grant (or a connected person of his within *CTA 2010, s 1122*) provides or makes available (directly or indirectly) 'services related to hairdressing' for use by the grantee (*VATA 1994, Sch 9, Group 1, Notes 17, 19*). For this purpose, services related to hairdressing means the services (either solely or shared) of a hairdresser's assistant or cashier, the booking of appointments, the laundering of towels, the cleaning of facilities subject to the grant, the making of refreshments and other similar services typically used in connection with hairdressing, but does not include the provision of utilities or the cleaning of shared areas in a building (*Note 18*). It is unclear whether services related to hairdressing require the provision of more than one item on this list or if a single service will suffice. If a store licenses a hairdressing chain to operate a concession in-store on part of a floor, it is likely that the cleaning of the space occupied by the concession (which is not a 'shared area') will be included in the licence as it would be unrealistic to expect the licensee to provide a separate cleaner for its part of the floor. So, if 'services' can be construed in the singular, that would undermine the exception for the exclusiveness of a clearly defined area.

17.63 The anti-forestalling rule described at **9.22** applies to the grant of facilities for the self-storage of goods and the grant of a right to receive such a supply (*FA 2012, Sch 27, para 3(1)*). In applying that rule, the grant of a right to receive such a supply is linked to the post-change period if (and to the extent that) the services to which the grant relates are carried out or provided after 30 September 2012 (*FA 2012, Sch 27, para 4(3)*).

What is a Licence to Occupy?

17.64 HMRC draw a distinction between an exempt licence to occupy land and a taxable licence to do something that involves coming on to land. Thus a licence to allow someone to enter a field to see the view is not a licence to occupy land. It is a taxable supply. Examples of grants that HMRC consider to be exempt are a licence to occupy a particular room or office, the grant of a trading franchise inside particular premises, the grant of a catering or trading concession within specific premises, and the grant of permission to erect and maintain advertising hoardings on specific sites (C & E Notice 742, para 2.6). The provision of stand space at a UK exhibition is normally exempt (but see **17.90**).

17.65 In *International Trade and Exhibitions J/V Ltd (VTD 14212)*, where the ground space which the stand would occupy was not ascertained when the contract was entered into, the tribunal held that what was being provided to the exhibitor was advertising services, not the right to occupy the stand. HMRC have said that they accept this decision in the specific circumstances of this case but still consider that there is an exempt supply if both parties agree a specified site for the stand (Business Brief 24/96). In a later case, *Miller Freeman World-wide plc (VTD 15452)* the tribunal accepted this view that what had been supplied was a licence to occupy land. The use of tables by dealers at an antiques fair (*Mrs W B Enever (VTD 1537)*); a non-exclusive grazing licence (*J A King (1980 VATTR 60) (VTD 933)*); payments by taxi drivers for the use of a rest room (*Ferris and Budd t/a Z Cars (VTD 412)*); payments by driving instructors for non-exclusive use of an office at a driving *school (C W and J A Garner (VTD 1476)*); and the use by a hairdresser of a non-specific chair in a salon (*N and J Price (VTD 1443)*) are examples of things that have been found by VAT tribunals to fall into the second category and thus be taxable. In *International Antiques Collectors Fairs Ltd (2016 SFTD 979)*, the Tribunal held that the fact that the landlord retained a right of access did not prevent the agreement being a licence to occupy, as, applying *Belgium v Temco Europe SA (2005 STC 1451)* (see **17.88**), the right to use the premises for a specific purpose gave the company exclusive possession of the land for that purpose. However, that did not help the taxpayer as its supply to an exhibitor was not a licence to occupy but a supply of participation as a seller at an expertly organised and expertly run antiques and collectors fair. Mention should also be made of RCC Brief 22/12, which states that HMRC regards the supply of specific stand space at an exhibition or conference as a supply of land 'where the service is restricted to the mere supply of space without any accompanying services'. However, where stand space is provided with accompanying services as a package, this package (stand and services) will no longer be seen as a supply of land with land-related services but will be taxed under the general place of supply rule 'when supplied to business customers'.

17.66 Hairdressing salons were fraught with difficulty and gave rise to a great deal of litigation. HMRC's view was: 'Where, under a written agreement, stylists are able to conduct their entire business from a designated area of the premises, such as a separate room or a partitioned area, there is likely to be an exempt supply of a licence to occupy land. However, with the exception of some barber's shops, in practice it is unusual for stylists to conduct their business restricted to a particular area of a salon, especially if it is open plan. Commonly, in providing a full hairdressing service to clients (the stylist's business) basins, hairdryers, storeroom and reception facilities will be used which are outside of the designated area, even if that is itself clearly defined. In such cases, we see any taxable supply of the general right of the facilities of the salon as a whole' (C & E Manual V & V1-8, para 5.14). Most of the decided cases reflect this view. Eventually HMRC got tired of litigating the position repeatedly and *FA 2012, Sch 26, para 5(6)* introduced a new Note 17 to, *Sch 9, Group 1* from 1 October 2012 (see **17.62**). The previous cases are still of interest for what they say about licences, In *William Walker t/a Ziska (VTD 11825)* where a self-employed hair stylist entered into two agreements with a salon owner, one licensing her the exclusive use of two chairs in the salon and the other providing her with various services. The tribunal held that the reality of the arrangement was that the stylist obtained the right to carry on business using the general facilities of the salon so that, despite the separate agreements, her right to exclusive occupation of the chairs was a mere incident of the supply of business facilities and this attracted VAT. The same approach was taken by the tribunal in *Anthony Winder t/a Anthony & Patricia (VTD 11784)* and *Simon Harris Hair Design Ltd (VTD 13939)*. Following the latter case, HMRC told their local offices to assess VAT where it is clear that stylists working in open-plan salons are using the facilities of the premises as a whole (Business Brief 13/96). In the later case of *Herbert of Liverpool (Hair Design) Ltd (VTD 15949)*, the tribunal expressed the view that 'the provision of a reception area, juniors, gowns for customers, a provision for laundry and the sale of products would be sufficiently dissociable from a hairdressing business as to allow the licence to occupy land to stand alone and therefore be treated as an exempt supply'. Unfortunately for the company, its licence covered only a chair and mirror. The tribunal felt that without a specific licence to use a specific washbasin it would not be possible to carry on the business of hairdressing. As the supply of a washbasin is not dissociable from the supply of the chair and mirror, the use of the chair and mirror was subsumed into the hairdressing business in the general area of the salon. The decision may give a pointer as to the sort of agreement that is needed to establish the licence as exempt. In *Quinto & Marcello Olivieri (VTD 16991)* the partnership provided very little to the stylists other than the right to use the chair. Nevertheless the tribunal held that licence of the chair was not an end in itself but was ancillary to the principal supply that it identified as 'the general right to carry on business at Quinto & Mario's salon and to make use of its business facilities'. The appeal in *Mr & Mrs Broadley (t/a Professional Haircare) (VTD 16643)* was similarly dismissed on the basis that there 'was a single supply of the right to carry on a hairdressing business and the use of a designated area in the salon was an integral part of that supply'. A similar decision was reached in *D R Kirkman (VTD 17651)* albeit with hesitation. The tribunal there commented, 'the exemption for a licence to occupy land ... must be interpreted strictly ... there must clearly be circumstances where areas within properties can amount to a licence to occupy land. In the present case we consider that the tenancy agreement could have achieved that objective if it had been correctly drafted'. They later said 'we would add that it would be easier for an owner of the entire building to establish that there were two supplies [ie of a licence and separate services] if that owner was not himself carrying on the business with the stylists.

17.67 The cases show that there are very few circumstances where a licence to occupy land will be established'. Indeed in *W E Mallinson & M Woodridge t/a The Hair Team (VTD 19087)* the tribunal said that 'we do not doubt that, if the circumstances were right, the Appellants could grant to the stylists licences for the exclusive occupation of areas in their salons … but it seems to us to be beside the point. The Appellant's argument depends upon us accepting that, even with such a licence, the stylists could realistically be regarded as carrying on the business of hairdressing within the space … allocated to them. In our view, the answer to that question is plainly no'. To add insult to injury the tribunal also expressed the view that even though they had earlier been told by Customs that they were accounting correctly for VAT, the Appellants were not entitled to rely on that advice indefinitely, as there is an obligation on every citizen to keep himself advised of the current state of the law. Most of the other cases follow the single supply line. It is sometimes thought that the use of the guidelines drawn up by the National Hairdressers Federation in 1992 will avoid the problem. This is not the case. These guidelines were aimed at ensuring that the supply is by the stylist not by the salon owner. They do not deal with chair rentals; indeed HMRC view is that the use of these guidelines establish a single taxable supply. There was held to be an exempt licence to occupy in *The executors of M J Taylor (VTD 20323)*. However, the facts there were unusual and HMRC chose to offer no evidence. They relied virtually solely on the fact that the NHF Contractor Licence had been used. The tribunal held that this could not displace the reality of the situation. This was that they had licensed the entire premises jointly to two stylists. The fact that Mr & Mrs Taylor paid the utility fees, water and business rates, maintenance and repairs and laundry bills did not detract from this. The arrangement was in essence a furnished letting.

17.68 Very few appeals in this area reach the High Court. This is probably because it is primarily a question of fact. One case that did was *Byrom, Kane & Kane t/a Salon 24 v HMRC (2006 STC 992)*. This concerned a massage parlour. The Court upheld the decision of the tribunal that what was being supplied was a package which could be identified as a supply of massage parlour services; the other services were not merely ancillary to a licence to the masseuse to occupy a room (which was rented to a masseuse on a daily basis). Another is *HMRC v Bryce (trading as The Barn) (2011 STC 903)*. Mrs Bryce provided children's parties in a large hall referred to as 'the play barn'. A parent who wished to hold a party would be given exclusive use of the play barn for a period and would be provided with refreshments in an adjacent café area. The play barn contained a variety of equipment which the hirer was free to use but rarely did, as it was aimed at young children (the play barn hosted activity play for under 5's during the week) whereas the parties were mainly attended by older children. A member of Mrs Bryce's staff was also on hand to ensure that the parties ran smoothly. If a parent wanted a party entertainer he had to organise this himself. Before the First-tier Tribunal Mrs Bryce claimed that she made a single supply of a licence to occupy the play barn. HMRC contented that the use of the space was merely ancillary to the supply of a children's party. The First-tier Tribunal held that neither was right. There were two supplies, the exempt use of the play barn and a taxable supply of catering. The Upper Tribunal disagreed. It held that there was a single taxable supply. It did not attempt to define what that supply was, but felt that the fact that the customer did not pay a flat fee for rental of the barn but was charged for a play party on the basis of a fee per child – so if he paid for 20 children, could not bring 25 – was wholly inconsistent with a right to occupy 'as if that person was the owner'.

17.69 The supply in question in *Finnamore v HMRC (2011 SFTD 551)* was self-storage facilities. Mr Finnamore provided such facilities in transport containers which were located on open land which he owned. He had 184 such containers. They were of metal construction with metal doors at one end which can be secured with a padlock. The site was laid out so that there is vehicular access to each container. The site was fenced in and had security gates which are locked at night. A customer had unrestricted access to his container during business hours and could access it at other times by arrangement with Mr Finnamore's on-site security team. Mr Finnamore was held to have granted licences to occupy land. The fact that the containers were moveable (albeit only with lifting gear) was irrelevant, as the right to use the container was parasitic on the right to occupy the land on which it stood. A similar result was reached in *UK Storage Co (SW) Ltd v HMRC (2011 SFTD 1233)*. Both decisions were reversed on appeal. Both the Upper Tribunal in *Finnamore (2014 UKUT 336 (TCC))* and that in *UK Storage (2012 UKUT 359 (TCC))* said that it was clear that the storage units are not immovable property on the basis of the ECJ decision in *Maierhofer v Finanzamt Augsburg-Land (C-315/00) (2003 STC 564)* (see **16.112**). Accordingly the question is what is the single composite supply of the land plus the storage unit? Both Tribunals held that this was the provision of storage facilities, not a licence to occupy land. These two decisions have been overtaken by events (see **17.57**). In *Sibcas Ltd (2017 UKUT 298(TCC))*, modular temporary accommodation for a school was held by the FTT not to be fixed to the land but the UT disagreed. It felt the FTT's focus should have been on the building as a whole, not on individual units, as the temporary school was a single integrated building, both physically and functionally. It ought to then have 'looked objectively at the building's relationship with the ground. That should have involved taking a holistic view, looking cumulatively at all of the links between the building and the ground, and whether the building could be easily moved or easily dismantled and moved'. On a proper application of the law to the facts, the only reasonable conclusion is that the building was fixed to or in the ground. It had substantial foundations which were sunk into the ground. It was held very firmly in position on these foundations by the very large compressive force which it exerted on them. It was connected to services that run through the ground. The building could not feasibly be moved without being dismantled and it could not easily be dismantled and moved. Curiously, the units (temporary classrooms) had previously been supplied to a different customer so had actually been moved.

17.70 In *HMRC v Denyer (2008 STC 633)*, a hairdressing case, the tribunal accepted that Mr Denyer had created exempt interests in land in return for his chair rentals and went on to hold that heat, light, water, use of telephone, laundering of towels and supplies of consumables were ancillary to the licence to occupy so that there was one single exempt supply. The facts in that case form a template of how to set up chair rental arrangements, albeit that Briggs J disagreed with the tribunal. He rejected HMRC's claim that the grant of an exclusive right to use a particular chair within the salon and the area immediately surrounding it was inherently incapable, viewed separately from the rest of the package of rights of which it formed an important part, of constituting the letting of immovable property. However, he thought that in Mr Denyer's case the tribunal had made a basic error in leaving out of account the shared use of washbasins and the waiting area in its analysis of the rights conferred by that package. 'Looked at in the round, the package in this case was the supply to the stylist of all the facilities requisite for the carrying on by him or her of the business of a hairdresser, including importantly the provision of an exclusive chair and allocated area, but including significantly also the facilities shared in common within the salon as a whole. It is one of those cases, expressly contemplated by Warren J in *Salon 24* (see **17.68**), where the correct VAT classification of the package as a whole is not to be derived from the identification of one, or even the most important of its elements'.

17.71 The arguments may have been brought to a close, at least as far as hairdressers' chairs are concerned, by the judgment of Blackburne J in the conjoined cases of *Holland (t/a The Studios Hair Co) v HMRC and Vigdor Ltd v HMRC (2009 STC 150)*. He did not spend much time on whether or not there was a licence to occupy. Instead he concentrated on the single or multiple supply question, noting that in *Levob Verzekermagen BV v Staatssecretaris van Financien (Case C-41/04; 2006 STC 766)* the ECJ had posed the test whether the elements or acts supplied 'are so closely linked that they form, objectively, a single indivisible economic supply which it would be artificial to split'. Oddly, for an interpretation of an EU law, he dismissed fairly brusquely the argument that 'instances of a single supply comprising a number of elements which it would be artificial to split may be extremely rare in mainland Europe' on the basis that, 'that does not mean that I should approach a supply containing several elements with a predisposition to conclude that it is a series of separate supplies'. He also felt himself bound by the analysis of Warren J in *Salon 24* (see **17.68**). It is unclear how important this decision is likely to be as Blackburne J was upholding the decision of the tribunal in both cases, so needed to do no more than hold that it had not misdirected itself. In *Holland* the tribunal identified the single supply as 'the services of a hairdressing business' and in *Vigdor* as 'salon facilities'. The fact that two different tribunals should find different labels for essentially the same thing shows how difficult this single supply concept can be to apply. In relation to the licence to occupy question, Blackburne J commented, 'the essence of the matter, as it seems to me, is that … the exemption (which is to be strictly interpreted) does not extend to a licence to occupy land which is but one element of a package of supplies made by the taxpayer/lessor to his customer in consideration of a payment or payments by that customer where the supplies in question are commercial in nature or are best understood as the provision of a service and not simply that making available of property'. However, this seems to go no further than saying where one has identified a single supply consisting of a package of elements, that package cannot be labelled a licence to occupy. He also pointed out that the judgement of Briggs J in Denyer 'demonstrates why hairdressers' arrangements such as those arising on these appeals cannot properly be characterised as the letting of immovable property. He also noted that 'Taylor … is the only tribunal decision which … went the other way but said that the position in that case was significantly different. It is difficult to reconcile this line of UK cases with the recent ECJ decision in *RLRE Tellmer Property sro* (see **16.181**). HMRC have eventually resorted to legislation to correct what they call the anomaly that it is possible for a licence to be granted over part of a hairdressing salon. From 1 October 2012 the grant of facilities which the grantee uses to supply hairdressing services is specifically taxable at 20% (see **17.27**(ix)). *Article 135* of the Principal *VAT Directive* permits a Member State to restrict the scope of the exemption for the grant of an interest in land, so this is probably consistent with EU law.

17.72 There is a growing number of cases on a similar theme in relation to adult entertainment clubs. Of particular interest is the FTT decision in *Dazmonda Ltd (TC 3473).* The club was on two floors. The club is on the second floor. The ground floor contains a number of small booths, each with a small sofa. They are dimly lit. The music playing in the upstairs area also plays downstairs. Each booth has a curtain that can be drawn across its entrance. The ground floor also contains lavatories and a make-up room and lockers for the dancers. There is CCTV in each booth, linked to the club's office upstairs. A dancer books a booth for anything between five minutes and several hours. She is given total control of the booth and told she can exclude anyone from it (although such use would be terminated immediately if the booth was used for drug-taking or other illegal purposes). The principal source of dancer's income was from private dances in the booths. A dancer paid a commission of 25% on income from private dances to use the booth. Eighty per cent of dancers would pre-book a booth, then not find a customer at the club (although the Tribunal had doubts about the evidence of this). It was held that even though many did not use the upstairs dance floor, the dancer received the right to use it, the benefit of music, lighting, heating and cleaning, the benefit of the security and management oversight provided by the club, the benefit of the club's advertising and, if required, an escort to her car at the end of the evening's work, in addition to the right to use the booth. This was a composite supply of facilities, not a supply of land. The Tribunal did say that without the other elements, they would have regarded use of the booth as a supply of land, even though the time for which it was used was short and not specified in advance as a number of hours or days or weeks.

17.73 An alternative method succeeded in *Catherine Hunter, Arlene Kiernan, Martine Wigglesworth and Lesley Ann Wright (t/a Blues Hairshop) (VTD 16558)*. The four individuals jointly leased the salon in which each had her own workstation. They shared many of the expenses but not their income. HMRC contended that this amounted to a partnership but this was rejected by the tribunal. This arrangement does not involve a licence at all as the individuals were joint owners of the interest in land.

17.74 HMRC's contention that a licence must be exclusive to constitute an interest in land was successfully challenged in *Abbotsley Golf and Squash Club Ltd (VTD 15042)*. The company granted a non-exclusive licence to Abbotsley Country Club Ltd of the occupation of its golf course. HMRC claimed that the agreement was not a licence over land but merely a contractual right for the Club's members to play golf on Abbotsley's land. The taxpayer drew to the tribunal's attention the decision of the House of Lords in *Street v Mountford (1985 1 AC 809)*, a landlord and tenant case, which held that an exclusive licence was normally a lease, claiming that exclusivity therefore could not be the test of a licence. Whilst expressing disagreement with this decision, HMRC opted not to appeal against it because, on reflection, they believed that 'in substance and reality' the Club had *de facto* an exclusive licence as no one else was licensed to use the golf course. In other words, they accepted the decision but not the tribunal's reasoning (Business Brief 25/97). HMRC reiterated their faith in the decision by a different tribunal in *P J Lamb t/a Footloose (VTD 15136)*. Mr Lamb was a shoe retailer. He entered into an agreement with a Mr Johnson under which Mr Johnson would sell watches from the same premises and pay Mr Lamb 12½% of his gross takings as a contribution towards the shop running costs. Mr Lamb allocated one display window to Mr Johnson who also installed a display unit in the centre of the shop and another on one wall. Mr Lamb and Mr Johnson shared the shop counter. The tribunal held that Mr Johnson had been granted the use of facilities at the premises, not a licence. It was influenced by the facts that customers of Mr Johnson had to use the other areas of the shop in order that he could conduct his business, the agreement did not refer to rent and the use of the non-exclusive areas meant that Mr Johnson did not have actual physical enjoyment of the land as land. The tribunal does not appear to have been referred to the *Abbotsley* decision, however.

17.75 Substance and reality seems to be a one way street. In *The Trustees of the Lyndon David Hollinshead SIPP and Others ([2009] UKFTT 92 (TC); TC 60)* the trustees had granted leases to a number of associated companies. In reality the companies did not use the space in the building designated by the leases and other associated companies without leases also used the building. The trustees contended that in substance and reality there were a number of licences to occupy. HMRC retorted (and the tribunal agreed) that by granting the leases the trustees no longer had any control over the premises and the reality was that the lessees were simply disregarding their legal rights.

17.76 In *Owen v HMRC (2015 SFTD 711)* the taxpayer provided cattle sheds. Each customer was allocated a specific shed for their own exclusive use. The taxpayer provided feed for the cattle (or placed the customer's own feed where the cattle could eat it) and water where necessary but provided no other services. HMRC contended that the taxpayer was providing animal husbandry. The FTT held that the services provided by the taxpayer were ancillary to its exempt supply of the right to occupy the shedIn *Zombory-Moldovan (trading as Craft Carnival) v HMRC (2016 STC 2436)*. Mrs Zombory-Moldovan organised craft fairs around Dorset. The fair would be held within a marquee with a separate refreshment tent. She also provided portable toilets and engaged staff to act as ticket sellers and car park marshalls. A fair attracts between 40 and 110 stallholders. She charged a VATable admission fee to customers and an exempt stall fee to exhibitors. HMRC contended that she provided stallholders with either a taxable licence to use land or a taxable package of services. The FTT held that the facilities were provided for the customers, not the stallholders. All that the stallholders got was the exclusive right to occupy the stall throughout the day. Sadly, the UT disagreed. It held that what was being provided was the right to participate in a high-quality, expertly organised fair and that this was a single standard-rated supply. In *Fareham Borough Council (TC 4129)*, the grant of a concession to park an ice-cream van in a car park and trade from it was held to be the taxable grant of a catering concession. Although there was a specific space marked, 'Reserved ice-cream van' the Tribunal said that if a car parked in that space, the concessionaire would not be able to force the driver to move it. An alternative HMRC claim that the charge was taxable as car-parking was dismissed by the Tribunal on the basis that the real subject matter of the supply was the right to trade rather than the right to be parked in a particular spot. In contrast, *International Antiques and Collectors Fairs Ltd (TC 4538)*, the Tribunal held that the pitch fee was in reality payment for participation in the fair and as such was a supply of services, not of an interest in land. The Tribunal thought that the company's activities generated significant added value which prevented the supply being of a passive interest in land (see **17.88**).

17.77 This issue has been considered by the ECJ briefly in *E C Commission & UK (2000 STC 777) (Case C-359/97)*, in a little more detail in *Sweden v Stockholm Lindopark AB (2001 STC 103) (Case C-150/99)* and again in *Sinclair Collis Ltd. V C & E Commrs (2003 STC 898) (Case C-275/01).*

17.78 The EC Commission case (see **17.254**) concerned road tolls. The UK argued that providing access to roads on payment of a toll represented a letting of immovable property within the meaning of *Article 13B(b)* of the *EC Sixth Directive*, the provision from which the exemption for letting land arises. The ECJ, whilst recognising that the letting of immovable property under *Article 13B* is wider than the concept of letting under some national laws, held that it 'cannot be considered to cover contracts where, as here, the parties have not agreed on any duration for the right of enjoyment of the immovable property, which is the essential element of a contract to let'.

17.79 The question in *Stockholm Lindopark* was whether the operation of a golf course fell within *Article 13B(b)*. The ECJ said that was a matter for the national courts to decide in the light of the facts. It acknowledged that 'it is certainly not impossible that in certain circumstances a supply of premises for the practice of sport or physical education may constitute the letting of immovable property' but held that it was not permissible for Sweden to grant a general exemption for such supplies. It also pointed out that the running of a golf course generally entails not only the passive activity of making the course available but also a large number of commercial activities, such as supervision, management, and maintenance and that 'in the absence of quite exceptional circumstances, letting out a golf course cannot therefore constitute the main service supplied'. The Advocate-General (Jacobs) was more forceful. He felt that the exemption in *Article 13B(b)* 'cannot extend to all transactions granting access, or for any other purpose, regardless of the characteristics of such access, but must in my view be limited by certain of the characteristics inherent in a contract of leasing or letting'. He pointed out that in *E C Commission v UK* (see **17.254**) the court had stressed in particular the need that the agreement between the parties should take account of the duration of the enjoyment of the property. He also pointed out that the concept and letting of immovable property is neither defined in the directive, nor comprehensively defined by the court. He felt that the type of broad definition argued for in the case by the UK government could not be accepted (which may suggest that UK jurisprudence in this area may not be wholly correct). He expressed the view that, apart from the duration of the contract, a lease or let 'necessarily involves the grant of some right to occupy the property as one's own and to exclude or admit others, a right which is, moreover, linked to a defined piece or area of property'.

17.80 *Sinclair Collis* was concerned with the placing of cigarette machines in public houses, etc. The VAT position of such machines had previously been considered by the VAT tribunal in 1990 in *Wolverhampton & Dudley Breweries (VTD 5351)* where the tribunal, looking at the substance and reality of the matter, had concluded that the use and enjoyment of the land was not a significant factor; the real subject of the agreement was the availability of the machine to customers which was not a licence to occupy land. Despite this case, HMRC had ruled that *Sinclair Collis* was granting licences to occupy land when it installed a cigarette machine. The company challenged this ruling and HMRC agreed that the licences were VATable. The company promptly put in a claim for repayment of past disallowed input tax, at which point HMRC changed their mind and said that the supply was of licences to occupy land. The VAT tribunal agreed with the company for the same reason as in the *Wolverhampton and Dudley* case, but both the High Court and the Court of Appeal held that the dominant element of the supply was the right to install, operate and maintain machines on the premises, which they felt amounted to a licence to occupy land.

17.81 The House of Lords reverted to the VAT tribunal's approach. Lord Slynn of Hadley thought it plain that 'the words, licence to occupy land, in the 1994 Act cannot go wider than the words, letting of immovable property, in the Sixth Directive'. He felt that 'the essential purpose of this agreement was to enable the company to bring its machines into the club owner's premises and to have them there for two years'. He felt that the letting of immovable property includes transactions which go beyond what are leases in the ordinary sense of the term and that, on balance, 'an agreement by which a machine may be fixed to a wall or put, free standing, in a particular place in a club for a sustained period is capable of amounting to the occupation of a portion of the land. It is a right given to the exclusion of all others and an individual putting it there is occupying the land by the machine'. Lord Steyn agreed with him. An opposing view was taken by Lord Nicholls of Birkenhead. He accepted that the machine occupies space on the site owner's premises and is located there 24 hours every day, so the use made of the premises by the tobacco company is not intermittent. However, he did not feel these factors conclusive. 'Occupation of space is a feature of every physical object. The grant of a right to occupy space by placing an object on the supplier's premises is not conclusive even if the right is of some duration. If it were, a licence to place any object on the licensor's property would be within the exemption; for example permission to display a picture for sale on the walls of a picture gallery. That cannot be correct'. The Sinclair Collis licence was 'more naturally to be regarded as a licence to use land rather than a licence to occupy land'. Lord Millett reached a similar conclusion by a different route, namely by construing the agreement itself. This did not contain the terms of a lease but the terms on which vending machines may be positioned on the premises. It did not specify the number of machines to be covered, leaving that to be determined by agreement. It did not identify any defined areas or even the rooms where machines were to be installed; that was left in the first instance to the site owner. Sinclair Collis was given no control over access to the machines (other than an express right to itself access them). Lord Millett thought the agreement far removed from the letting of land. 'The company cannot sensibly be described as occupying any part of the premises by its machine. Such a concept can hardly apply where the part of the premises in question has no independent existence of its own, being defined by the dimensions of the machine and its location from time to time .... The agreement ... is not an agreement for the letting of defined areas of land with a right to place machines on them, but a right to bring machines into the site owner's premises and place them in a suitable position there. The site owner remains in sole occupation of the whole of his premises including the areas from time to time occupied by machines'. Lord Scott of Foscote took a similar view. He thought it clear, 'as a matter of common sense as well as of authority that not all licences that transform a use of the land of another from what would otherwise have been trespass into a lawful use are to be regarded as licences to occupy land'. Whether a licence creates a relationship between the licensee and the land is a question of fact and degree. He felt that there are two characteristics that distinguish a licence to occupy from a mere licence to use, namely possession and control. If neither is present he felt it difficult to understand how a licensee can be said to 'occupy'. There is authority for this view in UK land law. He also pointed out that 'A licence to occupy is something to be enjoyed by persons, whether natural or corporate. It is people or companies who must be in possession or exercise control, not inanimate objects like tables, kiosks, cars or vending machines'. He pointed out that in this case the owner of the premises remains in possession and control of the whole of the room in which the vending machine is placed. It is unnatural to treat the room as being partly occupied by the owner and partly by Sinclair Collis.

17.82 The ECJ took a robust view. The agreement did not give Sinclair Collis any right over the land. It gave them a right of access only to the machine itself, not a right of access to that part of the premises where the machine is situated. Furthermore even that right was restricted to the opening hours of the premises and could not be exercised without the site owner's consent. Furthermore third parties had access to the machine within the practical perimeters imposed by the site owner, not according to limits determined by Sinclair Collis. The installation of the machines accordingly did not amount to a letting of immovable property. It seems likely that as a result the decision of the VAT tribunal in *British Telecommunications plc (VTD 16244)* is wrong. It was held there that where a payphone is affixed to premises, its occupation of the space is a licence to occupy land as the site owner supplies to BT the right to have on its premises what is in effect a vending machine. HMRC there accepted that where the payphone was not attached to the premises, such as a payphone in a hotel bedroom or fixed to a hospital trolley, there is no licence to occupy land. In *Ministero delle Finanze-Ufficio IVA di Milano v COGEP Srl (Case C-174/07; 2008 STC 2744)* the ECJ held that the grant of a concession to use a warehouse on payment of a fee which gave the company the right to occupy and use, including exclusively, public property for a specified period and against payment, is covered by the concept of leasing or letting of immovable property.

17.83 In another ECJ case, *Staatssecretaris van Financien v VOF Coffeeshop Siberie (Case C-158/98) (1999 STC 742)* Advocate General Fennelly opined (albeit obiter) that he would not be inclined to regard the renting of a table in a coffee shop from which to sell soft drinks as amounting to the letting of immovable property. What might be called the Slynn/Steyn view in *Sinclair Collis* does not fit well with that decision, and the concept that Sinclair Collis is primarily renting space offends common sense.

17.84 HMRC expressed the view a few years ago that a licence to occupy land exists where it relates to a clearly defined area or piece of land which in substance and reality permits the licensee an exclusive right of occupation during the times prescribed in the licence, ie the exclusive occupation need not be continuous, it could for example be every Thursday afternoon. In the light of the *Abbotsley* decision they also accept that a licence can exist where the land is not occupied exclusively by the licensee provided that the licence relates to a clearly defined area or piece of land, in substance and reality it allows the licensee to physically occupy the land and the rights granted are in relation to the occupation of the land thereby providing for the licensee's physical enjoyment or exploitation for the land (Business Brief 22/98).

17.85 They think that the following are likely to be licences to occupy land:

(*a*) the provision of a specific area of office accommodation, such as a bay, room or floor, together with the right to use shared areas such as reception, lifts, restaurant, rest rooms, leisure facilities and so on;

(*b*) the provision of a serviced office but only where the use of phones, computer systems, photocopiers, etc is incidental to the provision of office space;

(*c*) granting a concession to operate a shop within a shop, where the concessionaire is granted a defined area from which to sell their goods or services;

(*d*) granting space to erect advertising hoardings;

(*e*) granting space to place a fixed kiosk on a specified site, such as a newspaper kiosk or flower stand at a railway station;

(*f*) hiring out a hall or other accommodation for meetings or parties and so on (but not wedding or party facilities where the supplier does more than supplying accommodation, for example by assisting with entertainment and arranging catering). The use of a kitchen area, lighting and furniture can be included;

(*g*) granting a catering concession, where the caterer is granted a licence to occupy a specific kitchen and restaurant area, even if the grant includes use of kitchen or catering equipment;

(*h*) granting traders a pitch in a market or at a car boot sale; or

(*i*) granting a specific space for the installation of a 'hole in the wall' cash machine (ATM).

(C & E Notice 742, para 2.6.)

17.86 They think the following are unlikely to amount to a licence to occupy:

(*a*) the rental by a hairdressing salon of chair spaces to individual stylists, unless a clearly demarcated area is provided (such as a floor or whole salon) and no other services;

(*b*) the hire of tables in nail bars to self employed manicurists;

(*c*) providing another person with access to office premises to make use of facilities, such as remote sales staff away from home having access to photocopiers and the like at another office;

(*d*) allowing the public to tip rubbish on your land;

(*e*) storing someone's goods in a warehouse without allocating any specific area for them;

(*f*) granting of an ambulatory concession, such as an ice cream van on the sea front or a hamburger van at a football match;

(*g*) allowing the public admission to premises or events, such as theatres, historic houses, swimming pools and spectator sports events;

(*h*) wedding facilities (including, for example, use of rooms for a ceremony, wedding breakfast and evening party);

(*i*) hiring out safes to store valuables; or

(*j*) granting someone the right to place a free standing or wall mounted vending or gaming machine on your premises, where the location is not specified in the agreement.

(C & E Notice 742, para 2.7.)

17.87 This interpretation seems too restrictive in the light of the ECJ decision in *Belgian State v Temco Europe SA (case C284/03) (2005 STC 1451).*

Temco Europe owned and refurbished a property in Belgium. It entered into three contracts with three associated companies under which it allowed each of them to carry on its activities in the property as allocated by the board of directors of Temco Europe, without the licensee having individual rights over any specific parts of the property. Temco Europe had the right at any time without notice to require the licensee to vacate the premises. The Court held that such transactions constitute the letting of immovable property.

17.88 In reviewing its previous case law the ECJ stressed that the letting of immovable property within the meaning of the Sixth Directive is essentially the conferring by a landlord on a tenant, for an agreed period and in return for payment, of the right to occupy property as if that person were the owner and to exclude any other person from enjoyment of such a right. It commented that the period of letting is relevant only in order to distinguish a transaction comprising the letting of immovable property, which is usually a relatively passive activity linked simply to the passage of time and not generating any significant added value, from other activities which are industrial or commercial in nature. It felt that it is not essential for the period to be fixed at the time the contract is concluded; it is necessary to take into account the reality of the contractual relations. The period of letting can be shortened or extended by the mutual agreement of the parties during the performance of the contract. Also whilst a payment to the landlord which is strictly linked to the period of occupation appears best to reflect the passive nature of a letting transaction it is not to be inferred from that that a payment which takes into account other factors (usage of gas and electricity in the *Temco* case) has the effect of precluding the transaction being a letting of immovable property, particularly where those other factors are plainly accessory. Finally it stated that the tenant's right of exclusive occupation can be restricted in the contract concluded with the landlord. It pointed out that a contract of letting may relate to certain parts of the property which must be used in common with other occupiers and that that 'does not prevent that occupation being exclusive as regards other persons not permitted by law or by the contract to exercise a right over the property'.

17.89 In *Regie communale autonome du stade Luc Varenne v Belgium*, the ECJ held that there is not a letting of immovable property where a football stadium was made available under a contract reserving certain rights and prerogatives to the stadium owner, and providing for the supply by the owner of various services (including services of maintenance, cleaning, repair and upgrading) representing 80% of the charge agreed to be payable. The case involved the grant by a local authority to a football club for the club to use the facilities of the stadium. It charged a flat fee of £1,750 per day for the use of the playing surface, the changing rooms, the bar and the caretaking, surveillance and monitoring services for the facilities as a whole. The parties had agreed that 20% of the charge represented the right of access to the football pitch and the rest of the charge to other facilities. The Court felt that the economic value of the services indicated that the landlord remained present at the premises throughout (through its caretaker) and the need for the facilities was suggestive of a single composite supply of services.

17.90 Where an exhibition organiser supplied the use of a 'conversation' table on a stand and shared use of storage and meeting facilities, it was held that it was providing a taxable package of facilities not a licence to occupy land. The conversation table had a chair on each side, was separated from adjoining tables by a partition and had a hanging sign showing the name of the organisation. Nevertheless, the tribunal held that, although an organisation was entitled to occupation of its allocated table and chairs, it did not have exclusive occupation of any part of the exhibition stand (*Swiss National Tourist Office (VTD 13192)*). Similarly it was held in *Leander International Pet Foods Ltd t/a Arden Grange (VTD 18870)* that the supply of kennel space, either for quarantine or for boarding cats and dogs, was not the supply of an interest in land. In *John Window (VTD 17186)* the tribunal held that a supply of stabling with livery is a composite supply and that the stabling is the dominant of the two elements so the entire supply was exempt as a licence to occupy land. HMRC stated in the later case of *Halsall Riding and Livery Centre (VTD 19342)* that they accept that decision was correct.

17.91 *Pethericks and Gillard Ltd (VTD 20564)* is an interesting case. The licence fee there was for the use of a room in an office. The licence fee included some minor secretarial services, sorting of the mail (there were three licensees and only one letterbox) use of photocopier and fax, cleaning, use of kitchen, heating and lighting, use of toilets, use of telephone systems, and use of reception. The tribunal felt that most of these facilities were ancillary to the right to use the room. Even though Mr Gillard, the licensee, gave evidence that he did not use the other facilities the tribunal felt that when Mr Gillard was in his room it was 'impossible to view him as operating without the knowledge that he could and would use these services; they were an integral part of the benefit of being able to be there even though their provision … may not have been absolutely necessary' to Mr Gillard. Applying the test in Byron (see **17.68**) the tribunal held that there was a single supply and that on balance that supply was not a passive supply of land. The other elements, although less significant than in Byron, meant that the passive supply did not dominate the package enough for it to fall within an exemption (which needs to be strictly construed). Accordingly, the supply was taxable.

Virtual Assignments

17.92 In early 2000 Abbey National decided to enter into a sale and leaseback of its property portfolio to Mapeley Columbus Ltd. Abbey had a large number of leases, which gave rise to two problems. Firstly, it would take time to obtain the necessary consents to assign; and secondly, landlords would be reluctant to give consent to an assignment to Mapeley, which was a new company with no track-record of financial strength. The concept of a 'virtual' assignment was developed to overcome these problems. Under this, Abbey transferred all the economic benefits and burdens of the leases to Mapeley, remained in possession of the premises and paid a 'principal fee' to Mapeley similar to the rent that it would have paid under a leaseback. Two issues arose. HMRC took the view that the principal fee was not exempt rent, but a standard-related supply of agency and property management services. Also, where a property had been sublet so that the tenant paid its rent to Mapeley after the assignment that was also consideration for such a zero-rated supply by Mapeley to Abbey HMRC appealed in relation to the leases but not in relation to the subleases, as they consider that the effect of *VATA 1994, Sch 10, para 40,* formerly *para 8* (see **16.8**) is that Mapeley is deemed to make the supply to the subtenants as the benefit of the consideration (their rent) accrues to it.

17.93 The Court of Appeal (*Abbey National plc v HMRC, 2006 STC 1961*) (reversing the decision of Hart J) had no difficulty in holding that the principal fee was not exempt rent. 'The Community law authorities … leave no room for doubt that a right of occupation is an essential and fundamental element of a transaction of leasing or letting for the purposes of *Article 13B(b)* (of the *Sixth Directive*). It follows that, since … Mapeley acquired no right of occupation of the properties the subject of the virtual assignment, and hence was never in a position to transfer such a right back to Abbey, the supply made by Mapely to Abbey under the contractual arrangements in question is not a supply of 'leasing or letting' … The Commissioners are correct in characterising the supply by Mapely as a standard-rated supply of agency and property management services'. HMRC did not appeal against Hart J's decision that the subleases were exempt.

Other Problem Areas

17.94 It appears that a contract to acquire land is, in HMRC's view, itself an interest in land. In *Margrie Holdings Ltd v C & E Commrs (1991 STC 80)*, a Scottish case, it was held that the equivalent right under Scottish law was not an interest in land. As a result the wording of the legislation was changed by the *VAT (Buildings and Land) Order 1991* to exempt, in relation to land in Scotland, any personal right to call for or be granted an interest in land. This suggests that HMRC felt that no similar clarification was needed in relation to land in England and Wales. It was accepted by HMRC in *C & E Commrs v Latchmere Properties Ltd (2005 STC 731)* (see **17.108**) that an equitable interest in land is sufficient to create an interest although the facts of that case were unusual and it is not wholly clear whether the equitable interest in question was the contract itself or the bundle of obligations arising under it. The VAT tribunal decision in *Higher Education Statistics Agency Ltd (VTD 15917)* also points to a contract being an interest in land (see **17.219**). Nevertheless the position does not seem clear. If a contract to acquire land is entered into and the benefit of that contract sold, it might be advisable to obtain confirmation from HMRC that the sale will be exempt from VAT.

17.95 In *R H Carter t/a Protheroe Carter & Eason (VTD 12047)* the VAT tribunal held that the grant of an interest in, or right over, land was confined to the grant of a legal or equitable interest, and therefore an agreement with a developer to allow a crane jib to pass through the air space over the appellant's premises was neither a right over land nor a licence to occupy land and so was taxable.

17.96 HMRC initially considered that the first supply of a building after development determines whether input tax on the construction costs is recoverable. If that first supply was an exempt supply, no part of the input tax was recoverable. The draftsman of the 1989 legislation was presumably of the same view when he deemed the first receipt of rent from letting residential accommodation to be a zero-rated supply (see **16.120** above) in order to trigger the right to recover input tax in respect of the construction of the property. However, it was held in *C & E Commrs v Briararch Ltd* and *C & E Commrs v Curtis Henderson Ltd (1992 STC 732)* that where a person constructs a building with the intention on completion of selling it as soon as a buyer can be found, he is entitled to credit for an apportioned amount of the input tax incurred on building the house notwithstanding that he lets the house on a short let before selling it. Briararch Ltd converted a property into offices in 1988 intending to let them on a 25-year lease. It could not find a tenant. Badly needing money to meet its interest obligations, it let the property on a four-year lease, still intending to grant the 25-year lease on the expiry of that short lease. Curtis Henderson Ltd built a house intending to sell it. It could not find a buyer. An opportunity arose to let it for a short period and it did so to provide a contribution towards the burden of interest charges. The house was let for nine months and then remained empty for a further nine months until a buyer was found. The court held that *Article 20* of the *EC Sixth Directive*, which begins 'the initial deduction shall be adjusted according to the procedures laid down by the Member States, in particular *(a)* when that deduction was higher or lower than that to which the taxable person was entitled', gives authority for necessary adjustments according to intention. What is now *reg 107* of the *VAT Regulations 1995* provides the procedures for such adjustment. A taxable person had deducted input tax which had been attributed to an intended taxable supply of the building; during the following six years it had used the building in making an exempt supply; so it became necessary to determine how much of that input tax was attributable to the exempt supply. In the *Briararch* case the VAT tribunal had allowed 25/29ths of the input tax. Hutchinson J felt this was probably an incorrect basis of apportionment – it would not work if the intention had been to sell the property freehold – and that a more satisfactory basis would be 'to make a comparison between the values, adjusted if necessary, of the respective disposals'. HMRC said in response to this decision that they were 'considering an amendment to the legislation to prevent intention being used as a basis for determining input tax recovery' (Business Brief 15/92). However, they have as yet taken no action over this.

17.97 HMRC issued guidance on this area in September 2008 (VAT Information Sheet 07/08). This confirms that (except where the partial exemption de minimis limit applies – see **16.112**) the previously made input tax claims must be adjusted. HMRC say that the clawback adjustment must be based on the housebuilder's realistic expectation judged at the time that his original plans were changed. They might want evidence to support the adjustment, such as 'the business plan showing the price originally expected; reports of estate agents showing this price to be unobtainable and maybe estimating when a sale will be achievable; board minutes from the time of the decision to grant short leases, or any other commercial documentation that backs up the estimated use'. HMRC's expectation that such information is likely to be available may well be misplaced in many cases! HMRC's policy is to apply a 10-year 'economic life' for buildings when preparing time-based clawback adjustments. This is obviously completely unrealistic. The economic life of the average house is probably over 100 years! Accordingly HMRC 'strongly discourage housebuilders from basing their clawback adjustment on the anticipated number of years that a dwelling is likely to be let'. If the housebuilder estimates it will be let for five years that would disallow half of the total input tax. They suggest that the builder should base his estimate on the anticipated rents received and the anticipated sale proceeds. For example, if the housebuilder intends to let the house for five years at £12,000 p.a. and then sell it for £300,000, his new intention would be to use the building costs 16.67% for making £60,000 of exempt supplies and 83.73% for making £300,000 of taxable supplies. If the housebuilder actually manages to sell the house after it has been let for only one year there will be another change of intention and there seems no reason why he should not re-adjust the input tax again. This is, however, subject both to the three-year cap (which will not allow an adjustment of a deduction more than three years previously) and the six-year period in *reg 108* (see **16.22**).

17.98 In *Cooper and Chapman (Builders) Ltd v C & E Commrs (1993 STC 1)* the company converted a house into ten flats which it intended to let as holiday accommodation. It let some of them but, three months after completion of the conversion, granted a one-year lease of the entire building, which was of course an exempt supply. The VAT tribunal held that the expenditure on conversion had to be apportioned between the ten flats because the taxable supply which the company had intended to make was of letting the flats singly, so that only the expenditure on an individual flat would relate to the supply of that flat. The company could recover the input tax in respect of those flats which had actually been let as holiday accommodation. It could not recover input tax in relation to the other flats as the first supply of those flats was an exempt supply. This was upheld by the High Court on appeal.

17.99 Care may sometimes need to be taken to evidence whether a developer is acting as a principal or an agent. In *Drexlodge Ltd (VTD 5614)* a property development company entered into an agreement with the Cooperative Insurance Society Ltd for the development of two sites owned by the Society. Despite the fact that the invoices were addressed to Drexlodge Ltd, HMRC contended that supplies by subcontractors had been made to the Society through the agency of Drexlodge and sought to disallow relief for the input tax. The VAT tribunal held that the 'flavour' of the agreement was that of a joint venture not of an agency. Provisions in it which required Drexlodge to obtain the approval of the Society's surveyor for certain works were not evidence of agency. There was no evidence that the suppliers were aware of the existence of a principal other than Drexlodge with whom they had contracted.

17.100 This should be contrasted with the position in *Peter Anthony Estates Ltd (VTD 13250)*. In that case, the company managed the letting of properties on assured shorthold tenancies on behalf of the owner. The leases were entered into in the name of the company, not that of the owner, and contained no indication that the company was acting as an agent. The arrangement with the owner was that the company would pay him a guaranteed weekly amount and retain for its own benefit the balance of the rents. The company contended that the substance of the transaction was that the company had leased the properties from the owner for the guaranteed rent and subleased them to the tenants. It was held that, as there was a formal property management agreement between the company and the owner, the company was letting the properties as an undisclosed agent of the owner, and its share of the rents were fees for managing the properties and VAT was chargeable.

17.101 It is also important to identify exactly what is being supplied. In two cases relating to *Haringey Borough Council (VTD 8820, VTD 12050, VTD 12462)* the Council, as Trustees of Alexandra Palace, carried out extensive repairs to Alexandra Palace and were anxious to deduct as much of the input tax as possible. They contended that when they hired out the building in the course of a business, some of the supplies made to hirers were VATable supplies separate from the licence to use the building. The VAT tribunal held that if a service is necessary to the licence, such as heating and light and water, it has to be considered as an integral part of the supply of the licence, following *British Airways plc v C & E Commrs (1990 STC 643)*. Where, however, items could reasonably have been not supplied, or the customer would expect an extra charge to be made for them, they are a separate supply. It held that the provision of floral decorations, a courtesy bus service, off-site posters, and leaflet distribution were separate taxable supplies. So were the staffing of cloakrooms (as a separate charge could instead be made to visitors) and the cleaning of exhibition stands for which a specialist contractor was engaged. The box office, turnstiles and ticket machines and the provision of staff to run these and the car parking were integral to the supply. So was the removal of rubbish, general cleaning of common areas, the staffing and stocking of toilets, the services of a stand-by electrician, and crowd control. The tribunal observed that the lack of any rational basis for apportioning consideration could be indicative of an integral supply. The tribunal decision also covered other points. An HMRC appeal against certain aspects, but not including the above basis of apportionment, was dismissed by the High Court *(1995 STC 830*). Clearly if it is intended to contend that services are separate to the right to use the land, it is advisable to charge separately for them, although the omission to do so is not necessarily fatal.

17.102 However, in *Rayner & Keeler Ltd (VTD 5803, VTD 9349)* a contractor was required both to construct and provide goods (shop fittings) and to install them. The VAT tribunal held that it would be unrealistic to separate the obligation to provide an item from the obligation to fit it and to classify them as two separate supplies. There was therefore a single supply of services, not a composite supply of goods and services. On appeal, Owen J held that the tribunal had misdirected itself *(1994 STC 724*) and remitted the case to it 'to consider and analyse first the individual supplies of goods taking into account the principles laid down in *Sch 2* and asking the question whether each supply of goods has become an integral part of a supply of services or vice versa'. This seems to reaffirm that it is a matter of impression whether a supply of goods is separable from the service of installing them or whether there is the provision of a single service.

17.103 In *J E Greves & Sons (VTD 9777)* the taxpayer had squatted on land and claimed possessory title. Following a consent order made in High Court proceedings it agreed to vacate the land, to remove a caution registered against the title, and to abandon its claim to the land in return for a payment of £450,000. HMRC contended that it could not be inferred from the order that the taxpayer had given up a right in land; accordingly the receipt was consideration for a taxable supply. The taxpayer contended that it was exempt as being for the surrender of possession of the land. It was established that, had the proceedings continued, the taxpayer would probably have established title to the land. Accordingly the VAT tribunal held that the taxpayer could be regarded as having an interest in land which it had disposed of. It felt that a consent order needs to be examined with particular care and in its context to ascertain its effect. It differs from a contract because, in a document evidencing a compromise to settle a dispute, the supply is less likely to be described in clear terms.

17.104 In *Cullens Holdings plc (VTD 12376)* the group licensed some of its retail food stores to operators. The licence agreement gave the operator a licence to carry on business at the store premises using the group's name and business systems. HMRC contended that this was a single exempt supply, namely licences to occupy land. The company contended that there was a single composite standard-rated supply of business facilities. The tribunal held that the right to carry on business using the group's name and system was clearly an important part of the agreement. It was not a normal incident of a licence to occupy land and could not be regarded as physically or economically in-dissociable from the licences. Accordingly there were two supplies, albeit part of a single contract, an exempt licence to occupy and a taxable supply of business rights. This decision seems to fit uneasily with the hairdresser cases referred to at **17.66**. That line of cases identified a supply of business facilities but refused to regard it as separable from the licence to occupy, instead subsuming the licence as being an integral part of the single supply of business facilities.

17.105 In *Grantham Cricket Club (VTD 12287, VTD 12863)* the club entered into an agreement with a developer under which it would surrender its tenancy to its landlord and take a new lease of alternative premises on which it would itself prepare a cricket pitch and construct a pavilion. It was paid £110,000 by the developer and an additional £70,000 by its landlord for the surrender of the lease. The club contended that the entire payment related to a single exempt supply, the vacation of its former ground. It was held that the payment from the developer clearly imposed two requirements on the club, to vacate the old premises and adapt the alternative site. The £110,000 therefore had to be apportioned between the two, the part relating to the surrender being exempt and the balance taxable.

17.106 The importance of identifying correctly the supply for which the consideration is paid is well illustrated by *Terard Ltd (VTD 16949)*. Terard converted a commercial property into flats, which it leased to the Hyde Housing Association (HHA). In addition to the rent payable under the lease HHA agreed to pay Terard £20,000 as 'grant funding for the conversion works on their completion and the completion of the lease'. The £20,000 grant was made to HHA by the Housing Corporation under a scheme to encourage living accommodation over shops being used for housing homeless families. Normally HHA engaged contractors to carry out such work on its own properties. Terard claimed the payment was for zero-rated conversion work. It pointed out that that was the only thing for which the Housing Corporation was prepared to make a grant. HMRC contended that it was for the supply of the exempt lease. The tribunal held in favour of HMRC. It was strongly influenced by the fact that none of the documents actually obliged Terard to carry out the conversion work; they merely made clear that HHA would not be willing to lease the flats until that had been done to its satisfaction. They could not find any direct link between the conversion work and the consideration received. This case also illustrates two other important facets of VAT, the need to get the documents right and the need to be able to evidence what happened where there are staff changes so that the people involved in a transaction are not available to give evidence when it reaches the VAT tribunal. A similar conclusion was reached by the tribunal in *West Devon Borough Council (VTD 17107)* on fairly similar facts.

17.107 The question of what was being supplied was also an issue in *McCarthy & Stone (Developments) Ltd v HMRC (2014 SFTD 625)*. The company sold retirement flats. The lease granted the occupant the right to use the common parts. Two such parts were a resident's lounge and a community guestroom. These were furnished by McCarthy & Stone. A purchaser of the lease made a payment of £500 'towards the communal fittings'. McCarthy & Stone contended that the £500 was part of the premium for the lease and thus formed part of a single zero-rated supply, so it was entitled to recover the VAT on the furnishings. HMRC then contended that even where there is a single supply, zero-rating applies only to elements that fall within the express terms of *VATA 1994, Sch 8*. Furniture does not fall within the Schedule. They relied on the CJEU judgement in *Talacre* (see **16.27**). Accordingly the £500 was for the exempt element of the supply of land. The Tribunal felt that following *Talacre* what is required is an understanding of what would have been understood in 1991 (when the zero-rating derogation came in) to be the purpose and effect of the UK legislation. It felt that there would have been a single supply and the £500 was clearly part of the consideration for the grant of the lease. It was accordingly a premium that attracted zero-rating. This decision needs to be approached with caution. HMRC intended to appeal it but were not able to do so solely because they missed the time limit for appealing.

17.108 An interesting issue arose in *C & E Commrs v Latchmere Properties Ltd (2005 STC 731)*. The company entered into a building agreement with a landowner, Burhill Estates Co. Ltd. The agreement provided that Latchmere should convert, refurbish and extend a property owned by Burhill to form five residential units. Latchmere was granted a licence over the property for this purpose. It also provided that Burhill would sell the property to Latchmere, subject to the issue of a certificate of practical completion and subject to the provisions of clause 5.2. Clause 5.2 provided that completion was not to take place until 12 months after completion of the works. Latchmere was not required to complete in respect of any unit for which in the interim it and Burhill had entered into a contract with a purchaser for a sale of that unit. The sale contract with purchasers of the unit described Burhill as Owner and Latchmere as Developer. It provided that the purchaser would pay part of the price to Burhill 'in respect of the transfer of the unit' and the balance to Latchmere 'in respect of the works carried out to the dwelling on the unit'. Latchmere contended that it was selling an exempt interest in land. HMRC, whilst accepting that

Latchmere had an equitable interest in the land, contended that what it was selling was construction services. It was held that the answer depended on the proper construction of the agreement. Under that, it was Latchmere that took the development risk, Latchmere that was responsible for arranging sales and Latchmere that was obliged to buy any unsold units after 12 months. The agreement in reality set out the terms of a joint project for the development of the building, to which each contributed for their own separate benefit and from which each took a share of the sale proceeds, not of a supply of construction services by Latchmere to Burhill. Accordingly, Latchmere received its share of the proceeds as consideration for the release or the supply to the purchaser of the unit of its equitable interest in the unit.

17.109 The question in *Sandwell Metropolitan Borough Council (TC 2554)* was whether a 10-year lease of a memorial in a crematorium and a right to an inscribed plaque was an interest in land. It was held that a memorial consisting of a marble slab with a flower holder sunk into the top and a sloping face into which an inscribed tablet fitted and which was cemented to the ground alongside a path edge was immovable property and that the intention was that the customer should have the use of that particular marble vase complete with the affixed tablet. Similarly a memorial which provided a chamber for the storage of ashes was the letting of an interest in immovable property. However, where the memorial was a plastic plaque attached to a rose bush, or a wall mounted plaque that could be moved during the term of the lease, it did not constitute immovable property.

17.110 It should also be mentioned that there are a large number of cases on whether there is a single mixed supply or a number of separate supplies. Most of these involve property as they are attempts to dissect the provision of a service that involves the use of land into the use of that land and a separate supply of services. Most of these attempts fail! These types of cases are considered at **17.66** onwards.

Variations of Leases

17.111 Many variations of leases involve in law the surrender of the existing lease and the grant of a new lease. HMRC have agreed that, where no monetary consideration passes from the landlord to the tenant as a result of (or in connection with) the variation, they will accept that the old lease is not surrendered for a non-monetary consideration (ie the value of the new lease) if either:

(*a*) the new lease is for the same building but for an extended term;

(*b*) the new lease is for a greater area of the same building as the old lease and for the same or an extended term; or (*c*) the new lease is for the same land as the old and for an extended term.

This concession does not apply to ground leases or to building leases (ie where the lessee will develop the land) as HMRC consider that in most such cases the new lease is likely to be more valuable than the old.

17.112 If the landlord makes a payment to the tenant for a variation, HMRC will 'normally' regard that payment as the sole consideration for the surrender (ie they will not regard the value of the new lease as being part of the consideration for the surrender of the old). However, they reserve the right to treat the value of the new lease as additional consideration if the terms are significantly more favourable than could have been negotiated by a lessee with no existing lease to surrender.

17.113 If the tenant pays the landlord for a variation, HMRC will normally look on that payment as consideration for the grant of a new lease, and thus exempt, not as consideration for the surrender of the old lease. This will not apply if the circumstances suggest that the payment is consideration for the landlord's taxable supply of the acceptance of the surrender of an onerous lease from the tenant (Law Society Press Release 1 May 1991).

17.114 HMRC do accept that variations to leases should be treated as part of the original supply of the lease so that the VAT liability follows that of the original lease (Business Brief 16/94 & Notice 742, para 10.5). They also accept that the lifting of a restrictive covenant on land is also exempt unless the person lifting the restriction has elected to waive exemption on the land. They instance the lifting of a restriction to permit development which was previously forbidden, but the exemption will apply to the lifting of any restriction (Business Brief 17/94 and Notice 742, para 10.6).

17.115 Where none of these concessionary exclusions apply, consideration could be given to the landlord granting to an associated company of the tenant ('Newco') a headlease on the new terms subject to the existing lease. The tenant would remain in occupation as sub-tenant of its new 'landlord', Newco, until its lease expires, and Newco would then go into occupation. However, it is likely that this would result in loss of tax relief for Newco on the difference between the rent paid under the new head lease and that received under the sub-lease as the letting by Newco, ie its succession to the existing lease, would not be a lease at full rent. This corporation tax disadvantage would need to be weighed against the VAT saving. It may be possible to achieve the best of both worlds by Newco being a nominee of the existing tenant. However, particularly in the light of the decisions in *Kildrummy (Jersey) Ltd v CIR (1990 STC 657)* and *Lady Ingram's Executors v CIR (1997 STC 1234)* (see **18.62** below), care may be needed in choosing the nominee.

Wholly Artificial Transactions

17.116 In the past HMRC seemed relatively tolerant of artificial transactions designed to enhance the recoverability if input tax. However, their attitude has hardened in recent years and in 2006 culminated in the ECJ decision in *Halifax plc, Country Wide Property Investments Ltd* and *Leeds Permanent Development Services Ltd (Case C–255/02) ([2006] STC 919)*. Halifax makes mainly exempt supplies. It owned four sites on which it wished to construct call centres. It entered into a scheme designed to increase the recoverable VAT on its construction costs. It accepted the scheme had no other commercial purpose but was purely a tax avoidance scheme. It consisted of the following steps:

(*a*) Halifax entered into an agreement to lease the sites to Leeds Permanent Development Services (LPDS) and on the same days LPDS entered into an agreement with a third company, Halifax Property Investments Ltd (HPIL) to sell the leases to HPIL with completion to take place as and when each site had been developed.

(*b*) LPDS entered into an agreement with Country Wide Property Investments (CWPI) for CWPI to construct the call centres.

(*c*) CWPI engaged builders to carry out the work.

(*d*) During the prescribed accounting period in which LPDS entered into the contract with CWPI it made a small supply of taxable construction services to Halifax. It would therefore be able to recover the whole of the input tax charged by CWPI as its only outputs in that period were taxable outputs.

(*e*) In its next prescribed accounting period LPDS assigned its lease to HPIL in pursuance of the agreement at (*a*). This was an exempt supply, but as LPDS was undoubtedly a property dealing company this would not trigger any recovery of VAT under the capital goods scheme.

(*f*) Halifax provided interest free finance for the entire scheme. All of the companies were Halifax subsidiaries.

HMRC contended that a tax avoidance transaction is not a supply or alternatively that the EC doctrine of abuse of rights applied so as to disallow the claim for recovery of input tax.

17.117 The ECJ dismissed the contention that a tax avoidance transaction is not a supply. Indeed it specifically said that the fact that a transaction is carried out for the sole purpose of obtaining a tax advantage is wholly irrelevant in determining whether it constitutes a supply. However, it went on to hold that 'the Sixth Directive must be interpreted as precluding any right of a taxable person to deduct input VAT where the transaction from which that right derives constitutes an abusive practice. For it to be found that an abusive practice exists, it is necessary, first that the transactions concerned, notwithstanding formal application of the conditions laid down by the relevant provisions of the Sixth Directive and of national legislation transposing it, result in the accrual of a tax advantage the grant of which would be contrary to the purpose of those provisions. Second, it must also be apparent from a number of objective factors that the essential aim of the transactions concerned is obtain a tax advantage.' It almost immediately added that Community legislation must be certain and its application foreseeable by those subject to it and that the requirement of legal certainty 'must be observed all the more strictly in the case of rules liable to entail fiscal consequences, in order that those concerned may know precisely the extent of the obligations impose don them'. The court also affirmed that 'taxpayers may choose to structure their business so as to limit their tax liability'. Interestingly the ECJ also said that a finding of abusive practice must not lead to a penalty, that the transactions involved must be redefined so as to establish the situation which would have prevailed in the absence of the transactions constituting the abusive practice, and that, whilst the tax authorities can demand repayment of amounts deducted abusively, they must allow a taxable person to deduct the VAT that he could have deducted had a non-abusive transaction been adopted instead. The First-tier Tribunal in *Moorbury Ltd v Revenue and Customs Commrs (TC 135)* held that, if the neutrality of the VAT system is to be maintained, relief for input tax must happen automatically without risk that the trader might be denied repayment by having to make a claim that might be out of time. The Upper Tribunal agreed.

17.118 The ECJ heard the case of *The University of Huddersfield Higher Education Corporation v C & E Commrs (Case C-223/03) (2006 STC 980)* at the same time as the Halifax case. That case involved a lease and leaseback transaction where there was an intention eventually to collapse the leases to generate a permanent VAT saving. The tribunal did not refer the question of abuse of rights in that case so the Court did not address it but merely held that the transactions must be regarded as constituting supplies provided that they satisfy the objective criteria on which the concepts of supplies and economic activity are based, even if they are carried out with the sole aim of obtaining a tax advantage, without any other economic objective. It took until 2013 for the *University of Huddersfield* case to return to the FTT (Judge Demack). The Tribunal allowed the University's appeal. As the option to tax is specifically provided for in EU law, it follows that its use could not be an abuse of rights if all it achieves is a tax deferral as that end result is not contrary to either UK or EU legislation. The Upper Tribunal and Court of Appeal both disagreed *(2016 STC 1741)*. They thought that the FTT had not given proper weight to the fact that the scheme was intended not only to allow the University to defer tax but also to enable it to obtain an absolute VAT saving by collapsing the scheme. It was wrong to look on that collapse as a completely separate transaction. The scheme was abusive and the transaction should be redefined by disregarding both the lease by the University to the trust and the underlease from the Trust to the University so that the University is not required to account for any output tax but can reclaim input tax only to the extent that the refurbishment was undertaken for the University's general purposes. Halifax subsequently withdrew its appeal (HMRC Brief 30/07) and the *University of Huddersfield* case was ultimately resolved in HMRC's favour in the Court of Appeal (*2015 STC 1741*).

17.119 The Halifax VAT tribunal decision was followed in *J E & H Laurie (t/a the Peacock Montessori Nursery) (VTD 17219)* where a lease and leaseback transaction was created to generate taxable supplies and allow recovery of the VAT on building works in advance of making the exempt supply of education. The tribunal in *Capital One Developments Ltd (VTD 18642)* followed the *Halifax* principle but recognised that their findings might not be sufficient to dispose of the appeal and gave the parties permission to apply for the hearing to be continued if the ECJ decision in *Halifax* does not resolve all outstanding matters. Capital One Developments (COD) is a special purpose vehicle owned by Capital One Bank. A number of intra-group transactions were entered into which purported to result in input VAT on the construction of a new office building for occupation by the bank becoming recoverable. The tribunal held that those transactions were carried out purely for tax avoidance purposes but held that there is no single correct way 'to reconstruct the arrangements so as to reflect their true economic substance', although HMRC's preferred construction (of direct supplies to an exempt financial institution) 'would not have occurred even in the absence of the tax saving plan'. When the *Huddersfield* case returned to the Upper Tribunal (*2015 STC 307*) the Tribunal said that '*Weald* [*(C-103/09) HMRC v Weald Leasing (2011 STC 596)*] is not authority for the proposition that where a tax mitigation scheme is devised to create an absolute entitlement to deduct input tax but also generates a liability to account for output tax, one must wait to see how much output tax is in fact accounted for before the scheme runs its course'. On the contrary, the CJEU in *Halifax* clearly envisaged that output tax may need to be refunded to the taxable person once the abusive practice has been set aside. It felt that the FTT had given insufficient weight to its earlier finding that the scheme had been designed not only to defer tax but also to enable the University to obtain an absolute VAT saving by collapsing the arrangements. Also the FTT failed to look at the scheme as a whole. Looked at as a whole, it was apparent that the advantage sought was contrary to the purposes of the VAT legislation. The scheme was therefore an abuse of right. Accordingly the transactions had to be redefined so as to re-establish the situation that would have prevailed in the absence of the transactions constituting the abusive practice. The way to do this is to ignore the lease and underlease in their entirety.

17.120 The tribunal in *RBS Property Developments Ltd* and the *Royal Bank of Scotland Group plc (VTD 17789)* refused to refer that case to the ECJ, differentiating it from Halifax. The scheme in that case involved RBS selling a site to Developments, Development constructing a building thereon and selling it back to RBS with the consideration payable by instalments. The tribunal found that there was a business purpose in the development being carried out in this way so it could not be said that the 'sole' purpose of the transaction was tax avoidance. Even if the predominant purpose was tax avoidance, that could not prevent the transaction being an economic activity unless it was *de minimis*.

17.121 *HMRC v Gracechurch Management Services Ltd (2008 STC 795)* involved a prepayment scheme. Gracechurch was a member of a group VAT registration. It entered into a development agreement with another group company, Patriges Gracechurch SA, to undertake development work for it. Patriges paid Gracechurch an advance payment of £20 million. Gracechurch then left the VAT group and registered separately. It subsequently invoiced Patriges for the balance of the contract price, roughly £10.5 million, plus VAT of £1.75 million. HMRC contended that the input tax paid by Gracechurch was deductible only to the extent of the £1.75 million VAT charged by Gracechurch, as the balance of roughly £5 million related to the initial £20 million out-of-the-scope receipt. Sir Andrew Morritt agreed. Input tax is deductible only in so far as the services are used for the purpose of taxable transactions. Where inputs are used only to some extent in making taxable supplies it is deductible only to that extent. In *HMRC v Weald Leasing Ltd (Case C-103/09) (2011 STC 596)*, a non-property case, the ECJ held that leasing rather than buying assets from a third party did not constitute an abusive practice provided that the contractual terms correspond to arm's-length terms and that the involvement of an intermediate third party in the transaction is not such as to preclude the application of the appropriate provisions of the Directive.

17.122 The decision of the First-tier Tribunal in favour of HMRC in *Lower Mill Estate Ltd and Conservation Builders Ltd (2010 STC 636)* suggested that abuse of rights may have very wide application. This was reversed by the Upper Tribunal but HMRC are taking it to the Court of Appeal. Lower Mill Estate (LME) owned land with planning permission for holiday homes. Conservation Builders Ltd (CBL) was a building company under common control. LME sold standard-rated plots of land to customers. The customer could contract with CBL to erect a dwelling on the site. Alternatively he could instruct a different builder or construct the house himself. In practice the customer had always used CBL. Evidence was given that this two company structure was commonly used by house builders in both Australia and the USA. HMRC contended that the supply of the zero-rating building work was ancillary to the sale of the land. The tribunal dismissed this on the basis that the construction services business could not be ancillary to the land sales as it was a substantial business in its own right. HMRC next claimed that LME and CBL made a joint supply to the customer. The tribunal dismissed this, partly on the basis that it could not see how the time of supply rules could apply to such a joint supply and partly because 'consideration' arises from a legal relationship providing for reciprocal performance and the customer had got what he had paid for. Finally HMRC contended that the arrangements amounted to an abusive practice. The First-tier Tribunal agreed. It agreed despite the fact that good commercial reasons were shown for the separation, that the customer had the right to use a different builder, that the ECJ in Halifax had confirmed that 'taxpayers may choose to structure their business so as to limit their tax liability, and that it is hard to see how the Halifax condition that the accrual of the tax advantage must be contrary to the provisions of the VAT Directive is met (bearing in mind that zero-rating arises under a derogation from the Directive and that the Directive itself deals separately with sales of land and the provision of construction services). It is clear that the tribunal did not like the transaction. A number of phrases in the judgment give the appearance of sarcasm. The decision also seems to conflict with the later judgement of the ECJ in *RLRE Tellmer Property sro Financni reditelstvi v Usti nad Labem* (see **16.181**).

17.123 The Upper Tribunal started by confirming that, apart from any abuse or sham, it is not possible to combine supplies by two suppliers under two contracts to result in one supply for VAT purposes. It went on to say that the starting point to considering whether transactions result in a VAT advantage to the trader which is contrary to the purposes of the VAT Directive is to identify an appropriate corporator. It pointed out that:

> 'Even accepting that the Tribunal did so hold [That the substance or reality of the matter was different to the legal analysis], it must be remembered that such a categorisation does not necessarily lead to the conclusion that there is abuse. First, the substance or reality thus identified is that the purchaser has entered into agreements as the result of which he obtains a completed holiday home. But there are different ways in which that result could be achieved. For instance, a land-owner could build a house and sell it together with the plot; he could contract to sell the house with a yet-to-be-built house on it; he could adopt the self-build route using his captive associated builder; he could adopt the self-build route using an associated builder (as in the present case); or he could make arrangements with a non-associated builder under which they shared an on-site office where the land-owner was able to put the purchaser in contact with the builder but took no interest in the contractual relationships between purchaser and builder. Those are all transactions which it is easy to envisage in the real world. The substance or reality of them all is in this sense the same, namely that the purchase in all cases will end up with a completed holiday home. And yet the

> VAT consequences at least of the first and last transactions are clear and different. In each of those examples, it is necessary to see what the consequences of the substance and reality are. Is there abuse or is the choice which Halifax and Part Service recognise one which is available in the particular case?'

It then pointed out that the onus is on HMRC to establish that there is an abuse and thus that transactions under the self-build model are not normal commercial operations for a developer such as Lower Mill Estates. The evidence was that this model had been adopted for commercial reasons and was a permissible course open to the taxpayer. In any event the development model is not a valid comparator. A similar scheme was held to be ineffective in *Fairway Lakes Ltd v HMRC (2016 UKUT 340)* where the split was structured differently (see **17.45**).

17.124 Abuse of rights was also in issue in *HMRC v Atrium Club Ltd (2010 STC 1493*). The company originally carried on a gym and sporting facilities. A new company AAB Sports Ltd, a company limited by guarantee whose articles prohibited it from distributing surpluses, was set up to take advantage of the sporting exemption. Atrium granted AAB the non-exclusive right to occupy the premises and carry on the Atrium Club business in return for a monthly licence fee of £2,000 plus 50% of net turnover, which resulted in AAB making little profit. In fact AAB was held not to be eligible for the sporting exemption so no VAT benefit was received. However, by the time this was discovered the payment of the licence fee had deprived AAB of funds to meet its VAT liability. Roth J held that, 'an arrangement which results in that situation is contrary to the purpose of the exempting provision of the Sixth Directive'. He redefined the supplies made by AAB as supplies made by Atrium. HMRC do not always succeed on abuse of rights. In the non-property case of *Pendragon plc v HMRC (2009 UKFTT 192; 2010 SFTD 1)* the scheme adopted was held not to be abusive as the essential aim of the scheme was to obtain finance. The Tribunal commented that, 'What was done was done in a tax-efficient manner but that does not make the essential aim of the scheme to obtain a tax advantage'.

17.125 HMRC have said that if a house builder is unable to sell dwellings so decides to let them short-term while the market recovers, but before doing so grants a major interest in them to a connected person outside its VAT group so as to avoid a loss of input tax relief, they would not consider it abusive. HMRC believe that Parliament intended that the construction of new dwellings should be relieved from VAT. If the first grant provision does not achieve this then it is acceptable to enter into arrangements 'to ensure that a transaction of the kind Parliament envisaged will actually take place'. HMRC would, however, regard as abusive the grant of a major interest 'with the essential aim of deducting VAT on costs such as repair, maintenance and refurbishment of dwellings' as the relief of those kinds of costs does not fall within the policy objective as HMRC see it. They warn that such types of arrangement are likely to be challenged (HMRC Brief 54/08). It is interesting to note that HMRC did not claim abuse of rights in *Community Housing Association Ltd v HMRC* (see **16.244**). In that case the Housing Association restructured its operations so that input tax that was not deductible would in future become deductible. On the face of it that looks far more abusive than to create a structure initially so as to achieve a particular tax effect. The tax is unworkable if abuse of rights is a concept that is applicable when HMRC do not like the taxpayer but inapplicable where they think that it is a nice person. It is fundamental that a person needs to know the VAT effect of a transaction at the time that he enters into it.

The 'Option to Tax'

17.126 An election can be made to bring rent and other supplies – including subsequent disposals of the building – within the VAT net (*VAT 1994, Sch 10, para 2*). It can be made by anyone who lets property, including a pension fund and a local authority (*Finanzamt Augsburg v Marktgemeinde Welden (Case C-247/95) (1997 STC 531)*). The election can be made in relation to bare land, an individual building (which includes the land on which it stands) or, prior to 1 June 2008, on a global basis, ie the taxpayer could opt to tax all the land and buildings that he currently owns or acquires in the future. The relevant legislation is contained in *VATA 1994, Sch 10.*

17.127 The effect of the election is that any supply made by the taxpayer in relation to the building or land at a time when the election is in force must be regarded as not falling within *VATA 1994, Sch 9, Group 1*, ie as not being exempt, and therefore as being taxable at the standard rate of 20% (*VATA 1994, Sch 10, paras 1, 2*). Supply, of course, covers not only rents but also the disposal proceeds when the building is sold. It is obviously important to remember that the election has been made. Prior to the setting up of their Option to Tax Unit, HMRC did not maintain a central record of options. This was simply filed on the relevant files. HMRC's practice for many years has been to destroy files after six years, but to carry forward important documents to the new file. A few years ago, HMRC digitised their VAT files and destroyed the remaining originals. Misfiling, failure to identify that a letter contained an option to tax, etc has meant that in many cases options have been mislaid by HMRC, so they are unable to identify whether an election was made. Many businesses seem to have a similar problem of not being able to locate an election. For a rental property, the VAT treatment of the rents is indicative of the VAT status but for owner-occupied properties, there is nothing to suggest whether or not an election was made. If one was made and it has been misfiled by HMRC, there is always a risk that it will come to light at some stage.

17.128 It is equally important to deal with the option in the contract when a property is sold. Vendors have had mixed results in trying to recover VAT where the purchase price in the contract did not refer to VAT. In *Hostgilt v Megahart Ltd (1999 STC 141)*, the agreement stated, 'In this agreement the Purchase Price means £400,000', but included a clause providing 'Sums payable under this agreement for the supply of goods and services are exclusive of VAT on the payment'. The purchaser was held liable to pay the VAT in addition to the £400,000. In *Wym Realisations Ltd (in administration) v Vogue Holdings Inc (1999 STC 524)* the purchase price was expressed to be '£2,935,000 exclusive of VAT'. The agreement also provided that 'the vendor undertakes and warrants that no election to charge VAT has been or will be made'. It subsequently transpired that VAT arose on the sale because it was a new building. The words 'exclusive of VAT' were held to make the purchaser liable for this undisclosed VAT. In *CLP Holdings Company Ltd v Singh (2015 STC 214)* the sale price was expressed to be £130,000. No mention of VAT was made in the contract itself, but clause 4 of the general conditions of sale stated, 'An obligation to pay money includes an obligation to pay any VAT chargeable in respect of that payment, as sums made payable by the contract are exclusive of VAT'. When the option to tax subsequently came to light, the Court of Appeal held that the liability for VAT fell on the vendor despite this provision, because the general course of conduct in relation to the transaction would have led 'a reasonable person who has all the background knowledge which would reasonably have been available to all the parties in the situation in which they were at the time of the contract' would have concluded that the parties intended that nothing was or could become payable by the purchaser over and above the specific purchase price of £130,000.

17.129 Where the person making the election is a company, the election will apply not only to rents, etc. received by the company but also to those received by any relevant associate – broadly, a member of the same VAT group – in relation to the same land or building (*VATA 1994, Sch 10, para 2(2),*). For this purpose a relevant associate is any company which is either:

(*a*) a member of the same VAT group as the electing company at the time the election was made;

(*b*) a member of the same VAT group at any subsequent time at which the electing company continues to have an interest in, right over or licence to occupy the building or land (or any part of it); or

(*c*) a member of the same VAT group as another company that is itself within (*a*) or (*b*) above at a time when that company has an interest in, right over or licence to occupy the building or land.

(*VATA 1994, Sch 10, para 3.*)

17.130 An example may make head (*c*) clearer. Suppose A Ltd owns a building and has granted a lease of part to B Ltd which is in the same VAT group. An election by A Ltd will force B Ltd to charge VAT (and one by B Ltd would force A Ltd to do so). A Ltd sells its interest to C Ltd which is not a member of the VAT group (but is a wholly-owned subsidiary of B Ltd). C Ltd is not bound by A's election and this transfer does not affect B's obligation to charge VAT on its rents. A Ltd is sold and subsequently C Ltd is grouped with B Ltd for VAT purposes. C Ltd will from then on be bound by the election made by A Ltd because B Ltd, another member of the VAT group, is bound by that election.

17.131 A company will cease to be a relevant associate of the company if all of the following conditions are met:

(*a*) it has disposed of such an interest and the supply has already taken place (prior to 1 August 2009 the test was that of having no interest in, right over or licence to occupy the building or land (or any part of it) and no part of any consideration payable in respect of a disposal by the company of any such interest was unpaid);

(*b*) either the company or the opter ceases to be a member of the group; and

(*c*) the company is not connected with the opter or another relevant associate of the opter who has such an interest in the land or any part of it.

(*VATA 1994, Sch 10, para 3(3),(4),(6)*) – this provision did not apply prior to 1 June 2008.)

17.132 HMRC also have power to allow a company to cease to be a relevant associate if:

(*a*) it meets conditions specified in a public notice and has notified HMRC that it has done so in the form specified in the notice; or

(*b*) it gets the prior permission of HMRC (by applying in the form specified in a public notice); HMRC can grant such permission retrospectively but only where the application was deficient and the grounds which it did not meet were insignificant – presumably this is to enable the company to make a fresh application and for HMRC to give effect to it from the time that they would have approved the original application had it satisfied all of the relevant conditions.

(*VATA 1994, Sch 10, para 3(5), 4.*)

17.133 If the taxpayer has made, or intends to make, an exempt grant in respect of the land within the previous ten years (at any time prior to 1 June 2008) the prior written consent of HMRC to the election is needed. HMRC can permit the election only if they are satisfied that a fair and reasonable attribution of the input tax in relation to the land will be achieved between exempt and taxable supplies over the entire period of ownership of the land (*VATA 1994, Sch 10, para 3(9)*). From 1 June 2008, in deciding what is fair and reasonable, HMRC must have regard to all of the circumstances of the case but, in particular, the total value of any exempt supply to which any grant in relation to the land gives rise and is (or will be) made before the option is to have effect; the total value of any supply to which any grant in relation to the land gives rise that would be taxable under the option; and the total amount of input tax incurred, or likely to be incurred, in relation to the land (*VATA 1994, Sch 10, para 28(5),(6)*). HMRC are empowered to specify in a Notice conditions for which automatic permission can be assumed (*VATA 1994, Sch 10, para 28(2)(a)*). They have done so in paragraph 5.2 of Notice 742A.

17.134 Prior permission is not needed where either:

(*a*) the development is a mixed use one and the only exempt supplies have been in relation to the dwellings;

(*b*) the taxpayer does not wish to recover any input tax on goods, services or acquisitions received before the option to tax has effect, the consideration received for exempt supplies prior to that time has been solely by way of rent or service charges, and the only input tax the taxpayer wishes to recover after the option to tax takes effect is in relation to day-to-day overheads (which does not include a refurbishment of the building);

(*c*) although the taxpayer wishes to recover input tax incurred before the option to tax takes effect, this relates solely to tax charged by tenants on surrender of a lease, the relevant part of the building has been unoccupied since that surrender, there will be no further exempt supplies of the property and the taxpayer does not expect to occupy the building for an exempt or partly exempt purpose; or

(*d*) the exempt supplies have been incidental to the main use of the property, such as the siting of an advertising hoarding within the curtilage of a building, granting space for the erection of a radio mast or receiving income from an electrical substation.

17.135 An application for permission must be made in a form specified in a public notice. Notice 742A specifies form 1614H. HMRC can give permission subject to conditions being met. If HMRC give permission the option to tax takes effect from the start of the day on which the application is made or such later day as may be specified in the notice (*VATA 1994, Sch 10, para 29(1)–(3)*). If prior permission is needed but is not obtained, HMRC can dispense with the need to notify, in which case the option will take effect from the start of the day on which the option was exercised (or, if later, the date specified in the election) (*VATA 1994, Sch 10, para 30*).

17.136 The taxpayer challenged whether a country is entitled to impose a requirement for prior approval to the exercise of the option to tax in *Luxembourg v Vermietungsgesellschaft Objekt Kirchberg SARL (Case C-269/03) (2005 STC 1345)*. The taxpayer (VOK) had let a building since 1 January 1993. In Luxembourg, the exercise of the option is subject to prior approval of the tax authorities. VOK applied for approval on 29 June 1993. This was granted with effect from 1 July 1993. The tax authorities refused relief for input tax paid from 1 January to 29 June on the grounds that although VOK had charged VAT on the rents the letting was exempt. The ECJ held that the Sixth Directive does not preclude a member state that exercises the power to allow the option to tax from adopting legislation which make the deduction conditional on non-retroactive, prior approval of the tax authorities.

17.137 In *C & E Commrs v Trustees of R & R Pension Fund (1996 STC 889)*, the trustees of a pension fund had constructed a commercial building and reclaimed the whole of the input tax on the building costs. They granted a 15-year lease of the building from 1 August 1993. This triggered a self-supply charge under *VATA 1994, Sch 10, para 6(1)*. On 12 December 1994 they notified their election to waive exemption. They proposed that 99.1% of the tax on the self-supply should be allowed as input tax. This was calculated as 16 months exempt out of the expected 150-year life of the building. It was agreed that the building was within the capital goods scheme. HMRC refused permission for the election on the grounds that it did not give a fair and reasonable attribution of the input tax having regard to the application of the capital goods scheme. The VAT tribunal saw no reason why HMRC could not agree an initial attribution of input tax in lieu of adjustment under the capital goods scheme, but the High Court reversed this decision and held that HMRC were justified in refusing the election, as *VATA 1994, Sch 10, para 3(9)* did not permit them to allow an election unless a fair and reasonable attribution could be secured. Following this decision HMRC said that *para 3(9)* (which was added from 1 January 1992) was introduced 'with the primary purposes of removing the block for capital items to allow the capital goods scheme to run its course' (Business Brief 17/96).

17.138 In *The Island Trading Co Ltd (VTD 13838)*, the company used the property partly for its own business and partly for letting, and the input tax that HMRC wanted repaid as a condition of accepting the election was fully recoverable under the *de minimis* provisions. HMRC claimed that the *de minimis* limit did not apply where a special method of apportionment is used in respect of partially exempt supplies. The VAT tribunal rejected this, and also held that HMRC could only require an adjustment to past input tax relief if this was necessary to secure a fair and reasonable attribution, and as the input tax was fully deductible under the *de minimis* rules if no election were made, HMRC could not require any adjustment in that case as a condition of consenting to the election. This ruling was given before the High Court decision in *R & R Pension Fund* and may therefore be unreliable.

17.139 *British Eventing Ltd v HMRC (2011 SFTD 18)* was an appeal against HMRC's refusal to allow an option to tax. British Eventing leased Tweseldown Racecourse from the Ministry of Defence. It allowed a company, Tweseldown Equisport Ltd (TEL) to occupy the racecourse as a tenant at will on payment of a rent equal to that payable to the MoD. Neither the MoD nor the company charged VAT. One of the buildings at the racecourse was destroyed by fire. British Eventing received compensation of £140,000. However, it was told that it would cost £350,000 to fulfil all its reinstatement obligations to the MoD under the lease. British Eventing assigned the lease to TEL for the sum of £10. It also agreed to pay TEL £200,000 for TEL to assume its obligations under the lease and the £140,000 insurance monies for TEL to reinstate the destroyed building, in both cases plus VAT. HMRC refused to allow British Eventing to opt to tax as there was no intended taxable use of the property once the lease was assigned. The company purported to opt to tax on the day that the assignment was entered into. They were of course seeking to recover input tax of £59,000 against the output tax of £1.75 that would be payable on the £10. The Tribunal held that the assignment of the lease was not a supply at all. There was no disposal of an 'asset' as the lease was a liability as shown by the need to pay £140,000 to get rid of it. Accordingly the £59,000 VAT was not attributable to a supply of the lease; it was attributable as a general overhead to the business as a whole. Accordingly HMRC had not considered the correct attribution of input tax when exercising its discretion to refuse the option to tax. However, it would not set aside that decision as it was clear that there would be no taxable supplies at all of the land, so they would have refused permission in any event. The finding that the assignment was not a supply is questionable (see **17.20**).

17.140 An interesting scheme was tried in *C & E Commrs v Robert Gordon's College (1995 STC 1093)*. The appellant was an educational charity. It charged fees to pupils which were exempt. It spent some £3.4 million in developing some disused land and buildings as a playing field. It formed a company to exploit the playing field commercially and rented the land to the company, retaining a non-exclusive licence to use it itself. Both the charity and the company exercised the option to tax. The charity reclaimed the VAT on the development costs as directly attributable to the generation of the VATable rent. The company entered into a charitable deed of covenant under which it paid the whole of its profits to the charity. HMRC contended that the arrangement was a circular transaction within the *Furniss v Dawson* principle so that the lease to the company was not a business activity. This was rejected by the VAT tribunal on the basis that the recovery of input tax is a business purpose and also that the lease was intended to enable a particular area of the college's activities to be conducted in a more efficient manner and was therefore clearly in furtherance of a business. HMRC secondly claimed that the first occasion on which the school used the playing fields constituted occupation of them by the college when not a fully taxable person within ten years of completion of the works and therefore gave rise to a self-supply charge (see *s 5(6)(b)*). The House of Lords held that, whilst this might follow from the usual principles of construction used in the UK, it was incompatible with the *Sixth Directive*. As the use the College made of the playing field was pursuant to services (ie the licence) supplied to it by a third party (the company) 'there could be no room for a self-supply charge within the terms of the *Sixth Directive*'. HMRC did not appeal on the *Furniss v Dawson* point. This and similar arrangements have been blocked by legislation from 29 November 1994 (see **17.133** and **17.153**), so that this scheme will no longer work.

Exclusions

17.141 An election cannot take out of exemption a supply in relation to:

(*a*) A building or part of a building intended for use solely as a dwelling or number of dwellings or for a relevant residential purpose (and the appropriate certificate under *VATA 1994, Sch 8, Group 5, Note 12* – see **16.82** – has been given (*VATA 1994, Sch 10, para 5(1)(2)*). From 1 June 2008 this exclusion also applies if the purchaser or lessee certifies that the building or part of the building is intended for use for such a purpose. Such a certificate must be given within the period specified in a public notice or, if the seller agrees, at any later time before the seller makes a supply to which the grant gives rise. The relevant public notice, Notice 742A, states that the certificate must be given on form VAT 1614D and must be given before the price for the grant to the purchaser is legally fixed, eg before exchange of contracts, ie before completion in the case of a sale and in the case of a lease it can only apply to rent received after the certificate has been given. The purchaser/lessee must either:

   (i) intend himself to use the building for the specified purpose,

   (ii) intend to convert the building (or part) with a view to its being used for such a purpose, or

   (iii) intend to dispose of the whole of his interest to another person and that other person has given him a certificate stating either that he intends to convert the premises into a dwelling or he holds a certificate from a prospective purchaser of his who has such an intention.

(*VATA 1994, Sch 10, para 6(1)–(7)*.)

(*b*) A building (or part) cannot be regarded for this purpose as intended for use as a dwelling or number of dwellings if it is intended to be used for some other purpose before being so used (*VATA 1994, Sch 10, para 6(8)*).

(*c*) A building or part of a building intended for use solely for a relevant charitable purpose, *other than as an office* (*VATA 1994, Sch 10, para 7*).

(*d*) A grant to a registered housing association (within the meaning of *Part 1* of the *Housing Act 1996*, the *Housing (Scotland) Act 2001*, or *Part 2* of the *Housing (Northern Ireland) Order 1992*) where the association has given the grantor a certificate stating that the land is to be used for the construction of a dwelling or dwellings or for a relevant residential purpose (*VATA 1994, Sch 10, para 10(1)*). From 1 April 2010 this provision also applies where the grant is to a private registered provider of social housing (*VATA 1994, Sch 10, para 1(3)(2A)*). Until the coming into force of a provision defining a private registered provider of social housing that term means a person (other than a local authority) listed in the register under the *Housing and Regeneration Act 2008, Pt 2, Ch 3 (para 4(2)* of the *Order*), The certificate must be given in the form specified in a public notice and (unless the seller agrees otherwise) within the period specified in the notice (*VATA 1994, Sch 10, para 10(2)*). Notice 742A specifies that the notice must be given on form VAT 1614G and must be given before the price is legally fixed – but the seller can accept a later certificate if he wishes although it can apply only to rent payable after receipt of the certificate.

(*e*) A grant to an individual where the land is to be used for the construction of a building intended for use by him as a dwelling and the construction is not carried out in the course of furtherance of a business carried on by that individual (*VATA 1994, Sch 10, para 11*).

(*f*) A pitch for a residential caravan or facilities for mooring (or anchoring or berthing) a residential houseboat (ie a boat or other floating decked structure designed or adapted for use solely as a place of permanent habitation not having means of (or capable of being readily adapted for) self-propulsion) residence in which is not prevented throughout the year by the terms of a covenant, statutory planning consent or similar permission (*VATA 1994, Sch 10, paras 8, 9*).

(*g*) There is also an anti-avoidance provision that disapplies the option to tax in specific circumstances. This is considered at **17.147**.

17.142 Where an election is nullified by **17.141**(*a*) above, the person making the grant and the person to whom it is made can enter into a joint written declaration at or before the time of the grant that the election is to have effect. The grantee must intend, at the time the supply to him is made, to use the land for the purpose only of making a zero-rated supply by virtue of *VATA 1994, Sch 8,*

Group 5, item 1(b), ie converting a non-residential building into a dwelling or dwellings or into a building intended for use solely for a relevant residential purpose (see **16.6**(1)(*b*) above) (*VATA 1994, Sch 10, para 5,*). HMRC will allow VAT to be charged (and recovered by the purchaser) where the option to tax has been exercised in respect of a commercial building and the building is sold to a person who intends to convert it to residential use and make a zero-rated supply of the building (ie to sell it or let it on a long lease) and this will enable the vendor to recover VAT on the selling costs. The purchaser will of course be able to recover the VAT only if he ultimately makes a zero-rated supply of the building. To benefit from this concession, a vendor needs the co-operation of the purchaser, as he cannot force him to pay VAT that is not legally due. It should not be assumed that such consent will be automatically forthcoming as the election will obviously have an adverse cash flow effect for the purchaser.

17.143 This head was in issue in *Enterprise Inns plc and Unique Pub Properties Ltd v HMRC (2012 UKUT 240) TCC*). The two companies leased out a number of pubs on which they had opted to tax. Most of the pubs contain residential accommodation which was occupied by the lessees and their families. The appellants originally allocated 10% of the rents to the residential accommodation. This is a standard percentage that HMRC have agreed with the Brewers Society. In 2008, they contended that this was incorrect and the whole of the rent related to the commercial area, the residential accommodation being provided free of charge. They pointed out that the lease normally obliged the tenant to live in the pub. While accepting that the mere fact that a lease includes residential accommodation does not necessarily mean that part of the rent must be attributed to it, as it may have no value, the Upper Tribunal held that the First-tier Tribunal were entitled to attribute some of the rent to it and, having decided to do so, the amount so attributable was the agreed 10% figure. It thought the fact that the rent was fixed by reference to barrelage was irrelevant. The contract was not conclusive. The apportioned amount should have regard to the subjective views of both landlord and tenant. In a later case, *D J & P E Matthews (TC 5426)*, the appellant sold the pub without charging VAT. HMRC contended that 90% of the proceeds was VATable, but the Tribunal said that this standard figure was not binding on the appellant and split the consideration on the basis of usable space, attributing 33% to the residential flat.

17.144 It should particularly be noted that the determining factor under (*b*) is intention, not the use ultimately made of the building, although such use might well be evidence of the intention at the time of the supply. The case of *J Watters (VTD 13337)* illustrates the problem. Mr Watters purchased a disused public house from a brewery company which had elected to waive exemption. HMRC accepted that he had always intended to use the building as a dwelling, but argued that the purchase was not exempt as he had not sufficiently communicated that intention to the company. The VAT tribunal was satisfied that the building was intended for use as a dwelling at the time the supply was made and that the brewery had been told of that fact but had disregarded it as neither party realised that it affected the VAT position. It held that it was therefore unnecessary for it to decide whether a buyer's failure to communicate his intention to the seller would render the waiver of exemption ineffective. In the light of the clear wording of the legislation, it is unclear why HMRC pursued this case, as it seems clear that it is the intention of the future user, not that of the vendor, that matters.

17.145 An interesting issue in relation to (*d*) arose in *Langstane Housing Association Ltd (VTD 19111)*. The Housing Association bought a property in October 2001 with two sitting tenants. In February 2002 it sought to issue a certificate retrospectively to the vendor. HMRC stated it was too late to issue the certificate. The Association appealed against that decision. The tribunal agreed that the certificate could not be issued retrospectively. *Note 12* to *Group 5* (see **16.82**) (which is applied to *Sch 10* by *Note 9* (see **16.184**)) requires a certificate to be given before the supply takes place. This protects the vendor. Although in *Langstane's case* the vendor was prepared to accept a retrospective certificate there is no power in the legislation to permit it to do so.

17.146 In *SEH Holdings Ltd (VTD 16771)* the company (through another group company) contracted to purchase a former public house and on the same day agreed to resell it to two purchasers who intended to convert the property into new dwellings. The company contended that the sale to it was an exempt supply so the vendor had not been entitled to charge input tax. *Para 2(2)(a)* (head **17.141**(*a*) above) refers to the intended use of the property. On the face of it, that is not restricted to the intended use by SEH, the immediate purchaser. The tribunal decided that as VAT is a tax chargeable on each transaction the exclusion must apply only to the intended use by the immediate purchaser. A vendor is contractually in a position to determine the intention of his purchaser but might be unable to ascertain the intention of a future purchaser, which would make it impossible to ascertain the tax to be charged if the wording was intended to cover such an intention. It also held that for the exemption to apply the vendor had to be aware of the intended use of the property at the time of sale and that the appellant had to show on the balance of probabilities that the vendor knew of the intention to use the property as a dwelling. As there was no evidence before the tribunal to show this, the supply to SEH was held to have been correctly charged at the standard rate. Following this case HMRC said that where the immediate purchaser of a building (which the vendor had opted to tax) does not intend to use the building himself as a dwelling nor to convert the building into dwellings for sale or rent, their policy is that the vendor must account for VAT on the sale of the building. They accept that there are particular problems with auction sale where the vendor is not aware of the identity of the purchaser prior to the auction. They are reviewing this area. In the meantime they suggest that the purchaser should discuss with the vendor any problem he is facing prior to completion (Business Brief 8/01, 2 July 2001). Presumably they mean that if the purchaser does not wish to suffer VAT he must make his intentions known to the vendor. Or perhaps not. In *PJG Developments Ltd (VTD 19097)* the tribunal held that it was not necessary for the purchaser to make his intentions known to the vendor. In that case as the vendor has advertised the land (a public house) as suitable for residential development it ought to have been aware of the purchaser's intention. The tribunal also held that the intention is subjective, ie it is not necessary for the purchaser to use the land for the residential purpose. This conflicts with the SEH decision. The government have subsequently said that they intend to introduce legislation to give effect to the SEH decision.

17.147 The election cannot take a supply out of exemption if the grant giving rise to it was made by a developer of the land (see **17.148** below) and at the time of the grant it was the intention or expectation of either the grantor), that the land would become 'exempt land' (see **17.149** below) (either immediately or eventually and whether by reason of the grant or of some other transaction) or, if it was already exempt land, that it would continue (for a period at least) to be such land (*VATA 1994, Sch 10, para 12(1)–(3)*).

17.148 A developer is not defined. That probably does not matter as the word does not bear its normal meaning; a grant made by any person in relation to land is regarded as a grant made by a developer of that land if:

(*a*) the land (or a building, or part of a building, on it) falls to be treated by that person as a capital item within the capital goods scheme (see **17.205** below); and

(*b*) that person (or a person financing his development of the land for exempt use) intended or expected that the land or building or part of a building on (or to be constructed on) the land would become an asset falling to be treated as a capital item within the capital goods scheme (in relation either to the grantor or some other person to whom it was to be transferred in the course of a supply or a TOGC) unless the grant was made at a time falling after the asset's adjustment period under the scheme.

(*VATA 1994, Sch 10, para 13.*)

17.149 The sort of transaction this is aimed at is exemplified by *The Principal and Fellows of Newnham College in the University of Cambridge (2008 STC 1225)*. The College wished to renovate and extend its library. It sought to avoid VAT by creating a wholly owned subsidiary (NCLCL), opting to tax the College building, granting a lease of the library building to NCLCL for 11 years, selling the library books to NCLCL and seconding to it the library staff, and NCLCL agreeing with the College for an annual fee (based on usage) of around £167,000 to provide library services to the College. Customs attacked this by seeking to disallow the option to tax under *para 2(3AA)* on the basis that the College remained in occupation of the library, so it was intended for use to make exempt supplies. The College contended it was not in occupation of the building but that NCLCL was making a taxable supply to it of providing library facilities for its students. The tribunal gave a wide meaning to 'occupation' and held that the College was in occupation of the library in the course and furtherance of its exempt supply of education. This is the same decision as that reached by the tribunal in *Brambletye School Trust* (see **17.162**).

17.150 Both the Court of Appeal and the House of Lords disagreed, albeit the latter by a three to two majority. Lord Hoffmann felt that the word 'occupy' must be interpreted in its EU sense, as described in *Sinclair Collis* (see **17.77**), as meaning the right to occupy as if the person were the owner and to exclude any other person from enjoyment of that right. Accordingly the College and NCLCL could not both be in occupation simultaneously. Which is in occupation must be determined by an examination of the arrangements under which the members of the College are able to use the library. These pointed to control by NCLCL. Following this decision HMRC had said:

> 'HMRC now accept that physical presence alone is not the correct test of occupation for the purposes of what is now VATA 1994 Schedule 10 Paragraphs 12 to 17 (the 'anti-avoidance test'). Following the House of Lords judgment, a person is considered to be 'in occupation' if, in addition to physical presence which occupation normally entails, they have the right to occupy the property as if they are the owner and to exclude others from enjoyment of such a right. This means a person must have actual possession of the land along with a degree of permanence and control. Such a right will normally result from the grant of a legal interest or licence to occupy. Occupation could also, however, be by agreement or *de facto* and it is therefore necessary to take account of the day-to-day arrangements, particularly where these differ from the contractual terms. An exclusive right of occupation is not a requirement; an agreement might, for example, allow for joint occupation. Equally, it is not necessary for a person to be utilising all of the land for all of the time for them to be considered as occupying it.
>
> A person whose interest in land is subject to an inferior interest, such as to prevent him from having rights of occupation for the time being, is not 'in occupation' for the purposes of the anti-avoidance test until the inferior interest expires. It should be noted, however, that an important feature of the test is that it is forward looking and takes account of the intended or expected occupation of the building at any time during the Capital Goods Scheme (CGS) adjustment period (see **17.205**). As a result, a person who has granted an inferior interest but intends during that adjustment period to occupy the land himself would intend to be

'in occupation' for the purposes of the anti-avoidance test and so must consider whether his intended occupation was for eligible purposes.

However, a person can ignore the following types of occupation for the purposes of the test:

1. Occupation which is purely for the purpose of making his rental supplies under the grant, since those are the very supplies whose liability he is trying to determine by applying the test. For example:

   (*a*) occupation by the grantor between the date of the grant and the start of occupation by the tenant which is for the purpose of undertaking refurbishment or repairs;

   (*b*) occupation by maintenance, security or reception staff (or similar), unless it is for the purpose of providing ongoing services separate from the letting itself.

2. Occupation at a future date, but within the CGS adjustment period, which is solely for the purpose of re-letting the property or making a fresh grant.' (HMRC Brief 33/2009).

17.151 *Grimsby College Enterprises Ltd v Revenue and Customs Commrs ([2009] UKFTT 167 (TC) (TC 129)* demonstrates that care needs to be taken when using such a structure. In that case the College has contracted with the builder before the structure was put in place. The First-tier Tribunal held that the fact that the subsidiary, Enterprises, paid the builder could not affect the contractual position. The supply by the builder would remain a supply to the College in the absence of evidence that the contract has been novated. Even where Enterprises had ordered equipment itself it could not recover the input tax because the College was in occupation of the building and the licence to occupy the building by Enterprises to the College was an exempt licence.

17.152 It will be seen that *para 12* (see **17.147** above) will not apply to a grant made more than ten years after the building was acquired or constructed by the owner or after a substantial alteration, extension or refurbishment. Where a development was initially zero-rated, the ten-year period starts only from the change of use, so in such a case the *paragraph* could apply to a grant up to 20 years after the building was constructed.

17.153 The option to tax is also disapplied where the supply is made by a person other than the one who made the grant that gave rise to it. In such circumstance the person making the supply is treated as the grantor for the purpose of *Sch 10, para 12,* and the grant is treated as having been made when the supplier made his first supply arising from the grant (*VATA 1994, Sch 10, para 12(6)*). In addition, if that deemed grantor is not a developer because the period has expired, he is deemed to be a developer (*VATA 1994, Sch 10,* *para 13(7)*). This is aimed at the sort of situation where a developer carries out a development through a subsidiary, reclaims the input VAT, grants a lease to a subsidiary of an exempt occupier (S) and then sells the reversion to its parent. The developer will be the grantor but as his lease is not to the exempt occupier he does not have an intention that the land will become exempt land. *Paragraph 12(6)* treats S as the grantor, so that when S first charges rent to the exempt occupier that supply will trigger the disapplication of the option to tax. It will do so retrospectively (see **17.217**) so the input tax previously reclaimed will become repayable to HMRC. Without this provision the input tax would effectively have been clawed back under the capital goods scheme but it would have taken ten years to do so. A variant of this scheme is for the developer to carry out the development in a subsidiary company, cause the subsidiary to grant a lease and sell that subsidiary to the exempt end-user as a transfer of a business as a going concern. To prevent this, the TOGC rules (see **17.215**) are themselves disapplied where the transferor intends to use the property for exempt supplies. This makes the transfer taxable and, as it will give rise to a deemed grant, under the capital goods scheme will trigger an immediate clawback of the input tax previously relieved. In *Nora Harris (TC 4460),* the Tribunal accepted that charging rent to a tenant was evidence of the option having been exercised. That did not help the tenant though as it was a TOGC (see **17.201**) which requires the option to have been notified prior to the transaction.

17.154 A person is a development financier, ie responsible for financing the grantor's development of the land for exempt use, if he has provided finance for the development or has entered into any agreement, arrangement or understanding (even if not legally enforceable) to do so with the intention that (or in the expectation that) the land will become exempt land (or if it is already exempt land it will continue to be so for a period at least) (*VATA 1994, Sch 10, para 14(2)*).

17.155 All of the following (whether direct or indirect) constitute the provision of finance for this purpose:

(*a*) providing funds for meeting any part of the cost of the grantor's development of the land;

(*b*) procuring the provision of such funds by another;

(*c*) providing funds for discharging (in whole or part) any liability that has been incurred (or may be incurred) by any person for (or in connection with) the raising of funds to meet the costs of the grantor's development of the land; and

(*d*) procuring that any such liability will be discharged by another.

(*VATA 1994, Sch 10, para 14(3).*)

17.156 The provision of funds includes (but is not limited to):

(*a*) making a loan;

(*b*) guaranteeing a loan or giving security for a loan;

(*c*) providing any of the consideration for the issue of shares or securities which are issued wholly or partly to raise funds for the development;

(*d*) from 18 March 2004 the provision of any consideration for the acquisition by a person of any such shares or securities); and

(*e*) any other transfer of assets or value as a consequence of which any funds are made available for the purpose of the development.

(*VATA 1994, Sch 10, para 14(4).*)

17.157 An example of the width of this provision is given by *Winterthur Life UK Ltd (VTD 15785)*. Pension contributions by a partnership of insurance brokers were made to a Self-Invested Personal Pension Plan. It was intended that the pension plan would buy a property and lease it to the partnership. The VAT tribunal felt it obvious that the payment of pension contributions intended to provide pension benefits were 'transfers of assets' within **17.156**(*d*). It made no difference that their purpose was to provide pensions or that they were not conditional on the trustees acquiring the property as 'the funds were clearly 'made available' in consequence of the contributions'. It was also irrelevant that the contributions were not for the avoidance of tax in that both the contributions and the investment were planned before it was ever appreciated that there was a VAT problem.

17.158 Reference in **17.147** above to the grantor's development of the land means the acquisition by him of an asset which consists of the land, or a building (or part of a building) on the land, and which (in relation to the grantor) is within the capital goods scheme (see **17.205**) (or is intended or expected to be within that scheme) (*VATA 1994, Sch 10, para 14(5)*). The acquisition of an asset for this purpose includes its construction or reconstruction and the carrying out of any other works which cause it to be treated as a capital item, ie acquisition is used in the sense of 'comes to possess' rather than 'purchases' (*VATA 1994, Sch 10, para 14(6)*).

17.159 Exempt land is land which either:

(*a*) the grantor; or

(*b*) a person responsible for financing the grantor's development of the land for exempt use; or

(*c*) a person connected with one within (*a*) or (*b*) above (within *ITA 2007, s 993* – see Appendix 1), occupies the land at a time when it is within the capital goods scheme and such occupation is not wholly or substantially wholly for eligible purposes (*VATA 1994, Sch 10, para 15(1)–(3)*). A company is not, however, connected with another only because both are under the control of the Crown, a government department or the Northern Ireland department (*VATA 1994, Sch 10, para 34(2A)*). Wholly or substantially wholly must be interpreted in accordance with criteria specified in a public notice (*VATA 1994, Sch 10, para 15(5)*). The relevant notice, 742A, states that land is occupied wholly for eligible purposes if it is 100% so occupied and substantially wholly if it is occupied at least 80% for eligible purposes. Prior to 1 June 2008 the test was 'wholly or mainly' and HMRC normally interpreted mainly as meaning at least 80%, but that was not a hard and fast rule. Occupation includes occupation jointly with one or more other persons and also occupation of part only of the land (*VATA 1994, Sch 10, para 16(10)*). Land can be exempt land only during the owner's capital goods scheme adjustment period (*VATA 1994, Sch 10, para 15(2)*).

17.160 From 1 April 2010, a development financier (ie within (*b*) above) or a person connected with such a person (or from 1 March 2011 the grantor or a connected person), who is in occupation of the land at any time within 'the adjustment period' is treated as not being in occupation of it if the 'building occupation conditions' are met at that time (*VATA 1994, Sch 10, para 15(3A)*). The adjustment period is the ten-year capital goods scheme adjustment period (see **17.208**) (*VATA 1994, Sch 10, para 15(4)*). The building occupation conditions are met at any time if the grant consists of (or includes) the grant of a relevant interest in a building and either the financier or connected person (or a connected person of either) does not at that time occupy any part of the land that is not a building or more than 10% of any relevant building included in the grant or, from 1 March 2011, the grantor or a connected person does not occupy more than 2% (*VATA 1994, Sch 10, para 15A(1)(2)*). For this purpose a relevant building is any building which is included in the grant, other than any part of such a building in which neither the grantor nor a connected person of his held an interest immediately before the grant. Occupation of land used for parking cars or other vehicles, and of land within the curtilage of a building, is disregarded if such occupation is ancillary to the occupation of a building (not necessarily the same building) (*VATA 1994, Sch 10, para 15A(3)*). The way in which occupation of a building is measured under the 10% test must be determined in accordance with conditions specified in a public notice (*VATA 1994, Sch 10, para 15A(6A)*). This is a reference to Notice 742A (Opting to Tax Land and Buildings), para 13.8.5. From 1 March 2011 a person's occupation can also be ignored where it arises solely in respect of an automatic teller machine (*VATA 1994, Sch 10, para 15(3A)*).

17.161 A person is only in occupation of land for eligible purposes if he is a taxable person and even then only to the extent that he uses it for the purpose of making fully taxable supplies (*VATA 1994, Sch 10, para 16(1)–(4)*). If a person occupies land in order to be able to use it for an eligible purpose at a later date, he is treated as already occupying it for that eligible purpose provided that he is not occupying it in the interim for some other purpose (*VATA 1994, Sch 10, para 16(8)*). For example, if a fully taxable trader rents a factory to which he will move his business in six months' time, that is deemed to be use for an eligible purpose if it is left empty, but if he lets it temporarily (without opting to tax) the intended future use will not suffice to qualify the factory as being currently occupied for an eligible purpose. If the owner is not a taxable person but his supplies are treated for VAT purposes as made by someone else who is a taxable person, the owner and the taxable person are treated as a single person (*VATA 1994, Sch 10, para 16(9)* formerly *para 3A(12)*). The most obvious (if not the only) example is where the owner is acting as a nominee for a taxable person. From 1 June 2008 to 28 February 2011 if a person's occupation arose mainly by reference to an automatic teller machine of the person which was fixed on the land (ie a cashpoint) such occupation could be treated as occupation for eligible purposes (*VATA 1994, Sch 10, para 16(7)*). This provision has been replaced by *para 15(3A)* – see **17.160**.

17.162 *Brambletye School Trust Ltd (VTD 17688)* sought to get round the provision when it erected a new sports hall. It leased it to a subsidiary company which ran a club. All pupils of the school were members of the club, a separate fee being charged for the membership (which was collected with the school fees by the school as agent). There were few other members. The school contended that it did not occupy the sports hall. This was rejected by the tribunal. It regarded 'occupation' as a less formal concept than possession. It felt that the facts that priority was given to the use of the hall by pupils in term time, that when pupils used the hall they were supervised by the school staff, that such use was for school purposes, that the school remained responsible for the pupil while he used the hall and that whilst the hall was being used by pupils the control (through its staff's supervision) rested with the school, established occupation by the school. The tribunal added that if it were wrong in holding that the school, not the pupils, occupied the hall the school at least occupied it together with the pupils, which was sufficient to negate the option to tax. A similar scheme by Newnham College Cambridge failed on this point (see **17.150**).

17.163 Occupation of land by a government department (or other body within *VATA 1994, s 41*, ie one exercising functions on behalf of a Minister of the Crown) is also occupation for an eligible purpose. So is occupation by a local authority (or another body falling within *VATA 1994, s 33*) except to the extent that it uses the land for the purposes of a business carried on by it (*VATA 1994, Sch 10, para 16(5)(6)*).

17.164 This anti-avoidance provision was introduced to block 'lease and leaseback' schemes such as that used in *C & E Commrs v Robert Gordon's College* (see **17.140** above). However, its wording goes much wider. For example, it applied if a taxable property was transferred intra-group in the course of a group reorganisation made for sensible commercial reasons and the transferee company owned a number of properties not all of which have been opted in. Such transfers are not uncommon where a property investment group carries out developments. The property will frequently be owned by a separate company during the development phase but after completion, when the development risk is past, transferred to a group investment company for ease of administration.

17.165 The Minister indicated to Parliament that there would be an extra-statutory concession to let out innocent cases from the 1994 legislation. Two concessions were in fact announced. A person could be treated as fully taxable if, at the end of the prescribed accounting period in which the grant was made, he was able to recover 80% or more of his input tax (or would have been able to do so were it not for other exempt supplies of land) (News Release 62/95). A small self-administered pension scheme could be treated as a fully taxable person irrespective of what proportion of its input tax it could recover (News Release 11/96). Both of these concessions were retrospective to 30 November 1994. It appears from the fact that HMRC pursued *Winterthur Life* before the VAT tribunal (see **17.157**) that by 1997 the concept of letting out the innocent had been abandoned.

17.166 Although this was intended as an anti-avoidance provision, it had the side effect of allowing a taxpayer to avoid an option to tax. He could grant an interest in the building to a connected person. That would be an exempt supply. There would not even be a clawback of the input tax previously claimed (Notice 742, para 8.4(b)). The connected person would not be bound by the transferor's option to tax provided that the two do not form a VAT group.

17.167 The provisions referred to at **17.141** to **17.165** above do not mean that the election is invalid; merely that it is ineffective as far as such supplies are concerned. If the use of the building were subsequently to change, the election would take effect in relation to the new supplies. It should be noted that where part of an office building is used by a charity for relevant charitable purposes, the charity will nevertheless have to pay VAT if the landlord opts to bring the building into the VAT net. The reason for this is that it would place an undue burden on the landlord if he had to ascertain each quarter how much of the building was being used by the charity for relevant and how much for non-relevant purposes (Hansard, Standing Committee G, 16 May 1989, Col 92).

17.168 If a taxpayer has opted to tax land and later begins to construct a building on the land (the 'new building') (and no land within the curtilage of the new building is within the curtilage of an existing building) the taxpayer can give a notice to HMRC that he wishes to exclude the new building (and the land within its curtilage) from the option to tax (*VATA 1994, Sch 10, para 27(1)(2)*). The notice must begiven within 30 days from the date on which it is to have effect (or such longer period as HMRC may allow), must be in the form specified in a public notice, and must state the time from which it is to have effect (*VATA 1994, Sch 10, para 27(4)* as amended by the *VAT (Buildings and Land) Order 2009, SI 2009 No 1966*). It has effect from the earliest of the time that the new building is completed, the time any part of it is first used and the time when the grant of an interest in any part of it is made (*VATA 1994, Sch 10, para 27(3)*). Notice 742A requires the notice to be given on form 1614F. A building cannot be excluded before construction begins. HMRC are empowered by public notice to define when construction begins and have prescribed that it begins when construction progresses above the level of the building's foundations (*VATA 1994, Sch 10, para 27(7)* and Notice 742A para 2.7.2).

Notification

17.169 Notification of the election must normally be given to the Option to Tax National Unit and HMRC must also be supplied with such other information as they may require. The notification should be sent to 'Option to Tax National Unit HM Revenue & Customs, Cotton House, 7 Cochrane Street, Glasgow, G1 1GY rather than the taxpayers' local VAT office. Alternatively it can be faxed to 0141 555 3367. Where a business becomes liable to register for VAT solely as a result of the election, the election should instead be sent to the appropriate VAT Registration Unit at Wolverhampton for UK registration or Aberdeen for overseas ones, together with the application to register (Business Brief 16/03). HMRC have produced a notification form, VAT 1614A, which can be downloaded from their website. However, this does not need to be used; the requisite information can be provided in any form (Business Brief 3/06). In *C & E Commrs v McMaster Stores (Scotland) Ltd (1995 STC 846)*, it was accepted that failure to notify the election meant that it was invalid. The London tribunal had previously taken a different line, since in both *Fencing Supplies Ltd (VTD 10451)* and *Resource Maintenance Ltd (VTD 13204)* an election to waive exemption was held to be valid even though it had not been notified to the Commissioners. Indeed, this was agreed to be the position in *Copthorn Holdings Ltd v HMRC (2014 SFTT 1)* (see **17.171**) although the Tribunal stressed that there needs to be evidence, such as a Board Minute or correspondence, that the election was made. The election cannot be made retrospectively, albeit that it can be notified late.

17.170 In *Norbury Developments Ltd (VTD 14482)* the company bought land with planning permission for mainly residential development and resold it to a developer. It was charged VAT on its purchase but did not charge VAT on its sale. It subsequently sought to waive exemption but this was rejected by HMRC. HMRC refused relief for any of the input tax on the purchase as, no election having been made, the land was not used to make taxable supplies. The company contended that the land was clearly 'building land' which could not be exempted under *Article 13B(h)* of the *Sixth Directive (now Article 135(1)(k)* of the *VAT Directive)*. The tribunal referred this point to the *European Court of Justice (Case C-136/97) (1999 STC 511)*, which held that a Member State is entitled to exempt a supply of building land under *Article 28(3)(b)* of the *EC Sixth Directive* (which permits the retention of pre-*Sixth Directive* exemptions) notwithstanding that since the adoption of the directive it has introduced an option to tax and has reduced the scope of that exemption. Accordingly this confirms that even supplies of building land are exempt unless the option to tax is exercised (see Business Brief 22/96).

17.171 Notification of the election must normally be given within 30 days from the date the election is made (*VATA 1994, Sch 10, para 21(2),* formerly *para 3(6)(b)*). HMRC have power to extend this period. They have said that they will usually accept a belated notification if a trader provides evidence, such as a minute or correspondence referring to the decision, that the decision was made on the date specified in the notification. If no evidence exists, they will normally accept a statement from a responsible person if output tax has been accounted for and input tax claimed from the date of the election. They will obviously not normally accept late notification if there has been an investigation into the supplies in question during which no mention was made of the election, or if the trader has previously put forward a different explanation for the charging of output tax (Business Brief 13/05). In practice, people are likely to send an election to HMRC immediately it is made. Indeed, although the *Act* draws a distinction between the election and its notification, in most cases the letter to HMRC is likely to be the only document brought into being to evidence the election. In *Copthorn Holdings Ltd v HMRC (2014 SFTD 1)* the Tribunal held that it could overturn an HMRC refusal to accept a late election only if HMRC could not reasonably have been satisfied that there were grounds for the refusal. In that case, the company bought land and immediately resold it to another under the mistaken belief that the purchaser was part of its VAT group. HMRC refused to accept late notification because that was an exempt disposal (as it was not part of the group and the election had not been notified). The election must be accompanied by such information as HMRC may require. From 1 June 2008 HMRC have power to specify the form that notification must take (*VATA 1994, Sch 10, para 20(3)*). They have not yet specified a form but the use of their form VAT 1614A should ensure that all of the relevant information is provided.

17.172 The issue in *Marlow Gardner & Cooke Ltd Directors Pension Scheme v HMRC (2006 STC 2014)* was whether the election needs to be notified to

HMRC after the land has been sold. Net Support Ltd acquired a property in 1998. It let part of the premises to an associated company and made a decision to charge VAT on the rent from the outside. It regularly accounted for such VAT. In January 2004 Net Support sold the property to Marlow Gardner. The sale contract provided for a price of £400,000 plus VAT. On 27 February 2004 Net Support wrote a letter to HMRC which they accepted as notification of the election in 1998. Marlow Gardner challenged both whether an election had ever been made and whether the notification had been effective. Mann J held that the first point was a question of fact and that there was no manifest error in the VAT tribunal's decision. He then pointed out that notification is separate to the election and can be given after it. Notification gives the election effect retrospectively to the date it was made. Accordingly the tribunal had been entitled to conclude that there was a valid election. This did not make the position of Marlow Gardner uncertain as when it entered into the contract it had made a commercial decision to pay any VAT due. In practice it is unlikely that HMRC will now accept a late notification after a disposal has taken place if VAT was not charged on that disposal. In *Hills v HMRC (TC 3770)* HMRC confirmed to the Tribunal that they have no power to retrospectively grant permission to opt and, if there has been an exempt supply, a late notification cannot be effective as the option would not have been implemented so could not have been effective. In that case the taxpayer was seeking to void the option. However, the Tribunal held that the exempt supply had taken place after the date of the option. The vendor was a SIPP (Mr & Mrs Hills were the purchaser) and it was also unsuccessfully claimed that the sole beneficiary, Mrs Patel, had bought the SIPP to an end under the rule in *Saunders v Vautier*, so the disposal was by her and she had not elected.

17.173 In some cases the prior written permission of HMRC is needed before an election can be made (see **17.133** above). The distinction between electing and notifying the election is well illustrated by the VAT tribunal decision in *Blythe Limited Partnership (VTD 16011)*. The partnership took over 16 properties from a previous partnership. It intended to elect in respect of four of them. The solicitor to one of the parties wrongly notified HMRC that the partnership had elected in respect of all 16. The tribunal found as a fact that the partnership had only elected in respect of the four properties. HMRC contended that the partnership was bound by the notification but the tribunal held that such notification had no effect in relation to the other 12 properties as it was a purported notification of an election that had never been made. HMRC have since said that they fully agree with the tribunal's approach (Business Brief 16/99). A similar conclusion was reached in *D S Talafair & Sons (VTD 16144)* where the election purported to apply to three properties and the evidence showed that it was intended to apply only to one. However, in cases where there was only one property involved the VAT tribunals have consistently taken the view that the notification is prima facie evidence of the election and it is for the taxpayer to displace the inference that the option was exercised. The taxpayer has to date failed to overturn that inference, in *Hammersmith & West London College Ltd (VTD 1540), Rathbone Community Industry (VTD 18200)* and *Windsor House Investments Ltd (VTD 19666).*

17.174 It was held in *Chalegrove Properties Ltd (VTD 17151)* that notification of an election is given at the time that it is posted to HMRC. In that case the company gave notice of its option to tax on 21 August 1996 and sold its property on 30 August. The tribunal thought that the normal rule that service is effected when the letter would be delivered in the normal course of post is displaced by a contrary intention in the legislation, namely that it would require purchasers in a competitive auction to despatch notification of an election in advance of the auction (see *Higher Education Statistics Agency v C & E Commrs 2000 STC 332* – **17.219**). HMRC have said that they accept this decision. It is sufficient where property is purchased as a TOGC (see **17.215**) that on the relevant date the buyer has properly addressed, pre-paid and posted the letter. They suggest retaining evidence of posting. Where this has been done in the last three years and TOGC treatment was refused they will now accept that the transaction was a TOGC (Business Brief 11/01 21 Aug 2001). The lack of formality required for an election is emphasised by *Classic Furniture (Newport) Ltd (VTD 10451).* The company purchased a property with completion on 31 July 1999. On 29 July the sole director became aware that the vendor proposed to charge VAT. He contacted his professional advisors who told him that he would have to elect to waive exemption in order to recover the VAT. Based on this and the oral evidence of the professional advisor that he had given the advice and of the director that he had intended to accept it, the tribunal held that the company had opted to tax. The company had a further problem that the option had not been notified in the 30-day period. It was not until 10 November, following a VAT control visit and a resultant letter from HMRC rejecting relief for the input tax, that notification was given. The tribunal held that the reasons that led HMRC to reject the application to accept late notification were unjustified because they had misunderstood the facts. It effectively told HMRC to accept the late notification unless it had other reasons not to do so. It is doubtful if the tribunal has power to usurp in this manner the discretion given to HMRC.

17.175 The election normally takes effect from the beginning of the day on which it is made, not from the date that it is received by HMRC. The taxpayer can specify a later effective date in the election, in which case it will not take effect until that date (*VATA 1994, Sch 10, para 19(1),* formerly *para 3(1)*). The election can be made at any time but cannot have retrospective effect except where it is made in the circumstances outlined in **17.184** below. HMRC do not normally allow elections to be backdated even where there has been a genuine error as they have no statutory power to do so. They have, however, been known to allow a notification to be backdated where there is a good reason for doing so.

17.176 In the past it was possible to elect by accident! *Fencing Supplies Ltd (VTD 10451)* charged VAT on rents, apparently due to a misunderstanding of the VAT position. Subsequently, on granting a new lease to the same tenant it confirmed that it did not propose to elect to waive exemption. It did not charge VAT on the premium it received for the new lease. The VAT tribunal held that by demanding and receiving VAT to which it would only be entitled if it had waived exemption, the company had clearly indicated a decision to waive exemption. This 'decision' was not altered by the fact that it was based on a misunderstanding. The tribunal's decision in that case was followed by a subsequent tribunal in *Resource Maintenance Ltd (VTD 13204)*, but was not followed (or even referred to) in *McMaster Stores (Scotland) Ltd* (see **17.169** above), where the CS held that an election that was not notified to HMRC was invalid. In an earlier case, *Hi-Wire Ltd (VTD 6204)*, the company intended to opt to tax in 1989 but did not notify HMRC until September 1990. The VAT tribunal held that the election did not become effective until September 1990. This may be because there was no evidence to establish an earlier intention to elect. The law was changed from 1 March 1995 to make the validity of the election conditional upon notification so these cases are probably no longer operative except where an election was made before that date but not notified to HMRC. In *Mill House Management UK Ltd (TC 960)*, the company's book-keeper had mistakenly believed that because VAT had been paid on acquisition of the property the company was obliged to charge VAT to its tenants. However, it had not accounted for such VAT to HMRC and was not VAT registered. In these circumstances the Tribunal held that it could not have opted to tax at the time of acquisition because it did not know that it had to do so. The failure to register and opt was particularly unfortunate as the rental income had been spent on refurbishments, so the company not only was liable to hand over the £167,000 output tax charged to tenants but could not reclaim the £138,300 input tax on the refurbishments.

17.177 In *Euro Properties (Scotland) Ltd (VTD 15291)* the receipt by the purchaser of a tax invoice (issued after the vendor had deregistered) did not help. The tribunal firmly retorted that 'notice cannot be deemed to have been given'. To add insult to injury, it told the poor purchaser that a contract for the purchase of property would normally be exempt, so a tax invoice in relation to property 'could not be regarded as a standard tax invoice' and therefore he should have checked it. This seems harsh. If he had checked it, it is unlikely that he would have discovered that the vendor had failed to notify his election to HMRC.

17.178 One taxpayer claimed that the *EC Sixth Directive* allowed the deduction of input tax incurred before the election was made and so the bar on retrospectiveness was ineffective (*Lawson Mardon Group Pension Scheme (VTD 10231)*). The VAT tribunal disagreed. Until the election is made the property is not being used in making taxable supplies, and so earlier input tax cannot be attributed to any such supply. However, the facts in *Lawson Mardon* were that the company was trying to keep its options open. That decision is not authority for a proposition that one cannot have an intention to make taxable supplies before the option to tax is made. What is one's intention must be a question of fact independent of any election. This was confirmed by the VAT tribunal in *Beaverbank Properties Ltd (VTD 18099)* where the tribunal held that, in the circumstances of that case, there had always been an intention to opt to tax and that the absence of the election did not negate that intention. Mention should also be made of *Macaw Properties (TC 1863)* (see **16.205**) where the tribunal reviewed the law on intention.

17.179 Following this decision and that of the House of Lords in *Royal & Sun Alliance Insurance Group v C & E Commrs (2003 STC 832)* (see **16.246**) HMRC have said that they now accept that a taxpayer can have an intention to make taxable supplies before an option to tax is in place even though the taxable supply cannot occur until the option is exercised (see **16.248**). However, it should be noted that eight years later they argued to the contrary in *Macaw Properties Ltd (TC 1803)* (see **16.205**).

Revocation

17.180 The election cannot normally be revoked. There are two exceptions. It can be revoked:

(*a*) Within six months of making the election, but only if the taxpayer has not used the land since the option took effect, no tax has become chargeable as a result of the option, and there has been no supply under a TOGC (*VATA 1994, Sch 10, para 23(1)(2)*). The notification must be in a form specified in a public notice (*VATA 1994, Sch 10, para 23(3)*). Notice 742A requires the revocation to be given a form VAT 1614C. HMRC have power to publish a notice providing that a revocation is effective only if either the conditions specified in the notice are met, or the taxpayer obtains the prior permission of HMRC (*VATA 1994, Sch 10, para 23(4)*). Notice 742A specifies that the option is effective only if none of the input tax of the person who made the option (or of another group company) is deductible as being attributable to taxable supplies by virtue of the option. If this condition is not met the permission of HMRC to revoke the election must be sought within the six-month period. The rules were slightly different prior to 1 June 2008. The revocation had to be made within three months of making the election, it always required the consent of HMRC and could be made only if no tax has become chargeable, no credit for input tax has been claimed, and no grant constituting a transfer as a going concern has taken place, ie the election can only be revoked if it has not yet had any effect – which is likely to be a rare occurrence.

(*b*) More than 20 years after it has effect – which cannot occur until after 1 April 2009. The revocation must be notified to HMRC, must be in the specified form, state the day from which it is to be revoked (which cannot be before the day it is notified), contain a statement by the taxpayer certifying the conditions specified in the public notice are met and give certain other information specified in the public notice (*VATA 1994, Sch 10, para 25(1)–(3)*). Notice 742A requires the revocation to be notified on form VAT 1614J. The conditions are either:

(i) the taxpayer (and other group companies) has no relevant interest in the building or land at the time of the revocation, or

(ii) the taxpayer (or group company) held an interest in the building or land 'which is after the time from which the option has effect and more than 20 years before the option is revoked' [sic – this does not make sense as an interest is not a time]; no land or building that is subject to the option when it is revoked is within the capital goods scheme (or if it is the VAT repayable to HMRC as a result of the revocation does not exceed £10,000); the taxpayer (or group company) has made no supply of an interest in, right over or licence to occupy the building or land (or any part of it) in the ten years preceding the revocation – at less than market value or which is likely to give rise to a supply subsequent to the revocation; and no part of a supply of goods or services made to the taxpayer (or a group company) before the option is revoked will be attributable to a supply or other use of the land or buildings by the taxpayer more than 12 months after the option is revoked. If these conditions do not apply permission to revoke must be obtained from HMRC. In such a case the revocation takes effect from the day on which HMRC grants permission (or such later day as they specify) or from the time of a specified event, eg they could grant permission to revoke with reference to a sale of a building so the revocation would not take effect if the sale falls through. An application for permission must be made on form VAT 1614J (*VATA 1994, Sch 10, para 25(5), (6)*). If a taxpayer believes that he meets the conditions for automatic revocation and it is subsequently discovered that they were not met, HMRC can treat the option as if it had been validly revoked if they consider that the grounds on which those conditions are not met are insignificant. They can treat the revocation as effective from the date on which it would have had effect had it been valid (*VATA 1994, Sch 10, para 25(4),(7)–(9)*).

(*c*) An option to tax is also treated as having been revoked once the taxpayer has ceased to have any interest in, right over or licence to occupy the building or land (or any part of it) for a continuous period of six years (*VATA 1994, Sch 10, para 24*). The revocation is not effective if either:

(i) the opter (or a member of its VAT group) disposes of an interest in the building or land before the time from which the option would otherwise have been treated as revoked and at that time a supply for VAT purposes in respect of the disposal has yet to take place (or would be yet to take place if one or more conditions were to be met);

(ii) the opter is a body corporate that was (at any time previously) treated as a member of a VAT group and before the revocation would otherwise have taken effect another member of the opter's VAT group who had an interest in the land left the VAT group while holding an interest in the land (or where it had disposed of its interest but the supply for VAT purposes had not yet taken place); or

(iii) the opter is a body corporate and at the time that the revocation would otherwise have taken effect another member of its VAT group is treated under *VATA 1994, ss 43A–43D* as a member of the same group as that as the opter and holds a relevant interest in the building or land (or has held such an interest at any time in the previous six years).

(*VATA 1994, Sch 10, para 26.*) Head (*a*) is intended to ensure that the option cannot be automatically revoked where, for example, overages might arise subsequent to the revocation.

17.181 Revocation requires the consent of HMRC and in the case of (*b*) such consent cannot be given retrospectively (*VATA 1994, Sch 10, para 3(4),(5)*). An HMRC consultation paper of July 1993 suggested that the option might be revocable after ten years, so this appears to be a rare instance of the bulk of consultees protesting that HMRC did not want to tax them heavily enough!

Miscellaneous

17.182 A person can make as many elections as he likes for different buildings or areas of land. However, if he elects in relation to part only of a building (except where his entire interest in the building is in that part only) his election extends to the whole of his interest in the building (and the interest of any other member of the same VAT group in the building – see **17.130**) (*VATA 1994, Sch 10, para 18(2)*) and from 1 June 2008 includes an enlarged or extended building, an annexe to a building and a planned building (*VATA 1994, Sch 10, para 18(6)*). For this purpose a building also includes all land within its curtilage (*VATA 1994, Sch 10, para 18(2)*). Furthermore, buildings linked internally or by a covered walkway, and complexes consisting of a number of units grouped around a fully enclosed concourse must be taken to be a single building even if they would otherwise not be (*VATA 1994, Sch 10, para 18(4)*). Prior to 1 June 2008 the extension to certain complexes also applied to parades and precincts (although a complex probably includes a precinct). From 1 June 2008 buildings which are linked internally are not treated as a single building if the internal link is created after the buildings are completed. Similarly buildings linked by a covered walkway are not treated as a single building if the walkway starts to be constructed after the buildings are completed (*VATA 1994, Sch 10, para 18(5)*). From 1 June 2008 a covered walkway does not create a single building if it is one to which the general public has reasonable access (*VATA 1994, Sch 10, para 18(7)*).

17.183 This creates a number of uncertainties which may need to be resolved in advance with HMRC, or perhaps decided by a VAT tribunal. For example, can two buildings be regarded as a single building if they are owned by different companies which are both in the same VAT group? In *C & E Commrs v Kingfisher plc (1994 STC 63)* the QB held that *VATA 1994, s 43* intended to treat all the companies in a VAT group as a single person, so HMRC may well regard the two as a single building in such circumstances, particularly because treating the two as separate buildings tends to cast doubt on the efficacy of **17.130** above.

17.184 From 1 June 2008 a taxpayer can elect in relation to all relevant interests in any buildings or land which he (and all other members of his VAT group) acquires subsequent to the election to be treated as if he had exercised an option to tax in relation to each such interest with effect from the start of the day on which the interest was acquired. Such an election is called a 'real estate election' (*VATA 1994, Sch 10, para 21(1)(2)*). A relevant interest for this purpose is any interest in, right over or licence to occupy the buildings or land (or any part of it) (*VATA 1994, Sch 10, para 21(12)*). A real estate election is irrevocable (*VATA 1994, Sch 10, para 21(9)*). The election must be notified to HMRC within 30 days (or such longer period as HMRC may allow) and must be in the form specified in a public notice (*VATA 1994, Sch 10, para 21(7)*). Notice 742A specifies form VAT 1614E. HMRC can also require a person by public notice to provide other information at the same time (*VATA 1994, Sch 10, para 21(8)*). Note 742A sets out at para 14.8 the information that they require (broadly, details of all of the properties held at the time). If the person fails to provide such information, HMRC can revoke the election with retrospective effect (*VATA 1994, Sch 10, para 21(9)*). If they do so the prior permission of HMRC is required to make a fresh election (*VATA 1994, Sch 10, para 21(11)*). The time at which a relevant interest in a building or land is acquired is the time at which a supply is treated as taking place for VAT purposes or, if there is more than one such time, the earliest of them (*VATA 1994, Sch 10, para 21(13)*).

17.185 A real estate election does not apply to any property which the taxpayer or another group company opted to tax at a time prior to making the real estate election (*VATA 1994, Sch 10, para 21(3)*). Nor does it apply to any property in which the taxpayer or another group company held any interest prior to the real estate election (*VATA 1994, Sch 10, para 21(4)*). Nor does it apply to any building or land in which a relevant interest is acquired after making the election and, if the election had not been made, the permission of HMRC would have been required to opt to tax the property (*VATA 1994, Sch 10, para 21(5)(6)*).

17.186 Unless heads (*a*) or (*b*) of the anti-avoidance rule in para 26 applies (see **17.180**), where a real estate election is made any existing election in relation to land in which the opter (or its group) no longer holds an interest is deemed to be revoked (*VATA 1994, Sch 10, para 22(2)–(5)*). If the taxpayer who makes a real estate election wishes, an election can be made in relation to global options (see **17.126**) (or any other options that covers more than one property) in respect of existing land in circumstances covered in a public notice. Notice 742A specifies that details of the land concerned must be given to HMRC. The global option is not merged into the real estate election. Instead it is treated as if each property or site covered by the option had been opted separately from the date of the global option (*VATA 1994, Sch 10, para 22(6)–(13)*; Notice 742A, para 14.6).

17.187 The VAT tribunal in *A J White (VTD 15388)* held that the election even extended to goodwill. The property for which exemption had been waived was a public house. Mrs White contracted to buy it for £140,000 of which £7,000 was allocated to goodwill, £8,000 to fixtures and fittings and the balance to the property. The business was acquired on a transfer of a going concern. The vendor had opted to waive exemption but Mrs White did not do so. The effect was that the property itself attracted VAT but none of the other assets acquired did so (see **17.215** below). It appears that the vendor had assumed – wrongly – either that Mrs White had opted to waive exemption or that the TOGC rules applied to the entire transfer. He had not charged any VAT. Nevertheless Mrs White claimed as input tax 7/47ths of the £140,000. She claimed first that, even though the agreement specifically stated that she would carry on the same kind of business as the vendor, the transaction was not a TOGC at all. HMRC challenged this, also claiming that:

(*a*) only 56% of the premises was given over to commercial use, the remainder (the first floor flat) being residential and thus non-business; and

(*b*) the part of the price attributed to fixtures and fittings did not attract VAT because of the TOGC rules.

The election referred to 'the premises known as the Dog and Duck'. The tribunal felt that this must mean the whole of the property comprised in the registered title. This included the flat. That was not used exclusively for residential purposes as it was a condition of the licence that there should be a live-in manager, and in any event was not a dwelling as it was not self-contained living accommodation. Most of the fittings, being trade fixtures, did not form part of the land and would thus not be covered by the election (but landlord's fixtures would be). Goodwill is capable of existing as an intangible asset. However, in some cases, in the tribunal's view, it is not severable from the land. That was the position here. The goodwill is an attribute of the venue and attaches to the land. Accordingly the election to waive exemption 'covered the goodwill so long as the trade of public house was conducted from the Dog and Duck'. This decision is a potential nightmare. One man's VAT recoverability is another man's liability to HMRC. If expressly attributing a separate value to goodwill in the agreement will not be recognised as establishing that it is a separate asset, and goodwill may be part of the land but equally may not, the vendor of any property-based business will be vulnerable unless he finds a way to ensure that the purchaser has properly opted to tax the premises.

17.188 A property owner does not have to wait until he lets a property before he makes the election. He can do so immediately he acquires the building or land. If a developer expects to sell or let the building within three years of construction, he should be able to register for VAT as an intending trader (if he is not already registered) as he expects to make taxable supplies. If he is building for his own occupation he may well already be VAT-registered. In any other case, such as where the property is being developed as a long-term property investment, it appears vital to at least register, if not make the election, prior to incurring any development costs, even architects or planning fees, as input tax on services supplied more than six months prior to registration is not reclaimable (*VAT Regulations 1995, SI 1995 No 2518, reg 111(2)(c)*).

17.189 Indeed, HMRC have indicated that they will not allow registration of a developer of a potentially exempt building unless the election is made at the same time. In *Denise Jerzynek (VTD 18767)* HMRC sought to disallow VAT on rent paid during the six-month period on the grounds that it had been consumed prior to registration. However, the tribunal held that all that *reg 111* requires is for the service to have been supplied to a taxable person for the purpose of a business which was carried on (or to be carried on) by him and that, as at the time of the supply Mrs Jerzynek was a taxable person (albeit one not required to be registered), this test was satisfied. Although it could be argued that some of the purpose for which the premises were used was in respect of supplies prior to the registration, some of it was in respect of holding stock and in respect of the general development of the business and the *Regulation* contains no provision for apportionment.

17.190 Para 9.4, Notice 742A (Opting to tax land and building) states that the six-month restriction 'may lead to inequitable treatment compared with a business carrying out similar activities, but who was already VAT registered when the tax was incurred'. In these circumstances HMRC are prepared to override the restriction. *R (on the application of Argyll House Developments Ltd) v HMRC (2009 STC 2698)* concerned a judicial review against HMRC's refusal to apply this concession. Argyll House incurred input tax from July 2006. It registered for VAT from 1 August 2007. At that time HMRC sent it a form VAT 1614 (option to tax) as part of its questionnaire to consider whether it was carrying on a business. The company told HMRC that its intention was to develop the property for sale. It submitted a form VAT 1614 opting to tax the property from 1 January 2008. At the same time it lodged its VAT return for the initial period to 30 November 2007. HMRC disallowed the input tax between July 2006 and February 2007 citing the six-month rule. The company contended before the Court of Session that the concession should apply as it had gained no advantage from the delay in opting to tax and it would be unfair, discriminatory and offend the principle of fiscal neutrality not to allow it to recover the input tax. The court felt that the company was the author of its own misfortune. It did not come within the terms of the concession which required the need to register to flow from the option to tax. HMRC's decision to refuse to apply the concession could not be described as irrational.

17.191 HMRC have always taken the view that if the building is demolished the election falls away. The basis of this is that the election is in relation to the building. Although in law this includes the land on which it stands once the building ceases to exist the land is a different asset and a fresh decision as to whether or not to elect can be made. Doubt has been cast on this by the ECJ case of *Finanzamt Goslar v Breitsohl* (Case C-400/98) *(2001 STC 355)*. Mrs Breitsohl commissioned a construction company to construct a building on land that she owned and which she intended to use as a vehicle repair workshop. As building costs escalated she became unable to finance its completion so the building company ceased work. In November 1990 she sold the building works to a third party for a price including VAT and in December 1990 sold the land to the same purchaser without VAT. The German tax authorities claimed that Mrs Breitsohl was not a taxable person as she had not carried out any economic activity. They sought to distinguish the case from *Intercommunale voor Zeewaterontzilting* (see **17.175**) on the grounds that Mrs Breitsohl had no legitimate expectation of an input tax deduction as she never had the status of a taxable person. The ECJ dismissed this, holding that 'the right to deduct the VAT paid on transactions carried out with a view to the realisation of a planned economic activity still exists even where the tax authority is aware, from the time of the first tax assessment, that the economic activity envisaged, which was to give rise to taxable transactions, will not be taken up'. The German government secondly argued that as *Article 13C* of the *Sixth Directive (*now *Article 137* of the *VAT Directive)* expressly allows member states to fix the details of the use of the option to tax the question as to whether a taxpayer can exercise the option solely in relation to buildings, to the exclusion of the land on which they stand, is a question of national law. The ECJ rejected that concept. *Article 4(3)(a)* of the *Sixth Directive* (now *Article 12(2)* of the

VAT Directive) which refers to the 'supply ... of buildings or parts of buildings and the land on which they stand' needs to be interpreted in a uniform manner in all member states. As that *Article* distinguishes between building land on one hand and buildings and the land on which they stand on the other the court concluded that for VAT purposes buildings (or parts of buildings) and the land on which they stand cannot be dissociated from each other. The option to tax must therefore relate inseparably to the two. It seems a logical conclusion from this that the option must apply both to the building and to the land so that the destruction of the building would leave the option still attaching to the land.

17.192 HMRC have said that where, because of a tenant's default, the landlord collects the rent from the sub-tenant under *Law of Distress Amendment Act 1908, s 6*, this does not affect the VAT position. The supply is still made by the landlord to the tenant and a separate supply by the tenant to the sub-tenant. If the option to tax has been exercised the landlord can issue a VAT invoice only to the tenant, and the sub-tenant who wishes to reclaim VAT which he had paid to the landlord can do so only if he holds a VAT invoice from the tenant (Business Brief 17/93 & Notice 742, para 7.5.1). This seems reasonable. HMRC's approach suggests that *s 6*, in effect, merely provides a collection machinery for the money; it does not create a new legal relationship.

17.193 Where the option to tax is exercised and a grant in relation to the land would be taken to have been made (in whole or in part) before the time the election takes effect, the election is to have effect in relation to supplies to which the grant gives rise which are treated as taking place after that time, as if the grant had been made after that time (*VAT 1994, Sch 10, para 31*). Accordingly the reference to grants being exempt or taxable must be construed as references to supplies to which a grant gives rise being exempt or taxable (*VATA 1994, Sch 10, para 31*). What this is saying is merely that, in order to ensure that supplies made after the election to tax rents, etc. are taxable, the assumption must be made that the lease was entered into after that time. The reason for the clarification is that the draftsman has used the word 'grant' in *Sch 10* to mean a supply in pursuance of the grant. It might have been clearer to have substituted a different word for 'grant' in those two places rather than introduce this deeming to neutralise the effect of the draftsman having intended the word to have a different meaning to its normal use.

17.194 Rent for a period which bridged the date the election took effect had to be apportioned and the taxable part treated as relating to a supply made on the date the election takes effect (*VATA 1994, Sch 10, para 4(2)*).

17.195 If a supply took place after an election took effect but the first rent payment pursuant to it covered a period beginning prior to the election, the rent was again apportioned so that only the part attributable to the period after the election took effect was taxable (*VATA 1994, Sch 10, para 4(4)*).

17.196 To minimise administration, it is possible to issue a single tax invoice at the beginning of each year to cover all the rental payments due in the coming year. This must show the VAT-exclusive amount of rent, the dates on which each payment is due, the rate of VAT and the VAT payable. If the rate of tax changes, a new VAT invoice must be issued for the balance of the year. Where this procedure is adopted the tax point will be the due date of each payment or the date of actual payment if earlier (*VAT Regulations 1995, reg 85*).

17.197 Where the owner has a lease and grants a sublease, and following the expiry or termination of the sublease he continues to pay rent under the headlease, he is entitled to remain VAT-registered in order to recover VAT on outgoings in relation to the property as the decision in *I/S Fini v Skatteministeriet (2005 STC 903)* (see **12.45**) will apply. In contrast, where the trustee of an Enterprise Zone Property Trust (see **Appendix 4**) ceased to receive rent because it granted a 999-year leasehold interest in its building, but retained the freehold reversion, expenses incurred after the grant of the long lease were held not to be a cost of the letting business. The taxpayer had ceased that business and commenced a new activity of holding the freehold reversion (*Royal Bank of Canada Trust Corporation Ltd as Trustee of the Matrix Dudley Trust – VTD 20520*).

17.198 HMRC consider that if arrears of rent are received after the option to tax is in place, but in relation to a period before that time, VAT has to be charged (Notice 742A, para 10.3). They also consider that VAT has to be charged even if the rent arrears relate to a time before the owner acquired the building, ie he acquired the building with a tenant in place owing rent for earlier periods and subsequently collected those arrears (see example in VAT Land and Property Manual 22600). This view is based on the fact that Reg 85 of the VAT Regulations treats the supplies as taking place 'separately and successively' at the earlier of each time a payment is received or each time the supplier issues a VAT invoice. However, it is hard to see how this can make a supply by a previous landlord become a supply by the new landlord merely because the consideration is received after a sale of the property. It is particularly puzzling where the vendor retains the right to collect and retain the rent arrears. The HMRC view seems to nevertheless make the VAT on such arrears a liability of the purchaser even though he will never receive the money.

The VAT (Self-Supply of Construction Services) Order 1989

17.199 Where an exempt trader does his own building work, engaging his own staff instead of using a contractor, the labour element of the work would escape VAT without special provisions. The Treasury therefore issued a statutory instrument (*SI 1989 No 472*), under their general powers to deem a self-supply to be a taxable transaction, to impose VAT on a self-supply of a building.

17.200 This provides that if a person in the course or furtherance of his business:

(*a*) constructs a building;

(*b*) extends or alters a building or constructs an annexe to it such that additional floor area is created of 10% more than the original area;

(*c*) constructs any civil engineering work; or

(*d*) in connection with the above, carries out any demolition work contemporaneously or preparatory thereto,

those services must be treated as supplied to him for the purpose of his business and supplied by him in the course of it.

17.201 If he is a fully taxable person, this will not matter, as the output tax on the deemed supply by him will be cancelled out by the input tax on the deemed supply to him. If he is not VAT-registered, or is an exempt or partly exempt trader, it will create a VAT liability – and apparently an obligation to register for VAT if he is not already registered – as he will not be in a position to claim relief for the input tax.

17.202 This provision only applies if the value of the services is £100,000 or more and the deemed supply would not have been zero-rated if made by a taxable person.

17.203 The value of the deemed supply is the market value of the services (ie the labour). If the performance of the services bridged 1 April 1989, only the part arising after that date is taken into account, both for arriving at the tax charge and applying the £100,000 minimum limit. It should be noted that the charge applies only to the direct labour, as the materials will already have borne tax. As a contractor normally makes a combined charge to cover both materials and his construction services, it is likely to be difficult to establish a market value for the services alone.

17.204 If a VAT group registration is in force, all of the companies in the group must be treated as if they were a single person for the purpose of the *Order.*

Capital Goods Scheme

17.205 Where a taxpayer is partly exempt, the proportion of its input tax that is deductible will vary year by year. If heavy capital expenditure is incurred in a year when the deductible proportion is low the taxpayer could be unfairly penalised; if it is incurred in a year when it is high he may obtain relief for what the Government consider to be too high a proportion of the VAT. The capital goods scheme seeks to avoid such consequences by making the deduction more equitable. The relevant legislation is now contained in *regs 112–116* of the *VAT Regulations 1995*.

17.206 The capital goods scheme applies only to capital expenditure on:

(*a*) computers and items of computer equipment worth £50,000 or more;

(*b*) land and buildings (or parts of buildings or from 3 July 1997 a civil engineering work) worth £250,000 or more;

(*c*) a building (or part of a building) the owner's interest in which (or right over or licence to occupy) is taxed under the rules relating to the change of use of a residential or charitable building (see **16.122**) where the value taxed under those rules is £250,000 or more;

(*d*) a building (or part of a building) to which the developer's self-supply charge applied and the value of that supply was £250,000 or more;

(*e*) a building not falling within (*c*) or (*d*) which was constructed by the owner and first brought into use by him if the value of all taxable supplies of goods or services made to him after that date in connection with the construction are £250,000 or more;

(*f*) a building which the owner alters (including constructing an extension) if the value of all taxable supplies of goods or services made to him after that date in connection with the alteration are £250,000 or more (prior to 1 January 2011 additional floor area of 10% or more had to be created but this requirement was removed by the *VAT (Amendment) (No 4) Regulations 2010 (SI 2010, No 3022)*);

(*g*) a civil engineering work constructed by the owner and first brought into use by him if the aggregate value of taxable supplies to the owner after the date relating to the land or in connection with the construction of the work is £250,000 or more; and

(*h*) a building which the owner refurbishes or fits out where the value of capital expenditure on the taxable supplies of services and goods affixed to the building made to the owner in connection with the refurbishment is £250,000 or more.

17.207 The references to taxable supplies in each case exclude zero-rated supplies. In applying head (*b*) so much of the value of a supply as consists of rent (including charges reserved as rent) can be ignored, unless either the amount is payable more than 12 months in advance or it is invoiced for a period in excess of 12 months. The legislation is seeking to prevent capital expenditure incurred at the time of purchase from being classified as an advance payment of rent. Curiously, although a service charge is caught by this restriction if it is reserved as rent it is not caught if it is simply payable under a covenant in the lease. Head (*b*) includes freehold and leasehold interests in buildings and certain extensions and alterations to buildings, and includes buildings constructed by the owner for his own use. Costs incurred prior to 1 April 1990 are not taken into account. There is no definition of refurbishment for the purpose of head (*h*). As the expenditure needs to be capital, it is first necessary to differentiate refurbishment expenditure between capital and revenue as it is only if the capital element is at least £250,000 that the head can apply. HMRC's view is that they will follow the treatment adopted in the taxpayer's accounts. Conceptually in accounting terms most refurbishment work is revenue, but any element of improvement may be capital. Where a refurbishment is carried out, the capital goods scheme implications need to be borne in mind when deciding on the accounting treatment where in accounting terms it is permissible to treat expenditure as either capital or revenue. In practice in the past the Inland Revenue frequently challenged this apportionment for direct tax purposes. If it is agreed with HMRC that the accounting treatment is incorrect, this could have an impact on the capital goods adjustment. HMRC have indicated that they would not expect any adjustment to be made unless the agreement with the Revenue cast strong doubt on whether proper consideration had been initially given at all to the split between capital and revenue.

17.208 The scheme requires the deductible proportion of the tax on land and buildings to be re-calculated over a ten-year adjustment period, with tax being paid or repaid each year to correct the position in relation to the 10% of the cost notionally attributed to that year. In the case of computers and computer equipment (and from 1 January 2011, ships and aircraft) the adjustment period is five years. If the property is sold during that period by way of a taxable supply, the use for the rest of the period is deemed to be fully taxable; if it is sold by means of an exempt supply, the use for the balance of the period is deemed to be exempt use. The period can be less than ten years if during that period there is a transfer of a business as a going concern (see **17.213** below) or the owner joins or leaves the VAT group as such transactions trigger the end of an adjustment period. It is only the first transaction that will bring an adjustment period to an end – with subsequent periods ending on each anniversary of that shortened period. An interesting point arose in *Witney Golf Club (VTD 17706)*, namely when does the adjustment period start? An extension to the clubhouse was completed in the year to 31 March 1999. The company was fully taxable in that year. The final invoice for the building work of £600,000 was dated

30 April 1999. The club was partly exempt in the year to 31 March 2000. It was held that although the 'goods' (the extension) was brought into use in March 1999, on the wording of *reg 114(1)* the first adjustment period could not start earlier than the time the taxpayer was entitled to a deduction for the input tax, which in that case was in the year to 30 April 2000. From 1 January 2011 if a person was not VAT registered at the time the property was acquired, they can still make the adjustment in the periods after registration (*VAT Regulations 1995, reg 114*). Prior to 1 January 2011, the same treatment was allowed by concession.

17.209 Particular problems arise in relation to refurbishments. For example, if a person refurbishes one floor of a building at a cost of £150,000 and three months later refurbishes a second floor is that two separate refurbishments each costing under £250,000 or one costing over £250,000? HMRC say it depends on the facts and each case needs to be looked at on its merit. Another problem is that it is often not easy to distinguish goods affixed to a building from the value of other goods. HMRC have therefore introduced a concession, which allows a business to include goods not affixed to the premises in arriving at the £250,000 figure. To use the concession businesses must 'keep a record of the concessionary value of the capital expenditure including full details of the supplies on which the value was determined' (Business Brief 2/00). As the purpose of the concession is to avoid the costs of distinguishing the value of affixed goods from other goods the need to keep 'full details' seems to detract somewhat from its usefulness.

17.210 'Save as the Commissioners may otherwise allow', on a disposal of a capital goods item during the adjustment period there is a final adjustment to limit the total input tax deducted over the adjustment period to the output tax charged on the disposal. This is an anti-avoidance provision. It operates capriciously and unfairly in many cases. The intention is that it will not be applied to bona fide commercial disposals but that the taxpayer will need to ask HMRC to exercise this discretion not to charge tax for each individual disposal.

Example 17.1

A company with a 30 April VAT year buys a property for £300,000 plus VAT in March 2014. It uses it 80% for taxable purposes in the period to 30 April 2015, 30% for taxable purposes in the year to 30 April 2016 and 40% for taxable purposes in the year to 30 April 2017. It sells the property on 1 May 2017 for £200,000 plus VAT, the value having slumped as the area has become blighted by a motorway proposal.

The VAT position is:

Year to 30 April 2015: Input tax £300,000 × 20%	£60,000	
70% attributable to taxable use		£48,000
Year to 30 April 2016: Adjustment for the year (to restrict input tax for the year to 30% use)		(3,000)
£60,000 × 1/10th × (80–30)%		
year to 30 April 2017: Adjustment for the year		
£60,000 × 1/10th × (80– 40)%		(2,400)
years 4–10: deemed fully taxable so no adjustment		–
Net input tax allowed		53,400
Final adjustment to limit input tax to £200,000 × 20%		(2,600)
		40,000

In practice, HMRC will almost certainly agree not to require the £2,600 of 'excessive' input tax to be repaid in these circumstances. It should be noted that where the rate of VAT changes the adjustment is still at the original rate because *reg 115* calculates the adjustment in terms of the original input tax. In other words, what the adjustment does is to retroactively adjust the allowable input tax incurred on the acquisition of the item, albeit that the adjustment is given effect to in a later VAT period.

Example 17.2

The company in *Example 17.1* uses the property for making fully taxable supplies throughout the period of ownership.

Year to 30 April 2015: Input tax £300,000 × 20%	60,000
2 years to 30 April 2017: No adjustment	–
Years 4–10: deemed fully taxable so no adjustment	–
Final adjustment	(25,000)
	35,000

It will be seen that the greater the taxable use the more harshly the taxpayer is treated!

Example 17.3

The company in *Example 17.1* uses the property in its trade for fully taxable purposes. It does not exercise the option to tax.

Year to 30 April 2015: Input tax as before	60,000
2 years to 30 April 2017: No adjustment	–
Years 4–10: deemed wholly exempt so restrict input tax by	
60,000 × 7/10ths (ie remaining 7 years)	(42,000)
	18,000
Final adjustment to limit input tax to	
£200,000 × NIL (as no VAT on sale)	(18,000)
	NIL

17.211 HMRC issued a Business Brief on 19 December 1997 setting out how they intend to operate these rules (Business Brief 30/97). This states that the disposal test will not be applied:

(*a*) to sales of computer equipment;

(*b*) where an owner disposes of an item at a loss due to market conditions (such as a general downturn in property prices);

(*c*) where the value of the item has depreciated;

(*d*) where the value of the item is reduced for other legitimate reasons (such as accepting a lower price to effect a quick sale);

(*e*) where the amount of output tax on disposal is less than the total input tax claimed due only to a reduction in the VAT rate; and

(*f*) where the item is used only for taxable (including zero-rated) purposes throughout the adjustment period (including the final disposal) (para 5.1).

HMRC say that where there is no unjustified tax advantage a business should not apply the disposal test, but should not apply to HMRC for a specific ruling either. 'A business need only apply the disposal test where it has entered into arrangements for tax mitigation affecting the particular capital item or its disposal' (para 5.2). This leaves the problem of being able to recognise tax mitigation, particularly as that seems to be a concept that looks very different through the eyes of HMRC than most others perceive. HMRC warn that where they think the provision ought to have been applied it will be 'vigorously enforced', which suggests that there is a heavy risk of a misdeclaration penalty for getting it wrong.

17.212 The statement also indicates that even where the provision needs to be applied the trader will need to calculate the 'net tax advantage' (ie 'the overall benefit from the avoidance device') and then work out how much of it is unjustified. The net tax advantage will normally be the input tax secured by the sale less any output tax due on the sale. An apportionment will be needed to work out how much of this is unjustified. Normally, this should be done by using 'the ratio' that the value of the final taxable sale bears to the value of both the exempt supply and the final taxable sale (para 5.3). Where there have been other taxable supplies the ratio of exempt to taxable supplies (including the final sale) appears more reasonable.

17.213 An interesting issue arose in *Centralan Property Ltd v C & E Commrs (Case C-63/04) (2006 STC 1542)*. This was an avoidance scheme adopted by a university to seek to avoid the input tax disallowance in relation to the exempt supply of education. Centralan was wholly owned by the university. The university constructed a building which it sold as a VATable transaction to Centralan. Centralan leased the building back to the university for a term of 20 years. Two years later it granted a 999-year lease of the building at a substantial premium and a nominal rent to Infoco 546 Ltd, another company owned by the university. This sale was exempt because Centralan and Infoco were connected persons so the option to tax was disapplied. Three days later Centralan sold the freehold reversion of the building to the university for £1,000. This was a taxable transaction because it was a sale of a building less than three years old. Customs contended that the supply given rise to the disposal was the 999-year lease and that the sale of the reversion should be ignored as *de minimis*. The VAT tribunal held that the disposal was by two linked supplies. The ECJ held that in circumstances where two transactions are inextricably linked the property had to be regarded until the expiry of the adjustment period or having been used in business activities which are partly taxable and partly exempt in proportion to the respective value of the two transactions.

17.214 In *Gateshead Talmudical College v HMRC (2011 STC 1593)* the College set up a subsidiary, Starburst Properties Ltd, to which it granted a lease of its premises. Starburst granted it back a sublease. Both elected to waive exemption. After two years the two companies stopped paying one another rent and Starburst was struck off the Companies Register a year later. The College claimed that the capital goods scheme did not apply. The leases had continued as a matter of law to exist (and had become *bona vacantia* on the striking off). The Upper Tribunal retorted that for the purpose of the Directive the fundamental characteristics of a letting of immovable property is the 'conferring on the person concerned, for an agreed period, and for payment, the right to occupy property as if that person were the owner and to exclude any other person from enjoyment of such a right' (para 25 of the decision in *Sinclair Collis Ltd v HMRC (Case C-275/01) (2003 STC 898)*). Accordingly the letting had come to an end when the payments stopped. The College also contended that the capital goods scheme was looking at whether there was a change in the use between taxable and exempt supplies and the complete absence of supplies did not create exempt supplies. The Tribunal rejected that too. It held that after the cessation of rents, either the leases had been used other than for taxable use, which was a change of use, or the College had used the premises solely for making its own exempt supplies of education which was again a change of use. This case was concerned with a transaction which took place in 1966. Nowadays the option to tax would have been disapplied (see **17.133**).

Transfer of a Business as a Going Concern

17.215 The transfer of a business or part of a business as a going concern is neither a supply of goods or a supply of services and thus does not attract VAT (*VAT (Special Provisions) Order 1995* (*SI 1995 No 1268*) *Article 5*) provided that certain conditions are met – one of which is that 'the transferee is already, or immediately becomes as a result of the transfer, a taxable person'. This does not apply to a VATable transfer of a building or land (whether because the option to tax has been exercised or the building is a new building) unless the transferee has exercised the option to charge VAT in respect of the building concerned with effect from the date on which his acquisition takes place has given written notice of his election to HMRC before that date and has notified the transferor that *Article 5(2B)* (see **17.216**) does not apply to him (*Articles 5(2), (2A)*). Many people seem to think that where a building is exempt but the input tax on repairs, etc is being recovered because it is used wholly for the purposes of a taxable business, it is necessary to opt to tax the building in order to have a TOGC of the business. This is not correct. Where an exempt asset is transferred with the TOGC that transfer has no VAT effect. It should particularly be noted that the option to tax needs to be made before the first date on which the grant would have been treated as made if the transfer were not a TOGC. HMRC take the view that this is normally on completion, except where a deposit is received (other than as stakeholder) when it is the date of receipt of that deposit. However, it may be dangerous to rely on this view (see **17.219** below). Curiously, a formal election under *VATA 1994, Sch 10, para 2* is required even if the purchaser is a fully taxable person who will use the building in his business or if the building is new and will be sold on by the purchaser within the three-year period, so that he will in any event be a taxable person. If the transferee does not exercise the option to tax but acquires as a going concern a business which includes a VATable property, only the property will attract VAT; the going concern exclusion will still apply to the other assets (C & E Press Release 75A/91). See **17.172** above for a salutary lesson in what can go wrong unless the vendor satisfies himself that the purchaser has done all that is required of him.

17.216 *Article 5(2B)* applies to a transferee if:

(*a*) the supply of the asset being transferred would become a capital item for the purpose of the capital goods scheme (see **17.205**) if the TOGC rules applied to it (irrespective of whether or not they do); and

(*b*) his supplies of that asset will be exempt supplies under *VATA 1994, Sch 10, para 2 (3AA)* (see **17.149**).

17.217 *Articles 5(2A)* and *(2B)* are aimed at schemes which use TOGCs to avoid the disapplication of the option to tax in relation to exempt land. Removing the de-supply of the TOGC allows *para 2(3AA)* to disapply the option to tax at the date of the transfer.

17.218 The notice to the transferor under *Article 5(2B)* does not have to take any particular form. Nor does it need to be sent to HMRC. Its purpose is to be able to prove to HMRC, if called upon to do so, that at the time of the transfer the transferor was not aware of any intention to use the building for exempt purposes. HMRC are likely to want to see the notice if the building in fact comes to be used for an exempt purpose after the transfer. If the notice cannot be produced HMRC will seek to disapply the TOGC rules and collect from the transferor the resultant tax. If it is produced they will not proceed against the transferor but will seek to impose the tax liability on the transferee. In practice the notice is normally incorporated in the sale contract as a warranty.

17.219 Despite their view on time as stated above, in *Higher Education Statistics Agency Ltd v C & E Commrs (2000 STC 332)*, where a property was bought at auction, HMRC argued that a contract for the sale of land is concluded when the final bid at the auction is accepted by the auctioneer, that the result of a binding contract for the sale of land of which specific performance would be granted (ie that is enforceable) is that the purchaser becomes the equitable owner of the property, and therefore at the time of the auction the company acquired a beneficial or equitable interest in the land which amounts to the grant of an interest in the land and this was at a time when it was agreed that no election was in place. The High Court held that the receipt of the deposit was deemed by *Article 5* to be a taxable supply. HMRC said subsequent to the tribunal decision that there was nothing explicit in the tribunal decision to suggest that the relevant date could be the contract date (Business Brief 16/99). The tribunal decision actually states:

> '48 … It is unclear what the draftsman had in mind … although in property law the result of a binding contract for the sale of land of which specific performance would be granted is a transfer of an equitable interest in the land there are many reasons why such a contract might not be completed and accordingly a contract is a circumstance that a

grant could be said to have been treated as having been made, if for some reason it was not completed …

54 … largely for the reason that it is the decision which gives more meaning to the words 'the date of which the grant would have been treated as made' (see para 48), I have decided the matter in favour of the Respondents.'

That looks fairly explicit to this author. Moses J doubted whether the draftsman ever envisaged these provisions applying in the circumstances of an auction where the auctioneer acts as agent for the vendor but felt that the words of the order could not bear any alternative construction. Although not addressed by Moses J, there is probably an inference from his judgment that no problem arises where a deposit is received as stakeholder, which is HMRC's long-held view.

17.220 HMRC consider that where a person owns a portfolio of buildings, each building can be regarded as a separate business (including a separate property letting business) and thus a sale of a letting building can be a transfer of a business as a going concern if:

(*a*) the property is to be used by the purchaser for carrying on the same kind of business as the vendor, ie he will continue to let it, not necessarily to the same tenant or tenants; and

(*b*) the 'business' transferred is capable of operation as an independent business – which will apply to virtually any letting property.

It is not clear if head (*a*) is met if the property was previously let, is empty at the time of transfer, and will be relet by the purchaser only after refurbishment. The safe course is to seek to clear the position in advance with HMRC. In *Golden Oak Partnership (VTD 7212)* it was held that a sale of a development site on which the vendor had intended to build accommodation to be let on zero-rated leases and on which it had installed drainage, widened the road, and constructed electricity and gas substations, and which it sold to another developer together with a building that it had used as its administrative offices, was a transfer of a going concern and not an exempt supply of land. The VAT tribunal were influenced by the facts that at the time of the sale the land was in the course of active development, the purchaser had continued the development without a break (this was not strictly correct as he obtained and implemented a new planning consent) and on completion had granted zero-rated leases. However, in *Gulf Trading and Management Ltd (VTD 16847)*, where the only work done prior to resale was to fence the land, carry out soil inspection and prepare drawings with a view to obtaining planning consent, the tribunal said such works did not relate to active development so the appellant's ownership of the site did not constitute a business.

17.221 HMRC do not consider there to be a transfer of a going concern where:

(*a*) the purchaser of a property rental business is a member of the same VAT group as the existing tenant (as letting to oneself cannot be a business); or

(*b*) a member of a VAT group sells to a third party a property which is being rented to another member of the group (as the letting is not a business whilst the property is within the group).

However, they did not take this point in relation to transactions before 1 January 1999. Where the tenant which is a member of the VAT group is only one of a number of tenants, the presence of outside tenants will, however, qualify the building as a TOGC (Business Brief 26/98). *In Morton Hotels Ltd (VTD 20039)* sold three hotels to Swallow Hotels Ltd. Immediately after completion Swallow did a sale and leaseback of the hotel properties to finance the acquisition. HMRC contended that the sale and leaseback prevented the transfer from Morton being a TOGC as Swallow sold the hotels without having carried on the trade. At no time did it operate as owner-occupier of the hotels. Nor did the new purchaser from Swallow operate the hotels. The tribunal dismissed this, holding that the only requirement is for the transferee to be carrying on the same kind of business as the transferor; there is not a further requirement either that the assets must be used in the same way or that any proprietorial interest acquired must be retained in the same form. Looking at the substance of the transaction the same business is being run in the same way after the transfer as before.

17.222 The tribunal was fairly scathing of HMRC in the subsequent case of *Dartford Borough Council (VTD 20423)*. Dartford owned a site. In January 2003 it entered into a Development Agreement with Prologis to develop it. The agreement recited that it was intended to cover the master planning, marketing, development and disposal of the site in accordance with Dartford's legal obligation to obtain best consideration for it. In November 2004, Dartford and Prologis entered into a conditional lease agreement with Sainsbury's for two units on the site. It provided for leases to be executed and held in escrow until practical completion which was anticipated to be in April 2007. In August 2005 the agreement became unconditional. In December 2005 Dartford sold the land to G P Nominees Ltd with G P warranting that on completion it would let the units to Sainsbury's in accordance with the agreement for lease. At that time no work had been done on the Sainsbury's sites. Dartford contended that its sale to G P was a TOGC. HMRC disagreed. It said that Dartford had always intended to sell the plots whereas G P intended to receive rent from them; that is not the same kind of business. Furthermore for there to be a TOGC some actual development must have taken place (see the contrast between *Gulf* and *Golden Oak* in **17.220**

above). The tribunal rejected both of these arguments. In doing so it made some interesting points.

(*a*) It is necessary to identify only whether an economic activity is being carried on. Labelling that activity – Dartford said it was a rental business whereas HMRC described it as a future rental business – had caused considerable confusion. The question to be asked was whether the business included an intention to sell the plots before rent was received on completion of the building and, if so, whether it was a different business from G P's which intended to hold the plots and receive rent from them.

(*b*) The development agreement could not be construed as requiring Dartford to sell the land rather than lease it. It was free to do either. The agreement for lease with Sainsbury's made a sale a viable option. However, even if Dartford had been committed to sell the plots the sale of the site to G P would still have been a TOGC as once there is an agreement for lease the fact that no rents are currently receivable becomes irrelevant to determining the type of business. Accordingly from that time both Dartford and G P had an intention to generate rent from the land.

(*c*) HMRC's argument, taken to its logical conclusion, must mean that a dealer in land could never make a TOGC to an investor. That has never been their practice in the past. If they intended to change their practice they should have made a public statement to that effect.

(*d*) Once an agreement for lease is in place it becomes irrelevant whether there has been any development work. The decision in *Golden Oak Partnership* did not require there to be development; it was merely that factually some work has been done in that case. In any event that was a sale to a developer and the vendor had not contracted for any development.

The tribunal expressed concern about HMRC's misunderstanding of the nature of an agreement for lease.

17.223 In *ACS Hordern (VTD 8941)* the taxpayer bought and planted forestry land. He registered for VAT as an intending trader. Before making any taxable supplies he sold the land. HMRC sought to recover the input tax provisionally repaid on the planting, etc. costs. They contended that a business could not be a going concern until some supplies had been made. The VAT tribunal disagreed. It thought the business had been a going concern from the time the trees were planted and that, as the business was of a continuing nature and the purchaser was able to take it over and carry it on as before, there had been a transfer of a going concern.

17.224 There is a particular problem where the property is acquired in the name of a nominee. For example, a property acquired by a partnership of more than four members will normally be registered in the name of four of them as nominees for all the partners. Similarly, if property is held for an unincorporated association it will be registered in the name of nominees. The nominee will not be carrying on the business and therefore the transfer of a going concern rules do not technically apply. HMRC are prepared to treat the beneficial owner as the transferee (if the parties wish) if the nominee holds the land for a named beneficial owner (Business Brief 10/96). They will not do so if the identity of the beneficial owner is not disclosed to the vendor. The vendor is expected to check that the beneficial owner is VAT-registered and, where necessary, has opted to tax the property. The concession looks only at a nominee for the purchaser. HMRC interpret the *VAT (Special Provisions) Order 1995* as requiring the transferee to carry on the business but there is no specific requirement for the transferor to do so. The problems of joint ownership are considered at **16.263**.

17.225 The decision of the ECJ in *Finanzamt Offenbach am Main-Land v Faxworld Vorgrundung sgesellschaft Peter Hunning Lausen und Wolfgang Klein GbR (Case C-137/02) (2005 STC 1192)* casts doubt on whether that part of the Special Provisions Order is consistent with EC law and, accordingly, whether there is a concession at all. In that case, Faxworld was established with the sole object of setting up a business and transferring it to a limited company, Faxworld AG. It was held that although Faxworld GbR made no supplies and never had any intention of doing so, Faxworld AG must be treated as its successor and Faxworld GbR, as the transferor, must be entitled to take account of the taxable transactions of the recipient, ie Faxworld AG, so as to be entitled to deduct the VAT paid on input services which have been procured for the purposes of the recipient's taxable operations. On that basis, it does not appear necessary for a nominee to itself carry on the business.

17.226 So do the arguments put forward on behalf of HMRC and accepted by the VAT tribunal in *MPH Leisure Ltd (VTD 19778)*. In that case Mr & Mrs Iredale operated a private members club in Cleveland. On 4 November 2004 they sold the club to Easington Greyhound Station Ltd. VAT was included in the sale price. With effect from 5 November 2004 Easington granted a lease of the premises to MPH. MPH also took on staff formerly employed by Mr & Mrs Iredale and also seems to have taken over her membership list. It was held that there had been a TOGC as MPH was put in possession of the business formerly carried on by Mr & Mrs Iredale. The tribunal pointed out that the legislation and case law did not prescribe a method for transferring a going concern and that it is not necessary for the transfer to be effected in a single transaction. Nor is there any requirement for the transferee to purchase the business or its assets for there to be a TOGC. There was no break in trading and no fundamental change in the business from Mr & Mrs Iredale to MPH.

The tribunal clearly placed no weight on the fact that Easington never carried on the business or indeed on who carried it on. They looked merely at whether the business carried on at 5 November was the same as that on 4 November. A similar decision was reached in *Sam's Bistro Ltd (VTD 19973)* where the premises had been acquired by Mr Barker who had then licensed the company to carry on the business.

17.227 HMRC have given some further guidance on their views of the application of the TOGC rules in relation to buildings (Technical Note, 3 March 2008).

(*a*) The surrender of a lease to the landlord is not normally a TOGC as there is no asset that passes to the landlord; it ceases to exist. However, it can be a TOGC if the lease is not extinguished (the freehold and leasehold interest do not merge) and the lease continues to be exploited by receiving rent from sub-tenants.

(*b*) If the owner of an undertaking ceases to trade and lets the premises to someone who will carry on the same trade it is not a TOGC as the property has not been transferred; a new asset, the lease, has been created.

(*c*) If a pub tenant surrenders his lease to his landlord (typically a brewery) who grants a new lease to an incoming tenant, that is not a TOGC, as no asset has been transferred – although if the old tenant sells furniture and equipment to the new tenant, that transaction can be a TOGC.

(*d*) The grant of an intermediate lease out of a freehold and the sale of that lease is not a TOGC, even if the tenant in occupation remains the same, as the lease is a different asset from the freehold – even if it is for 999 years, even if it is done simply to avoid triggering a balancing charge under the capital allowance rules and even if it is done simply as a mechanism to impose service charges on occupiers.

(*e*) If a person acquires a head lease which is subject to an occupational lease and at the same time acquires the freehold and allows the two to merge there is not a TOGC as although the rent continues to be received from the same tenant it is rent from a different asset (this seems questionable).

(*f*) If a property that has been let out for many years is vacant at the time of the sale it cannot be a TOGC even if the purchaser is seeking a new tenant as 'when the lease ended the property rental business carried on by former freeholder ceased' (this seems highly questionable; it seems to assume that each lease is a separate 'business' whereas most people would regard them as being a single continuing business of renting out the property).

(*g*) If a holding company acquires a business on a share for share exchange and immediately transfers the shares to a subsidiary there is not a TOGC.

(*h*) HMRC's policy is that a partially let property is capable of being a property rental business provided that the letting constitutes economic activity. The letting of electricity sub-stations or space for advertising hoarding may be sufficient provided that there is a lease in place. However, each case will be unique and depend on the precise circumstances.

In a later HMRC Brief (27/2014) they added:

(i) The surrender of a lease can be a TOGC where, for example, a tenant subletting premises surrenders its interest together with the benefit of the sub-tenants, or where a retailer sells its retailing business to its landlord. This will apply even where the landlord's interest is held via one or more nominees so that the transaction involves a transfer to the nominee for the landlord's benefit.

17.228 Curiously (*c*) above is precisely what happened in *Tom Carr t/a The Princess Royal Public House (VTD 20507)* where HMRC argued – unsuccessfully – that there was a TOGC. Head (*b*) is roughly what happened in *Robinson Family Ltd (TC 2046)* where HMRC refused TOGC treatment. The transferor had a 125-year lease of the premises but, by virtue of restrictions on alienation in it could not transfer the lease but had to transfer the business by granting a sub-lease for the term of the lease less three days. The FTT held that it was a TOGC. Following that case HMRC issued Business Brief 30/12 saying that they accept that the retention of a small reversionary interest in the property concerned does not prevent the transaction from being a TOGC, 'provided that the interest retained is small enough not to disturb the substance of the transaction'. It is questionable whether this small concession properly reflects EU law. They subsequently confirmed that where the lease was part of a building, the 1% must be applied only to that part of the building (HMRC Brief 27/2014).

17.229 In *Finanzamt Ludenscheid v Christel Schriever (Case C-444/10) (2012 STC 633)* the CJEC held that 'there is a transfer of a totality of assets, or part thereof, for the purpose of [Article 5(8) of the Sixth Directive] where the stock and fittings of a retail outlet are transferred concomitantly with the conclusion of a contract of lease, to the transferee of the premises of that outlet for an indefinite period but terminable at short notice by either party, provided that the assets transferred are sufficient for the transferee to be able to carry on an independent economic activity on a lasting basis'. In that case the lease could be terminated by both landlord and tenant on three months' notice. It can also be noted that the judgment recites that 'in the order for reference … the Bundezfinanzhof observes that it has found a 10-year lease to be sufficient for a long-term transfer of use of such important component elements, while the *Finanzgericht Baden-Württemburg* has held, in a judgment which has become final, that a lease of premises owned by a transferor for a five-year period was insufficient to support a finding that the business activity was being continued'. Whilst these German cases are not of direct relevance in the UK they do illustrate that Germany, at least, takes a more relaxed interpretation of the EU legislation than HMRC. *Christel Schriever* was concerned with the transfer of a retail business but there is no logical reason why a different rule should apply to a property rental business.

17.230 Where the sale of a building constitutes the transfer of a business as a going concern VAT incurred on the legal and other costs of the transfer relates to overheads of the business. It is therefore fully deductible if the business is fully taxable and partially deductible if it is partly exempt (unless there is a direct and immediate link with a clearly defined part of the business so that the overheads relate only to that part). This was confirmed by the ECJ in *Abbey National plc v C & E Commrs (Case C-408/98) (2001 STC 297)*. The logic is that in principle the various services used by the transferor for the purpose of the transfer have a direct and immediate link with the whole economic activity of the taxable person. The court did not consider the position of the transferee but that logic seems equally applicable to the transferee. In *London & Exmoor Estates Ltd (VTD 16707)*, in contrast, legal fees on the abortive purchase of a property were held not to be a cost component of any taxable supply or intended taxable supply. This decision is questionable in the light of the Abbey National decision.

17.231 *Scottish Homes (VTD 16644)* was established as a statutory body to take over management of residential properties in the public sector. It carried out improvement works including electrical rewiring, replacement of windows and doors, major roof repairs, new kitchens and central heating systems. It claimed that it had used the improvement work in making taxable as well as exempt supplies because it carried out the improvements partly to encourage tenants to exercise their statutory right to buy. This was accepted by the tribunal. The cost of the improvement work was part of the costs of the supplies made by the business as a whole, including both sales and lettings, and there was a sufficient and immediate link to its taxable transactions to justify apportionment of the input tax.

Transfers of Estate Roads, etc

17.232 If a developer of a housing or industrial estate transfers the basic amenities of estate roads and footpaths, communal parking, and open space to a management company which will maintain them, no taxable supply is regarded as taking place but the input tax in relation to such items is regarded as attributable to the houses, warehouses or factories on the estate (C & E Notice 742, para 8.2). HMRC have said that this does not, however, apply to any other transfer of land or buildings, such as a management office (Notice

742A, para 19F – now withdrawn). The logic behind this distinction is not readily apparent. It is not repeated in the current edition of Notice 742.

Domestic Accommodation for Directors and Employees

17.233 Input tax incurred by a company in relation to goods or services in connection with the provision of accommodation to be used for domestic purposes by a director of the company (or a connected person, ie his spouse, or a relative, or the spouse of a relative of either the director or his spouse) is treated as incurred for non-business purposes, and is accordingly not deductible. Up to 31 December 2010 this was achieved by *VATA 1994, s 24(3)*, but this was repealed by *F(No 3)A 2010*.The *s 24(3)* disallowance was wider than simply domestic accommodation, as it would cover, for example, an office provided for the use of personal staff of the director who he engages for his domestic purposes. 'Relative' is not defined. There was no similar restriction on accommodation provided for employees, but it should not be assumed that input tax will be recoverable in relation to building work on a house owned by a company and occupied by an employee. Prior to the introduction of this provision in 1990 the approach of the VAT tribunals to accommodation used partly for business purposes and partly as living accommodation for a director had been to regard it as being partly for business and partly for non-business purposes and to require an apportionment of the input tax. *VATA 1994, s 24(3)* does not affect the deductibility of expenditure in relation to accommodation occupied by a sole trader or partner in a partnership, but again the practice has been to treat a portion of such expenditure as having been incurred for non-business purposes even if a primary business purpose for the expenditure could be established.

17.234 A further difficulty is that on an appeal against a decision of HMRC in relation to the allowance of input tax on the supply of 'something in the nature of a luxury, amusement or entertainment', the VAT tribunal is prohibited from altering the decision of HMRC unless it considers it was unreasonable, or would have been unreasonable if at that time they had been aware of information that became available between the time of determination and the time of the hearing (*VATA 1994, s 84(4)*, deriving from *FA 1993, s 46*). During the course of the Finance Bill debates the Minister declined to elaborate on the words in inverted commas, saying that their meaning depends on the facts of each case. In *Durnell Marketing Ltd (VTD 17813)*, the company sought to argue that work on a director's house had a business purpose, namely to provide a bonus to the director, but the tribunal dismissed this, holding that the cost of the work was far in excess of what a company in that financial position would vote as a bonus. The 2011 changes curiously extend the disallowance to staff but no longer seem to cover private use by a connected person of a director if that person is not a member of the company's staff. The *F(No 3)A 2010* changes also repealed the definitions of both a director and a connected person. The Finance Bill Explanatory Notes say the definition is unnecessary following the repeal of *s 24(3)*.

17.235 Now where goods or services supplied to a taxable person are used partly for the purpose of his business and partly for other purposes, the VAT must be apportioned so that only the part referable to the business use counts as input tax (*VATA 1994, s 24(5)*). For this purpose a relevant asset held for the purposes of a business carried on by a taxable person cannot, in any circumstances, be regarded as used for the purposes of the business to the extent that it is used (or to be used) for that person's private use or the private use of his staff (*VATA 1994, s 24(5A)*). A relevant asset includes:

(*a*) any interest in land;

(*b*) any building or part of a building;

(*c*) any civil engineering work or part of such a work; and

(*d*) any goods incorporated or to be incorporated in a building or civil engineering work (whether by being installed as fixtures or fittings or otherwise).

(*VATA 1994, s 24(5B)*.)

17.236 HMRC are given power by regulation to make such supplementary, incidental, consequential and transitional provisions as appear to them to be necessary (*VATA 1994, s 24(6A)*). They have done so by *reg 11* of the *VAT (Amendment) (No 4) Regulation 2010 (SI 2010, No 3022)* which extends the capital goods scheme to also cover changes between business and non-business use of assets. This will apparently enable taxpayers to adjust VAT initially deducted on expenditure if there is a subsequent increase in the extent to which it is used for business purposes (2010 (No 3) Finance Bill Explanatory Notes). The same rule applies to services (*VATA 1994, Sch 4, para, 5(4A)* inserted by *F(No 3)A 2010, Sch 8, para 3*).

17.237 What happens where part of a building is used as a private residence and part as business premises? The ECJ has consistently held that the taxpayer has the choice of (i) allocating that item wholly to the assets of his business, (ii) retaining it wholly within his private assets, thereby excluding it entirely from the VAT system, or (iii) integrating it into his business only to the extent to which it is actually used for business purposes. The leading cases on the first two options are *Bakcsi v Finanzamt Furstenfeldbruck (Case C-415/98, 2002 STC 802)* which involved a car, and *Seeling v Finanzamt Starnberg (Case C-269/00, 2003 STC 805* – see **17.243**) and *Lennartz v Finanzamt Munchen III (Case C-97/90, 1995 STC 514* (see **17.239**) which held that the principle applies equally to construction services. The leading case on option

(iii) is probably *Finanzamt Ulzen v Armbrecht (Case C-291/92, 1995 STC 997* – see **17.244**).

17.238 There is normally a deemed supply of services where goods (which includes a major interest in land) held for the purpose of a business are put to private use unless either there is no consideration or no right to deduct input tax arises *(VATA 1994, Sch 4, para 5(4)(5))*. This did not apply to an interest in land, a building or part of a building, any civil engineering work or part of such work or goods incorporated or to be incorporated into a building or civil engineering work except to the extent that the taxpayer or a predecessor was entitled to a deduction for input tax prior to that date *(VATA 1994, Sch 4, para 5(4A)* (as originally enacted) inserted by *FA 2003, s 22* and repealed by *FA 2007, s 99(2))*. Instead the *VAT (Supply of Services) Order 1993* (which provides that where a person carrying on a business puts services which have been supplied to him to private use he is treated as supplying those services in the course of his business) applies to those items.

17.239 This was intended to reverse the effect of the judgment of the European Court of Justice in *Lennartz v Finanzamt Munchen III (Case C-97/90) (1995 STC 514)*, where it was held that a business is entitled to deduct the full amount of input tax on an asset acquired partly for non-business purposes, however small the proportion of business use, but must then treat as a supply of services for a consideration the private use of the asset, so triggering an output tax charge by reference to the use. By preventing a deemed supply arising, the government believed that the initial right to deduct would be limited to the anticipated business proportion of the use of the building. The government believed that they were entitled to do this under *Article 6(2)* of the *Sixth Directive* (power to derogate where it will not lead to distortions of competition). The subsequent ECJ decision in *Charles and Another v Staatssecretaris van Financien (Case C-434/03) (2006 STC 1429)* showed this to be wrong.

17.240 Accordingly, in Business Brief 15/05, HMRC accepted that what they call the *Lennartz* mechanism was available for the purchase of land, buildings and civil engineering works with mixed business and non-business use. It could also be used for construction services on buildings or civil engineering works which result in the construction of a new building or a major refurbishment or extension of an existing building. HMRC require the output tax charge under the *Lennartz* principle to be calculated over a maximum of 20 years and based on straight-line depreciation (unless a shorter period is indicated, eg a lease has less than 20 years to run). For example, if a building cost £500,000 and business use is 10%, VAT needs to be accounted for each year on a notional £2,500 supply, ie 10% of 5% of £500,000 (Business Brief 15/05). The exclusion by *Sch 4, para 5(4A)* was repealed by *FA 2007, s 99(2)* and the extension of the Supply of Services order to land and construction was repealed by the

VAT (Supply of Services) (Amendment) Order 2007 (SI 2007 No 2173). At the same time HMRC were given power, by Statutory Instrument, to make regulations to determine how the full cost to the taxable person of providing such services is to be calculated (*FA 2007, s 99(4)(5)*). They did so by the *VAT (Amendment) (No 7) Regulations 2007 (SI 2007 No 3099)* with effect from 1 November 2007. These reduced the 20-year period referred to above to ten years following the decision of the ECJ in *Wolley & Wollny v Finanzgericht Landshut (Case C-72/05).* In that case the German court was seeking a ruling as to whether the 'full cost of providing the services' (the deemed supply under *Lennartz*) in respect of construction costs must be calculated by reference to depreciation for wear and tear of the building or on the basis of the length of the adjustment period under the capital goods scheme. The ECJ held that 'a member state does not misconstrue the discretion which it enjoys in providing that the rules relating to the adjustment of deductions apply for the purpose of establishing the taxable amount for the private use of business goods', ie that a country can require the capital goods scheme adjustment period to be used. The *Regulations* insert new *regs 116A–116N* into the *VAT Regulations 1995.* These provide that where the economic life of a person's interest in goods (which includes land), commencing on the day when they are first used for any purpose exceeds ten years, the adjustment period is ten years (five years for goods other than land, buildings or part of a building). If the economic life is less than ten years from first use the adjustment period is limited to the number of months remaining to the expiry of the interest. If a subsequent supply of goods or services is made to the owner in respect of the goods the economic life of that subsequent expenditure is determined separately. The *VAT (Special Provisions) (Amendment) Order 2007 (SI 2007 No 2923)* excludes the operation of *VATA 1994, Sch 4, para 5(4)* (goods put to private use) once their economic life for adjustment purposes has expired, so as to avoid a double tax charge.

17.241 HMRC announced on 22 January 2010 that the ECJ case of *Vereniging Noordelijke Land-en Tuinbouw Organisatie v Staatssecretaris van Financien (Case C-515/07)(2009 STC 935)* made clear that the legislation does not give, and has never given, a right to use *Lennartz* accounting for economic activities that give rise to supplies that are outside the scope of VAT. It will only be available where the goods are used in part for making taxable supplies in the course of an economic activity that gives a right to input VAT deduction, and they are also used in part for the private purposes of the trader or his staff (or, exceptionally, for other uses which are wholly outside the purpose of the taxpayer's enterprise The issue in the *Lennartz* case was membership subscriptions the greater part of which were used to fund activities which promoted the general interest of the members. This change is most likely to affect charities and members organisations. HMRC said that businesses which were already using *Lennartz* accounting at 22 January 2010 could either continue to do so or reverse the position retrospectively (HMRC Brief 02/2010).

EU Council Directive 2009/162/EU, which took effect from 1 January 2011, requires Member States to restrict VAT recovery in relation to the private use of land and property expenditure. *F(No 3)A 2010, s 19* and *Sch 8* (which are considered at **17.219**) give effect to this Directive. This effectively blocked the use of the *Lennartz* mechanism in relation to property.

17.242 Where a person carrying on a business (or a predecessor of his) was allowed a deduction before 22 January 2010 in respect of such assets on the basis that the *Lennartz* principle applied, and the credit has not been fully reversed (by being repaid to HMRC or offset against overpaid output tax), the deduction must be treated as having been made pursuant to *VATA 1994, Sch 4, para 5(4)* thus triggering future deemed supplies by reference to use *(F(No 3) A 2010, Sch 8, para 4* and *VAT Regulations 1995, reg 102ZA*). In *Stichting Goed Wonen v Staatssecretaris van Financien (Case C-326/99) (2003 STC 1137)* it was held that, as a country has a discretion under *Article 5(3)* of the *Sixth Directive* to treat as tangible property interests in commercial property and rights *in rem* giving the holder a right of use over immovable property, it must also be entitled to lay down conditions to restrict such treatment. The case was concerned with usufruct, which is a right *in rem* common in Europe but which has no equivalent in English law. The ECJ held that the right has fundamental attributes in common with leasing so such a right can be treated as the leasing or letting of immovable property. It should be noted that the taxpayer needs to be a taxable person (registered or registerable) at the time of acquisition. No input tax can be claimed if a property initially used for private purposes is later used for the business unless the business use was contemplated at the time of acquisition *(Klub OOD v Direcktor na Direktsia Obzhalvanei upravlenie na izpalnenieto – 2012 STC 1129).*

17.243 The German Government sought to achieve the same effect by a different route in *Seeling v Finanzamt Starnberg (Case C-269/00) (2003 STC 805).* They contended that the private use by Mr Seeling was a letting of immovable property which was an exempt supply. The ECJ disagreed. The letting of immovable property essentially involves the landlord of property assigning to the tenant, in return for rent and for an agreed period, the right to occupy his property and to exclude other persons from it. The private use by the taxable person of a dwelling in the building does not satisfy those conditions. Not only is no rent paid but also there is no genuine agreement either on the duration of the right of enjoyment or to exclude third parties. In that case the court also stressed that 'it must first be pointed out that it is settled case law that a taxable person may choose whether or not to integrate into his business, for the purpose of applying the Sixth Directive, part of an asset which is given over to his private use.' It is this settled case law that *s 22* seeks to exclude.

17.244 In *Finanzamt Ülzen v Armbrecht (Case C-291/92)(1995 STC 997)* the European Court of Justice held that where a taxable person performs transactions in a private capacity he does not act as a taxable person, and there is nothing in the *Sixth Directive* which precludes a taxable person who wishes to retain part of an item of property amongst his private assets from excluding it from the tax system. Input tax attributable to such excluded part is of course not deductible. This principle was followed by the VAT tribunal in *Wellright Ltd (VTD 14646)*. In *Dysart Developments Ltd (VTD 17333)*, where the company, which is a property development company, occupied premises in the grounds of the residence of its managing director, HMRC sought to disallow 50% of the costs of reconstructing a fountain, reducing its circumference to produce additional car parking and remodelling a pond 'to promote the Appellant's landscaping ability and its environmental concerns'. The tribunal allowed the entire input tax, finding that the goods or services which were supplied to the Appellant company were wholly for the purpose of its business. It is doubtful whether this decision is of general application. Evidence was given by the managing director that she in fact derived little personal benefit from the works. The works to the fountain were necessitated by the needs of the company to accommodate its business visitors; she had been happy to keep topping up the pond, and the work to reline it was done to protect the company's reputation.

17.245 In *Finanzamt Bergisch Gladback v HE (Case C-25/03, 2007 STC 128)* HE and his wife purchased a plot of land on which they constructed a dwelling. The land and dwelling were owned 25% by HE and 75% by his wife and the invoices for the construction services were addressed to them jointly. HE used one room in the house as an office in connection with his activity as an author which was ancillary to his salaried employment. He claimed a deduction for 12% of the VAT on the construction costs on the basis that the room was 12% of the whole house. The German tax authorities sought to restrict the claim to 25% of 12% as ME only had a 25% interest in the house. Advocate General Tizzano agreed, but the ECJ disagreed and held that ME was entitled to deduct the full 12%: 'Given that the community formed by the spouses is not a taxable person … any such entitlement to deduct must be granted to the spouses taken individually insofar as they have the status of taxable person … It is necessary to bear in mind … that the home office is used by HE personally and wholly for the purposes of his business and that he has decided to allocate this room entirely to his business. Hence it is evident that he in fact disposes of this room as owner and therefore fulfils the condition' to deduct the VAT. The ECJ considered that *Article 5(1)* of the *Sixth Directive* covers any transfer of tangible property by one party which empowers the other party to dispose of it as if he were the owner of the property and the purpose of the Directive might be jeopardised if the requirements for there to be a supply of goods were to differ according to the civil law of the Member State concerned. The Court did, however, say that HE was entitled to deduct the whole of the input tax attributable to the business room only in so far as the amount deducted does not exceed the limits of the taxable person's interest in the co-ownership of the item. It also held that an invoice issued to the co-owning spouses without distinguishing between them and without reference to the proportion of the interest of each in the property is sufficient to enable the taxable co-owner to exercise his right to deduct. This seems reasonable. Suppose the two had bought the land 75% for the purpose of a business carried on by Mrs HE and 25% for that carried on by HE. Logically all of the VAT ought to be deductible by one or the other. However, the German Government's argument would have disallowed 25% of Mrs HE's VAT and 75% of Mr HE's.

17.246 HMRC and the National Farmers Union have agreed guidelines for the recovery of input tax on repairs, maintenance, renovation, etc. of farmhouses – although HMRC say that these do not give any automatic entitlement:

(*a*) in the case of a normal working farm where the VAT-registered person is actively engaged in running it, 70% of the input tax may be recovered;

(*b*) where the building work is more associated with an alteration (eg building an extension) it is necessary to look at the purpose for the construction; if the dominant purpose is a business one, the 70% figure will apply, but if the dominant purpose is a personal one, then the recoverable amount is unlikely to exceed 40% and in some cases will be nil;

(*c*) where farming is not a full-time occupation for the VAT-registered person, HMRC expect that the recoverable portion will be somewhere between 10% and 30% only; and

(*d*) if the occupant of the farmhouse is a director of a company (or a connected person) then **17.233** above will apply and nothing will be recoverable.

Rent-free Periods

17.247 There was concern for a time that where a landlord granted a tenant a rent-free period, HMRC might seek to exact VAT on the rent foregone. The then Minister, Mrs Gillian Shephard, explained in a House of Commons Written Answer on 17 December 1991 (Hansard, Vol 201, Col 119) that 'rent-free periods are outside the scope of VAT unless services are performed in return by the tenant for the landlord. As this is uncommon, in practice only a few cases will lead to VAT being charged'. This probably means that for a rent-free period to give rise to a VAT liability, an obligation must be imposed on the tenant to carry out works on the premises; it would not be sufficient for it to be allowed to give a tenant time to carry out such works or for it to be negotiated as one of the terms of the lease – although it would obviously be dangerous to express the rent-free period as an inducement to take the lease.

17.248 Where a tenant was granted a lease with a rent-free period and agreed to carry out specific works to the property, a VAT tribunal held that, in carrying out the works, the tenant had made a taxable supply of the works to the landlord for a consideration (*Ridgeons Bulk Ltd (1992 VATTR 169) (VTD 7655)*). The tenant contended that the tribunal should look only at the lease, which contained no reference to the works, and that the motives for entering into it should be disregarded, but the tribunal held that the two were directly linked in a letter from the landlord to the tenant. Although this case went to appeal *(1994 STC 427)*, the appeal was concerned solely with procedural matters and the admissibility of the landlord's letter as evidence. In any case the CJEU rules in *Serebryannay vek EOOD v Direktor na Direktsia ObzLalvane I uptavlenie na izpalnenieto (C-283/12) (2014 STC 427)* that where a company agreed to fit out and furnish an apartment in return for being able to rent it out for a fixed period without being required to pay rent, and the owner recovers the improved apartment at the end of the contract, there is a supply to the owner for consideration of the services of fitting out and furnishing.

Building Regulation Fees

17.249 The *Building Act 1984* enabled the private sector to apply for approval as inspectors for the purpose of the *Building Regulations*. NHBC (Building Control Services) Ltd was approved to carry out certain work on residential development, but in the case of flats not exceeding eight storeys in height. From 13 January 1997, other private sector bodies have been approved to cover the whole range of building control work. Local authorities have to charge VAT on building regulation fees for such work. (Business Briefs 26/95, 5/97 and News Release 10/96).

Rent Guarantees, etc

17.250 If a developer, vendor or lessor of a property guarantees to the purchaser that it will pay the commercial rent until a tenant or sub-tenant is found, the guarantee (and payments under it) are may well be outside the scope of VAT as the tenant is not making a supply of anything to the landlord. This does not apply if the documents clearly show that it is part of the consideration for the purchaser taking on the building. In most cases such an undertaking is likely to be part of the consideration. The same practice is likely to apply when the vendor agrees to pay the purchaser's mortgage interest to the extent it exceeds an agreed cap. These views were expressed by HMRC in an earlier version of Notice 742, but seem to have been dropped from the current version.

Dilapidations

17.251 HMRC regard a payment for dilapidations on the expiry of a lease as outside the scope of VAT, as in their view it represents a claim for damages by the landlord against the tenant's 'want of repair' (C & E Notice 742, para 10.12). As the dilapidations are normally payable under a specific provision in the lease and a claim for damages is not normally outside the scope of VAT if it merely quantifies the value of a supply, it is difficult to follow the logic of this, particularly where the option to tax has been exercised. Where a landlord has opted a building into the tax net and the tenant is prepared to pay an amount to terminate the lease prematurely, it is worth considering whether a reduced termination payment plus a payment for dilapidations should be demanded instead of simply a taxable termination payment.

Road and Bridge Tolls

17.252 The UK initially believed that toll charges levied by local authorities and by bodies operating under PFI (private finance initiative) or PPP (public private partnership) concessions were not payment for a supply and are thus outside the scope of VAT and that other toll charges were exempt from VAT as the grant of a right over land (Business Brief 26/99). Unfortunately, the EC Commission and the European Court of Justice did not agree and consider tolls levied by private operators to be taxable supplies, although the ECJ accepted that tolls levied by local authorities are not (*EC Commission v United Kingdom, CJEC Case C-359/97)(2000 STC 777)*.

17.253 The concept of a right to pass over a stretch of road being an exempt grant of a right over land fits uneasily with a right to go on to a tennis court being a right to make use of the facilities and with HMRC's' concept of a licence (see **17.73** above).

Local Authorities

17.254 Local authorities (and certain other public bodies) need to register for VAT if they make taxable supplies in the course of a business. The registration threshold does not apply to a local authority (*VATA 1994, s 42*). However, local authorities and other bodies governed by public law cannot be regarded as taxable persons in respect of activities and transactions in which they engage as public authorities even where they collect dues, fees, contributions or payments in connection with those activities or transactions, except to the extent that their treatment as non-taxable persons would lead to significant distortions of competition (*Article 13* of the *Principal VAT Directive*).

17.255 Isle of Wight Council and three other local authorities challenged whether the provision of off-street car parking for a parking charge by a local authority leads to a significant distortion of competition with private car park operators. The High Court referred this question to the ECJ (*Isle of Wight Council v HMRC, 2008 STC 614*) which held that 'significant distortion' must be evaluated 'by reference to the activity in question, as such, without such evaluation relating to any local market in particular', and that 'would lead to' must be interpreted 'as encompassing not only actual competition but also potential competition'. The High Court remitted the case to the tribunal for a rehearing, saying that the decision 'appears to involve an enquiry as to the impact upon local authorities' car-parking activities on markets said to be affected by them without any investigation into actual markets'. The judge admitted to 'an unawareness of how the type of exercise expected by the ECJ might be carried out'! The FTT held both that charges for off-street parking were in competition with commercial car parks and that to exempt such charges would be a deterrent to outsourcing local authority services, so VAT was payable. The Upper Tribunal and the Court of Appeal both agreed *(2015 STC 460; 2016 STI 65).*

17.256 Another interesting case is *Finanzamt Oschatz v Zweckverband zur Trinkwasserverseitigung Torgau-Westelbien (Case C-442/05) (2008 STC 1).* The Zweckverband, an association governed by public law, supplies drinking water and treats waste water. In addition to supplying its customers with water it carries out household water connections to its water mains. The issue was the charge for such connections. It claimed that the reduced rate of 9% which applies to the supply of water in Germany should also be applicable to the connection charge as the connection is exclusively intended to ensure the supply of water to the house. The ECJ agreed. It decided that laying the mains connection forms part of the supply of water, as without that connection it is impossible to make water available to the owner or occupier of the building and that in doing so the Zweckverband was acting as a taxable person even if it is acting as a public activity in laying the mains itself. It is interesting to note that the Advocator General said that:

> 'It is clear from the case law of the court that a service must be regarded as ancillary to a principle service, and thus share the tax treatment of the principle service, if it does not constitute for customers an aim in itself, but a means of better enjoying the principal service supplied … The laying of a household water connection does not constitute an aim in itself … The only purpose of laying a household water connection from the point of view of the person requesting it … is to enable the delivery of water from a water distribution network to a dwelling … The fact that the connection is laid only once while water may be delivered to a dwelling over an extended period of time does not … alter the above analysis given the on-going necessity of the connection in order to obtain

water …' He also said that the fact that laying the connection incurred a substantial up-front fee as compared to the monthly water charges did not sever 'the intrinsic, fundamental link between the laying of the connection and the supply of water.'

17.257 It was subsequently held in *Finanzamt Dusseldorf-Sud v SALIX Grundstucks-Vermietungsgesellschaft mbH & Co Object Offenbach KG (Case C-102/08) (2009 STC 1607)* that bodies governed by public law must be considered taxable persons if their treatment as non-taxable would lead to significant distortions to their own detriment. SALIX let an office property to a local Chamber of Industry and Commerce (IHK), a body governed by public law in Germany. IHK occupied the building and sublet part. SALIX waived exemption to be able to recover VAT on its building costs. The Finanzamt sought to disallow the VAT attributable to the sublet part on the basis that IHK was not acting as a taxable person in making the subletting, as subletting was not a 'commercial purpose' under German law as only short-term letting qualified as such. The ECJ said that 'the right to deduct is, in principle, applicable to the entire chain of supply of goods and services performed by taxable persons acting as such for the purpose of the economic activities of other taxable persons'. However, it is for the German courts to determine whether in making the sub-letting IHK was acting as a taxable person, ie whether treating it as non-taxable would lead to significant distortions of competition.

17.258 Local authorities and certain other statutory bodies are entitled to reclaim the VAT that they suffer on its acquisition of goods and services for their non-business activities (*VATA 1994, s 33*). Accordingly it should be largely irrelevant to a local authority whether or not it is charged VAT by its suppliers. It is only to the extent that such VAT is used for exempt business activities, primarily the supply of welfare services, the supply of ambulance services, and cultural services, that it is irrecoverable.

Chapter 18

Inheritance Tax

18.1 Inheritance tax was introduced as a combined estate and gift tax, although it does not now apply to most gifts. It is chargeable on the assets held by a person on death and on the following gifts:

(*a*) those made within seven years prior to the transferor's death;

(*b*) those where the donor reserves or enjoys a benefit; and

(*c*) gifts into settlement (with some exceptions) or to companies.

The tax is payable on the worldwide assets of an individual domiciled in the UK (or treated as domiciled in the UK) and on UK assets of one domiciled outside the UK. A person is treated as domiciled in the UK if he is domiciled outside the UK but has been tax resident in the UK for 17 out of the previous 20 years, or he has ceased to be UK domiciled within the previous three years. The government propose from 5 April 2017 to reduce the 17-year period to 15, to extend the three-year period to four and to treat a person who was born in the UK with a UK domicile of origin but subsequently acquired a foreign domicile of choice as domiciled in the UK in any year in which he is resident here. From 6 April 2017, they also intend to treat the shares in an overseas company or other entity that owns UK residential property as a UK asset to the extent its value derives from such property.

18.2 There are a number of exemptions. The most important are gifts between spouses (which includes a gift on death but only to the extent of £325,000 (£55,000 prior to 6 April 2013) if the deceased is UK domiciled but the spouse is not and does not elect to be treated as UK domiciled) and gifts to individuals (including to a non-UK domiciled spouse) and gifts to individuals provided that the donor survives for at least seven years after making the gift. The inter-spouse exemption also applies to a gift in settlement which creates an interest in possession in favour of the spouse. The first £325,000 of assets is technically taxable at nil per cent, but for all practical purposes can be looked on as exempt. The excess is taxed at a single rate of 40%. Lifetime gifts (including gifts to individuals but not those to a spouse) in the seven years before death are, in effect, brought back into the estate on death. The tax on such gifts is payable by the donor, but such gifts utilise the £325,000 nil rate band in priority to the deceased estate, so in reality they increase the tax on the estate. If a person leaves at least 10% of his estate on death to charity the tax on the remainder of the estate is reduced to 36%. The rules are complex and are not considered here. They can be found in *FA 2012, Sch 33*. Where a house is owned jointly by husband and wife, conventional planning is for the one who dies first to leave his interest in the house to the children (at least to the extent that this can be done within the £325,000 nil rate band). Such planning in relation to the private residence is considered at **13.57** onwards. A UK domiciled individual is chargeable to IHT on worldwide assets (subject to any relief under the small number of double tax agreements that the UK has entered into in relation to IHT). A non-UK domiciled individual is liable to IHT on UK assets only.

18.3 Obviously where a gift is made by one individual to another it cannot be known whether or not a charge to tax will arise in respect of the gift as the exemption is conditional upon the donor surviving for the seven-year period. Such a gift is known as a 'potentially exempt transfer'. Where the donor does die in that period, so that the gift generates an inheritance tax charge, business property relief, agricultural property relief, and the right to pay the tax by instalments will be granted only if the conditions set out in **18.4**, **18.34** and **18.53** below are met.

Agricultural Property Relief

18.4 A gift of agricultural property is effectively either exempted from inheritance tax or taxed on only 50% of its value. This is because the legislation provides that on a gift or other transfer of agricultural property which has been either:

(*a*) occupied by the transferor for the purpose of agriculture throughout the two years ending with the date of the transfer (or if it replaced other agricultural property they were together so occupied for at least two out of the five years to the date of the transfer); or

(*b*) owned by the transferor throughout the seven years ending with the date of transfer and occupied throughout that period (by anyone) for the purpose of agriculture (or if it replaced other agricultural property they were together so occupied for at least seven out of the ten years to the date of transfer),

the amount of the value transferred is to be reduced by:

(1) 100% if either:

    (A) the interest of the transferor immediately before the transfer carries the right to vacant possession or the right to obtain it within the next twelve months (or, if it is a joint interest or interest in common, that of the joint co-owners does so); or

    (B) the transferor has been beneficially entitled to the interest since before 10 March 1981, and both:

(i) if he had disposed of his interest immediately before 10 March 1981 and made the appropriate claim he would have been entitled to agricultural property relief, and such relief would not have been restricted by the old £250,000 or 1,000 acres limitation; and

(ii) at no time after 9 March 1981 has the interest conferred a right to vacant possession or to obtain vacant possession within twelve months (or could have done but for any act or omission of the transferor); or

(C) the property is let on a tenancy beginning after 31 August 1995, eg one under the *Agricultural Holdings Act 1995* (including in Scotland one acquired after that date by right of succession),

(2) 50% in any other case.

(IHTA 1984, ss 116–118.)

Where the transferor is a settlement, the trustees (who are the legal owners of the land) are, of course, deemed to be the transferor (*IHTA 1994, s 115(1)(b)*). Where the land is in an EEA country references to rights and obligations under UK law must be interpreted as referring to an equivalent right or obligation under the law governing the disposition of the property (*IHTA 1994, s 116(8)*).

18.5 HMRC have confirmed that head (C) covers any tenancy starting after 31 August 1995 including a statutory succession to one starting before that date (Tax Bulletin, Issue 18, August 1995).

18.6 In *Exors of G W Harrold decd v CIR (1996 STC (SCD) 195)* the Special Commissioner held that a farmhouse which had been empty but undergoing renovations for a number of years was agricultural property (see **18.12** for the definition) but was not occupied for the purpose of agriculture – or indeed for any purpose – and thus did not qualify for the 100% relief.

18.7 For the purpose of head (C), if the tenant dies and a new tenancy is subsequently entered into between the landlord and a person in whom the tenancy vested under the deceased tenant's Will or intestacy (or by virtue of an enactment such as the *Agricultural Tenancies Act*), the new tenancy is treated as starting from the date of death (*IHTA 1984, s 116(5A), (5B)*). Accordingly, if the landlord also dies in the interim, the 100% relief will apply, not the 50% relief that would otherwise have been due because the property is legally subject to the old pre-September 1995 tenancy. Similarly, if the tenant dies after having given notice of his intention to retire in favour of a new tenant, the new tenancy is related back to the date of death provided that it is entered into within 30 months of the date the notice of intention to retire was given (*IHTA 1984, s 116(5D)*).

18.8 Following ESC F16 the minimum period of ownership or occupation conditions in **18.4**(*a*) and (*b*) is regarded as satisfied in respect of an agricultural tied cottage occupied by a retired farm employee or their surviving spouse if either:

(*a*) the occupier is a statutorily protected tenant; or

(*b*) as part of the farm employee's contract of employment, occupation of the cottage is granted under a lease for the employee for life and for the life of their surviving spouse.

18.9 By concession (ESC F17) the 100% relief under head (B)(ii) above is also given if either:

(*a*) the interest carries a right to vacant possession within 24 months of the date of transfer; or

(*b*) notwithstanding the terms of the tenancy, the transferor's interest is valued at an amount broadly equivalent to the vacant possession value (HMRC Press Release 13.2.1995).

Head (*a*) covers two common situations: *Gladstone v Bower ([1960] 3 All ER 353)* tenancies (ie one for between one and under two years) and tenancies where there is a right to terminate within 12 months but under the *Agricultural Holdings Act 1986* it may take a further 12 months to gain possession. Head (*b*) is only likely to arise where the tenant and landlord are so closely connected that the landlord could dispose of both interests, eg land let to a company controlled by the landlord.

18.10 Where, because of the donor's death within the seven-year period, tax becomes payable on an *inter vivos* transfer that was a potentially exempt transfer, three further conditions need to be met. It has to be shown that:

(i) the transferee has retained the ownership of the property throughout the period from the date of the gift to the date of the donee's death; and

(ii) the property is agricultural property at the date of the donor's death and has been occupied for the purposes of agriculture (not necessarily by the transferee) throughout the period from the date of the gift to the date of the donor's death; and

(iii) if the property gifted was shares in a company, the agricultural land must have continued to be owned by the company and occupied for the purpose of agriculture throughout the period to the date of the donor's death.

If the donee predeceases the donor, the period for which the above conditions must be satisfied terminates on the donee's death. If the above conditions are met in respect of part only of the property gifted, the relief applies to that part (*IHTA 1984, s 124A*). If condition (i) is not satisfied but the donee disposed of the original property and applied the whole of the consideration in acquiring replacement agricultural property, the relief can still be claimed (*IHTA 1984, s 124B*). The replacement property must be bought within three years of the disposal of the original property or such longer period as HMRC may allow.

18.11 The relief is calculated on the actual value transferred before grossing up for any tax payable by the donor (*IHTA 1984, s 116(7)*). If the condition in (B)(i) above is not met because the limit is exceeded (calculated before grossing up by the tax payable), the 100% deduction will still apply on the first £250,000 or 1,000 acres but the deduction will be limited to 50% on the remainder of the land (*IHTA 1984, s 116(4)*).

18.12 The relief applies to agricultural property in the UK, the Channel Islands and the Isle of Man and an EEA member country (*IHTA 1984, s 115(5), 122(3)*). Agricultural property means agricultural land or pasture. It includes woodland and any building used in connection with the intensive rearing of livestock or fish if such woodland or building is occupied with (and its occupation is ancillary to) agricultural land or pasture. It also includes such cottages, farm buildings and farmhouses (together with the land occupied with them) as are of a character appropriate to the property (*IHTA 1984, s 115(2)*).

18.13 In *Starke v CIR (1995 STC 689)*, it was held that a 2.5-acre site containing a substantial house and a number of buildings used for egg production, for producing heavy hogs, for housing cattle and storing feed, and in connection with the rearing of cattle and sheep was not agricultural land or pasture. The site was used as part of a 171-acre mixed farm, the remainder of which was owned by a farming company. The judge felt that 'land' has to be construed with 'pasture' and must therefore be given the limited meaning of bare land without buildings on it. Any other meaning would render much of the rest of the definition – in particular, buildings of a character appropriate to the property – largely pointless. This reasoning was approved by the Court of Appeal. In *Dixon v CIR (2002 STC (SCD) 53)*, there was a small amount of sales of fruit from the orchard of a cottage, hens were kept in the garden for eggs and poultry meat, and in the summer months a neighbouring farmer was allowed to graze six ewes and lambs in the orchard. It was held that, although these activities come within the definition of agriculture, the orchard and garden were not agricultural land or pasture within the meaning of *s 115(2)*.

18.14 It should be stressed that the relief applies only to the agricultural value of the property, ie its value on the assumption that it is subject to a perpetual covenant prohibiting its use otherwise than as agricultural property, or, if the land is in an EEA country, its value if it were subject to provisions having the same effect as such a covenant (*IHTA 1984, s 115(3)*). Any excess of the market value of the land over its agricultural value is taxed in full. In *Lloyds TSB (Personal representative of Antrobus decd) v CIR (2002 STC*

(SCD) 468) HMRC claimed that the house, albeit the farmhouse to the surrounding 162-acre farm, was not of a character appropriate to the property. The Special Commissioners applied a four-stage test derived from the above cases: 'First one should consider whether the house is appropriate, by reference to its size, content and layout, with … the area of farmland being farmed; secondly one should consider whether the house is proportionate in size and nature to the requirement of the farming activities …; thirdly that although one cannot describe a farmhouse which satisfies the 'character appropriate' test, one knows one when one sees it; fourthly, one should ask whether the educated rural layman would regard the property as a house with land or a farm; and finally, one should consider the historical dimension.' In that case the house had been the farmhouse for 100 years!

18.15 Mr Higginson's Executors *(Higginson's Executors v CIR (2002 STC (SCD) 483)* were less fortunate. The house was held not to be of a character appropriate – largely, it appears, on the basis that after the death it was sold for £1 million which would be 'an appalling investment, in terms of yield from the farm', so one is driven to the conclusion that the property was 'a house with farmland going with it (and not vice versa)'. The house was similarly held not to be of a character appropriate to the agricultural property in *Rosser v CIR (2003 STC (SCD) 311)*. In that case the farm had originally been 41 acres but the deceased had gifted 39 acres to her daughter some years earlier, and at the date of death the daughter and her husband farmed that land. It was held that the test had to be applied solely by reference to the two acres of land still owned by the deceased, as that was the land passing on death. A barn was held to be of a character appropriate to the two acres even though it performed functions in relation to the 39 acres of gifted land as well as the two retained acres. In *Williams v HMRC (2005 STC (SCD) 782)*, it was held that land housing broiler houses used for the intensive rearing of poultry did not qualify. Although it was used for the intensive rearing of livestock there was no other activity of the farm to which it was ancillary. Curiously land housing an adjoining barn which was used for storage of materials for the broiler houses was held to be agricultural property as being agricultural land. The Commissioner effectively treated *s 115(2)* as containing three distinct tests, agricultural land, buildings for intensive rearing, and cottages and farm buildings. He held that the barn qualified as a farm building, albeit that its use was clearly ancillary to the occupation of the broiler houses.

18.16 In *Arnander (McKenna's Executors) v HMRC (2006 STC (SCD) 800)*, the Commissioner felt that the educated rural layman would conclude that the property was primarily an estate with a large country house and some farmland and held that the house was not a farmhouse at all. In *Atkinson v Revenue and Customs Commrs ([2012] STC 289)*, Mr Atkinson had lived in the house from 1966 but in 2002 he had become ill and had had to go into a care home where he remained until his death in 2006. His possessions remained in the house and his family regularly visited it to pick up post and access the water supply. They occasionally brought him to visit the house. The taxpayer remained a partner in the farming partnership that operated the farm and took part in weekly discussions about the farm. The Upper Tribunal held that the property was not in occupation for the purposes of agriculture up to the date of Mr Atkinson's death as it was apparent that he would never be able to return there to live. The fact that it was still used to accommodate his diminishing needs did not constitute occupation.

18.17 One issue that has surprisingly not been much litigated is the requisite nexus between the land and the farmhouse. *IHTA 1984, s 115(2)* states, 'it also includes such … farmhouses … as are of a character appropriate to the property'. To what does 'the property' refer? HMRC's view has always been that it refers to the property included in the estate of the deceased. Accordingly the agricultural land and the farmhouse both have to have been owned and occupied by the deceased. This view was approved by the Special Commissioner in *Rosser v CIR (2003 STC(SCD) 311)* (see **18.15**). However, in the later case of *Hanson (As trustee of the William Hanson 1957 Settlement) v HMRC (2012 SFTD 705)* the First-tier Tribunal declined to follow that decision. It may be worth noting that in *Rosser* the appellant was represented by her husband, not by Counsel. The Tribunal in *Hanson* could see no justification for requiring common ownership. As Parliament has defined 'agricultural property' in *IHTA 1984, s 115(2)*, it felt that the meaning is intended to be found from a construction of the words of the definition rather than by inferences drawn from other areas of the legislation. It accordingly held that the required nexus was that of occupation only. In *Hanson* the farmhouse was held by the settlement occupied under licence by the deceased, and the land was owned partly by the deceased and partly by the deceased jointly with his brother. HMRC told the Tribunal that they regard the point as an important one, so it is likely that either they will appeal the decision or look to re-argue the point in another case.

18.18 The cultivation of short rotation coppice (see **23.19**) is regarded as agriculture. Accordingly, land on which such coppice is cultivated is agricultural land, and buildings used in connection with such cultivation are farm buildings (*FA 1995, s 154(2)*).

18.19 On the other hand, land used solely for grazing horses used by the grazier for leisure purposes has been held by the Special Commissioners not to be agricultural land as the horses had no connection with agriculture (*Wheatley & Anor v CIR (1998 STC (SCD) 60*). The Commissioner expressed an opinion that 'grazing by draught animals, for example, might qualify'.

18.20 Land in a habitat scheme is treated as agricultural land, management in accordance with such a scheme is regarded as agriculture, and buildings used in connection with such management are treated as farm buildings. Land is in a habitat scheme if an application for aid under the *Habitat (Water Fringe) Regulations 1994,* the *Habitat (Former Set-Aside Land) Regulations 1994*, or the *Habitat (Salt-Marsh) Regulations 1994* (or their Scottish or Northern Irish equivalents) has been accepted in respect of the land and the undertakings given in relation to the scheme are still in force (*IHTA 1984, s 124C*).

18.21 Where land is occupied by a company and the land is owned by a person who controls the company (within the meaning of *IHTA 1984, s 269*), or it is occupied by a partnership and the land is owned by a person who controls the partnership, it will be treated as being occupied by that person to ascertain whether or not relief is due (*IHTA 1984, s 119(1)*). If land is occupied by a Scottish partnership it is to be treated as being occupied by the partners for the purposes of *s 117* (minimum period of ownership) and *s 118* (replacement property) but not for any other purpose (*IHTA 1994, s 119(2)*). In particular, HMRC do not consider that it applies for the purpose of *s 121* which provides an alternative test to *s 117* (see **18.27**) (*IHTA 1984, s 119*). Where replaced property is taken into account to meet the qualifying conditions, the relief is not to exceed what it would have been if the replacement had not taken place (*IHTA 1984, s 118(3)*). This appears to require the agricultural value of the previous property to be ascertained at the date of the gift rather than at the date that the property was disposed of. If it is less than the agricultural value at the date of the gift of the new property (ie the one gifted) the relief will be calculated on that lower amount.

18.22 Changes resulting from the conversion of a sole tradership to a partnership or vice versa or in the composition of a partnership are to be ignored (*IHTA 1984, s 118(4)*). This presumably means that any restriction is to be simply by reference to any difference in value between the old property and the new, and no further restriction (or relaxation of the restriction) needs to be made if the taxpayer's share of the old property differs from his share of the new.

18.23 The sole tests are whether the land is used for the purpose of agriculture and how long it has been owned. The relief is 100% of the agricultural value if the land has vacant possession at the time of disposal (or will have within 12 months), irrespective of whether it has been let out during the preceding seven years or occupied by the owner himself. If it is let land at the time of disposal the relief is only 50%. The reason for this distinction is to eliminate double relief. The tenanted value of agricultural land is well below its vacant possession value and the government felt that, as this discount already confers a substantial benefit, the full 100% relief should not be given in addition. As a transitional measure a person who owned tenanted land (as well as some land he farmed himself) prior to 10 March 1981 and who would have expected to get the old 50% deduction for a working farmer will keep his right to the 100%

deduction for as long as the land remains tenanted (or until he is in a position to bring the tenancy to an end).

18.24 Where the transferor became entitled to his interest in the agricultural property on the death of his spouse after 9 March 1981, in looking at whether the 100% relief is due:

(*a*) he will be treated as beneficially entitled to the interest at any time his spouse was so entitled;

(*b*) if the land qualifies as let land before 10 March 1981, it must have so qualified by virtue of the spouse's ownership; and

(*c*) if the land qualifies as let land before 10 March 1981, it must not have become vacant possession land at any time after that date whilst in the ownership of either spouse.

(*IHTA 1984, s 120(2).*)

18.25 Where the transferor became entitled to the agricultural property on the death of another person (or on the death of his spouse before 10 March 1981) he is treated as both owning and occupying it (provided he subsequently occupies it) from the date of the death. If the deceased was his spouse, he is also to be treated as having occupied it for agricultural purposes and to have owned it for any period for which his spouse so occupied or owned it (*IHTA 1984, s 120(1)*).

18.26 If:

(*a*) a transfer (the earlier transfer) was eligible for relief (or would have been had the relief existed at the time) and on that transfer the property passed to a person who makes a subsequent chargeable transfer of it (the subsequent transfer) or to his spouse; and

(*b*) at the time of the subsequent transfer it is occupied for the purposes of agriculture by either the owner or the personal representatives of the transferor on the earlier transfer; and

(*c*) either the earlier or the subsequent transfer is a transfer on death; and

(*d*) the property does not qualify for relief on the subsequent transfer only because the transferor cannot meet the requisite length of ownership,

he can be treated as having owned it (and where appropriate occupied it) for the requisite period to attract the relief (*IHTA 1984, s 121*).

18.27 In other words, if land is transferred by A to B during A's life and B dies at a time when it is occupied for the purpose of agriculture either by

B or by the personal representatives of A, but B has not held the property long enough to qualify for relief in his own right, the qualifying period for the transfer on B's death is treated as having been met provided that A's transfer itself qualified for agricultural property relief. Similarly, if the property is transferred to B on A's death and B makes a subsequent transfer of the land (either during his lifetime or on death) at a time when the property is occupied for the purpose of agriculture either by B or by the personal representatives of A (eg because they are still in the course of administering the estate), B is again treated as having owned the property for the requisite period if the transfer on A's death attracted agricultural property relief.

Example 18.1

John, a widower, owned a farm in Sussex since 1969. It was farmed by him in partnership with his two sons. John died in December 2015. He left the land to his daughter, Jane, and the partnership interest passed to his sons. In November 2016 the daughter joined the partnership. Two months later she gifted an interest in the land to her two brothers.

The land qualified for agricultural property relief on John's death. Jane's gift in January 2017 would not normally qualify for the relief as she had owned the land for less than two years. However, as she was farming the land (in partnership) in January 2017, *s 121* grants the relief. (If the partnership had been a Scottish partnership, HMRC would have denied the relief unless Jane controlled the partnership (so that *IHTA 1994, s 119(1)* deemed her to be the occupier) as she did not occupy the land.

18.28 Relief can also be given on the disposal of shares or securities of a company to the extent that the value of those shares represents the agricultural value of agricultural property. The agricultural property must form part of the company's assets and the shares or securities must give the transferor control of the company immediately before the transfer. The definition of control in *IHTA 1984, s 269* applies with the exception that shares or securities cannot be taken into account in determining control if they are valued as separate property under *IHTA 1984, s 176* (shares disposed of within three years of death) (*IHTA 1984, s 122*).

18.29 To qualify for relief either:

(*a*) the agricultural property must have been occupied by the company (or by a person who subsequently controls the company) for the purpose of agriculture throughout the two years ending with the date of transfer, and the shares must have been owned by the transferor for the same period; or (*b*) the agricultural property must have been owned by the company throughout the period of seven years ending with the date of the transfer and occupied (by anyone) for the purposes of agriculture throughout that period, and the shares must also have been owned by the transferor for the same period.

(*IHTA 1984, s 123(1)*.)

18.30 The replacement property provisions set out earlier also apply for this purpose (*IHTA 1984, s 123(2)*). If the shares or securities replaced other eligible property (ie either agricultural property or shares or securities attracting agricultural property relief) the ownership requirements in (*a*) in **18.29** above will be satisfied if the shares and the replaced property were together owned for at least two of the last five years of ownership and those in (*b*) in **18.29** above will be satisfied if they were owned for at least seven of the last ten years of ownership (*IHTA 1984, s 123(3)*).

18.31 The relief cannot be claimed if, at the time of the transfer, the transferor has entered into a binding contract for the sale of the property unless that sale is to a company and is wholly or mainly in consideration of the issue of shares or securities which will give the transferor control of the company. Similarly, no relief will be given on a disposal of shares or securities where a binding contract for their sale exists, unless the sale is merely for the purpose of reconstruction or amalgamation (*IHTA 1984, s 124*).

18.32 Agricultural property relief (and also business property relief – see **18.34** below) is deducted from the value of the agricultural property if that property is the subject of a specific gift. This means that if, for example, the agricultural property is gifted to the deceased's widow the benefit of the relief will be lost. If the agricultural property is included in the residue the relief is apportioned on a pro rata basis between exempt and chargeable parts of the residue – so part of the benefit will be lost to the extent that the widow has an interest in the residue (*IHTA 1984, s 39A*). Previously, the relief was given in calculating the overall liability and that liability was, in general, apportioned pro rata between the exempt and chargeable parts of the estate. Clearly assets qualifying for these reliefs are not appropriate subjects of specific gifts to the surviving spouse.

Grant of Tenancies of Agricultural Property

18.33 The grant of a tenancy of agricultural property in the UK, the Channel Islands or the Isle of Man (but not elsewhere) for use for agricultural purposes does not constitute a transfer of value if it is made for full consideration in money or money's worth (*IHTA 1984, s 16*). This ensures that the grant of an agricultural tenancy to a connected person even if made for full consideration, cannot give rise to a transfer of value because the reduction in value of the interest retained exceeds the consideration received.

Business Property Relief

18.34 Land and buildings can qualify for 100% business property relief where they form part of the assets of a business carried on, either alone or in partnership, by the transferor (*IHTA 1984, ss 104(1)(a), 105(1)(a)*). They can alternatively qualify for 50% relief in two circumstances:

(*a*) where immediately before its transfer the land was used wholly or mainly for the purposes of a business carried on by a company of which the transferor had control, or for the purposes of a business carried on by a partnership of which the transferor was a partner (*IHTA 1984, s 105(1)(d)*); or

(*b*) where immediately before its transfer the land was used wholly or mainly for the purposes of a business carried on by the transferor, and was settled property in which he was beneficially entitled to an interest in possession (*IHTA 1984, s 105(1)(e)*).

18.35 A business of property dealing does not qualify for relief (*IHTA 1984, s 105(3)*). A business consisting wholly or mainly of the making or holding of investments does not qualify for relief either (*IHTA 1984, s 105(3)*). This wording does not exclude a business of property development for resale, such as housebuilding. This has been clearly distinguished in other legislation, eg EIS and EIS reinvestment relief.

18.36 Where the business sells a mixture of the use of property and the provision of services it can be difficult to discern whether it amounts to the holding of investments or the carrying on of a trade. This problem is considered in an income tax context at **2.86–2.102**. What is said there is equally relevant to inheritance tax – although in *Powell v CIR (1997 STC (SCD) 181)* the Special Commissioner said 'the income tax status of the income of the business is irrelevant in the context of inheritance tax ... The availability of business property relief depends entirely on the interpretation of the provisions of the *IHTA 1984* and I do not believe that the past income tax treatment of the income of the business necessarily throws any light on the inheritance tax position'. There are a number of decisions of the Special Commissioners on *s 105(3)*. In *Martin & Horsfall v CIR (1995 STC (SCD) 5)*, the ownership and management of a number of industrial units was held to be the making or holding of investments. So was the letting of four flats (*Burkinyoung v CIR (1995 STC (SCD) 29)*. The ownership and operation of a caravan park was held to be the making and holding of investments in *Hall v CIR (1997 STC*

(SCD) 126) and also in *Powell v CIR (1997 STC (SCD) 181)*. However, in *Furness v CIR (1999 STC (SCD) 232)*, the operation of a caravan park was held to qualify for relief. The taxpayer was able to show the income from caravan sales and other trading activities exceeded the site rents and a considerable amount of work (including 80% of Mr Furness's time) was undertaken in looking after the welfare of the residents of the park and maintaining the park and its structures. Such considerable activity did not suggest a business concerned wholly or mainly with the holding of investments.

18.37 This decision was distinguished fairly forcefully in a later case, *Weston v CIR (2000 STC (SCD) 30)* so may be of limited application: 'The caravan park in *Furness* was not a residential park but a holiday park … Unlike the company's park … [it] was situated in beautiful countryside and offered considerable facilities to its residents.' It was held there, looking at the matter in the round, that the pitch fees were not ancillary to caravan sales but that caravan sales were, if anything, ancillary to pitch fees. The Commissioner appears to have been influenced by a letter from the specialist valuers who, in order to compare the level of return from a residential caravan park with that from commercial property, stated: 'It would not be unreasonable to assume that the trading activities (such as commission and sales) serve to cover the running costs of the park', although the valuer seemed to envisage this statement merely as a rough and ready way to justify basing the yield on the pure pitch fees. This decision was affirmed in the *High Court (2000 STC 1064)* where Lawrence Collins J said three questions need to be asked: Does the company have investments? Is it 'holding' investments? Does its business consist 'wholly or mainly' of 'holding' investments? The cases show that the meaning of investment depends on its context but that property may be held as an investment even if the person who holds it has to take active steps in connection with it. Adopting the definition of investment in *Cook v Medway Housing Society Ltd (1997 STC 90)* (see **7.13**) the Commissioners were entitled to answer the first question in the affirmative. Whether a person is holding investments and whether a business consists wholly or mainly of holding investments are questions of fact. It was clear that the Commissioners had taken all of the relevant matters into account and reached a conclusion which was justified by the evidence. The executors sought to take a fresh point in the High Court that the reality was that pitch holders were paying for the services provided rather than for the mere right to enjoy the pitch, but the judge refused to let them do so on the basis that new evidential issues would need to be explored to test this claim.

18.38 Nevertheless, whether or not a caravan park qualifies for relief still depends very much on the facts. In a later case, *CIR v George and another (executors of Stedman decd) (2004 STC 147)*, the taxpayer put forward an argument that had not been used before, but that found favour with the Commissioners, namely that the investment business was limited to the grant of the rights to station mobile homes on particular plots (including access rights) and the physical connections to services. Everything else, including not only the services which produced a profit in their own right such as the supply of gas and electricity, but all the activities involved in running the site, including maintenance of the common parts, lighting, grass-cutting, refuse-removal, etc, was the provision of services, which is not the business of holding investments. The Commissioner accepted this although holding that the storage of caravans for owners was also investment business. On that basis he held that the investment activity amounted to only 40% of turnover and 20% of gross profits so that the business of the company was not wholly or mainly the holding of investments. The Court of Appeal thought that 'the Commissioner's overall approach was correct in law and he reached a view which was open to him on the facts'. Carnwath LJ emphasised that 'the most important point about each of the [Cook and Weston] decisions is that the court was upholding the decision of the fact-finding tribunal', so the particular formulation of those decisions ought not to be relied upon.

18.39 Although most of the litigation has related to caravan parks, the principle can apply to other assets too. For example, copyrights are capable of being held either as investments or as the assets of a trade; the extent to which they are actively exploited may well determine whether they are trading assets or investments (see *Noddy Subsidiary Rights Company Ltd v CIR (43 TC 458)*). The Upper Tribunal, reversing the decision of the FTT, took a similar approach to that in *George* (see **18.38**) in *HMRC v Exors of Pawson decd (2013 STC 976* This involved a bungalow used for holiday letting. The FTT had held that the letting of the bungalow was 'a serious undertaking earnestly pursued' (which is a definition of a business – see **11.105**). The Tribunal reviewed the above cases and was very much influenced by the judgment of Carnworth LJ in *CIR v George* (see **18.38**). It concluded that,

> 'In any normal property letting business, the provision of additional services or facilities of a non-investment nature will either be incidental to the business of holding the property as an investment, or at least will not predominate to such an extent that the business ceases to be mainly one of holding the property as an investment. ... Nevertheless ... the imprecision of the statutory test is such that no test can be applied in a mechanical fashion.'

The Tribunal went on to note that:

> 'I take as my starting point the proposition that the owning and holding of land in order to obtain an income from it, is generally to be characterised as an investment activity. Further, it is clear from the authorities that such an investment may be actively managed without losing its essential character as an investment. ... It is clear from George that the provision of ... additional services and facilities is not to be regarded as part

> of the maintenance of the property as an investment and that their characterisation as services is unaffected by the fact that no separate charge was made for them. The critical question, however, is whether those services were of such a nature and extent that they prevented the business from being mainly one of holding investments.'

This emphasises that the provision of services is capable of turning an investment business into a trade, but that in order to do so the services will need to be very extensive. In *Green v HMRC (2015 SFTD 711)*, the taxpayer's business was the letting of five units of self-contained holiday accommodation in a single building on the coast. The work was held to be insufficient to demonstrate that the business was anything other than mainly one of holding the property as an investment.

18.40 The decision of the Commissioner in the *Weston* case was also much influenced by that in *Farmer & another v CIR (1999 STC (SCD) 321)*. That case involved a farmer who clearly carried on a farming business but also let properties on the farm which were surplus to requirements. HMRC contended that the business at the farm consisted 'mainly' of making or holding investments, not mainly of farming. The Commissioner accepted that the farm was conducted on a business-like basis. There were 23 tenancies, mostly for a year or less. Farmer did not want to grant long-term leases, which might affect the future use of the estate. Farmer was aged about 80. The farm manager spent 90% of his time on the farm and 10% on lettings. His assistant spent 95% of his time on the farm. Farmer's son, a retired solicitor, spent one and a half days a week on the farm, 30% of which was on farming and 70% on lettings. The rents received varied between 33% and 53% of turnover (mainly because the farming income fluctuated). HMRC argued that one should look at profits not turnover but the Commissioner thought that the test must be 'of what the business consists', which indicates that all relevant factors of what a business consists requires consideration. He identified five relevant factors: the overall context of the business, the capital employed, the time spent by the employees, the turnover and the profits, and commented, 'When these factors have been considered it will then be necessary to stand back and consider in the round whether the business consisted mainly of making or holding investments'. On doing so he held that the business consisted mainly of farming.

18.41 A similar approach was taken in *Clark v HMRC (2005 STC (SCD) 823)*. A company owned 122 properties from which it received rent and also managed 141 other properties on behalf of their owners in return for a fee. It had its own workforce for carrying out maintenance and refurbishment of all of the properties. Both sets of properties required extremely active management. The investment activity was greater than the building and management activities in terms of turnover and profits. It was smaller in terms of time spent, but the Commissioner dismissed this on the somewhat odd grounds that 'apportioning the time spent on this basis gives a large loss for the non-investment activity and so cannot be justified'. It is unclear why a real loss on one activity should be regarded as unjustified and so ignored.

18.42 *McCall and another (PRs of McClean decd) v HMRC (2009 STC 990)* suggests that showing that the whole of the activities carried on constitute a business is not enough. Mrs McCall inherited land on her husband's death in 1983. One of her daughters, Mrs Mitchell, lived next door to her. Mrs McLean did not farm the land herself but it was let on conacre or agistment agreements (Northern Irish land tenures) to local farmers. As Mrs McLean grew older her mental capacity diminished. In 1992 (seven years before her death) she was taken for a short visit to her other daughter in Tipperary but her mental state continued to diminish and she never returned home to Antrim. The land continued to be looked after by her son-in-law, Mr Mitchell. HMRC first contended that the operation of the land did not amount to a business. The Special Commissioner held that Mr Mitchell spent about 100 hours a year on the operation, the letting of the land was earnestly pursued and the work tending the land was modest but serious. To his mind the Lord Fisher indicia (see **17.63**) pointed towards a business – just! HMRC then claimed that it was Mr Mitchell, not Mrs McLean who carried on the business, but the Special Commissioner held that he did so as a bare trustee for Mrs McLean. The final question was whether the business was one of holding investments. The executors fell at this hurdle. Albeit that under agistment what is sold is the grass, not the use of the land, the activities of the business did not involve the cutting of the grass; the income arose from making the land available for grazing, not for any other activity associated with it or from selling separately the fruits of the asset. It is not like a 'pick-your-own' fruit farm where after months of work customers are licensed to enter to take the produce. Mrs McLean's fields were let for the accommodation of the cattle as well as for grazing and the rent was paid by the acre not by the ton of grass eaten. It was not a business consisting of the provision of the grass but of the provision of the (non-exclusive) use of the land. The Northern Ireland Court of Appeal thought that this was a decision which the Commissioner was entitled to reach.

18.43 What happens on the ground may supplant the legal niceties as *Brander v HMRC (2010 STC 2666)* illustrates. Lord Balfour enjoyed a life rent over a Scottish landed estate. He farmed part on his own behalf. The trustees rented out the remainder of the estate but in practice they delegated everything to Lord Balfour, doing little, it appears, other than meeting annually and signing whatever documents Lord Balfour asked them to. Although the farm and the rental properties were separately registered for VAT (the farm in the name of Lord Balfour and the land in that of the trustees) in practice Lord Balfour ran both as if they constituted a single business. When Lord Balfour died, the question arose as to what attracted business property relief.

The First-tier Tribunal held that everything did. So did the Upper Tribunal. Lord Balfour carried on a single business even though part of that business may have been in a separate ownership. Looking at that single business it was primarily a farming business. 'The management of a landed estate, even where a significant amount of the income is derived from letting income is, overall, mainly a trading activity. That is where the preponderance of activity and effect lies.' Accordingly, it did not consist wholly or mainly of making or holding investments.

18.44 The nature of a company's business is a question of fact. In *Executors of the Will of Brown (Deceased) v CIR (1996 STC(SCD) 277)*, the taxpayer had a 99% ordinary shareholding in an unquoted company which operated a night club. The remaining share was owned by the taxpayer's brother and co-director. In 1985 the nightclub was sold and the sale proceeds were placed in an interest-bearing short-term deposit account because the taxpayer wanted access to these funds for the purposes of the business. Neither director considered that the company should cease trading and the taxpayer was actively investigating the purchase of other night clubs. Following the taxpayer's death in 1986, business property relief was claimed, but HMRC denied the relief under *IHTA 1984, s 105(3)* arguing that the company's business since the disposal of the nightclub in 1985 consisted wholly or mainly of the holding of investments. Looking at the evidence as a whole, the Special Commissioner did not accept HMRC's argument that the nature of the business had changed and business property relief was therefore allowed.

18.44A The FTT decision in *Vigne decd (TC 6068)* is interesting. Mrs Vigne owned 30 acres of land from which she ran livery stables. She provided part livery, where the day-to-day care for the horses is shared between they livery operator and the site owner, but the package that she provided was significantly more than is normal. HMRC contended that the business 'amounts to no more than a land-owner letter or licensing land for the use of others', which is an investment business. They also argued that little time was spent on the services, but the Tribunal regarded their calculations as unrealistic. The Tribunal accepted that Mrs Vigne had been carrying on a trade and accordingly BPR applied. It is interesting that HMRC seems to have approached the case on an all-or-nothing basis, ie they were contending that despite the fact that they had treated the activities as trading for income tax, there was actually no trade at all.

18.45 In contrast, in *Barclays Bank Trust Co v CIR (1998 STC(SCD)125)* where at the time of the deceased's death in 1990 the company had £300,000 of cash which it claimed was needed to acquire a business property – and subsequently spent over that sum in buying a property although not until 1997 – the Special Commissioners decided that the cash did not qualify for business property relief. It felt that in 1990 it could not be said that there was 'some imperative that the money will fall to be used upon a given project or for some palpable business purpose'. *Executors of Piercy (decd) v HMRC (2008 STC (SCD) 858)* involved a property development company with substantial rental income but little or no dealing activity in recent years. HMRC contended that as the bulk of the income was from rents, the business was making or holding investments, but this was dismissed by the Commissioner who accepted that all of the land owned by the company was held as trading stock notwithstanding the receipt of income, so the business could not consist of making or holding investments.

18.46 For the purposes of (*a*) and (*b*) in **18.34** above the transferor's interest in the business or the company, as the case may be, must itself be relevant business property in relation to the transfer (*IHTA 1984, s 105(6)*). This may mean that the relief is given only if the land is transferred in conjunction with the business or the shares in the company. The business, or, in the case of the 50% relief, the property, must have been owned by the transferor for at least two years prior to the transfer (*IHTA 1984, s 106*). If this test is not met but the property replaced other property, relief will be given (up to the value of the former property only) if the former property had been owned for at least two years and the two together were held for an aggregate period of at least two out of the five years up to the date of the transfer (*IHTA 1984, s 107*). Where the replaced property was agricultural property of a farming business the period of ownership of such property can be taken into account, as it also constitutes business property (Tax Bulletin, Issue 14, December 1994). If the transferor inherited the property on the death of his spouse, the spouse's period of ownership can be taken into account (*IHTA 1984, s 108*).

18.47 An asset cannot qualify for relief if it is an excepted asset, ie one which is neither used wholly or mainly for the purposes of the business concerned throughout at least the two years prior to the transfer nor required at the time of the transfer for future use for such purposes (*IHTA 1984, s 112(1)(2)*). If part only or any land or buildings is used exclusively for the purposes of the trade or business and the building would otherwise be an excepted asset, the value must be apportioned in such manner as may be just, and relief can be given on the business element only (*IHTA 1984, s 112(4)*). Where the 100% relief applies, a further restriction will be necessary if the property was not in business use throughout the two years up to the time of the transfer (*IHTA 1984, s 112*). The relief does not apply if a binding contract for the sale of the property has been entered into at the time of the transfer (other than on the incorporation of a business wholly or mainly for shares or securities) (*IHTA 1984, s 113*).

18.48 The issue in *Exors of Eighth Marquess of Hertford decd v CIR (Sp C 444, 2005 STC (SCD) 171)* was whether an apportionment was applicable where a building is not an accepted asset. The legislation contains no provision for apportionment in such circumstances and it was accepted that the building was mainly used for the purpose of the business. Ragley Hall is an historic Grade I listed building from which a business of opening the hall to the public is conducted. In November 1991, the Eighth Marquess gifted the business to his son. It was common ground that at least 78% of the value of Ragley Hall attracts relief. HMRC claimed, however, that 22% of the house was not open to the public so was not used for the purpose of the business. The executors retorted that the whole of the exterior is available for viewing by the public. It was held that the entire building qualified for relief. The Hall is plainly important as a single structure, the whole building is a vital backdrop to the business and there is, in any event, no sensible way to divide the Hall if a split had to be made.

18.49 The issue in *Re the Nelson Dance Family Settlement; Trustees of the Nelson Dance Family Settlement v HMRC (2009 STC 802)* was whether business property relief can apply on the transfer of an asset of a business as the Trustees contended, or only on the transfer of a business or part of a business. Mr Dance simply transferred part of his farmland to the Trustees without transferring any part of his business to it. John Avery Jones thought the position clear. If the definitions in *IHTA 1984, ss 105(1)(a)* and *110* (which deals with the value of a business) are imported into *s 104(1)* it reads, 'Where the whole or part of the value transferred by a transfer of value is attributable to the net value of a business (i.e. the value of the assets used in the business (including goodwill) reduced by the aggregate amount of any liabilities incurred for the purpose of the business), the whole or that part of the value transferred shall be treated as reduced – (a) in the case of property consisting of a business … by 100%'. The *section* is looking at value. The value of an individual asset transferred is clearly attributable to 'the value of the assets used in the business' as it is one of those assets. On this basis the purpose of *s 110* is to put a ceiling on the relief to prevent a transferor giving away all of the assets, retaining the liability, and claiming 100% relief on the unreduced value of the assets. Sales J agreed.

18.50 As with agricultural property relief (see **18.4** above), business property relief will be given only if the property gifted (or qualifying replacement property) is retained by the donee throughout the period from the date of the gift to the date of the donor's death (or the donee's death if earlier) and it would have been relevant business property if it had been retained by the donor and gifted by him immediately before his death. Even if the original property is retained, the question as to whether the relief is 100% or 50% seems to depend on what shares are retained by the transferee at the time of his death.

18.51 An interesting point on **18.34**(*a*) above arose in *Walkers Executors v CIR (2001 STC (SCD) 86)*. The deceased owned land held for the business of a company in which she was a 50% shareholder and chairman of the board of directors and as such entitled to a casting vote under the company's articles. It was held that she controlled the company by virtue of her casting vote, so that the property qualified for business property relief, even though when casting that vote she owed a fiduciary duty as an officer of the company.

18.52 If assets do not constitute business property because they are wholly or mainly held as investments this does not preclude claiming agricultural property relief where appropriate. However, if assets which constitute agricultural property can qualify for business property relief it is usually preferable to claim it. Agricultural property relief can apply only to those assets that meet the tests at **18.4** onwards whereas business property relief applies to all of the assets of the business. Agricultural property relief is given only on the agricultural value of the land but business property relief is given on the full value including any development value or hope value element.

Payment of IHT by Instalments

18.53 Land (wherever situated) is one of the types of assets on which IHT can be paid by ten equal annual instalments. The instalments carry interest, however, unless the property forms part of a business or an interest in a business (*IHTA 1984, ss 227(3), 234(1)*). Where the tax is payable because a potentially exempt transfer becomes a chargeable transfer, the instalment provisions apply only if the donee still owns the property at the date of the donor's death (*IHTA 1984, s 227(1A)*) or has replaced it by property that itself qualifies for business property relief or agricultural property relief (*FA 1987, Sch 8, para 15(3)*).

Transfers of Land within Seven Years before Death

18.54 Where property was transferred *inter vivos* and the transferor dies within the following seven years, the recipient becomes liable to pay IHT if the gift was a potentially exempt transfer (or additional IHT if it was not) to bring the tax charge to the rate that applies on death (subject to a tapering relief for gifts more than three years prior to the death). If the value of the property has fallen between the date of the gift, etc. and the date of death, the tax (or additional tax) is based on the lower figure only (*IHTA 1984, s 131(1)(a)*). If the transferee (or his spouse) has sold the property prior to the date of death it can be based on the sale proceeds if these are below the value at the time of the gift and the sale is an arm's length sale (at a price freely negotiated at the time of sale) to an unconnected person with no right to buy back any part of the property sold (*IHTA 1984, s 131(1)(b)(3)*).

18.55 In the case of land or an interest in land, special rules apply if either the interest sold or held at the date of death was not the same in all respects and with the same incidents as at the date of the gift, or the land in which the interest subsists was not in the same state and with the same incidents at both dates (*IHTA 1984, s 137(1)(2)*). The market value of the property at the date of death or sale must be increased by the difference between the market value of the interest at the time of the gift and what the market value at the time would have been if the circumstances prevailing at the date of the death or sale had existed at the time of the gift (*IHTA 1984, s 137(1)*). If the change in circumstances reduced rather than increased the value of the property, the value at the date of the death or sale must obviously be reduced by the difference between the values on these two assumptions at the date of the gift (*IHTA 1984, s 137(4)*).

18.56 If compensation became payable under any enactment to the transferee or his spouse between the two dates because of the imposition of a restriction on the use or development of the land or because the value of the interest is reduced for any other reason, the imposition of that restriction is ignored (both in deciding whether the special rules apply and, if they do, the effect of their application), but the compensation received must be added to the market value of the interest at the date of death or earlier sale (*IHTA 1984, s 137(3)*).

18.57 If the property gifted was a lease of 50 years or less its market value at the date of death (or prior sale) must be increased by the 'appropriate fraction' of the market value of the interest at the time of the gift (*IHTA 1984, s 138(1)*). The appropriate fraction is based on the capital gains tax wasting asset table (see **11.32** above) and is:

$$\frac{\text{table figure for duration of lease at date of gift-table figure for duration of lease at date of death (or prior sale)}}{\text{table figure for duration of lease at date of gift}}$$

(*IHTA 1984, s 138(2)*.)

Sale of Land from Deceased Estate

18.58 Relief is also given where an interest in land (other than an interest by way of mortgage or other security) comprised in a person's estate immediately before his death is sold by the 'appropriate person' at less than probate value within the three years following the death (*IHTA 1984, s 191*). The 'appropriate person' will normally be the personal representative. It means the person liable for the inheritance tax attributable to the value of the interest. If there is more than one such person it is the one who, in fact, pays the tax. The relief must be claimed by the appropriate person (*IHTA 1984, s 191(1)(b)*). No specific time limit for making a claim is given so the normal six-year limit will apply. Property sold in the fourth year after death for a price at or below its value on death, is deemed to have been sold in the three-year period unless the sale is to an authority having compulsory purchase powers (see **18.71**) (*IHTA 1984, s 197A*). In *Stonor v CIR (2001 STC (SCD) 199)*, it was held that a claim under *s 191* is not possible where no inheritance tax is payable on the death, as there is no 'appropriate person' if there is no person liable to pay the tax because no tax is payable. In that case the bulk of the assets went to charity, leaving the balance within the nil rate band. The executors sought to substitute the sale value of the properties for their probate value in order to increase their capital gains tax base cost.

18.59 The relief is given by reference to the aggregate sale proceeds of all the land sold (note the use of 'sold', not 'disposed of') by the appropriate person (in his capacity as personal representative) in the three-year period. It is given by reducing the aggregate value of the land at the date of death to its 'sale value', that is, the aggregate sale proceeds (or, if greater, the best consideration that could reasonably have been obtained for the land at the time of sale) adjusted in accordance with such, if any, of the provisions considered below as are appropriate (*IHTA 1984, ss 190, 191*). The sale proceeds for this purpose are the gross proceeds before deduction of commission, stamp duty or other expenses which are incidental to the sale (*IHTA 1984, s 190(4)*).

18.60 No relief will be given for a fall in the value of an interest if the amount involved is small, that is, if it is less than £1,000 (or 5% of the probate value if that is under £20,000) (*IHTA 1984, s 191(2)*). Neither will any reduction be allowed in relation to land sold:

(*a*) by a personal representative or trustee to:

- (i) a person who is (or at any time since the death had been) beneficially entitled to the property or to an interest in possession in the property (or would be when the administration of the estate is completed); or
- (ii) the spouse, child, or remoter descendant of a person within (i); or
- (iii) the trustees of a settlement under which a person in (i) or (ii) has an interest in possession in property comprising the interest sold; or

(*b*) under a transaction in connection with which either the vendor or a person within (*a*)(i) to (iii) obtains a right to acquire either the interest sold or another interest in the same land.

(*IHTA 1984, s 191(3)*.)

18.61 It should be noted that the relief will be given where land is sold to the parent of a person having an interest in possession in the property or to a brother, sister, cousin, etc. No indication is given as to whether or not 'a child' includes an adopted child, an illegitimate child or a step-child. It is safest to assume it includes all three. A sale to a discretionary beneficiary will not debar the relief. A sale to trustees of a settlement in which a person within (*a*) in **18.60** above had an interest in possession at the time of the death, but gave up that interest prior to the sale, is apparently also alright. The reason for these distinctions is not readily apparent.

18.62 A sale to a connected person of the deceased not falling within (*a*) or (*b*) in **18.60** above, or a non-arm's length sale, will still attract the relief. If such a sale is at less than market value, though, the undervalue will be excluded from relief by the general rule substituting the best consideration that could reasonably be obtained for the land for the sale proceeds. This seems a very open-ended provision. If land is sold at arm's length by auction HMRC could apparently contend that it could have fetched a higher price if sold privately or if sold in a number of small lots, and thus reduce the relief.

18.63 Identical rules to those in *IHTA 1984, ss 137, 138* (see **18.55–18.57** above) apply where there is a change in the interest sold or in the land in which it subsists between the death and the sale (*IHTA 1984, s 193*) and where the interest at the date of death was a lease with 50 years or less unexpired (*IHTA 1984, s 194*).

18.64 If any other interests (whether or not in the same ownership) were taken into account in determining the value at the date of death of the interest sold, the sale price must be increased by the difference between the probate value and what that value would have been if no interests other than the interest sold had been taken into account (*IHTA 1984, s 195*). This will apply, for example, where another interest is related property.

Example 18.2

Mark (dec'd) owned an 80-year lease which was worth £70,000 at the date of his death. The freehold was owned by Mrs Mark and at the date of Mark's death was worth £30,000. The unencumbered freehold was worth £150,000 at the time of Mark's death. Three years after the death Mark's executors sold his lease for £60,000.

As the lease and freehold are related property the value taken into account on the death for IHT purposes will not be £70,000 but:

$$\frac{£70{,}000}{£70{,}000 + £30{,}000} \times £150{,}000 = £105{,}000$$

		£
The relief will be:		
Sale proceeds		60,000
Addition		
IHT value at death	105,000	
Value at death of lease only	70,000	35,000
		95,000
IHT value at death		105,000
Relief due		£10,000

18.65 If the 'appropriate person', acting as such, either:

(*a*) sells an interest which would have qualified for relief but for the fact that the transaction falls within (*a*) or (*b*) in **18.60** above (sales to certain beneficiaries or with an option to reacquire an interest in the land); or

(*b*) exchanges within three years after the death (with or without any cash adjustment) an interest in land which was comprised in the deceased's estate at the time of death,

(called below, for convenience, the 'non-qualifying land') and the sale price of the interest disposed of (or its market value where (*b*) applies) is higher than the value at death, the sale price or prices of interests to which the claim relates (which will normally be interests in other land) must be increased by 'the appropriate fraction' of the rise in value of the non-qualifying land (*IHTA 1984, s 196(1), (2)*). The 'appropriate fraction' is that which the fall (or, apparently where applicable, the rise, as the legislation refers to the difference between the two figures) in value of each interest affected (after taking account of adjustments in **18.63** and **18.64** above) bears to the aggregate falls (or rises) in value of all of the interests affected (*IHTA 1984, s 196(3)*). Where there are both falls and rises these must apparently always be added, never subtracted, ie rises will not count as negative figures. It should be noted that although the term 'appropriate fraction' is used in both *ss 194* and *196*, its meaning is not the same in both cases. The logic of *s 196* is not readily apparent. The following examples illustrate how it appears to work, however.

Example 18.3

Rupert owned the following freehold land at the date of his death, all of which was disposed of at market value within three years of the death.

	Value at death	*Sale proceeds*
	£	£
Whiteacre	10,000	8,000
Blackacre	11,500	9,000
Greenacre	18,500	20,000
Redacre	22,000	21,500
Blueacre	24,000	26,000
Yellowacre	30,000	–

Notes. Blueacre was sold to the residuary beneficiary of the estate. Yellowacre was exchanged for land at Brownacre, which was worth £24,000 at the date of exchange.

Before applying *section 196* the relief will be as follows:

	Sale proceeds	*Value at death*	*Relief*
	£	£	£
Whiteacre	8,000	10,000	
Blackacre	9,000	11,500	
Greenacre	20,000	18,500	
	£37,000	£40,000	£3,000

Blueacre and Yellowacre do not qualify for the relief. Nor does Redacre as its fall in value is under £1,000.

An adjustment is required under *s 196* in respect of Blueacre – of £2,000 (£26,000 – £24,000). No adjustment is required in respect of Yellowacre as there had been no increase in the value of that land since Rupert's death. It would clearly have been better for Yellowacre to have been sold instead of being exchanged as no relief will be obtained for the fall in value.

The difference in value of the other land is:

	£	£
Whiteacre	(10,000 – 8,000) =	2,000
Blackacre	(11,500 – 9,000) =	2,500
Greenacre	(20,000 – 18,500) =	1,500
		£6,000

The adjustment in respect of Blueacre must be apportioned between the three sites in the above proportions, eg the amount by which the sale proceeds of Blackacre must be increased is:

$$£2{,}000 \times \frac{2{,}500}{6{,}000} = £833$$

The claim will therefore now become:

	Sale proceeds	*Adjustments*	*Adjusted Sale Proceeds*	*Value at death*	*Relief*
	£	£	£	£	£
Whiteacre	8,000	667	8,667	10,000	
Blackacre	9,000	833	9,833	11,500	
Greenacre	20,000	500	20,500	18,500	
	£37,000	£2,000	£39,000	£40,000	£1,000

18.66 It is not clear why it should be necessary to apportion the £2,000 between the three interests to which the claim relates instead of merely deducting it from the total claim. It appears that if the effect had been to reduce the difference between the figures for any property to less than £1,000 (or 5% of probate value) then that property would fall out of the claim.

18.67 If any land is purchased by the 'appropriate person' (acting as such) in the period between the date of death and four months after the date of the last sale covered by *s 191* (other than one brought in by *IHTA 1984, s 197A*), an adjustment to the relief is required. If the aggregate purchase prices of all such purchases equal or exceed the aggregate prices (adjusted in accordance with *ss 193–195* but not *s 196*) of the interest covered by *s 191*, no relief will be given. In other cases the sale proceeds of each interest affected will be increased (or reduced if the value has fallen since the death) by the fraction of the difference in the values of that interest between the dates of death and sale (the latter being adjusted in accordance with *ss 193–196*, note including *s 196*) which the aggregate purchase prices bear to the aggregate sales prices. Where the value at death of any interest is less than its sale price (adjusted in accordance with *ss 193–196*, the sale price must be decreased instead of increased (*IHTA 1984, s 192*).

Example 18.4

Suppose that Rupert's executors in *Example 18.3* purchase land for £20,000. As this is less than the £37,000 aggregate sale prices before applying *IHTA 1984, s 196*, an adjustment must be made. This will be done by increasing or decreasing the various sale proceeds by the following amounts.

Whiteacre	$10{,}000 - 8{,}667 = 1{,}333 \times \frac{20{,}000}{37{,}000}$	=	£721
Blackacre	11,500 – 9,833 = 1,667 × 20/37	=	£901
Greenacre	18,500 – 20,500 = (2,000) × 20/37	=	(£1,081)

The adjusted claim now becomes

	Adjusted sale proceeds as before	*Adjustment under section 192*	*Adjusted sale proceeds*	*Value at death*	*Relief*
	£	£	£	£	£
Whiteacre	8,667	721	9,388	10,000	
Blackacre	9,833	901	10,734	11,500	
Greenacre	20,500	(1,081)	19,419	18,500	
			39,541	40,000	
Less Greenacre			19,419	18,500	
			£20,122	£21,500	£1,378

18.68 As the difference between the value at death and the adjusted sale proceeds is in the case of Greenacre less than 5% of £18,500, *s 191(2)* (see **18.60** above) will now exclude this from *s 191(1)*. It accordingly no longer affects the relief.

18.69 It should particularly be noted that, subject to the special rules contained in *s 196*, only sales of land need to be taken into account. Other disposals, such as exchanges of land or distributions to beneficiaries, do not affect the relief.

18.70 The date of a sale or purchase will normally be the contract date (*IHTA 1984, s 198(1)*). However, if the sale or purchase results from the exercise of an option which was granted within the previous six months, the option date must be adopted instead (*IHTA 1984, s 198(2)*). If the land is disposed of to a local authority (or other body possessing compulsory purchase powers) in pursuance of a notice to treat, the date of sale will be the earlier of the date on which compensation is agreed or the date on which the local authority enters into possession. Where the land is acquired under the vesting declaration procedure the last day of the period specified in the vesting declaration will be treated as the date of sale (*IHTA 1984, s 198(3)(4)*). The question for decision in *Jones and another (Balls' Administrators) v CIR (1997 STC 358)* was whether a contract that was not completed was nevertheless a sale for this purpose. Lightman J said that the meaning of 'sold' (like 'paid') depended on the context. It could mean 'agreed to be sold' and it could mean 'conveyed or transferred on completion of a sale'. In the context of *s 191* it clearly had the latter meaning. There was no machinery for dealing with multiple contracts in the three-year period, no guidance as to what would constitute a contract and the intention was clearly that tax should not be payable on a greater price than the amount actually received.

18.71 Where land is acquired in pursuance of a notice to treat, served before the death or within the three-year period, these rules cannot be used to deny relief by taking the sale outside the scope of *s 191*, however. In such circumstances the three-year period will be deemed to be extended to include the date of sale to the local authority (*IHTA 1984, s 197(1)*). This only applies to bring that sale into *s 191*; it will not extend the four-month period under *s 192* within which acquisitions have to be taken into account (see **18.67**) (*IHTA 1984, s 197(3)*). This provision operates in the taxpayer's favour only. If the sale proceeds exceed the probate value the normal three-year rule applies (*IHTA 1984, s 197(2)*).

Heritage Property

18.72 Heritage property attracts a number of exemptions from inheritance tax.

18.73 The general exemptions from inheritance tax for gifts to charity and for gifts to specified national heritage bodies, such as The National Trust, of course also apply to heritage property in the same way as other assets.

18.74 HMRC can also grant conditional exemption for certain private gifts (*IHTA 1984, s 30*). A conditionally exempt gift will be treated as exempt whilst certain undertakings remain in force, but a tax charge will crystallise if the building is sold or the undertakings broken. A building for the preservation of which special steps should in the opinion of HMRC be taken by reason of its outstanding historic or architectural interest qualifies for this relief. So does land where it is essential for the preservation of the character and amenities of such a building. Such land does not have to be in the same ownership. The undertakings required are that until the death of the donee, or the property is disposed of, reasonable steps will be taken for the maintenance, repair, and preservation of the property and for securing access to it by the public (*IHTA 1984, s 31(2)(a)*). Access by prior appointment only is not adequate except where the transfer was before 1 August 1998. HMRC can require publication of details of the undertakings and other information about the property (*IHTA 1984, s 31(4FA)*). In the cases of land, in addition to the normal undertakings, every person owning any part of the property must agree with HMRC what specific steps are required for the maintenance, repair, and preservation of the land and the historic building, and must give an undertaking to do such work. Such an undertaking can only be required in relation to the historic building itself and any land falling between the building and the land for which exemption is sought (*FA 1985, Sch 26, paras 1, 2*).

Example 18.5

Jack's family trust owns an historic building. To the south is a field owned by Jack personally and to the south of that is another field owned by Joe. Both Jack and Joe claim exemption in respect of their land.

Jack can be required to give a repairs undertaking in respect of the historic building and his land. He cannot be required to give an undertaking in relation to Joe's land as it is not between Jack's land and the building. Joe can be required to give an undertaking in respect of the building, his own land, and Jack's land.

18.75 HMRC can, if they think it appropriate, require separate undertakings from different people (*IHTA 1984, s 31(4B)*). For instance, in the above example they either might require the trustees to give the undertaking in respect of the building, and the undertakings by Jack and Joe to be restricted to their own land, or they might require the undertakings to extend to the building but place a ceiling on their financial obligations.

18.76 An undertaking under these provisions can be varied between HMRC and the person who gave it. If that person does not agree to a proposed variation HMRC can apply to the Special Commissioners who are empowered to direct that it be varied (*IHTA 1984, s 35A*). This applies even if the undertaking was given before 31 July 1998, although in such a case the variation must be limited to greater access and publication of details of the property (*FA 1998, Sch 25, para 10*).

18.77 *Re applications to vary to undertakings of A and B (2005 STC (SCD) 103)* is the first such appeal. A and B were each the owner of heritage property chattels which they kept in their own homes, which were not open to the public. Their pre-31 July 1998 undertakings required them to give 'by appointment' access to the chattels. HMRC's proposed variation was to require A to give access to 49 specified objects without appointment on a minimum of 15 days per year, and for B to give access to 51 specified objects without appointment on a minimum of ten days per year, and for them each to arrange for a minimum of four daily tours of up to 25 people in A's case, and up to ten in B's. Alternatively, they could exhibit the objects for a minimum of three months at a public gallery. They also required A and B to provide details to local tourist offices of the arrangements for access on public access days, to provide photographs of the listed objects and notification that these are available for loan to specified local and national museums and to allow the Revenue to publicise these access arrangements. The Special Commissioner, Stephen Oliver QC, held that as the scheme was changed by parliament, the owners had no legitimate expectation that their undertakings would remain unaffected, that the open access proposals were, on the facts of the two cases, onerous and intrusive and would involve a real disruption to the lives of the families and that the museum or gallery option was not a reasonable alternative condition as such exhibition space is not readily available. He did not feel that the public interest in the right to view being more freely available would outweigh the impact on the owners, and concluded that it would not be just and reasonable in the circumstances to order a variation.

18.78 Where a conditionally exempt transfer has taken place, a tax charge will arise on the first occurrence of a breach of an undertaking (unless HMRC opt to excuse it), or a disposal of the property – other than a disposal by way of gift to a person from whom HMRC are prepared to accept fresh undertakings, or one by private treaty to one of the specified national heritage bodies. The government have said that where a part disposal of a conditionally exempt property results solely from leasehold enfranchisement and there is no breach of undertaking in respect of the retained property the disposal will not give rise to a review of designation of the retained property (IR Press Release 7.5.1993). They indicated that a new clause to this effect would be added to the Finance Bill but, as this was not done, presumably the government felt on reflection that it was unnecessary to legislate for this concession. The death of the donee will also crystallise a tax charge if the property is sold by his executors, but not if it is left to an heir who is prepared to give the necessary undertakings. In the latter case the exemption granted to the deceased will have become absolute. This is, accordingly, an effective method of passing on heritage property within a family – which is, of course, what it is designed to allow. Where a tax charge crystallises it will be on the value of the property at the time of the breach or the sale, not on the value at the time of the original gift. As this can produce a significantly greater liability than if the exemption had never been claimed, the relief should not automatically be claimed without due consideration being given as to whether a future disposal is likely.

18.79 If there is a breach of any of the undertakings given in relation to the building and associated land, or in relation to historic objects associated with the building, that breach will crystallise the inheritance tax liability in relation to the whole of the associated items. Similarly, the disposal of any of the associated items or the death of any of the owners (without his heirs themselves giving the appropriate undertakings or the property being sold to one of the heritage bodies (within *IHTA 1984, Sch 3*) or being given in satisfaction of the inheritance tax on death) will crystallise the deferred tax on all the items (*IHTA 1984, s 32A*). HMRC have power to allow the conditional exemption of owners who are not in breach to continue if it appears to them that the entity consisting of the associated properties has not been materially affected by the breach or disposal (*IHTA 1984, s 32A(10)*). The Minister has given an assurance that when considering the application of the provision in individual cases HMRC will examine all relevant factors in the light of advice from the appropriate advisory bodies. A relevant factor to which weight will be given will be whether what remains of the entity after the sale or breach of the undertaking might qualify for exemption as a viable heritage unit looked at on its own merit.

18.80 Where conditional exemption applies to heritage property, HMRC can also grant exemption from the IHT trust charges for funds put into a trust for the maintenance, repair or preservation of the building. The detailed rules are outside the scope of this book. They can be found in *IHTA 1984, ss 77–79A* and *Sch 4*.

Gifts with Reservation

18.81 If on a gift either:

(*a*) possession and enjoyment of the property is not bona fide assumed by the donee at least seven years before the donor's death (or by the date of the gift if later); or

(*b*) at any time in the seven years prior to his death (or the period from the date of the gift) the property is not enjoyed to the entire exclusion, or virtually to the entire exclusion, of the donor and of any benefit to him by contract or otherwise,

the property is treated for inheritance tax purposes as remaining part of the donor's estate (*FA 1986, s 102*). This wording is similar, but not identical, to that which used to apply for estate duty purposes, namely 'property taken under any gift, whenever made, of which property bona fide possession and enjoyment shall not have been assumed by the donee immediately upon the gift and thenceforth retained, to the entire exclusion of the donor, or of any benefit to him by contract or otherwise'. If the property ceases to be subject to the reservation subsequent to the gift but prior to the donor's death it is treated as a gift at that time.

18.82 A gift of part of an interest in a private residence would be caught by this provision as the donor would still be entitled to occupy the property by virtue of ownership of the remainder of his interest (but see **18.86** below). Similarly, a gift of the entire property subject to a right would constitute a reservation. An understanding falling short of a right may also do so, although in *Attorney-General v Seccombe ([1911] 2 KB 688)*, it was held that the 1889 wording, which is identical in this respect, required some legally enforceable arrangement as opposed to a merely casual one. However, it is specifically provided that retention or assumption by the donor of an incorporeal right over land is to be disregarded if it is for full consideration in money or money's worth (*FA 1986, Sch 20, para 6(1)(a)*). A gift of a private residence subject to the retention of a right to remain in occupation at a full market rent should therefore be effective (but it must be remembered that a right of occupation for one's life is treated as a settlement in which the donor has a life interest, which would render the gift ineffective). HMRC consider that the rent paid needs to be reviewed at appropriate intervals to reflect market changes if a gift with reservation is not to arise. They do, however, accept that full consideration can cover 'a range of values reflecting normal valuation tolerances' and that any amount within that range is acceptable (Tax Bulletin Issue 9, Nov 1993, page 98). Similarly, a gift of the property subject to the grant of a lease to the donor at a market value premium plus a nominal annual rent would suffice.

18.83 In a 1952 case, *St Aubyn v Attorney-General ([1952] AC 15)*, Lord Radcliffe said 'it is the possession and enjoyment of the actual property given that has to be taken account of, and… if that property is, as it may be, a limited equitable interest or an equitable interest distinct from another such interest which is not given, or an interest in property subject to an interest that is retained, it is of no consequence for this purpose that the retained interest remains in the beneficial enjoyment of the person who provides the gift'. It was also pointed out in the Privy Council in *Chick v Commissioners of Stamp Duties ([1958] AC 435)* in relation to similar wording that it must often be a matter of fine distinction what is the subject matter of a gift. If the gift is of a property shorn of certain rights which appertain to complete ownership, the donor cannot be said not to have been excluded from possession and enjoyment of that which he has given, eg if he carves out a lease and gifts only the freehold reversion, occupation by virtue of the lease should not constitute a reservation of benefit in relation to the property gifted, namely the reversion – unless the associated operations rules catch the creation of the lease (as they may well do). *FA 1986, s 102A* (see **18.91**) is designed to prevent this in most cases where the donor wishes to contrive to reside in the property. It is still relatively easy with investment property where the donor does not wish to gift his entire interest.

18.84 Care may need to be taken in splitting the property into a lease and a reversion. In a Scottish case *Kildrummy (Jersey) Ltd v CIR (1990 STC 657)* it was held that a person cannot grant a lease to himself and such a transaction was therefore a nullity. However, in *Ingram v CIR (1999 STC 37)*, the House of Lords held that the position is different under English law as splitting does not treat a nominee or trustee as an agent for his beneficiary; he contracts in his own name with a right of indemnity against the beneficiary for the liabilities he incurs. The nominee incurs real obligations so cannot be regarded as a mere puppet. In the *Ingram* case the House of Lords accepted that the *St Aubyn* principle applies for inheritance tax as well as estate duty. There was no reservation of benefit. What was comprised in the gift by Lady Ingram was the freehold shorn of her leasehold interest. The effect of the *Ingram* decision has been significantly restricted by *IHTA 1984, s 102A* (see **18.90**). In Scotland it may be possible to avoid the effect of *Kildrummy* by transferring the property jointly to a nominee for the donor and a relative who will take a small beneficial interest in the property.

18.85 Where the property is itself a leasehold interest, not a freehold, the contrasting decisions in *Buzzoni (executors of Kamhi decd) v HMRC ([2013] STC 262)* and Viscount Hood (Executor of Lady Diana Hood) v HMRC (2017 STC 1707) merit a read. In March 2004, Mrs Kamhi was granted a long lease of a flat. In November 2007, with her landlord's consent, she granted an underlease for the entire remaining term of the lease less one day to Ovalap Nominees Ltd as nominee of a settlement created by Mrs Kamhi. Mrs Kamhi died in 2008. At the date of her death her lease (subject to the sub-lease) was worth £50,000, whereas the head-lease with vacant possession would have been worth around £2.1 million. The terms of the sub-lease largely mirrored those of the head-lease, the main exception being that the sub-lease did not require Ovalap to pay rent. It did, however, covenant to pay Mrs Kamhi an amount equal to the amount of service charge payable under the head-lease. The First-tier Tribunal held that the covenants in the lease provided a benefit to Mrs Kamhi as they indemnified her against her liabilities to her landlord under the head-lease. Similarly the reimbursement of the service charge was a benefit even though it mirrored the payment she made to her landlord as she had the liability to make such a payment. Accordingly Ovalap did not enjoy the property to the entire exclusion of any benefit to Mrs Kamhi. Fortunately the Court of Appeal analysed the transaction differently. The first question is 'whether it can be said that these positive covenants should be regarded as rights which Mrs Kamhi enjoyed by virtue of her reversionary interest which was never comprised in the gift, or whether they were enjoyed by virtue of the interest, the underlease, of which she did make a gift'. They held that the rights conferred by the covenants were obtained by virtue of the underlease. However, they went on to hold that there was no benefit to Mrs Kamhi because, if her landlord sued for breach of the covenants, the under-lessees were under an obligation to indemnify her where the breaches were a result of their omission (*Moule v Garrett* 1872 LR 7 Ex 101). Accordingly the covenants gave her no additional benefit. Unfortunately in the *Hood* casethere was held to be a reservation of benefit. The distinction made between the two was that, unlike in *Buzzoni*, the sub-licencees in *Hood* gave no direct covenants to the head-lessor; their only positive covenants were to Lady Hood, the sub-lessor. Berner J felt that *Buzzoni* held that the statutory criterion is the exclusivity of enjoyment of the gifted property. If the donor's benefit makes no difference to the donee's enjoyment of that property, it is not possible to say that the donee's enjoyment was other than to the exclusion of any benefit to the donor. As Moses LJ said in *Buzzoni*, in that case the under-lessees were already under obligations to the head lessor, in the licence to sublet, which precisely matched the obligations into which they entered with Mrs Kamhi. Their obligations to her did not in any way detract from the enjoyment of the sub-lease as they did not in any way add to the obligations already imposed by the licence. Lady Hood, in contrast, was the only one to whom the head landlord was entitled to look to perform the covenants. Accordingly, the sub-lessee's covenants to her gave her a real benefit as they indemnified her against that obligation. There was a world of difference between obligations to which a sub-lessee might be subject by way of direct covenant to a head lessor and the actions which might have to be taken in practice by a sub-lessee to avoid or obtain relief from forfeiture in the event that the head lessee failed to observe covenants in the head lease and the head lessor took steps to forfeit the head lease. The Upper Tribunal agreed: 'The gift by Lady Hood of the sub-lease estate in the premises is the gift of the whole sub-lease estate and the benefits of the covenants entered into by her sons was a benefit she received back from them and not something that was carved out of the estate which she granted to them.'

18.86 There is a statutory exemption in relation to a gift of land (such as a house) if the donor initially gives up possession but later occupies the property:

(*a*) as a result of a change in the donor's circumstances which was unforeseen at the time of the gift and which was not brought about by the donor to receive the benefit of the exemption; and

(*b*) at a time when he has become unable to maintain himself through old age, infirmity, or otherwise; and

(*c*) where such occupation represents a reasonable provision by the donee for the care and maintenance of the donor; and provided that

(*d*) the donee is a relative of the donor or his spouse ('relative' does not appear to be defined for this purpose).

(*FA 1986, Sch 20, para 6(1)(b).*)

18.87 There is also a statutory exemption if, or to the extent that, the disposal of property by way of gift is an exempt transfer by virtue of *IHTA 1984, s 18* (transfers between spouses), *s 20* (small gifts), *s 22* (gifts in consideration of marriage), *s 23* (gifts to charities), *s 24* (gifts to political parties), *s 24A* (gifts to housing associations), *s 25* (gifts for national purposes), *s 27* (maintenance funds for historic buildings), or *s 28* (employee trusts) (*FA 1986, s 102(5)*). In *CIR v Eversden (2003 STC 989)* a settlor gave a 95% interest in her house to trustees on trust to pay the income to her husband for life, and after her death to hold the capital and income on discretionary trust for a class of beneficiary including herself and her issue, and subject thereto for her issue. The husband died in 1992 and the settlor in 1998. It was held that, as the creation of the settlement was an exempt transfer within *IHTA 1984, ss 18, 102(5)* took the 95% interest out of the reservation of benefit provisions. The Commissioner also opined that if he was wrong on this point, the whole of the trust property was not enjoyed to the entire exclusion of the settlor, though not because she resided in the house until her death (he accepted that she did so by virtue of her 5% interest albeit that the trustees did not seek to enforce their right to permit one of the beneficiaries to occupy it with her) but because she was one of the class of discretionary beneficiary. The decision that there was no reservation of benefit was affirmed by both the high court and the Court of Appeal.

18.88 Not surprisingly, the legislation was amended in the *Finance Act 2003*. There is now a reservation of benefit where *s 18* (transfers between spouses) applies if the property becomes settled property by virtue of the gift, the donor's spouse becomes entitled to an interest in possession in the settled property, that interest in possession comes to an end at some time before the donor's death and on its termination the spouse does not become beneficially entitled to the settled property (or to another interest in possession in respect of it) (*FA 1986, s 185(5)(5A)*) as amended by *FA 2003, s 185*). The gift is treated as being made not when the property was settled but when the spouse's interest in possession terminates (*FA 1986, s 185(5B)*). This change prevents avoidance of inheritance tax by granting an interest in possession to the spouse, waiting a short while and then revoking the interest in possession and leaving the trust as a discretionary trust of which the donor's children are the beneficiaries.

18.89 At the time of the introduction of these rules the then Minister gave an assurance that 'the gift with reservation rules will not be applied to an unconditional gift of an undivided share in land merely because the property is occupied by all the joint owners or tenants in common, including the donor'. For example 'if elderly parents and the children occupy the property as their family home, each owner bearing his or her share of the running costs… the parents' occupation and enjoyment of the part of the house that they have given away is in return for similar enjoyment of the children of the other part of the property. Thus, the donor's occupation is for a full consideration' (Hansard, Standing Committee G, 10 June 1986, Col 425). This reasoning would seem to apply equally where the children are not living regularly in the property provided that they are not specifically excluded from the ability to do so. However, it seems likely that HMRC would seek to challenge a gift if it does not fall squarely within the minister's wording. If the children do not occupy the property at all they would probably not have assumed possession and enjoyment of it.

18.90 The Minister also stated that the legislation does not prevent a man giving away an asset and reserving a benefit to his wife. However, if a person does this and then shares the spouse's enjoyment or benefit of the reservation without paying her for it, HMRC take the view that he has not been excluded from enjoyment of or benefit from the gifted property (Hansard, Standing Committee G, 10 June 1986, col 420).

18.91 For gifts after 8 March 1999 a gift of an interest in land is treated as giving rise to a reservation of benefit if at any time in the relevant period (the seven years before the donor's death or, if shorter, the period from the date of the gift to the date of the donor's death) the donor or his spouse enjoys a significant right or interest in relation to the land or is party to a significant arrangement in relation to the land (*FA 1986, ss 102A(1)(2), 102C(1)*). A right, interest or arrangement is significant for this purpose if (and only if) it entitles or enables the donor to occupy all or part of the land, or to enjoy some right in relation to all or part of the land, otherwise than for full consideration in money or money's worth (*FA 1986, s 102A(3)*). A right, interest or arrangement is not significant if either:

(*a*) it does not (and cannot) prevent the enjoyment of the land to the entire exclusion (or virtually the entire exclusion) of the donor; or

(*b*) it does not entitle or enable the donor to occupy all or part of the land immediately after the disposal, but would do so were it not for the interest disposed of; or

(*c*) in the case of a right or interest, that right or interest was granted or acquired more than seven years prior to the date of the gift (*FA 1986, s 102A(4)(5)*).

If the donor gifts more than one interest in the land (whether or not at the same time and whether or not to the same donee) *s 102A* applies separately in relation to each interest (*s 102A(6)*).

18.92 It will be apparent that *s 102A* goes far wider than merely to attack the creation of a lease and reversion as happened in the *Ingram* case. It will also catch variants such as the creation of a lease in favour of the beneficiary to take effect at a future date after the death of the donor (so that the value of the property at that date would be reduced by the value of the lease). It should be noted that a right for the donor's spouse to occupy will not be a significant right if it does not enable the donor himself to occupy the land. Accordingly a holiday home which the donor himself rarely visits but is used by other members of the family could still be passed on using the *St Aubyn* principle. It would be dangerous for the donor to in fact occupy the property in such a case though (unless he pays a full rent for such usage) as that might well constitute an arrangement enabling him to occupy the property.

18.93 The exclusion where the right was granted more than seven years prior to the date of the gift is intriguing. The effect is to allow the *St Aubyn* principle to apply if after the transfer of the property to the nominee and the grant of the lease to the donor, the donor waits for seven years before gifting the reversionary interest. If the gift is a potentially exempt transfer this means that the donor will have to live for 14 years after splitting the freehold (or long leasehold) interest. Apart from the costs, there is not normally any adverse consequence of splitting the interest into two. In particular both interests will qualify for the capital gains private residence relief during the period in which both are beneficially owned by the donor. Accordingly there may be merit in splitting the interest in a property in this way now so as to give the owner the ability to gift a reversionary interest at some future time without triggering a reservation of benefit.

18.94 It should also be noted that the provision applies only where the donor disposes of an interest by way of gift. A sale at an undervalue does not appear to trigger the provision. It is possible that the Courts would regard the undervalue as a 'gift' but the ordinary meaning of that word is not apt to do so and it would, in any event, be a gift of the undervalue not of the interest in land. *Section 102A* would also not apply if the property is split on purchase. For example when a person moves house he could arrange with the vendor to sell him a lease for a period of 50 years at a nominal rent and at the same time to sell to the purchaser's children the reversionary interest in the property. The vendor would probably be unwilling to do this for a lease of under 50 years as that would trigger an income tax charge (see **3.2**) so this is unlikely to be workable if the 'donor' is already elderly. The shift in value to the children is brought about by the reduction in the value of the lease due to the effluxion of time between creating the lease and the donor dying. It probably does not affect the position if the parent gifts cash to the child to enable him to pay for the reversion provided that the gift is not conditional on the money being used to make the purchase.

18.95 A gift of an undivided share of an interest in land similarly gives rise to a deemed reservation of benefit unless either:

(*a*) the donor does not occupy the land at any time in the relevant period (as defined in **18.91**); or (*b*) he occupies it to the exclusion of the donee for full consideration in money or money's worth; or

(*c*) both the donor and the donee occupy the land and the donor does not receive any benefit, other than a negligible one, which is provided by or at the expense of the donee for some reason connected with the gift.

(*FA 1986, s 102*.)

Head (*c*) above will be satisfied if the donor simply gifts the share of the interest so that the donee receives a benefit. It is only if the donee in turn provides a benefit to the donor that *s 102B* will be triggered.

18.96 Neither *s 102A* nor *s 102B* applies:

(*a*) to the extent that the disposal is an exempt transfer by virtue of any of the provisions of *s 102(5)* (transfers between spouses and other exempt transfers such as for small gifts, gifts in consideration of marriage, gifts to charity, etc.) (*FA 1986, s 102C(2)*); or

(*b*) where occupation of the land by the donor would be disregarded under *FA 1986, Sch 20, para 6(1)(b)* (change in donor's circumstances – see **18.86**) (*FA 1986, s 102C(3)*).

18.97 Overall, therefore, HMRC say that neither *ss 102A* nor *102B* will apply in the following circumstances:

(*a*) the gift is to a spouse or covered by another IHT exemption;

(*b*) the retained right or interest is negligible so that the donor is virtually entirely excluded from any enjoyment of the land;

(*c*) the donor pays full consideration for his occupation of the land;

(*d*) the occupation of the land is effectively forced on the donor by some unforeseen downturn in his financial circumstances;

(*e*) the gift is made more than seven years after the right, interest or arrangement concerned is created or entered into;

(*f*) the donor may occupy the land or enjoy some right in relation to it only on the determination of the interest that he has given away; eg the donor gives away a leasehold interest and retains the freehold reversion which entitles him to re-occupy the land when the lease expires; or

(*g*) the gift is of a share in land, which the donor then occupies jointly with the other owner (the donee) provided the donor receives no other benefit at the donee's expense in connection with the gift.

18.98 The detailed rules on reservation of benefit contained in *FA 1986, Sch 20* also apply for *ss 102A* and *102B* with the exception of *para 6* (exclusion of benefit – but similar rules apply for *ss 102A* and *102B*) (*FA 1986, s 102C(4)*). Any question which falls to be answered under *s 102A* or *102B* in relation to an interest in land is to be determined by reference to the interest which is treated as property comprised in the gift (*FA 1986, s 102C(4)*). It is not clear if this applies generally or only for the purpose of *Sch 20*. If property other than an interest in land is treated as comprised in a gift under *Sch 20, para 2* (substitutions and accretions), *s 102* (not *102A* or *102B*) applies to that property even if the original gift was of an interest in land (*FA 1986, s 102C(5)*). Where two or more of *ss 102, 102A* and *102B* potentially apply only *s 102B* will apply (*FA 1986, s 102C(6)*). Where both *ss 102* and *102A* could apply the charge will be under *s 102* (*FA 1986, s 102C(7)*).

18.99 HMRC have indicated that they consider the words 'virtually to the entire exclusion' in **18.81**(*b*) as covering cases where the benefit to the donor is insignificant in relation to the gifted property. They say that they operate the provision in such a way that donors are not 'unreasonably prevented from having limited access to property they have given away and a measure of flexibility is adopted in applying the test'. Examples of the sort of things they consider will not give rise to a gift with reservation in relation to a gift of a house which becomes the donee's residence are:

(*a*) 'house-sitting' for up to two weeks a year in the donee's absence;

(*b*) staying with the donee for less than a month a year;

(*c*) social visits to the donee as his guest which are no more than might be expected had the house not been gifted to the donee;

(*d*) a temporary stay at the house for a short term purpose such as to convalesce after medical treatment, to nurse the donee after medical treatment, or while the donor's own house is undergoing redecoration;

(*e*) visits to the house for domestic reasons such as to babysit for the donees' children;

(*f*) if the house includes a library which is included in the gift, visits of less than five times in any year to consult or borrow a book; and

(*g*) visits to the grounds or other land given away by the donor to walk his dogs or for horse riding (provided such visits do not restrict the donee's own use of the land).

It should be stressed that these examples are intended for guidance. Whether or not a gift is a gift with reservation will depend on the exact facts of each individual case.

18.100 The sort of thing HMRC consider does give rise to a reservation of benefit are:

(*a*) staying in the house most weekends;

(*b*) staying there for a month or more each year;

(*c*) use of the house on an occasional basis if it is a second home or a holiday home which is only used on an occasional basis by the donee;

(*d*) use of the house to keep a library that is retained by the donor; and

(*e*) use of the house on a regular basis, for example, because it is necessary for the donor's work.

(Tax Bulletin, Issue 9, Nov 93, p 98.)

18.101 Where there is not a reservation of benefit the pre-owned asset rules (see **13.50**) also need to be considered. These can impose an annual income tax charge on the use of an asset where a transaction has taken place that sought to avoid a reservation of benefit arising, usually as a result of a series of transactions designed to bypass the rules.

Debts

18.102 Debts can be deducted in calculating the amount liable to inheritance tax on death. A debt that is secured on a specific asset must be deducted as far as possible from the value of that asset. Accordingly, up to 6 April 2013, it was relatively easy for a UK domiciled individual to significantly minimise his IHT liability by keeping his UK property fully mortgaged.

18.103 However, from 17 July 2013, a liability that arises after that date can be taken into account on death only to the extent that it is discharged in money or money's worth on or after death out of the estate or from excluded property (non-UK property of a non-UK domiciled individual) owned by the individual immediately before death (*IHTA 1984, s 175A(1)* inserted by *FA 2013, Sch 36, para 4(1)*). It can also be deducted if it is not so discharged but there is a 'real commercial reason' for its not being discharged; securing a tax advantage is not a main benefit of leaving it undischarged. There is a real commercial reason only if it can be shown that the debt (or other liability) is to a person dealing at arm's length or, if it is not, that, if it were, that person would not require the liability to be discharged (*IHTA 1984, s 175A(2)(3)*).

18.104 From the same date a liability that arises after 6 April 2013 similarly cannot be taken into account to the extent that it is attributable to financing (directly or indirectly) the acquisition of any excluded property (or the maintenance or enhancement of such property). This does not apply if (or to the extent that) the excluded property has been disposed of for full consideration in money or money's worth (provided that it has not subsequently itself become excluded property (ie invested in non-UK assets) and has not been used (directly or indirectly) to acquire, maintain or enhance the value of excluded property or to discharge another liability incurred for such a purpose) (*IHTA 1984, s 162A(1)(2)*). Accordingly, whilst taking a mortgage to meet the purchase price of a UK property can still reduce the IHT for a non-UK domiciled individual, if the mortgage is subsequently topped up to keep the net value of the property within the £325,000 nil rate band the additional borrowing will not be deductible if it is used to acquire overseas assets (which includes being put on bank deposit overseas). However, if the borrowed money is taken overseas and gifted to a family member the top up borrowing appears to remain deductible.

18.105 Where property qualifies for IHT business property relief (see **18.34**) and the transferor has a liability that is attributable (wholly or partly) to financing (directly or indirectly) the acquisition, maintenance or enhancement of the property, the liability must be deducted, as far as possible, from the value of that property before applying the relief (*IHTA 1984, s 162B(1)(2)*). This rule also applies to liabilities that relate to agricultural property (*IHTA 1984, s 162B(3)(4)*) and to forestry land where the value of the growing property is left out of account under *IHTA 1984, s 125(2)(a)* (see **23.26**) in determining the value on death (*IHTA 1984, s 162B(5)(6)*).

Other Matters

18.106 An interesting issue arose in *Oakley and another (as PRs of Jossaume decd) v CIR (2005 STC (SCD) 343)*. Mrs Jossaume died in 1990. Under a deed of variation to the will of her late husband, Mrs Jossaume had a life interest in all of the real property held in his estate (other than one in which she had an absolute interest and three which passed to their three children). One of the properties was a contractor's yard and premises at Saffron Walden occupied by John F Jossaume Ltd. The will directed that 'during the subsistence of the trust hereof my trustees shall not require any payment by way of rent from John F Jossaume Ltd in respect of the use of the premises occupied by it at Saffron Walden'. Mrs Jossaume's estate contended that this gave the company an interest in possession in the yard with the result that Mrs Jossaume could not have had any interest in it. The Special Commissioners agreed.

18.107 Another interesting issue arose in *Moggs v CIR (2005 STC (SCD) 394)*. Mr Moggs died in 2001. In 1996, following the death of his wife, he invited his niece Miss Green to stay with him. He suggested that she stay with him initially until the end of March 1997, but each year they extended the arrangement for a further year. In late 1996, Mr Moggs drafted a will stating that if Miss Green was still permanently resident in the property at his death she could continue to reside there for her life, but he did not execute the will. In 1997 or 1998 Mr Moggs extended the house to provide a bedroom and en suite bathroom for Miss Green. Miss Green was divorced in November 1999. In August 2000, Mr Moggs transferred a half interest to Miss Green as joint tenant, the delay between November 1999 and August 2000 being due to the need to amalgamate the title to the property with that of the next door land that he had previously bought for the extension. Miss Green's impression was that if it had not been for her divorce Mr Moggs would have transferred a joint interest in the property to her earlier. Miss Green contended that Mr Moggs' actions showed that he was making a gift to her of an interest in the property on the basis of proprietary estoppel on account of her commitment of care to him. HMRC accepted that it was possible that the deceased made a promise to Miss Green which would have had the effect of Mr Moggs having made the gift earlier than 2000. The Special Commissioners felt that there were a number of contrary indications – in particular that the draft will had envisaged only a life interest to her not a gift of the property – and that in August 2000 neither Miss Green nor Mr Moggs had told his solicitor that the transfer was to give effect to a earlier gift, and concluded that there had been no such gift.

18.108 A disposition is not a transfer of value, and so does not attract inheritance tax, if it is made in favour of a dependent relative and is a reasonable provision for his care or maintenance (*IHTA 1984, s 11(3)*). It is easy to think of this exception as requiring payments in the nature of income. However, that is not so. In *McKelvey (executor of McKelvey decd) v HMRC (2008 STC (SCD) 944)* the transfer of two properties was held to be covered by this exemption. Dolores McKelvey (Dolores) had never married and lived all her life with her mother (Mary) who was widowed in 1983. In late 2002, Dolores was told by her doctor that she had terminal cancer and had six months to live. At that time Mary was aged 85, registered blind and in frail health. She was dependent on Dolores for most of her needs. In 2003 Dolores gifted two houses which she held as investments to Mary. These were valued at £169,000. Dolores died in 2005. Dolores' executors said that Dolores, knowing that she had only a short time to live and that her ability to care for her mother would soon come to an end, transferred the two properties to her to provide her with the financial resources to pay for her future care, either in her own home or, should it be necessary, in a care home. HMRC accepted that, in principle, a gift in kind is capable of falling within *s 11(3)* as being intended for the care of the beneficiary, but contended that there had to be an immediate or imminent need for the gift so that it, or the proceeds of its sale, would be used for that purpose within a fairly short period. Mere contingency was not enough. Dolores in fact lived for a further two years after the gift and Mary for two more years. Neither of the properties was sold during that four-year period. The Special Commissioners felt that the test had to be applied at the time of the gift. However, it is a subjective test, not what Dolores considered reasonable but what in fact was reasonable. He decided that at the time of the gift, £140,500 would have been reasonable, leaving the remaining £28,500 of value taxable. It should be noted that although HMRC accepted that the transfer of a property could be a reasonable provision for care, they distinguished care from maintenance. Accordingly, the case is not necessarily a basis for assuming that the transfer of a property would be excluded by *IHTA 1984, s 11(1)* which is concerned only with maintenance, although it would probably cover *s 11(2)* which refers to maintenance, education or training of a child.

18.109 The special rules in *IHTA 1984, s 161* which deal with the valuation of property where it is related to property held by the taxpayer's spouse or civil partner are dealt with at **23.91**.

18.110 There are two specific IHT reliefs for forestry. These are considered at **23.25** onwards. The ownership and management of woodlands on a commercial basis is treated as a business, and there is a specific relief for IHT on woodlands on a death, although with 100% business property relief this is unlikely to apply at present.

The Residence Nil Rate Amount

18.111 A new relief, the residence nil rate amount applies on a death after 5 April 2017. This relief in theory enables a married couple to pass up to £1million of the value of their house to their children. Each has a £325,000 nil rate band so an additional £175,000 residence nil rate band will mean that the first £500,000 gifted by each parent will pass tax-free. However, the rules are very restrictive and in many cases this relief will be limited or not available at all. The relief applies only on death.

18.112 The relief is being phased in. The £175,000 figure will not actually be reached until after 5 April 2020. The proposed allowance is as follows:

2017/18	£100,000
2018/19	£125,000
2019/20	£150,000
2020/21	£175,000

(*IHTA 1984, s 8D(5)(a)* inserted by *F(No 2)A 2015, s 9(4)*).

The £175,000 increases in line with inflation after 2020/21 unless Parliament decides otherwise (*IHTA 1984, s 8D(3), (7)*).

18.113 The relief applies only if the person's estate immediately before his death includes a 'qualifying residential interest' (see **18.115**) and a percentage of that interest is inherited (see **18.92**) by a lineal descendant of that person (*IHTA 1984, s 8E(1)*). For this purpose a stepchild and a foster-child are treated as children and can continue to be treated as children until the time of death. An adopted child is treated as a child both of his natural parents and of his adoptive parents. If an individual is appointed as guardian of a person who is under 18 at the time of the appointment and the appointment is under the *Children Act 1989, s 5* (or the corresponding law in Scotland or Northern Ireland) or the corresponding law in any other country, the child is treated as a child of the guardian (and will continue to be regarded as his child when the guardianship ceases). Similarly, where a person is appointed by the court as a special guardian of a person under 18 under the *Children Act 1989, s 14A*, that person is regarded as the child's parent. Children and grandchildren of such deemed children are, of course, then regarded as lineal descendants of the person who is treated as being the parent (*IHTA 1984, s 8K*). HMRC have said that where a person gifts his home but continues to occupy it, so that there is a reservation of benefit, the residence nil-rate band may be available if it is given away to a direct descendant (Guidance Note 8.11.2016). That guidance also makes clear that the relief is given to the estate, so the benefit is not given to the donee of the home but is spread across the whole estate (subject to any other allocation in the will). It also stresses that the relief does not apply to lifetime gifts, even if made in the seven years prior to the death. Accordingly, the residence nil rate band might be available on death even where lifetime gifts utilised the whole of the normal nil rate band. It also says that the home does not have to be in the UK, but it must be included in the person's estate.

18.114 Property is inherited for this purpose if there is a disposition of it (whether effected by will, under an intestacy or otherwise). However, it does not apply if under the disposition the property becomes comprised in a settlement unless either:

(*a*) the disposition is a Will Trust under which the beneficiary becomes entitled to an interest in possession (such as a life interest) which is either an immediate post-death interest (ie the interest in possession takes effect from the date of death) or a disabled person's interest (as defined in *IHTA 1984, ss 89B, 89C*); or

(*b*) under the disposition, the property becomes settled property to which *IHTA 1984, ss 71A* (trusts for bereaved minors) or *74D* (age 18-25 trusts) applies.

(*IHTA 1984, s 8J(1)–(4)*.)

If the property forms part of the parent's estate because it is a gift with reservation, the relief applies provided that the child or grandchild who holds the property at the date of death is the person to whom the gift was made (*IHTA 1984, s 8J(5)*).

18.115 A residential interest is an interest in a dwelling-house which has been the person's residence at a time when he owned either that or another interest in the dwelling-house (*IHTA 1984, s 8H(2)*). If a person's estate at the time of his death includes such an interest in only one dwelling, the person's interest in that dwelling is a qualifying residential interest (*IHTA 1984, s 8H(3)*). If it includes interests in each of two or more dwellings, the executors (or other personal representatives) can nominate one (and only one) of them as the qualifying residential interest (*IHTA 1984, s 8H(4)*). If the person's estate includes an interest in a dwelling-house, but at the time of his death he was living in job-related accommodation (as defined in *TCGA 1992, s 222(8A)–(8D)* but ignoring *s 222(9)*) and intended in due course to occupy the dwelling-house as his residence, it can be treated as if it were occupied by him as a residence (*IHTA 1984, s 8H(6)*).

18.116 For this purpose, a dwelling-house includes any land occupied and enjoyed with it as its garden or grounds, but does not include any trees or underwood in relation to which an election is made under *IHTA 1984, s 125* (to defer the tax on it – see **23.26**) (*IHTA 1984, s 8H(5)*). When he announced the legislation, the Chancellor indicated that the relief could extend to a former dwelling-house that was no longer owned at the date of death. However, he appears to have changed his mind as no such provision is included in the legislation.

18.117 Subject to a taper relief, the relief does not apply where the value of the estate on death exceeds £2 million. It should particularly be noted that the £2million looks at the value of the deceased's entire estate, not merely at the value of the property. The £2 million is indexed for 2018/19 onwards (*IHTA 1984, s 8D(5)(b), (6), (7)*).

18.118 In some circumstances if the allowance is not used on the death of the first spouse or civil partner to die, it can be carried forward and added to the residence nil rate band on the second death. If an interest in the house goes to children or other descendants, the value of the estate of the first to die does not exceed the taper threshold at the person's death (ie the £2 million for 2017/18) and the percentage of the interest in the property that passes to the children, etc, on the first death is less than the default allowance (the £1 million for 2017/18) the shortfall can be utilised on the second death (*IHTA 1984, s 8E(1)(2)*). If the value of the estate exceeds the taper threshold and the percentage of the interest in the property that passes to the children is less than the person's 'adjusted allowance' the shortfall can also be carried forward (*IHTA 1984, s 8E(4)*). The adjusted allowance is the default allowance less half of the excess of the value of the estate over the default allowance (*IHTA 1984, s 8D(5)(g)*).

The Chancellor put it rather more simply. If the value of the estate exceeds £2 million, the default allowance is reduced by 50% of the excess. This means that if the default allowance is £175,000, no relief is due if the value of the estate exceeds £2.35 million (as 50% of £350,000 = £175,000). For 2017/18, where the default allowance is £100,000, no relief is due if the value of the estate exceeds £2.2 million (as 50% of £200,000 = £100,000).

18.119 The calculation gets a little more complicated where there is a brought-forward allowance from an earlier death. The brought-forward allowance becomes part of the default allowance on the second death (*IHTA 1984, s 8D(5)(f)*). The brought-forward allowance is the sum of the amounts available for carry forward from the earlier death of a spouse or civil partner expressed as a percentage of the residential enhancement (the £175,000) at the death of the previous spouse. Where there is more than one previous spouse (eg the surviving spouse remarried and was widowed for a second time) it is then necessary to calculate the percentage that is the total of the individual percentages. That total percentage is the residential enhancement on the last death. If the percentage exceeds 100%, the brought-forward allowance is the residential enhancement on the last death (*IHTA 1984, s 8G(1)–(3)*).

Example 18.6

Mary was married to Peter who died in 2017/18. Peter left an interest in the matrimonial home value at £30,000 to his children. Mary then married John who died in 2018/19. John had previously been married and left an interest in his previous matrimonial home worth £50,000 to the children of his first marriage. Mary died in 2020/21. The value of Peter's estate was £1.8 million and that of John's estate £2.1 million.

On Peter's death he would have used £30,000 of his £100,000 residential enhancement leaving 70% to carry forward. On John's death, his residence nil rate band would have been £125,000 reduced by 50% of the excess of his estate over £2 million (£50,000) giving an adjusted allowance of £75,000. He used £50,000 leaving £25,000 to carry forward. This is 20% of the residential enhancement of £125,000.

Accordingly, on Mary's death, she has a 50% residential enhancement brought-forward from Peter plus a 20% residential enhancement brought-forward from John, a total of 70%. As that is less than 100%, the nil rate band on Mary's death is:

	£
Mary's residential enhancement	175,000
Brought-forward residential enhancement	
70% of £175,000	122,500
Default allowance	297,500

18.120 Where the value of the person's estate exceeds £2.8 million, the reduction applies to both the deceased's own and any brought-forward allowance (*IHTA 1984, s 8D(5)(f)(g)*).

Example 18.7

Suppose that Mary in the above example had an estate of £2.4 million. Her default allowance is reduced by 50% of the excess of her estate over £2 million. It is accordingly:

	£
Default allowance	297,500
Less 50% of £400,000	200,000
Adjusted allowance	97,500

18.121 If the estate at the first death does not exceed the taper threshold but the value of the property passing to descendants equals or exceeds the person's default allowance (including any brought-forward allowance), the gift will obviously fully utilise the default allowance leaving nothing to be carried forward (*IHTA 1984, s 8E(3)*). If the estate exceeds the taper threshold, the amount available for carry forward is obviously limited to the unused part of the adjusted allowance (*IHTA 1984, s 8E(4)(5)*). If the value of the residence given to the children exceeds the net value of the estate, the residence nil rate band is restricted to that value but the excess of the default allowance over that amount is available for carry forward (*IHTA 1984, s 8E(7)*).

18.122 If a person's estate at the time of death does not include a qualifying residence, or it does so and no interest in the residence goes to descendants, the whole of that person's default allowance (or adjusted allowance if less) is available for carry forward (*IHTA 1984, s 8F*).

18.123 If the first spouse or civil partner dies before 6 April 2017, the carry forward amount is deemed to be £100,000 (ie 100% of the default amount for that year) if the estate of the first spouse did not exceed £2 million. If it did, the default amount must be reduced by 50% of the excess in the normal way (*IHTA 1984, s 8G(4)(5)*).

18.124 The brought-forward allowance must be claimed. This must be done within two years from the end of the month in which the person whose executors wish to use the allowance dies or, if later, within three months from the date on which the personal representatives first act as such (or such longer period as HMRC may allow) (*IHTA 1984, s 8L(1)(2)*). If the executors or other personal representatives do not make the claim, any other person who is liable to tax chargeable on the person's death (such as trustee or the donee of a failed PET) may do so. Such a person must make the claim within such later period as HMRC may in a particular case allow (*IHTA 1984, s 8L(1)(2)*). It does not appear that HMRC are required to allow any such period though. Once made, a claim can be withdrawn, but only during the claim period or the one month following it (*IHTA 1984, s 8L(3)*).

18.125 If no claim is made and, had that been done it would have affected the IHT liability on a later death, the personal representatives (or some other person) of that other person can make the claim. They must do so within the above time limits but as if they had applied by reference to the second death (*IHTA 1984, s 8L(4)–(6)*).

Example 18.8

Jane leaves her house to her son. On his death it passes to her grandson.

If the son's executors do not make the claim, the grandson's executors can do so. It appears that the effect of such a claim is to re-open the IHT position on the son's death. The unused relief does not pass direct to the grandson's estate.

Downsizing Addition

18.126 There is also an entitlement to an additional downsizing relief where –

(*a*) not all of the value transferred is attributable to the person's qualifying residential interest;

(*b*) the person has a qualifying former residential interest;

(*c*) the value of that qualifying former residential interest exceeds the part of the residence nil-rate band already utilised by the property in the estate; and

(*d*) at least some of the remainder of the estate is closely inherited.

(*IHTA 1984, s 8FA(1)–(6)* inserted by *FA 2016, Sch 15, para 5*.)

The relief is, of course, the lesser of the utilised residence nil-rate band and the value of the remainder of the estate which is closely inherited (*ITA 1984, s 8FA(8)*). The relief must be claimed (*IHTA 1984, s 8FA(7)*). Where the downsizing occurred before 6 April 2017, HMRC treat the maximum available residential nil-rate band at that time as £100,000 (Guidance Note 8.11.2016).

18.127 If no residential property interest is held at death, the relief can still be claimed provided that there is a qualifying former residential interest and at least some of the estate is closely inherited. The relief is the lesser of the last relievable amount or the amount of the estate that is closely inherited (*IHTA 1984, s 8FB(1)–(7)*).

18.128 An interest is a qualifying former residential interest if it is a residential property interest in the nominated dwelling house which the person disposed of during his lifetime but after 7 July 2015, after it became his residence and after having ceased to occupy it as his residence (or two or more such interest in that dwelling house), provided that the person did not dispose of some other interest in that house during his lifetime (*IHTA 1984, ss 8H(4B), AH(4F)*). For example, if a person moves out of his property and sells a ten-year lease and later sells the reversion, the relief does not appear to be due. The concept is to grant relief only where the deceased sold and bought a smaller house. However, if there are two separate disposals, the executors can nominate one to be treated as the qualifying former residential interest (*IHTA 1984, s 8H(4C)*). So, in the above example, they could nominate either the leasehold interest or the reversion. The nominated dwelling house is that nominated by the executors (or other personal representatives). It should be noted that they have to make a nomination even if there was only one disposal by the deceased (*IHTA 1984, s 8H(4A)*).

Example 18.9

John sold his house for £400,000 and moved into a flat. He decided he did not like it and sold the flat for £350,000 to move into a second house. He sold the house when he went into a nursing home, but received only £250,000 because of a fall in the property market. The executors do not have to nominate the £250,000 property; they can nominate the £400,000 one.

18.129 Downsizing relief does not apply if the disposal of the nominated property was by way of gift which was subject to a reservation of benefit. However, if the property subsequently ceases to be subject to the benefit, a disposal is treated as taking place at that time (*IHTA 1984, s 84(4D)*). If the disposal is a conditionally exempt transfer (heritage property, etc) and no chargeable event has occurred in relation to the property by the time of the donor's death, the relief cannot be claimed (*IHTA 1984, s 84(4E)*).

18.130 A property held by a settlement will be a qualifying former residential interest in relation to the beneficiary if he had a beneficial entitlement to a qualifying interest in possession in the property and the trustees disposed of the property (other than to that beneficiary) at a time when he had an interest in possession in it (*IHTA 1984, s 8HA(1)–(4)*). An interest qualifies only if the interest in possession arose before 22 March 2006 (and if *IHTA 1984, s 71A* does not apply) or the interest is an immediate post-death interest, a disabled person's interest, or a transitional serial interest (or the interest falls within *IHTA 1984, s 5(1B)*). In other words, an interest in possession qualifies only if it deems the beneficiary to own the property for IHT purposes. It will not apply if the property is within the relevant property regime.

18.131 Where the estate on death includes a relevant residential property, the downsizing addition is added to its value to calculate the relief due (*IHTA 1984, s 8FC*). Where no such property was held at death, the person's residence nil-rate amount is of course the downsizing addition (*IHTA 1984, s 8FD*).

18.132 If the estate of a person who dies after 5 April 2017 includes a qualifying residential interest and all or part of the interest is conditionally exempt (ie it is heritage property – see **18.74**) the exempt part is treated as being not closely inherited. Where only part of the interest is exempt, the exempt part is proportionate to the value of the estate (*IHTA 1984, s 8M(1)–(21) as amended by FA 2016, Sch 15, para 12*). The effect is that the residence nil rate band is not utilised against that exempt value, but is available for carry forward. If the conditional exemption is subsequently lost (eg on a sale of the property or a failure to comply with the undertakings given) the carry forward amount can be utilised against the tax that becomes chargeable at the time of that trigger event (*IHTA 1984, s 8M(3)*). If a claim to use the carry forward amount was made on the death of a spouse occurring between the first death and the cessation of the conditional exemption, the amount transferred on that second death must be deducted from the carry forward amount on the first death (*IHTA 1984, s 8M(4)(5)*). If the cessation of the conditional exemption occurs before the second death, the amount of relief utilised on that trigger event obviously reduces the amount that can be brought forward on the second death (*IHTA 1984, s 8M(6)(7)*). The legislation is very complex and recourse must be had to it when dealing with conditionally exempt property.

Chapter 19

Stamp Duty Land Tax

Introduction

19.1 Stamp duty was often described as a voluntary tax. It was a tax on documents, so was not normally payable if a transaction could be carried out without bringing a document into existence. Even where it was payable the only penalty for non-payment was that the document could not be recognised by the Land Registry or used in evidence in court proceedings.

19.2 It was replaced by stamp duty land tax (SDLT) in relation to property transactions from 1 December 2003. SDLT is a more conventional tax. It is a tax on transactions and there are monetary penalties (and criminal penalties for fraudulent evasion of the tax) where the tax is not duly paid.

The Basic Rules

19.3 SDLT is chargeable on UK land transactions (other than where the land is in Scotland), namely any acquisition of a 'chargeable interest' in land (*FA 2003, s 42(1), 43(1)*). It is payable irrespective of whether there is a document effecting the transaction, irrespective of whether or not the document is executed in the UK and irrespective of whether the acquirer (or any other party) is UK-resident or physically present in the UK (*FA 2003, s 42(2)*). Subject to specified exceptions, it is payable however the acquisition is effected, whether by an act of the parties or by a court order, by compulsory acquisition or otherwise under any statutory provision or by operation of law (*FA 2003, s 43(2)*). From 1 April 2015, SDLT in Scotland was devolved to the Scottish Parliament, which replaced it by their own land and buildings transaction tax (see **19.444**). It is proposed that SDLT on land in Wales will be devolved to the Welsh Assembly from 1 April 2018.

19.4 A chargeable interest means:

(*a*) an estate, interest, right or power in or over land in the UK; or (*b*) the benefit of an obligation, restriction or condition affecting the value of any such estate, interest, right or power.

(*FA 2003, s 48(1)*.)

19.5 The creation of a chargeable interest, a surrender or release of such an interest, and the variation of a chargeable interest are all treated for SDLT purposes as an acquisition and disposal of that chargeable interest although the variation of a lease is an acquisition and disposal of a chargeable interest only if it constitutes a new lease or is deemed to do so (*FA 2003, s 43(3)*). For convenience the terms purchaser and vendor are used in the Act to describe the parties to a land transaction. It needs to be remembered though that an acquisition of a chargeable interest is a land transaction even though it does not take place by purchase or sale, and even if no consideration is given for the transaction (*FA 2003, s 43(4)*). However, a person is not treated as a purchaser unless he has either given consideration for the transaction or is a party to it (*FA 2003, s 44(5)*).

Exceptions

19.6 However, the following are not land transactions:

(*a*) a security interest, ie an interest or right (other than a rent charge – or feu duty in Scotland) held for the purpose of securing the payment of money or the performance of any other obligation;

(*b*) a licence to use or occupy land;

(*c*) a tenancy at will;

(*d*) in England and Wales an advowson, franchise (ie a grant from the Crown such as the right to take tolls or to hold a market or fair) or manor; and

(*e*) such other descriptions of interest or rights as the Treasury may by regulation provide.

(*FA 2003, s 48(2)–(5)*). HMRC also accept that a land pooling arrangement, ie a transfer by a number of landowners into a bare trust, as happened in the CGT case of *Jenkins v Brown (62 TC 226)* – see **11.145**, does not attract SDLT.

19.7 In addition, the following partnership transactions are treated as if they were not land transactions:

(*a*) The transfer of an interest in land by a partner into a partnership or by a prospective partner in return for an interest in the partnership. The exemption applies in any case where an interest in land that was not partnership property (see below) becomes partnership property. It applies both where the transfer is in connection with the formation of a partnership and where the partnership already *exists* (*FA 2003, Sch 15, para 10*).

(*b*) The acquisition of an interest in a partnership (*FA 2003, Sch 15, para 11*).

(*c*) The transfer of an interest in land out of a partnership to a person in consideration of his either ceasing to be a member of the partnership or reducing his interest in the partnership (including any transaction under which an interest in land that was partnership property ceases to be such property). Where a partnership is dissolved or otherwise ceases to exist any partnership property is treated as remaining partnership property until it is distributed (*FA 2003, Sch 15, para 11*).

For the purpose of *(a)* to *(c)*, references to an interest in land include any interest or right that would be a chargeable interest but for being excluded from SDLT; a transfer of an interest in land includes the grant or creation of an interest, the variation of an interest and the surrender or release of an interest; and partnership property means any interest or right held by or on behalf of the partnership, or the members of the partnership, for the purposes of the partnership business (*FA 2003, Sch 15, paras 9, 14*). There are, however, a number of anti-avoidance provisions in relation to partnerships that need to be considered. These are outlined at **19.303** onwards.

19.8 There are also a number of exemptions:

(*a*) A land transaction for which there is no chargeable consideration (*FA 2003, Sch 3, para 1*). An important exception to this is that SDLT applies on a gift to a company, calculated on the market value of the property, and on some gifts by companies (see **19.134**).

(*b*) The grant of a lease of a dwelling if it is for an indefinite term (or is terminable by notice of a month or less), and is granted by a registered social landlord to one or more individuals in accordance with arrangements between the landlord and a housing authority under which the landlord provides temporary rented accommodation for individuals nominated by the authority in pursuance of its statutory housing function. The freehold of the accommodation must not be owned by the landlord though; the exemption applies only if it is leased to the landlord for a term of five years or less. A housing authority is a local council (or a Northern Irish housing authority) (*FA 2003, Sch 3, para 2*).

(*c*) A transaction between the parties to a marriage which is effected in pursuance of either:

  (i) an order of a court made on granting a decree of divorce, nullity or judicial separation;

(ii) an order of a court made in connection with the dissolution or annulment of the marriage, or of the parties' judicial separation, subsequent to the granting of the decree of divorce, etc;

(iii) an order made at any time under *ss 22A, 23A* or *24A* of the *Matrimonial Causes Act 1973* or under *s 8(2)* of the *Family Law (Scotland) Act 1985* by virtue of *s 14(1)* of that Act; or

(iv) an agreement of the parties made in contemplation of, or otherwise in connection with, the dissolution or annulment of their marriage, their judicial separation, or the making of a separation order in respect of them.

(*FA 2003, Sch 3, para 3.*)

(*d*) The acquisition of a property without consideration (other than the assumption of a secured debt) by a person in or towards satisfaction of his entitlement under the will or intestacy of a deceased person. A debt is secured for this purpose only if immediately after the death of the deceased it is secured on the property. If the beneficiary pays any consideration such a secured debt is excluded from the chargeable consideration (*FA 2003, Sch 3, para 3A, Sch 4, para 8A(1)*).

(*e*) A transaction following a person's death that varies a disposition (whether under a will, or intestacy or otherwise) of property of which the deceased was competent to dispose. The transaction must be carried out within two years of the death and there must be no consideration in money or money's worth given for it (other than the variation of another such disposition) (*FA 2003, Sch 3, para 4*). If any consideration is given the making of the variation itself is not treated as consideration (*FA 2003, Sch 4, para 8A(2)*).

(*f*) A land transaction under which the purchaser is any of a Minister of the Crown, the Scottish Minister, a Northern Ireland Department, the Corporate Officer of the House of Lords or of the House of Commons, the Scottish Parliamentary Corporate Body, the Northern Ireland Assembly Commission or the National Assembly for Wales (*FA 2003, s 107*). SDLT applies to the Crown apart from this exemption but the Crown is not liable to prosecution for an offence (*FA 2003, s 107(1), (4)*).

(*g*) A land transaction entered into on (or in consequence, or in connection with) a reorganisation effected by or under a statutory provision where the purchaser and vendor are both public bodies. These are the bodies in (f) above plus local authorities, health authorities, planning authorities, statutory bodies and such other persons as the Treasury may prescribe. The Treasury can by order exempt other types of land transactions under statutory provisions. From 25 May 2007 they have exempted transfers of land to a local education authority under the *Schools Standards and*

Framework Act 1998, and transfers of land from foundation governors under the *Education and Inspections Act 2006* where one of the parties is a public body (*FA 2003, Section 66 (Prescribed Statutory Provisions) Order 2007 (SI 2007 No 1385)*). This exemption for public bodies extends to a company which is 100% owned by such a body and 100% subsidiaries of such companies (*FA 2003, s 66*).

(*h*) Such a description of land transactions as the Treasury may by regulation specify (*FA 2003, Sch 3, para 5*). They have specified by the *SDLT (Open-ended Investment Companies) Regulations 2008 (SI 2008 No 710)* the conversion of an authorised unit trust to an OEIC and the amalgamation of an authorised unit trust with an OEIC. They also granted a temporary exemption by the *SDLT (Exemption of Certain Acquisitions of Residential Property) Regulations 2008 (SI 2008 No 2339)*. This applied to land transactions whose effective date was in the period from 3 September 2008 to 31 December 2009. It exempted from SDLT the acquisition of a major interest in land which consisted entirely of residential property where the chargeable consideration (including that for linked transactions) did not exceed £175,000. It did not, however, apply to the grant of a lease of under 21 years or the assignment of a lease which had less than 21 years to run. It did not apply to property such as a flat above a shop which is partly residential and partly non-residential even though the tax on such a property is calculated by apportioning the consideration between the two parts. The relief had to be claimed in an SDLT return. An obligation to notify such transactions was imposed by the *SDLT (Variation of Part 4 of the FA 2003) Regulations 2008 (SI 2008 No 2338)*. These *Regulations* were repealed by *FA 2009, s 10* which re-enacted the £175,000 threshold and extended it to 31 December 2009.

19.9 There are also specific exemptions for:

(*a*) non-residential property in disadvantaged areas (see **19.172**);

(*b*) residential exchanges by individuals with house-builders (see **19.174**);

(*c*) certain residential sales to relocation companies (see **19.184**);

(*d*) compulsory purchase facilitating development (see **19.186**);

(*e*) certain transactions to comply with planning obligations (see **19.188**);

(*f*) transactions within a group of companies (see **19.189**);

(*g*) company reconstructions (see **19.209**);

(*h*) incorporation of a limited liability partnership (see **19.224**);

(*i*) disposals to charities (see **19.243**);

(*j*) the demutualisation of an insurance company or building society (see **19.250** and **19.194**);

(*k*) the reorganisation of a public body or parliamentary constituency (see **19.250**);

(*l*) acquisitions by certain national heritage bodies (see **19.250**);

(*m*) acquisitions by a registered social landlord (see **19.250**);

(*n*) certain transactions in relation to alternative property finance (see **19.270**);

(*o*) the leaseback element of a sale and leaseback (see **19.285**);

(*p*) prior to 22 March 2006, the initial transfer of assets to a unit trust scheme;

(*q*) new zero-carbon homes (see **19.286**).

Most of these transactions are subject to conditions or limitations and are accordingly considered separately below. It will be seen that there is no exemption for transfers between spouses, although such transfers are normally by way of gift, which is outside the scope of SDLT. The tax needs to be considered on a transfer by sale or for other consideration in money or money's worth though.

Rate of Tax

19.10 The tax for residential and non-residential property is based on different scales. Both are now based on a progressive system (ie one rate applies to the first slice of consideration, a higher rate to the second, a still higher rate for the third, etc).

There are two rate scales, one for residential and one for non-residential property. The meaning of residential property is considered at **19.19**. There are two exceptions. The non-residential rates apply to mixed properties, ie where the acquisition is of a combination of residential and non-residential property, such as the purchase of a shop with a flat above (see **19.13**). The non-residential rates also apply (subject to the possibility of claiming multiple dwellings relief – see **19.291**) to the purchase of six or more dwellings as a single transaction (see **19.24**). A surcharge of three percentage points applies to the residential rates where the purchaser already has an interest in a residential property, and to purchases by companies and by most trusts (see **19.54** and **19.65**). Transactions which attract the surcharge are called Higher Rate transactions. A 15% rate applies to purchases by a company of residential property costing over £500,000 (see **19.26**).

19.11 The rates are as follows:

Residential	%	%
	First property	*Additional properties*
The first £125,000	0	3
The next £125,000	2	5
The next £675,000	5	8
The next £575,000	10	13
The excess over £1.5 million	12	15
Non-residential		
The first £150,000	0	
The next £100,000	2	
The excess over £250,000	5	

(FA 2003, s 55.)

The 3% surcharge did not apply to transactions before 1 April 2016. Its effect is significant. For example the SDLT on a £300,000 property is £5,000 without the surcharge and £14,000 with it, an increase of 163%. Curiously the charge is regressive, ie it has a greater impact on the poor than the rich. The tax on a £925,000 house is £35,250 without the surcharge and £63,000 with it, an increase this time of only 79%. This surcharge is considered at **19.53** onwards.

A new relief for first-time buyers, which exempts from SDLT completely the first £300,000 of value of a residential property costing up to £500,000, will be introduced with effect from 22 November 2017. This relief appears to be fairly restrictive. As the relevant legislation is yet to be approved by parliament the draft legislation is considered at the end of this chapter, but needs to be approached with a degree of caution.

The non-residential rates were calculated differently prior to 17 March 2016 (see **19.11**). As there is no obligation to notify most transactions to HMRC where the consideration is under £40,000 (see **19.352**(a)(ii)) such transactions are effectively exempt from SDLT.

19.12 If the transaction consists entirely of residential property and the transaction is one of a number of linked transactions (see **19.81**), the tax is calculated as follows:

(*a*) calculate the tax for each transaction;

(*b*) add together the tax for all of the linked transactions; and (*c*) apportion that amount between the transactions in the proportion that the consideration for each transaction bears to the aggregate consideration.

(*FA 2003, s 55(1C)*.)

19.13 If the land included in a transaction is not wholly residential property, the non-residential property rate applies to the entire transaction (*FA 2003, s 55(2)* as amended by the *Stamp Duty Land Tax Act 2015, s 1(4)*).

19.14 The rates which applied to residential property up to 3 December 2014 (when the rate scale shown above came into effect), and to non-residential property up to 16 March 2016 were as follows:

Chargeable consideration	*Rate*
Up to £125,000 (£150,000 for non-residential or mixed use property)	0%
£125,001 to £250,000	1%
£250,001 to £500,000	3%
£500,001 to £1 million	4%
Over £1 million (from 6 April 2011) (residential property only)	5%
Over £2 million (from 22 March 2012)(residential property only)	7%
Over £500,000 (£2 million from 22 March 2012 to 19 March 2014) (residential property bought by a company, etc)	15%

These rates were not graduated. The size of the consideration determined the rate applicable to the entire consideration (*FA 2003, s 55(1)(2)* as amended by *FA 2010, s 7(1)*). The first band went up to £60,000 until 16 March 2005 and £120,000 until 22 March 2006. The 5% band did not apply to transactions before 6 April 2011 (or to a later transaction effected and substantially performed before 25 March 2010 or effected before that date and not varied, assigned, sub-sold or effected in consequence of an option or similar right after that date)(*FA 2010, s 7(2)(4)*). The 7% rate applied only to transactions entered into after 22 March 2012, with exclusions for contracts entered into and substantially performed before that date, or entered into before that date and not varied (or assigned or an option exercised), after it (*FA 2012, s 213*). It should be noted that the reduction to £500,000 for the 15% rate applied from 20 March 2014 even though the corresponding ATED reduction does not take place until 1 April 2016 (*FA 2014, s 111*). It did not, however, apply to a transaction effected in pursuance of a contract entered into and substantially performed before 20 March 2014, a contract effected before 20 March which was not varied or assigned after that date (provided that the transaction was not effected in consequence of the exercise of an option or similar right after that date and there was no transaction under which a third party became entitled to call for a conveyance), or a partnership transaction within *FA 2003, Sch 15, para 17(2)* or *17A(4)* (see **19.316** and **19.317**) if the effective date of the land transfer was before 20 March 2014 (*FA 2014, s 111(5)–(7)*). If six or more residential properties were bought together for over £1 millon the 5% rate applied to the acquisition, not the residential property rate (see **19.24**).

19.15 For transactions during the 16 months to 31 December 2009 there was an exemption for residential property where the chargeable consideration (before any other reliefs) did not exceed £175,000. The detailed conditions for this exemption are dealt with at **19.8**(*h*). During the two years to 24 March 2012 there was an exemption for first-time buyers where the consideration did not exceed £250,000. The details are considered at **19.289**.

19.16 If a post-3 December 2014 transaction is effected in pursuance of a contract entered into and substantially performed before 4 December 2014, the purchaser can elect to apply the pre-4 December system and rates. Such an election can also be made if the contract was entered into before 4 December 2014 (but not substantially performed before that date) provided that: there is no variation of the contract or assignment of rights under the contract after that date; the transaction is not effected in consequence of the exercise of any option, right of pre-emption or similar right after that date; and there has not been any assignment, subsale or other transaction relating to all or part of the property after that date as a result of which someone other than the purchaser under the contract becomes entitled to call for a conveyance (*Stamp Duty Land Tax Act 2015, s 2(3)(5)*). Such an election must be included in the land transaction return in respect of the transaction (or is an amendment to the return) and must comply with any requirements as to its form specified by HMRC (*Stamp Duty Land Tax Act 2015, s 2(4)*).

19.17 The chargeable consideration for a transaction is any consideration in money or money's worth given directly or indirectly for the subject matter of the transaction by the purchaser or by a person connected with him (within *ITA 2007, s 993*) (*FA 2003, Sch 4, para 1*). If the transaction in question is one of a number of linked transactions (see **19.81**), the chargeable consideration is the aggregate of the consideration for all of those transactions (*FA 2003, s 55(4)*). Where linked transactions take place at different times SDLT is of course paid on each as it occurs, but the second such transaction may trigger additional tax in relation to the first. It is not clear what the effective date is for the purpose of such additional tax. It is probably the effective date of the latest of the linked transactions. Any VAT chargeable in respect of the transaction forms part of the consideration (but not any VAT payable as a result of the exercise of the option to tax if the election is made after the 'effective date' of the transaction (see **19.88**) (*FA 2003, Sch 4, para 2*). HMRC consider that the calculation should reflect the VAT position known at the effective date of the transaction (HMRC Notice, 11 Oct 2010). Accordingly where the effective date is on or after 27 July 2010 (when *F (No 2) A 2010* came into force) the VAT needed to be calculated at 17.5% on rents payable up to 4 January 2011 and at 20% on later rents (which meant that if rent was payable a quarter in advance, the whole of the payment due on 25 December used the 17.5% rate even though most of it related to a period after 4 January 2011).

19.18 The consideration must be determined without any discount for postponement of the right to receive any part of it (*FA 2003, Sch 4, para 3*). If a single consideration is attributable to two or more land transactions (or partly in relation to a land transaction and partly to something else), it must be apportioned on a just and reasonable basis. If there is in substance one bargain, such an apportionment needs to be made even if separate consideration is attributed to different elements of the bargain and even if the bargain is given effect to by separate transactions in respect of different elements (*FA 2003, Sch 4, para 4*). There is a particular vulnerability where land and chattels are bought at the same time. *Gill Orsman v HMRC (TC 1921)* bought a house for £250,000 together with chattels for a further £8,000. She expected to pay 1% SDLT. HMRC looked at the list of chattels and noticed that these included two items that they considered fixtures. They attributed £800 of the £8,000 to them and contended that, as fixtures were part of the building, the building had been bought for £250,800, so the SDLT was at the 2%. The Tribunal agreed!

Meaning of Residential Property

19.19 Reference to residential property means:

(*a*) a building, or part of a building, that is used, or suitable for use, as a dwelling (or which is in the process of being constructed or adapted for such use);

(*b*) land that is, or forms part of, the garden or grounds of a building within (a) (including any building or structure on such land); or

(*c*) an interest in, or right over, land that subsists for the benefit of a building within (a) or land within (b).

(*FA 2003, s 116(1), (6)*.)

19.20 For this purpose a building used for any of the following purposes is used as a dwelling:

(*a*) residential accommodation for school pupils;

(*b*) residential accommodation for students (other than a hall of residence for students in further or higher education);

(*c*) residential accommodation for members of the armed forces; or

(*d*) an institution that is the sole or main residence of at least 90% of its residents (provided that it does not fall within any of paragraphs **19.21**(*a*)–(*f*) below).

(*FA 2003, s 116(2)*.)

19.21 A building used for any of the following purposes is not used as a dwelling though:

(*a*) a home or other institution providing residential accommodation for children;

(*b*) a hall of residence for students in further or higher education;

(*c*) a home or other institution providing residential accommodation with personal care for persons in need of such care by reason of old age, disablement, past or present dependence on alcohol or drugs or past or present mental disorder;

(*d*) a hospital or hospice;

(*e*) a prison or similar establishment; or

(*f*) a hotel, inn or similar establishment.

(*FA 2003, s 116(3)*.)

19.22 Where a building is used for one of these purposes no account is to be taken for the purpose of *s 116(1)(a)* (see **19.19**(*a*)) of its suitability for any other use (*FA 2003, s 116(4)*).

19.23 If a building, or part of a building, that is not in use is suitable for at least one use within **19.20** and one within **19.21** and there is one use for which it is most suitable (or several such uses which all fall within the same paragraph) no account is to be taken of the fact that it is also suitable for a different use. If there is no most suitable use, the building (or part) is treated as suitable for use as a dwelling (*FA 2003, s 116(5), (6)*).

19.24 Where six or more separate dwellings are the subject of a single transaction involving the transfer of a major interest in (or the grant of a lease over) them, eg a sale of a block of flats, those dwellings must be treated as not being residential property (*FA 2003, s 116(7)*).

19.25 The Treasury have power by regulation to amend *s 116(2)* and *(3)* to change or clarify what falls within either, or to amend or repeal *s 116(7)* (*FA 2003, s 116(8)*).

Expensive Residential Property bought by a Company, etc

19.26 The 15% rate applies where the transaction is a 'high-value residential transaction' and the purchaser is either a company, a partnership one or more of whose members is a company, or a collective investment scheme (*FA 2003, Sch 4A, para 3(1)–(3)* inserted by *FA 2012, Sch 35, para 4*). For this purpose a company does not include a company which acts in a capacity as trustee of a settlement (*FA 2003, Sch 4A, para 3(4)*). In the case of joint purchases, the 15% rate applies if any of them are companies (*FA 2003, Sch 4A, para 3(5)*). Where a transfer of an interest in a partnership is a chargeable transaction by virtue of *FA 2003, Sch 15, para 17(2)* (see **19.316**) or *para 17A(4)* (see **19.317**) the 15% rate applies if the 'purchasers' (as defined in *para 17(3)* or *17A(5)*) include a company (*FA 2003, Sch 4A, para 3(6)(7)*). Where a person acquires an interest, or is granted a lease, as bare trustee, the act of the trustee is treated as the act of the principals, so if the principal or one of them is a company, the 15% rate applies. The exceptions from the basic rule in *FA 2003, Sch 15, para 3* are disapplied for this purpose (*FA 2003, Sch 4A, para 3(8)*). The Treasury have power by statutory instrument to limit (but not increase) the circumstances in which the 15% rate applies (*FA 2003, Sch 4A, para 3(10)*). If the whole or part of the chargeable consideration for a transaction is rent, *para 3* is subject to *FA 2003, Sch 5* (amount of tax chargeable: rent) (*FA 2003, Sch 4A, para 3(a)*). This appears to mean that the consideration is calculated in accordance with *Sch 5* and the 15% rate applied to the amount so calculated.

19.27 A high value residential transaction is a transaction (other than one to which *FA 2003, s 74* (collective enfranchisement) or *s 75* (crafting community right to buy) applies) whose subject matter is a higher threshold interest, together with any appurtenant rights (*FA 2003, Sch 4A, para 2(5)(9)*). A higher threshold interest is an interest in a single dwelling (ie so much of the subject matter of a chargeable transaction as consists of a chargeable interest in or over a single dwelling, together with appurtenant rights) to which chargeable consideration of more than £500,000 (£2 million prior to 20 March 2014) is attributable (*FA 2003, Sch 4A, para 1*). If the main subject matter of a transaction consists entirely of higher threshold interests, the entire transaction is a high-value residential transaction. If the main subject matter includes other interests, it is treated as two separate chargeable transactions, one consisting of all of the higher threshold interests together with any appurtenant rights, and the other consisting of the remaining interests (*FA 2003, Sch 4A, para 2(2)(3)*). This split into two transactions applies for the purposes of *FA 2003, Sch 4A, paras 3* and *5*, *s 55* (amount of tax chargeable: general), *Sch 5* (amount of tax chargeable: rent), *Sch 6B* (transfers involving multiple dwellings) and any other SDLT provision so far as it is necessary because of any of these provisions (*FA 2003, Sch 4A, para 2(6)*). If the transaction is notifiable both of the deemed separate transactions are notifiable and separate SDLT returns need to be submitted for each (*FA 2003, Sch 4A, para 2(7)(8)*).

Example 19.1

Megacorp plc buys an investment property for £100 million. The property building consists of retail premises on the ground floor, offices on the next six floors and 12 floors of flats. The top floor consists of two penthouse flats each worth £5 million. None of the other flats has a value of £2 million or more.

The purchase must be treated as two separate transactions, namely –

1. The purchase of two penthouse apartments for £10 million, and
2. The purchase of the remainder of the building for £90 million.

The tax payable is –

£10 million at 15%	£1,500,000
£90 million at 4%	3,600,000
	£5,100,000

19.28 A dwelling (for the purpose of *Sch 4A* only) is a building or part of a building which is used as, or suitable for use as, a single dwelling, or which is in the process of being constructed or adapted for such use (*FA 2003, Sch 4A, para 7(2)*). Land that is, or is to be, occupied or enjoyed with a dwelling as its garden or grounds (including any building or structure on such land) is part of that dwelling. So is any other land that subsists, or is to subsist, for the benefit of the dwelling (*FA 2003, Sch 4A, para 7(3)(4)*). The subject matter of a transaction must be taken to include an interest in a dwelling if substantial performance of a contract constitutes the effective date of the transaction by virtue of a relevant deeming provision, the main subject matter of the transaction consists of (or includes) an interest in a building or part of a building that is to be constructed or adapted under the contract for use as a single dwelling, and construction or adaptation of the building, or part of the building, has not begun by the time the contract is substantially performed. For this purpose 'contract', 'relevant deeming provision' and 'substantially performed' have the same meaning as in *FA 2003, Sch 6B, para 7(5)* – see **19.294** (*FA 2003, Sch 4A, para 7(5)(6)*). A building or part of a building used for a purpose specified in *FA 2003, s 116(2)(3)* (institutional residences) is not used as a dwelling for the purpose of *Sch 4A* and no account is to be taken of the suitability of such a building for a different use (*FA 2003, Sch 4A, para 7(7)(8)*). The Treasury have power by statutory instrument to amend *para 7* to specify other cases in which a building is to be treated as a dwelling (*FA 2003, Sch 4A, para 8*).

19.29 If the subject matter of a chargeable transaction (other than one to which *s 74* (collective enfranchisement) or *s 75* (crafting community right to buy) applies) includes a chargeable interest in or over a dwelling, one or more land transactions (the subject matter of each of which includes a chargeable interest in or over the dwelling) are linked to that chargeable transaction, and the total consideration attributable to those interests (and to any appurtenant rights but ignoring any rent) exceeds £500,000 (£2 million prior to 20 March 2014), each of those chargeable interests must be treated as a higher threshold interest (*FA 2003, Sch 4A para 4(1)(2)*). If the purchaser is a company (or other person within *FA 2003, Sch 4A, para 3(a)*, the 15% rate applies to each of the deemed transactions (*FA 2003, Sch 4A, para 4(3)*). This deals with the position where interests in the same dwelling are acquired by means of different transactions. The transactions are linked, no matter how far apart in time they are, so as to prevent the avoidance of the 15% rate by acquiring a property in slices, eg a lease, a head-lease and a freehold reversion each worth under £2 million, so as to effectively have acquired at the end of the day a freehold property worth over £2 million. Apart from this special rule, a transaction to which the 15% rate applies is not linked to any other transaction for the purpose of *FA 2003, s 55(4)* (see **19.17**) (*FA 2003, Sch 4A, para 3(1)(b)*).

Exceptions

19.30 The 15% rate does not apply, to the extent that the subject matter of the transaction consists of a higher threshold interest (one with a value exceeding £2 million) that is acquired exclusively for one or more of the following:

(*a*) exploitation as a source of rents or other receipts (other than excluded rent as defined in *FA 2013, s 133* – see **20.36**) in the course of a qualifying property rental business (as defined in *FA 2013, s 133*);

(*b*) from 1 April 2016, use as business premises for the purposes of a qualifying property rental business (other than one which gives rise to income consisting wholly or mainly of excluded rents);

(*c*) from 1 April 2016, use for the purposes of a relievable trade, ie one that is run on a commercial basis and with a view to profit;

(*d*) development or redevelopment and resale in the course of a property development trade, or development or redevelopment and exploitation falling within (*a*) or use falling within (b) or (c) (prior to 1 April 2016 the exclusion was of development or redevelopment and resale in the course of a property development trade (a trade that consists of or includes buying and developing or redeveloping for resale residential or non-residential property, and which is run on a commercial basis and with a view to profit));

(*e*) resale in the course of a property development business but only if the chargeable transaction is part of a qualifying exchange (as defined in *FA 2013, s 139(4)* – see **20.43**);

(*f*) resale (as stock of the business) in the course of a property trading business (one that consists of or includes activities in the nature of a trade of buying and selling dwellings and is run on a commercial basis and with a view to profit).

(*FA 2003, Sch 4A, para 5(1)(3)* as substituted by *FA 2013, Sch 40, para 2* and amended by *FA 2016, s 129(2)*). HMRC have indicated that they interpret 'developing' for this purpose as simply doing work on the building. Buying, redecorating and reselling should be sufficient. A token amount of work, such as painting one door, will probably not be accepted as development. There is, however, a potential problem with joint venture companies and consortium companies. Even if both (or all) of the shareholders are qualifying property development companies, as the consortium company is not a subsidiary of any of them it cannot piggyback onto its shareholders' qualifying period.

19.31 These exemptions do not apply if it is intended that a non-qualifying individual will be permitted to occupy a dwelling on the land (*FA 2003, Sch 4A, para 5(2)* as amended by *FA 2016, s 129(2)*). A non-qualifying individual is:

(*a*) the purchaser (other than a purchaser entering into the transaction as a member of a partnership);

(*b*) a purchaser who enters into the transaction as a member of a partnership and has a major share in the partnership (an entitlement to 50% or more in the income profits of the partnership or the partnership assets);

(*c*) an individual who is connected with the purchaser;

(*d*) a relevant settlor (the settlor of a settlement where a person, in the capacity of trustee, is connected with the purchaser (or one of the purchasers));

(*e*) the spouse or civil partner of a connected person of the settlor;

(*f*) a relative (brother, sister, ancestor or lineal descendant) of a connected person, or of a relevant settlor, or the spouse or civil partner of such a person;

(*g*) a relative of the spouse or civil partner of a connected person or a relevant settlor;

(*h*) the spouse or civil partner of a person within (*g*); and

(*i*) an individual who is a major participant in a relevant collective investment scheme, or is connected with such a major participant.

(*FA 2003, Sch 4A, para 5A(1)(2)(6)(7)* inserted by *FA 2013, Sch 40, para 2*.)

Reference above to the purchaser in relation to a chargeable transaction means any of the purchasers if there are more than one (*FA 2003, Sch 4A, para 5A(9)*). The *CTA 2010, s 1122* definition of connected persons applies (see Appendix 1) but ignoring *s 1122(7)* or *(8)* (*ITA 2007, s 993(4)*) and with the extension in *FA 2013, s 172(3)–(7)* (which defines connected person in the context of a collective investment scheme – see **20.118**) (*FA 2003, Sch 4A, para 5A(10)*). For the purpose of (*d*), if there would otherwise be no trustee any person in whom the property comprised in the settlement is for the time being vested or to whom the management of the property is for the time being vested must be treated as a trustee (*FA 2003, Sch 4A, para 5A(8)*). For the purpose of (*i*) an individual who participates in a collective investment scheme is a major participant if he is entitled to at least 50% of all of the profits or income arising from the acquisition, holding, management or disposal of the property subject to the scheme (or of any profits or income arising from the scheme that may be distributed to participants) or he would be entitled to at least 50% of the assets of the scheme that would then be available for distribution among the participants in the event of a winding up (*FA 2003, Sch 4A, para 5A(3)–(5)*).

19.32 The 15% rate also does not apply to a chargeable transaction so far as its subject matter consists of a higher threshold interest which is acquired with the intention that it will be exploited as a source of income in the course of a trade which is carried on on a commercial basis and with a view to profit and which involves (in its normal course) offering the public the opportunity to make use of (or stay in, or otherwise enjoy) the dwelling as customers of the trade on at least 28 days in any calendar year (and reasonable commercial plans have been formulated to carry out that intention without delay – except so far as delay may be justified by commercial considerations, or cannot be avoided) (*FA 2003, Sch 4A, para 5B(1)–(3)*). For this purpose, persons are able to make use of, stay in or otherwise enjoy a dwelling only if the areas they have the opportunity to use include a significant part of the interior of the dwelling. The size (relative to the size of the whole dwelling), nature and function of the area or areas in a dwelling must be taken into account in determining whether they form a significant part of the interior of the dwelling (*FA 2003, Sch 4A, para 5B(4)(5)*).

19.33 The 15% rate also does not apply to a chargeable transaction so far as its subject matter consists of a higher threshold interest that is acquired by a financial institution (see **19.135**) carrying on a business that involves the lending of money, provided that the interest is acquired in the course of that business for the purpose of resale in the course of the business and in connection with those lending activities (*FA 2003, Sch 4A, para 5C*). This exemption does not apply to a person who is a financial institution only because it is a regulated home purchaser plan provider (*FA 2003, Sch 4A, para 9* as amended by *FA 2015, s 68(3)*).

19.34 Nor does it apply to a chargeable transaction after 31 March 2016 if (and so far as) the purchaser is an authorised plan provider (one authorised under *FSMA 2000* as a provider of regulated home reversion plans) who acquires the subject-matter of the chargeable transaction under a regulated home reversion plan which the purchaser enters into as plan provider. A regulated home reversion plan for this purpose is an arrangement which is a regulated home reversion plan for the purposes of the *Financial Services and Markets (Regulated Activities) Order 2001 (SI 2001 No 544), Ch 15A, Pt 2* (*FA 2003, Sch 4A, para 5CA* inserted by *FA 2016, s 130(2)*).

19.35 The 15% rate also does not apply where the purchaser (or another member of its group – as defined for group relief) carries on (or is to carry on) a relievable business, (a trade or property rental business that is carried on on a commercial basis and with a view to profit) and the interest is acquired for the purpose of making the dwelling available to one or more qualifying employees or qualifying partners for use as living accommodation for purposes that are solely or mainly purposes of the relievable business (*FA 2003, Sch 4A, para 5D(1)(2)(4)(6)* as amended by *FA 2016, s 131(2)*). The individual or individuals do not need to be identified at the time of purchase (*FA 2003, Sch 4A, para 5D(3)*). Making a dwelling available to a qualifying employee or partner includes making it available to persons who are to share it with him as his family (*FA 2003, Sch 4A, para 5D(5)*). A qualifying employee is an individual employed for the purpose of the relievable business. A qualifying partner is an individual who is a member of the partnership that carries on the relievable business (*FA 2003, Sch 4A, para 5E(1)(2)* as amended by *FA 2016, s 131(6)*). However, the exemption does not apply if the individual or class of individuals to whom it is proposed to make the dwelling available includes (or is likely to include) an employee or a partner who is (or at the relevant time will be) entitled to 10% or more of the income profits of the partnership, of a company that is beneficially entitled to the interest in the dwelling, or of the interest in the property itself (*FA 2003, Sch 4A, para 5E(3)(4)*). Nor does it apply if the employee or class of employee includes a person whose duties include the provision of domestic services in connection with the actual (or intended) occupation of the dwelling (or of a linked dwelling) by an individual who is connected with a person who is (or is to be) beneficially entitled to the interest in the dwelling (*FA 2003, Sch 4A, para 5E(5)(6)*). For this purpose dwellings are linked if they are linked for the purpose of *FA 2013, s 116(2)* (see **20.18**) or *s 117(1)* (see **20.19**) (*FA 2003, Sch 4A, para 5E(7)*). In determining whether an individual is beneficially entitled to an interest in the dwelling, beneficial joint tenants must be treated as tenants in common (*FA 2003, Sch 4A, para 5E(8)*). *FA 2013, s 147* (meaning of 10% or greater share in a company – see **20.49**) also applies (*FA 2003, Sch 4A, para 5E(9)*). Prior to 1 April 2016, the relief did not extend to property investment.

19.36 From 1 April 2016, the 15% rate does not apply to the acquisition of a flat which is one of at least three flats contained in the same premises and is acquired by a tenant's management company for the purpose of making the flat available for use as caretaker accommodation, ie it makes it available to an individual for use as living accommodation in connection with the individual's employment as caretaker of the premises. Premises for this purpose can constitute the whole or part of a building. A company is a tenants' management company if the tenants of two or more other flats contained in the premises are members of the company and the company owns (or it is intended that it will acquire) the freehold of the premises. However, a company that carries on a relievable business (see **19.35**) is not a tenants' management company (*FA 2003, Sch 4A, para 5EA* inserted by *FA 2016, s 131(4)*). It should be noted that the company needs to own the freehold; a 999-year lease would not be sufficient.

19.37 The 15% rate also does not apply to a chargeable interest in a dwelling that is (or is to be) a farmhouse (ie that forms part of land that is to be occupied (or continue to be occupied) for the purpose of a qualifying trade of farming (one carried on on a commercial basis and with a view to profit)) if it (or part of it) is to be occupied for the purpose of that trade by a qualifying farm worker (*FA 2003, Sch 4A, para 5F(1)–(3)(5)(6)*). A qualifying farm worker is an individual who occupies the dwelling for the purposes of the farming trade and has a substantial involvement in either the day-to-day work of the trade or the direction and control of the conduct of the trade (*FA 2003, Sch 4A, para 5F(4)*). The exclusion applies only if reasonable commercial plans have been formulated under which the occupation by the farm worker is either to continue from the effective date of the chargeable transaction or to begin without delay (except so far as delay may be justified by commercial consideration or cannot be avoided) and occupation by a qualifying farm worker is then expected to continue as part of the normal way in which the trade is carried on (*FA 2003, Sch 4A, para 5F(3)*). The definition of farming in *CTA 2010, s 1125* (see **23.10**) applies, but also includes market gardening (as defined in *CTA 2010, s 1125(5)*) (*FA 2003, Sch 4A, para 5F(7)*).

19.38 Although these exclusions broadly follow the ATED reliefs (see **20.35**) they are not identical. Accordingly it should not be assumed that because a relief applies to one of these taxes, it will automatically apply to the other.

19.39 Where the effective date of the transaction was prior to 17 July 2013, the exemption was far more limited as it applied only to the extent that the company acquired the property in the course of a bona-fide property development business and for the sole purpose of developing and reselling the land and the company had carried on that business for at least two years before the effective date of the transaction (*FA 2003, Sch 4A, para 5(1)* as originally enacted). For this purpose a property development business was a business that consisted of, or included, buying, and redeveloping for resale, residential property (*FA 2003, Sch 4A, para 5(5)* as originally enacted). A property development business was treated as having been carried on by a company at any time when it was carried on by a member of the same group of companies (as defined for group relief purposes) (*FA 2003, Sch 4A, para 5(6)(8)*). This enabled a newly formed single purpose company to qualify for the exemption if its parent company or a fellow subsidiary had carried on a property development business for the requisite two-year period. If the purchaser is a partnership, the partnership acquired the property in the course of a bona-fide property development business and for the sole purpose of developing and reselling the land, and the partnership had carried on the business for at least two years before the effective date of the transaction, the transaction was exempted from the 15% rate even if one of the partners was a company (*FA 2003, Sch 4A, para 5(2)* as originally enacted). Similarly the 'purchasers' were treated as not including a company in relation to a transfer of an interest in such a partnership that is a chargeable transfer by virtue of *FA 2003, Sch 15, para 17(2)*, or an event that was a chargeable transaction by virtue of *FA 2003, Sch 5, para 17A(4)*, provided that the partnership wa still carrying on the property development business at the effective date of the partnership transfer and the acquisition effected by the land transfer referred to in *para 17(1)(a)* or *17A(1)(a)* as the case may be was made in the course of the property development business and for the sole purpose of developing and reselling the land (*FA 2004, Sch 4A, para 5(3)(4)* as originally enacted).

19.40 The above reliefs under *para 5* (see **19.31**) are withdrawn if throughout the three years from the effective date of the chargeable transaction (the control period) either:

(*a*) the interest (if still held by the purchaser) ceases to be held exclusively for one or more of the purposes within *para 5*;

(*b*) any chargeable interest derived from the higher threshold interest that may be held by the purchaser ceases to be held exclusively for one or more of those purposes; and

(*c*) if the interest (or a chargeable interest derived from it) is held by the purchaser, a non-qualifying individual (as defined in *para 5A* – see **19.31**) is permitted to occupy a dwelling on the land,

(*FA 2003, Sch 4A, para 5G(1)–(3)(7)* as amended by *FA 2016, s 129(3)*.)

A breach of (*a*) or (*b*) can be ignored in relation to times when it is not reasonable to expect the purposes for which the interest was acquired to be carried out because of a change of circumstances that is unforeseen and beyond the purchaser's control (*FA 2003, Sch 4A, para 5G(4)*). If the interest was acquired for a purpose within *para 5* but at any time in the control period the activity in question has not yet begun or has ceased, it can be regarded as held for the purpose in question only if reasonable steps are being taken to ensure that purpose is carried out (*FA 2003, Sch 4A, para 5G(5)(6)*).

19.41 Similarly the relief under *para 5B* (trades involving making a dwelling open to the public – see **19.32**) will be withdrawn if at any time within the three-year control period the interest (if still held by the purchaser) or any chargeable interest derived from it that is held by the purchaser is not being exploited as a source of income in the course of a qualifying trade (*FA 2003, Sch 4A, para 5H(1)–(3)*). Again a breach can be ignored where it is not reasonable to expect the interest to be so exploited because of a change of circumstances that is unforeseen and beyond the purchaser's control, and, if at a time in the control period the exploitation has not yet begun or has ceased, the exploitation is treated as occurring if reasonable steps are being taken to ensure that the interest in question begins to be so exploited or that such exploitation is resumed (*FA 2003, Sch 4A, para 5H(4)–(6)*).

19.42 The relief under *para 5C* (financial institutions acquiring dwellings in the course of lending – see **19.33**) is withdrawn if during the three-year control period the purchaser ceases to be a financial institution carrying on a business that involves the lending of money or the interest ceases to be held for the purpose of resale in the course of the business and at that time the purchaser still holds either the interest or a chargeable interest that is derived from it (*FA 2003, Sch 4A, para 5I(1)–(4)*). Such a cessation is again ignored in relation to times when it is not reasonable to expect those conditions to be met because of a change of circumstances that is unforeseen and beyond the purchaser's control (*FA 2003, Sch 4A, para 5I(5)*).

19.43 The relief under *para 5CA* (regulated home reversion plans – see **19.33**) is withdrawn if at any time during the three-year control period the purchaser held the higher threshold interest otherwise than for the purposes of the regulated home reversion plan (*FA 2003, Sch 4A, para 5IA(1)(2)*). This clawback does not apply if after ceasing to hold the interest for such purpose the purchaser sells it without delay (except insofar as delay is justified by commercial considerations or cannot be avoided), and at no time when the interest was held other than as plan provider is the dwelling (or any part of it) occupied by a non-qualifying individual (*FA 2003, Sch 4A, para 5IA* inserted by *FA 2016, s 130(3)*).

19.44 The relief under *para 5D* (dwellings for occupation by certain employees, etc – see **19.34**) is withdrawn if during the three-year control period and at a time when the purchaser still holds the interest or a chargeable interest that is derived from it, either the purchaser (or all members of its group) ceases to carry on the relievable business on a commercial basis with a view to profit, the dwelling ceases to be made available solely to qualifying employees or partners, or the dwelling is made so available other than solely or mainly for purposes of the trade concerned (*FA 2003, Sch 4A, para 5J(1)–(4)* as amended by *FA 2016, s 131(7)*). The clawback does not apply to times when it is not reasonable to expect these requirements to be met because of a change of circumstances that is unforeseen and beyond the purchaser's control (*FA 2003, Sch 4A, para 5J(5)*). The requirements (other than that for the trade to be carried on on a commercial basis) are treated as met at a time when the dwelling has not begun, or has ceased, to be made available if reasonable steps are being taken to ensure that the dwelling will begin to be (or return to being) made available (*FA 2003, Sch 4A, para 5J(5)*).

19.45 The relief under *para 5EA* (see **19.36**) is withdrawn if at any time during the three-year control period the purchaser comes to hold the interest otherwise than for the purpose of making the flat available for use as caretaker accommodation (*FA 2003, Sch 4A, para 5JA* inserted by *FA 2016, s 131(5)*).

19.46 The relief under *para 5F* (farmhouses – see **19.37**) will be withdrawn if during the three-year control period and at a time when the purchaser continues to hold the interest or a chargeable interest derived from it, the land is occupied other than for the purposes of a qualifying trade of farming or the dwelling ceases to be occupied for the purposes of that trade by a qualifying farm worker (*FA 2003, Sch 4A, para 5K(1)–(4)*). The clawback does not apply in relation to times when it is not reasonable to expect these requirements to be met because of a change of circumstances that is unforeseen and beyond the purchaser's control (*FA 2003, Sch 4A, para 5K(5)*). The requirements are treated as being met at a time in the control period when they have not yet begun to be met (or have ceased to be met) if reasonable steps are being taken to ensure that the requirements will be met (or met again) (*FA 2003, Sch 4A, para 5K(6)(7)*).

Other Exemptions

19.47 *FA 2003, Sch 4A, para 2(3)–(8)* do not apply if the subject matter of the transaction includes a higher threshold interest and the result of applying *paras 2(3)* and *(4)* (apportionment of the consideration) would be to attribute £2 million or less of the consideration to the higher threshold interest (*FA 2003, Sch 4A, para 6(3)*). For this purpose the subject matter (and the main subject matter) of a transfer of an interest in a partnership that is a chargeable transfer under *FA 2003, Sch 15, para 14(2)* is the relevant partnership property as defined in *para 14(5)* for a Type A transfer or as defined in *para 14(5A)* for a Type B transfer (*FA 2003, Sch 4A, para 6(4)*). The subject matter of a transfer of an interest in a partnership that is a chargeable transfer under *FA 2003, Sch 15, para 17* is the subject matter of the land transfer referred to in *para 15(1)(a)* and of one that is treated as occurring under *FA 2003, Sch 15, para 17A* is that referred to in *para 17A(1)(a)* (*FA 2003, Sch 4A, para 6(5)(6)*).

19.48 For transactions from 17 July 2013 where any of *FA 2003, ss 71A, 72* or *73* (alternative finance arrangements) (see **19.270**) applies and the major interest in land purchased under the first transaction (as defined in the relevant section), consists of or includes a higher threshold interest, the condition in *FA 2003, Sch 4A, para 3(3)* (that the purchaser is a company, a partnership one of the partners of which is a company or is a collective investment scheme – see **19.26**) is to be treated as being met with respect to the first transaction only if it is met with respect to the second transaction (as defined in the relevant provision (*FA 2003, Sch 4A, para 6A(1)–(3)(6)*). If the second transaction would qualify for relief under any of *paras 5* (see **19.30**), *5B* (see **19.32**) *5D* (see **19.35**) or *5F* (see **19.37**) (disregarding the exemptions in *FA 2003, ss 71A(3), 72(3)* and *73(3)* and assuming that the subject matter of the second transaction is a higher threshold interest) the first transaction is regarded as qualifying for relief under the same provision, but if the second transaction does not qualify for such relief, the first cannot do so either (*FA 2003, Sch 4A, para 6A(4)(5)*).

19.49 Similarly where *FA 2003, s 72A* applies (land in Scotland sold to financial institution and person in common – see **19.277**) and the major interest in land purchased under the first transaction (as defined in that provision) consists of, or includes, a higher threshold interest, in determining whether the first transaction meets the conditions in *FA 2003, Sch 4A, para 3* (see **19.26**) it must be assumed that the financial institution is not one of the persons acquiring the interest in land under that transaction (*FA 2003, Sch 4A, para 6B(1)(2)*). *FA 2003, Sch 4A, paras 5–5F* have effect in relation to the first transaction as they would have done if the financial institution were not a purchaser under that transaction (*FA 2003, Sch 4A, para 6B(3)*). For the purposes of *paras 6A–6H*, a financial institution includes a regulated home purchase plan provider from 26 March 2015 (*FA 2007, Sch 4A, para 9* as amended by *FA 2015, s 68(3)*).

19.50 Where *paras 6A* or *6B* (the modifying paragraph) apply and the first transaction is treated under *para 2(3)* (see **19.27**) as two separate transactions (because the whole subject matter is not a higher threshold interest), reference in the modifying paragraph to the first transaction includes those separate transactions (*FA 2003, Sch 4A, para 6C(1)*). If the subject matter of the second transaction includes a chargeable interest other than a higher threshold interest, that fact is ignored in determining whether the transaction meets the conditions of *FA 2003, Sch 4A, para 3(3)* and whether it would qualify for relief under any of *paras 5, 5B, 5D* and *5F* (*FA 2003, Sch 4A, para 6C(2)*).

19.51 If relief from the 15% rate is claimed under *para 5* (see **19.30**) by virtue of *paras 6A* or *6B*, it will be withdrawn if either at any time within three years (the control period) a relevant interest held by the relevant person (the person other than the financial institution who entered into the arrangements) ceases to be held by him exclusively for one or more of the purposes within *para 5*, or if at a time when a relevant interest is held by a relevant person a non-qualifying individual (see **19.31**) is permitted to occupy a dwelling on the land (*FA 2003, Sch 4A, para 6D(1)–(3)(7)* as amended by *FA 2016, s 129(4)*). Where the relief is allowed by virtue of *para 6A* (see **19.39**), a relevant interest is the interest acquired under the second transaction, any interest transferred to the relevant person as a result of the exercise of the right referred to in *FA 2003, ss 71A* (see **19.271**), *72* (see **19.276**) or *73* (see **19.275**), and any chargeable interest derived from any of them (*FA 2003, Sch 4A, para 6D(5)*). Where the relief is allowed by virtue of *para 6B* (see **19.33**) it is the interest purchased under the first transaction, any interest transferred to the relevant person as a result of the exercise of the right in *FA 2003, s 72A* (see **19.277**) and any chargeable interest derived from either of them (*FA 2003, Sch 4A, para 6D(6)*). The clawback is the same whether the relevant interest is held jointly or in common (*FA 2003, Sch 4A, para 6D(4)*). A breach of the requirement to hold the interest solely for the qualifying purpose at a time when it is not reasonable to expect the interest to be held for the purpose for which the relevant person acquired his initial interest (the interest acquired under the second transaction where *ss 71A, 72* or *73* apply or under the first transaction where *s 72A* applies) because of a change of circumstances that is unforeseen and beyond the relevant person's control is ignored (*FA 2003, Sch 4A, para 6E(1)(4)*). If at some time in the control period the qualifying activity has not begun (or has ceased) the relevant interest is treated as being held for the purpose in question if reasonable steps are then being taken to ensure that such purpose is carried out (*FA 2003, Sch 4A, para 6E(2)(3)*).

19.52 Where the relief is under *para 5B* (see **19.32**) it is withdrawn (subject to the above caveats) if the dwelling ceases to be exploited as a source of income in the qualifying trade during the control period (*FA 2003, Sch 4A, para 6F*). If the relief is under *para 5D* (see **19.35**) it is withdrawn (subject to the above caveats) if during the control period, the relevant person (or a member of its group) ceases to carry on the relievable business, ceases to make the dwelling available to qualifying employees or partners, or makes it available for purposes that are not solely or mainly purposes of the relievable business (*FA 2003, Sch 4A, para 6G* as amended by *FA 2016, s 131(8)*). If the relief is under *para 5H* (see **19.41**) it is withdrawn if, during the control period, the land is not occupied for the purposes of the qualifying trade of farming or the dwelling ceases to be occupied for the purposes of the trade by a qualifying farm worker. The above caveats again apply (*FA 2003, Sch 4A, para 6H*).

Higher Rate Transactions (the 3% Surcharge)

19.53 The 3% surcharge applies to the purchase of a major interest (see **19.57**) in a single dwelling (see **19.72**) by an individual if:

(*a*) the chargeable consideration for the transaction is £40,000 or more;

(*b*) on the effective date of the transaction (see **19.88**) that dwelling is not subject to a lease upon which the interest being purchased is reversionary – or if it is, the lease has an unexpired term of 21 years or less (ie the surcharge does not apply to the purchase of a reversion unless the lease will expire within the next 21 years);

(*c*) at the end of the day that is the effective date of the transaction the purchaser has a major interest in a dwelling other than the one being purchased, that interest has a market value of at least £40,000 and it is not a reversionary interest where the lease has 21 years or less unexpired); and

(*d*) the purchased dwelling is not a replacement for the purchaser's only or main residence (see **19.59**).

(*FA 2003, Sch 4ZA, para 3* inserted by *FA 2016, s 128.*)

HMRC say that the second interest held at the end of the day must be an interest in another dwelling. The purchase of a further interest in a dwelling will not trigger the surcharge if that is the owner's only dwelling (HMRC Guidance Note, November 2016). The Note also says that an individual holding a mixed residential and non-residential property will meet condition (*c*) if the property contains a dwelling (eg a self-contained flat above a shop or public house with access). There is probably an inference that if there is no separate access, ie it can only be accessed through the shop or pub, it is not a dwelling. The Note also points out that the extension of a lease normally takes the form of a surrender of the existing lease and payment of a sum in return for the grant of a fresh lease. The value of the old lease is not regarded for SDLT as consideration for the new one, but where (as will normally be the case) the new lease has a term of more than seven years and the amount paid is at least £40,000, the surcharge will apply if conditions (*c*) and (*d*) are met in respect of the purchase. HMRC say that the payment is a reservation fee, or the acquisition of an option to purchase a property that has not yet been built would not normally constitute a contract and so could not benefit from the transitional rules (HMRC Guidance Note, November 2016). A number of fairly minor changes are proposed to the surcharge with effect from 22 November 2017. The proposals are set out at **19.448**. As these have not yet been considered by parliament they need to be approached with a degree of caution.

19.54 The surcharge also applies to a purchase of a major interest in a single dwelling by anyone other than an individual if conditions (*b*) and (*c*) above are met (*FA 2003, Sch 4ZA, para 4*).

19.55 If there are two or more purchasers, the surcharge applies if any of them meet the above conditions (*FA 2003, Sch 4ZA, para 2(2)*).

19.56 If two or more dwellings are purchased together by an individual, the surcharge applies if two or more of them meet conditions (*a*) and (*b*) in **19.53** and they are not subsidiary to any of the other dwellings included in the purchase (*FA 2003, Sch 4ZA, para 5(1)–(4)*). For this purpose a dwelling is subsidiary to another if:

(*a*) it is situated within the grounds of the other (or within the same building); and

(*b*) the amount of the chargeable consideration attributable (on a just and reasonable apportionment) to the main dwelling is at least two-thirds of the combined values of the two dwellings and any other of the dwellings being purchased that are also situated in the same grounds (or building).

(*FA 2003, Sch 4ZA, para 5(5)*.)

If only one of the dwellings meets these conditions, the surcharge applies unless that one is a replacement for the purchaser's only or main residence (*FA 2003, Sch 4ZA, para 6*). In other words, the purchase together of more than one dwelling can be treated for the purpose of the surcharge as the purchase of a single dwelling, but only if the value of the principal dwelling is at least two-thirds of the value of the transaction. A transaction involving more than one dwelling will either attract the surcharge or not. Part only of a single transaction cannot do so. Accordingly if none of the dwellings being purchased meet conditions (*a*) and (*b*), the surcharge cannot apply.

19.57 If a major interest in two or more dwellings is purchased by someone other than an individual and at least one of them is not subject to a lease with less than 21 years to run and has an apportioned value of over £40,000, the surcharge applies (*FA 2003, Sch 4ZA, para 7*).

19.58 The normal definition of a major interest in land (see **19.87**) is modified for the purpose of the 3% surcharge to exclude a leasehold interest whose term does not exceed seven years on the date of its grant (*FA 2003, Sch 4ZA, para 2(4)*).

19.59 A dwelling being purchased is a replacement for the purchaser's only or main residence if:

(*a*) on the effective date of the transaction, the purchaser intends that dwelling to be his only or main residence;

(*b*) in another land transaction the effective date of which fell within the previous three years, the purchaser (or his spouse or civil partner) disposed of a major interest in another dwelling;

(*c*) at some time within that three-year period, that previous dwelling was the purchaser's only or main residence; and (*d*) at no time between the effective date of the two transactions has the purchaser (or his spouse or civil partner) acquired a major interest in another property with the intention of it being the purchaser's only or main residence.

(*FA 2003, Sch 4ZA, para 3(6)*.)

Where the effective date of a transaction is before 27 November 2018, (*b*) and (*c*) above have effect as if the reference to the previous residence being sold in the prior three years was to it being sold on the same day as the purchase of the new, or at an earlier time, and as if that other previous property being the person's main residence at some time in the previous three years were to any earlier time (*FA 2016, s 128(3)*). HMRC say that the purchaser (or his spouse) must have disposed of either the freehold of the previous main residence or a lease which had a term of more than seven years when it was purchased; terminating a shorthold tenancy would not count as a disposal of a previous main residence (HMRC Guidance Note, November 2016). The Note also states that renting a new main residence in the time between disposal and purchase will not prevent the purchase from being a replacement of a main residence unless the period of the tenancy agreed is more than seven years. It also stresses that the main residence is a question of fact but says that this is not necessarily the residence where the individual spends the majority of his time. *Frost v Feltham 55 TC 10* (see **16.119**) is cited as a useful summary of the criteria to be applied. The Note also points out that the test in respect of the new dwelling purchased is a question of intention and acknowledges that: 'There may be rare cases of the purchaser's genuine intention at the time of purchase being frustrated by events.'

19.60 A dwelling being purchased is not, but may become, a replacement for the purchaser's only or main residence if:

(*a*) on the effective date of the transaction the purchaser intended the dwelling to be his only or main residence;

(*b*) in another land transaction that takes place within three years after the effective date of the purchase, the purchaser (or his spouse or civil partner) disposes of a major interest in another dwelling; and

(*c*) at some time during that three-year period that other dwelling was the purchaser's only or main residence.

(*FA 2003, Sch 4ZA, para 3(7)*.).

19.61 In other words, a dwelling is a replacement main residence if the previous residence was sold within the previous three years or the current residence is sold within the following three years. Which property is a person's only or main residence is a question of fact. The capital gains tax rules do not apply for this purpose.

19.62 If a purchase within **19.60** does become a main residence and so the transaction ceases to be a higher rate transaction, that purchase cannot be treated as a transaction within **19.59**(b) in determining whether any other transaction is a higher rate transaction (*FA 2003, 4ZA, para 8(2)*).

Example 19.2

Joe sells his only residence, Homeland 1, on 5 October 2016. He purchases a replacement residence, Homeland 2, on 10 August 2018. He sells Homeland 2 and buys Homeland 3 on 5 June 2021.

On the purchase of Homeland 2 Joe intends it to become his main residence. As the purchase is within three years of the sale of Homeland 1, the purchase of Homeland 1 ceases to be a higher rate transaction.

The purchase of Homeland 3 will be a higher rate transaction because, ignoring Homeland 2, he did not have another sole residence land transaction in the prior three years.

Example 19.3

Suppose that Homeland 2 had been burgled in December 2018 and Joe decided to put it on the market and was able to sell it and buy Homeland 3 on 5 July 2019.

On the purchase of Homeland 2, Homeland 1 again ceases to be a higher rate transaction.

On the purchase of Homeland 3, the acquisition of Homeland 2 is ignored. Although Homeland 1 was sold within the three-year period, the purchase of Homeland 2 during that period prevents Homeland 3 escaping the surcharge (see **19.59**(*d*)).

19.63 Where the new main residence is purchased before the sale of the old, the purchaser has to treat the new residence as a higher rate transaction and pay the 3% surcharge. On the disposal of the old residence, he becomes entitled to file an amended land transaction return to reduce the tax by excluding the surcharge. There is a very tight time limit for filing the amended return, namely within three months from the effective date of the disposal of the old residence (or, if later, within 12 months of the filing date of the original return) (*FA 2003, Sch 4ZA, para 8(3)*).

19.64 If the purchaser of a residential property is married (or in a civil partnership) and living with his spouse (or civil partner) on the effective date but the spouse is not a party to the purchase, it must be treated as a higher rate transaction if it would have been one had the purchaser's spouse or civil partner been the purchaser, ie if the purchaser does not own another dwelling but his spouse does the purchaser's acquisition will attract the surcharge (*FA 2003, Sch 4ZA, para 9(1), (2)*). *ITA 2007, s 1011* applies to determine whether a couple are living together (*FA 2003, Sch 4ZA, para 9(3)*). This provides that they are living together unless either:

(*a*) they are separated under an order of a court of competent jurisdiction;

(*b*) they are separated by deed of separation; or

(*c*) they are, in fact, separated in circumstances in which the separation is likely to be permanent.

Settlements and Bare Trusts

19.65 If the main subject of a land transaction consists of a major interest in one or more dwellings, the purchaser (or one of them) as acting as trustee of a settlement, and under the terms of the settlement a beneficiary will be entitled to occupy the dwelling or dwellings for life (or will be entitled to income earned in respect of the dwelling or dwellings) that beneficiary must be treated as the purchaser for the purpose of applying *Sch 4ZA* (*FA 2003, Sch 4ZA, para 10(1), (3)*). Similarly on a purchase by a trustee of a bare trust, the beneficiary is treated as the purchaser (*FA 2003, Sch 4ZA, para 10(2), (3)*). Accordingly if the dwelling is the beneficiary's replacement residence, the surcharge will not apply and if the beneficiary has an interest in another dwelling, the surcharge will apply even though the trustees do not hold a second dwelling. Curiously if the beneficiary is not entitled to occupy the property but is entitled to the income earned in respect of the dwelling, a short-term interest in possession seems to suffice to avoid the surcharge (unless the beneficiary has an interest in another property).

19.66 If a person is a beneficiary of a settlement, the settlement owns a major interest in trust property and under the terms of the settlement the beneficiary is entitled to occupy the dwelling for life (or to income earned in respect of the dwelling) the beneficiary is similarily treated for the purpose of the surcharge as holding the interest in the dwelling (so if the trustees dispose of the interest, the beneficiary is treated as having disposed of it). The same applies where a person is a beneficiary under a bare trust of a term of years absolute in a dwelling (*FA 2003, Sch 4ZA, para 10*). This deeming will enable the beneficiary to claim relief on the replacement of his only or main residence if the existing residence is in the trust. It should be noted that the beneficiary must have a life interest rather than an interest in possession. An interest in possession for a fixed term, or based on someone else's life, or a revocable life interest will not be sufficient to deem the disposal as being by the beneficiary.

19.67 If under **19.66** (or *FA 2003, Sch 16, para 3(1)* – see **19.278**) a child under 18 would otherwise be treated as being the purchaser in relation to a land transaction, as holding an interest in a dwelling or as having disposed of an interest in a dwelling, the child's parent (and any spouse or civil partner of the parent who is living together with the parent) is treated as being the purchaser (or disposer or holder of the interest) instead of the child (*FA 2003, Sch 4ZA, para 12*). This seems to apply even if the child is not living with the parent.

19.68 Where a beneficiary under a settlement does not have a life interest (or a life entitlement to income earned in respect of the dwelling) and the trustee is an individual, the fact that he is an individual must be ignored to determine whether the 3% surcharge applies by virtue of *para 4* (see **19.54**) or *para 7* (see **19.56**) (*FA 2003, Sch 4ZA, para 13*).

Other Special Situations

19.69 If the purchaser (or one of them) is a partner in a partnership but he does not enter into the transaction for the purposes of the partnership, any major interest in another dwelling that is held by (or on behalf of) the partnership for the purpose of a trade carried on by the partnership is not to be treated as held by (or on behalf of) the purchaser. This overrides *FA 2003, Sch 18, para 2(1)(a)* which treats partnership property as being owned by the partners (*FA 2003, Sch 4ZA, para 14*). It should be noted that this exclusion will not apply to a partnership carrying on an investment business. The partnership has to be carrying on a trade.

Example 19.4

Mike does not own any property personally but is a partner in the family partnership, which carries on a buy-to-let business. Mike decides to buy a lease as his private residence. He has never previously owned any property.

The 3% surcharge applies because Mike is deemed by *FA 2003, Sch 15, para 2(1)(a)* to own an interest in the partnership properties for SDLT purposes, so his acquisition of his own first home is a second property.

19.70 In relation to the first transaction under an alternative finance arrangement entered into between a person and a financial institution (see

19.271 and **19.275**), that person and not the financial institution is treated as the purchaser in relation to the transaction (*FA 2003, Sch 4ZA, para 15*). This does not apply in relation to a land transaction of which the effective date is on or before 15 September 2016 if the effect of its application would be to make the transaction a higher rate transaction when it would not otherwise have been one. The government is aware that this does not work properly and have said that the rules will be amended with retrospective effect to 1 April 2016, the next Finance Act to treat the purchaser under the first transaction (ie the intended 'owner') as the purchaser under the second transaction, rather than the institution, for the purpose of these provisions. That will mean that the surcharge will apply only if the individual owns another property at the end of the day of the effective date of the institution and the purchase is not a replacement of the individual's previous or main residence.

19.71 If by virtue of an inheritance a person becomes jointly entitled with one or more others to a major interest in a dwelling and that person's beneficial share in the interest does not exceed 50%, he is treated as not having the major interest at any time within three years of the date of the inheritance (*FA 2003, Sch 4ZA, para 16(1), (2)*). If he becomes the only person beneficially entitled to the whole of the interest (or his beneficial share comes to exceed 50%) he must, however, be treated as having the interest from that time (*FA 2003, Sch 4ZA, para 16(3)*). An inheritance means the acquisition of an interest in (or towards) satisfaction of an entitlement under the will of a deceased person, or on the intestacy of a deceased person (*FA 2003, Sch 4ZA, para 16(5)*). Unfortunately, it is not readily apparent when a person becomes so entitled. This might be at the time of the death of the deceased, or it might be when the executors assent to the gift. HMRC say that an interest in an unadministered estate is not an interest in land and so usually the date the individual acquires the interest is the date it is transferred to him. However, in a jurisdiction where property devolves directly on heirs the date of inheritance will be the date of death (HMRC Guidance Note, November 2016). A person's share in the interest exceeds 50% if either he is beneficially entitled as a tenant in common or coparcener to more than half of the interest, he and his spouse or civil partner are together so entitled to over 50%, or if he and his spouse or civil partner are beneficially entitled as joint tenants to the interest and there is no more than one other joint tenant (NB joint tenant not tenant in common) who is entitled to the interest (*FA 2003, Sch 4ZA, para 16(4)*). It is not readily apparent what this last test is aimed at. It seems to mean that if, say, 20% of a property is left to each of the person and his spouse under a will and the deceased only owned 50% of the property with the other 50% being owned by his surviving spouse, the person is treated as owning over 50%. The logic may be that he and his spouse inherit 100% of the deceased's interest or it might be that on the death of the co-owner the person and his spouse will become beneficially entitled to the entire property.

Meaning of a Dwelling

19.72 A building or part of a building is a dwelling for the purpose of *Sch 4ZA* if:

(*a*) it is used or suitable for use as a single dwelling; or

(*b*) it is in the process of being constructed or adapted for such use

(*FA 2003, Sch 4ZA, para 18(2).*)

Land that is (or is to be) occupied or enjoyed with a dwelling as a garden or grounds (including any building or structure on that land) must be regarded as part of the dwelling. So must land that subsists (or is to subsist) for the benefit of a dwelling (*FA 2003, Sch 4ZA, para 18(3), (4)*). HMRC say that a detached garage must be taken to be part of the dwelling (Guidance Note November 2016). This is questionable. Although such a garage is to be enjoyed with the dwelling, it is doubtful if it is to be enjoyed as garden or grounds unless it is on the same site as the house. The Guidance Note also makes clear that the purchase of a detached garden or part of the garden or grounds of a dwelling without the purchase of the actual dwelling does not attract the higher rate. It says that a dwelling has its everyday meaning, which HMRC interpret as a building or part of a building that affords to those who use it the facilities required for day-to-day private domestic existence. In particular HMRC say that it includes a holiday home and furnished holiday lettings. HMRC also say that caravans, houseboats and mobile homes do not attract the surcharge (and instead are normally chattels and, as such, not liable to SDLT) unless they become sufficiently fixed as to become part of the land.

19.73 The main subject matter of a transaction must also be taken to consist of (or include) an interest in a dwelling if:

(*a*) substantial performance of a contract (which includes an agreement) constitutes the effective date of a transaction under *FA 2003, ss 44–45A* (see **19.88**) or *Sch 2A, para 5(1), (2)* (see **19.107**) or *Sch 17A, para 12A* (see **19.162**);

(*b*) the main subject-matter of the transaction consists of (or includes) an interest in a building, (or a part of a building), that is to be constructed or adapted under the contract for use as a single dwelling; and

(*c*) construction or adaptation of the building, or part of a building, has not begun by the time the contract is substantially performed.

(*FA 2013, Sch 4ZA, para 18(5)(6).*)

This will ensure that the 3% applies on an off-plan purchase. Care may need to be taken to ensure that it does not apply in other circumstances.

Example 19.5

Nigel buys a disused pub intending to convert it into a house. The 3% surcharge does not apply as it is not used or suitable for use as a dwelling.

Nigel agrees with the vendor that he will engage the vendor to convert the pub into a house after he has purchased the property. The 3% surcharge does not apply.

Nigel agrees with the vendor that the vendor will convert the pub into a dwelling before completion but that Nigel will pay 80% of the agreed consideration up-front. The 3% surcharge applies. Payment of the 80% triggers substantial performance and at the time of that payment the conversion work has not begun.

19.74 A building used for a purpose within *FA 2003, s 116(2)* (which treats residential accommodation for school children and other groups of people as being used as a dwelling) or *s 116(3)* (which treats children's homes, care homes and other institutional-type accommodation as not used as a dwelling – see **19.20** and **19.21**) is not used as a dwelling for this purpose and no account is to be taken of its suitability for any other use (*FA 2003, Sch 4ZA, para 18(7), (8)*).

19.75 References to a dwelling in *Sch 4ZA* include references to a dwelling situated outside England and Wales and Northern Ireland. In applying the schedule to a foreign dwelling, references to a major interest are to an equivalent interest under the laws of the other country or territory; reference to persons being beneficially entitled as joint tenants, tenants in common or coparceners are to persons having an equivalent entitlement to the interest in the dwelling under the laws of that country; references to a land transaction are to the acquisition of an interest in the dwelling under the laws of that country; references to the effective date of a transaction are to the date on which the interest in the dwelling is acquired under the laws of that country; and references to inheritance are to the acquisition of an interest from a deceased's person's estate in accordance with the laws of that country (*FA 2013, Sch 4ZA, para 17(1), (2)*). If an infant child has an interest in a dwelling situated in a foreign country (or Scotland), the child's parent (and any spouse or civil partner of the parent living together with him) is treated as having that interest (*FA 2003, Sch 4ZA, para 17(4)–(6)*).

Miscellaneous

19.76 The Treasury have power by Regulation to amend or modify *Sch 4ZA* for the purpose of preventing certain chargeable transactions from being higher rate transactions (*FA 2003, Sch 4ZA, para 19(1), (2)*).

19.77 The 3% surcharge does not apply where the effective date of the transaction was before 1 April 2016 or if it is after that date, the transaction is effected in pursuance of a contract entered into and substantially performed before 26 November 2015 or entered into before 26 November 2015 and not varied or assigned on or after that date. The surcharge does apply if the contract was entered into before 26 November 2015 but the transaction is effected in consequence of the exercise of an option, right of pre-emption or similar right after that date or there is an assignment, sub-sale or other transaction after that date relating to the whole or part of the subject-matter of the contract as a result of which someone else becomes entitled to call for a conveyance (*FA 2016, s 128(5)–(8)*).

19.78 There are no exemptions from the surcharge. It will apply to a purchase of a residential property by a developer who intends to refurbish and resell it. It will also apply to the purchase of a main residence by, for example, someone living in employer-provided accommodation, if he owns another property.

Exchanges

19.79 If a land transaction is entered into by the purchaser (alone or jointly) wholly or partly in consideration of another land transaction being entered into by him (alone or jointly) as vendor, each transaction is taxed as if it were distinct or separate from the other (*FA 2003, s 47*). In the case of such an exchange of one piece of land for another (ie where one or more land transactions are entered into by a person as purchaser (alone or jointly) wholly or partly in consideration of one or more other land transactions being entered into by him (alone or jointly) as vendor):

(*a*) if the subject matter of any of the transactions is a major interest in land (see **19.87**) and a single relevant acquisition is made by the purchaser, the chargeable consideration for that acquisition is the market value of the subject matter of the acquisition (and if it is the grant of a lease at a rent, that rent) or, where the effective date is after 23 March 2011, the amount which would be the chargeable value ignoring *FA 2003, Sch 4, para 5*. If two or more relevant acquisitions are made by the purchaser, the chargeable consideration for each is the market value (and rent) of each;

(*b*) if the subject matter of none of the transactions is a major interest in land and a single acquisition is made in consideration of one or more disposals, the chargeable consideration for the acquisition is the amount or value of any chargeable consideration given for the acquisition other than the disposal or disposals, ie if the subject matter of all of the transactions are minor interests then there will be no consideration other than any payment of equality money or similar consideration. If there are two or more acquisitions any chargeable consideration needs to be apportioned by reference to the respective market values of the interests acquired.

(*FA 2003, Sch 4, para 5* as amended by *FA 2011, Sch 21, para 4*.)

The effect of the 2011 change is that the chargeable consideration becomes the greater of what it would have been under the old rules and what it would be in the absence of the rules for exchanges. This ensures that SDLT avoidance will not be possible by the manipulation of the market value of the interest acquired. It has to be charged on at least market value (Finance Bill 2011 Explanatory Notes).

19.80 It should particularly be noted that SDLT is payable on both sides of a property exchange. This is different to the stamp duty position where only one side of the transactions attracted duty. There is an exception for PFI contracts (see **19.298**). HMRC initially regarded exchanges as linked transactions (see **19.81**) with the result that the consideration for each had to be aggregated to fix the rate of tax. This was clearly unfair so the law was amended from 19 July 2007 by *FA 2007, s 76* to make clear that the transactions are not linked.

Linked Transactions

19.81 Where there are two or more linked transactions with the same effective date the purchaser (or all of the purchasers if there is more than one) can make a single land transaction return as if all of those transactions which are notifiable were a single transaction. Where two or more purchasers make such a single return *s 103* applies as if the transactions were a single transaction and the purchasers were acting jointly. Transactions are linked for this purpose if they form part of a single scheme, arrangement or series of transactions between the same vendor and purchaser or persons connected with either (*FA 2003, s 108*). Where transactions are linked the rate of tax is determined as if they formed a single transaction (see **19.9**).

Foreign Currency

19.82 The value of any chargeable consideration other than money (whether in sterling or a foreign currency) or a debt must be taken as its market value at the effective date (see **19.88**) of the transaction (*FA 2003, Sch 4, para 7*). If the consideration is in a foreign currency the amount of the consideration is of course the sterling equivalent ascertained by reference to the London closing exchange rate on the effective date of the transaction – but if the parties have used a different exchange rate for the purposes of the transaction that different rate is used (*FA 2003, Sch 4, para 9*).

19.83 If any part of the consideration consists of the satisfaction or release of a debt due to the purchaser (or owed by the vendor), or the assumption of an existing debt by the purchaser, the consideration is the amount satisfied, realised or assumed, unless that would produce a consideration in excess of the market value of the property, in which case the chargeable consideration is limited to that value (*FA 2003, Sch 4, para 8*). If a debt is secured on the land at the time of the land transaction (ie both immediately before and after it) and the rights or liabilities in relation to that debt of any party to the transaction are charged by it, the debt must be added to the chargeable consideration (*FA 2003, Sch 4, para 8(1A)*). If either there were joint owners of the property prior to the transaction or there are joint purchasers, the amount of secured debt assumed must be determined as if the amount of the debt owned by each were the proportion of it corresponding to his undivided share of the property – and for this purpose each joint owner is treated as holding an equal undivided share of the property (*FA 2003, Sch 4, para 8(1B) and (1C)*).

Joint Purchasers

19.84 If there are two or more purchasers who are or will be jointly entitled to the interest acquired:

(*a*) any SDLT obligation of a purchaser is an obligation of the purchasers jointly but can be discharged by any one of them;

(*b*) anything required by the legislation to be done in relation to the purchaser must be done by, or in relation to, all of them;

(*c*) any liability of the purchaser in relation to the transaction is a joint and several liability;

(*d*) a single land transaction return is required if the transaction is a notifiable one but the declaration required by *Sch 10, para 1(1)(c)* (that a return is complete and correct) must be made by all of them;

(*e*) if HMRC enquire into the return the enquiry notice and closure notice must be given to each of the joint purchasers but the powers to require the production of documents and information are exercisable separately (and differently) in relation to each of them and any one of the joint purchasers can apply for a direction that a closure notice should be given;

(*f*) an HMRC determination or discovery assessment relating to the transaction must be made against all of the joint purchasers and is not effective unless notice of it is given to each of them whose identity is known to HMRC;

(*g*) an appeal may be brought by any of the purchasers but the others must be notified of it and are entitled to appear and be heard as they will be bound by it; and

(*h*) an appeal can be settled by agreement only with the agreement of all of the joint purchasers.

(*FA 2003, s 103.*)

Carrying out of Works

19.85 If the whole or part of the consideration consists of the carrying out of works of construction, improvement or repair of a building (or other works to enhance the value of the land) the value of such works must be regarded as part of the chargeable consideration. Such value is of course the amount that would have to be paid in the open market for the carrying out of such works. This obviously does not apply to the extent that:

(*a*) the works are carried out after the effective date of the transaction;

(*b*) they are carried out on land acquired (or to be acquired) under the transaction or on other land held by the purchaser or a person connected with him (within *ITA 2007, s 993*); and

(*c*) it is not a condition of the transaction that the works are carried out by the vendor or a person connected with him.

If head (*a*) is satisfied in relation to the conveyance it is deemed to be also satisfied in relation to the contract (*FA 2003, Sch 4, para 10(2A)*).

(*FA 2003, Sch 4 para 10.*)

If all or part of the consideration consists of the provision of any other form of services, the value of such consideration is the amount that would have to be paid in the open market to obtain such services (*FA 2003, Sch 4, para 11*).

19.86 It was held for stamp duty that where land was sold or leased and at the same time related arrangements to erect a building on the land was entered into, the cost of the building works can be part of the consideration for the disposal of the land or the grant of the lease (*M'Innes v CIR (1934 SC 424)*). In *Paul v CIR (1936 SC 443)* Lord Normand felt that the *M'Innes* principle could not apply unless both the vendor of the land and the building contractor were one and the same person (or one was the agent or nominee of the other) and the contracts were so interlocked that if default was made in one the other would not be enforceable by either party. In *Prudential Assurance Co Ltd v CIR (1992 STC 863)* it was held that the *M'Innes* principle could not apply unless the completion of one contract was dependent on the performance of the other. The Prudential contracted to buy a partially completed building (with the benefit of pre-lets agreements) and at the same time entered into a development agreement with the developers under which it agreed to pay the developers each month (up to a maximum) the sum the developers had already contracted to pay the builder. The conveyance of the partially completed building was executed six months later at a time when £4 million of work was still to be done. HMRC contended that there was a single contract for sale of the completed building contained in two instruments. It was held that albeit that the two were part of one transaction, of which the intended result was that the Prudential would become the owner of the land together with the new building being constructed by the developer, that was not the legal shape of the transaction; the sale agreement was, as the parties intended, completed independently of the carrying out of the building work under the development agreement. HMRC's view following this case was that, to avoid stamp duty on the combined consideration, the two contracts had to be genuinely independent of each other and capable of being completed independently. They did not regard them as being independent if in the event of default on one contract the other became unenforceable. In any event, even if there were two contracts the consideration for the sale of the land would have included the amount payable under the second contract for any building work on the land completed at the date of execution of the land sale – the Prudential accepted that the value of such work attracted duty (SP 8/93). HMRC have confirmed that where there are separate agreements between the same parties to sell the land and to carry out works the Prudential decision applies to the same extent as for stamp duty (HMRC Press Release 5.4.2004).

Definitions

Major Interest in Land

19.87 A major interest in land for SDLT purposes means a freehold or a lease for a term of years absolute, whether subsisting at law or in equity (*FA 2003, s 117(2)*). In Scotland it is the interest of an owner of land and the tenant's right over (or interest in) a property subject to a lease, and in Northern Ireland it is any freehold or leasehold estate (*FA 2003, s 117(3)(4)*). It is unfortunate that the draftsman chose to adopt the expression 'major interest' which already has a well established meaning for VAT purposes to describe something very different to that established meaning. Minor interest is not defined. It is presumably anything that is not a major interest. It appears that a lease at will or a lease for life are not major interests even if it is likely that the lease will subsist for a number of years.

Effective Date

19.88 The effective date of a transaction is the date of completion (*FA 2003, s 119(1)*). There are a number of exceptions. If a contract is substantially performed without having been completed, the effective date of the transaction is when the contract is substantially performed (*FA 2003, s 44(4), 119(2)*). The effective date for the acquisition of an option or right of pre-emption (which is itself deemed to be a land transaction (see **19.133**)), is the date that the option or right is acquired not the time it becomes exercisable (*FA 2003, s 46(3), 119(2)*). In addition *ss 44A(3)* (see **19.131**), *45A(8)* (see **19.132**), *Sch 17A, para 12A(2)* (see **19.161**) and *Sch 17A, para 19(3)* (leases in Scotland) provide their own effective dates. Subject to this, a person is not regarded as entering into a land transaction when he enters into a contract, but the contract and completion are treated as a single land transaction the effective date of which is the date of completion (*FA 2003, s 44(2)(3)*). In the case of an agreement for a lease entered into after 17 March 2004 *Sch 17A, para 12A* (see **19.162**) applies in place of *s 44(4), (8)* and *(9)* (*FA 2003, s 44(9A)*).

Substantial Performance

19.89 A contract is substantially performed when either:

(*a*) the purchaser (or a person connected with him within *ITA 2007, s 993*) takes possession of the whole (or substantially the whole) of the subject matter of the contract (whether under the contract or under a licence or lease of a temporary character), eg he goes into occupation or receives, or becomes entitled to receive, rents and profits; or

(*b*) a substantial amount of the consideration is paid or provided, ie if none of it is rent, when the whole or substantially the whole is paid, if it is wholly rent when the first payment of rent is made, and if it is partly rent and partly not when either the first payment or rent is made or the other consideration is substantially paid (*FA 2003, s 44(5)–(7)*).

19.90 What is substantially the whole for the purpose of (*b*) is a question of fact. HMRC's rule of thumb is apparently an amount equal to or greater than 90% (Hansard, SCB, 36 2003 Col 315). Possession includes receipt of rents and profits or the right to receive them. It is immaterial for this purpose whether possession is taken under the contract or under a licence or lease of a temporary character (*FA 2003, s 44(6)*).

19.91 Where SDLT is triggered by substantial performance and the contract is subsequently completed, both the contract and the completion are notifiable transactions. Tax is chargeable on the conveyance to the extent (if any) that the amount of tax on the conveyance exceeds that chargeable on the contract (*FA 2003, s 44(8)*). In effect the tax on the contract is a payment on account. If the rate is increased in the interim, or something else happens to increase the liability, an extra amount will be payable on completion. If the contract is not completed (ie between the same parties and in substantial conformity with the contract), but after payment of the tax by reference to substantial performance the contract is rescinded or annulled or for any other reason not carried into effect, the tax paid becomes repayable. The repayment must be claimed by amendment of the land transaction return made in respect of the contract (*FA 2003, s 44(8)–(10)*).

19.92 In *Peter Bone Ltd v CIR (1995 STC 921)*, a stamp duty case, a family partnership entered into an agreement to sell the business as a going concern to a company. The deed included a provision that the partnership was to hold the land as nominee for the company and execute such assignments, transfers or conveyances of the property to such persons as the company might require. It was intended that in due course the company would sell on the land and stamp duty would be paid by the ultimate purchasers. It was held that the agreement was stampable by reference to the value of the land either as a sale or as a conveyance on sale of the equitable estate. Following completion of the contract nothing further needed to be done so there was nothing capable of being specifically performed. Accordingly the partnership did not have the same rights as the vendor under an uncompleted contract would have of requiring the purchaser to take a conveyance and relieve it of a potentially burdensome legal title. This case seems equally applicable to SDLT to treat the transaction as substantially performed. The taxpayer also lost in *Allchin v HMRC (TC 2613)*. That case involved a novation and the Tribunal held that there was no evidence to support the novation and, in any event, a novation brings the original contract to an end, whereas it has to remain in existence for *s 45* to apply.

Companies

19.93 For SDLT purposes references to a company mean a body corporate or unincorporated association (but do not include a partnership). Anything required to be done by a company can be done by the proper officer (the secretary, a director, or a liquidator or administrator) or by any other person having for the time being express, implied or apparent authority to act for the company (*FA 2003, s 100*). The SDLT provisions apply to a unit trust scheme as if the trustees were a company and the rights of the unit-holders were shares in the company. Each of the parts of an umbrella scheme is regarded for this purpose as a separate unit trust (*FA 2003, s 101*). The Treasury are empowered to make regulations to ensure that the SDLT legislation applies to open-ended investment companies (*FA 2003, s 102*). Tax due from a company that is not a body corporate, or that is incorporated outside the UK, can be recovered from the proper officer (*FA 2003, s 100(4)*).

Co-ownership Authorised Contractual Schemes

19.94 The SDLT legislation (other than *Sch 7* (group relief, reconstruction relief and acquisition relief) applies to a co-ownership authorised contractual scheme (COACS) as if the scheme were a company and the rights of the participants (as defined in *FSMA 2000, s 235*) were shares in the company (*FA 2003, s 102A(2), (10)*) inserted by *FA 2016, s 133* and *Sch 16*). A COACS is a co-ownership scheme which is authorised under *FSMA 2000, s 261D(1)*. A co-ownership scheme has the same meaning as in *FSMA 2000, s 235A* (*FA 2003, s 102A(8)*). The Treasury has power by Regulation to exclude a scheme from being a COACS for SDLT purposes (*FA 2003, s 102A(9)*). References to a COACS are treated as including a collective investment scheme which is constituted under the law of an EEA State, is managed by a body corporate under the law of an EEA State, and is authorised under the law of the EEA State in which it is incorporated in a way which (under that law) makes it the equivalent of a COACS as defined above (*FA 2003, s 102A(7)*).

19.95 An umbrella COACS means a COACS whose arrangements provide for separate pooling of the contributions of the participants and the profits or income out of which payments are made to them (pooling arrangements) and under which the participants are entitled to exchange rights in one pool for rights in another (*FA 2003, s 102A(3)*). A sub-scheme in relation to an umbrella COACS is such of the pooling arrangements as relate to a separate pool (*FA 2003, s 102A(4)*). Each of the sub-schemes of an umbrella COACS is regarded as a separate COACS (and the umbrella COACS as a whole is not regarded as a COACS (*FA 2003, s 102A(5)*). In relation to a sub-scheme, references to chargeable interests means those chargeable interests that under the pooling arrangements form part of the separate pool to which the sub-scheme relates. References to the scheme documents means such part of the documents as apply to the sub-scheme (*FA 2003, s 102A(6)*).

19.96 In relation to a land transaction in respect of which a COACS is treated as the purchaser by these rules, references to the purchaser in *FA 2003,* *ss 76, 80, 81, 81A, 108(2)* and *Sch 10* (land transactions returns, enquiries etc), *s 85* (liability for tax) and *s 90* (application to defer payment in cases of contingent or unascertained consideration) must be read as references to the operator of the scheme. The operator under a UK regulated COACS is the person given by *FSMA 2000, s 237(2)*. In relation to an equivalent EEA scheme, it is the corporate body responsible for the management of the scheme (*FA 2003, s 102A(11)(12)*).

Other Definitions

19.97 *Major interest in land*: This is dealt with at **19.87** above.

Market value: Market value is determined as for capital gains tax purposes under *TCGA 1992, ss 272–274* (*FA 2003, s 118*).

Effective date: This is dealt with at **19.88** above.

Lease: A lease means:

(*a*) an interest or right in or over land for a term of years (whether fixed or periodic); or

(*b*) a tenancy at will or other interest or right in or over land terminable by notice at any time (*FA 2003, Sch 17A, para 1*).

Jointly entitled: Jointly entitled in England and Wales means beneficially entitled either as joint tenants or tenants in common. In Scotland it means entitled as joint owners or owners in common. In Northern Ireland it means beneficially entitled as joint tenants, tenants in common or coparceners (*FA 2003, s 121*).

Land: Land includes buildings and structures and also land covered by *water* (*FA 2003, s 121*).

Assignments, Sub-sales, etc

19.98 Following a growing number of attempts to avoid SDLT by exploiting the rules on assignments, sub-sales and similar transactions, the rules on such transactions were recast in *FA 2013*. The new rules retain the basic concept, namely that where the person who completes a transaction is different to the one who entered into the contract, there should be only one charge to SDLT but that this should be based on the aggregate of the purchase price and any additional sum paid for the assignment or other change in the identity of the purchaser.

19.99 The new rules are contained in a new *FA 2003, Sch 2A*, which was inserted in that Act by *FA 2013, Sch 39*. They apply where a person (the original purchaser) enters into a contract (the original contract) to acquire a chargeable interest (which is to be completed by a conveyance) and at a time after 16 July 2013 there is a 'pre-completion transaction' (*FA 2003, Sch 2A, para 1(1)*). A transaction is a pre-completion one if:

(*a*) as a result of the transaction someone other than the original purchaser (the transferee) becomes entitled to call for a conveyance to himself of the whole or part of the subject matter of the original contract; and

(*b*) immediately before the transaction took place, a person was entitled under the original contract to call for that conveyance,

(*FA 2003, Sch 2A para 1(2).*)

For this purpose the reference in (*a*) to a contract does not include a contract that is an assignment of rights in relation to another contract (*FA 2003, Sch 2A, para 1(6)*). Reference to part of the subject matter of the original contract are to a chargeable interest that is the same as the chargeable interest under the original contract other than that it relates to part only of the land concerned, but the expression also includes (so far is appropriate) interests or rights appurtenant or pertaining to the chargeable interest (*FA 2003, Sch 2A, para 1(7)*). *Sch 2A* does not apply if *FA 2003, Sch 17A, para 12B* (assignment of agreement for lease) applies (*FA 2003, Sch 2A, para 1(8)*).

19.100 A transaction that gives effect to a person's acquisition of the whole or part of the subject matter of the original contract is not a pre-completion transaction. Nor is the grant or assignment of an option (*FA 2003, Sch 2A, para 1(3), (4)*). The fact that a transaction has the effect of discharging the original contract does not prevent it being a pre-completion transaction (*FA 2003, Sch 2A, para 1(5)*).

19.101 Where the provisions apply, the transferee is not regarded as entering into a land transaction by reason of the pre-completion transaction (*FA 2003, Sch 2A, para 3*). Instead the following provisions apply. There are separate rules for assignments of rights (**19.102**) and freestanding transfers (**19.117**).

Assignment of rights

19.102 If the pre-completion transaction is an assignment of rights and the subject matter of the original contract is conveyed to the transferee, the conveyance is taken to effect the completion of the original contract (despite the fact that *FA 2003, s 94(10)* defines completion as completion between the same parties) (*FA 2003, Sch 2A, para 4(1)(2)*). As a result (where the subject matter of the original contract is conveyed to the transferee or the original contract is substantially performed by the transferee – see **19.109**) the transferee is taken to be the purchaser under the land transaction referred to in *FA 2013, s 14(3)* (or treated as effected under *s 44(4)* (substantial performance – see **19.88**). However, for the purpose of determining the chargeable consideration for that land transaction, it is taken to give effect to a contract the 'consideration' (see **19.101**) under which is the aggregate of the consideration under the original contract and any consideration paid or given for the assignment of rights (*FA 2003, Sch 2A, para 4(3)–(5)*).

19.103 If there is a relevant connection between parties the chargeable consideration for the land transaction is calculated as if in *FA 2003, Sch 4, para 1(1)* the words 'or a person connected with him' were omitted (*FA 2003, Sch 2A, para 4(6)*). The effect of this is to ignore any consideration provided directly or indirectly by a connected person of the purchaser under the original contract. This is because *Sch 2A, para 12(2)* provides that where there is a relevant connection the consideration given by the purchaser for the subject matter of the land transaction is the higher of:

(*a*) the consideration under *para 4(5)*;

(*b*) the first minimum amount (see **19.106**); and

(*c*) the second minimum amount (see **19.108**).

(*FA 2003, Sch 2A, para 12(1)*.)

The *CTA 2010, s 1122* definition of connected person (see Appendix 1) applies (*FA 2003, Sch 2A, para 20*).

19.104 There is such a relevant connection if either:

(*a*) the transferor and transferee in relation to the pre-completion transaction are connected with each other, or are not acting at arm's length – (*FA 2003, Sch 2A, para 13(2)*); or

(*b*) if the implemented transaction is one of a chain of successive transactions (all of which have at least part of their subject matter in common) that are pre-completion transactions in relation to the original contract, and the transferee in relation to a pre-completion transaction that precedes the implemented transaction (ie for an earlier transaction in the chain) is connected with the transferee under the implemented transaction (or not acting at arm's length in relation to him) (*FA 2003, Sch 2A, para 12(3)(4)*).

19.105 Where the implemented transaction is a pre-completion transaction in relation to both:

(*a*) a contract for a land transaction that is not itself a free-standing transfer in relation to any other contract; and

(*b*) a contract (or two or more successive contracts) that is itself a free-standing transfer in relation to the contract referred to in (*a*),

'the original contract' is that at (*a*) and does not include any of the contracts at (*b*) (*FA 2003, Sch 2A, para 12(5)*).

19.106 If the chargeable interest acquired (or treated as acquired) under the land transaction referred to at **19.103** is the whole subject matter of the original contract, the 'first minimum amount' is the amount of any consideration (in money or money's worth) agreed to be given for the acquisition of that subject matter under the terms of the original contract. If it is not the whole subject matter, the first minimum amount is so much of such consideration as is referable, on a just and reasonable apportionment, to the chargeable interest acquired (*FA 2003, Sch 2A, para 13(1)*).

19.107 If:

(*a*) the pre-completion transaction referred to at **19.102** is one of a chain of successive transactions (all having at least part of their subject matter in common) that are pre-completion transactions in relation to the original contract;

(*b*) a person (T) is the transferor under a pre-completion transaction that forms part of that chain and is connected with (or not acting at arm's length in relation to) either the transferee under that transaction or the transferee under a subsequent transaction in the chain; and

(*c*) having regard to all the circumstances it would not be reasonable to conclude that the obtaining of a tax advantage (for any person) was one of the main purposes of T in entering into any pre-completion transaction in the chain (or any arrangements of which such a transaction forms part),

the first minimum amount is the amount of any consideration (in money or money's worth) agreed, under the terms of the transfer to 'the first T', to be given in respect of the subject matter of that transaction (including any consideration relating to an obligation of the transferor under the transfer to the first T) (*FA 2003, Sch 2A, para 13(2)(3)*). For this purpose 'the first T' means the transferor in relation to the first of the pre-completion transactions in the chain in relation to which head (*b*) is met if it is met in relation to more than one transaction (otherwise it means T). The transfer to the first T means the pre-completion transaction under which the first T is the transferee (or the original contract if T is the original purchaser) (*FA 2003, Sch 2A, para 13(4)(5)*).

19.108 The second minimum amount is the aggregate of the net amount of consideration given by the 'relevant parties' (*FA 2003, Sch 2A, para 14(1)*). The net amount of consideration given by any relevant party is that given by that party either for the acquisition of the chargeable interest or as consideration for a pre-acquisition transaction, less the consideration given to that party by another relevant party (or other relevant parties) as such consideration. If the consideration received exceeds that paid, the net amount of consideration is zero (*FA 2003, Sch 2A, para 14(2)*). The relevant parties are the original purchaser and the transferee. Where there is a chain of such transactions the relevant parties are:

(*a*) the transferor and transferee in relation to the implemented transaction;

(*b*) the transferor in relation to a preceding transaction if that person is connected with (or not acting at arm's length to) the transferee under the implemented transaction; and

(*c*) the transferee under a pre-completion transaction if the transferor under that transaction is a relevant party (whether by virtue of this paragraph or otherwise).

(*FA 2003, Sch 2A, para 14(3)(4)*.)

In determining the consideration, amounts given by (or to) a person connected with a relevant party are treated as given by (or to) that relevant party (but, to avoid double counting, if a person connected with a relevant party is himself a relevant party, he is not treated as a connected person for this purpose) (*FA 2003, Sch 2A, para 14(5)*). If the subject matter of the implemented transaction is not the whole subject matter of the original contract, the amounts that are taken into account as consideration for the acquisition of the chargeable interest are to be determined on a just and reasonable basis, and only so much of the consideration for a preceding transaction as if referable, on a just and reasonable apportionment, to the subject matter of the implemented transaction is to be taken into account (*FA 2003, Sch 2A, para 14(6)*).

19.109 For the purpose of **19.102**, the original contract is substantially performed by the transferee where the contract is treated under *FA 2003, s 44(4)* (substantial performance) as itself being the transaction by reason of either:

(*a*) the transferee under the assignment of rights (or a person connected with him) taking possession of the whole (or substantially the whole) of the subject matter of the original contract;

(*b*) a substantial amount (ie over 80%) of the consideration being paid or provided by the transferee (or a person connected with him); or (*c*) consideration paid or provided by a person within (*b*), together with consideration paid or provided by another person, amounting in total to a substantial amount of the consideration.

(*FA 2003, Sch 2A, para 4(7)*.)

The consideration in relation to the land transaction means the amount taken to be the consideration for the acquisition of the subject matter of the land transaction. In relation to the original contract, it means the consideration for the acquisition of the subject matter of that contract, and in relation to the assignment of rights it means the consideration for the transferee's acquisition of the rights to which that contract relates (*FA 2003, Sch 2A, para 4(9)*).

19.110 Where the original contract is completed or substantially performed, SDLT applies as if the effective date of the land transaction (at **19.102**) (the transferee's land transaction) were also the effective date of another land transaction (the notional land transaction) and the original purchaser were the purchaser under that notional land transaction (*FA 2003, Sch 2A, para 5(1)*). If the assignment of rights at **19.102** (the implemented assignment of rights) was preceded by one or more related assignments of rights (a transaction that is an assignment of rights in relation to the original contract and has some subject matter in common with the implemented assignment of rights – *para 5(7)*), there must be taken to be (for each assignment of rights (other than the first) in the chain) an additional land transaction for which the effective date is the effective date of the transferee's land transaction and the purchaser is the transferor under that assignment of rights (*FA 2003, Sch 2A, para 5(2)*). *FA 2003, Sch 4, para 1(1)* (chargeable consideration) does not apply to the notional land transaction or any additional land transaction but instead the consideration for the notional transaction is the total of amounts A and B below and that for an additional transaction is the total of amounts A, B and C (*FA 2003, Sch 2A, paras 5(3)(4)*).

19.111 Amount A is the total of any consideration in money or money's worth given (directly or indirectly) as consideration under the original contract by:

(*a*) the transferee under the assignment of rights with which the notional land transaction, or (as the case requires) the additional land transaction, is associated (for this purpose the notional land transaction is associated with the assignment of rights under which the purchaser is the transferor and an additional land transaction is associated with the assignment of rights);

(*b*) where that assignment of rights is one in a chain of successive transactions that are pre-completion transactions in relation to the original contract, the transferee under any subsequent pre-completion transaction in the chain; or

(*c*) a person connected with someone within (*a*) or (*b*).

19.112 Amount B is the total of any other consideration in money or money's worth given as consideration under the original contract (directly or indirectly) by the purchaser (under the notional land transaction or an additional land transaction) or a person connected with him.

19.113 Amount C is the amount of any consideration (in money or money's worth) given for the preceding assignment of rights (the one as a result of which the purchaser became entitled to call for a conveyance of what became the subject matter of the assignment of rights associated with the additional land transaction) by the purchaser (under the additional land transaction) or a person connected with him (*FA 2003, Sch 2A, para 5(5)(6)*).

19.114 If *para 5* applies by virtue of the substantial performance by the transferee of the original contract, and the original contract is (to any extent) subsequently rescinded or annulled (or for any other reason is not carried into effect) the tax paid on the notional land transaction and any tax paid on an additional land transaction must (to that extent) be repaid by HMRC. The repayment must be claimed by amendment of the land transaction return made in respect of the notional or additional land transaction (*FA 2003, Sch 2A, para 6*).

19.115 Where the transferee under the assignment of rights at **19.102** is entitled to call for a conveyance of part only of the subject matter of the original contract, **19.102–19.110** apply as if the original contract so far as relating to that part were a separate contract (*FA 2003, Sch 2A, para 7*).

19.116 Where the pre-completion transaction is an assignment of rights and the subject matter of the original contract is conveyed to the transferee (or the original contract is substantially performed by the transferee, references to the vendor means the vendor under the original contract, except where the original contract was substantially performed before the transferee became entitled to call for a conveyance – in which case the vendor means the person who was the purchaser under the original contract at the time when it was substantially performed (*FA 2003, Sch 2A, para 8(1)(3)(4)*). However, in relation to the land transaction effected by the conveyance or the substantial performance (and the notional land transaction and any additional land transaction) it means either the vendor under the original contract or the transferor under the assignment of rights (or any other transaction that is an assignment of rights in relation to the original contract and has some subject matter in common with the assignment of rights that gave rise to the conveyance (or substantial performance). This does not apply for the application of *FA 2003*:

(*a*) *s 61(1)(a)* (compliance with planning obligations conditions for exemption – see **19.205**);

(*b*) *s 66(1)(2)* (transfers involving public bodies – see **19.250**);

(*c*) *Sch 4, para 8(1)(a)* (debt as consideration – see **23.170**);

(*d*) *Sch 4, para 10(2)(c)* (carrying out of works – see **19.75**); or

(*e*) *Sch 4, para 16* (indemnity given by vendor – see **19.440**).

In applying these provisions, references to the vendor must be read as including the vendor under the original contract and the transferee under any relevant assignment of rights (*FA 2013, Sch 2A, para 8(5)–(7)(9)*). In determining under *FA 2013, s 108(1)* (see **19.134**) whether or not such a land transaction is linked to another transaction, it can be assumed that the vendor includes both the vendorunder the original contract and the transferor under the assignment of rights (or other transaction mentioned above) (*FA 2003, Sch 2A, para 8(8)*).

Free-standing Transfers

19.117 If the pre-completion transaction is a free-standing transfer (anything other than an assignment of rights – *FA 2003, Sch 2A, para 2(2)*) and the transferee acquires the subject matter of that free-standing transfer, the consideration for the transaction effecting that acquisition includes the consideration given for the free-standing transfer (if that would not otherwise be the case) (*FA 2003, Sch 2A, para 9(1)(2)*). For this purpose an acquisition includes an acquisition deemed to take place under *FA 2003, s 44(4)* (substantial performance) (*FA 2003, Sch 2A, para 9(3)*). An action taken by the transferee or a person connected with him (or by an assignee of the transferee, or a person connected with him) that would (if taken by the original purchaser) constitute the taking of possession of the whole or substantially the whole of the subject matter of the original contract is treated as effecting the substantial performance of the original contract (*FA 2003, Sch 2A, para 9(4)(6)*). If a transaction that is a free-standing transfer in relation to a contract is also a free-standing transfer in relation to another contract (in particular, where there have been successive free-standing transfers) each of those contracts can be regarded as the 'original contract' for the purposes of separate applications of *para 9(4)* (*FA 2003, Sch 2A, para 9(5)*). References in *para 9* to an assignee of the transferee are to any person who (as a result of a transaction that is an assignment of rights in relation to the free-standing transfer) is entitled to call for a conveyance of the whole or part of the subject matter of the free-standing transfer (*FA 2003, Sch 2A, para 9(7)*).

19.118 Where a land transaction is effected (or treated as effected) by an acquisition under a free-standing transfer, or *para 8(1)* (meaning of vendor where the transferee is the assignee under an assignment of rights – see **19.116**) would apply but for the exclusion of cases where the original contract is itself a free-standing transfer, the vendor in relation to the relevant land transaction (the free-standing transfer referred to above or, in the case of an assignment of rights, the land transaction effected by the conveyance to the transferee of the subject matter of the original contract (or its substantial performance by the transferee)) is the vendor or (as the case may be) transferor under the first appropriate transaction (see **19.119**) (*FA 2003, Sch 2A, para 10(1)(3)(4)*). This general rule does not apply for the provisions set out at (*a*) to (*e*) in **19.116**, where the vendor is treated as being any of the vendor under the first appropriate transaction and each person who is the transferee in the case of a relevant pre-completion transaction (ie the free-standing transfer, the original contract the subject matter of which is conveyed to the transferee (or substantially performed by the transferee – see **19.16**) (together called the specified transaction) and any other transaction that is a pre-completion transaction in relation to the original contract and has some subject matter in common with the above transactions (*FA 2003, Sch 2A, para 10(3)(5)(6)(8)*). In determining under *FA 2003, s 108(1)* (see **19.134**) whether or not the relevant land transaction is linked to another transaction, it can be assumed that the vendor is any of the vendor, the transferor under the first appropriate transaction or the transferor under the transaction concerned or under any other pre-completion transaction that has some subject matter in common with that transaction (*FA 2003, Sch 2A, para 10(7)*).

19.119 For this purpose the first appropriate transaction means the original contract, but if that contract is not performed at the same time as (and in connection with the performance of) the specified transaction, it means that pre-completion transaction in relation to the original contract that meets the following conditions:

(*a*) it is performed at the time when the specified transaction is performed and (if it is not itself the specified transaction) is performed in connection with the performance of the specified transaction;

(*b*) it is a transaction on which the entitlement of the transferee to call for the conveyance of the subject matter of the specified transaction depends; and

(*c*) it is not preceded by another pre-completion transaction that meets conditions (*a*) and (*b*),

(*FA 2003, Sch 2A, para 11(1)–(3)*.)

For this purpose a contract for a land transaction is performed when it is substantially performed or completed (whichever is the earlier). A free-standing transfer other than a contract is performed when the transferee under that transfer (or an assignee of that transferee, ie a person who, as a result of a transaction that is an assignment of rights in relation to the free-standing transfer, is entitled to call for a conveyance of the whole or part of the subject matter of the free-standing transfer) acquires the subject matter of the transfer (*FA 2003, Sch 2A, para 11(4)*). Where the specified transaction is a pre-completion transaction in relation to each of two or more contracts to which *Sch 2A* applies that together form a series of such contracts (each having some subject matter in common with all the others), references to the original contract mean the first contract in that series (*FA 2003, Sch 2A, para 11(5)*).

19.120 *FA 2003, Sch 2A, paras 12–14* (which determine the consideration where there is a relevant consideration between parties) apply to a free-standing transfer in the same way as to an assignment of rights (*FA 2003, Sch 2A, para 12(1)*). These provisions are dealt with at **19.103–19.108**.

Relief for Transferor

19.121 If a person would otherwise be liable to pay tax in respect of a notional land transaction deemed to take place under *para 5(1)*, or an additional land transaction deemed to take place under *para 5(2)* (see **19.110**) and the original contract had not been substantially performed when the assignment of rights was entered into, no liability to tax arises in respect of the notional or additional transaction provided that the purchaser claims relief (which must be done in a land transaction return or an amendment of such a return). No claim is needed if the land transaction is exempt from charge under any of *FA 2003, ss 71A–73* (alternative property finance – see **19.274**) (*FA 2003, Sch 2A, para 15*).

Relief for Original Purchaser

19.122 If:

(*a*) the pre-completion transaction is a qualifying sub-sale (a contract under which the original purchaser contracts to sell the whole or part of the subject matter of the original contract to the transferee);

(*b*) the original purchaser would otherwise be liable to pay tax in respect of a land transaction effected by the completion (or substantial performance) of the original contract;

(*c*) the performance of the qualifying sub-sale takes place at the same time as (and in connection with) the performance of the original contract; and

(*d*) relief is claimed in a land transaction return or an amendment of such a return in respect of the land transaction at (*b*),

no liability to tax arises in respect of that transaction if it relates to the whole of the subject matter of the original contract (*FA 2003, Sch 2A, para 16(1)(2)(6)*). If it relates to part only of the subject matter, the consideration for the land transaction is reduced by so much of it as is referable to the subject matter of the qualifying sub-sale – and can be reduced more than once if there is more than one qualifying subsale (*FA 2003, Sch 2A, para 16(3)(4)*). Neither of those reliefs apply if the original contract had been substantially performed when the qualifying sub-sale was entered into, or the transaction effected by the performance of the qualifying sub-sale is exempt from charge by virtue of any of *FA 2003, ss 71A–73* (alternative property finance) (*FA 2003, Sch 2A, para 16(5)*). For the purposes of *para 16*, a contract is performed when it is substantially performed or completed (whatever is the earlier) (*FA 2003, Sch 2A, para 16(7)*). If a transaction is a qualifying sub-sale in relation to more than one original contract, *para* 16 is to be applied separately in relation to each such original contract for the purpose of determining what relief may be available with respect to the land transaction in question (*FA 2003, Sch 2A, para 17*).

Tax Avoidance Arrangements

19.123 Relief cannot be claimed under either *paras 15* or *16* if the assignment of rights or the qualifying sub-sale (as the case may be) forms part of a tax avoidance arrangement (*FA 2003, Sch 2A, para 18(1)*). Arrangements are tax avoidance arrangements if, having regard to all the circumstances, it would be reasonable to conclude that the obtaining of a tax advantage for the original purchaser or any other person was the main purpose (or one of the main purposes) of the original purchaser entering into the arrangements (*FA 2003, Sch 2A, para 18(2)*). A tax advantage is a relief (or increased relief) from tax; a repayment (or increased repayment) of tax; the avoidance or reduction of a charge to tax; or the avoidance of a possible assessment to tax (*FA 2013, Sch 2A, para 18(3)*). Tax for this purpose is limited to SDLT (*FA 2003, s 121*). Arrangements includes any agreement, understanding, scheme, transaction or series of transactions (whether or not legally enforceable) (*FA 2003, Sch 2A, para 18(4)*). Nothing in *paras 12–14* (minimum consideration rule – see **19.103–19.108**) or *para 18* affects the breadth of the application of *FA 2003, ss 75A–75C* (anti-avoidance – see **19.239**) (*FA 2003, Sch 2A, para 18(5)*).

19.124 The Treasury have power by regulation to amend *Sch 2A* or any provisions relating to the making of returns so as to:

(*a*) exempt a relevant purchaser (ie the person who is the transferor under a pre-completion transaction) of any specified description, or in specified circumstances, from the duty to deliver a land transaction return;

(*b*) provide for relief under *Sch 2A, paras 15* or *16* (see **19.121** and **19.122**) to be available without a claim in the case of any specified class of transactions; or

(*c*) provide that *Sch 2A, para 5* (see **19.110**) does not apply in specified cases (*FA 2003, Sch 2A, para 19*).

Pre-17 July 2013 Transactions

19.125 Up to 20 March 2012, if a contract for a land transaction was assigned (or there was a sub-sale or other transaction as a result of which someone other than the original purchaser became entitled to call for a conveyance), SDLT applied as if there were a contract for a land transaction (the secondary contract) under which the transferee was the purchaser and the consideration was the sum of the consideration payable by the transferee (or a person connected with him within *ITA 2007, s 993*) under the original contract and the consideration given for the transfer of rights (*FA 2003, s 45(1)(3)*). From 21 March 2012 this does not apply to the grant or assignment of an option or to an agreement for the future grant or assignment of an option.(*FA 2003, s 45(1A)* inserted by *FA 2012, s 212* and amended by *FA 2013, s 194(2)*). Where there are successive transfers, the provision has effect in relation to each of them (*FA 2003, s 45(4)*). However, *s 45(3)* provides that if the substantial performance or completion of the original contract takes place at the same time as the substantial performance or completion of the secondary one the original contract is disregarded. This preserves sub-sale relief in the normal case where at the time of a sub-sale or assignment the original contract has not been performed but all that has been paid is a deposit. If the assignment relates to part only of the property under the contract, the provision obviously applies by reference to that part only (and the remainder of the contract is treated as a separate contract) (*FA 2003, s 45(5)*). This does not apply if the secondary contract is exempt from SDLT under *FA 2003, s 73(3)* (alternative property finance – see **19.307**). Where the effective date of the transaction is after 23 March 2011, it does not apply where any of the alternative property finance legislation applies (*FA 2003, s 45(3)* as amended by *FA 2011, Sch 21, para* 2). This makes clear that the sub-sales rules and the alternative property finance rules cannot be combined to remove all SDLT charges on the purchase of an interest in land (Finance Bill 2011 Explanatory Notes). St Matthews (West) Ltd sought to challenge the retrospective application of the legislation by way of judicial review (*R (on the application of St Matthews (West) Ltd and others v HM Treasury and another (2015 STC 2272)*) but both the High Court and the Court of Appeal refused the application. The only basis to challenge primary legislation would be that it is incompatible with human rights. But it was held by the Court of Appeal in *R (on the application of Heutson) v HMRC (2011 STC 1860)* that there is no obligation on the State to test the efficacy of a tax avoidance scheme in the courts before enacting retrospective legislation.

19.126 The interaction of *FA 2003, s 45* with *FA 2003, Sch 15, para 10* (see **19.307**) was in issue in an SDLT avoidance scheme in *DV3 RS Limited Partnership v HMRC (TC 1012)*. This is considered at **19.309**. Another attempt to exploit sub-sale relief was made in *Vardy Properties (an unlimited company) and Vardy Properties (Teeside) Ltd v HMRC (2012 SFTD 1398)*. This involved a complex scheme. As the rules for sale relief have been altered, it is not proposed to explain it here. Suffice to say that Teeside was a shareholder in Vardy Properties. Vardy Properties contracted to buy a property and before completion resolved to distribute it by way of dividend to Teeside immediately after completion. The companies claimed that *s 45* applied so the acquisition by Vardy Properties fell to be ignored and that the acquisition by Teeside was exempt because there was no consideration. The tribunal felt that from a tax point of view, the taxpayer was correct but that the dividend was unlawful on a technicality as the way it had been declared did not properly comply with the requirements of the *Companies Act 1985*. Accordingly Teeside never became entitled to call for a conveyance, so *s 45* was not engaged. The tribunal added that it been engaged, the scheme would still not have worked as the consideration on the transfer of rights would have been £7.25 million, as that was an amount of consideration that had been indirectly provided by Teeside for the acquisition (it was actually the amount that it subscribed for its shares in Vardy Properties). HMRC have said that the scheme used here was 'a widely-marketed scheme used by homebuyers and others who have tried to get out of their responsibilities to pay SDLT' (HMRC Press Release 20.9.2012). It should be noted that it took place before the enactment of *FA 2003, s 75A* (see **19.339**), which would probably now apply to such a transaction. A similar scheme was used in *Crest Nicholson (Wainscott) Ltd v HMRC (2017 SFTD 451)*. In that case, the distribution was in a reduction of capital by a transfer of the right to call for the property transfers. The FTT held that transfer did not attract SDLT. There was, however, a further issue. The money paid on completion did not emanate from the transferee, South East, it came from another group company, Operations. HMRC contended that South East must have acted as an agent for Operations throughout. The Tribunal disagreed, but instead held that South East had acted as principal and, as such, was liable for the tax on completion of the contract. As HMRC had raised assessments on all three companies, that on South East was accordingly upheld. This makes sense. The purpose of *s 45* is to eliminate a double SDLT charge, not to enable SDLT to be completely avoided.

19.127

Example 19.6

Peter contracts with Paul to sell him a property for £200,000 and pays a deposit of £10,000. Paul assigns the benefit of the contract to Simon for £20,000. Before completion Simon reassigns the contract to Sheila for £30,000. On completion Sheila pays Peter the balance of £190,000.

On completion the only charge will be on Sheila. This will be on £220,000 as the deemed price is the amount of £30,000 payable by Sheila to Simon plus the amount payable by Sheila under the original contract, namely £190,000. As Peter's contract for £200,000 is completed at the same time as Sheila's it is ignored so does not attract SDLT. Similarly Simon's secondary contract for a consideration of £210,000 (£20,000 paid to Simon plus £190,000 payable to Peter) is ignored and does not attract SDLT.

19.128 Substantial performance can of course trigger the tax on some or all of the contracts. Suppose that the price in the above example was £21,000. On the assignment to Simon, Paul would obtain £20,000 out of the £21,000 consideration on his deemed contract, which would probably mean that the deemed contract was substantially performed at that stage. That would trigger a SDLT charge on Paul, but not on Peter as his contract would not have been substantially performed.

19.129 During the period 20 March 2012 to 16 July 2013, *FA 2003, s 45* as originally enacted applied with modifications. The substantial performance or completion of the original contract could not be disregarded if:

(*a*) the secondary contract was substantially performed at the same time as (and in connection with) the substantial performance or completion of the original contract but was not completed at that time (the relevant time);

(*b*) the original purchaser (or a connected person) was in possession of the whole or substantially the whole, of the subject matter of the transfer of rights at any time after the relevant time; and

(*c*) having regard to all the circumstances, it would be reasonable to conclude that the obtaining of a tax advantage (a relief (or increased relief) from SDLT, a repayment (or increased repayment) of SDLT, or the avoidance or reduction of a charge to SDLT) for the original purchaser was the main purpose or one of the main purposes, of the original purchaser in entering into the transfer of rights,

(*FA 2003, s 45(3A)(3B)* inserted by *FA 2013, s 194*.)

Nothing in this provision affects the breadth of the application of *FA 2003, ss 75A–75C* (see **19.389**) (*FA 2003, s 45(3C)*). This provision applied also to successive transfers within *FA 2003, s 45(4)* as if the reference to the original contract was a reference to the secondary contract arising from the transfer of rights, the reference to the original purchaser was a reference to the transferee under the earlier transfer of rights, and the reference to the transfer of rights were a reference to the subsequent transfer of rights (*FA 2003, s 45(4A)* inserted by *FA 2013, s 194(6)*).

19.130 Where, as a result of the exclusion of an agreement for the future grant or assignment of an option, *FA 2003, s 45* does not apply to a contract (the original contract), the original contract was substantially performed or completed at the same time as (and in connection with) the substantial performance or completion of an agreement for the grant or assignment of an option, and that time fell before 17 July 2013:

(*a*) *FA 2003, s 76* (duty to deliver land transaction return) had to be regarded as requiring the purchase under the original contract to deliver a return relating to the land transaction by 30 September 2013;

(*b*) 30 September 2013 became the filing date for the return relating to the transaction; and

(*c*) If the purchaser under the original contract had delivered a return relating to the transaction before 17 July 2013, he had to amend the return by 30 September 2013 (without prejudice to his right to make further amendments),

(*FA 2013, s 194(8)(10–12)*.)

These requirements also applied where *FA 2003, s 45* applied in relation to the contract for a land transaction (the original contract), as a result of the amendments described at **19.129** the substantial performance or completion of the original contract could not be disregarded, and the relevant time referred to at **19.129**(*a*) fell before 17 July 2013 (*FA 2013, s 194(9)*).

Contracts Providing for Conveyance to a Third Party

19.131 If a chargeable interest is to be conveyed to a third party (C) under a contract (or to either a third party or the purchaser under the contract) at the direction or request of the purchaser (B), the purchaser is not regarded as entering into a land transaction unless either the contract is substantially performed or the property is in fact conveyed to the purchaser (*FA 2003, s 44A(1)–(3)* and *(6)*). If the contract is later rescinded or annulled, or for any other reason not carried into effect, the tax paid on substantial performance becomes repayable – but only if an amended return is filed (*FA 2003, s 44A(4)*). Any contract between the purchaser under the main contract and the third party to whom the land is conveyed is a land transaction to which the normal rules fixing the effective date (see **19.88**) apply (*FA 2003, s 44A(7)*). This is intended to apply to such things as a development agreement where the developer has a right to enter on the land, build houses and then direct the conveyance of the plot to the purchaser of the house.

19.132 If the purchaser (B) assigns or otherwise transfers his rights under such a contract to someone else (D) (either in respect of all or part of the land), so that D becomes the person entitled to call for the conveyance to C, the assignment is not taxed as a land transaction but instead D is treated as having entered into a contract on the same terms as B's original contract other than that the consideration is the aggregate of the consideration for the transfer of the rights and so much of the consideration under B's original contract as is due to be paid (directly or indirectly) by D or a person connected with him (within *CTA 2010, s 1122*) to the original vendor (A) (*FA 2003, s 45A(1)–(3)*). If there are successive transfers this provision applies to each of them (*FA 2003, s 45A(5)*). Where the transfer relates to part only of the land (or to only some of the rights) the deemed contract between A and D obviously extends only to that part and the contract between A and B is treated as if it related to the part not transferred (*FA 2003, s 45A(7)*). The effective date of D's deemed land transaction cannot be earlier than the date of transfer of the rights (*FA 2003, s 45A(8)*). The substantial performance of the original contract between A and B is of course ignored if it takes place at the same time (and in connection with) the substantial performance of the deemed contract between A and D (except insofar as it relates to land or rights not transferred). If D assigns to E his contract with B, (which will create a deemed contract between A and E) substantial performance by E similarly does not also trigger tax on D (*FA 2003, s 45A(4),(6)*).

Options

19.133 The acquisition of an option is a separate land transaction to that effected by its exercise (*FA 2003, s 46(1)(a)*). So is the acquisition of a right of pre-emption preventing the grantor from entering into a land transaction or restricting his right to enter into such a transaction (*FA 2003, s 46(1)(b)*). The effective date of that transaction is the time that the option or right is acquired, not when it becomes exercisable (*FA 2003, s 46(3)*). The acquisition of an option is a land transaction even if the grantor has the choice either to enter into the land transaction if the option is exercised or to discharge his obligations in some other way such as paying a sum of money (*FA 2003, s 46(2)*).

19.134 The *section* notes that the grant and exercise could be linked transactions – and indeed the explanatory notes to the Finance Bill indicate that it is probably a 'linked' transaction. Transactions are linked for SDLT purposes if they form part of a single scheme, arrangement or series of transactions between the same vendor and purchaser or, in other case, persons connected with them (within *CTA 2010, s 1122*) (*FA 2003, s 108(1)*). The grant of an option and its subsequent exercise would normally be a series of transactions between the same parties (unless the option is assignable and is, in fact, assigned).

19.135 Where two or more transactions are linked, for the purpose of determining the duty payable, duty is chargeable only on the interest in land which is the main subject matter of any of the transactions (ie the chargeable interest acquired – *s 43(6)*), but the consideration on which duty is chargeable is the total of the chargeable consideration for all of those linked transactions (*FA 2003, s 55(4)*). In other words, the exercise of the option merges the grant of the option and the conveyance in pursuance of its exercise into a single transaction taking place at the time of conveyance (as the land is the main subject matter of both the option and the sale) for a deemed consideration equal to the total of the option money and the purchase price of the land.

19.136 It appears, however, that a SDLT return needs to be made on the grant of the option and, if appropriate, tax paid on the option money at that stage. Presumably, credit for such tax will be given in calculating the tax payable at the time of exercise, although the statutory authority to permit this is not readily apparent.

19.137 *Section 46* does not apply to so much of an option or right of pre-emption as constitutes or forms part of a land transaction apart from the section (*FA 2003, s 46(4)*). It is unclear what this is intended to cover. The explanatory notes to the Bill state that it 'confirms that if an option or right of pre-emption is chargeable as a land transaction in its own right, or because it is part of a wider transaction, then it is dealt with as such, rather than dealt with under the clause'. For an option to be chargeable as a land transaction in its own right it must constitute a chargeable interest, ie it must confer the benefit of an obligation, restriction or condition affecting the value of an interest of land in the UK (*FA 2003, s 48(1)(b)* – see **19.4**). It may well be such an obligation but, if so, it is hard to see at what *s 46* is aimed. The purpose of *s 46* is to prevent avoidance by attributing the bulk of the consideration to the grant of the option and very little to the land itself.

Contingent, Uncertain and Unascertained Consideration

19.138 If the whole or part of the chargeable consideration for a transaction is contingent, the value of the consideration must be determined on the assumption that the outcome of the contingency will be such that the consideration will be payable (or will not cease to be payable as the case may be), ie the contingency is ignored (*FA 2003, s 51(1)*). Consideration is contingent for this purpose if it is to be paid only if some uncertain future event occurs (or if it is to cease to be paid if some uncertain future event occurs (*FA 2003, s 51(3)*).

19.139 If the whole or part of the chargeable consideration for a transaction is uncertain or unascertained, its value must be determined on the basis of a reasonable estimate (*FA 2003, s 51(2)*). Consideration is uncertain if its amount or value depends on uncertain future events (*FA 2003, s 51(3)*). It is unclear how one is expected to estimate an unascertainable amount. It is equally unclear what happens if HMRC's view of a reasonable estimate differs from the taxpayer's. Presumably they will amend the taxpayer's SDLT return and trigger his right of appeal against that amendment.

19.140 The purchaser can apply to HMRC to defer payment of SDLT where the amount payable depends on the value of contingent or uncertain consideration, provided that all or part of that consideration is payable more than six months after the effective date of the transaction (*FA 2003, s 90(1)*). HMRC have power to provide by statutory instrument how such an application is to be made, the procedure for their making a decision on it, and the taxpayer's right of appeal against a refusal of the application (*FA 2003, s 90(2)(3)*). They have done so in *regs 10–28* of the *SDLT (Administration) Regulations 2003 (SI 2003 No 2837)*. These require the sort of information that one would expect. It also gives the purchaser a right of appeal against a refusal of the application. The only possible controversial provision is that HMRC can refuse the deferral if there are tax avoidance arrangements in relation to the transaction, ie arrangements the main object (or one of the main objects) of which is either to enable payment of the tax in respect of the transaction to be deferred or to avoid the amount of the whole or part of the chargeable consideration for the transaction being determined. An application to defer payment of the tax cannot be made to the extent that the consideration has already been paid, is not contingent, or an amount is ascertained or ascertainable at the time of the payment (*FA 2003, s 90(5)*).

19.141 In any event the return is provisional. The transaction needs to be reconsidered if the contingency occurs or it becomes clear that it will not occur or, in the case of uncertain or unascertainable consideration, an amount relevant to the calculation of the consideration (or of any instalment of the consideration) becomes ascertained (*FA 2003, s 80(1)*). The taxpayer may then need to make a return, or further return, and pay any additional tax due as a consequence of the new information becoming known (*FA 2003, s 80(2)*).

19.142 It is not always clear whether consideration is unascertainable or merely difficult to quantify. In *Underground Electric Railways Company v CIR ([1906] AC 21)*, a stamp duty case, where part of the consideration for the sale of the company was to be based on a future dividend payable on paid-up issued share capital at that time, it was held that for stamp duty purposes the consideration should be ascertained on the amount of share capital paid up at the time of the transfer. This decision was followed in *LM Tenancies 1 plc v CIR (1998 STC 326)*. Two properties were leased to a company and under the terms of the leases the consideration payable was fixed by reference to the price of the holding of government stock at the close of business on the 25th business day following the execution of the leases. The company argued that the consideration was unascertainable for stamp duty purposes and therefore the leases should be chargeable with fixed duty of £2 only. The stamp duty office contended that the consideration was ascertainable as at the date of execution of the leases, and any subsequent variation in the price of government stock should be ignored. Applying the reasoning in *Underground Electric*, it was held that it was permissible to calculate stamp duty by reference to the price of the government stock at the date the leases were executed. These decisions seem equally applicable to SDLT.

Annuities, etc

19.143 If all or part of the chargeable consideration for a land transaction consists of an annuity (or other payment, other than rent, that falls to be paid periodically) payable for life, in perpetuity, for an indefinite period or for a definite period exceeding 12 years, the consideration is treated as equal to 12 years' annual payments. If the amount payable varies (or can vary) from year to year, it is the 12 highest annual payments – but a provision for adjustment of the amount payable in line with the retail price index is ignored (*FA 2003, s 52(1)–(3), (6)*). *Section 51* – but not *ss 80* and *90* (see **19.138**) – applies for this purpose in the same way as with contingent or unascertained consideration (*FA 2003, s 52(5)(7)*). In other words a reasonable estimate must be made at the time of the transaction but this cannot be adjusted subsequently if, for example, the life tenant dies in less than 12 years or the annuity payments otherwise come to an end prematurely.

Transfers to Connected Companies

19.144 Normally, if there is no consideration for a transaction, no SDLT is payable and if property is sold at an undervalue SDLT is payable only on the price paid. There is no requirement to substitute an open market value. However, there is a major exception where the purchaser is a company and either the vendor is connected with it (within *CTA 2010, s 1122*), or some or all of the consideration for the transaction consists of the issue or transfer of shares in a company with which the vendor is connected. In such a case the chargeable consideration for the transaction must be taken to be not less than the market value of the land in question at the effective date of the transaction. If the acquisition is the grant of a lease at a rent it must similarly be taken to be not less than that rent (*FA 2003, s 53*). Furthermore the exemption for gifts (or other transactions for which there is no chargeable consideration) does not apply unless either:

(*a*) immediately after the transaction, the company holds the property as trustee in the course of a business carried on by it that consists of or includes the management of trusts;

(*b*) immediately after the transaction, the company holds the property as trustee and the only reason it is connected with the vendor is that the vendor is the settlor, a connected person of the settlor or a company connected with the settlement; or

(*c*) the vendor is a company and both:

 (i) the transaction is (or is part of) a distribution of assets of the company (either in a winding up or by way of dividend); and

 (ii) neither the subject matter of the transaction or another interest from which it is derived has been the subject of a transaction within the previous three years in respect of which group relief was claimed by the vendor.

(*FA 2003, s 54.*)

Note the use of the phrase 'not less than'. This is a one-way adjustment. If the price is below market value SDLT is based on the market value, but if it exceeds market value the SDLT is based on the actual price paid. It should be remembered that 'vendor' is defined to mean disposer under a land transaction (see **19.5**). As a result this provision will impose SDLT in some unexpected circumstances.

Leases

19.145 If the chargeable consideration for a transaction is, or includes, rent, the SDLT is 1% of the net present value of the rent payable over the term of the lease. No SDLT is payable on the first £125,000 if the property is residential (£120,000 prior to 22 March 2006 and £60,000 prior to 16 March 2005), or £150,000 if it is non-residential or mixed, ie if it includes land that is not residential property (*FA 2003, s 56* and *Sch 5, para 2*). Where VAT is payable on a lease and the landlord opted to tax on or before the effective date of the transaction the VAT is part of the amount of the rent. However, if he opts subsequently the VAT on the future rents does not constitute chargeable consideration (Stamp Duty Land Tax Manual, SDLT3800). When the standard rate of VAT increased from 17.5% to 20% on 4 January 2011 HMRC said that the 17.5% rate should be used to calculate NPV where the effective date of the lease was between those two dates and the 20% rate if it was on or after 4 January 2011. However, they would treat the NPV calculation as being based on rents that are uncertain (see **19.155**).

19.146 If the lease is one of a number of linked transactions for which the chargeable consideration consists of or includes rent the tax is calculated as if all of these transactions were a single transaction and the resulting figure is apportioned over the leases concerned by reference to the net present value of the rent payable over the term of the leases for each of such leases (*FA 2003, Sch 5, para 2(5)–(7)*). The net present value is the sum of the present value of the rent payable for each year of the lease discounted at 3.5% (the temporal discount rate) (*FA 2003, Sch 5, paras 3, 4*).

19.147 In applying SDLT to a lease for a fixed term, no account is taken of any contingency as a result of which the lease might end before the end of the fixed term or of any right of either party to determine or renew the lease (*FA 2003, Sch 17A, para 2*). Where a lease is for a fixed term and thereafter until determined (or a lease for a fixed term that may continue by operation of law) it is treated as if it were a lease for the original fixed term only. If it in fact continues beyond the fixed term it is regarded as a lease for a fixed term of one year longer than the fixed term (and if it continues for more than a year, then as being a lease for a fixed term of two years longer than the original term and so on). If extra tax is payable as a result of such deeming for a period (or further period) of one year the purchaser must make a fresh SDLT return within 30 days after the end of that one-year period. Prior to 17 July 2013 the return did not have to be delivered until 30 days after the end of the extended term. The tax payable is at the rates in force at the effective date of the transaction, ie normally of the grant of the original lease (*FA 2003, Sch 17A, para 3* as amended by *FA 2013, Sch 41, para 2*). From 17 July 2013, no tax (or additional tax) is payable as a result of the continuation of a lease for a period (or further period) of one year under *para 2* if, during that one-year period, the tenant is granted a new lease of the same (or substantially the same) premises in circumstances where *para 9A* applies (see **19.191**) (*FA 2003, Sch 17A, para 3(3)* inserted by *FA 2013, Sch 41, para 2*). Where a lease is treated as continuing for a period (or further period) of one year under *para 2* but it actually terminates during that one-year period, it is instead treated under *para 2* as continuing only until the date of its termination. The references in *paras 3* and *4* to the one-year period are then to be read as referring to the period until the termination (*FA 2003, Sch 17A, para 3(6)* inserted by *FA 2013, Sch 41, para 2*).

19.148 Where:

(*a*) *para 3* would apply to treat a lease (the original lease) as if it were a lease for a fixed term one year longer than the original term;

(*b*) during that one-year period the tenant is granted a new lease of the same (or substantially the same) premises;

(*c*) the term of the new lease begins during that one-year period; and

(*d*) *para 9A* (backdated lease granted to tenant holding over) does not apply, *para 3* does not apply to treat the lease as continuing after the original term, but the term of the new lease is instead treated for SDLT as beginning immediately after the original term. Any rent which would be regarded as payable under the original lease in respect of that one-year period is treated as payable under the new lease (and *FA 2003, Sch 5, para 1A* does not apply to it) (*FA 2003, Sch 17A, para 3A(1)–(4)* inserted by *FA 2013, Sch 41, para 3*). Where the fixed term of a lease has previously been extended (on one or more occasions) under *para 3, para 3A* applies as if references to the original term were to that term as so extended (*FA 2003, Sch 17A, para 3A(5)*).

19.149 A lease for an indefinite term (other than a tenancy at will, etc which is not a land transaction – see **9.5**) is treated as being for a fixed term of a year. If it continues beyond a year it is treated as being for a fixed term of two years and so on. Again, if any additional tax is payable as a result of this deeming a return must be made and the tax paid within 30 days after the end of the previous deemed term (*FA 2003, Sch 17A, para 4*).

19.150 If successive leases are granted (or treated as granted) whether at the same or different times of the same (or substantially the same) premises and those grants are linked transactions (see **19.25**) the series of leases is treated for SDLT purposes as if it were a single lease granted at the time of the first lease in the series, for a term equal to the aggregate of those of all the leases and in consideration of the rent due under all the leases (*FA 2003, Sch 17A, para 5*).

19.151 Where a premium (or other chargeable consideration other than rent) is payable, the 0% band does not apply in relation to the premium (so SDLT at 1% is payable on it if it falls within that band) if the relevant land is wholly non-residential and the relevant rent is £1,000 or more). If the relevant land is partly residential the relevant rent (and the consideration) must be apportioned on a just and reasonable basis between the two types of land. If the part apportioned to the non-residential property is £1,000 or more, the transaction is treated as two separate transactions so that the 1% charge applies only to the non-residential element (*FA 2003, Sch 5, paras 9, 9A*). For this purpose, the relevant rent is the average annual rent over the term of the lease (or if the lease provides for different amounts of rent to be payable for different parts of the term and those amounts are ascertainable at the time of the transaction, over the period for which the highest ascertainable rent is payable). If the transaction is one of a number of linked transactions for which the chargeable consideration includes rent, the relevant rent is the total of the average annual rent for all of those transactions (*FA 2003, Sch 5, para 9A(6), (7)*). The relevant land is the land an interest in which is the main subject matter of the transaction (or in the case of a series of linked transactions any land an interest in which is the main subject matter of any of the transactions) (*FA 2003, s 55(3)(4)), Sch 5, para 9A(8)*). For land transactions prior to 12 March 2008 the de minimis figure was £600 p.a.

19.152 The relevant rental figure is the annual rent in relation to the transaction in question or, if it is one of a number of linked transactions, the total of the annual rents in relation to all of those transactions. The tax payable in such a case is the sum of the SDLT on the premium and the SDLT on the rent (*FA 2003, Sch 5, para 9*). The rent element will of course still attract the exempt slice, but if the sum of the premium and the net present value of the rent is below the exemption limit SDLT will be payable on the premium. The annual rent for this purpose is the average annual rent over the term of the lease. If the rent is different for different parts of the term it is the average annual rent over the period for which the highest ascertainable amount is payable (*FA 2003, Sch 5, para 9(3)*). If such a lease is one of a number of linked transactions, only the premium is taken into account in determining the relevant consideration for the purpose of *s 55* (*FA 2003, Sch 5, para 9(5)*). This does not appear to mean that the rent is ignored but rather that the lease bears its own SDLT on the rent.

19.153 The value of the following items does not count as chargeable consideration:

(*a*) any undertaking by the tenant to repair, maintain or insure the deemed premises;

(*b*) any undertaking by the tenant to pay an amount in respect of services, repairs, maintenance, insurance or the landlord's costs of management;

(*c*) any obligation undertaken by the tenant that does not affect the rent that a tenant would be prepared to pay in the open market;

(*d*) any guarantee of the payment of rent or the performance by the tenant of his obligation under the lease;

(*e*) any penal rent, or increased rent in the nature of a penal rent, payable in respect of the breach of any obligation of the tenant;

(*f*) any payment made in discharge of any of the above obligations; and

(*g*) the release of any of the above obligations.

(*FA 2003, Sch 17A, para 10*.)

19.154 A single sum expressed to be payable in respect of rent and other matters but not apportioned must be treated as entirely rent (*FA 2003, Sch 17A, para 6*). Where separate sums are expressed to be payable in respect of rent and other matters a reapportionment may be required under *Sch 4, para 4* (see **19.17**). However, any chargeable consideration for the grant of a lease that is payable in respect of a period before such grant is specifically excluded from constituting rent (*FA 2003, Sch 5, para 1A*).

19.155 If the rent payable under a lease varies in accordance with provisions in the lease (or is contingent, uncertain or unascertained) the normal rules apply for the first five years of the term, ie the tax has to be recalculated each year when the actual rent is ascertained (see **19.138–19.141**). The annual rent for each subsequent year is deemed to be equal to the highest amount of rent payable in respect of any consecutive 12-month period in the first five years of the term (*FA 2003, Sch 17A, para 7*). Any reduction in that rent as a result of applying *FA 2003, Sch 17A, para 9(2)* (see **19.178**) or *9A* (see **19.171**) is of course ignored for this purpose (but not where the transaction took place prior to 22 July 2004) (*Reg 8, Stamp Duty and SDLT (Variation of the Finance Act 2003) (No 2) Regulations 2003 (SI 2003 No 2816)*). Where there is a possibility of the rent under a lease granted after 19 July 2006 being varied under the *Agricultural Holdings Act 1086, ss 12, 13 or 33* or the *Agricultural Holdings Act 1995, Part 2* (or their Scottish equivalents) the rent payable under the lease must be treated as uncertain for this purpose (*FA 2003 Sch 17A, para 7(4A)*).

9.156 If the initial rent is contingent, uncertain or unascertained the rent payable under the lease is reviewed at the end of the fifth year of the term (or on any earlier date on which the rent ceases to be uncertain, ie the contingency crystallises or it becomes clear that it will not do so, or the amount of rent becomes ascertained). If as a result of that review further tax is payable a return must be made, and the tax paid, within 30 days of the end of the fifth year (or earlier date on which the rent becomes ascertained) (*FA 2003, Sch 17A, para 8(1)–(4)*). If the review results in a reduction in tax the purchaser can amend his return if he is in time to do so. If he is not, he can make a claim outside the return for repayment of the amount overpaid (*FA 2003, Sch 17A, para 8(5)*).

19.157 If a lease contains provisions under which the rent can be adjusted, the first (or only) such adjustment is to an amount that (before the adjustment) is uncertain and that adjustment has effect from a date (the review date) that is expressed as falling five years after a specified date (which itself falls within the three months before the start of the term of the lease) the adjustments that are normally made for the first five years are made only up to the review date (*FA 2003, Sch 17A, para 7A*).

19.158 If a lease is surrendered in consideration of the grant of a new lease of the same premises to the tenant by the landlord (the rent payable under the new lease in relation to any period falling within the overlap period (the period between the date of grant of the new lease and what would have been the end of the term of the old lease if it had not been terminated) is treated as reduced by the rent that would have been payable for that period under the old lease. The rent that would have been payable under the old lease for this purpose is the amount on which SDLT was calculated, not the actual rent payable. If the rent under the new lease for the overlap period is less than that under the old, the rent is treated as nil; the calculation cannot produce a negative amount (*FA 2003, Sch 17A, para 9*). This effectively gives credit for the SDLT already paid on the rent for the overlap period.

19.159 This provision also applies if an overlap period arises by reason of the grant of a new lease under *Part 2* of the *Landlord and Tenant Act 1954*, or the grant of a new lease to a subtenant on the termination of the headlease in pursuance of a court order on a claim for relief against re-entry or forfeiture (or of a contractual entitlement arising in the event of the headlease being terminated), or the grant of a lease to a guarantor under a lease that has been terminated (*FA 2003, Sch 17A, para 9(1)(c), (d)*).

19.160 If the grant of a lease is exempt from SDLT under *FA 2003, s 57A* (sale and lease back arrangements), *Sch 7* (group relief or reconstruction or acquisition relief), *Sch 7A* (PAIF and COACS seeding relief), *s 66* (transfers involving public bodies) *Sch 8* (charities) regulations and *s 123(3)* (to mirror stamp duty exemptions) or *FA 2009, Sch 61, Pt 3 paras 6* and *8* (alternative finance investment bond relief) the first assignment of the lease that is not exempt is treated as the grant of a new lease by the assignor for a term equal to the unexpired term of the exempt lease and on the same terms as those on which the assignee holds the lease (*FA 2003, Sch 17A, para 11*). This treatment does not apply where the assignment of the lease would otherwise be exempt from SDLT by virtue of *FA 2009, Sch 61* (alternative finance investment bonds) (*SDLT (Alternative Finance Investment Bonds) Regulations 2010; SI 2010 No 814*).

19.161 Where a lease is assigned any obligations of the assignor under *FA 2003, s 80* (see **19.141**), *s 81A* (see **19.368**), *Sch 17A para 3* or *4* (see **19.147** and **19.149**) or *Sch 17A, para 8* (see **19.156**) obviously pass to the assignee if the adjustment or return requirement occurs after the effective date of the assignment (*FA 2003, Sch 17A, para 12*).

19.162 If an agreement for a lease is entered into and the agreement is substantially performed (within the meaning of *s 44* – see **19.89**) without having been completed the agreement is treated as if it were the grant of a lease in accordance with the agreement and beginning with the date of substantial performance. If a lease is subsequently granted in pursuance of the agreement the notional lease is treated as if it were a lease granted on the date the agreement was substantially performed, for a term which begins with that date and ends at the end of the term of the actual lease, and in consideration of the total rent payable over that term. The actual lease is disregarded for SDLT purposes other than *FA 2003, s 81A* (return or further return in consequence of later linked transaction). For the purpose of *s 81A*, the grant of this notional lease and the grant of the actual lease are linked, the lessee under the actual lease (rather than that under the notional lease) is liable for any tax or additional tax, and the purchaser under the earlier transaction is the lessee under the actual lease (*FA 2003, Sch 17A, para 12A(3)(3A)(3B)* as amended by *FA 2013, Sch 41, para 6*). Prior to 17 July 2013, the notional lease was treated as surrendered at that time and the actual lease was treated as having been granted in consideration of that surrender (so as to trigger the overlap relief under *para 9* – see **19.158**). In such a case *para 5* (see **19.150**) obviously does not apply so as to treat the notional lease and the actual lease as a single lease. If the agreement is (to any extent) rescinded, annulled or not carried into effect subsequent to the deemed grant of the lease the land transaction return can be amended to reclaim the tax paid. It appears that no refund can be claimed if it is too late to amend the return (*FA 2003, Sch 17A, para 12A*.

19.163 If an agreement for a lease is assigned before it is substantially performed, *s 44* (see **19.91**) applies as if the contract were with the assignee not the assignor and as if the consideration given by the assignee for entering into the contract included any consideration given by him for the assignment. If the assignment occurs after the agreement has been substantially performed the assignment is treated as a separate land transaction whose effective date is the date of the assignment (*FA 2003, Sch 17A, para 12B*).

19.164 Up to 17 July 2013, if a lease was varied so as to increase the rent as from a date before the end of the fifth year of the term the variation was treated for SDLT purposes as the grant of a lease in consideration of the additional rent (*FA 2003, Sch 17A, para 13* as amended by *FA 2006, Sch 25, para 6*). There was an exception where the increase was in pursuance of a provision in the lease (although *para 14* could apply instead) or, from 19 July 2006, a statutory provision within *para 7(4A)* (see **19.155**). Similarly if the rent payable under a lease increased (whether in accordance with the provisions of the lease or otherwise) at some time after the first five years and that increase was 'abnormal', the increase in rent was treated as if it were the grant of a lease in consideration of the excess rent (ie the difference between the new rent and the rent previously taxed). This deemed lease was treated as made on the date on which the increased rent first becomes payable, as being for a term equal to the unexpired term of the original lease and as being linked with the original lease (*FA 2003, Sch 17A, para 14*). This provision was repealed by *FA 2013, Sch 41, para 7*.

19.165 Broadly speaking, an 'abnormal' increase was one where the annualised increase in rent since the later of the grant of the lease or the last time *para 14* applied was greater than 20% per year. It was calculated as follows:

(*a*) Find the start date. This was the beginning of the term of the lease or the beginning of the period by reference to which the rent assumed to be payable after the fifth year was determined under *para 7(3)* (see **19.155**).

If *para 14* has previously been applied it was the date of the last increase in relation to which it applied.

(*b*) Find the number of whole years in the period between the start date and the date on which the new rent first became payable.

(*c*) the rent increase was abnormal if the excess rent was greater than

$$\frac{R \times Y}{5}$$

where R is the rent previously taxed and Y is the number of whole years found under Step 2.

(*FA 2003, Sch 17A, para 15.*)

This provision was also repealed from 17 July 2013 by *FA 2013, Sch 41, para 7.*

19.166 Where the increase in rent occurred before 19 July 2006 an increase was abnormal if it exceeded the percentage increase in the retail price index plus 5%. The calculation was as follows.

(*a*) Find the start date as above.

(*b*) Divide the period between the start date and the date on which the new rent first becomes payable (the reference period) into 12-month periods (and a period consisting of any balance of the reference period).

(*c*) Find the factor by which the retail price index has increased over each of those periods. This is a figure expressed as a decimal (rounded to three decimal places) and determined by the formula:

$$\frac{RD - RI}{RI}$$

Where RD is the RPI for the month in which the last day of the period falls and RI is the RPI for the month in which the first day in that period falls. If RD is equal to or less than RI the income is nil.

(*d*) Find the relevant factor for each period. This is a figure expressed as a decimal (to three decimal places) and determined by the formula:

$$1 + \left(0.05 \times \frac{m}{12}\right) + r$$

Where m is the number of months in the period (treating a part of a month as a whole month) and r is the factor by which the RPI has increased in the period, ie the figure at step (*c*).

(*e*) Find the uplift factor for the reference period (expressed to three decimal places). If there is only one period at step (*b*) the uplift factor for the reference period is the relevant factor (the figure at (*d*)) for that period. If there are two it is the relevant factor for the first period multiplied by that for the second. If there are three it is the relevant factor for the first period multiplied by that for the second multiplied by that for the third, and so on.

(*f*) The rent increase is abnormal if the new rent is greater than the rent previously taxed multiplied by the uplift factor for the reference period.

19.167 If a lease is varied so as to reduce the rent, the variation is treated as an acquisition of a chargeable interest by the lessee. A variation that reduces the term is treated as an acquisition of a chargeable interest by the lessor (*FA 2003, Sch 17A, para 15A*). If the variation takes place after 19 May 2005 and any consideration in money or money's worth (other than an increase in rent) is given by the lessee for the variation (and it is not a variation of the amount of the rent or the term of the lease) the variation must be treated as an acquisition of a chargeable interest by the lessee (*FA 2003, Sch 17A, para 15A*).

19.168 If a lease is granted in consideration of the surrender of an existing lease between the same parties the grant of the new lease is not chargeable considerations for the surrender of the old and the surrender is not chargeable consideration for the grant of the new lease (*FA 2003, Sch 17A, para 16*). In the case of an assignment of a lease, the assumption by the assignee of the obligation to pay rent or to perform the obligations under the lease is not chargeable consideration for the assignment (*FA 2003, Sch 17A, para 17*). A reverse premium paid on the grant, assignment or surrender of a lease is not chargeable consideration. For this purpose a reverse premium is a payment by the landlord to the tenant on a grant, by the assignor to the assignee on an assignment, or by the tenant to the landlord on a surrender.

19.169 If under arrangements made in connection with the grant or assignment of a lease:

(*a*) the lessee or assignee (or any person connected with him – within *CTA 2010, s 1122* – or acting on his behalf) pays a deposit or makes a loan to any person;, and

(*b*) the repayment of all or part of the deposit or loan is contingent on anything done or omitted to be done by the lessee or assignee (or on the death of the lessee or assignee),

the amount of the loan or deposit (disregarding any repayment) must be treated as consideration other than rent given for the grant or assignment of the lease (*FA 2003, Sch 17A, para 18A(1)(2)*).

19.170 This does not apply in relation to a deposit if the total deemed consideration under *para 18(1)(2)* does not exceed twice the relevant maximum rent, ie the highest amount of rent payable in respect of any consecutive 12-month period in the first five years of the term (or in the case of an assignment the first five years remaining outstanding at the date of the assignment) (*FA 2003, Sch 17A, para 18A(3)(4)*). Tax is not chargeable under this provision merely because of the exclusion of the nil rate band under *Sch 5, para 9(2)* or *Sch 6, para 5(4)(b)* or *6(6)(b)* or *9(4)(b)* or *10(6)(b)* (*FA 2003, Sch 17A, para 18A(5)*).

19.171 If the tenant continues in occupation after his lease terminates and is subsequently granted a new lease of the same (or substantially the same) premises which is expressed to begin immediately after the termination of the old one, the term of the new lease is treated for SDLT purposes as beginning on the date on which it is expressed to begin and the rent payable in respect of any period falling before the actual date of the lease is treated as reduced by any amount of the actual rent as has already been taken into account for SDLT purposes (*FA 2003, Sch 17A, para 9A*).

Reliefs, etc

Disadvantaged Area Relief (to 5 April 2013 only)

19.172 If the subject matter of a land transaction was wholly situated in a disadvantaged area:

(*a*) If all of the land was non-residential property the transaction was exempt from SDLT.

(*b*) If all of the land was residential property the transaction was exempt if the consideration did not exceed £150,000 and either did not include rent or was wholly rent. If it was partly rent and partly other consideration, such as a premium, and the value of the rent did not exceed £150,000, the rent did not count as chargeable consideration. Prior to 12 March 2008 if the annual rent did not exceed £600 and the premium on other consideration did not exceed £150,000, then the premium did not count as chargeable consideration. If the rent exceeded £600, the premium was taxable even if it was under £60,000. This further restriction was abolished by *FA 2008, s 95(4)(5)*.

(*c*) If the land was partly non-residential property and partly residential, the consideration had to be apportioned on a just and reasonable basis. The part attributed to the non-residential element was exempt from SDLT and the residential element was taxed as in (*b*) above.

(*FA 2003, Sch 6, paras 3–6.*)

This relief was repealed by *FA 2012, Sch 39, para 8* where the effective date was after 5 April 2013. Any claim for relief in respect of earlier transactions had to be made before 6 May 2014 (*FA 2012, Sch 39, para 13*).

19.173 A disadvantaged area was one designated as such by regulations made by the Treasury (*FA 2003, Sch 6, para 1*). The regulations designating disadvantaged areas for stamp duty purposes under *FA 2000, s 92* which were in force at 1 December 2003 were treated as if they were regulations made for SDLT purposes (*FA 2003, Sch 6, para 2*). Disadvantaged areas relief was regarded by the EU as a State Aid. Accordingly it could be restricted if the recipient was in receipt of a State aid from other sources, such as a Regional Development Agency as there was a ceiling on the total State aid for a particular project (HMRC Press Release 21.12.2004).

19.174 If the subject matter of a land transaction was partly in a disadvantaged area and partly not, the consideration had be apportioned between the two areas of land on a just and reasonable basis. The part attributed to the land in the disadvantaged area was then taxed as above with that attributable to the balance of the land being chargeable to SDLT in the normal way (*FA 2003, Sch 6, paras 7–10*). HMRC Statement of Practice SP1/2004, which gives detailed guidance on the operation of this relief.

Exchanges with House Builders and Property Traders

19.175 If a dwelling (the old dwelling) is acquired from an individual (either alone or with other individuals) by a house-building company (or a company connected with a house-building company) the acquisition is exempt if:

(*a*) the individual (alone or with other individuals) acquires a new dwelling from the house-building company;

(*b*) the individual occupied the old dwelling as his only or main residence at some time in the two-year period ending with its disposal and intends to occupy the new dwelling as his only or main residence;

(*c*) the disposal of the old residence is entered into in consideration of the acquisition of the new one; and

(*d*) the area of land acquired by the house-building company or connected company (ie the area of the old dwelling and its garden or grounds) does not exceed the permitted area, namely a half hectare (inclusive of the site of the dwelling) or such larger area as is required for the reasonable enjoyment of the dwelling as a dwelling having regard to its size and character.

(*FA 2003, Sch 6A, paras 1(1), (2), 7(3).*)

19.176 For the above purposes:

(i) A dwelling includes land occupied and enjoyed with the building as its garden or grounds (*FA 2003, Sch 6A, para 7*).

(ii) A building or part of a building is a new dwelling if either it has been constructed for use as a single dwelling and has not previously been occupied or it has been adapted for use as a single dwelling and has not been occupied since its adaptation (*FA 2003, Sch 6A, para 7*).

(iii) A house-building company is a company that carries on the business of constructing or adapting buildings or parts of buildings for use as dwellings (*FA 2003, Sch 6A, para 1(4)*). It appears that an individual or partnership cannot qualify for the relief.

(iv) *ITA 2007, s 993* applies for determining whether a company is connected with a house-building company (*FA 2003, Sch 6A, para 10*).

(v) If conditions (*a*) to (*c*) above are met but the area occupied by the old dwelling exceeds the permitted area, the chargeable consideration is the market value of the old dwelling less the market value of the permitted area, ie SDLT is payable on the acquisition only by reference to the excess land (*FA 2003, Sch 6A, para 1(3)*). The permitted area is taken to consist of that part of the old dwelling that would be the most suitable for occupation and enjoyment with the dwelling as its garden or grounds if the rest of the land were separately occupied (*FA 2003, Sch 6A, para 7*).

(vi) The acquisition of a dwelling means acquisition by way of grant or transfer of a major interest in the dwelling and references to the market value of the old dwelling and to the permitted area means the market value of that major interest and the area covered by that major interest (*FA 2003, Sch 6A, para 1(5)*).

19.177 SDLT is of course still payable on the acquisition of the new dwelling. As condition (*c*) does not require the exchange to be the sole consideration, the relief will apply even though – as will normally be the case – cash consideration is payable to the house-builder in addition to the transfer of the old dwelling.

19.178 This relief is of course to facilitate the housing market. House-builders who sell a new house will often take in exchange (and resell on the market) the purchaser's existing house to prevent the sale of the new house falling through because of the inability of the purchaser to sell his existing house. The government feel it reasonable to continue the relief for exchanges in such circumstances.

19.179 This exemption also applies if the old dwelling is acquired by a property trader in the course of a business that consists of or includes acquiring dwellings from individuals who acquire new dwellings from housebuilding companies, and the individual (alone or with other individuals) acquires a new dwelling from a housebuilding company. The conditions at **19.175**(*b*) and (*d*) obviously need to be met. The property trader must not intend to:

(*a*) spend more than £10,000 (or if greater 5% of the purchase price subject to a maximum of £20,000) on refurbishment, ie on the carrying out of works that are intended to enhance the value of the dwelling (but excluding cleaning and works required solely to ensure that the dwelling meets minimum safety standards);

(*b*) grant a lease or licence of the old dwelling (other than to an individual for a period of no more than six months for transactions after 22 July 2004); or

(*c*) permit any of its principals or employees (or any person connected with them) to occupy the old dwelling.

(*FA 2003, Sch 6A, paras 1, 9.*)

19.180 For this purpose 'property trader' means a company, a limited liability partnership (LLP) or a partnership whose members are all companies or LLPs and which carries on the business of buying and selling dwellings (*FA 2003, Sch 6A, para 8(1)*). It should be noted that the relief does not apply if the trader is an individual or a partnership which includes an individual. A principal of a property trader is a director of the company or a member of the LLP (*FA 2003, Sch 6A, para 8(2)*). Curiously it appears that there is no objection to allowing a shareholder of a company who is not a director or shadow director to occupy the property. Anything done by (or in relation to) a company connected with a property trader (within *CTA 2010, s 1122*) is treated as done by the trader. A principal or employee of such a company is treated as a principal or employee of the trader (*FA 2003, Sch 6A, para 8(3)*).

19.181 If the business of a property trader includes acquiring dwellings from personal representatives, the exemption also applies provided that the deceased person occupied the dwelling as his main residence at some time in the two years ending with his death (*FA 2003, Sch 6A, para 3*). In this case there is no requirement for anyone to acquire a new dwelling from a housebuilder but the other conditions still need to be met.

19.182 The exemption for a property trader again applies where a dwelling is acquired from an individual (whether alone or with other individuals) who had made arrangements to sell the dwelling and acquire another dwelling and the acquisition by the property trader is made, following the failure of those arrangements, for the purpose of enabling the individual's acquisition of the new dwelling to proceed (*FA 2003, Sch 6A, para 4*). The appropriate conditions at **19.175** onwards obviously need to be met. It should be noted that there is no requirement in this case that the new dwelling should be acquired from a builder. The purpose of *para 4* is to encourage the dealer to step in where a house-buying chain breaks down so that the whole chain does not collapse.

19.183 A breach of any of the conditions (*a*) to (*c*) at **19.179** will result in a withdrawal of the relief (*FA 2003, Sch 6A, para 11*).

Relocation Relief

19.184 If a dwelling is acquired from an employee or prospective employee (either alone or with other individuals) by his employer (or by a property trader) the acquisition by the employer or trader is exempt from SDLT if:

(*a*) the individual occupied the dwelling as his only or main residence at some time in the two years ended with the date of the acquisition by the employer;

(*b*) the acquisition is made in connection with a change of residence by the individual resulting from relocation of employment;

(*c*) the consideration for the acquisition does not exceed the market value of the dwelling; and

(*d*) the area of land acquired does not exceed the permitted area.

(*FA 2003, Sch 6A, para 5.*)

19.185 For this purpose:

(i) Relocation of employment means a change in the individual's place of employment due to his becoming an employee of the employer or to an alteration in the duties of his employment or in the place where he normally performs those duties (*FA 2003, Sch 6A, para 5(4)*).

(ii) A change of residence results from relocation of employment if it is made wholly or mainly to allow the individual to have his residence within a reasonable daily travelling distance of his new place of employment (ie where he normally performs, or is normally to perform, the duties of his employment after the relocation) and his former residence is not within a reasonable daily travelling distance of that place (*FA 2003, Sch 6A, para 5(5)*).

(iii) A building or part of a building is a new dwelling if it has either been constructed for use as a single dwelling and has not previously been occupied or it has been adapted for use as a single dwelling and has not been occupied since its adaptation (*FA 2003, Sch 6A, para 7(2)*).

(iv) A dwelling includes land occupied and enjoyed with the dwelling as its garden or grounds (*FA 2003, Sch 6A, para 7(1)*).

(v) The permitted area has the same meaning as in **19.175**(*d*) above. If the area occupied by the old dwelling exceeds the permitted area, the consideration for the acquisition is limited to the value of the excess (arrived at by deducting the value of the permitted area from the value of the entire dwelling) (*FA 2003, Sch 6A para 7(3)*).

(vi) In the case of an acquisition by a property trader conditions (*a*) to (*c*) at **19.179** obviously have to be met (*FA 2003, Sch 6A, para 6(2)(e)*). Any breach of these conditions will trigger a withdrawal of the relief in the same way as the housebuilder relief (see **19.150**).

Compulsory Purchase Facilitating Development

19.186 A compulsory purchase facilitating development is exempt from SDLT. This is the acquisition by a person of a chargeable interest in respect of which that person has made a compulsory purchase order (CPO) for the purpose of facilitating development (as defined in *Town and Country Planning Act 1990, s 55* or the corresponding enactments in Scotland and Northern Ireland) by another person. It does not matter how the acquisition is effected, ie the relief will still apply if the acquisition is effected by agreement rather than pursuant to the CPO (*FA 2003, s 60*).

19.187 This is an odd provision. It will not confer exemption if the local authority itself intends to develop the land. Nor will it do so if the vendor is threatened with a CPO and agrees to sell the land to the local authority to avoid its having to go through the CPO procedure. If the disposal is effected by agreement the agreement must be with the local authority not with the developer.

Compliance with Planning Obligations

19.188 A land transaction that is entered into in order to comply with a planning obligation, such as a *section 106* agreement, or with a modification of a planning obligation, is exempt from SDLT if that obligation (or modification) is enforceable against the vendor, the purchaser is a public authority and the transaction takes place within five years of the date that the planning obligation or modification was entered into (*FA 2003, s 61(1)*). A planning obligation is one entered into in accordance with *ss 106(9)* or *299A(2)* of the *Town and County Planning Act 1990* (or its Scottish or Northern Irish equivalents) (*FA 2003, s 61(2)*). Public authorities are government departments, local authorities,

Transport for London, Health authorities and trusts, and any other authority that is a local planning authority under the *Town and County Planning Act 1990*. A full list is contained in the legislation. The Treasury have power by Regulation to add other bodies (*FA 2003, s 61(3)*).

Group Relief

19.189 A transaction between members of a group (75% subsidiaries) is exempt from SDLT (*FA 2003, s 62* and *Sch 7, para 1(11)*).

19.190 To constitute a group there must not only be beneficial ownership of at least 75% of the ordinary share capital but the shareholder company must also be beneficially entitled to at least 75% of any profits available for distribution to equity holders and to at least 75% of any assets available for distribution to equity holders on a winding up (*FA 2003, Sch 7, para 1(3)*). The test looks at the aggregate of direct ownership and indirect ownership through another company or companies. *ICTA 1988, s 838(5)–(10)* apply to determine ownership. *ICTA 1988, Sch 18* (equity holders and profits or assets available for distribution) also apply for this purpose but with the omission of *paras 5(3)* and *5B–5E* (*FA 2003, Sch 7, para 1(4)(6)*). Ordinary share capital means all of the issued share capital of the company other than capital which has a right to a dividend at a fixed rate but has no other right to share in the profits of the company. HMRC accept that a 'body corporate' includes a limited liability partnership for the purposes of SDLT group relief (HMRC Notice, 12 Oct 2010). Accordingly an LLP can be a parent company in a group structure. However, an LLP cannot meet the definition of a subsidiary of another company as it does not have issued ordinary share capital. HMRC also consider that the insertion of an LLP in a group structure will prevent the LLP's subsidiaries being grouped with the corporate members of the LLP. As an LLP is regarded as transparent, this means that if one of its members is a member of a group, its share of the partnership transaction can be grouped. However, if the LLP transfers land to or from one of its own subsidiaries, group relief cannot apply as a member of the LLP cannot form a group with the LLP's subsidiaries.

19.191 The exemption does not apply if at the effective date of the transaction arrangements exist by virtue of which (at that or some later time) a person (or persons together) has or could obtain control of the purchaser but not of the vendor (*FA 2003, Sch 7, para 2(1)*).

19.192 Arrangements entered into with a view to the acquisition of shares by a company in relation to which *FA 1986, s 75* (stamp duty acquisition relief) applies and as a result of which the purchaser will be a member of the same group as the acquiring company will not forfeit the relief though.

Unfortunately *s 75* is a very limited relief. About the only thing it covers is a share exchange that puts a new UK holding company on top of an existing company. The only grounds on which an appeal against a determination can be made are that the purchase did not take place, the interest in land to which it relates has not been purchased, the contract has not been substantially performed or the land transaction is one which is not itself notifiable (*FA 2003, Sch 10, para, 36(5A)*).

19.193 The exemption also does not apply if the transaction is effected in pursuance of (or in connection with) arrangements under which:

(*a*) the consideration (or any part of it) is to be provided or received, directly or indirectly, by a person other than a member of the group; or

(*b*) the vendor and purchaser will cease to be members of the same group by reason of the purchaser ceasing to be a 75% subsidiary of either the vendor or another member of the group.

(*FA 2003, Sch 7, para 2(3)*.)

19.194 Arrangements under which the vendor or purchaser (or another group company) is able to provide (or part with) any of the consideration by (or in consequence of) carrying out a transaction involving a payment or other disposition by a person other than a group company fall within (*a*) above (*FA 2003, Sch 7, para 2(3)*).

19.195 For the purpose of both of these restrictions 'arrangements' includes any scheme, agreement or understanding whether or not legally enforceable, and the *ICTA 1988, s 840* definition of control applies (*FA 2003, Sch 7, para 2(5)*). However, the exclusion does not apply to arrangements for the purpose of facilitating the transfer of the whole or part of the business of a company to another company on the demutualisation of an insurance company provided that the conditions of *FA 1997, s 96* are met (*FA 2003, Sch 7, para 2(3A)*).

19.196 Group relief does not apply on a transaction that either was not effected for bona fide commercial reasons, or forms part of arrangements of which the main purpose or one of the main purposes is the avoidance of liability to SDLT, stamp duty, income tax, corporation tax or CGT (*FA 2003, Sch 7, para 2(4A)*).

19.197 Where group relief applies the relief will be withdrawn if:

(*a*) the purchaser ceases to be a member of the same group as the vendor within three years of the effective date of the transaction – or subsequently in pursuance of, or in connection with, arrangements (as defined above) made during the three-year period; and (*b*) at the time the purchaser ceases to be a member of the group it (or a relevant associated company) still holds the chargeable interest acquired under the transaction or an interest derived from that interest.

(*FA 2003, Sch 7, para 3(1)*.)

19.198 A relevant associated company for this purpose is a member of the same group as the purchaser which ceases to be a member of the same group as the vendor in consequence of the purchaser leaving that group (*FA 2003, Sch 7, para 3(4)*). If the interest held when the purchaser leaves the group was acquired at full market value subsequent to the original transaction under a chargeable transaction for which group relief was available but was not claimed there is no claw-back of the relief (*FA 2003, Sch 7, para 3(1)*). This is because the subsequent transaction will in effect already have triggered a claw-back of the original relief.

19.199 Where the relief is withdrawn the tax that has to be paid is of course that which would have been paid on the original transaction if group relief had not applied. If the relief is only partially withdrawn, eg because part of the land acquired has been sold or will remain within the vendor's group, an appropriate proportion of the tax that would have been so chargeable becomes payable (*FA 2003, Sch 7, para 3(2), (3)*).

19.200 The following transactions will not trigger a claw-back of the relief:

(*a*) If the two cease to be in the same group (*FA 2003, Sch 7, para 4ZA(1)*). For this purpose the vendor is regarded as leaving the group if the two cease to be members of the same group by reason of a transaction relating to shares either in the vendor or in another company that is above the vendor in the group structure (a 75% parent) and which as a result of the transaction ceases to be a member of the same group as the purchaser (*FA 2003, Sch 7, para 4ZA(2),(3)*). Prior to 13 March 2008, the vendor had to leave the group by virtue of a transaction in relation to shares in the vendor or in another company that was above the vendor in the group structure and as a result of the transaction ceases to be a member of the same group as the purchaser (*FA 2003, Sch 7, para 4(2),(3)*).

(*b*) If the purchaser ceases to be a member of the group by reason of anything done for the purposes of, or in the course of, winding up the vendor (or another company that is above the vendor in the group structure, ie one of which the vendor or another company that is above the vendor is a 75% subsidiary) (*FA 2003, Sch 7, para 4(4)*).

(*c*) If the purchaser ceases to be a member of the same group as the vendor as a result of an acquisition by another company to which *FA 1986* applies (stamp duty acquisition relief) where the purchaser is immediately after the acquisition a member of the same group as that acquiring company (*FA 2003, Sch 7, para 4(6)*).

(*d*) From 22 March 2006 If the purchaser ceases to be a member of the same group as the vendor as the result of the transfer of the whole or part of the vendor's business to another company on the demutualisation of an insurance company to which *FA 1997, s 96* applies (*FA 2003, Sch 7, para 4(6A)*).

19.201 Where (*a*) above applies, if there is a change in the control of the purchaser after the vendor leaves the group the group relief claw-back rules must be applied as if at that time the purchaser had ceased to be a member of the same group as the vendor (*FA 2003, Sch 7, para 4ZA(4)*). For this purpose there is a change of control if a person who controls the purchaser (alone or with others) ceases to do so, a person obtains control of the purchaser (alone or with others) or the purchaser is wound up (*FA 2003, Sch 7, para 4ZA(5)*). However, a person does not control (or obtain control of) the purchaser if that person is itself under the control of another person or persons (*FA 2003, Sch 7, para 4ZA(6)*). There is also no change of control if the change in the control of the purchaser arises because a loan creditor obtains control of (or ceases to control) the purchaser provided that the other person who controlled the purchaser before the change continues to do so (*FA 2003, Sch 7, para 4ZA(7)*). *CTA 2010, s 493* definition of control applies (*FA 2003, Sch 7, para 4ZA(8)*).

19.202 This ensures that the claw-back cannot be avoided by the vendor being sold immediately after the transfer and the purchaser subsequently being sold within the three-year period and claiming that at the time of its sale it was not in the same group as the vendor. It treats the vendor as remaining part of the group for the three-year period. HMRC have said that they will not regard the appointment of a liquidator to a holding company in a group (or the eventual liquidation of that company) as giving rise to a change of control provided that the liquidation can be shown to be part of a scheme of reconstruction for which reconstruction or group relief is given or where the economic ownership of the relevant assets remains within the group (HMRC Guidance Note 26.11.2008). The Guidance Note also states that HMRC will apply a minimum controlling combination test, ie if a company has three equal shareholders A, B and C and A leaves there is technically a change of control as the company was previously under the control of A and B jointly (or of A and C jointly). However, as it was also under the control of B and C jointly and they still control it they will regard no change of control as taking place. HMRC also say that an option over shares will not be taken into account in determining whether there has been a change of control of the purchaser.

19.203 If **19.200**(*c*) above applies and the purchaser ceases to be a member of the same group as the acquiring company within three years of the effective date of the property transaction (or later if it is in pursuance of arrangements made during the three-year period) at a time when it, or a relevant associated company, holds a chargeable interest that was acquired under the property transaction, or that is derived from an interest so acquired, the group relief is clawed back as if at that time the purchaser had ceased to be a member of the same group as the vendor. The definitions of 'arrangements' and 'relevant associated company' in **19.198** and **19.200** apply (*FA 2003, Sch 7, para 4(7)(8)*).

19.204 If there is a change in control of the purchaser within three years of the effective date of the intra-group transaction (or at any time in pursuance of, or in connection with) arrangements made in that three-year period), group relief would not otherwise fall to be withdrawn, the intra group transaction accrued after 19 May 2005, and there was an earlier transaction within three years preceding the change of control affecting all or part of the same land which qualified for group relief, reconstruction relief or acquisition relief, then the tests as to whether or not group relief falls to be withdrawn must be applied as if the vendors under the earlier transaction were the vendor under the later one (*FA 2003, Sch 7, para 4A(1)(2)*).

19.205 There is a change of control for this purpose if any person who controls the company (within *CTA 2010, s 493*) (either alone or with others) ceases to do so, a person obtains control (alone or with others), or the company is wound up. If there is more than one earlier transaction it is the vendor under the earliest who becomes the deemed vendor. If two or more such transactions were effected simultaneously it is any person who was a vendor under any of those transactions (*FA 2003, Sch 7, para 4A(3)(4)*). For example, suppose subsidiary A transfers land to subsidiary B which transfers it to C which transfers it to its own subsidiary D all within the three-year period. Company C is then sold. There is no clawback of group relief under the normal rules as purchaser D remains in the same group as its vendor C. *Paragraph 4A* then asks if D remains in the same group as A and if it does not the group relief claimed by D is withdrawn. If there is a transfer in the chain where relief was not claimed earlier transactions to that one are ignored (*FA 2003, Sch 7, para 4A(2)(d)*). From 13 March 2008 *para 4A* does not apply where the change in control of the purchaser is brought about by a loan creditor obtaining control, or ceasing to control, the purchaser, provided that the other persons who controlled the purchaser before that change continue to do so (*FA 2003, Sch 7, para 4A(3A)*).

19.206 Where all or part of a contract has been assigned references in *Sch 7* to the vendor must be read as referring to the vendor under the original contract not to the deemed vendor under the secondary contract, ie the assignment (see **19.125**) (*FA 2003, s 45(5A)*).

19.207 Where group relief is withdrawn and the purchaser does not pay the tax within six months of the due date it can be collected from any of the vendor, any company that was a member of the same group as the purchaser and was above it in the group structure at any time between the effective date of the property transaction and the purchaser leaving the group, or any person who at such a time was a controlling director of either the purchaser or a company having control of the purchaser (*FA 2003, Sch 7, para 5(1)–(3)*). A controlling director is a director (including a shadow director) who has control of the company within the meaning of *CTA 2010, s 493* (*FA 2003, Sch 7, para 5(4)*).

19.208 If they decide to collect the tax from such a third party HMRC must serve a notice on him within three years from the date of the final determination of the tax chargeable. The notice must state the amount required to be paid by the person on whom it is served and must require him to pay the unpaid amount within 30 days of the service of the notice. Such a notice has effect for the purpose of collecting the tax and interest thereon and for the purpose of appeals as if it were an assessment and as if the amount demanded was tax due from that person (*FA 2003, Sch 7, para 6(1)–(4)*). Once the third party has paid the tax he has a right of recovery from the purchaser (*FA 2003, Sch 7, para 6(5)*). He cannot claim a deduction for such tax in computing his own income, profits or losses for any tax purpose though (*FA 2003, Sch 7, para 6(6)*).

Reconstruction Relief

19.209 If one company acquires the whole or part of the undertaking of another in pursuance of a scheme for the reconstruction of another, and:

(*a*) the consideration for the acquisition consists wholly of the issue of non-redeemable shares in the acquiring company to all of the shareholders of the target company (or partly of the issue of such shares and partly of the assumption or discharge by the acquiring company of liabilities of the target company);

(*b*) after the acquisition each shareholder of each of the companies is a shareholder of the other and the proportion of shares of one of the companies held by any shareholder is the same (or as nearly as may be the same) as the proportion held by that shareholder in the other; and

(*c*) the acquisition is effected for bona fide commercial reasons and does not form part of a scheme or arrangement of which the main purpose, or one of the main purposes, is the avoidance of liability to SDLT, stamp duty, income tax, corporation tax, or capital gains tax,

then a land transaction entered into for the purposes of (or in connection with) that transfer of the undertaking is exempt from SDLT (*FA 2003, Sch 7, para 7*).

19.210 This is a limited relief. It will apply where a new holding company is inserted on top of an exsiting company by means of a share exchange. It will also cover a split of a company where a new company is formed specifically to acquire part of the business of an existing company wholly for shares and each shareholder is allocated shares in both companies in proportion to his shareholding. It does not apply, however, if the new company has existing shareholders. This seems to be the case even if the existing shareholders are subscribers who took a £1 share to get the company formed. It may be that in practice HMRC will not take this point if the subscribers are existing shareholders and the new shares issued to them together with their subscriber shares have no effect on the proportionate shareholdings. However, as there is a specific exemption for subscriber shares in the enterprise investment scheme legislation, the courts could take that as an indication that parliament did not intend that exception to apply more widely.

19.211 The relief will be withdrawn if a disqualifying event occurs in the next three years (see **19.216**) (*FA 2003, Sch 7, para 7(6)*).

Acquisition Relief

19.212 If a company acquires the whole or part of the undertaking of another, and:

(*a*) the consideration for the acquisition consists either:

- (i) wholly of the issue of non-redeemable shares in the acquiring company to either the target company or to all or any of that company's shareholders; or

- (ii) partly of the issue of such shares with the balance being either (or both):

  - (1) cash not exceeding 10% of the nominal value of the non-redeemable shares issued on the acquisition; or

  - (2) the assumption or discharge by the acquiring company of liabilities of the target company;

(*b*) the acquiring company is not associated with another company that is a party to arrangements with the target company relating to any of the shares of the acquiring company that are issued in connection with the transfer of the undertaking;

(*c*) the undertaking (or part acquired) has as its main activity the carrying on of a trade that does not consist wholly or mainly of dealing in chargeable interests (ie it is not a property dealing trade); and (*d*) the acquisition is effected for bona-fide commercial reasons and does not form part of arrangements of which the main purpose or one of the main purposes is the avoidance of tax (ie SDLT, stamp duty, income tax, corporation tax or CGT),

then the tax chargeable on a land transaction entered into for the purposes of (or in connection with) the transfer of the undertaking is limited to 0.5% (*FA 2003, Sch 7, para 8* as amended by *Stamp Duty Land Tax Act 2015, Sch 1, para 8*). The exclusion for a property dealing trade did not apply to an acquisition before 20 May 2005 and that for tax avoidance to one before 20 July 2005.

19.213 For the purposes of (*b*) above, companies are associated if one has control of the other (within *CTA 2010, s 493*) or both are controlled by the same person or persons. Arrangements include any scheme, agreement or understanding, whether or not legally enforceable (*FA 2003, Sch 7, para 8(5), (5C)*).

19.214 As with reconstruction relief, the relief is withdrawn if a disqualifying event occurs within the following three years (*FA 2003, Sch 7, para 8(6)*).

19.215 This provision will grant relief where an outside company either buys all or part of a company's business in exchange for issuing shares to the company or it does so in exchange for issuing shares direct to the shareholders of that company. Such a transaction is not possible under UK company law other than in the course of a liquidation, when *Insolvency Act 1986, s 110* permits it. It must, however, be noted that the shares must be issued to all of the target company's shareholders. Accordingly, while it will facilitate a split of one company into two companies with identical shareholders, it will not apply where *s 110* is used to divide an existing company between two groups of shareholders each of which ends up owning a company that carries a distinct part of the original company's business. This contrasts with the CGT reconstruction rules where *TCGA 1992, Sch 5AA* was introduced to ensure that such a reconstruction attracted relief.

Withdrawal of Reconstruction or Acquisition Relief

19.216 Both of the above reliefs will be withdrawn if:

(*a*) control of the acquiring company changes within three years from the effective date of the transaction (or subsequent to that time in pursuance of (or in connection with) arrangements made during (or before) that three year period; and (*b*) at the time of that change of control the acquiring company (or a relevant associated company) holds a chargeable interest that was acquired under the relevant transaction or that is derived from an interest so acquired (unless that derived interest was acquired at market value under a chargeable transaction in relation to which reconstruction or acquisition relief was available but not claimed).

(*FA 2003, Sch 7, para 9(1)*.)

19.217 Where relief is withdrawn the tax that would have been due had the relief not applied becomes payable. If the whole of the property acquired under the original transaction is not still held at the time of the change of control only an appropriate proportion of the relief (having regard to the subject matter of the original transaction and what is still held at the time of the change of control) is withdrawn (*FA 2003, Sch 7, para 9(2),(3)*).

19.218 For this purpose control of a company changes if it becomes controlled (within *CTA 2010, s 493*) by a different person, by a different number of persons, or by two or more persons at least one of whom is not the person (or one of the persons) who previously controlled it (*FA 2003, Sch 7, para 9(5)(c)*). A relevant associated company is one that is controlled (within *CTA 2010, s 493*) by the acquiring company immediately before control of that company changes and whose control also changes in consequence of the change of control of the acquiring company (*FA 2003, Sch 7, para 9(4),(5)(b)*). Arrangements includes any scheme, agreement or understanding whether or not it is legally enforceable (*FA 2003, Sch 7, para 9(5)(a)*).

19.219 The following events do not trigger a withdrawal of the relief:

(*a*) If control of the acquiring company changes as a result of a share transaction that is exempt from SDLT under *FA 2003, Sch 3, para 3* (see **19.8**(*c*)) as being in pursuance of a split of property on a divorce, nullity of marriage or judicial separation (*FA 2003, Sch 7, para 10(2)*).

(*b*) If control of the acquiring company changes as a result of a share transaction in pursuance of the variation of a deceased estate that attracts exemption under *FA 2003, Sch 3, para 4* (see **19.8**(*d*)) (*FA 2003, Sch 7 para 10(3)*).

(*c*) If control of the acquiring company changes as a result of an intra-group transfer of shares which is exempt from stamp duty under *FA 1930, s 42* or its Northern Irish equivalent (*FA 2003, Sch 7, para 10(4)*).

(*d*) If control of the acquiring company changes as a result of one transfer of shares to another company which is exempt from stamp duty under *FA 1988, s 77* (*FA 2003, Sch 7, para 10(5)*).

(*e*) If control of the acquiring company changes as a result of a loan creditor (within *ICTA 1988, s 417(7)–(9)*) becoming, or ceasing, to be treated as controlling that company, provided that the other persons who also were previously treated as controlling it continue to do so (*FA 2003, Sch 7, para 10(6)*).

19.220 Where (*c*) or (*d*) above applies the SDLT becomes payable if:

(*a*) within three years of the original property transaction (or subsequently under arrangements entered into before that time) a company holding shares in the acquiring company to which the intra-group transaction related (or that are derived from such shares) ceases to be a member of the same group as the target company or, in the case of (*d*) above control of the other company referred to in (*d*) so changes; and

(*b*) at that time the acquiring company (or a relevant associated company – see **19.218**) holds a chargeable interest that was transferred to the acquiring company by the relevant transaction or is derived from an interest that was so transferred (and the derived interest was not acquired at market value by a chargeable interest in relation to which reconstruction or acquisition relief was available but was not claimed).

(*FA 2003, Sch 7, para 11(1)(2).*)

19.221 Paragraphs **19.217** and **19.218** above apply for this purpose also (*FA 2003, Sch 7, para 11(3)–(6)*).

Recovery of Reconstruction or Acquisition Relief from Third Party

19.222 If the acquiring company does not pay the tax it can be recovered from:

(*a*) any company that was a member of the same group as the acquiring company and above it in the group structure at any time between the effective date of the original property transaction and the change of control which triggers the withdrawal of the relief; or

(*b*) any person who at any time in that period was a controlling director (ie one who controlled it within *ICTA 1988, s 416*) of the acquiring company or of a company having control of the acquiring company.

(*FA 2003, Sch 7, para 12.*)

19.223 The procedure is the same as that described at **19.209** (*FA 2003, Sch 7, paras 12, 13*).

Incorporation of Limited Liability Partnership

19.224 The transfer of a chargeable interest to a limited liability partnership in connection with its incorporation is exempt from SDLT, provided that:

(*a*) the effective date of the transaction is within 12 months of the date of incorporation of the LLP;

(*b*) immediately before the incorporation of the LLP (or if later at the time the transferor acquired the interest) the transferor was a partner in a partnership which comprised all the persons who are to be members of the LLP (and no one else) (or was a nominee or bare trustee for one or more such partners); and

(*c*) the proportions of the interest transferred to which the persons in (*b*) are entitled immediately after the transfer are the same as those to which they were entitled immediately before the incorporation of the LLP (or, if later, the time they acquired the interest).

(*FA 2003, s 65.*)

19.225 The effect of these conditions is that the exemption will apply only where the property is transferred to the LLP from a predecessor partnership. It will, however, apply to a property owned wholly by one or more of the partners provided that there is no change in the entitlement to the ownership of the property. The relief is also given if the interests in the property before and after incorporation differ and it can be shown that no such difference has arisen as part of a scheme or arrangement of which one of the main purposes is the avoidance of any duty or tax (*FA 2003, s 65(4)(b)*).

PAIF Seeding Relief and COACS Seeding Relief

19.226 A land transaction after 14 September 2016 is exempt from SDLT if:

(*a*) the purchaser is a property AIF (PAIF – see below);

(*b*) the main subject matter of the transaction consists of a major interest in land;

(*c*) the only consideration for the transaction is the issue of units in the PAIF to a person who is the vendor; and

(*d*) the effective date of the transaction is a day within the seeding period (see **19.228**).

(*FA 2003, Sch 7A, para 1* inserted by *FA 2016, s 133* and *Sch 16, para 4.*) A PAIF is an open-ended investment company (as defined in the *Authorised*

Investment Funds (Tax) Regulations 2016 (SI 2006 No 964) to which *Pt 4A* of those Regulations apply. A company incorporated under the laws of an EEA State and authorised in a way that makes it the equivalent of a PAIF must also be treated as a PAIF (*FA 2003, Sch 7A, paras 2, 21*).

19.227 A land transaction by a COACS (see **19.94**) is similarly exempt if the above conditions are met (obviously substituting COACS for PAIF) (*FA 2003, Sch 7A, para 10*). The reference to units in a PAIF include, where the PAIF is a part of an umbrella company, units in the separate pool to which that part of the umbrella company relates, and units in a feeder fund of the PAIF. The reference to units in a COACS include, where the COACS is a sub-scheme of an umbrella COACS (see **19.95**), units in the separate pool to which that sub-scheme relates, and units in a feeder fund of the scheme. Units mean the rights or interests (however described) of the participants in the PAIF or COACS. A feeder fund is a unit trust scheme in the case of a PAIF (or an open-ended investment company, offshore fund or unit trust scheme in the case of a COACS), one of the main objects of which is investment in the PAIF (or COACS) and which is managed by the same person as the PAIF (or COACS) (*FA 2003, Sch 7A, para 20*).

19.228 The seeding period is the shorter of the period beginning with the first property seeding date and ending with the date of the first external investment into the PAIF (or the COACS), or 18 months from the property seeding date. The PAIF (or COACS) can elect to shorten the seeding period by specifying an earlier date. Such an election can be made either by including it in a notice accompanying a claim for PAIF (or COACS) seeding relief or by separate notice to HMRC (*FA 2003, Sch 7A, paras 3(1)–(3), 11(1)–(3)*). For this purpose the first property seeding date is the earliest effective date of a transaction in respect of which (*a*) to (*c*) in **19.226** are met. External investment means a non-land transaction in which the investor is an external investor. A non-land transaction is a transaction by which the PAIF (or COACS) acquires assets which do not consist of (or include) a chargeable interest. An external investor is any person other than a vendor in a transaction which was on or before the date of the non-land transaction in which conditions (*a*)–(*c*) were met (*FA 2003, Sch 7A, paras 3(4), (5); 11(4), (5)*).

19.229 PAIF (and COACS) seeding relief is not available unless (at the effective date of the transaction) the PAIF (or COACS) has arrangements in place requiring a person who is the vendor to notify the authorised corporate director of the PAIF (or the operator of the COACS scheme) of:

(*a*) the identity of the beneficial owner of the units in the PAIF (or COACS) received in consideration of the transaction; and (*b*) any disposal of units in the PAIF (or COACS) on or after the effective date of that transaction by that owner (or where it is a company, a group company) which is, or could be, a relevant disposal (see **19.234**).

(*FA 2003, Sch 7A, paras 4(1), (2); 12(1), (2).*)

A group company for this purpose is a company which is a member of the same group of companies as the person mentioned in (*a*) for the purposes mentioned in *FA 2003, Sch 7, para 1* (group relief – see **19.190**).

19.230 PAIF (or COACS) seeding relief is also not available if either:

(*a*) at the effective date of the transaction there are arrangements in existence by virtue of which, at that or some later time, a person who is the vendor makes (or could make) a disposal of units in the PAIF (or COACS) which is or could be a relevant disposal; or

(*b*) the transaction is not effected for bona-fide commercial reasons, or forms part of arrangements of which one of the main purposes is the avoidance of liability to tax (ie stamp duty, income tax, corporation tax, CGT or SDLT).

(*FA 2003, Sch 7A, paras 4(3), (4); 12(3), (4).*)

19.231 There are a number of circumstances when seeding relief can be withdrawn. If the purchaser ceases to be a PAIF (or COACS) at any time after the effective date of the transaction that attracted the relief but within the seeding period, or at any time in the control period (ie the three years following the end of the seeding period, or in pursuance of (or in connection with) arrangements made before the end of the control period. The relief is withdrawn only if at the time when the purchaser ceases to be a PAIF (or COACS) it still holds the chargeable interest that it acquired under the relevant transaction or a chargeable interest that is derived from the interest. The amount chargeable to SDLT is the amount that would have been chargeable on the relevant transaction but for the seeding relief. If the purchaser still holds part of the interest acquired, only an appropriate proportion of the tax becomes chargeable, having regard to the subject-matter of the relevant transaction and what is held by the purchaser at the time it ceases to be a PAIF (or COACS) (*FA 2003, Sch 7A, paras 5, 13*).

19.232 The relief is also withdrawn if the portfolio test is not met immediately before the end of the seeding period. The PAIF (or COACS) has to meet either the non-residential portfolio test or the residential portfolio test. Under the non-residential portfolio test, it has to hold at least 10 seeded interests, these must be worth in aggregate at least £100 million, and the total chargeable consideration attributable to interests in or over residential property must not exceed 10% of the seeded portfolio. The residential portfolio test requires the total chargeable consideration attributable to all the seeded interests held by the PAIF (or COACS) to be valued at least at £100 million and for at least 100 of the seeded interests held by the PAIF (or COACS) to be interests on or over residential property. In applying these tests a seeded interest is a chargeable interest acquired by the PAIF (or COACS) in a transaction for which seeding relief was allowed (whether or not it is subsequently withdrawn), and the total chargeable consideration is the total of the chargeable consideration for all such transactions. For this purpose *FA 2003, s 116(7)* (purchase of six or more dwellings treated as non-residential – see **19.24**) does not apply, ie the dwellings must be treated as residential property (*FA 2003, Sch 7A, paras 6(1), (7)–(11); 16(1), (7)–(11)).*

19.233 The amount chargeable is the amount that would have been chargeable on the transaction had seeding relief not applied. If the portfolio test is met at the end of the seeding period but not at the end of the control period (or at a subsequent time when the failure is pursuant to (or in connection with) arrangements made before the end of that period) only an appropriate proportion of the seeding relief needs to be withdrawn having regard to the subject-matter of the relevant transaction and what is held by the PAIF (or COACS) at the time when the portfolio test is not met. This partial clawback of relief is subject to the proviso that it applies only if the PAIF (or COACS) still hold the chargeable interest that was acquired under the relevant transaction (or a chargeable interest derived from that interest) at the time that the portfolio test needs to be met (*FA 2003, Sch 7A, para 6(2)–(6); 16(2)–(6)*).

19.234 Relief is partially withdrawn where a person (V) makes a relevant disposal of one or more units in a PAIF (or COACS) at any time in the seeding period or the control period, or in pursuance of (or in connection with arrangements made before the end of the control period) and there is a relevant seeding transaction in relation to that disposal. For this purpose V's disposal of units is a relevant disposal if, in relation to that disposal A exceeds B, where A is the total of the chargeable consideration for all relevant seeding transactions (or if the value of V's investment in the PAIF or COACS immediately before the disposal is a lower figure, A is the value of V's investment in the PAIF or COACS immediately before the disposal) and B is the value of V's investment in the PAIF or COACS immediately after the disposal. A seeding transaction for this purpose is a transaction in respect of which seeding relief was allowed (whether or not it is subsequently withdrawn) and a relevant seeding transaction in relation to a disposal of units by V is a seeding transaction (the effective date of which is on or before the date of disposal) in which the PAIF or COACS is the purchaser and in which V (or a group company of V) is a vendor. The value of V's investment at a particular time is the market value of all units in the PAIF or COACS held at that time by V or, if V is a company, a company which is a group company at that time and which before that time has been a vendor in one or more seeding transactions of which the PAIF or COACS was the purchaser. The market value of units on a particular date is an amount equal to the buying price (ie the lower price) published by the authorised corporate director (or by the operator in the case of a COACS) on that date (or if no such price is published on that date, on the latest date before it (*FA 2013, Sch 7A, para 7(1)–(4), (6), (7); 17(1)–(4), (6), (7)*).

19.235 The amount chargeable is:

$$\frac{C \times SDLT}{CCRST}$$

Where: C = the difference between A and B,

CCRST = the aggregate chargeable consideration for all relevant seeding transactions, and

SDLT = the tax that would have been chargeable in respect of relevant seeding transactions but for seeding relief, less any amount of tax charged under para 7 (or 17 in the case of a COACS) in relation to an earlier disposal of units by V,

(*FA 2003, Sch 7A, paras 7(5), 17(5)*.)

19.236 Relief is also withdrawn if seeding relief has been allowed in respect of a transaction, the main subject-matter of the transaction consists of a chargeable interest in or over land which is or includes a dwelling, and a non-qualifying individual (see **19.237**) is permitted to occupy the dwelling (referred to as the disqualifying dwelling) at any time after the effective date of the transaction (*FA 2003, Sch 7A, paras 8(1), 18(1)*). The relief (or an appropriate proportion of it) is withdrawn only if at the time that the non-qualifying individual is permitted to occupy it, the PAIF (or COACS) holds a chargeable interest in or over the disqualifying dwelling that it acquired under the relevant transaction (or is derived from an interest so acquired). If the non-qualifying individual is first permitted to occupy the disqualifying dwelling after the end of the control period, relief is withdrawn only if at that time the PAIF fails to meet the genuine diversity of ownership condition. In the case of a PAIF this is set out in the *Authorised Investment Funds (Tax) Regulations 2006 (SI 2006 No 964)*. In the case of a COACS, it is defined in *Sch 7A, para 15* (see **19.239**). The chargeable amount is the amount that would have been chargeable but for the seeding relief, or an appropriate proportion of that amount having regard to the extent to which the subject-matter of the relevant transaction was an interest in or over land other than the disqualifying dwelling (*FA 2003, Sch 7A, paras 8, 18*).

19.237 The following are non-qualifying individuals:

(*a*) an individual who is a major participant in the PAIF or COACS;

(*b*) an individual who is connected with a major participant;

(*c*) an individual who is connected with the PAIF (or in the case of a COACS, with the operator of the scheme or the depository of the scheme);

(*d*) a relevant settlor;

(*e*) the spouse or civil partner of an individual within (*a*)–(*d*);

(*f*) a relative (brother, sister, ancestor or lineal descendant) of an individual within (*b*), (*c*) or (*d*), or the spouse or civil partner of such a relative;

(*g*) a relative (brother, sister, ancestor or lineal descendant) of the spouse or civil partner of an individual within (*b*), (*c*) or (*d*); and

(*h*) the spouse or civil partner of an individual within (*g*).

(*FA 2003, Sch 7A, paras 9(1), 19(1).*)

19.238 For the purpose of **19.237**, an individual who participates in a PAIF (or COACS) is a major participant in it if he is entitled to a share of at least 50% either of all the profits or income arising from the PAIF (or COACS) or of any profits or income arising from it that may be distributed to participants, or if in the event of a winding up of the PAIF (or COACS) he would be entitled to 50% or more of the assets that would then be available for distribution among the participants. For this purpose, profits or income arising from the PAIF (or COACS) means profits or income arising from the acquisition, holding, management or disposal of the property subject to the PAIF (or COACS) (*FA 2003, Sch 7A, paras 9(2), (3), 19(2), (3)*). A relevant settlor in relation to a land transaction is an individual in relation to a relevant settlement. A settlement is a relevant settlement if a trustee of the settlement is connected with a person who is the purchaser under the land transaction. The definition of a settlement in *ITTOIA 2005, s 620* applies. Trustee must be read in accordance with *CTA 2010, s 1123(3)* (connected persons supplementary) and *CTA 2010, s 1122* (connected persons) has effect for the purpose of this provision (but disregarding *s 1122(7), (8)* (application to partnerships) (*FA 2003, Sch 7A, paras 9(4)–(7), 19(4)–(7)*). In the case of a COACS a depository is the person to whom the property subject to the scheme is entrusted for safekeeping (*FA 2003, Sch 7A, para 19(4)*).

19.239 In the case of a COACS, only, seeding relief is also withdrawn if the genuine diversity of ownership condition (see **19.240**) is not met either immediately before the end of the seeding period, at a time during the control period, or at a time after the end of the control period where the failure is pursuant to (or in connection with) arrangements made before the end of that period. The requirement to meet this condition applies only to times when the COACS hold the chargeable interest that was acquired by it under the relevant transaction, or a chargeable interest derived from the interest. The amount chargeable is the amount that would have been chargeable had the seeding relief not applied, or an appropriate proportion of that amount having regard to the subject-matter of the relevant transaction and what is held by the COACS at the time when the genuine diversity of ownership condition is not met (*FA 2003, Sch 7A, para 14(1)–(4)*). The operator of a COACS can apply to HMRC for clearance that the scheme meets the genuine diversity of ownership conditions. Where such an application is made, HMRC must notify the COACS of its decision within 28 days of the receipt of all of the information that is needed to make the decision. Such a clearance has effect only for so long as the information on which HMRC relies in granting clearance is materially unchanged and the scheme is operated in accordance with it (*FA 2003, Sch 7A, para 14(5), (6)*).

19.240 For the purpose of *paras 11* and *18(4)* (see **19.228** and **19.236**), a COACS meets the genuine diversity of ownership test if:

(*a*) the scheme documents which are available to investors and to HMRC contain: a statement specifying the intended categories of investor; an undertaking that units in the scheme will be widely available; and an undertaking that units in the scheme will be marketed and made available sufficiently widely to reach the intended categories of investors and in a manner appropriate to them;

(*b*) the specification of the intended categories of investor does not have a limiting or deterrent effect, and any other terms or conditions governing participation in the scheme do not have a limiting or deterrent effect; and

(*c*) units in the scheme are marketed and made available sufficiently widely to reach the intended categories of investors, and in a manner appropriate to attract those categories of investors and a person who falls within one of the intended categories of investors can (on request to the operator) obtain information about the scheme and acquire units in it.

(*FA 2003, Sch 7A, para 15(1)–(6).*)

A COACS is not regarded as failing to meet condition (*c*) at any time by reason of it having at that time no capacity to receive additional investments, unless that such capacity is fixed by the scheme documents (or otherwise) and a pre-determined number of specific persons, or specific groups of connected persons (as defined in *CTA 2010, s 1122*) make investments in the scheme which collectively exhaust all (or substantially all) of that capacity (*FA 2003, Sch 7A, para 15(7)*).

19.241 A COACS also meets the genuine diversity of ownership condition at any time when:

(*a*) there is a feeder fund in relation to the COACS; and

(*b*) conditions (*a*) to (*c*) above (**19.240**) are met in relation to the scheme after taking account of the scheme documents relating to the feeder fund and the intended investors in the feeder fund.

(*FA 2003, Sch 7A, para 15(8).*)

A feeder fund of a COACS is an open-ended investment company (as defined in *FSMA 2000, s 236*), an offshore fund (as defined in *TIOPA 2010, s 355*), or a unit trust scheme (as defined in *FSMA 2000, s 237(11)* one of the main objects of which is investment in the COACS and which is managed by the same person as the COACS (*FA 2003, Sch 7A, para 20*).

19.242 These seeding reliefs have effect in relation to land transactions of which the effective date is after 14 September 2016. However, they do not apply to a transaction effected in pursuance of a contract entered into or substantially performed before that date. Nor do they apply to a transaction effected in pursuance of a contract entered into before that date unless there is any variation of the contract, or assignment of rights under it, after that date; or the transaction is effected in consequence of the exercise after that date of an option, right of pre-emption or similar right; or there is an assignment, sub-sale or other transaction relating to the whole or part of the subject-matter of the contract after that date as a result of which a person other than the purchaser under the contract becomes entitled to call for a conveyance (*FA 2016, Sch 16, para 15*).

Charities

19.243 A land transaction is exempt from SDLT if the purchaser is a charity provided that:

(*a*) it intends to hold the subject matter of the transaction either for use in furtherance of its charitable purposes (or for those of another charity) or as an investment the profits of which will be used for its charitable purposes (but oddly not those of another charity); and

(*b*) the transaction is not entered into for the purpose of avoiding SDLT (either by the charity or some other person.

(*FA 2003, s 68* and *Sch 8, para 1.*)

The relief also applies to a purchase by a 'charitable trust', ie a trust all the beneficiaries of which are charities or a unit trust scheme in which all the unitholders are charities. In such a case the charitable purposes that need to be looked at are those of the beneficiaries (*FA 2003, Sch 8, para 4 as amended by FA 2014, Sch 23, para 4*). For this purpose, a charity holds a chargeable interest for qualifying charitable purposes if it holds it either for use in furtherance of its charitable purposes (or those of another charity) or as an investment from which the profits are applied to its own charitable purposes (*FA 2003, Sch 8, para 1(3A)* inserted by *FA 2014, Sch 23, para 2*).

19.244 The FTT and Upper Tribunal in the *Pollen Estate Trustee Co Ltd v HMRC ([2013] STC 1479)* held that where a property is bought jointly by a charity and a non-charity, the exemption does not apply. The Court of Appeal disagreed. It held that the wording 'if the purchaser is a charity' should be interpreted as 'to the extent that the purchaser is a charity'. That was a permissible interpretation and the Court could see no policy reason why parliament should have intended not to grant relief on a joint purchase but to grant relief if the charity bought a part interest separately.

19.245 As a result the law was changed to provide that where there is more than one purchaser under a land transaction, the purchasers acquire as tenants in common, at least one of them is not a 'qualifying charity', and no purchaser enters into the transaction for the purpose of the avoidance of SDLT (whether for himself or any other person) the tax chargeable is reduced by the proportion of the tax that the aggregate consideration given by qualifying charities bears to the total consideration (or if lower, the proportion in which the parts of the property acquired by qualifying charities bears to the whole). A charity is a 'qualifying charity' for this purpose if it intends to hold its undivided share of the property interest for qualifying charitable purposes (*FA 2003, Sch 8, para 3A* inserted by *FA 2014, Sch 23, para 2*). This gives statutory effect to the decision in *Pullen Estates*, albeit on a much more restrictive basis. It should particularly be noted that it applies only where the purchasers are tenants in common; it will not apply if the relationship of the purchasers as joint tenants (presumably because that might create scope for avoidance).

19.246 Where relief is given under *para 3A*, it will be withdrawn if the charity ceases to be established for charitable purposes only or the chargeable interest acquired by the charity under the transaction (or any interest or right derived from it) is used or held by the charity otherwise than for qualifying charitable purposes either within three years from the effective date of the transaction or in pursuance of (or in connection with) arrangements made before the end of that three-year period (which would accordingly include arrangements made prior to the acquisition) (*FA 2003, Sch 8, para 3B(1)–(4)*). If the acquirers included more than one charity, only the portion of the relief applicable to the interest acquired by the charity concerned is withdrawn (*FA 2003, Sch 8,* *para 3B(5)–(9)*). Where only part of the charity's interest ceases to be used or held for qualifying charitable purposes, only the relief applicable to that part is withdrawn (*FA 2003, Sch 8, para 3B(10)*). If the charity is not a qualifying charity but it intends to hold the greater part of its undivided share of the property for qualifying charitable purposes, the relief is given in full but, in addition to the two above as qualifying events, the relief will be withdrawn if within the three-year period the charity transfers the whole (or any part) of the chargeable interest acquired by it or grants a low-rental lease of the whole or any part of the chargeable interest at a premium (as defined in *para 3(2)(b)(ii)* – see **19.249**). The date of such an event is the effective date of the transaction (*FA 2003, Sch 8, para 3C*).

19.247 The relief is withdrawn if at some time during the three years from the effective date of the transaction (or later as a result of arrangements made during that three-year period or earlier) and while the charity still holds the property (or an interest derived from it) either:

(*a*) the purchaser ceases to be a charity (ie established for charitable purposes only); or

(*b*) the charity ceases to hold the property (or any interest or other right derived from it) otherwise than for qualifying charitable purposes (ie within (*a*) in **19.243** above).

(*FA 2003, Sch 8, para 2(1)–(3)*.)

19.248 The tax payable in such circumstances is of course that which would have been due if the relief had never applied or, if at that time it no longer owns the entire interest in what was acquired, an appropriate proportion of such tax having regard to what was initially acquired, what is held by the purchaser at the time of the disqualifying event and the extent to which what is still held becomes used for non-charitable purposes (*FA 2003, Sch 8, para 2(4),(8)*).

19.249 If the disposal is precluded from exemption because the purchaser does not intend to hold the land for qualifying charitable purposes (within **19.243**(*a*)) but the purchaser intends to hold the greater part of it for such purposes, the exemption applies but any transfer by the charity of a major interest in the whole or any part of the land, or any grant by it at a premium (or for any consideration other than rent) of a lease of all or part of the land at an annual rent of £1,000 p.a. or less (£600 prior to 12 March 2008), that is not made in furtherance of the charity's charitable purposes will be a disqualifying event which could trigger a withdrawal of the relief under *para 2* (see **19.247**). The date of the disqualifying event is the effective date of the transaction. (*FA 2003, Sch 8, para 3*).

Miscellaneous Exemptions

19.250 The following types of transactions are also exempt from SDLT.

(1) One entered into for the purposes of, or in connection with, a qualifying transfer of the whole or part of the business of a mutual insurance company to a company that has share capital (ie a transaction on the demutualisation of an insurance company) (*FA 2003, s 63*).

(2) A land transaction effected by the *Building Societies Act 1986, s 97(6)* or *(7)* on the demutualisation of a building society (*FA 2003, s 64*).

(3) A land transaction entered into on, or in connection with, a reorganisation under a statutory provision where both the purchaser and vendor are public bodies (*FA 2003, s 66(1)*. Broadly speaking, a public body for this purpose is a government department, local authority, health authority or trust, NHS Foundation trust, planning authority, or other statutory body. The full list is contained in *s 66(4)* as amended by *FA 2003, Section 66 (Prescribed Persons) Regulations 2005 (SI 2005 No 83)*.The Treasury have power by statutory instrument to extend the relief to transactions entered into under a statutory provision where only one of the parties is a public body (*FA 2003, s 66(2)*). They have done so in relation to nuclear transfer schemes by the *FA 2003, Section 66 (Prescribed Transactions) Order 2005 (SI 2005 No 645)*. Where the exemption would apply if the transaction had been entered into by a public body it will also apply if the party is a company all of the shares of which are held by the public body, or a wholly owned subsidiary of such a company (*FA 2003, s 66(5)*).

(4) A transfer in consequence of the reorganisation of parliamentary constituencies by an Order in Council under the *Parliamentary Constituencies Act 1986*. The detailed rules are contained in *FA 2003, s 67*.

(5) An acquisition by the Historic Buildings and Monuments Commission for England, the National Endowment for Science, Technology and the Arts, the British Museum, the National Heritage Memorial Fund or the National History Museum (*FA 2003, s 69*).

(6) An acquisition by a registered social landlord, but only if either that landlord is controlled by its tenants, the vendor is a qualifying body or the transaction is funded with the assistance of a public subsidy (*FA 2003, s 71(1)*).

(7) From 21 July 2009 a purchase by a profit-making registered provider of social housing if the transaction is funded with the assistance of a public subsidy (*FA 2003, s 71(A1)*).

19.251 A registered social landlord for the purpose of (6) above is a body registered as a social landlord under the *Housing Act 1996, s 1(1)* (or the corresponding Scottish and Northern Irish enactments) (*FA 2003, s 121*). A registered social landlord is controlled by its tenants if the majority of its board members (or committee of management if it is not a company) are tenants occupying properties owned or managed by it (*FA 2003, s 71(2)*). A qualifying body means a registered social landlord, a housing action trust within *Part 3, Housing Act 1988*, a principal council under the *Local Government Act 1972*, the Common Council of the City of London and certain similar Scottish and Northern Irish bodies (*FA 2003, s 71(3)*). A public subsidy is a grant or other financial assistance under the *National Lottery Act 1993, s 25*, the *Housing Act 1996, s 18* (social housing grants), the *Housing Grants, Construction and Regeneration Act 1996, s 126* (financial assistance for regeneration and development), the *Housing (Scotland) Act 1988, s 2*, or the *Housing (Northern Ireland) Order 1992, Article 33* (*FA 2003, s 71(4)*).

Right to Buy Transactions

19.252 On a right to buy transaction, ie the sale of a dwelling at a discount or the grant of a lease of a dwelling at a discount by a relevant public sector body (or in pursuance of the preserved right to buy), any consideration that would be payable only if a contingency were to occur (or is payable only because it has occurred) is ignored for SDLT purposes (*FA 2003, s 70* and *Sch 9, para 1(1), (2)*). Accordingly *FA 2003, s 51(1)* (see **19.138**) does not apply to such a transaction. Where the vendor is a registered social landlord, any grant under the *Housing Act 1996, ss 20, 21* is also ignored for a right to buy transaction (*FA 2003, Sch 9, para 1(5)*).

19.253 Broadly speaking, a relevant public sector body is a government department, a local housing authority, a county council, the Housing Corporation, a registered social landlord, a housing action trust, the Commission for the New Towns, a New Towns development corporation, an urban development corporation, the Welsh Development Agency, a police authority, the UK Atomic Energy Authority, and their Scottish and Northern Irish equivalents. The full list is set out in *FA 2003, Sch 9, para 1(3)*. The Treasury have power by statutory instrument to add other bodies.

19.254 The transfer of a dwelling (or grant of a lease) is made in pursuance of the preserved right to buy if:

(*a*) the vendor is a person against whom the right to buy is exercisable by virtue of the *Housing Act 1985, s 171A* or the *Housing (Scotland) Act 1987, s 81A* (both of which preserve the right to buy on a disposal of the property to a private sector landlord);

(*b*) the purchaser is the qualifying person for the purpose of the above provisions; and

(*c*) the dwelling is under those provisions the qualifying dwelling-house in relation to the purchaser.

(*FA 2003, Sch 9, para 1(4)*.)

Shared Ownership Leases

19.255 If a lease is granted by a qualifying body in pursuance of the preserved right to buy the purchaser can elect to treat the chargeable consideration for SDLT as the amount stated in the lease in accordance with (*e*) below (*FA 2003, Sch 9, para 2(1)(4)*). In effect he can choose to pay SDLT initially on the then value of the property or to pay SDLT on the lease plus further SDLT when he buys the top slice of the equity. The lease must:

(*a*) be of a dwelling;

(*b*) give the lessee or lessees exclusive use of the dwelling;

(*c*) provide for the lessee or lessees to acquire the dwelling;

(*d*) be granted partly in consideration of rent and partly in consideration of a premium calculated by reference to the market value of the dwelling (or to a sum calculated in accordance with that value); and

(*e*) contain a statement of the market value (or other sum) by reference to which the premium is calculated.

(*FA 2003, Sch 9, para 2(2)*.)

19.256 The election must be included in the land transaction return made in respect of the grant of the lease (or in an amendment to that return) and is irrevocable (*FA 2003, Sch 9, para 2(3)*). *FA 2003, s 118* (meaning of market value – see **19.97**) does not apply for the purpose of (*e*) above (*FA 2003, Sch 9, para 2(5)*). As it still appears to apply for the purpose of (*d*) it is unclear what this is trying to do. It does not offer an alternative meaning of market value.

19.257 Where such an election is made on the grant of the lease (and the tax chargeable on the lease duly paid) the transfer of the reversion to the lessee or lessees under the terms of the lease is exempt from SDLT (*FA 2003, Sch 9, para 3*).

19.258 A shared ownership scheme is an arrangement which enables a tenant to buy (sometimes at below market value – which is why the legislation refers to a sum calculated by reference to the premium) gradually from a 'qualifying body', (a housing association, local authority or new town development corporation) by not having to pay the full price initially (*FA 2003, Sch 9, para 5*). The housing association, etc, grants a long lease for a premium equivalent to the value of the share acquired with rent payable on the remaining portion. Sometimes the tenant is entitled to acquire the reversion or a full leasehold interest. Some arrangements allow the purchase of the freehold in two or more steps. For example, the tenant may initially buy a 50% share and pay rent for the other half but might be entitled to pay a further amount at a later date to acquire a further 25% and as a consequence have his rent reduced. Such arrangements are known as 'staircasing provisions'.

19.259 Where staircasing is allowed, the effect of the election is that:

(*a*) the rent in consideration of which the lease is granted must be taken to be the maximum rent stated in the lease; and

(*b*) the chargeable consideration for the grant other than rent must be taken to be the amount stated in the lease as the premium obtainable on the open market (or sum calculated by reference to that premium) by reference to which the premium is calculated.

(*FA 2003, Sch 9, para 4(1)(4)*.)

19.260 For this to apply the lease must:

(*a*) be of a dwelling;

(*b*) give the lessee or lessees exclusive use of the dwelling;

(*c*) provide that the lessee or lessees can, on the payment of a sum, require the terms of the lease to be altered so that the rent payable under it is reduced;

(*d*) be granted partly in consideration of rent and partly in consideration of a premium calculated by reference to that obtainable on the open market for the grant of a lease containing the same terms as the lease but with the substitution of the minimum rent (ie the lowest rent which could become payable if it were altered in accordance with (*c*) at the date when the lease is granted) for the rent payable under the lease (or by reference to a sum calculated by reference to such a premium); and

(*e*) contain a statement both of the minimum rent and of the premium obtainable on the open market (or the sum calculated by reference to that premium) by reference to which the premium is calculated.

(*FA 2003, Sch 9, para 4(2)*.)

19.261 If under a shared ownership lease, the lessee or lessees have the right to pay an amount to reduce the rent payable under the lease and by exercising that right the lessee acquires an interest additional to that already held, calculated by reference to the market value of the dwelling and expressed as a percentage of the dwelling or its value, the acquisition of that additional interest is exempt from SDLT if the acquisition takes place after 17 March 2004 and:

(*a*) an election was made for tax to be charged on the grant of the lease in accordance with *para 2* (see **19.255**) or *para 4* (see **19.259**) and that tax was duly paid, or

(*b*) immediately after the acquisition the total share of the dwelling held by the lessee or lessees does not exceed 80%.

(*FA 2003, Sch 9, para 4A*.)

In other words, SDLT is payable only by reference to the initial grant of the lease and then on any additional payments that bring the purchaser's interest above 80% (*FA 2003, Sch 9, para 2(1),(4),(4A)* as amended by *FA 2007, s 78*. For the purpose of determining the rate of SDLT chargeable on the grant of a shared ownership lease of a dwelling where the transaction is after 11 March 2008, the grant must be treated as if it were not linked to either any acquisition of an interest in the dwelling to which *para 4A* applies or to any transfer of the reversion to the lessee or lessees under the terms of the lease (*FA 2003, Sch 9, para 4B* inserted by *FA 2008, s 95(8)*).

19.262 For the purpose of the above provisions, a qualifying body means a local housing authority under the *Housing Act 1985*, a housing association within the meaning of the *Housing Associations Act 1985* or the *Housing (Northern Ireland) Order 1992*, a housing action trust under the *Housing Act 1988*, the Northern Ireland Housing Executive, the Commission for the New Towns, a development corporation established under the *New Towns Act 1981* or, from 21 July 2009, a registered provider of social housing that is not a housing association (*FA 2003, Sch 9, para 5(2)* as amended by *FA 2009, s 81*). A registered provider of social housing is only a qualifying body in relation to a lease of premises if the purchase or construction of the premises (or their adaptation for use as a dwelling) by that provider (or a person connected with it – within *CTA 2010, s 1122*) has been funded with the assistance of a grant or other financial assistance under the *Housing and Regeneration Act 2008, s 19* (*FA 2003, Sch 9, para 5(2A) (2B)*). Paragraph **19.254** above applies to determine if a lease is granted in pursuance of the preserved right to buy (*FA 2003, Sch 9, para 5(3)*). The return form SDLT1 is not wholly suitable to deal with shared ownership leases. HMRC have accordingly issued guidance as to how it should be completed in a Press Release of 31 August 2004.

Shared Ownership Trusts

19.263 Shared ownership trusts have developed as a way of providing affordable housing under 'commonhold' ownership. Shared ownership leases are not feasible for commonhold. The legal title to the dwelling is held by trustees. A declaration of trust gives the purchaser a beneficial interest in the property and the exclusive right to occupy it in return for making regular payments to reflect the equity interest of the other beneficiary, a social landlord. The purchaser can also make capital payments which will increase his share of the equity in the property (so that eventually he can own it outright) and thus reduce the regular payments he has to make.

19.264 To qualify as a shared ownership trust there has to be a trust of land where the trust property is a dwelling in England or Wales, one of the beneficiaries ('the social landlord') is a qualifying body (within **19.262** above), and the terms of the trust:

(*a*) provide for one or more of the individual beneficiaries ('the purchaser') to have exclusive use of the trust property as his only or main residence;

(*b*) require the purchaser to make an initial payment to the social landlord ('the initial capital');

(*c*) require the purchaser to make additional payments to the social landlord under *Trusts of Land and Appointment of Trustees Act 1996, s 13(6)(a)* ('rent equivalent payments');

(*d*) enable the purchaser to make other additional payments to the social landlord ('equity acquisition payments');

(*e*) determine the initial beneficial interests of the social landlord and of the purchaser by reference to the initial capital;

(*f*) specify a sum, equating or relating to the market value of the dwelling (the actual market value not the deemed value under *s 118* (see **19.26**)), by reference to which the initial capital was calculated; and

(*g*) provide for the purchaser's beneficial interest in the trust property to increase and the social landlord's to diminish as equity-acquisition payments are made.

A dwelling for this purpose includes a building which is being constructed or adapted for use as a dwelling and land which is to be used for the purpose of the construction of a dwelling or is, or is to become, the garden or grounds of a dwelling (*FA 2003, Sch 9, para 7(1)–(6)*). A registered provider of social housing is only a qualifying body in relation to a shared ownership trust if it meets the conditions set out at **19.262** above (*FA 2003, Sch 9, para 7(8)*).

19.265 For this purpose, 'the purchaser' (not the social landlord) is treated as the purchaser of the trust property, the initial capital is treated as chargeable consideration other than rent, and any rent-equivalent additional payments are treated as rent (*FA 2003, Sch 9, paras 8, 11*). The equity-acquisition payments are exempt from SDLT provided that the payment does not bring the total interest of the purchaser above 80% of the overall equity (*FA 2003, Sch 9, para 10*). This mirrors the position for shared ownership leases (see **19.261**). In effect, SDLT is chargeable on only the first and last instalments of the purchase price. Alternatively the purchaser can elect (irrevocably) for the chargeable consideration to be the amount at **19.264**(*f*), ie the initial market value of the dwelling, and for the rent equivalent payments to be ignored (*FA 2003, Sch 9, para 9*). Where that election is made no SDLT is chargeable on equity-acquisition payments even above the 80% ceiling. The election can be beneficial if the first payment is large and it is almost certain that the final 20% slice of the equity will in time be acquired as it crystallises the SDLT by reference to current value, albeit of a 100% interest, (which may well be under £125,000) rather than risk a heavy SDLT charge on the final 20% slice. In practice the Treasury say that it is rare for the purchaser's interest to go above the 80% figure (Finance Bill 2007 Explanatory Notes).

19.266 For the purpose of determining the rate of SDLT chargeable on the declaration of a shared ownership trust after 11 March 2008, the declaration is treated as if it were not linked to either any equity-acquisition payment under the trust (see **19.264**(*d*)) or any consequent increase in the purchaser's beneficial interest in the trust property, or to a transfer to the purchaser of an interest in the trust property upon the termination of the trust (*FA 2003, Sch 9, para 12*).

Rent to Shared Ownership

19.267 In calculating the chargeable consideration for transactions forming part of a rent to shared ownership lease scheme, or a rent to shared ownership trust scheme, after 20 July 2009 the following transactions must be treated as if they were not linked to each other:

(*a*) the grant of the assured shorthold tenancy;

(*b*) the grant of the shared ownership lease (or the declaration of the shared ownership trust; and

(*c*) any other land transaction between the qualifying body and the tenant, or any of the tenants, entered into as part of the scheme.

(*FA 2003, Sch 9, paras 13(1)(3), 14(1)(3).*)

For the purpose of determining the effective date of the grant of the lease (or the declaration of the trust) the possession of the dwelling by the tenant or tenants pursuant to the assured shorthold tenancy is disregarded (*FA 2003, Sch 9, paras 13(4), 14(4)*).

19.268 A rent to shared ownership lease scheme is a scheme or arrangement under which a qualifying body (within **19.258**) grants an assured shorthold tenancy (as defined in *Part 1* of the *Housing Act 1988*) of a dwelling to a person or persons and subsequently grants a shared ownership lease (see below) of the dwelling (or another dwelling) to that tenant or to one or more of those tenants (*FA 2003, Sch 9, para 13(2)(5)*). A shared ownership lease is a lease granted by a qualifying body, or in pursuance of the preserved right to buy, which meets the conditions in **19.255** or **19.260** above (*FA 2003, Sch 9, paras 4A(3), 13(5)*). A rent to shared ownership trust scheme is a scheme or arrangement under which a qualifying body grants an assured shorthold tenancy of a dwelling to a person or persons and the tenant (or one or more of the tenants) becomes the purchaser under a shared ownership trust of the dwelling (or of another dwelling) under which the qualifying body is the social landlord. The above definitions again apply (*FA 2003, Sch 9, para 14(2), (5)*).

Rent to Mortgage and Rent to Loan

19.269 The chargeable consideration for a rent to mortgage transaction is the price which would be payable under the *Housing Act 1985, s 126* for a transfer of the dwelling (where the transaction is a transfer) or for the grant of a lease of the dwelling (where the transaction is the grant of a lease) if the acquirer were exercising the right to buy under *Part 5* of that Act (*FA 2003, Sch 9, para 6(1)(3)*). A rent to mortgage transaction for this purpose is the transfer of a dwelling to a person, or the grant of a lease of a dwelling to that person, pursuant to his exercise of the right to acquire on rent to mortgage terms under *Part 5* of the *Housing Act 1985* (*FA 2003, Sch 9, para 6(2)*). The same rules apply to the execution of a heritable disposition in Scotland pursuant to the exercise of the right to purchase a house by way of the rent to loan scheme under the *Housing (Scotland) Act 1987* (*FA 2003, Sch 9, para 6(4)(5)*).

Alternative Property Finance (eg Islamic Mortgages)

19.270 Islamic law prohibits the lending of money at interest. Accordingly, an Islamic mortgage often takes the form of either the individual purchasing the property and immediately reselling it to the financial institution, or the institution purchasing the property under terms that the individual will be granted a lease and be given a right to repurchase or purchase the property at the expiry of the lease. In such a case the rent is generally equivalent to the interest on a conventional mortgage and the term of the lease is equivalent to the term of such a mortgage. Where the individual buys and resells it is fair that all of the transactions other than the initial purchase should escape SDLT as the overall effect of them is the same as the grant and redemption of a conventional mortgage and a mortgage does not attract SDLT. If the initial purchase by the institution is direct that transaction (the first transaction) will attract SDLT (as the vendor is not the individual) but the subsequent ones will not do so. Again that is fair, as with a conventional mortgage the purchase of the property attracts SDLT even though the mortgage which generates the bulk of the property consideration does not do so. The products eligible for relief were extended by the *Finance Act 2005* to cover the situation in Scotland where the financial institution and the individual become beneficial tenants in common.

19.271 The relief applies where arrangements are entered into between an individual (or other person) and a financial institution (as defined at **19.272**) under which:

(*a*) the institution purchases a major interest in land (or an undivided share of a major interest) ('the first transaction');

(*b*) where the interest is an undivided share, the major interest is held on trust for the institution and the individual as beneficial tenants in common;

(*c*) the institution (or trustee at (*b*)) grants a lease (or sub-lease) ('the second transaction'); and

(*d*) the institution and the individual enter into an agreement under which the individual has the right to require the institution or its successor in title to transfer to the individual (in either one or a series of transactions) the whole interest purchased by the institution under the first transaction ('a further transaction').

(*FA 2003, s 71A(1)*.)

19.272 The first transaction is exempt from SDLT provided that the vendor is either the individual concerned or another financial institution by whom the interest was acquired under the same type of arrangement entered into between it and the individual (*FA 2003, s 71A(2)*). In other words there initially has to be a taxable purchase by the individual as a prelude either to entering into the transaction or a previous transaction which is being refinanced. The second transaction is also exempt but only if the SDLT rules relating to the first transaction are complied with, eg the SDLT return was duly filed and any tax chargeable paid (*FA 2003, s 71A(3)*). Any transfer to the individual that results from the exercise of the right at **19.271**(*d*) is exempt if the SDLT rules in relation to both the first and second transactions are complied with and at all times between the second transaction and the further transactions in question the interest purchased under the first transaction (so far as not transferred to the individual by a previous further transaction) is held by a financial institution and the lease or sub-lease granted under the second transaction is held by the individual (*FA 2003, s 71A(4)*).

19.273 The agreement at **19.276**(*c*) is not to be treated as substantially performed (see **19.89**) unless and until the whole interest purchased by the institution under the first transaction has been transferred (*FA 2003, s 71A(5)(a)*). Nor is that agreement to be treated as a distinct land transaction by virtue of *FA 2003, s 46* (options etc – see **19.133**) (*FA 2003, s 71A(5)(b)*). A further transaction that is exempt under *s 71A(4)* is not a notifiable transaction if after it the institution still has an interest in the land. The transfer under which the institution completes the transfer to the individual of the whole interest that it purchased under the first transaction is notifiable though (*FA 2003, s 71A(7)*). References in this provision to an individual in relation to a time after his death include his personal representatives (*FA 2003, s 71A(9)*). The provision is slightly different where the land is in Scotland, The Scottish rules are considered at **19.276** and **19.277**.

19.274 A financial institution is:

(*a*) a bank within *ICTA 1988, s 840A*;

(*b*) a building society within the meaning of the *Building Societies Act 1988*;

(*c*) a wholly-owned subsidiary of a bank or building society;

(*d*) to 24 March 2011 only, a person licensed under the *Consumer Credit Act 1974, Part 3* to carry on a consumer credit business or consumer hire business;

(*e*) a bond issuer (as defined in *ITA 2007, s 564G*) but only in relation to specified bonds;

(*f*) a person authorised in a jurisdiction outside the UK to receive deposits or other repayable funds from the public and to grant credit on its own account; or

(*g*) an insurance company (within *ICTA 1988, s 431(2)*) or a person authorised to carry out similar business in a jurisdiction outside the UK.

(*FA 2003, s 73BA*; *ITA 2007, s 564B*.)

The removal of head (*d*) was to assure that the relief 'cannot be abused by purchasers setting themselves up as a financial institution by acquiring a Consumer Credit Licence' (Finance Bill 2011, Explanatory Notes). From 26 March 2015, a person who has permission under the *Financial Services and Markets Act 2000, Pt 4A* to carry on the regulated activity specified in Art 63F(1) of the *Financial Services and Markets Act (Regulated Activities) Order 2001 (SI 2001/544)* is also a financial institution for the purposes of *FA 2003, ss 71A, 73AB* and *73B* (*FA 2003, s 73BA(3)* inserted by *FA 2015, s 68*). This extends the provision to home purchase plan providers.

19.275 An alternative type of Islamic mortgage is for the institution to purchase the property and resell it for a consideration that is paid in instalments making a profit equivalent to the total interest on a conventional mortgage. *Section 73* deals with this type of transaction. It provides that where arrangements are entered into with a financial institution under which:

(*a*) the institution purchases a major interest in land (the first transaction);

(*b*) the institution sells that interest to another person (the second transaction); and

(*c*) that person granted the institution a legal mortgage over that interest; then:

- (i) the first transaction is exempt from SDLT if the vendor is the person concerned or another financial institution by whom the interest was acquired under other arrangements of the kind mentioned in *FA 2003, s 72(1)* entered into between it and that person (ie it is a refinancing of an existing Islamic mortgage); and
- (ii) the second transaction is exempt from SDLT if the financial institution complies with the SDLT rules relating to the first transaction on a chargeable consideration that is not less than the market value of the interest and, in the case of a lease, the rent.

(*FA 2003, s 73(1)–(3)*.)

A legal mortgage means a legal mortgage as defined in the *Law of Property Act 1925, s 205(1)(xvi)*, namely a mortgage by demise or subdemise or a charge by way of legal mortgage. In Scotland it means a standard security and in Northern Ireland a mortgage by conveyance of a legal estate or by demise or sub-demise or a charge by way of legal mortgage (*FA 2003, s 73(5)*).

19.276 In Scotland it is usual for the individual to purchase the property and enter into a sale and leaseback with the institution. Accordingly, the Scottish version states that where arrangements are entered into between an individual (or another person) and a financial institution under which the institution:

(*a*) purchases a major interest in land (the first transaction);

(*b*) grants to the individual out of that interest a lease or sub-lease (the second transaction); and (*c*) enters into an agreement under which that individual has a right to require the institution (or its successor in title) to transfer the major interest purchased by the institution under the first transaction, then:

   (i) the first transaction is exempt from SDLT provided that the vendor is the individual or another financial institution which originally entered into a similar arrangement with the individual;

   (ii) the second transaction is exempt from SDLT provided that the SDLT provisions relating to the first transaction (including the payment of any tax due) are complied with; and

   (iii) a transfer that results from an exercise of the right at (*c*) above (the third transaction) is exempt from SDLT provided that the transfer is to the same person, the SDLT provisions relating to the first and second transactions have been complied with, and at all times between the second and third transactions the interest purchased under the first transaction is held by a financial institution and the lease or sub-lease granted under the second is held by the individual.

(*FA 2003, s 72(1)–(4)*.)

The other person had to be an individual in relation to arrangements for which the effective date of the first transaction was before 19 July 2006. The agreement is not to be treated for SDLT purposes as substantially performed unless and until either the third transaction is entered into, and it is not to be treated as being a distinct land transaction by virtue of *FA 2003, s 46* (options and rights of pre-emption) (*FA 2003, s 72(5)*). A major interest in land is the freehold or a lease for a term of years absolute (*FA 2003, s 117*) (see **19.87**). The reason that all three transactions are exempt is, of course, because the SDLT charge arises on the initial purchase by the individual.

19.277 An alternative type of Scottish transaction is for the institution and the individual to purchase as owners in common, with an agreement that the individual has a right to occupy the property exclusively and a right to acquire the institution's interest at a future date. In such a case the first transaction (the initial purchase), the second transaction (the agreement for exclusive occupation) and the third transaction (on the exercise of the right) are all exempt from SDLT (subject to the conditions in **19.276**) (*FA 2003, s 72A*).

19.278 From 19 July 2006, *ss 71A–73* do not apply to arrangements in which the first transaction is exempt by virtue of *Sch 7* (group, reconstruction and acquisition reliefs) see **19.189** onwards (*FA 2003, s 73A*).

19.279 An interest held by a financial institution as a result of the first transaction within *s 71A* (see **19.271**), *72* (see **19.272**) or *72A* (see **19.277**) is an exempt interest for SDLT purposes in relation to further dealings with it by the institution (unless it qualifies for group relief). It will, however, cease to be an exempt interest if the lease or agreement ceases to have effect or the right ceases to have effect or becomes subject to a restriction (*FA 2003, s 73B*).

Exercise of Collective Rights by Tenants of Flats

19.280 One of the conditions for the leaseholder of a flat to be able to acquire the freehold is that the purchase has to be made in conjunction with other leaseholders. A company is normally used for this purpose.. The consideration payable on an enfranchisement is, of course, the aggregate consideration for all the freeholds being purchased. This could attract a higher rate of SDLT than would be payable if an individual tenant could have bought his own interest in the freehold.

19.281 To avoid this, where a chargeable transaction is entered into in pursuance of a right of collective enfranchisement the rate of tax is determined by reference to the fraction of the total consideration produced by dividing that consideration by the number of flats in respect of which the right to collective enfranchisement is being exercised. That rate is then applied to the chargeable consideration (*FA 2003, s 74(1)–(3)*).

9.282 The provision applies where a chargeable transaction is entered into by a person or persons nominated or appointed by qualifying tenants of flats in exercise of a right under either *Part 1* of the *Landlord and Tenant Act 1987* (right of first refusal) or *Chapter 1* of *Part 1* of the *Leasehold Reform, Housing and Urban Development Act 1993* (right to collective enfranchisement) (*FA 2003, s 74(1)* as substituted). The tax is calculated by first determining the tax that would have been chargeable had the consideration been the appropriate fraction of the actual consideration, and multiplying that figure by the number of qualifying flats in the premises (*FA 2003, s 74(1B)* inserted by *Stamp Duty Land Tax Act 2015, Sch 1, para 2(3)*). The appropriate fraction is that derived from dividing the consideration by the number of 'qualifying flats' in the premises (*FA 2003, s 74(1A)*). A qualifying flat is one held by a qualifying tenant (as defined in the relevant enfranchisement act) who is participating in the exercise of the right (*FA 2003, s 74(4)* as substituted). For transactions prior to 4 December 2014, the rate of tax for a single flat was calculated by reference to the fraction of the consideration produced by dividing the consideration by the number of 'qualifying flats' in the premises (and that rate was applied to the total consideration (*FA 2003, s 73(1A)(2)(3)* as amended by *FA 2013, Sch 35, para 5* and *FA 2014, s 112*).

19.283 If the calculation produces a figure of more than £500,000 (£2 million before 1 July 2014) and the purchaser is a company (or other body within *FA 2003, Sch 4A, para 3(3)* (see **19.26**), tax is charged at 15% on the chargeable consideration for the transaction. There is a saving for certain contracts entered into before 20 March 2014 where the consideration is between £500,000 and £2 million. This is the same as that considered at **19.10** (*FA 2014, s 112(3)(4)*). Curiously if a block consists of one flat worth £3 million and five worth £50,000 each, a total of £3,250,000, the 15% rate will apply to the total even though that is clearly not the spirit of the 15% charge. That rate is then applied to the chargeable consideration for the transaction (*FA 2003, s 74(3)*). For this purpose the definition of 'flat' and 'qualifying tenant' in the relevant Act are used, and a qualifying flat is defined as a flat held by a qualifying tenant who is participating in the exercise of the right (*FA 2003, s 74(4)* as substituted).

Crofting Community Right to Buy

19.284 A similar problem arises in respect of the right to buy by a crofting community body under *Part 3* of the *Land Reform (Scotland) Act 2003*. In this case the rate of tax is determined by reference to the fraction of the chargeable consideration produced by dividing that consideration by the number of crofts being bought and applying that rate to the total consideration (*FA 2003, s 75*). The calculation is the same as that at **19.283** (*FA 2003, s 75* as amended by *Stamp Duty Land Tax Act 2015, Sch 1, para 1A*).

Sale and Leaseback Arrangements

19.285 The leaseback element of a sale and leaseback is exempt if:

(*a*) the sale is entered into wholly or partly in consideration of the leaseback being entered into;

(*b*) the only other consideration (if any) for the sale is the payment of money or the assumption, satisfaction or release of a debt (or both);

(*c*) the sale is not a transfer of rights within the meaning of *s 45* (see **19.125**) or *s 45A* (see **19.132**); and

(*d*) if the transferor and transferee are both companies they are not members of the same group for the purposes of group relief (see **19.189**).

A sale and leaseback for this purpose is a transaction under which A transfers or grants a major interest in land to B and out of that interest B grants a lease to A (*FA 2003, s 57A*).

New Zero-Carbon Homes (to 30 September 2012 only)

19.286 The Treasury have power by Regulation to exempt from SDLT the first acquisition of a dwelling (a building or part of a building which has been constructed for use as a single dwelling) at a time when it has not previously been occupied) or to reduce the tax chargeable on such a dwelling (*FA 2003, s 58B*). They did so by the *SDLT (Zero-Carbon Homes Relief) Regulations 2007 (SI 2007 No 3437)*. It should be noted that the relief was available only on the first purchase and only if the dwelling had not been used. The intention was to exempt such houses if they cost less than £500,000 and to reduce the tax on more expensive houses by £15,000. The relief applied only to acquisitions up to 30 September 2012.

19.287 The government said that 'A zero-carbon home is one that does not consume fossil fuels for heat and power. It is highly insulated and uses renewable energy to power its needs over a year through microgeneration. Heat and power technologies include ground source heat pumps, photovoltaic cells, solar water heaters and wind turbines' (Budget 2007 RIA).

19.288 The relevant regulations, the *SDLT (Zero-Carbon Homes Relief) Regulations 2007* and the *SDLT (Zero-Carbon Homes) (Amendment) Regulations 2008 (SI 2008 No 1932)*, applied to acquisitions after 1 October 2007. They exempted consideration other than rent from SDLT where the chargeable consideration other than any rent was up to £500,000 and reduced the SDLT by £15,000 where the consideration exceeded £500,000 (*reg 4*). The relief had to be claimed in the land transaction return or an amendment of such a return (*reg 8*). A zero-carbon home is one that is energy efficient in relation to each of its heat loss parameter, dwelling carbon-dioxide emission rate and net carbon-dioxide emissions. Whether those requirements are met must be ascertained by an accredited assessor (under the Building Regulations) using a methodology approved by the Secretary of State as meeting the standards set out in the Regulations (*regs 2, 5, 7*). The assessor must issue a zero-carbon home certificate containing specified information. That certificate must be obtained from the assessor by the vendor and given to the purchaser on or before the acquisition (or for acquisitions before 7 December 2007 as soon as practicable after that date (and for acquisitions of part of a building prior to 13 August 2008 as soon as practicable after that date) (*reg 6*). HMRC were not bound by the certificate but could refuse the relief if they had reason to believe that the dwelling was not a zero-carbon home (*reg 4(5)*). If the first acquisition of a zero-carbon home was one of a number of linked transactions *FA 2003, s 55(4)* (which aggregates the consideration) did not apply for the purpose of granting this relief but the acquisition continued to form part of the set of linked transactions for other purposes – such as determining the tax due on the aggregated transactions (*reg 9*). The accredited assessor was of course entitled to charge a reasonable fee for the assessment of the building and the issue of the certificate.

First-time Buyers (to 24 March 2012 only)

19.289 A land transaction between 25 March 2010 and 24 March 2012 was exempt from SDLT if:

(*a*) it was an acquisition of a major interest in land (other than the grant of a lease of under 21 years or an assignment of a lease which has less than 21 years to run);

(*b*) the land consisted entirely of residential property;

(*c*) the consideration (other than rent) was under £250,000;

(*d*) the purchaser (or, in the case of joint purchasers, all of them) was a first time buyer who intended to occupy the property as his only or main residence; and

(*e*) the transaction was not one of a number of linked transactions (unless the only reason that they were linked was by reason of the connection with the same building).

(*FA 2003, s 57AA(1)(3)(4).*)

19.290 A first-time buyer was a person who had not previously been a purchaser in relation to any acquisition of an interest in land which consisted of (or included) residential property; had not previously acquired such an interest under the laws of another country or territory; had not previously been 'the person' under *FA 2003, ss 71A–73* (Islamic finance); and would not have been such a person if those provisions had always been in force (*FA 2003, s 57AA(2)*). Curiously a person who inherited an overseas property seems to have been excluded but a person who inherited a UK one does not. The conditions were very restrictive. The equivalent Islamic finance transaction (see **19.271** onwards) was similarly exempt (*FA 2003, s 73AC*). The exemption did not, however, apply to the acquisition of a shared ownership lease of a dwelling (within *FA 2003, Sch 9, para 2, 4, or 4A* – see **19.255–19.262**), or where a shared ownership trust was declared (within *FA 2003, Sch 9, para 9* – see **19.265**), or an equity-acquisition payment was made under a shared ownership trust and the consequential increase in the purchaser's beneficial interest was not exempt under *FA 2003, Sch 9, para 10*) and no election was made under these provisions (*FA 2003, Sch 9, para 15*).

Transfers Involving Multiple Dwellings

19.291 Where the main subject matter of a transaction the effective date of which is after 18 July 2011 consists of either:

(*a*) an interest in at least two dwellings (with or without other property); or

(*b*) an interest in a single dwelling (with or without other property) which is one of a number of linked transactions, at least one of the other of which consist of an interest in another dwelling or dwellings,

the SDLT charge is a percentage of the consideration attributable to dwellings (plus a percentage of the remaining consideration (if any)) (*FA 2003, s 58D* and *Sch 6B, paras 2(1)–(3), 4(1)* inserted by *FA 2011, Sch 22*).

19.292 For this purpose the consideration attributable to dwellings is the sum of the tax related to the consideration attributable to dwellings and the tax (if any) related to the remaining consideration (*FA 2003, Sch 6B, paras 2(1)–(3), 4(1)* as substituted by *Stamp Duty Land Tax Act 2015, Sch 1, para 7*). For this purpose the tax related to the consideration attributable to dwellings is calculated by determining the tax that would be chargeable if the land had consisted entirely of residential property and the consideration were the fraction produced by dividing total dwellings consideration by total dwellings; and then multiplying that amount by total dwellings (*FA 2003, Sch 6B, para 5* as substituted). For transactions after 31 March 2016, account must be taken of *FA 2003, Sch 4ZA, para 1* (higher rate transactions – see **19.53**), ie where the 3% surcharge applies to a dwelling that surcharged rate needs to be used in the calculation (*FA 2003, Sch 6B, para 6A* inserted by *FA 2016, s 128(4)*). If the calculation produces an amount of less than 1% of the consideration attributable to dwellings, the chargeable amount is 1% (*FA 2003, Sch 6B, para 5(2)* as substituted). Prior to 4 December 2014 it was so much of the chargeable consideration as was attributed (on a just and reasonable basis) to dwellings (*FA 2003, Sch 6B, para 4(2)(6)*). The percentage attributable to dwellings was the rate that would apply under *FA 2003, s 55* if the relevant land consisted entirely of residential property and the relevant consideration were the fraction produced by dividing 'total dwellings consideration' by total dwellings, but subject to the rate not falling below 1% (*FA 2003, Sch 6B, para 5(1)(2)*). Total dwellings consideration for a single transaction is the consideration attributable to dwellings on that transaction. Where there are linked transactions, the consideration attributable to dwellings under each of them is aggregated together with any further amount that is attributable to the dwellings by reference to which the calculation is made (*FA 2003, Sch 6B, para 5(3)(4)*). Total dwellings is of course the total number of dwellings by reference to which total dwelling consideration is calculated (*FA 2003, Sch 6B, para 5(5)*). In determining the percentage, no account can be taken of *FA 2003, s 116(7)* (which treats some dwellings as not being residential property – see **19.24**) or *Sch 5, para 9A(4)* (consideration to be split where land is partly residential – see **19.151**) (*FA 2003, Sch 6B, para 5(6)*).

19.293 A building or part of a building counts as a dwelling if either:

(*a*) it is used or suitable for use as a single dwelling; or

(*b*) it is in the process of being constructed or adapted for such use.

(*FA 2003, Sch 6B, para 7(2).*)

Land that is (or is to be) occupied or enjoyed with a dwelling as its garden or grounds (including any structures on it) is regarded as part of that dwelling. So is land that subsists for the benefit of a dwelling (*FA 2003, Sch 6B, para 7(3)(4)*). *FA 2003, s 116(2)–(5)* (see **19.19–19.23**) also applies for the purpose of *para 7* (*FA 2003, Sch 6B, para 7(7)*).

19.294 The main subject matter of a transaction is treated as consisting of or including an interest in a dwelling if:

(*a*) substantial performance of a contract constitutes the effective date of the transaction by virtue of any of *FA 2003, ss 44* (contract and conveyance – see **19.88–19.89**), *44A* (contract providing for conveyance to a third party – see **19.131**) *45* (assignments, sub-sales etc – see **19.125**) or *45A* (effect of transfer of rights – see **19.132**) or of *Sch 17A, para 12A* (agreement for lease – see **19.161**) or *19(3)* (Scottish agreements)),

(*b*) the main subject matter of the transaction consists of or includes an interest in a building (or a part of a building) that is to be constructed or adapted under the contract for use as a single dwelling; and

(*c*) construction or adaption of the building (or part) has not begun by the time the contract is substantially performed.

(*FA 2003, Sch 6B, para 7(5)(6).*)

This will extend the relief to off-plan purchases.

19.295 The relief must be claimed (*FA 2003, Sch 6B, para 4(1)*). HMRC say that the claim has to be included in an SDLT return or an amendment to such a return. It cannot be claimed on a transaction to which *FA 2003, ss 74* or *75* applies or for which group or reconstruction relief or charities relief is available (or would be if it were claimed) (*FA 2003, Sch 6B, para 2(4)*). For the purpose of the relief an interest in a dwelling means any chargeable interest in or over a dwelling other than an interest that is reversionary on a lease that was granted for an initial term of over 21 years (*FA 2003, Sch 6B,* *para 2(5(6))*. From 26 March 2015, this exclusion for a reversionary interest does not apply if the vendor is a qualifying body within *FA 2003, Sch 9, para 5* (a housing association, etc), the transaction is a sale under a sale and leaseback arrangement within *FA 2003, s 7A(2)* (see **19.285**), that sale is the grant of a leasehold interest, and the leaseback element of that arrangement is exempt under *s 57A* (*FA 2003, Sch 6B, para 2(7)* inserted by *FA 2015, s 69*). If the whole or part of the chargeable consideration is rent, the percentage needs to be calculated in accordance with *FA 2003, s 56* and *Sch 5* (leases – see **19.145**).

Example 19.7

Investor plc acquired for £3.1m a block consisting of 30 flats with a commercial gym on the ground floor. £100,000 of the consideration is attributable to the gym.

The rate under *s 55* is 4% so the SDLT is	£124,000
Applying *Sch 6A* the consideration is split	
consideration attributable to gym	£200,000
consideration attributable to flats	£2,900,000
Consideration per flat	£96,667

As the consideration per flat is below the 1% threshold of £125,000, the flats attract SDLT at 1%.

The SDLT payable is accordingly

on the flats £2,900,000 @ 1%	£29,000
on the gym 200,000 @ 4%	£8,000
	£37,000

19.296 The tax related to the remainder of the consideration (if any) is the appropriate fraction of the tax that would have been due had *Sch 6B* not applied. The appropriate fraction is the proportion that the consideration for the non-residential element bear to the sum of that amount and the total dwellings consideration, ie tax is calculated on the full consideration but only the proportion of that tax which is attributable to the non-residential element is brought into account (and added to the amount calculated for the residential element) (*FA 2003, Sch 6B, para 5(7)–(9)* as substituted). Where there is linked consideration, the aggregate consideration has to be used (*FA 2003, Sch 6B, para 5(10)* as substituted). Prior to 4 December 2014, the tax related to the remainder of the consideration was the tax payable on the consideration under the normal rules less the proportion thereof attributable to dwellings (*FA 2003, Sch 6B, para 5(4)(6),(7)* as originally enacted).

19.297 If after relief has been claimed an event occurs within three years of the effective date of the relevant transaction (or if earlier before the purchaser disposes of the dwelling or dwellings to an unconnected purchaser) and more tax would have been payable had the event occurred immediately before the effective date of the transaction, the tax must be recalculated as if that event had occurred before the transaction on which the relief was claimed took place (*FA 2003, Sch 6B, para 6(1)(2)(5)*). The purchaser has to file an SDLT return and pay the extra tax within 30 days of that event (*FA 2003, Sch 6B, para 6(3)*). If the original transaction was substantially performed before completion, the three-year period runs from the date of substantial performance (*FA 2003, Sch 6B, para 6(6)*). The definition of connected person in *CTA 2010, s 1122* (see Appendix 1) applies to determine whether a disposal is to an unconnected person (*FA 2003, Sch 6B, para 6(8)*). The relief applies even if the 4% non-residential SDLT rate applies to the transaction (see **19.24**).

Arrangements Involving Public or Educational Bodies (PFI Transactions)

19.298 Where:

(*a*) a qualifying body (A) transfers (or grants or assigns) a lease of land (the transferred land) to a non-qualifying body (B);

(*b*) in consideration (in whole or part) for that transfer B grants to A a lease, or an underlease or sub-lease of the whole or substantially the whole of the transferred land;

(*c*) B undertakes to carry out works or provide services to A; and

(*d*) some or all of the consideration given by A to B for such works or services is in money,

the market value of the transfer, lease, underlease or sub-lease (and any transfer or lease of surplus land not assigned to B) is regarded as nil (so in effect conferring exemption from SDLT) (*FA 2003, Sch 4, para 17(1), (3)*). Similarly, neither the provision of the works or services or the consideration at (*d*) is regarded as rent (*FA 2003, Sch 4, para 17(4)*). Nevertheless, such a transaction is still notifiable to HMRC (*FA 2003, Sch 4, para 17(4A)*). This deals with PFI (Private Finance Initiative) transactions. The effect is that there is no charge on the qualifying body for the lease back and the only chargeable consideration for the transfer of the land (or the grant of a lease of it) or of any surplus land transferred is any cash premium or rent paid by the private sector supplier. These rules replace the rules on exchanges (see **19.79**), which would otherwise have applied.

19.299 The qualifying bodies are:

(*a*) public bodies within *FA 2003, s 66*;

(*b*) institutions within the further or higher education sectors within *Further and Higher Education Act 1992, s 91*;

(*c*) further and higher education corporations within *ss 17* or *90* of that Act;

(*d*) persons who undertake to establish, maintain and carry on (or provide for the carrying on) of an Academy within *Education Act 1996, s 482*; and

(*e*) in Scotland, institutions funded by the Scottish Further or Higher Education Councils.

(*FA 2003, Sch 4, para 17(2)*.)

Partnerships

19.300 A chargeable interest held by or on behalf of a partnership (including a limited partnership, a limited liability partnership and their overseas equivalents) is treated as held by, or on behalf of the partners. A land transaction entered into for the purposes of a partnership is treated as entered into by the partners. This is so even where a partnership is treated as a separate legal person in the place where it is formed. In particular a partnership is not to be treated as a unit trust scheme or OEIC (*FA 2003, s 104* and *Sch 15, paras 1, 24*). A partnership is treated as the same partnership if any person who was a member before a partnership change is still a partner after that change (*FA 2003, Sch 15, para 3*).

19.301 Anything required to be done by (or in relation to) the purchaser is required to be done by all the responsible partners where the purchaser is a partnership. Everyone who was a partner at the effective date of the transaction or becomes one subsequently is a responsible partner (*FA 2003, Sch 15, para 6*). A majority of the partners can, however, nominate a representative partner or partners to undertake this responsibility. Such a nomination is ineffective until it has been notified to HMRC (*FA 2003, Sch 15, para 8*). In the case of a transfer of a chargeable interest to a partnership, the responsible partners are those who were partners immediately before the transfer and remained partners after it and anyone who became a partner as a result of (or in connection with) the transfer (*FA 2003, Sch 15, paras 10(7), 17(7)*).

19.302 SDLT (and interest and penalties thereon) is a joint and several liability of the responsible partners, but tax and interest cannot be recovered from a person who did not become a responsible partner until after the effective date of the transaction to which it relates and a penalty (or interest thereon) cannot be recovered from a person who was not a responsible partner at the time of the act or omission that caused the penalty to become payable (although for daily penalties the omission is deemed to occur daily so a person who was a partner at the beginning of a day is responsible for the daily penalty from that day*)* (*FA 2003, Sch 15, para 7)*. Where a representative partner is appointed it appears that the other partners remain liable for the tax and any interest or penalties.

Transfers of Partnership Interests

19.303 The acquisition of an interest in a partnership is not normally chargeable to SDLT even if the partnership property includes land (*FA 2003, Sch 15, para 29*). However, this is subject to major exceptions. These are contained in *Sch 15, paras 10, 14* and *17*. Furthermore, a transfer of a partnership interest is liable to stamp duty as a transfer on sale (*FA 2003, Sch 15, para 31*). To avoid double taxation, where a charge to SDLT arises on such a transfer a proportion of the consideration for the transfer is excluded from stamp duty. If the person acquiring the interest was not previously a partner, the excluded part is his partnership share of the net market value of the partnership land (subject to the exclusions at **19.318**) immediately after the transfer (but of course excluding any land transferred to the partnership in connection with the transfer). If he was a partner, it is the increase in his partnership share. The net market value of land is the market value less any loan secured solely on it. If the loan exceeds the value it is nil. If the excluded amount exceeds the actual consideration the consideration is also nil (*FA 2003, Sch 15, para 32*). If a person simply withdraws his accumulated capital account there is no rational reason for an SDLT charge. Unfortunately, one can arise. The chargeable consideration is deemed to be the appropriate proportion (relating to the partnership share) of the market value of the interests in land held by the partnership (but ignoring any interest that was transferred to the partnership in connection with the transfer).

Transfers to a Partnership

19.304 If:

(*a*) a partner transfers an interest in land to the partnership; or

(*b*) a person transfers an interest in land to a partnership in return for an interest in a partnership; or (*c*) a person connected with a partner or prospective partner transfers an interest in land to the partnership,

the chargeable consideration for the transaction is a percentage of the market value of the interest transferred. The relevant percentage is 100 minus the sum of the lower proportions (see **19.305**).

(*FA 2003 Sch 15, paras 10(1)* and *(2)*.)

In a simple case of a partner transferring a property to the partmership, the lower proportion is his share in the partnership. So, for example, if his share is 40% he will reduce his interest in the property from 100% to 40%, a reduction of 60%. That is the proportion of the market value on which SDLT is charged.

19.305 The sum of the lower proportions (SLP) is determined by the following process.

(*a*) Identify the relevant owner or owners, ie every person who immediately before the transaction was entitled to a proportion of the chargeable interest and immediately after it was a partner or connected with a partner.

(*b*) For each relevant owner, identify the corresponding partner or partners. A person is a corresponding partner in relation to a relevant owner if immediately after the transaction he is a partner and is the relevant owner or is an individual connected with the relevant owner.

(*c*) For each relevant owner find the proportion of the chargeable interest to which he was entitled immediately before the transaction and apportion that proportion between that relevant owner's corresponding partners.

(*d*) Find the 'lower proportion' for each person who is a corresponding partner in relation to one or more relevant owners. This is the lower of the proportion of the chargeable interest attributable to that partner or that partner's partnership share immediately after the transaction. If a person is a corresponding partner in relation to only one relevant owner the proportion of the chargeable interest attributable to him is the proportion apportioned to him at step (c). If he is a corresponding partner in relation to more than one relevant owner, it is the sum of the proportions apportioned to him at (c) in respect of each of those owners.

(*e*) Add together the lower proportions of each person who is a corresponding partner in relation to one or more relevant owners.

For the purpose of this calculation, persons who are entitled to a chargeable interest as beneficial joint tenants must be assumed to be entitled to the chargeable interest as beneficial tenants in common in equal shares (*FA 2003,*

Sch 15, para 12). If there is no relevant owner with a corresponding partner at (b) the sum of the lower proportion is nil. For the purpose of (*b*) a company must be treated as an individual connected with the relevant owner if it holds property as trustee and is connected with the relevant owner only because of *CTA 2010, s 1122(6).*

19.306 What happens where a transfer within *FA 2003, Sch 15, para 10* is combined with a sub-sale? In *DV3 RS Limited Partnership v HMRC (TC 1012)* the First-tier Tribunal said that it results in exemption from tax. DV3 Regent Street Ltd (BB) contracted to acquire a leasehold interest in a property from Legal & General Assurance Society Ltd (AA) for £65.1 million. DV3 RS Limited Partnership (CC), in which BB had an entitlement to 98% of the income, then contracted to acquire the leasehold interest from BB, also for £65.1 million. Both contracts were completed (by separate transfers) on the same day. *Paragraph 10* applied because BB transferred its interest in the lease to a partnership of which it was a member. BB was entitled to 100% before the transfer and 98% after, so only 2% of the consideration on the transfer to CC is taxable (in this case they were connected parties, leaving nothing taxable). At the time *FA 2003, s 45(5)* (see **19.125**) provided that if there is a subsale or other transaction as a result of which some other person is entitled to call for a transaction and the two contracts are completed at the same time, the original contract is disregarded. Accordingly there is no SDLT on the AA to BB contract and SDLT is only 2% of the consideration on the BB to CC contract. There is nothing in *s 45* that says that the first contract is disregarded for all purposes, so it is still a contract for the purpose of *Sch 15.* Not surprisingly, HMRC appealed this decision but the Upper Tribunal upheld it. It was pointed out that had the transaction taken place a few months later it would probably have been caught by *FA 2003, s 75A* (see **19.337**). The Court of Appeal disagreed *([2013] EWCA Civ 907).* It said that the effect of disregarding the contract between BB and AA is that *s 44(3)* does not apply to the completion of that contract. Accordingly BB must be deemed not to have entered into a land transaction for SDLT. That means it never acquired a chargeable interest. Accordingly it had no chargeable interest to transfer to CC, so *Sch 15* could not apply. This left CC with an SDLT liability on its deemed acquisition under *s 44(3).*

19.307 The position gets more complicated if the whole or part of the chargeable consideration for the transaction is rent. *Schedule 5* (see **19.144** onwards) is then applied to the relevant chargeable proportion of the rent (ie 100 – SLP). If there is chargeable consideration other than rent, that chargeable consideration must be taken to be equal to the relevant chargeable proportion (ie SLP%) of the market value of the interest transferred plus the relevant chargeable proportion of the actual consideration other than rent. If there is no actual chargeable consideration other than rent there is deemed additional consideration equal to the relevant chargeable proportion (ie SLP%) of the market value of the interest transferred (*FA 2003, Sch 15, para 11*).

19.308 The purchaser can elect to disapply *para 10* in relation to a transfer of a chargeable interest to a 'property investment partnership' (see **19.309**) (*FA 2003, Sch 15, paras 10(8), 12A(1)*). Where such an election is made the chargeable consideration for the transaction is the market value of the chargeable interest transferred, and the transaction is treated as a normal partnership transaction so that *paras 5–8* of *Sch 15* apply to it instead of the special rules in *paras 10–15* (*FA 2003, Sch 15, para 12A(2)*). Where the election is made *para 18* (which deals with a transfer out of a partnership – see **19.318**) is also disapplied if it would otherwise apply to the other side of the transaction (*FA 2003, Sch 15, para 12A(2)(a)*). The election must be included in the land transaction return (or an amendment to it), it is irrevocable and a land transaction return cannot be amended so as to withdraw it (*FA 2003, Sch 15, para 12(3)(4)*). Where a return is amended by making the election it has effect as if it had been made on the date of the original return and any other return in respect of a *para 14* transaction (see **19.310**) made subsequent to the elected transaction can also be amended to reflect the election (*FA 2003, Sch 15, para 12A(5)(6)*). For transactions prior to 21 July 2008 the purchaser can amend the return in order to incorporate the election (and can amend any related return to reflect the election) at any time up to 20 July 2008. In such a case the election has effect from the date of the return even though *para 12A* was not then in force (*FA 2008, Sch 31, para 11*).

Property-investment Partnerships

19.309 If there is a transfer of an interest in a property-investment partnership and the partnership property (see **19.323**) includes a chargeable interest the transfer must be treated both as a land transaction and a chargeable transaction (*FA 2003, Sch 15, para 14(1)(2)*). A 'property-investment partnership' is a partnership whose sole or main activity is investing or dealing in chargeable interests (whether or not that activity involves the carrying out of construction operations on the land in question (*FA 2003, Sch 15, para 14(8)*). Prior to 19 July 2007 this provision normally applied only if consideration was given for the transfer (*FA 2007, s 72(13),(14)*). Consideration was given for the transfer in relation to such a transfer if either consideration in money or money's worth is given by or on behalf of the person acquiring the interest or there was a withdrawal of money or money's worth from the partnership by a person who reduced his interest or ceased to be a partner (*FA 2003, Sch 15, para 14(4)*).

19.310 The purchaser under the deemed transaction is the person who becomes a partner or acquires an increased partnership share in consequence of the transfer. There is a transfer of an interest in a partnership if arrangements are entered into under which either a partner transfers the whole or part of his interest as a partner to another person (who could be an existing partner), or a person becomes a partner and an existing partner reduces his interest in the partnership or ceases to be a partner (*FA 2003, Sch 15, para 36*). The chargeable consideration for the transaction is the proportion of the market value of the relevant partnership property (see **19.312** and **19.313**) attributable to the partnership share acquired by the incoming partner (or the increase in the partnership share of an existing partner) (*FA 2003, Sch 15, para 14(6)* and *(7)*). An interest transferred in accordance with paragraph 14 must be treated as a chargeable interest for the purpose of *FA 2003, Sch 7, para 3(1)* (withdrawal of group relief) to the extent that the relevant partnership property consists of a chargeable interest (*FA 2003, Sch 15, para 14(9)*).

19.311 Transfers after 18 July 2007 that fall within *para 14* are split into two categories, Type A and Type B. A transfer is a Type A transfer if either:

(*a*) it takes the form of arrangements (see **19.323**) under which the whole or part of a partner's interest as a partner is acquired by another person (who could be an existing partner) and consideration in money or money's worth is given by (or on behalf of) the person acquiring the interest; or

(*b*) it takes the form of arrangements under which a person becomes a partner, the interest of an existing partner in the partnership is reduced (or an existing partner ceases to be a partner), and there is a withdrawal of money or money's worth from the partnership by the partner who leaves or reduces his share (see **19.323**) (other than if that withdrawal is paid from the resources available to the partnership prior to the transfer).

(*FA 2003, Sch 15, para 14(3A)(3B)*.)

Every other transfer within *para 14* is a Type B transfer.

19.312 The 'relevant partnership property' in relation to a Type A transfer is every chargeable interest that is held as partnership property immediately after the transfer with the exception of any chargeable interest that was transferred to the partnership in connection with the transfer, any lease to which *para 15* (exclusion of market rent leases – see **19.315**) applies and any chargeable interest that is not attributable economically to the interest in the partnership that is transferred (*FA 2003, Sch 15, para 14(5)*).

19.313 The 'relevant partnership property' in relation to a Type B transfer is every chargeable interest held as partnership property immediately after the transfer other than:

(*a*) any chargeable interest that was transferred to the partnership in connection with the transfer (or for Type A);

(*b*) a lease to which *para 15* applies (as for Type A);

(*c*) a chargeable interest that is not attributable economically to the interest in the partnership that is transferred (as for Type A);

(*d*) any chargeable interest that was transferred to the partnership on or before 22 July 2004;

(*e*) any chargeable interest in respect of whose transfer to the partnership an election is made under *para 12A*; and

(*f*) any other chargeable interest whose transfer to the partnership did not fall within *para 10* (ie which was not transferred to the partnership by a partner (or in return for becoming a partner) or a connected person – see **19.323**).

(*FA 2003, Sch 15, para 14(5A).*)

19.314 The Explanatory Notes to the 2008 Finance Bill state that the *FA 2008* changes ensure that where there is a transfer of an interest in a property within an investment partnership there will be no charge to SDLT.

19.315 A lease is excluded from being relevant property as being a market rent lease if:

(*a*) no chargeable consideration other than rent has been given in respect of the grant of the lease (and no arrangements are in place at the time of the transfer for any such consideration to be given);

(*b*) the rent payable under the lease as granted was a market rent at the time of the grant;

(*c*) either the term of the lease is five years or less or it provides for a rent review at least once every five years to a market rent at the review date; and

(*d*) there has been no change to the lease since it was granted such as reduces the market rent.

The market rent at any time is the rent which the lease might reasonably be expected to fetch at that time in the open market (*FA 2003, Sch 15, para 15*). It should particularly be noted that a lease with upward only rent reviews will not satisfy head (*d*). Nor, it appears, would one that provides for the rent on a review to exclude any increase attributable to tenant's fixtures.

19.316 If after a transfer of a chargeable interest to a partnership ('the land transfer' which falls within *para 10(1)* – see **19.304**) there is a later transfer of an interest in the partnership ('the partnership transfer') which is made by the partner who made the land transfer (or by one who is connected with the land transferor) and the partnership transfer is made pursuant to arrangements that were in place at the time of the land transfer, the partnership transfer must be treated for SDLT purposes as a land transaction (and a chargeable transaction) if it would not otherwise be one (*FA 2003, Sch 15, para 17(1)(2)*). The partners are the deemed purchasers under that deemed transaction. The chargeable consideration is the proportion of the market value at the date of the transaction (ie the partnership transfer) of the interest transferred by the land transfer attributable to the decrease in the partnership share of the person making the partnership transfer. The partnership transfer and the land transfer are deemed to be linked transactions (see **19.325**) (*FA 2003, Sch 15, para 17(3)–(6)*). This is an anti-avoidance provision to prevent the rules being circumvented by separating the acquisition of the land by the partnership from the payment to the outgoing partner.

19.317 If money is withdrawn from the partnership by a 'qualifying event' within three years of a transfer of a chargeable interest to a partnership within **19.304** that qualifying event must be deemed to be a land transaction under which the partners are the purchasers and the chargeable consideration for which is equal to the lower of the money or money's worth (or loan repayment or value) withdrawn from the partnership and the market value of the interest in land at the effective date of the land transfer (reduced by any amount previously chargeable to tax) (*FA 2003, Sch 15, para 17A(1)(4)(5)(7)*). This does not apply where the effective date of the land transaction was before 20 May 2005 or if at the time of the qualifying event an election has been made under *para 12A* (see **19.304**). If a qualifying event that occurs after 19 July 2006 gives rise to a charge under this provision and also a charge under *para 14* (see **19.310**) the charge under this provision is reduced by the *para 14* charge (*FA 2006, Sch 15, para 17A(8)*).

19.318 A qualifying event for this purpose is:

(*a*) a withdrawal from the partnership of money or money's worth which does not represent income profit by the person who made the land transfer (or the partner concerned or connected person under **19.304**(c)) withdrawing capital from his capital account, reducing his interest, or ceasing to be a partner; or

(*b*) if the person who made the land transfer had made a loan to the partnership, the repayment (to any extent) of that loan by the partnership or a withdrawal by that person from the partnership of money or money's worth which does not represent income profit (*FA 2003, Sch 15, para 17A(2)(3)*).

Transfers from a Partnership

19.319 Where a chargeable interest in land is transferred from a partnership to a partner or former partner (see **19.323**), or to a person connected with a partner or former partner, the chargeable consideration is deemed to be equal to the market value of the interest transferred multiplied by (100 minus SLP). The effect of this is that no SDLT is normally payable on the incorporation of a partnership because the company will be a connected person of all of the partners and it is acquiring 100% of the land (so SLP will be 100 for each of the partners). This will not apply if the partners share capital profits in a different ratio to income as partnership shares for SDLT are based on the income-sharing ratio (see **19.323**(b)) and the shares will normally be issued in capital-sharing ratios which will give rise to transfers of interests in the effective ownership of the property between partners. Prior to 19 July 2006 the chargeable consideration was the relevant chargeable proportion of the market value of the interest concerned plus the relevant chargeable proportion of the actual consideration for the transaction (*FA 2003, Sch 15, para 18(1)(2)*). The market value of a lease is determined as explained at **19.323**(*f*). *Paragraphs 195* and *196* above apply to the ascertainment of SLP in the same way as for transfers of land into a partnership with the exception that at **19.305**(a) and (b) one looks at the position immediately before the transaction instead of immediately after it and special rules apply to determine the partnership share attributable to the partner at **19.305**(d) (*FA 2003, Sch 15, paras 18(3)–(6), 19* and *20*). Property that was partnership property before a partnership was dissolved or otherwise ceased to exist must be treated as remaining partnership property until it is distributed (*FA 2003, Sch 15, para 18(7)*). *Paragraph 18* does not apply if the purchaser has elected under *para 12A* (see **19.304**) to disapply *para 10*.

19.320 For the purpose of determining the partnership share attributable to a partner for the purpose of *para 20* (but not *para 12*), ie at (*d*) in **19.305**, the partnership share attributable to the partner is zero. The relevant chargeable interest for this purpose is the interest which ceased to be partnership property as a result of the paragraph 18 transaction or, if the transaction was the grant or creation of a chargeable interest, the interest out of which it was granted or created (*FA 2003, Sch 15, paras 20, 21*).

19.321 Where a chargeable interest is transferred from one partnership to another, *para 18* (see **19.320**) must be applied to the transferor partnership and *para 10* (see **19.304**) to the transferee partnership. If none of the chargeable consideration is rent the chargeable consideration for both sides of the transaction is the greater of that calculated under *paras 10(2)–(5)* in relation to the transferee partnership and that calculated under *para 18(2)–(5)* for the transferor partnership. If the consideration includes rent the chargeable consideration for the transaction is the greater of whichever of *para 11* (see

19.310) or *para 19* (see **19.319**) produces the larger figure (*FA 2003, Sch 15, para 23*).

19.322 If immediately before the transaction all of the parties are bodies corporate and the sum of the lower proportions is 75 or more, the chargeable consideration for the transaction must be regarded as equal to the full market value of the interest transferred (*FA 2003, Sch 15, para 24*).

Interpretation

19.323 The following definitions apply for the purpose of these partnership provisions:

(*a*) 'Partnership property' means an interest or right held by or on behalf of a partnership (or the members of a partnership) for the purposes of the partnership business (*FA 2003, Sch 15, para 34(1)*).

(*b*) A person's 'partnership share' at any time is the proportion in which he is entitled at that time to share in the income profits of the partnership (*FA 2003, Sch 15, para 34(2)*).

(*c*) There is a 'transfer of a chargeable interest to a partnership' if a chargeable interest in land (see **19.4**) becomes partnership property (*FA 2003, Sch 15, para 35*).

(*d*) Where a person acquires or increases a partnership share there is a 'transfer of an interest in the partnership' to that partner and from the other partners. Prior to 6 December 2006 there was a 'transfer of an interest in a partnership' if arrangements were entered into under which a partner transferred all or part of his interest to another person or an existing partner reduced his interest in the partnership or ceased to be a partner (*FA 2003, Sch 15, para 36*).

(*e*) There is a 'transfer of a chargeable interest from a partnership' if a chargeable interest that was partnership property ceases to be such property or a chargeable interest which is not partnership property is granted or created out of partnership property (*FA 2003, Sch 15, para 37*).

(*f*) In determining the 'market value of a lease' an obligation of the tenant under the lease can be taken into account only if it is either an obligation such as is mentioned in *FA 2003, Sch 17A, para 10(1)* (see **19.153**) or it is an obligation to make a payment to a person. This rule applies if the grant of the lease is or was a transaction to which either *FA 2003, Sch 15, para 10* (see **19.6**) applies or applied (or would have done so had it been in force at the time of the grant), or *FA 2003, Sch 15, para 18* (see **19.219**) applies (*FA 2003, Sch 15, para 38*).

(*g*) 'Connected persons' has the same meaning as under *CTA 2010, s 1122* with the exception that partners are not connected persons (*FA 2003, Sch 15, para 39*). From 6 December 2006 for the purpose only of *para 12* or *20* a trustee is not connected with a body corporate which is connected with the settlement (*FA 2003, Sch 15, para 39(3)*).

(*h*) 'Arrangements' includes any scheme, agreement or understanding, whether or not legally enforceable (*FA 2003, Sch 15, para 40*).

Exemptions and Reliefs

19.324 The above rules obviously override the exemption of transactions for which there is no chargeable consideration (as they create deemed chargeable consideration) but the other exemptions apply to partnership transactions subject to the following modifications (*FA 2003, Sch 15, para 25*).

19.325 Disadvantaged area relief (see **19.172**) applies to a transfer of an interest in a partnership that is deemed to be a chargeable land transaction by *para 14* (see **19.309**) or *para 17* (see **19.316**) if every chargeable interest in land held by the partnership (other than those excluded at **19.309**) is wholly situated in a disadvantaged area. It also applies if the relevant consideration does not exceed £150,000. When the land is partly residential the non-residential proportion (the part that on a just and reasonable apportionment is attributable to non-residential property) of the chargeable consideration does not count as chargeable consideration, and if the residential proportion does not exceed £150,000 there is deemed to be no chargeable consideration. If the land held by the partnership is partly situated in a disadvantaged area and partly not, the deemed consideration under *paras 14* and *17* must be apportioned on a just and reasonable basis between land inside disadvantaged areas and that outside and the exemption will apply only to the disadvantaged area proportion of the consideration (*FA 2003, Sch 15, para 26*). This *paragraph* is subject to any election under *para 12A* (see **19.304**).

19.326 Group relief (see **19.189**) can apply to both a transfer of land to a partnership within *para 10* (see **19.304**) and a transfer within *para 17* (see **19.316**) but the relief will be withdrawn if a person who was a partner at the effective date of the relevant transaction ceases to be a partner within the following three years, at the time that partner ceases to be a member of the same group as the vendor a chargeable interest is held by (or on behalf of) the members of the partnership and that chargeable interest was acquired by (or on behalf of) the partnership under the relevant transaction (or is derived from a chargeable interest so acquired) and has not subsequently been acquired at market value under a chargeable transaction for which group relief was available but was not claimed (*FA 2003, Sch 15, para 27*). If in calculating the sum of the lower proportions in relation to a transaction under *para 12* (see **19.305**) a company ('the connected company') would have been a corresponding partner of a relevant owner ('the original owner') but for the fact the connected persons are included only if they are individuals, and the connected company and the original owner are members of the same group, the charge in respect of the transaction must be reduced by the amount that would have been payable had the connected company been a corresponding partner of the original owner for the purpose of *para 14*. The group relief rules in *Sch 7* apply to group relief under this provision with the omission of *para 2(2)(a)* (consideration) and the substitution for the purchaser in *para 3(1)(a)* of a partner who was at the effective date of the transaction a partner and a member of the same group as the transferor (*FA 2003, Sch 15, para 27A*).

19.327 The relief for a transfer to a charity extends to the deemed transfer on the disposal of a partnership share if the disposal of that share is to a charity. The relief is clawed back if at the time of a disqualifying event the partnership includes a chargeable interest in land that was held as partnership property at the time of the transfer of the partnership interest or was derived from land held at that time. A disqualifying event for this purpose is if either the charity ceases to be established for charitable purposes only or a chargeable interest held as partnership property at the time of the transfer (or property derived from it) is used, or held, otherwise than for charitable purposes. If part of the property ceases to qualify there is a clawback of an 'appropriate proportion' of the relief (*FA 2003, Sch 15, para 28*).

Trustees

19.328 Where a person acquires a chargeable interest or an interest in a partnership, as bare trustee SDLT applies as if the interest were vested in the person or persons for whom he is trustee and as if the acts of the trustee were acts of the beneficiary (*FA 2003, Sch 16, para 3(1)*). This does not apply in relation to the grant of a lease. Instead where a lease is granted to a bare trustee he is treated as the purchaser of the whole of the interest acquired, and where it is granted by a bare trustee he is treated as the vendor of the whole of the interest disposed of (*FA 2003, Sch 16, para 3(2)–(4)*). A bare trustee is one under a trust where the property is held for a person who is absolutely entitled as against the trustee (or would be so entitled but for being a minor or other person under a disability) or for two or more persons who are jointly so entitled (*FA 2003, Sch 16, para 1(2)*). A person is absolutely entitled as against the trustee if he has the exclusive right, subject only to satisfying any outstanding charge, lien or other right of the trustee, to resort to the property for payment of duty, taxes, costs or other outgoings or to direct how the property is to be dealt with (*FA 2003, Sch 16, para 1(3)*). A nominee is a bare trustee.

19.329 If persons acquire a chargeable interest, or after 6 December 2006 an interest in a partnership, as trustees of a settlement (which is defined as a trust that is not a bare trust) they are treated for SDLT purposes as purchasers of the whole of the interest acquired (including the beneficial interest) (*FA 2003, Sch 16, paras 1(1)(4)*).

19.330 Where the trustees of a settlement (but not bare trustees) are liable to make a payment of SDLT (including a recovery of an excessive payment) or interest or penalties thereon that amount can be recovered from any one of the responsible trustees, ie the persons who were trustees at the effective date of the land transaction or become trustees subsequently. A penalty (and interest thereon) cannot be recovered from a person who was not a trustee at the time of the act or omission that caused it to become payable (but a daily penalty can be recovered from anyone who was a trustee at the beginning of the day) (*FA 2003, Sch 16, para 5*).

19.331 A return in relation to a land transaction can be made or given by any one or more of the responsible trustees in relation to the transaction but the declaration required by *Sch 10, para 1(1)(c)* must be made by all of the relevant trustees (*FA 2003, Sch 16, para 6(1)(2)*).

19.332 If HMRC enquire into a trust return they must serve an enquiry notice on, and give a closure notice to, each of the relevant trustees. However, their power to require the production of documents and provide information can be exercised separately (and differently) in relation to each of the relevant trustees and any such trustee can apply for a direction that a closure notice should be given (*FA 2003, Sch 16, para 6(3)*). A HMRC determination or discovery assessment must be made against all of the relevant trustees and is not effective against any of them unless notice of it is given to each of those whose identity is known to HMRC (*FA 2003, Sch 16, para 6(4)*). Appeals can be brought by any relevant trustee but the agreement of all of them is required if an appeal is to be settled by agreement. Where an appeal is not brought by all of the trustees notice of the appeal must be given to the others, who are entitled to appear and be heard and will be bound by the decision (*FA 2003, Sch 16, para 6(5)*).

19.333 Where a chargeable interest is acquired by virtue of the exercise of a power of appointment or the exercise of a discretion vested in trustees of a settlement, any consideration given for the person in whose favour the appointment was made (or discretion exercised) becoming an object of the power or discretion must be treated as consideration for the acquisition of the interest or right obtained by virtue of the exercise of the power or discretion (*FA 2003, Sch 16, para 7*). In other words consideration paid for the exercise of a power or discretion is treated as consideration for any land transaction that results from the exercise. If with the consent of a beneficiary the trustees reallocate trust property in such a way that he acquires an interest in certain trust property and ceases to have an interest in other trust property the giving of consent does not constitute consideration for the acquisition (*FA 2003, Sch 16, para 8*).

19.334 If property is held in trust under the law of Scotland or of a country outside the UK on terms such that, if the trust had effect under the laws of England and Wales, a beneficiary would be regarded as having an equitable interest in the trust property, that beneficiary must be treated as having such an interest even though no such interest is recognised by the law governing the trust. An acquisition of the interest of a beneficiary under the trust must accordingly be treated as involving the acquisition of an interest in the trust property (*FA 2003, Sch 16, para 2*). The acquisition of an equitable interest in land is of course a land transaction (see **19.4**).

Persons Acting in a Representative Capacity

19.335 The parents or guardian of a minor is responsible for discharging the minor's obligation under the SDLT legislation if the minor does not do so himself (*FA 2003, s 106(2)*). The personal representatives of a deceased purchaser under a land transaction are responsible for discharging his obligations under the Act and can deduct any payment they make out of the assets of the deceased estate (*FA 2003, s 106(3)*). In the case of an incapacitated person it is the person having the direction, management or control of his property who is responsible for discharging that person's obligations. He is empowered to retain money coming into his hands on behalf of the incapacitated person to meet any SDLT payments he makes. If there is not enough money coming in he is still liable for the tax but is entitled to an indemnity from the incapacitated person (*FA 203, s 106(1)*). A receiver appointed by a UK court having the direction and control of any property is responsible for discharging the SDLT obligations in relation to a transaction affecting that property as if it were not under the direction and control of the court (*FA 2003, s 106(4)*).

Targeted Anti-Avoidance Rule

19.336 A broadly drawn anti-avoidance provision, *FA 2003, s 75A* was introduced from 6 December 2006. This was initially introduced by the *SDLT (Variation of the Finance Act 2003) Regulations 2003 (SI 2003 No 3237)* and has subsequently been re-enacted, with some changes, by *FA 2007, s 71.* It applies where one person (the vendor) disposes of a chargeable interest, another person (the purchaser) acquires either the same interest or one deriving from it and a number of transactions (including the disposal by the vendor and the acquisition by the purchaser) are involved in connection with the disposal and acquisition ('the scheme transactions') (*FA 2003, s 75A(1)*).

19.337 If the sum of the amounts of SDLT payable in respect of the scheme transactions is less than that which would be payable on a notional land transaction effecting the acquisition of the vendor's chargeable interest by the purchaser, then SDLT is payable on that notional transaction (and any of the scheme transactions which give rise to an SDLT liability are not then chargeable to SDLT and any SDLT paid on them is treated as a payment on account of that due on the notional transaction) (*FA 2003, ss 75A(1)(4), 75C(10)*). The deemed consideration on the notional land transaction is the largest amount (or aggregate amount) given by or on behalf of any one person by way of consideration for the scheme transactions, or the largest amount received by or on behalf of the vendor (or a person connected with the vendor (within *CTA 2010, s 1122*)). The effective date of the notional transaction is the last date of completion of any of the scheme transactions or, if earlier, the last date on which a contract in respect of the scheme transactions is substantially performed (*FA 2003, s 75A(6)*). In calculating the chargeable consideration, consideration for a transaction is ignored if (or insofar as) the transaction is merely incidental to the transfer of the chargeable interest from the vendor to the purchaser. In particular a transfer is likely to be incidental if it is undertaken only for a purpose relating to either:

(*a*) the construction of a building on property to which the chargeable interest relates (provided that it does not form part of a process or series of transactions by which the transfer is effected and that the transfer of the chargeable interest is not conditional on the completion of the transaction);

(*b*) the sale or supply of anything other than land (provided that it does not form part of a process or series of transactions by which the transfer is effected); or

(*c*) a loan to the purchaser secured by a mortgage (or any other provision of finance to enable the purchaser, or another person, to pay for part of a process, or series of transactions, by which the chargeable interest transfers) (provided that it does not form part of a process or series of transactions by which the transfer is effected and that the transfer of the chargeable interest is not conditional on the transaction).

(*FA 2003, s 75B(3)(4)*.)

19.338 Any other type of transaction cannot be regarded as incidental to the transfer of the chargeable interest if, or insofar as, it forms part of a process or series of transactions by which the transfer is effected; or the transfer of the chargeable interest is conditional on the completion of the transaction (*FA 2003, s 75B(2)*).

19.339 The legislation gives a number of examples of things that the scheme transactions might include, namely:

(*a*) the acquisition by a purchaser of a lease deriving from the freehold owned or formerly owned by the vendor;

(*b*) a sub-sale to a third person;

(*c*) the grant of a lease to a third person subject to a right to terminate;

(*d*) the exercise of a right to terminate a lease or to take some other action;

(*e*) an agreement not to exercise a right to terminate a lease or to take some other action; and

(*f*) the variation of a right to terminate a lease or to take some other action.

(*FA 2003, s 75A(3)*.)

The consideration for the above types of transaction cannot be ignored as merely incidental (*FA 2003, s 75B(2)*).

19.340 For the purpose of the provision a transaction includes in particular:

(*a*) a non-land transaction;

(*b*) an agreement, offer or undertaking not to take specified action;

(*c*) any kind of arrangement whether or not it could otherwise be described as a transaction; and

(*d*) a transaction which takes place after the purchaser's acquisition of the chargeable interest.

(*FA 2003, s 75A(2)*.)

19.341 The section does not, of course, apply if the only reason that the SDLT on a notional transaction would be greater is that the actual transaction is an alternative property finance transaction or a transaction within *FA 2003, Sch 9* (right to buy, shared ownership leases and rent to mortgage or rent to loan transactions) (*FA 2003, s 75A(7)*). A transfer of shares or securities is ignored if it would be the first of a series of scheme transactions (*FA 2003, s 75C(1)*). The notional transaction attracts any relief that would be due if it were a real transaction (*FA 2003, s 75C(2)*). If any of the scheme transactions is entered into for the purpose of, or in connection with, the transfer of an undertaking to which reconstruction or acquisition relief (within *FA 2003, Sch 7, para 7* or *8*) applies, the notional transaction is treated as entered into for that purpose (*FA 2003, s 75C(3)*). The notional consideration is not to include any amount paid as consideration in respect of a transaction to which any of *FA 2003, ss 60, 61, 63, 64, 65, 66, 67, 69, 71, 74* or *75* or *Sch 6A, 7A* or *8* applies (*FA 2003, s 75C(4)*). References to an amount of consideration include a reference to the value of consideration given as money's worth and where a transaction involves a connected company *FA 2003, s 53* (market value to be substituted for the actual consideration if higher – see **19.144**) and *Sch 4, para 5* (exchanges – see **19.79**) apply to the notional transaction (*FA 2003, s 75C(5),(6),(9)*). Any necessary apportionment is to be done on a just and reasonable basis (*FA 2003, s 75C(5)*). An interest in a property-investment partnership (within *FA 2003, Sch 15, para 14* – see **19.309**) is a chargeable interest insofar as it concerns land owned by the partnership (*FA 2003, s 75C(8)(a)*).

19.342 Up to 23 March 2010, if either the vendor or purchaser was a partnership, *FA 2003, Sch 15, paras 9–40* (see **19.253** onwards) applied to the notional transfer in the same way as to the transfer of a chargeable interest to and from a partnership (*FA 2003, s 75C(8)(b)*). This provision was repealed by *FA 2010, s 55* but continues to apply in relation to a notional transaction if any scheme transaction was completed before that date or effected before that date and not varied, assigned, sub-sold or effected in consequence of an option exercised at some time after that date. (*FA 2010, s 55(2)–(4)*).

19.343 From the same date nothing in *FA 2003, Sch 15, paras 9–40* (transactions in relation to partnerships to which special provisions apply (see **19.300** onwards) applies to the notional transaction under *s 75A* (*FA 2003, s 75C(8A)* inserted by *FA 2010, s 55*). The Treasury have power by statutory instrument to provide for *s 75A* not to apply in specified circumstances (*FA 2003, s 75C(10)*). The rules in *s 75C* do not apply where the vendor's disposal took place before 19 July 2007 if, or insofar as, it would make a person liable for a higher amount of tax than would have been chargeable under the Regulations which the statutory provision replaces (*FA 2007, s 71(3)(b)*).

19.344 The first *s 75* case to come before the Tribunals was *Project Blue Ltd v HMRC (2016 STC 2168)*. This was a complex scheme. It relied on a combination of sub-scale relief and alternative finance relief. The taxpayer contended that *s 75A* should not apply; it is an anti-avoidance provision and the transactions in the appeal were wholly commercial. The structure of the financing was driven by Project Blue, not by its bankers. Sharia compliant finance was a requirement of the parties. The FTT said that following the House of Lords decision in *Barclays Mercantile Business Finance Ltd v Mawson (76 TC 446)* tax statutes have to be construed purposively. The heading to *s 75A* and the *Finance Bill 2007, Explanatory Notes* make it clear that the purpose of the provision is to combat the avoidance of SDLT, It also felt that *s 75A* does not give HMRC a discretion whether or not to apply the statute. The provision does not contain a motive test. This was clearly deliberate. Accordingly *s 75A* is capable of being engaged where the transactions have commercial motives and are not part of an avoidance scheme. The Upper Tribunal agreed that *s 75A* operates even where there is no purpose of avoiding tax. It thought *ss 75A–75C* very difficult to construe. The judge commented, 'I regard the possibility of there being more than one person who is V and more than one person who is P as being unsatisfactory' and said that he would be reluctant to accept that interpretation.

19.345 The Court of Appeal decided the case in favour of the taxpayer on a different basis so had no need to consider *s 75A*. They analysed the transactions in the same way as the company, namely that sub-sale relief applied at the first stage and the later transactions fell within the Islamic finance rules in *FA 2003, s 71A* (see **19.270**). Patten LJ thought that: 'The much more obvious construction of *s 71A* … is that cases falling within *s 45(3)* [sub-sales] were intended to be treated as direct acquisition by the financial institution from the third party vendor in terms of their tax consequences.' The result of this was not to exempt the transaction but to make the bank (which HMRC were out of time to assess) liable for SDLT on completion of the secondary contract under *s 45(3)*, not Project Blue liable on the Islamic finance transaction. Patten LJ did in passing make two points about *s 75A* though. First, HMRC do not have to show tax avoidance; the provisions 'operate according to their terms and nowhere in s *75A* is there any reference to the purposes of the scheme transactions being tax avoidance or any requirement to establish the existence of such a purpose or objective as a pre-condition to the operation of the section'. Secondly, he dealt with the identification of P: 'What has first to be identified is the disposal and acquisition of a chargeable interest or a chargeable interest deriving from it. Those and any other transactions involved in connection with the disposal and acquisition are then taken into account as part of the comparative exercise under *s 75A(1)(c)*.' The notional land transaction imposed by *s 75A(4)* relates to P's acquisition of V's chargeable interest and not a derivation from it. If V's interest is acquired by a person in the chain, then one need look no further. 'It would be very strange in my view to ignore the acquisition of V's interest by [the bank] as an acquisition by P and instead to regard Project Blue as P by virtue of the lease'. The anomaly disappears if it is recognised that the bank is a real purchaser of the freehold and for tax purposes has to be treated as such. It is the bank that he identified as P in the transaction in question.

19.346 HMRC say that as *s 75A* is an anti-avoidance provision, it applies only where there is avoidance of tax. They will not seek to apply the transaction where they consider transactions have already been assessed appropriately. HMRC also say that the section uses a three-step process – first identify a disposal and the relevant person who is V (vendor); secondly identify an acquisition and the relevant person who is P (purchaser); and thirdly consider whether a number of transactions are 'involved in connection with' the disposal and acquisition. In deciding whether *s 75A* applies, HMRC say it is necessary to look at the arrangements as a whole rather than at each individual step in isolation (HMRC Guidance Note 1, March 2011).

19.347 The guidance note sets out a number of situations where 'in general' HMRC accept that, to the extent that the situation described genuinely stands alone, the transactions will be taxed appropriately under the normal SDLT rules:

1. X, Y and Z are individuals who decide to establish a partnership to manage their investment portfolio. They transfer investment property and cash into that partnership at value. HMRC considers this to be a straightforward establishment of and transfer of property into a partnership.

2. X, Y and Z are the partners of a partnership. The purpose of the partnership is to acquire and develop a large residential property into six flats. When the development is complete they disagree as to how to manage the completed development so the partnership is dissolved and the partnership property (the flats and any partnership monies) is divided among the partners. It is assumed here that the agreements and documents relating to the creation of the partnership demonstrate that the intention was for the partnership to manage the property after development and that the dissolution of the partnership arises from an unforeseen disagreement. HMRC would not seek to apply *s 75A* to this situation as long as the general Stamp Duty Land Tax legislation has been applied to the creation and dissolution of the partnership.

3. A property investment business is carried on by a company owned in equal shares by four family members. The company is to be sold to an unconnected third party. The four individuals establish a partnership to hold the properties that were held by the company but that aren't included in the sale. There is a clear commercial reason for the properties to be transferred out of the company that is to be sold to the unconnected third party.

4. A property lettings business is carried on by three individuals X, Y and Z through a partnership. X, Y and Z consider that, commercially, the best way to continue to carry on their business is through a company. They therefore decide to incorporate the business. X, Y and Z subscribe for shares in a new company in the same proportion as their respective partnership holdings. The properties are transferred to the company.

5. X and Y are corporate partners in a joint property-letting venture. They are unconnected except through their shares in the partnership. The partnership owns one property. Y's shareholders have accepted an offer from a third party, Z, to acquire all of its share capital. Z does not wish to continue to operate the business with X so the decision is taken to distribute the property to Y. There is a clear commercial reason for the transactions. The normal Stamp Duty Land Tax rules applied to the original acquisition of the property by the company.

6. V sells land to X and at the same time X sells the land to P. P pays Stamp Duty Land Tax based on the full amount of consideration received by V.

7. V sells land to X and at the same time X sells the land to P. P pays Stamp Duty Land Tax based on the full amount of consideration received by V. At a later date P sells the land to Y and Y pays the full amount of Stamp Duty Land Tax that arises from the consideration that P received.

8. V sells two properties at arm's length to third party purchasers N1 and N2. Subsequently, and in transactions which are not connected in any way with the purchases by N1 and N2, P buys both properties at arm's length. It is assumed that there is no connection between the sale by V and the purchase by P.

9. V grants a long lease to X. At a later stage, and in a transaction which is not connected in any way with the grant of the long lease, X assigns the lease to an unconnected third party P. P exercises a statutory right of enfranchisement. *Section 75A* does not apply as regards to disposal by V and the acquisition by P because it is taxed appropriately under the normal Stamp Duty Land Tax rules.

10. V grants an option to X to purchase land. Subsequently, and in a transaction which is not connected in any way with the grant of the option, X assigns the benefit of the option to an unconnected third party P. P exercises the option. There is no connection between the transactions.

19.348 The guidance note also sets out a number of situations where they consider that *s 75* applies, namely:

1. V agrees to sell land to X, and X agrees to sell the same land to P which is a partnership where the partners are X and persons connected to him. At the same time as the completion of the V-X contract, the X-P contract completes, this acquisition is effected by means of a 'transfer of rights'. X argues that no Stamp Duty Land Tax is due as his contract is disregarded by *s 45*, whilst P argues that no Stamp Duty Land Tax is due per *FA 2003, Sch 15* given its connection with X. *Section 75A* applies because HMRC considers that the conditions of *s 75A 1(a)–(c)* are met and that the notional transaction V-P could have been achieved in a more straightforward manner that would not have satisfied *s 75A(1)(c)*; Stamp Duty Land Tax is due on the notional consideration which is the full amount of consideration received by V.

2. V grants a 999-year lease to Nominee for no premium and a peppercorn rent. V assigns the freehold reversion to P for a nominal sum. P pays Nominee £x in consideration of Nominee's agreement to vary the lease by the insertion of a provision giving the landlord the right to terminate the lease for no payment. P exercises the right to terminate. Under *s 75A*, the

notional transaction is the acquisition of the unencumbered freehold by P and the notional consideration chargeable is £x given by P to Nominee.

3. V grants a 999-year lease to Nominee for no premium and a peppercorn rent. The lease includes a right for the landlord to terminate the lease on payment of £x to the tenant. V assigns the freehold reversion to P for a nominal sum. P exercises the right to terminate and pays Nominee £x. Under *s 75A*, the notional transaction is the acquisition of the unencumbered freehold by P from V, and the notional consideration chargeable is £x given by P to Nominee.

4. V grants a 999-year lease to P for no premium and a peppercorn rent. The lease gives the landlord a right to terminate it within 14 days of the date of grant. P offers to pay V £x if V allows the 14 days to elapse without exercising the right to terminate. V does so. Under *s 75A*, the notional transaction is the grant by V of a 999-year lease to P and the notional consideration, which is the chargeable consideration, is £x, the amount paid by P and received by V.

5. V agrees to sell property to X Ltd for £10 million. X Ltd declares a dividend in favour of P, the dividend to consist of the property and to be paid at the same time as completion of the V-X Ltd contract. The contract is completed and the property transferred to P. X argues that the £10 million is not chargeable to Stamp Duty Land Tax as his contract is disregarded under *s 45*. P argues that there is no Stamp Duty Land Tax charge on the transfer of the property to him because a dividend in specie is a transaction that does not constitute consideration for the purposes of the Stamp Duty Land Tax legislation. Under *s 75A*, the notional transaction is the acquisition of the property by P, and the notional consideration, which is the chargeable consideration, is £10 million, the amount received by V.

6. V agrees to sell land to X, and X agrees to sell the same land to P which is a partnership where the partners are X, X1 Ltd and X2 Ltd companies connected to X which manage a trust for which X is the beneficiary. V and X enter an arrangement where V settles a nominal amount into X's trust, thereby creating a connection between V and X as per *CTA 2010, s 1122*. The V-X contract completes and at the same time and simultaneously the X-P contract completes. X claims that no Stamp Duty Land Tax is due as his contract is disregarded by *FA 2003, s 45*, whilst P claims that no Stamp Duty Land Tax is due per *FA 2003, Sch 15* given its connection with X. *Section 75A* applies and the notional transaction involved is V-P. Stamp Duty Land Tax is due on the notional consideration which is the full amount of consideration received by V.

19.349 The *Furniss v Dawson (55 TCF 324)* principle may also apply to SDLT as it was held to apply to the predecessor tax, stamp duty, in *Ingram* *v CIR (1985 STC 835)*. In that case it was wished to convey a house for £145,500. In order to avoid the duty (at 1%) of £1,455, this was done in two steps. An agreement for a 999-year lease was entered into for a premium of £145,000 payable immediately. At the time an agreement for a lease of over 35 years was not dutiable (this exemption was removed by the *Finance Act 1984*). The freehold was sold, subject to the agreement, for £500 to a third party who resold it to Mr Ingram for £600. He volunteered to pay duty of £6 on the acquisition. He would not of course need to enter into the lease itself, so it was hoped that HMRC would never collect duty on the £145,000. It was held that there was a pre-ordained series of transactions designed to transfer the unencumbered freehold to Mr Ingram and HMRC were entitled to duty on the real transaction, a freehold sale at £145,600, of £1,456.

19.350 A dividend in specie of a property and a distribution in specie to shareholders in a liquidation are normally outside the scope of SDLT as the shareholder gives no consideration for the transfer. He is simply receiving a return to which his shares entitle him. However, if the property is subject to a mortgage, they regard the assumption of the liability under the mortgage as consideration. Because of the impact of ATED (see **Chapter 20**), many taxpayers are seeking to take a property out of a company by one of these means. HMRC have issued guidance on the circumstances in which it will not regard the 'developing' of a property by a company through a capital distribution in a liquidation as giving rise to 'consideration' for SDLT (HMRC Notice 20.12.2013). There will be no change if the company is free from debt or its only debt is due to the shareholder. The reference to 'the' shareholder suggests that HMRC are looking at the position only where there is a single shareholder or possibly where all of the shareholders have lent the company money equivalent to their shareholding. Where there is a third party loan secured on the property and as a result of shareholder action (either through the subscription for more issued share capital or by replacing the third party debt with shareholder debt) prior to the liquidation, *s 75A* could apply. They point out that in Project Blue (see **19.344**) the FTT stated that the section does not require a tax avoidance motive as a precondition or defence; parliament obviously intended that the provision should apply regardless of motive. The Tribunal went on to say, 'for a transaction to be "involved" in connection with the disposal, the linkage must be more than simply being a party in a chain of transactions and the test must be more than a "but for" test (or, as the classicists would put it, a "sine qua non test") otherwise the word "involved" would be deprived of significant meaning'. This is not particularly helpful. It says no more than each case needs to be considered on its merits. It does suggest that if at stage 1, a third party loan is secured on the property and at the end of the day a third party loan is secured on the property but there was no such security at the date of the transfer, the transaction is vulnerable to attack.

Administrative Rules

Land Transaction Returns

19.351 The purchaser must both deliver a land transaction return to HMRC and pay the tax due within 30 days of the effective date of a notifiable transaction (*FA 2003, s 76(1)*). The return must include a calculation (a self-assessment) of the tax chargeable in respect of the transaction. Prior to 19 July 2007, it also had to be accompanied by payment of the tax (*FA 2003, s 76(3)*). HMRC have power by statutory instrument to reduce the 30-day period (*FA 2003, s 76(2)*).

19.352 Notifiable transactions are:

(*a*) An acquisition of a major interest in land, other than:

- (i) an acquisition that is exempt under *Sch 13*,
- (ii) an acquisition (other than the grant, assignment or surrender of a lease) where the chargeable consideration (including that for any linked transaction) is under £40,000,
- (iii) the grant of a lease for seven years or more where the chargeable consideration other than rent is under £40,000 and the relevant rent (the annual rent within *FA 2003, Sch 5, para 9A* (or, if *FA 2003, Sch 15, paras 11* or *19*) applies, the relevant proportion of the annual rent) is under £1,000,
- (iv) the assignment or surrender of a lease where the lease was originally granted for a term of seven or more years and the chargeable consideration for the assignment or surrender is under £40,000,
- (v) the grant of a lease for a term of under seven years where the chargeable consideration does not exceed the zero-rate threshold (the level at which tax at 1% would become chargeable but for any relief), or
- (vi) the assignment or surrender of a lease which was originally granted for a term of less than seven years and the chargeable consideration for the assignment or surrender does not exceed the zero-rate threshold.

(*b*) An acquisition of a chargeable interest other than a major interest in land where any part of the consideration is chargeable at a rate of more than 0% or would be so chargeable but for a relief (but taking account of any exemption under *FA 2003, Sch 3*).

(*c*) A land transaction that a person is treated as entering into by virtue of *FA 2003, s 44A(3)*.

(*d*) A notional land transaction under *FA 2003, s 75A*.

(*FA 2003, ss 77, 77A.*)

19.353 However, there is no need to notify any of the above transactions if it is exempt from SDLT under *FA 2003, s 71A(4)* (or in Scotland *s 72A(7)*) (alternative finance-arrangements) unless it involves the transfer of the whole of the interest purchased by the institution under the first transaction, or if it is a partnership transaction the consideration for which is taxed at a rate other than 0% under *FA 2003, Sch 15, para 30* (*FA 2003, s 77(2)* as amended by *Stamp Duty Land Tax Act 2015, Sch 1, para 16*).

19.354 The effect of the *Finance Act 2008* changes is that it is no longer necessary to complete any SDLT form where the chargeable consideration for non-leasehold transactions is below £40,000 or where either the chargeable consideration for a lease for seven or more years is below £40,000 and the annual rent is below £1,000.

19.355 It should be stressed that the acquisition of a freehold or leasehold interest in land (other than a lease of under seven years) needs to be notified unless an exemption applies even if the consideration is less than £120,000. There is no duty to notify if there is no consideration though. A gift subject to the donee taking over a mortgage is notifiable as the assumption of the loan is consideration (HMRC Press Release 11.11.2003). A lease for an indefinite term is treated as a lease for a term of under seven years, so there is no obligation to notify the grant (*FA 2003, Sch 17A, para 4(4A)*). This includes a periodic tenancy or other interest or right terminable by a period of notice, a tenancy at will, and any other interest or right terminable by notice at any time (*FA 2003, Sch 17A, para 4(5)*). A lease for a fixed term and thereafter until determined (or which may continue beyond the fixed term by operation of law) is a lease for the fixed term only (*FA 2003, Sch 17A, para 3(5)*). A transaction in a disadvantaged area had to be notified even if *FA 2003, Sch 6* (see **19.172**) exempted it from tax (*FA 2003, Sch 6, para 13*).

19.356 A land transaction return must:

(*a*) be in the form prescribed by regulations made by HMRC (who can make different provision for different kinds of return) (*FA 2003, Sch 10, para 1(1)(a)–(3)*);

(*b*) contain the information prescribed by regulations made by HMRC (*FA 2003, Sch 10, para 1(1)(b)(4)*); and

(*c*) include a declaration by the purchaser (or each of them) that the return is to the best of his knowledge correct and complete (*FA 2003, Sch 10, para 1(b)*).

(*FA 2003, s 78 and Sch 10, para 1.*)

19.357 HMRC have prescribed that the return must be in writing and completed in black ink. It must be made on HMRC's form SDLT 1 or in a form approved by HMRC, and where necessary must be accompanied by forms SDLT 2 (additional vendor/purchaser details), SDLT 3 (additional details about the land) and SDLT 4 (additional details about the transaction, including leases). These forms can be downloaded from HMRC's website (*reg 9, SDLT (Administration) Regulations 2003 (SI 2003 No 2837*). The return has to be signed by the purchaser personally; it cannot be signed on his behalf by a solicitor or accountant. However, it can be signed by the holder of a Power of Attorney (*FA 2003, s 81B*). As an alternative to meeting head (c) above, the purchaser can authorise an agent to complete the return, with the agent declaring in it that the effective date shown therein is correct and complete and the client signing a separate letter confirming that the information shown in the return is to the best of his information correct and complete. However, a special form must be used (*FA 2003, Sch 10, para 1A).* This will enable the return to be filed more quickly as the purchaser can review a draft or an e-mail copy and electronically authorise the agent to file the return. If the purchaser is under a disability and the Official Solicitor is acting, the Official Solicitor can sign the return but a special form must be used (*FA 2003, Sch 10, para 18*).

19.358 A photocopy cannot be used as each form has a unique reference number. If the purchaser (or one of the purchasers) is an individual it requires his National Insurance number (if he has one). HMRC ask for the National Land and Property Gazetteer Unique Property Reference Number if that is known. Plans need to be submitted with the form for development land, agricultural land and small 'garden' plots (Stamp Duty Information Bulletin, Issue 4, 24.9.2003). The return must be submitted to HMRC, SDLT, Netherton, Merseyside L30 4RN.

19.359 HMRC have a general power under *FA 1999, ss 132* and *133* to make subordinate legislation in relation to the delivery of information and making payments. They have used this to enable SDLT returns and payments to be made electronically. The detailed rules are contained in the *SDLT (Electronic Communications) Regulations 2005 (SI 2005 No 844)* as amended .

19.360 The return is treated as containing any information provided by the purchaser for the purpose of completing it (*FA 2003, Sch 10, para 1(5)*). Failure to deliver a return attracts a penalty of £100 if it is delivered within three months of the filing date and £200 if it is delivered later (*FA 2003, Sch 10, para 3*). If the return is not filed within 12 months of the due date a tax-related penalty of up to 100% of the SDLT on the transaction is payable in addition to this fixed penalty (*FA 2003, Sch 10, para 4*). In *De Nemethy v HMRC (2008 STC (SCD)* 136) which related to the purchase of a house in the stamp duty era the Special Commissioner held that although lack of funds was capable of being a reasonable excuse it was not one in that case as the taxpayer could have bought a smaller house or rented and that a penalty of £100% (£12,600) on a return made six years late was not excessive. It was held in *Browne v HMRC (2011 SFTD 67)* that the taxpayer had a reasonable excuse as she had relied on her solicitor to make the return and could have expected this to have been done as part of the conveyancing process. The current legislation (*FA 2008, Sch 41, para 20*) states that 'where P relies on any other person to do anything, that is not a reasonable excuse unless P took reasonable care to avoid the relevant act or failure', so it seems likely that the same decision would be reached under the current law.

19.361 If HMRC believe that a purchaser is required to deliver a land transaction return and that he has not done so by the due date they can issue a notice requiring him to deliver the return. The notice must specify the transaction to which it relates and the period allowed for complying with the notice (which must be at least 30 days from the date of issue of the notice). Failure to comply with such a notice attracts a penalty of up to £60 for each day on which the failure continues after the day on which the purchaser is notified that the First-tier Tribunal has directed that the penalty should apply (*FA 2003, Sch 10, para 5*). This daily penalty is in addition to the penalties under *paras 3* and *4* for failure to deliver the return.

19.362 The purchaser can amend a land transaction return by notice to HMRC. This must be in such form, and contain such information, as HMRC may require. Such an amendment must normally be made within 12 months after the filing date (*FA 2003, Sch 10, para 6*). HMRC have power to amend a land transaction return to correct obvious errors or omissions in the return. They must do so by notice to the purchaser within nine months of the day on which the return is delivered (or of the day on which an amendment is made if the correction is to that amendment). The amendment has no effect if the purchaser either amends the return so as to reject the correction or, if it is too late to make an amendment, gives notice to the Officer who gave him notice of the correction rejecting the amendment within three months from the date of issue of the notice of correction.

19.363 A purchaser who either:

(*a*) fraudulently or negligently delivers a land transaction return which is incorrect; or

(*b*) discovers that a land transaction return that he submitted is incorrect and does not remedy the error without unreasonable delay,

is liable to a penalty of up to 100% of the tax understated on the return (*FA 2003, Sch 10, para 8*).

19.364 Where *FA 2003, s 51* (contingent, uncertain or unascertained consideration) applies in relation to a transaction and a transaction subsequently becomes notifiable when new information becomes known which increases the tax payable (or creates a SDLT liability where none previously existed) (see **19.141**) the purchaser must deliver a SDLT return to HMRC within 30 days. The return must contain a self-assessment of the additional tax chargeable (by reference to the rates in force at the effective date of the transaction) and up to 17 July 2007 had to be accompanied by payment of the tax or additional tax due. The tax also has to be paid within that 30-day period (*FA 2003, s 80*). If the effect of the new information is to reduce the tax payable the purchaser can amend his return if he is still in time to do so or, if not, can make a claim for repayment of the tax paid (*FA 2003, s 80(4)*). The administrative provisions in relation to claims for repayment are considered at **19.402–19.403**. Where the transaction is the grant or assignment of a lease no claim for repayment can be made in respect of the repayment of any loan or deposit that it treated by *FA 2003, Sch 17A, para 18A* (see **19.169**) as being consideration given for the relevant transaction, or in respect of the refund of any of the consideration given for the relevant transaction if it is made under arrangements made in connection with the transaction and it is contingent on the determination or assignment of the lease or on the grant of a chargeable interest out of it (*FA 2003, s 80*).

19.365 A return must similarly be delivered and the tax paid within 30 days after the date on which the disqualifying event occurs if that event triggers a claw-back of group relief (see **19.189**), reconstruction relief (see **19.209**) acquisition relief (see **19.212**), PAIF or COACS seeding relief (see **19.238**) charities relief (see **19.249**) or housebuilder or relocation relief (see **19.184**), or if one of the reliefs against the15% tax rate on dwellings costing over £2 million ceases to apply (*FA 2003, s 81* as amended by *FA 2013, Sch 40, para 3*). If a relief against the 15% tax rate is withdrawn and alternative finance arrangements apply, a return must again be delivered within 30 days of the disqualifying event (the first day in the control period on which disqualification is triggered). This must contain a self-assessment of the additional tax chargeable as a result of the withdrawal of the relief, calculated by reference to the rates in force at the effective date of the transaction in respect of which the relief was allowed (*FA 2003, s 81ZA* inserted by *FA 2013, Sch 40, para 4*). The provisions of *FA 2003, Sch 10* (returns, enquiries, assessments and other matters) apply to all of these returns in the same way as to one under *FA 2003, s 76* but with the adaptation that references to the effective date of the transactions must be read as references to the disqualifying event (*FA 2003, ss 81(3)(5), 81ZA(2)*). In the case of alternative finance arrangements, references to the purchaser must also, as far as necessary, be read as references to the relevant person (*FA 2003, s 81ZA(2)(b)*).

19.366 Where SDLT becomes payable, or becomes payable at a higher rate, as a result of a later linked transaction the purchaser needs to submit a further

SDLT return in respect of the earlier transaction or transactions. The return has to be delivered within 30 days from the effective date of the later transaction. The tax due must be calculated by reference to the rates in force at the effective date of the earlier transaction (*FA 2003, s 81A*).

19.367 If a return delivered to HMRC (or any other document relating to tax made by or provided to HMRC) is lost or destroyed or so defaced or damaged as to be illegible or otherwise useless, HMRC can treat the return as not having been delivered (or the document as not having been made or provided) (*FA 2003, s 82(1),(2)*). If, as a result, HMRC require a fresh return to be submitted and the purchaser proves to the satisfaction of the First-tier Tribunal that he has already paid the tax in respect of the transaction, relief against double taxation is to be given by reducing the charge on the new return or by repayment as the case may require (*FA 2003, s 82(4)*).

Duty to Keep Records

19.368 A purchaser who is required to deliver a land transaction return must keep such records as may be needed to enable him to deliver a correct and complete return (including relevant instruments relating to the transaction – particularly any contract or conveyance and any supporting maps, plans or similar documents – and records of relevant payments, receipts and financial arrangements) (*FA 2003, Sch 11, para 9(1)(3)*).

19.369 The records must be preserved for six years after the effective date of the transaction, and until any later date on which an enquiry into a return is completed or HMRC no longer have power to enquire into the return (*FA 2003, Sch 11, para 9(2)*). The duty to preserve records can be satisfied by preservation of the information contained in them. Where this is done a copy of any document forming part of the records is admissible in evidence before the Commissioners to the same extent as the records themselves (*FA 2003, Sch 11, para 10*).

19.370 A purchaser under a non-notifiable transaction must similarly keep such records as may be needed to enable him to demonstrate that the transaction is not notifiable and preserve such records for six years from the effective date of the transaction (*FA 2003, Sch 11, para 4(2)*).

19.371 A penalty of up to £3,000 can be imposed for failure to keep the appropriate records for the requisite period (*FA 2003, Sch 10, para 11(1), Sch 11, para 6(1)*). No penalty arises if HMRC are satisfied that any facts that they reasonably require to be proved (and would have been proved by the records) are proved by other documentary evidence available to them (*FA 2003, Sch 10, para 11(2), Sch 11, para 6(2)*).

Enquiry into Return

19.372 HMRC are entitled to enquire into a land transaction return. They must give the purchaser notice of their intention to do so within nine months after the filing date (ie the last day of the period within which the return must be delivered). If the return is delivered late, the nine months runs from the date the return was delivered. If the return is amended by the purchaser it runs from the date of the amendment (*FA 2003, Sch 10, para 12(1)(2)*). If the return is a further return under *s 80* (contingent and unascertained consideration) *81* (withdrawal of group etc relief) or *81A* (linked transactions), HMRC can open an enquiry into the original return also if at the time they have an open enquiry into the further return (*FA 2003, Sch 10, para 12(2A)*).A return that has been the subject of one notice of enquiry cannot be the subject of another, other than one given in consequence of an amendment (or another amendment) by the purchaser (*FA 2003, Sch 10, para 12(3)*).

19.373 An enquiry into a return can extend to anything contained in the return (or required to be contained in it) that relates to the question whether tax is chargeable in respect of the transaction or that relates to the amount of tax chargeable (*FA 2003, Sch 10, para 13(1)*). If notice of enquiry is given as a result of an amendment of the return at a time when the enquiry window into the return has closed the enquiry is limited to matters to which the amendment relates or which are affected by the amendment (*FA 2003, Sch 10, para 13(2)*). An enquiry into a self-certificate extended to anything contained in the certificate (or required to be contained in it) that related to the question whether the transaction was chargeable or notifiable or that related to the amount of tax chargeable in respect of the transaction (*FA 2003, Sch 11, para 8*).

19.374 Where HMRC give a notice of enquiry, they may by notice in writing require the purchaser:

(*a*) to produce to them such documents as are in his possession or power; and

(*b*) to provide them with such information, in such form as they may reasonably require for the purposes of the enquiry.

The notice must specify the time within which the purchaser must comply with it, which must not be less than 30 days. Copies (rather than the originals) can be produced in response to such a notice provided that such copies must be photographic or other facsimiles. HMRC can by notice require sight of the original. HMRC can take copies of, or make extracts from any documents produced to them. Such a notice does not oblige the purchaser to produce documents, or provide information relating to the conduct of any pending appeal by him (or any pending referral to the First-tier Tribunal – see **19.379**) (*FA 2003, Sch 10, para 14*).

19.375 The purchaser can appeal to the First-tier Tribunal against a requirement imposed by the notice. Notice of appeal must be given to HMRC in writing within 30 days of the issue of the notice. On appeal, the Tribunal must set aside the notice if it appears to them that the documents or information is not reasonably required for the purpose of the enquiry. They must confirm the notice if it appears to them that it is reasonably required. Where a notice is confirmed the purchaser has 30 days from the determination of the appeal in which to comply with it. The decision of the Tribunal on an appeal against such a notice is final (*FA 2003, Sch 10, para 15*).

19.376 A person who fails to comply with a notice to produce documents, etc, is liable to a penalty of £50 and, if the failure continues after that fixed penalty is imposed, to a further daily penalty up to £30 a day if the penalty is determined by HMRC, or up to £150 a day if it is determined by the court, for each day on which the failure continues. No penalty can be imposed in respect of a failure at any time after that failure has been remedied (*FA 2003, Sch 10, para 16*).

19.377 If during the course of enquiry into a return (but not one into a self-certificate) HMRC form the opinion that the tax declared is insufficient and that unless the assessment is immediately amended there is likely to be a loss of tax to the Crown, they can by notice in writing to the purchaser amend the assessment (*FA 2003, Sch 10, para 17*). The taxpayer has a right of appeal against the amendment (*FA 2003, Sch 10, para 35(1)* – see **19.395**).

19.378 If the purchaser amends his return during the course of an enquiry that amendment does not restrict the scope of the enquiry but can be taken into account in the enquiry (*FA 2003, Sch 10, para 18(1)(2)*). If such an amendment affects the amount of tax payable it does not take effect until the closure notice is issued (*FA 2003, Sch 10, para 18(3)*).

19.379 During the course of an enquiry the purchaser and HMRC can jointly refer to the First-tier Tribunal for their determination any question arising in connection with the subject matter of the enquiry. More than one such notice of referral can be given in relation to an enquiry (*FA 2003, Sch 10, para 19*). Either party can withdraw a notice of referral at any time before the first hearing by the Tribunal in relation to it by giving notice in writing to both the other party and the Tribunal (*FA 2003, Sch 10, para 20*). This procedure is designed to enable disputes on a specific aspect of an enquiry to be resolved without waiting for the enquiry to be completed.

19.380 A closure notice cannot be given in relation to the enquiry while proceedings on a referral are in progress, ie until the referral has been determined by the First-tier Tribunal and there is no further possibility of the determination being varied or set aside (disregarding any power to grant permission to appeal out of time) (*FA 2003, Sch 10, para 21*).

19.381 The determination of a question by the Tribunal on a referral is binding on the parties in the same way, and to the same extent, as a decision on a preliminary issue on an appeal. The determination must be taken into account by HMRC in reaching their conclusions on the enquiry and formulating any consequential amendments to the return. The right of appeal against the assessment is not to be exercised so as to reopen the question determined except to the extent (if any) that it could be reopened if it had been determined as a preliminary issue in that appeal (*FA 2003, Sch 10, para 22*).

19.382 An enquiry is completed when HMRC issue a closure notice informing the purchaser that they have completed their enquiries and stating their conclusions. The notice in relation to a return must either state that in their opinion no amendment of the return is required or amend the return to give effect to their conclusions (*FA 2003, Sch 10, para 23*). A closure notice in relation to a self-certificate must state whether in the opinion of HMRC the self-certificate was correct. If their opinion is that it was not it must also state whether in their opinion the transaction to which it relates was chargeable or notifiable (*FA 2003, Sch 10, para 16*). A closure notice in relation to a return takes effect when it is issued (*FA 2003, Sch 10, para 23*). There is no corresponding provision in relation to a self-certificate. In *Portland Gas Storage Ltd v HMRC (2014 UKUT 270 (TCC))* the Upper Tribunal held that neither a notice of enquiry or a closure notice need be in any particular form, the only requirement being that an enquiry notice must give notice of an intention to enquire into a land transaction return. It accordingly held that correspondence by HMRC constituted a notice of enquiry and a later letter constituted a closure notice, so as to give the company a right of appeal against the HMRC decision to which the correspondence related.

19.383 The purchaser is entitled (at any time during the course of the enquiry but not whilst proceedings on a referral under *para 19* (or *12*) is in progress) to apply to the First-tier Tribunal for a direction that HMRC gave a closure notice within a specified period (*FA 2003, Sch 10, para 24(1)*). Such an application is to be heard and determined in the same way as an appeal. The Tribunal hearing the application must give the direction unless it is satisfied that HMRC have reasonable grounds for not giving a closure notice within a specified period (*FA 2003, Sch 10, para 24(2)(3)*).

19.384 There is a right of appeal against a conclusion stated, or amendment made, by a closure notice (*FA 2003, Sch 10, para 35(1)(b)* – see **19.395**). This appears to apply equally to a closure notice following an enquiry into a self-certificate.

HMRC Determination

19.385 If no land transaction return is delivered by the filing date, HMRC have power to make a determination to the best of their information and belief of the amount of tax chargeable in respect of the transaction (*FA 2003, Sch 10, para 25(1)*). Notice of such an HMRC determination must be served on the purchaser stating the date on which it is issued (*FA 2003, Sch 10, para 25(2)*). An HMRC determination cannot be made more than six years after the effective date of the transaction (*FA 2003, Sch 10, para 25(3)*). An HMRC determination has effect for enforcement purposes (ie collection and recovery of unpaid tax, interest, and tax related penalties) as if it were a self assessment by the purchaser, but does not affect any liability of the purchaser to a penalty for failure to deliver a return (*FA 2003, Sch 10, para 26*).

19.386 If after a determination is made the purchaser delivers the land transaction return that return supersedes the determination – but only if the return is delivered within six years after the day on which the power to make the determination first became exercisable or, if later, within 12 months after the date of the determination. If before the land transaction return is delivered proceedings have begun for the recovery of the tax charged by an HMRC determination those proceedings can be continued as if they were proceedings for the recovery of so much of the tax charged by the self-assessment (ie shown as payable on the return) as is due and payable and has not been paid (*FA 2003, Sch 10, para 27*).

Discovery Assessments

19.387 If HMRC discover as regards a chargeable transaction that tax that ought to be assessed has not been assessed, an assessment is insufficient or a relief that has been allowed is excessive they can make an assessment in the amount that they believe is needed to make good the loss of tax (*FA 2003, Sch 10, para 28*). They can also make such an assessment to recover any over-repayment of tax and any interest paid thereon (*FA 2003, Sch 10, para 29*).

19.388 Where a land transaction return has been submitted a discovery assessment can be made only if either:

(*a*) the tax lost is attributable to fraudulent or negligent conduct on the part of the purchaser, a person acting on his behalf or a partner of the purchaser; or

(*b*) before the enquiry window closed HMRC could not have been reasonably expected on the basis of the information made available to them before that time, to be aware of the loss of tax.

(*FA 2003, Sch 10, para 30(1)–(3)*.)

19.389 For the purpose of (*b*) above information is regarded as having been made available to HMRC if it is contained on a land transaction return by the purchaser, it is contained in any documents produced or information provided in relation to an enquiry into a land transaction return, or it is information the existence of which and the relevance of which was notified to HMRC by the purchaser or someone on his behalf or could reasonably be expected to be inferred from the above information (*FA 2003, Sch 10, para 30(4)*).

19.390 A discovery assessment cannot be made if the loss of tax is attributable to a mistake in the return as to the basis on which the tax liability ought to have been computed and the return was made in accordance with the practice generally prevailing at the time it was made (*FA 2003, Sch 10, para 30(5)*).

19.391 A discovery assessment cannot normally be made more than six years after the effective date of the transaction to which it relates but in a case involving fraud or negligence the time limit is extended to 21 years (*FA 2003, Sch 10, para 31(1)*). An assessment to recover an excessive tax repayment is not out of time if it is made during the course of an enquiry or within one year after the over-repayment was made (*FA 2003, Sch 10, para 31(2)*). Where the purchaser has died any assessment on the personal representatives must be made within three years of his death and if fraud or negligence is involved can only cover a transaction the effective date of which was within six years before the death (*FA 2003, Sch 10, para 31(4)*).

19.392 Notice of an assessment must be served on the purchaser. It must state the tax due, the date on which the notice is issued and the time within which an appeal can be made. The officer who decides to make the assessment can entrust to another officer responsibility for making the assessment and serving notice of it (*FA 2003, Sch 10, para 32*). An objection to an assessment on the ground that it is out of time can be made only on an appeal against the assessment (*FA 2003, Sch 10, para 31(5)*).

Relief from Excessive Assessments

19.393 If a person believes that he has been assessed to tax more than once in respect of the same matter, he can make a claim to HMRC for relief against any double tax charge (*FA 2003, Sch 10, para 33*). The provisions on claims considered at **19.402–19.404** will apply to the claim. There does not appear to be any time limit for making such a claim.

19.394 If a person believes he has overpaid tax under an assessment that was excessive by reason of a mistake in a land transaction return he can similarly claim relief. Such a claim must be made within six years of the effective date of the transaction. In determining such a claim HMRC, and on appeal the Tribunal, must have regard to all the relevant circumstances of the case and must in particular consider whether the granting of relief would result in amounts being excluded from tax. Relief cannot be given in respect of either a mistake as to the basis of calculation if the return was made in accordance with the practice generally prevailing at the time it was made, or a mistake in a claim or election included in the return (*FA 2003, Sch 10, para 34*). From a date to be announced *para 34* is replaced by more detailed rules. Where a person overpays or is over-assessed in respect of SDLT (including under a contract settlement with HMRC) he will be able to reclaim the tax (or to reduce the assessment) only if there were no other means of reclaiming the overpayment in the SDLT legislation when he first became aware (or ought to have become aware) that he could recover it. No relief is due if the overpayment is due to a mistake relating to a claim for another relief. Nor is it due if the payment was calculated in accordance with the practice generally prevailing at the time. The claim must be made within four years of the effective date of the transaction. The person must have exhausted all of the appeal rights that were available to him. The claimant must qualify for the amount repayable subject to HMRC's right to enquire into the claim. This is now the only method of claiming relief. Legal action for repayment or restitution is no longer an option. If the grounds for a claim are also grounds for a discovery assessment, HMRC can make such a discovery if they are otherwise out of time to do so (*FA 2003, Sch 10, para 34–34E*).

Appeals

19.395 An appeal can be brought to the First-tier Tribunal against:

(*a*) an amendment of a self-assessment under *Sch 10, para 17* (amendment by HMRC during an enquiry to prevent loss of tax) – but in such a case the appeal is not to be heard and determined until the enquiry is completed;

(*b*) a conclusion stated, or amendment made, by a closure notice;

(*c*) a discovery assessment;

(*d*) an assessment to recover an excessive repayment; or

(*e*) from 8 December 2004, a Revenue determination under *para 25*.

(*FA 2003, Sch 10, para 35*.)

19.396 Notice of appeal must be given in writing to the Officer who gave the notice of assessment or by whom the closure notice was issued within 30 days of the date on which the notice of the closure, assessment determination or amendment was issued. The notice must specify the grounds of appeal, although on hearing the appeal the First-tier Tribunal can allow the appellant to put forward grounds not specified in the notice if they are satisfied that their omission was not deliberate or unreasonable (*FA 2003, Sch 10, para 36*). The only permitted grounds of appeal against a determination that has been made in the absence of a return are that the purchase did not take place, the interest in land specified has not been purchased, the contract has not been substantially performed or the transaction is not notifiable (*FA 2003, Sch 10, para 36(5A)*).

Settling of Appeals by Agreement

19.397 If before an appeal is determined the appellant (or his agent) and HMRC reach an agreement as to what the position should be the same consequences follow as if the Tribunal had determined the appeal. If the agreement is not in writing that applies only if the fact of the agreement and its terms are confirmed in writing by one party to the other. In such a case the agreement is deemed to be reached at the time such confirmation is given (*FA 2003, Sch 10, para 37(1)(3)*). The appeal is not deemed to have been determined if the taxpayer notifies HMRC within 30 days of the date of the agreement that he wishes to withdraw from it (*FA 2003, Sch 10, para 37(2)*). If the appellant notifies HMRC that he does not wish to proceed with the appeal (and if he does so orally it is confirmed in writing) the parties are treated as having agreed that the decision under appeal should be upheld without variation unless HMRC give the appellant notice in writing within 30 days of the notice of withdrawal that they are unwilling that the appeal should be withdrawn (*FA 2003, Sch 10, para 37*).

Postponement of Tax Pending an Appeal

19.398 Where there is an appeal to the Tribunal the tax charged remains due and payable as if there had been no appeal (*FA 2003, Sch 10, para 38*). However, the appellant can by notice apply to the Tribunal for a direction that payment of an amount of tax should be postponed pending the determination of the appeal. The notice must be given to HMRC within 30 days of the date of the assessment, closure notice or amendment and must state the amount by which he believes himself to be overcharged and the grounds for such belief. The notice can be given outside the 30-day period if there is a change in the circumstances of the case as a result of which the appellant has grounds for believing that he is overcharged (*FA 2003, Sch 10, para 39(1)–(3)*). Such an application is to be determined by the Tribunal in the same way as an appeal. If after a determination there is a change in circumstances either the appellant or HMRC can apply for a further determination (*FA 2003, Sch 10, para 39(4)–(6)*).

19.399 Where the Tribunal determines that some tax is to be paid, the due and payable date for such tax becomes the date of its determination (*FA 2003, Sch 10, para 39(7)*). When the appeal is ultimately determined the due date for any further tax is the date that HMRC issues to the appellant a notice of the total tax payable in accordance with the determination (unless he appeals the decision to the High Court). Any tax overpaid becomes repayable (*FA 2003, Sch 10, para 39(8)*). The appellant and HMRC can agree what tax should be postponed in which case the same consequences follow as if the appeal had been determined by the Tribunal (*FA 2003, Sch 10, para 40*).

Formal Requirements as to Assessments, etc

19.400 An assessment, determination, notice or other document used in assessing or collecting SDLT or penalties must be in the form prescribed from time to time by HMRC (*FA 2003, s 83(1)*). However, such a document is not ineffective for want of form, or by reason of any mistake, defect or omission in it, if it is substantially in conformity with the SDLT legislation and its intended effect is reasonably ascertainable by the person to whom it is directed (*FA 2003, s 83(2)*). The validity of an assessment or determination is not affected by any mistake in it as to the name of the person liable or the amount of any tax charged. Nor is its validity affected by reason of any variance between the notice of assessment or determination and the assessment or determination itself (*FA 2003, s 83(3)*). The Tribunal in *Coolatinney Developments Ltd (TC 1116)* held that this provision validated letters that wrongly stated that HMRC intended to enquire into 'your self-certificate' as opening enquiries into the SDLT returns.

Delivery and Service of Documents

19.401 A notice or other document to be 'served' on a person can be delivered to him or left at his usual or last known place of abode. If the notice is to be 'given, served or delivered' it can be served by post. Such a notice is regarded for the purposes of the *Interpretation Act 1978, s 7* (general provisions as to service by post) as properly addressed if it is addressed to that person at his usual or last known place of residence or his place of business if he is an individual, or in the case of a company at its principal place of business, the address for the purpose of the liquidation if a liquidator has been appointed or at a place prescribed by Regulations made by HMRC (*FA 2003, s 84*).

Claims not Included in Returns

19.402 A claim must be made in such form as HMRC may determine and must contain a declaration to the effect that all of the particulars given in the form are correctly stated to the best of the claimant's information and belief. No claim for a repayment can be made unless the claimant has documentary evidence that the tax has been paid (*FA 2003, Sch 11A, para 2*). A person who wishes to make a claim must keep such records as may be needed to enable him to make a correct and complete claim. The records must be preserved for 12 months from making the claim (or, if later, until any enquiry has been completed or, if the claim is amended, when the enquiry window for the amendment closes) (*FA 2003, Sch 11A, para 3*). It seems odd that the normal six-year period (see **19.369**) does not apply to such records. Paragraphs **19.369** and **19.371** (which impose a penalty of up to £3,000) apply to the records in the same way as records supporting a return.

19.403 A claim can be amended by notice to HMRC but only within 12 months of making the claim (or during the period during which any enquiry into the claim is open) (*FA 2003, Sch 11A, para 4*). HMRC can themselves amend a claim so as to correct any obvious errors or omissions, but only within nine months of the claim being made or in the course of an enquiry into the claim. The taxpayer can reject an HMRC correction by notice to HMRC within three months of the date of issue of the notice of correction (*FA 2003, Sch 11A, para 5*). HMRC must give effect to a claim by discharge or repayment of tax as soon as is practicable (but obviously do not need to give effect to it whilst they are enquiring into the claim) (*FA 2003, Sch 11A, para 6*).

19.404 HMRC can enquire into a claim. Their powers (and taxpayers' rights) are identical to those which apply to enquiries into returns (see **19.372–19.384**) with the exception that the £150 daily penalty for non-compliance does not apply (*FA 2003, Sch 11A, paras 7–15*).

Payment of Tax

19.405 The purchaser is liable to pay the tax in respect of a chargeable transaction (*FA 2003, s 85(1)*). In the case of joint purchasers they are jointly and severally liable (*FA 2003, s 103(2), (3)*). So are partners and trustees if they are partners or trustees at the effective date of the transaction (*FA 2003, Sch 15, para 7, Sch 16, para 5*). Where relief against the 15% rate of tax is withdrawn and alternative finance arrangements apply, the relevant person (ie the person other than the financial institution that entered into the arrangements), not the purchaser, is liable for the additional tax (*FA 2003, s 85(3)(4)* inserted by *FA 2013, Sch 40, para 5)*.

19.406 The tax payable must be paid within the same timeframe as the making of the land transaction return. Tax that becomes payable as the result of a withdrawal of group relief, reconstruction relief, acquisition relief, PAIF or COACS seeding relief or charities relief must be paid at the same time as the return in respect of the withdrawal is made. Tax payable as a result of the amendment of a return must be paid forthwith unless the amendment is made before the filing date for the return in which case it must be paid by the filing date. Tax payable on an HMRC determination or assessment must be paid within 30 days of the determination or assessment (*FA 2003, s 86*). Tax payable as a result of the withdrawal of a relief from the 15% rate of tax under *FA 2003, Sch 4A, paras 6D, 6F, 6G* or *6H* (see **19.37** onwards) must be paid by the filing date for the return relating to the withdrawal under *FA 2003, s 81ZA* (see **19.364**) (*FA 2003, s 86(2A)* inserted by *FA 2013, Sch 40, para 6*).

Interest

19.407 Interest is payable on any tax unpaid 30 days after the relevant date at the rate applicable under *FA 1989, s 178*. HMRC have power by regulation to shorten the 30-day period. The relevant date is normally the effective date of the transaction (which is normally the date of completion). In the case of the withdrawal of a relief it is the date of the disqualifying event and where a later linked transaction triggers tax on an earlier transaction it is the effective date of the later transaction. Where HMRC agreed that tax should be deferred in the case of contingent or uncertain consideration (see **19.140**) it is the date when the deferred payment becomes due. If no application for deferment is made and additional tax is due when the contingency ceases or the amount becomes ascertainable, the due date for such additional tax is the effective date of the transaction not the date the amount due is ascertained. If an amount is lodged with HMRC in respect of the tax the amount on which interest is payable is reduced by that amount (*FA 2003, s 87*). In the case of an amount payable under *FA 2003, Sch 17A, para 3(3)* (leases that continue after a fixed term – see **19.147**) by reason of the continuation of a lease, the relevant date is the final day of the extended period (*FA 2003, s 87(3)(aaa)* inserted by *FA 2013, Sch 41, para 4*).

19.408 Interest at the rate applicable under *FA 1989, s 178* is also payable on SDLT penalties. Such interest runs from the date that the penalty is determined until payment (*FA 2003, s 88*).

19.409 Where HMRC make a repayment of tax or of a penalty such repayment also carries interest at the rate applicable under *FA 1989, s 178* from the date on which the payment was made to the date when the order for repayment is issued.

19.410 If the purchaser lodges an amount with HMRC in respect of a transaction and part of that amount becomes repayable the interest runs from the date on which the amount was lodged (*FA 2003, s 89(1)–(3)*). No interest is payable in respect of a payment made in consequence of an order or judgment of a court having power to allow interest on the payment (*FA 2003, s 89(4)*).

19.411 The interest paid by HMRC is not income of the recipient for any tax purposes (*FA 2003, s 89(5)*).

Collection and Recovery of Tax

19.412 Where tax is due and payable a collector can demand it (*FA 2003, Sch 12, para 1(1)*). If so requested 'on payment of the tax' he must give a receipt (*FA 2003, Sch 12, para 1(2)*). The practice seems to be that HMRC regard 'on payment' literally. If a receipt is not requested with the cheque their practice in relation to other taxes is to refuse to give a receipt but to write a letter confirming that they have received the money. The legality of this practice seems questionable.

19.413 If the amount due is not paid, HMRC can distrain upon the taxpayer's goods and chattels. They can ask a JP to issue a warrant authorising them to break open, in the daytime any house or premises. The Collector must personally attend a distraint. The goods seized must be held for five days. If the taxpayer does not pay the tax in that period the goods will be sold by public auction. The taxpayer is liable for the costs of both the distraint and the auction (*FA 2003, Sch 12, para* 2). The Treasury have power to prescribe the fees chargeable in connection with distraint and the costs and charges that are recoverable where distraint has been levied. They have done so by *regs 29–32* of the *SDLT (Administration) Regulations 2003 (SI 2003 No 2837).*

19.414 If the tax due is £2,000 or less HMRC can sue for the debt in the magistrates court as a civil debt, but they must do so within 12 months of the time that 'the matter complained of' (whatever that may mean) arose (*FA 2003, Sch 12, para 4*). They can also sue for the debt, irrespective of the amount, in a county court or in the High Court (*FA 2003, Sch 12, paras 5, 6*). In any proceedings, a certificate of an HMRC official that the tax is due and payable, and that to the best of his knowledge and belief has not been paid, is sufficient evidence that the sum is due (*FA 2003, Sch 12, para 7*). This does not mean that such a certificate is conclusive but merely that HMRC do not have to bring additional evidence. The taxpayer is entitled to bring evidence to rebut the presumption.

19.415 Where the tax is paid by cheque it is deemed to be paid on the day the cheque was received by HMRC provided that it is met on first presentation (*FA 2003, s 92*).

Information Powers

19.416 HMRC's information powers have been aligned across the taxes. They can be found in *FA 2008, Sch 36* and apply to SDLT from 1 April 2010 by virtue of *FA 2009, s 96* and *Sch 46* and the *Finance Act 2009 Section 96 and Schedule 46 (Appointed Day, Savings and Consequential Amendments Order 2009 (SI 2009 No 3054)*. Because these are of general application to all taxes they are not considered here. Prior to 1 April 2010 the SDLT legislation contained information powers limited to SDLT. HMRC could by notice require a person to deliver to them within a specified period of at least 30 days such documents as were in his possession or power, and to provide them with such information as in the officer's reasonable opinion might contain information relevant to any tax liability of that person. The person had first be given a reasonable opportunity to produce the information voluntarily (*FA 2003, Sch 13, paras 1, 3*). If HMRC decided to issue a formal notice they needed the prior consent of the First-tier Tribunal (*FA 2003, Sch 13, para 2*). HMRC had to give the taxpayer a written summary of their reasons for applying for consent – and the Tribunal had to be satisfied that they had reasonable grounds for believing that the information in question would assist the collection of tax (*FA 2003, Sch 3, para 4*). HMRC could take copies of, or extracts from, the documents delivered under such a notice (*FA 2003, Sch 13, para 5*).

19.417 With the consent of the First-tier Tribunal HMRC could also by notice require a person to deliver to them (or, if the person preferred, make available for inspection by them) such documents as in their reasonable opinion might be relevant to the tax liability of some other person (including a deceased taxpayer or a company that no longer existed). Such a notice had to specify the documents to which it related, the period allowed for complying with it (which had to be at least 30 days) and, unless the Tribunal decided otherwise, the name of the taxpayer to whom it related (*FA 2003, Sch 13, paras 8, 11*). HMRC had no power to seek information (as opposed to documents) from a third party. A copy of a third party notice and a summary of the reasons for applying for consent to issue it normally had to be given to the taxpayer (*FA 2003, Sch 13, paras 9, 10*).

19.418 If a 'tax accountant' (which does not appear to be defined but is probably intended to have the same meaning as in *TMA 1970, s 20D(2)*) is convicted in the UK of an offence in relation to tax, or has a penalty imposed on him under *s 96* (see **19.427**), HMRC can, with the consent of a circuit judge, require him to deliver to them such documents as are in his possession and power as they reasonably believe contain information relevant to a tax liability of any client of his (*FA 2003, Sch 13, paras 14–16*). This provision still applies.

19.419 None of these powers extend to:

(*a*) personal records or journalistic material;

(*b*) information in relation to a pending appeal;

(*c*) information held by a barrister, advocate or solicitor, unless the Board of HMRC itself issues the notice;

(*d*) requiring the delivery of original documents, copies are sufficient – but HMRC can insist on inspecting the original;

(*e*) documents which originate more than six years before the date of the notice (but the First-tier tribunal can override this restriction);

(*f*) documents held by a barrister, advocate or solicitor which they believe are subject to legal privilege; and

(*g*) documents created by an auditor or tax adviser (acting as such) that are his property and were created by him (and in the case of a tax adviser are communications for the purpose of giving tax advice) – but HMRC are entitled to any part of such documents which explain information already delivered to HMRC.

(*FA 2003, Sch 13, paras 19–27.*)

19.420 Up to 1 April 2010, the Board of HMRC had power to require the production of information relating to the taxpayer himself without obtaining the consent of the First-tier Tribunal if they believed that the failure to make a return was likely to lead to serious prejudice to the proper collection of tax (*FA 2003, Sch 13, paras 28–31*).

19.421 A circuit judge can require documents to be produced to HMRC within ten working days (or such shorter period as he may specify) if he is satisfied that a serious fraud in relation to SDLT has been, or is about to be, committed. The taxpayer is normally entitled to notice of an application for such an order and to appear before the judge to oppose it (*FA 2003, Sch 13, paras 32–34*). Failure to comply with such an order is a contempt of court (*FA 2003, Sch 13, para 40*). The procedural rules regarding such an application are contained in *regs 33–38* of the *SDLT (Administration) Regulations 2003 (SI 2003 No 2837)*.

19.422 A circuit judge can issue a search warrant if he is satisfied that there are reasonable grounds for suspecting that an offence involving serious fraud in relation to tax has been, or is about to be, committed and evidence of such fraud can be found on the premises in question (*FA 2003, Sch 13, para 43*). A search warrant cannot be issued in relation to premises occupied for the purposes of the Crown (*FA 2003, s 107(2)*).

19.423 It is a criminal offence to intentionally falsify, conceal, destroy or otherwise dispose of a document for which one of the above orders has been made (or the person has been given an opportunity to deliver to avoid the making of such an order) (*FA 2003, Sch 13, para 53*). Failure to comply with an order renders the person liable to a penalty of up to £200 plus £60 a day if the failure continues after the day on which the penalty is imposed. The penalty for fraudulently or negligently delivering an incorrect document or information is up to £3,000 (*FA 2003, s 93*).

19.424 Up to 1 April 2010 HMRC were empowered to inspect any property for the purpose of ascertaining its market value or any other matter relevant to SDLT. The penalty for wilfully delaying or obstructing an official from doing so was a fine of up to level 1 (£200) (*FA 2003, s 94*). The new standard information powers contain a right to inspect premises, so this provision no longer applies.

19.425 HMRC have power to disclose information to listing officers to facilitate the completion and maintenance of council tax valuation lists, to a valuation tribunal as evidence in an appeal and to such other persons as the Treasury may by regulation prescribe (*FA 1983, s 78A).* From 21 August 2009 such information can also be disclosed to the corresponding people in Northern Ireland and NI Department for Finance (the *SDLT (Use of Information Contained in Land Transaction Returns) Regulations 2009, SI 2009 No 2095*).

Penalties, etc

19.426 A person who is knowingly concerned in the fraudulent evasion of SDLT (by himself or any other person) is liable to six months imprisonment or a fine of up to the statutory maximum (£5,000) or both on summary conviction or imprisonment for up to seven years (or a fine, or both) on conviction on indictment (*FA 2003, s 95*).

19.427 A person who assists in, or induces the preparation or delivery of, any information, return or other document that he knows is likely to be used for any SDLT purpose and he knows to be incorrect is liable to a fine of up to £3,000 (*FA 2003, s 96*).

19.428 For SDLT purposes a person is deemed not to have failed to do anything required to be done within a limited time if he did it within such further time, if any, as HMRC may allow. If a person has a reasonable excuse for not doing something he is deemed not to have failed to do it unless the excuse ceased and he did not do it without unreasonable delay thereafter (*FA 2003, s 97*). In

Runham v HMRC (TC 933) the taxpayer was held to have a reasonable excuse by relying on her solicitor to submit the return within the time limit.

19.429 Statements made or documents produced to HMRC are not inadmissible in proceedings merely because it had been drawn to the attention of the person making it that where serious fraud had been committed the Board may accept a monetary settlement and not pursue a criminal prosecution if he makes a full confession of all SDLT irregularities (*FA 2003, s 98*).

19.430 Penalties for incorrect returns and documents have also been aligned across the taxes, mainly from 1 April 2009, by *FA 2008, s 122* and *Sch 40* and the *FA 2009, Sch 40 (Appointed Day, Savings and Consequential Amendments) Order 2009 (SI 2009 No 571).* These general rules are not considered here. Prior to that SDLT had its own rules. HMRC could impose penalties without recourse to the First-tier Tribunal. Notice of the penalty had to be given to the person liable, who had the normal right of appeal to the First-tier Tribunal against the determination (*FA 2003, Sch 14, para 1(4)*). There is a right of appeal to the High Court against a penalty determined by the Tribunal (*FA 2003, Sch 14, para 6*). Where HMRC believe that the liability to a penalty arises by reasons of fraud they can bring penalty proceedings in the High Court (*FA 2003, Sch 14, para 7*). HMRC had power to mitigate a penalty or stay or compound any proceedings for the recovery of a penalty, and could mitigate or remit a penalty even after judgment had been given (*FA 2003, s 99*). However, the acceptance of a penalty did not affect any criminal proceedings for an offence (*FA 2003, s 99(3)*). If a person was liable to more than one tax-related penalty in relation to the same transaction, the total liability was limited to the largest of those penalties (*FA 2003, s 99(2A)*). In *Ryan v HMRC ([2012] UKUT 9 (TCC))* the Upper Tribunal (Judge Bishopp) held that a taxpayer should be entitled to expect his solicitor not merely to advise him of his obligations to submit a return but to perform the obligation for him. Nevertheless it held that the solicitor's failure to do so did not give the taxpayer a reasonable excuse for not having submitted the return.

No Deduction for other Tax Purposes

19.431 Interest and penalties in relation to SDLT are not allowable as a deduction for income tax, corporation tax or any other tax purpose (*CTA 2009, s 1313*).

Disclosure of SDLT Avoidance Schemes

19. 432 It should be mentioned that there is an obligation on both promoters and users of tax avoidance schemes that satisfy such criteria to notify HMRC of details of the scheme – normally before the time at which it is first used (*FA 2004, ss 306–319* and the *Stamp Duty Land Tax Avoidance Schemes (Prescribed Description of Arrangements) Regulations 2005 (SI 2005 No 1868)*). From 1 April 2010 this applies to arrangements whose subject matter is either–

(*a*) wholly non-residential property in respect of which the aggregate value is at least £5 million;

(*b*) wholly residential property in respect of which the aggregate value is at least £1 million;

(*c*) a mixture of residential and non-residential property where either the value of the residential property is at least £1 million or the overall value is at least £5 million.

(*Reg 2* as amended by the *SDLT Avoidance Schemes (Prescribed Description of Arrangements) (Amendment) Regulations 2010 (SI 2010 No 407)*.)

There are a number of exceptions. There are also heavy penalties for non-compliance with this obligation. HMRC have power to extend the disclosure requirements to other proposals or arrangements that might be expected to enable a person to obtain an advantage in relation to SDLT (*FA 2012, s 215*). They have prescribed 'arrangements which involve the acquisition of chargeable interests', ie everything, but then excluded arrangements falling within most SDLT reliefs and arrangements first marketed before 1 April 2010. (*SDLT (Tax Avoidance Schemes Prescribed Description of Arrangements) (Amendment) Regulations 2012 (SI 2012 No 2395)*). This broad approach replaced (*a*) to (*c*) above from 1 November 2012. The detailed rules are outside the scope of this book. They are set out in *Anti-Avoidance Provisions* (Bloomsbury Professional).

Miscellaneous

19.433 Where a land transaction gives effect to a partition or division of a chargeable interest to which persons are jointly entitled, the share of the interest held by the purchaser immediately before the partition or division does not count as chargeable consideration (*FA 2003, Sch 4, para 6*).

19.434 If a land transaction is entered into by reason of the purchaser's employment (or that of a person connected with him within *CTA 2010, s 1122*) and that transaction gives rise to an income tax charge under *ITEPA 2003, s 102* (taxable benefit: living accommodation) and no rent is payable by the purchaser or the rent is less than the cash equivalent of the benefit under *ITEPA 2003, ss 105* or *106*, SDLT on the lease must be calculated as if rent equal to that cash equivalent were payable (*FA 2003, Sch 4, para 12(1)(a)*). If the transaction does not give rise to an income tax charge because it is exempt under *ITEPA 2003, s 99* (beneficial occupation, etc.) the consideration for the transaction is the actual consideration (if any), ie no SDLT is payable if the accommodation is provided rent free and the SDLT is based on the actual rent if it is let to the employee at a preferential rate (*FA 2003, Sch 4, para 12(1)(b)*). In any other circumstance the consideration for the transaction is the higher of the actual consideration and the market value of the accommodation at the effective date of the transaction (*FA 2003, Sch 4, para 12(1)(c)*).

19.435 None of the following counts as chargeable consideration for the grant of a lease:

(*a*) any undertaking by the tenant to repair, maintain or insure the property;

(*b*) any undertaking by the tenant to pay a service charge in respect of services, repairs, maintenance, insurance or the landlord's costs of management;

(*c*) any other obligation undertaken by the tenant that is not such as to affect the open market rent of the property;

(*d*) any guarantee of the payment of rent or the performance of any other obligation of the tenant under the lease;

(*e*) any final or increased rent payable in respect of the breach of any obligation of the tenant under the lease;

(*f*) a payment made in discharge of any of the above obligations; or

(*g*) the assumption or release of any of the above obligations.

(*FA 2003, Sch 4, para 13*.)

19.436 If a lease is granted in consideration of the surrender of an existing lease of the same (or substantially the same) premises of which the unexpired term is substantially the same as the term of the new lease, and the terms are the same or substantially the same, the grant of the new lease is not chargeable consideration for the surrender and the surrender is not chargeable consideration for the grant of the new lease (*FA 2003, Sch 4, para 14*). The government intend to clarify this further. The surrender of any lease will not be consideration for the grant of another and the grant will not be consideration for the surrender. When a new lease is granted SDLT will be payable on the premium and rent due, not on the value of any interest surrendered. If a lease at a fixed rent is surrendered to the landlord credit will be given in calculating the SDLT on the new lease for the amount of rent that was due under the old for the surrendered years (Technical Note 20.10.2003, para 24).

19.437 A reverse premium is not chargeable consideration for the grant, assignment or surrender of a lease. A reverse premium for this purpose means:

(*a*) a payment paid by the landlord to the tenant for the grant of a lease;

(*b*) a payment by the assignor to the assignee for the assignment of a lease; or

(*c*) a payment from the tenant to the landlord to accept a surrender of a lease.

(*FA 2003, Sch 4, para 15.*)

19.438 If the purchaser agrees to indemnify the vendor in respect of liability to a third party arising from the breach of an obligation by the vendor in relation to the land that is the subject of the transaction, neither the agreement nor any payment made in pursuance of it constitutes chargeable consideration (*FA 2003, Sch 4, para 16*).

19.439 There is no relief for SDLT on the incorporation of a business. There used to be a relief on the initial transfer of assets to a unit trust but this was abolished in 2006. The basic rules operate capriciously. If a partnership is incorporated and the partners receive shareholdings in the company in proportion to their holdings in the partnership, there is no SDLT irrespective of whether the partnership business is acquired by the company for shares or for cash. This is because the company will be a connected person of each of the former partners and the 'sum of the lower parts' will be 100, so that the formula becomes:

$$\text{market value} \times (100 - 100) = \text{nil}$$

However, where a sole trader is incorporated, there will be a disposal by the individual to the company which will attract SDLT on the market value of the property (see **19.144**). In theory a sole trader could bring in a partner before incorporating but such a device is likely to fall foul of s *75A*.

General Regulation-Making Power

19.440 In addition to specific regulation-making powers the Treasury have a general power, if they think it expedient in the public interest, to vary by Regulation the SDLT legislation in its application to land transaction of any description. In particular they can alter the description of land transactions that are chargeable or notifiable, the descriptions of land transactions in respect of which tax is chargeable at any existing rate of amount or in respect of which tax is calculated under any particular provision, and the conditions for the application of the 15% tax rate (other than that the transaction must be a high-value residential transaction). The only limitation is that they cannot vary the thresholds, rate or amounts specified in *s 55* (amount of tax chargeable) or *Sch 5* (amount of tax chargeable in relation to rent) (*FA 2003, s 109(1)–(3)* as amended by *FA 2012, Sch 35, para 6 and Stamp Duty Land Tax Act 2015, Sch 1, para 11*).

19.441 Such Regulations must be laid before the House of Commons after being made and lapse if they are not approved by the House within 28 days after they are made (ignoring any period in which parliament is prorogued or dissolved or is adjourned for more than four days) (*FA 2003, ss 109(4), 110*). Such Regulations will in any event lapse after 18 months or such shorter period as they may specify (*FA 2003, s 109(5)*). This effectively requires parliament to re-enact the Regulations in the next Finance Act if it is intended to be permanent. If such Regulations lapse because they are not approved by parliament a taxpayer who has paid tax under them is entitled to claim repayment of such tax (and any interest or penalties paid), with interest. Such a claim must be made within two years of the effective date of the transaction (*FA 2003, s 111*). The fact that such non-approved regulations automatically lapse is without prejudice to anything done in reliance on them (*FA 2003, s 110(5)*).

19.442 HMRC have a separate power to amend *Sch 5* and *s 55(2)* so far as it relates to the thresholds at which different rates of tax become payable but only before the implementation date – which is intended to be 1 December 2003 (*FA 2003, s 112*). HMRC are still discussing with interested parties the best way to deal with leases. The purpose of this power is to allow the rules to be amended before the legislation comes into force if a better solution than that in the Act can be reached. The Treasury have power under *FA 2003, s 123(2)* to make consequential amendments to other legislation. They have done so by the *SDLT (Consequential Amendment of Enactments) Regulations 2003 (SI 2003 No 2867)*. This reflects specific exemptions and reliefs from stamp duty under various non-tax Acts. They have also made further amendments by the *Stamp Duty and SDLT (Consequential Amendment of Enactments) Regulations 2003 (SI 2003 No 2868)* in relation to the imposition of SDLT and the abolition of stamp duty and by the *SDLT (Consequential Amendment of Enactments) Regulations 2005 (SI 2005 No 82)* in relation to NHS trusts and Northern Ireland.

19.443 HMRC also have a general power under *FA 1999, ss 132* and *133* to make subordinate legislation in relation to the delivery of information and making payments. They have used this for SDLT purposes in the *SDLT (Electronic Communications) Regulations 2005 (SI 2005 No 844)* as amended in relation to Scotland by the *SDLT (Electronic Communications) (Amendment) Regulations 2006 (SI 2006 No 3427)*.

Land in Scotland

19.444 The Scottish Parliament introduced its new Land and Buildings Transactions Tax (LBTT) from 1 April 2015. From that date, SDLT ceased to apply to land in Scotland. LBTT returns need to be made to Revenue Scotland, the new Scottish tax authority, not to HMRC. ATED will continue to apply to Scottish residential property and will continue to be payable to HMRC as ATED has not been devolved to the Scottish Parliament. The LBTT rules are similar, but not identical, to those of SDLT. In particular LBTT does not contain a sub-sale relief. Unlike with SDLT which uses a slab system, ie the size of the transaction determines which single rate applies, LBTT uses a progressive system, ie the rate on the first slice of the consideration is less than that on the next slice, and so on. Whilst LBTT is based on SDLT, the detailed rules are not identical. A detailed consideration of those rules is outside the scope of this work. It does, however, need to be borne in mind that the rules in relation to Scottish land differ from those in the rest of the UK.

19.445 The rates of LBTT for 2015/16 to 2017/18 are as follows:

Residential property

	£	%
First	145,000	Nil
Next	105,000	2
Next	75,000	5
Next	425,000	10
Excess over	750,000	12

As with SDLT, a 3% Additional Dwellings Supplement applies on the purchase of second homes and rentqal properties from 1 April 2016.

Non-residential property

	£	%
First	150,000	Nil
Next	100,000	3
Excess over	250,000	4.5

The rates on the capitlised amount of rent payable under leases is the same as for SDLT, but residential leases are exempt from LBTT.

19.446 As they are separate taxes, if a portfolio of properties is purchased some of which are in England and some in Scotland, the Scottish properties will be ignored in determining the rate of SDLT on the English properties.

Land in Wales

19.447 The Welsh Assembly takes on responsibility for taxing transfers of land from 1 April 2018. Up to that date the above SDLT rules apply. Transfers after 31 March 2018 will attract the new Welsh Land Transactions Tax (LTT). This is based on SDLT, but is not identical, albeit the rules are closer to those of SDLT than those governing Scottish LBTT.

19.448 The rates for LTT for 2018/19 have already been announced as follows:

Residential property	*First residence*	*Subsequent residences*
	£	%
First £150,000	nil	nil
Next £100,000 (to £250,000)	2.5	5.5
Next £150,000 (to £400,000)	5	8
Next £350,000 (to £750,000)	7.5	10.5
Next £750,000 (to £1.5 million)	10	13
Excess over £1.5 million	12	15

As with SDLT, an additional three percentage points will be charged where a person buys a second residence.

Non-residential property	
	%
First £150,000	nil
Next £100,000 (to £250,000)	1
Next £750,000 (to £1 million)	5
Excess over £1 million	6

The rates on the capitalised value of rents under leases will be nil up to £150,000, 1% on the next £1.85 million and 2% on the excess over £2 million.

Chapter 20

Annual Tax on Enveloped Dwellings

Introduction

20.1 The annual tax on enveloped dwellings (ATED) was brought in by the *Finance Act 2013* with effect from 1 April 2013. It is an unusual tax insofar as it contains so many exemptions that it rarely applies. At the time that it was introduced, the government estimated that there were only around 5,300 enveloped properties and only about 1,000 of these were expected to pay the tax, the rest being covered by exemptions (Hansard Public Bill Committee, 13.6.2013, cols 494, 501).

20.2 The reason for this is that, although it is a completely separate tax which has its own system of administration and involves 82 pages of primary legislation, the entire tax was conceived as an SDLT anti-avoidance provision.

20.3 The tax is imposed on companies that own residential property valued at more than £500,000 and which, broadly speaking, are occupied by a person who is connected with the owner. The tax initially applied only to properties worth over £2 million. From 1 April 2015 it was extended to properties worth more than £1 million and from 1 April 2016 to those worth more than £500,000. 1 April 2015 and 1 April 2016 are not valuation dates (see **20.21**). Accordingly, the £1 million and £500,000 figures relate to the value at 1 April 2012. A property worth more than the £1 million figure at 1 April 2015, but below it at 1 April 2012, does not come into ATED until 1 April 2018 when the 2017 revaluation figures come into effect. The government were concerned that such properties were being bought through companies to avoid the then 5% SDLT charge (since increased to 7%) on the purchase of the property. By buying through a company, SDLT would have to be paid only once, as on future sales the shares could be sold instead of the property (assuming that a purchaser would be prepared to take on the risk of unknown liabilities to save 5%), attracting stamp duty of 0.5% on the shares (or nil in the case of an overseas company in a country which does not itself impose a transfer tax). In practice, it was hard to find an SDLT practitioner who had come across a client willing to adopt such a strategy. Accordingly, the tax is in the nature of a sledgehammer to crack a non-existent nut!

20.4 Ironically the tax has had a significant effect on a different class of people, namely overseas residents and short-term UK residents who have traditionally bought their UK house through an overseas company to keep it outside the scope of UK inheritance tax in the event of their death. It might accordingly create a disincentive to wealthy overseas entrepreneurs from setting up businesses in the UK.

20.5 ATED is part of a three-pronged attack on the purchase of expensive properties through companies. The other two prongs are a 15% rate of SDLT on the purchase of a property costing more than £2 million through a company (see **19.10**) and the introduction of a 28% CGT charge on the disposal of such a property by a company (whether it is UK or non-UK resident) (see **11.37**). It seems likely that the cumulative effect of these three imposts is intended to deter people from acquiring expensive properties through companies, rather than to raise a significant amount of tax.

20.6 ATED is chargeable in respect of a 'chargeable interest' (see **20.7**) if on one or more days in a fiscal year (the year to 31 March) the interest is a 'single-dwelling interest' (see **20.8**) with a taxable value of over £500,000 and a company, partnership or collective investment scheme (such as a unit trust) is entitled to the interest (*FA 2013, s 94(1)–(6), (8)*). A partnership is within the scope of ATED only if it has a corporate partner (*FA 2013, s 94(5)*). Where an interest is jointly owned, the company (or partnership or collective investment scheme) is regarded for this purpose as entitled to the entire interest (even if the joint ownership is a tenancy in common) (*FA 2013, s 94(7)*). 'Entitled' means beneficially entitled, whether solely or jointly with another person, and whether as a member of a partnership or otherwise (*FA 2013, s 95(1)*). It does not include entitlement as trustee or personal representative or entitlement as a beneficiary under a settlement (as defined in *FA 2003, Sch 16, para 1*, ie for SDLT purposes, namely a trust that is not a bare trust (see **19.329**)) (*FA 2013, s 95(2)*).

20.7 A chargeable interest is any estate, interest, right or power in or over land in the UK, or the benefit of an obligation, restriction or condition affecting the value of any such estate, interest, right or power (*FA 2013, s 107(1)*). Where two or more persons are jointly entitled to a chargeable interest, the chargeable interest cannot be treated as consisting of separate interests corresponding to the shares that those persons have by virtue of their joint entitlement; the entire interest is the chargeable interest (*FA 2013, s 107(2)*). There are a few exemptions, namely:

(*a*) a security interest, ie an interest or right (other than a rent-charge) held for the purpose of securing the payment of money or the performance of any other obligation;

(*b*) a licence to use or occupy land;

(*c*) a tenancy at will; and

(*d*) any other description of interest or right in or over a dwelling that the Treasury may by Regulation provide.

(*FA 2013, s 107(3)–(7)*.)

20.8 A single-dwelling interest is a chargeable interest that is exclusively in or over land consisting of a single dwelling (see **20.14**) (*FA 2013, s 108(2)*). If a person is entitled to a chargeable interest that is exclusively in or over land consisting of two or more single dwellings, he must be treated as having a separate chargeable interest in or over each dwelling, so that each will be regarded as a single-dwelling interest (*FA 2013, s 108(3)*). If a person is entitled to a chargeable interest that consists of one or more single dwellings and non-residential land, he is treated as having a separate chargeable interest in or over the non-residential land (*FA 2013, s 108(4)*). For example, suppose a company purchases an office block for £100 million and there are two penthouse flats on top and a caretaker's flat in the basement. The company is treated as owning four separate interests, namely each of the penthouse flats, the caretaker's flat and the offices. A single-dwelling interest in one dwelling is distinct from any single-dwelling interest in another dwelling even if they stand successively on the same land (*FA 2013, s 108(6)*). For example, if a house is demolished and a new house built on the site, the two are separate single-dwelling interests. References above to a dwelling include part of a dwelling, and non-residential land means land that is not a dwelling or part of a dwelling (*FA 2013, s 108(7)*).

20.9 If a company is entitled to two or more single-dwelling interests in the same dwelling, those separate interests must be treated as one single-dwelling interest whose value is equal to the aggregate of the values of the separate interests (*FA 2013, s 109(1)(2)*). For this purpose the market value of each interest must be determined in accordance with *TCGA 1992, s 272* on the assumption that all of the interests are placed together on the open market at the same time (*FA 2013, s 109(3)*).

20.10 If on any day a company is entitled to a single-dwelling interest in a dwelling and a person connected with it (see **20.120**) is entitled to a different single-dwelling interest in the same building, the company must be treated as being entitled to the connected person's interest in addition to its own (*FA 2013, s 110(1)*). If the connected person is a company, this results in both companies being treated as entitled to the combined interests. In such a case they are both chargeable on the full value, but HMRC can collect only one lot of tax from the two of them (*FA 2013, s 104*). This also applies with the necessary modifications where either or both of the landowner and the connected person are collective investment schemes (*FA 2013, s 110(3)(4)(6)*).

20.11 There is an exception to such aggregation. If the connected person is an individual, his interest is treated as owned by the company only if the company's own interest (or the aggregate of interests treated as owned by the company apart from that of the individual) is a freehold or leasehold interest with a taxable value of over £500,000. If the value of the company's interest is below £2 million, the exemption applies only if the company's interest is under £250,000 (*FA 2013, s 110(2–(2B)* as amended by *FA 2015, s 72*). This prevents a company that simply owns a reversionary interest in a long lease, perhaps arising from the leasehold enfranchisement legislation, from being treated as also owning the occupational lease, when the reversion has a small value only.

20.12 There is also no need to aggregate such interests where the connected person is either:

(*a*) a public body or a body established for national purposes (see **20.57** and **20.58**);

(*b*) a provider of social housing which is relievable under *FA 2013, s 150* (see **20.53**);

(*c*) a charitable company where the ownership condition is treated as rent met under *FA 2013, s 151* (see **20.53**); or

(*d*) a person who has entered into an undertaking by virtue of which the dwelling is conditionally exempt from inheritance tax (and whose value is treated as zero under *FA 2013, s 155*) (see **20.59**).

(FA 2013, s 111(1)(2).)

20.13 If the separate interests that fall to be aggregated and treated as owned by the company under **20.9** or **20.10** include a freehold or leasehold interest and a leasehold interest (the inferior interest) granted out of that interest, and the inferior interest is the most inferior relevant interest (ie none of the other interests is a leasehold interest granted out of it), the combined interest and the dwelling itself are regarded for the purposes of *FA 2013, ss 132–150* (reliefs) as being exploited in the same way as the inferior interest is exploited (*FA 2013, s 111(3)(4)(6)(7)*). For example, suppose Company A owns a leasehold reversion, Company B owns a lease granted out of it and Company C holds its interest as trading stock. The interest of Company C is the most inferior interest. Accordingly although all three companies are treated as owning all three interests, they are all treated as holding them as trading stock, so that the exemption under *FA 2013, s 141* is treated as applying to all three companies. If the inferior interest is in part only of the land, this deeming obviously applies only to the extent of that part (*FA 2013, s 111(5)*). Reference in *s 111* to a leasehold interest includes the interest of a lessee under an agreement for lease (*FA 2013, s 111(8)*).

20.14 A dwelling is defined as a building or part of a building which is either used, or suitable for use, as a single dwelling, or is in the process of being constructed or adapted for such use (*FA 2013, s 112(1)*). Land that is (or is at any time intended to be) occupied or enjoyed with a dwelling as its garden or grounds (including any building or structure on such land) is regarded as part of that dwelling (*FA 2013, s 112(2)*). Land that subsists (or is at any time intended to subsist) for the benefit of a dwelling must also be taken to be part of the dwelling (*FA 2013, s 112(3)*). This might, for example, bring in as part of the dwelling the value of a nearby garage that is used by the occupant of the dwelling if the two are in the same ownership. A building that is used as a dwelling under *FA 2013, s 116(2)* (see **20.18**) is not used (or suitable for use) as a dwelling for the purpose of *s 112(1)* (*FA 2013, s 112(4)(5)*), ie it is not treated as a separate dwelling. If a building or part of a building becomes temporarily unsuitable for use as a dwelling for any reason (including accidental damage, repairs or any other physical change to the building or its environment) that temporary unsuitability must be ignored in determining whether it is a dwelling during the period in question (*FA 2013, s 112(6)*).

20.15 If a contract or agreement is entered into for the acquisition of a chargeable interest in or over land that consists of or includes a building (or part of a building) that is to be constructed or adapted for use as a single dwelling (eg it is bought 'off plan'), substantial performance is treated as constituting the acquisition of the chargeable interest (under *FA 2013, s 122* – see **20.29**), and construction or adaptation of the building (or part) has not begun by the time that the contract is substantially performed, the chargeable interest acquired is deemed to be an interest in a dwelling (*FA 2013, s 113(1)(2)(5)*). If at any time after the substantial performance of the contract the obligation to carry out the construction or adaptation ceases to have effect without the work having been begun, the interest will cease to be an interest in a dwelling at that time (*FA 2013, s 113(3)*). Substantially performed has the same meaning as for SDLT (see **19.89**).

20.16 The Treasury have power by statutory instrument to specify cases where use of a building is to be treated as use as a dwelling (*FA 2013, s 114*).

20.17 The fact that part of a building is suitable for use as a dwelling does not prevent that part forming part of a larger single dwelling. Similarly, the fact that a building or structure in the garden or grounds of a dwelling and occupied with that dwelling may itself be suitable for use as a single dwelling does not prevent it being treated as part of the main dwelling (*FA 2013, s 115*).

20.18 If a company is entitled to a chargeable interest in a dwelling (the main dwelling) and it or a connected person is entitled to a chargeable interest in an 'associated dwelling' the two together must be treated as suitable for use as a single dwelling (*FA 2013, s 116(3)(4)*). A dwelling is an associated dwelling if it stands within the garden or grounds of the main dwelling, it does not have separate access and is not part of the same building as the main dwelling, and it is not occupied or enjoyed with the main dwelling (*FA 2013, s 116(1)(2)*). This aggregation does not apply if either of the interests is covered by one of the reliefs (see **20.35**) or falls within *FA 2013, s 151* (charitable companies) (*FA 2013, s 116(5)(6)*). A public body or body established for national purposes (see **20.57** and **20.58**) is regarded as not being a connected person for this purpose (*FA 2013, s 116(7)*). For the purpose of *s 116*, an associated dwelling has separate access only if either there is access to it directly from a highway (in Scotland, a road) that the main dwelling adjoins, or the person entitled to possession of the associated dwelling has access to it from a highway exclusively by passing over land that he is entitled to pass over by reason of one or more rights of way (or other interests in land) to which he is separately entitled (*FA 2013, s 116(9)*). Garden or grounds means land occupied or enjoyed with the dwelling as its garden or grounds. A person entitled to possession of a dwelling means a person so entitled by reason of an estate or interest held by that person and separately entitled means entitled otherwise than by reason of a chargeable interest in or over the main dwelling (*FA 2013, s 116(10)*).

20.19 If two parts of a building constitute 'linked dwellings' the two parts must together be treated as suitable for use as a single dwelling (*FA 2013, s 117(3)*). Two parts of a building are linked dwellings if each of them counts as a dwelling, there is private access between the two, the two are not together used (or suitable for use) as a single dwelling, a company is entitled to a chargeable interest in one of the dwellings and it or a person connected with it is entitled to a chargeable interest in the other, and each of the two dwellings is occupied (or usually occupied) by a 'relevant individual' (see below), or is intended to be so occupied or is not occupied (*FA 2013, ss 117(1)(2), 118(4)*). A relevant individual is an individual who is connected with the company, or who occupies (or will occupy) the dwelling concerned otherwise than on commercial terms, or an individual who is employed wholly or partly in connection with the occupation by such a person of a dwelling in the building (or provides services in connection with such a person's occupation of a dwelling in the building) (*FA 2013, s 118(5)*). If two dwellings in a building are linked and one of them is linked with a third dwelling, all three must be treated as suitable for use as a single dwelling (and so on) (*FA 2013, s 117(7)*). The exceptions in *s 116* where a relief applies, and where the connected person is a public body or body established for national purposes also apply for this provision (*FA 2013, s 117(4)–(6)*). For the above purpose there is private access between two dwellings if the person entitled to possession of each dwelling (by reason of an estate or interest held by that person) is entitled, by reason of a right of way or other interest in land, to have access to his dwelling from the other dwelling, without passing over any part of a building (or any other land) in which a third party has an interest entitling that third party to enter it (*FA 2013, s 118(2)(6)*). A third party for this purpose is any person other than the person entitled to possession of the dwellings concerned (by reason of an estate or interest held by that person) and persons connected with any of them (*FA 2013, s 118(3)*). Any structure (such as a terrace of houses or a pair of semi-detached houses) that is composed of (or includes) dwellings is a building for the purposes of *ss 117, 118* (*FA 2013, s 119*).

Amount of Tax

20.20 The tax is a fixed annual amount based on the value of the single-dwelling interest:

Taxable value of interest		*Annual tax*	
	2015/16	2017/18	2018/19
£	£	£	£
500,000 to 1,000,000	3,500	3,500	3,600
1,000,001 to 2,000,000	7,000	7,050	7,250
2,000,001 to 5,000,000	23,250	23,550	24,250
5,000,001 to 10,000,000	54,450	54,950	56,550
10,000,001 to 20,000,000	109,950	110,100	113,400
over £20 million	218,200	220,350	226,950

*Prior to 1 April 2016 the starting point was £1 million so the £3,500 rate did not apply for 2015/16 (*FA 2014, ss 109, 110*).

Where the interest is not held throughout the tax year (year to 31 March) the amount is pro-rated by reference to the number of days for which the interest is owned (*FA 2013, s 99* and the *ATED (Indexation of Annual Chargeable Amounts) Order 2014 (SI 2014 No 854)*. The above amounts will be increased (but not reduced) by reference to the increase in the consumer prices index. The Treasury must make an order before the start of the tax year setting out the rates for the following year (*FA 2013, s 101*). However, for 2015/16, the government decided to increase the rates by 50% plus inflation (*FA 2015, s 70*).

20.21 The taxable value of a single dwelling interest on any day is its market value at the end of the last valuation date falling prior to that day (*FA 2013, s 102(1)*). The valuation dates are:

1 April 2012

1 April 2017

1 April 2022

and so on for each further multiple of five years

(*FA 2013, s 102(2)*.)

In addition, if the company (or partnership or collective investment scheme) makes a substantial acquisition of a chargeable interest in the dwelling concerned or a substantial disposal (see **20.20**) of part of its interest (but not a disposal of its entire interest) the effective date of that acquisition or disposal is also a valuation date (*FA 2013, s 102(3)–(5)*). The effective date of an acquisition or disposal is the completion date (or such other date as HMRC by regulation may prescribe) (*FA 2013, s 121(4)(5)*). For this purpose the grant of a chargeable interest (such as a lease) out of the single-dwelling interest is treated as a disposal but the grant of an option is not (*FA 2013, s 102(6)(7)*). From 26 March 2015, a day that is a valuation date only because of the five-yearly revaluation is treated as if it were not a valuation date for the year beginning with that date (*FA 2013, s 102(2A)* inserted by *FA 2015, s 71*). This corrects an anomaly which required the new valuation to be notified to HMRC within 30 days of the valuation date, whereas the intention was that it should be notified a year later when the tax based on the value first becomes due.

20.22 For the above purpose the acquisition of a chargeable interest in a dwelling is a substantial acquisition only if the 'chargeable consideration' for the acquisition is £40,000 or more, and the disposal of part (but not the whole) of a single-dwelling interest (or the grant of a chargeable interest out of such an interest) is a substantial disposal only if the chargeable consideration for the acquisition by the person acquiring it is £40,000 or more (*FA 2013, s 103(1)(9)*). Chargeable consideration is as defined for SDLT (*FA 2013, s 103(9)*). It is broadly any consideration in money or money's worth given (directly or indirectly) for the subject matter of the transaction by the purchaser or by a person connected with him (see **19.12**) but there are a number of circumstances in which this definition is modified. The chargeable consideration for the acquisition includes the chargeable consideration for any linked acquisition of a chargeable interest in the same dwelling, and that for the disposal includes the chargeable consideration for any linked disposal or part (but not the whole) of the single-dwelling interest concerned (*FA 2013, s 103(4)(7)*). Transactions are linked for this purpose if they form part of a single scheme, arrangement or series of transactions between the same vendor and purchaser or (in either case) persons connected with them (*FA 2013, s 103(8)*).

20.23 The tax must be paid on or before the filing date for the return (*FA 2013, s 163(1)*). This is 30 April in the tax year, ie the tax is payable largely in advance (*FA 2013, s 159(1)*). For 2013/14 only, the return had to be delivered by 1 October 2013 (or, if later, 30 days after the company first came into charge to ATED) and the tax had to be paid by 31 October 2013 (or if later, the filing date for the return) (*FA 2013, Sch 35, paras 4, 5*). Similarly, the 2015/16 return on properties valued at between £1million and £2 million had to be made by 1 October 2015 if the charge applied from 1 April 2015, and from the later of that date and 30 days after the property was brought within ATED if it occurred after that date, and the tax paid by 31 October 2015 (or if later, by the filing date for the return) (*FA 2014, s 109(5)–(7)*). There was no similar transitional rule on the reduction to £500,000 because taxpayers had two years warning of the charge. Any additional tax payable on an amendment to a return is payable at the time of the amendment (*FA 2013, s 163(3)*). Where the tax charge increases during the fiscal year (eg because the acquisition of an additional interest in the dwelling triggers a valuation date – see **20.21**) the additional tax is payable on the filing date of return of adjusted chargeable amount (see **20.64**) (*FA 2013, s 163(2)*). If the tax is assessed or determined by HMRC it must be paid within 30 days of the issue of the assessment or determination (*FA 2013, s 163(5)*).

20.24 The person liable for the tax is the company (or the responsible partners or the trustees (in the case of a unit trust, an OEIC, UCITS, or other entity) or the managers of the collective investment scheme (*FA 2013, s 96(1)–(3)*). In the case of a partnership, the responsible partners are everyone who is a member of the partnership on the first day in the tax year on which the partnership is entitled to the interest in the dwelling (*FA 2013, s 96(5)*). They are jointly and severally liable for the tax (*FA 2013, s 96(4)*). In the case of joint ownerships, the company and the other joint owners are jointly and severally liable for the tax (*FA 2013, s 97(1)(2)*). If the dwelling is jointly owned by a partnership and another person, that person and the responsible partners are all jointly and severally liable for the tax (*FA 2013, s 97(3)(4)*). In the case of a collective investment scheme, any person who is a major participant in the scheme on the first day in the fiscal year in which the chargeable interest is held is jointly and severally liable with the trustees or manager (as the case may be) (*FA 2013, s 98(1)(2)*). The liability of a major participant is, however, limited to the market value of his holding in the scheme (*FA 2013, s 98(3)*). A person is a major participant if he is entitled to at least 50% of all of the profits or income of the scheme, or of any profits or income that can be distributed to participants, or of the assets available for distribution to participants in a winding up (*FA 2013, s 136(5)*). The tax can also be recovered from the depositary (if any) of a collective investment scheme, but only up to the amount or value of any money or other property subject to the scheme that has been entrusted to the depositary for safekeeping (*FA 2013, s 98(5)*).

20.25 If the 'adjusted chargeable amount' for a chargeable period is less than the initial charged amount (the amount charged under *s 99* – see **20.20**) a claim can be made to reduce the tax to the adjusted chargeable amount (*FA 2013, s 106(3)(4)*). The claim must be made by 31 March following the end of the fiscal year to which it relates, ie within 12 months, and can be claimed only on an ATED return or by amending an ATED return (*FA 2013, s 106(5)(6)*). The adjusted chargeable amount is the total of the daily amount for all the days in the fiscal year on which the chargeable person is within the charge to tax with respect to the interest. The daily amount is the annual chargeable amount for the interest divided by the number of days in the fiscal year (*FA 2013, s 105*). In other words if the chargeable person is not liable for tax for the whole year (eg he sells the dwelling during the year) he can claim to be taxable only on a proportionate part of the annual charge by reference to the part of the year in which it held the interest. However, the excess must be reclaimed within the tight one-year time limit.

20.26 Relief (interim relief) can alternatively be claimed in the fiscal year itself if:

(*a*) a relief (see **20.35**) applies with respect to the interest on one or more days in the fiscal year;

(*b*) the person is not within the charge to ATED in respect of the interest for one or more days in the fiscal year (after the first day in that year on which he comes within the charge); or

(*c*) the taxable value of the chargeable interest decreases,

(*FA 2013, s 100(1)*.)

The relief must be claimed in an ATED return or by amending an ATED return (*FA 2013, s 100(2)*). Where interim relief is claimed, the tax payable becomes the sum of all of the daily amounts (see **20.25**) up to the day before the day of the claim, plus the sum of all of the revised daily amounts from the date of the claim to the end of the fiscal year (or nil if the claim is for a relief or is that the chargeable person has ceased to be within the scope of ATED) (*FA 2013, s 100(3)–(8)*). This is an odd procedure. An interim claim can reduce the tax only from the date of the claim, not from the earlier date of the event that gave rise to the claim.

Acquisitions and Disposals of Chargeable Interests

20.27 A person who acquires a chargeable interest in or over land that consists of or includes a dwelling is treated as acquiring it on the effective date of the acquisition and therefore as entitled to it with effect from that date (*FA 2013, s 121(1)*). Similarly, a person who disposes of such a chargeable interest is treated as ceasing to be entitled to it on the effective date of the disposal and therefore as not being entitled to it on that day – because in determining whether or not a state of affairs obtains on a particular day it must be assumed that the state of affairs obtaining at the end of the day persisted throughout that day – *FA 2013, s 173* (*FA 2013, s 121(2)*). The effective date of an acquisition or disposal is the date on which it is completed (or any alternative date that HMRC may by regulation prescribe) (*FA 2013, s 121(4)(5)*). If a person's acquisition and disposal of a chargeable interest are completed on the same day, the acquisition is ignored if it precedes the disposal and the disposal is ignored if it precedes the acquisition (*FA 2013, s 121(3)*). It is not clear what this is intended to do. Ignoring the disposal seems to leave the company owning the dwelling indefinitely, but that is clearly not the intention.

20.28 References to an acquisition of a chargeable interest includes any acquisition, however effected (including one effected by the act of parties to a transaction, by order of a court or other authority, by or under any statutory provision, or by operation of law (*FA 2013, s 120(1)*). The surrender or release of a chargeable interest is an acquisition of that interest by any person whose interest or right is benefited or enlarged by the transaction (and a disposal by the person ceasing to be entitled to the interest) (*FA 2013, s 120(2)*). The variation of a chargeable interest is an acquisition of a chargeable interest by the person benefiting from it (and a disposal by the person whose interest is subject to or limited by, the variation) (*FA 2013, s 120(3)*).

20.29 If a person enters into a contract (or other agreement) to acquire a chargeable interest in or over land which includes a dwelling, and the acquisition is to be completed by a conveyance (or other instrument), entering into the contract is not the acquisition of a chargeable interest, but if the contract is substantially performed (within *FA 2003, s 44* – see **19.89**) the substantial performance is regarded as the completion of the acquisition and the actual completion by conveyance is ignored (*FA 2013, s 122(3)(4)(9)*). If the contract is subsequently rescinded or annulled (or performance of the contract is otherwise terminated before it has been carried fully into effect) the person is treated as having disposed of the chargeable interest at that time (*FA 2013, s 122(5)(6)*). If the contract is varied (or partially rescinded, or the parties act as if it had been varied) between substantial performance and completion of the conveyance, so that the chargeable interest to be acquired under the contract is not the same as the chargeable interest to which the contract originally related, the variation must be treated as giving rise to the disposal of the chargeable interest originally contracted for and the substantial performance of the contract as varied (*FA 2013, s 122(7)(8)*). The same rules obviously apply to the vendor (*FA 2013, s 123*).

Special Situations

20.30 If a new dwelling is being (or has been) constructed (whether or not as part of a larger building, the earlier of the completion day (under *Local Government Finance Act 1992, s 17*, ie normally the date of service of the completion notice), or the day on which the dwelling is first occupied, is a valuation date in the case of a single-dwelling interest in that dwelling (*FA 2013, s 124(1)(3)*). For this purpose the construction of a new dwelling includes the production of a new dwelling by the alteration (whether structural or otherwise) of an existing building, but does not include a case within *s 125* (see **20.31**) or *s 128* (see **20.32**) (*FA 2013, s 124(2)*).

20.31 If an existing dwelling or dwellings (the old dwelling) becomes a different dwelling or dwellings (the new dwelling) as a result of structural alterations the old dwelling is regarded as ceasing to exist and the new dwelling as coming into existence only when the conversion is completed (as defined in *Local Government Finance Act 1992, s 17*) (*FA 2013, s 125(1)(2)(4)*). The day after the conversion is completed is a valuation date in the cases of any single-dwelling interest in the new dwelling (*FA 2013, s 125(3)*).

20.32 If a building (or part of a building) that is a dwelling is demolished after 1 April 2013 any question as to whether a person has a single-dwelling interest in it must be determined as if the dwelling had not been demolished (*FA 2013, s 126(1)(2)(4)*). A building is demolished after 1 April 2013 only if the demolition begins after that date and, as a result, the building is no longer suitable for use as a dwelling (*FA 2013, s 126(3)*). If a person entitled to a single-dwelling interest in the old building notifies HMRC that to the best of his knowledge there is no proposal to construct any dwelling or dwellings on the land on which the old dwelling stood, any question as to whether a person (not necessarily the same person, ie if there are a number of different single-dwelling interests in the building, only one notification is required) has a single-dwelling interest in the old dwelling will instead be determined on the assumption that the old dwelling ceases (or ceased) to exist with effect from the end of the first day on which the demolition has begun and as a result the building in question is no longer suitable for use as a dwelling (*FA 2013, s 127(1)–(3)(5)*). Such a notification must be given in an ATED return or by amending such a return (*FA 2013, s 127(4)*). If one or more dwellings (the new dwellings) are constructed (wholly or jointly) on the land on which the old dwelling stood after the demolition, any question as to whether a person has a single-dwelling interest at any time in either the old or new dwelling must be determined on the assumption that the old dwelling ceases to exist and the new dwelling comes into existence only when the rebuilding is completed, ie on the earlier of the completion day (as defined in *Local Government Act 1992, s 17*) or the day on which the last of the new dwellings to be occupied is first occupied (*FA 2013, s 128(1)(2)(4)–(6)*). The day after the rebuilding is completed is a valuation date in the case of any single-dwelling interest in a new dwelling (*FA 2013, s 128(3)*). If a building is constructed (wholly or partly) on the land on which the old dwelling stood after the demolition and *s 128* does not apply, any question as to whether a person has a single-dwelling interest in the old dwelling must be determined on the assumption that the old dwelling ceases to exist on the day after the change of use is approved or, if later, the day on which the old dwelling ceased to be occupied (*FA 2013, s 129*).

20.33 If a building or part of a building has been suitable for use as a dwelling and is altered for the purpose of making it suitable for use other than as a dwelling, it will not be regarded as having become unsuitable as a result of the alterations at any time unless any planning permission or development consent required for the alterations has been granted (and the alterations have been made in accordance with any such permission or consent) (*FA 2013, s 130(1)(3)*). Whether or not alterations make the building or part unsuitable for use as a dwelling is a question of fact (*FA 2013, s 130(2)*).

20.34 If a building (or part of a building) is damaged so as to be temporarily unsuitable for use as a dwelling, the unsuitability for use can be taken into account in applying the definition of a dwelling only if:

(*a*) the damage is accidental, or otherwise caused by events beyond the control of the person entitled to the single-dwelling interest (and the damage does not occur in the course of work that is done for the purpose of altering or partially demolishing the dwelling (or a building of which it forms part) and that itself involves (or could be expected to involve) making the building unsuitable for use as a dwelling for 30 days or more); and

(*b*) as a result of the damage, the building concerned is unsuitable for use as a dwelling for at least 90 consecutive days.

(*FA 2013, s 131(1)–(4)(6)*.)

The 90-day period in (*b*) can start before 1 April 2013 (*FA 2013, s 131(8)*). In such a case the entire period of unsuitability for use as a dwelling (including the first 90 days) can be taken into account. In applying the definition of dwelling any work done in that period to restore the building to suitability for use as a dwelling does not count as construction or adaptation of the building for use as a dwelling for the purpose of *ss 112* or *113* (for meaning of dwelling – see **20.14**, and substantial performance of 'off plan' purchase – see **20.15**) (*FA 2013, s 131(5)*).

Reliefs

20.35 Where tax is charged in respect of a single-dwelling interest for a fiscal year that includes one or more days that are relievable, the adjusted chargeable amount is to be calculated on the basis that the chargeable person is not within the charge with respect to the interest on any such relievable day (*FA 2013, s 132(1)(2)*). A day is a relievable one if the interest is being used for an exempt purpose on that day. These are:

(*a*) property rental business (see **20.36**);

(*b*) dwellings open to the public (see **20.40**);

(*c*) property developers (see **20.41**);

(*d*) property traders (see **20.43**);

(*e*) financial institutions acquiring dwellings in the course of lending (see **20.46**);

(*f*) occupation by certain employees or partners (see **20.48**);

(*g*) caretaker flat owned by management company (see **20.50**)

(*h*) farmhouses (see **20.51**); or

(*i*) providers of social housing (see **20.53**).

These reliefs (or, effectively, exemptions) have to be claimed. Where a relief applies throughout a fiscal year, an ATED return still needs to be completed in order to claim the relief. Like the tax itself, the reliefs are expressed in terms of days to reflect the fact that the use of a property might change during the fiscal year.

Property Rental Business

20.36 A single-dwelling interest is exempt if it is being exploited as a source of rents or other receipts (other than excluded rents) in the course of a qualifying property rental business carried on by a person entitled to the interest (*FA 2013, s 133(1)(a)*). A qualifying rental business is run on a commercial basis and with a view to profit (*FA 2013, s 133(3)*). However, the exemption does not apply on days on which a non-qualifying individual is permitted to occupy the dwelling (*FA 2013, s 133(2)*). A non-qualifying individual is any of:

(*a*) An individual who is entitled to the interest (otherwise than as a member of a partnership).

(*b*) An individual who is connected with a person entitled to the interest. The *CTA 2010, s 1122* definition of a connected person (see Appendix 1) applies but as if *s 1122(7)* and *(8)* (application of rules to partnerships) were omitted (*FA 2013, s 136(6)*).

(*c*) If a person is entitled to the interest as a member of a partnership, an individual who either is a qualifying member of the partnership or connected with such a person. A qualifying member of a partnership is one who is entitled to 50% or more of the income profits of the partnership or of the partnership assets (*FA 2013, s 136(2)*).

(*d*) An individual who is the settler in relation to a settlement of which a trustee (in his capacity as trustee) is connected with a person who is entitled to the interest. The *ITTOIA 2005, s 620* definitions of settlement and settlor, and the *CTA 2010, s 1122(3)* extension of the meaning of trustee (a person in whom the property comprised in the settlement is for the time being vested or in whom the management of the property is for the time being vested) apply (*FA 2013, s 136(7)(8)*).

(*e*) The spouse or civil partner of a person within (*b*) above or of a settlor within (*d*) above.

(*f*) A relative (brother, sister, ancestor or lineal descendant) of a person within (*b*) above or of a settlor within (*d*) above, or the spouse or civil partner of such a relative.

(*g*) A relative (brother, sister, ancestor or lineal descendant) of the spouse or civil partner of a person within (*b*) or a settlor within (*d*).

(*h*) The spouse or civil partner of a person within (*g*) above.

(*i*) An individual who is a major participator in a collective investment scheme that owns the interest, or who is connected with such a major participant. A major participant is a person who is entitled to at least 50% of either all the profits or income arising to the scheme from the acquisition, holding, management or disposal of the property subject to the scheme (or of any profits or income arising to the scheme that are available for distribution among participants) or who would in the event of the winding up of the scheme be entitled to 50% or more of the assets of the scheme that would be available for distribution among the participants (*FA 2013, s 136(4)(5)*).

20.37 The exemption also applies on any day on which steps are being taken to secure that the interest will (without undue delay) be exploited as a source of rents or other receipts in the course of a qualifying property rental business that is being carried on (or is to be carried on) by a person entitled to the interest (*FA 2013, s 133(1)(b)*). This ensures that the relief continues where a rental property is undergoing repairs or refurbishment and in void periods between letting. Without undue delay means without delay except so far as a delay is justified by commercial considerations or cannot be avoided (*FA 2013, s 133(5)*). This proviso is probably intended to prevent a day being a qualifying day where there is only a vague intention of letting the property some time in the future.

20.38 The exemption also applies where:

(*a*) the dwelling is unoccupied and either–

(i) steps are being taken to sell the interest without undue delay;

(ii) steps are being taken to demolish the dwelling without undue delay, and if it is intended that a new dwelling will be constructed on the site of the existing dwelling, that new dwelling will qualify for one of the exemptions for letting, dwellings open to the public, occupation by certain employees or partners, or farmhouses;

(iii) steps are being taken to secure that the dwelling will be converted into a different dwelling without undue delay and it is intended that that different dwelling will qualify for exemption under one of the above heads; or

(iv) steps are being taken to secure that the dwelling will be converted into a building, other than a dwelling without undue delay,

(*b*) the property was previously used in a qualifying property rental business carried on by the person entitled to the interest (or where a person is entitled to the interest as a member of a partnership, by a person who was carrying on the qualifying rental property business concerned as a member of that partnership); and

(*c*) all of the days since the property was previously let fall within (*a*) above (*FA 2013, s 134*). It should be particularly noted that where a rental property is left vacant preparatory to its being rebuilt or converted into a new dwelling that will be sold, this exemption does not apply even though the rebuilding or conversion and onward sale may itself qualify for exemption under the property developer or property trader heads. This creates a timing issue. The property development or property dealing trade needs to start immediately the letting ceases in order to maintain the exemption. This can conflict with the income and corporation tax position under which it can be favourable to delay transferring an investment property into trading stock for as long as possible.

20.39 If a single-dwelling interest to which a person (the landlord) is entitled is being let in the course of a qualifying property rental business and a non-qualifying individual is permitted to occupy the dwelling the relief described at **20.37** cannot apply to the landlord and for the remainder of the fiscal year or for any of the three subsequent fiscal years, ie the taxable period extends up to the time when the dwelling is next let (*FA 2013, s 135(1)(2)*). Similarly, if a non-qualifying individual occupies a dwelling the reliefs at **20.37** and **20.38** cannot apply to the landlord at any earlier time in the same or the previous fiscal year from the time when the property was last let to someone other than a non-qualifying individual (*FA 2013, s 135(4)–(8)).*

Dwellings Open to the Public

20.40 A single-dwelling interest is exempt if either:

(*a*) it is being exploited as a source of income in the course of a qualifying trade in the normal course of which the public are offered the opportunity to make use of, stay in, or otherwise enjoy the dwelling as customers of the trade on at least 28 days in any year; or

(*b*) steps are being taken to secure that the dwelling will at a future date be exploited as a source of income in the course of such a qualifying trade and that it will be so exploited without delay (except so far as delay is justified by commercial considerations or cannot otherwise be avoided).

(*FA 2013, s 137(1)–(3)*.)

A qualifying trade is carried on on a commercial basis and with a view to profit (*FA 2013, s 137(4)*). Persons have an opportunity to make use of, stay in or enjoy a dwelling only if the areas that they are permitted to use include a significant part of the interior of the dwelling. The size (relative to the size of the whole dwelling), nature and function of the area or areas concerned must be taken into account in determining whether they form a significant part of the interior of the dwelling (*FA 2013, s 137(5)(6)*).

Property Developers

20.41 A single-dwelling interest is exempt on any day on which a person carrying on a property development trade is entitled to the interest and it is held exclusively for the purpose of developing and reselling the land in the course of that trade (*FA 2013, s 138(1)*). A property development trade is one that consists of, or includes, buying and developing (or redeveloping) for resale residential or non-residential property, and which is run on a commercial basis and with a view to profit (*FA 2013, s 138(4)(5)*). It should be noted that this does not appear to cover developing with a view to letting the developed dwellings. It is not readily apparent why, particularly in the light of the national need for more rental properties. It may be that the intention is to relieve only housebuilders who do not normally let their properties other than where they are forced to do so because of a market downturn.

20.42 If the property developer holds an interest for the purpose of developing and reselling any additional purpose that he may have of exploiting the interest as a source of rents or other receipts in the course of a qualifying property rental business (after developing the land and before reselling it) is treated as not being a separate purpose (*FA 2013, s 138(2)*). For example, an intention to let a block of flats and then sell it does not prevent the property being held exclusively for development. Any day on which a non-qualifying individual (see **20.36**) is permitted to occupy the dwelling does not qualify for exemption (*FA 2013, s 138(3)*).

20.43 The relief also applies where a property developer (within **20.41**) is entitled to a single-dwelling interest that was acquired by the relevant person in the course of his property development trade as a reverse acquisition as part of a qualifying exchange (the returned interest) (*FA 2013, s 139(1)*). A qualifying exchange is one made by way of transfer whereby the person from whom the acquisition was made itself acquired (by way of grant or transfer) a chargeable interest in or over a new dwelling from the relevant person and each of those acquisitions was entered into in consideration of the other (*FA 2013, s 139(4)*). A building (or part of a building) is a new dwelling if it has been constructed (or adapted) for use as a single dwelling and has not previously been occupied (or not occupied since its adaption (*FA 2013, s 139(5)*). A relevant person is the property developer, any person who acquired the returned interest (the single-dwelling interest) jointly with the property developer, or, if the property developer is entitled to the returned interest as a member of a partnership, the persons who acquired the interest as members of the partnership (ie the partnership as such) (*FA 2013, s 139(3)*). This is aimed at the situation where a housebuilder takes over the customer's existing home in part-exchange for a newly built house. As he is likely to resell the acquired property, its acquisition and sale is not itself property development, but clearly ought to form part of the property development trade. Any day on which a non-qualifying individual (see **20.36**) is permitted to occupy the dwelling does not attract exemption (*FA 2013, s 139(2)*).

20.44 If a person carrying on a property development trade is entitled to a single-dwelling interest that has been acquired in the course of the trade and a non-qualifying individual (see **20.36**) is permitted to occupy the dwelling (or part of it), no subsequent day qualifies for the exemption for the rest of the fiscal year or the following three fiscal years (or until the property developer disposes of his interest or ceases to use it for his trade) (*FA 2013, s 140(1)–(3)*). In addition the exemption does not apply for any earlier part of that fiscal year or for the previous fiscal year (*FA 2013, s 140(4)–(7)*). If the property business exemption applies at any time in that earlier period (ie it is let to a qualifying individual) the disallowance does not apply to any period before that qualifying letting.

20.45 A single-dwelling interest is exempt if a person carrying on a property trading business is entitled to the interest and it is held as trading stock of the business and for the sole purpose of resale in the course of that trade (*FA 2013, s 141(1)*). A property trading business is one that consists of or includes activities in the nature of a trade of buying and selling dwellings and it is carried on on a commercial basis and with a view to profit (*FA 2013, s 141(3)*). A single-dwelling interest must be treated as not held for the sole purpose of resale at any time when a non-qualifying individual is permitted to occupy the dwelling (*FA 2013, s 141(2)*). The disallowance explained at **20.44** for the following three fiscal years and the previous fiscal year (or until a qualifying letting intervenes) also applies to the property dealing exemption (*FA 2013, s 142*).

Financial Institutions Acquiring Dwellings in the Course of Lending

20.46 There is an exemption where the single-dwelling interest is held by a financial institution (within *ITA 2007, s 564B*, but ignoring *s 564B(1)(d)*) carrying on a business that involves the lending of money if that interest was acquired by it in the course of its business and in connection with its letting activities and is held with the intention that it will be sold in the course of that business without delay (except so far as delay is justified by commercial considerations or cannot be avoided) (*FA 2013, s 143(1)(3)*). The exemption does not apply at a time where a non-qualifying individual is permitted to occupy the dwelling (*FA 2013, s 143(2)*). The disallowance explained at **20.44** again applies for the purpose of the financial institution exemption (*FA 2013, s 144*).

Regulated Home Reversion Plans

20.47 From 1 April 2016 there is an exemption for a single dwelling interest held by an authorised plan provider if he has, as plan provider, entered into a regulated home reversion plan relating to that interest and the occupation condition is met (*FA 2013, s 144A(1)* inserted by *FA 2016, s 134*). An authorised plan provider is a person authorised under *FSMA 2000* to carry on the activity of entering into regulated home reversion plans. A regulated home reversion plan is an arrangement for the purposes of the *Financial Services and Markets (Regulated Activities) Order 2001 (SI 2001 No 544)*. The occupation condition is that a person who was originally entitled to occupy the dwelling (or any part of it) under the regulated home reversion plan is still entitled to do so. If a qualifying termination event (as defined in *art 63B* of the Order – the occupier dies or wants to move home) has occurred, the occupation condition is instead that the single dwelling interest is being held with the intention that it will be sold without delay (except insofar as delay is justified by commercial considerations or cannot be avoided), and no non-qualifying individual (see **20.36**) is permitted to occupy the dwelling or any part of it (*FA 2013, s 144A(2)–(5), (7)*). An arrangement which the plan provider entered into before 6 April 2007 (or in relation to which he acquired rights or obligations before that date) is treated as a regulated home reversion plan if it would be so treated for the purpose of *art 63B(1)* of the Order (*FA 2013, s 144A(6)*).

Occupation by Certain Employees or Partners

20.48 An exemption applies where a person entitled to a single-dwelling interest, or a member of the same group (as defined in *FA 2013, Sch 7, para 1*), carries on a qualifying trade or property rental business on a commercial basis and with a view to profit, and the interest is held for the purpose of making the dwelling available to one or more qualifying employees (or office-holders) or qualifying partners (and their families) for use as living accommodation, for purposes that are solely or mainly purposes of the trade or property rental business (*FA 2013, s 145* as amended by *FA 2016, s 135*). A property rental business qualifies only from 1 April 2016. A qualifying business is one that is run on a commercial basis and with a view to profit (see **20.36**). A qualifying employee is an individual employed for the purpose of the qualifying trade or property rental business and who neither:

(*a*) is entitled to a 10% or greater share in the income profits of the trade, or in the company that is entitled to the single dwelling interest, or in the single dwelling interest; or

(*b*) is a person the duties of whose employment include the provision of services in connection with the (actual or intended) occupation by a person connected with the person entitled to the single-dwelling interest, of the dwelling or a linked dwelling.

(*FA 2013, s 146(2)–(4).*).

A dwelling is linked if it falls within *FA 2013, s 116* (dwelling in grounds of another dwelling – see **20.18**) or *s 117* (dwelling in the same building – see **20.19**) (*FA 2013, s 146(5)*). A qualifying partner is an individual who is a member of a partnership that carries on the trade or property rental business and who is not entitled to 10% or more of the income profits of the partnership, or in a company that is entitled to the single-dwelling interest, or in the partnership's assets (*FA 2013, s 146(1)*). Persons who are entitled to a chargeable interest as beneficial joint tenants must be treated for the purpose of *s 146* as being entitled to the joint interest as beneficial tenants in common in equal shares (*FA 2013, s 146(7)*).

20.49 For this purpose an individual is entitled to 10% or more in a company if he possesses (directly or indirectly) or is entitled to acquire:

(*a*) 10% or more of its share capital;

(*b*) 10% or more of its issued share capital;

(*c*) 10% or more of the voting power in the company;

(*d*) so much of the issued share capital as would, if the whole of the company's income were distributed among its participators, entitle him to receive 10% or more of the amount so distributed; or

(*e*) such rights as would entitle him on a winding up, or in any other circumstances, to receive 10% or more of the assets of the company that would then be available for distribution among the participators.

(*FA 2013, s 147(1)(2)*.)

Any rights that the individual or any other person has as a loan creditor are to be ignored for the purpose of (*d*) (*FA 2013, s 147(3)*). A person is treated as entitled to acquire anything which he is entitled to acquire at a future date or at a future date will become entitled to acquire (*FA 2013, s 147(4)*). If a person possesses any rights or powers on behalf of another person, or can be required to exercise any rights or powers at the direction of, or on behalf of, another person those rights or powers must be attributed to that other person (*FA 2013, s 147(5)*). A person must also be treated as entitled to:

(*a*) the rights and powers of any company of which he (or he and associates of his) has control;

(*b*) the rights and powers of any two or more companies within (i); and

(*c*) the rights and powers of any associate of his (or of any two or more associates).

(*FA 2013, s 147(6)*.) The rights and powers so attributable include those attributed to a company or associate under *s 147(5)* but not those attributed to an associate under *s 147(6)* itself (*FA 2013, s 147(7)*). A person is also treated as having 10% or more of the company if he exercises, or is able to exercise, or is entitled to acquire, direct or indirect control over the company's affairs (*FA 2013, s 147(8)*). For the purpose of *s 147*, the *CTA 2010, s 448* definition of associate applies but with the omission of 'partner' in *s 448(1)(a)* (*FA 2013, s 147(9)*). Control, loan creditor, and participator adopt the definitions in *CTA 2010, s 450, 453* and *454* respectively (*FA 2013, s 147(9)*).

Caretaker Flat Owned by Management Company

20.50 From 1 April 2016, a single-dwelling interest is exempt if the dwelling in question is a flat in relation to which:

(*a*) a company (the management company) holds the single-dwelling interest for the purpose of making the flat available as caretaker accommodation;

(*b*) the flat is contained in premises which also contain two or more other flats;

(*c*) the tenants of at least two of the other flats in the premises are members of the management company;

(*d*) the management company owns the freehold of the premises; and

(*e*) the management company is not carrying on a trade or property rental business.

(*FA 2013, s 147A(1),(2)* inserted by *FA 2016, s 135(7)*.)

For this purpose the management company makes a flat available as caretaker accommodation if it makes it available to an individual for use as living accommodation in connection with the individual's employment as caretaker of the premises. Premises can constitute the whole or part of a building (*FA 2013, s 147A(3),(4)*). It should be noted that the company needs to own the freehold; a long lease is not sufficient. The caretaker needs to be an employee. He does not need to be employed by the management company. He could, for example, be employed by a firm of estate agents that manage the premises. On the face of it, the exemption can rarely apply as in most cases the freehold owning company will have a property rental business as it will receive ground rents from the leaseholders. It will be interesting to see if HMRC ignore this. It is not clear if the caretaker has to be employed solely to look after the premises or if he can be caretaker of other premises in addition.

Farmhouses

20.51 A single-dwelling interest is exempt if the dwelling forms part of land occupied for the purpose of a trade of farming (carried on on a commercial basis and with a view to profit), a person carrying on the trade is entitled to (or connected with a person who is entitled to) the interest, and the dwelling (or part of it) is occupied by a farm worker who occupies it for the purposes of the trade (or by a former long-serving farm worker, or the surviving spouse or civil partner of a former farm worker (not necessarily a long-serving one)) (*FA 2013, ss 148(1)–(3), 149(4)*). Farming has the same meaning as in

CTA 2010, s 1125 (see **23.10**) but also includes market gardening (as defined in *CTA 2010, s 1125(5)*) (*FA 2013, s 148(4)*).

20.52 For this purpose an individual is a farm worker in relation to the trade of farming if he has a substantial involvement in the day-to-day work of the trade or in the direction and control of the conduct of the trade (*FA 2013, s 149(1)*). A person is a former long-serving farm worker if he had been a farm worker in the trade for a period of three or more years (or periods which together amount to three or more years within a five-year period) and during that period:

(*a*) the individual occupied the dwelling for the purpose of the trade;

(*b*) the land of which the dwelling forms part was occupied for the purposes of the trade;

(*c*) the trade was carried on by a person who is entitled to the single-dwelling interest at the time that the exemption is claimed (or by a connected person of his); and

(*d*) a person who is entitled to the single-dwelling interest in the dwelling at that time was entitled to that interest during the three-year period.

(*FA 2013, s 149(2)(3).*)

Providers of Social Housing

20.53 A single dwelling interest is exempt if either:

(*a*) a profit-making registered provider of social housing is entitled to the interest and its acquisition of the interest (or any part of it) was funded with the assistance of public subsidy (as defined in *FA 2003, s 71*); or

(*b*) a relevant housing provider (ie a non-profit registered provider of social housing or a registered social landlord) is entitled to the interest and–

  (i) the relevant housing provider is controlled by its tenants (in accordance with *FA 2003, s 71* – see **19.251**);

  (ii) the person from whom the relevant housing provider acquired the interest (or any part of it) is a qualifying body (as defined in *FA 2003, s 71(3)*); and

  (iii) the relevant housing provider's acquisition of the interest (or any part of it) was funded with the assistance of a public subsidy.

(*FA 2013, s 150.*)

Charitable Companies

20.54 A charitable company that is entitled to a single-dwelling interest is treated as not meeting the ownership conditions (and thus being outside the scope of the tax) with respect to the interest if it is held by the company:

(*a*) for use or furtherance of the charitable purposes of the charitable company or of another charity; or

(*b*) as an investment from which the profits are (or are to be) applied to the charitable purposes of the charitable company.

(*FA 2013, s 151(1)(2).*)

20.55 The exemption does not apply though where:

(*a*) a person (the donor) has made, or agreed to make, a gift to the charitable company (or to a charity that is connected with it);

(*b*) there exists arrangements under which (or as a result of which) the donor (or a person who was an associate of the donor (see below) when the arrangements were entered into) is permitted, or may in the future be permitted, to occupy the dwelling (or any part of the dwelling); and

(*c*) it is reasonable to assume from either or both of–

   (i) the likely effects of the gift and the arrangements; or

   (ii) the circumstances in which the gift was made and the arrangements were entered into,

   that the gift would not have been made and the arrangements would not have been entered into independently of one another.

(*FA 2013, ss 151(3)(4), 152(4).*)

In (*a*) above, connected means connected in a matter relating to the structure, administration or control of the charitable company, not a connected person (*FA 2013, s 151(8)*). In (*b*) an associate in relation to a donor is any of:

(i) an individual who is connected with the donor (see **20.120**) (a connected person);

(ii) an individual who is the settlor (as defined in *ITTOIA 2005, s 620*) in relation to a settlement of which a trustee (as defined *in CTA 2010, s 1123(3)*) is (in the capacity of trustee) connected with the donor;

(iii) the spouse or civil partner of such a connected person or of a relevant settlor;

(iv) a relative (brother, sister, ancestor or lineal descendant) of a connected person or of a relevant settlor, or the spouse or civil partner of a relative of a connected person or relevant settlor;

(v) a relative of the spouse or civil partner of a connected person or of a relevant settlor; or

(vi) the spouse or civil partner of a person within (*v*).

(*FA 2013, s 152(1)–(3)*.)

Head (*b*) does not apply if the gift was made before 17 July 2013 or an agreement to make it was entered into before that date (*FA 2013, s 152(5)*). Arrangements entered into before 17 July 2013 can also be ignored unless a material alteration (ie one affecting anything in the arrangements that relates to the individual's having (at any time), or potentially having, permission to occupy the dwelling) is made to them on or after that date (*FA 2013, s 152(6)*). References to a gift include the disposal of an asset for less than its market value (*FA 2013, s 152(7)*). Arrangements include any scheme, arrangement or understanding of any kind, whether or not legally enforceable, involving a single transaction or two or more transactions (*FA 2013, s 152(8)*).

20.56 This exclusion does not apply (so the exemption applies) if either:

(*a*) the activities undertaken for carrying out the primary purposes of the charitable company include (or normally include) opening the dwelling to the public; or

(*b*) the dwelling is being exploited through commercial activities that involve (or normally involve) opening the dwelling to the public; or

(*c*) steps are being taken to secure that either (*a*) or (*b*) will be met without undue delay (except so far as delay is justified by commercial consideration or for the sake of a primary purpose of the charitable company) or that the single-dwelling interest will be sold without undue delay (except so far as it is justified for the above reasons).

(*FA 2013, s 151(5)(6)*.)

For this purpose a dwelling is open to the public only if the public is offered the opportunity to make use of (or stay in or otherwise enjoy), on at least 28 days in any year, areas that constitute a significant part of the interior of the dwelling or of the dwelling's garden or grounds (*FA 2013, s 151(6)*). The size (relative to the size of the whole dwelling or of the whole garden or grounds), nature and function of the areas concerned must be taken into account in determining whether they form a significant part of the interior of the dwelling or of the garden or grounds (*FA 2013, s 151(7)*).

Public Bodies

20.57 A public body is not regarded as a company for the purposes of ATED. For this purpose a public body is a body corporate that is a public body or company (as defined by *Companies Act 2006, s 1*) wholly owned by such a body. The power of the Treasury to prescribe persons as a public body under *FA 2003, s 66(4)* can be exercised so as to make different provisions for SDLT and ATED (*FA 2013, s 153*).

Bodies Established for National Purposes

20.58 The following bodies are not regarded as companies for the purposes of ATED:

(*a*) The Historic Buildings and Monuments Commission for England.

(*b*) The Trustees of the British Museum.

(*c*) The Trustees of the National Heritage Memorial Fund.

(*d*) The Trustees of the Natural History Museum.

(*FA 2013, s 154.*)

Dwellings Conditionally Exempt from Inheritance Tax

20.59 If the whole or part of the dwelling has been designated under *IHTA 1984, s 31* (buildings of outstanding historic or architectural interest, etc), an undertaking has been made with respect to the dwelling under *IHTA 1984, s 30* (conditionally exempt transfers) and a transfer of value is exempt from IHT by virtue of that designation and undertaking, the taxable value of a single-dwelling interest in the dwelling is treated as zero if no chargeable event under *IHTA 1984, s 32* has occurred with respect to the dwelling since the transfer of value (*FA 2013, s 155(1)(2)(5)*). The value is similarly treated as zero where the undertaking with respect to the dwelling has been given under *IHTA 1984, s 78* (settled property: conditionally exempt occasions) and a transfer of property or other event is a conditionally exempt occasion under *IHTA 1984, s 78* by virtue of the designation and that undertaking (*FA 2013, s 156(3)(4)(5)*).

Modification of Reliefs

20.60 The Treasury have power by regulation to provide for further reliefs or exemptions (including by modifying an existing relief or exemption) or to amend or repeal any of *ss 132–155* and to make any amendment of any other ATED provision that may be necessary in consequence of such an amendment or repeal (*FA 2013, s 156*).

Alternative Property Finance

20.61 Where *FA 2003, s 71A* (land sold to financial institution and leased to person – see **19.272**) applies in relation to arrangements entered into between a financial institution (as defined in *FA 2003, s 73BA*) and another person (the lessee), land in which the institution purchases a major interest under the first transaction (as defined in *FA 2003, ss 71A* or *72*) consists of (or includes) one or more dwellings (or parts of dwellings), and the lessee is a company, ATED has effect in relation to times when the arrangements are in operation as if:

(*a*) the interest held by the financial institution were instead held by the lessee; and

(*b*) the lease or sub-lease granted under the second transaction (as defined in *FA 2003, ss 71A* or *72*) had not been granted.

(*FA 2013, s 157(1)(2)(7)*.)

20.62 For this purpose times when the arrangements are in operation means times when the lessee holds the major interest granted to it under the second transaction and the interest purchased under the first transaction (except so far as transferred by a further transaction) is held by a financial institution (*FA 2013, s 157(3)*). A company treated as holding an interest under this provision is treated as holding it as a member of a partnership if it holds the leasehold interest as a member of the partnership (*FA 2013, s 157(4)*). In relation to times when the arrangements operate for the benefit of a collective investment scheme, ATED applies as if the interest held by the financial institution were held by the lessee for the purposes of a collective investment scheme (instead of being held by the institution) and the lease or sub-lease granted under the second transaction had not been granted. Times when the arrangements operate for the benefit of a collective investment scheme mean times when the lessee holds the leasehold interest for the purposes of a collective investment scheme and the interest purchased under the first transaction (except as far as transferred by a further transaction) is held by the financial institution (*FA 2013, s 157(5)(6)*). Where the lessee is an individual, the references in *s 157(5)(6)* to the lessee includes his personal representatives after his death (*FA 2013, s 157(9)*). Reference to a major interest in land must be read in accordance with *FA 2003, s 117* (see **19.14**) (*FA 2013, s 157(8)*). This provision does not apply in Scotland in cases where UK SDLT has been disapplied by the *Scotland Act 2012, s 29* (*FA 2013, s 157(10)*).

20.63 From 1 April 2016, if:

(*a*) arrangements are entered into between a person (the lessee) and a financial institution under which the institution purchases a major interest in land (the first transaction), grants to the lessee out of that interest a lease or a sub-lease (the second transaction), and enters into an agreement under which the lessee has a right to require the institution to transfer the major interest purchased by the institution under the first transaction;

(*b*) the land is in Scotland and consists of or includes one or more dwellings or parts of dwellings; and

(*c*) the lessee is a company,

ATED applies in relation to times when the arrangements are in operation as if the interest held by the financial institution were held by the lessee (and not the institution) and the lease or sub-lease granted under the second transaction had not been granted (*FA 2013, s 157A(1)–(4)* inserted by *FA 2016, s 136(7)*). The reference to times when the arrangements are in operation is to times when the lessee holds the interest granted to it under the second transaction and the interest purchased under the first transaction is held by the financial institution (*FA 2013, s 157A(5)*). A company treated under this provision as holding an interest at a particular time is treated as a partnership interest (*FA 2013, s 157A(6)*). Similarly, at times when the arrangements operate for the benefit of a collective investment scheme, ATED applies as if the interest held by the financial institution were held by the lessee for the purposes of a collective investment scheme instead of by the financial institution) and the lease or sub-lease granted under the second transaction had not been granted (*FA 2013, s 157A(7),(8)*). References above to a major interest in land are to ownership of the land, or the tenant's right over, or interest in, land subject to a lease (*FA 2013, s 157A(10)*). Where the lessee is an individual, references *in s 157A(7),(8)* to the lessee must be read in relation to time after his death as references to his personal representatives (*FA 2013, s 157A(11)*).

Administration

Returns

20.64 A person who is liable to ATED with respect to a single-dwelling interest has to submit an ATED return to HMRC within 30 days of the start of the period for which he is liable (*FA 2013, s 159(1)(2)*). This is normally 30 April in the fiscal year (year to 31 March) but if the interest is acquired or something else triggers a valuation date (see **20.21**) during the course of a fiscal year it will be 30 days from the date of the acquisition of the interest or of that event. If a valuation date arises because of *FA 2013, ss 124* (new dwellings – see **20.30**) or *125* (dwellings produced from other dwellings – see **20.31**) the return must instead be delivered within 90 days of the charge to ATED arising (*FA 2013, s 159(3)*). From 1 April 2015, if a person would be required to deliver returns in respect of a property under *s 159(1)* for the current year and at a later date under *s 159(3)* for the previous year, the *s 159(3)* time limit applies to both returns (*FA 2013, s 159(3A)* inserted by *FA 2015, s 73(2)*). It should be stressed that a return is required if the value of a property exceeds the threshold even if no ATED is payable because one of the reliefs applies. This gives HMRC the opportunity to check that it does apply. Where a person has more than one property within ATED, a separate return is required for each. However, HMRC have said that where the same relief is being claimed for more than one dwelling, they will accept a single return provided that the requisite details for each property (title and/or number, if any; address and postcode; date of acquisition; actual value of dwelling; whether this is a professional valuation obtained in the return period; date of valuation; and any relevant PRBC reference – see **20.66**) are provided in a PDF file attached to the return which is e-mailed to HMRC at the same time as the return is filed and which includes 'ATED RELIEF' in the title (Guidance Note, 3 March 2014). For 2015/16 and 2016/17, a longer filing window applied for properties under £2 million and £1 million respectively (see **20.23**). This extended period also applied to a relief declaration return (see **20.69**) (*FA 2015, s 73(7)(8)*).

20.65 If either:

(*a*) the adjusted chargeable amount (see **20.25**) exceeds the amount charged under *FA 2013, s 99* (see **20.20**) and the taxpayer has not made a claim for interim relief in respect of the interest for the chargeable period; or

(*b*) the person has made a claim or claims for interim relief and the sum of amounts referred to at **20.26** in connection with the latest such claim is less than the adjusted chargeable amount,

the taxpayer must submit a further return to HMRC (called a return of the adjusted chargeable amount) within 30 days of the fiscal year following that to which the return relates (*FA 2013, s 160(1)(2)(4)–(6)*). If the return is required because of (*b*) and the adjusted chargeable amount is affected by an event occurring after the end of the fiscal year, the return must be submitted within 30 days of the occurrence of that event (*FA 2013, s 160(3)*).

20.66 An ATED return (other than a relief declaration return (see **20.68**) must include a self-assessment of the amount chargeable and if it includes a claim for interim relief, the tax payable after the relief (*FA 2013, s 161(1)–(3)* as amended by *FA 2015, s 73(4)*). A return of the adjusted chargeable amount must include a self-assessment of the adjusted chargeable amount and the additional tax payable (*FA 2013, s 161(1)(2)(4)*). In both cases the return also needs to include a statement of the amount taken to be the market value of the interest on each valuation date that is relevant for the purpose of the assessment (*FA 2013, s 161(5)*). It is up to the taxpayer to determine the value of the property and he is subject to penalties if he gets it wrong. HMRC are, however, prepared to consider the taxpayer's valuation in advance of the submission of the ATED return (a pre-return banding check or PRBC) if the taxpayer's valuation falls within 10% of a banding threshold and the taxpayer is not claiming a relief that will reduce the tax to nil. The HMRC PRBC application form must be used and HMRC will not agree a value; they will simply say whether or not they consider that the taxpayer's valuation falls within the correct band (Guidance Note, 3 March 2014).

20.67 HMRC can by regulation make provision about the method of delivering a return and the form and content of a return. They can make different provisions for different purposes (*FA 2013, Sch 33, para 1(1)(2)*). Every return must include a declaration by the person completing it that the return is correct and complete to the best of that person's knowledge. A return is treated as containing any information provided by the person for the purpose of completing it (*FA 2013, Sch 33, para 1(3)(4)*).

20.68 A person who has delivered a return can amend it by notice to HMRC. HMRC can require such a notice to be in a specified form and contain specified information. The amendment must be made by 31 March of the fiscal year following the end of the fiscal year to which the return relates (or if it is delivered after 31 December in the fiscal year, within three months of the date on which it was delivered) (*FA 2013, Sch 33, para 3*). HMRC can correct any obvious error (such as a mathematical mistake or an error of principle) or omission in a return by notice to the taxpayer. Such a correction is regarded as an amendment of the return. Any such correction must be made within nine months of the date the return was delivered (or if it relates to an amendment by the taxpayer within nine months of the date the amendment was made (*FA 2013, Sch 33, para 4(1)–(4)*). Such an HMRC amendment has no effect if the chargeable person amends the return so as to reject the correction or, if the notice is issued in the last three months of the period in which the taxpayer can amend the return, gives a notice rejecting it within three months from the date of issue of the notice of correction (*FA 2013, Sch 33, para 4*). HMRC say that the online ATED return form should be used to notify them of a change of circumstances which may result in a repayment. They also say that to claim a repayment, the taxpayer must amend his ATED return and must enter on it a reason for the repayment (eg he has sold the property) (Guidance Note, 3 March 2014).

20.69 From 1 April 2015, a 'relief declaration return' can be made in respect of one or more single dwelling interest. Such a return must state that it is a relief declaration return, must relate to only one type of relief and must specify the type of relief to which it relates, ie:

Type 1:	*ss 134* or *135* (property rental business – see **20.36**)
Type 2:	*s 137* (dwellings open to the public – see **20.40**)
Type 3:	*ss 138* or *139* (property developers – see **20.41**)
Type 4:	*s 141* (property traders – see **20.43**)
Type 5:	*s 143* (financial institutions acquiring dwellings – see **20.46**)
Type 5A	*s 144A* (regulated home reversion plans – see **20.47**)
Type 6:	*s 145* (occupation by certain employee etc– see **20.48** and **20.50**)
Type 7:	*s 148* (farmhouses – see **20.51**)
Type 8:	*s 150* (providers of social housing – see **20.53**)

(*FA 2013, s 159A(1)(2)(9)* inserted by *FA 2015, s 73(3)* and amended by *FA 2016, s 134(6)*.) It should be noted that there is no requirement to specify the properties concerned. The return is itself treated as a claim for interim relief (see **20.26**) with respect to the interest or interests to which it relates (*FA 2013, s 159A(5)*). A relief declaration return is treated as being a return in relation to all single dwelling interests owned by that person to which the relief in question applies (*FA 2013, s 159A(3)(4)*). If the taxpayer subsequently acquires another chargeable interest (eg he buys another property) during the year to which the return relates and the same relief applies to the new property, the return is regarded as relating to the new property also (*FA 2013, s 159A(6)(7)*). If the person has failed to make ATED returns in relation to two or more single-dwelling interests and he could have discharged his duty to make a return by filing a single relief declaration in respect of them all, the failure can be regarded for penalty purposes as the failure to make a single return (*FA 2013, s 159A(10)*). This is obviously a simplification measure. It enables HMRC to verify the existence of the relevant business while relieving the taxpayer of the need to make multiple returns.

Duty to Keep and Preserve Records

20.70 A person who is required to deliver a return must keep any records that may be needed to enable him to deliver a correct and complete return and must preserve those records until the later of six years after the end of the fiscal year (or any earlier date that may be specified in writing by HMRC), the date on which any enquiry into the return is completed, and (if there is no enquiry) the end of the enquiry window (*FA 2013, Sch 33, para 5(1)–(3)*). The records that must be kept and preserved include details of any relevant transaction (including any contract or conveyance and supporting maps, plans or similar documents and records of relevant payments, receipts and financial arrangements) and records of any valuation of the single-dwelling interest relevant to its value on any day in the fiscal year (*FA 2013, Sch 33, para 5(5)*). HMRC have power by regulation to provide that records to be kept do or do not include specified items and to specify supporting documents (including accounts, books, deeds, contracts, vouchers and receipts) that are required to be kept (*FA 2013, Sch 33, para 5(6)–(8)*).

20.71 The duty to preserve records can be satisfied by preserving them in any form and by any means, or by preserving the information contained in them by any form and by any means but subject to any conditions or exceptions specified in writing by HMRC (*FA 2013, Sch 33, para 6*).

20.72 A person who fails to comply with these record-keeping requirements is liable to a penalty of up to £3,000 (*FA 2013, Sch 33, para 7(1)*). No penalty can be imposed if HMRC is satisfied that any facts that it is reasonable to require to be proved to HMRC and would have been proved by the records have been proved by other documentary evidence (*FA 2013, Sch 33, para 7*).

20.73 HMRC can enquire into an ATED return. If they wish to do so they must first issue an enquiry notice to the taxpayer within 12 months of the filing date of the return or, if later, of the date on which the return was submitted (or if the return is an amended return, of the date of the amendment). HMRC can normally issue only one enquiry notice into a return, but can issue a subsequent notice (or notices) in consequence of an amendment (or amendments) to the return (*FA 2013, Sch 33, para 8*). An enquiry extends to anything contained in the return (or required to be contained in the return) that relates to whether the person is chargeable to ATED with respect to the interest to which the return relates or to the amount of tax chargeable (*FA 2013, Sch 33, para 9(1)*). If a notice of enquiry is given as a result of an amendment at a time when it is too late to enquire into the return itself (or after an enquiry has been completed) the enquiry is limited to matters to which the amendment relates and matters affected by the amendment (*FA 2013, Sch 33, para 9(2)(3)*).

20.74 If during the course of an enquiry the HMRC officer forms an opinion that the amount stated in the self-assessment is inadequate and that, unless it is immediately amended, there is likely to be a loss of tax to the Crown, he can (by notice in writing to the taxpayer) amend the assessment to make good the deficiency. If the enquiry relates only to an amendment this power applies only so far as the deficiency is attributable to the amendment (*FA 2013, Sch 33, para 10*).

20.75 During the course of an enquiry any question arising in connection with the subject-matter of the return can be referred to the First-tier Tribunal (or the Upper Tribunal in accordance with the Tribunal Procedure rules) for determination. Such a referral must be made jointly by the taxpayer and HMRC. More than one referral can be made if necessary (*FA 2013, Sch 33, paras 11, 15*). If the question relates to the market value of any single-dwelling interest, the referral must be made to the Upper Tribunal not the First-tier Tribunal (FTT) if the land is in England or Wales (or to the Lands Tribunal for Scotland or for Northern Ireland if it is in one of those countries) (*FA 2013, Sch 33, para 15*). Such a referral is presumably to the Upper Tribunal (Lands Chamber) not the Tax and Chancery Chamber. Either party can withdraw a notice of referral; it does not need to be done jointly (*FA 2013, Sch 33, para 12*).

20.76 Where such a referral is made, HMRC cannot issue a closure notice (and the taxpayer cannot ask for one to be given) until after the questions referred have been finally determined by the Tribunal and there is no possibility of it being varied on appeal (ignoring the possibility of an appeal being allowed out of time) (*FA 2013, Sch 33, para 13*). A determination on a referral is binding to the same extent as a decision on a preliminary issue in an appeal and cannot be reopened on an appeal except to the extent that a preliminary issue could be reopened. HMRC must take the determination into account in reaching conclusions on the enquiry and amending the return to give effect to those conclusions (*FA 2013, Sch 33, para 14*).

20.77 An enquiry into a return is closed by HMRC issuing a closure notice to the taxpayer and stating the conclusions reached in the enquiry. A closure notice must either state that no amendment is required or must amend the return to give effect to the HMRC officer's conclusions. The notice takes effect when it is issued (*FA 2013, Sch 33, para 16*). The taxpayer can apply to the FTT for a direction that a closure notice must be given within a specified period. If he does so, the Tribunal must make such a direction unless it is satisfied that HMRC have reasonable grounds for not giving a closure notice within that period (*FA 2013, Sch 33, para 17*).

20.78 If an HMRC officer has reason to believe that a person is chargeable to ATED in respect of a single-dwelling interest (or that additional tax is payable as a result of an amendment under *FA 2013, s 163(2)* – see **20.23**) and that he has not submitted an ATED return (or amended return) by the due date, he can make a determination to the best of his information and belief of the amount of tax to which that person is liable. Notice of such a determination must be given to the person concerned. This must state the date it is issued. Any determination must be made within four years from the end of the fiscal year to which it relates (*FA 2013, Sch 33, para 18*). Such a determination has effect for enforcement purposes (ie for the purposes of *FA 2013, s 165* and *FA 2003, Sch 12* (collection and recovery of tax) – see **20.113**) as if it were a self-assessment made by the person concerned (but does not absolve that person from a penalty for failure to submit the return)

(*FA 2013, Sch 33, para 19*). Unlike with income tax, an appeal can be made against such a determination but only on very limited grounds – see **20.94** (*FA 2013, Sch 33, para 35(1)(c)*).

20.79 If the taxpayer subsequently submits an ATED return within 12 months of the date of the determination (or, if later, within four years after the power to make a determination first became exercisable – which is probably the filing date for the return) the self-assessment included therein supersedes the determination (*FA 2013, Sch 33, para 20(1)(2)*). If proceedings have begun for the recovery of tax charged by an HMRC determination and before those proceedings are concluded, the determination is displaced by a self-assessment, the proceedings can be continued as if they were to recover the tax charged by the self-assessment (or so much of it as has not been paid) (*FA 2013, Sch 33, para 20(3)*).

20.80 If an HMRC officer discovers that either an amount of tax that ought to have been assessed to ATED has not been assessed, an ATED assessment is insufficient or a relief given is excessive, he can make an assessment (a discovery assessment) in the amount (or further amount) that in his opinion ought to be charged in order to make good the loss of tax to the Crown (*FA 2013, Sch 33, paras 21, 23*). If an amount of tax that ought not to have been repaid has been repaid to the taxpayer that amount (plus any interest paid on the repayment) can also be assessed and recovered as if it were unpaid tax (*FA 2013, Sch 33, para 22*).

20.81 If the taxpayer has delivered an ATED return, a discovery assessment can be made only if either:

(*a*) the loss of tax was brought about carelessly or deliberately by the taxpayer, a person acting on his behalf or a person who was a partner of the taxpayer at the time when HMRC completed their enquiry or ceased to be entitled to open an enquiry; or

(*b*) it could not reasonably have been expected that an HMRC officer in possession of the information made available to HMRC before the enquiry window closed would be aware of the loss of tax (or excessive repayment).

(*FA 2013, Sch 33, para 24(1)–(4).*)

20.82 For the purpose of (*b*) above, information is regarded as made available to HMRC if either:

(*a*) it is contained in an ATED return delivered by the taxpayer;

(*b*) it is contained in any documents produced (or information provided) to HMRC for the purposes of an enquiry into such an ATED return;

(*c*) it is information the existence and relevance of which officers of HMRC could reasonably have been expected to infer from information within (*a*) or (*b*); or

(*d*) it is information the existence and relevance of which was notified to an HMRC officer by the taxpayer or someone acting on his behalf.

(*FA 2013, Sch 33, para 24(5)(6).*)

20.83 A discovery assessment (or an assessment to recover excess relief) cannot be made if the underpayment is attributable to a mistake in the return as to the basis on which the tax liability ought to have been calculated, and the return was made on the basis prevailing, or in accordance with the practice generally prevailing, at the time it was made (*FA 2013, Sch 33, para 24(7)*).

20.84 An ATED assessment must normally be made within four years after the end of the fiscal year to which it relates (*FA 2013, Sch 33, para 25(1)*). The period is increased to six years if the assessment involves a loss of tax brought about carelessly by the taxpayer or a 'related person' and to 20 years if it is brought about deliberately by the taxpayer or a related person or it is attributable to a failure by the taxpayer to make an ATED return (or amended return) or it is attributable to arrangements in respect of which the person has failed to comply with an obligation under DOTAS (*FA 2013, Sch 33, para 25(2)–(4)*). An assessment to recover an excessive repayment (see **20.80**) is not out of time if it is made while an enquiry into the relevant return is in progress or it is made within 12 months from the date of the repayment (*FA 2013, Sch 33, para 25(5)(6)*). An assessment on the personal representatives of a deceased person must be made within four years of the death and, if it relates to a loss of tax brought about carelessly, must not relate to a fiscal year ending more than six years before the death (*FA 2013, Sch 33, para 25(7)*). An objection to the making of an assessment on the grounds that the time limit for making it has expired can only be made on an appeal against the assessment (*FA 2013, Sch 33, para 25(8)*).

20.85 For the above purposes a related person is someone acting on the taxpayer's behalf, or a person who was a partner of the taxpayer at the relevant time (which is not defined but is presumably the time that the careless or fraudulent action occurred) (*FA 2013, Sch 33, para 25(9)*). A loss of tax is brought about carelessly by a person if that person fails to take reasonable care to avoid bringing about the loss. If information is provided to HMRC and the person who provided the information (or the taxpayer) subsequently discovers that the information was inaccurate and does not take reasonable steps to inform HMRC, any loss of tax brought about by the inaccuracy must be treated as having been brought about carelessly (*FA 2013, Sch 33, para 26(2)–(4)*). A loss of tax brought about as a result of a deliberate inaccuracy in a document given to HMRC by or on behalf of a person is regarded as having been brought about deliberately by that person (*FA 2013, Sch 33, para 26(5)*).

20.86 A notice of assessment must be served on the taxpayer. It must state the tax due, the date it is issued and the time within which any appeal must be made. Once an assessment has been served on the taxpayer, it can be altered only in accordance with the express provision of the ATED legislation. After an HMRC officer has decided to make an ATED assessment and has taken all other decisions needed for arriving at the amount of the assessment he can delegate responsibility for completing the assessing procedure to another HMRC officer (*FA 2013, Sch 33, para 27*).

20.87 A person who believes that ATED has been assessed on him more than once in respect of the same matter can make a claim to HMRC for relief against any double charge. *FA 2003, Sch 11A* applies to such a claim (*FA 2013, Sch 33, para 28*).

20.88 If a person has paid an amount of tax, or been assessed to such an amount, or an HMRC determination has been made that he is chargeable to an amount of tax, he can make a claim to HMRC for the amount to be repaid or discharged (*FA 2013, Sch 33, para 29(1)(2)*). For this purpose an amount paid by one person on behalf of another is treated as paid by that other person (*FA 2013, Sch 33, para 29(4)*). HMRC are not liable to give relief for such a claim except as provided under the ATED legislation (*FA 2013, Sch 33, para 29(3)*).

20.89 HMRC do not have to give effect to such a claim if (or to the extent that):

(*a*) the amount of tax paid (or payable) is excessive because of a mistake in a claim or a mistake consisting of making a claim or failing to do so;

(*b*) the claimant can (or will be able to) seek relief by taking other steps under the ATED legislation;

(*c*) the claimant could have sought relief by taking such steps within a period which has expired and knew, or ought reasonably to have known, before the end of that period that the relief was available;

(*d*) the claim is made on grounds that have been put to a court or Tribunal in the course of an appeal by the claimant relating to the amount paid or payable (or have been put to HMRC in the course of an appeal by the claimant relating to that amount that has been settled by agreement);

(*e*) the claimant knew, or ought reasonably to have known, of the grounds for the claim before the latest of–

(i) the date on which an appeal relating to the amount paid or payable in the course of which the ground could have been put forward was determined by a court or Tribunal (or treated as so determined by an agreement entered into with HMRC),

(ii) the date on which the taxpayer withdrew such an appeal to a court or Tribunal, or

(iii) the end of the period in which the taxpayer was entitled to make such an appeal to a court or Tribunal,

(*f*) the amount in question was paid (or is liable to be paid) in consequence of proceedings enforcing its payment brought against the claimant by HMRC (or in accordance with an agreement between the claimant and HMRC settling such proceedings); or

(*g*) unless the amount paid or payable is contrary to EU law, it is excessive by reason of a mistake in calculating the claimant's liability to tax and that liability was calculated in accordance with the practice generally prevailing at the time.

(*FA 2013, Sch 33, para 30(1)–(9).*) For the purpose of head (*g*), an amount is contrary to EU law if, in the circumstances in question, the charge to tax is contrary to the provisions relating to the free movement of goods, persons, services or capital in Titles II and IV of Part 3 of the Treaty on the Functioning of the European Union (or the provisions of any subsequent treaty replacing those provisions) (*FA 2013, Sch 33, para 30(10)*).

20.90 A claim for relief under *para 29* must be made within four years of the end of the fiscal year to which the payment, assessment or determination relates (*FA 2013, Sch 33, para 31(1)*). Such a claim cannot be made by being included in an ATED return (*FA 2013, Sch 33, para 31(2)*). *FA 2003, Sch 11A* (claims not included in a return – see **19.402**) applies in relation to such a claim (*FA 2013, Sch 33, para 31(3)*). Where the claim is by a partnership, the claim can be made only by a person who has been nominated to do so by all of the persons who would have been liable as responsible partners (see **20.24**) to pay the amount in question had the payment been due or the assessment or determination been correctly made (*FA 2013, Sch 33, para 32*).

20.91 If a claim is made under *para 29* and the grounds for giving effect to the claim also provide grounds for a discovery assessment on the claimant in respect of the single-dwelling interest, but such an assessment cannot be raised either because of the restrictions in *para 24* (see **20.81–20.83**) or the expiry of a time limit for making the assessment, those restrictions must be disregarded and the discovery assessment will not be out of time if it is made before the claim is finally determined (ie before the amount can no longer be varied, whether on appeal or otherwise) (*FA 2013, Sch 33, para 33*).

20.92 References in *para 29* to an amount paid by way of tax include an amount paid under a contract settlement (ie an agreement made in connection with any person's liability to make a payment to HMRC under, or by virtue of, any enactment) in connection with tax believed to be due (*FA 2013, Sch 33, para 34(1)(7)*). If the person who paid the amount under the contract settlement (the payer) and the person from whom the tax was due (the taxpayer) are not the same person:

(*a*) references above to the claimant include the taxpayer (or as appropriate have effect as if they were a reference to the taxpayer);

(*b*) references to tax in *FA 2003, Sch 11A* include the amount paid under the contract settlement; and

(*c*) if the grounds for giving effect to a claim by the payer in respect of the amount also provide grounds for a discovery assessment on the taxpayer, HMRC can set-off any amount repayable to the payer as a result of the claim against any amount payable by the taxpayer on the discovery assessment (and the obligations of HMRC and the taxpayer are discharged to the extent of any such set-off).

(*FA 2013, Sch 33, para 34(2)–(6)*.)

Reviews and Appeals

20.93 An appeal can be brought against:

(*a*) an amendment of a self-assessment under *para 10* (amendment during enquiry to prevent loss of tax – see **20.74**);

(*b*) a conclusion stated or amendment made by a closure notice (see **20.77**);

(*c*) an HMRC determination under *para 18* (determination of tax chargeable if no return is delivered – see **20.78**);

(*d*) a discovery assessment – see **20.80**; or

(*e*) an assessment under *para 22* (assessment to recover excessive repayment – see **20.80**).

(*FA 2013, Sch 33, para 35(1)*.)

20.94 Notice of an appeal must be given to HMRC in writing within 30 days of the date on which the notice of amendment (or the closure notice or HMRC determination or notice of assessment, as the case may be) was issued and must specify the grounds of appeal (*FA 2013, Sch 33, para 36(1)–(3)*).

20.95 Where an HMRC determination has been made under *para 18* as to the amount of tax to which a person is chargeable with respect to a single-dwelling interest, the only grounds on which an appeal lies are:

(*a*) that the condition in *FA 2013, s 94(2)(a)* (nature and value of interest – see **20.6**, ie that it is a single-dwelling interest with a value of over £500,000) is not met in relation to the interest in question on any day to which the determination relates;

(*b*) that the person, partnership or scheme that the determination identifies as meeting the ownership condition on one or more days does not meet that condition on any day in the fiscal year;

(*c*) if the determination is on a partnership, that a person identified in the determination as one of the responsible partners is not a responsible partner in relation to any tax chargeable for the period in question; and

(*d*) if the determination is on a collective investment scheme, that the person identified in the determination as the chargeable person in relation to the collective investment scheme concerned is not the chargeable person.

(*FA 2013, Sch 33, para 36(4).*)

20.96 HMRC have the power to accept a late notice of appeal. They must do so if they are satisfied that there was a reasonable excuse for not giving the notice before the expiry of the time limit and that the request for them to accept a late appeal was made without unreasonable delay. HMRC must notify the taxpayer whether or not they agree to the request. If HMRC decline to accept a late appeal, the FTT has power to give permission for the taxpayer to give a late notice of appeal (*FA 2013, Sch 33, para 37*).

20.97 If notice of appeal has been given to HMRC, the taxpayer can require an HMRC review to be carried out (see **20.98**). HMRC can offer a review (see **20.98**) or the appellant can notify the appeal to the Tribunal – in which case the Tribunal must determine the matter in question (*FA 2013, Sch 33, para 38(1)(2)*). If the appeal is against an amendment of a self-assessment under *para 10* (amendment during enquiry to prevent loss of tax), none of these three steps can be taken until the enquiry is completed (*FA 2013, Sch 33, para 35(2)*).

20.98 If the taxpayer requires a review, HMRC must notify the appellant of their view of the matter in question within 30 days of their receiving the notification from the taxpayer or such longer period as is reasonable. They must then review the matter in question (unless the taxpayer has previously asked for a review, HMRC have offered a review or the taxpayer has notified the appeal to the Tribunal (*FA 2013, Sch 33, para* 29). If HMRC offer a review, the offer must include a statement of HMRC's view of the matter in question. If the taxpayer accepts the offer within 30 days of the date of the offer document,

HMRC must review the matter in question. They cannot offer a review if they have previously offered one in relation to the matter in question, the taxpayer has already required a review or he has notified the appeal to the Tribunal. If the taxpayer does not accept the offer of a review, he can notify the appeal to the Tribunal within the 30-day period (*FA 2013, Sch 33, para 46*) (see **20.101**). The Tribunal (but not HMRC) has power to extend the 30-day period (*FA 2013, Sch 33, para 44(3)(4)*).

20.99 Where HMRC are required to carry out a review under either of these provisions, the nature and extent of the review are to be such as appear appropriate to HMRC in the circumstances, having regard, in particular, to steps taken before the beginning of the review by HMRC in deciding the matter in question, and by any other person in seeking to resolve disagreement about the matter in question (such as whether ADR has been tried). The review must take account of any representations made by the taxpayer at a stage which gives HMRC a reasonable opportunity to consider them (*FA 2013, Sch 33, para 41(1)–(4)*). The reviewer can uphold, vary or cancel the HMRC decision, etc (*FA 2013, Sch 33, para 41(5)*). HMRC must notify the appellant of the conclusions of the review and their reasoning within 45 days of the day when HMRC notified the taxpayer of their (pre-review) view of the matter in question or, if HMRC offered the review, within 45 days of their receipt of the taxpayer's acceptance. HMRC and the taxpayer can agree a different notification period – which in practice is likely to mean a longer period than 45 days (*FA 2013, Sch 33, para 41(6)(7)*). If HMRC do not give notice of the conclusions of the review within the specified period, the review is treated as upholding HMRC's view and HMRC must notify the taxpayer of this deemed conclusion (*FA 2013, Sch 33, para 41(8)(9)*).

20.100 This procedure for internal reviews is based on that which applies for income tax, corporation tax and CGT. For those taxes the review is normally carried out by specialist review teams in a different office, so ought to produce a genuine second opinion. It is unlikely that this will apply to ATED reviews as ATED is likely to be administered by a small specialist team, so the only people with the technical knowledge to carry out a review are likely to be in the same office as the original decision-maker. Indeed the reviewer could well be the decision-maker's superior and, as such, may well have been consulted on the matter by the decision-maker prior to his forming his conclusion. Accordingly, while conceptually an internal review is normally an attractive extra step in seeking to reach an agreement without involving the Tribunal, this will not necessarily apply to ATED as the review may simply be re-looking at a decision which the reviewer was involved in making. Accordingly the efficacy of the ATED review process remains to be seen. There is little downside in using it, but if in practice it normally upholds the HMRC view, there may turn out to be little benefit either.

20.101 Once the taxpayer has asked for a review he cannot notify his appeal to the Tribunal during the 45-day review period (or other agreed period) but, if he wishes to do so, must notify it to the Tribunal within 30 days of the date of the document in which HMRC give notice of their conclusion of the review (or of the notice in which they explain that the HMRC view is deemed to be upheld because they did not make a review decision within the specified period) (*FA 2013, Sch 33, para 43*). The same rule applies if HMRC offer the review (*FA 2013, Sch 13, para 44*). The Tribunal can give permission for an appeal to be notified to it outside the 30-day period, ie to accept a late notification of the appeal (*FA 2013, Sch 33, para 44(2)(b),(3)(b)*).

20.102 If the taxpayer either does not accept the offer of a review and does not notify his appeal to the Tribunal within the 30-day period, or he requires or accepts a review and after its conclusion does not notify his appeal to the Tribunal within the 30-day period (or such extended period as the Tribunal may permit) HMRC's view of the matter in question is deemed to have been agreed and becomes binding as if it had been contained in a settlement agreement (see **20.105**). The taxpayer has no right to withdraw from such a deemed agreement (*FA 2013, Sch 33, paras 40(4)(5), 42(1)*).

20.103 The taxpayer (or his agent) and HMRC can enter into an agreement (a settlement agreement) at any time before the appeal is determined to the effect that the decision appealed against should be upheld without variation, varied in a particular manner or discharged or cancelled (*FA 2013, Sch 33, para 46(1)(7)*). The consequences of entering into a settlement agreement are the same (for all purposes) as if, at the time the agreement was entered into, the Tribunal had decided the appeal in the same way as has been agreed (*FA 2013, Sch 33, para 46(2)*). This does not apply if within 30 days of entering into the settlement agreement the taxpayer (or his agent) gives notice in writing to HMRC that it wishes to withdraw from the agreement (*FA 2013, Sch 33, para 46(3)(7)*). If the settlement agreement is not in writing, it has no effect unless the fact that it was entered into and the terms agreed are confirmed in writing by either party to the other. In that event the taxpayer's right to withdraw from the agreement applies to the 30 days from the date that such confirmation is given (*FA 2013, Sch 33, para 46(4)*).

20.104 If after giving notice of appeal to HMRC the taxpayer notifies HMRC (orally or in writing) that he does not wish to proceed with the appeal and HMRC do not give the taxpayer notice in writing within 30 days after that notification that they are unwilling that the appeal should be withdrawn, the parties are deemed to have entered into a settlement agreement that the decision appealed against should be upheld without variation (*FA 2013, Sch 33, para 46(5)(6)*).

20.105 Where an appeal is made, the tax charged remains due and payable unless the taxpayer makes a postponement application (*FA 2013, Sch 33, para 47*). The taxpayer can apply in writing to HMRC within 30 days of the date of the notice of amendment, closure notice, determination or assessment (as the case may be) for a determination by HMRC of the amount of tax the payment of which should be postponed pending the determination of the appeal. The taxpayer can make such an application only if he has grounds for believing that the amendment, assessment, etc overcharges him to tax. The application must state the amount believed to be overcharged and the grounds for that belief (*FA 2013, Sch 33, para 48(1),(2)(9)*). An application can be made outside the 30-day period if there is a change of circumstances as a result of which the taxpayer has grounds for believing that he is overcharged to tax (*FA 2013, Sch 33, para 48(3)*).

20.106 If the taxpayer does not agree with the determination made by HMRC he can refer the application for postponement to the FTT within 30 days of the document notifying the taxpayer of HMRC's determination (*FA 2013, Sch 33, para 48(1)(b)*). Such an application is subject to *TMA 1970, s 48(2)(b)* (proceedings before Tribunal other than an appeal against an assessment) (*FA 2013, Sch 33, para 48(6)*). The amount of tax payment of which is to be postponed pending the determination of the appeal is the amount (if any) by which it appears that there are reasonable grounds for believing that the taxpayer is overcharged (*FA 2013, Sch 33, para 48(7)*). Once a postponement application has been determined, *FA 2013, s 163* (payment of tax – see **20.23**) has effect in relation to tax the payment of the amount which has not been postponed as if that tax were payable in accordance with an assessment issued on the date on which the postponement application was determined and against which there was no appeal (*FA 2013, Sch 33, para 48(8)*). If after a postponement application has been determined there is a change of circumstances, both the taxpayer and HMRC have a right to apply to the FTT for a revised determination of the amount to be postponed. Such an application can be made at any time before the determination of the appeal (*FA 2013, Sch 33, para 48(4)(5)*).

20.107 If the taxpayer (or his agent) and HMRC agree that payment of an amount of tax should be postponed pending the determination of the appeal, the consequences are the same (for all purposes) as if the FTT had made a direction to the same effect as the agreement at the time the agreement was entered into (*FA 2013, Sch 33, para 49(1)–(3)*). If the agreement is not in writing this does not apply unless the fact that an agreement was entered into, and the terms agreed, are confirmed in writing by one party to the other (*FA 2013, Sch 33, para 49(2)*).

20.108 When an appeal has been notified to the FTT, if it decides that the taxpayer is overcharged by an assessment it must be reduced accordingly.

Otherwise the assessment is to stand good. If it appears to the FTT that the taxpayer is undercharged by the assessment, it must be increased accordingly (*FA 2013, Sch 33, para 50*). The determination of the Tribunal in relation to ATED is final and conclusive except as otherwise provided in the *Tribunals, Courts and Enforcement Act 2007, ss 9–14* (appeals to Upper Tribunal and Court of Appeal) and the ATED provisions (*FA 2013, Sch 33, para 51*).

20.109 On the determination of an appeal, any tax overpaid must be repaid (*FA 2013, Sch 33, para 52(1)*). Any tax that has been postponed, and any increase in tax as a result of the determination becomes payable within 30 days of the issue by HMRC of a notice of the total amount payable in accordance with the determination (*FA 2013, s 163(5), Sch 33, para 52(2)(3)*). The tax is payable even if there is a further appeal against the Tribunal's decision (*FA 2013, Sch 33, para 53(1)*). If the amount payable is subsequently altered by the Upper Tribunal or a court, any resultant overpayment must be refunded together with any interest allowed by the order or judgment. If the amount payable is subsequently increased, the balance becomes payable within 30 days of the issue by HMRC of a notice of the total amount payable as a result of the order or judgment (*FA 2013, Sch 33, para 53(2)*).

Information and Inspection Powers

20.110 *FA 2008, Sch 36* (information and inspection powers) applies for the purposes of ATED (*FA 2008, Sch 36, para 63(1)(ha)* inserted by *FA 2013, Sch 14, para 5*). The power to inspect property for valuation purposes extends to ATED (*FA 2008, Sch 36, para 12A(3)(f)* inserted by *FA 2013, Sch 34, para 2*).

20.111 Where a person has delivered an ATED return or a return of the adjusted chargeable amount for a fiscal year with respect to a single-dwelling interest a taxpayer notice (ie a notice to provide information or to produce a document if the information or document is reasonably required by HMRC for the purpose of checking the taxpayer's tax position – *FA 2008, Sch 36, para 1*) cannot be given for the purpose of checking that person's ATED position as regards the matters dealt with in that return unless either:

(*a*) an enquiry notice has been given in respect of the return (or of a claim or amendment made by the person in relation to the fiscal year and the enquiry has not been completed);

(*b*) an HMRC officer has reason to suspect (as regards that person) that an amount that ought to have been assessed to ATED for the fiscal year may not have been assessed, an assessment to ATED may have become insufficient, or relief from ATED may have become excessive; or (*c*) the notice is given for the purpose of obtaining any information or document that is also required for the purpose of checking that person's position as regards a tax other than ATED.

(*FA 2008, Sch 36, para 21B* inserted by *FA 2013, Sch 34, para 3.*)

20.112 Where in respect of a single-dwelling interest to which one or more companies are (or were) entitled as members of a partnership, any member of the partnership has delivered an ATED return, or a return of the adjusted chargeable amount, or made a claim in relation to ATED, *FA 2008, Sch 36, para 21B* (restrictions where the taxpayer has delivered a return) has effect as if that return had been delivered (or the claim made) by each member of the partnership (*FA 2008, Sch 36, para 37(2B)* inserted by *FA 2013, Sch 34, para 4*).

Penalties

20.113 The penalty provisions in *FA 2007, Sch 24* (penalties for errors), *FA 2009, Sch 55* (penalty for failure to make returns etc) and *FA 2009, Sch 56*, are extended to cover ATED (both ATED returns and returns of adjusted chargeable amount) with effect from 17 July 2013 (*FA 2013, Sch 34, paras 6,7*). *FA 2009, Sch 56* (penalty for failure to make payments on time) is also extended to ATED from the same date. The penalty date under *para 1* of that *Schedule* is 30 days after the date on which the tax must be paid under *FA 2013, s 163(1)(2)* (see **20.23**) or 30 days after the filing date for the return where no return is submitted and an HMRC determination of the tax payable is made (*FA 2013, Sch 34, paras 8–12*). In *Chartridge Developments Ltd (TC 5493)*, the first reported ATED case to have come before the FTT, HMRC quoted the wrong dates for the start of the penalties in the penalty notices. It was held that this invalidated the fixed penalty notices as it was a gross error likely to mislead the taxpayer. A tax-related penalty was upheld, though, as the notice contained a detailed description of how the penalties are calculated, so the notice was in substance and effect in conformity with the intent of the legislation.

Collection and Recovery of Tax

20.114 *FA 2003, Sch 12* (SDLT collection and recovery of tax) applies to ATED as it has effect in relation to SDLT (*FA 2013, s 165*). These provisions are considered at **19.204–19.206**.

Miscellaneous

Companies

20.115 For ATED purposes a company means a body corporate, but does not include a corporation, sole practitioner or a partnership (*FA 2013, s 166(1)*). Nor does it include a public body (see **20.57**) or a body established for national purposes (see **20.58**) (*FA 2013, s 166(10)*). Everything to be done by a company in relation to ATED must be done by the company acting through the 'proper officer' of the company or (unless the company is in liquidation) another person who has the express, implied or apparent authority of the company to act on its behalf for this purpose (*FA 2013, s 166(2)(7)(a)*). Service of a document on a company can be effected by serving it on the proper officer (*FA 2013, s 166(3)*). Tax due from a company that is incorporated outside the UK can be recovered from the proper officer of the company as well as by any means available to HMRC in the absence of this provision (*FA 2013, s 166(4)*). The proper officer is entitled to retain out of any money that may come into his hands on the company's behalf enough money to pay that tax and to be fully reimbursed by the company for tax or other amounts paid by the officer under *s 166(4)* (*FA 2013, s 166(5)*). For these purposes, unless a liquidator or administrator has been appointed, the 'proper officer' is the company secretary or a person acting as secretary of the company or, if there is no such person, the treasurer or a person acting as treasurer of the company. If a liquidator has been appointed, the proper officer is the liquidator, and if an administrator has been appointed, it is the administrator. If two or more persons are appointed to act jointly or concurrently as the administrator of a company, they can choose, by notice given to HMRC, which of them is to be the proper officer. If they do not give such a notice, HMRC can designate one of them as the proper officer (*FA 2013, s 166(6)–(9)*).

Partnerships

20.116 For the purposes of ATED, a partnership means:

(*a*) a partnership within the *Partnership Act 1890*;

(*b*) a limited partnership registered under the *Limited Partnerships Act 1907*;

(*c*) a limited liability partnership formed under the *Limited Liability Partnerships Act 2000* or the *Limited Liability Partnerships Act (Northern Ireland) 2002*; or

(*d*) a firm or entity of a similar character to any of the above formed under the law of a country or territory outside the UK.

(*FA 2013, s 167(1)*.)

20.117 In relation to a partnership (such as a UK LLP) that is itself capable of being entitled to (or of acquiring or disposing of) a chargeable interest:

(*a*) transactions entered into on behalf of the partnership must be treated as entered into by or on behalf of the partners; and

(*b*) where the partnership is entitled to a single-dwelling interest, the ATED legislation has effect as if the partners were jointly entitled to the interest (instead of the partnership).

(*FA 2013, s 167(2)*.)

20.118 A partnership is treated as the same partnership despite a change in membership if any person who was a member before the change remains a member after it (*FA 2013, s 167(3)*). A collective investment scheme is not regarded as a partnership. Accordingly a member of a partnership by or on whose behalf a single-dwelling interest is held for the purposes of a collective investment scheme is not regarded as entitled to the interest as a member of the partnership (*FA 2013, s 167(4)*).

20.119 In relation to a return delivered by the responsible partners for a partnership, anything required or authorised under *FA 2013, ss 159* (ATED return) or *160* (return of adjusted chargeable amount) or *Sch 33*, to be done by the responsible partners (see **20.24**) is required or authorised to be done by all the responsible partners (*FA 2013, Sch 33, para 56*). However, this seems to be subject to *s 167* which provides that anything required or authorised to be done by (or in relation to) the responsible partners for a partnership can instead be done by any representative partner or partners. A representative partner is a partner nominated by a majority of the partners to act as the representative of the partnership for the purposes of ATED. Any such nomination, or the revocation of such a nomination, has effect only after notice of it has been given to HMRC (*FA 2013, s 167(5)–(7)*).

Connected Persons

20.120 The definition of connected person in *CTA 2010, s 1122* (see Appendix 1) applies for ATED (*FA 2013, s 172(1)*).

20.121 In addition for ATED a person is regarded as connected with a collective investment scheme if he is a participant in the scheme who is:

(*a*) entitled to a share of at least 50% of either of all of the profits or income arising from the scheme or of any profits or income arising from the scheme that may be distributed to participants; or (*b*) would be entitled, in the event of a winding up of the scheme, to 50% or more of the assets of the scheme that would then be available for distribution among the participants.

(*FA 2013, s 172(2)*.)

For this purpose the reference to a collective investment scheme does not include a unit trust scheme (as *CTA 2010, s 1123(2)* already defines connected persons in relation to such a scheme) (*FA 2013, s 172(3)*). Profits or income arising from the scheme means profits or income arising from the acquisition, holding, management or disposal of the property subject to the scheme (*FA 2013, s 172(4)*). In applying the 50% tests, a person is regarded as having any rights or powers that he is entitled to acquire at a future date, or will at a future date be entitled to acquire, and the rights and powers of any associate (or any two or more associates) of his (as defined in *CTA 2010, s 448* but omitting the reference to a partner) must be attributed to that person (*FA 2013, s 172(5)–(7)*).

20.122 A person is connected to a cell company where, if any cell were a separate company, he would be connected to that separate company (*FA 2013, s 173(1)*). A company is a cell company for this purpose if either:

(*a*) under the law under which the company is incorporated or formed, or under the Articles of Association or other document regulating the company, or under arrangements entered into by or in relation to the company–

  (i) some or all of the assets of the company are available only, or primarily, to meet particular liabilities of the company, and

  (ii) some or all of the members of the company, and some or all of its creditors, have rights only, or primarily, in relation to particular assets of the company, or

(*b*) the company's Articles of Association (or other documents regulating it) establish an entity (by whatever name known) which, under the law under which the company is incorporated or formed, has legal personality distinct from that of the company and which is not itself a company.

(*FA 2013, s 173(2)–(4)*.) A cell in relation to a cell company is either an identifiable part of the company (by whatever name known) that carries on distinct business activities and to which particular assets and liabilities of the company are wholly or primarily attributable, or the entity referred to at (*b*) above (*FA 2013, s 173(5)*).

Other Matters

20.123

(*a*) Orders and regulations in relation to ATED are to be made by statutory instrument (*FA 2013, s 169(1)*). An order or regulation can make different provisions for different purposes and can include consequential or transitional provision or savings (*FA 2013, s 169(5)*).

(*b*) Where *FA 2013, s 97(2)* applies (joint ownership – see **20.24**) and the other joint owners include a company, or *FA 2013, s 97(4)* (partnerships – see **20.24**) applies and one of the partners is a company, any obligation to deliver a return with respect to the single-dwelling interest for the fiscal year concerned is a joint obligation of the persons who are jointly and severally liable. A single return is required (*FA 2013, Sch 33, para 55*).

(*c*) ATED has been added to the definition of 'tax' in the DOTAS (disclosure of tax avoidance schemes) rules (*FA 2013, Sch 35, para 2*).

(*d*) The standard definitions of charity, charitable company and charitable trust in *FA 2010, Sch 6, para 7* apply to ATED (*FA 2013, Sch 35, para 3*).

(*e*) In relation to the fiscal year to 31 March 2013, the ATED return must be delivered by 1 October 2013 if the days on which the person is within the charge to tax include 1 April 2013. If they do not include that day it must be delivered within 30 days of the first day in the fiscal year on which the person is within the charge with respect to the interest if that is later than 1 October 2013 (*FA 2013, Sch 35, para 4*). The tax for that fiscal year must be paid by 31 October 2013, or, if later, by the filing date for the return (*FA 2013, Sch 35, para 4*).

(*f*) The phrase 'fiscal year' has been used above to describe the ATED tax year. The legislation uses the phrase 'chargeable period'. However, as in other tax contexts, a chargeable period can normally vary in length and for ATED the chargeable period is always the 12 months to 31 March, so the author feels that 'fiscal year' is less likely to cause confusion.

Chapter 21

The Council Tax

21.1 In addition to central government taxation local authorities impose two property taxes, the council tax and non-domestic rates (except in Northern Ireland). The council tax replaced the community charge, a form of local authority taxation of individuals known colloquially as the poll tax. It is imposed by the *Local Government Finance Act 1992* and section references below are to that Act unless otherwise stated.

21.2 The rate of tax is fixed locally by each 'billing authority' and will vary from year to year depending on the billing authority's budget requirements and whether or not the Secretary of State for the Environment exercises his power to limit, or cap, the rate chosen by an individual authority. District councils and London borough councils are billing authorities (*s 1*). Liability to pay the tax is determined on a daily basis and is based on the facts prevailing at the end of each day (*s 2*).

The *Localism Act 2011, s 72* introduced new *ss 52ZA–52ZY* to the *Local Government Finance Act 1992*. These provide that if a local authority fixes a rate of council tax which is excessive (in accordance with a set of principles to be determined by the Minister), it must hold a referendum of its local electorate. If they do not approve the proposed rate, the council tax is limited to the amount calculated in accordance with the Ministerial principles. The conduct of such referendums is governed by the *Local Authority (Conduct of Referendums) (Council Tax Increases) (England) Regulations 2012 (SI 2012 No 444)* as amended by the *Local Authority (Conduct of Referendums) (Council Tax Increases) (England) (Amendment and Amendment No 2) Regulations 2014 (SI 2014 Nos 231 and 925)*.

21.3 The tax is payable in respect of any dwelling that is not an exempt dwelling (*s 4*). The exemptions are set out in **21.8**. In calculating the tax certain categories of people are granted discounts of either 25% or 50% (see **21.21** below). In addition, a social security benefit, council tax benefit, has been introduced to help those who cannot afford to pay the full tax. Responsibility for council tax in Scotland and Wales has been devolved to the Scottish Parliament and the Welsh Assembly. This chapter accordingly deals with the legislation only as it applies in England.

What is Domestic Property?

21.4 A dwelling is defined as any property which would have been a hereditament for the purpose of the *General Rate Act 1967* had it remained in force and which is not covered by a local or central non-domestic rating list (or exempt from local non-domestic rating under *Part III* of the *Local Government Finance Act 1988*). The *Local Government Finance Act 1988, s 42* excludes from rating domestic property and *s 66* defines such property as:

(*a*) property used wholly for the purposes of living accommodation;

(*b*) a yard, garden, outhouse or other appurtenance belonging to or enjoyed with property within (*a*);

(*c*) a private garage used wholly or mainly for the accommodation of a private motor vehicle;

(*d*) private storage premises used wholly or mainly for the storage of articles of domestic use;

(*e*) a caravan pitch on a protected site used as the sole or main residence of an individual;

(*f*) a mooring occupied by a boat which is the sole or main residence of an individual; or

(*g*) property not in use where it appears that its next use will be domestic.

Property which is wholly or mainly used in the course of a business for the provision of accommodation for short periods (with domestic or other services) to individuals whose sole or main residence is elsewhere is not domestic through *s 66(2)*. Nor is time-share accommodation or property wholly or mainly used in the course of a business for the provision of short-stay accommodation, ie (subject to exceptions) accommodation which is provided for short periods to individuals whose sole or main residence is elsewhere and which is not self-contained catering accommodation provided commercially (*Standard Community Charge and Non-Domestic Rating (Definition of Domestic Property) Order 1990* (*SI 1990 No 162*) and *Non-Domestic Rating (Definition of Domestic Property) Order 1993* (*SI 1993 No 542*)). From 1 April 2013, property is also domestic if it is situated in or on a property which is used wholly for the purpose of living accommodation (or a yard, garden, outhouse or other appurtenance belonging to, or enjoyed with, such property) and is used wholly or mainly for microgeneration (small scale energy generation using sustainable technologies such as solar or wind) of electricity or heat for use mainly in the property (*Non-Domestic Rating and Council Tax (Definition of Domestic Property and Dwelling) (England) Order 2013 (SI 2013 No 468)*.

21.5 A composite residence, ie one used partly as a dwelling and partly for some other purpose, is also included (*s 3(1)–(3)*). However, the *Council Tax*

(Situation and Valuation of Dwellings) Regulations 1992 (SI 1992 No 550) provides that the value of a dwelling which is a composite hereditament is that portion of the value of the hereditament which can reasonably be attributed to domestic use of the dwelling. The balance of the value is of course liable to non-domestic rating. A yard, garden, outhouse or other appurtenance belonging to, or enjoyed with, property used wholly for the purpose of living accommodation, private garage which either has a floor area of 25 square metres or less or is used wholly or mainly for accommodation of a private motor vehicle, and private storage premises used wholly or mainly for the storage of articles of domestic use, are specifically excluded from themselves constituting dwellings (*s 3(4)*).

21.6 The Minister is given power to amend the definition of a dwelling and to prescribe that one dwelling should be treated as two or more and vice versa (*s 3(5)(6)*). He has provided in the *Council Tax (Chargeable Dwellings) Order 1992 (SI 1992 No 549)* (as amended by the *Council Tax (Chargeable Dwellings, Exempt Dwellings and Discount Disregards) Amendment Order 1997 (SI 1997 No 656)* and the *Council Tax (Chargeable Dwellings, Exempt Dwellings and Discount Disregards) (Amendment) (England) Order 2003 (SI 2003 No 3121)*) that where a single property contains more than one self-contained unit each such unit must be treated as a separate dwelling, and where a multiple property, ie one that would otherwise be two or more dwellings, consists of a single self-contained unit (or of such a unit plus premises constructed or adapted for non-domestic purposes) and is occupied as more than one unit of separate living accommodation the listing officer (see **21.34** below) can, if he thinks fit, having regard to all the circumstances including the extent if any to which the property has been structurally altered, treat the property as a single dwelling. A self-contained unit is defined as a building or part of a building, a caravan, or a boat which has been constructed or adapted for use as separate living accommodation. (The Order fell to be considered by the court in *Clement (Listing Officer) v Bryant and others.* This appeal related to 11 bedsits in a dwelling occupied by elderly persons. The Valuation Tribunal had held that the bedsits formed a single dwelling. Each unit had its own front door, washbasin, wc and kitchen. The tribunal were also influenced by the facts that there was only one TV licence for the premises and there were shared bathrooms, lounge and laundry facilities 'which pointed to a high degree of communality and dependency' and that there was only one access point which would pose a difficulty if the units were to be sold separately on the open market. It therefore felt that they were not self-contained. The court held that although this was a question of fact, the tribunal had misdirected itself and that 'these units were undoubtedly constructed or adapted for use as separate living accommodation'. The judge said that the fact that there was only one access point 'cannot assist in deciding whether those units are or are not self-contained'. He also felt that neither communal living nor the fact that the bedsits happened to be occupied by elderly people were relevant considerations. The court similarly reversed the decision of the tribunal in *Beasley (Listing Officer) v National Council of YMCAs (2000 RA 429)* holding that bedsits were again self-contained. The judge there said that 'when looking at *arts 2* and *3* of the *1992 Order*, one focuses not upon the use that is actually made of the building, but upon whether it has been constructed for use as separate living accommodation'.

21.7 A particular problem can arise with 'granny flats' and similar annexes to a house. A number of valuation tribunals have held that these are part of the main house. HMRC appealed four of these cases – *Rodd v Ritchings, Gilbert v Childs, Batty v Burfoot* and *Batty v Merriman* – on the basis that the *Chargeable Dwellings Order* required a granny flat to be treated as a separate dwelling to the main house. In each case it was held that the valuation tribunal had misdirected itself and its decision in favour of the taxpayer must be quashed and the case remitted for reconsideration (*The Times*, 21 June 1995). In *Rodd v Ritchings* the valuation tribunal's decision had been based on the fact that the granny flat could not be used as a separate unit without breaching the planning consent. In *Gilbert v Childs* the tribunal had looked not at whether the annexe was built or adapted as a separate dwelling, which is the test applied by the *Order*, but whether those living in it in fact shared access to services and shared family life with the occupants of the main house. In *Batty v Burfoot* and *Batty v Merriman* the tribunal had reasoned that it was not practical to sell the granny flat on the open market separate from the house, which ignored the statutory presumptions imposed by the *Order*. It should be stressed that these decisions do not necessarily mean that the *Chargeable Dwellings Order* prevents a granny flat from being part of the main building. That is a question of fact to be decided in the light of each individual case. They probably make it likely that in most cases it will fall to be treated as a separate building.

The Minister has also provided that, from 1 January 2004 a registered care home (within the meaning of the *Care Standards Act 2000*) is to be treated as one plus as many separate dwellings as there are self-contained units provided for the purpose of accommodating the persons registered in respect of it under the *Care Standards Act 2000*. For example, if the home is registered to accommodate 20 persons and currently has 17 residents, it will be treated as comprising 21 dwellings (*Council Tax (Chargeable Dwellings) Order 1992, Article 3A* inserted by the *Council Tax (Chargeable Dwellings, Exempt Dwellings and Discount Disregards) (Amendment) (England) Order 2003*).

Classes of Exempt Dwellings

21.8 The *Council Tax (Exempt Dwellings) Order 1992* (*SI 1992 No 558*) as amended on a number of occasions, most recently by the *Council Tax (Exempt*

Dwellings) (Amendment) (England) Order 2006 (SI 2006 No 2318) sets out the categories of dwelling that are exempted from the council tax. These cover student and armed forces accommodation and certain unoccupied buildings. The detailed exemptions are:

Class A: A vacant dwelling (ie one which is unoccupied and substantially unfurnished) which either:

- (*a*) requires, or is undergoing, major repair works (including structural works) to render it habitable;
- (*b*) is undergoing structural alteration; or
- (*c*) has been vacant for a continuous period of under six months following the substantial completion of works within (*a*) or (*b*),

but only for the first 12 continuous months (in total) in which such conditions apply.

Class B: An unoccupied dwelling owned by a charity and which was previously occupied in furtherance of the objects of the charity. Again the exemption applies only for the first six months of a period that the property is empty.

Class C: A vacant dwelling which has been empty for a continuous period of less than six months.

Class D: An unoccupied dwelling which, but for his detention, would be the sole or main residence of a person detained in a prison, hospital or any other place by virtue of an order of a UK court (or of a Standing Civilian Court under the *Armed Forces Act 1976*) or detailed under *Sch 3, para 2* of the *Immigration Act 1971* (awaiting deportation) or *ss 46–48* or *136* of the *Mental Health Act 1983* or their Scottish equivalents and who is the owner or tenant of the dwelling. Imprisonment for default in paying the council tax itself or for default in payment of a fine will not attract the exemption though. This exemption also extends to a dwelling which was previously the sole or main residence of the qualifying person provided that he has been in detention for the entire period since it was last occupied. A dwelling is unoccupied under this head only if all of its occupants are in detention.

Class E: An unoccupied dwelling which was previously the sole or main residence of a qualifying person whose current one is in a hospital (but not a private hospital), a registered residential care home, registered nursing home or registered mental care home in which he is receiving care or treatment (or both) as a patient and who is an owner or tenant of the dwelling. The person must have been in the hospital or home for the whole period since he last occupied the house as his sole or main residence.

Class F: A dwelling which has been unoccupied since the death of a person who either:

(i) owned the freehold or a lease of over six months (from the grant) and there is no other person (other than the personal representative) who is a qualifying person, ie a person who is liable for the council tax in respect of the dwelling as an owner; or

(ii) was a tenant under a lease of less than six months, a secure or statutory tenant, or a contractual licensee of the dwelling at the time of his death and his personal representative (acting as such) is the person liable for the rent or licence fee.

The exemption applies only until six months after probate or letters of administration have been granted. A single period of temporary occupation of up to six weeks can be ignored in determining whether the property is unoccupied.

Class G: An unoccupied dwelling, the occupation of which is restricted by a condition which prevents occupancy and is imposed by any planning permission or the occupation of which is otherwise prohibited by law (or which is kept unoccupied by reason of the exercise of powers under any Act of Parliament with a view to prohibiting its occupation or to acquiring it). (The wording was slightly different prior to 1 April 2007.)

Class H: An unoccupied dwelling held for occupation by a minister of religion as a residence from which to perform the duties of his office.

Class I: An unoccupied dwelling which was previously the sole or main residence of a person who is an owner or tenant of the dwelling and who both has his main residence in another place (other than a hospital, private hospital, care home or hostel) for the purpose of receiving personal care required by him by reason of old age, disablement, illness, past or present alcohol or drug dependence or past or present mental disorder; and who has been a relevant absentee for the entire period since the dwelling was last his main residence (*Council Tax (Chargeable Dwellings, Exempt Dwellings and Discount Disregards) (Amendment) (England) Order 2003 (SI 2003 No 3121)*).

Class J: An unoccupied dwelling which was previously the sole or main residence of a person who currently has his sole or main residence elsewhere for the purpose of providing (or better providing) personal care for someone else who requires such care by reason of old age, disablement, illness, alcohol or drug dependence or mental disorder. This head will cover, for example, the house of someone who moves in with an elderly parent to care for him leaving his own house temporarily unoccupied. The person must have been living in the other residence since he last occupied his own house as his residence and must be an owner or tenant of the dwelling.

Class K: An unoccupied dwelling which was last occupied as their main residence by one or more students (as defined in *Sch 1, para 4*), and in relation to which every qualifying person is a student and either has been one since the last occupier ceased to occupy the building as his sole or main residence or became one within six weeks of that date.

Class L: An unoccupied dwelling where a mortgagee is in possession under the mortgage.

Class M: A dwelling comprising a hall of residence provided predominantly for the accommodation of students which is owned or managed by a prescribed educational establishment (within *Sch 1, para 5*) or a charity or is the subject of an agreement allowing such an establishment to nominate the majority of the persons to occupy the accommodation.

Class N: A dwelling which is occupied by one or more residents all of whom are students, or which is occupied only by one or more students as term-time accommodation (in which case the dwelling is deemed to also be occupied as student accommodation during any vacation in which the student has an interest in the property or licence to occupy it, provided that he has previously used or intends to use the dwelling as term-time accommodation. Student for this purpose includes a college or school leaver within Class C of *SI 1992 No 2942* – see **21.23**(9)). It also includes a spouse or dependent of a student, provided that such a person is not a British citizen, who is prevented by immigration laws from taking paid employment or claiming benefits, etc. in the UK (*Council Tax (Discount Disregards and Exempt Dwellings) (Amendment) Order 1995* (*SI 1995 No 619*)).

Class O: A dwelling owned by the Minister of Defence and held for the purposes of armed forces accommodation other than accommodation for visiting forces.

Class P: A dwelling in respect of which at least one person who otherwise would be liable to pay council tax has a relevant association under the *Visiting Forces Act 1952* with a body, contingent or detachment of the forces of a country covered by the *Act*.

Class Q: An unoccupied dwelling owned by a trustee in bankruptcy.

Class R: A dwelling consisting of a pitch or mooring but which is not occupied by a caravan or boat.

Class S: A dwelling occupied only by persons aged under 18.

Class T: An unoccupied dwelling which forms part of a single property which includes another dwelling if the two cannot be let separately without a breach of planning consent.

Class U: A dwelling occupied only by persons who are severely mentally impaired (see **21.25**) and who but for this exemption would be liable to pay the council tax. From 1 April 1999 this exemption also applies if the dwelling is owned or occupied by one or more students (within Class N).

Class V: A dwelling at least one occupier of which is entitled to Diplomatic (and some similar statutory) privileges and immunities and is not a British citizen (or British Dependent Territories citizens British National (Overseas) citizen, British Overseas citizen, British subject or British protected person) nor a permanent resident of the UK. Where such a person has more than one UK dwelling the exemption applies only to his main UK residence.

Class W: A dwelling which forms part of a single property (ie one which would otherwise be one dwelling) consisting of more than one dwelling and which is the sole or main residence of a dependent relative of a person who resides in the other dwelling (or one of them). For this purpose, relative covers the person's spouse, 'common-law' spouse, civil partner, person living as a civil partner, parent, grandparent, child, child of the person's civil partner, stepchild, grandchild, brother, sister, uncle, aunt, nephew or niece, or a parent or child of any of these people. It also includes a great (or great-great) grandparent, grandchild, uncle, aunt, nephew or niece. It also includes such a relative of the person's spouse or civil partner or of someone living together with that person as husband and wife or as civil partners. It probably includes a former spouse (or live-in partner); the *Order* states a relationship by marriage shall be treated as a relationship by blood, which suggests that the relationship will survive a termination of the marriage. A relative is dependent if he is 65 or over or is severely mentally impaired or substantially and permanently disabled (whether by illness, injury, congenital deformity or otherwise).

Valuation Bands

21.9 For the purpose of the tax all dwellings in the local authority area have been allocated into eight categories, bands A to H. Band D represents an average property. Band A contains properties worth less than 50% of average value and Band H those worth more than 400% of the average. The values are as at 1 April 1991. In theory, the large fluctuations in house prices since then should not have an adverse effect as the tax differentials are effectively based on relative values rather than actual prices. In practice, as changes in value have not been uniform, it will probably have an effect on houses near the margin of a band. However, as a taxpayer will be told only which band his house falls into, not the value placed on it, no one can be sure whether or not the arbitrary choice of 1 April 1991 as a reference date has prejudiced them.

21.10 The council tax payable in respect of all dwellings in a billing authorities area must be allocated in the ratios 6 (band A):7:8:9:11:13:15:18 (band H) (*ss 5* and *74*). The bands are as follows:

Band	*England*	*Wales*	*Scotland*
A	Up to £40,000	Up to £44,000	Up to £27,000
B	£40,001–£52,000	£44,001–£65,000	£27,001–£35,000
C	£52,001–£68,000	£65,001–£95,000	£35,001–£45,000
D	£68,001–£88,000	£95,001–£123,000	£45,001–£58,000
E	£88,001–£120,000	£123,001–£162,000	£58,001–£80,000
F	£120,001–£160,000	£162,001–£223,000	£80,001–£106,000
G	£160,001–£320,000	£223,001–£324,000	£106,001–£212,000
H	Over £320,000	£324,001–£424,000	Over £212,000
I	–	Over £424,000	–

The Minister is given power to substitute other bands, to change the ratios in which the tax is allocated between the bands and to change the number of bands (*s 5(4)* and *(4A)*). He has not yet done so. However, the National Assembly for Wales has done so by the *Council Tax (Valuation Bands) (Wales) Order 2003 (SI 2003 No 3046)* which changed the valuation bands in Wales from 1 April 2005. Prior to that date the bands ran from Band A (up to £30,000) to Band H (over £240,000). The Minister also has power by regulation to make provision for smoothing changes in liability resulting from any such change or from a revaluation (*s 13B* inserted by *Local Government Act 2003, s 79*). The value of a dwelling for the purpose of allocating it to a band is the value as shown in the billing authorities' valuation list (*s 5(6)*).

21.11 It will be seen that the tax bill as percentages of those for band A and for band D (the average value) is as follows in England:

Band	*% of band A*	*% of band D*
A	100.0	66.7
B	116.7	77.8

Band	*% of band A*	*% of band D*
C	133.3	88.9
D	150.0	100.0
E	183.3	122.2
F	216.6	144.4
G	250.0	166.7
H	300.0	200.0

21.12 It should be stressed that the grading is applied by reference to the values in the country as a whole. Thus, if the rate of tax levied by each local authority were the same (which will not, of course, be the case), a £5 million property in Hampstead would attract three times the tax of a £14,000 one in Cleveland. When the tax was introduced the then government indicated that in the South East, 40% or more of the properties in Barnet, the City of Westminster and South Buckinghamshire, and 30% or more of those in Camden, Islington, Kensington and Chelsea, Richmond and Kingston-on-Thames, would fall within Bands G or H, while in the rest of the country very few houses would be in those bands. As a Band G property attracts two-and-a-half-times, and a Band H property three times, the tax produced by a Band A property, local authorities with a high proportion of Band G and Band H properties will in theory need to levy a much smaller basic charge (ie for Band D properties) than councils in, say, Cleveland, which apparently has no Band G or Band H properties, to raise the same amount of revenue.

21.13 The intention was that this disparity would be corrected by the allocation of government grant. It was intended that the total amount of central government general grants to local authorities would be distributed so that the local authorities in each area can finance spending at a standard level by levying the same Band D charge. It is not wholly clear what this means, nor indeed if it still actually happens. Previously grants were distributed so that authorities could finance spending at a standard level by levying a common community charge, yet not only did the levels of community charge vary enormously across the country, but so did the government's estimates of what local authorities would need to charge to provide a standard level of service. In practice Band D charges vary enormously.

Liability

21.14 The person who is liable to pay the tax in respect of a chargeable dwelling for a particular day is:

(*a*) the owner of the freehold (of all or any part of it) if he resides there;

(*b*) a leaseholder (of all or any part of it) who resides in the dwelling, unless another resident has a superior interest (in which case it will be that person who will be liable);

(*c*) if none of the residents holds a lease, a statutory or secure tenant (of all or part of the dwelling) who resides in it;

(*d*) if there is no such person, a resident who has a contractual licence to occupy the whole or any part of the dwelling;

(*e*) if there are none of the above, any person who is resident in the dwelling;

(*f*) if no one is resident in the dwelling, the owner of it; or

(*g*) from a date to be determined, a mortgagee in possession of the owner's interest in the property.

(*Section 6(1),(2)* as amended by *LGFA 2012, s 13.*).

21.15 If two or more people meet one of these tests they are jointly and severally liable for the tax unless one or more of them is severely mentally impaired (within *Sch 1, para 2* see **21.25**), in which case the other or others is solely liable (*s 6(3)(4)*). A person under 18 cannot be liable for the tax as a resident (although he could be under head (*f*) as an owner). A person is resident in a property only if it is his sole or main residence (*s 6(5)*). A statutory tenancy for the purpose of head (*c*) is one under the *Rent Act 1977* or the *Rent (Agriculture) Act 1976*. A secure tenancy is one within *Part IV* of the *Housing Act 1985* (*s 6(6)*). For the purpose of head (*f*) the owner means any person who has a material interest in the whole or any part of the house (the freehold or a lease of six months or more) where at least part of that interest is not subject to a material interest that is inferior to his own (*s 6(5)(6)*).

21.16 In the case of a pitch occupied by a caravan, or a mooring occupied by a boat, the owner of the caravan or boat is liable for the tax – other than for any day for which he is not resident in the caravan or boat but someone else is, in which case that other person is liable for the tax for that day (*s 7(1)–(3)*). Permanent holiday caravans and boats are not liable to council tax. They were instead subjected to business rates (see **21.86**) by the *Rating (Caravans and Boats) Act 1996*. If two or more persons are liable for the tax on a particular day they are jointly and severally liable for it, any severely mentally impaired person again being excluded (*s 7(4)(5)*). If a caravan or boat is subject to a hire purchase or conditional sale agreement the owner is, of course, the person in possession under the agreement. If it is subject to a bill of sale or mortgage it is the person entitled to the asset apart from the bill or mortgage (*s 7(7)*).

21.17 The above rules do not apply to six specified classes of dwellings (*s 8(1)*). These are as follows.

Class A: A registered care home (within the meaning of the *Care Standards Act 2000*), a building or part of a building in which residential accommodation is provided under *National Assistance Act 1948, s 21* or a hostel within the meaning of *Sch 5, para 7* to that Act. Prior to 1 January 2004 the wording was wider.

Class B: A dwelling inhabited by a religious community whose principal occupation consists of prayer, contemplation, education, the relief of suffering, or any combination of these.

Class C: A dwelling which is in multiple occupation, ie one which was constructed or adapted for occupation by persons who do not constitute a single household or ('and' prior to 1 April 1995) which is inhabited by a person (or persons) who is a tenant of part only of the dwelling, or has a licence to occupy part, or has a licence to occupy the dwelling as a whole but is not liable to pay rent or a licence fee in respect of the whole dwelling.

Class D: A dwelling in which at least one of the residents is employed in domestic service and resides in the dwelling wholly or mainly for the purpose of his employment, the other residents are all either similarly employed or are members of the family of such employee, and which is occupied from time to time by that person's employer, ie a dwelling occupied by resident domestic staff and their families, such as a housekeeper's flat. Domestic service is not defined. It would probably include a gardener as well as servants actually working in the house.

Class E: A dwelling which is inhabited by a minister of religion as a residence from which he performs the duties of his office.

Class F A dwelling provided to an asylum seeker under (or under arrangements made under) the *Immigration and Asylum Act 1994, s 95.*

(The *Council Tax (Liability for Owners) Regulations 1992 – SI 1992 No 551* as amended on a number of occasions, most recently by the *Council Tax (Liability for Owners) (Amendment) (England) Regulations 2003* (*SI 2003 No 3125*).

21.18 In these cases the owner of the dwelling is liable to pay the tax. If there are two or more such owners they are jointly and severally liable (except for one who is a severely mentally impaired person). In the case of a dwelling in multiple occupation, the person liable to pay the tax is the person with the lowest interest, freehold or leasehold, extending to the entire building (*s 8(3)–(5)*). In the case of a dwelling within Class E if a minister of the Church of England is the inhabitant and the owner and is in receipt of a stipend the person liable for the tax is the Diocesan Board of Finance. The owner is also liable for the tax in respect of other dwellings of a prescribed class if the billing authority so decides in relation to all dwellings of that class situated in its area (*s 8(2)*). No regulations prescribing such classes have yet been made though.

21.19 A husband and wife are jointly and severally liable for the tax if one is the person liable under *ss 6–8* and the other is resident in the dwelling but would not otherwise be liable (and is not a severely mentally impaired person) (*s 9(1)(2)*). This joint and several liability applies not only to married couples but also to unmarried persons living together as husband and wife (*s 9(3)*). In *Gardiner v Swindon Borough Council (2003 EWHC 515 (Admin))* Mr Gardiner challenged the decision of the Valuation Tribunal that a Ms Rouse who lived with him was liable for council tax. He contended that Ms Rouse was his housekeeper. The tribunal had held that they lived together as husband and wife, largely on the basis that in an application for transfer of a council property she had referred to him as her partner, she had included him and his son in a box prefaced 'family' and that she had named her child Matthew Edward Rouse-Gardiner. The judge also noted that the council had repeatedly asked Mr Gardiner and Ms Rouse for evidence that she was his housekeeper but none had been produced. Not surprisingly, the court held that the decision was not one that no reasonable tribunal could have reached.

Amount of Liability

21.20 The amount for which a person is liable for any day is, of course, the annual amount fixed by the billing authority for a house in the appropriate band divided by the number of days in the financial year (to 31 March) (*s 10(1)*). In practice the authority will (and are entitled to) assume that he will remain in the house through the financial year, a retrospective adjustment being made subsequently if this assumption proves unfounded. If a billing authority fixes different rates for different parts of its area, the Minister is empowered to introduce rules for ascertaining in which part of the authority's area each dwelling is situated and he has done this in the *Council Tax (Situation and Valuation of Dwellings) Regulations 1992* (*SI 1992 No 550*) (*s 10(2)*).

Discounts

21.21 In some cases the taxpayer will be entitled to a discount of either 25% or 50% based on the number and status of the adult occupants (ie over 18). The tax assumes an average of two adults per household. If there is only one adult in the household on a particular day the discount is 25% for that day. If there are no adults the discount is 50%. Certain categories of people are disregarded for this purpose (see **21.23**). If all of the adults in a household fall to be disregarded the discount is accordingly 50% (ie as if there are no adults). If all but one fall to be disregarded the discount is 25%. The Minister is empowered to alter the 25% and 50% figures.

21.22 A local authority must also give a 50% discount for a second home where the taxpayer is provided with accommodation because of the nature of his employment, eg a tenant publican or a clergyman. It must give a discount of between 10% and 50% on other second homes. A council can also give a discount of up to 50% for empty property but need not do so. Councils are also authorised to give discounts to groups of their choice, such as pensioners, but such discounts will be ignored in calculating contributions by central government.

21.23 A person falls to be disregarded for days on which he meets the appropriate conditions for the purpose of determining the discount to be given if he is either:

1. a person in detention (**21.24**);
2. severely mentally impaired (**21.25**);
3. a person over 18 in respect of whom child benefit is payable (or would be payable but for *Social Security Contributions and Benefits Act 1992, Sch 9, para 1(c)* (*Sch 1, para 3*);
4. a student (**21.26**);
5. a hospital patient – but only if the hospital is a health service hospital within the meaning of the *National Health Service Act 1977* (or its Scottish equivalent) or a military, air-force or naval unit or establishment at which medical or surgical treatment is provided, and the hospital has become his sole or main residence (*Sch 1, para 6*);
6. a patient in a home (**21.27**);
7. a care worker (**21.28**);
8. a resident of a hostel, night shelter, etc. where the accommodation is predominantly provided otherwise than in separate and self-contained sets of premises for persons of no fixed abode and no settled way of life, and under licences to occupy which do not constitute tenancies (*Sch 1 para 10*);
9. other persons that the Minister may prescribe (*Sch 1, para 11*). By the *Council Tax (Additional Provisions for Discount Disregards) Regulations 1992* (*SI 1992 No 552*) as amended by the *Council Tax (Additional Provisions for Discount Disregards) (Amendment) Regulations 1993* (*SI 1993 No 149*) he has prescribed members of International Headquarters and Defence Organisations; members of

religious communities who have no income or capital of their own and are dependent on the community; and a school leaver who is under 20 and has ceased a qualifying or full time course of education (within *SI 1992 No 548* – see **21.26**) between 1 May and 31 October in that year; by the *Council Tax (Additional Provisions for Discount Disregards) (Amendment) Regulations 1992* (*SI 1992 No 2942*) he has prescribed persons having a relevant association with a body, contingent, or detachment of the forces of a country covered by the *Visiting Forces Act 1952*; by the *Council Tax (Liability for Owners and Additional Provisions for Discount Disregards) (Amendment) Regulations 1995* (*SI 1995 No 620*) he has prescribed the spouse (or from 10 December 2005 civil partner or person of the same sex living as if he were a civil partner) or dependant of a student (as defined in *Sch 1, para 4*) if that person is not a British citizen and is prevented by his immigration status from taking paid employment or from claiming benefits; and by the *Council Tax (Additional Provisions for Discount Disregards) Amendment Regulations 1997* (*SI 1997 No 657*) he has prescribed persons entitled to Diplomatic (and some similar statutory) privileges and immunities who are not British citizens (or British Dependent Territories citizens, British National (Overseas) citizens, British Overseas citizens, British subjects, nor British protected persons) nor permanent residents of the UK.

21.24 A person in detention is one detained in a prison, a hospital, or elsewhere by order of a UK court or a Standing Civilian Court established under the *Armed Forces Act 1976*; one detained under *Immigration Act 1971, Sch 3, para 2* awaiting deportation; one detained under *Part II* or *ss 46–48* or *136* of the *Mental Health Act 1983* (or the equivalent Scottish legislation); or if the Minister so prescribes one imprisoned, detained or in custody under the *Army Act 1955*, the *Air Force Act 1955* or the *Naval Discipline Act 1957*. He has so prescribed by the *Council Tax (Discount Disregards) Order 1992* (*SI 1992 No 548*) provided that the detention is not under open arrest and forms part of a continuous period of arrest exceeding 48 hours. A person temporarily discharged or temporarily released under *s 28* or *47(5)* of the *Prison Act 1952* (or its Scottish equivalent) is treated as still detained. However, a person who is detained under Regulations made under *Sch 4, para 8*, ie for not paying his council tax, or for default in payment of a fine does not count as a person in detention and thus cannot attract any discount (*Sch 1, para 1*).

21.25 To qualify as severely mentally impaired a person must be entitled to one of several specified Social Security benefits (or would be so entitled if he had not reached pensionable age) and must produce a certificate from a registered medical practitioner that he is (or is likely to be) severely mentally impaired, ie he has a severe impairment of intelligence and social functioning (however caused) which appears to be permanent (*Sch 1, para 2* and *Council Tax (Discount Disregards) Order 1992, reg 3* as amended on a number of occasions, most recently by the *Council Tax (Chargeable Dwellings, Exempt Dwellings and Discount Disregards) Amendment Order 2003* (*SI 2003 No 3121*)).

21.26 The disregard of students applies to a student, student nurse, apprentice or youth training trainee who meets such conditions as the Minister may impose. The Minister is also empowered to define the expressions student, etc. The institution at which a student or student nurse is studying must, if so requested by the student, give him a certificate, containing such information as the Minister may prescribe, provided that he asks for it within a year after the completion of the course (*Sch 1, paras 4, 5*). He has prescribed all of these things by *regs 4, 5* of the *Council Tax (Discount Disregards) Order 1992* (*SI 1992 No 548*) as amended by the *Council Tax (Exempt Dwellings and Discount Disregards) (Amendment) Order 1998* (*SI 1998 No 291*) and the *Council Tax (Discount Disregards) (Amendment) Order 2011 (SI 2011 No 948).* A student is defined as a person attending a full-time course of education at a specified educational establishment or a person under 20 attending a qualifying course at such an establishment, and a foreign language assistant (ie an overseas student on an educational/teaching assignment). A course is full time only if the student is required by the educational establishment to undertake periods of study, tuition or work experience of at least 24 weeks in each calendar or academic year and which when taken together average at least 21 hours a week. This does not apply to an initial teacher training course. It also includes a youth trainee under 25 whose course is being funded by the Learning and Skills Council for England. (*Council Tax (Discount Disregards and Exempt Dwellings) (Amendment) Order 1995* (*SI 1995 No 619*)). A student ceases to qualify if he abandons his course or is expelled (*Council Tax (Discount Disregards) (Amendment) Order 1996* (*SI 1996 No 636*)). An apprentice qualifies only if they are earning less than £195 per week (£130 before 1 April 1998 and £160 before 1 April 2007).

21.27 The disregard for patients in homes applies to those in a residential care home (one required to be registered under *Part 1* of the *Registered Homes Act 1984* or exempted from registration under *s 1(4), (5)(j)* of that *Act*, a building in which residential accommodation is provided under *National Assistance Act 1948, s 21*, or a building run by the Abbeyfield Society); a nursing home (required to be registered under the *Registered Homes Act 1984* or exempted from registration under *s 21(3)(a)* of that *Act*); a mental nursing home (within the meaning of the *Registered Homes Act 1984*); or hostel (as defined in *Regulation 6* of the *Council Tax (Discount Disregards) Order 1992*, ie from 1 January 2004, premises approved under the *Criminal Justice and Court Services Act 2000, s 9(1)* or a building or part of a building which is not a care home or independent hospital but which is solely or mainly used for the provision of residential accommodation in other than separate and self contained premises, together with personal care for persons who require such care by reason of old age, disablement, past or present alcohol or drug dependence or past or present mental disorder. The person must be receiving care or treatment at the home and it must have become his sole or main residence (*Sch 1, para 7*). Similar rules apply to Scotland (*Sch 1, para 8*).

21.28 A person is a care worker if he is engaged in providing care or support (or both) to another person or persons, and meets the conditions contained in *Council Tax (Additional Provisions for Discount Disregards) Regulations 1992, Sch 1* as amended on a number of occasions, most recently by the *Council Tax (Discount Disregards) (Amendment) Regulations 2013* (*SI 2013 No 725*).

21.29 A Welsh billing authority (but not an English or Scottish one) can decide in relation to dwellings or classes of dwelling in their area that may be specified by the Minister, either to grant a 25% discount for empty dwellings or not to allow any discount for such dwellings in place of giving the normal 25% discount for a dwelling with only one adult resident (*s 12*). Such a decision must be advertised within 21 days of its determination in a local newspaper.

21.30 The Minister is empowered, by regulation, to specify payment of a lower amount of council tax than that to which a person is liable under *ss 10–12* (*s 13*). The *Council Tax (Reductions for Disabilities) Regulations 1992* (*SI 1992 No 554*) as amended by the *Council Tax (Reduction for Disabilities) (Amendment) Regulations 1999* (*SI 1999 No 1004*) does so in respect of certain houses that have been adapted to meet the needs of a severely disabled resident by deeming the house to fall into the next lower valuation band (or reducing the bill proportionately for a dwelling within Band A). From 1 April 2014, the *Council Tax (Reductions for Annexes) (England) Regulations 2013 (SI 2013, No 2977)* prescribe a 50% reduction in the tax payable for people living in annexes (on top of any discounts under *ss 11 or 11A* and any premiums under *s 11B*) provided that they are related to the person liable to pay the council tax on the main dwelling, and also for an annexe that is unoccupied and being used as part of the main residence. A relative for this purpose is a spouse or civil partner, parent, child, grandparent, grandchild, brother, sister, uncle, aunt, nephew, niece, great-grandparent, great grandchild, great-uncle, great-aunt, great-niece or nephew or great-great grandparent, etc. A relationship by marriage is treated in the same way as a relationship by blood. A common-law marriage is treated in the same way as an actual marriage.

Section 11A (inserted by *Local Government Act 2003, s 75*) allows the Deputy Prime Minister by regulation to allow individual local authorities in England to reduce the normal 50% discount on unoccupied dwellings for a financial year in relation to prescribed lasses of dwellings. A similar provision applies in Wales (*new s 12*). The Deputy Prime Minister has prescribed three classes of dwelling by the *Council Tax (Prescribed Classes of Dwellings) (England)*

Regulations 2003 (SI 2003 No 3011) as amended by the *Council Tax (Prescribed Classes of Dwellings) Regulations 2004 (SI 2004 No 926)* and *2005 (SI 2005 No 416)* and the *Council Tax (Civil Partners) (England) Regulations 2005 (SI 2005 No 2866)*. A local authority can reduce the discount on the first two to a minimum of 10% and on the third to nil (or any intermediate level).

Class A:	A chargeable dwelling which is not the sole or main residence of an individual, which is furnished and the occupation of which is restricted by a planning condition preventing occupancy for a continuous period of 28 days or more.
Class B:	A chargeable dwelling which is not the sole or main residence of an individual, which is furnished and the occupancy of which is not restricted to 28 days.
Class C:	A dwelling which is unoccupied and substantially unfurnished.

Classes A and B do not, however, include any dwelling which consists of a pitch occupied by a caravan or a mooring occupied by a boat. Nor do they include a dwelling of which the intended occupant is in job-related accommodation. The definition of 'job-related accommodation' is broadly the same as that for representative occupation in *ITEPA 2003, s 99* (see **23.62–23.64**) but excludes a dwelling provided wholly or partly by a third party with whom the worker or his spouse (or a common law spouse or, from 10 December 2005, civil partner or person of the same sex living as a civil partner) carries on a trade or business in partnership and includes a property occupied by a minister of religion as a residence from which he performs the duties of his office.

A local authority also has power from 2005/06 to reduce the tax for any dwelling or class of dwelling to such extent as it thinks fit (including to nil) (*s 13A* inserted by *Local Government Act 2003, s 76*).

21.31 A new *s 13A* was introduced by the *Local Government Finance Act (LGFA) 2012, s 10* with effect from 1 April 2013. A local authority must make a reduction scheme by 31 January 2013 in relation to persons whom the local authority considers to be in financial need (or persons in classes consisting of persons considered to be in general financial need). The authority can reduce the council tax for such persons to such extent (including to nil) as it thinks fit. A local authority is also given power to refuse a discount (or fix it at a different amount to normal) for classes of dwellings that may be prescribed by the Minister. It is intended to prescribe unoccupied and unfurnished dwellings (*LGFA 2012, s 11*). Such local schemes replaced council tax benefit from 1 April 2013. A local authority can also provide that no discount (or a lower discount than 50%) is to apply to a long-term empty dwelling, ie one that has been unoccupied and substantially unfurnished for at least two years (*LGFA 2012, s 12*). A scheme must include persons whose capital exceeds £16,000, persons not habitually resident in the UK and persons subject to immigration controls (*The Council Tax Reduction Schemes (Prescribed Requirements) (England) Regulations 2012 (SI 2012, No2885)* as amended most recently by the *Council Tax Reduction Schemes (Prescribed Requirements)(England) (Amendment) Regulations 2016 (SI 2016 No 1262)*). The Regulations contain detailed rules as to what a local authority is permitted to do.

21.32 From 1 April 2013, a local authority can provide that the discount for empty dwellings does not apply to a long-term empty dwelling but instead the charge for that dwelling is to be increased by up to 50%. A dwelling is a long-term empty dwelling if it has been unoccupied for a continuous period of at least two years and it has been substantially unfurnished (periods of up to six weeks when it is occupied or furnished are ignored for this purpose) (*s 11B* inserted by *Local Government Finance Act 2012, s 12*).

Administration

21.33 The administrative provisions are contained in *Schedule 2* but this is little more than a series of enabling provisions. The real provisions are contained in secondary legislation: the *Council Tax (Administration and Enforcement) Regulations 1992 (SI 1992 No 613)* as amended, most recently by the *Council Tax and Non-Domestic Rating (Amendment)(England) Regulations 2012 (SI 2012 No 3086)*. From 31 October 2012, HMRC have power to supply to a local authority information which they hold for tax purposes for prescribed purposes relating to council tax (*LGFA 1992, s 15A–15C* inserted by *LGFA 2012, s 17*). The local authority must not disclose such information to anyone else (*s 15D*).

21.34 A local authority has power to make regulations requiring the provision of information and to provide arrangements for access to electronic records (*LGFA 1992, s 14A* inserted by *LGFA 2012, s 14*). A local authority can also provide for the creation of offences that may be committed by a person in prescribed circumstances, but cannot provide for a fine in excess of level 3 on the standard scale (£1,000) or a daily fine of more than £40 a day (*LGFA 1992, s 14B*). It can, of course, also make regulations about penalties (*LGFA 1992, s 14B*).

Preparation of Valuation Lists

21.35 HMRC are responsible for the preparation of valuation lists. They must appoint a listing officer for each billing authority (*s 20*). It appears that the listing officer must be an HMRC employee (*s 26(5)*). They must also carry out such valuations as they think necessary or expedient for facilitating the compilation and maintenance of valuation lists and must furnish to listing officers information obtained in carrying out such valuations or in the exercise of their powers under *s 27* (see **21.40** below) and such information contained in particular delivered forms (which are sent to them for stamp duty purposes) as they think expedient (*s 21(1)*). The valuations must be done by reference to values at 1 April 1991 (*s 21(2)*). HMRC can appoint people other than civil servants to assist them in carrying out valuations and can disclose to such persons any survey report obtained for the purpose of rating (including non-domestic rating) or obtained in exercise of their powers under *s 27.* If such a person uses such information for any purpose other than council tax valuation he is liable to imprisonment for up to two years or a fine or both (*s 21(3)–(5)*). To carry out the 1991 general revaluation the Inland Revenue in exercise of this power appointed a number of firms of valuers to carry out valuations under the guidance of the Revenue's own Valuation Branch.

21.36 The listing officer compiles and maintains the valuation list. The initial list had to be compiled on 1 April 1993 and came into force on that date. The valuations were by reference to 1 April 1991. *The Local Government Act 2003* inserted a new *s 22B* to the *1992 Act* which required new valuation lists to be compiled on 1 April 2007 and 10-yearly thereafter. This requirement was amended in relation to England by the *Council Tax (New Valuation Lists for England) Act 2006* to give the Secretary of State power to fix revaluation date by Order. No such order has yet been made so the 1993 lists still apply. New lists for Wales came into force on 1 April 2005. Whenever the listing officer subsequently compiles a list he must as soon as reasonably practicable send a copy to the billing authority who must deposit it at its principal office (*s 22(8)*). The valuation list must show, for each day for which it is in force, each dwelling which is situated in the billing authority's area, the valuation band applicable to the dwelling, the reference number ascribed to the dwelling by the listing officer (where relevant) an indication that the dwelling is a composite one, and where the entry on the list has been altered an indication of the day from which (or period for which) the alteration has effect and whether the alteration was made pursuant to the order of a valuation tribunal or the High Court (but the omission of any matter required to be included will not of itself invalidate the list) (*s 23* and *Council Tax (Contents of Valuation List) Regulations 1992 (SI 1992 No 553)*).

Alteration of Valuation Lists

21.37 The Minister is empowered to make regulations to deal with the alteration of valuation lists (*s 24*). He has duly done so, most recently, by the *Council Tax (Alteration of Lists and Appeals) (England) Regulations 2009 (SI 2009 No 2270)* as amended by the *Council Tax (Alteration of Lists and Appeals) (England)(Amendment) Regulations 2013 (SI 2013 No 467)*).

A proposal to alter the list can be made by either a billing authority or by an interested person such as the person liable for the tax. The proposal must be made in writing to the listing officer and must contain specified information (*regs 4, 5*). It must be made within six months of the entry on the list being made. The listing office must acknowledge receipt within 28 days and send the proposer a statement setting out the procedure for agreeing such proposals (*reg 6*). The grounds on which a proposal can be made are limited, namely:

(*a*) the property is not a dwelling – which would include that it should be shown as several buildings;

(*b*) a dwelling has been omitted from the list;

(*c*) the dwelling has been included in the wrong valuation band –a person who becomes the taxpayer in relation to the dwelling after the list was initially compiled can make a proposal within six months of becoming the taxpayer (provided that he was not the taxpayer at an earlier time since the list was compiled, a proposal has not previously been determined by a valuation tribunal, the new taxpayer is not a subsidiary, fellow subsidiary or parent company of the previous one and the new taxpayer is not a 'new' partnership resulting from a partnership change but an alteration can be made only if the valuation officer is convinced that the property was put in the wrong band at the revaluation date);

(*d*) since the dwelling was included on the list in its current valuation band building or demolition work (other than as part of a redevelopment) has been carried out on it, and the building has become or ceased to be a composite hereditament, or there has been a change in the domestic element if it was such an hereditament; and

(*e*) account has not been taken of a decision made within the previous six months by the local valuation tribunal or the High Court (*reg 4*).

21.38 Following receipt of a proposal the listing officer has six weeks to send a copy of it to the taxpayer and (if so requested generally by the authority) the billing authority (*reg 8*). If he thinks the proposal is well founded he must serve notice on the proposer and the taxpayer that he proposes to alter the list and must alter it within six weeks (*reg 9*). A proposer may withdraw his proposal by written notice – but if he was the taxpayer and has moved, only with the consent of the current taxpayer. Any interested person who is aggrieved by the withdrawal can be substituted as proposer provided that he was competent to make the original proposal (*reg 10*). If the listing officer, the proposer, the current taxpayer, the taxpayer at the date of the proposal and any person who has served notice on the listing officer asking to be a party to the proceedings agree how the list should be altered, the valuation officer must make the alteration and the proposal is treated as withdrawn (*reg 13*). If the listing officer considers the proposal is not well-founded and the parties cannot reach agreement under *reg 12* there is a right of Appeal to the Valuation Tribunal for England. An appeal must be made within three months of the service of the decision notice by the listing officer (*reg 10*). The procedure on such a reference is considered in **21.81**.

21.39 An alteration has effect from the date of the event that gave rise to the need for it, not the date of the proposal or the date of any agreement (*reg 16*). This does not apply where a valuation tribunal orders a valuation band to be increased; it is to be altered only with effect from the date their decision is given (*reg 29*). Nor from 1 April 2007 does it apply where the alteration moves the dwelling into a higher band or is to correct an entry which treated two or more dwellings as a single dwelling. In both of these cases it takes effect from the date of entry in the list (*Council Tax and Non-Domestic Rating (Amendment) (England) Regulations 2006 (SI 2006 No 3395), reg 6*). The listing officer must notify the billing authority (subject to specified exemptions) and the taxpayer within six weeks of making an alteration to the list (*reg 12*). Within six months of the service of the notice under *reg 15* the billing authority or any interested person can make a fresh proposal to restore the list to its original state or to alter it further (*reg 4(6)*). An alteration to a valuation band can only be made where either one of the events in **21.37** has occurred, the listing officer is satisfied that the property is in the wrong valuation band, or an order of a valuation tribunal or the High Court requires the alteration to be made (*reg 3*). If the valuation list is altered because a property has been improved and subsequently sold or has been split into more than one dwelling the valuation must be based on the value at the date of sale or the date the new living accommodation has been created (*Council Tax (Situation and Valuation of Dwellings) Regulations 1992 (SI 1992 No 550, reg 6* as amended by the *Council Tax (Valuations, Alteration of Lists and Appeals) Regulations 2008 (SI 2008 No 315)*).

21.40 If the Minister makes an order changing the valuation bands such an order must specify a date by which the new valuation list is to be prepared and the date that it is to come into force, a new reference date, and new dates for the listing officer to send to the billing authority two drafts of the list (*s 25*).

21.41 If a valuation officer (ie any listing officer or any other HMRC officer appointed by HMRC to carry out any of his functions – but not a private sector valuer appointed to assist him) needs to value a dwelling he (and any servant of the Crown authorised by him in writing) is empowered to enter, survey and value the dwelling. Three clear days' notice of such a visit must be given, disregarding a Saturday, Sunday, Christmas Day, Good Friday and any Bank Holiday. From 1 October 2015, the Valuation Officer must obtain the prior approval of the First-tier Tribunal before he can exercise the power of entry. The FTT needs to be satisfied that the Valuation Officer needs to value the dwelling (*Council Tax and Non-Domestic Rating (Powers of Entry: Safeguards) (England) Order 2015, SI 2015 No 982*). Any person who intentionally delays or obstructs a person in the exercise of these powers is liable, on summary conviction, to a fine up to level 2 (£500) (*s 26*).

Requests for Information

21.42 A listing officer or HMRC can require a charging authority (under *s 144(1)* of the *Local Government Finance Act 1988*), a billing authority, a community charges registration officer or any other person prescribed by the Minister to supply him with such information relating to property as he reasonably believes will assist him in carrying out his council tax functions (*s 27(1)*). A valuation officer can also serve on the owner or occupier (or any former owner or occupier) of any dwelling a notice requesting him to supply any information specified in the notice which he believes will assist him in carrying out his function. Provided that the information is in the person's possession or control, such a notice must be complied with within 21 days. Failure to do so without reasonable excuse renders him liable on summary conviction to a fine of up to level 2 (£500). Knowingly or recklessly supplying false information in response to such a request can attract a term of imprisonment of up to three months, or a fine up to level 3 (£1,000) or both (*s 27(2)–(5)*). If in the course of carrying out its functions information comes to the notice of a charging or billing authority which it considers would assist a listing officer it must inform him (*s 27(6)*). A listing officer and HMRC are also empowered to use for council tax purposes any other information available to them, whatever its source, and whether or not obtained under statutory powers (*s 27(7)*).

21.43 A billing authority will wish to satisfy itself that the valuation lists are complete and accurate and that they are kept up to date – as the greater the number of taxpayers the lower the rate of tax it needs to impose and errors in the list can lead to a shortfall in its budgeted income. An authority can require, by written notice, any person who it believes to be a resident, owner or managing agent (ie a person authorised to arrange lettings of the dwelling) of a particular dwelling to supply to it such information (as is in that person's possession or control) as it requests for the purpose of identifying who is liable for the council tax for any period in respect of the dwelling (*Council Tax (Administration and Enforcement) Regulations 1992, reg 3*). Such information must be supplied within 21 days of the request and must be in such form as the billing authority specify. An authority can also seek information from any other billing authority, a precepting authority, any levying authority or the electoral registration officer for any area of Great Britain. The information it can ask such a body for is limited to the name, address and any past or present place of residence of a person and the dates during which he is known or thought to have resided there. The request for information must be in writing and the information must be supplied within 21 days of its being requested provided, of course, that it is in the possession or control of the person asked.

Such a body cannot be asked to supply information obtained by it, or by one of its committees, in its capacity as police authority (or as a constituent council of such an authority), or as an employer. It can also ask community charge registration officers for the name and any past or present address of any person, the days on which he resided at an address, the days on which he was an exempt individual, and any information relevant to his status as such a person. A billing authority can also if it wishes volunteer to another billing authority or a levying authority any information that it obtains in exercising its council tax functions and that it thinks will be useful to that other authority for collecting the council tax (*reg 4*). Precepting authorities are county councils, metropolitan county police authorities, the Northumbria Police Authority, Metropolitan County fire and civil defence authorities, the London Fire and Civil Defence Authority, the Receiver for the Metropolitan Police District, the sub-treasurer of the Inner Temple, the under-treasurer of the Middle Temple, parish and community councils, the chairman of a parish meeting and the charter trustees (*s 39*). A levying authority is a Scottish islands authority or Scottish regional authority (*s 97*).

21.44 A Registrar of Births and Deaths has to supply the billing authority within seven days of the registration of the death of a person aged 18 or over with the name and surname of the deceased, the date of his death and his usual address (*reg 5*). The billing authority can, of course, also utilise for the purpose of the council tax information that it itself obtains under any other enactment other than in its capacity as a police authority (*reg 6*).

21.45 Anyone, including a billing authority, can require a listing officer to give him access to such information as is needed to establish the state (or past state) of a list maintained by him which has been in force at any time in the previous five years (*s 28(1)*). A taxpayer can also require a billing authority to give him access to such information as will enable him to establish the state of the copy of such a list which was deposited with it under *s 22(8)* or of a proposed list that has been deposited with it under *s 22(6)* but is not yet in force (see **21.35** above) (*s 28(2) (3)*). Such requests must be complied with at a reasonable time and place and without payment being sought, but the information can be provided in such form as the listing officer or billing authority thinks fit (*s 28(8)*). If it is provided in documentary form the enquirer can, on payment of a reasonable charge, either make copies of the document or require the person having custody of it to supply him with a photographic copy. If the information is not provided in documentary form, eg it is provided by accessing a computer terminal, he is entitled on payment of a reasonable charge either to make a transcript of it or to require the person having control of access to the information to supply him with a copy in documentary form (*s 28(5)–(7)*). If without reasonable excuse a person having custody of the information intentionally obstructs a person exercising a right under the section he is liable to a fine of up to level 2 (£500) (*s 28(8)*).

21.46 Any person can, similarly, at a reasonable time and without payment also inspect any proposal made or notice of appeal given under regulations made under *s 24* if they relate to a list currently in force or in force at any time within the previous five years and make, or ask to be provided with, copies of all or part of the document on payment of a reasonable charge (*s 29*).

Exempt Dwellings

21.47 When a billing authority received the copy of the proposed valuation list sent to it under *s 22(5)(b)* (see **21.33**) it had to notify the 'taxpayers' concerned (other than for forces accommodation) by 31 March 1993 if it considered that any of the dwellings were exempt dwellings (see **21.8**) on that date.

21.48 Every billing authority is required to take reasonable steps each year to check whether any dwellings in its area are exempt dwellings for any part of the year (*reg 8*). Having done that it must assume for billing purposes that every dwelling that it has reason to believe is exempt is in fact exempt and that all other dwellings are chargeable dwellings (*reg 9*). When it treats a dwelling as exempt for all or part of the year it must notify the relevant person (ie the one or ones who would be liable to pay the council tax if it were not exempt) of that fact. The notice must be given as soon as is reasonably practicable and must show the valuation band into which the dwelling falls and the tax that would be payable if it were not exempt (or an estimate if at the time the rate has not been fixed) ignoring council tax benefit and social security benefits; must summarise the effect of the *s 24 Regulations* for altering the list; and give a summary of the classes of dwelling that are exempt. If there is more than one relevant person the billing authority can choose to which of them to give the notice. It does not have to repeat any information that it has previously notified to that relevant person under *reg 7* (see **21.47**) (*reg 10*).

21.49 If at any time during the financial year concerned or the following year a person who has been notified by the billing authority that a dwelling is exempt, has reason to believe that it is a chargeable dwelling for any part of the year, he must notify the billing authority within 21 days of forming that opinion. If two people are both jointly and severally liable for the tax notification but one satisfies the obligation of both, it appears that if the authority serves the *reg 10* notice on one only the other does not have any obligation to notify as he is not a person who 'has been informed' in accordance with *reg 10 (reg 11)*. As the penalty for not notifying is only £50 (*Sch 3, para 1*) it seems unlikely that many people will comply with this obligation.

21.50 The billing authority can serve notice on any person who it believes is resident in, or the owner or managing agent of, a dwelling that it believes is an exempt dwelling requesting such information as it needs to ascertain the identity of the relevant person in relation to it. If the information is in that person's possession or control he must supply it within 21 days of the request (*reg 12*).

Discounts

21.51 Before calculating an individual's liability to council tax, the billing authority must take reasonable steps to ascertain whether the property attracts a discount under *ss 11* or *12* (see **21.21** and **21.29**) (*reg 14*). If it believes it does, it must allow that discount in calculating the tax payable (*reg 15*). If a person is given a discount to which he is not entitled (or a larger discount than is due) he must notify the billing authority within 21 days of first having reason to believe that he is not entitled to it (*reg 16*). Again the penalty is only £50. There is no obligation to notify the authority if too little discount has been granted but it is obviously in the taxpayer's interest to do so.

Billing

21.52 The *Regulations* contain a rigid procedure that must be followed. For each financial year the billing authority must send a demand notice to the liable person. If a person is liable for the tax in respect of more than one dwelling a separate demand note must be issued for each dwelling (*reg 18*). The demand notice must be served as soon as is practicable after the billing authority fixes the rate of tax. The *Council Tax and Non-Domestic Rating (Demand Notices) (England) Regulations 2003 (SI 2003 No 2613)* as amended, most recently by the *Council Tax and Non-Domestic Rating (Demand Notices) (England) (Amendment) Regulations 2016 (SI 2016 No 396)* and supplemented by the *Council Tax (Demand Notices)(England) Regulations 2011 (SI 2011 No 3038)* as amended most recently by the *Council Tax (Demand Notices)(England) (Amendment) Regulations 2017 (SI 2017 No 13)* set out very extensive information that needs to be shown in a council tax demand. However, a failure to do so, if due to a mistake, does not affect the collectability of the tax. A single demand notice can cover several financial years. Demand notes can be served electronically to an e-mail address notified to the billing authority by the taxpayer or the demand or the information required to be shown on the demand note can simply be posted on the authority's website with reference being made to it on the demand note. Where notice of legal proceedings is served electronically it is deemed to be served on the second business day after it is e-mailed or posted on the website (*Council Tax and Non-Domestic Rating (Electronic Communications) (England) Order 2003 (SI 2003 No 2604)* as amended by the *Council Tax and Non-Domestic Rating (Electronic Communications) (England) (No 2) Order 2003 (SI 2003 No 3052)* and the *Council Tax (Electronic Communications) (England) Order 2008 (SI 2008 No 316)*).

21.53 Unless the demand note is issued after the end of the financial year concerned, the amount demanded must be calculated on the assumption that the chargeable person will remain liable for the tax throughout the year, the property will remain in the same valuation band, any reduction will continue to apply, the building will continue to be a chargeable dwelling, any discount will continue at the same rate and any entitlement to council tax benefit will continue (*reg 20(1)–(3)*). If the demand notice is issued during the year and the person is not liable for the tax on the day it is issued it must only demand payment of tax up to the last day for which he was liable (*reg 20(4)*). This obviously assumes that the demand notice will be issued only after he ceases to be liable, which seems an odd assumption. If the demand notice is issued after the end of the financial year it must be for the tax actually payable (*reg 20(5)*).

21.54 The tax is payable by instalments except where a demand notice is issued after 31 December in the financial year in which case it is payable 'as a single instalment' on such day as the authority specifies in the demand notices. Except where a *Part II* Scheme is operated (see below), it is normally payable in ten consecutive monthly instalments. It is up to the authority to choose which ten. It appears that if it wishes it can adopt different payment dates for different dwellings and which day in the month the amount is payable on. If the demand notice is issued after 30 April the number of instalments is one less than the number of whole months remaining. For example, if it is issued on 4 June, there are nine whole months to the following 31 March so the tax is payable by eight instalments. If the tax divided by the number of instalments does not result in an exact pound the monthly instalments other than the first are rounded up or down to the nearest pound, and the first is adjusted to the balance needed to collect the exact amount due over the year. From 1 April 2013 the taxpayer can elect to pay by 12 instalments instead of ten. Such an election can be made either during the year or in the preceding year. Where it is done during the year, the revision to the instalments starts only from the following month. If the total tax is less than £10 the authority can demand the whole amount in a lump sum. If it exceeds £10 but the instalments would be less than £5 per month it can require the tax to be paid by the number of £5 instalments necessary to collect the amount payable (*reg 21* and *Sch 1, Part I*). It can also require the first two instalments to be paid together, and if it revises a person's tax liability during the year must take into account any tax prepaid (*Council Tax (Administration and Enforcement) (Amendment) Regulations 1995* (*SI 1995 No* 22)).

21.55 The authority can opt to use a *Part II* Scheme to collect the council tax from its council tenants, but not from other people – although if a house ceases to be a council house during the year it can remain in the scheme until the end of the financial year. If it adopts such a scheme it must continue to use it each year until it decides to vary or revoke it. It cannot be varied after the rate for the financial year has been fixed and cannot be revoked later than

31 December of the prior year, eg if the scheme is to be revoked for 2011/12 this must be done by 31 December 2010. Such a scheme must provide for the tax to be payable by between ten and 52 instalments. The first instalment cannot be due less than 14 days after the issue of the demand and they must all be payable during the financial year, but subject to this the authority has complete flexibility. The idea is of course to allow it to collect the tax at the same time as the rent (*reg 21* and *Sch 1, Part II*).

21.56 A taxpayer and the authority can agree that the tax should be payable in some other manner, eg as a single payment (*reg 21(6)*). This will enable an authority to offer an early payment discount to speed up and simplify collection (see **21.60**). If a demand note is issued after the end of the year, or during the year and after the taxpayer has ceased to own or occupy the property, the tax can be demanded either in one sum or by such instalments as the authority may decide (*reg 21(7)*).

21.57 No one can be required to make a payment in respect of the tax unless a formal demand notice has been issued (*reg 22*). Assuming that this has been duly done, if a person fails to pay any instalment for which he is liable the billing authority must serve a reminder notice stating the instalments owing, and the effect of not paying. If the outstanding instalments are not paid within seven days from the issue of the reminder, the whole of the balance for the year will become payable in a further seven days. If the notice is the second reminder notice to be issued to him in respect of the same year, late payment of any further instalment will cause the whole of the balance of the year to automatically become payable the day after that instalment fell due. The reminder notice procedure obviously does not apply after all of the instalments have fallen due or after the tax has ceased to be payable by instalments (*reg 23*). The *Council Tax (Administration and Enforcement) (Amendment) Regulations 1997* (*SI 1997 No 393*) makes clear that this procedure also applies where tax is payable by instalments under *reg 21* (see **21.54**).

21.58 If the tax actually due proves to be more than was estimated when the demand notice was issued, the excess is payable in one sum 14 days after the issue by the billing authority of a notice of the actual chargeable amount (*reg 24(1)*). If the estimate was excessive the billing authority must notify the taxpayer. He can then claim repayment unless the reduction is because he moved house within the same district so that he owes tax to the same billing authority on another house – in which case the billing authority can credit the overpayment against the tax due. If the taxpayer does not claim repayment the billing authority can either repay it or credit it against any subsequent liability of the liable person to its council tax, eg the following year's tax (*reg 24(2)(6)*). If after the issue of a demand notice but before the tax actually due can be calculated (which cannot be done until after the end of the financial year) it becomes apparent that the estimate was wrong, the billing authority can recalculate the tax and require an interim payment of any underpayment or make an interim refund. It must do this if the taxpayer so requires (*reg 24(3)*). It must, in any event, recalculate the instalments due for the remainder of the year and serve notice of these on the taxpayer (*Sch 1, para 10*).

21.59 If after a demand notice is served on a person he ceases to be the liable person, the authority cannot enforce subsequent instalments. It must serve a notice on him showing the actual tax due for the period that he was liable and demand payment of the balance or make a refund (if the taxpayer so required) or set off the balance owing against another council tax liability the taxpayer owes it (*Sch 1, para 9*).

21.60 A billing authority can accept payment in one sum (and issue a demand notice for the tax in one sum) of such lesser amount as it may determine than the tax due, ie it can give a cash discount for prompt payment, provided that it decides on the discount not later than when it fixes the rate of tax, it makes the same offer to all its taxpayers who are entitled to pay the same number of instalments, and that the tax would otherwise have been payable by at least two instalments (*reg 26(1),(2)*). If the estimated tax due is subsequently increased, the balance is payable as a single payment within 14 days of being calculated but subject to the same percentage discount (*reg 25(4),(6),(9)*). If it is reduced, any repayment (if claimed) or amount set against another liability is also reduced in the same proportion (*reg 25(5),(6),(9)*). Notice of the difference must be served on the taxpayer. A billing authority is also empowered to accept a discounted amount in satisfaction of any instalment to induce payment to be made otherwise than in coin or bank notes, eg it can offer a discount for payment by cheque, provided that it decides the circumstances in which it is prepared to do so not later than when it fixes the rate of tax (*reg 26*).

21.61 *Regulation 27* contains rules for ascertaining the amounts for which persons are jointly and severally liable if they are not so liable throughout the year – these seem merely to certify what common sense would dictate by apportioning the total tax on a daily basis. No amount can be collected from such a person unless the authority has served a notice on him showing the amount due (*reg 28*). There are provisions for adjusting the amount thought to be due if circumstances change or the original estimate proves incorrect (*reg 28*).

Enforcement

21.62 As with administration, the enforcement powers are not contained in the Act but were left to the Minister to deal with by statutory instrument and are contained in the *Council Tax (Administration and Enforcement)*

Regulations 1992 (as amended on a number of occasions). These provide a variety of methods of enforcement, namely:

(*a*) attachment of earnings orders;

(*b*) distress;

(*c*) commitment to prison; and

(*d*) charging orders.

21.63 The billing authority first applies to a magistrates' court for a liability order. Before doing so it must serve on the taxpayer a final notice showing the amount in respect of which it proposes to make the application – unless it is seeking the order in relation to an unpaid instalment and has already served him with a reminder notice (*reg 33*). It must allow seven days from the service of the final notice before applying for the order. This is then done by making a complaint to a Justice of the Peace, and requesting the issue of a summons directing the taxpayer to appear before the magistrates' court. The application must be made within six years of the sum in question becoming due. The authority then serves the summons on the taxpayer either by delivering it to him or leaving it at, or posting it to, his usual or last known place of abode (or the registered office of a company). If, before the application is heard, the taxpayer tenders to it the sum specified in the summons plus an amount equal to the authority's reasonable costs up to that time the authority cannot proceed with the order. Subject to that, the magistrates must make a liability order if they are satisfied that the amount demanded has become payable and it has not been paid and that the summons was served at least 14 days earlier. The order must cover both the tax and the authority's costs. If the tax has been paid before the hearing and the billing authority so requests, the magistrates must still make an order in relation to costs. The magistrates can make separate liability orders on each individual or can deal with more than one person (eg all the cases they hear at a sitting) in a single order (*regs 34, 35*).

21.64 When a liability order has been made the debtor must supply the billing authority with the following information within 14 days of the authority requesting it, provided that it is in his possession or control:

(*a*) the name and address of his employer;

(*b*) information about his earnings or expected earnings;

(*c*) information about deductions therefrom for income tax, national insurance, and superannuation scheme payments;

(*d*) his work or identity number or other information to enable his employer to identify him;

(*e*) information as to sources of his income other than from an employer; and (*f*) whether another person is jointly and severally liable for the tax (*reg 36*).

A local authority has power to apply to the magistrates' court to quash a liability order if it considers that it should not have been made or to reduce the amount of such an order (*s 12A*).

Attachment of Earnings Orders

21.65 Based on this information the authority can then itself make an attachment of earnings order requiring the employer to make deductions in respect of the council tax from the debtor's net earnings (earnings less tax, national insurance and pension scheme contributions) and pay them over to the authority (*reg 37*). It must send a copy of the order to the debtor (*reg 41(3)*). It should particularly be noted that the authority does not have to return to court. The liability order triggers its right to serve an attachment of earnings order. From 1 October 1998, it cannot make an order if it already has two such orders in force against the debtor.

21.66 Where an attachment of earnings order is made the employer must deduct the following percentage from the employee's net salary, ie salary less PAYE, national insurance and pension contributions (*reg 38* as amended by the *Council Tax and Non-domestic Rating (Amendment) (England) Regulations 2006 (SI 2006 No 3395)* and the *Council Tax and Non-domestic Rating (Amendment) (England) Regulations 2007 (SI 2007 No 501)*).

Daily Earnings	*Weekly Earnings*	*Monthly Earnings*	*Deduction Rate*
£	£	£	
Up to 11	Up to 75	Up to 300	0%
11.01–20	75.01–135	300.01–550	3%
20.01–27	135.01–185	550.01–740	5%
27.01–33	185.01–225	740.01–900	7%
33.01–52	225.01–355	900.01–1420	12%
52.01–72	355.01–505	1,420.01–1,2020	17%
Over 72	Over 505	Over 2,020	17% of first £1,480 (or £53 or £270) + 50% of the excess.

The earnings limits were lower prior to 1 April 2007.

21.67 Special rules apply where a person is paid at other intervals (*reg 38(1)(c),(4)(10)*). Where he receives an advance against pay the deduction must be made from the advance as well, although not as if it were part of the salary for the period in which it is paid (*reg 38(2)*). If the employer is entitled to recoup an earlier advance against pay from the salary this deduction must be ignored in arriving at net earnings, ie the council tax deduction is to be calculated before making the loan deduction (*reg 38(3)* as amended by the *Council Tax (Administration and Enforcement) (Amendment) Regulations 1995 (SI 1995 No 22)*). From 15 April 2003 tax credits under the *Tax Credits Act 2002* are disregarded as earnings, ie they cannot be attached (*Council Tax (Administration and Enforcement) (Amendment) (England) Regulations 2003 (SI 2003 No 768)*).

21.68 The employer can also, if he wishes, add (and retain) a further pound to each deduction he makes, towards his administrative costs (*reg 39(1)*). He must provide the employee with a statement at the same time as his payslip showing both the total deductions to date and the further deductions he is required to make. If he does not in fact employ the debtor, he must tell the billing authority within 14 days of receiving the order. He must also tell it within 14 days of ceasing to employ him (*reg 39(2)–(6)*). The debtor is also obliged to tell the billing authority within 14 days if he changes his job or becomes re-employed (*reg 40*). If he changes job and the new employer is aware of the existence of the order and which billing authority made it, it must notify the authority within 14 days that it has become the debtor's employer – so that the authority can then serve it with an attachment of earnings order (*reg 39(7)*).

21.69 Once the debt has been paid in full the billing authority must notify the employer so that he can stop deducting. It can, if it wishes, discharge the order. If it does so it must of course notify the employer (*reg 41(1)(2)*). If two or more attachment of earnings orders for any of council tax, community charge, or under the *Attachment of Earnings Act 1971* or the *Child Support Act 1991* are served on an employer in respect of the same employee he must give effect to them in the order in which they were made. An attachment of earnings order in respect of the payment of a judgment debt or of payment under an administration order should not be dealt with until all other orders have been settled though (*reg 42*). There is no bar to an attachment of earnings order being served on a government department (*reg 43*). If the defaulter is a local councillor (of a billing or precepting authority) an attachment of earnings order can be made against his local authority attendance and special responsibility allowances. In such circumstances the deduction is at a flat rate of 40% (*reg 44*).

Detection of Fraud in Relation to Council Tax Reductions

21.70 From 7 March 2013, the authority has power to require information from specified persons for the purpose of preventing, detecting and securing evidence of the commission of offences connected with a reduction under the council tax reduction scheme. It can also require such a person to give it access to electronic records which are likely to contain such information. It is a criminal offence to intentionally delay or obstruct an officer exercising such a power, or to fail to comply with a requirement of access to electronic records (unless there is a reasonable excuse), or to make a statement or representation or to provide (or knowingly cause to be provided) a document or information which the person knows to be false in a material particular, for the purpose of obtaining a council tax reduction. It is also an offence not to notify the authority of a change of circumstances. The penalty for obstruction, etc is a fine of up to level 3 on the standard scale (£1,000) and that for the other offences, a fine of up to level 4 (£2,500) or imprisonment for up to three months or both. The authority can invite the person to accept a penalty of between £100 and £1,000 as an alternative to prosecution. It can also charge a penalty of £70 on a person who negligently makes a false statement or fails to notify a change of circumstances (*Council Tax Reduction Scheme (Detection of Fraud and Enforcement) (England) Regulations 2013 (SI 2013, No 501)*). HMRC's power to provide information to a local authority is extended to enable them to supply information to an authority for the purpose of these regulations (*Council Tax (Administration and Enforcement) (Amendment) (England) Regulations 2013 (SI 2013, No 590)*).

Distress

21.71 Where a liability order has been made the billing authority can also distrain on the debtor's goods for both the outstanding tax and the costs of the distress (but *Schedule 5* places limits on some of those costs). If the debtor pays the full amount due (including costs) before the sale of the goods they must not be sold. They need not be returned to the debtor though; they must 'be made available for collection' by him. A distress can be levied anywhere in England and Wales, but the bailiff must produce written authorisation from the authority and must give the debtor a copy of *reg 45* and *Schedule 5* to the Order. Distress cannot be levied on goods which general law protects from distress (*reg 45*). Nor can it be levied on tools, books, vehicles and equipment which are necessary to the debtor for personal use by him in his work or on clothing, bedding, furniture, household effects and provisions which are necessary for satisfying the basic domestic needs of the debtor and his family (*reg 45*). From 1 October 1998 distress can be levied only by a certified bailiff and only if the billing authority has served at least 14 days earlier written notice on the debtor stating that a liability order has been made and its amount, and warning that distress may be levied if the amount is not paid within 14 days and that this will attract costs.

21.72 A person aggrieved by the levy of distress (or an attempt to do so) has a right of appeal to a magistrates' court. This is done by making a complaint to a Justice of the Peace requesting the issue of a summons against the billing authority. The court can order the goods to be returned or if they have been sold can order compensation to be paid. If it feels that an attempted levy was irregular it can require the authority to desist from proceeding in its proposed manner (*reg 46*).

Imprisonment

21.73 If the authority has sought to levy distress but was unable to find sufficient goods, and the debtor is an individual over 18, it can apply to a magistrates' court for the issue of a warrant committing the debtor to prison. The court may inquire into the debtor's means and whether the failure to pay was due to wilful default or culpable neglect. If the court decides that it was, it can issue a warrant to commit him to prison immediately, or postpone the issue of the warrant until such time and on such conditions as it thinks fit. The court must make the enquiries in the debtor's presence, so cannot proceed with the hearing if the debtor does not turn up. However, a Justice of the Peace can then issue a warrant for his arrest to force him to attend. If the outstanding tax and reasonable costs (up to the limit specified by the *Council Tax (Administration and Enforcement) (Amendment) Regulations 1994* (*SI 1994 No 505*)) are paid before the debtor is imprisoned the warrant must not be executed. If it is paid while he is in prison he must be released. The term of imprisonment cannot exceed three months. If after the committal order is made part of the debt is paid, the term imposed is reduced proportionately (*reg 47*). If the magistrates do not issue a warrant or fix a term of imprisonment they can remit all or part of the debt. If circumstances change, the billing authority can make a fresh application for imprisonment on the first application (*reg 48*).

Charging Order

21.74 If the tax due under the liability order (ie excluding cost) is £1,000 or more, the authority can apply to the county court for a charging order on the debtor's interest in the dwelling concerned to secure the debt (*reg 50*).

Other Matters

21.75 When a liability order is made, the amount is deemed to be a debt, thus entitling the authority to petition as a creditor for the debtor's bankruptcy or winding-up (*reg 49*).

21.76 Once a warrant committing the debtor to prison is made no further steps can be taken by way of attachment of earnings, distress, bankruptcy or a charging order or under the *Council Tax (Deductions for Income Support) Regulations 1993* (*SI 1993 No 494*) (*reg 52(1)*). The authority can only use one of the other remedies at any one time, but can resort to attachment of earnings, distress and, from 1 April 1994, deduction under the Income Support regulations more than once and in any order it chooses (*reg 52(2),(3)* and *reg 7, Council Tax (Administration and Enforcement) (Amendment) Regulations 1994* (*SI 1994 No 505*)). An application for an order under *SI 1993 No 494* cannot be made while steps to enforce payment are being taken under this provision (*reg 52(2A)*). If the enforcement remedy is an income support deduction, simultaneous action can, however, be taken against another person who is not a member of the other's family (*Reg 8* of the *Council Tax (Administration and Enforcement) (Amendment) Regulations 1994* (*SI 1994 No 505*)).

21.77 Where two or more persons are jointly and severally liable for the tax a liability order can be obtained against one or both. If it is made against both, the authority does not need to choose the same enforcement remedies against both. However, it cannot enforce remedies against one while it is already in the course of enforcing remedies against the other. Nor can it apply to have one imprisoned unless distress has been unsuccessfully tried against all of them and once it seeks imprisonment of one of them it cannot seek an order under *SI 1993 No 494* in relation to any of them (*reg 54*).

Appeals

21.78 A person can apply to the Valuation Tribunal for England if he is aggrieved by:

(*a*) any decision of a billing authority that a dwelling is a chargeable dwelling or that he is liable to pay council tax in respect of it;

(*b*) any calculation made by the authority (including an estimate) of the tax that he is liable to pay (*s 16(1)(2)*).

The procedure for alterations to the valuation list, which is not technically an appeal against the listing, is considered at **21.37**. The appeals procedure where such a proposal is rejected is dealt with at **21.81**.

21.79 The Minister is empowered to prescribe matters against which no appeal can be made (*s 16(3)*). He has done so in the *Council Tax (Administration and Enforcement) Regulations 1992, reg 30* which prevents an appeal on the grounds that an assumption as to the future that has been made in the calculation of the tax may prove to be inaccurate.

21.80 Before appealing to the tribunal a person must serve a written notice on the billing authority stating what aggrieves him and his grounds for being upset (*s 16(4)–(6)*). He must then wait until either:

(*a*) the authority notifies him in writing that it believes his grievance is not well-founded and sets out the reasons for that belief;

(*b*) the authority notifies him in writing that steps have been taken to deal with his grievance, and what those steps are; or

(*c*) it does not give either notification within two months of being served with the notice of appeal (*s 16(4)(7)(8)*).

The idea is, of course, to give the billing authority an opportunity to try to resolve the dispute before resorting to the tribunal.

21.81 In the absence of agreement (see **21.36**) there is a right of appeal against a proposal to alter the valuation list to the Valuation Tribunal for England (or its Welsh or Scottish equivalent). The procedure on appeals is set out in the *Valuation Tribunal for England (Council Tax and Rating Appeals) (Procedure) Regulations 2009 (SI 2009 No 2269)* as amended by the *Valuation Tribunal for England, Non-Domestic Rating and Council Tax (England) (Amendment) Regulations 2011 (SI 2011 No 434),* the *Valuation Tribunal for England (Council Tax and Rating Appeals) (Procedure) (Amendment) Regulations 2013 (SI 2013 No 465) and the Valuation Tribunal for England (Council Tax and Rating Appeals)(Procedure)(Amendment) Regulations 2017 (SI 2017 No 156).*

21.82 No appeals can be made against the following matters except by way of judicial review:

(*a*) the specification by the Minister of a class of 'exempt dwelling' (see **21.8**);

(*b*) a determination by a billing authority under *s 8(2)* or, in Wales, *s 12(1)*;

(*c*) the calculation by a billing authority of its budget or of the rate of tax it proposes to levy;

(*d*) the calculation by a precepting authority of its budget (*s 66*).

Penalties

21.83 The penalty for failure to supply information when so requested, for failing without a reasonable excuse to give notice to a billing authority (or in Scotland a laying authority) or for knowingly providing inaccurate information is a fixed amount of £50. The penalty can be imposed by the authority – it does not need to take court action. It can also be quashed by the authority. Curiously an English or Welsh authority can revoke the penalty on any ground but in Scotland the taxpayer has to show that he had a reasonable excuse for his failure. If after imposing a penalty for failing to provide information or giving incorrect information, the authority again requests the person to supply the same information, the penalty for not doing so the second time is £200. It can ask for the information as many times as it likes until it is provided, each further refusal attracting another £200 penalty (*Sch 3, paras 1, 2*). An appeal against a penalty can be made to a valuation tribunal (see **21.81**) or in Scotland a valuation appeal committee. This is the case even if the ground of appeal is that there was no power to impose a penalty (*Sch 3, para 3*).

21.84 Where a person is convicted of an offence he cannot also be charged a penalty for the same default (*Sch 3, para 4*). The Treasury have power to change the £50 or £200 figure, but only to adjust for the effect of inflation (*Sch 3, para 5*). The Minister is empowered to make regulations for the collection of penalties and has done so in the *Council Tax (Administration and Enforcement) Regulations 1992*. These permit the authority to collect the penalty either by treating it as part of the tax (and thus collecting it by instalments) or by serving a notice on the taxpayer demanding payment within 14 days (*reg 29(1)*). They cannot add it to the tax where the taxpayer is jointly liable with someone else for the tax (*reg 27(2)(e)*).

21.85 Penalties up to level 2 (£500) can also be imposed on a debtor who fails to supply information following the making of a liability order (see **21.64**), or on the debtor or an employer who fails to notify a billing authority of a change of employment or fails to give the debtor the requisite notification in relation to an attachment of earnings order. They can be imposed up to level 3 (£1,000) on a debtor who provides false information, on an employer who fails to comply with an attachment of earnings order (unless he proves that he took all reasonable steps to do so), and on an employer who knowingly or recklessly gives a false statement in relation to an attachment of earnings order (*reg 56*).

21.86 Payment of a penalty cannot be demanded while any appeal or arbitration over it is outstanding, that is, until it is finally disposed of by the tribunal or is abandoned or fails for non-prosecution (*reg 29(2)–(4)*). If a penalty is paid and subsequently quashed by the authority, or by the valuation tribunal or the High Court, the authority can use the money against any other liability of the payer to council tax or penalty but must repay the excess (*reg 29(5)*).

21.87 Most of the penalties are fixed by reference to the standard scale of penalties which was introduced by *s 35* of the *Criminal Justice Act 1982* as amended by *s 17* of the *Criminal Justice Act 1991*. The current penalty levels are as follows:

Level 1	£200
Level 2	£500
Level 3	£1,000
Level 4	£2,500
Level 5	£5,000

Level 5 is sometimes referred to as the 'statutory maximum'.

Miscellaneous

21.88 The Minister is empowered to make regulations to deal with what happens when a person dies owing council tax, including as the spouse of someone who owes the tax, or penalties (*s 18*). The *Council Tax (Administration and Enforcement) Regulations 1992, reg 58* make his executors or personal representatives liable for such tax and, if the billing authority serves a notice on them requiring payment, for future tax that would have been due from the deceased but for his death. The executors are entitled to deduct the amount out of the estate. Unfortunately, their liability is not limited to assets in the estate. It may, accordingly, in future be dangerous to accept appointment as personal representative of an insolvent estate.

21.89 *Sections 30–38* and *65* of the *Act* contain the rules billing authorities must follow in settling the level of the tax and are not considered here. *Sections 39–52* contain similar rules for precepting authorities. *Sections 53–64* deal with the Minister's capping powers. Because of the difference in land and other law in Scotland, the government have opted to enact separate legislation for Scotland. This is contained in *ss 70–99* and is broadly similar to the provisions in respect of England and Wales. A new social security benefit, council tax benefit, was introduced to shield the poorest sections of society from the impact of the tax. This is enacted in *Sch 9* and outside the scope of this book.

Non-Domestic Rating

21.90 Property which is not liable to the council tax attracts non-domestic rating (which previously used to be called the Uniform Business Rate). That is a more descriptive name as rates are imposed on commercial and industrial premises at a rate fixed nationally by the government, which redistributes the yield between local authorities. The rateable value of such properties is based on their rental value on a letting from year to year (on the basis that the tenant undertook to pay all usual tenant's rates and taxes and to bear the cost of repairs and insurance and other expenses (if any) necessary to maintain the hereditament in a state to command that rent) (*Local Government Finance Act 1988, Sch 6, para 2*). In *Benjamin v Anston Properties (11.3.1998)* the Lands Tribunal held that this does not require an assumption that the property has been put into a reasonable state of repair at the valuation date and a property should therefore be valued in its existing state. The effect of this decision was reversed by the *Rating (Valuation) Act 1999* which requires three assumptions, namely that the tenancy begins on the valuation date, immediately before that date the property was in a state of reasonable repair (other than any repairs which a reasonable landlord would regard as uneconomic) and the tenant undertakes to bear all usual tenant's rates and taxes and to bear the cost of repairs insurance and any other expenses necessary to maintain the property in a state to command the rent (*section 1*). Properties liable to the uniform business rate (UBR) were valued at 1 April 1988 by local valuation officers and are required to be revalued every five years (*LGFA 1988, s 41*). The most recent revaluation was to 1 April 2015 and applies for 2017/18 onwards (*Rating Lists (Valuation Date) (England) Order No 216)*).

21.91 There are exemptions for:

(*a*) agricultural land and agricultural buildings;

(*b*) fish farms;

(*c*) registered places of religious worship (including church halls);

(*d*) certain property of Trinity House;

(*e*) sewers;

(*f*) property of drainage authorities;

(*g*) parks;

(*h*) property used for the training or welfare of the disabled;

(*i*) air-raid protection works;

(*j*) swinging moorings;

(*k*) property in enterprise zones;

(*l*) such other categories as the Minister may determine.

(*LGFA 1988, Sch 3.*)

21.92 There are a number of other reliefs:

(*a*) Empty properties: No business rates are payable for the first three months, and after that full business rates are payable from 1 April 2008, but the Minister has power by Order to reduce the rate by up to 50% (*Local*

Government Finance Act 1988, s 45 as amended by the *Rating (Empty Properties) Act 2007*). The three-month exempt period increases to six months for industrial and warehouse property. No rates are chargeable if the ratepayer is a charity or a community amateur sports club and it appears that when next in use the building will be wholly or mainly used for charitable purposes (or for the purposes of the club or of the club and another registered club) or on a property with a rateable value of up to £2,600. Listed buildings and small properties with a rateable value of under £2,200 pay no rates for the entire period that they are empty and unused.

(*b*) Charities: A charity or a Community Amateur Sports Clubs that is registered with HMRC is entitled to a deduction of 80% of the normal bill for non-domestic property which is wholly or mainly used for charitable purposes. A charity shop gets this only if it is mainly used for the sale of donated goods. Local authorities can also grant relief to a non-profit organisation that is not a charity but this is wholly at the discretion of the local authority. They can also increase the charity relief up to 100% (*LGFA 1988, s 41*).

(*c*) Rural villages with a population of under 3,000: Business premises are entitled to a 50% rates reduction if the property is the only village general store or post office and has a rateable value of under £8,500or the only village pub or the only petrol station and has a rateable value of less than £12,500. This relief was first introduced in 1998 and was initially limited to post offices and general stores, but its scope has since been broadened and the *Non-Domestic Rating (Designation of Rural Areas) (England) Order 2001* (*SI 2000 No 3916*) has designated the whole of England as rural apart from certain urban areas. The billing authority can increase this exemption to up to 100% if it wishes. A billing authority has discretion to remit all or part of the rates of any other building in such a settlement if its rateable value is £16,500 or less and the property is used for a purpose which benefits the local community (*LGFA 1988, ss 42A–43* as amended by the *Local Government Rating Act 1997*). The Minister confirmed this can cover public houses and garages.

(*d*) Retail relief: This is a discretionary relief for small retail premises. It is up to individual billing authorities whether to grant it. The relief was introduced at £1,000 for 2014/15 and increased to £1,500 for 2015/16. It is given only for properties with a rateable value of up to £50,000. It does not vary with the rateable value and there is no taper relief. The relief is not given for premises used to sell financial services (including payday lenders, betting shops and pawnbrokers); medical services (eg vets, dentists, doctors, osteopaths and chiropractors); professional services (eg solicitors, accountants, insurance agents, financial advisors or tutors); other services (such as estate agents and employment bureaux);

or post office sorting offices, Nor is it given for any premises that are not reasonably accessible to visiting members of the public.

(*e*) Small businesses: There is a 100% relief from business rates for 2017/18 where a business owns only one property and it has a rateable value of under £6,000. A 50% relief applies where the rateable value exceeds that sum but is less than £12,000. If a business uses more than one property, the rateable values must be aggregated. Relief is then given from the rates on the main property only, but based on that aggregate amount.

(*f*) Properties in enterprise zones (see **23.189**) qualify for rate relief at a level determined by the individual local authority.

21.93 The rate for a building is arrived at by multiplying the rateable value of the property by a standard rate multiplier (or poundage) which is fixed annually, not by the local authority like council tax, but by the government – which gave rise to the name of uniform business rate. There are two multipliers, a standard multiplier which for 2017/18 is 47.9p and a small business multiplier which for 2017/18 is 46.6p. This applies to eligible businesses with rateable values up to £17,999 (£25,499 in London). Eligible businesses with a rateable value below £6,000 get a 50% rate relief (100% during the five-and-a-half years to 31 March 2016). A lower reduction is given for larger properties. The relief decreases by 1% for every £120 of extra rateable value, disappearing when the rateable value reaches £12,000. Eligible ratepayers are those with one property (or with one main property and others all of which have an individual rateable value of under £2,600 provided that the total does not exceed £18,000 (£25,500 if the main property is in London), although in such a case only the main property attracts the relief). Eligible ratepayers have to apply for the relief but, once granted, the application continues automatically until the end of the five-yearly valuation period. A claim must be made not later than 30 September following the fiscal year, eg for the year to 31 March 2018 the last date for applications was 30 September 2017. There was also a 50% business rate relief for 18 months where, during the year to 31 March 2015, a business moved into retail premises that had been empty for a year or more.

21.94 Following devolution, the Scottish and Welsh Assemblies fix the rate in those countries. For 2017/18 it is nominally 46.6p in Scotland, but if the rateable value of a property is over £51,000 there is a small business surcharge to fund reduced rates for small businesses, bringing the effective rate to 49.2p. The discount for small businesses is 100% where the rateable value is under £10,000, 50% if it is under £12,000 and 25% if it is under £18,000. The rate in Wales for 2017/18 is 49.9p. There is no small business rate in Wales. A 50% relief applies where the rateable value is £2,000 or less and a 25% relief where it is between £2,001 and £5,000. Enhanced relief applies during the year to 30 November 2011 if the rateable value is up to £11,000. The City of London sets its own rate. This is 48p for 2017/18 with a small business rate of 47.1p.

21.95 Properties are normally revalued every five years to reflect changes in the relative valuations of properties in an area. 2015 was a revaluation year. The values at 1 April 2015 will be used in determining business rates from 1 April 2017 onwards. In England the rate poundage for subsequent years (other than revaluation years) is increased in line with inflation. It is determined by the formula:

$$\text{poundage for the preceding year} \times \frac{\text{RPI for September of the preceding year}}{\text{RPI for September of the year before the preceding year}}$$

In revaluation years the figure arrived at by this formula is adjusted by:

$$\frac{\text{total rateable values in the valuation list on the last day of the preceding financial year}}{\text{estimated rateable values in the next valuation list}}$$

21.96 Business rates are allocated to local authorities (and precepting authorities) in proportion to their adult populations.

21.97 Rating revaluations tend to bring about major changes in the rate burden for different business sectors and in different areas. Accordingly transitional arrangements are normally introduced to cushion businesses most seriously affected.

21.98 A transitional relief on the 2015 revaluation limits the percentage by which a property's rates liability can increase each year. This is: applies to a property for which the 'notional chargeable amount' exceeds its 'base liability' multiplied by 'the appropriate fraction'. For this purpose, the notional chargeable amount is the rateable value at 1 April 2015 multiplied by the small business multiplier for the relevant year, eg for 2017/18 multiplied by 47.9p. The base liability is the 2014/15 liability (annualised if the building was not rated for the entire year) for 2017/18 and for subsequent years it is the previous year's base liability times the previous year's appropriate fraction. The appropriate fractions are:

Year	*Small business*	*Medium*	*Large*
2017/18	5%	12.5%	42%
2018/19	7.5%	17.5%	32%
2019/20	10%	20%	49%
2020/21	15%	25%	16%
2021/22	15%	5%	6%

These caps are on the increase as compared with the previous year. A small business is one with a rateable value of under £20,000 (£28,000 in London). A medium business is one with a rateable value of up to £100,000. To offset this relief, reductions will also be capped as follows:

Year	*Small business*	*Medium*	*Large*
2017/18	20%	10%	4.1%
2018/19	30%	15%	4.6%
2019/20	35%	20%	5.9%
2020/21	55%	25%	5.8%
2021/22	55%	25%	4.8%

21.99 On the 2010 revaluation the figures were:

Year	*Small business*	*Large business*
2010/11	5%	12.5%
2011/12	7.5%	17.5%
2012/13	10%	20%
2013/14 and 2014/15	15%	25%

If the rates bill for a property decreased following the revaluation, the benefit of the decrease was similarly phased in. The percentage limitation was:

Year	*Small business*	*Large business*
2010/11	20%	4.6%
2011/12	30%	6.7%
2012/13	35%	7%
2013/14 and 2014/15	55%	13%

Business Improvement District Levies

21.100 A local authority can charge a levy, the BID levy, on non-domestic ratepayers in a business improvement district. The amount of the levy must be determined in accordance with the BID arrangements (*Local Government Act 2003, s 46*). A local authority can make arrangements (BID arrangements) with respect to a business improvement district comprising all or part of its area to enable the projects specified in the arrangements to be carried out for the benefit of the business improvement district (or those who live, work or carry on any activity in it) and for those projects to be financed in whole or part by a BID levy imposed on the non-domestic ratepayers (or a class of them) in the district (*s 41*).

21.101 BID arrangements cannot be brought into force unless proposals for the arrangement have been approved in a ballot of the non-domestic ratepayers in the proposed business improvement district who are liable for the proposed levy. The proposals have to be approved by a majority of those voting and the aggregate rateable values held by those in favour must exceed those in relation to those voting against (*s 50*). If the ballot is passed, the local authority can itself veto the arrangements in some circumstances. If it does so anyone who was entitled to vote in the ballot can appeal to the Secretary of State (*ss 51, 52*).

21.102 BID arrangements have effect for such period as is specified in the arrangements but this cannot exceed five years. However, the arrangements can be renewed for successive five-year periods but only if a fresh ballot is held for each renewal (*s 54*).

Business Rate Supplements

21.103 The *Business Rate Supplement Act 2009* (as amended by the *Localism Act 2011*) gives local authorities power to impose a levy, the business rate supplement (BRS) on non-domestic ratepayers in its area to raise money for expenditure on a project that the authority considers will promote economic development in the area (*s 1*). It must first publish its proposal for the project and consult those persons liable to pay business rates (*ss 4–6*). A BRS cannot be imposed for any period before 1 April 2010. However, it can raise money for a project started before that date but only if it started to do so in the year to 31 March 2011, 2012 or 2013 (*s 27*).

21.104 If the amount that the local authority hopes to raise for the project from the BRS is more than a third of the anticipated cost of the project it must hold a ballot. The only persons entitled to vote on a ballot are business rate payers (and potential payers). If a ballot needs to be held the BRS can be levied only if both it is passed by a majority of those voting and the aggregate rateable values of those who vote in favour of the proposition exceeds that of those who vote against it (*ss 7, 8*). The local authority can grant such relief in relation to the BRS as it thinks appropriate (*s 15(1)*). However, if it wishes to grant reliefs it must specify them in the original prospectus for the project (*s 15(3)*).

21.105 If a person who is liable for BRS is also liable for BID levy (see **21.100**) for the same year in relation to the property, the local authority must set down rules to deal with the position. The rules must allow all or part of the BID levy to be offset against the BRS. They must apply uniformly, be consistent in relation to bid levies and be specified in the prospectus for the BRS (*s 16*).

21.106 The Secretary of State has the power to give guidance as to the type of projects for which it may, or may not be, appropriate to levy a BRS and on various other matters. The local authority must have regard to such guidance when proposing a BRS (*s 26*). The Secretary of State also has the power to cancel a BRS if he thinks that the local authority has acted in a way that is materially inconsistent with information provided by it in the prospectus for the BRS, or a consultation document, or in connection with the holding of the ballot. He can also direct the local authority to repay money collected under the BRS (*s 24*).

21.107 The Greater London Authority has used this power to impose a supplement of 2p from 1 April 2010 on all business premises in Greater London of over £70,000 rateable value in order to help to finance Crossrail, a major infrastructure project. It expects to continue with this supplement for 24–30 years. It says that it will apply to only 15% of business premises in London and that premises that are exempt under non-domestic rating will not have to pay the levy. It was not required to hold a ballot as the project started before 1 April 2010 (see **21.103**) and has said that it does not intend to do so voluntarily. It also does not intend to introduce transitional arrangements for the levy, irrespective of what the government decides to do for non-domestic rating.

Chapter 22

Landfill Tax

22.1 A special tax on landfill waste disposal applies to all waste disposal operations at landfill sites in the UK. It is imposed on the site operator. In addition, VAT is payable on the landfill tax-inclusive price, ie if the operator makes a charge for disposal of £1,000 and landfill tax is £200 he will have to charge the customer £1,440 (£1,000 + £200 + 20% of £1,200). The customer will be able to treat the VAT as input tax in the normal way but will not be able to reclaim any part of the landfill tax – although if the waste disposal is a revenue expense the full £1,200 VAT-exclusive figure will be a business expense attracting a corporation tax deduction. From 1 April 2015, landfill tax was devolved to the Scottish Parliament. Accordingly, landfill tax has been replaced by Scottish Landfill Tax, which is payable to Revenue Scotland, not to HMRC. The initial standard rate of Scottish Landfill Tax is £82.60 per tonne with a reduced rate of £2.60 a tonne for inert waste. This is the same as the rates in the remainder of the UK (see **22.14**). As Scottish Landfill Tax is under the control of the Scottish Parliament, the detailed rules in Scotland will not necessarily reflect those outlined below.

22.2 HMRC have confirmed that where a trader generates waste and pays landfill tax on it, the landfill tax will qualify as a deductible expense in calculating profit for income or corporation tax purposes provided that the other costs of disposing of the waste, eg the carriage and the waste disposal charge, are themselves deductible. Where a landfill site operator makes a payment to an environmental body (see **22.47**) that payment will be deductible provided that it meets the test of being wholly and exclusively for the purpose of the trade. *Prima facie* this test will normally be met (Tax Bulletin 23, June 1996).

22.3 The tax is under the control of HMRC. It applies to all forms of landfill disposal which involve the deposit of waste in or on land. There is no *de minimis* exemption. Landfill site operators will normally account for the tax quarterly by reference to deliveries to the site during the quarter.

22.4 Although the professed objectives of the tax are to promote greater efficiency in the waste management market by ensuring landfill waste disposal is properly priced, and to encourage the production of less waste and a greater emphasis on recycling, as it does not apply to incineration there were fears that it could instead encourage that alternative method of disposal which many feel more environmentally damaging. However, the government stated in 1998 that research shows that already almost a third of companies began, or were considering, waste recycling, re-use or minimisation as a result of the tax. (Business Brief 9/98).

Disposal as Waste

22.5 The tax applies to a disposal of materials as waste made by way of landfill at a landfill site (*FA 1996, s 40(2)*). For this purpose material is disposed of as waste if the person disposing of it (or if the person on whose behalf or at whose request, it is being disposed of) does so with the intention of discarding it. The fact that someone else could, or does, benefit from, or make use of, the materials will not prevent there being a disposal as waste (*FA 1996, s 64*). ICI Chemicals and Polymer Ltd manufacture hydrogen fluoride, a by-product of which is dehydrous calcium sulphate (Andricite). It discovered that Andricite can be used for encapsulating mercury waste and used it as such in its landfill site. HMRC contended that the Andricite was waste, ie something that ICI intended to discard or throw away, and felt that the fact that it was also able to be used for site engineering purposes was irrelevant. The VAT and Duties Tribunal (*L00002*) noted that Andricite had a saleable value and that ICI did not have the intention of disposing of it as useless but intended to use it for encapsulating mercury. It was therefore not 'waste' within the meaning of *s 64*.

22.6 A similar decision was reached by the tribunal in *Darfish Ltd (L00005)* where soil was brought onto a landfill site specifically to be used for site engineering purposes. However, on appeal (*2000 All ER (D) 361*) Moses J held that in deciding whether the material was waste the tribunal should have looked at the intention of the disposers of the material (topsoil and sub-soil), Hallamshire and Wilson Bowden, not that of Darfish, the site operator, and remitted the case to the tribunal to decide this point. In that case Moses J thought that disposal cannot be confined to the moment of deposit. It is a term wider than 'discarding', and wider than 'deposit'. Disposal will include, but not be confined to, any of the processes of removal, transport and deposit. It must include deposit because the deposit triggers the tax and also identifies the time when the landfill site operator must be identified as such, but disposal is not limited to the process of deposit'.

22.7 In *C & E Commrs v Parkwood Landfill Ltd (2002 STC 417)* Sir Andrew Morritt V-C thought it clear that in *Darfish* Moses J had regarded the disposal of waste as different from the disposal by way of landfill. In the *Parkwood* case, a joint venture company, Parkwood Recycling Ltd, acquired domestic waste from Sheffield City Council, crushed, sorted, and graded it and separated it into saleable materials and other which went to landfill (and on which tax was presumably paid). The saleable materials included aggregates and fines, which were sold to Parkwood Landfill which used them at its landfill site for road-making and landscaping. Parkwood contended that such materials were not Parkwood Recycling's waste. HMRC contended that tax was due as the Council had discarded the material as waste. The judge agreed, but his decision was reversed by the Court of Appeal *(2002 STC 1536)* which held that, 'the natural meaning of *s 40(2)* requires a disposal which is a taxable disposal to satisfy the conditions in sub-sections *(a),(b),(c)* and *(d)* at the same time … the disposal has to be made at a landfill site by way of landfill and also to be a disposal of material as waste. The tax is a landfill tax, not a landfill and recycling tax. The tax is to be paid when waste material is disposed by way of landfill in a landfill site; not on waste material (eg fines) which has been recycled (eg into blocks) which may be used in a landfill site (eg to build a wall or hard standing). The disposal referred to in *s 40(2)* is a particular disposal'.

22.8 In *Waste Recycling Group Ltd v HMRC (2009 STC 200)* 11 different categories of inert material deposited as 'daily cover' over the waste and used for site engineering were considered separately, namely:

(*a*) purchased material bought from a supplier of inert material – HMRC accepted that this was not disposed of as waste;

(*b*) free tips, ie where the company (WRG) did not charge for tipping as it wanted to use the waste for daily cover or site engineering;

(*c*) uneconomic tips, ie where WRG makes a charge which is less than the landfill tax (if any is due);

(*d*) break-even tips, ie where the charge simply covers the landfill tax;

(*e*) discounted tips, ie where the charge is more than £2 per tonne but is below the market rate;

(*f*) civic amenity site deposits, ie where WRG is paid by a local authority to take away inert waste from a recycling site;

(*g*) transfer station deposits, ie where WRG takes away inert waste from another site for payment;

(*h*) procured material, ie where WRG sources inert waste from a known supplier of such material;

(*i*) sorted material, ie where the waste has already been sorted, so attracting a lower charge from WRG;

(*j*) site engineering, ie waste already owned by WRG used for site engineering;

(*k*) daily cover, ie waste already owned by WRG used for daily cover.

The Court of Appeal held that none of these categories attract tax to the extent that they were acquired for site engineering or daily cover. It cast doubt on whether there is a 'disposal by way of landfill' at all if it is not intended as waste. It also indicated that the test as to whether material is waste should be applied at the time that it is brought onto the site. In this case, title to all of the waste had passed to WRG by that stage. Accordingly, the disposal, if any, was made by WRG on its own behalf. WRG did not intend to discard the material as 'discard' does not comprehend the retention and use of the material for the purposes of its owner. An interesting question arose in *Patersons of Greenoakhill Ltd v HMRC (2017 STC 225)*. A landfill site produces landfill gas (mainly methane) as landfilled biomass decomposes. Patersons collected this gas and used it to generate electricity, which it sold to the national grid. Relying on *Waste Recycling*, it claimed that the biomass waste was not waste at all as it used it for the production of electricity. Although such material was mixed with non-biodegradable waste, it claimed that a reasonable apportionment could be made based on a mathematical formula. The Upper Tribunal held that Patersons intended to discard the biomass materials at the point they were put in landfill. The electricity generated did not arise from the 'use' of the biomass. Patersons does nothing to bring about the decomposition. The methane production is an inevitable consequence of tipping biomass and will occur irrespective of whether it is flamed off or is harnessed to use for a different purpose. Patersons' licence required it to do something with the gas and converting it to electricity is simply its means of disposing of that gas. The Court of Appeal agreed, but on a different ground. In the context used, the word 'material' does not include future by-products and means material in the form in which it exists or the date of deposit on the landfill site. HMRC have subsequently decided that reverse or top fluff (the careful placement of soft waste) is not covered by the *Waste Recycling Group* decision and is disposed of with the intention of discarding it. It does not fulfil any engineering purpose or any regulatory requirement. As such, it has not been 'used' but is simply carefully placed and well-managed waste. They said that an FTT case on this was pending (HMRC Brief 2/2014, now withdrawn) but it does not appear to have proceeded.

22.9 A disposal is by way of landfill if either:

(*a*) the material is deposited on the surface of land or on a structure set into the surface; or

(*b*) the material is deposited under the surface of land.

(*FA 1996, s 65(1)*.)

22.10 Material means material of any kind and includes objects, substances and products of all kind (*FA 1996, s 70(1)*). Placing the material in a container before disposal will not prevent it being by way of landfill (*FA 1996, s 65(2)*).

Depositing the material and later covering it with earth (or with similar matter such as sand or rocks) and depositing material in a cavity such as a cavern or mine are both caught (*FA 1996, s 65(3)(8)*). If material is deposited within (*a*) with a view to it later being covered with earth (so that it will fall within (*b*)) the charge arises under (*a*) when it is deposited, not under (*b*) when it is later covered (*FA 1996, s 65(4)*). Land covered by water is within *s 65* if it is above the low water mark of ordinary spring tides (*FA 1996, s 65(7)*). The Treasury have power by statutory instrument to amend these rules (*FA 1996, s 65(5)(6)*). A site is a landfill site only if it has been granted a site licence under Part II of the *Environmental Protection Act 1990* (or its Scottish or Northern Ireland equivalent) (*FA 1996, s 66* as amended by the *Pollution Prevention and Control Act 1999, Sch 2, para 19*), although the tribunal in *Lancashire Waste Services Ltd (L00008)* held that where a site licence was amended to restrict disposals to a small part of the site only, the entire site remained a landfill site. Due to an error the definition did not reflect the need for a change in the law as it applied to Scotland, but this was corrected by *FA 2012, s 206* with retroactive effect to 2000. In *McIntosh Plant Hire (L00010)* the tribunal held that the site included the access roadway so that waste material deposited on the road to upgrade what was an unsurfaced track was liable to tax. Where a company brought soil onto a landfill site and paid a tipping fee to the site operator the soil was held to be waste notwithstanding that it was set aside by the operator and later used in the site restoration, as it was material deposited on the surface of the site (*F L Gamble & Sons Ltd L00004*).

22.11 HMRC have said that they accept that if a material is processed it is not necessary for the process to change the material's chemical properties (as they previously contended) in order for it to be regarded as having been recycled. Where waste is recycled (which would include composting) the original producer's intention becomes irrelevant to the question of whether the material is waste. What matters is the recycler's intention – which will be evidenced by the nature of the transaction. If a landfill site operator can demonstrate that the material he uses in site engineering is not discarded by the producer it will not attract tax (Business Brief 10/04).

22.12 HMRC consider that material used to create a 'reverse fluff layer' or 'top fluff layer' (material used to protect or provide a suitable stable substrate for the overlying layers at the top of a landfill cell) is liable to landfill tax as the waste material is disposed of with the intention of discarding it and the disposal does not constitute a use of that material. However, material placed to form the regulating layer (by providing protection to the overlying geo-synthetic engineering cap) did constitute using that material up to 31 August 2009. After that date head (*g*) above makes them taxable (HMRC Brief 15/2012). Such material could attract the lower rate of tax if it can be clearly evidenced that it can only consist of materials within **22.13** below. Rocks and soil can fall into this category, but only if they are not contaminated with materials such as asbestos, metal, wood and plastic and do not contain elevated levels of chemical contaminants (heavy metals, hydrocarbons) (HMRC Brief 18/2012).

22.13 In response to the decision in *Waste Recycling Group Ltd*, the Treasury were given power by regulation to prescribe landfill site activities that should be treated:

(*a*) as a disposal at the landfill site of the material involved in the activity;

(*b*) as a disposal of that material as waste; and

(*c*) as a disposal of that material by way of landfill.

(*FA 1996, s 65A* inserted by *FA 2009, Sch 60, para 2*.)

They have done so by the *Landfill Tax (Prescribed Landfill Site Activities) Order 2009 (SI 2009 No 1929)*. This prescribes the following activities with effect from 1 September 2009 unless they use material that has already been chargeable to landfill tax or exempted from the tax:

(*a*) the use of material to cover the disposal area (any area of a landfill site where any landfill disposal takes place) during a short-term cessation in landfill deposit activity;

(*b*) the use of material to create or maintain a temporary haul road (any road within a landfill site which gives access to a disposal area);

(*c*) the use of material to create or maintain temporary hard standing (a base within a landfill site on which any landfill activity such as sorting, treatment, processing storage or recycling is carried out);

(*d*) the use of material to create or maintain a cell bund (a structure within a disposal area which separates units of waste);

(*e*) the use of material to create or maintain a temporary screening bund (any structure on a landfill site, whether above or below ground, put in place to protect or conceal any landfill site activity or to reduce nuisance from noise), except where the material so used is naturally occurring material extracted from the landfill site in which the bund is located;

(*f*) the temporary storage of ashes (including pulverised fuel ash and furnace bottom ash);

(*g*) the use of material placed against the drainage layer or liner of the disposal area to prevent damage to that layer or liner; and

(*h*) any other landfill activity if *FA 1996, Sch 5, para 1B* (see **22.39**) requires a person to notify or give information or, under the *Landfill Tax Regulations 1996, reg 16A*, a person is required to designate a part of a landfill site as an 'information area' (see **22.26**), give information or maintain a record in respect of that area, and that requirement to notify is not complied with.

Rates of Tax

22.14 The tax is based on weight. The standard rate is £86.10 per tonne for 2017/18 but will increase to £88.95 for 2018/19 and again to £91.35 for 2019/20 (£48 before 1 April 2011, £64 before 1 April 2013, £72 before 1 April 2014, £80 before 1 April 2015, £82.60 before 1 April 2016 and £84.40 for 2016/17), reduced proportionately for parts of a tonne after the first or, if less than a tonne is disposed of, a proportionately reduced sum (*FA 1996, s 42(1)*). A reduced rate of £2.70 per tonne applies for 2017/18 increasing to £2.80 for 2018/19 and £2.90 for 2019/20 (£2.50 prior to 1 April 2014, £2.60 for 2015/16 and £2.65 for 2016/17) applies to inactive or inert waste (called 'qualifying material') and also from 1 April 2015 to qualifying fines (see **22.18**). The Treasury is given power by statutory instrument to determine what qualifies for the reduced rate. From 1 April 2011 the Treasury must set criteria for determining what material qualifies, publish such criteria and keep it under review (*FA 1996, s 42(4)* as amended by *FA 2015, Sch 15, para* 2). Previously the Treasury had to have regard to the object of ensuring that the material listed was inactive or inert. It is still the government's intention that the reduced rate should apply only to inert waste even though that obligation has disappeared. Landfill tax is one of the devolved taxes so does not apply in Scotland and from 1 April 2018 will not apply in Wales, but both countries will impose a similar tax at their own rates (see **22.56**).

22.15 The current criteria are that the material must be–

(*a*) non-hazardous;

(*b*) having a low potential for greenhouse gas omissions; and

(*c*) having a low polluting potential in the landfill environment.

(Notice LFT1: A general guide to landfill tax.)

The *Landfill Tax (Qualifying Material) Order 2011 (SI 2011, No 1017)* as amended by the *Landfill Tax (Qualifying Material) (Amendment) Order 2012 (SI 2012 No 940)* sets out what qualifies for the reduced rate from 1 April 2011, namely:

Group 1 Rocks and soils: rock, clay, sand, gravel, sandstone, limestone, crushed stone, china clay, construction stone, stones from the demolition of buildings or structures, slate, sub-soil, silts and dredgings. However, the material can be treated as qualifying only if it is naturally occurring.

Group 2 Ceramic or concrete materials: glass, including fritted enamel, ceramics including bricks, bricks and mortar, tiles, clayware, pottery, china and refractories, concrete, including reinforced concrete, concrete blocks, breeze blocks and aircrete blocks. However, the group does not include glass fibre and glass reinforced plastic or concrete plant washings.

Group 3 Minerals (processed or prepared): moulding sands, including used foundry sand; clays, including moulding clays and clay absorbents (including Fuller's earth and bentonite), mineral absorbents, man-made mineral fibres, including glass fibres; silica; mica; and mineral abrasives. The group does not include moulding sands containing organic binder or man-made mineral fibres made from glass reinforced plastic and asbestos.

Group 4 Furnace slags: vitrified wastes and residues from thermal processing of minerals where, in either case, the residue is both fused and insoluble; and slag from waste incineration.

Group 5 Ash: bottom ash and fly ash produced only from the combustion of wood or waste or both, and bottom ash and fly ash from the combustion of coal or petroleum coke or both (including when burnt together with biomass but only if put into a separate cell) deposited in a cell containing the product of that combustion alone. The group does not include fly ash from sewage sludge, municipal, clinical and hazardous waste incinerators. The requirement for separate cells did not apply prior to 1 April 2012.

Group 6 Low activity organic compounds: calcium based reaction wastes from titanium dioxide production; calcium carbonate, magnesium carbonates, magnesium oxide; magnesium hydroxide; iron oxide; ferric hydroxide; aluminium oxide; aluminium hydroxide; and zirconium dioxide.

Group 7 Calcium sulphate: including calcium sulphate, gypsum and calcium sulphate based plasters; but not including plasterboard. The reduced rate applies only if the disposal is in landfills for non-hazardous waste in a cell where no biodegradable waste is accepted.

Group 8 Calcium hydroxide and brine: but only if deposited in a brine cavity.

Notes

1 The detailed items against Groups 1 to 6 are an exhaustive definition of what falls within the group.

2 If the owner of the material immediately prior to disposal is not the site operator, the reduced rate applies only if there is a transfer note under the *Environmental Protection (Duty of Care) Regulations 1991* (or its Northern Irish equivalent) which contains a description of the material which accords with either one of the above group headings or one of the detailed items on the group.

22.16 Prior to 1 April 2011 the *Landfill Tax (Qualifying Material) Order 1996* (*SI 1996 No 1528*) applied. This applied the reduced rate to the deposit of:

(1) Naturally occurring rocks and soils (including clay, sand, gravel, sandstone, limestone, crushed stone, china clay, construction stone, stone from the demolition of buildings or structures, slate, topsoil, peat, silt and dredgings).

(2) Glass, ceramics and concrete (including fritted enamel, bricks, tiles, clayware, pottery, china, bricks and mortar, refractory bricks, reinforced concrete, concrete blocks, breeze blocks and aircrete blocks – but not glass-fibre or glass-reinforced plastic or concrete plant washings).

(3) Unused processed or prepared minerals (namely moulding sands, clays, clay absorbents such as Fuller's earth, bentonite and other mineral absorbents, man-made mineral fibres, glass fibre, silica, mica and mineral abrasives – but not sand containing organic binders, glass-reinforced plastic or asbestos).

(4) Furnace slags (including vitrified wastes, fused and insoluble residues from thermal processing of minerals, and slag from waste incineration).

(5) Bottom ash and fly ash from wood or coal combustion (but not fly ash from municipal, clinical and hazardous waste incinerators or sewage sludge incinerators).

(6) Low-activity inorganic compounds (namely titanium dioxide, calcium carbonate, magnesium carbonate, magnesium oxide, magnesium hydroxide, iron oxide, ferric hydroxide, aluminium oxide, aluminium hydroxide, and zirconium dioxide).

(7) Calcium sulphate (including gypsum and calcium sulphate based plasters – but not plasterboard) if it is either disposed of at a site licensed to take only non-putrescible (inactive) waste or is landfilled in a separate containment cell within a mixed site.

(8) Calcium hydroxide and brine which is deposited in brine cavity.

(9) Water which contains any of the above qualifying materials in suspension.

22.17 To qualify for the lower rate, the transfer note (as defined in the *Environmental Protection (Duty of Care) Regulations 1991* (*SI 1991 No 2839*) must describe the materials in accordance with the above list and in the case of water must also describe the material held in suspension (*art 6*). The waste must not contain or be contaminated with other unqualifying material subject to a *de minimis* limit where that material does not lead to any potential for pollution. Unfortunately, HMRC have defined that limit as 'a small quantity of non-qualifying material'. They told the tribunal in *Cleanaway Ltd (L00017)* that they had no official view as to what percentage was small, but considered that the 27 disputed loads in that case did not meet the test. The tribunal adopted a yardstick of under 5% being small and, applying that, held that 16 of the 27 disputed loads qualified for the lower rate as containing under 5% non-qualifying material. HMRC have also said that where a load contains some incidental active waste this will in general be ignored if it is ignored for environmental regulatory purposes (HMRC report on responses to consultation, April 1996). HMRC say that, as it is normally impossible to determine the origin and exact source of residues from treated transfer station waste, these cannot be qualifying materials (HMRC Brief 15/2012). However, if it can be evidenced that the waste can only result from materials subject to the lower rate of tax, the waste will attract that rate (HMRC Brief 18/2012) *F(No 3)A 2010, s 24* requires the Treasury, in relation to disposals made after 31 March 2011, to set criteria to be considered in determining from time to time what materials to prescribe, to keep such criteria under review and to revise them when they consider it appropriate to do so. They will have to publish that criteria and must have regard to such published criteria and to any other factors they consider relevant in determining what materials to prescribe.

22.18 Qualifying fines are a mixture of fines that consist of such qualifying material as is prescribed by order and material that is not qualifying fines provided that the mixture satisfies the requirement prescribed in the order (*FA 1996, s 43(3A)* inserted by *FA 2015, Sch 15, para 2*). The Treasury has provided that the mixture must contain no more than an incidental amount of non-qualifying material and must not be hazardous waste. They have also provided that the mixture must not result from any deliberate or artificial blending or mixing with any quantity of material (including fines) prior to disposal at a landfill site (the *Landfill Tax (Qualifying Fines) (No 2) Order 2015, (SI 2015, No 1385), Art 3*). The Treasury can by statutory instrument lay down conditions to qualifying fines (*FA 1996, s 63A* inserted by *FA 2015, Sch 15, para 4*). They have provided that fines cannot be treated as qualifying fines unless all of the following conditions are met:

(*a*) if the owner of the fines immediately prior to the disposal is not the site owner, the site owner holds a transfer note in respect of the quality of material being landfilled;

(*b*) the site owner holds such evidence as is specified in a public notice that the fines are qualifying fines;

(*c*) where an LOI test has been conducted on any part of the fines in accordance with any published notice, the LOI percentage determined by that test does not exceed 15% (10% for disposals after 1 April 2016); and (*d*) where HMRC has directed the site owner to conduct an LOI test of a quantity of material proposed to be disposed of as qualifying fines, he conducts that test.

(*Landfill Tax (Qualifying Fines) (No 2) Order 2015, Art 4(1).*)

The LOI percentage is the amount of non-qualifying material contained in fines as indicated by the percentage of the mass of those fines lost on ignition. An LOI test is a test to determine that percentage conducted in accordance with the terms of a public notice. Qualifying material is material that attracts the lower rate of landfill tax (*Art 1*). Fines are particles produced by a waste treatment process that involves an element of mechanical treatment (*FA 1996, s 70(1)*). Hazardous waste is as defined in *EC Directive 2008/98/EC* (*Art 1*). Where HMRC have required the site operator to carry out an LOI test, material received by him for disposal as fines cannot be treated as qualifying fines between the date of the requirement and that on which the test is carried out (*Art 4(2)(3)*). The public notice is, of course, LFT1, 'A General Guide to Landfill Tax'. The *Landfill Tax (Qualifying Fines) Order 2015*, was introduced from 1 April 2015, but repealed from 14 June 2015 by the *No 2 Order*. The only change seems to be the addition of a definition of a transfer note.

22.19 Where a site owner has carried out an LOI test on any fires, he must retain a representative sample of at least one kilogram from the load of fires tested for a month after the end of the quarter following that in which the test was carried out and must notify HMRC within a month of the quarter in which it was carried out of any test result in which the LOI percentage exceeds the 15% limit, giving the name of the person responsible for the waste treatment of the fires and the address at which such treatment took place. There is a penalty of £250 for non-compliance (*Landfill Tax Regulations 1996, Reg 16ZA* inserted by *Landfill Tax (Amendment) (No 2) Regulations 2015 (SI 2015, No 846), Reg 2(c)*).

22.20 HMRC have power to make regulations to determine weight. They have done so by the *Landfill Tax Regulations 1996* (*SI 1996 No 1527*). The weight of material disposed of must normally be ascertained by weighing it at the time of disposal (unless that is a deemed time under *FA 1996, s 61*). If there is no weighbridge at the landfill site – or, although there is one, it would be costly to use it, eg because the waste does not normally pass near it or it is out of order – an alternative method of calculating the waste can be agreed with HMRC. For example, the maximum permitted weight for the lorry could be used, or the volume of waste could be measured or otherwise ascertained and converted to weight. HMRC Information Note, 4/96, 'Calculating the weight of waste' contains conversion factors for various categories of waste (Information Note 1/96, paras 7.1 and 7.2). The authority for this is *reg 44* which allows the registrable person to agree a special method with HMRC and *reg 43* which provides that if they publish a notice specifying rules for determining weight it must be followed. HMRC can withdraw from an agreement at any time (*reg 44(3)*). In *D W Thomas (L00012)* the waste was not weighed and no method of ascertaining weight was agreed with HMRC as it was not realised that the site was a landfill site. The taxpayer engaged a geologist to calculate the volume to weight ratio of the site (by which time tipping had ceased). HMRC objected that the geologist had not used one of their standard methods – he had felt this impractical as the site sloped. HMRC adopted a method which gave a significantly higher tax liability than the maximum produced by any of their standard methods. The tribunal felt this unreasonable and held that their assessment had not been made to their best judgment.

22.21 HMRC can lay down rules to discount the weight of any water if water is present in waste only because either:

(*a*) it has been added to enable the material to be transported for disposal, eg moved by pipeline;

(*b*) it has been used for the extraction of a mineral;

(*c*) it has arisen or has been added in the course of an industrial process; or

(*d*) the material is the residue from the treatment of effluent or sewage by a water treatment works.

The water cannot be discounted under (*a*) to (*c*) unless it forms 25% or more of the weight of the material at the time of the disposal. In all cases the water cannot be discounted if the material is capable of escaping from the landfill site by leaching, unless either it is likely to do so in the form of water only or the leachate will be collected on the site and treated to eliminate any potential it has to cause harm (*reg 44(6)(7)*).

Where the material falls within (*d*) above, the water cannot be discounted unless it has been added prior to disposal. Naturally occurring water (such as rain or snow) cannot be discounted. It appears that if there is any such water in a load even the added water cannot be discounted although this is clearly not the intention.

22.22 The person liable for the tax is the landfill site operator, ie the person who at the time of disposal holds the licence for the landfill site concerned (*FA 1996, s 41*). There is no obligation on the site owner to issue a landfill tax invoice but if he chooses to do so this must contain specific information, which is set out in *reg 37* of the *Landfill Tax Regulations 1996* (*SI 1996 No 1527*). As bad debt relief is dependent on there being a landfill invoice it is likely that most site operators will choose to issue one. Landfill tax is not recoverable by the customer either by repayment or by being offset against VAT. It is, however, an expense which is deductible in calculating taxable profits for income or corporation tax.

Exemptions

22.23 There are a number of exemptions.

(1) *Material removed from water (dredging, etc).* The disposal of material removed from a river, a canal or watercourse (natural or artificial) or a dock or harbour (natural or artificial) and which before its removal formed part of or projected from the bed of the water concerned is exempt from the tax. This exemption extends to material removed from water within the approaches of a harbour and which was moved in the interests of navigation and to naturally occurring mineral material that has been removed from the sea in the course of commercial operations to obtain sand, gravel or other substances from the seabed (*FA 1996, s 43*). From 30 October 2008 it also extends to cases where other material has been added to the waste in order to solidify it (*FA 1996, s 43(5)*).

(2) *Mining and quarrying.* There is an exemption for the disposal of naturally occurring material extracted from the earth in the course of either commercial mining operations (both deep and open-cast) or commercial quarrying operations. The material must not have been subjected to, or resulted from, any process separate from the mining or quarrying or any process which has permanently altered the material's chemical composition (*FA 1996, s 44*).

(3) *Pet cemeteries.* A cemetery is not normally within the scope of the tax as the burial of human remains is not the disposal of waste. However, a pet cemetery is licensed as a landfill site under the *Environmental Protection Act 1990* or from 21 March 2000, is granted a permit under the *Pollution Prevention and Control Act 1999* so a specific exemption from the tax is needed for pet cemeteries. For the exemption to apply the only landfill disposals made at the site since 1 October 1996 must have been of the remains of dead domestic pets (*FA 1996, s 45*).

(4) *Material removed from contaminated land.* There is an exemption for the disposal of waste removed from contaminated land for which a certificate was issued by HMRC. The certificate must be in force at the time the waste is removed and any conditions attached to the certificate must be met. The material must be removed before construction of any building or civil engineering work commences on the part of the land in question, or in the case of other qualifying land reclamation when the pollutants have been cleared from the relevant part of the site (*FA 1996, s 43A*). In other words, the exemption will not cover building waste or waste arising from landscaping, fencing or general site clearance. It is not clear when construction of a building commences for this purpose. It is probably not when a start is made on a foundation trench as logically the exemption needs to cover not merely contamination of the topsoil but

the removal of deep contamination which is unearthed in the course of the construction of the foundations of a building.

The exemption does not apply if at the time the material is removed an enforcement notice has been served in relation to any part of the land in question requiring clearance of the pollution – unless the person carrying out the removal is a local authority, a development corporation under *s 135, Local Government, Planning and Land Act 1980* or its Scottish equivalent, the Environment Agency, the Scottish Environment Protection Agency, English Partnerships, Scottish Enterprise, Highland and Islands Enterprise or the Welsh Development Agency (*FA 1996, s 43A(4),(5)*). An enforcement notice for this purpose means a works notice under *s 46A, Control of Pollution Act 1974*, an enforcement, prohibition, order or remediation notice under the *Environmental Protection Act 1990* or a works notice under *Water Resources Act 1991, s 161A*. The purpose of this exclusion is to deny relief to the person who has himself created the contamination. The government has given notice that this exemption is to be withdrawn. *Section 43A* will be repealed with effect from 1 April 2012 (*The Landfill Tax (Material from Contaminated Land) (Phasing out of Exemption) Order 2008, SI 2008 No 2669*).

A certificate of contamination is issued by HMRC on the application in writing by a person either carrying out or intending to carry out a reclamation of the land in question once HMRC are satisfied that the reclamation qualifies for exemption (*FA 1996, s 43B*). A reclamation qualifies if:

(*a*) it is (or will be) carried out with the object of either facilitating development, conservation, the provision of a public park or other amenity, or the use of the land for agriculture or forestry, or of reducing or removing the potential of pollutants to cause harm;

(*b*) it constitutes (or includes) clearing the land of pollutants which are causing harm or have the potential for causing harm;

(*c*) unless removed the pollutants would prevent the development or other purpose being carried out; and

(*d*) all activities that have at any time resulted in the presence of pollutants on the land by the applicant or a connected person or by any other person on the land in question have either ceased or have ceased to create pollution (*FA 1996, s 43B(7),(8)*).

For the purpose of head (*d*), any activities carried out without the consent of the then occupier (or if the land is unoccupied, the person entitled to occupy it) can be ignored, as can the presence of pollutants which were borne onto the land by air or water. So can any activities not carried on by the applicant or a connected person of his (within

ITA 2007, s 993 – see Appendix 1) or carried out by someone else but not on the land in question. The clearing of some pollutants can still be qualifying reclamation even though not all the pollutants on the land are removed (*FA 1996, s 43B (9)–(11)*). The application for a certificate has to be made at least 30 days before it is to take effect. By concession dated 27 May 1997 HMRC agreed to remit tax paid before 30 June 1997 where the waste clearly qualified for exemption and at least some of the waste from the reclamation site had been certified. HMRC refused to apply this concession to *Zenith Builders (L00001)* which appealed to the VAT and Duties Tribunal. The tribunal held that it had no jurisdiction and suggested the company should approach the HMRC Adjudicator, although it expressed the view that the officer did not seem to have acted unreasonably. HMRC appear to have refused the concession because there had been no previous certified waste from the site. They thought the company ought to have stockpiled it until HMRC could inspect it. When HMRC withdrew a contaminated land certificate because they formed the opinion that the soil was removed because of its engineering properties not because it was contaminated, the VAT and Duties Tribunal held that it was sufficient for one object of the removal to be because the land was contaminated, so the two motives were not mutually exclusive, and that the soil had been removed with the object of facilitating development with (*a*) above. It accordingly restored the certificate (*Taylor Woodrow Construction (Northern) Ltd – L00003*). The restrictive nature of this exemption is demonstrated by *Augean plc v HMRC (2008 STC 2894)*. Augean bought a landfill site on which almost 1 million tonnes of waste had been deposited, landfill activity had ceased in 1993 many years earlier but the site had not been capped. The local authority were concerned about pollutants leaching from the site. Augean reached an agreement with the local authority that it would remove all of the waste to another site, would build a modern containment landfill for hazardous waste with low leachate potential, and when the site was filled would cap the site. HMRC refused a *s 43B* certification on the grounds that relevant activity had not ceased on the site within (*d*) above. It was held that they were justified in doing so, as although the project involved removing the existing pollutants it also involved the presence of new pollutants. Augean pointed out that this refusal made it uneconomic to reclaim the site, so the construction placed by the court on *s 43B* seems to undermine its purpose. This exemption is being phased out. New applications for certificates have not been accepted since 30 November 2008 and the benefits from existing ones will cease to apply from 1 April 2012 (*Landfill Tax (Material from Contaminated Land)(Phasing Out of Exemption) Order 2008 (SI 2008 No 2669)*).

(5) *Temporary disposals.* A landfill site operator can designate part of his site as set aside for temporary disposals pending the material being either:

(*a*) recycled or incinerated;

(*b*) used (other than being taken to another landfill site) either:

(i) at a place other than a relevant site; or

(ii) for site restoration purposes at the landfill site itself; or

(*c*) sorted pending either:

(i) its use for a purpose within (*a*) or (*b*) above; or

(ii) its disposal.

The definition of site restoration for the purpose of (*b*) and (*c*) above is the same as for *FA 1996, s 43C(1)* (see (6) below).

Landfill tax will not be payable on such materials provided that they are actually dealt with in one of these three ways within 12 months of being deposited (three years in the case of site restoration). The landfill site operator needs to maintain specified records in respect of materials deposited in a designated area. If the material is not used or removed in the 12-month (or three-year) period it is deemed to have been deposited for landfill at the end of that period so as to trigger liability for the tax. HMRC can nullify the designation either by notice in writing, or if materials not intended to be dealt with as in (*a*) to (*c*) above are deposited in the designated area, or if material not dealt with in the 12-month or three-year period is not removed from the designated area within a further seven days. If they do so, all material in that designated area is deemed to have been landfilled at that time (*regs 38–40, Landfill Tax Regulations 1996* (*SI 1996 No 1527*) as amended by the *Landfill Tax (Amendment) Regulations 2002* (*SI 2002 No 1*)). The power to designate part of a site to hold qualifying materials pending site restoration was introduced by *FA 2000, s 141* but the amending regulation did not come into effect until 1 February 2002. HMRC allowed relief on an extra-statutory basis in the interim.

(6) *Site restoration.* For disposals between 30 September 1999 and 31 August 2009, the disposal of qualifying material within *s 42* (see **22.14**), ie inactive or inert waste, by depositing it on and using it in the restoration of the site or part thereof (*FA 1996, s 43C(1)*). The site operator had to notify HMRC in writing prior to the disposal that he was commencing the restoration of all or a part of the site and had to provide such other written information (again, it appears, before the disposal) as HMRC may require either generally or in a particular case (*FA 1996, s 43C(1)(b)*). Restoration for this purpose means work which is required to be carried out to restore a landfill site to use on completion of waste disposal operations under either a planning consent, a waste management licence, or a resolution (presumably by a local authority)

or permit authorising the disposal of waste on or in land. It does not, however, include work to cap the landfill site (*FA 1996, s 43C(2),(3)*). In *C & E Commrs v Ebbcliff Ltd (2004 STC 1496)* the tribunal held that the deposit of qualifying material underneath the capping layer was work carried out to restore the site to use and was thus part of the restoration. This was rejected by Etherton J who held that *sub-s 43C(2)* 'is directed at work to land which, prior to the commencement of that work, has received disposals of waste as an operational licensed landfill site, and has not changed its use since then, and which work is carried out to restore the land to use for a purpose other than the disposal of waste by way of landfill'. He went on to say that there are three phases: the filling of the site, the construction of the cap and finally the work of restoration. The relief is restricted to that final operation. The was confirmed by the Court of Appeal which pointed out that parliament had specifically excluded capping and 'it is hard to see what possible reason there would be for excluding the capping layer from the exemption while including both the waste below and the soil above in the exemption'. *Section 43C* was repealed by *FA 2009, Sch 60, para 10.* Apparently following the *Waste Recycling Group* case (see **22.8**) it is clear that temporary holding of waste on a landfill site for certain purposes and the use of material for site restoration are, in any case, not taxable. Accordingly the relief has been removed as being unnecessary and creating confusion (Finance Bill 2009 Explanatory Notes).

(7) *Quarries.* The disposal after 30 September 1999 of qualifying material within *s 42* (see **22.14**), ie inactive or inert waste, at a qualifying landfill site (*FA 1996, s 44A*). A qualifying landfill site for this purpose is one which at the time of the disposal is (or was) a quarry for which it was a requirement of planning consent that it be wholly or partially refilled and the waste management licence (or resolution or permit) authorising disposals on or in the land comprising the site permits only the disposal of qualifying materials (*FA 1996, s 44A(2)*). If a waste management licence does not permit only the disposal of qualifying material and an application is made to vary the licence so that it does so, the variation will be treated as effective from the making of the application provided it is finally resolved within two years. If it is not, the variation is deemed to have effect for the two years from the application, then to cease to have effect until the application is disposed of and then to have effect again (*FA 1996, s 44A(4)*). The logic of backdating the variation for two years from the application rather than for the two years preceding disposal of the application is not readily apparent. An application is disposed of for this purpose if it is granted, it is withdrawn, it is refused and there is no right of appeal against the refusal, it is refused and the time limit for appeal expires without an appeal being made, or an appeal against refusal is dismissed or withdrawn and there is no further right of appeal

(*FA 1996, s 44A(5)*). Effectively this allows inactive or inert waste to be deposited on the site free of landfill tax for two years (or until rights of appeal are exhausted if earlier) even if at the end of the day the licence is not varied. If the application is not granted within two years there seems no point from a landfill tax point of view of continuing to pursue it; the application or any pending appeal might as well be abandoned. Neither this exemption nor that for site restoration extends to site engineering activities such as the construction of cells, haul roads, daily cover, etc. (Business Brief 9/98), presumably as such operations do not amount to site restoration or the refilling of a quarry.

(8) *Power to vary.* The Treasury has power by statutory instruments both to grant new exemptions and to withdraw existing ones (*FA 1996, s 46*).

Registration

22.24 Anyone who carries out taxable activities has to register for landfill tax (*FA 1996, s 47(1)*). There is no *de minimis* exemption. A person carries out a taxable activity if either:

(*a*) he makes a taxable disposal in respect of which he is liable to pay tax, ie he is the holder of the site licence of a landfill site;

(*b*) he is liable to pay tax in respect of a taxable disposal made with his permission by another person, eg a lorry driver; or

(*c*) he is the person liable to pay tax (because he is the site operator) in relation to a taxable disposal made by some other person even though that disposal is made without his knowledge (*FA 1996, s 69*).

If at any time a person who is not registered forms the intention of carrying out taxable activities he must notify HMRC of his intention (*FA 1996, s 47(3)*). A registrable person will be registered with effect from the time he begins to carry out taxable activities, irrespective of when he notifies HMRC (*FA 1996, s 47(5)*).

22.25 Application for registration needs to be made on a statutory form (LT1 plus LT2 if the applicant will operate more than one site and LT3 if it is a partnership). Application must be made within 30 days of the earliest date on which the person has the intention to carry out taxable activities (*reg 4, Landfill Tax Regulation 1996* (*SI 1996 No 1527*)). If a person discovers an inaccuracy in his application form or any of the information shown on the form changes he must notify HMRC within 30 days. Such notification must not only reveal what was wrong and the date a change occurred, but why any information provided was inaccurate and the date on which the inaccuracy was discovered (*reg 5*).

22.26 A person who at any time ceases to have the intention of carrying out taxable activities must also notify HMRC within 30 days of that change, giving the date on which he ceased to intend to carry out taxable activities and, if different, the date on which he in fact ceased to do so. HMRC must then deregister him from the earliest practicable time after he ceases to carry out taxable activities – but only if they are satisfied that he will not carry out any further taxable activities, he has paid all the tax for which he is liable and there are no outstanding credits due to him. HMRC can in any event at their discretion deregister a person who has ceased to carry out taxable activities and must deregister someone if they are satisfied that he never fulfilled his intention to carry out taxable activities and has decided not to do so (*FA 1996, s 47(4)(6)(7)(8)* and *reg 6*).

22.27 Where the right to carry on a taxable business is transferred, it is transferred as a going concern, and the registration of the transferor has not already been cancelled but as a result of the transfer it will fall to be cancelled, the transferor and transferee can jointly apply (on form LT4) for the registration of the transferor to be cancelled and for the transferee to be registered with the transferor's registration number. As with the transfer of a VAT registration number, the transferee takes over any outstanding liabilities of his predecessor to pay tax or to make a return, and all past actions of the predecessor are deemed to be the actions of the transferee (*reg 7*).

22.28 In the case of a partnership all the partners are jointly and severally liable for landfill tax responsibilities but once they have been complied with the obligation of the other partners is released (*reg 8(3)*). There is similar joint and several liability for the responsibilities of other unincorporated bodies. The persons liable are the president, chairman, treasurer, secretary or any similar office holder. If there are no office holders it is the members of the management committee and if there is no such committee it is the members (*reg 8(1)(2)*). If a registrable person becomes bankrupt or incapacitated (or in the case of a company goes into liquidation, receivership or administration) HMRC can treat any person who carries on the business as if he were the registrable person. Such person must notify HMRC of the bankruptcy or incapacity and the date on which it began, within 30 days of commencing to carry on the business (*reg 9*).

22.29 A body corporate that carries on business in divisions can apply to register the divisions separately (*FA 1996, s 58(3)*). A group of companies can opt for a single group registration. If they do so, all the tax is due from the representative members but all other members of the group are jointly and severally liable. Companies can form a group if one controls the others or one person (or two or more individuals carrying on business in partnership) control them all. HMRC can refuse a group registration if it appears to them necessary to do so for the protection of the revenue (*FA 1996, s 59*).

Accounting for the Tax

22.30 The landfill site operator must make a quarterly return, and pay the tax shown as due on it, by the end of the month following the period to which it relates. HMRC will decide what accounting quarter a particular operator should use so as to spread their work load (*regs 2, 11*). The return requires details both of tax payable and weight of materials deposited. If an operator does not submit his return, HMRC have power to assess him in estimated figures (*FA 1996, s 50*). There is an obligation to keep and preserve accounting records for six years (*reg 16*).

22.31 Interest is, of course, payable on tax paid late. This is at a penal rate – 10 percentage points above the normal HMRC rate for unpaid tax, ie if the HMRC rate is 7.5% the interest on overdue tax is 17.5% Furthermore it is compounded with monthly rests. Where an assessment is made by HMRC in the absence of a return the penal rate again applies. Where a return is made but an assessment is raised to recover further tax, eg HMRC believe there is an underdeclaration, interest is at the normal rate until the date the assessment is notified to the taxpayer and at the penal rate thereafter (*FA 1996, Sch 6, paras 26, 27*). HMRC or the VAT and Duties Tribunal both have power to reduce or waive the interest (*Sch 5, para 28*). Interest on repayments is payable by HMRC – at the normal rate only (*Sch 5, para 29*).

22.32 Interest (and penalties) in respect of landfill tax are not deductible for income or corporation tax purposes (*CTA 2009, s 1303*).

22.33 Deductions can be claimed for various 'credits'. These fall into three categories: removal of material from the site, bad debts, and contributions to bodies concerned with the environment (Environmental Trusts and Companies) (see **22.46**). A removals credit arises in three circumstances only. The first is where the site operator notifies HMRC before the waste is landfilled that some or all of it will be recycled, incinerated or removed for use (not to another landfill site) and the removal of the material takes place within twelve months of its being landfilled (five years where water was added to facilitate disposal) (*reg 21(2)*). The second is where the Environment Agency (or its Scottish or Northern Irish counterpart) order the material to be removed because the deposit was in breach of the site licence or permit, the material has been landfilled elsewhere and the site operator has paid landfill tax in relation to the new deposit of the material (*reg 21(4)*). In both cases the amount of the credit is the tax originally paid on the material actually removed (*reg 21(6)*). The third is where the materials are removed after 1 September 2009 for use in restoration of a relevant site and the material involved has previously been used to create or maintain temporary hard standing, to create or maintain a temporary screening bund or to create or maintain a temporary haul road (all of which trigger a tax charge – see **22.13**).

22.34 In the case of a transfer of a going concern any credits that become payable will be given to the transferee, not the transferor, irrespective of whether or not he has opted to take over the transferor's registration number (*reg 7(5)*).

22.35 A credit for a bad debt can be claimed only if the person who deposited the material was not a connected person (within *ITA 2007, s 993* – see **Appendix 1**) of the site operator, the operator has accounted for tax on the deposit, the debt is written off in his accounts as bad, he issued a landfill invoice in respect of the debt within 14 days of the material being deposited (or such other period agreed with HMRC) and the invoice has remained unpaid for a period of at least 12 months. The Regulations lay down detailed record-keeping requirements. Where there are several amounts owing by the same customer any receipts from him must be set against the earliest invoices first unless a payment was both allocated to a different invoice by the customer at the time of payment and that invoice was settled in full. Writing-off of the debt needs to have been done both in the operator's annual accounts and in a 'landfill tax bad debt account' which is required by the Regulations to be maintained (*regs 22–29*).

22.36 The 'controller', ie the person in actual control of the landfill site, is liable for the tax if the holder of the waste management disposal licence, the 'operator', does not pay it. In some cases the operator is not involved in the day-to-day running of the site. For example, he may be a farmer who has leased out the site to the operator. A person is the controller of all or part of a site at a given time if he is entitled to determine what disposals of materials can be made at that site or that part of it (unless he does so only as an employee or agent) (*FA 1996, Sch 5, para 48*). Where the controller controls part of the site he is, of course, only liable for the tax on disposals on that part. If the operator is entitled to offset credits (see **22.33**) the controller can take the benefit of them in proportion to the amount of the operator's tax to which he is liable (*FA 1996, Sch 5, para 50*). HMRC can collect tax from the controller only if they serve notice on him of the amount payable within two years of the end of the accounting period by reference to which the tax is due (*FA 1996, Sch 5, para 51*). HMRC can similarly collect from the controller tax assessed under *FA 1996, s 50* (see **22.30**). They must notify him that they intend to do so within two years of the issue of the assessment (*FA 1996, Sch 5, para 52*). Where HMRC decide to assess the controller that does not relieve the operator of liability; both are jointly and severally liable but HMRC cannot collect in total more than is due (*FA 1996, Sch 5, para 57*). The Controller is, of course, also liable for interest on the tax (*FA 1996, Sch 5, para 58*). He has a right of appeal to the VAT and Duties Tribunal against a notice or against a decision that he is the controller (*FA 1996, Sch 5, para 59*). When a person ceases to be the controller, they and the operator must together ensure that notice of that fact is given to HMRC (*FA 1996, Sch 5, para 57*).

22.37 In addition, *FA 1996, s 51* provides that regulations may provide that where a person has paid or is liable to pay tax and prescribed conditions are fulfilled, he is entitled to credit of such amount as is prescribed. The prescription is in regs 19 and 20 of the *Landfill Tax Regulations 1996 (SI 1996, No 1527)*. In *Harley v HMRC (TC 2239)* the taxpayer accounted for landfill tax but subsequently reclaimed it on the basis that all of the material deposited on his site was used for site engineering. He claimed a credit under *s 51*. The Tribunal refused this on the grounds that, as he was claiming not to be taxable, the amount paid to HMRC could not have been 'tax'. He could have claimed repayment under *FA 1996, Sch 5, para 14* (see **22.40**) but was out of time for such a claim; *s 51* has no time limit as it does not require a claim.

Administration

22.38 The administrative provisions are set out in *FA 1996, Sch 5*. They broadly follow the VAT rules. HMRC have the power to inspect documents (*para 3*); to enter and inspect business premises (*para 4*); to enter and search premises and remove anything thereon and to search any person on the premises who they reasonably believe to be in possession of any relevant documents or other things when they suspect a fraud offence of a serious nature and obtain a search warrant from a Justice of the Peace (*para 5*); to arrest anyone who they have reasonable grounds for suspecting has committed a fraud offence (*para 6*); to obtain access to records of third parties if a Justice of the Peace so orders because he believes that an offence (not necessarily a fraud offence) has been or is about to be committed (*para 7*); and to take samples from material that has been or is intended to be landfilled if they suspect either a mistake or fraud (*para 10*). A fraud offence is one for which criminal penalties can be imposed under *para 15(1)* to *(5)* – but not *para 15(6)* which makes it a criminal offence to enter into a landfill tax contract (or make arrangements for someone else to do so) with reason to believe that the tax in respect of the disposal will be evaded, or *para 15(7)* which makes it a criminal offence to operate a landfill site without giving any security for the tax that may have been required by HMRC. HMRC have power by regulation to require a registrable person to keep and preserve such records as they may require (*para 2*). From 1 September 2009, these can relate to all or part of a site (*para 2A* inserted by *FA 2009, Sch 60, para 9*). Any person who is concerned (in any capacity) with a landfill disposal must furnish to HMRC such information relating to the disposal as HMRC may reasonably require (*para 1*). From 1 September 2009, HMRC also have specific power by regulation to require a person to designate a part of a site as an information area and to require prescribed descriptions of material to be deposited in an information area (*para 1A* inserted by *FA 2009, Sch 60, para 7*). They have done so by the *Landfill Tax (Amendment) Regulations 2009 (SI 2009 No 1930)*. These insert a new *reg 16A* into the *Landfill Tax Regulations 1996* which provide that where material at a landfill site is not going to be disposed of as waste and HMRC consider there to be a risk to the revenue the material must be deposited in an information area and the registrable person must keep a record of the weight and description of all material deposited there, the intended destination or use of all such material (and its actual destination or use) and the weight and description of any such material sorted or removed.

22.39 The operator of a landfill site must notify HMRC in writing that site restoration is to commence and must provide such other written information as HMRC may require. Restoration for this purpose means work (other than capping waste) which is required to be carried out to restore the site on completion of waste disposal operations by a planning consent, a waste management licence or a permit authorising the disposal of waste on or in land (*FA 1996, Sch 5, para 1B*).

22.40 Landfill tax is a preferential debt in an insolvency to the extent that it fell due in the six months prior to the insolvency (*para 12*). HMRC have a right of set-off against any amount owed by them in respect of other taxes, but cannot set a debt arising before the commencement of insolvency procedures against one arising subsequent to that time (*regs 45–47, Landfill Tax Regulations 1996* (*SI 1996 No 1527*)). They also have power to distrain on goods and chattels of the site operator (but in the case of assessed tax (other than an assessment made in the absence of a return) cannot distrain until the period for appeal against the assessment had ended) (*para 13* and *regs 48* and *49*). If tax is overpaid there is no obligation on HMRC to repay it unless the operator makes a claim in such form and supported by such documentary evidence as they may specify – and even then they need not repay it if to do so would unjustly enrich the site operator (*para 14*).

22.41 There are both criminal and civil penalties for landfill tax evasion. The criminal penalty on summary conviction is up to six months' imprisonment, a fine of up to the statutory maximum (£5,000) or three times the tax if greater, or both. On indictment it is up to seven years' imprisonment, an unlimited fine, or both (*para 16*). HMRC have power to mitigate these penalties (*para 17*). The civil penalty for evasion is an amount equal to the tax evaded or sought to be evaded (*para 18*). In the case of a body corporate, HMRC can switch the penalty from the company to a director or manager whose conduct gave rise to the dishonesty (*para 19*). There is a 5% serious misdeclaration penalty which is not payable if the understatement of tax is disclosed before HMRC begin enquiries (*para 20*). The penalty for late registration is the greater of 5% of the tax or £250 (*para* 21). For failure to furnish information required by HMRC the penalty is £250 plus £20 a day after the imposition of the initial penalty (*para 22*). The penalty for a regulatory breach is £250 and that for breach of a walking possession agreement is 50% of the tax (*paras 23* and *24*). HMRC have power to mitigate (or reduce to nil) all the civil penalties (*para 25*).

22.42 HMRC can require a taxable person to give security (or further security) for landfill tax as a condition of his running a landfill site (*para 31*). HMRC have power to disclose information to the Environment Agency and similar regulatory bodies (*para 35*). They also have the right to publish the Landfill Tax register (*para 36*) and have done so. If a person issues a landfill tax invoice and no tax is, in fact, chargeable, the amount shown thereon is nevertheless recoverable as a debt due to the Crown (*para 44*). If a landfill invoice is issued within 14 days after material has been deposited, the invoice date is treated as the date of the landfill unless the site operator notifies HMRC in writing that he wants to adopt the actual landfill date. HMRC have power to extend the 14-day period at the request of a site operator (*FA 1996, s 61*). HMRC have power to direct that where material is disposed of it must be regarded as qualifying material if it would in fact be such material but for a small quantity of non-qualifying material. The direction may be made, either generally or at the request of a site operator in relation to a specific site (*FA 1996, s 63*).

22.43 There is no general right of appeal against decisions of HMRC. However, a right of appeal is specifically given in relation to most such decisions (*FA 1996, s 54(1)*). Experience with VAT suggests that the VAT and Duties Tribunal will lean over backwards to try to bring something within their jurisdiction if they can. An appeal cannot be brought unless the decision has first been reviewed within HMRC. An application for a review must be made within 45 days of written notification of the original decision having been given and HMRC have 45 days from the day on which the review was required to give a decision (if they do not respond within that time they are deemed to have confirmed the decision (*FA 1996, s 54(3)–(8)*). A person who is under a duty to make landfill tax returns cannot pursue an appeal (but can request a review) unless he has made all the returns due and paid all the tax shown as payable in those returns. Similarly, an appeal as to whether tax is chargeable in respect of a disposal (or how much) or against an HMRC assessment cannot be entertained unless either the tax in dispute has been paid or HMRC or the tribunal accepts that it would cause hardship to do so (*FA 1996, s 55*). It should be noted that the relief for hardship does not apply where a return has been made and the disputed tax is shown as payable on that return. The VAT rules for settling appeals by agreement and for the enforcement of tribunal decisions also apply to landfill tax (*FA 1996, s 56*). Curiously, the VAT power to leap-frog an appeal from the tribunal direct to the Court of Appeal does not apply; a landfill tax appeal must proceed via the High Court.

22.44 The *Provisional Collection of Taxes Act 1968* has been extended to landfill tax. This will enable changes to rates to take effect provisionally from the time of the appropriate budget resolution (*FA 1998, s 148*).

Adjustment of Contracts

22.45 Where a lease or other agreement for the use of land entered into before 30 November 1994 provided for a rent or royalty or some other sum to be calculated by reference to the turnover of a business, landfill tax is to be ignored in calculating turnover if it can reasonably be expected that such a provision would have been included had the agreement been entered into after that date (*FA 1996, Sch 5, para 47*). This ensures that the landlord of a landfill site does not benefit from the introduction of the tax and his rent will be based on what it would have been had landfill tax not been introduced (ignoring, of course, the behavioural changes that the tax aims to bring about).

22.46 If the rate of landfill tax changes (including a change from no tax to tax becoming chargeable) after the making of a contract under which materials are to be landfilled, the contract is to be adjusted to reflect the landfill tax that actually falls to be paid (unless the contract provides otherwise). It is immaterial when the contract was made or whether or not it relates solely to the landfill or covers other things also (*FA 1996, Sch 5, para 45*).

Environmental Bodies

22.47 To encourage the restoration of the environment a landfill site operator is allowed to deduct from his landfill tax liability 90% of a contribution that he makes to a qualifying environmental body but only up to a percentage of his tax liability (*FA 1996 s 53* and *reg 31, Landfill Tax Regulations 1996* (*SI 1996 No 1527*) as amended, most recently by the *Landfill Tax (Amendment) Regulations 2017 (SI 2017 No 332)*). Not only can he deduct contributions during the quarter to which the return relates but he can also deduct contributions made in the month following the end of the quarter (but before the return for that quarter has been submitted). Prior to 1 January 2000 he could only deduct contributions made in the month following the end of his landfill tax year from the tax due in the last quarter of that year. He could not carry back contributions during the year. The total deductions for contributions during any one landfill tax year is limited to 5.3% of the tax payable (less any amount repayable) for the operator's tax year to 31 March 2018 and 31 March 2019 (5.5% prior to 1 April 2011, 6.2% for 2011/12, 5.6% for 2012/13, 6.8% for 2013/14, 5.1% for 2014/15, 5.7% for 2015/16, 4.2% for 2016/17) (*reg 31(3)(7)*). The contribution year for all is the year to 31 March.

22.48 A person can still deduct from his landfill tax liability a payment that he makes to a qualifying environmental body if he does not bear the cost because it has been reimbursed by a contributing third party, ie a person who has made or agreed to make a payment to him to induce him to make a qualifying contribution or to reimburse in whole or in part a contribution he has made. He needs to maintain and pass on to both The Environmental Trust Scheme Regulatory Body Ltd (ENTRUST) (see **22.53**) and the qualifying body specified details of contributing third parties. The qualifying body is deemed to have received the funds from the third party, not from the company that makes the payment, although the third party itself is not entitled to a deduction for its contribution (*reg 32*). A contribution after 31 March 2016 does not attract relief if it is an investment contribution, ie a payment made to an approved body subject to a condition that it may only be invested for the purposes of generating interest (*reg 32* as amended by the *Landfill Tax (Amendment) Regulations 2016, SI 2016, No 376*).

22.49 A qualifying environmental body is a company, trust partnership or other incorporated body that meets the following conditions.

1. Its objects are (or include):

   (*a*) Reclamation, remediation, restoration or any other operation intended to facilitate economic, social or environmental use of any land the use (for such a purpose) of which has been prevented or restricted because of the previous carrying on of an activity on the land which has ceased.

   (*b*) Carrying out operations to prevent or reduce the potential for pollution, or to remedy or mitigate the effects of pollution in relation to land which is (or may have become) polluted as a result of some activity previously carried out on it which has ceased.

   (*c*) Research and development, education or the collection and dissemination of information either about:

      (i) waste management practices in order to encourage the use of more sustainable waste management practices (including waste minimisation, minimisation of pollution and harm from waste, reuse of waste, water recovery activities and the clearing of pollutants from contaminated land); or

      (ii) the development of products from waste or the development of markets for recycled waste in order to encourage the development or use of such waste.

   (*d*) The provision, maintenance or improvement of a public park or other public amenity in the vicinity of a landfill site (other than one that is to be run with a view to profit) where it is for the protection of the environment, and is not work required by a planning or other statutory consent or under a *s 106, Town and Country Planning Act 1990* agreement.

   (*e*) The maintenance, repair or restoration of a building which is either a place of religious worship or of historic or architectural interest, is open to the public, is not operated with a view to profit and is in the vicinity of a landfill site, where such work is for the protection of the environment.

(*f*) The provision of financial administration and other similar services to other qualifying environmental bodies (but not to anyone else).

(*g*) The conservation or preservation of biological diversity (as defined in the UN Environmental Programme Convention on Biological Diversity of 1992) through the provision, conservation, restoration or enhancement of a natural habitat, or the maintenance or recovery of a species in its natural habitat, on land or water situated in the vicinity of a landfill site where it is for the protection of the environment.

An object does not, however, fall within head (*a*) or (*b*) if the operation to be carried out by the environmental body either is such that any benefit from it will accrue to any person who carried out or knowingly permitted the pollution, etc., involves work that is required to be carried out by an order under the *Control of Pollution Act 1974*, the *Environmental Protection Act 1990* or the *Water Resources Act 1991*, or which is wholly or partly required to be carried out under the terms of a planning or other statutory consent or an agreement under *s 106, Town and Country Planning Act 1990*. In other words, work can qualify only if there is no one else that can be required to do it or that has a vested interest in doing it. An object is similarly excluded from heads (*d*) and (*g*) if it is required to be carried out in accordance with the above orders or an agreement made (or obligation) under the *National Parks and Access to the Countryside Act 1949*, the *Countryside Act 1968*, the *Wildlife and Countryside Act 1981*, a planning or other statutory condition, a *s 106* agreement or if the work is carried out with a view to profit.

2. It is precluded from distributing and does not distribute any of its profits or other income.

3. It applies any profit or other income to the furtherance of its objects (whether or not falling within (1) above).

4. It is precluded from applying any of its funds for the benefit of any of the persons who make qualifying contributions (ie those attracting a landfill tax deduction) to it or where qualifying third parties make contributions to these parties in relation to such contributions (except where those persons may benefit because they belong to a class of persons that benefits generally).

5. It is not controlled by one or more local authorities (or companies under local authority control) or by landfill site operators who are registered for landfill tax

6. It is not controlled by either:

   (*a*) one or more of a local authority, a company controlled by a local authority or authorities, a registered person, or a person connected with one of the above;

   (*b*) a person who was concerned in the management of another approved body whose approval has been revoked, a person convicted of an indictable offence, a person who is disqualified from being a trustee for a charity, or a person connected with any of them; or

   (*c*) a person who is incapable by reason of any mental disorder.

7. No one within 6(*b*) above is concerned in its management.

8. It has been approved by the regulatory body (see **22.53** below) and pays its required fee (which must not exceed £100).

(Regulation 33.)

22.50 An approved body must apply its contributions only to approved objects, must not benefit (except incidentally) persons who have made contributions to it, must keep specified records and notify the regulatory body within seven days of any transfer of contributions to another approved body, must pay a fee of 5% of all qualifying contributions to the regulatory body and must comply with other specified conditions *(reg 33A)*.

22.51 In *Twizell v Entrust; re Groundwork Community Forests North East Developments (in administration) (2010 STC 37)* Entrust sought to prevent the administrators of Groundwork from selling and distributing the proceeds of land purchased with funds provided out of the Landfill Communities Fund. Entrust contended that the sale of the land would infringe the Regulations so that HMRC would become entitled to claw back from the relevant landfill site operators the tax credits originally granted to them – as a result of which those operators might sue the landfill funds which they paid the money to Groundwork. Entrust thought that income derived from the sale of the land would constitute income derived from the funds, and even paying the fees of the administrators would not be compliant. The Court of Appeal conferred that the proceeds of sale of the land would not be 'income' and therefore could not be 'income derived from the contributions'. Accordingly Entrust's objections were unfounded. It appeared to the court that Entrust's real concern was how to police and enforce the obligations of an approved body; Sir Andrew Morritt, V-C retorted that Entrust simply needs to consider the body's Memorandum of Association and revoke its approval if the body acts *ultra vires*.

22.52 The use of contributions to pay running costs of the body is treated as use for a qualifying purpose but only if these do not exceed the proportion of qualifying contributions from landfill site operators (plus the income produced from such contributions) that such contributions bear to the total funds at the body's disposal, eg if an environmental body derives £100,000 of income from qualifying contributions and £50,000 from elsewhere, not more than two-thirds of the £100,000 can be used to meet running costs. The use of contributions to contribute towards the running costs of the regulatory body (see below) is also treated as a qualifying purpose.

22.53 To qualify for a deduction the environmental body has to have been approved by a regulatory body – which is in turn approved by HMRC. The regulatory body can charge an application fee to environmental bodies that seek approval and can require them to make a contribution to its running costs. It can give approval subject to conditions, including as to records and accounts. It can revoke approval at its discretion. It must maintain a register of approved bodies and their registered numbers, which it must publish and keep up to date. Its main function though is to satisfy itself that the qualifying contributions received by an environmental body have been used only in the furtherance of its objects falling within head (1) above (*reg 34*). HMRC can only approve one regulatory body at any time. They can revoke the approval and appoint a different body in its place. If HMRC revoke approval and do not approve a replacement body they must notify all the approved environmental bodies in advance that when the revocation takes effect HMRC itself will take over the functions of the regulator. If they do not do so the approval of all the environmental bodies lapses on the revocation (*regs 34(2) and 35*). HMRC have approved a non-profit company, The Environmental Trust Scheme Regulatory Body Ltd (ENTRUST), for this purpose. By December 1997 Entrust had enrolled over 750 environmental bodies.

22.54 A contribution to an approved environmental body qualifies for a landfill tax deduction only if it is made subject to a condition that the body will spend the sum paid and any income derived from it in the course or furtherance of its approved objects (ie objects within (1) in para **22.49**). A transfer to another approved body subject to a condition that it will only use it for its approved objects is also permissible.

22.55 If HMRC believe that an approved environmental body has not spent a contribution or the income therefrom on its approved objects they have power to require the landfill site operator who claimed the deduction to pay over the tax he saved (*reg 36(1)*). If a contribution is repaid to the contributor by the environmental body or by the contributor to a contributing third party he must account to HMRC for the tax saved, ie repay to them 90% of the amount refunded (*reg 36(3)*). HMRC also have power (instead of ENTRUST) by regulation to withdraw the approval of an environmental body enrolled under the scheme if it breaches the statutory requirements. It is intended that they should use this in the event of serious non-compliance. There is a right of appeal against such withdrawal (*FA 1996, s 53(4)*).

Scotland and Wales

22.56 Scottish Landfill Tax replaced landfill tax in relation to waste disposed of at a landfill site in Scotland from 1 April 2015. For 2015/16 and 2016/17, the standard rate was £84.40 per tonne with a reduced rate of £2.65 per tonne. The rates from 1 April 2017 are £86.10 and £2.70 respectively. Landfill tax continues to apply in Wales, but will cease to apply on 31 March 2018 and will be replaced by Welsh Landfill Disposals tax from 1 April 2018 where the landfill site is in Wales. This is to be initially at the rates of £88.95 and £2.80 per tonne (the same as in England). These will increase to £91.70 and £2.90 respectively from 1 April 2019. There will also be an unauthorised disposal rate of 150% of the standard rate, namely £133.45 for 2018/19 and £137.55 for 2019/20.

Chapter 23

Miscellaneous

Is a Company the Best Vehicle?

23.1 Many people considering property transactions automatically adopt a corporate vehicle. This is frequently a mistake. As much consideration ought to be given to the structure of a property transaction as to the carrying out of the transaction itself. There are two basic considerations; the protection of limited liability may be vital, but a company is an inefficient way to hold appreciating assets from a capital gains tax point of view.

23.2 To what extent is limited liability needed in a property situation? Clearly if a taxpayer buys land with his own funds which he will resell later without having carried out significant improvements, limited liability is unlikely to be very important. It is difficult to envisage any likelihood of sizeable liabilities ever arising. If part of the funds are borrowed, limited liability becomes of greater importance, but except where the price includes a substantial element of hope value, there may still be little risk that the property cannot be resold at a price that will at least cover the borrowing. Where a property is being developed there is a far greater element of risk and the protection of limited liability in such circumstances may well outweigh the tax disadvantages of holding an investment property in a corporate form. Obviously one needs to consider how real the limited liability is before opting for a corporate structure for protection. If the development is being wholly financed by an 'institution' and the developer is required to give personal guarantees to the institution it will be wholly illusory. If the developer has to give a personal guarantee to the main contractor a company may not be worthwhile to provide protection from other creditors as the amounts involved may be comparatively small. Limited liability can, in many cases, be obtained without having to suffer the capital gains tax (CGT) disadvantage by the use of a limited liability partnership (LLP).

23.3 The capital gains tax problem is not merely the rate of tax but also that if an appreciating asset such as a property is held through a company there are two levels of capital gains tax; an increase in value of the property will bring about an increase in the value of the shares in the company as well. This effectively means that in order to pass the gain through to the shareholders a total tax charge of up to 35.2% will be borne – 19% in the company and a further 16.2% (20% of the 81% left in the company after payment of the tax) at shareholder level. Indexation relief within the company is a help to alleviate this burden but property investments very rarely increase in value in line with the retail prices index. If there is a spread of shareholdings the £11,300 CGT annual exemption may alleviate the problem but this is frequently not of great significance in the context of increases in property values.

23.4 Some other factors that can influence the decision whether or not to use a company are the following.

(*a*) The taxpayer's objective. If he is trying to build up a vehicle that he can sell or float, the limited company is often the only practical form to adopt. However, if a likely purchaser for the building is a pension fund, a corporate form is not necessarily attractive. If the individual is trying to build up a 'pension fund' for his old age, personal ownership is likely to be more sensible to avoid two levels of tax on the income – where possible, ownership by a self-administered pension fund may be even better. If he is trying to build up assets for his children, a family trust may be the preferred solution.

(*b*) If the property transaction being entered into is a dealing transaction a company will pay tax at 19%. On the other hand, 55% of the profit available in personal hands (assuming a 45% personal tax rate), where it can be spent or invested as the taxpayer wishes, can often be of far greater use than 81% of it locked inside a company. Once a profit is made in a company, the total effective tax rate to get it into personal hands increases to around 53% if the profit is extracted as salary. This ignores employee's NIC (other than at the unlimited 2% rate) as it assumes that the individual has already reached the NIC limit through other income. If it is extracted as dividend the effective total tax for a 45% taxpayer is 30.9% on the excess over £2,000) with profits taxed at 19%. It also needs to be borne in mind that, depending on the choice of accounting date, an unincorporated business can pay one-half of its tax up to almost nine months after the year end and the other half up to 15 months after it. To the extent that profits exceed those of the previous year, tax on the excess is payable up to nearly 21 months after the year end. With a company, the tax on undistributed profits and profits distributed as dividends is payable nine months after the year end with that on profits distributed as salary payable within a maximum of six weeks of the distribution. A further point to bear in mind is that trading losses of an individual can be set against other income. Although this also applies in a company, an individual is more likely to have other income than a company. However, in many cases CGT entrepreneurs' relief will tip the balance the other way if the shareholders are prepared to wait for their money. Property dealing is a trade. Accordingly, the shares in a property-dealing company can qualify for the relief. Curiously the exclusion for a property or share dealing company that is normally made when granting tax reliefs for trading companies does not apply to entrepreneurs' relief.

(*c*) Once an individual has been labelled as a property dealer it may be difficult to convince HMRC that all future property transactions are not also dealing. Accordingly a decision to carry out dealing transactions as an individual should not be taken too lightly.

A discretionary trust pays income tax at a rate of 45% but income of an interest in possession trust is taxed at the beneficiary's tax rate. A trust may therefore be a good vehicle for property dealing activities. A possible problem is that as trustees are personally liable for debts of the trust it may be difficult to find trustees willing to enter into such transactions, although family members, who might be willing to take that risk could be the trustees. A trust can also be a sensible vehicle in which to hold property investments. It avoids the inheritance tax problems of appreciating assets being held by individuals and also avoids the double capital gains tax problem of a company. It needs to be realised though that most trusts do not qualify for CGT entrepreneurs' relief. The IHT treatment of a trust is also different. A trust (other than some pre-22 March 2016 trusts) pays a ten-yearly charge at a maximum rate of 6% instead of the 40% charge on the death of an individual.

(*d*) It is easier to spread value around one's family if a company is used as shares can readily be gifted. On the other hand, an interest in a limited liability partnership can also be easily gifted and a trust is equally a very effective inheritance tax planning tool. A limited partnership can in some circumstances also be an attractive tax-planning vehicle, as this can give children or trustees most of the tax benefits of trading as an individual without taking on the risks of unlimited liability. Again CGT entrepreneurs' relief needs to be considered. Each shareholder or member will need to satisfy the qualifying conditions.

(*e*) It should be remembered that interest payable by an individual or a trust is not deductible for CGT purposes. However, it will be deductible in computing rental income in many cases. A company can set interest payments against its capital gains as deficits on loan relationships.

(*f*) Because the limited company is the normal form of business organisation in this country many bankers are reluctant to lend substantial sums of money to other types of organisation, particularly where the money is needed for general purposes, not to buy a specific property on which it can be secured. It may sometimes be necessary to use a company in order to be able to raise finance regardless of whether or not this is a sensible structure from a tax viewpoint. This problem can sometimes be solved by drawing up a *pro forma* consolidated balance sheet for the whole of a person's business interests so that his banker can appreciate what his business activities embrace in a form with which he is familiar.

Group Structures

23.5 If a corporate structure is to be used, a subsidiary question that arises is, 'How many companies are needed?' In some cases it may also be desirable to keep certain companies or individual properties outside any form of group structure which is used for the main part of a person's property interests.

23.6 The decision is likely to be very much influenced by the owner's individual circumstances. There is no 'best' structure for a group of property companies. There are, however, a number of basic principles that should be borne in mind. Dealing and investment activities should normally be segregated into separate companies. Although in theory a company can carry out both dealing and investment activities, it is in practice far more difficult to establish that a property that is sold at a substantial profit was bought as an investment if the company carries out dealing transactions than if it has never done so. There is something to be said for initially putting each investment property into a separate company. If one is sold shortly after purchase and HMRC dispute that it was acquired as an investment, a relabelling of that property as a dealing property is unlikely to affect other properties, whereas if the company owning it also owned other properties the reclassification of one is likely to cast doubt on the status of the others. If, at the time of acquisition of a property, it is uncertain whether it will be retained or sold, there may be merit in putting it into a new property investment company to preserve as much flexibility as possible. It can also be commercially attractive to put developments into separate companies to isolate the development risk from other investments, although a large number of separate investment companies is unlikely to be attractive in the long term.

23.7 There is not normally any tax advantage to be obtained by putting dealing properties in separate companies. Indeed, as there are restrictions in setting losses in one company against profits of another, it is not normally desirable to have more than one dealing company in a group.

23.8 Another question to be asked is whether the companies should be grouped or whether each should be held direct by the shareholders. Direct holdings have the merit that one company can be sold and the proceeds passed direct to the ultimate shareholders. The main benefit of grouping is that losses/deficits on loan relationships and excess management expenses in one company can be set against profits of another in the same year under the group relief provisions. There may also be legal problems in one associated company pledging its assets to support borrowings by another, whereas if they are both members of a group there is far more commercial logic for doing so. The Plant and Machinery Annual Investment Allowance, which gives a 100% initial allowance on the first £200,000 p.a. of plant and machinery from 1 January 2016 also points towards parallel companies rather than a group as non-group associated companies can sometimes each have their own £200,000 but a group of companies will have to share one £200,000 between them. The structure to adopt is likely to depend on the facts of each individual case. If in doubt, it is worth remembering that if companies start life as parallel, it is relatively easy to form them into a group at a later date without adverse tax consequences; if they start as members of a group it may be difficult, if not impossible, to separate them at a later date without a heavy tax charge on an unrealised profit, which would need to be funded from somewhere. It should also be borne in mind that the definition of a group for VAT purposes is different to that for corporation tax. It is possible for associated companies to register as a VAT group while remaining parallel companies for income and corporation tax purposes.

Farming and Agricultural Land

23.9 All farming and market gardening in the UK is to be treated for income tax and corporation tax on income purposes as the carrying on of a trade and is therefore taxable as trading income (*ITTOIA 2005, s 9(1)*; *CTA 2009, s 36(1)*). All the farming – but not, apparently, market gardening – carried on by a single taxpayer must be treated as one trade (*ITTOIA 2005, s 9(2)*; *CTA 2009, s 38*). Accordingly, if a farmer in, say, Somerset sells his farm and acquires a new farm in, say, Northumbria he will not have a cessation of one trade and a commencement of another. It is not clear what happens if there is a gap of several years between the sale of the first farm and the purchase of another. It is possible that the farming activities could be regarded as one continuing trade that was in suspension during the intervening period. The problem does not appear to have come before the courts. HMRC normally contend that there is a cessation of trade and the later start of a new farming trade if the gap exceeds twelve months. In *Bispham v Eardiston Farming Co (1919) Ltd (40 TC 322)*, where a company operating two farms sold one of them, it was held that the *sub-section* allowed losses on the farm sold to be carried forward against future profits from the retained one. Short rotation coppicing (see **23.19**) is treated as farming (*ITTOIA 2005, s 876(3)*; *CTA 2010, s 1125(3)(4)* formerly *FA 1995, s 154*). This deeming does not apply to the other taxes. It is solely an income tax provision; it does not apply for capital gains tax.

23.10 Farming means the occupation of land wholly or mainly for the purposes of husbandry, but does not include market gardening (*ITA 2007, s 996(1)*; *CTA 2010, s 1125(1)*). Husbandry includes hop growing and the breeding and rearing of horses (and the grazing of horses in connection with those activities) (*ITA 2007, s 996(2); CTA 2010, s 1125(2)*). The cultivation of short rotation coppice is regarded as husbandry, not as forestry (*ITA 2007, s 996(3); CTA 2010, s 1125(3)*). Short rotation coppice means a perennial crop of tree species planted at high density, the stems of which are harvested above ground at intervals of less than 10 years (*ITA 2007, s 996(6); CTA 2010, s 1125(6)*). Market gardening is the occupation of land in a garden or nursery for the purpose of growing produce for sale (*ITA 2007, s 996(5); CTA 2010, s 1125(5)*). In the past HMRC generally accepted that two-thirds of the running costs of a farmhouse relate to business use and the balance to personal use. They are no longer prepared to do so; the split will be based on the facts of the case for each year (Tax Bulletin, Issue 6). An interesting issue arose in *Thorne v HMRC (2016 UKUT 349)*. Mrs Thorne described her activities as 'equestrian breeder and farming'. The equestrian activities were the breeding and rearing of event horses. The farming was the growing and selling of asparagus. HMRC considered that the two together constituted a single composite trade (as Mrs Thorne had shown on her tax return) and that this composite trade was not carried out on a commercial basis. In the Upper Tribunal Mrs Thorne contended that the asparagus growing was not farming at all, but market gardening. The Upper Tribunal set out some helpful tests to distinguish the two but ultimately decided that the case would have to go back to the FTT to resolve the issue.

23.11 It has been held that compensation for disturbance under *Agricultural Holdings Act 1948, s 34* is also not liable to capital gains tax (*Davis v Powell (51 TC 492)*). HMRC regard grants under the Arable Payments Scheme as income, whether or not there is a set-aside requirement and, if there is, whether or not the set aside land is left fallow or is used to grow eligible non-food crops (Tax Bulletin, Issue 10, February 1994, page 108). They similarly regard 'SLOM compensation', which is paid by the European Community to certain milk producers unfairly deprived of milk quota because they were participating in an EC non-production of milk scheme in 1984, as income (Tax Bulletin, Issue 11, May 1994, p 126). A sum payable to an individual by virtue of a scheme under *Agriculture Act 1967, s 27* (grants for relinquishing occupation of uncommercial agricultural units) was specifically excluded from capital gains tax (*TCGA 1992, s 249*), but this provision was repealed by *FA 2012, Sch 39, para 49* with effect from 6 April 2013.

23.12 HMRC have agreed that under a share farming agreement based on the Country Land and Business Association model, both parties can be regarded as carrying on a farming trade provided that the landowner takes an 'active' part in the venture, at least to the extent of concerning himself with details of farming policy and exercising his right to enter onto his land for some material purpose even if only for the purpose of inspection and policy making (CLA Press Release 19.12.1991). This means not only that the landowner's income will be taxable as trading income, not as property business income, but also that the landowner will qualify for capital gains tax roll-over relief and business asset taper relief. In share farming a landowner enters into a joint venture with an operator under which the operator farms the land and the two share the profit generated. If the landowner does not take an active part in the venture his share of the profit will be a UK property business receipt and the land will probably not qualify for business asset taper relief.

23.13 As mentioned in **23.19** the cultivation of short rotation coppicing is farming not forestry. HMRC regard the initial cultivation of the land including spraying, ploughing, fencing and planting of the cuttings as capital. Costs following planting are revenue but direct costs such as weeding, disease prevention, harvesting and the cost of the first cut should be reflected in the annual stock valuation. Further details of HMRC's views can be found in Tax Bulletin, Issue 19, October 1995.

23.14 The ECJ has held that compensation paid to a farmer in return for an undertaking not to harvest at least 20% of his potato crop is not a supply for VAT purposes (*Landbuden-Agrardienste v Finanzamt (Case C-384/95) (1998 STC 171)*). This is because there is no consumption (and VAT is a general tax on consumption). The farmer does not supply goods or services to an identifiable consumer. Nor does he provide any benefit capable of constituting a cost component of the activity of some other person in the commercial chain. A similar result was reached in *Mohr v Finanzamt Bad Segeberg (Case C-215/94) (1996 STC 328)* in relation to milk quotas. Statutory compensation generally is dealt with at **16.261**. In *HMRC v Frank A Smart & Son Ltd (2016 STC 1956)* the UTT upheld the FTT's decision that VAT on the purchase of Single Farm Payment Entitlement units was wholly incurred for the purpose of the farming business and thus fully recoverable.

23.15 There is a restriction on claiming sideways loss relief for losses from farming and market gardening (*ITA 2007, s 67*). Such relief can be given for losses after the first five tax years of trade only if it can be shown that the reasonable expectation of profit test is met. This requires the taxpayer to prove that a competent person carrying on the activities in the current year would reasonably expect future profits and that such a person carrying on the activities when the loss-making permit started would not have expected the activities to become profitable until after the end of the current tax year (*ITA 2007, s 68*). In *Henderson v HMRC (TC 4730)* Mr Henderson sought to reduce his losses by including income he received from an excavation licence as part of his farming income. The FTT held that that income fell within *ITTOIA 2005, s 335* (see **23.37**) and as such could not be part of the farming profits.

23.16 HMRC have agreed some guidelines with the National Farmers Union in relation to VAT input tax recovery on repairs, maintenance, renovation, etc of a farmhouse.

(*a*) In the case of a normal working farm where the VAT registered person is actively engaged in running it, 70% of the input tax can normally be claimed.

(*b*) In the case of an alteration, such as building an extension, the recoverable amount will depend on the purpose of the work. If the dominant purpose is a business one 70% can be claimed; if it is a personal one HMRC would expect the claim to be 40% or less – possibly none, depending on the circumstances.

(*c*) Where farming is not a full-time business and is the occupation of the VAT-registered person the amount claimable will be significantly less. VAT tribunals have tended to adopt a figure between 10% and 30%.

(*d*) If the farming trade is carried on by a company and the occupant of the farmhouse is a director (or a connected person) only tax on supplies used for other than domestic purpose is claimable. Where a room is used partly for business a proportion can be recovered but only if suitable records are kept to justify the business portion being claimed.

(Business Brief 18/96). These are guidelines only. They are not binding on the taxpayer and will not necessarily be applied by HMRC if the facts suggest a lower business element. When, in reliance on (*b*) above, *Mrs Walthall and Mrs Crisp (15976)* who formed a partnership claimed 40% of the tax on the conversion of a building within the curtilage of the farmhouse to form a residence for Mrs Walthall (under a planning consent that permitted it to be used only in connection with the residential part of the farmhouse) HMRC restricted the claim to 10%. The VAT tribunal upheld this, although mainly on the basis that the facts put before it were so sparse that it was not possible for it to say that HMRC were wrong. HMRC's 10% figure was based on the fact that there was already a farmhouse on the land and the dominant purpose of the conversion appeared to be to provide a second residence, although it was accepted that some business activity was carried on from it.

23.17 There is a special VAT flat rate scheme for farmers. A person who registers as a flat rate farmer cannot recover input tax. However he can add 4% to his sales to VAT registered customers and retain it to compensate for the loss of input tax relief. The 4% cannot be added to sales of machinery or land or the repair and maintenance of farm buildings belonging to others. Nor can it be charged on sales to people not registered for VAT or to other flat rate farmers. The customer can treat the 4% addition as input tax. A farmer cannot join the scheme if his non-farming income exceeds the VAT threshold. The 4% is not added to non-farming income. (*VATA 1994, s 54* and *VAT (Flat Rate Scheme for Farmers) Designated Activities Order 1992). Article 25* of the *Sixth Directive*, which is the authority for the scheme, was considered by the ECJ in *Finanzamt Rendsburg v Harbs (Case C-321/02) (2006 STC 340).*

Mr Harbs farmed 92 hectares. In 1992 he leased his dairy operation on 31 hectares to his son for 12 years. He took the view that the rental income from his son fell within the flat rate scheme so no output tax fell to be declared in respect of it. The German tax authorities considered that letting the land was an exempt supply and that leasing the milk quota and cows did not arise from farming within the meaning of the flat rate scheme so tax fell to be accounted in respect of it. The ECJ confirmed that the scheme applies only to farming activities and that accordingly VAT was chargeable on the leasing income under the normal VAT rules.

23.18 HMRC have given guidance on the capital allowance treatment of slurry storage facilities. Their view is that slurry storage systems that are used for the temporary storage of slurry qualify as plant. However, any building or structure that is part of such a facility does not do so. For example, if a slurry storage facility consists of an above ground circular store, a reception pit and an open ended shed which provides shelter to the tank (and the circular store), the store and pit and any channels or pipes associated with them will qualify as plant but the shed will not do so as it is a structure, which is excluded from being plant (HMRC Brief 66/2008).

Woodlands

23.19 Income from the occupation of woodlands in the UK is exempt from income tax. *ITTOIA 2005, ss 11, 768* and *CTA 2009, s 37* exclude the occupation of woodlands (or land being prepared for forestry purposes) from constituting taxable income and *ITTOIA 2005, s 10* and *CTA 2009, s 208* excludes all occupation of land from the rules on taxing income from property). This tax exemption applies to sales of both felled and growing timber, underwoods, thinnings and all other such receipts. The exemption extends not only to woodlands but also to land which is being prepared for use for forestry purposes (*ITTOIA 2005, s 10(3)(b)*; *CTA 2009, s 38(3)*). It was held in *Jaggers (t/a Shide Trees) v Ellis (1997 STC 1417)* that a Christmas tree plantation is not woodland and therefore does not fall within the exemption. The Special Commissioner felt that what is woodland or forestry is to a large extent a matter of impression. He felt that the land was not woodland because no timber was being produced and the spacing of the trees was in accordance with Christmas tree production rather than timber production. The Special Commissioner seems to have rejected the dictionary definition of woodland, ie land covered with trees, and invented his own definition, which appears to be land used for timber production, but did not make clear his basis for doing so. In the High Court the judge said that the word 'woodlands' is an ordinary word of the English language. The taxpayer can upset the Commissioners' decision only if she can show that on any reasonable use of the English language a

Christmas tree plantation must fall within the description 'woodlands'. He said she clearly could not do this, as for the purposes of *ICTA 1988, s 53(4)* (now *ITTOIA 2005, ss 11, 768* and *CTA 2009, s 37*)('the occupation of land which comprises woodlands or is being prepared for forestry purposes') woodlands and land used for forestry purposes 'are to be treated as synonymous'. Why? Because, he felt 'the sub-section provides for protection for land being prepared for forestry purposes and … land used for forestry, ie woodlands'. He reinforced his view by saying that when the dictionary defines 'woodland' as 'land covered with trees' it cannot mean that, as to his mind 'woodland' denotes a wood, a sizeable area of land to a significant extent covered by growing trees of some maturity'. How much maturity? Well, he thought 'there is something to be said for the rule of thumb that their wood should be capable of being used for timber'. Ergo, if woods do not produce timber they cannot be woodlands. The cultivation of short rotation coppice is regarded as farming not forestry and is therefore taxable (*ITTOIA 2005, s 876(2)*; *CTA 2010, s 1125(3)(4)*). Such coppicing means a perennial crop of tree species planted at high density, the stems of which are harvested above ground level at intervals of less than ten years (*ITTOIA 2005, s 876(6)*; *CTA 2010, s 1125(6)*). Typically, willow or poplar is planted at high density and cut back to ground level after a year to produce shoots which are harvested every three years to be made into chips for fuel.

23.20 Special rules apply to the purchase and sale of woodlands in the UK by property dealers. So much of the cost of such land as is attributable to trees or saleable underwood growing on the land is disregarded on purchase, and on a subsequent sale the same figure (correspondingly reduced where some of those trees have been felled in the interim) is deducted from the sale proceeds (*ITTOIA 2005, s 156(2)(3)*; *CTA 2009, s 134*). The effect is to exclude the timber purchased and not felled from the dealer's trading profits whilst leaving within charge to tax as trading income both the value of any new trees planted by the dealer during the period that he held the land as trading stock and also the increase during his ownership in the value of the original trees. It should be noted that if the property dealer fells trees, or sells the right to cut standing timber, during his ownership he will be in a disadvantageous position, as the proceeds will constitute trading income but he will obtain no relief for the cost of that timber (ie its value at the time of acquisition of the woodland).

23.21 The part of the cost and sale proceeds of woodlands in the UK which is attributable to trees or saleable underwood growing on the land is disregarded for capital gains tax purposes (*TCGA 1992, s 250(3)(4)*). Where woodlands are managed by the occupier on a commercial basis and with a view to the realisation of profits the proceeds of felled timber or of the right to fell standing timber, and insurance proceeds for the destruction of, or damage to, trees by fire or other hazards, is also disregarded (*TCGA 1992, s 250(1)(2)*). This provision is, of course, necessary merely to ensure that income receipts which are not taxed as such cannot be subjected to capital gains tax. It appears, however, that this relief for timber applies irrespective of whether the woodlands are in the UK.

23.22 The effect of *s 250(4)* is that on a purchase and sale of woodlands the price needs to be apportioned between the value of the land, which is chargeable to capital gains tax, and the value of the growing timber, which is not.

23.23 The Forestry Commission Bulletin 84 (formerly Leaflet 12) 'Taxation of Woodlands' (HMSO) (1989 edition), compiled by the Forestry Commission with the authority of HMRC, indicated that the exclusion of the value of growing timber under *sub-ss 250(3)* and *250(4)* applies only where the woodlands are run on a commercial basis (para 2.4). It is not clear why, as *s 250* does not contain such a limitation. However, this booklet is highly recommended. It is out of print but can still be found on the Forestry Commission website. Where woodlands are not run on a commercial basis the sale of felled timber or the grant of the right to fell and remove growing timber is not taxable as income and does not fall within *s 250(1)*. It will accordingly be chargeable to capital gains tax. However, felled trees are treated as chattels and a chargeable gain can only arise if an individual tree is sold for over £6,000 (*TCGA 1992, s 262* and Forestry Commission Bulletin 84, para 2.5).

23.24 Although no longer taxable as a business for income tax purposes, the occupation of woodlands on a commercial basis is still accepted as a business for capital gains tax purposes. Accordingly the reinvestment of the proceeds of the sale of business assets in such woodlands still qualifies for roll-over relief. Obviously the gain on the old assets can only be rolled over against the cost of land and infrastructure work, such as drainage, roads and fences, not against the cost of growing timber. Nevertheless with planting land or a young plantation such items are likely to form a significant part of the cost of a forest.

23.24A The commercial occupation of woodlands attracts inheritance tax business property relief. Where this does not apply, there is a special relief from IHT on death (but not on lifetime gifts) provided that the land is in the UK and has been held for at least five years (or was received as a gift). The beneficiary can elect for the value of the trees and underwood to be left out of account in determining the IHT on death. However the IHT has to be paid if the trees are disposed of by the beneficiary (*IHTA 1984, ss 125–130*). This election is unlikely to be attractive unless the trees are hardwoods that are unlikely to be ready for harvesting until after the beneficiary's death because in most cases the tax will be a higher amount than if it had been paid on the death (because the sale proceeds will almost always exceed the value at death, if only because the trees will be more mature when they are sold). There was a similar relief for estate duty which applied to deaths before 18 March 1986.

23.25 There are two specific inheritance tax reliefs for forestry. The more important is that the ownership and management of woodlands on a commercial basis is accepted as qualifying for IHT business relief. The normal business property relief rules apply (see **18.34**). The property must have been held for at least two years (or have replaced other business property, the two together having been held for at least two out of the five years before the transfer) and a binding contract for disposal must not have been entered into at the time of the taxpayer's death or *inter vivos* gift. The relief is normally 100%, thus effectively conferring total exemption.

23.26 There is a specific relief for woodlands from IHT payable on a death although the 100% business property relief effectively renders this inoperable in most cases. An election can be made to leave the value of growing trees and underwood out of account in determining the IHT on the death. The deceased must have beneficially owned the land for at least five years or become entitled to it by gift or inheritance (*IHTA 1984, s 125*). The land must be in the UK, Channel Islands or Isle of Man or another EEA country, at the time of the person's death (*IHTA 1984, s 125(1A)*). Where tax has been paid it is repayable with interest. See **18.12** for the detailed requirements.

23.27 Accordingly, the relief will not apply to any part of the value of shares in forestry-owning companies. The election must be made within two years after the death (or such longer time as HMRC may allow) (*IHTA 1984, s 125(3)*). The snag of such an election is that when the whole or any part of the trees or underwood so left out of account is disposed of (including on a sale of the land including growing timber but excluding a transfer between spouses), IHT is charged on the net disposal proceeds – if the sale is for full consideration in money or money's worth – or the net value at the time of the disposal in other cases (*IHTA 1984, s 127*). The net proceeds or net value is the proceeds or value less any expenses incurred either:

(*a*) in disposing of the trees or underwood; or

(*b*) in replanting to replace the trees or underwood disposed of – to the extent that the expenditure is incurred within three years after the disposal (or such longer time as HMRC may allow); or

(*c*) in replanting to replace trees or underwood previously disposed of to the extent that the expense was not allowable on the previous disposal, eg because it was incurred more than three years after that disposal,

but only to the extent that such expenditure is not allowable for income tax purposes (*IHTA 1984, s 130(1)(b)(2)*).

23.28 The IHT charge is at the rate or rates at which it would have been charged on the death if the net disposal proceeds or net value (and any previous amount of disposal proceeds, etc.) had been included in the deceased's estate at the date of his death and had formed the highest part of the value of the estate (*IHTA 1984, s 128*). The effect is, of course, that more IHT may well be payable at the end of the day than if the election had not been made – although this is offset by the cash flow effect of deferring the tax until the money to pay it is generated by a sale. If the rates of IHT have reduced between the death and the sale, the rate table to be used is not that in force on death but normally that in force at the time of the disposal – it is actually the rates at the last preceding reduction (*IHTA 1984, Sch 2, para 4*).

23.29 If more than one death of an owner of the woodlands occurs before the sale, etc. takes place, the charge under *s 128* is made only by reference to the second death (*IHTA 1984, s 126(1)*). In such circumstances there will have been a real saving of IHT on the first death. Once a charge has crystallised under *s 126* a further charge will not of course arise on a later disposal of the same trees or underwood (*IHTA 1984, s 126(3)*). The 1985 edition of the Forestry Commission booklet stated that in the case of underwood a charge to tax is made only in respect of the first cutting of underwood subsequent to the death. This is not repeated in the 1989 edition but may follow from *s 126(3)*. If the 50% business property relief applied on the death, only 50% of the net proceeds of the trees or underwood is charged (*IHTA 1984, s 127(2)*). If the disposal which gives rise to the charge under *s 126* is itself an *inter vivos* gift that is not a potentially exempt transfer, the IHT payable under *s 126* is deducted from the value of the trees to calculate the IHT on the gift (*IHTA 1984, s 129*). A disposal of an interest in trees or underwood generates a *s 126* charge in the same way as a disposal of the trees themselves (*IHTA 1984, s 130(1)(c)*). Timber cut for use on the estate will not generate a *s 126* charge as it will not have been disposed of (Forestry Commission Bulletin 84, para 3.16).

23.30 Where woodlands transferred on death 'can be divided into clearly distinct geographic areas' the election can be made for some of the separate areas only (Forestry Commission Bulletin 84, para 3.8). HMRC regard the election once made as irrevocable.

23.31 In the case of hardwoods which are many years from maturity the election will in many cases be worthwhile if the 100% business property relief applies. Deep consideration of the pros and cons needs to be given in other cases. The election will not normally be advisable if the woodland is likely to come to maturity within the next five to ten years. Strangely, although the person eligible to make the *s 125* election is the person liable for the whole or part of the tax, which would normally be the deceased's personal representative, the only person liable for the tax payable under *s 126* is the beneficiary who is entitled to the sale proceeds (or who would have been so entitled if the *s 126* disposal were a sale) (*IHTA 1984, s 208*).

23.32 Woodlands may well of course qualify for national heritage property relief under *IHTA 1984, s 30* (see **18.74** above).

23.33 The IHT on woodlands can be paid by ten annual instalments in the same way as tax on other disposals of land (see **18.53**) (*IHTA 1984, s 227*). Tax on an *inter vivos* gift of growing timber which was excluded on a previous death can also be paid by ten equal yearly instalments (the first payable six months after the end of the month in which the transfer is made) if the gift is a potentially exempt transfer (*IHTA 1984, s 229*). It appears that this applies only to the tax on the gift and not to the charge under *s 126* which is crystallised by the gift. It is difficult to discern the logic of this. It should not be overlooked that where an election for instalments is made the instalments attract interest on overdue tax (*IHTA 1984, s 233*) except where the woodlands constitute the asset of a business or *s 229* applies (*IHTA 1984, s 234(1)*).

Estate Duty

23.34 Estate duty, the forerunner of capital transfer tax, applied on deaths before 13 March 1975. Where a person's estate at the time of death included growing timber, *F(1909–10)A 1910, s 61* allowed an election to be made to defer the tax on growing timber. The value of the timber was left out of account and a subsequent sale crystallised tax – but, unlike under the IHT rules, only up to the value of the growing timber at the date of death. The rate at which tax was charged on the subsequent sale of the growing timber was the estate rate, the average rate of estate duty payable on the death. This deferred charge can still crystallise. It will be crystallised by a transfer of value for IHT purposes other than a transfer between spouses (*FA 1975, s 49(4)*) (or eliminated if that transfer is a transfer on death) as well as by a sale of the timber. A transfer which crystallises the deferred charge cannot be a PET. Strictly speaking no part of a gift can be a PET if a small part carries a deferred charge. However HMRC will apportion the gift and levy tax only on the woodlands (Inland Revenue Press Release, 5 December 1990).

Mines, Quarries, etc

23.35 Profits or gains arising out of land are taxed as trading income – although they are not specifically to be treated as the carrying on of a trade – if they derive from one of the following 'concerns':

(*a*) mines and quarries (including gravel pits, sand pits and brickfields);

(*b*) ironworks, gasworks, salt springs or works, alum mines and works, and water works and streams of water;

(*c*) canals, inland navigations, docks, and drains or levels;

(*d*) fishing;

(*e*) rights of markets and fairs, tolls, bridges and ferries;

(*f*) railways and other ways; and

(*g*) other concerns of a like nature to those in (*b*) to (*e*) above.

(*ITTOIA 2005, s 12*; *CTA 2009, s 39*).

23.36 It has been held that the receipt by the owner of a foreshore of payments by a contractor to remove shingle did not constitute the carrying on of a 'concern' (*Duke of Fife's Trustees v Geo Wimpey & Co Ltd (1943 SC 377)*). Similarly, payments by a quarry-master for taking stone from spoil banks adjoining the quarry were held to be rents not payments for trading stock (*Craigenlow Quarries Ltd v CIR (32 TC 326)*). A farmer was held not to be carrying on a mining concern within *s 55* when he received from a mineral merchant payments for material excavated from old lead mining dumps on the farm (*Rogers v Longsdon (43 TC 231)*). Receipts from such activities are accordingly taxable as property income.

23.37 Rent payable in respect of any land or easement which is used, occupied or enjoyed in connection with one of the above concerns, or where the lease (or other agreement under which the rent is payable) provides for the recoupment of the rent by way of reduction of royalties or similar payments in the event of the land or easement being so occupied, is taxed as if it were trading income not property income (*ITTOIA 2005, ss 12(4), 337*; *CTA 2009, ss 39(4), 271*). A rent could alternatively constitute a 'mineral royalty' (see **23.42**) which is taxed less heavily. In *Bute v HMRC (2008 STC (SCD) 258* – see **23.44**) it was held to do so.

23.38 For the purpose of *ss 337* and *271* 'rent' includes payments in respect of a licence to occupy or otherwise use land, payments in respect of the exercise of any other right over land, rentcharges and other annual payments reserved in respect of (or charged on or issuing out of) land and any other receipt in the nature of rent (*ITTOIA 2005, s 336(3); CTA 2009, s 271(3)*). *ICTA 1998, s 119(3)* from which these derive, stated that it included a rent service, rentcharge, fee farm rent, feu duty, or other rent, toll, duty, royalty, or annual or periodical payment in the nature of rent, whether payable in money or money's worth or otherwise; and that 'easement' includes any right, privilege or benefit in, over, or derived from, land, but these types of receipt are no longer specifically referred to.

23.39 For income tax purposes, if rights to work minerals in the UK are let for a year of assessment the lessor is entitled to deduct in calculating his rental income sums wholly and exclusively disbursed by him as expenses of management or supervision of those minerals in that year to the extent that such sums have not otherwise been allowed as a deduction for income tax purposes (*ITTOIA 2005, s 339*).

23.40 Similarly, a company is entitled to deduct any sums disbursed by it wholly, exclusively and necessarily as expenses of management or supervision of the minerals in the accounting period in computing its taxable income from the letting of rights to work minerals in the UK (*CTA 2009, s 272* (formerly *ICTA 1988, s 121(1)*)). It should be noted that under *ICTA 1988, s 121* the expenditure also had to have been necessarily incurred – which is far tighter than the normal trading income test for deductibility.

Aggregates Levy

23.41 It should also be mentioned that a special tax, the Aggregates Levy, applies to the sale of sand, gravel and rock (together with whatever substances are for the time being incorporated in them or naturally occur mixed with them) extracted from land in the UK or imported into the UK. The tax is a flat rate of £2.00 per tonne (£1.60 prior to 1 April 2008, £1.95 prior to 1 April 2009). It applies only when the aggregate is subjected to commercial exploitation. There are exceptions for aggregate removed from a building site in the course of excavations in connection with the modification or erection of a building (including laying foundations or pipes and cables); from the bed of a river or canal in the course of dredging or creating, restoring, improving or maintaining the river canal or watercourse; from the ground in the course of highway excavations (provided that they are not carried out for the purpose of extracting the aggregate); from the extraction of china clay or ball clay (with exceptions); or from a process for mining coal, lignite or slate (or shale to 1 April 2014) and, from 1 August 2007, aggregates removed from ground along the line of a railway, tramway or monorail in the course of excavation for constructing, manufacturing or improving the railway (*FA 2007, s 22*). In *Hochtief (UK) Construction Ltd v HMRC ([2009] UKFTT 321; [2010] SFTD 268)* rock was removed from a quarry on the site of a dam and used in the construction of the dam. It was held there was no commercial exploitation of the aggregate as it again became part of the land on the site from which it was won. In *Northumbrian Water Ltd v HMRC (2015 STC 1458)* where the company took gravel from one part of a site and used it in construction elsewhere on the site – up to three km away – the Tribunals similarly held that the word 'site' should be given a sensible working meaning and held that in the particular circumstances, taking account of the size and scale of the construction project, the gravel was won and used on the same site so no levy way payable. A similar decision was reached in *Hanson Quarry Products Ltd (TC 4814)*. In that case part of the site had been sold to a developer and the aggregate was moved from the unsold to the sold part. HMRC accepted that ownership of the land, while relevant, was not determinative of whether there was a single site. *P J Thory Ltd (TC 5317)* was concerned with the exemption for aggregate extracted from the bed of a river. The project was the creation of a marina on the river out of a field adjoining the river, which involved dredging part of the river. The company contended that was the creation of a harbour. The Tribunal held that the word dredging could not describe the whole of the activities and the marina was not a watercourse or channel. Accordingly the claim failed. The person liable for the tax is the quarry or other site operator, construction company, importer or dealer in aggregates. Such people are required to register for the tax with HMRC. The detailed rules are outside the scope of this book. They are mainly contained in *FA 2001, ss 16–48* and *Schs 4–10*.

Taxation of Mineral Royalties (to 5 April 2013 only)

23.42 Where a person who is resident or ordinarily resident in the UK was entitled to receive mineral royalties under a mineral lease or agreement:

(*a*) only 50% of the royalties were chargeable to income tax (or corporation tax on income) and only 50% of any management expenses available for offset against the royalties could be deducted; and

(*b*) the other 50% of the royalties receivable under the lease in the year of assessment or accounting period was chargeable to capital gains tax (or corporation tax on chargeable gains).

(*ITTOIA 2005, ss 157, 319* and *340*; *CTA 2009, ss 135, 258, 273*). This provision overrode *ITTOIA 2005, s 337* and *CTA 2009, s 271* (see **23.33** above). These provisions were repealed from 5 April 2013 by *FA 2012, Sch 39, paras 43, 44*.

23.43 For the purpose of this provision 'minerals' meant all minerals and substances in or under land which are ordinarily worked for removal by underground or surface working, other than water, peat, top-soil and vegetation. A mineral lease or agreement meant:

(*a*) a lease, profit *à prendre*, licence or other agreement conferring a right to win and work minerals in the UK;

(*b*) a contract for the sale, or a conveyance, of minerals in or under land in the UK; or

(*c*) a grant of a right under *Mines (Working Facilities and Support) Act 1966, s 1* (other than an ancillary right).

(*ITTOIA 2005, s 341*; *CTA 2009, s 274(1)*).

23.44 'Mineral royalties' meant the part of any rent receivable under a mineral lease or agreement as related to the winning and working of minerals (*ITTOIA 2005, s 341(2); CTA 2009, s 274(2)*). In *Bute v HMRC (2008 STC (SCD) 258)* trustees granted wayleaves to various mining companies to work coal under the surface of their land. The right to coal is vested in the Coal Authority by the *Coal Industry Act 1994*. HMRC contended that the wayleaves were rent within what is now *ITTOIA 2005, s 337*,(see **23.37**) as the trustees could not grant a right to 'work' the coal. The taxpayer argued that the correct charging provision was *s 122* (so only 50% was taxable as income). The taxpayer contended that the phrase 'win and work' was a composite phrase and that a right to enter and disturb the surface of the land was a necessary precondition for the winning and working of minerals. The Special Commissioner agreed that *s 122(5)* applied as its wording 'does not … demand any more than that the agreement has a clear connection to the winning and working'. The Court of Session agreed (*2009 STC 2138*). HMRC were empowered to make regulations to provide whether and to what extent payments made under a mineral lease or agreement that related only partly to the winning and working of minerals were to be treated as mineral royalties (*ITTOIA 2005, s 343*; *CTA 2009, s 276*). These regulations, the *Mineral Royalties (Tax) Regulations 1971*, limited the mineral royalty element to the royalty value of the land (excluding any buildings, etc. on it) on the basis that it could only be used for the working of minerals. The entire royalty could, however, be treated as a mineral royalty if at least 90% of it qualified under this test.

23.45 The amount taxed as a capital gain in **23.24** above was 50% of the gross royalties. No deduction could be made in calculating the gain for expenditure incurred (*TCGA 1992, s 201(3)*). Where a capital loss accrued during the currency of a mineral lease or agreement, the following special rules applied (*TCGA 1992, ss 202, 203*). They operated only where, on the expiry or termination of a mineral lease or agreement or on the disposal (or a deemed disposal under any provision of *TCGA 1992*) of the 'relevant interest' the person who immediately before the occurrence of that event was entitled to receive mineral royalties under the lease or agreement had an interest in the land to which that lease or agreement related (ie the relevant interest) (*TCGA 1992, ss 202, 203*). If the relevant event was the expiry or termination of the mineral lease or agreement, the taxpayer could elect to be treated for CGT (or corporation tax on chargeable gains) purposes as if he had disposed of and re-acquired the relevant interest at its market value. The election (or one under *para* 6, see below) had to be made within six years of the relevant event and could only be made if an allowable capital loss would accrue to the taxpayer on this deemed disposal (*TCGA 1992, ss 202, 203*). Such loss was called 'the terminal loss'. The election could not be made if the expiry or termination of the lease already gave rise to a *TCGA 1992* disposal. The terminal loss could either be treated as an allowable capital loss for the year of assessment or accounting period in which the lease or agreement expired, or be carried back and set against the capital gains element of the royalties received under the lease in years of assessment or accounting periods falling wholly or partly within the preceding 15 years. The election had to specify which of these options the taxpayer wished to adopt. If the relevant event was a *TCGA 1992* disposal of the relevant interest the taxpayer could similarly elect to spread it back over the previous 15 years. He could not elect to treat it in any other way as it was, of course, already a capital loss for the current year under the normal *TCGA 1992* rules. If the election to carry back the loss was made, the loss was set against the gains of the latest possible years. The loss could only be carried back against the capital gains element of mineral royalties under the mineral lease or agreement in question. This probably prevented it being set against gains arising from a prior lease of the same site even if it was to the same operator. If the carry-back did not exhaust the loss the balance was treated as an allowable loss arising in the year of assessment in which the relevant event occurred (*TCGA 1992, ss 202, 203*). This relief was initially introduced to avoid arguments as to whether a receipt was income or capital. Its repeal will presumably resurrect that problem.

Rent in Respect of Electric Line, etc Wayleaves

23.46 Rent payable in the UK in respect of an easement enjoyed in the UK in connection with any electric, telegraphic, or telephonic wire or cable is taxed separately on the recipient unless the recipient has a UK property business, in which case the wayleave rent is included as a receipt of that business (*ITTOIA 2005, ss 344, 346; CTA 2009, ss, 278, 279*).

23.47 If a wire or cable is used by the payer of the rent in carrying on a trade which includes the provision of a radio relay service, the rent is deductible as a trading expense Similarly receipts of wayleave rent in the course of a trade are taxable as trading income if the trader does not have a UK property business (*ITTOIA 2007, s 22; CTA 2009, s 45*).

23.48 For the above purpose the definitions of rent and easements in **23.37** above again apply; the reference to easements enjoyed in connection with any electric, telegraphic, or telephonic wire or cable includes easements enjoyed in connection with any pole or pylon supporting the wire or cable or in connection with any apparatus – such as a transformer – used in connection with any such wire or cable.

Tied Premises

23.49 Rent receivable from the lessee of tied premises is treated as part of the lessor's trading receipts, not taxed as property business income or, if the property is outside the UK, overseas property business income (*CTA 2009, s 42*). The lessor can deduct as a trading expense any rent that he pays for those premises but cannot claim a deduction for notional rent payable where he owns the premises. Premises are tied for this purpose only if in the course of his trade the lessor is concerned (either as principal or agent) in the supply of goods sold or used on those premises and he deals with his interest in those premises as property employed for the purposes of that trade (*ITTOIA 2005, s 19(1)(2)*; *CTA 2009, s 42(1)*).

23.50 Where part of a property is tied and part not the rent received must be apportioned on a fair and just basis, the non-tied portion being taxable as property business income (*ITTOIA 2005, s 19(3)*; *CTA 2009, s 42(3)*).

23.51 The trader is also treated for capital gains tax roll-over relief purposes as occupying as well as using the premises for the purposes of his trade (*TCGA 1992, s 156(4)*).

Other Occupation of Land

23.52 The occupation of land in the UK (other than for farming or market gardening) is treated as the carrying on of a trade if managed on a commercial basis and with a view to the realisation of profits, unless the land comprises woodlands or is being prepared for use for forestry purposes (*ITTOIA 2005, s 10*; *CTA 2009, ss 37, 38*).

Housing Associations, etc

23.53 Special rules apply to approved co-operative housing associations. The rent received from members is ignored and interest payable by the association is apportioned amongst the members who were tenants during the year and deemed to be payable by them personally – so that they can claim relief for such interest against their personal incomes. There is also an exemption from corporation tax on capital gains on the sale of a property which was occupied by a tenant of the association. The detailed rules and the conditions for approval are not considered here. They can be found in *CTA 2010, ss 642–649*. The tax position where a housing association which is a registered social landlord under the *Housing Act 1996* enters into a 'VAT arrangement' when acquiring properties from a local authority is considered at **16.197**.

23.54 An approved self-build society is similarly exempted from tax on its rents and on chargeable gains accruing on the disposal of land to a member of the society. The conditions for approval and the detailed rules are contained in *CTA 2010, ss 650–654*.

23.55 Special rules also apply to chargeable gains arising on a disposal of land between the Housing Corporation, Housing for Wales or Scottish Homes and a housing society. The sale is deemed to take place at such a price as would secure that neither a gain nor a loss accrues on the disposal (*TCGA 1992, s 218*). This also applies where the Housing Corporation, etc. disposes of land to a registered housing association, one registered housing association disposes of land to another, or a registered housing association or unregistered self-build society disposes of land to the Housing Corporation, etc. (*TCGA 1992, s 219*).

Housing Grants

23.56 A grant or other contribution to expenses made to any person under any enactment relating to the giving of financial assistance for the provision, maintenance, or improvement of housing accommodation or other residential accommodation is not to be treated as a receipt in computing income for any tax purpose (except to the extent that it is made in respect of expenditure which gives rise to a deduction) (*ITTOIA 2005, s 769*; *CTA 2009, s 1284*). Such a receipt may of course still be within the scope of capital gains tax.

Annual Value of Land

23.57 *ICTA 1988, s 837* used to contain a definition of annual value. However this was repealed by *ITA 2007* and not re-enacted. Presumably it was felt relevant only for the purpose of employment income and *ITTOIA 2003* introduced its own definition for that purpose. The *ITEPA 2003* definition for the purpose of the provisions considered at **23.51** is:

> The 'annual value' of living accommodation is the rent which might reasonably be expected to be obtained on a letting from year to year if the tenant undertook to pay all taxes, rates and charges usually paid by a tenant, and the landlord undertook to bear the costs of the repairs and insurance and the other expenses (if any) necessary for maintaining the property in a state to command that rent. That rent is to be calculated on the basis that the only amounts that may be deducted in respect of services provided by the landlord are amounts in respect of the cost to the landlord of providing any services other than the repair, insurance or maintenance of the accommodation of any other premises. If living accommodation is of a kind that might reasonably be expected to be let on terms under which the landlord is to provide such services (or the repair, insurance or maintenance of any premises which do not form part of the accommodation but belong to or are occupied by the landlord) for which a service charge is payable the rent in respect of the accommodation is to be increased by any profit element in the service charge and by any amount that relates to other premises.

Meaning of United Kingdom

23.58 The UK means Great Britain and Northern Ireland (*Interpretation Act 1978, Sch 1*). For all income tax, capital gains tax and corporation tax purposes the territorial sea of the UK is also deemed to be part of the UK (*TCGA 1992, s 276(1)*; *CTA 2010, s 1170*). For certain purposes any 'designated area' under *Continental Shelf Act 1964, s 1(7)* is treated as UK property (*TCGA 1992, s 276(3)–(8)*; *ITTOIA 2005, s 874*; *CTA 2009, s 1313*). This is intended to enable the UK to tax North Sea oil profits.

Meaning of Land

23.59 Land includes buildings and other structures, land covered with water, and any estate, interest, easement, servitude or right in or over land (*Interpretation Act 1978, Sch 1*). For CGT purposes 'land' includes messuages, tenements, and hereditaments, houses and buildings of any tenure (*TCGA 1992, s 288(1)*). This extends the above definition; it does not displace it. For inheritance tax, 'land' is expressed to exclude any estate, interest or right by way of mortgage or other security (*IHTA 1984, s 284*). Again this definition does not displace the *Interpretation Act* definition but supplements it.

Income Tax Charge on Occupation of Living Accommodation

23.60 Where a person (or members of his family or household) is provided with living accommodation by reason of his employment he is treated as if he had received additional salary equal to the value to him of the accommodation for the period for which it is provided, less so much as is properly attributable to the accommodation of any sum made good by him to the person providing the accommodation (eg the rent, if any, that he pays) (*ITEPA 2003, ss 97, 104*). The value of the accommodation is the greater of the annual value (see **23.43** above) or the rent payable for the accommodation by the person providing it (who will, of course, normally be the employer) (*ITEPA 2003, ss 105, 106)*). In practice the charge is normally based on the old gross rateable value of the property, which is far below the current rental value as it is the rental value in 1973. Special rules apply in Scotland where there was a rating revaluation in 1985. Where a property does not have a rateable value, which will apply where it was built or substantially altered after 1 April 1989, the employer is expected to provide an estimate of what that value would have been had rating continued. The annual value will then be agreed with the District Valuer on that basis (HMRC Press Release, 19 April 1990). This probably means what the value would have been had the building existed in that state at 1 April 1973, although this is not clear from the Press Release.

23.61 Where the employer rents the property and the lease is entered into after 21 April 2009 the rent payable for the accommodation is the sum of the actual rent and any amount attributable to the period in respect of a lease premium (*ITEPA 2003, s 105(4)–(4B)*). For this purpose an amount is attributed in respect of a lease premium if a premium was paid by the employer either under the lease or otherwise under the terms on which the lease was granted, the lease is for a term of 10 years or less and the premises are not mainly used by the employer for a purpose other than the provision of living accommodation to employees (*ITEPA 2003, s 105A(1)(5)*). The amount attributed is the proportion of the premium that the relevant period in days bears to the terms of the lease in days, ie the premium is spread on a daily basis over the term of the lease (*ITEPA 2003, s 105A(2)*). If a lease contains a break clause that will enable it to be terminated to shorten the term to 10 years or less, it must be assumed for this purpose that it will be exercised in such a way that the term of the lease is as short as possible (*ITEPA 2003, s 105B(2)(3)*). If the break clause is not in fact exercised, the parties to the lease are treated for the purpose of *s 105A* as entering into a second lease which starts at the time the actual lease is deemed to terminate under the above rule and ends at the earlier of the time that the original lease would be deemed to end if another break clause under the actual lease continues to be exercisable, and the tenth anniversary of the beginning of the term of the actual lease (*ITEPA 2003, s 105B(4),(5)*). If any further premium is payable under the original lease it is treated as being a premium for the notional lease (except to the extent, if any, that it has already been taken into account in calculating the benefit under the original lease). If the notional lease is deemed to end on the tenth anniversary of the original lease only a proportion of that notional premium is brought into account, namely the proportion that the term of the notional lease (in days) bears to that term plus the number of days by which the term of the original lease would exceed 10 years on the assumption that no break clause is exercised (*ITEPA 2003, s 105B(6)–(8)*). For the purpose of *s 105A* the amount of the premium payable by the employer is the total amounts that have been paid, or is, or will become, payable by the employer in relation to the lease by way of premium less any part of that amount that has been repaid or is, or will become, repayable (*ITEPA 2003, s 105A(4)*).

23.62 The charge is restricted to the extent that a claim could be made under *ITEPA 2003, ss 336* or *351* (allowable expenses of an employment) in respect of business use of the premises. No charge at all will arise if the employee is in 'representative occupation', ie where either:

(*a*) it is necessary for the proper performance of the employee's duties that he should reside in the accommodation (*ITEPA 2003, s 99(2)(a)*);

(*b*) the accommodation is provided for the better performance of the duties of the employment, and it is employment of a kind in which it is customary for employers to provide accommodation for employees (*ITEPA 2003, s 99(2)(b)*); or

(*c*) there is a special threat to the employee's security and he resides in the accommodation as part of special security arrangements (*ITEPA 2003, s 100*).

In addition no charge will apply to living accommodation provided for an employee of a local authority if the terms on which it is provided are not more favourable than those on which accommodation is provided to non-employees in similar circumstances (*ITEPA 2003, s 98*). This will exempt a local authority employee who happens to occupy a council house the rent for which is subsidised.

23.63 A company director cannot come within (*a*) or (*b*) above if he owns a material interest in the company; or if his employment is not as a full-time working director (unless the company is non profit-making or is established for charitable purposes only) (*ITEPA 2003, s 100(3)*).

23.64 *Toronto-Dominion Bank v Oberoi (75 TC 244)* is an interesting case. The bank rented property from Mr Oberoi for occupation by an executive of the bank. It was advised that if instead of paying rent it were to pay a premium for the grant of a short lease, that would reduce the benefit on the executive (as the combined charge at **23.56** would be less than the rent). Accordingly, on the expiry of the then current lease of a year less two days, the bank paid a premium for a two-year lease, calculated as the discounted value of the rent that would have been paid had the earlier arrangement continued. The lease contained a break provision after a year. Unfortunately instead of drafting the new lease from scratch, the parties altered the old tenancy agreement and omitted to make some crucial changes. As a result, the legal nature of the 'premium' was unclear. The bank accordingly applied to the court for rectification of the lease. This was opposed by HMRC. The court ordered the lease to be rectified by substituting 'premium' for 'rent' in one clause of the lease. The court pointed out that it is ultimately for the court to determine whether the payment provided for in the agreement has the character of rent or the character of a consideration which is not rent, irrespective of what label the parties attach to the payment. It is interesting to note that HMRC accepted that it is possible to grant a tenancy of property, even for as short as two years, for a premium and without a rent by ensuring that the consideration is given contractually for the grant of the lease and that the tenancy contains no provision which results in the payment being related to the occupation of the property.

23.65 If the employee is a director or is in higher-paid employment he is also taxable as remuneration on the whole of any expenses in relation to the property borne by the employer or some other person, including rates, utilities, repairs and maintenance. Where, however, he is in representative occupation, the aggregate charge in respect of heating, lighting, cleaning, repairs, maintenance, decoration and the provision of furniture and other effects which are normal for domestic occupation is limited to 10% of the employee's salary less certain deductions (*ITEPA 2003, s 315*). HMRC have said that the exemption for rates also applies to council tax (IR Press Release, 16 March 1993). This concession also applies for national insurance purposes (DSS Press Release, 9 November 1993). As stated at **15.4** above, HMRC consider that, in the majority of cases, where a UK house is owned by an overseas company but occupied by a UK resident the UK resident is likely to be a shadow director of the company (irrespective of whether or not the company is owned by trustees). Such a claim, if successful, will bring these provisions and, more importantly, *ITEPA 2003, s 146* into play. There may well be a similar risk where a UK property is occupied by a person who is non-UK resident – as the benefit could be taxable as UK source income.

23.66 If the employer pays the employee's council tax the full amount is assessable as a benefit, and a payment in respect of council tax following a move to a more expensive housing area cannot attract relief. Reimbursement of council tax on a second home where that is temporary accommodation while the employee is working away from home will not necessarily give rise to a benefit though. (IR Press Release, 16 March 1993).

23.67 Where a charge in relation to the use of accommodation arises under *ITEPA 2003, s 97* (or would arise if the employee paid no rent for the use of the accommodation) and the cost of providing it exceeds £75,000, an additional income tax charge on employment income also arises. This is the rent which would have been payable for the period of occupation if the premises had been let to the employee at an annual rent equal to the appropriate percentage of the amount by which the cost of providing the accommodation exceeds £75,000 (*ITEPA 2003, s 106*)). The appropriate percentage is the rate of interest prescribed for beneficial loans at the beginning of the year of assessment in question (*ITEPA 2003, s 106(2)*). This is 3.25% for 2014/15. It was 5% for 2002/03 to 2007/08 and 6.25% for 2008/09, 4.75% for 2009/10 and 4.00% for 2010/11 to 2013/14. The cost of providing the accommodation is the expenditure on acquiring the property (ie the estate or interest in the property held by the person providing the accommodation) plus any expenditure on improvements to it prior to the start of the year of assessment (*ITEPA 2003, s 104*)). If the employee reimburses all or part of the cost of the property or of the improvements or pays a premium for a grant of a tenancy of the premises, the amount reimbursed or paid is deducted. So is any rent paid by the employee (*ITEPA 2003, s 104*).

Example 23.1

Norman was provided throughout 2017/18 with the use of a London flat by his employer, Opeequeue Ltd at a rent of £2,000 p.a. The gross rateable value used to be £1,500. The flat cost £100,000. In 2008/09 Opeequeue carried out improvements at a cost of £24,000. As part of the work was done at Norman's insistence he agreed to reimburse one-third of the cost of such works.

Norman's assessable benefit in kind 2017/18 is:

	£	£
Basic charge		
annual value		1,500
additional charge		
Cost of flat	100,000	
Cost of improvements	24,000	
	124,000	
Less reimbursement by Norman	8,000	
	116,000	
Less first £75,000	75,000	
	£41,000	
2.75% thereof		1,127
		2,627
Less rent paid by Norman		2,000
Assessable benefit		£627

23.68 If the property was held by either the person providing the accommodation, the employee's employer or any connected person (within *ITA 2007, s 993* – see Appendix 1) of either, throughout the six years prior to the time that the employee first occupied the property (and this was after 30 March 1983), the value of the accommodation will be the market value of the property at the date of such first occupation plus expenditure on improvements since that date (*ITEPA 2003, s 107*). The market value for this purpose is the price which the property might reasonably be expected to fetch on a sale in the open market with vacant possession, no reduction being made in estimating the market value on account of any option in respect of the property held by the employee or a person connected with him or by the employer or a connected person (within *ITA 2007, s 993*) of the employer or, if different, of the person providing the accommodation (*ITEPA 2003, s 107(3)(4)*).

23.69 If the employer provides more than one property to the employee, the £75,000 threshold is applied separately to each property. If the same living accommodation is provided to more than one employee at the same time the aggregate charge on them is limited to what would have been paid had the property been provided to a single employee (*ITEPA 2003, s 108*).

23.70 The charge under *ITEPA 2003, ss 105, 106* can be reduced by a claim for business use under *ITEPA 2003, ss 336* or *351* to the extent to which the relief exceeds the charge under *ss 105* or *106* (*ITEPA 2003, s 364*).

23.71 It is arguable that if a property is owned jointly by the company and the employee no charge can arise under *s 105* or *106* as living accommodation is not 'provided for' the employee – he is already entitled to occupy the property by virtue of his joint ownership. *Sections 105* and *106* apply even if the provision of accommodation is taxable under some other provision, but the tax charge under that other provision is then limited to any excess over the *s 105* or *106* charge (*ITEPA 2003, s 109*). This prevents the application of the *Heaton v Bell (46 TC 211)* principle under which it might have been contended that no charge could arise under *s 105* or *106* if the employee takes a small salary reduction in return for the right to live in the house, with the ability to increase the salary by surrendering the right.

23.72 Where an interest in premises belongs to a charity or an ecclesiastical corporation and in right of that interest a person (or persons) holding a full-time office as clergyman or minister of any religious denomination has a residence in those premises from which to perform the duties of the office, the following special rules apply to determine the amount of the emoluments assessable on the clergyman as employment income:

(*a*) the making good to him as holder of the office of statutory amounts payable in connection with the premises (or statutory deductions falling to be made in connection with them) are to be disregarded except to the extent, if any, to which they are attributable to a part of the premises in respect of which he receives rent;

(*b*) so is the payment on his behalf (except as in (*a*)) of any such statutory amounts;

(*c*) unless he is in director's or higher-paid employment, expenses incurred in connection with the provision in the premises of living accommodation for him are to be disregarded provided that they are incurred in consequence of his being the holder of the office;

(*d*) 25% of any expenses borne by him on maintenance, repairs, insurance or management of the premises can be deducted from his salary; and

(*e*) if he rents a dwelling-house any part of which is used mainly or substantially for the purposes of his duty as clergyman, up to 25% of the rent can be deducted from his salary.

(*ITEPA 2003, ss 290, 351.*)

23.73 For 2010/11 onwards no liability to income tax arises in respect of a person in lower-paid employment as a minister of religion by virtue of the payment or reimbursement of heating, lighting or cleaning premises within *s 290* or maintaining a garden forming part of such premises (*ITEPA 2003, s 290A*)). This gives statutory effect to a previous concession, ESC A61. The exemption does not apply if the minister is paid an allowance intended to be used wholly or partly to pay such outgoings, except to the extent that the allowance is actually used to pay such outgoings (*ITEPA 2003, s 290B*).

23.74 When considering the provision of living accommodation by a company for a major shareholder the capital gains tax position also needs to be borne in mind. The company is not entitled to the benefit of the private residence exemption and a company is in general an undesirable vehicle for holding investment property because of the double capital gains tax effect. The CGT indexation allowance is some help but house prices tend not to rise in line with inflation. Some people feel that the problem can be overcome by granting the employee an option to buy the house at a future date at its current value. They contend that such an option has no – or very little – value at the time it is granted and that when it *is* exercised the benefit is obtained *qua* option holder not *qua* employee. The author is sceptical as to both of these claims. Many property dealers would in all probability be prepared to pay a significant sum in 2015 for an option to buy for £500,000 at any time prior to, say, the year 2025 a house which is worth £500,000 in 2015. If such an option is given to a director for no consideration the author considers that its value would be a perquisite of the employment taxable under *ITEPA 2003, s 62*. It is also felt that the benefit obtained when the option is exercised is obtained by reason of the employment and is thus taxable under the benefit in kind provisions (see *Cheatle v CIR (56 TC 111)*).

23.75 For 2016/17 onwards, no benefit in kind charge arises in respect of the provision of board or lodging (or both) to an individual employed as a home care worker if the provision is on a reasonable scale, is at the recipient's home and is provided by reason of the individual's employment as a home care worker. A person is a home care worker for this purpose if the duties of his employment consist wholly or mainly of the provision of personal care to another individual (the recipient) at the recipient's home and the recipient is in need of personal care because of old age, mental or physical disability, past or present dependence on alcohol or drugs, past or present illness or past or present mental disorder (*ITEPA 2003, s 306A* inserted by *FA 2014, s 14*).

Homes Abroad Owned Through a Company

23.76 It is very common for holiday homes abroad to be owned through overseas companies. This is not done to avoid UK tax but because of foreign inheritance laws and transfer taxes. Many people expressed concerns that such homes might fall within the above provisions, albeit that to do so HMRC would need to contend that the owner is a shadow director of the company. In response to such concerns the Chancellor announced in his 2007 budget that legislation would be introduced to ensure that no benefit-in-kind charge applies. This legislation, *ITEPA 2003, s 100A*, was inserted by *FA 2008, s 45* as always having had effect (*FA 2008, s 45(2)*) ie it is retrospective to the start of the charge under *ICTA 1988, s 145* (5 April 1998) although it is of course too late to seek a refund for most of that period. It excludes from the benefit charge living accommodation outside the UK provided by a company for a director or other officer of the company (or a member of his family or household) if:

(*a*) the company is wholly owned by that person or by him and other individuals (and no interest in the company is partnership property); and

(*b*) the company has been the 'holding company' of the property at all times since the company first owned an interest in the property that gave it a right to exclusive possession of the property at all times or at certain times (eg if the property is a time-share) (or if the company owned an interest in the property when the individual first acquired shares in it from the time that he first acquired shares – but this does not apply if he acquired the shares directly or indirectly from a connected person).

(*ITEPA 2003, s 100A(1),(4)–(6)*.)

23.77 Holding company in this context does not bear its normal meaning. It means a company that holds its interest in the property as its main or only asset and the only activities of which are ones that are incidental to the ownership of that interest (*ITEPA 2003, s 100A(2)*). A company can also qualify as a holding company if it is itself the parent company of a wholly-owned subsidiary, the subsidiary meets the above conditions, the interest in the subsidiary (which appears to include loans as well as the shares) is the parent company's only or main asset and the only activities of the parent company are ones that are incidental to its ownership of the subsidiary (*ITEPA 2003, s 100A(3)*). Receiving rents from letting the property when it is not required for use by the directors would of course be incidental to ownership of the property.

23.78 The exemption does not apply if either:

(*a*) the company's interest in the property was acquired (or granted to it) directly or indirectly from a connected company at an undervalue (*ITEPA 2003, s 100B(1),(2)(a),(4)*);

(*b*) the company's interest in the property derives from an interest that was acquired directly or indirectly from a connected company at an undervalue (*ITEPA 2003, s 100B(1),(2)(b),(4)*);

(*c*) at any time after the company acquired the property (or if later after the director acquired the shares from an unconnected person) expenditure in respect of the property has been incurred directly or indirectly by a connected company (*ITEPA 2003, s 100B(1),(3)(a)*);

(*d*) at any time after the company acquired the property (or the individual acquired the shares) any borrowing by the company directly or indirectly from a connected company has been outstanding (but any borrowing at a commercial rate, or which results in the individual being taxed on notional interest on a beneficial loan, can be ignored) (*ITEPA 2003, s 100B(1),(3)(b),(7)*); or

(*e*) the living accommodation is provided in pursuance of an arrangement (including any scheme, agreement or understanding whether or not enforceable) the main purpose, or one of the main purposes of which is the avoidance of tax or NIC.

(*ITEPA 2003, s 100B(1),(4)(8)*.)

23.79 For the purpose of (*a*) and (*b*) above an interest is acquired at an undervalue if the total consideration is less than that which might reasonably have been expected to be obtained on the open market. Consideration for this purpose means consideration provided at any time and includes payments of rent (*ITEPA 2003, s 100B(6)*).

23.80 For the purpose of these provisions a connected company means a company connected with the individual, with a member of the individual's family or with an employer of the individual (such as a company of which he is a director) or a company which is connected with such a company (*ITEPA 2003, s 100B(9)*). The meaning of connected person in *ITA 2007, s 993* (see Appendix 1) applies for this purpose (*ITEPA 2003, s 718*). It is irrelevant whether the company is resident in the UK or elsewhere.

23.81 It should be noted that this exemption is fairly limited. In particular it cannot apply if either:

(*a*) some or all of the shares are held by a family trust (even if this was only at a time before anyone was aware of this legislation);

(*b*) some (but not all) of the shares are held by a company;

(*c*) the shares are partnership property;

(*d*) the company has other assets – for example it may have cash which was required to support a mortgage although it is possible that such cash would be incidental to the ownership of the property);

(*e*) the structure is company A wholly owns company B which wholly owns company C which owns the property (such a structure may have been created to acquire the property via a purchase of the shares in B);

(*f*) the company owns interests in two or more properties both of which are used by the individual, such as time-shares in different countries;

(*g*) other transactions have been put through the company in the past in ignorance of this legislation;

(*h*) the property is jointly held by the company and another person so that the company does not have exclusive possession;

(*i*) the company acquired the property before the individual acquired any shares in it and did not meet the qualifying conditions prior to his acquisition, and the shares were acquired from a connected person of the individual, eg he was gifted them some years ago by his father, or he bought the company jointly with his former wife and at some time in the past she transferred her shares to him as part of a divorce settlement;

(*j*) the individual's UK trading company initially contracted to buy the property and paid the deposit but the deposit was reimbursed to it by the holding company of the property and there was an increase in value between contract and completion; or

(*k*) a payment in respect of running expenses of the property was accidentally made by the individual's UK trading company albeit that when the mistake was discovered it was reimbursed by the holding company of the property.

23.82 HMRC said in March 2007 that they would not seek to charge anyone to a benefit-in-kind where:

(*a*) the property is owned by a company that is owned by individuals;

(*b*) the company's only activities are ones that are incidental to its ownership of the property (which would include letting it out);

(*c*) the property is the company's only or main asset; and

(*d*) the property is not funded directly or indirectly by a connected company.

(2007 Budget Notice 50.)

Employees' Household Expenses

23.83 No income tax is chargeable on a payment by an employer to an employee in respect of reasonable additional household expenses which the employee incurs in carrying out duties of the employment at home under homeworking arrangements (*ITEPA 2003, s 816A*). Household expenses for this purpose are expenses connected with the day to day running of the employee's home (*ITEPA 2003, s 316A(3)*). It should be noted that relief is given for additional expenses, not for a proportion of items such as repairs or council tax, which the employee would have had to incur irrespective of the arrangements. HMRC have said though that they will not question payments of up to £2 a week. Homeworking arrangements are any arrangements between an employer and employee under which the employee regularly performs some or all of the duties of the employment at home (*ITEPA 2003, s 316A(3)*).

Small Profits Rate of Tax (to 31 March 2015 only)

23.84 Up to 31 March 2015, UK resident company whose profits were 'small' paid corporation tax at the small companies rate of tax, which was 20% for 2014/15 (*CTA 2010, s 18*). A small company for this purpose was one whose taxable profits for the accounting period do not exceed £300,000. The usual definition of a small company did not apply. Where a company had associated companies (companies under common control within *CTA 2010, s 450*) the £300,000 limit was divided equally between all of the associated companies, eg if a company had five associated companies the small companies rate threshold for each was £50,000 (one sixth of £300,000). A marginal relief applied to profits in the band from £300,000 to £1.5 million. For 2013/14 this had the effect of taxing profits in that band at an effective rate of 23.75%, as compared with the main corporation tax rate on profits over that level of 23%. The £1.5 million limit again had to be divided amongst associated companies so a company with five associated companies would have had a threshold of £250,000. For 2014/15 the marginal rate was 21.25%, so the excess was very small.

23.85 From 1 April 2011, if the relationship was not one of substantial commercial interdependence, rights did not need to be attributed to a person under *CTA 2010, s 451(4)* (rights of associates) to determine whether companies were associated for the purposes of the small profits rate of tax (*CTA 2010, s 27* as substituted by *FA 2011, s 55*). In determining whether there was substantial commercial interdependence between two companies, account had to be taken of the degree to which the companies were financially interdependent, economically interdependent or organisationally interdependent (*Corporation Tax Act 2010 (Factors Determining Substantial Commercial Interdependence) Order 2011(SI 2011 No 1784)*).

23.86 In determining the number of associated companies in an accounting period a company that had not carried on any trade or business at any time in the accounting period was disregarded *(CTA 2010, s 26)*. In *HMRC v Salaried Persons Postal Loans Ltd (2006 STC 1315)* the High Court held that a company in receipt of rental income was not carrying on a trade or business and could therefore be disregarded, although this decision may be of limited importance as it depended on its facts. An associated company carried on a trade of making loans from premises in Glasgow. In 1966 it vacated its premises in West Regent Street and moved to Union Street. It ceased trading in 1995 and vacated its premises at Union Street. However it continued to hold the West Regent Street property which it had let out. Since the company ceased trading it had done nothing other than receive its rents through its agents. In particular it had not negotiated any rent reviews. The premises had been let to the same tenant since 1966 and the rent reviews had taken place automatically as, although the lease contained a rent review clause, it provided for a 20% minimum increase in rentals at the three-yearly review dates and the company had been content to accept that minimum. The Special Commissioners inferred that the company performed its obligations under the lease each year such as paying the insurance and recovering it from the tenant. It also incurred accountancy fees and paid its tax on the rents. The Commissioners placed particular emphasis on the fact that the company did not purchase the premises as an investment but as an asset of its trade, that the same tenant occupied the property throughout, the lease was a tenant's repairing lease, the company did nothing other than pay the insurance and collect the rents and the value of the property, £90,000, was a small part of the company's assets of £1.4 m, the balance of which had been lent interest free to an associated company. This decision needs to be borne in mind in cases where the facts are similar. It is unlikely that it will apply where a company ceases its trade and makes a positive decision to invest some of its surplus cash in a rental property.

Valuation

23.87 For CGT purposes the 'market value' of an asset is the price that it might reasonably be expected to fetch on a sale in the open market. In estimating such value no reduction is to be made on account of the estimate being made on the assumption that the whole of the assets are to be placed on the market at one and the same time (*TCGA 1992, s 272(1)(2)*). However, if inheritance tax is chargeable on a person's death (on his personal estate) and the value of an asset forming part of his estate has been ascertained for inheritance tax purposes, the value so ascertained must be taken as the market value for capital gains tax purposes at the date of death (*TCGA 1992, s 274*). HMRC consider that a value has not been 'ascertained' where the 100% business property relief applies. It is arguable whether this is right as the relief takes the form of a deduction and it is questionable whether a deduction can be made from an unascertained amount. They have also expressed the view that if an asset is wholly exempt or relieved from IHT neither the deceased's personal representative nor HMRC can require the value to be ascertained. Even where tax is payable they also see a distinction between their 'considering' the value and its being ascertained (Tax Bulletin, Issue 16, April 1995). It seems unreasonable that a person's CGT liability should vary dependent on whether HMRC choose to ascertain a different person's liability, or to merely consider it, or to simply ignore it because it does not affect the amount of a tax liability. Nevertheless their view has found favour with the Special Commissioners in *Stonor v CIR (2001 STC (SCD) 199),* where the view was expressed that, for a value to be ascertained there is an implication that some formality or agreement is required and also that if a transfer of value is exempt (in that case as a gift to charity), tax was not 'chargeable'. That case was concerned primarily with *s 191, IHTA 1984* (see **18.37**), not *s 274* though. When considering a 5 April 1965 or 1 March 1982 valuation, the asset needs to be valued as it stood at the relevant date. This is not always easy to ascertain as is apparent from the case of *Henderson v Karmel's Exors (58 TC 201)* which is considered at **11.91**.

23.88 HMRC take the view that the inheritance tax decision in *Lady Fox's Exors v CIR (1994 STC 360)* applies equally for capital gains tax where the statutory hypothesis on which the valuation is based deems the assets to be disposed of together, eg an acquisition of assets by personal representatives under *TCGA 1992, s 62*, or a beneficiary of a trust becoming absolutely entitled to the settled property under *TCGA 1992, s 71(1)*. Where the statutory hypothesis requires the disposal of a number of single assets, eg rebasing to 6 April 1965 (see *Henderson v Karmel's Exors (58 TC 201)* at **11.79**) or 31 March 1992, or a non-arm's-length disposal under *TCGA 1992, s 17*, each asset must be valued separately (Tax Bulletin 24, Aug 1996).

23.89 Market value for inheritance tax is the price that the property might reasonably be expected to fetch if sold in the open market at the time it falls to be valued. That price must not be assumed to be reduced on the ground that the whole property is to be placed on the market at one and the same time (*IHTA 1984, s 160*). In an estate duty case (the forerunner of inheritance tax) it was held that knowledge of local conditions and requirements – including the existence of a 'special purchaser', ie someone who has a special reason for wanting the property and would be prepared to pay above market value to get it – are factors properly to be taken into account in determining the open market value of a house (*CIR v Clay ([1914–15] All ER 882)*). In another estate duty case it was held that a large estate should be divided into its natural units for valuation purposes if such 'lotting' would produce a greater aggregate value than if the entire estate were placed on the market at the same time (*Duke of Buccleuch & Another v CIR ([1967] All ER 129)*). If a property acquired under the 'right to buy' provisions of the *Housing Act 1980* falls to be valued for inheritance tax purposes during the period in which repayment of part of the discount would be triggered by a sale, it must be assumed that the hypothetical purchaser could acquire the property without triggering any repayment, but would acquire it subject to having to make the repayment if he were to resell it during the five-year period, ie he will stand in the shoes of the previous owner (*Alexander v CIR (1991 STC 112)*). As the open market would include potential occupiers as purchasers it seems unlikely that the value on that assumption would be much below the market value shorn of any obligation to repay. In *Alexander* the District Valuer was prepared to accept a discount of around 20% because he found that 75% of purchasers of flats in the block concerned resold within two to six years of purchase. The Lands Tribunal held in *Executors of G A Baird v CIR* (14 June 1990) that a non-assignable agricultural tenancy has a value. The District Valuer assessed this at 25% of vacant possession value. This was accepted by the tribunal as no alternative value (other than nil) had been put forward by the taxpayer. In the circumstances it should not necessarily be taken as indicative of the value of such a tenancy in other cases, particularly as it was effectively rejected by the Court of Appeal in the *Walton* case considered below. In practice, the same basis is normally adopted for income and corporation tax purpose. However for some employee shareholding valuation HMRC have been known to take the view that the employee himself, not a deemed person, is the purchaser. It is questionable whether that is a correct approach.

23.90 It is important to identify correctly what needs to be valued. This is what was actually held at the valuation date. If, for example, a person held a tenanted building at 1 April 1982 the building has to be valued at that date subject to the tenancy even though at the time of sale the taxpayer may have had vacant possession. A discount may well be appropriate where a property is jointly owned. In *Walton decd v CIR (1995 STC 68)* the deceased held a one-third interest in a farm which was let under an agricultural tenancy to a farming partnership of which the deceased and his son were the partners sharing equally. The vacant possession value of the farm was agreed at £400,000 and the value of the freehold subject to the tenancy at £150,000. In dispute was the value of the partnership's tenancy. HMRC valued this at half the marriage value, namely £130,000. It was held to be the profit rent to the next rent review, a mere £12,645. This was because the value of a tenancy depends on the circumstances of the parties. The marriage value could be realised only if the landlord wished to obtain vacant possession at an early date and the tenant was prepared to stop farming the land. Although the buyer and seller are hypothetical it is not necessary for the operation of the statutory hypothesis of a sale in the open market of an interest in a tenancy that the landlord should be a hypothetical person, and similarly regard should be had to the actual intention of the actual surviving partner, not to a hypothetical partner. A purchaser of the deceased's interest in the partnership could not unlock the marriage value without the consent not only of the other partner but also of the freeholders.

23.91 Normally what has to be ascertained for inheritance tax purposes is the fall in value of a person's estate. Where part only of an asset is disposed of this is effectively the difference between the value of the asset concerned prior to the disposal and its value after the disposal. For example, if the owner of a freehold property gifts a 20-year lease, what needs to be valued is not the 20-year lease but the freehold and the freehold reversion on the lease, the difference between the two being the reduction in the donor's estate.

23.92 Where the value of any property comprised in a person's estate would be less than the appropriate portion of the value of it and any related property, its value must be taken to be the appropriate portion of that aggregate (*IHTA 1984, s 161(1)*). Property is related if it is owned by the transferor's spouse or if it has within the previous five years been owned by a charity or a National Heritage body and was gifted to it by the transferor (or spouse) by way of an exempt transfer (*IHTA 1984, s 161*). If other assets owned by the transferor himself affect the value of what is being transferred, they are not related property but are automatically taken into account as such in determining the value being transferred.

Example 23.2

Roger owns a freehold field worth £10,000 together with a lease worth £3,000 of an adjoining field. His wife, Rita, owns the freehold reversion on the second field valued at £5,000. The unencumbered freehold of the second is worth £10,000. Roger transfers his freehold field to a discretionary settlement. The value of the two fields together would be £25,000 if they had both been freehold.

	£	£
The amount of the gift is		
Value of 2 freehold fields		25,000
Value of field settled	10,000	
Value of lease of other field owned by Roger	3,000	
Value of reversion owned by Rita	5,000	
	£18,000	
Value of assets in Roger's estate		
prior to gift 13/18ths of £25,000	18,056	
Value of assets in Roger's estate		
after gift 3/8ths of £10,000		
(value of second field)	3,750	
	£14,306	

23.93 *IHTA 1984, s 161(4)* provides that 'the proportion which a smaller number of shares of any class bear to the value of a greater number shall be taken to be that which the smaller number bears to the greater; and similarly with stock, debentures and units of other description of property'. In *Arkwright and Another v CIR (2004 STC 1323)* (see **23.79**) the Special Commissioners held that this provision could not apply to property and HMRC did not pursue that point when it appealed the case to the High Court. However after the Arkwright decision had become final so it was too late for the courts to consider this point HMRC announced that they consider the Special Commissioners' decision on this point to be wrong and intend to apply *s 161(4)* when valuing shares of land in related property after 28 November 2007 – and will consider litigating in appropriate cases (R & C Brief 28 November 2007). In *Price v CIR (2011 SFTD 52)* the taxpayer argued that the deeming merely requires an assumption that both items of property are on the market at the same time. Thus if the asset owned by the deceased is an undivided half-share of a property as tenant in common, the related property is the other undivided half-share and what has to be valued is the two undivided shares, not the freehold property in which they are shares. This was rejected by the Tribunal. The appellant was a tax QC and the Tribunal's reasoning is not wholly convincing, so this decision could well go to appeal.

23.94 In *Lady Fox's Exors v CIR (1994 STC 360)* the Court of Appeal held that the hypothetical sale must be supposed to take the course which would get the largest possible price provided that does not entail undue expenditure of time and effort. Lady Fox had a 92.5% interest in a farming partnership and also held the freehold reversion in the land that was subject to the partnership's agricultural tenancy. It was held that the two should be valued as a package.

23.95 In determining the value of a person's estate immediately before his death, changes in the value of his estate brought about by the death must be taken into account (as if they had occurred immediately prior to the death) but the termination on the death of any interest (or its passing by survivorship) is not to be taken into account (*IHTA 194, s 171*). In *Arkwright and another v CIR (2004 STC 1323)* Gloster J held that where land is held by two people as tenants in common the death does not terminate the deceased's interest in the land but that the deceased's death converted the possibility that he would die before his co-tenant into a certainty and that this was a factor that devalued the interest for inheritance tax purposes. In that case, the surviving co-tenant had a significantly greater life expectancy than the deceased and a prospective purchaser would be aware that she had a right of continuing occupation – whereas before the death there was at least the upside to a prospective purchaser that she might die first.

23.96 For inheritance tax purposes, where the right to dispose of any property has been excluded or restricted by a contract made at any time, that exclusion or restriction is to be ignored in valuing the property except to the extent that consideration in money or money's worth was given for the restriction. If the contract was itself a chargeable transfer an allowance will be given against the inheritance tax on the transfer of the property for the value transferred by the prior contract (*IHTA 1984, s 163*).

23.97 In valuing for inheritance tax purposes agricultural property that includes cottages occupied by people who are employed solely for agricultural purposes in connection with that property, any additional value attributable to the fact that they might also be suitable for residential occupation generally must be ignored (*IHTA 1984, s 169*).

23.98 The Law Society has discussed with HMRC the valuation of agricultural tenancies. HMRC's normal approach is to adopt a percentage of the vacant possession value. In arriving at the value, account needs to be taken of the benefits attaching to the tenancy, such as residential accommodation, compensation for disturbance, improvements, manurial rights, together with any favourable level of the rent, the consideration of who might be in the hypothetical market for the tenancy, and the principle that there should be no automatic presumption that the value of a tenancy could be arrived at by a method based on a standard percentage of the vacant possession premium or value. If the taxpayer believes that the likelihood or otherwise of a bid by the landlord is a factor to take into account, he should adduce evidence of this at an early stage (Law Society's Gazette 18.3.1992). The statement of course predates the *Walton* decision (see **23.90**).

23.99 HMRC operate a sampling scheme, the Multiple Land Valuation scheme, where a taxpayer disposes of 30 or more interests in land in an accounting period or year of assessment. For this purpose a group of companies is regarded as a single taxpayer. The scheme is operated by a special unit, the Capital Gains Tax Sampling Unit (CGTSU). The CGTSU selects a sample – usually between 25% and 50% of the properties – and refers these to the local District Valuers. The CGTSU will then discuss the DVs' valuations with the taxpayer, and reach agreement on those valuations. Based on the changes, if any, to the taxpayer's figures in respect of those valuations, the CGTSU may suggest changes to the valuations of non-sampled properties, if the sample produces a reliable pattern of differences. If it does not, the sample may be enlarged – up to 100% if all the valuations look suspect – and non-sampled properties that appear to give rise to particular difficulties may also be valued individually. If the valuations of the sampled properties support the taxpayer's valuations the remainder are of course accepted unchallenged (Tax Bulletin, Issue 12, August 1994).

23.100 Where property is held jointly HMRC normally accept a discount of 10% in valuing one of two joint interests. This derives from the 1917 decision of *Cust v CIR (91 EG 11)*. In the 1982 decision in *Wight and Moss v CIR (264 EG 935)* a deduction of 15% was given. The Valuation Office Agency Manual Practice Note 2 contains a useful discussion on the appropriate discount to use. While this does not endorse any figure it indicates that a 15% discount for a 50% interest is not necessarily unreasonable. A 10% discount reflects the likelihood that an order for sale would be granted but a 15% discount might be appropriate where an order is less likely such as:

(i) where it would involve displacing a co-owner entitled to possession; or

(ii) where the purpose of the trust for sale has not been fulfilled but is still capable of being fulfilled.

23.101 If the matter in dispute on an appeal in relation to capital gains tax or corporation tax on chargeable gains relates to or includes the question of the value of land or of a lease of land that question must be decided by the Upper Tribunal (which since 1 June 2009 has incorporated the Lands Tribunal) if the land is in the UK (*TMA 1970, s 46D*). However, it was held in *Arkwright and another v CIR (2004 STC 1323)* that a dispute as to what is to be valued is a question of law for determination by the Special Commissioners (or now by the First-tier Tribunal (Tax Chamber)). An issue in that case was whether the value of a deceased tenant in common's share of property was a mathematical one half of the vacant possession value. Gloster J held that it was less than such a figure and that the interest should be valued taking into account the rights given to the surviving tenant in common under the *Trusts of Land and Appointment of Trustees Act 1996*. If the land is not in the UK jurisdiction apparently remains with the First-tier Tribunal (Tax).

23.102 Curiously, it appears that where a question as to the value of land arises in an appeal in relation to income tax or corporation tax on income it must be decided by the First-tier Tribunal. Where there is no right of appeal to the Upper Tribunal (Property) a reference by consent can be made under *s 1(5)* of the *Lands Tribunal Act 1949*. HMRC have said that for stamp duty purposes they will normally consent but where questions of both law and valuation arise in relation to an appeal they would wish to resolve the legal issue prior to any determination of value by the Upper Tribunal (Tax Bulletin, Issue 18, August 1995). It seems likely that they would similarly normally agree to a reference in other valuation issues. Inheritance tax appeals on the question of the value of land are made to the Upper Tribunal. If the value of the land is relevant to the settlement of a dispute before the Special Commissioners or the High Court they must refer the valuation questions to the Upper Tribunal (*IHTA 1984, s 222*). Before that date the taxpayer had to run two appeals, to the Commissioners and to the Lands Tribunal, with it being unclear how the two interacted. This problem was highlighted in *Alexander v CIR (1991 STC 112)* – see **23.63**. Following the incorporation of the Lands tribunal into the Upper Tribunal there is probably no longer a need for such a concession as the

Tribunal rules allow for transfers with the consent of the Upper Tribunal. The special valuation issues that arise in relation to trade-related properties are considered at **23.193**.

Interest on Compulsory Purchase

23.103 Where property is compulsorily acquired it frequently takes months or even years to agree the compensation payable. Interest on the compensation is payable from the date the authority enters on to the land. Such interest is not income for income tax purposes until it is received. However, when it is received the whole amount is taxable as income of the year of receipt even though the figure may represent interest for several years. This can adversely affect the tax payable and needs to be watched. HMRC adopt the view that the taxpayer can avoid the problem by asking for an interim payment on account of the compensation, and if he does not do so he must accept any resultant distortion of his tax position. For corporation tax interest is recognised on an accruals basis so this is not a problem for companies.

Transactions at Other than Market Value

23.104 For capital gains tax purposes, transactions between connected persons (see *TCGA 1992, s 286*) are treated as made other than by way of bargains made at arm's length (*TCGA 1992, ss 17(1)(a), 18*) and therefore must be deemed to be at market value. The legislation clearly envisages a distinction between the two, so it is undoubtedly possible to have a transaction which is not between connected persons and is nevertheless not at arm's length. Indeed, HMRC may well draw an inference that any transaction not at market value is not at arm's length. Having said that, the market price of a site is what an arm's-length purchaser will pay for it, and in the absence of any indication to the contrary the price paid by a non-connected purchaser could well be the market price of the site even though it may differ considerably from the value put on the land by a valuer. If an asset which is disposed of to a connected person is subject to any restriction or right enforceable by the disposer, or a connected person of his, the market value is the value ignoring that restriction, minus the market value of the restriction (or, if less, the amount by which its extinction would enhance the value of the asset). If the right is of such a nature that it would destroy or substantially impair the value of the asset without giving any corresponding benefit to the disposer or the connected person, or it is an option or other right to acquire the asset (or to extinguish it by forfeiture, merger, etc.) the value of the right is ignored completely, ie capital gains tax is payable by reference to the unencumbered value of the asset (*TCGA 1992, s 18(6)(7)*). A mortgage or other charge or a right to forfeit a lease exercisable on a breach of a covenant does not trigger this restriction (*TCGA 1992, s 18(8)*).

23.105 Other points to bear in mind from a CGT point of view are that a loss on a disposal to a connected person can be used only against gains on disposals to that same connected person (*TCGA 1992, s 18(3)*); and that where a disposal at an undervalue is between individuals and/or trusts or is a disposal of assets by an individual an election can sometimes be made to roll over the gain to the purchaser (*TCGA 1992, ss 165, 260*). It is not always sensible to make such an election.

23.106 If a transaction takes place at other than market value, *TIOPA 2010, ss 146–217* (transfer pricing) need to be considered. These are aimed at transactions between associated companies, although the test of association is wider than normal. However, the provision does not apply to a small company (one with fewer than 50 employees and either turnover or assets of less than 10 million euro) unless the other party is resident in a tax haven (or a country with which the UK does not have a full double tax agreement). Nor does it normally apply to a medium-sized company (one with fewer than 250 employees and either turnover of less than 50 million euro or assets of less than 43 million euro). HMRC have power to require a medium-sized company to apply the transfer pricing rules – effectively with retrospective effect as it is exercisable only when HMRC decide to do so in the course of an enquiry into the company's tax return. HMRC have said that they will use this power only in 'exceptional circumstances' but have given no guidance as to what such circumstances might be.

23.107 Where *TIOPA 2010, ss 146–217* apply to increase the profits of one UK company and the other party is also within the charge to UK tax, that other person can claim a corresponding reduction in its own taxable profits (*TIOPA 2010, s 174*). If the adjustment relates to a transfer of trading stock or work in progress it will not affect the valuation of that stock in the transferee's hand for accounting periods ending on or after the end of the transferor's accounting period in which the transfer took place, ie the stock will be valued in later periods at the actual transfer price (*TIOPA 2010, s 180*).

Example 23.3

A Ltd ceases to trade on 28 December 2016 and transfers a property held as trading stock to an associated company B Ltd for its original cost of £100,000. The property is worth £400,000 at the time. B Ltd prepares accounts to 31 March each year.

A Ltd is treated as having sold the stock for £400,000 so its profit for its accounting period to 28 December 2016 is increased by £300,000 (the cessation of a trade triggers the end of an accounting period). B Ltd can claim to increase its cost of the property to £400,000. However it must still value it in its accounts at 31 March 2017 at £100,000 so creating a £300,000 reduction in its taxable profit for that year, eliminating the effect of the increase on the acquisition.

23.108 Without *TIOPA 2010, s 180* the increase in deemed cost would reflect in an increase in closing stock so the relief would be deferred until the property were sold. It is not clear what would happen if B Ltd had acquired the property as an investment. A Ltd is deemed under *TCGA 1992, s 173(2)* (see **8.16**) to have appropriated the asset otherwise than as trading stock immediately before its disposal to B Ltd. It is unclear how the deeming under *s 173(2)* interacts with that under the transfer pricing rules. If *s 173(2)* is applied first, the effect will be to increase the profits of A Ltd by £300,000 and to deem the property as sold to B Ltd for £400,000. Accordingly no adjustment will fall to be made under the transfer pricing rules.

23.109 Particular problems in relation to transfer pricing arise in relation to loan interest. These are considered at **4.65** onwards.

23.110 It was confirmed in *Ametalco UK v CIR (1996 STC (SCD) 399), (SpC 94)* that *s 770* (the predecessor to *TIOPA 2010, ss 146–217*) could apply to impute interest on an interest free loan. This is because *ICTA 1988, s 773(4)* extended it, with the necessary adaptations, to lettings and hirings of property, grants and transfers of rights, interests and licences and the giving of business facilities of whatever kind. Many people doubted that an interest-free loan fell within any of these categories. In practice HMRC rarely applied *s 770* where both parties to a transaction were UK resident. If they were to do so the imputed interest would be taxable or deductible on an accruals basis as interest under either a loan relationship or a deemed loan relationship (*FA 1996, s 100(3)*). *TIOPA 2010, ss 146–217* is more widely drawn. It refers to transactions which differ from those which would have applied had the parties been at arm's length rather than to purchases and sales. This is clearly wide enough to tax imputed interest on an interest free loan.

23.111 Where the transfer pricing rules do not apply this does not necessarily mean that no adjustment need be made. In *Petrotim Securities Ltd v Ayres (41 TC 389)* the court held that a transaction had taken place at such a substantial undervalue that it was not in the course of the company's trade. The company had therefore appropriated the item of trading stock for a non-trading purpose and the item needed to be taken out of stock at market value under the principle in *Sharkey v Wernher (36 TC 275)*. A similar finding was made in *Coates v Arndale Properties Ltd (59 TC 516)*. The *Sharkey v Wernher* principle was given statutory effect by what is now *ITTOIA 2005, ss 172A–172F* and *CTA 2009, ss 156–161* (formerly *FA 2008, s 37* and *Sch 15)*. It was felt that then current accounting principles permitted stock to be appropriated at cost and the government wished to preserve the *Sharkey v Wernher* principle by requiring a statutory adjustment to accounts that adopt a different basis.

23.112 The courts will not necessarily adopt such a view unless the transaction is clearly not at market value. In *Jacgilden (Weston Hall) Ltd v Castle (45 TC 685)* they declined to allow a company to substitute market value which it estimated at £150,000 for the price of £72,000 paid to buy property from its shareholders.

23.113 If trading stock is sold at arm's length to another UK trader, at other than market value on the discontinuance of the vendor's trade, *CTA 2009, ss 164–166* specifically provide that the consideration is the price actually paid. It has been held that no adjustment to market value was competent in such circumstances in *Moore v R J Mackenzie & Sons Ltd (48 TC 196)* and *Bradshaw v Blunden (No 2) (39 TC 73).*

23.114 However if the parties are connected with each other the arm's length price must normally be substituted. If the aggregate market value on the transfer exceeds both the vendor's acquisition value of the properties sold and the price actually obtained for them on the transfer, a joint election can be made (within two years after the end of the year of assessment or accounting period in which the trade is discontinued) to treat the transfer as taking place at the higher of the vendor's acquisition value of the stock or the price actually paid on the transfer (*CTA 2009, ss 165–168*). The acquisition value is the amount that would have been deductible in calculating profits had the stock been sold (*CTA 2009, s 167(5)*). This is, of course, cost unless the value of the property has been written down in an earlier year. The purchaser must of course acquire the property as trading stock. If stock is sold on the discontinuance of a trade to someone who does not acquire it as trading stock, (whether or not it is a connected person) market value must be substituted in calculating the vendor's profits if it differs from the actual sale price (*CTA 2009, s 164(4)*).

23.115 A transaction at an undervalue will normally be an occasion of charge to inheritance tax as the undervalue will result in a reduction in the value of the transferor's estate. The main exception is if it can be shown both that the transaction was not intended to confer a gratuitous benefit on any person and that the transaction was either one made between unconnected persons or was 'such as might be expected to be made in a transaction at arm's length between persons not connected with each other' (*IHTA 1984, s 10(1)*). In *CIR v Spencer-Nairn (1991 STC 60)* a disposal was unwittingly made to a connected person, ie the vendor did not know the purchaser was a connected person. The vendor had taken advice on the value – albeit not from a valuer. The adviser, mistakenly as it turned out, had thought that a liability for improvements of £80,000 attached to the land and had advised a sale at around £100,000. It was held that in determining whether a transaction is such as might be expected to be paid in a transaction between unconnected persons the price was only one of the factors to be taken into account. In all the circumstances, particularly the taxpayer's mistaken belief that he was dealing with an unconnected person, the Commissioners were entitled to find that the exemption conferred by *s 10(1)* applied.

Special Returns

23.116 From 1 April 2012 HMRC can, by giving a notice, require a 'relevant data-holder' to provide information (within the categories set out below only) to assist with the efficient discharge of HMRC's tax functions. Failure to comply with such a notice attracts an initial penalty of £300 with further penalties if the default continues (*FA 2011, Sch 23, para* 30). The notice must specify the information required. It cannot relate to a period ending more than four years before the date of the notice. HMRC can, and normally do, specify the form in which the data is to be provided (*FA 2011, Sch 23, paras 1–4*). The list of relevant data-holders includes the following who are likely to be involved with property transactions:

(*a*) A person who carries on a business in connection with which payments are likely to be made for services provided by persons other than employees of the business (*FA 2011, Sch 23, para 9*). Such people can be asked to provide information relating to the payments (but not in relation to payments to any one person of under £500).

(*b*) A person who (in any capacity) is in receipt of money or value belonging to another (*FA 2011, Sch 23, para 13*). Such a person can be required to provide information relating to the money or value received, and the name and address of the beneficial owner.

(*c*) A lessee (or successor in title of a lessee), an occupier of land, a person having the use of land, and a person who (as agent) manages land or is in receipt of rent or other payments arising from land (*FA 2011, Sch 23, para 18*). Such a person can be required to provide information relating to the terms applying to the lease, occupation or use of land; information relating to any consideration given for the grant or assignment of the tenancy; and information relating to any person on whose behalf the land is managed or the payments received, including particulars of payments arising from the land.

(*FA 2011, Sch 23* and the *Data-gathering Powers (Relevant Data) Regulations 2012, SI 2012 No 847.*)

23.117 HMRC had similar powers prior to 1 April 2012. These were contained in *TMA 1970, s 19*. HMRC could use those powers only for the purpose of obtaining particulars of amounts taxable as profits of a property business or in respect of premiums, etc taxable as miscellaneous income by virtue of *CTA 2009, ss 217–226* (see **3.2–3.22** above). HMRC could not require a mortgagee to provide such information (*TMA 1970, s 19(3)*). Where a householder takes in lodgers HMRC could also require from him a return containing 'to the best of his belief' the name of every lodger or inmate resident in his house, and if any of those people has another ordinary place of residence at which they wish to be assessed to tax the address of that residence (*TMA 1970, s 14*). The provision applied only to a property which is a dwelling-house. These provisions were repealed when *FA 2011, Sch 23* was enacted.

Power to Enter Premises

23.118 HMRC can obtain a warrant to search, if necessary by force, any premises in which there is reasonable grounds for suspecting that there will be found evidence of any indictable offence, such as tax fraud (*Police and Criminal Evidence Act 1994, s 8* as applied by the *Police and Criminal Evidence Act (Application to Revenue and Customs) Order 2007, SI 2007 No 3175*). The search warrant must be granted by a Justice of the Peace. The officer authorised by the warrant to make the search can seize and remove anything found on the premises for which a search has been authorised (*PACE 1994, s 8(2)*). If so requested he must, however, provide the occupier of the premises (or any person having custody of the items taken before their seizure) with a list of the items taken (*PACE, s 21(1)*). This list does not have to be provided at the time of seizure nor within any particular time after seizure; it has to be provided within a reasonable time of its being requested. In *CIR & Another v Rossminster Ltd and Others (52 TC 106)* it seems clear that at the time of seizure under this provision HMRC simply stuffed into sacks every piece of paper they could lay their hands on and did not themselves know exactly what they had taken until some days after the raid.

23.119 It should particularly be noted that the power is to forcibly enter any premises in which it is thought evidence may be found. There is no need for HMRC to show that the owner or occupier of the premises is involved in, or knows of, the suspected fraud. The only limitation is that if HMRC raid a solicitor's office or barrister's chambers they cannot remove any document to which professional privilege attaches.

23.120 Up to 1 April 2010 HMRC also had specific powers to enter premises to value the premises or items in them. However such powers have been superseded by *FA 2008, Sch 36 para 10* which empowers an HMRC officer to enter business premises and inspect the premises, business assets and documents on the premises if the inspection is reasonably required for checking the occupier's tax position. Under this power HMRC cannot enter any part of the premises used solely as a dwelling. Business premises is defined as any premises (or part of any premises) that an HMRC officer has reason to believe are used in connection with a business (*FA 2008, Sch 36, para 10(3)*). There is no penalty for refusing access to HMRC unless they first obtain permission from the First-tier Tribunal, in which case there is a fine of £300 for refusing access (*FA 2008, Sch 36, para 39*). HMRC have somewhat wider powers in relation to VAT. They can also enter business premises of third parties if they have reason to believe that such premises are used in connection with the supply of taxable goods and that such goods are on those premises, or that the premises are used in connection with the acquisition of goods from other EU countries and such goods are on the premises, or the premises are used as a fiscal warehouse (*FA 2008, Sch 36, para 11*).

23.121 *Finance Act 2008, Sch 36* only gives HMRC power to come in and look around; they cannot open cupboards and drawers. To do that they need to obtain a search warrant.

Property Investment under the EIS Scheme

23.122 The Enterprise Investment Scheme legislation is designed to encourage individuals to invest in risk ventures. It does so by reducing the investor's tax liability by 30% of the amount invested (20% up to 2010/11) – up to a maximum of £1,000,000 p.a. (£500,000 up to 5 April 2012) – provided that certain conditions are met. The EIS scheme is not in general suitable for property investment. The company must be carrying on a trade and most trades with a substantial property element have been excluded from the scheme. Property dealing, property development, farming, market gardening, holding, managing or occupying woodlands, any other forestry activities or timber production, operating or managing hotels or comparable establishments or managing property used as a hotel or comparable establishment, operating or managing nursing homes or residential care homes, and managing property used as a nursing home or residential care home are all excluded from the relief. The operation of public houses is still acceptable, but if a pub incorporates residential accommodation it might be excluded as a comparable establishment to a hotel. It is not clear if property development includes housebuilding. The indications are that it does not, although most people would describe housebuilding as development.

23.123 Receiving royalties and licence fees is also an excluded activity. HMRC have pointed out that licences may be granted as a means of exploiting an interest in land. If the grant of the licence is merely incidental to an activity of supplying services (eg a cinema ticket confers a licence to occupy the seat but is primarily an opportunity to see the film) they accept that the exclusion does not apply. On the other hand making sports facilities available to the general public with no provision of services (a rare occurrence) would be an activity of receiving licence fees. Even if there is no provision of services, eg a fee to use a tennis court or a ticket to view an ancient monument, if continuous work is required to keep the property in a fit state for use by customers the fee may relate primarily to the cost of such work in which case it would not be regarded as a licence fee (Tax Bulletin 54, August 2001). HMRC also consider that the provision of self-storage warehousing facilities is an excluded activity as constituting leasing. They consider that such exclusion applies in any case where, subject to reasonable conditions imposed by the trader, the customer is free to use the property for the purpose for which it is intended (Tax Bulletin 54, August 2001).

23.124 EIS relief is withdrawn or reduced if the investor obtains a benefit from the company during the qualifying period. There are exceptions for business expenses for certain directors' fees, for dividends not exceeding a normal return on the capital invested, for rent for a property occupied by the company which does not exceed a reasonable and commercial return and for interest not exceeding a commercial rate (*ITA 2007, ss 167–169*).

Gifts of Real Property to Charity

23.125 A gift of land to charity attracts a tax deduction against total income for the year of assessment in which the gift is made (*ITA 2007, ss 431(1), 433; CTA 2010, ss 189, 203(1)(2)*). Where property is sold to a charity at an undervalue the amount of the undervalue is a gift for this purpose (*ITA 2007, s 434(2); CTA 2010, s 206(2)*).

23.126 The amount deductible is 'the relevant amount'. This is not necessarily the value of the asset gifted. It is the value of the 'net benefit' to the charity at the time of the gift (or immediately after the gift if that is a lower figure). In the case of a sale at an undervalue it is the amount, if any, by which the net benefit exceeds the consideration given. The net benefit is normally the market value of the land. However it is the market value reduced by the amount of the 'related liabilities' of the charity if the charity is (or becomes) subject to an obligation to any person (not necessarily the donor) and either:

(*a*) taking into account all the circumstances (including in particular the difference in the value of the net benefit to the charity if the obligation did not exist) it is reasonable to suppose that the property would not have been given to the charity in the absence of the obligations, or

(*b*) the obligation wholly or partly relates to (or is formed by reference to or is conditional on) the charity receiving the land or a related investment (*ITA 2007, ss 431, 434, 437* and *439*; *CTA 2010, ss 203–212*).

23.127 A 'related liability' is of course the liability of the charity under the above obligations. If an obligation is contingent and the contingency occurs the amount of the related liability is the amount actually payable in consequence of the occurrence of the contingency. If the contingency does not occur the amount of the liability is nil (*ITA 2007, ss 439, 440; CTA 2010, ss 211, 212*). It is unclear how this is expected to operate in practice. It seems unlikely that the government intend to give relief by reference to the market value of the property and claw back part of that relief if and when the obligation crystallises, but that appears to be the effect of the legislation. An 'obligation' includes any scheme, arrangement or understanding of any kind (whether or not legally enforceable) and a series of obligations (whether or not between the same parties) (*ITA 2007, s 439(7); CTA 2010, s 211(7)*).

23.128 A 'related investment' means any of:

(*a*) an asset of the same class or description as the qualifying investment (ie the land gifted);

(*b*) an asset derived from (or representing) the qualifying investment (in whole or in part and directly or indirectly); and

(*c*) an asset from which the qualifying investment is derived (or which it represents).

(*ITA 2007, s 439(6); CTA 2010, s 211(6)*.)

23.129 The charity is treated, for capital gains tax purposes, as acquiring the property at nil cost or, in the case of a gift at an undervalue, at the price it actually paid reduced by the relevant amount (or at nil cost if the relevant amount exceeded the price paid) (*TCGA 1992, s 257(2A)–(2C)*). This is not relevant in most cases as a charity is not liable to capital gains tax unless and until it ceases to be a charity. The sub-sections claw back the relief if that eventually crystallises.

23.130 The relief also extends to the incidental costs of making the disposal (as defined at **11.11**) (*ITA 2007, s 435; CTA 2010, s 207*). In the case of a sale at an undervalue, incidental costs are relieved only to the extent that the sale proceeds are below the vendor's capital gains tax base cost (*ITA 2007, s 434(1)*; *CTA 2010, s 206(1)*).

23.131 If the donor (or a connected person) receives any benefit in consequence of making the disposal, the amount eligible for relief is reduced by the value of that benefit (*ITA 2007, s 432(1)(2); CTA 2010, s 206(1)(2)*). The legislation gives no guidance as to how the benefit is to be calculated.

23.132 The relief applies only to a gift of UK land which is either a freehold or a lease for a term of years absolute (*ITA 2007, s 433(1); CTA 2010, s 205(1)*).

The gift must be of the whole of the donor's beneficial interest in the land (*ITA 2007, s 431(1); CTA 2010, s 203(1)*). If a person makes a qualifying gift of land and also gifts to the charity an easement, servitude right or privilege so far as benefiting that land, the gift of the easement, etc. also qualifies for relief (*ITA 2007, s 433(2); CTA 2010, s 205(2)(3)*). The gift of a qualifying lease while retaining the freehold reversion or head lease qualifies as it is regarded as a gift of the whole of the beneficial interest in the lease (*ITA 2007, s 433(4); CTA 2010, s 205(4)(6)*). An agreement to acquire a freehold interest and an agreement for lease are not qualifying interests in land (*ITA 2007, s 433(5); CTA 2010, s 205(5)*). Accordingly, if for example a person were to contract to buy land and passed the benefit of the contract to the charity when the land increased significantly in value between contract and completion, he could not obtain relief for the amount of the increase.

23.133 If the qualifying interest in land is held jointly by two or more people either as joint tenants or tenants in common, no relief is due unless all of the joint owners gift their interest to the charity (it has to be to the same charity) (*ITA 2007, s 442(2)(3); CTA 2010, s 214*). The reason for this restriction is not readily apparent. Curiously, if one of the joint owners is the charity itself it appears to prevent the relief applying completely. Where all of the joint owners do gift a property it appears that the relief does not need to be claimed in proportion to beneficial ownership but rather that the donors can – indeed, must, as it appears that no relief will be given if they do not – decide amongst themselves how the relief is to be split (*ITA 2007, s 442(3)–(7); CTA 2010, s 215*). The logic of this is also not readily apparent.

23.134 The relief must be claimed (*ITA 2007, s 445(1); CTA 2010, s 203*). The normal four-year time limit applies. A claim cannot however be made unless the charity has given the donor a certificate specifying the land concerned and the date of the gift and containing a statement that the charity has acquired the land (*ITA 2007, s 441; CTA 2010, s 213*).

23.135 The relief is withdrawn if at any time within the six years following the disposal (five years and ten months for income tax – ie 31 January following the fifth anniversary of the end of the tax year in which the gift was made) the donor or a connected person either:

(*a*) becomes entitled to any interest or right in relation to all or part of the land; or

(*b*) becomes party to an arrangement under which he enjoys some right in relation to all or part of the land

unless he pays full consideration in money or money's worth for such interest, right or enjoyment. In the case of a joint gift the relief is withdrawn from all the donors if one of them or a person connected with one of them receives the interest, right or enjoyment (*ITA 2007, s 444; CTA 2010, s 216*). There is no clawback of relief if the person inherits or becomes entitled to the interest or right (but not an arrangement under which he enjoys a right) on a death of someone else (*ITA 2007, s 444(6); CTA 2010, s 216(6)*).

Property Held by Investment-Regulated Pension Schemes

23.136 The taxation of pension schemes was completely recast from 6 April 2006. The new rules do not seek to limit the type of investments that can be made by a registered pension scheme, as the previous regime did, but instead impose tax charges where scheme investments are used to provide a benefit to members or their relatives. The one exception is investment in residential property by small pension schemes. This was introduced to prevent small pension schemes investing in overseas holiday homes for use by their members or investing in buy-to-let properties which would create unfair competition for such properties with potential owner occupiers.

23.137 A registered pension scheme is an investment-regulated scheme if one or more of its members (or persons related to the member) is (or has been) able directly or indirectly to direct, influence or advise on the manner of investment of any of the assets of the pension scheme (*FA 2004, Sch 29A, paras 1, 2*). An occupational pension scheme with over 50 members is investment-regulated only if 10% or more of the members have such control. Related persons are ignored in applying this test (*FA 2004, Sch 29A, para 2(1)(b)*). If a scheme with over 50 members has separate self-controlled sections and any member is able to exercise such control or influence over those assets which are linked to that member (ie are held specifically for the purpose of his pension or fund) then that part of the main fund is treated as an investment-regulated pension scheme. The Treasury can amend this rule by statutory instrument (*FA 2004, Sch 29A, para 3*). A related person of the member is someone who is a connected person of him within *ITA 2007, s 993*) or who acts on behalf of the member or of a connected person of the member (*FA 2004, Sch 29A, para 4*).

23.138 An investment-regulated pension scheme is treated as making an unauthorised payment to a member of the scheme if it acquires an interest in 'taxable property' (see **23.139**) and that interest is held as part of the assets relating to the member (*FA 2004, s 174A(1)*). It is similarly treated as making an unauthorised payment to the member if it carries out improvements to a 'taxable property' that it owns or if a property that it owns which is not a residential one is converted or adapted to become residential property (*FA 2004, s 174A(2)(3)*). An unauthorised payment to a member attracts a tax charge of 40%. It can also attract a 15% surcharge if the total unauthorised payments to the member in a 12-month period exceed 25% of the fund.

23.139 In addition the pension scheme is treated as making a scheme chargeable payment if it holds an interest in taxable property in a tax year (*FA 2004, s 185A(1)*). Such a payment attracts a 40% scheme sanction charge on the scheme administrator. If the interest in the taxable property is a direct one the charge is on the greater of the rent from the property and the deemed profit from the interest in the property during the year. This is 10% of the deemed market value of the property for the year, pro-rated on a daily basis if it was not held for the entire tax year (*FA 2004, ss 185A(3)(4), 185B*).

23.140 The deemed market value of a property is its market value when it first becomes scheme-held taxable property (which will be 6 April 2006 for existing properties) plus the cost of any improvements during the year, and increased by the increase in the RPI during the year (or the part of the year for which the property is owned by the pension scheme) (*FA 2004, s 185C(1)(2)*). In practice there are unlikely to be direct investments in any such properties owned at 6 April 2006 as small pension schemes were not allowed to invest in residential property. There can be indirect investments, such as a shareholding in a property company, though. For years after 2006/07 if the property was held at the end of the previous year the deemed market value is the value at the end of the previous year plus the cost of any improvements during the year increased in line with the RPI during the year (up to the date of sale if it is held for only part of the year) (*FA 2004, s 185C(1)(2)*). It will be seen that the deemed market value is actually cost plus improvements increased in line with increases in the RPI, not the value of the property.

23.141 If the interest in the property is leasehold, the deemed market value of the interest is the relevant rental value on the assumption that the lease was granted when the property first became scheme-held, the term of the lease is 50 years, a fully commercial rent is payable for the first five years of the term and thereafter the rent is reviewed on an upwards only basis (*FA 2004, s 185C(3)*). The relevant rental value is calculated in the same way as for SDLT (see **19.145**) (*FA 2004, Sch 29A, para 34*).

23.142 If the property interest is an indirect one through a vehicle wholly owned by the pension scheme (or by a 100% subsidiary of such a vehicle), the annual profit is again calculated by reference to the higher of the actual rent or 10% of the deemed market value of the property. For any other indirect holding the annual profit is calculated as a whole and then apportioned by reference to the extent of the pension scheme's interest in the vehicle (or indirectly in the underlying vehicle which owns the property). The apportionment is made on a just and reasonable basis by reference to whichever of share capital, voting rights, income, the amounts distributed on a distribution, the percentage of assets of the company on a winding up or the percentage of any particular asset in which the pension fund has an interest, gives the pension fund the greatest interest in the company (*FA 2004, ss 185D* and *Sch 29A, paras 41–43*).

23.143 If the extent of the scheme's interest in the property changes during a tax year the calculation must be done by reference to the average interest that the scheme had in the property during the year (*FA 2004, s 185D(3)*).

23.144 Where the property is held indirectly and the person who holds it directly has paid tax on the income that tax (or the part of it relating to the amount apportioned to the pension scheme), is allowed as a credit against the tax payable on the scheme sanction charge (*FA 2004, s 185E*).

23.145 An investment regulated pension scheme is also treated as having made a scheme chargeable payment (so as to trigger a scheme sanction charge) if it holds an interest in taxable property, during the tax year it realises a capital gain in respect of its taxable interest and that gain exceeds any CGT losses arising to the scheme in that tax year. The amount of the chargeable payment is of course that difference (*FA 2004, s 185F*). This provision overrides the normal pension fund exemption for chargeable gains (*TCGA 2004, s 271(1B)*). Where the interest is an indirect interest the gain made by the vehicle (or the appropriate part thereof) is apportioned through to the pension fund. The detailed rules are contained in *FA 2004, s 185E*. They are similar to those at **23.114** above.

23.146 If the pension scheme disposes of an interest in a vehicle through which it holds a taxable interest indirectly, it is deemed to realise a capital gain within *s 185F*. For this purpose the deemed disposal proceeds is the reduction in the market value of the taxable interest apportioned to the pension scheme in accordance with *FA 2004, Sch 29, paras 41–43* (see **23.114**) brought about by the disposal (*FA 2004, s 185G*). The deemed acquisition price is the total amount of unauthorised payments treated as made by the pension scheme in respect of the taxable interest up to the time of the disposal (less any part utilised against prior disposals of interests in the vehicle) (*FA 2004, s 185H*).

23.147 Again credit against the tax on the scheme sanction charge is allowed for tax paid by the property owning vehicle (or the part thereof attributable to the pension fund's interest) (*FA 2004, s 185I*).

23.148 The Treasury have power to make regulations to deal with the situation where the pension scheme is non-UK resident and the property is not situated in the UK (*FA 2004, s 273ZA*). The intention is to make the member liable for the scheme sanction charge in place of the scheme administrator.

Taxable Property

23.149 Property is taxable property if it is residential property or tangible moveable property (*FA 2004, Sch 29A, para 6*). The Treasury are given power by regulation to exclude specific descriptions of tangible moveable property from being taxable property (*FA 2004, Sch 29A, para 11*).

23.150 Residential property is defined as:

(*a*) a building that is used, or suitable for use, as a dwelling;

(*b*) land forming (or forming part of) the garden or grounds of such a dwelling which is used or intended for use in connection with the enjoyment of the building; or

(*c*) a beach hut,

whether in the UK or elsewhere (*FA 2004, Sch 29A, para 7(1)*).

23.151 For this purpose a building includes a structure and part of a building or structure (*FA 2004, Sch 29A, para 7(2)*). A building used or a home or other institution providing residential accommodation for children; a hall of residence for students; a home or other institution providing residential accommodation with personal care for persons in need of such care by reason of old age, disability, past or present dependence on alcohol or drugs or past or present mental disorder; a hospital or hospice; and a prison or similar establishment are not residential property (*FA 2004, Sch 29A, para 8(1)*). Where a building is used (or was last used) for such a purpose, or has never been used but is more suitable for use for such a purpose than any other, its suitability for use as a dwelling is ignored (*FA 2004, Sch 29A, para 8(2)*). The Treasury have power by regulation to amend these rules and to specify other descriptions of building that are, or are not, to be regarded as residential property (*FA 2004, Sch 29A, para 9*).

23.152 Residential property which is either:

(*a*) occupied by an employee (of anyone) who is required to occupy the property as a condition of his employment and who is not a member of the pension scheme or connected (within *ITA 2007, s 993*) with either a member or the employer (which presumably means the employer of the member not that of the occupier) or

(*b*) used in connection with business premises held as an investment of the pension scheme and is not occupied by a member of the scheme or a person connected with such a member

is excluded from being taxable property, ie it is a permissible investment for the pension scheme. If the property is unoccupied the exemption applies if its intended occupation meets one of the above tests (*FA 2004, Sch 29A, para 10*).

23.153 Even where a property is residential, there are a number of exclusions from it being taxable property (see **23.128** and **23.136**).

23.154 An investment-regulated pension scheme or any other person holds an interest in taxable property directly if under the law of any country or territory it, whether jointly, in common or alone:

(*a*) holds the property or any estate, interest, right or power in or over the property;

(*b*) has the right to use the property, or a description of property to which that property belongs, or to participate in arrangements relating to such use;

(*c*) has the benefit of any obligation, restriction or condition affecting the value of any estate, interest, right or power in or over the property; or

(*d*) it is entitled to receive payments determined by reference to the value of, or the income from, the property (*FA 2004, Sch 29A, para 14*).

23.155 There are a number of exceptions.

(*a*) A person does not held an interest in residential property consisting of hotel accommodation unless he holds (or has rights over) part only of the hotel accommodation (and, as a result, any person has a right to use or occupy that or any other part of the hotel), or he has a right to use (or participate in arrangements relating to the use of) part only of the hotel (or a description of property to which that part belongs) (*FA 2004, Sch 29A, para 14*).

(*b*) A person does not hold an interest in property by virtue of **23.116** if he is entitled to receive the payment by virtue of a life insurance policy, life annuity contract or capital redemption policy issued by an insurance company; the property does not constitute a linked asset and has not been appropriated by the insurance company to an internal linked fund; and the policy or contract does not entitle the person, either alone or together with one or more associated persons, to receive payments representing 10% or more of the market value of the property or the income from the property (or if the person is the pension scheme the policy or contract, either by itself or with one or more associated policies, does not entitle the pension scheme (or in the case of a non-occupational scheme any pension arrangement under the scheme) to do so) (*FA 2004, Sch 29A, para 15*).

23.156 Exception (*b*) above does not apply if the purpose or one of the purposes for which the person holds rights under the policy or contract is to enable a member of the pension scheme (or a person connected with him) to occupy or use the property (*FA 2004, Sch 29A, para 15(5)*). For the purpose of exception (*b*) an associated policy is one which entitles an associated person to receive payments determined by reference to the value of (or the income from) the policy (*FA 2004, Sch 29A, para 15(6)*). An associated person in relation to a scheme is any member of the scheme, any person connected with such a member, any arrangements (under that or another pension scheme) relating to a member of the pension scheme, any arrangements relating to a person connected with a member of the scheme and any associated pension scheme.

23.157 A pension scheme is associated with another scheme if members representing at least 10% of the value of one pension scheme or members of the other or connected with members of the other. The definition (but excluding an associated pension scheme) apply to determine associated persons in relation to an arrangement under a pension scheme but by reference only to the member of the scheme to which the arrangements relate rather than to all members of the scheme (*FA 2004, Sch 29A, para 30*). Capital redemption policy, internal linked fund, linked assets and life annuity are defined in *FA 2004, Sch 29A, para 15(8)(9)*.

23.158 An investment-regulated pension scheme (or some other person) holds an interest in property indirectly if (whether jointly, in common or alone) it holds an interest in the person who holds the interest in the property, or if it holds an interest in another person who holds the interest indirectly (ie, if it holds an interest in any entity in a chain of holdings the last one of which holds the interest) (*FA 2004, Sch 29A, para 16(1)*). A person holds an interest in another person if he holds an interest, right or power in or over that other person or he lends money to that other person to fund the acquisition by it of an interest in taxable property (unless the loan is an authorised employer loan made by a pension scheme to a sponsoring employer, the interest in the property is acquired by that employer so that it can be used for the purpose of its trade, profession or vocation and after the acquisition the property is not occupied or used by a member of the pension scheme or a person connected with such a member) (*FA 2004, Sch 29A, para 16(2)(3)*).

23.159 Some further rules apply to determine whether a person holds an interest in a company, a collective investment scheme or a trust. A person holds an interest in a company if:

(*a*) he has (or is entitled to acquire) share capital or voting rights in the company;

(*b*) he has (or is entitled to acquire) a right to receive or participate in distributions of the company;

(*c*) he is entitled to secure that income or assets (whether present or future) of the company will be applied directly or indirectly for his benefit; or (*d*) he has control of the company (within *CTA 2010, s 450*) either alone or together with other persons.

For this purpose a person must be treated as being entitled to do anything that he will become entitled to do at a later date (*FA 2004, Sch 29A, para 17*).

23.160 A person has an interest in a collective investment scheme (as defined in the *Financial Services and Markets Act 2000, s 235*) if he is a participant in that scheme (within *s 235(2)*) (*FA 2004, Sch 29A, para 18*).

23.161 A pension scheme holds an interest in a trust if either:

(*a*) it has a 'relevant interest' in the trust and the pension scheme, a member of the scheme or a person connected with such a member (within *CTA 2010, s 1122*) has made a payment to the trust on or after the acquisition of the interest (other than one made as part of an arm's length transaction by which property or a benefit is to be provided in return for the payment and which is made otherwise than to enable a member of the pension scheme or a connected person to occupy or use any property); or

(*b*) a member of the pension scheme (or a connected person) has a relevant interest in the trust and the pension scheme has made a payment to the trust (other than such an arm's length payment as is mentioned in (a)) on or after the acquisition of the interest.

(*FA 2004, Sch 29A, para 19(1)–(3),(7).*)

23.162 A person other than a pension scheme holds an interest in a trust (other than a unit trust scheme which is a collective investment scheme) if he has a relevant interest in the trust and he has made a payment to the trust (other than such an arm's length payment as is mentioned in **23.161**(*a*)) on or after the acquisition of the interest (*FA 2004, Sch 29A, para 19(4)(9)*).

23.163 A person has a relevant interest in a trust if any property which may at any time be comprised in the trust or any derived property) is, or will or may become, payable or applicable for his benefit in any circumstances whatsoever, or he enjoys a benefit deriving directly or indirectly from any property which is comprised in the trust or from any derived property (*FA 2004, Sch 29A, para 19(5)*). Derived property is income from the property – and any other property directly or indirectly representing proceeds of, or income from, the property (*FA 2004, Sch 29A, para 19(6)*).

23.164 There are a number of exceptions. Subject to the detailed rules set out below a pension scheme does not hold an interest in property indirectly if it holds it through a vehicle (the person through whom it holds the interest in property) which either:

(*a*) carries on trading activities

(*b*) is a REIT (see **7.38**)

(*c*) is a multiple property company (see **23.58**)

holds the interest in the property directly by virtue of *para 14(3)* (receipt of payments determined by reference to value of, or income from, property – see **23.143**(d). (*FA 2004, Sch 29A, para 20*).

23.165 The exception for trading companies (or other vehicles) applies where the company's main activity is the carrying on of a trade, profession or vocation, the pension scheme does not, whether alone or together with one or more associated persons control the company (within *CTA 2010, s 450*), and neither a member of the pension scheme nor a person connected with such a member is a controlling director of it (one who, on his own or with one or more associates or associated persons, is the beneficial owner of, or able to control directly or indirectly, 20% or more of the ordinary share capital of the company). A pension scheme (or an arrangement under a pension scheme) has control of a vehicle if it would do so were it a person (*FA 2004, Sch 29A, para 21*).

23.166 The exception for an investment in a REIT applies if the vehicle is a REIT (or a member of a group to which the REIT legislation applies), and the purpose or one of the purposes for which the pension scheme holds the interest in the REIT is not to enable a member of the pension scheme, or a connected person (within *ITA 2007, s 993*), to occupy or use the property (*FA 2004, Sch 29A, para 22*).

23.167 The exception for a multiple property company applies if:

(*a*) either the total value of the assets held directly by the company (or other vehicle) is at least £1 million or the vehicle holds directly at least three assets which consist of an interest in residential property, and in either case no interest in taxable property held by the company has a value in excess of 40% of the total value of the assets held directly by the vehicle;

(*b*) if the vehicle is a company it is not a close company (and if it is non-UK resident would not be close if it were resident in the UK;

(*c*) the vehicle does not have as its main purpose or one of its main purposes, the direct or indirect holding of an animal or animals used for sporting purposes (such as a racehorse syndicate);

(*d*) the pension scheme must not hold its interest in the vehicle for the purpose of enabling a member of the scheme or a connected person (within *CTA 2010, s 1122*) to occupy or use the property; and (*e*) the pension scheme (or any arrangement under the scheme) must not, either alone or together with one or more associated persons (as defined at **23.156**), directly or indirectly hold an interest in the vehicle consisting of either:

   (i) 10% or more of the share capital or issued share capital of the vehicle,

   (ii) 10% or more of the voting rights in the vehicle,

   (iii) a right to receive 10% or more of the income of the vehicle,

   (iv) such interest in the vehicle as gives an entitlement to 10% or more of the amounts distributed on a distribution by the vehicle,

   (v) such interest in the vehicle as gives an entitlement to 10% or more of the assets of the vehicle on a winding up (or in any other circumstances), or

   (vi) such interest in the vehicle as gives rise to income or gains from a specific property.

(*FA 2004, Sch 29A, paras 23(1)–(4), 24.*)

23.168 For the purpose of **23.167**(*a*) assets must be valued in accordance with UK GAAP or IAS, no account is to be taken of liabilities secured against (or otherwise relating to) assets, either generally or specifically, and where GAAP offers a choice of valuation between cost and fair value, fair value must be used (*FA 2004, Sch 29A, para 23(5)*). The Treasury have power by statutory instrument to increase the £1 million and 40% figures (*FA 2004, Sch 29A, para 23(6)*).

Amount and Timing of Unauthorised Payment

23.169 If the unauthorised payment is the acquisition of an interest in taxable property it is treated as made when the property is acquired. The amount of the payment is the consideration paid plus any fees and costs incurred in connection with the acquisition (*FA 2004, Sch 29A, para 32 (2),(3)*).

23.170 If the pension scheme acquires an interest in taxable property which is an estate, interest, right or power in or over land in the UK or the benefit of an obligation, restriction or condition affecting such an estate, it is acquired before the pension scheme (or some other person) comes to hold the interest directly and the whole or part of the consideration is something other than rent, then the following SDLT rules apply for determining the amount of the consideration: *FA 2003, Sch 4, paras 2–8* and *9–16* (chargeable consideration – see **19.17** onwards), *s 51* (contingent, uncertain or unascertained consideration – see

19.138) and *s 52* (annuities etc – see **19.143**). The Treasury can, by regulation, modify these rules (*FA 2004, Sch 29A, para 33*). If in the case of such an acquisition the whole or part of the consideration is rent the consideration (or that part of it) must be determined in accordance with *FA 2003, Sch 5, paras 2(4)(a), 3* and *8* (leases – see **19.145** onwards), *Sch 17A, paras 2, 5–7A, 9* and *16* (further provisions relating to leases – see **19.147** onwards) in addition to the above SDLT provisions. The Treasury have power to amend these provisions also (*FA 2004, Sch 29A, paras 34*).

23.171 If the taxable interest is acquired at an undervalue and tax relief under *FA 2004, ss 188* (tax relief for pension contributions by an individual) or *199* (tax relief for pension contributions by an employer) is available in respect of the transfer of the interest, the consideration for the acquisition is the market value at the date of acquisition (or if the property is a lease at a rent) the consideration that would have been treated as arising under **23.141** if it had been assigned at that time (*FA 2004, Sch 29A, para 35*).

23.172 If the interest in taxable property is acquired indirectly (because the pension scheme or another person comes to hold an interest in a company or in some other person who directly or indirectly holds the interest in the taxable property), the amount of the unauthorised payment is the market value of the interest in the property held by the person who owns it at the date the pension fund acquires its interest in the vehicle. If the interest in a property is a lease at a rent the rules in **23.141** apply to determine the consideration (*FA 2004, Sch 29A, para 32(5)*). If the acquisition is a deemed acquisition under *Sch 29A, paras 27* or *28* it is of course the market value at the date the property is deemed to be acquired (*FA 2004, Sch 29A, para 32(6)*). The Treasury have power by regulation to lay down rules to determine the amount of the consideration (*FA 2004, Sch 29A, para 36*).

23.173 The Treasury also have power by regulation to provide for a further unauthorised payment to arise in cases where the amount of the consideration for the acquisition was determined on the basis of a reasonable estimate and the actual consideration turns out to be higher or, in the case of a lease, there is a variation in the rent payable, or the consideration for the acquisition was based on an assumption about the term of a lease and the lease continues beyond the end of that assumed term (*FA 2004, Sch 29A, para 37*).

23.174 If the unauthorised payment is improvements to taxable property the amount is the cost of the improvement works and it is deemed to arise each time a payment is made in connection with such works.

23.175 If the unauthorised payment is the conversion or adaptation of a non-residential property into a residential one it is treated as made on the earlier of the substantial completion of the works of conversion or adaptation or the disposal of the interest in the property by the pension fund. If the property becomes residential property more than three years from the date of the first payment in connection with those works the unauthorised payment is instead treated as made when the property becomes residential property (*FA 2004, Sch 29A, para 39(1)–(3)*). If the works began within 12 months of the acquisition of the property the taxable amount is the consideration for the acquisition of the interest see **23.169–23.172**) (including the acquisition costs) plus 'the development costs', ie the total cost of the conversion or adaptation works up to the time the unauthorised payment is treated as made (*FA 2004, Sch 29A, para 39(4)(7)*). It is not clear if 'works' is limited to construction costs or include professional fees for obtaining planning consent and/or architects fees for designing and supervising the alterations. The former is a more natural meaning of 'works' but the latter seems more logical. If the conversion begins more than 12 months after the acquisition of the interest in the property the amount of the unauthorised payment is the market value of the interest in the property held by the pension fund (or person who holds it) at the date the work begins (valuing a lease in accordance with **23.141**) plus the development costs (*FA 2004, Sch 29A, para 39(5)–(7)*).

23.176 If, at the time the unauthorised payment is treated as made, part of the cost is contingent on an uncertain future event the development costs must be calculated on the basis that it will have to be paid (*FA 2004, Sch 29A, para 39(8)*). If at that time the amount of the payment depends on uncertain future events or cannot be ascertained a reasonable estimate must be made (*FA 2004, Sch 29A, para 39(9)*). In such a case a further unauthorised payment equal to the difference is treated as made when the amount is ascertained if the estimate turns out to be too low (*FA 2004, Sch 29A para 40*). At least that is the intention. The legislation actually refers to *para 39(8)* instead of *39(9)* so it may be ineffective.

23.177 The whole of the amount ascertained above is taxable where the taxable interest is held by the pension fund itself, by a vehicle wholly owned by the pension fund or by a chain of wholly owned vehicles. Where the property interest is held by a vehicle that is not wholly owned then only the proportion what would otherwise have been the unauthorised payment that is attributable to the pension scheme's interest in the property constitutes the unauthorised payment (*FA 2004, Sch 29A, para 41(1)–(6)*). If the interest is held through more than one chain of vehicles the pension fund's overall interest is of course the aggregate of its interests held through each chain (*FA 2004, Sch 29A, para 41(7)*). The amount of the pension fund's interest is calculated in accordance with *FA 2004, Sch 29A, paras 41–43*. These rules are considered at **23.114**.

23.178 Where a pension fund is treated as acquiring an interest in taxable property by virtue of *Sch 29A, para 28* (increase in extent of interest in vehicle

– see **23.172**) the amount of the unauthorised payment is the difference in what would have been an unauthorised payment had immediately before and immediately after the increase, ie it is the increase in the value of the pension fund's interest, not the value of the extra interest acquired (*FA 2004, Sch 29A, para 44*).

23.179 If the taxable property interest is held by the pension scheme for the purposes of arrangements under the scheme relating to more than one member, the unauthorised payment is apportioned on a just and reasonable basis to determine the amount taxable on each (*FA 2004, Sch 29A, para 45*).

23.180 HMRC are given power by regulation to make provision for a transfer member of a relevant non-UK scheme (a scheme that has entered into an agreement with HMRC to comply with certain information requirements and for the scheme administrator to accept liability to scheme sanction charges) to be liable to the unauthorised payment charge in the same or similar circumstances to which a member of a registered pension scheme would have been so liable or the scheme administrator of a registered pension scheme would be liable to a scheme sanction charge (*FA 2004, s 7A*).

Transitional Provisions

23.181 If the pension scheme held an interest in taxable property at 6 April 2006 (and was not prohibited from holding it by the legislation in force at that time) none of the above provisions apply to the property. This applies both to direct and indirect holdings. It also applies to an interest acquired after 6 April 2006 in pursuance of a contract entered into before that date, provided that the pension scheme was not prohibited from holding the interest in the property (or the interest in the vehicle through which that interest was held) immediately before 6 April 2006 (*FA 2004, Sch 36, para 37A*).

23.182 The exemption is lost if after 6 April 2006 either there is a change in the occupation or use of the property which would have made it a prohibited investment had it occurred before that date, improvement works had begun, or there is a change in the pension scheme's interest in the vehicle which owns the property interest which would have made it a prohibited investment had the change occurred before 6 April 2006. In such circumstances the exemption is only from the date of the change in occupation or use, the substantial completion of the improvement works, or the change in the pension fund's interest. The pension fund (or owner of the interest) is treated as acquiring the property on the date of that trigger event (*FA 2004, Sch 36, para 37B(1)–(6)*). The amount of the unauthorised payment is the market value of the interest in the property at the date of the trigger event (applying **23.141** above in relation to rent) (*FA 2004, Sch 36, para 37B(7)*).

23.183 Where a deemed scheme chargeable payment arises under *FA 2004, s 185F* the pension scheme is treated as having acquired its interest at 6 April 2006 for the purpose of applying the special rules in *s 185G* (*FA 2004, Sch 36, para 37B(8)*).

23.184 For the purpose of these provisions improvement works are works which naturally improve the property and which are not carried out for the purpose of complying with a statutory requirement (or one imposed by a government department, a statutory body or a person holding a statutory office); a property is materially improved only if the market value on the date the works are substantially completed exceeds what would have been its market value on that date in the absence of such works by over 20%; and improvement works are treated as begun before 6 April 2006 only if a binding contract for such works was entered into before that date or a substantial amount (not defined) of the works had been carried out before that date (*FA 2004, Sch 36, para 37B(9)–(12)*).

23.185 If the works were not completed by 6 April 2006 then *para 37B* (see **23.182**) applied as if the works were begun on or after that date (*FA 2004, Sch 36, para 37D*). If immediately before 6 April 2006 the pension scheme was a retirement benefit scheme but it was not approved by HMRC until after 5 December 2005, the exemption under *para 37A* again did not apply and *para 37C (3)–(5)* applied instead (*FA 2004, Sch 36, para 37E*). 5 December 2005 is the date of the pre-budget report in which the *FA 2006* changes were announced.

23.186 If a pension scheme held the interest in taxable property at 6 April 2006 and immediately before that time it was prohibited from holding the investment (whether it was direct or indirect) it is treated as acquiring the interest in the property at 6 April 2006 (*FA 2004, Sch 36, para 37C(1)–(3)*). This triggered an unauthorised payment on 6 April 2006 the amount of which was the market value (or appropriate proportion of such value) on that date of the interest in the property held by the person who held it directly (applying the rules in **23.141** in the case of a lease where rent is payable) (*FA 2004, Sch 36, para 37C(4)*). Similarly the pension scheme was treated having acquired the property at its market value on 6 April 2006 for the purpose of *FA 2004, s 185G* (see **23.146**).

23.187 None of the above unauthorised payment provisions apply where after 5 April 2006 an investment-regulated pension scheme is treated as acquiring an interest in residential property because a vehicle in which it held an interest at 6 April 2006 does so; immediately before that date the pension scheme was not prohibited from holding the interest in the vehicle; the business of the vehicle involved the holding and letting of residential property (and it held directly five or more assets consisting of interests in residential property for the purposes of that business); at no time between 6 April 2006 and the acquisition by the pension fund of its interest in the post 6 April 2006 property had the fund's interest in the vehicle been such that it would have been prohibited from holding it prior to 6 April 2006; the vehicle acquires the post 6 April 2006 property for the purpose of its property rental business; and after its acquisition the property is not occupied or used by a member of the pension scheme or a person connected with such a member (within *CTA 2010, s 1122*) (*FA 2004, Sch 36, para 37H*).

23.188 However if after 6 April 2006 there is either a change in the pension fund's interest in the vehicle such that the fund would have been prohibited from holding the interest had it occurred prior to 6 April 2006, the property ceases to be used for the purpose of the vehicle's property rental business or the property is occupied or used by a member of the pension scheme or a connected person, the pension scheme is treated for the purpose of the taxable property provisions as acquiring its interest in the property on the date of that trigger event (*FA 2004, Sch 36, para 37I(1)–(4)*). The amount of the unauthorised payment is the appropriate proportion of the value of the property on the date of the trigger event (applying **23.141** in the case of a lease at a rent) (*FA 2004, Sch 36, para 37I(5)*).

2011 Style Enterprise Zones

23.189 In his 2011 Budget the Chancellor announced the setting up of a number of 'enterprise zones'. These do not currently attract any tax benefits other than a reduction in council tax. The location of the zones is shown in Appendix 2. However the zones are closely defined and reference to the relevant detailed designation is needed if one wishes to locate in such a zone. It will be seen that a number of further zones were added by the *Capital Allowances (Designated Assisted Areas) Order 2014 (SI 2014 No 3183)* on 23 December 2014. This treats the new designated areas as having been designated on 1 April 2012. The *Capital Allowances (Designated Assisted Areas (Order) 2015 (SI 2015 No 2047)* added 25 further zones, most with effect from 1 April 2012 but one with effect from 1 April 2015. The benefits are:

(*a*) a 100% business rate discount of up to £275,000 over a five-year period for those businesses that move into the zone during the life of the current parliament (ie up to May 2015);

(*b*) the local authority will share the growth in business rates within the zone for 25 years, to reinvest locally;

(*c*) the government will help to develop 'radically simplified planning approaches' for the zone; and (*d*) the government will support the roll out of superfast broadband throughout the zone (but mainly by 'guaranteeing the most supportive regulatory environment').

23.190 The government will also consider, on a zone-by-zone basis:

(i) enhanced capital allowances in place of the business rate discount in zones where there is a strong focus on manufacturing;

(ii) Tax Increment Finance to support the long-term viability of the area; and

(iii) UK Trade & Investment (UKTI) support for investment or trade opportunities within the zone.

Finance Act 2012, Sch 11 enacts (*i*). It inserts *CAA 2001, ss 45K–45N* which grant a first-year allowance for qualifying expenditure incurred in a designated assisted area within an enterprise zone, initially during the five years from 1 April 2012 to 31 March 2017. From 15 September 2016 the relief applies to expenditure incurred in the eight years from the date on which the area is (or is treated as) designated as an enterprise zone (*FA 2016, s 69*). As designation has sometimes been backdated this appears to mean that where that happens the eight years runs from that prior date, not from the date of the designation. It is a very restrictive relief. It applies only for corporation tax and only to new investment. The Treasury have power to extend the qualifying period (*CAA 2001, s 45K(1A)* inserted by *FA 2014, s 64*).

Property Authorised Investment Funds

23.191 A property authorised investment funds (PAIF) is an open-ended investment company which meets certain requirements and has given notice to HMRC that it wants to come within the PAIF regime (*Authorised Investment Funds (Tax) Regulations 2006 (SI 2006 No 964), reg 69D*). The company's investment objectives must be to carry on property investment business and to manage cash raised from investors for investment in the property investment business (*reg 69E*). Property investment business for this purpose means both direct investment in rental properties and owning shares in UK REITs (see **Chapter 7**) or an overseas listed property company or unit trust scheme that is not within the charge to corporation tax and is equivalent to a UK REIT in the jurisdiction in which it is incorporated or carries on business (*reg 69F*). A PAIF cannot carry on a trade (*reg 94(5)*) or be a member of a group of companies (*reg 107*). No body corporate must own (directly or indirectly) 10% or more of the net asset value of the PAIF, and any company that invests in it must give an undertaking that it holds its shares as beneficial owner and that it will not acquire more than 10% of the PAIF (*reg 69K*). A PAIF must not borrow money on terms which tie the interest to either the results of the PAIF's business or the value of its assets, or require interest to be paid that exceeds a reasonable commercial rate on the money lent, or require a repayment of an amount that exceeds the money lent (unless it is reasonably comparable with the amounts generally repayable under the terms of issue of securities issued on a recognised stock exchange). At least 60% of the fund's income in the accounting period must be derived from its property investment business (but excluding dividends from UK REITs) and at the end of the accounting period at least 60% of the assets must be assets of the property investment business.

23.192 Like a REIT, a PAIF is exempt from corporation tax on the profits of its property investment business (*reg 69Y*). However the investor is taxed on any distribution out of the tax exempt part of the fund (and his share of any REIT dividend paid out of its tax exempt funds) as if it were income of a UK property business (*reg 69Z18*). The non-exempt income is likely to be interest received or dividend income. The PAIF is taxed on the interest but can deduct dividends paid out of such income, with the dividend being treated as investment income in the hands of the recipient (*regs 69Z16, 69Z19*). The PAIF must deduct income tax at source at the basic rate both from dividends paid out of its exempt property business and dividends paid out of investment income (except where a REIT would not need to deduct tax) (*reg 69Z22*). The concept is to place the investor as near as possible in the same tax position as if he had invested directly into property. The detailed rules can be found in the *Authorised Investment Funds (Tax) Regulations 2006 (SI 2006, No 964)* (*regs 69A–69Z41*). They are not considered here as they are not of general interest. They broadly follow the REIT rules.

Goodwill and Trade-Related Property

23.193 When valuing a property, the valuation is of the property alone; it does not reflect the value of any business carried on from the property. However in HMRC's view, the position is different with trade-related property, ie buildings and other structures that are purpose built (or altered) for a specific type of business activity. Trade-related properties include hotels, theatres, petrol stations, nursing homes, hospitals, bars, clubs and pubs, and many other types of healthcare and leisure properties. As a trade-related property can normally only be used for a particular activity, the value of the property interest is normally intrinsically linked to the trading potential for that activity in that location, unless some alternative use is more valuable.

23.194 HMRC consider that the value of a trade-related property is the price that would be paid by a reasonably efficient economic operator who wishes to carry on the business for which the property is used. They base this view on the guidance note issued to its members by the Royal Institution of Chartered

Surveyors which says that surveyors should value the economic entity rather than the property. Whilst this makes sense in the context that a sale of such properties normally takes place only as part of a sale of the business, it is not wholly clear that HMRC are correct in equating the value of the economic entity – broadly the value of the property and the business assuming that the property is fitted out and that the business can be operated from it – with the value of the property. The issue is significant in the context of the corporation tax intellectual property rules which allow a deduction (normally spread over a period) for goodwill, but not for the value of a property – so the HMRC approach denies relief for what most accountants would regard as goodwill – and for stamp duty land tax which is charged on property values but not on goodwill, so the HMRC approach effectively charges it on goodwill in trade-related properties.

23.195 It seems clear that anyone who wishes to challenge HMRC's view will have to pursue an appeal before the Tribunal – and probably be prepared for HMRC to appeal if the taxpayer wins. The HMRC approach does not mean that there cannot be any goodwill separate from the property, but that in most cases there is unlikely to be any. If the business actually carried on generates greater profits than the valuer assesses would be generated by a reasonably competent economic operator, ie someone with expertise in the business concerned, the capitalised value of excess is attributable to goodwill. When purchasing a trade-related property, it is accordingly sensible to instruct a valuer to consider whether the profits on which the purchase price is based simply reflect what could be generated by a reasonably efficient economic operator or whether part of the purchase price represents the goodwill in the exceptional expertise of the vendor.

Contributions to Flood and Coastal Erosion Risk Management Projects

23.196 Relief is allowed as a trading expense or a property business expense (as the case may be) for qualifying contributions paid or provided after 31 December 2014 to a qualifying flood or coastal erosion risk management project (if a deduction would not otherwise be allowed) (*ITTOIA 2005, ss 86A(1)(3), 272; CTA 2009, ss 86A(1)(3), 210, 124A*). A qualifying flood or coastal erosion risk management project (ie one within the *Flood and Water Management Act 2010, ss 1–3*) is one where either an English risk management authority (as defined in *s 6(14)* of the Act has applied to the Environment Agency for a grant under *s 16* of that Act in order to fund the project, or the Environment Agency has itself decided to carry out the project, and the Environment Agency has granted funding to the project (*ITTOIA 2005, s 86B(2); CTA 2009, s 86B(2)*). A contribution is a qualifying one if it is made for the purpose of the project and under an agreement between the person making the contribution and the applicable authority under that Act (or the Environment Agency) or between those two persons and others (*ITTOIA 2005, s 86B(3)(4), CTA 2009, s 86B(3)(4)*). A contribution can be a sum of money or the provision of services (*ITTOIA 2005, s 86B(3), CTA 2009, s 86B(5)*).

23.197 A deduction can be claimed even if the expenditure qualifies for capital allowances (*ITTOIA 2005, s 86A(2); CTA 2009, s 86A(2)*).

23.198 However no deduction is due if the contributor receives a disqualifying benefit (or is entitled to receive such a benefit), either from the carrying out of the project itself or from any person (*ITTOIA 2005, s 86A(4)(5); CTA 2009, s 86A(4)(5)*). A disqualifying benefit is a benefit consisting of money or other property, other than:

(*a*) a refund of the contribution (if it is money);

(*b*) compensation for the contribution (if it is services);

(*c*) a structure, road, path, pipes earthwork, or plant or machinery (or an addition to a structure, etc) that is for (or is to be used for) the purposes of flood or coastal erosion risk management and is put in place in carrying out the project; or

(*d*) land (or a right over land), plant or machinery that is to be used in the realisation of the project for the purposes of the project

(*ITTOIA 2005, s 86A(8); CTA 2009, s 86A(8)*.)

23.199 If a deduction is allowed under this provision and the contributor or a connected person receives a refund of any part of the contribution (or compensation for any part if the contribution is the provision of services) the amount is obviously income on the date of receipt (or as a post-cessation receipt if the trade has ceased) (*ITTOIA 2005, s 86A(6)(7); CTA 2009, s 86A(6)(7)*).

Business Investment Relief

23.200 An individual who is resident but not domiciled in the UK can elect to be taxed in relation to overseas income and capital gains on a remittance basis (*ITA 2007, s 809B*). If he does so, he is taxed only when the income or gain is brought into the UK. From 6 April 2017 those resident in the UK for 15 out of the previous 20 tax years (and those born in the UK with a UK domicile of origin) cannot use the remittance basis for income and gains arising in earlier years that have not yet attracted UK tax. The remittance basis rules are widely drawn and treat amounts indirectly used in the UK or remitted by certain related persons as if they had been remitted by the taxpayer. There are however some exceptions and reliefs.

23.201 One of those is business investment relief. This enables overseas money to be remitted temporarily to the UK to invest in a UK company (the target company). The company needs to be an eligible trading company (or its holding company). The significance of this for property is that an eligible trading company is defined as a private limited company that carries on one or more commercial trades (or is preparing to do so within the next two years) and for which carrying on commercial trades is all, or substantially all, of what is does (or of what it is reasonably expected to do once it begins trading) (*ITA 2007, s 809VD(1), (2)*). A commercial trade is one conducted on a commercial basis and with a view to the realisation of profit (*ITA 2007, s 809VE(3)*). A trade is defined to include 'anything that is treated for corporation tax purposes as if it were a trade, and a business carried on for generating income from land (as defined in *CTA 2009, s 207*)' (*ITA 2007, s 809VE(2)*). *Section 207* is the charging provision for property businesses. Accordingly the provision allows overseas money to be used to invest temporarily in a company that carries on either a property dealing trade or a property investment business.

23.202 There are some other conditions that must be met. The investment must be made within 45 days of the money being brought into the UK (*ITA 2007, s 809VB*). The investment must be either in shares in, or in a loan (secured or unsecured) to, the company (*ITA 2007, s 809VC*). The individual (and certain related persons) must not obtain or expect to obtain any 'related benefit', ie a benefit directly or indirectly attributable to the making of the investment or something that it is reasonable to assume would not be available in the absence of the investment. Something provided in the ordinary course of business and on arm's length terms is not a benefit (*ITA 2007, s 809VF*). If the shares are sold or the loan is repaid (in whole or in part) the money (up to the amount of the initial investment) has to be sent overseas again within 45 days of the sale (or of certain other disqualifying events) (*ITA 2007, s 809VG*).

23.203 There is no maximum shareholding. The non-resident could own the whole company. The capital gain on disposal and any interest or dividends from the investment are, of course, taxable in the UK. Those income and gains do not need to be sent overseas. As they are taxable here, they can be used here.

Appendix 1

Meaning of 'Connected Persons'

ITA 2007, s 993

(1) This section has effect for the purposes of the provisions of the Income Tax Acts which apply this section.

(2) An individual ('A') is connected with another individual ('B') if—

(*a*) A is B's spouse or civil partner,

(*b*) A is a relative of B,

(*c*) A is the spouse or civil partner of a relative of B,

(*d*) A is a relative of B's spouse or civil partner, or

(*e*) A is the spouse or civil partner of a relative of B's spouse or civil partner.

(3) A person, in the capacity as trustee of a settlement, is connected with—

(*a*) any individual who is a settlor in relation to the settlement,

(*b*) any person connected with such an individual,

(*c*) any close company whose participators include the trustees of the settlement,

(*d*) any non-UK resident company which, if it were UK resident, would be a close company whose participators include the trustees of the settlement,

(*e*) any body corporate controlled (within the meaning of section 995) by a company within paragraph (c) or (d),

(*f*) if the settlement is the principal settlement in relation to one or more sub-fund settlements, a person in the capacity as trustee of such a sub-fund settlement, and

(*g*) if the settlement is a sub-fund settlement in relation to a principal settlement, a person in the capacity as trustee of any other sub-fund settlements in relation to the principal settlement.

(4) A person who is a partner in a partnership is connected with—

(*a*) any partner in the partnership,

(*b*) the spouse or civil partner of any individual who is a partner in the partnership, and

(*c*) a relative of any individual who is a partner in the partnership.

But this subsection does not apply in relation to acquisitions or disposals of assets of the partnership pursuant to genuine commercial arrangements.

(5) A company is connected with another company if—

(*a*) the same person has control of both companies,

(*b*) a person ('A') has control of one company and persons connected with A have control of the other company,

(*c*) A has control of one company and A together with persons connected with A have control of the other company, or

(*d*) a group of two or more persons has control of both companies and the groups either consist of the same persons or could be so regarded if (in one or more cases) a member of either group were replaced by a person with whom the member is connected.

(6) A company is connected with another person ('A') if—

(*a*) A has control of the company, or

(*b*) A together with persons connected with A have control of the company.

(7) In relation to a company, any two or more persons acting together to secure or exercise control of the company are connected with—

(*a*) one another, and

(*b*) any person acting on the directions of any of them to secure or exercise control of the company.

[For the purpose of (2) above a relative means a brother or sister, an ancestor, or a lineal descendant (ITA 2007, s 994(1))]

CTA 2010, s 1122

Section 1122 is identical to section 993 subject to

(1) The ordering of the sub-paragraphs is different as section 1122 deals with connected companies before connected individuals.

Section 993	*Section 1122*
(2)	(5)
(3)	(6)
(4)	(7) & (8)
(5)	(2)
(6)	(3)
(7)	(4)

(2) The reference to ITA 2007, s 995 in s 993(3)(e) is replaced by a reference to CTA 2010, s 1124 in s 1122(6)(e).

TCGA 1992, s 286

The persons treated as associated for the purpose of s 286 are identical to those in s 993, although the wording is slightly different. The only difference that might be significant is that the proviso to para (4) of s 286 refers to bona fide commercial arrangements in place of genuine commercial arrangements, although the difference is probably simply due to more modern drafting.

Appendix 2

Enterprise Zones

1981 Series Enterprise Zones

An 'enterprise zone' was an area designated as such by the Secretary of State (or Department of the Environment for Northern Ireland). There are no zones still currently in force. Designation was for a ten-year period.

Former zones where the ten-year period has expired are set out below

Arbroath, see Tayside (Arbroath)

Belfast (expired 20 October 1991, *SR 1981 No 309*)

Chatham, see North West Kent

Clydebank (expired 2 August 1991, *SI 1981 No 975*)

Corby (expired 21 June 1991, *SI 1981 No 764*)

Dearne Valley (6 zones) (expired 2 November 2005, *SI 1995 No 2624*)

Delyn (expired 20 July 1993, *SI 1983 No 896*)

Dudley (expired 9 July 1991, *SI 1981 No 852*)

Dudley (Round Oak) (expired 3 October 1994, *SI 1984 No 1403*)

Dundee, see Tayside (Dundee)

East Durham (6 zones) (expired 29 November 2005, *SI 1995 No 2812*)

East Midlands (Ashfield) (expired 20 November 2005, *SI 1995 No 2758*)

East Midlands (Bassetlaw) (expired 15 November 2005, *SI 1995 No 2738*)

East Midlands (North East Derbyshire) (3 zones) (expired 2 November 1995, *SI 1995 No 2625*)

Flixborough, see Glanford (Flixborough)

Gateshead (expired 24 August 1991, *SI 1981 No 1070*)

Glanford (Flixborough) (expired 12 April 1994, *SI 1984 No 347*)

Glasgow (expired 17 August 1991, *SI 1981 No 1069*)

Hartlepool (expired 22 October 1991, *SI 1981 No 1378*)

Inverclyde (expired 28 February 1999, *SI 1989 No 145*)

Invergordon (expired 6 October 1993, *SI 1983 No 1359*)

Isle of Dogs (expired 25 April 1992, *SI 1982 No 462*)

Kent (NW) (expired 30 October 1993, *SI 1983 No 1452*)

Lanarkshire (Hamilton) (expired 31 January 2003)

Lanarkshire (Monklands) (expired 31 January 2003)

Lanarkshire (Motherwell) (expired 31 January 2003)

Lancashire (NE) (expired 6 December 1993, *SI 1983 No 1639*)

Liverpool (Speke) (expired 24 August 1991, *SI 1981 No 1072*)

London, see Isle of Dogs

Londonderry (expired 12 September 1993, *SR 1983 No 226*)

Lower Swansea Valley (expired 10 June 1991, *SI 1981 No 757*)

Lower Swansea Valley (No 2) (expired 6 March 1995, *SI 1985 No 137*)

Middlesbrough (Britannia) (expired 7 November 1993, *SI 1983 No 1473*)

Milford Haven Waterway (North Shore) (expired 23 April 1994, *SI 1984 No 443*)

Milford Haven Waterway (South Shore) (expired 23 April 1994, *SI 1984 No 444*)

Newcastle (expired 24 August 1991, *SI 1981 No 1071*)

North West Kent (Chatham) (expired 9 October 1996, *SI 1986, No 1557*)

Rotherham (expired 15 August 1993, *SI 1983 No 1007*)

Salford Docks (expired 11 August 1991, *SI 1981 No 1024*)

Scunthorpe (Normanby Ridge and Queensway (expired 22 September 1993, *SI 1983 No 1304*)

Speke, see Liverpool (Speke)

Sunderland (Castletown and Doxford park) (expired 26 March 2000, *SI 1990 No 794*)

Sunderland (Hylton Riverside and Southwick) (expired 26 March 2000, *SI 1990 No 795*)

Tayside (Arbroath) (expired 8 January 1994, *SI 1983 No 1816*)

Tayside (Dundee) (expired 8 January 1994, *SI 1983 No 1817*)

Telford (expired 12 January 1994, *SI 1983 No 1852*)

Trafford Park (expired 11 August 1991, *SI 1981 No 1025*)

Tyne Riverside (North Tyneside) (6 zones) (expired 25 August 2006, *SI 1996 No 1981*)

Tyne Riverside (North Tyneside and South Tyneside) (4 zones) (expired 20 October 2006, *SI 1996 No 2435*)

Wakefield (Dale Lane and Kinsley) (expired 22 September 1993, *SI 1983 No 1305*)

Wakefield (Langthwaite Grange) (expired 31 July 1991, *SI 1981 No 950*)

Wellingborough (expired 25 July 1993, *SI 1983 No 907*)

Workington (Allerdale) (expired 3 October 1993, *SI 1983 No 1331*)

See **10.164** above as regards capital allowances for commercial buildings in enterprise zones.

See **21.87** above as regards exemption from the uniform business rate for properties in enterprise zones.

2011 Series Enterprise Zones

The current series of enterprise zones have different benefits to the 1981 series (which no longer carry tax benefits except in relation ot developments carried out during the currency of the loan which have not yet been fully let). The main benefit is an exemption from business rates, but there can also be capital allowance advantages.

Nottingham (Boots campus)	24.3.2011
Liverpool Waters	24.3.2011
Manchester Airport	24.3.2011
London (Royal Docks)	24.3.2011
Birmingham and Solihull (seven sites within Birmingham City Centre)	28.7.2011
Leeds (four sites within Lower Aire Valley)	28.7.2011
Bristol (Temple Meads Rail Station)	28.7.2011
Sheffield (various sites along the M1 Motorway)	28.7.2011

Humber Estuary Renewable Energy Super Cluster	17.8.2011
Warrington & Runcorn (Daresbury Science Campus)	17.8.2011
Cornwall (Newquay Aerohub)	17.8.2011
Gosport (Daedalus Airfield – the Solent Enterprise Zone)	17.8.2011
Hinchley (MIRA Technology Park)	17.8.2011
Hereford (Rotherwas Enterprise Zone)	17.8.2011
Sandwich (Discovery Park)	17.8.2011
Harlow (Enterprise West Essex)	17.8.2011
Oxfordshire (Science Vale UK)	17.8.2011
Northampton Waterside	17.8.2011
Huntingdon (Alconbury Airfield)	17.8.2011
Great Yarmouth	17.8.2011
Lowestoft	17.8.2011
Black Country (Wolverhampton North and Darlaston)	17.8.2011
Lancashire (Warton and Samlesbury)	29.11.2011
Hull and Humber (Green Port Corridor)	29.11.2011
Deeside	23.12.2014
Ebbw Vale	23.12.2014
Haven Waterway (Milford East and Newland West)	23.12.2014
Low Carbon/Renewables East (East Port Dundee Port)	23.12.2014
Low Carbon/Renewables East (East Port, Camperdown, Dundee)	23.12.2014
Low Carbon/Renewables East (Longhaugh, Claverhouse, Dundee)	23.12.2014
Low Carbon/Renewables North (Nigg Seaboard)	23.12.2014
Life Sciences (Irvine Townhead)	23.12.2014
Humber Green Port Corridor (Paull S W Holderness)	23.12.2014
Tees Valley (Headland and Harbour, Hartlepool Port)	23.12.2014
Humber Renewable Energy Super Cluster	23.12.2014
(Queen Elizabeth Dock South, Marfleet)	23.12.2014
North East (Neptune Yard Walkergate)	23.12.2014
Humber Renewable Energy Super Cluster (Able Marine Energy Port)	23.12.2014
North East (Port of Blyth – Bates)	23.12.2014

North East (Port of Blyth – East Sieekburn)	23.12.2014
North East (North Bank of the Tyne, Port of Tyne)	23.12.2014
Tees Valley (New Energy and Technology Park, Billingham South)	23.12.2014
Aerohub Extension (Cornwall & Isles of Scilly)	7.1.2016
Aylesbury Vale	7.1.2016
Bristol Temple Quarter	7.1.2016
Birmingham Enterprise Zone Curzon Street	7.1.2016
Cambridge Compass	7.1.2016
Carlisle Kingsmoor Park	7.1.2016
Ceramics Valley (Stoke)	7.1.2016
Cheshire Science Corridor	7.1.2016
Didcot Growth Accelerator	7.1.2016
Dorset Green	7.1.2016
Enterprise M3	7.1.2016
Enviro-Tech (Hertfordshire)	7.1.2016
Great Yarmouth and Lowestoft	7.1.2016
Greater Manchester Life Science	7.1.2016
Heart of the South West	7.1.2016
Hillhouse Chemicals and Energy	7.1.2016
Humber EZ Extension	7.1.2016
Infinity Park Derby Extension	7.1.2016
Luton Airport	7.1.2016
M62 Corridor (Leeds)	7.1.2016
N E Round 2	7.1.2016
New Anglia	7.1.2016
Newhaven	7.1.2016
North Kent Innovation Zone	7.1.2016
Tees Valley Enterprise Zone (from 1.4.2015)	7.1.2016
York Central	7.1.2016

Appendix 3

Disadvantaged Areas

Items marked † were included only up to 21 July 2014

*Items marked * are included only from 22 July 2014*

For areas included in both the 2007 and 2014 designation the individual wards are not necessarily identical even though an area is on both lists

The Local Authority areas of:

Caradon†
Carrick†
Cornwall*
Isles of Scilly
Kerrier†
Na h-Eileanon an lar*
North Cornwall†
Penwith†
Restormel†

Specified wards in the following local authority areas (the full list as contained in the *Assisted Places Order 2007 (SI 2007 No 107)*:

North East

Blyth Valley†
Castle Morpeth†
Chester-le-Street†
Darlington
Derwentside†
Durham
Easington†
Gateshead
Hartlepool
Middlesbrough
Newcastle-upon-Tyne
Northumberland*

North West

Allerdale
Barrow-in-Furness
Blackburn with Darwen
Blackpool*
Bolton
Burnley
Bury*
Carlisle*
Cheshire West & Chester*
Copeland
Fylde*
Halton*

North Tyneside

Redcar & Cleveland

Sedgefield†

South Tyneside

Stockton-on-Tees

Sunderland

Teesdale†

Tees Valley: South Bank

Tees Valley: Wilton

Tees Valley: Prairie (from 1 April 2015 only)

Wansbeck†

Wear Valley†

Hyndburn

Knowsley

Lancaster*

Liverpool

Mersey Waters: Wirral Waters

Manchester*

Oldham

Pendle*

Rochdale

Rossendale*

Salford*

Sefton

South Lakeland

St Helens

Tameside*

Trafford*

West Lancashire

Wigan†

Wirral†

Wyre*

Yorkshire & Humber

Barnsley

Bradford*

Calderdale*

Doncaster

East Riding of Yorkshire

Kingston upon Hull

Kirklees*

Leeds*

North East Lincolnshire

North Lincolnshire

East Midlands

Amber Valley

Ashfield

Bassetlaw

Bolsover

Broxtowe*

Corby*

Chesterfield

Derby*

East Northamptonshire*

Erewash*

Rotherham
Selby
Sheffield
Wakefield

Gedling
High Peak
Kettering*
Leicester*
Mansfield
Newark and Sherwood
North East Derbyshire
Nottingham
South Derbyshire*
Wellingborough*

West Midlands
Birmingham
Black Country: George Dyke
Black Country: Gasholder
Black Country: Phoenix 10
Bromsgrove
Cannock Chase*
Coventry
Dudley
East Staffordshire*
Lichfield*
Newcastle-under-Lyne
North Warwickshire*
Nuneaton & Bedworth*
Redditch*
Rugby*
Sandwell
Shropshire*
Solihull
South Staffordshire
Stafford*
Staffordshire Moorlands*

East
Babergh*
Central Bedfordshire*
Great Yarmouth*
Luton
Ipswich*
South Bedfordshire[†]
Tendring*
Waveney*

Stoke-on-Trent UA
Telford & Wrekin*
Walsall
Warwick*
Wolverhampton
Wyehaven*
Wyre Forest*

London

Barking and Dagenham
Bexley
Greenwich
Havering†
Newha

South East

Dover
Gosport*
Hastings*
Isle of Wight*
Medway*
Portsmouth*
Rother*
Swale*
Thanet

South West

North Devon*
Plymouth
Teignbridge*
Torbay*
Torridge*
South Hams

WALES

The Local Authority Areas of

Blaenau Gwent
Bridgend
Caerphilly
Carmarthenshire
Ceredigion
Isle of Anglesey
Merthyr Tydfil
Neath Port Talbot
Pembrokeshire
Rhondda Cynon Taff

Disadvantaged Areas

Conwy

Denbighshire

Gwynedd

Swansea

Torfaen

Specified wards in the Local Authority Areas of

Cardiff

Flintshire

Newport

Powys

Vale of Glamorgan*

SCOTLAND

The Local Authority Areas of

Highland†

Western Isles†

Orkney Islands†

Shetland Islands†

The former Argyll and Bute District Council†

Part of Moray†

The Islands of Arran, Great Cumbrae and Little Cumbrae†

Specified wards in the Local Authority Areas of

Argyll and Bute*

Clackmannanshire

Dundee City

East Ayrshire

East Dunbartonshire

Falkirk

Fife

Renfrewshire

Shetland Islands*

South Ayrshire

South Lanarkshire

Stirling

The Islands of Arran, Great Cumbrae and Little Cumbrae*

West Dunbartonshir

Glasgow City
Highland*
Inverclyde
North Ayrshire
North Lanarkshire
Orkney*

Appendix 4

Obsolete Capital Allowances Provisions

Introduction

App 4.1 A large number of items that used to qualify for special types of capital allowance were removed from qualification for allowances, generally from 5 April 2011. The explanation of these provisions has been removed from **Chapter 10** but is reproduced below as it may still be helpful in relation to dealing with questions on earlier years.

App 4.2 *Sections 352–353* of the *CAA 2001* extended the relief for capital allowances in a property letting business to include industrial buildings allowances. Such allowances were given as a trading expense of the deemed UK property business in the same way as in an actual trading business. For corporation tax, the initial allowance was given by reference to the date the expenditure was incurred, if it was let at that time, or when the building was used for any purpose, if later. Writing-down allowances were given on the balance at the end of the chargeable period for which the allowance was made together with any balancing allowances or charges arising on disposals. The rules effectively relieved 'pre-trading' expenditure by creating a loss in the deemed business which could be carried forward until the real UK property business commenced. The same procedure applied where an industrial building was temporarily disused (*CAA 2001, s 354*). Similar rules applied to agricultural buildings allowances (given on expenditure incurred before 15 March 1988 only) under *CAA 2001, s 392* and to capital allowances for assured tenancies (on expenditure incurred before 15 March 1988 only).

App 4.3 Industrial buildings allowances were initially 4% They were phased out over the period from 27 March 2007 to 31 March 2011. As a first step balancing allowances and charges did not arise on a disposal after 27 March 2007 *(FA 2007, s 36)*. The rate of annual allowance for the year to 31 March 2009 reduced to 3%, that for the year to 31 March 2010 it was 2% and that for the year to 31 March 2011 it was 1%, after which no further allowances were given (*FA 2008, ss 84, 85*).

Industrial Buildings (to 5 April 2011 only)

Introduction

App 4.4 Expenditure on the construction of an industrial building (or, to be more precise, a building which will become an industrial building), or on the cost of improvements to such a building, used to attract a writing-down allowance of 4% of the cost each year. These allowances were phased out over four years. On expenditure before 31 March 1986 an initial allowance of 25% could be claimed in the first year in addition. The total allowances could not exceed the cost. Accordingly, (subject to the 31 March 2011 cut-off) writing-down allowances continued for 25 years where no initial allowance was given or for 19 years where the initial allowance was due and claimed in full. Initial allowances at the rate of 20% were reintroduced briefly for expenditure incurred between 1 November 1992 and 31 October 1993 provided that the building was first used before 1 January 1995. Where a building was intended to be used by that date the allowance was given provisionally and withdrawn if not so used. Expenditure was incurred in the year to 31 October 1993 for this purpose if it was either contracted for during that year or was payable under a contract entered into subsequently for the purpose of securing that a contract entered into during that year was complied with (*CAA 2001, Sch 3, para 77*). Where some of the vendor's expenditure fell within *para 77* and some did not, the purchaser's deemed expenditure was apportioned on a proportionate basis into a *para 77* element and a residual element, and the initial allowance given only on the *para 77* element. If the vendor traded as a property developer the restriction by reference to the vendor's cost did not apply (*CAA 2001, Sch 3, para 77*).

App 4.5 If the relevant interest was purchased before the building was brought into use but after 31 October 1993 (during a year in which the conditions of *para 77* are not met), the purchaser was deemed to have incurred expenditure equal to the lower of his cost or the vendor's expenditure on the building.

Definition of Industrial Building or Structure

App 4.6 An industrial building is a building or structure in use for the purposes of:

(*a*) a trade (or part of a trade) carried on in a mill, factory or similar premises;

(*b*) a trade (or part of a trade) which consists in the manufacture of goods or materials or the subjection of goods or materials to any process;

(*c*) a trade (or part of a trade) which consists in the storage

(i) of goods or materials to be used in the manufacture of other goods or materials,

(ii) of goods or materials which are to be subjected in the course of a trade to any process,

(iii) of goods or materials which have been subjected to a process but have not yet been delivered to any purchaser, or

(iv) of goods or materials on their arrival in any part of the UK from a place outside (prior to 1 May 1995 the storage had to be by sea or air into the UK);

(*d*) a trade (or part of a trade) which consists of the maintaining or repairing of any goods or materials (other than those employed by the trader in a trade or undertaking which itself is not a qualifying process);

(*e*) a transport, dock, inland navigation, water, sewerage, electricity or hydraulic power undertaking; a tunnel undertaking; a bridge undertaking; a toll road undertaking; the working of any mine, oil well or other source of mineral deposits or of a foreign plantation; ploughing or cultivating land, the doing of any other agricultural operation or the threshing of the crops of another person; or the catching or taking of fish or shellfish.

(*CAA 2001, ss 271(1), 274*).

App 4.7 The meaning of 'part of a trade' for this purpose was considered by the High Court in *Bestway (Holdings) Ltd v Luff (70 TC 512)*. Lightman J thought that at a minimum the expression must constitute 'a significant, separate and identifiable part' of the company's trade. He thought its primary purpose is to make provision for use of a building in a composite trade; use for that trade might not qualify but if use for one of the two or more component parts did that would give a right to the allowance.

App 4.8 Prior to that case HMRC used to take the view that anything done in the course of a trade was part of the trade. They now say that the activities in question need to be a 'significant, separate and identifiable part of the trade carried on.' They say that this revised view should be applied to claims for capital allowances for chargeable periods ending after 31 December 1999. They will also apply their new view to open claims for earlier periods but will not seek to re-open agreed claims for such earlier periods (unless of course there is some other change in the nature and conduct of the trade that may affect entitlement to IBA for those periods) (Tax Bulletin 44, December 1999). This is a major change. It is likely that many buildings that used to qualify for allowances will no longer do so.

App 4.9 HMRC similarly changed their views on storage in the light of the *Bestway* case. They now consider that a building is only used for storage if the purpose of keeping goods there is their storage as an end in itself. The building will not qualify if the goods are kept there for some other purpose. 'Storage which is merely a necessary and transitory incidence of the conduct of the business is not sufficient.' They believe the main impact is likely to be on the wholesale trades. For example, it has previously been accepted that premises used by a builders' merchant for storing goods or materials that are to be used in the manufacture of other goods and materials would qualify but, depending on the facts, now think that it may no longer do so (Tax Bulletin 44, December 1999). It is not at all clear what this means. The shoes in the *Lilley & Skinner* case (see **App 4.17**) were not stored in the company's warehouse 'as an end in itself'. They were stored there as a necessary and transitory incidence of the conduct of the company's business of selling shoes. That was a House of Lords decision which clearly cannot be overturned by the High Court. Indeed Lightman J actually said, 'The authorities make clear that there may be "storage" where goods are kept or held for a limited period… In *Saxone* the shoes were held to be stored in a warehouse though they remained there for 10 to 13 weeks or less.' He later says:

> 'The determining factor must be the purpose for which the goods are kept or held. If goods are delivered for safe keeping to a depository … so long as the goods remain in the possession of the depository they may be described as "stored", but this would not be the apt description of goods handed over in the course of his business to a repairer or pawnbroker.'

The reference to storage being an end in itself was in the context of:

> 'All the stock in the present case is kept in the buildings, not for storage but for sale. No goods are reserved or withheld for future use: they are all likewise available for sale and intended to be sold as soon as the turnover allows. For practical reasons only part of the stock can be made physically available for self-service by customers; but that does not alter the fact that the back-up stock is intended to be made immediately available as soon as required to meet demand … Far from being kept in reserve, the stock is in the process or in the course of being made available to purchasers at the buildings.'

App 4.10 A building which was occupied by a person carrying on a trade and used as a sports pavilion for the welfare of all or any of the workers employed in that trade was treated as if it were an industrial building (*CAA 2001, ss 271(1)(b)(iii), 280*). There was no requirement that the trade should be an industrial trade. It did, however, have to be a trade, not a profession or vocation.

App 4.11 Occupying a highway concession, embracing both the right to charge tolls and the right to receive 'rent' from the government under its Design Build Finance and Operate initiative – under which the person incurring the expenditure would never own the road; so he was building it on behalf of the government – was deemed to be carrying on a trade (*CAA 2001, s 341*).

App 4.12 Even if it could be brought within one of the above heads, a building or structure in use as, or as part of, a dwelling house, retail shop (including any premises of a similar character where retail trade or business – including repair work – was carried on), showroom, hotel, or office, or for any purpose ancillary to such a purpose, was specifically excluded from industrial buildings allowances (other than certain buildings for the welfare of employees of a mine or oil well, and certain similar activities, which would have no value when the mine was exhausted or the foreign plantation ceased to be worked) (*CAA 2001, s 277*). It should be noted that the restriction was by reference to use. Accordingly, if, for example, part of a dwelling house was set aside to be used for a qualifying purpose, expenditure on it qualified for relief provided that it ceased to be used as part of the dwelling house, even though it still physically formed part of the house.

App 4.13 This exclusion was considered in *Sarsfield v Dixons Group plc (1998 STC 938)*. A warehouse was constructed by Dixons Investments Limited (DIL). It was initially occupied by a retail subsidiary but from May 1981 it was used by Dixons Group Distribution Ltd (DGDL) which HMRC accepted carried on a transport undertaking, receiving, storing and delivering the goods purchased by the Dixons group for sale from their retail shops. The Court of Appeal, reversing the decision of the High Court, said two questions needed to be asked:

(i) Is it sufficient that the use of the warehouse was ancillary to the purposes of the Dixon Group retail shops; and

(ii) whether the use of the warehouse for the purposes of DGDL's transport undertaking constituted use for a purpose ancillary to the purposes of the Dixon Group retail shops.

They answered both questions in the affirmative. The purpose of the warehouse was exclusively that of receiving, storing and distributing to the retail shops the goods necessary for them to operate as retail shops. The use of the warehouse was subservient and subordinate, and therefore ancillary, to the purposes of the retail shops. The fact that DGDL had a separate undertaking was not inconsistent with the purpose to which it put its building being ancillary to a retail shop. If, as in the *Kilmarnock* case (see **App 4.14**), the use of the building served the purpose both of retail shops and the company's wholesale business, the use would be merely preliminary to that of the shop, but that was not the case with Dixons.

App 4.14 The drawing-office of a business of structural engineers was held to be an industrial building and not an office or ancillary to an office

(*CIR v Lambhill Ironworks Ltd (31 TC 393)*). It was predominantly used for the preparation of plans for the workshop. The screening and packing of coal in paper bags was held to constitute a process within what is now *s 274, item 2* (see **para 6**(*b*) above) and not to be ancillary to a retail shop. The process took place in a separate building but the sacks of coal were sold retail by the processor (*Kilmarnock Equitable Co-operative Society Ltd v CIR (42 TC 675)*). A laundry constructed by an NHS trust which serviced the needs of a number of hospitals was found to be used for the purpose of a trade and thus an industrial building in *HMRC v Thompson (2015 UT 341)*. Mr Thompson was a member of an Enterprise Zone Property Trust (see **App 4.79**) which funded the construction and fitting out of the laundry. Where any process whatever was carried on in a building, the possibility of the building being an industrial building needed to be considered as the scope of *item 2* was very wide. *Crusabridge Investments Ltd v Casings International Ltd (54 TC 246)* is an interesting case which illustrates the need to consider all of the heads of *s 274* before deciding whether a trade qualified. Casings' business was the purchase of used car tyre casings, examining and grading them and reselling them to remoulders. It also sold remoulds on a commission basis. Its claim that it was subjecting goods to a process within *item 2* was rejected. It was, however, held that the storage of the used casings fell within *s 274, item 3(b)* and the storage of the remoulds within *s 274, item 3(c)* (see **App 4.6**(*c*)(ii) and (iii) above respectively). Accordingly the building was an industrial building. It did not matter for the purpose of *item 3(b)* that the trade in which the goods will be processed is not that of the storer.

App 4.15 Things that were held not to be qualifying activities are a warehouse owned by selling agents for a number of manufacturers (*Dale v Johnson Bros (32 TC 487)*); an inland warehouse for goods imported in containers (*s 274, item 3(d)*) (see **App 4.6**(*c*)(iv) above) was held to be restricted to goods in transit and does not include goods which have reached their purchaser) (*Copol Clothing Ltd v Hindmarch (57 TC 575)*); a crematorium – bodies are not goods (*Bourne v Norwich Crematorium Ltd (44 TC 164)*); a building used for making up wage packets – money is not goods (*Buckingham v Securitas Properties Ltd (53 TC 292)*); the depot of a plant hire contractor where plant was repaired and maintained as well as being stored between hirings – process implies a substantial measure of uniformity or a system of treatment and the individual nature of the repairs to each individual item of equipment could not be regarded as a process (*Vibroplant Ltd v Holland (54 TC 658)*); quarantine kennels – although dogs and cats might possibly fall within the expression goods or materials in the context of *s 274, item 3* (see **App 4.6**(*c*)(iv) above) and are undoubtedly taken directly to the quarantine kennels from the seaport or airport of arrival, a quarantine business exists not as part of the ordinary process of physical transportation, but because of statutory restrictions, and thus the facility does not fit 'happily' into the wording (*Carr v Sayer (65 TC 15)*); a document and data processing centre of a bank – although documents are goods and they were subjected to a process the building was an 'office' as the operations carried on at the centre were of a kind that one would expect to be carried on in or by a bank in its back office (*Girobank plc v Clarke (1998 STC 182)*); and two cash and carry warehouses (which HMRC accepted were not retail shops) – the trade carried on was not one of storage of goods or materials, it was the sale by wholesale of groceries and other products; and the checking and sorting of goods, repackaging them, labelling them, unpacking them, and the reading of product codes on the goods did not amount to the subjection of goods to a process; they were mere preliminaries to the trade of selling (*Bestway (Holdings) Ltd v Luff (1998 STC 357)*); a warehouse and distribution building used by an importer of manufactured products which it sold in the UK mainly to wholesalers, and which was used for the receiving, breaking down of bulk deliveries, storing, retrieving, packaging and dispatch of products (*Maco Door & Window Hardware (UK) v HMRC (2008 STC 2594)*); and the purchase of products (mainly electronic components) in large quantities, breaking them down into smaller units, boxing them and storing them – the trade was the purchase and sale of goods by way of distribution, not the subjection of goods to a process (*Fornell Electronics Components Ltd (TC 1440)*, and a highly sophisticated warehouse in which bulk goods were broken down into smaller quantities (the goods were the individual items not the bulk, so were not subjected to a process and the storage was not an end in itself per Bestway) (*Next Distribution Ltd v HMRC (TC 2100)*).

App 4.16 A building outside the UK could qualify for allowances only if it was used for the purpose of a trade the profits of which were 'assessable in accordance with the rules that apply in calculating trade profits for income tax purposes or for corporation tax purposes', ie the trade was carried on in the UK (*CAA 2001, s 282*).

App 4.17 It will be seen that the test as to whether a building was an industrial building was applied by reference to the use to which the building was put, not the use to which the taxpayer put it. Accordingly a taxpayer who uses a building to generate rental income was nevertheless entitled to claim allowances provided that the occupier (who was not necessarily his tenant but could be a sub-tenant or a licensee) used the building for a qualifying purpose. If a building was used by more than one licensee of the same person it could qualify as an industrial building only if each of those licensees used it for a qualifying purpose (*CAA 2001, s 278*). On the other hand, where a single person used the entire building for more than one purpose, one of which was qualifying and the other or others of which were not, the entire building was an industrial building provided that an identifiable part was not set aside for the non-qualifying use (*Saxone, Lilley & Skinner (Holdings) Ltd v CIR (44 TC 122)*). In that case a warehouse was used to store shoes, one-third of which had been manufactured by a group company (and fell within *s 274, item 3 (c)* (see **App 4.6**(c)(iii) above)) and two-thirds of which had been purchased from other suppliers (storage of which was not a qualifying purpose). If an identifiable part of a building was the only part used for qualifying purposes then only that part qualified for allowances (*CAA 2001, ss 283, 571*).

App 4.18 In *Maco Door & Window Hardware (UK) Ltd v HMRC (2008 STC 2594)*, which the HMRC won in the House of Lords by a three to two majority, Lord Walker opined that

> '"a part of a trade" must be not simply one of the activities carried out in the course of a trade, but a viable section of a composite trade which would still be recognisable as a trade if separated from the composite whole ... it is not enough ... to be able to isolate (by horizontal division as it were) some activity carried out in the course of a vertically integrated trade, even if that activity is (in the words of Lightman J in the Bestway case) "significant, separate and identifiable" .... Storage was not a part of the wholesale cash and carry trade considered in the case, not so much because it was insignificant as because you cannot trade by selling your own goods.'

He instanced as a part of a trade a garage business that sells cars from its showroom and services and repairs cars in its workshop. If the proprietor were to close one of those activities it would still have part of its original trade.

App 4.19 Where part of a building did not qualify as an industrial building, allowances were nevertheless given on the entire cost if the capital expenditure on the non-qualifying part did not exceed 25% of the total capital expenditure on the entire building or structure (*CAA 2001, s 283(2)*). For this purpose it was necessary to look at all the expenditure since the building was constructed. Accordingly, the cost in 2010 of, say, an office extension to a factory needed to be compared with the cost of the factory when it was built. If it was built in 1930 even a very small extension in 2010 was likely to cost more than 25% of the total.

Allowable Expenditure

App 4.20 The right to allowances crystallised at the time when the expenditure was incurred (*CAA 2001, s 309(1)*). However, it could not be known whether the building qualified as an industrial building until it was physically occupied. Occupation by either the owner, a tenant, or a licensee is sufficient (*CAA 2001, s 271*). In practice, allowances were always given on a provisional basis pending occupation of the building. If it were to remain unoccupied for six years they would almost certainly be withdrawn at that stage although it is not wholly clear how HMRC would do this. They would need to make a 'discovery' that the building had not been used for the qualifying purpose. However, if the accounts or tax return for the year that the expenditure was incurred clearly showed that the building was not yet occupied for the qualifying purpose it is by no means clear that they would be entitled to make a discovery.

App 4.21 Where a building was bought unused, ie before it had been used, the purchaser was deemed to have incurred expenditure on the construction of the building equal to the lower of his purchase price or the vendor's construction cost (*CAA 2001, s 295*). If the vendor was a person carrying on a trade consisting of the construction of industrial buildings with a view to their sale, the purchaser's allowances were based on his purchase price (which included the vendor's profit element) (*CAA 2001, s 296*). (See **App 4.4** above).

App 4.22 IBAs could also be claimed for capital expenditure on repairs to an industrial building if these did not qualify as a revenue deduction for tax purposes (*CAA 2001, s 272*). If capital expenditure was incurred on preparing, cutting, tunnelling, or levelling land to prepare it as a site for the installation of plant or machinery and that expenditure did not attract allowances as plant and machinery it could be treated as if it were expenditure on an industrial building (*CAA 2001, s 273*). Where a building included plant or machinery, expenditure on the provision of such items did not qualify for industrial buildings allowance (*CAA 1990, s 21(8)*). In practice, HMRC normally allowed the taxpayer to claim allowances on such expenditure either as plant or as industrial building expenditure, as he chose.

App 4.23 Problems could sometimes arise with architects' fees and other professional fees. These were not specifically catered for in the legislation and Inspectors of Taxes were known to contend that they did not constitute expenditure 'on the construction of a building'. The probability is that they are part of the cost of construction and that allowances were due on such fees. It was generally accepted by HMRC that construction costs included the costs of preparing, cutting, tunnelling or levelling the land. It is interesting to note that in *Associated Restaurants Ltd v Warland (61 TC 51)* the Commissioners regarded an apportioned part of the engineers' and architects' fees as forming part of the capital expenditure incurred in the installation of plant, and of the planning fees as being in principle expenditure on plant. HMRC did not appeal against this ruling. That case was concerned with allowances for plant and machinery rather than IBAs, but it is likely that the same principle applies. An interesting discussion on this subject can be found in Taxline, January 1996, p 4.

App 4.24 IBAs could not be claimed in respect of expenditure on the acquisition of, or of rights in or over, land (*CAA 2001, s 272(1)*). The sum paid on a sale of the relevant interest in a building (or any other sale, insurance, salvage or compensation monies payable in respect of the building) were deemed to be reduced by the amount which on a just apportionment was attributable to items not qualifying for allowances, eg land (*CAA 2001, s 356*). The reference only to sales is confusing. The provision undoubtedly required a similar apportionment to be made on purchase (which was of course a sale by the previous owner). There is an argument that where a building was bought unused from a developer allowances were claimable on the land element. This is because *CAA 2001, s 296(2)* deemed the purchaser to have incurred expenditure on the construction of the building equal to the price paid by him on the purchase from the developer. This price would include the land element. As it was a deemed construction cost, one was not claiming the cost of land as such; one was merely claiming a deemed cost of construction work which happened to be statutorily calculated as a figure equal to the purchase price of the relevant interest. Accordingly *CAA 2001, s 21* could have no application. This argument was firmly rejected by Sir John Vinelott in *Bostock v Totham (1997 STC 764)* who held that in the context the 'relevant interest' must mean the interest relevant to the capital allowance, not the legal interest in the land, so a 'just apportionment' was required under *CAA 2001, s 356*. He also supported the Special Commissioner's view that the just apportionment was the part of the purchase price that the cost of the building bore to the combined cost of the land and the construction work, not the purchase price less the value of the site at the date of the construction.

App 4.25 The allowances were restricted where a building was bought unused if arrangements had been entered into which contained a provision having an artificial effect on pricing (*CAA 2001, s 357*). The vendor's balancing charge was similarly restricted. The arrangements which triggered this provision were:

(*a*) any arrangements relating to, or

(*b*) any other arrangements made with respect to,

any interest in (or right over) the building concerned (whether granted by the person entitled to the relevant interest or by someone else) which were entered into between any two or more persons before the sale price of the building was agreed and the effect of which was to enhance the value of the relevant interest in the building. Such arrangements have an artificial effect on pricing to the extent that they go beyond what (at the time they were entered into) it was reasonable to regard as required by the market conditions then prevailing for persons dealing with each other at arm's length in the open market. The comparison was to be made with transactions involving interests in or rights over buildings or structures of the same or a similar description (*CAA 2001, s 357(4),(5)*).

App 4.26 This was an anti-avoidance provision. It was introduced to combat schemes similar to one devised in 1994 by Matrix Securities to seek to regenerate the London Docklands property market, but to which the government took exception. Matrix wanted to sell via an Enterprise Zone Property Trust (see **App 4.79**) a building at its tenanted value, which because of the recession was far in excess of its vacant possession value, and entered into a scheme to create an artificial tenant. Such a scheme will now be an arrangement having an artificial effect on pricing – at least if the arm's-length value is for a vacant possession building, although it is not at all clear that that is what *s 357(4)* required in such circumstances. Very many enterprise zone buildings have rent guarantees, often from a local authority desperate to bring employment to the area. Is such a guarantee reasonably required by the market conditions? In most cases the building could be sold without it, albeit at a lower price. What incentives is it reasonable to expect might be required by market conditions? Reverse premiums, rent-free periods, customised fitting out, etc. are very common and are all designed to create a higher value for the tenanted building than it would otherwise have. This provision is accordingly likely to be extremely difficult to apply in practice.

Relevant Interest

App 4.27 A person was entitled to claim a writing-down allowance for a particular year only if at the end of his accounting period (or the income tax base period) the building was an industrial building, and he was entitled to 'the relevant interest in it' (*CAA 2001, s 309*). The relevant interest was the interest held by the person who incurred the expenditure at the time at which it was incurred (*CAA 2001, s 286*). If he had more than one interest in the building at that time, it was whichever of those interests is reversionary on all the others, ie the one nearest to the freehold (*CAA 2001, s 286(3)*). If the relevant interest wais a leasehold one, and the lease was extinguished by becoming merged with its immediately superior interest, that merged interest became the relevant interest (*CAA 2001, s 289*). If the lease expired, the interest which was immediately reversionary to it (ie the landlord's interest) became the relevant interest.

App 4.28 If, on a termination of a lease, the tenant remained in possession with the consent of the landlord but without entering into a new lease, his old lease was treated as continuing whilst he remained in possession (so that if that lease was the relevant interest he preserved his right to allowances) (*CAA 2001, s 359(2)*). If a lease contained an option to renew which was exercised, the new lease was similarly treated as if it were a continuation of the old (*CAA 2001, s 359(3)*). If a new lease was granted to a different lessee, and in connection with the transaction the new lessee made a payment to the old, the new lease was treated as if it were a continuation of the old and as if it had been assigned in consideration of that payment (*CAA 2001, s 359(5)*). This passed the right to the allowance to the new lessee, not the landlord, if the old lease was the relevant interest. If, on the termination of a lease which was the relevant interest, the landlord made a payment to the tenant in respect of a building comprised in the lease, the lease had to be treated as if it had been surrendered in consideration of that payment (*CAA 2001, s 359(4)*). This of course brought *CAA 2001, s 289* (see **App 4.27** above) into play.

App 4.29 A person who incurred expenditure on the construction of a building was deemed to have the same interest at that time as he would have had if construction had been completed (*CAA 2001, s 287*). It is not clear what this provision was intended to do. It may have been intended to cover a building lease where the owner was granted his lease only after completion, but in most such cases the leasehold interest would not automatically come into existence on completion so it is doubtful whether in such circumstances this statutory presumption would have the effect of deeming the leasehold interest to have existed at the date the expenditure was incurred.

Disposal of an Industrial Building

App 4.30 Up to 20 March 2007 if at a time when the building was (or had in the past been) an industrial building, either:

(*a*) the relevant interest was sold or transferred; or

(*b*) the relevant interest came to an end on the expiration of a foreign concession on which it was dependent; or

(*c*) if the relevant interest was a lease, the lease came to an end other than by the owner acquiring the immediately superior interest and merging the two; or

(*d*) the building was demolished or destroyed or ceased altogether to be used (but not if it merely ceased to be used for a qualifying purpose and began to be used for some other purpose);

a balancing allowance or charge was made to or on the owner at that time of the relevant interest – but only if that event occurred within 25 years of the building having been first used (50 years where the expenditure was incurred before 6 November 1962) (*CAA 2001, s 314*). Once a charge or allowance was triggered under *s 314*, the occurrence of a subsequent event without the building having been used as an industrial building in the interim could not, of course, generate a second charge. No balancing charges or allowances arose where the trigger event was after 20 March 2007. Instead the purchaser or other successor to the relevant interest was entitled to claim the writing down allowance to which the vendor or transferor would have been entitled (*FA 2007, s 36(2)*). There were two exceptions. The old rules continued to apply to a disposal before 1 April 2011 if it was made in pursuance of a written contract entered into before 21 March 2007, that contract was unconditional at that date, all of its terms had been agreed and it was not varied in a significant way after 20 March 2007(*FA 2007, s 36(1),(3),(7)*). The second was that the old rules continued to apply to enterprise zone buildings ((*FA 2007, s 36(1),(3)*).

App 4.31 A building did not cease altogether to be used merely by falling temporarily out of use. Indeed, it was treated as remaining an industrial building during the period of temporary disuse (*CAA 2001, s 285*).

App 4.32 If after 11 March 2008 there was a sale of a relevant interest in an industrial building which was a balancing event (ie one to which the old rules continued to apply up to 31 March 2011), the buyer and seller were connected persons or under common control (see **App 4.34**) and had different accounting periods, and the purpose or one of the main purposes of the sale wais for the buyer to obtain a tax advantage under these provisions, the buyer's writing-down allowance was restricted (*CAA 2001, s 313A(1)(2)* inserted by *FA 2008, s 87*). Its writing-down allowance for the period in which the sale took place was limited to the proportion of the allowance that would otherwise be due that the number of days for which it held the relevant interest in the accounting period bore to the length of the accounting period (*CAA 2001, s 331A(2)*). This restriction did not apply if the sale was in pursuance of a contract in writing made before 12 March 2008 provided that the contract was unconditional (or all of the conditions had been satisfied before that date), no terms remained to be agreed on, and it was not varied in a significant way on or after that date (*FA 2008, s 87(3)*).

App 4.33 A balancing allowance also arose if the sale, insurance, salvage or compensation monies were less than the 'residue of expenditure' – namely in most cases (see **App 4.40** below for the full definition) the cost less the initial expenditure (if any) and writing-down allowances given (*CAA 2001, s 318(2),(3)*). If the sale proceeds, etc. exceeded the residue of expenditure, a balancing charge equal to the difference was made – but limited to the allowances given (*CAA 2001, ss 314, 318(4),(5)*). If the building was not an industrial building (nor used for scientific research nor deemed to be an industrial building under *CAA 2001, s 285*) throughout the whole of its period of use and the sale proceeds, etc. were less than the 'capital expenditure', ie the initial expenditure qualifying for allowances (the cost of construction or the residue of expenditure at the time of purchase where the taxpayer was not the original owner), the balancing allowance was restricted, and could even be transformed into a balancing charge. The 'adjusted net cost' of the building first needed to be ascertained. This was the capital expenditure minus any sale proceeds, etc., reduced in the proportion that the aggregate period for which the building was an industrial building bore to the whole of the period from its first use (or from its acquisition by the taxpayer if later). The adjusted net cost was then compared with the allowances given, the difference between the two figures being the balancing charge or allowance (*CAA 2001, s 318*).

Example App 4.1

Bloggs Ltd constructed a warehouse during its accounting period to 31 March 1994, at a cost of £100,000, and first occupied it on 1 January 1994. It used it for a qualifying purpose until 30 June 1997. It was then used for a non-qualifying purpose for nine months, before being let on 1 April 1998 to a tenant who used it for a qualifying purpose. The tenant went into liquidation on 30 September 2002. The building was empty thereafter until it was relet on 19 June 2003 to a new tenant who used it for a non-qualifying purpose until 31 December 2005 when it burned down. It was not insured, and only £1,000 net salvage proceeds were received.

	£
Allowances given	
20% initial allowance	20,000
4% writing-down allowance, year to 31.3.94	4,000
year to 31.3.95	4,000
year to 31.3.96	4,000
year to 31.3.97	4,000
year to 31.3.99	4,000
year to 31.3.00	4,000
year to 31.3.01	4,000
	48,000
notional writing-down allowance for periods when not in use as an industrial building (see **App 4.38** below) ie 5¼ years @ £4,000 pa	21,000
	£69,000
Residue of expenditure (£100,000 – £69,000)	£31,000

There is therefore an apparent balancing allowance of £30,000 (ie £31,000 – £1,000). As the building was not used as an industrial building throughout the period of ownership an adjustment may be necessary.

Usage	*Total period (years)*	*Period for which an industrial building (years)*
1.1.94 – 30.6.97	3½	3½
1.7.97 – 31.3.98	¾	–
1.4.98 – 30.9.00	2½	2½
1.10.00 – 31.12.05	5¼	¾
	12	6¾

Adjusted net cost (*s 4(9)*):

£100,000 (cost) less £1,000 (salvage)	£99,000
6¾/12ths thereof	£55,687
Allowances given	48,000
Adjusted net cost as above	55,687
Balancing allowance	£7,687

Notes.

(i) No writing-down allowance is due for the year to 31 March 1998 as the building was not in use as an industrial building on that date.

(ii) Although the building was not actually used as an industrial building between October 2000 and June 2001, it is deemed to be one by virtue of *CAA 2001, s 285*.

(iii) Curiously it appears that notional allowances must be calculated for 5¼ years (and not 5 as might be expected) as *CAA 2001, s 336(3)* refers to amounts equal to writing-down allowances made for chargeable periods of a total length equal to the period for which the building was not in use (or deemed to be in use) as an industrial building. The effect is to bring into account allowances for 10¼ years instead of 10. This arises because *CAA 2001, s 310(1)* allowed for a full year's allowance for the year to 31.3.86 even though the building was used for only ¼ of that year, and denied any allowance for the year to 31.3.98 and for the year to 31.3.02 even though it was used as an industrial building for ¼ of both years, so that in effect allowances were given for 3 months more than the period of industrial use.

(iv) If the disposal proceeds, etc. had equalled or exceeded the capital expenditure, a balancing charge equal to the whole of the allowances given would have arisen irrespective of the proportion of the period of ownership for which the building was an industrial building (*CAA 2001, s 319(4)(5)*).

App 4.34 Where an industrial building was sold to a connected person or one under common control (ie where one controlled the other or both were controlled by the same person or persons), or it appeared that the sole or main benefit which might be expected to accrue from the sale (or from transactions of which the sale is one) was the obtaining of a tax advantage by any of the parties in relation to capital allowances (other than plant and machinery allowances), the sale had to be treated as being made at market value (*CAA 2001, s 568*). Alternatively an election could be made to treat the building as having been sold for a price equal to its residue of expenditure

(CAA 2001, s 569). Such an election overrode the above special rules under *s 319 (CAA 2001, s 569(5))*. It had to be made within two years after the sale. This election could not be made unless both buyer and seller were within the scope of capital allowances *(CAA 2001, s 570(2))*. There was some confusion whether this provision applied for the purpose of the application of the industrial buildings allowances rules to qualifying hotels, enterprise zone buildings and research and development expenditure, but *FA 1994, s 119* made clear that it did (and always had).

App 4.35 Subject to the possibility of the *Furniss v Dawson* principle being applicable, it was relatively easy to avoid a balancing charge by selling a lesser interest than the relevant interest. For example, if the relevant interest was the freehold, a 999-year lease could be granted at a premium and a nil or nominal ground rent. If it was a lease with 56 years 1 month unexpired, a sublease for 56 years 28 days could be granted at a premium. It was held in *Woods v R M Mallen (Engineering) Ltd (45 TC 619)* that the grant of a sublease for three days less than the head lease was not equivalent to a disposal of the relevant interest. It seems doubtful whether HMRC could substantiate a claim to apply the *Furniss v Dawson* principle on the grant of a sublease unless an agreement to sell the reversion subsequently was entered into at that time, as it ishard to discern a composite transaction – although their Lordships indicated in *McGuckian v CIR (1997 STC 908)* that a composite transaction might not be crucial to the *Furniss v Dawson* principle. Additionally, the grant of a sublease may be commercially more attractive than an assignment of the lease as the sublessor can retake possession in the event of default and has control over variations of the lease, whereas he loses such rights with an assignment whilst remaining liable to the head landlord. Accordingly, even if HMRC could categorise the grant of the sublease as an inserted step, they may have difficulty in showing that it has no commercial purpose. Where a building contains items of plant and machinery, the carving out of a lesser interest or the retention of a nominal reversion can also be used to avoid the balancing charge under the plant and machinery rules, as there will not have been a disposal of the asset in question. It is in any event implicit in the special rules for enterprise zone buildings in *CAA 2001, ss 327–331* and the HMRC press releases issued at the time that HMRC accepted that this device was effective (see **App 4.7**).

App 4.36 The balancing allowance on a sale was restricted if the relevant interest was sold subject to a subordinate interest and either:

(*a*) the vendor, the purchaser and the grantee of the subordinate interest (or any two of them) were connected persons (within *ITA 2007, s 993*, see Appendix 1); or

(*b*) it appeared with respect to the sale, or the grant of the lease, or related transactions, that the sole or main benefit that might have been expected to accrue to the parties or any of them was the obtaining of an allowance (not merely the balancing allowance);

(*CAA 2001, s 325*).

App 4.37 The vendor had to add to his net proceeds of the sale any premium received by him for the grant of the subordinate interest (or any other capital consideration he had received for its grant or variation) – and if the rent payable under the subordinate interest was below a commercial rent (bearing in mind any premium) the additional premium that could have been obtained if the transaction had been at arm's length (*CAA 2001, s 325(4)(5)*).

Example App 4.2

Exwye Ltd owns a freehold industrial building. It grants a lease to its subsidiary, Wyezed Ltd, for a premium of £1 million. It then sells the freehold reversion to a second subsidiary, Exzed Ltd, for its market value of £500. Exwye's residue of expenditure at the time it sold its reversion was £600,000.

	£
Exwye Ltd's tax position is	
Sale proceeds	500
Residue of expenditure	600,000
Balancing allowance	£599,500
But limited to	
Sale proceeds	500
Premium received on grant of lease	1,000,000
	1,000,500
Residue of expenditure	600,000
Balancing charge that would have arisen	£400,500
Therefore the balancing allowance is	£ nil

App 4.38 The adjustment under *CAA 2001, s 325* could not give rise to a balancing charge. It merely eliminated the balancing allowance (*CAA 2001, s 325(5)*). Where the restriction operated, the vendor's residue of expenditure immediately after the sale (on which the purchaser of the relevant interest was entitled to allowances) was calculated as if the full balancing allowance had been given (*CAA 2001, s 325(7)*). This effectively resulted in a complete loss of allowances on the expenditure. It is possible that HMRC could contend that (*b*) in **App 4.35** above applied if a long lease was granted to take advantage of the *Mallen Engineering* case (see **App 4. 35** above) and the reversion was

subsequently sold – although it is doubtful whether the sole or main benefit test is satisfied in such circumstances. As *s 325* could not create a balancing charge there was no real problem if the provision did apply in such a case.

Purchase of an Existing Building

App 4.39 Where a person purchased an existing industrial building (other than one which has not previously been used – as to which see **App 4.21** above) before 1 April 2007 the rules were modified. His writing-down allowance was not 4% of cost. Instead his allowances were based on the vendor's 'residue of expenditure' and the age of the building.

App 4.40 The vendor's residue of expenditure was his original cost (the amount on which he was entitled to claim IBAs) plus any balancing charge and less the aggregate of his initial allowance (if any), writing-down allowances or research and development allowances, a notional writing-down allowance for years when the building was not an industrial building, and any balancing allowance (*CAA 2001, s 311*). Initial allowances were given on expenditure between 6 April 1944 (when the allowances were introduced) and 31 March 1986 with the exception of that in two short periods, 6 April 1952 to 14 April 1953 and 7 April 1954 to 17 February 1956. The rate of allowance fluctuated between 5% and 75% (100% for certain small buildings – 'small workshops'). Allowances were also given at 20% for expenditure between 1 November 1992 and 31 October 1993 (see **App 4.15**).

App 4.41 The notional allowance where the building was not used as an industrial building was the writing-down allowance that would have been due if it had been so used. If a balancing charge arose under *CAA 2001, s 314* (see **App 4.33** above) the normal rules did not apply but the residue of expenditure was instead treated as equal to the net proceeds (*CAA 2001, s 337*). 'Net proceeds' was not defined. It probably meant the sale proceeds less any part thereof attributable to land or other non-qualifying expenditure.

App 4.42 The purchaser calculated his writing-down allowance by spreading the amount of the vendor's residue of expenditure over the balance of the period of 25 years from the date that the building was first used (50 years if this was prior to 6 November 1962) (*CAA 2001, s 311*).

Example App 4.3

Suppose that the building in *Example 10.6* had instead been sold to a purchaser with a 30 June accounting date on 31 December 1997 for £170,000, of which £60,000 was attributed to the land element.

The purchaser's writing-down allowances would be calculated as follows:

Bloggs Ltd's residue of expenditure:

	£	£
Sale proceeds (£170,000 – £60,000)	110,000	
but limited to original cost		100,000
Less allowances given	53,000	
deduct balancing charge	53,000	—
Notional allowances as before		21,000
Residue after sale		£79,000

Period remaining from 31 December 1997 to 25th anniversary of date of first use (1 January 2011) is 13 years.

Annual writing-down allowances (£79,000/13)		£6,077
Allowed in year to 30.6.98 (6/12 × £6,077)	£3,038	
12 years to 30.6.2010 (12 × £6,077)	£72,924	
year to 30.6.2011	£3,038	

For simplicity the above example ignores the gradual withdrawal of industrial buildings allowances. This phasing out applies to *CAA 2001, s 311* as to the basic writing-down allowance under *s 310.* The allowances for the years to 30 June 2008 onwards in the above example will actually be:

Year to 30.6.2008		
	To 31.3.2008	
	¾ × £6,077	£4,558
	¼ × £6,077 × 75%	£1,139
		£5,697
Year to 30.6.2009		
	¾ × £6,077 × 75%	£3,418
	¼ × £6,077 × 50%	£759
		£4,177
Year to 30.6.2010		
	¾ × £6,077 × 50%	£2,279
	¼ × £6,077 × 25%	£379
		£2,658

Year to 30.6.2011

	¾ × £6,077 × 25%	£1,139
	¼ to 30.6.2011	Nil
		£1,139

App 4.43 Where additions to a building took place at different times, each addition was regarded as if it were a separate building and, strictly speaking, the residue of expenditure and the purchaser's writing-down allowances had to be computed separately in respect of each addition. In practice this was rarely done, the whole of the allowances normally being given over the remainder of the period from the time the building was erected.

App 4.44 Normally a purchaser was entitled to claim a writing-down allowance only if he purchased the relevant interest in the property (see **App 4.27** above). If he purchased an interest carved out of the relevant interest – which the vendor might have wanted to avoid a balancing charge – he was not entitled to claim IBAs. Instead, the 'vendor' continued to be entitled to claim his 4% pa for the balance of the 25-year period.

App 4.45 Where a person paid a premium for a lease of over 50 years an election could be made for the right to allowances to be transferred to him from the landlord (*CAA 2001, s 290*). The property business rules (see **3.23** above) applied to determine whether a lease exceeded 50 years (*CAA 2001, s 291(3)*). The election had to be made jointly by the landlord and tenant within two years after the date on which the lease took effect – which was not necessarily the date it was granted but was often earlier (*CAA 2001, ss 290, 291(4)*). It should be noted that this time limit was not tied to a year of assessment or accounting period. It was therefore easily overlooked. The landlord himself had to own the relevant interest (or be deemed to own it by virtue of an election that he and his own landlord made under *s 290*). The election was to treat the relevant interest as having been sold for a price equal to the premium received (*CAA 2001, s 290(2)*). An election could not be made in respect of part only of the expenditure incurred by the landlord (*CAA 2001, s 290(3)*). He needed to give up his right to allowances entirely.

App 4.46 The election could, of course, result in a balancing charge arising on the lessor so he was generally unwilling to make it. If he had available losses he might be prepared to do so but would no doubt have wanted to reflect in the amount of the premium the benefit he was passing to the tenant. The landlord did not, however, have to be a person who had claimed IBAs on the building. It could be a local authority which was outside the scope of tax in relation to the building, or a pension fund which was exempt from tax on its rental income, or a property dealer who was not entitled to allowances because his expenditure on the building was not capital expenditure.

App 4.47 The election could not be made if the lessor and lessee were connected with one another (*CAA 2001, s 291(1)*), although there was an exception for statutory bodies. Not surprisingly, it also could not be made if the sole or main benefit which might be expected to accrue to the lessor from the grant of the lease and the making of the election was the obtaining of a balancing allowance (*CAA 2001, s 291(2)*).

Agricultural Buildings and Works (to 5 April 2011 only)

Introduction

App 4.48 Agricultural buildings allowances were granted where the owner or tenant of agricultural land incurred capital expenditure on the construction of farmhouses, farm buildings, cottages, fences, or other works. It should particularly be noted that the allowance was not restricted to buildings. It could also be claimed on such things as estate roads, fences, drainage, shelter belts of trees, water and electricity installations, glasshouses on market garden land, and even the reclamation of former agricultural land (HMRC Pamphlet CA3 (withdrawn)). For expenditure after 31 March 1986 allowances were given only to a person having a major interest in the land, ie the freehold (or an agreement to acquire it) or a lease (of any duration). An agreement for a lease or any tenancy or licence falling short of a lease did not carry a right to allowances (*CAA 2001, s 361(1)(b)*).

Allowances Available

App 4.49 The allowance was previously an annual allowance of 4% of the qualifying expenditure. As with industrial buildings allowances the allowances were phased out over the period to 5 April 2011 (see **App 4.15**). The rate of allowance for the year to 5 April 2009 was 3%, that for 2009/10 2%, and for 2010/11 1%. For expenditure prior to 1 April 1986 an initial allowance of 20% of the expenditure and an annual writing-down allowance of 10% for eight years was given (*CAA 2001, s 372*). Where an agricultural building was acquired before being brought into use special rules applied on the lines of those for industrial buildings (see **App 4.21** above) (*CAA 2001, s 370*). Balancing adjustments did not automatically arise on the disposal of agricultural buildings – instead the right to allowances passes to a purchaser or other transferee of the land (*CAA 2001, s 375*). If the transfer takes place during a chargeable period the writing-down allowance (but not any initial allowance) for that period – including any expenditure by the new owners – was apportioned on a time basis. Accordingly in the absence of special provisions full relief for such expenditure would not be obtained unless the building – or rather the land on which it stood as there was no requirement for the building to continue to exist at the time the allowance was claimed – was retained for 25 years. An initial allowance at the rate of 20% was temporarily reintroduced for expenditure contracted for in the period 1 November 1992 to 31 October 1993 (or for later expenditure incurred for the purpose of complying with such a contract). The expenditure had to be incurred for the purposes of husbandry on the land. If it was expenditure on the construction of a building, fence or other work it had to be used before 1 January 1995. If the expenditure was on a farmhouse (or other asset used partly for use) only the business proportion qualified. The allowance could be disclaimed in whole or part. Where the initial allowance was claimed a writing-down allowance could be claimed for the same period, but only if the building or works is in use at some time in that period (*CAA 1990, s 124A*).

App 4.50 If any building, fence or other works on the construction of which qualifying expenditure was incurred was destroyed or demolished the owner could elect for balancing adjustments to apply unless the expenditure was incurred before 1 April 1986 (or before 1 April 1987 under a contract entered into before 14 March 1984) or the balancing event occurred after 20 March 2007. He would normally do so as, except where insurance proceeds were received, such an adjustment would almost always be a balancing allowance. On the disposal of the relevant interest in an agricultural building (the interest, or the most superior interest, held by the person who incurred the expenditure at that time (*CAA 2001, s 364*), the former and the new owner could jointly elect for balancing adjustments to apply. The election had to be made for corporation tax purposes within two years after the end of the chargeable period and for income tax purposes within twelve months after 31 January following the tax year in which the accounts concerned ended. An election could not be made by a person who was not within the charge to tax in the UK, nor if the transaction was one the sole or main benefit of which was the obtaining of agricultural buildings allowances – although somewhat surprisingly it could be made if the object was to crystallise a balancing charge (*CAA 2001, ss 380–382*). Balancing adjustments could not arise on a disposal after 20 March 2007 unless it arose under a pre 21 March 2007 contract. The detailed rules were the same as for industrial buildings allowances (see **para 30**) (*FA 2007, s 36(4),(6),(7)*).

App 4.51 The amount of a balancing allowance or charge was, of course, the difference between the residue of expenditure – the expenditure qualifying for allowances less the allowances given (including any given to a previous owner who did not make the election under **App 4.50** above) – and any sale proceeds or insurance, salvage or compensation monies (*CAA 2001, s 385*). Where only part of the expenditure qualified for allowances only a proportionate part of the sale proceeds, etc. was taken into account (*CAA 2001, s 384(2)*). A balancing charge could not exceed the writing-down allowances given to the person on whom it was made (*CAA 2001, s 387*). This needed to be watched.

Suppose A owned an agricultural building for ten years and sold it to B who retained it for four years and sold it to C. The building cost A £10,000. B and C elected for balancing adjustments but A and B did not. There was a clawback of the £1,600 writing-down allowances given to B but no clawback of those given to A. However C's writing-down allowances, which would have been spread over the balance of the 25-year writing-down period in the same way as with IBAs, were based on the residue of expenditure at the time of the sale (£10,000 – 14 years at 4% = £4,400) less the balancing allowance or plus the balancing charge made on B (*CAA 2001, s 376*). He would therefore have been entitled to allowances on £6,000 only – which would have been given at the rate of £545 pa for eleven years. This is not unreasonable as A would have had – and kept – the allowances on the remaining £4,000. As with IBAs, market value had to be substituted for the sale proceeds on a disposal between connected persons or on a transaction the main purpose of which was to obtain an agricultural buildings allowance or reduce a balancing charge (*CAA 2001, ss 567–573*). The special provisions which restricted the balancing allowance on industrial buildings in certain circumstances (see **App 4.38** above) were repeated in virtually identical terms for agricultural buildings allowances purposes (*CAA 2001, s 389*). As with IBAs (see **App 4.24** above), allowances could not be claimed on the land element of any expenditure.

Meaning of Agricultural Land

App 4.52 Agricultural land meant land, houses or other buildings in the UK occupied wholly or mainly for the purpose of husbandry (*CAA 2001, s 361*). Prior to 1968 there was no definition of husbandry. In *CIR v Cavan Central Co-operative Agricultural and Dairy Society Ltd (12 TC 10)*, Madden J defined it as tilling and cultivating the soil, the raising of livestock or poultry and sometimes extended to that of silkworms, etc. He added that the word would certainly include the conversion by a husbandman of milk produced on his farm into butter or cheese. In *Lean and Dickson v Ball (12 TC 341)*, where poultry farming was held to be husbandry, Lord Clyde felt that land is occupied for husbandry if the trade or business carried on by the occupier depends to a material extent on the industrial or commercial use of the fruits (natural or artificial) of the land so occupied. Husbandry specifically included any method of intensive rearing of livestock or fish on a commercial basis for the production of food for human consumption (*CAA 2001, s 362*).

Qualifying Expenditure

App 4.53 To qualify for allowances it had to be shown that the expenditure was incurred for the purposes of husbandry on the land in question, eg that it was not for personal non-business reasons (*CAA 2001, s 361(1)(b)(ii)*).

Only a third of the expenditure on a farmhouse could qualify for relief. If 'the accommodation and amenities of the farmhouse are out of due relation to the nature and extent of the farm', the one-third figure was reduced to such proportion of the expenditure as may be just (*CAA 2001, s 369*). In *Lindsay v CIR (34 TC 289)* it was held that a dwelling house occupied by the head shepherd on a sheep farm which was managed by agents was a farmhouse, so the restriction applied. On the other hand where land was farmed by a father and son in partnership and the son moved to a new house built on the farm by the partnership it was held that the house was a cottage so that the one-third restriction did not apply (the father's house being the farmhouse) (*CIR v Whiteford & Son (40 TC 379)*). Where expenditure on an asset other than the farmhouse was incurred partly for the purpose of husbandry and partly for some other purpose the expenditure had to be apportioned in such manner as may be just.

Transfer of Interest in Land

App 4.54 As mentioned in **App 4.50** above, if, in the absence of an election, the whole of the taxpayer's interest in the land (or in any part of it) was transferred to some other person, the transferee took over the right to the future allowances in relation to that land (or part) (*CAA 2001, s 375*). It was held that a farmer, who after incurring considerable capital expenditure, conveyed the freehold in his farm to trustees and the following day took back a lease from them, had not disposed of his whole interest in the farm and therefore retained the right to allowances (*Sargaison v Roberts (45 TC 612)*). Megarry J there felt that he should look at the realities at the expense of the technicalities. It is difficult to reconcile this decision with that in the *Mallen Engineering* case (**App 4.35** above) which was decided in the same year.

App 4.55 If the interest in land attracting the allowance was a lease, on its expiry it was treated as having been acquired by the incoming tenant if he made a payment to his predecessor in respect of the expenditure, or by the landlord in any other case (*CAA 2001, s 375*).

Qualifying Hotels (to 5 April 2011 only)

App 4.56 The allowances in respect of qualifying hotels were based on the industrial buildings allowances rules and as such have also been phased out. To qualify for the allowance a hotel had to:

1. provide accommodation in a building or buildings of a permanent nature;
2. be open for at least four months in the period April to October ('the season') during the year for which the allowance is being claimed; and

3. when it is open in the season:

   (*a*) have at least ten letting bedrooms (ie private bedrooms available for letting to the public generally and not normally in the same occupation for more than one month);

   (*b*) offer sleeping accommodation consisting wholly or mainly of letting bedrooms; and

   (*c*) normally provide for guests:

      (i) breakfast,

      (ii) an evening meal,

      (iii) bed-making, and

      (iv) cleaning of rooms,

(*CAA 2001, s 279*).

App 4.57 HMRC regarded the tests at (*c*)(i) and (ii) as satisfied if the offering of breakfast and dinner was a normal event in the running of the business. They did not regard them as met if the service of either breakfast or dinner was only available on request or in exceptional circumstances (HMRC Statement of Practice SP 9/87). The hotel did not have to be in the UK but one in a different climate might have difficulty in meeting the test at (2) above if it did not open throughout the year.

App 4.58 If the hotel was in use throughout the 12 months ending with the last day of the accounting period (or basis period in the case of an individual) of the person claiming the allowances, the above tests had to be applied by reference to that accounting period (*CAA 2001, s 279(3)*).

App 4.59 If a hotel had fewer than ten letting bedrooms until a date too late for it to qualify for relief under the normal test it could instead apply the tests by reference to the period of 12 months starting from the date from which it first qualified for relief (*CAA 2001, s 279(5)*).

Example App 4.4

A company erected a hotel which it opened on 1 March 2000 as a residential hotel for long-stay (over three months) guests. It prepares accounts to 30 June. On 31 January 2008 there was a change of policy and thenceforth the hotel catered only for short-term (under a month) guests.

The hotel does not qualify for relief up to the year to 30 June 2007. The year to 30 June 2008 must be looked at to decide whether allowances are due for that year as the hotel was in use for the purpose of the trade throughout the year. It did not qualify in the months July to October 2007. It does do so in the months April to June 2008 but as this is under three months, allowances are not due under the normal test.

Under the alternative test one looks at the twelve months from 1 February 2008. In that period it meets the necessary conditions for six months, April to October 2008, and can thus claim the allowances.

App 4.60 Where the hotel was first used for the purpose of the trade during the accounting period, the tests were again applied by reference to the first twelve months of use (*CAA 2001, s 279(4)*).

App 4.61 Under the normal IBA rules the building had to be a qualifying building on the last day of the accounting period to attract a writing-down allowance. The application of the above tests could not be used to make a building a qualifying hotel at a time after it ceased altogether to be used (*CAA 2001, s 279(6)*). It appears, however, that if it ceased to qualify but did not cease to be used altogether it could be deemed to qualify, as once it was found that the qualifying tests were met the effect seems to be to have deemed it a qualifying hotel for the entire accounting period. For example, suppose a hotel company preparing accounts to 31 December qualified until 30 September 2007 and then changed to a residential hotel for long-term residents. Allowances were still due for the year to 31 December 2007 even though at that date it no longer had ten letting bedrooms.

App 4.62 Where a hotel was a qualifying hotel allowances could also be claimed on any building provided by the hotel operator for the welfare of workers employed by the hotel (eg a staff hostel) (*CAA 2001, s 279(7)*). Where the hotel was operated by an individual (including as a partner) expenditure on living accommodation of the proprietor did not qualify (*CAA 2001, s 279(8)*). How this exclusion was to be done was not specified. If a hotel was constructed with 50 bedrooms, one of which was used by the owner-manager, it is not on the face of it feasible to arrive at a cost of that bedroom. This specific exclusion appears to override the normal 25% non-qualifying rule (see **App 4.19** above).

App 4.63 The allowance was a writing-down allowance of 4% pa On expenditure before 1 April 1986 an initial allowance was also given (*FA 1995, s 66*). If a hotel ceased to be a qualifying hotel (other than on sale, demolition, or expiry of lease) and did not again become one within the next two years it had to be treated as having been sold at its open market value at the end of the two-year period if nothing had happened in the interim to trigger a balancing adjustment (*CAA 2001, s 317*). For chargeable periods ending before 27 July 1989, expenditure on fire and safety which qualified for allowances as plant and machinery could not qualify for hotel allowances (*CAA 1990, s 7(1)* *(b), (3)*). There was no option to choose which allowances to claim. As with industrial buildings allowances (see **App 4.4** and **App 4.30**) the writing down allowance was phased out over the period to 5 April 2011 and no balancing adjustments arise on a disposal after 20 March 2007

App 4.64 The definition section of the IBA rules (*CAA 2001, s 271*) did not of course apply. The provision (*CAA 2001, s 284*) allowing the whole of a building to be treated as a qualifying building if at least 75% of the expenditure qualified did, however, apply (although this seems to be subject to *CAA 2001, s 279(8)* – see **App 4.48**) as did the exclusion of buildings outside the UK unless they were used for the purpose of a trade that was taxable in the UK (*CAA 2001, s 282*).

Commercial Buildings in 1980 Style Enterprise Zones (to 5 April 2011 only)

Introduction

App 4.65 Enterprise zones were initially set up under the *Local Government Planning and Land Act 1980.* No new zones were designated under that Act after October 1996. These enterprise zones gave a number of benefits for 10 years after the zones were designated. A new type of enterprise zone was created in 2011. These give different benefits to the 1980 style zones. They are dealt with at **App 4.68**. The provisions considered at **App 4.65 –App 4.78** relate only to buildings in the 1980 style zones. These allowances ceased to apply to expenditure after 31 March 2011. The enterprise zone allowances were also based on the IBA rules. Capital expenditure on qualifying buildings in an enterprise zone attracted an initial allowance of 100% (*CAA 2001, s 306*). If the taxpayer preferred he could take a lower initial allowance (*CAA 2001, s 306(2)*). He was then entitled to a writing-down allowance of 25% pa of the cost instead of the normal 4% (*CAA 2001, s 310*). Enterprise zone building allowances were not phased out like other industrial buildings allowances. Instead the right to claim allowances simply ceased on 1 April 2011 (6 April for income tax). Where an accounting period bridged that date the writing-down allowance was the proportion of 25% that the days in the accounting period up to that date bore to the length of the accounting period (*FA 2008, s 86*). The definition of an industrial building was extended to include a qualifying hotel (within **App 4.56** above) and a 'commercial building'. A commercial building was any building which was used for the purposes of a trade, profession or vocation, or any building used as an office, provided that it did not form part of a dwelling house (*CAA 2001, s 281*). The expenditure had to be contracted for within ten years of the zone being designated (*CAA 2001, s 298*). There was no clawback of allowances if the building ceased to be used for a qualifying purpose without being sold. There was an anomaly where a building was destroyed outside the ten-year period. The destruction gave rise to a disposal at a price equal to the insurance proceeds or compensation. Normally the balancing charge this generated would have been offset by the allowances on the rebuilding costs, but it created a real tax liability in this case as the rebuilding did not qualify for enterprise zone building allowances; indeed if it was not an industrial building or qualifying hotel it did not qualify for allowances at all.

Plant and Machinery Installed in the Building

App 4.66 Expenditure on the provision of plant or ot eligible for enterprise zone buildings allowance. Nevertheless, by concession, HMRC allowed the taxpayer to elect to treat such expenditure as eligible for the enterprise zone buildings allowance instead of for capital allowances on plant and machinery (HMRC Press Release 6 January 1987).

Current List of Enterprise Zones

App 4.67 A list of the enterprise zones that were designated is given in Appendix 2. No new zones were designated between December 1985 and March 1990. Further ones were designated between 1993 and1996 but they have all now expired.

Purchase of Building in Zone

App 4.68 Where expenditure was incurred on the construction of a building or structure (the actual expenditure), and at the time some of the expenditure was incurred (or contracted for) the building was in an enterprise zone, but before the building was brought into use the relevant interest in it was sold, the purchaser was deemed to have incurred expenditure on the construction of the building on the date his purchase price became payable equal to the lesser of his net purchase price or the actual expenditure (and the actual expenditure was ignored) (*CAA 2001, ss 295–297*). If the whole of the actual expenditure was not incurred within ten years of the site first being included in the enterprise zone, the deemed expenditure was split into enterprise zone and non-enterprise zone elements. The enterprise zone element was:

$$\text{deemed expenditure} \times \frac{\text{part of actual expenditure incurred in the ten-year period}}{\text{total actual expenditure}}$$

(*CAA 2001, s 302*).

App 4.69 For the purpose of calculating capital allowances only, the enterprise zone element of the expenditure was then deemed to have been incurred at a time when the building was in the enterprise zone (*CAA 2001, s 302(2)*). If there was more than one sale before the building was first used the above modification applied only to the last sale, as the intermediate one would not have triggered a right to allowances because of *CAA 2001, s 295(4)*. If the actual expenditure was incurred by a property dealer, the actual expenditure was, as for industrial buildings allowances, treated as equal to his selling price (*CAA 2001, ss 296, 297*). The anti-avoidance rule attached to *s 295* expenditure (see **App 4.25**) also applied for the purpose of *ss 296* and *297*.

App 4.70 HMRC took the view that where a person bought an uncompleted building with the benefit of an existing building contract the purchase price consisted of two elements, the purchase of the relevant interest in relation to the construction expenditure already incurred (the *section 10A* element) and the developer's obligation to complete the building (the *section 1* element). Both elements attracted the 100% allowances. HMRC said that they believed that some agreements they had seen might be ineffective to grant to the purchaser the *section 1* element as the terms of the contract were insufficient to enable the purchaser to 'step into' the construction contract and thereby incur the future construction expenditure. This particularly applied if the vendor agreed to complete the building at his own cost which was later to be reimbursed by the purchaser or the vendor retained an interest in the property during the construction period. They therefore recommended a clear contractual separation of the purchaser's obligations to purchase the partially completed building and the purchaser's arrangements with the vendor to secure the completion of the building by the purchaser incurring construction expenditure on his own account (Tax Bulletin 35, June 1998).

Disposal of Building in Zone

App 4.71 If an enterprise zone building or structure was sold within two years after its first being used, the purchaser could also claim the 100% allowance as if the building had not been used (but only if it was the first such sale) (*CAA 2001, s 301*). This applied irrespective of whether there were previously sales of the building before it was first used. The allowances were, of course, based on the lower of his net purchase price or the actual expenditure on the construction of the building. If all of the actual expenditure on the construction was not incurred during the life of the enterprise zone, the deemed expenditure had to be split into an enterprise zone element and a non-enterprise zone element as outlined in **App 4.68** above (*CAA 2001, s 303*). Although the allowances were calculated on the lower of the purchaser's cost or the actual construction costs, any balancing allowance or charge on the vendor was calculated in the normal way (*CAA 2001, s 301(2)*). This relaxation was particularly useful where a building was in multi-occupation as it effectively allowed a developer a two-year period in which to let tenants gradually into occupation and to sell the fully-let building to an investor.

App 4.72 Expenditure incurred under a contract entered into at a time when the site of a building was not in an enterprise zone did not qualify for allowances unless it was actually incurred within 20 years after the site in question was first included in the enterprise zone (*CAA 2001, s 298(1)*). This was an anti-avoidance provision. Without it a developer could have contracted to incur expenditure before the ten-year enterprise period expired, and gradually carry out his development in pursuance of the contract over a very long time scale while retaining the right to the allowances. *Section 298* still enabled the allowances to be preserved on expenditure for up to ten years after the enterprise zone expired by contracting for such expenditure during the ten-year enterprise zone period.

App 4.73 In addition to the events set out in **App 4.30** above, a balancing charge (but not a balancing allowance) also arose in relation to enterprise zone buildings if any capital value was realised in relation to the relevant interest (*CAA 2001, s 328*). This did not apply if the relevant interest in the building was acquired under a contract entered into before 13 January 1994 (other than a conditional contract which became unconditional after 25 February 1994).

App 4.74 For this purpose capital value was realised if, within seven years of the expenditure having been incurred and either while the building was an industrial building or after it has ceased to be one, an amount of capital value was paid which was attributable to an interest in land (the subordinate interest) to which the relevant interest was (or would become) subject (*CAA 2001, s 328(5)–(7)*). Capital value meant a capital sum (or something that would have been a capital sum if it had taken the form of a money payment). Rent or the part of a premium taxable under *CTA 2009, s 217* (see **3.2**) was excluded. If the disposal was not on arm's length terms the premium or other capital sum that could have been demanded at arm's length would be a capital sum (*CAA 2001, s 331(1)*). The amount of capital realised was, of course, the capital sum. Capital value was attributable to a subordinate interest if it was paid in consideration of the grant of such an interest (eg a premium for the grant of a lease or a sublease); it was paid in lieu of rent payable by the person entitled to the interest or in consideration of the assignment of such rent (eg a lease was granted at a market rent but such rent was then commuted into the payment of a capital sum); or it was paid in consideration of the surrender of the subordinate interest or the variation or waiver of any of the terms on which it was granted (*CAA 2001, s 329(1)*). A substantial advance payment of rent did not constitute capital value. Nor did an amount in respect of which an election was made under *s 290* (see **App 4.45**) (*CAA 2001, s 329(6)*).

App 4.75 Where the acquisition of the relevant interest included arrangements for its subsequent sale, and the subsequent grant out of it of some other interest, or any other event on which capital value attributable to the subordinate interest would be paid (or treated as paid), and those arrangements either required that subsequent sale or other transaction to take place, or made it substantially more likely to occur than if the arrangements had not been entered into, *s 330* applied even where the disposal was more than seven years after the acquisition (*CAA 2001, s 330(3)(4)*).

App 4.76 An interest in land included a lease, an easement and a licence. Agreeing to grant an interest was equivalent to granting it. If an agreement to pay an amount of capital value was made within the seven-year period but the transaction did not take place until after seven years it was deemed to occur in the seven-year period (*CAA 2001, s 331(2)(3)*).

App 4.77 This prevented the avoidance of a balancing charge on an enterprise zone building under the *Woods v RM Mallen (Engineering) Ltd* principle (see **App 4.35**). It imposed a charge only where the long lease, etc was disposed of within seven years or anti-avoidance arrangements were entered into, eg to give guaranteed exit arrangements. The then government initially intended that this provision should apply to all industrial buildings but relented on the basis that 'the weakness in the capital allowances legislation was not significant in the case of buildings eligible for normal industrial buildings allowances' (HMRC Press Releases 13.1.1994 and 25.2.1994).

App 4.78 Where enterprise zone allowances were claimed and an event occurred after 31 March 2011 which would have been a balancing event had the allowances not been abolished, a balancing charge still arises if that event occurs within seven years after the building was first used (or if the allowance was made in respect of a building which was intended to be a qualifying building but was not used, seven years after the end of the chargeable period for which the allowance was made) (*FA 2008, Sch 27, paras 31, 32*).

Enterprise Zone Property Unit Trusts

App 4.79 An enterprise zone property trust was an authorised unit trust investing in enterprise zone properties. The assets of the trust had to consist wholly of land (including buildings or structures on the land) substantially the whole of which was situated in enterprise zones when it was acquired by the trust, and any part which was not in an enterprise zone had to be contiguous to land held by the trust which was in the zone. Land which was previously situated in an enterprise zone and the construction cost on which qualified for enterprise zone allowances when it was expended or contracted for, was treated as if it was in such a zone for this purpose. Contributions by participants had to be expended on the acquisition of the land or interests in land, the construction of (or the purchase of interests in) buildings or structures on that land (eligible for enterprise zone capital allowances), and the provision of machinery and plant which was an integral part of such buildings. A temporary holding of cash or of assets held in connection with the trust property, and the use of participant's contributions for expenditure incidental to (or arising out of) the permitted expenditure was also allowed. The terms of the trust had tot ensure that:

(i) a contribution by all the participants was made in the same tax year;

(ii) the expenditure by the trust was incurred wholly in that same tax year;

(iii) the nature of the rights and interests of all participants was the same;

(iv) the rights and interests of participants could not be purchased, redeemed or cancelled by the trustees in whole or part other than by way of a distribution to participants generally; and

(v) the trustees were irrevocably authorised and obliged to take responsibility for agreeing with HMRC the amount of capital expenditure attributable to each participant, the amount of any receipt to be taken into account by each participant for calculating balancing charges or allowances, the property business income from the building and any interest income attributable to each participant, and for giving each participant, within three months after the end of each accounting period, a statement showing such information.

The trustees had to submit to HMRC every year a return showing the names, addresses, tax office reference, and, in the case of an individual who was UK resident at any time in the preceding tax year, national insurance number, and their interests in the scheme (*Income Tax (Definition of Unit Trust Scheme) Regulations 1988* (*SI 1988 No 266*) and *Income Tax (Definition of Unit Trust Scheme) (Amendment) Regulations 1992* (*SI 1992 No 571*)). As far as the investor was concerned, an investment in an enterprise zone property trust gave the same tax benefit as a direct investment in an enterprise zone building. In addition, in theory at least, investment in an enterprise zone through such a trust spread the risk as the trust could invest in a range of properties. In practice, most did not; they invested in a single building. During the last recession a number of such trusts got into financial difficulties, largely because they had invested in unlet buildings on the basis of an initial rent guarantee by the developer and the developer was unable to meet the guarantee. An enterprise zone property trust also allowed small investors who could not afford to invest large amounts to invest in enterprise zone properties and enables those that could afford to do so to take instead a share in a far more substantial building which might have an institutional value.

App 4.80 EZPUTs largely disappeared in the 1990s following a number of spectacular collapses of trusts whose properties proved to be unlettable. It was held in *Smallwood v HMRC (2007 STC 1237)* that the capital allowances did not fall to be deducted from the loss on the units under *TCGA 1992, s 41(2)*. The expenditure to which that section refers must be the expenditure comprised in the consideration given for the acquisition of the relevant asset and the consideration that Mr Smallwood had given was for his units in the EZPUT, not for the acquisition of the property by the EZPUT on which the capital allowances arose. The Court of Appeal emphasised that *TCGA 1992, s 99* treated a unit trust scheme as if the rights of the unit holders were shares in a company so Mr Smallwood's loss was a loss on a disposal of deemed shares.

Flat Conversion Allowances (to 5 April 2013 only)

App 4.81 Flat conversion allowances were given on expenditure on the conversion of parts of business premises into flats (*CAA 2001, s 393A*). There was an initial allowance of 100% of qualifying expenditure (*CAA 2001, s 393H*). This could be disclaimed in whole or in part and the balance claimed in subsequent years as a writing-down allowance of 25% of the expenditure (which could also be disclaimed in whole or part) (*CAA 2001, ss 393J, 393K*). A writing-down allowance could be claimed only if at the end of the accounting period or year of assessment the person who incurred the expenditure remained entitled to the relevant interest in the flat and had not granted a long lease of it out of that interest for a capital sum (*CAA 2001, s 393J(1)*). A long lease for this purpose was one the duration of which exceeded 50 years (*CAA 2001, s 393J(2)*). The special rules in *ITTOIA 2005, s 303* and *CTA 2009, s 243* (see **3.23**) applied to determine the length of the lease but *CAA 2001, s 393V(3)* (see **App 4.90**), which treated a new lease granted in pursuance of an option as a continuation of the old lease, did not (*CAA 2001, s 393J(3)*). The relevant interest was the interest in the flat to which the person who incurred the expenditure was entitled when it was incurred. If the relevant interest was a lease the legislation contained similar rules to those in *CAA 2001, ss 286–289* (see **App 4.26**) (*CAA 2001, s 393F*). If the person who incurred the expenditure became entitled to his interest only on completion of the conversion he was treated as having had that interest when the expenditure was incurred (*CAA 2001, s 393G*). The allowance was repealed by *FA 2012, Sch 39, paras 36, 37* in relation to expenditure incurred after 5 April 2013.

App 4.82 There were no balancing adjustments unless a relevant balancing event occurred within seven years of the time when the flat was first suitable for letting as a dwelling. There were six such events:

(*a*) a sale of the relevant interest;

(*b*) the grant of a long lease in consideration of the payment of a capital sum;

(*c*) if the relevant interest was a lease, its coming to an end other than by the holder acquiring the headlease;

(*d*) the death of the taxpayer;

(*e*) the demolition or destruction of the flat;

(*f*) the flat ceasing to be a qualifying flat (without being demolished or destroyed).

(*CAA 2001, s 393N*).

App 4.83 The balancing adjustment was of course the difference between the residue of expenditure and the proceeds. In the case of the grant of a long lease the proceeds was the premium or, if greater, the commercial premium, ie the amount that would have been given if the transaction had been at arm's length. Curiously there appears to have been no similar need to substitute an arm's length price on a sale at an undervalue. The proceeds on the termination of a lease appears to be nil (even if compensation for its termination was received) unless the landlord (or any superior landlord) was a connected person in which case the proceeds was the market value of the relevant interest at the time the lease was terminated. This was likely to be nil unless the lease was surrendered. Logically if the parties were not connected and the lease was surrendered the proceeds ought to be any amount received on the surrender. However, *s 393O* stated that the proceeds were 'the amounts received or receivable in connection with the event, as shown in the *Table*'. The *Table* did not cover the case where a lease between unconnected parties came to an end. It is possible that the wording quoted above could be interpreted by the courts as the amount received in connection with the event even where nothing is shown in the *Table* in *s 393O*, with the words after the comma being taken to apply only where there is an entry in the *Table*. However, that would be a strained interpretation of the wording.

App 4.84 If the owner died the proceeds was the residue of expenditure immediately before the death (*CAA 2001, s 393O*). This always resulted in a nil balancing adjustment. It is accordingly unclear why death should have triggered an adjustment. As allowances could be claimed only by the person who incurred the expenditure, the personal representatives would not have been entitled to allowances in any event.

App 4.85 In the case of demolition or destruction of the flat the proceeds were the amount received for the remains of the flat together with any insurance money received in respect of the demolition or destruction and any other capital sum received as compensation (*CAA 2001, s 393O*). If the flat was rebuilt by the owner there did not appear to be any requirement to bring in the market value of the remains. It is not clear what is meant by demolition or destruction. Is a flat demolished if the interior of two adjoining flats is gutted so that the flats can be rebuilt as a single (non-qualifying) flat within the outer shell? Is a flat destroyed if it is vandalised so as no longer to be fit for human habitation? There seems little logic in parliament rushing to grant a balancing allowance in either of such circumstances.

App 4.86 If the flat ceased to be a qualifying flat the proceeds was the market value of the relevant interest at that time (*CAA 2001, s 393O*). If a flat was not a qualifying flat at the time it was first suitable for letting as a dwelling no initial allowance was due and any such allowance previously given were withdrawn (*CAA 2001, s 393I*). Similarly a writing-down allowance could not be claimed if it was not a qualifying flat at the end of an accounting period or year of assessment (*CAA 2001, s 393J(1)*).

App 4.87 Where more than one balancing event occurred a balancing adjustment was made only on the first of them (*CAA 2001, s 393M(5)*). As with other capital allowances, a balancing charge was limited to the amount of allowances previously given (*CAA 2001, s 393P(5)*).

Qualifying Expenditure

App 4.88 Qualifying expenditure was capital expenditure incurred on (or in connection with) either:

(*a*) the conversion of part of a qualifying building into a qualifying flat;

(*b*) the renovation of a flat (which was or would become a qualifying flat) in a qualifying building; or

(*c*) repairs to a qualifying building to the extent that such repairs were incidental to expenditure within (*a*) or (*b*).

(*CAA 2001, s 393B(1)*).

Head (*c*) appears on the face of it a little strange. How can repairs be capital expenditure? The answer is that repairs were deemed for this purpose to be capital expenditure if it would not be allowed to be deducted in calculating the profits of a property business (*CAA 2001, s 393B(4)*). In other words it was only 'repairs' that were capital under the *Law Shipping* principle (see **9.4**) that could fall within (*c*).

App 4.89 There were a large number of conditions that needed to be met.

(*a*) The part of the building (or the flat) in respect of which the expenditure was incurred must have been either:

   (i) unused; or

   (ii) used only for storage throughout the twelve months ending immediately before the date on which the conversion or renovation work began (*CAA 2001, s 393B(2)*).

(*b*) The expenditure could not be on:

   (i) the acquisition of land or rights in or over land;

   (ii) the extension of a qualifying building (except to the extent required for the purpose of providing a means of getting to or from a qualifying flat – such as the erection of an external stairwell or lift shaft);

   (iii) the development of land adjoining or adjacent to a qualifying building; or

   (iv) the provision of furnishings or chattels (no guidance is given as to when non-allowable furnishings become allowable fixtures).

   (*CAA 2001, s 393B(3)*).

(*c*) The building in which the flat was situated had to be a qualifying building. This was one where:

   (i) all or most of the ground floor of the building was authorised for business use (ie within *class A1*, shops, *A2*, financial and professional services, *A3*, food and drink, B1, business (which can be carried on in a residential area) or D1(a), medical or health services (not attached to the residence of the practitioner) of the *Schedule* to the *Town and Country Planning (Use Classes) Order 1987 (SI 1987 No 764)* (or the corresponding Scottish or Northern Irish legislation);

   (ii) it appeared that, when the building was constructed, the storeys above the ground floor were for use primarily as one or more dwellings;

   (iii) the building has no more than four storeys above the ground floor (ignoring any attic unless it was or has been in use as a dwelling or part of a dwelling);

   (iv) the construction of the building must either have been:

      1. completed before 1 January 1980; or

      2. if it was extended after 31 December 1980, the extension must have been completed before 1 January 2001.

   (*CAA 2001, s 393C*).

This definition gave rise to a great many uncertainties. These are considered at **App 4.56**.

(*d*) The flat had to be suitable for letting as a dwelling (see **App 4.90**) (*CAA 2001, s 393D(1)(b)*).

(*e*) The flat had to be held for the purpose of 'short-term letting', ie letting as a dwelling on a lease of not more than five years (*CAA 2001, s 393D(1)(c), 2*).

(*f*) It had to be possible to gain access to the flat without using the part of the ground floor of the building that was authorised for business use (see (*c*) above) (*CAA 2001, s 393D(1)(d)*).

(*g*) The flat could not have more than four rooms. For this purpose a kitchen or bathroom did not count as rooms. Nor did any closet, cloakroom or hallways not exceeding five square metres in area (*CAA 2001, s 393D(1)(e), 3*). It is not clear whether one of the above expressions was intended as a polite word for a toilet or if a toilet is to be regarded as a room. It is probably not.

(*h*) The flat could not be a high value flat. This meant that the rent that could reasonably be expected for the flat on the date on which the first qualifying expenditure on the conversion was incurred and on the assumption that:

(i) the conversion or renovation had been completed;

(ii) the flat was let furnished;

(iii) the lease dId not require the tenant to pay a premium (or make any other payments (presumably other than rent although the legislation does not say so) to the landlord or a connected person);

(iv) the tenant was not connected with the taxpayer;

(v) the flat was let on an assured shorthold tenancy (a short assured tenancy in Scotland),

could not exceed the following limits:

	Greater London	**Elsewhere**
1 or 2 room flat	£350	£150
3 room flat	£425	£225
4 room flat	£480	£300

The Treasury had power by regulation to amend these limits.(*CAA 2001, s 393D(f), 393E*). They never did so despite property values having moved significantly since the allowances were introduced in May 2001.

It is not clear precisely what assumption (i) required where, as often happens with building work, the specification of the works changed during the construction period. Did one assume the conversion that was intended to be carried out at the valuation date or did one use hindsight and assume the conversion that was actually carried out? It should be noted that the actual rent was irrelevant. That would not be received until a later date (ie after completion) so was not necessarily of assistance in arriving at a notional rental value some months or even years earlier. There was a potential question mark over expenditure on obtaining planning consent. This appears to be qualifying expenditure as it is 'in connection with' the conversion (see *s 393B(1)* – **para 83**) but is probably not expenditure 'on' the conversion, so such expenditure would not trigger the valuation date.

(*i*) The flat could not be (or have been) created or renovated as part of a scheme involving the creation or renovation of one or more high value flats (*CAA 2001, s 393D(1)(3)*). This was an odd exclusion. Suppose that for example the space above a shop was converted into three storeys of low value flats and one high value flat on the fourth storey. This condition excluded the whole of the expenditure not merely that relating to the high value flat.

(*j*) The flat could not be let to a person connected with the taxpayer (within *ITA 2007, s 933* – see Appendix 1) (*CAA 2001, s 393D(i)(h), 575(1)*).

App 4.90 For the purpose of these allowances a dwelling was defined as a building or part of a building occupied or intended to be occupied as a separate dwelling (*CAA 2001, s 393A(4)*). A flat was a dwelling which formed part of a building, was a separate set of premises (whether or not on the same floor) and was divided horizontally from another part of the building (*CAA 2001, s 393A(3)*). A qualifying flat was one that met all of the conditions at **App 4.89**(*i*) (*CAA 2001, s 393D(i)*). If a qualifying flat became temporarily unsuitable for letting as a dwelling it was nevertheless treated as continuing to be a qualifying one during that period (*CAA 2001, s 393D(4)*).

App 4.91 A lease included a tenancy and also an agreement for a lease but only at a time when the term to be covered by the lease had begun (*CAA 2001, s 393W(1)*). If a lease was terminated with the consent of the lessor and the lessee remained in possession without a new lease being granted to him the lease was treated as continuing as long as the lessee remained in occupation (*CAA 2001, s 393V(2)*). If the lease contained an option for a new lease, the exercise of that option was treated as a continuation of the old lease (*CAA 2001, s 393V(3)*). If on the termination of a lease the landlord made a payment to the tenant in respect of a flat comprised in the lease, it was treated as having been surrendered in consideration of that payment (*CAA 2001, s 393V(4)*). If the tenant received a payment not from the landlord but from an incoming tenant he was treated as having assigned his lease in consideration of that payment and the new tenant's lease was treated as a continuation of the old tenant's one *(CAA 2001, s 393V(5))*.

App 4.92 For a short, narrowly targeted provision a lot was left for secondary legislation. The Treasury was given power to alter the definition of qualifying expenditure (*s 393B(5)*), to alter the definition of a qualifying building (*s 393C(5)*), to alter the meaning of a qualifying flat (*s 393D*) and to alter the notional rent limits (*s 393E(6)*). That does not leave very much that the Treasury could not touch. As can be seen from **App 4.89** there were a great many conditions that already had to be met before the relief applied.

App 4.93 There were also a great many potential practical problems in applying the legislation. Certainty is of especial importance in relation to a tax incentive, because taxpayers who cannot tell whether or not their particular project will qualify for that incentive are unlikely to proceed on the off chance that it might do so. The ground floor of the building had to have planning permission for business use, all the other floors had to have been constructed as dwellings but it did not matter what any basement was or was not used for. In these circumstances identifying the ground floor was pretty crucial. There are a lot of buildings where the lowest floor (to use a neutral term) is half above ground level and half below. One goes down a flight of steps to reach that floor and up a flight of steps to reach the next. If the lower floor is a basement the next floor must have a commercial use. If the lower floor is the ground floor the next floor must have been originally for residential use. See the problem? Fortunately this is one of the issues that was raised in the Parliamentary debates. Unfortunately the then Minister's answer (Dawn Primarolo – the Paymaster General) was less than helpful:

> 'People are reasonably sensible and understand the ground floor to be the level at which one enters the property – unless one has tunnelled one's way in.'

When it was pointed out that an awful lot of buildings are on hillsides, she added:

> 'In Bristol, one enters the house in which I live on the ground floor, but that has become the first floor by the time one reaches the back of the house. However capital allowances and assistance have worked perfectly well in relation to the issue. The Committee is making a meal of the proposition that people … cannot, when looking at a property, determine the ground floor from the first floor. The distinction is clear'.

Unfortunately no one pointed out that prior to this legislation capital allowances did not depend on identifying the ground floor. And is there not a risk that the man on the Bristol Omnibus passing the Minister's back door might regard that as on the ground floor and the other entrance as in the basement? The Minister then made the quite extraordinary statement:

> 'We expect people to be sensible. The tax system cannot be absolute and is not designed to be. The Schedule gives clear indicators of the type of development that we want'.

Assuming that it does, which is questionable, this seems a novel approach to tax. When the Inspector says that the development does not meet the statutory conditions, is the taxpayer really entitled to respond: 'Forget the conditions, I don't need to meet them precisely, they are only intended as an indication of the type of development that attracts allowances?'

App 4.94 That was not the only area of uncertainty. An attic was not a storey unless it has been in use as part of a dwelling. What if it has been used for storing household goods? Is that use as part of a dwelling? And if the building is very old who knows what the attic was used for in 1640 or whatever. The provision appeared to mean use at any time. The construction of the building must have been completed before 1 January 1980. What is meant by completed? Although the flats had to be held out for letting could they be temporarily occupied by the owner? Could they be let to staff at a nominal rent? As a bathroom is not a room could it be assumed that a toilet was not one either? The notional rent limit was by reference to a notional letting furnished amount. What is meant by furnished in this context? Was the condition that a flat must have been unused for a year met if it was occupied by squatters for part of that period? The demolition or destruction of the flat was a balancing event. What is destruction? Is the flat destroyed if it is trashed by vandals? Or made uninhabitable by fire? Can one demolish a flat without demolishing the rest of the building?

App 4.95 Also the reasons for many of the restrictions was not apparent, so it was hard to identify precisely what it was aimed at. For example why did the relief not apply if the original building had two floors of shops and two of dwellings? Why did it apply if the shop basement was used for storage ancillary to a shop but did not apply if the shop did not have a basement so part of the first floor was designed for use for such storage? Why did it not allow the conversion of a disused shop to residential use? If a building had four storeys above the ground floor why did it allow the conversion of all four but if it had only three would not allow the construction of a fourth? Why did it not cover the construction of garages on vacant space behind the shop so as to make the flats more readily lettable? Were fitted kitchen cupboards intended to be allowable development or non-allowable furnishings? Why could the flat not be let to a connected person even at a full market rent? Indeed why could it not be occupied by the owner? If the idea was to increase the housing stock, that is achieved as much by releasing an existing house as by bringing a new one onto the letting market. Why could the allowances not be transferred, particularly on a transfer to the purchaser of the shop itself on the sale of the business? Why could access to the flat not be through the shop? If a conversion resulted in the creation of six qualifying flats and one high value penthouse why was no relief given for the qualifying flats? Why did a flat have to be available for letting for at least seven years but an individual lease of it could not exceed five?

Index

[*All references are to paragraph number*]